7a WORD BIBLICAL COMMENTARY

Joshua 1–12
Second Edition

TRENT C. BUTLER

Old Testament Editor: Nancy L. deClaissé-Walford
New Testament Editor: Peter H. Davids

These volumes (7a and 7b) are dedicated to delightful new members of the Butler/Spears clan.

New daughter-in-law Jill Butler has quickly become a daughter-in-love bringing joy, order, stability, and love to Curtis and Brynn.

Librarian Alexa Butler is multi-talented and proves more than able to challenge Curtis and Trent in travel and academic pursuits.

Jacob Butler throws balls, chases granddaddy, and laughs incessantly.

Future golf pro Cord Spears loves to hit golf balls and dig in the yard with his digger toys.

Recent addition Anna Spears runs and runs with grandpapa and then grabs hold of her momma.

God is so good to keep adding messengers of joy to our family.

ZONDERVAN

Joshua 1–12, Volume 7A
Copyright © 2014 by Trent C. Butler

This title is also available as a Zondervan ebook. Visit www.zondervan.com/ebooks.

Requests for information should be addressed to:

Zondervan, 3900 Sparks Dr. SE, Grand Rapids, Michigan 49546

ISBN 978-0-785-25268-9

Interior design: Matthew Van Zomeren

Printed in the United States of America

14 15 16 17 18 19 20 21 22 /DCI/ 20 19 18 17 16 15 14 13 12 11 10 9 8 7 6 5 4 3 2 1

Table of Contents

Editorial Preface

The launching of the Word Biblical Commentary brings to fulfillment an enterprise of several years' planning. The publishers and the members of the editorial board met in 1977 to explore the possibility of a new commentary on the books of the Bible that would incorporate several distinctive features. Prospective readers of these volumes are entitled to know what such features were intended to be; whether the aims of the commentary have been fully achieved time alone will tell.

First, we have tried to cast a wide net to include as contributors a number of scholars from around the world who not only share our aims, but are in the main engaged in the ministry of teaching in university, college, and seminary. They represent a rich diversity of denominational allegiance. The broad stance of our contributors can rightly be called evangelical, and this term is to be understood in its positive, historic sense of a commitment to Scripture as divine revelation and to the truth and power of the Christian gospel.

Then, the commentaries in our series are all commissioned and written for the purpose of inclusion in the Word Biblical Commentary. Unlike several of our distinguished counterparts in the field of commentary writing, there are no translated works, originally written in a non-English language. Also, our commentators were asked to prepare their own rendering of the original biblical text and to use the biblical languages as the basis of their own comments and exegesis. What may be claimed as distinctive with this series is that it is based on the biblical languages, yet it seeks to make the technical and scholarly approach to a theological understanding of Scripture understandable by—and useful to—the fledgling student, the working minister, and colleagues in the guild of professional scholars and teachers as well.

Finally, a word must be said about the format of the series. The layout, in clearly defined sections, has been consciously devised to assist readers at different levels. Those wishing to learn about the textual witnesses on which the translation is offered are invited to consult the section headed *Notes*. If the readers' concern is with the state of modern scholarship on any given portion of Scripture, they should turn to the sections on *Bibliography* and *Form/Structure/Setting*. For a clear exposition of the passage's meaning and its relevance to the ongoing biblical revelation, the *Comment* and concluding *Explanation* are designed expressly to meet that need. There is therefore something for everyone who may pick up and use these volumes.

If these aims come anywhere near realization, the intention of the editors will have been met, and the labor of our team of contributors rewarded.

General Editors:	*Bruce M. Metzger*†
	David A. Hubbard†
	Glenn W. Barker†
Old Testament Editor:	*Nancy L. deClaissé-Walford*
New Testament Editor:	*Ralph P. Martin*†
Associate Editor:	*Lynn Allan Losie*

Author's Preface
Joshua: An Evangelical-Critical Approach

The original edition of this commentary raised eyebrows and much more among my evangelical colleagues. The most interesting question came from Martin Woudstra, author of the at-that-time standard conservative commentary on Joshua. He asked whether the methods and presuppositions of my commentary would in any way become the norm within the evangelical community.

A to-the-point critique came in a kind way from David Howard, whose commentary is now the standard for evangelicals. Listing my work as number three under "The Best Commentaries on Joshua," Howard recommends its purchase with the note that the "work's major flaw is its too-easy acceptance of higher-critical orthodoxy concerning the history of traditions and sources that supposedly went into the composition of the book, so it must be used with some caution."

Such reception of the work requires a new clarification of the methodology and presuppositions behind this commentary. I tried to state my lifelong love affair with God's Word but found even that personal testimony to be misinterpreted as making me Barthian. So I will trace the writing of the commentary and the method behind it.

The series editors asked me to do extensive textual study. Doing this in Joshua revealed what was for me—at that time as a beginning scholar—an amazing fact. Joshua has been considered a work whose text was relatively easy to reconstruct with only a few major questions such as the placement of 8:30–35 and the bridge to Judges. I found such a description to be much too simplistic. Almost every verse raised questions of text from one angle or another. I was thus able to construct tables representing the various types of textual differences with hundreds of entities within the tables.

I could not solve a large number of the textual issues by simply repeating the normal response: a copyist made an obvious copying error. Rather, many of the textual differences had to be classified as literary improvements, homiletic interpretation and exegesis, or avoidance of unacceptable language. I began to recognize an unexpected freedom the early translators and scribes employed both in translation and transmission of the text. It appeared that concern for a final, standardized, unchangeable written text came into play at a quite late date in the literary, transmission, and translation work that went into developing the present text forms (i.e., Dead Sea Scrolls, Masoretic Text, Septuagint in its several manuscript forms, Old Latin, Vulgate, Targums, etc.).

If copyists and translators felt such freedom with the text in the later history of its transmission, why should I believe the early history of transmission did not reflect the same freedom of interpreting the text and passing it on to a new generation? Careful study then revealed how much of the language of Deuteronomy reappeared in Joshua. This gave some reason for adopting parts of Martin Noth's theory of a Deuteronomistic Historian playing a significant role in preserving, interpreting, and passing on the stories of Joshua and the first battles in Canaanite territory.

Similarly, removal of Deuteronomic language left complete stories moving from crisis to resolution, so that deeper literary study was required to understand the nature of the text and the literary genres that provided the core of the text.

In reporting such study, I evidently raised hackles from some of my friends and colleagues, who could not correlate my methodology with a strong commitment to an inerrant Scripture. Still, year after year I have committed myself to the Evangelical Theological Society by signing the statement of belief and by presenting papers in the annual sessions. I simply see from the evidence of the text a different method God used to create, preserve, interpret, and transmit his holy text than do some of my colleagues.

My commitment to the Word has never wavered. My method of interpreting the Word has gradually changed over the years. I remain convinced that the Word that led a small boy down the aisle of First Baptist Church in Sweetwater, Texas, so many years ago, still leads a retired editor in service to Christ and his church. I do not seek to change other peoples' statements of belief or practice of exegesis. I simply want to testify to the depth I find in the biblical text the deeper I dig into it with standard tools of investigation.

While reviews in more critical journals greeted the first "truly theological commentary" on Joshua, the more evangelical reviewers simply spoke of the dedication to critical method and literary development. My intent was and remains to use the critical methods—which I find justified by their results—and show how they lead to results more in touch with more conservative scholarship.

The spring 1998 issue of *Review and Expositor* published my article on the theology of Joshua. Unexpectedly, several of my harshest Joshua commentary critics wrote to say how much they appreciated and valued the article and the great change it showed in my perspective. The outline for the article came directly from the commentary and must have shown how a bit of more mature reflection on how to communicate validated the conclusions to which I came even if my methodology remained suspect.

In the meantime, evangelical, conservative scholars writing on Joshua and Judges, such as Block, Hess, and Hubbard, also have begun to recognize the ties to Deuteronomy but have talked more about what Daniel I. Block speaks of as "an independent literary composition, written in light of the authentically Mosaic theology of Deuteronomy."[1] K. Lawson Younger allows for an exilic date or afterwards for Judges.[2] Hubbard sees that Joshua "comprises an edited compilation of source materials. . . . Acceptance of a deuteronomistic historian does not deny the antiquity of the contents of much of Deuteronomy nor does it preclude the possibility that the DH, or at least part of it, may have found written form as early as the early monarchy."[3] Hubbard then concludes "one may tentatively regard the Deuteronomist as its author, whatever date one assigns him, since that person effectively wrote it drawing on earlier sources."[4] Such conservative opinions certainly do not verify the opinions of my Joshua commentary but do show that evidence is pushing conservatives to join in seeing a connection of an important kind between Joshua and Deuteronomy and between Joshua and Samuel/Kings.

---

1   *Judges, Ruth*, NAC 6 (Nashville: Broadman & Holman, 1999) 49.
2   *Judges and Ruth*, NIVAC (Grand Rapids: Zondervan, 2002) 23.
3   *Joshua*, NIVAC (Grand Rapids: Zondervan, 2009) 30–31.
4   Ibid., 32.

Interestingly, the same type of study when used to create my Judges commentary in this series did not lead to the same literary results, for I found very little reason to attribute Judges materials to a Deuteronomist. I hope this shows some objectivity on my part in using the various methods I employ to see the history of the transmission, preservation, and canonization of the text. At the same time as I was writing the Judges volume, many other scholars began questioning the existence and/or contributions of the Deuteronomistic editor. Most of them went in a direction quite distinct from my own as they pushed the date late into the Persian period and discovered more and more sources or editors or redactors for the book. This, in my view, is critical scholarship gone wild with their methods and assumptions. Each new theme, new vocabulary word, or new variation on a theme does not necessarily lead to a new editor. New study continues to tie Deuteronomistic language and Priestly language together at some late point in the process.

I cannot see how the small kingdom of the united monarchy or of Judah and of Israel could have developed competing scribal schools whose theological and cultic language and views were so nicely separated from one another. The assumed rather small number of literate scribes in Jerusalem would certainly understand and could utilize both the theological and the Priestly language of the day. The task of the exegete thus becomes a much simpler duty than to see how many contributors one can find in one brief text.

My view of the development of the present text of Joshua is quite simple, far too simple for the dedicated redaction critics of today. I have divided the task into the following sections for analysis, conscious that observations in one area influence conclusions in another. The exegete works in many methodological disciplines.

I. Text

An examination and comparison of the various Joshua manuscripts leads to decisions as to the reconstruction of a Hebrew text that comes as close as possible to the earliest Hebrew source, with the understanding that literary differences appeared early in the text's history and continued well into the postexilic period. Text notes attempt to show major manuscript variations, scholarly options, and the understanding of the current writer.

II. Translation

A study of lexicons, commentaries, grammars, and translations leads to decisions about how to render each Hebrew phrase or sentence into understandable English, which is more literal at most points in the commentary than in a translation one would produce for public and devotional reading. Here one seeks for consistency in the rendering of key literary and theological words and concepts, knowing that no English translation can reproduce exactly the meaning of Hebrew terms that by the nature of language have either broader or narrower semantic ranges than the English terms chosen. Text notes and comments attempt at key points to show the distinctive meanings.

III. Tradition History

Tradition study seeks to determine the earliest origin and use of the material behind a present unit of literature. The origin may be oral or written. Much of the material in Joshua fits the pattern that Nadav Na'aman describes for the Saul and David stories: "In my opinion, the pre-Deuteronomistic story cycle of Saul, David and Solomon was inspired by a genuine antiquarian and literary interest of the scribes and their audience, and rested on a cycle of oral narratives that were passed down orally to their authors in the court of Jerusalem."[5] Na'aman would date the writing after 800, while the current writer places the Joshua materials in the Solomonic period. At any date, oral tradition is involved in preserving and interpreting the materials.[6]

Tradition study assumes that biblical materials were not created in the final form of the present text. This is not so evident in Joshua, where only one generation appears on the stage. It is much more apparent in Genesis and in Judges, where centuries intervene between the narratives. Narratives were told and preserved individually before gradually being collected together to create a new literary whole that we call the Pentateuch. Tradition study seeks to isolate the appearance of the literary unit within the life of Israel prior to its compilation into a larger literary unit. Thus individual tribal boundary and/or city lists apparently began as written individual tribal lists before being united with other tribal lists to serve political, military, or religious interests. These were then joined into the present form combining both city lists and boundary lists with relations to each other and with summary and final totals being added. On the other hand, stories such as that of Rahab sound like fireside entertainment delivered by early Israelite storytellers. That most likely means we have one rendition of the story among several that storytellers used to bring fun and instruction to their audiences. Tradition study uses the best possible literary and oral tools to isolate elements of the oral narrative from material inserted by a compiler or editor to incorporate the story into the larger narrative. This shows us the sources available to those who put the biblical material together in its present form. Tradition history gives more place to the Hebrew community and less place to an individual writer in the creation of biblical narrative.

IV. Source and Redaction Study

Here is where I have written in ways that were easily misunderstood and opposed. To use the term *source* is to call to mind the critical source theories of JEDP. To hear

---

5   Nadav Na'aman, "Saul, Benjamin and the Emergence of 'Biblical Israel' [Part 2]," *ZAW* 121 (2009) 345.

6   For suggested criteria to differentiate texts that rest on oral literature from texts that were first composed in writing, see F. Polak, "The Oral and the Written: Syntax, Stylistics and the Development of Biblical Prose Narrative," *JANESCU* 26 (1999) 59–105; idem, "The Style of the Dialogue in Biblical Prose Narrative," *JANESCU* 28 (2002) 53–95; idem, "Style Is More than One Person: Sociolinguistics, Literary Culture, and the Distinction between Written and Oral Narrative," in *Studies in Chronology and Typology*, ed. I. Young, JSOTSup 369 (New York: T&T Clark, 2003) 38–103; idem, "Sociolinguistics: A Key to the Typology and the Social Background of Biblical Hebrew," *HS* 47 (2006) 115–62; idem, "Linguistic and Stylistic Aspects of Epic Formulae in Ancient Semitic Poetry and Biblical Narrative," in *Biblical Hebrew in Its Northwest Semitic Setting: Typological and Historical Perspectives*, ed. S. E. Fassberg and A. Hurvitz (Winona Lake, IN: Eisenbrauns, 2006) 285–304.

the term *priestly* is to categorize something as belonging to a very late, exilic/postexilic source. Neither of these understandings is what I mean now, nor is it precisely what I intended to convey in the first edition of this commentary. For me, a source may be oral or written. It may utilize cultic language at home among the priests, story language of the fireside entertainers, legal language of the courts, military language of the soldiers, etc. At a more complex level, a source may represent a compilation of oral or written materials. For this I should use *compilation* or some kindred term other than *source*. The assumption is that all Israel knew most of the priestly language at a very early time in the nation's history and did not have to put it to writing in the exile or later for the people to suddenly discover it. An author in any period after the development of the temple ritual could converse in and use most priestly terminology.

The same goes for deuteronomistic language. This may well have originated in northern Israel, perhaps among Levites at local shrines. Solomon's temple building or Jeroboam I's rebellion may have driven many Levites south, where their theology now supported the Jerusalem temple and called for worship of Yahweh alone. These Levitical priests may well have compiled the conquest stories into a whole.

Some of these northern Levites and their comrades may well have fled south even earlier to support David over against Saul and Mephibosheth. If so, they would have brought the northern traditions of Benjamin and Manasseh with them from Gilgal, Shechem, Shiloh, and Bethel. At this point they may well have combined the basic Judges narratives into a whole. Quite likely, the two sets of traditions—conquest and Judges—were joined into literary wholes during the Rehoboam/Jeroboam confrontations in support of a unified people of God.

The redaction part of the study seeks to determine the new emphasis of materials compiled together from the earliest written or oral souces into compilation and then into a complete "book." How does placing the individual narratives such as that of Rahab into the present order with theological transitions and literary connections between narratives create a meaning greater than the meaning of the individual original sources? How does becoming part of the canon of Scripture extend or interpret the meaning of the original narratives and the redacted book?

To see God working through generations, and at times centuries, to collect amazingly well-told stories into collections of stories and finally into canonical books sets us on the path to determine the meaning and the extension in meaning all along the path of storytelling, collection, and final redaction. That is source and redaction study.

V. Form

Form criticism determines the type or genre of literature a particular literary unit represents. We begin with the present piece of literature and attempt to trace it back to its earliest source. Comparison with other biblical and ancient Near Eastern literature reveals common components that make up an oral or written genre. Applied to a specific writing, this analysis shows how the individual unit compares to and contrasts with the genre in general. Analysis determines the function of the genre within ancient society and the setting within which the genre functions and is preserved. Thus individual battle reports can be incorporated into a larger conquest annal preserved in national military records or on monuments to support or memorialize a military and political leader. Taken up into a larger literary unit, the one-time battle report becomes a component of a conquest narrative preserving a nation's land claims against an opposing nation or tribe (cf. Judg 10).

VI. Structure or Narrative Criticism

Narrative study seeks to discover how components of a narrative are combined to show the literary movement from crisis to resolution. A storyteller or narrative writer retains the audience's attention and interest by utilizing (1) an introductory exposition, (2) leading to a crisis that introduces an unmistakable problem or tension that must be resolved, (3) introducing complications that deter the resolution, (4) building to a climax or turning point in the narrative, (5) that eases the tension and prepares for the (6) resolution that solves the crisis and provides the meaning of the narrative so that the storyteller or narrator can bring the story back to the (7) calm stage of the conclusion.

Narrative criticism often works with the final form of the text, removing it from a historical setting for the events related or for the lifetime of the author. In addition, narrative criticism can limit itself to one element of the narrative.

VII. Setting

The setting reasons out the historical or chronological and geographical/social setting in which a narrative unit was first created and preserved. This may be a cultic site like Gilgal, a social group such as Levites, a political unit such as David's court, or a chronological period such as the exile. Placing the narrative within such a setting helps determine why a literary unit was preserved, how it functioned, and its meaning as it is incorporated into larger literary units. Thus the ceremonies of Josh 8:30–35 and 24:1–28 relate closely to the cultic site(s) at Shechem and reveal Israel's control of that part of the land even without related conquest stories. Such cultic rites bring points of climax and resolution for a people called to obedience to God's law.

VIII. Comment

Comment sections dig into the text verse by verse to show the literary function and theological importance of each component of the narrative and to give deeper meanings and information about various items the text mentions. Here one finds information about archaeological discoveries, the nature of the Jordan River, the history and meaning of Passover, the meaning of the covenant relationship of God and Israel, and the various meanings and functions of important Hebrew words.

IX. Explanation

The final unit in each section of the commentary seeks to bring all the information gained in the above methodological steps together to show the meaning of the literary unit in its historical and literary settings.

The explanation of method presented above does not deal with history. The same method may be used to discuss and study a myth, a novel, an epic poem, a biography, and a historical annal. By arriving at a setting for the unit, the exegete determines whether the piece is intended strictly for entertainment and is thus fiction or whether it has roots in history and must be categorized with historical genres and understood as historical event. Here was the great weakness of my first edition in the eyes of many readers. I did not lay out my assumption of historicity for the materials. I assumed the larger portion of the readership shared and expected me to share in the belief in the historicity of the materials.

But one must ask what historicity means. Is it simply a fit into the practices of a certain period in history based on ancient Near Eastern parallels as produced particularly by Hess, Younger, and Kitchen? How much literary hyperbole is allowed in a work we want to identify as historical? Is it a complete presentation of Israel's conquest of the land? Is it simply a historian's presentation of his own view of the historical era seeking to teach a certain perspective on Israel's life? Is it the result of oral tradition that has gradually molded the materials into a canonical form with gradual changes along the way that are inherent in oral tradition? Is it merely an outline of historical "fact" shaped many centuries later into an apology, thereby creating an identity for a landless or powerless people?

To claim for an appreciative audience that something is historical and true generalizes the issue to far too great a perspective. One must deal with an understanding of narrative formation, author's intention, oral tradition transmission and preservation, textual accuracy, and narrative plot and function. No two human writers are going to tell the story the same way as seen in Chronicles and its work with Kings and Samuel or in the first three Gospels and their telling of the same stories with different vocabulary and literary and theological twists.

Thus my first edition sought to methodologically trace, as clearly as possible, the routes various elements in the biblical text took as they developed in oral tradition, cultic liturgy, battle reports, administrative lists, etc. Such developments of individual stories led to compilations of stories; to a book giving more concrete form to the compilations; to a collection of books like Joshua and Judges and then Joshua, Judges, Samuel, and Kings; and then the ultimate history adding these books to the Pentateuch; until finally the thirty-nine Hebrew testament books were united into one.

This preface must report that my beloved Mary fought cancer for four strong months before entering her eternal reward in April of 1996. Her loving strength will always form part of my identity. I can also report that God in grace and goodness brought another Mary into my life as on August 5, 1999, Mary Martin Spears became my wife and began showing an emotional strength and strong support as we blended our families. As of this writing together we have four adult sons, each with a lovely wife, a charming daughter, five granddaughters including two energetic twins, and two grandsons. This larger family, each person in an individual way, has accepted, loved, and encouraged me through the challenge of this second edition of Joshua.

Again, the work has strengthened my faith and brought me closer to our Lord even as it has continued to leave intriguing questions that I suppose I will research until the Father calls me away from the books and into his place prepared just for me.

Trent C. Butler
Gallatin, Tennessee
New Year's Day 2011

Preface to First Edition

What type of person would devote years in Switzerland to a study of the conflicts and conquests of the book of Joshua? Why would one look down from the majesty of the Swiss mountains to the horror of Hebrew "holy war"—ḥērem?

The answer lies, I suppose, in the "accidents" of human history under God. I drove out of the dusty heat of West Texas into the classrooms of Southern Baptist Seminary in Louisville, Kentucky, ready to put aside the pat answers of childhood because they no longer seemed to have meaning in the face of questions brought to the fore by the recent death of my adopted hemophiliac brother and a near-fatal accident that forced me to spend university graduation night unconscious in the hospital.

I began looking for answers in the normal places. Strangely, exegesis of Genesis, Galatians, John, seemed to join systematic theology in raising new questions rather than solving the old ones. Finally, Professor Don Williams offered a seminar course in Deuteronomy and the Deuteronomistic History. I joined a team including my roommate Paul Redditt, who also later joined the ranks of Old Testament professors. We explored the Hebrew Passover in enough depth to develop wild new theories on the most varied aspects of Hebrew worship, faith, and the origin of the Hebrew Scriptures. Actually, I learned few real answers in the seminar, but I learned something much more important. I learned how to ask significant questions of the biblical materials. I lost my preoccupation with the standard "unanswerable questions" and devoted my life to the excitement of biblical exegesis.

Then God introduced a new excitement into my life. Mary Burnett of Nashville, Tennessee, entered Southern Seminary. Soon she occupied more of my time than did the classroom excitement I had just discovered. The marvelous mystery of a trusting, loving personal relationship began to supply answers to many of the questions, whose answers I had sought in vain in my many books. After sixteen years of marriage and two exciting, loving sons, the excitement keeps increasing, and the answers continue to appear mysteriously when they are most needed.

The academic quest continued at Vanderbilt University with a seminar on methods in biblical scholarship, demanding research on historical method as illustrated in the study of Josh 1–12. Exploring the history of research revealed the flood of questions I had never asked, questions to which I would devote the next ten years of my life. Archaeological results, literary studies, sociological theories, textual investigations, linguistic developments, and other information all had to be sorted out and fitted into theological presuppositions to form a new theological perspective. The more study I devoted to Joshua, the more I became convinced that a solution to its problems would yield a solid foundation for constructing a literary and theological history of the Old Testament, if not of the entire Bible. Joshua offered the keys to understanding the time-honored Pentateuch/Hexateuch debate, the origin and nature of Israel's worship prior to the temple, the nature of premonarchical government, and the home and meaning of covenant theology. What was more, Joshua presented both the fulfillment of the promises to the ancestors and the establishment of the promises to the exiles.

Sad to report, the present commentary, as all others, cannot provide keys to the locks to all these tantilizing subjects. We must suffice with a report along the scholarly way. We can report that the years devoted to the venture have raised not only new questions but have raised new levels of personal faith for the author.

For this faith-provoking venture, I want to express personal thanks to the many compatriots who have helped and encouraged me along the way: church members at Hopewell Baptist Church, Springfield, Tennessee; Calvary Baptist Church, Lilburn, Georgia; Ruschlikon Baptist Church, Ruschlikon, Switzerland; and the several congregations of the European Baptist Convention, English Language. Further thanks are due the constantly questioning, yet supporting, students at Atlanta Baptist College (now Mercer University, Atlanta); Baptist Theological Seminary, Ruschlikon, Switzerland; Southern Baptist Theological Seminary, Louisville, Kentucky; and the many others at guest lectures throughout Israel, Yugoslavia, Germany, Poland, and Portugal.

The greatest gratitude goes to Mary, Curt, and Kevin, who have endured the lonely days while Daddy wrote "the Book." Their support and love have made the endeavor worthwhile.

A final word must be directed to John Watts and his editorial staff for enduring with me to the end.

Trent Butler
Nashville, Tennessee
September 21, 1982

Abbreviations

Periodicals, Reference Works, and Serials

AASF	Annales Academiae scientiarum fennicae
AASOR	Annual of the American Schools of Oriental Research
AB	Anchor Bible
ABD	*Anchor Bible Dictionary*. Ed. D. N. Freedman. 6 vols. New York, 1992.
ABLAK	*Aufsätze zur biblischen Landes- und Altertumskunde Acta orientalia*. M. Noth. 2 vols. Leiden, 1971.
ABRL	Anchor Bible Reference Library
AbrN	*Abr-Nahrain*
ACCS	Ancient Christian Commentary on Scripture
AcT	*Acta theologica*
ADPV	Abhandlungen des deutschen Palästina Vereins
AEHL	*Archaeological Encyclopedia of the Holy Land*. Ed. A. Negev. New York, 1972.
AER	*American Ecclesiastical Review*
AfO	*Archiv für Orientforschung*
ÄgAT	Ägypten und Altes Testament
AGJU	Arbeiten zur Geschichte des antiken Judentums und des Urchristentums
Aharoni, Land	Aharoni, Y. *The Land of the Bible: A Historical Geography*. Revised and enlarged edition. Philadelphia, 1979.
AION	*Annali dell'Istituto Orientali di Napoli*
AJA	*American Journal of Archaeology*
AJBA	*Australian Journal of Biblical Archaeology*
AJBI	*Annual of the Japanese Biblical Institute*
AJSL	*American Journal of Semitic Languages and Literature*

AmiCl	*Ami du Clergé*
AnBib	Analecta biblica
Andersen, Sentence	Andersen, F. I. *The Sentence in Biblical Hebrew*. The Hage, 1974.
ANEP	*The Ancient Near East in Pictures*. Ed. J. B. Pritchard. 2nd ed. with supplement. Princeton, 1969.
ANET	*Ancient Near Eastern Texts Relating to the Old Testament*. Ed. J. B. Pritchard. 3rd ed. Princeton, 1969.
AnOr	Analecta orientalia
AntSur	*Antiquity and Survival*
AOAT	Alter Orient und Altes Testament
AoF	Altorientalische Forschungen
APF	*Archiv für Papyrusforschung*
ArOr	*Archiv orientální*
ARWAW	Abhandlungen der Rheinisch-Westfälischen Akademie der Wissenschaften
ASOR	American Schools of Oriental Research
ASORDS	American Schools of Oriental Research, Dissertation Series
ASTI	*Annual of the Swedish Theological Institute*
ATANT	Abhandlungen zur Theologie des Alten und Neuen Testaments
ATAT	Arbeiten zu Text und Sprache im Alten Testament
ATD	Das Alte Testament Deutsch
AThR	*Anglican Theological Review*
AUSS	*Andrews University Seminary Studies*
AUU	Acta Universitatis Upsaliensis
AzTh	Arbeiten zur Theologie

BA	Biblical Archaeologist	BIES	Bulletin of the Israel Exploration Society (= Yediot)
BaghM	Baghdader Mitteilungen		
BAIAS	Bulletin of the Anglo-Israel Archeological Society	BIOSCS	Bulletin of the International Organization for Septuagint and Cognate Studies
BAR	Biblical Archaeology Review		
BASOR	Bulletin of the American Schools of Oriental Research	BJPES	Bulletin of the Jewish Palestine Exploration Society
BAT	Die Botschaft des Alten Testaments	BJRL	Bulletin of the John Rylands University Library of Manchester
BBB	Bonner biblische Beiträge		
BBET	Beiträge zur biblischen Exegese und Theologie	BJS	Brown Judaic Studies
		BK	Bibel und Kirche
BBLAK	Beiträge zur Biblischen Landes- und Altertumskunde	BKAT	Biblischer Kommentar: Altes Testament. Ed. M. Noth and H. W. Wolff.
BBR	Bulletin for Biblical Research		
BBRSup	Bulletin for Biblical Research, Supplement	BMik	Beit Mikra
		BN	Biblische Notizen
BDB	Brown, F., S. R. Driver, and C. A. Briggs. A Hebrew and English Lexicon of the Old Testament. Oxford, 1907. Corrected ed., 1962.	BO	Bibliotheca orientalis
		BR	Biblical Research
		BRev	Bible Review
		BRL2	Biblisches Reallexikon. 2nd ed. Ed. K. Galling. HAT 1.1. Tübingen, 1977.
BDS	BIBAL Dissertation Series		
BEAT	Beiträge zur Erklärung des alten Testamentes	BSac	Bibliotheca Sacra
		BT	The Bible Translator
BEATAJ	Beiträge zur Erforschung des Alten Testaments und des antiken Judentum	BTB	Biblical Theology Bulletin
		BTS	Bible et terre sainte
		BTZ	Berliner Theologische Zeitschrift
BeO	Bibbia e oriente	BurH	Buried History
BETL	Bibliotheca ephemeridum theologicarum lovaniensium	BWANT	Beiträge zur Wissenschaft vom Alten und Neuen Testament
BEvT	Beiträge zur evangelischen Theologie	ByzZ	Byzantinische Zeitschrift
		BZ	Biblische Zeitschrift
BFCTL	Bibliothêque de la Faculté Catholique de Thêologie de Lyon	BZAW	Beihefte zur Zeitschrift für die alttestamentliche Wissenschaft
BHH	Biblisch-historisches Handwörterbuch: Landeskunde, Geschichte, Religion, Kultur. Ed. B. Reicke and L. Rost. 4 vols. Göttingen, 1962–1966.	CA	Convivium assisiense
		CAH	Cambridge Ancient History
		CahRB	Cahiers de la Revue biblique
		CAT	Commentaire de l'Ancien Testament
BHK	Biblia Hebraica. Ed. R. Kittel. 16th ed. Stuttgart, 1973.	CB	Cultura bíblica
		CBC	Cambridge Bible Commentary
BHS	Biblia Hebraica Stuttgartensia. Ed. K. Elliger and W. Rudolph. Stuttgart, 1983.	CBQ	Catholic Biblical Quarterly
		CBR	Currents in Biblical Research
		CDOG	Colloquien der Deutschen Orient-Gesellschaft
Bib	Biblica		
BibInt	Biblical Interpretation	CHALOT	W. L. Holladay, A Concise Hebrew and Aramaic Lexicon of the Old Testament. Grand Rapids: Eerdmans, 1971.
BibOr	Biblica et orientalia		
BibS(N)	Biblische Studien (Neukirchen, 1951–)		

ConBOT	Coniectanea biblica: Old Testament Series	*EstBíb*	*Estudios bíblicos*
COS	*The Context of Scripture.* Vol. 1, *Canonical Compositions.* Vol. 2, *Monumental Inscriptions.* Vol. 3, *Archival Documents.* Ed. W. W. Hallo and K. L. Younger, Jr. Leiden, 1997, 1999, 2002.	*ETR*	*Etudes théologiques et religieuses*
		ETS	Erfurter theologische Studien
		EvQ	*The Evangelical Quarterly*
		EvT	*Evangelische Theologie*
		Exp	*The Expositor*
		ExpTim	*The Expository Times*
		FAT	Forschungen zum Alten Testament
Crux	*Crux*	FB	Forschung zur Bibel
CTJ	*Calvin Theological Journal*	*FF*	*Forschungen und Fortschritte*
CTM	*Concordia Theological Monthly*	FOTL	The Forms of the Old Testament Literature
CurBS	*Currents in Research: Biblical Studies*	FRLANT	Forschungen zur Religion und Literatur des Alten und Neuen Testaments
CV	*Communio viatorum*		
DBAT	*Dielheimer Blätter zum Alten Testament und seiner Rezeption in der Alten Kirche*	*FV*	*Foi et Vie*
		GAT	Grundrisse zum Alten Testament
DCH	*Dictionary of Classical Hebrew.* Ed. D. J. A. Clines. 7 vols. Sheffield, 1993–2007.	GBS	Guides to Biblical Scholarship
		GKC	*Gesenius' Hebrew Grammar.* Ed. E. Kautsch. Trans. A. E. Cowley. 2nd ed. Oxford, 1910. Repr. 1966.
DD	*Dor le Dor*		
DE	*Discussions in Egyptology*		
Diog	*Diogenes*	*Greg*	*Gregorianum*
DJD	Discoveries in the Judaean Desert	GTA	Göttinger theologischer Arbeiten
DOTHB	*Dictionary of the Hebrew Bible*	*GTJ*	*Grace Theological Journal*
DOTT	*Documents from Old Testament Times.* Ed. D. W. Thomas. London, 1958.	*GTT*	*Geereformeerd theologisch tijdschrift*
DTT	*Dansk teologisk tidsskrift*	*HALOT*	Koehler, L. W. Baumgartner, and J. J. Stamm. *The Hebrew and Aramaic Lexicon of the Old Testament.* Trans. and ed. under supervision of M. E. J. Richardson. 4 vols. Leiden, 1994–1999.
EA	El-Amarna tablets. According to the edition of J. A. Knudtzon. *Die el-Amarna-Tafeln.* Leipzig, 1908–1915. Reprint, Aalen, 1964. Continued in A. F. Rainey, *El-Amarna Tables, 349–379.* 2nd rev. ed. Kevelaer, 1978.		
		HAR	*Hebrew Annual Review*
		HAT	Handbuch zum Alten Testament
EAEHL	*Encyclopedia of Archaeological Excavations in the Holy Land.* Ed. M. Avi-Yonah. 4 vols. Jerusalem, 1975–1978.	*HBT*	*Horizons in Biblical Theology*
		HDR	Harvard Dissertations in Religion
EB	Echter Bibel	*Hen*	*Henoch*
EBC	Expositor's Bible Commentary	*Herm*	*Hermanthena*
EBib	Etudes bibliques	*HeyJ*	*Heythrop Journal*
EdF	Erträge der Forschung	*HIBD*	Brand, C., C. W. Draper, and A. England. *Holman Illustrated Bible Dictionary.* Rev. ed. Ed. T. C. Butler. Nashville: B&H, 2003.
EHS	Europäischen Hochschulschriften		
EncJud	*Encyclopaedia Judaica.* 16 vols. Jerusalem, 1972.		
ErIsr	*Ereṣ Israel*		

HKAT	Handkommentar zum Alten Testament	JBT	Jahrbuch für Biblische Theologie
HS	*Hebrew Studies*	*JCS*	*Journal of Cuneiform Studies*
HSM	Harvard Semitic Monographs	*JETS*	*Journal of the Evangelical Theological Society*
HSS	Harvard Semitic Studies		
HTR	*Harvard Theological Review*	*JHS*	*Journal of Hellenic Studies*
HUCA	*Hebrew Union College Annual*	*JJS*	*Journal of Jewish Studies*
HvTSt	*Hervormde teologiese studies*	*JNES*	*Journal of Near Eastern Studies*
HW	*Hebräische Wortforschung.* FS W. Baumgartner, ed. B. Hartmann et al. VTSup 16. Leiden, 1967.	*JNSL*	*Journal of Northwest Semitic Languages*
		JOTT	*Journal of Translation and Textlinguistics*
IB	*Interpreter's Bible.* Ed. G. A. Buttrick et al. 12 vols. New York, 1951–1957.	Joüon	Joüon, P. *A Grammar of Biblical Hebrew.* Trans. and rev. T. Muraoka. 2 vols. Subsidia biblica 14/1–2. Rome, 1991. Also *Grammaire de l'Hébreu biblique,* 2nd ed. Rome: Institut biblique pontifical, 1947.
IBHS	*An Introduction to Biblical Hebrew Syntax.* B. K. Waltke and M. O'Connor. Winona Lake, IN, 1990.		
IBS	*Irish Biblical Studies*		
IDB	*Interpreter's Dictionary of the Bible.* Ed. G. A. Buttrick. 4 vols. Nashville, 1962.	*JPOS*	*Journal of the Palestine Oriental Society*
		JQR	*Jewish Quarterly Review*
IDBSup	*Interpreter's Dictionary of the Bible: Supplementary Volume.* Ed. K. Crim. Nashville, 1976.	*JRefJ*	*Journal of Reformed Judaism*
		JSJ	*Journal for the Study of Judaism in the Persian, Hellenistic, and Roman Periods*
IEJ	*Israel Exploration Journal*	JSJSup	*JSJ* Supplements
Int	*Interpretation*	*JSNT*	*Journal for the Study of the New Testament*
IOS	*Israel Oriental Studies*		
IOSCS	International Organization for Septuagint and Cognate Studies	*JSOR*	*Journal of the Society of Oriental Research*
		JSOT	*Journal for the Study of the Old Testament*
IOSOT	International Organization for the Study of the Old Testament	JSOTSup	Journal for the Study of the Old Testament Supplement Series
Irén	*Irénikon*		
ITC	International Theological Commentary	*JSS*	*Journal of Semitic Studies*
		JSSEA	*Journal of the Society for the Study of Egyptian Antiquities*
ITQ	*Irish Theological Quarterly*		
JA	*Journal asiatique*	*JTS*	*Journal of Theological Studies*
JANESCU	*Journal of the Ancient Near Eastern Society of Columbia University*	*Jud*	*Judaica*
		KAT	Kommentar zum Alten Testament
JAOS	*Journal of the American Oriental Society*	KB	*Keilinschriftliche Bibliothek.* Ed. E. Schrader. 6 vols. Berlin, 1889–1915.
JARCE	*Journal of the American Research Center in Egypt*		
JBL	*Journal of Biblical Literature*	KBL	Koehler, L., and W. Baumgartner. *Lexicon in Veteris Testamenti libros.* 2nd ed. Leiden, 1958.
JBQ	*Jewish Bible Quarterly*		
JBS	Jerusalem Biblical Studies		

KHC	Kurzer Hand-Commentar zum Alten Testament		*NIDOTTE*	*New International Dictionary of Old Testament Theology and Exegesis.* Ed. W. A. VanGemeren. 5 vols. Grand Rapids, 1997.
KlSchr	*Kleine Schriften*			
KS	*Kirjath-Sepher*			
Lambdin,				
Introduction			NIVAC	NIV Application Commentary
to Biblical			*NRTh*	*La nouvelle revue théologique*
Hebrew	Lambdin, T. O. *Introduction to Biblical Hebrew.* New York: Scribner's, 1971.		OBO	Orbis biblicus et orientalis
			ÖBS	Österreichische biblische Studien
Laur	*Laurentianum*		OBT	Overtures to Biblical Theology
LBC	Layman's Bible Commentary		OLA	Orientalia lovaniensia analecta
LTQ	*Lexington Theological Quarterly*			
Maarav	*Maarav*		*OLP*	*Orientalia lovaniensia periodica*
MDAI	*Mitteilungen des Deutschen archäologischen Instituts*		*OLZ*	*Orientalistische Literaturzeitung*
			OTA	*Old Testament Abstracts*
MdB	*Le Monde de la Bible*		*OTE*	*Old Testament Essays*
MNDPV	*Mitteilungen und nachrichten des Deutschen Palaestina-Vereins*		OTL	Old Testament Library
			OTS	Old Testament Studies
			OtSt	Oudtestamentische Studiën
MSP	Monumenta sacra et profana		*PaVi*	*Parole di Vita*
MUSJ	*Mélanges de l'Université Saint-Joseph*		*PEFQS*	*Palestine Exploration Fund Quarterly Statement*
NAC	New American Commentary		*PEQ*	*Palestine Exploration Quarterly*
NBC	New Bible Commentary		*Per*	*Perspectives*
NBD	*New Biblical Dictionary.* Ed. J. D. Douglas. London, 1962.		PerlesII	Perles, F. *Analekten zur Textkritik des Alten Testaments.* NF. Leipzig: Engel, 1922.
NCB	New Century Bible [Commentary] (new ed.)		*PIBA*	*Proceedings of the Irish Biblical Association*
NEA	*Near Eastern Archaeology* (formerly *Biblical Archaeologist*)		PIHANS	Publications de l'Institut historique et archeologique neerlandais de Stamboul
NEAEHL	*The New Encyclopedia of Archaeological Excavations in the Holy Land.* Ed. E. Stern. 4 vols. Jerusalem, 1993.			
			PJ	*Palästina-Jahrbuch*
			PL	Patrologia latine Ed. J.-P. Migne. 217 vols. Paris, 1844–1864.
NEASB	*Near East Archaeological Society Bulletin*		*POTT*	*Peoples of Old Testament Times.* Ed. D. J. Wiseman. London, 1973.
NEchtB	Neue Echter Bibel			
NedTT	*Nederlands theologisch tijdschrift*			
NGTT	*Nederduitse gereformeerde teologiese tydskrif*		*Preliminary*	
			and Interim	
NIB	*The New Interpreter's Bible*		*Report*	*Preliminary and Interim Report on the Hebrew Old Testament Text Project.* Vol. 1, *Pentateuch.* Vol. 2, *Historical Books.* Ed. D. Barthélemy et al. 2nd rev. ed. New York, 1979.
NIBCOT	New International Biblical Commentary on the Old Testament			
NICOT	New International Commentary on the Old Testament			
NIDB	*The New Interpreter's Dictionary of the Bible.* Ed. Katharine Doob Sakenfeld. Nashville: Abingdon, 2009.		*Protest*	*Protestantesimo*
			PrWCJewSt	*Proceedings of the World Congress of Jewish Studies*

PTR	Princeton Theological Review	SBLTCS	SBL Text-Critical Studies
PUST	Pontifical University of St. Thomas Aquinas	SBOT	Sacred Books of the Old Testament
Qad	Qadmoniot	SBS	Stuttgarter Bibelstudien
QD	Quaestiones disputatae	SBT	Studies in Biblical Theology
RadRel	Radical Religion	SBTS	Sources for Biblical and Theological Study
RAr	Revue archéologique		
RB	Revue biblique	SC	Sources chrétiennes. Paris, 1943–.
RBL	Review of Biblical Literature		
RBR	Ricerche Bibliche e Religiose	ScEs	Science et esprit
RelS	Religious Studies	Schneider,	
ResQ	Restoration Quarterly	Grammatik	Schneider, W. Grammatik des biblischen Hebräisch: Ein Lehrbuch. Munich, 1974.
RevExp	Review and Expositor		
RevistB	Revista bíblica		
RevQ	Revue de Qumran	Scr	Scripture
RGG	Die Religion in Geschichte und Gegenwart. Ed. K. Galling. 7 vols. 3rd ed. Tübingen, 1957–1965.	ScrHier	Scripta hierosolymitana
		ScrVict	Scriptorium victoriense
		SEÅ	Svensk exegetisk årsbok
		Sef	Sefarad
RHPR	Revue d'histoire et de philosophie religieuses	Sem	Semitica
		SemeiaSt	Semeia Studies
RHR	Revue de l'histoire des religions	SFSHJ	South Florida Studies in the History of Judaism
RICP	Revue de l'Institut Catholique de Paris		
		SHANE	Studies in the History of the Ancient Near East
RivB	Rivista biblical italiana		
RSO	Rivista degli studi orientali	Shnaton	Shnaton: An Annual for Biblical and Ancient Near Eastern Studies
RST	Regensburger Studien zur Theologie		
		SJOT	Scandinavian Journal of the Old Testament
RTFL	Recueil de travaux publiépar la Faculté des Lettres		
		SÖAW	Sitzungen der österreichischen Akademie der Wissenschaften in Wien
RTP	Revue de théologie et de philosophie		
RTR	Reformed Theological Review	Sperber	Sperber, A., ed. The Bible in Aramaic. 4 vols. Leiden, 1992.
SA	Studia anselmiana		
Salm	Salmaticensis		
SANT	Studien zum Alten und Neuen Testaments	SR	Studies in Religion/Sciences Religieuses
SAOC	Studies in Ancient Oriental Civilization	SSN	Studia semitica neerlandica
		ST	Studia theologica
SBFLA	Studii biblici Franciscani liber annus	StC	Studia catholica
		STDJ	Studies on the Texts of the Desert of Judah
SBJT	Southern Baptist Journal of Theology		
		SThU	Schweizerische theologische Umschau
SBL	Society of Biblical Literature		
SBLABS	SBL Archaeology and Biblical Studies	STT	Suomalaisen tiedeakatemian toimituksia
		SWBA	Social World of Biblical Antiquity
SBLDS	SBL Dissertation Series		
SBLMS	SBL Monograph Series		
SBLSCS	SBL Septuagint and Cognate Studies	SWBASup	The Social World of Biblical Antiquity Supplement
SBLSP	SBL Seminar Papers	SwJT	Southwestern Journal of Theology
SBLSS	SBL Semeia Studies	TA	Tel Aviv
SBLSymS	SBL Symposium Series		

Tarbiz	*Tarbiz*	
TAVO	*Tübinger Atlas des Vorderen Orients.* 7 vols. Wiesbaden, 1977–1993.	
TB	Theologische Bücherei: Neudrucke und Berichte aus dem 20. Jahrhundert	
TBei	*Theologische Beiträge*	
TBT	*The Bible Today*	
TDOT	*Theological Dictionary of the Old Testament.* Ed. E. Jenni and C. Westermann. Trans. J. T. Willis, G. W. Bromiley, and D. E. Green. 8 vols. Grand Rapids, 1974–.	
TEH	Theologische Existenze heute	
TGl	*Theologie und Glaube*	
THAT	*Theologisches Handwörterbuch zum Alten Testament.* Ed. E. Jenni and C. Westermann. 2 vols. Stuttgart, 1971–1976.	
Them	*Themelios*	
ThSt	Theologische Studiën	
ThT	*Theologisch tijdschrift*	
ThTo	*Theology Today*	
ThV	*Theologische Versuche*	
ThViat	*Theologia viatorum*	
TJ	*Trinity Journal*	
T&K	*Texte & Kontexte*	
TLOT	*Theological Lexicon of the Old Testament.* Ed. E. Jenni and C. Westermann. Tr. M. E. Biddle. 3 vols. Peabody, MA, 1997.	
TLZ	*Theologische Literaturzeitung*	
TOTC	Tyndale Old Testament Commentaries	
TP	*Theologie und Philosophie*	
TQ	*Theologische Quartalschrift*	
Transeu	*Transeuphratène*	
TRev	*Theologische Revue*	
TRu	*Theologische Rundschau*	
TSK	*Theologische Studien und Kritiken*	
TT	*Teologisk Tidsskrift*	
TUAT	*Texte aus der Umwelt des Alten Testaments.* Ed. O. Kaiser. Gütersloh, 1984–.	
TvT	*Tijdschrift voor theologie*	
TWAT	*Theologisches Wörterbuch zum Alten Testament.* Ed. G. J. Botterweck and H. Ringgren. 5 vols. (incomplete).	

Stuttgart, 1970 = *Theological Dictionary of the Old Testament.* Trans. J. T. Willis et al. Grand Rapids, 1974–.

TWOT	*Theological Wordbook of the Old Testament.* Ed. R. L. Harris and G. L. Archer, Jr. 2 vols. Chicago, 1980.
TynBul	*Tyndale Bulletin*
TZ	*Theologische Zeitschrift*
UF	*Ugarit-Forschungen*
USQR	*Union Seminary Quarterly Review*
VD	*Verbum domini*
VF	*Verkündigung und Forschung*
VoxTh	*Vox theologica*
VT	*Vetus Testamentum*
VTSup	Vetus Testamentum, Supplements
WBC	Word Biblical Commentary
Williams' Hebrew Syntax	Williams, R. J. *Williams' Hebrew Syntax: An Outline.* Rev. J. C. Beckman. 3rd ed. Toronto, 2007.
WMANT	Wissenschaftliche Monographien zum Alten und Neuen Testament
WO	*Die Welt des Orients*
WTJ	*Westminster Theological Journal*
WUNT	Wissenschaftliche Untersuchungen zum Neuen Testament
WVDOG	Wissenschaftliche Veröffentlichungen der deutschen Orientgesellschaft
WW	*Word and World*
WZR	*Wissenschaftliche Zeitschrift der Universität Rostock*
ZABR	*Zeitschrift für altorientalische und biblische Rechtgeschichte*
ZÄS	*Zeitschrift fur ägyptische Sprache und Altertumskunde*
ZAW	*Zeitschrift für die alttestamentliche Wissenschaft*
ZBK	Zürcher Bibelkommentare
ZDMG	*Zeitschrift der deutschen morgenländischen Gesellschaft*
ZDPV	*Zeitschrift des deutschen Palästina-Vereins*
ZdZ	*Die Zeichen der Zeit*

ZKT	*Zeitschrift für katholische Theologie*	ZTK	*Zeitschrift für Theologie und Kirche*
ZIBBC	*Zondervan Illustrated Bible Backgrounds Commentary*		

Texts, Versions, and Ancient Works

1Q, 2Q, 3Q, etc.	Numbered caves of Qumran, followed by abbreviation of biblical or apocryphal book	KJV	King James Version
		LXX	Septuagint, Greek translation of the OT
B. Bat.	*Baba Batra*	LXX^A	LXX Codex, Alexandrinus
CEV	Contemporary English Version	LXX^B	LXX Codex, Vaticanus
		LXXL	LXX, Lucianic recension
DSB	Daily Study Bible	*m.*	Mishnah
DSS	Dead Sea Scrolls	Message	Contemporary rendering by E. H. Peterson
Dtn	Deuteronomic		
Dtr	Deuteronomistic, Deuteronomist	MT	Masoretic Text (as published in *BHS*)
DtrN	Nomistic Deuteronomist	NAB	New American Bible
DtrP	Priestly Deuteronomist	NASB	New American Standard Bible, 1995 Update
E	Elohist (supposed biblical literary source)	NEB	New English Bible
G	Greek translation: as published in *Septuaginta*, LXX ed. A. Rahlfs, 1935. In Daniel, G includes both OG and Th, as published in J. Ziegler's ed., 1954	NET	New English Translation (online NET Bible)
		NETS	A New English Translation of the Septuagint
		NIV	New International Version
		NJB	New Jerusalem Bible
GWT	God's Word Translation	NLT	New Living Translation
HCSB	Holman Christian Standard Bible	NRSV	New Revised Standard Version
J	Yahwist/Jahwist (supposed biblical literary source)	P	Priestly Source
		Q	Qere, Hebrew reading tradition
JB	Jerusalem Bible	REB	Revised English Bible
JPS	Jewish Publication Society translation	RSV	Revised Standard Version
		Tg(s).	Targum(s)
K	Kethib (the written consonantal Hebrew text of OT)	Theod.	Theodotion
		Vg.	Vulgate

Biblical and Apocryphal Books

Old Testament

Gen	Genesis	1–2 Sam	1–2 Samuel
Exod	Exodus	1–2 Kgs	1–2 Kings
Lev	Leviticus	1–2 Chr	1–2 Chronicles
Num	Numbers	Ezra	Ezra
Deut	Deuteronomy	Neh	Nehemiah
Josh	Joshua	Esth	Esther
Judg	Judges	Job	Job
Ruth	Ruth	Ps(s)	Psalm(s)

Prov	Proverbs	Amos	Amos
Eccl	Ecclesiastes	Obad	Obadiah
Song	Song of Solomon	Jonah	Jonah
Isa	Isaiah	Mic	Micah
Jer	Jeremiah	Nah	Nahum
Lam	Lamentations	Hab	Habakkuk
Ezek	Ezekiel	Zeph	Zephaniah
Dan	Daniel	Hag	Haggai
Hos	Hosea	Zech	Zechariah
Joel	Joel	Mal	Malachi

Apocrypha

Bar	Baruch	Ep Jer	Epistle of Jeremiah
Add Dan	Additions to Daniel	Jdt	Judith
PrAzar	Prayer of Azariah	1–2 Macc	1–2 Maccabees
Bel	Bel and the Dragon	3–4 Macc	3–4 Maccabees
SgThree	Song of the Three Young Men	Pr Man	Prayer of Manasseh
		Ps 151	Psalm 151
Sus	Susanna	Sir	Sirach/Ecclesiasticus
1–2 Esd	1–2 Esdras	Tob	Tobit
Add Esth	Additions to Esther	Wis	Wisdom of Solomon

New Testament

Matt	Matthew	1–2 Thess	1–2 Thessalonians
Mark	Mark	1–2 Tim	1–2 Timothy
Luke	Luke	Titus	Titus
John	John	Phlm	Philemon
Acts	Acts	Heb	Hebrews
Rom	Romans	Jas	James
1–2 Cor	1–2 Corinthians	1–2 Pet	1–2 Peter
Gal	Galatians	1–2–3 John	1–2–3 John
Eph	Ephesians	Jude	Jude
Phil	Philippians	Rev	Revelation
Col	Colossians		

Miscellaneous

abs.	absolute	Eg.	Egyptian
Aram.	Aramaic	EI	Early Iron
BCE	Before the Common Era	Eng.	English
c.	common	esp.	especially
ca.	*circa*, about	ET	English Translation
CE	Common Era	fem.	feminine
chap(s).	chapter(s)	frg.	fragment
consec.	consecutive	FS	*Festschrift*, volume written in honor of
const.	construct		
diss.	dissertation	Ger.	German
ed(s).	edition; edited by; editor(s)	Gk.	Greek
e.g.	*exempli gratia*, for example	Heb.	Hebrew

impf.	imperfect	pl.	plural
impv.	imperative	repr.	reprint, reprinted
ind.	indicative	rev.	revised, reviser, revision
inf.	infinitive	*seb.*	*sebir,* the usual form of the
LB	Late Bronze		word noted in the margin
lit.	literally	*Sef.*	*Sefarad*
M.R.	Map Reference	Sem.	Semitic
masc.	masculine	ser.	series
n(n).	note(s)	sg.	singular
NF	*Neue Folge,* new series	suff.	suffix
NS	new series	Syr.	Syriac language
NT	New Testament	TR	Textus Receptus
OG	Old Greek	trans.	translated by; translator
orig.	original, originally	Ugar.	Ugaritic
OS	old series	*var. lect.*	*varia(e) lectio(nes),* "variant
OT	Old Testament		reading(s)"
p(p).	page(s)	vb.	verb
part.	participle	v(v)	verse(s)
pers.	person	§	section/paragraph
pf.	perfect		

Commentary Bibliography

In the text of the commentary, references to commentaries on Joshua are by author's name only or by author's name and year of publication if the author has produced more than one commentary.

Abadie, P. *Le livre de Josué critique historique.* Cahiers Évangile 134. Paris: Cerf, 2005. **Abel, F.-M.** *Le livre de Josué.* Le Sainte Bible. Paris, 1950. **Ahituv, S.** *Joshua: Introduction and Commentary* (Heb.). Tel Aviv, 1995. **Alonso Schökel, L.** *Josué y Jueces.* Ed J. M. Valverde. Trans. M. Iglesias González and L. Alonso Schökel. Los Libros Sagrados 3. Madrid, 1973. **Auld, G.** *Joshua, Judges, and Ruth.* Daily Study Bible. Philadelphia: Westminister, 1984. **Auzou, G.** *Le Don d'une Conquêt:. Étude du Livre de Josué.* Paris, 1964. **Baker, D.** *Joshua: The Power of God's Promises.* Downer's Grove, IL: InterVarsity Press, 1988. **Baldi, D.** *Giosuè.* La Sacra Bibbia. Rome: Marietti, 1956. **Beda Venerabilis** (pseudo.). *Quaestiones super Jesu Nave Librum.* PL 93. 1862. Repr., Paris, 1950. 417–22. **Beek, M. A.** *Jozua.* De Prediking van het Oude Testament. Nijkerk, 1981. **Bennett, W. H.** *The Book of Joshua: Critical Edition of the Hebrew Text.* The Sacred Books of the Old Testament 6. Leipzig: Hinrichs, 1895. **Blair, E. P.** *The Book of Deuteronomy, the Book of Joshua.* LBC 5. Richmond: John Knox, 1964. **Boer, P. A. H. de.** *Zoals er gezegd is over de intocht (Jozua).* Bijbelcommentaren voor de moderne mens 7. Zeist: De Haan, 1963. **Boling, R.** *Joshua.* AB 6. Garden City, NY: Doubleday, 1982. **Bonfrerius, J.** *Josue, Judices et Ruth.* Paris, 1631. **Borrhaus, M.** *Josua.* Basel, 1557. **Bright, J.** "The Book of Joshua." In *IB.* Vol. 2. Nashville: Abingdon, 1953. 2:539–673. **Burmannus, F.** *De Rigteren Israels, of te uitlegginge ende betrachtinge van de boeken Josua, der Rigteren ende Ruth.* Utrecht, 1675. **Calmet, A.** *Josua, Commentarius literalis in omnes libros Veteris Testamenti, Tomus tertius: Josue, Judicium, Ruth, I+II Regum.* Würzburg, 1790. **Calvin, J.** *Commentaires sur le livre de Josue: Avec une préface de Th. De Besze. (Genève, 1564) / Commentaries on the Book of Joshua.* Grand Rapids: Eerdmans, 1948. Also published as *Commentarius in Librum Iosue.* Corpus Reformatorum. Brunsvigae: Schwetschke, 1882 (Calvina Opera 25) 421. Repr., New York: Johnson, 1964. Translated as *Commentaries on the Book of Joshua,* trans. H. Beveridge (Edinburgh: Calvin Translation Society, 1854). **Cetina, E. S.** "Joshua." In *The International Bible Commentary.* Ed. W. R. Farmer. Collegeville, MN: Liturgical Press, 1998. 525–47. **Chyträus, D.** *Josua.* Rostock, 1577. **Claire, Abbé.** *Le Livre de Josué.* Paris, 1877. **Cohen, A.** *Joshua and Judges.* Soncino Books of the Bible. London, 1976. **Cohen, M.** *Joshua and Judges* (Heb.). Ramat Gan, 1992. **Colenso, J. W.** *The Pentateuch and Book of Joshua Critically Examined.* Vols. 1–7. London, 1863–1879. **Constable, T. L.** *Notes on Joshua.* Sonic Light, 2010. Online: http://www.soniclight.com/constable/notes/pdf/joshua.pdf. **Cooke, G. A.** *The Book of Joshua in the Revised Version with Introduction and Notes.* The Cambridge Bible for Schools and Colleges. Cambridge: Cambridge UP, 1918. **Coornaert, V. J.** *Josuë, Rechters, Ruth, Koningen en Paaralipomenon volgens en met den latijnschen tekst der vulgata: In het vlaamsch vertaald en in doorlopende antekeningehn uitgeleid.* Bruge, 1897. **Coote, R. B.** "The Book of Joshua." In *NIB.* Vol. 2. Nashville: Abingdon, 1998. 553–719. **Creach, J. F. D.** *Joshua.* Interpretation Commentary. Louisville: John Knox, 2003. **Croceti, G.** *Giosuè, Giudici, Rut.* Leggere oggi la Bibbia 1.7. Brescia, 1981. **Crosby, H.** *Expository Notes on the Book of Joshua.* London, 1875. **Davidson, R. M.** *Joshua: In the Footsteps of Joshua.* Hagerstown, PA: Review and Herald Publishing, 1995. **Davis, D. R.** *No Falling Words: Expositions of the Book of Joshua.* Grand Rapids: Baker, 1988. **Deurloo, K. A.** *Jozua: Een praktische bijbelverklaring.* Tekst en toelichting. Kok: Kampen, 1994. ———. *Jozua: Verklaring van een bijbelgedeelte.* Kok: Kampen, 1981. **Dillmann, A.** *Die Bücher Numeri, Deuter-*

onomium und Josua. 2nd ed. Kurzgefasstes exegetisches Handbuch zum Alten Testament 13. Leipzig: Hirzel, 1886. **Earl, D. S.** *Reading Joshua as Christian Scripture.* Journal of Theological Interpretation Supplement 2. Winona Lake, IN: Eisenbrauns, 2010. **Ehrlich, A. B.** *Randglossen zur hebräischen Bibel: Textkritisches, Sprachliches und Sachliches.* Vol. 3, *Josua, Richter, I und II Samuelis.* Leipzig: Hinrichs, 1910. **Fernández, P. A.** *Commentarius in librum Iosue.* Cursus Scripturae Sacrae 5. Paris, 1938. **Franke, J. R.** *Joshua, Judges, Ruth, 1–2 Samuel.* ACCS, OT 4. Downers Grove, IL: InterVarsity Press, 2005. **Fritz, V.** *Das Buch Josua.* HAT 1.7. Tübingen: Mohr (Siebeck), 1994. **Garstang, J.** *Joshua-Judges.* Foundations of Bible History. New York: Smith, 1931. **Gelin, A.** "Le Livre de Josué." In La *Sainte Bible.* Paris: Alliance Biblique Française, 1949. **Görg, M.** *Josua.* NEchtB 26. Würzburg: Echter, 1991. **Gray, J.** *Joshua, Judges, Ruth.* NCB. London: Thomas Nelson and Sons, 1967. Repr., Grand Rapids: Eerdmans, 1986. **Gressmann, H.** *Die älteste Geschichtsschreibung und Prophetie Israels: Samuel bis Amos und Hosea.* 2nd ed. Die Schriften des Alten Testaments 2, vol. 1. Göttingen: Vandenhoeck & Ruprecht, 1921. ———. *Die Anfänge Israels: Mosis bis Richter und Ruth.* 2nd ed. Die Schriften des Alten Testaments 1, vol. 2. Göttingen: Vandenhoeck & Ruprecht, 1922. **Gutbrod, K.** *Das Buch vom Lande Gottes: Josua und Richter.* BAT 10. Stuttgart: Calwer, 1951. **Hamlin, E. J.** *Inheriting the Land: A Commentary on the Book of Joshua.* ITC. Grand Rapids: Eerdmans, 1983. **Harris, J. G.** "Joshua." In *Joshua, Judges, Ruth.* NIBCOT. Peabody, MA: Hendrickson, 2000. 1–119. **Harstad, A. L.** *Joshua.* Concordia Commentary. St. Louis: Concordia, 2004. **Hawk, L. D.** *Joshua.* Berit Olam. Collegeville, MN: Liturgical, 2000. ———. *Joshua in 3-D: A Commentary on Biblical Conquest and Manifest Destiny.* Eugene, OR: Cascade, 2010. **Hertzberg, H. W.** *Die Bücher Josua, Richter, Ruth.* ATD 9. Göttingen: Vandenhoeck & Ruprecht, 1953. **Hess, R. S.** *Joshua.* TOTC. Downers Grove, IL: InterVarsity Press, 1996. **Holzinger, H.** *Das Buch Josua.* KHC 6. Tübingen: Mohr (Siebeck), 1901. **Hoppe, L.** *Joshua, Judges.* Old Testament Message 5. Wilmington, DE: Glazier, 1982. **Howard, D. M., Jr.** *Joshua.* NAC. Nashville: Broadman & Holman, 1998. **Hubbard, R. L., Jr.** *Joshua.* NIVAC. Grand Rapids: Zondervan, 2009. **Hummelauer, E. V.** *Commentarius in librum Iosue.* Cursus Scripturae Sacrae. Paris: Lethielleux, 1903. **Keil, C. F.** *Joshua, Judges, Ruth.* Trans. J. Martin. Edinburgh: T&T Clark, 1868. Originally published as *Josua, Richter und Ruth,* vol. 1 of *Biblischer Commentar über die prophetischen Geschichtsbücher des Alten Testaments* (Leipzig: Düorffling und Franke, 1863). **Knauf, E. A.** *Josua.* ZBK AT 6. Zürich: Theologische Verlag Zürich, 2008. **Knobel, A.** *Die Bücher Numeri, Deuteronomium, und Josua.* Kurzgefasstes exegetisches Handbuch zum Alten Testament 13. Leipzig: Hirzel, 1861. **Koorevaar, H. J.** *De opbouw van het Boek Jozua.* Dissertation, Brussels/Heverlee, 1990. **Kroeze, J. H.** *Het Boek Jozua.* Commentaar op het Oude Testament. Kampen: Kok, 1968. **Madvig, D. H.** "Joshua." In *Deuteronomy, Joshua, Judges, Ruth, 1 and 2 Samuel.* Ed. F. E. Gaebelein. EBC 3. Grand Rapids: Zondervan, 1992. 239–371. **Masius, A.** *Iosuae imperatoris historia illustrata atq. explicata.* Antwerp: Plantinus, 1574. **McConville, J. G.** "Joshua." In *Oxford Bible Commentary.* Ed. J. Barton and J. Muddiman. Oxford: Oxford UP, 2001. 158–76. **McConville, J. G., and S. W. Williams.** *Joshua.* Two Horizons Old Testament Commentary. Grand Rapids: Eerdmans, 2010. **Miller, J. M., and G. Tucker.** *The Book of Joshua.* CBC. Cambridge: Cambridge UP, 1974. **Nelson, R. D.** *Joshua: A Commentary.* OTL. Louisville: Westminster John Knox, 1997. **Noth, M.** *Das Buch Josua.* 2nd ed. HAT 1.7. Tübingen: Mohr (Siebeck), 1953. **Nötscher, F.** *Josua, das Buch der Richter.* EB 3. Würzburg: Echter, 1950. **Oenig, S. B.,** ed. *The Book of Joshua: A New English Translation of the Text and Rashi with a Commentary Digest.* New York: Judaica, 1969. **Oettli, S.** *Das Deuteronomium und die Bücher Josua und Richter mit einer Karte Palästinas.* Kurzgefaßter Kommentar zu den heiligen Schriften Alten und Neuen Testamentes sowie den Apokryphen. Munich, 1893. **Ottosson, M.** *Josuaboken: En programskrift för davidisk restauration.* Studia Biblical Upsaliensia 1. Uppsala: Amqvist & Wiksell, 1991. **Pitkänen, P. M. A.** *Joshua.* Apollos Old Testament Commentary 6. Downers Grove, IL: InterVarsity

Press, 2010. **Pressler, C.** *Joshua, Judges, and Ruth.* Westminster Bible Companion. Louisville: John Knox, 2002. **Robinson, H. W.,** ed. *Deutronomy and Joshua.* Century Bible. Edinburgh: Jack, 1907. **Roussel, L.** *Le livre de Josué, premiére partie: L'invasion (chapitre 1–12): Texte, traduction, commentaire.* Publications de la Faculté des Lettres de l'université de Montpellier 8. Nimes: Barnier, 1955. **Schulz, A.** *Das Buch Josue.* Bonn: Hanstein, 1924. **Sicre, J. L.** *Josué: Historia.* Nueva Biblia Española. Estella: Verbo Divino, 2002. **Soggin, J. A.** *Le Livre de Josué.* CAT 5a. Neuchatel: Delachaux et Niestlé, 1970. Translated as *Joshua,* trans. R. A. Wilson, OTL (Philadelphia: Westminster Press, 1972). **Spronk, K.** *Jozua: Een praktische bijbelverklaring.* Tekst en Toelichting. Kampen: Kok, 1994. **Steuernagel, H.** *Das Deuteronomium: Das Buch Josua.* HKAT 1.3. Göttingen: Vandenhoeck & Ruprecht, 1900. **Wesley, J.** *John Wesley's Commentary on the Bible.* Ed. G. R. Schoenhals. Grand Rapids: Asbury, 1990. **Woudstra, M.** *The Book of Joshua.* NICOT. Grand Rapids: Eerdmans, 1981. **Younger, K. L., Jr.** "Joshua." In *Eerdmans Commentary on the Bible.* Ed. J. W. Rogerson and J. D. G. Dunn. Grand Rapids: Eerdmans, 2003. 174–89.

Introduction

I. Texts and Versions

Bibliography: Texts of Joshua

Abegg, M., Jr., P. Flint, and E. Ulrich. *The Dead Sea Scrolls Bible.* San Francisco: Harper San Francisco, 1999. 201–7. **Auld, A. G.** *Joshua: Jesus Son of Nauē in Codex Vaticanus.* Septuagint Commentary Series. Leiden: Brill, 2005. **Ben-Hayyim, Z.** "A Samaritan Text of the Former Prophet?" *Leš* 35 (1971) 292–302 (Heb.). **Bennett, W. H.** *The Book of Joshua: Critical Edition of the Hebrew Text Printed in Colours Exhibiting the Composite Structure of the Book with Notes.* SBOT 6.1–2. Leipzig, 1895. **Billen, A. V.** *The Old Latin Texts of the Heptateuch.* Cambridge: Cambridge UP, 1927. **Brooke, A. E., and N. McLean,** eds. *The Old Testament in Greek, according to the text of Codex Vaticanus.* Vol. 1, part 4, *Joshua, Judges and Ruth.* Cambridge: Cambridge UP, 1917. **Charlesworth, J.** "XJoshua." In *Miscellaneous Texts from the Judean Desert.* Ed. J. Charlesworth et al. DJD 38. Oxford: UP, 2000. 231–39. **Crane, O. T.** *The Samaritan Chronicle of the Book of Joshua.* New York, 1890. **Elliger, K., and W. Rudolph.** *Biblia Hebraica Stuttgartensia.* Stuttgart: Deutsche Bibelstiftung, 1976–1977. **Erbes, J.,** ed. *The Old Testament in Syriac according to the Peshitta Version Edited on behalf of the International Organization for the Study of the Old Testament by the Peshitta Institute Leiden.* Part 2, fascicle b. Leiden, 1991. ———. *The Peshitta and the Versions: A Study of the Peshitta Variants in Joshua 1–5 in relation to Their Equivalents in the Ancient Versions.* AUU. Studia Semitica Upsaliensia 16. Uppsala, 1999. **Field, F.** *Origenis Hexaplorum.* Vol. 1, *Prolegomena Genesis-Esther.* 1875. Repr., Hildesheim: Olms, 1964. **Gaster, M.** "Das Buch Josua in hebräisch-samaritanischen Rezension: Entdeckt und zum ersten Male herausgegeben." *ZDMG* 62 (1908) 209–79, 494–549. **Greenspoon, L. J.** "The Qumran Fragments of Joshua: Which Puzzle Are They Part of and Where Do They Fit?" In *Septuagint, Scrolls, and Cognate Writings: Papers Presented to the International Symposium on the Septuagint and Its Relations to the Dead Sea Scrolls and Other Writings, Manchester, 1990.* Ed. G. J. Brooke and B. Lindars. SBLSCS 33. Atlanta: Scholars Press, 1992. 159–94. **Holmes, S.** *Joshua, the Hebrew and Greek Texts.* Cambridge: Cambridge UP, 1914. **Kasser, R.,** ed. *Papyrus Bodmer XXI: Josué VI, 16–25, VII, 6–XI, 23, XII, 1–2,19–XIII,7, 15–XXIV,23.* Bibliotheca Bodmeriana. Cologne, 1965. **Kenyon, F. G.,** ed. *The Codex Alexandrinus in Reduced Photographic Facsimile.* Old Testament Part 1: *Genesis-Ruth.* London: British Museum, 1915. **Kittel, R.** *Biblia Hebraica.* Stuttgart: Württembergische Bibelanstalt, 1937. **Macdonald, J.** *The Samaritan Chronicle No. II; or, Sepher Ha-Yamim: From Joshua to Nebuchadnezzar.* BZAW 107. Berlin: De Gruyter, 1969. **Mager, H.** *Die Peschittho zum Buche Josua.* Freiburger Theologische Studien 9. Freiburg im Breisgau, 1916. **Margolis, M. L.** "Additions to Field from the Lyons Codex of the Old Latin." *JAOS* 33 (1913) 254–58. ———. *The Book of Joshua in Greek: According to the Critically Restored Text with an Apparatus Containing the Variants of the Principal Recensions and of the Individual Witnesses.* Part 5, *Joshua 19:39–24:33.* Publications of the Alexander Kohut Memorial Foundation. Paris: Librairie Orientaliste Paul Geuthner, 1931–38. Repr., Monograph Series. Philadelphia: Annenberg Research Institute, 1992. ———. "Corrections in the Apparatus of the Book of Joshua in the Larger Cambridge Septuagint." *JBL* 49 (1930) 234–64. ———. "The Grouping of the Codices in the Greek Joshua: A Preliminary Notice." *JQR* NS (1910–1911) 259–63. ———. "The K Text of Joshua." *AJSL* 28 (1911) 1–55. ———. "Specimen of a New Edition of the Greek Joshua." In *Jewish Studies in Memory of Israel Abrahams.* New York, 1927. 307–23. ———.

"The Washington MS of Joshua." *JAOS* 31 (1911) 365–67. **Rahlfs, A.** *Septuaginta.* Vol. 1, *Leges et historiae.* Stuttgart: Württembergische Bibelanstalt, 1935. **Rossi, J. B. de.** *Variae Lectiones Veteris Testamenti Librorum: Ex immensa manuscriptorum editorumque codicum congerie haustae et ad samaritanum textum, ad vetustissimas versiones, ad accuratiores sacrae criticae fontes ac leges examinatae.* Vol. 2, *Libri Numeri, Deuteronomium, Josue, Judices, Samuel, Reges.* Parmae, 1784–1798. **Shore, A. F.,** ed. *Joshua i–vi and Other Passages in Sahidic, Edited from a Fourth-Century Sahidic Codex in the Chester Beatty Library.* Chester Beatty Monographs 9. Dublin, 1963. **Sperber, A.** *The Bible in Aramaic.* Vol. 2, *The Former Prophets according to Targum Jonathan.* Leiden: Brill, 1959. **Talmon, S.** "Fragments of a Joshua Apocryphon: Masada 1039–1211." *JJS* 47 (1996) 128–39. **Ulrich, E.** "4QJoshua[a] and Joshua's First Altar in the Promised Land." In *New Qumran Text and Studies.* Ed. G. J. Brooke with F. G. Martinez. STDJ 15. Leiden: Brill, 1994. 89–104. **Ulrich, E., and E. Tov.** "Joshua." In *Qumran Cave 4. IX: Deuteronomy, Joshua, Judges, Kings.* DJD 14. Oxford: Clarendon, 1995. **Weber, R., et al.** *Biblia Sacra Iuxta Vulgatam Versionera.* Stuttgart: Württembergische Bibelanstalt, 1969. **Weber, R.,** ed. *Biblia Sacraiusta Vulgatam Versionem.* 3rd ed. Stuttgart, 1983.

Bibliography: Studies of the Text of Joshua

Arichea, B. C., Jr. "Restructuring: Some Examples from Joshua." *BT* 29 (1978) 438–43. **Auld, A. G.** "Joshua and 1 Chronicles." In *Studies in Historical Geography and Biblical Historiography Presented to Zechariah Kallai.* Ed. Z. Kallai and Moshe Weinfeld. VTSup. Leiden: Brill, 2000. 132–40. ———. *Joshua Retold: Synoptic Perspectives.* Edinburgh: T&T Clark, 1998. ———. "Joshua: the Hebrew and Greek Texts." In *Studies in the Historical Books of the Old Testament.* Ed. J. A. Emerton. VTSup 30. Leiden: Brill, 1979. 1–14. ———. "A Judean Sanctuary of Anat (Josh. 15:5)?" *TA* 4 (1977) 85–86. ———. "Judges 1 and History: A Reconsideration." *VT* 25 (1975) 261–85. ———. "The 'Levitical Cities': Texts and History." *ZAW* 91 (1979) 194–206. ———. "Reading Joshua after Kings." In *Words Remembered, Texts Renewed: Essays in Honour of John A. F. Sawyer.* Ed. J. Davies, G. Harvey, and W. G. E. Watson. JSOTSup 195. Sheffield: JSOT Press, 1995. 167–81. ———. *Studies in Joshua: Text and Literary Relationships.* Dissertation, University of Edinburgh, 1976. ———. "Textual and Literary Studies in the Book of Joshua." *ZAW* 90 (1978) 412–417. **Barthélemy, D.** *Critique Textuelle de l'Ancien Testament.* Vol. 1, *Josué, Juges, Ruth, Samuel, Rois, Chroniques, Esdras, Néhémie, Esther.* OBO 50. Göttingen: Vandenhoeck & Ruprecht, 1982. ———. *Les Devanciers d'Aquila.* VTSup 10. Leiden: Brill, 1963. ———. "Post-Scriptum: The 'Lucianic Recension.'" In *1972 Proceedings IOSCS Pseudepigrapha.* SBLSCS 2. Atlanta: Society of Biblical Literature, 1972. 64–89. **Benjamin, C. D.** *The Variations between the Hebrew and Greek Texts of Joshua: Chapters 1–12.* Thesis, University of Pennsylvania. Leipzig: W. Drugulin, 1921. **Bieberstein, K.** *Josua, Jordan, Jericho: Archäologie, Geschichte und Theologie der Landnahmeerzählung Josua 1–6.* OBO 143. Göttingen: Vandenhoeck & Ruprecht, 1995. ———. *Lukan und Theodotion im Josuabuch, mit einem Beitrag zu den Josuarollen von Khirbet Qumran.* Biblische Notizen Beiheft 7. Munich: Kaiser, 1994. **Billen, A. V.** "The Classification of the Greek MSS of the Hexateuch." *JTS* 26 (1925) 262–77. **Bodine, W. R.** *The Greek Text of Judges: Recensional Developments.* HSM 23. Chico, CA: Scholars Press, 1980. ———. "*Kaige* and Other Recensional Developments in the Greek Text of Judges." *BIOSCS* 13 (1980) 45–57. **Böhlig, A.** "Zur Anlage Koptischer Textausgaben (Jos: P. Bodmer XXI)." *MDAI* 21 (1966) 188–200. **Boling, R. G.** "Some Conflate Readings in Joshua-Judges." *VT* 16 (1966) 293–98. **Bratcher, R. G., and B. M. Newman.** *A Translator's Handbook on the Book of Joshua.* Helps for Translators. New York: United Bible Societies, 1983. **Bundy, D.** "The Peshitta and the Versions: A Study of the Peshitta Variants in Joshua 1–5 in relation to Their Equivalents in the Ancient Versions." *CBQ* 63 (2001) 106–7. **Burgmann, H.** *Der "Sitz im Leben" in den Josuafluch-Texten, in 4Q379 22 ii und 4Qtestimonia.* Mogilanensia 1. Krakow/Offenburg, 1990. **Ceriani, A. M.,** ed. *Pentateuchi et Josue quae ex prima Scriptura supersunt in codice Ambrosiano Graeco seculi fere V.* MSP 3. Milan, 1864. **Chesman, E. A.** "Sudies in the Septuagint Text of the Book of Joshua." Master's thesis, New York, Hebrew Union College, 1967. **Crown, A. D.** "The Date and Authenticity of the Samaritan Hebrew Book of Joshua as Seen in the Territorial Allotments." *PEQ* 96 (1964) 79–100. ———. "Some Traces of Heterodox Theology in the Samaritan Book of Joshua." *BJRL* 50 (1967–1968) 178–98. **Gottstein, M. H.** "Neue Syrohexaplafragmente." *Bib* 37 (1956) 162–83. **Greenspoon, L. J.** "The Book of Joshua—Part 1: Texts and Versions." *CurBS* 3 (2005) 229–61. ———. "The Qumran Fragments of Joshua: Which Puzzle Are They Part of and Where Do They Fit." In *Septuagint, Scrolls and Cognate Writings: Papers Presented to the International Symposium on the Septuagint and Its Relations to the Dead Sea Scrolls and Other Writings (Manchester, 1990).* Ed. G. J. Brooke and B. Lindars. SBLSCS 53. Atlanta: Scholars Press, 1992. 159–204. ———. *Textual Studies in the Book of Joshua.* HSM 28. Chico, CA: Scholars Press, 1983. ———. "Theodotion, Aquila, Symmachus, and the Old Greek of Joshua." Paper read to the one hundred fifteenth annual meeting of the Society of Biblical Literature in New York, November 15, 1979. **Hertog, C. G. den.** *Studien zur griechischen Übersetzung des Buches Josua.* Dissertation. Giessen, 1996. **Hollenberg, J.** "Der Charakter der alexandrinischen Übersetzung des Buches Josua und ihr textkritischer Werth. Moers, 1876: Zur Textkritik des Buches Josua und des Buches der Richter." *ZAW* 1 (1881) 97–105. **Lohfink, N.** "Textkritisches zu *jrš* im Alten Testament." In *Mélanges Dominique Barthélemy: Études bibliques offertes à l'occasion de son 60e anniversaire.* Ed. P. Casetti, O. Keel, and A. Schenker. OBO 38. Göttingen: Vandenhoeck & Ruprecht, 1981. 273–88. **Lucassen, B.** "Josua, Richter und CD." *RevQ* 18 (1998) 373–96. ———. "Possibility and Probability of Textual Reconstruction: The Transition from 4QJosh[b], frg. 2 to frg. 3 and the Transit of the Israelites through the Jordan." *Textus* 20 (2000) 71–81. **Margolis, M. L.** *The Book of Joshua in Greek, according to the Critically Restored Text.* Paris: Geuthner, 1931–1938. ———. "Corrections in the Apparatus of the Book of Joshua in the Larger Cambridge Septuagint." *JBL* 49 (1930) 234–64. ———. "The Groupings of the Codices in the Greek Joshua." *JQR* NS 1 (1910) 259–63. ———. "The K Text of Joshua." *AJSL* 28 (1911) 1–55. ———. "Specimen of a New Edition of the Greek Joshua." In *Jewish Studies in Memory of Israel Abrahams.* New York, 1927. 307–23. ———. "The Washington ms of Joshua." *JAOS* 31 (1911) 365–67. **Mazor, L.** "The Origin and Evolution of the Curse upon the Rebuilder of Jericho—A Contribution of Textual Criticism to Biblical Historiography." *Textus* 16 (1988) 1–26. ———. "The Septuagint Translation of the Book of Joshua." *BIOSCS* 27 (1994) 29–38. ———. "The Septuagint Translation of the Book of Joshua—Its Contribution to the Understanding of the Textual Transmission of the Book and Its Literary and Ideological Development" (Heb.). Dissertation, Hebrew University, Jerusalem, 1994. **Meer, M. N. van der.** *Formation and Reformulation: The Redaction of the Book of Joshua in the Light of the Oldest Textual Witnesses.* VTSup 102. Leiden: Brill, 2004. **Moatti-Fine, J.** *Jésus (Josué): Traduction du texte grec de la Septante, Introduction et notes.* La Bible d'Alexandrie 6. Paris: Cerf, 1996. ———. "La 'Tâche du Traducteur' de Josué/Jésus." In *Selon les Septante: Homage à Marguerite Harl.* Ed. G. Dorival and O. Munnich. Paris: Cerf, 1995. **Noort, E.** "4QJosh[a] and the History of Tradition in the Book of Joshua." *JNSL* 24 (1998) 127–44. ———. *Das Buch Josua: Forschungsgeschichte und Problemfelder.* EdF 292. Darmstadt: Wissenschaftliche Buchgesellschaft, 1998. **Orlinsky, H.** "The Hebrew *Vorlage* of the Septuagint of the Book of Joshua." In *Rome Congress Volume 1969.* VTSup 17. Leiden: Brill, 1969. 187–95. *Preliminary and Interim Report on the Hebrew Old Testament Text Project.* Vol. 2, *Historical Books.* Stuttgart: United Bible Societies, 1976. **Pretzl, O.** "Die griechischen Handschriftengruppen im Buche Josue untersucht nach ihrer Eigenart und ihrem Verhältnis zueinander." *Bib* 9 (1928) 377–427. ———. "Der Hexaplarische und tetraplarische Septuagintatext des Origenes in den Büchern Josua und Richter." *ByzZ* 30 (1929–1930) 262–68. **Rahlfs, A.,** ed. *Septuaginta: Id est Vetus Testamentum graece iuxta LXX interpretes.* Stuttgart: Württembergische Bibelanstalt, 1962. **Robert, U.** *Heptateuchi partis posterioris versio latina antiquissima e codice Lugdunensi: Version latine du Deutéronome, de Josué et des Juges antérieure à saint Jérôme publiée d'aprés le manuscrit de Lyon avec un facsimile, des observations paleographiques et philogique sur l'origine et la valeur de ce texte.* Lyon, 1900. **Rofé, A.** "The Editing of the Book of Joshua in the Light of 4QJosh[a]." In *New Qumran Texts and Studies*. Ed. G. Brooke and F. Martínez. STDJ 15. Leiden: Brill, 1994. 73–80. ———. "The End of the Book of Joshua according to the Septuagint." *Shnaton* 2 (1977) 217–27 (Heb.). ———. "The End of the Book of Joshua according to the Septuagint." *Hen* 4 (1982) 17–36. **Rösel, M.** "Die Septuagint-Version des Josua-Buches." In *Im Brennpunkt: Die Septuaginta. Studien zur Enstehung der Griechischen Bibel*. Ed. H.-J. Fabry and U. Offerhaus. BWANT 153. Stuttgart: Kohlhammer, 2001. 197–211 = "The Septuagint Version of the Book of Joshua." *SJOT* 16 (2002) 5–23. **Sipilä, S.** *Between Literalness and Freedom: Translation Technique in the Septuagint of Joshua and Judges regarding the Clause Connections Introduced by* w *and* yk. Publications of the Finnish Exegetical Society 75. Helsinki: Finnish Exegetical Society, 1999. ———. "John Chrysostom and the Book of Joshua." In *IX Congress of the International Organization for Septuagint and Cognate Studies, Cambridge, 1995*. Ed. B. A. Taylor. Atlanta: Scholars Press, 1997. 329–54. ———. "Max Leoppold Margolis and Origenic Recension in Joshua." In *Origen's Hexapla and Fragments: Papers Presented at the Rich Seminar on the Hexapla, Oxford Centre for Hebrew and Jewish Studies, 25th July–3rd August 1994*. Ed. A. Salvesen. Tübingen: Mohr Siebeck, 1998. 16–38. ———. "The Renderings of *yhyw* and *hyhw* as Formulas in the LXX of Joshua. In *VIII Congress of the International Organization for Septuagint and Cognate Studies Paris 1992*. Ed. L. Greenspoon and O. Munnich. SBLSCS 41. Atlanta: Scholars Press, 1995. 273–89. ———. "The Septuagint Version of Joshua 3–4." In *VII Congress of the International Organization for Septuagint and Cognate Studies. Leuven 1989*. Ed. C. E. Cox. SBLSCS 31. Atlanta: Scholars Press, 1991. 63–74. **Skeat, T.** "Sinaiticus, Vaticanus, and Constantine." *JTS* NS 50 (1999) 583–625. **Smith, G. V.** "An Introduction to the Greek Manuscripts of Joshua: Their Classification, Characteristics and Relationships." Dissertation, Philadelphia, Dropsie University, 1973. **Stipp, H.-J.** "Das Verhältnis von Textkritik und Literarkritik in neueren alttestamentlichen Veröffentlichungen." *BZ* NF 34 (1990) 16–37. **Tov, E.** "4QJosh[b]." In *Intertestamental Essays in Honour of Józef Tadeusz Milik*. Qumranica Mogilanensia 6. Kraków, 1992. 205–12. ———. *The Greek and Hebrew Bible: Collected Essays on the Septuagint*. VTSup 72. Leiden: Brill, 1999. ———. "The Growth of the Book of Joshua in the Light of the Evidence of the LXX Translation." In *Studies in the Bible*. Ed. S. Japhet. ScrHier 31. Jerusalem: Magnes, 1986. 321–39. ———. "Midrash-type Exegesis in the LXX of Joshua." *RB* 95 (1978) 50–61. ———. "The Rewritten Book of Joshua as Found at Qumran and Masada." In *Biblical Perspectives: Early Use and Interpretation of the Bible in Light of the Dead Sea Scrolls. Proceedings of the First International Symposium of the Orion Center for the Study of the Dead Sea Scrolls and Associated Literature. 12–14 May, 1996*. Ed. M. Stone and E. G. Chazon. STDJ 27. Leiden: Brill, 1998. 233–56. ———. "Some Sequence Differences between the MT and LXX and Their Ramifications for the Literary Criticism of the Bible." *JNSL* 13 (1987) 151–60. ———. *The Text-critical Use of the Septuagint in Biblical Research*. 2nd ed. Jerusalem, 1997. ———. *Textual Criticism of the Hebrew Bible*. 2nd ed. Minneapolis: Fortress, 2001. **Troyer, K. de.** "Reconstructing the OG of Joshua." Paper Delivered to 2007 SBL group. ———. *Rewriting the Sacred Text: What the Old Greek Texts Tell Us about the Literary Growth of the Bible*. Atlanta: SBL, 2003. **Winther-Nielsen, N.** *A Functional Discourse Grammar of Joshua: A Computer-Assisted Rhetorical Structure Analysis*. ConBOT 40. Stockholm: Almquist & Wiksell, 1995.

A. *The Text of the Book of Joshua*

The first step in the interpretation of the book of Joshua is to determine the basic text. This is necessary because virtually every verse of Joshua shows textual distinctions between the Hebrew or Masoretic Text (MT) and the earliest translation, the Greek Septuagint (LXX). The Hebrew text contains elements not attested in the Greek (Josh 6:3b–7:4; 8:11b–13, 26; 20:4–6). The reverse is also true. Greek elements are not present in the Hebrew (Josh 6:26; 16:10; 24:31, 33). Michaël van der Meer points out that Josh 5:2–9 has dramatically different readings and interpretations.[7] The Septuagint places Josh 8:30–35 after 9:2, while the Dead Sea Scroll manuscripts indicate that this section appears before 5:2. Overall, LXX is about 5 percent shorter than MT and in some places up to 20 percent shorter, with both texts receiving further editorial changes after their paths separated.[8] The indecision as to the priority of one tradition over the other remains unclear even after the Qumran evidence is considered.[9] Modern research thus puts the MT in the center of study, knowing it is also a part of the history of interpretation.[10]

Such obvious evidence forces the commentator to take a close look at the different readings and attempt to understand what processes were at work in the scribal and liturgical worlds that resulted in the differing textual readings. Van der Meer concludes from this evidence alone that "there is every reason to assume that the divergencies between the oldest textual witnesses of this biblical composition, LXX-Joshua, 4QJosh[a], and MT-Joshua, are the result of editorial activity."[11]

Since the first edition of this commentary, much work has been done in providing critical texts with which to work and in analyzing the textual history of Joshua. Van der Meer provides a strong introduction to the history of textual criticism of Joshua.[12] Klaus Bieberstein[13] defines the work of the text critic as beginning with the available multitude of text forms and asking about changes that are witnessed by different types of readings. He notes that the divergences among the available text forms have usually rested on textual changes that are relatively late in origin. Bieberstein finds that one cannot establish the "original text" because the texts of the Old Testament were constantly moving or changing. One seeks only to find the text that witnesses a stage in the ongoing development on which other readings can be based.[14] He decides the Greek translator has deliberately rewritten the text in a comprehensive manner, seeking to provide a more coherent and fluid narrative and to enhance the role of the priests.[15]

Van der Meer[16] summarizes and analyzes the Hebrew work of Mazor. Mazor finds differences in MT and LXX in "scope, order, and content."[17] Mazor attributes most of the differences between MT and LXX to the Hebrew *Vorlage* behind the LXX. The Greek translator did enrich the monotonous and repetitive Hebrew vocabulary and at times offered paraphrastic interpretations to avoid incomprehensible or stylistically unsatisfactory Greek. Mazor sees separate recensions in the MT and the Hebrew behind the LXX. Some changes were made to give the book more coherence; others came from ideological purposes. The latter resulted from theology, cult, law, territory, and national history concerns. The simple concluson for Mazor is that LXX and MT "represent two separate recensions of the book of Joshua."[18] "LXX and MT share a common source from which both eventually

---

7   *Formation and Reformulation*, 17.
8   E. Noort, *Das Buch Josua: Forschungsgeschichte und Problemfelder*, EdF 292 (Darmstadt: Wissenschaftliche Buchgesellschaft, 1998) 47.
9   Ibid., 57.
10 Ibid., 59.
11 *Formation and Reformulation*, 17.
12 Ibid., 1–114.
13 *Josua, Jordan, Jericho*, 73.
14 Ibid., 72.
15 Ibid., 230.
16 *Formation and Reformulation*, 65–78.
17 *BIOSCS* 27 (1994) 29.
18 Ibid., 36.

diverged and developed independently."[19] Van der Meer then points to quantative changes in LXX that lead to the conclusion that "they must be the result of deliberate literary initiatives," which he attributes to the Greek translator.[20]

The present work can only hope to show the necessity of the goal and the nature of the textual process. The work, like all current work on Joshua, is based on the Leningrad Codex B19A.[21] The manuscript itself dates from 1008 CE. I have limited my text-critical work to a rather thorough comparison of the Hebrew text with the earliest Greek translation, dating back to about the second century BCE but preserved only in manuscripts dating from the fourth century.[22]

Among the Dead Sea Scrolls, three manuscripts contain fragments of Joshua. 4QJosh[a], dated after 150 BCE, has twenty-two fragments and includes parts of Josh 5:2–7; 6:5–10; 7:12–17; 8:3–14; 8:34–35; and 10:2–5, 8–11 plus an additon to chap. 5 unknown in other witnesses. Ulrich understands the scroll as a unique composition, "disagreeing with both MT and Greek in significant readings."[23] Bieberstein states that 4QJosh[a] agrees more with MT than with LXX but must be reckoned as an independent third form of the text.[24] Van der Meer emphasizes the agreements of these fragments with MT over against LXX.[25]

Particularly significant is the scroll's apparent placing of MT Josh 8:34–35 in chap. 5. Ulrich sees the sequence in 4QJosh[a] to be "simple and unproblematic, since one would expect from Deut 27:1–3 that the altar would be built at Gilgal."[26] Ulrich also points to evidence from Josephus to support the originality and logic of the Qumran text.

4QJosh[b] consists of six fragments, dates about 50 BCE, and contains parts of Josh 2:11–12; 3:15–4:3; and 17:1–5, 11–15. It is closely connected to MT, according to Tov,[27] but it has several unique readings. Thus Richard Hess sides with Greenspoon: "The scribe(s) responsible for these scrolls were not reluctant to incorporate material of their own creation, material I judge to be 'in the spirit' of the MT."[28]

Van der Meer[29] summarizes the readings of the scrolls as well as XJoshua purchased by M. Schøyen without certainty as to its original location. XJoshua is about 446 words in length, representing Josh 1:9–12 and 2:4–15. It dates to the first century CE.[30] XJoshua has no significant differences from the MT, which it supports over against LXX.

Bieberstein discusses quotations from Joshua in nonbiblical Qumran texts.[31]

---

19 Ibid., 38. Moatti-Fine presents a French translation of the LXX of Joshua and shows a lexical richness and innovativeness in comparison with the LXX Pentateuch (*Jésus [Josué]: Traduction du texte grec de la Septante, Introduction et notes*).

20 *Formation and Reformulation*, 161.

21 Published in the critical edition *Biblia Hebraica Stuttgartensia*, edited by R. Meyer (1972).

22 *Septuaginta*, ed. A. Rahlfs (1935). I have also noted the data from the Dead Sea Scrolls as shown by Abegg, Flint, and Ulrich, *Dead Sea Scrolls Bible*, and by Ulrich and Tov in *Qumran Cave 4. IX: Deuteronomy, Joshua, Judges, Kings*, DJD 14.

23 *Qumran Cave 4*, 145.

24 *Josua, Jordan, Jericho*, 76.

25 *Formation and Reformulation*, 96.

26 *Qumran Cave 4*, 145–46.

27 Ibid., 154; see also Bieberstein, *Josua, Jordan, Jericho*, 77.

28 Hess, *Joshua* (1996), 19; see Greenspoon, "Qumran Fragments of Joshua," 175.

29 *Formation and Reformulation*, 93–113. See Charlesworth, "XJoshua."

30 Van der Meer, 104.

31 *Josua, Jordan, Jericho*, 74–75.

He claims that these texts, written in Hebrew, show that the book of Joshua in the Hasmonean/Herodian period was in circulation in a form quite distinct from the later Masoretic text. These texts stand closer to the shorter Septuagint and may be valued as the source for their translation.

The comparison leads to several interesting conclusions. The Greek shows numerous divergences from the Hebrew text in every chapter, at times in every verse of a chapter. Many of the divergences can be explained as simple mechanical errors that occur when a text is copied by hand. The majority of the differences cannot, however, be explained in this manner. A few of the changes result from translators who did not understand the precise nuance of Hebrew words, forms, or syntax. A greater number of the differences rest on attempts of the Greek translator to improve the style or continuity of the narrative itself. Here it becomes clear that the earliest translator did not feel himself obliged to reproduce an original text word for word.

Critical evaluation of such changes leads a step further. The changes are not limited to the Greek translator. Indeed, at points the Greek translation represents a better-preserved text than our Hebrew manuscripts. Schäfer-Lichtenberger concludes that the LXX translator had a Hebrew text that differed in many points from MT.[32] Van der Meer shows in his incisive study of Josh 1, 5, and 8 that much of the material in LXX results from the translator's creativity in producing a literary work in Greek rather than a weak direct reproduction of Hebrew syntax and word order. He specifically demonstrates that LXX does not use the same word or series of words to reproduce standard Hebrew phrases. Thus van der Meer speaks of "different editions of the same composition."[33]

Comparison shows that the Hebrew manuscripts behind our Greek texts were different from the Hebrew manuscripts we presently possess. This means that such literary changes do not reflect simply a change caused by going from one language and culture to another. Such changes were already occurring in the transmission of the Hebrew text. The discovery of the Dead Sea Scrolls has proved this point beyond a shadow of a doubt. Tov, one of the leading text critics of our generation, reminds would-be text critics of the close relationship between literary growth and textual transmission; he concludes, "If such readings belong to the area of the literary growth, textual evaluation should be avoided, but if they were created in the course of the scribal transmission, evaluation is essential."[34] He thus sees at least two with 4QJosh[a], possibly bringing the total to three literary strata in Joshua with the OG representing the earliest stratum.[35]

Recent work by Auld, Mazor, Rofé, and Tov, among others, has built on Holmes and swayed current discussions in favor of the shorter (by about 5%) LXX over against the MT. Seeing the Hebraistic diction of the LXX pluses, Tov concludes "it is not feasible for one translator to have faithfully rendered the text and at the same time omit significant elements. Moreover, no principle can be recognized for

---

32   Schäfer-Lichtenberger, *Josua und Salomo: Eine Studie zu Autorität und Legitimität des Nachfolgers im Alten Testament*, VTSup 58 (Leiden: Brill, 1995) 192.

33   *Formation and Reformulation*, 9.

34   *Textual Criticism of the Hebrew Bible*, 350.

35   Ibid., 327.

a supposed shortening by the translator."[36] Tov provides over five pages of examples of the superior text in the LXX. He then provides one page of illustrations of LXX pluses that do not belong to the original text.

K. Lawson Younger sides with Orlinksy "that the differences between the OG and the preserved Hebrew are due to the fact that behind the OG of Joshua lay a different Hebrew *Vorlage* from that of the preserved Hebrew and that the difference between these two texts are such that a third text must be assumed."[37] The emphasis on the reliablity of LXX and of early sources for its translators is commendable and needed; however, an ecclectic approach is still necessary, judging each incident on its own text-critical merits without imposing preconceived expectations on the text and without creating rules such as "the shorter text is to be preferred" and then following that rule without exception.

A frequent cause of distinction between the two text forms comes in the use of idiomatic phrases, particularly those that appear in variant forms. Thus at Josh 1:11 the Hebrew speaks of "Yahweh your God," while the Greek reads "Yahweh, the God of your fathers." Similarly, titles such as "servant of Yahweh" are often used at different places by the traditions, without a pattern being visible in either (e.g. 1:1, 15).

The most interesting changes are those with practical and theological relevance to the communities for which the Bible was preserved and translated. Here we see the copyists often bringing in material from other biblical texts or interpreting the material in a way to make it more relevant for their own times. This shows us that the Bible was not simply a book to be copied by the community. It remained a dynamic text to be preached and applied within the community. Such preaching and application were not confined to the teaching situation or the cultic worship. It took place even in the process of copying of the text. A final category that must be noted is that of obvious theological change made to avoid language that could be misinterpreted and thus dangerous for the new generation—thus the elimination of Baal in the Hebrew text of Josh 18:15. Such evidence leads Rösel to decide that "a high degree of uncertainty remains when judging about the problems of the text, whether differences have occurred in the process of the transmission of the text or whether they are a result of the rendering of one language into another."[38]

The following table seeks to summarize the most obvious changes discovered in the preparation of the commentary and to categorize them under the general classes named above. Such categorization is too simple, of course; each example is open to being placed in a different category. The purpose is to present in tabular form the quantity of the textual evidence involved and to provide a quick reference for those who would like to study further the interesting question of how the textual evidence leads to a history of the interpretation as well as the transmission of the text.

The material is arranged according to the tradition in which the textual differences appear to have arisen, either the Greek Septuagint (LXX) with the Hebrew tradition on which it is based or the Masoretic tradition (MT), which resulted in the present Hebrew text. We find complexity, not just two or three text traditions but several Hebrew and several Greek traditions.

---

36   "Growth of the Book of Joshua," 388.
37   K. Lawson Younger, 359.
38   *SJOT* 16 (2002) 9.

B. *Tendencies in Textual Transmission of Joshua*

Table 0.1. Textual Transmission in Joshua

	MT	LXX
Mechanical Errors in Copying	2:1, 3, 4; 6:13, 20; 7:17; 8:6, 13, 29, 33; 9:2, 27; 10:3, 10, 13; 11:6, 7; 12:5; 13:7–8, 9, 29–30; 14:12; 15:1, 12, 18, 23, 28, 32, 36, 47, 59; 17:7, 9, 11; 18:16, 18–19, 24, 28; 19:2, 4–5, 7, 10, 13, 14, 21, 28, 29, 34, 42, 45, 46; 21:8, 15, 16, 22, 25, 27, 31, 34, 36–37, 42; 22:7, 12, 16, 19; 23:5, 11, 12, 13; 24:6, 30, 32	1:11; 2:5, 13, 15, 21; 3:8; 6:10, 13; 7:2, 6, 17–18, 19; 8:15–16, 26, 29; 9:2, 10, 14, 18; 10:3, 10; 11:2, 4, 7, 10, 22; 12:1, 2, 3, 7, 13–14, 16, 20; 13:5, 9, 17–19, 26, 27, 29–30, 31; 14:2, 9, 15; 15:3, 5, 9–10, 14, 25, 59; 16:3; 17:7, 11; 18:4, 5, 15, 16, 18–19; 19:15, 19, 22, 29, 30, 35–36, 41, 50; 21:18, 20, 22, 29, 32, 40; 23:5, 14; 24:1, 14, 30, 33
Misunderstanding of Meanings, Forms, or Syntax	21:42	2:1, 4; 3:12; 4:3; 6:4; 7:5, 7, 21; 9:2, 7, 20; 10:25; 12:5; 13:3, 4, 9, 21, 22, 26; 14:4; 15:18; 17:14; 18:4; 19:8, 11; 21:42; 22:3, 8, 10, 14, 19, 20, 23; 23:11, 16; 24:6, 17, 20, 32
Literary Improvements	1:2; 2:4, 5, 22; 3:13; 5:9; 6:1, 2, 5, 15, 20; 7:2, 11, 15, 25–26; 8:1, 2, 9, 18, 20, 24, 28, 31, 32, 34; 9:6, 9, 12, 21; 10:1, 2, 11, 13, 15, 18, 26, 27, 28, 36, 43; 12:16, 18, 20, 23; 13:1, 10–11, 24; 15:20; 18:9; 19:1; 22:25; 24:30	1:1, 2, 4; 2:2–3, 4, 12, 13, 14, 15, 16; 3:10; 4:1–3, 5, 7, 11; 5:1, 10, 11, 14; 6:3, 12, 15, 20; 7:1, 13, 16–18; 8:1, 5, 11–14, 16, 21, 24, 32, 34, 35; 9:1, 5, 6, 9, 11, 20, 24, 25; 10:6, 11, 28, 30, 32, 33, 35, 37, 39; 11:2–3, 19; 12:4, 9, 18, 22, 24; 13:1, 2, 6, 12, 14, 16, 17, 23, 31, 33; 14:1, 4, 11, 12, 15; 15:4, 15, 18, 20; 16:1, 6–7, 10; 17:5, 14; 18:2, 6, 8, 9, 26–28; 19:8, 16, 25, 27, 31; 20:3; 22:9, 19, 22, 28, 33, 34; 23:3; 24:1, 4, 18, 19, 26, 33
Free Use of Familiar Phrases	6:1, 2; 8:7, 34; 12:6; 16:10; 17:15; 18:3, 11, 21; 19:41; 21:1, 5–6, 11, 13, 19, 20; 22:1, 4, 13, 16, 18, 29, 31–32; 23:13, 15; 24:3, 9, 17, 24	1:1, 11, 15; 2:10; 3:13; 4:8, 10; 6:17; 14:13; 18:7; 19:1, 8, 12, 16, 24, 32, 39, 40; 21:45; 22:1, 23; 23:2; 24:6, 7, 10, 11, 15, 33
Homiletic Interpretation and Exegesis	1:4, 7, 15; 2:3, 9, 14, 18; 3:1, 16; 4:3; 5:2; 6:3, 5, 8, 11, 20, 22; 7:11, 24, 25, 26; 8:1, 8, 9, 17, 18, 24, 31; 9:1, 5, 19; 10:2, 5, 13, 22–23, 24, 28, 35, 40, 41; 11:13, 14, 15; 13:1, 14, 21; 14:1–2; 15:14, 32, 36, 63; 17:2, 3, 4, 5; 18:10, 13, 28; 19:6; 20:3, 4–6, 8, 9; 21:10, 11, 21; 22:5, 30, 33; 23:5, 7, 12, 14, 16; 24:5, 8, 12, 13, 17, 22, 24, 27, 28–31, 32	1:7, 14; 2:10, 12, 15, 17, 19, 20; 3:3, 9; 4:7, 8, 10; 5:1, 4, 6; 6:3, 9, 21, 26; 7:22, 23; 8:30–35, 34, 35; 9:2, 18, 22, 23, 27; 10:1, 5, 10, 20, 21; 11:11, 19, 21, 22; 13:13, 14, 25, 26, 28; 14:2; 15:1, 5, 13, 14; 16:10; 17:6, 11, 16, 17, 18; 18:4–5, 9, 11, 17, 18, 28; 19:15, 22, 30, 38, 42–48; 20:3, 7, 9; 21:9, 12, 34–35, 42; 22:4, 8, 10, 13, 15, 19, 30, 32–34, 34; 23:4, 14; 24:1, 4, 5, 6, 13, 15, 18, 25, 27, 28–31, 30, 31, 32, 33
Avoiding Unacceptable Language	13:5; 18:15; 24:30	9:17; 10:14, 32; 17:9; 19:11; 24:10, 11, 26

Such a quantity of evidence raises problems for the biblical student. Should one work with the oldest manuscript, thus basing analysis on the Septuagint, which served as the Bible of the Christian church for much of its history? Or should one work with the text representing the language in which the book was originally written, thus choosing the Hebrew text? Or should the text critic attempt to remove the copyists' errors and work with the text that can be theoretically reconstructed as being closest to the source of the Masoretic or Septuagint tradition? Or should one be audacious enough to believe that through scholarly methods one can discover the "original" text, stripping away all of the later changes, the text's earliest interpretation and exegesis? Noort finds that a definitive decision favoring Greek or Hebrew over the other text tradition is not yet in sight.[39] The arbitrary choice here is to take the Masoretic Text, translate it and interpret it, and point out its divergences with the LXX and other transmission traditions.

II. Review of Critical Research

A. *Review of Major Modern and Postmodern Commentaries*

Carl Friedrich Keil (1863) presents a strongly conservative orientation, while thoroughly conscious of critical work up to its time. This remains the most thorough linguistic study available, without losing the theological dimension. H. Holzinger (1901) emphasizes literary source delineation. C. Steuernagel (1900) wrote the most thorough commentary early in the twentieth century with close attention to critical matters and language. Hugo Gressmann (1922) introduces form-critical methodology to Joshua with thorough analysis of strata in tradition and literary activity. Martin Noth (1938) has become the standard German commentary with detailed attention to matters of geography, literary analysis, and form criticism but little interest in theology. Félix-Marie Abel's (1950) is the standard French commentary for his generation. Hans Wilhelm Hertzberg (1953) presents more theological concern with the text than any of the other major commentaries, while still explaining the critical issues that arise. John Gray (1967) centers attention on sifting out the historical nucleus of the biblical traditions and illuminating details from the author's vast knowledge of the ancient Near East. Only brief attention is paid to theological concerns. Jan Hendrik Kroeze (1968) contributes an important commentary in Dutch. J. Alberto Soggin (1970) provides massive details on literary, geographical, archaeological, and history of tradition matters but seldom ties his information together into a theological whole. Marten H. Woudstra (1981) presents a massive contribution from the conservative side, aware of the problems raised by more critical scholars but intent on showing the reliability of the Joshua narrative, while identifying with the "German school" in the use of archaeological materials.

Commentaries and studies on Joshua appearing since my first edition of the Word Biblical Commentary on Joshua feature different methodologies, presuppositions, historical understandings, and thus exegetical and theological conclusions.

---

39 *Das Buch Josua*, 47.

The following synopsis summarizes the approach of the major commentaries and briefly states their conclusions.

Leslie Hoppe (1982), in a popular Catholic series, works from the final form of the text seen as Deuteronomic without addressing the issue of the number of Deuteronomistic editions. He maintains that the purpose of the book is to show how and why the land of promise was lost, thus attempting to shock exiled Israel to obedience. The Holy War theology within Joshua is much more ideology than history. Hoppe points out that Israel did occupy the land, partly through violence, and that "the ideology of Holy War is not any more difficult to explain than the necessity of Jesus' death. Both are attempts to describe the mysterious ways by which God uses human folly and sin as a means of salvation. . . . The wars that took place during the settlement period were evil—there is no denying that. . . . What the Bible does affirm is that God's purpose was served even by this evil."[40] "Any attempt to use this [archaeological] data to support the historicity of the Biblical narrative then is an exercise in circular reasoning."[41]

A. Graeme Auld (1984) offers a commentary in a popular format after having written a series of articles supporting the Septuagint text as closer to the original than the expansive Masoretic Text. He wants to address the texts from both the Christian and the Jewish viewpoint. He maintains that Joshua and Judges portray Israel's struggle with its Mosaic inheritance and expands the Deuteronomistic theory of Noth to include at least two Deuteronomistic editions, leading to the view that Joshua hardly represents any kind of historical records.

H. J. Koorevaar (1990) provides a new literary analysis.[42] Koorevaar sums up the message of Joshua by saying: "Because God took initiatives for the possession of the land of Canaan, the people of Israel were able to cross the Jordan and capture the land. As a result of these two initiatives Joshua was able to divide the land among the tribes of Israel on the basis of a third initiative from God. With the erection of the Tent of Meeting in Shiloh, God fulfilled his last promise, and Israel now has the task to serve Yahweh in the land and to stand fast in that service."[43]

Gordon Mitchell (1993) examines the contradictions in Joshua, especially that of the command to destroy all the foreigners through *ḥērem* (חרם) while maintaining the reality of foreigners like Rahab and the Gibeonites being incorporated into the people of Israel.[44] Mitchell follows Rolf Rendtorff in using *Kompositionsgeschicte*, joining traditional redactional criticism with structural analysis. Mitchell suggests that the literary use of ambiguity holds together unresolved tensions. The narrative moves between dream and reality for a postexilic audience that lives between disillusionment and hope. The Joshua narrative "is an attempt to reconcile the challenge of living together with others in the promised land, and the hope of their effective removal. . . . Tales set in a distant age before they have been alienated from their land and which describe the death of the kings, offer a vision of the future which makes the present bearable."[45]

---

40 Hoppe, 18.
41 Ibid., 19.
42 See R. Vannoy, "Joshua," *NIDOTTE* 4:813–14; see also Narrative Criticism below for a sketch of Koorevaar's work.
43 Koorevaar, 219.
44 *Together in the Land*, JSOTSup 134 (Sheffield: Sheffield Academic, 1993).
45 Ibid., 190.

Volkmar Fritz (1994) follows in the footsteps of Martin Noth, whose commentary he updates. He works from the model of a basic text given two extensive redactions by a Deuteronomist and a post-Priestly redactor, along with a large number of expansions from different hands. The exilic or early-Persian-period Deuteronomistic redaction shows the conquest and gift of the land as a fulfillment of Deuteronomy 12–26. The post-Priestly work comes from no earlier than the fifth century and harmonizes Joshua's cultic notations with those of the Priestly document. Later additions come from the fifth century. None of the material relies on ancient, premonarchical traditions, though the author did have some oral source materials available, but these are connected to an all-Israel conquest portrayal and so come only from the period of the later monarchy. The only historical data from these saga traditions is the name of the place, indicating where the narrative was at home. The literary picture of conquest comes from the impression left by Assyrian and Babylonian invasion campaigns. Israel originated from nomads who settled down in new villages in the hill country, the Negeb, and East Jordan.[46] Canaanites resettled cities destroyed in the twelfth century. Habiru and Shasu nomadic elements settled in Canaan in agricultural pursuits. A tribal structure marked Israel in the time before the monarchy, a structure Solomon used to create political districts.

Fritz encourages caution concerning recent claims for the originality of the Septuagint over against the Masoretic Text. He sees the literary structure as presenting a war of conquest and a peaceful gift of the land ending in Josh 19:49a, followed by Joshua's final speech in 24:1–28, with chaps. 20–23 being later insertions. The two parts are held together by a literary frame of biographical notices concerning the figure of Joshua. The picture of Joshua as the one and only leader after Moses is a creation of the Deuteronomistic Historian. The historical person is known only through his grave tradition in Josh 24:29–31. Originally, the gift of the land has no chronological limits. The Deuteronomistic redactor places demands for obedience to the holding of the land.

Richard Hess (1996) draws from "the exciting results of archaeology" to make available for the first time a "more complete understanding of how people lived, of where they lived, and of how many of them actually settled in the hill country and elsewhere" and thus to ground the book of Joshua "in the early Israelite world in a more accurate and detailed manner than was ever possible before."[47] Textually, he sees minor differences between LXX and MT that preserve "two separate editions of the text of Joshua" with "secondary elements in both texts."[48] He cautiously assigns Dead Sea Scroll materials of Joshua to a midrashic or parabiblical text.[49] The book presents Joshua as the chief character with a strong view of his appointment by God to be leader after Moses. He is the "model leader who anticipates the best kings of Judah."[50]

Many elements of the book can best be explained, according to Hess, by tracing their origins back to the second millennium. These include the border descriptions of Canaan, the spies of chap. 2; the Hivites, Perizzites, and Girgashites of Josh 3:10;

---

46   Fritz, 18.
47   Hess, 9.
48   Ibid., 18.
49   Ibid., 20.
50   Ibid., 33.

the bringing down of the walls of Jericho; the list of items Achan stole; the Gibeonites of Josh 9; the names of the defeated kings of chaps. 10 and 11; the Anakim names of Josh 15:14; and the covenant report of Josh 24:2–27.

Hess's perspective on the formation of the book begins with the presupposition of "difficulties with assumptions that deuteronomistic theology must be confined to the period of Josiah and with the analysis of the Joshua narratives divorced from their Ancient Near Eastern context."[51] For Hess, much of the conquest narratives and boundary lists can best be explained by ancient forms of conquest and treaties. Hess thus sees authenticity, cohesion, and textual and thematic unity in the book.

Theologically, Hess discusses holy war and the ban as concepts Israel shared with the other nations. Israel's distinctive thought might be that God did not approve of all wars and that mercy was extended to foreigners who joined God's covenant. The land as inheritance theme involves a constant tension between God's gift to families and Israel's challenge to occupy the land. Israel had the opportunity to use the land as part of covenant worship. But when misuse of the land signified breaking of covenant, then God's warnings came into effect. Using second-millennium covenant forms, Joshua sets "a standard of faith and unity that will seldom be attained in future generations."[52] In this "most nationalistic of books," the God of mercy and holiness finds room for foreigners within Israel and its worship.[53] The land distribution documents in chaps. 13–21 are part of the treaty tradition and show that "God uses the boundary descriptions to define the fulfilment of promises made to the nation's ancestors in the context of formal covenant ceremonies."[54]

Richard Nelson's (1997) Old Testament Library commentary on Joshua replaced that of Soggin (1972). According the Nelson, the land that remains in Josh 13:2–6 fills out the Egyptian province of Canaan. The map of Josh 1:4, taken from Deut 11:24, represents the language of royal myth as shown in Ps 72:8 and 1 Kgs 4:21 (5:1).

Theologically, says Nelson, Joshua's portraits of a Divine Warrior seem "incompatible with enlightened notions of religion."[55] Still, Joshua deals with contemporary issues: God's gift of peoplehood, responsibilities of peoplehood, kept and unfulfilled promises, and people and land.

As a literary work of theology, Joshua preserves little material useful for historical reconstruction, decides Nelson, who classifies it form critically as "historiography" and also as etiology.[56] Geographical lists and boundaries reflect the history of a much later age. Archaeology shows continuity of population rather than discontinuity, refuting the idea of infiltrators or invaders. The "emergence of Israel was an indigenous development. . . . A shared devotion to Yahweh played an important role in this process of ethnic formation."[57]

For Nelson, Josh 1:1–12:24; 21:43–22:6; 23:1–16; and 24:28–31 are part of the Deuteronomistic History, but the book has no evidence of a second Deuteronomist.

---

51   Ibid.
52   Ibid., 51.
53   Ibid., 52.
54   Ibid., 59.
55   Nelson, 2.
56   Ibid., 9, 11.
57   Ibid., 4.

The Deuteronomist found an independent collection of discontinuous stories to use in forming the history centered on the fear of the native inhabitants. The stories have an Ephraimite hero and a Benjaminite setting but a distinctly Judean outlook. Chaps. 13–21 for Nelson form a separate collection that was added later. Priestly touches appear in scattered places and especially in Josh 22:9–34. Chap. 24 is a purely literary chapter that remains the center of scholarly controversy.

Literarily, the character Joshua is the "chief unifying factor," but Yahweh is the most prominent literary character.[58] Theologically "the book seeks to give its readers the courage to meet whatever current challenges are brought on by their identity as Yahweh's people" and to "communicate hope for a future fulfillment of Yahweh's promises."[59] Major theological themes include land as Yahweh's gift on which Israel can depend; conquest testifying that Yahweh has fought for Israel and brings hope to a people threatened with losing their land or to exiles having already lost it; the enemy as opportunity, danger, and a potential source of threatened punishment; the ban as designating something or someone as a possession of Yahweh not to be used by humans; and obedience to Yahweh as the way to achieve success and avoid ruin.

For Nelson, Joshua does not take over Moses' office as lawgiver or as a prophet. He is "a forerunner for the ideological role played by later kings and especially for the expansionistic and reforming policies of Josiah."[60]

Textually, Nelson finds the Greek translation "a dependable translation of a form of the Hebrew text with textual value at least equal to MT."[61] Its shorter readings are to be seen as likely better than MT, and shorter MT readings point to a more original text.

Robert Coote (1998) fits Joshua into the Deuteronomistic History and argues for its opposition to Christian values. "Joshua's conquest of Canaan was taken as a precursor of Josiah's reconquest of Israel."[62] Much of Joshua, Judges, and Kings derives from Hezekiah's reign. "Joshua was an Israelite hero, probably introduced into wider popularity by Jeroboam I, the usurper of what had been Davidic Israel."[63] Minor changes to the book came in the exile, with materials related to the Priestly strand of the Pentateuch coming in the Persian period, though this did not represent any kind of comprehensive source.

According to Coote, Joshua presents "an orgy of terror, violence, and mayhem. . . . It forms a triumphant finale to the Bible's foundational epic of liberation, the savage goal toward which God's creation of Israel and delivery of Israel from slavery in Egypt appears to point from the start."[64] Thus "much about the book of Joshua is repulsive."[65] Only a "sidestepping approach" can rescue the stories of Joshua by letting them "illustrate reliance on the power of God, whose provision both short-term and long-run, does not fail. They illustrate the importance

---

58   Ibid., 14.
59   Ibid., 15.
60   Ibid., 22.
61   Ibid.
62   Coote, 556.
63   Ibid., 557.
64   Ibid., 555.
65   Ibid., 558.

of grace, allegiance, obedience to authority, community solidarity, the family, and deterring hasty revenge. . . . Joshua's values are not pure but are "multifaceted, mixed, and ambiguous."[66] The book may, however, "suggest to us our own affinities with the atrocities, violence, coercion, and prejudicial categorizing as means to social betterment."[67]

Coote finds "it is possible, but unlikely, that the story of the book of Joshua was recorded as it happened in history."[68] Instead the reader encounters set speeches, folk narratives, echoes of rituals, excerpts from supposed ancient sources, lists, territorial descriptions, material repeated elsewhere in the Bible but in different form, and a double ending. The presentation of the character of Joshua is sporadic, indicating he may not be an original part of much if any of the materials. Archaeological evidence does not support Joshua's conquests. The book is a gradual composition, preserved two to six hundred years after the events narrated in it supposedly occurred. It represents the viewpoint of the house of David. Israel was indigenous to Palestine, not attacking outsiders. The tribes of Israel are not genealogical creations but political ones seeking to centralize and reform government. Thus most of Josh 1–9 centers on Gilgal, Bethel, and Gibeon, important to the Davidic monarchy as places where Samuel decided to depose Saul, where Jeroboam I usurped the power of the Davidic kings, and where the overthrow of Saul took place.

For Coote, Deuteronomy and Joshua have no connection with an original Tetrateuch but begin the new Deuteronomistic History. Joshua's appearances in the Tetrateuch come from additions by scribes in the court of Hezekiah or that of Josiah.[69] "The Deuteronomistic History tells of how Israel under Joshua acquired its land in the first place, then how the house of David took it over, lost it, and under Josiah looked to recover it." Its purpose was either to refer to an actual reconquest or to set out the basis for a policy of reconquest. "Joshua . . . pre-figures Josiah and may be said to be modeled on Josiah."[70] The new history also supported Josiah's debt remission, his reputation as a ruler, his need to undermine the power and influence of national opponents, represented by the key word *Canaanites*, which basically meant "not Israelite."[71] The story of Joshua thus seeks to coerce and intimidate all of Josiah's opponents to submit to the king.

David Howard (1998) presents a strong theological exposition of Joshua from a firmly evangelical viewpoint. He accepts an early date for the Exodus and thus for the conquest and supports a modified conquest model for the events behind Joshua. He emphasizes that the battles were not really battles but works of God and that only three cities were destroyed. The thirteenth-century archaeological evidence points to participation in a widespread upheaval in the ancient Near East, not to the limited destruction of cities in Joshua. Rather, fifteenth-century archaeological evidence is more in line with the book of Joshua. This allows one to take seriously the biblical dating and allow for some overlapping in the period of the Judges. This places the exodus about 1446 BCE. Howard concludes "the biblical

---

66   Ibid., 578.
67   Ibid., 579.
68   Ibid., 556.
69   Ibid., 560.
70   Ibid., 565.
71   Ibid., 577.

picture of an 'Israel' descended from Abraham entering Canaan from without and engaging and defeating various Canaanite forces, but without causing extensive material destruction, is the most reasonable and defensible model."[72]

According to Howard, portions of the book come from Joshua's day, and the book was completed in David's time at the latest. Howard is willing to talk of a Deuteronomistic philosophy of history or even a Deuteronomistic History as long as that does not determine a date for the component parts and especially for Deuteronomy. The central theme of the book of Joshua is not battle but land. Other major themes include God's promises, the covenant, obedience, purity of worship (holiness), godly leadership, and rest.

L. Daniel Hawk (2000)[73] sees Joshua as a book about geographical, behavioral, and national boundaries. He was the first to point out the narrative tension of the book between God's desire for allegiance and human desire for security in the land.[74] Hawk finds two types of plots that create this tension. Ostensive plots feature obedience and integrity, while opposing plots feature disruptive disobedience and fragmentation.[75] The story remains "untidy and resistant" because other peoples still inhabit parts of the land and because Israel makes agreements with people like Rahab and the Gibeonites.[76]

"The impulse to fix and maintain these boundaries drives the story from start to conclusion, interweaving themes of land, behavior, and ethnicity into an intricate tapestry."[77] These boundaries give Israel an identity distinct from that of all other nations. Yet the narrative "antagonizes modern sensibilities. . . . [H]ow can readers in an age saturated with ethnic violence find meaning in a story that seems to endorse brutality against others?"[78]

The book of Joshua, however, has an extraordinary turn of events. "Boundaries of territory, race, and practice . . . are constantly subverted. . . . [E]ncounters with pious Canaanites and rebellious Israelites have collapsed the notion that Israel is somehow different than or superior to the surrounding nations."[79] Hawk centers his reading of Joshua on two questions: "How does Joshua construct an identity for the people of God?" and "What does Joshua hold to be the essential mark(s) of Israelite identity." To answer such questions, Hawk turns to a narrative approach, noticing structures, themes, allusions, and especially discontinuities that involve abrupt shifts and contradictory assertions. As Joshua executes the commandments of Moses, he represents the national ideal.

Hawk sees the basis as a collection of materials from diverse settings and times. The narrator pits commentary against narration, constructing a series of polarities: obedience/disobedience; success/failure; completion/openness; insider/outsider; ideal/real. Deuteronomic themes of devotion, obedience to the commandments,

---

72   Howard, 39–40.
73   Cf. Hawk's *Joshua in 3-D* (2010), which looks at Joshua as a forerunner of the United States' belief in manifest destiny.
74   See his *Every Promise Fulfilled: Contesting Plots in Joshua* (Louisville: Westminster John Knox, 1991) 141–45.
75   Ibid., 53.
76   Ibid., 144–45.
77   Ibid., ix.
78   Ibid., xii.
79   Ibid., xiii.

occupation of the land, and extermination of the indigenous peoples shape the narrative in Joshua.

A narrator's construction of identity is often at odds with the reality of Israel. The ideal identity says "Israel is one people bound by one covenant to one God and obedient to the whole law with a whole heart as they worship at one sanctuary. They take all the land and defeat all the kings so that Joshua can distribute all the land. The essence of Israelite identity . . . is . . . YHWH's exclusive choosing of Israel and Israel's exclusive choosing of YHWH (cf. 24:2–15)."[80]

Hawk's *Joshua in 3-D* speaks of a polarized text that both inspires and provokes. Centuries of reflection and composition have created multiple perspectives on Israel's success in taking the land. He draws out the motifs of national identity, divine destiny, and violent conquest for consideration and concludes, "Joshua provokes colonizing peoples to confront their past and its residue in the present and thus constitutes a powerful biblical resource for moving divinely destined nations to repentance."[81]

J. Gordon Harris (2000) focuses on "life situations and biblical theology." He maintains that the book of Joshua promises that "believers receive rest from enemies and security when they fight for God and God's chosen leader."[82] But God's sanction and command of violence, divine brutality, and the promise of material success for the nation and for individuals cause Christian readers problems. Theological themes, for Harris, must be approached by asking how the theme teaches about God. He then looks at leadership, land as gift, obedience and God's grace, and unity.

Harris follows Nelson in finding Joshua as the model of a royal figure and adopts a thirteenth-century date for the exodus. In a quite tentative discussion of the settlement, he suggests that "readers should not reject the historical quality of Joshua's narrative because archaeology does not directly support the book." Harris quickly dismisses Noth's tradition-history approach as circular, theoretical, and atomizing, preferring narrative analysis instead.[83]

Harris is concerned with worship in Joshua at various places, concluding that "worship during the settlement utilized symbols and worship places in Canaan to give birth to new faith in the Lord of the heavens and the earth." He also maintains that LXX is a "reliable translation of a Hebrew text that equals the value of the MT."[84]

Carolyn Pressler (2002) sees Joshua as "less an academic history than a people's colorful, complex of stories told to probe or proclaim a nation's identity and its faith . . . [with] array of earlier traditions . . . : spy stories, battle reports, hero legends, songs, liturgies, confessions, and administrative lists."[85] Pressler follows Cross in seeing two editions of the book, one under Josiah and one in the exile. The story justifies God's exile of Israel but still points to God's mercy extending beyond wrath to offer hope. Joshua shows that Israel is obedient, Joshua is faithful,

---

80   Ibid., xxxi.
81   Hawk, *Joshua in 3-D*, xxxii.
82   Harris, 9.
83   Ibid., 6–7.
84   Ibid., 9.
85   Pressler, 1.

and God fulfills God's promises.[86] Israel is seeking to avoid assimilation into the Assyrian and Babylonian empires. Its faith identity appears in Israel's assimilating Rahab and the Gibeonites. Pressler emphasizes listening to counter voices as well as dominant voices in the text and to read it as political and theological literature rather than mere historical report, though history is not irrelevant.

José Luis Sicre's commentary (2002) mirrors the Word Biblical Commentary in many ways. Sicre devotes substantial space to the history of research and to linguistic tables. He sees the text as a literary production of the Persian or Hellenistic age with little historical tradition behind it. Joshua is an unbelievable character in a quite theological book that devotes only a couple of chapters to warfare.

Jerome Creach (2003) finds the book of Joshua "pivotal to the theology and literature of the Old Testament, no matter how one configures the material" and focuses on theological issues and passages that provide theological fodder. Still, "some Christians reject Joshua because they think it primitive and brutal, promoting a violent god who is surely different from the Father of Jesus Christ."[87] Creach thus maintains that "the contemporary community of faith is impoverished theologically when it fails to attend to Joshua." Violence and warfare represent more of a modern problem than one of Israel's problems. A narrative approach to the canonical book is seen as the best method of interpretation, thus leaving textual issues and critical studies of authorship, date, and redaction to others for the most part.

As history, Joshua is part of its ancient environment; the Israelites are trying to establish national identity and support nationalistic goals. It is "composed for theological purposes, not to satisfy the intellectual curiosity of modern readers."[88] This brings a "primary challenge" for modern readers, namely, "to enter Joshua's world and to have *our* history and *our* future shaped by it."[89]

The book itself shows doublets that indicate a history of authorship and editing. Some form of chaps. 2–11 may have developed at Gilgal. An early form of the book was part of the Deuteronomistic History, whose editing appears clearly in chaps. 1, 12, and 23 and in 21:43–22:6. This early form, sponsored by King Josiah, was written just before the Babylonian exile. The book was completed during or after the exile. Priestly touches appear in chaps. 14–22. Such additions "temper Joshua's authority."[90] Other later additions to the book deal with the acquisition of land (Josh 1:7–9a; 13:1b–6; 23:6–13). These make possession of the land dependent on devotion to Torah.

Structurally, Creach sees that chaps. 1–12 have some parallels with chaps. 13–22, thus being intended "to depict Joshua's two primary roles, conquest and allotment of the land."[91]

Thematically, Creach seeks to show the different value and definition the Old Testament places on violence as opposed to modern conceptions. For Israel, violence "refers principally to actions that tear at the fabric of Israelite society by defying the sovereignty of God."[92] Israel's conquest is not violent because it seeks to

---

86   Ibid., 4.
87   Creach, 3.
88   Ibid., 5.
89   Ibid., 6.
90   Ibid., 11.
91   Ibid., 12.
92   Ibid., 15.

instill loyalty to God and address human justice on earth. As far as the ban (*ḥērem*) goes, the stories and reality part company, for "Israel did not in reality commit genocide."[93] Such stories seek to "present an Israel that was more powerful than was true historically."[94] The book presents Israel's warfare as mostly a defensive action initiated by the Canaanite enemies. The Canaanites had a chance for peace but rejected it (11:19).

Adolph Harstad (2004) offers a strongly traditional commentary, extending his exegetical findings to New Testament texts. He offers extensive notes on Hebrew terms, texts, and constructions and leans heavily on Martin Luther's commentary. The book of Joshua may be attributed to Eleazar or Phinehas, to Joshua himself, or to a slightly later writer in the second millennium who had to explain some things that lasted "until this day" or names that no longer applied. He dates the conquest itself to 1406 BCE and follows a historical-grammatical method of interpretation rather than a historical-critical one. Following in the tradition of Origen, he accepts four senses of Scripture—one historical and three spiritual. The latter include allegory (belief about Jesus), tropology (life as a disciple), and anagogy (future hope). For Harstad, the book's central theme is: The Lord fulfills his promise to give the land of Canaan to his covenant people Israel as an inheritance.[95]

Robert Hubbard (2009) accepts the later dating of a 1250 BCE Exodus but tries to give explanations of texts from both the earlier and later contexts. He accepts a Deuteronomist with earlier sources as author and notes: "whatever date one assigns him." Some sources may reach back into the premonarchical period. Hubbard follows K. L. Younger[96] in seeing a literary work using hyperbole and other literary devices. Central themes are Yahweh the Promise Keeper, Yahweh the Warrior, Joshua the Successor, the people of God, and Israel and the Peoples.[97]

Ernst Axel Knauf (2008) attempts to understand the book of Joshua in the milieu for which it was written in its canonical form.[98] This milieu or historical frame stretches wide, spanning the political and theological controversies from the end of the seventh to the beginning of the fourth century BCE. This far-reaching milieu is discovered only through extensive redaction-critical work on the text. The discovery, however, of tensions and contradictions in the text leads only to incorporating them in the reading of the text. Knauf reads the book as a "book about land," land that is God's gift to Israel.[99]

For Knauf, Joshua is a necessary narrative supplement to Torah but is also the first book of the historical narrative running from Joshua through 2 Kings. Josh 1 introduces the prophetic canon pointing ahead to Mal 3, while Josh 24 looks back at Gen 10 and 11. To read Exodus through Joshua as biography of Joshua, says Knauf, is to see him come out of Torah and then with Josh 24:26 return back in to Torah. Knauf finds Joshua to be a person who is tribally and genealogically isolated. This leads to the conclusion that his name, Joshua, is actually a constructed variant of

93   Ibid., 16.
94   Ibid., 17.
95   Harstad, 26
96   *Ancient Conquest Accounts,* JSOTSup 98 (Sheffield: JSOT Press, 1990).
97   Hubbard, 53–61. See below under Studies in Warfare and Conquest.
98   Knauf, 7.
99   Ibid., 9. All translations of Knauf are my own. See below, The Meaning of the Material.

the name of Josiah the king. This means, for Knauf, that the oldest edition of the story of Joshua comes from the reign of Josiah (640–609 BCE) or later.[100]

Gordon McConville and Stephen Williams (2010) represent a new challenge in commentary writing: "to interpret the book of Joshua in relation to Christian theology."[101] An exegete joins with a systematic theologian in trying to bridge the infamous gap between text and modern application. This leaves McConville a quite limited space for exegetical comments. McConville points to differences of meaning at different stages in Israel's history.[102] He accepts archaeology's evidence that the people Israel gradually emerged from the indigenous Canaanites. He struggles with the issue of how close to "historical" a book has to be to be theologically valid.[103] He concludes that one cannot be expected to answer the question, for such a demonstration of historicity cannot be exhibited. "Faith need not depend upon a fully worked out historical hypothesis."[104] McConville sets out land as the "central topic" of the book.[105] Williams begins his theological contribution with "The Question of the Land" before turning to genocide, idolatry, covenant, and the God of miracle and mystery.[106]

McConville relates the relationship of Joshua to each section of the Pentateuch and to the Deuteronomistic History. He then gives a biblical theologian's perspective on evil and violence in Joshua and in the rest of the Hebrew Bible. Williams closes with the question of history and the God of Joshua.

Douglas Earl (2010) seeks to answer the same type of issues that McConville and Williams explore—the use of Joshua as Christian Scripture. He approaches Joshua as a book of myth and provides a thorough investigation of myth from the ideological, psychological, existential and symbolic, and structuralist viewpoint. He then turns to hermeneutical issues, especially the place of testimony and symbols. Section II looks at "Making Joshua Intelligible as Discourse: Starting to Read Well." Here he speaks of Joshua's affinities with Deuteronomistic and Priestly thinking. He then compares Joshua with ancient Near Eastern conquest accounts. A look at ḥērem comes next. Finally, Earl reads each section of Joshua and offers conclusion drawing it all together.

Pekka Pitkänen (2010) also interprets the book as Christian Scripture.[107] He infers from Josh 12:7 that Joshua may have begun a long-term conquest process that the editors telescoped into a brief period.[108] Textually, according to Pitkänen, the tradition was transmitted reliably.[109]

Pitkänen attempts to incorporate into the conquest/settlement picture a slave group out of Egypt bringing ancestral traditions and Yahweh worship.[110] Indigenous groups joined these Yahweh worshipers in the central highlands into the period of

---

100   See Redaction History below.
101   McConville and Williams, 10.
102   Ibid., 3.
103   Ibid., 5.
104   Ibid., 8.
105   Ibid., 11.
106   Ibid., 95, 108, 124, 140, 154 (in sequence).
107   Pitkänen, 23.
108   Ibid., 25.
109   Ibid., 27.
110   Ibid., 31.

the monarchy. The incidents in the book of Joshua may plausibly be considered as historical, though this cannot be proven.[111] He does interpret archaeological data so that "just about all identifiable sites in both Transjordan and Cisjordan that relate to the book of Joshua can be seen to bear witness to occupation during the Late Bronze-Early Iron era."[112] Pitkänen leaves a date for the conquest open, though he points favorably to the thirteenth century. He denies Noth's theory of a Deuteronomistic Historian as author, seeing Joshua composed as a separate entity.[113] He argues that the book of Joshua reflects northern dominance and cannot be considered to be at home in Judah. The emphasis on the Transjordanian tribes must come before their deportation in the eighth century. All evidence put together, he argues for a writing date in the eleventh century, before the fall of Shiloh,[114] while admitting to later updating of some parts such as the lists of Josh 13–21. This creates a Hexateuch, not a Deuteronomistic History.

Theologically, Pitkänen points to Yahweh and his determination of success, to the ark of the covenant, to an all-Israel perspective, the insider/outsider emphasis, and the Deuteronomic slant of the theology. Covenant and Priestly theology also appear. The book is the product of a pro-Yahweh party that sought to mold the people of Israel into a nation living out their ideals.[115] Their rhetoric thus used hyperbole and strong persuasive language to gain their audience's assent.

Pitkänen shows particular interest in war, conquest, and genocide. Joshua seeks to establish in Canaan a pure, ideal society. Most other books except Deuteronomy do not deal with the issue. In New and Old Testaments an unresolved tension remains that can only be treated as one of the mysteries of God.[116] He apparently holds to a form of the just war theory but does not fully spell it out. Egocentrism and ethnocentrism explain the origin of most wars and of genocide efforts. These must be obliterated and societies totally changed if we are to achieve justice.

B. Basic Issues in Joshua

Select Bibliography

Abel, F. M. "Les stratagèmes dans le Livre de Josué." *RB* 56 (1949) 321–39. **Adoul, A.** *Josué.* A la Découverte de la Bible 6. Lausanne: Ligue pour la lecture de la Bible, 1983. **Alfrink, B. J.** *Josue.* Vol. 3 of *De Boeken van het Oude Testament.* Ed. A van den Born et al. Roermond: Romen & Zonen, 1952. ———. "Die Wundererzählungen des AT als 'Volkserzählung.'" *BK* 14 (1959) 87–88. **Alonso Schökel, L.** "Nota bibliográfica sobre el libro de Josué." *Bib* 39 (1958) 217–21. **Anbar, M.** "La 'reprise.'" *VT* 38 (1988) 385–98. **Angel, H.** "One Book, Two Books: The Joshua-Judges Continuum." *JBQ* 36 (2008) 163–70. **Bieberstein, K.** *Josua, Jordan, Jericho: Archäologie, Geschichte und Theologie der Landnahmeerzählung Josua 1–6.* OBO 143. Göttingen: Vandenhoeck & Ruprecht, 1995. **Budde, K.** "Richter und Josua." *ZAW* 7 (1887) 93–166. **Chirichigno, G. C.** "The Use of the Epithet in the Characterization of Joshua." *TJ* 8 (1987) 69–79. **Conder, C. R.** "Notes on the Antiquities of the Book of Joshua." *PEFQS* 31.2 (March 1899) 161–62. **Davies, J.** *Notes on the Book of*

---

111 Ibid., 40.
112 Ibid., 46.
113 Ibid., 53.
114 Ibid., 62.
115 Ibid., 71.
116 Ibid., 82.

Joshua. London, 1871. **Davis, J. J.** *Conquest and Crisis: Studies in Joshua, Judges, and Ruth.* Rev. ed. Eugene, OR: Wipf & Stock, 2001. **Ehrlich, C. S.** "Josua und das Judentum." In *Bibel und Judentum: Beiträge aus dem christlich-jüdischen Gespräch.* Zürich: Pano, 2004. 87–100. **Hess, R. S.** "Studies in the Book of Joshua." *Them* 20 (1995) 12–15. **Jaubert, A.**, ed. *Homélies sur Josué: Texte latin, introduction, traduction et notes.* SC 71. Paris: Cerf, 1960. **Kuenen, A.** "Bijdragen tot de critiek van Pentateuch en Jozua: III. De uitzendingdes verspieders." *TT* 11 (1877) 545–66. ————. "Bijdragen tot de critiek van Pentateuch en Jozua: V. De godsdienstige vergadering bij Ebal en Gerizim. (Deut. XI:29,30; XXVII; Joz. VIII:30–35." *TT* 12 (1878) 297–323. **Latvus, K.** *God, Anger, and Ideology: The Anger of God in Joshua and Judges in Relation to Deuteronomy and the Priestly Writings.* JSOTSup 279. Sheffield: Sheffield Academic, 1998. **Lindeque, G. C. B.** "Reading the Book of Joshua against a Post-exilic Background." *HvTSt* 58 (2002) 1761–94. **Lohfink, N.** "Eroberung oder Heimkehr? Zum heutigen Umgang mit dem Buch Joshua." In *Im Schatten deiner Flugel: Grosse Bibeltexte neu erschlossen.* Freiburg im Breisgau, 1999. 82–103. **Mowinckel, S.** *Tetrateuch, Pentateuch, Hexateuch: Die Berichte über die Landnahme in den drei altisraelitischen Geschichtswerken.* BZAW 90. Berlin: Töpelmann, 1964. **Nelson, R.** "Josiah in the Book of Joshua." *JBL* 100 (1981) 531–40. **Noort, E.** *Das Buch Josua: Forschungsgeschichte und Problemfelder.* EdF 292. Darmstadt: Wissenschaftliche Buchgesellschaft, 1998. ————. "Joshua: The History of Reception and Hermeneutics." In *Past, Present, Future: The Deuteronomistic History and the Prophets.* Ed J. C. de Moor and H. F. van Rooy. OtSt 44. Leiden: Brill, 2000. 199–215. **Noth, M.** *Überlieferungsgeschichtliche Studien: Die sammelnden und bearbeitende Geschichtswerke im Alten Testament.* 2nd ed. Tübingen: Niemeyer, 1957. **Otto, E.** *Das Mazzotfest in Gilgal.* BWANT 107. Stuttgart: Kohlhammer, 1975. **Ottosson, M.** *Josuaboken: En programskrift för davidisk restauration.* AUU: Studia Biblica Upsaliensia 1. Uppsala: AUU, 1991. ————. "Tradition and History with Emphasis on the Composition of the Book of Joshua." In *The Productions of Time: Tradition History in Old Testament Scholarship.* Ed. K. Jeppesen and B. Otzen. Sheffield: Almond, 1984. 81–106, 141–43. **Rösel, H. N.** "Studien zur Topographie der Kriege in den Büchern Josua und Richter." *ZDPV* 91 (1975) 159–90. ————. "Studien zur Topographie der Kriege in den Büchern Josua und Richter: Schluss." *ZDPV* 92 (1976) 10–46. **Rowlett, L. L.** *Joshua and the Rhetoric of Violence: A New Historicist Analysis.* JSOTSup 226. Sheffield: Sheffield Academic, 1996. **Rudolph, W.** *Der "Elohist" von Exodus bis Josua.* BZAW 68. Berlin: Töpelmann, 1938. **Schäfer-Lichtenberger, C.** *Josua und Salomo: Eine Studie zu Autorität und Legitimität des Nachfolgers im Alten Testament.* VTSup 58. Leiden: Brill, 1995. **Schmid, K.** *Erzväter und Exodus: Untersuchungen zur doppelten Begründung der Ursprünge Israels innerhalb der Geschichtsbücher des Alten Testaments.* WMANT 81. Neukirchen-Vluyn: Neukirchener Verlag, 1999. **Smend, R., Sr.** *Die Erzählung des Hexateuch auf ihre Quellen untersucht.* Berlin, 1912. **Vink, J. G.** "The Date and Origin of the Priestly Code in the Old Testament." In *The Priestly Code and Other Studies.* Ed. P. A. H. de Boer. OtSt 15. Leiden: Brill, 1969. **Wellhausen, J.** *Die Composition des Hexateuchs und der historischen Bücher des Alten Testaments.* 2nd ed. Berlin, 1889. **Winther-Nielsen, N., and E. Talstra.** *A Computational Display of Joshua: A Computer-Assisted Analysis and Textual Interpretation.* Applicatio 13. Amsterdam: VU UP, 1995. **Younger, K. L., Jr.** *Ancient Conquest Accounts: A Study in Ancient Near Eastern and Biblical History Writing.* JSOTSup 98. Sheffield: JSOT Press, 1990.

1. General Issues on the Formation of the Book

The purpose of this section is to outline the process by which the book received its present shape. This involves an attempt to study the history of the materials as they were used within Israel to celebrate the work of God and to proclaim the Word of God.

The long history of interpretation and exegesis that text-critical work reveals leads one to suppose that such scribal interpretative work did not begin with the first copyists of the completed book. The process began long before the material was reduced to a final written text. The text underwent slight variations and interpretations in each oral telling and in each new copying of it. This was the method by which Israel received the word of God and passed it on to ensuing generations.

Many scholars want to put the dating of the final, unchangeable text much earlier than will be noted in the following discussion. In so doing, they reduce its history of composition to a much simpler process than that about to be described. Woudstra, for example, lists scholars arguing for an early date and then decides on the earliest possible one, the days of Joshua and of the elders who outlived him.[117] Howard sees portions written in Joshua's lifetime and other parts in David's day "at the latest."[118]

The following discussion will attempt to show the strong distinction in literature between the age of the source materials and the age of the final literary product. Close study of the textual history of the book should show us that the text did not reach a final form until late in its history. Other types of critical study will attempt to demonstrate how oral literature, the major medium of transmitting tradition and history at the time of Joshua and Judges, can retain and transmit the items, issues, and ideology of earlier times even as the oral literature becomes popular written literature and court educational literature. An eyewitness may give a totally confusing rendition of an incident, while oral tradents may shape the materials into a form that both narrator and audience know, to the extent that it bears a much closer relationship to the actual event than does the eyewitness report. All the while, every telling of the narrative has purpose and agenda behind it. Each rendition of the story is done for more than entertainment and improving the narrative art.

Thus we will look at the process of creating a story-telling tradition by using typical forms to narrate a story. We will look at how the oral forms are integrated into literary works as source materials and how the literary works are shaped into final forms by editors incorporating them into larger literary works.

2. Form Criticism

Bibliography

See *Bibliography* on chap. 24 for specific covenant studies.
Alt, A. "Josua." In *Werden und Wesen des Alten Testaments.* Ed. J. Hempel et al. BZAW 66. Berlin: Töppelmann, 1936 13–29 (= *KS* [1953], 1:176–92). **Baltzer, K.** *Die Biographie der Propheten.* Neukirchen-Vluyn: Neukirchener Verlag, 1975. **Bright, J.** *Early Israel in Recent History Writing.* SBT 19. London: SCM Press, 1956. **Chapman, S. B.** "Joshua Son of Nun: Presentation of a Prophet." In *Thus Says the Lord: Essays on the Former and Latter Prophets in Honor of R. Wilson.* Library of Hebrew Bible/Old Testament Studies 502. London: T&T

---

117 Woudstra, 12–13.
118 Howard, 30. Hess points to Holland, *Das Buch Josua* (Wuppertaler Studienbibel, AT [Wuppertal/Zürich: Brockhaus, 1993]) and Koorevaar, *De Opbouw van het Boek Jozua* (Heverlee: Centrum voor Bijbelse Vorming België, 1990) as examples of early dating of the book, and then proceeds to show numerous examples of things from antiquity in the book without ever establishing a final date.

Clark, 2000. 13–26. **Childs, B. S.** "The Etiological Tale Re-examined," *VT* 24 (1974) 387–97. ———. "A Study of the Formula 'Until this Day.'" *JBL* 82 (1963) 279–92. **Coats, G.** "An Exposition for the Conquest Theme." *CBQ* 47 (1985) 47–54. ———. "The Book of Joshua: Heroic Saga or Conquest Theme?" *JSOT* 38 (1987) 16–32. **Conrad, E. W.** *Fear Not Warrior: A Study of 'al tîrā' Pericopes in the Hebrew Scriptures.* Chico, CA: Society of Biblical Literature, 1985. **Coogan, M. D.** "Archaeology and Biblical Studies: The Book of Joshua." In *The Hebrew Bible and Its Interpreters.* Ed. W. H. Propp, B. Halpern, and D. N. Freedman. Winona Lake, IN: Eisenbrauns, 1990. 19–32. **Dion, H. M.** "The 'Fear Not' Formula and Holy War." *CBQ* 32 (1970) 565–70. **Eslinger, L.** *Into the Hands of the Living God.* Bible and Literature 24. Sheffield: Almond, 1989. **Fichtner, J.** "Die etymologische Etiologie in den Namengebungen der geschichtlichen Bücher des Alten Testaments." *VT* 6 (1956) 372–96. **Geoghegan, J. C.** *The Time, Place, and Purpose of the Deuteronomistic History: The Evidence of "Until This Day."* BJS 347. Providence: Brown Judaic Studies, 2006. **Golka, F. W.** "The Etiologies in the Old Testament." Part 1, *VT* 26 (1976) 410–28; part 2, *VT* 27 (1977) 36–47. ———. "Zur Erforschung der Etiologien im Alten Testament." *VT* 20 (1970) 90–98. **Gunkel, H.** "Die israelitische Literatur." In *Die orientalischen Literaturen.* Ed. P. Hinneberg. KdG 1.7 Leipzig; Stuttgart: Teubner, 1906; 2nd ed., 1925. Reprinted separately in Darmstadt: Wissenschaftliche Buchgesellschaft, 1963. **Hess, R.** "The Book of Joshua as a Land Grant." *Bib* 83 (2002) 493–506. **Hoffmeier, J. K.** "The Structure of Joshua 1–11 and the Annals of Thutmose III." In *Faith, Tradition, and History.* Ed. A. R. Millard, J. K. Hoffmeier, and D. W. Baker. Winona Lake, IN: Eisenbrauns, 1994. 165–79. **Knoppers, G. N.** "Ancient Near Eastern Royal Grants and the Davidic Covenant: A Parallel?" *JAOS* 116 (1996) 670–97. **Lohfink, N.** "Geschichtstypologisch Orientierte Textstrukturen in den Büchern Deuteronomium und Josua." In *Deuteronomy and Deuteronomic Literature: Festschrift C. H. Brekelmans.* Ed. M. Vervenne and J. Lust. BETL 83. Leuven: Leuven UP, 1997. 133–60. **Long, B. O.** *The Problem of Etiological Narrative in the Old Testament.* BZAW 108. Berlin: Töppelmann, 1968. **Marconcini, B.** "Giosuè 1–12: Etiologia storica in prospettiva religiosa." *BeO* 14 (1972) 3–12. **Merling, D.** "The Book of Joshua: Its Structure and Meaning." In *To Understand the Scriptures: Essays in Honor of William H. Shea.* Ed. D. Merling. Berrien Springs, MI: Institute of Archaeology, Siegfried H. Horn Archaeological Museum, Andrews University, 1997. 7–28. ———. "The Book of Joshua, Part 1: Its Evaluation by Nonevidence." *AUSS* 39 (2001) 61–72. ———. "The Book of Joshua, Part 2: "Expectations of Archaeology." *AUSS* 39 (2001) 209–21. **Noth, M.** "Der Beitrag der Archäologie zur Geschichte Israels." In *Congress Volume: Oxford, 1959.* VTSup 7. Leiden: Brill, 1960. 262–82 (= *ABLAK,* 1:34–51). ———. "Hat die Bibel doch Recht?" In *Festschrift für Günther Dehn.* Neukirchen-Vluyn: Neukirchener Verlag, 1957. 7–22 (= *ABLAK,* 1:489–543). **Polzin, R.** *Moses and the Deuteronomist: Deuteronomy, Judges, Joshua.* New York: Seabury, 1980. **Rad, G. von.** "The Form-Critical Problem of the Hexateuch." In *The Problem of the Hexateuch and Other Essays.* New York: McGraw-Hill, 1966. 1–78. **Ramsey, G. W.** *The Quest for the Historical Israel.* Atlanta: John Knox, 1981. **Römer, T.** *The So-called Deuteronomistic History: A Sociological, Historical and Literary Introduction.* London: T&T Clark, 2005. **Rose, M.** *Deuteronomist und Jahwist.* Zürich: Theologischer Verlag, 1980. **Rowlett, L.** "Inclusion, Exclusion and Marginality in the Book of Joshua." *JSOT* 55 (1992) 15–23. **Schäfer-Lichtenberger, C.** *Josua und Salomo: Eine Studie zu Autorität und Legitimität des Nachfolgers im Alten Testament.* VTSup 58. Leiden: Brill, 1995. **Smend, R.** *Elemente alttestamentlichen Geschichtsdenkens.* ThSt 95. Zürich: EVZ-Verlag, 1968. **Soggin, J. A.** "Kultätiologische Sagen und Katachese im Hexateuch." *VT* 10 (1960) 341–47. **Van Seters, J.** *In Search of History: Historiography in the Ancient World and the Origins of Biblical History.* Winona Lake, IN: Eisenbrauns, 1997. ———. "Joshua's Campaign of Canaan and Near Eastern Historiography." In *Israel's Past in Present Research: Essays on Ancient Israelite Historiography.* Ed. P. Long. SBTS 8. Winona Lake, IN: Eisenbrauns, 1999. 170–80. **Westermann, C.** "Arten der Erzählung in der Genesis." In *Forschung am Alten Testament.* TB 24. Munich: Kaiser, 1964. 9–91 (= *Die Verheissungen an die Väter,* FRLANT 116 [Göttingen:

Vandenhoeck & Ruprecht, 1976] = *The Promises to the Fathers*, trans. D. Green [Philadelphia: Fortress, 1980]). **Younger, K. L., Jr.** *Ancient Conquest Accounts: A Study in Ancient Near Eastern and Biblical History Writing.* JSOTSup 98. Sheffield: JSOT Press, 1990.

Herman Gunkel taught scholarship to seek not only the literary history of a book but also the forms of the tradition used in its oral stage of development.[119] In his 1922 commentary Hugo Gressmann applied the work of Gunkel on etiological sagas in Genesis to the book of Joshua. Albrecht Alt[120] and Martin Noth, in his commentary, then carried the work further, isolating a series of narratives featuring the formula "unto this day," which seemed to have developed in the territory of Benjamin. Biblical authors, according to Alt and Noth, could thus explain various types of noteworthy phenomena in the "present" through narratives of the past. They noted that when the Joshua narrative retreats from the Gilgal area, the etiological formula fades.

John Bright opposed Alt and Noth with his claim that etiology was not a creative factor in the formation of tradition, being secondary rather than primary to the development of the tradition.[121] Noth later backed down somewhat to leave open a whole realm of possibilities for the relationship between historical event, developing tradition concerning the event, and the etiological form.[122]

Subsequent research has further analyzed the components of etiological narrative. Johannes Fichtner separated two forms of name-giving etiologies, which he shows to be at home in Israel's old saga material, not the later historical works.[123] Etiology is again seen as sometimes primary, sometimes secondary within the tradition.

J. Alberto Soggin analyzed the etiologies as children's questions and connected these to liturgical catechesis rather than family conversations.[124] Having some relationship to the early sanctuaries at Gilgal and Shechem, the form is seen to be at home in the early stages of the Deuteronomic movement.

Brevard Childs returned to the basic "until this day" formula.[125] The complete and pure form occurs only rarely (Josh 7:26; Judg 18:21; 2 Chr 20:26). In the great majority of the cases, the formula represents a redactional commentary on the tradition, giving personal testimony confirming the received tradition. In his second study of the problem,[126] Childs sought to clarify definitions and functions by showing that Gunkel's theory involved a mythical conception of cause and effect not present in the narratives of Joshua first analyzed by Gressmann. Childs argues for the distinction between the mythical act that alters the structure of reality and a non-mythical story establishing a precedent for the present. He warns against unwarranted mythologizing of Israel's historical tradition.

---

119   See Gunkel's "Die israelitische Literatur."
120   "Josua," 13–29.
121   See Bright's *Early Israel.*
122   See Noth, "Hat die Bibel doch Recht?"; "Der Beitrag der Archäologie zur Geschichte Israels."
123   *VT* 6 (1956) 372–96.
124   *VT* 10 (1960) 341–47.
125   *JBL* 82 (1963) 279–92.
126   *VT* 24 (1974) 387–97.

Burke O. Long studied the formal structure of various etiological clauses, finding them rarely related to a story.[127] He concluded that rarely in Israel did etiological interest play a strong role in building extensive narrative material. Only in studying narrative function could one properly discuss and isolate etiological narrative.

Rudolf Smend examined etiological function rather than form.[128] He showed that narrative continued to be used both etiologically and paradigmatically. Basic etiology had to grow beyond itself to survive. As narratives were assimilated into larger complexes, the complexes could also become etiological. In the book of Joshua, original narratives of the settlement as a military operation were fed by the ideology of Yahweh War, which bound together the narratives into a larger complex. They then functioned etiologically to justify Israel's possession of the land, or at least the piece of land under discussion in the individual narrative. Together they produced a paradigm of Yahweh as the glorious warrior who fights for Israel. The etiological function, however, did not disappear. The narrative complex demonstrated how Israel occupied Palestine. Even the original boundary documents of chaps. 13–21 functioned in this etiological fashion. Both when possession was not self-evident and when it was no longer self-evident, the stories fulfilled this etiological role.

Claus Westermann carefully studied the basic structure of narrative, noting that narrative plot runs from tension to resolution.[129] He distinguished between an etiological story in which the line of tension is identical with the line of the etiology on the one hand and an etiological notice concluding a story in a brief sentence or two at the end without a necessary connection to the line of narrative tension. According to Westermann the true etiological narrative answers real questions reliably rather than inventing answers to obscure questions.

Friedemann W. Golka attempted to apply Westermann's criteria to Old Testament historical narratives.[130] In Joshua he found true narratives in the story in chaps. 2 and 6 and in 7:1, 5b–26; 7:2–5a; 8:1–29; and 9:1–27. Only a narrative torso could be isolated in 5:2–9, while 6:25 represented an etiological motif. Etiological notes appear in 13:12, 15:63, and 16:10. Golka seems to have ignored his own distinctions along with many of the issues and cautions raised by Long and Childs when he sought a historical period for the etiologies. He found that etiology was alive among the tribes, not among the families, nor in Israel's history writing. It began to disappear at the organization of the national state, to be artificially revived in an "unreal existence" later.

Reviewing the study of etiological narrative in Joshua, George W. Ramsey concluded that the appearance of etiological narrative does not automatically prove that the narrative lacks historical value; determination of genre or form is incapable of answering historical questions.[131]

Jeffrey C. Geoghegan provides a strong history of research on the issue and then attempts to show that the "until this day" etiological formula has southern, Deuteronomistic roots and is the work of the Deuteronomistic editors under

---

127 *Problem of Etiological Narrative.*
128 *Elemente alttestamentlichen Geschichtsdenkens.*
129 "Arten der Erzählung in der Genesis," 9–91.
130 *VT* 20 (1970) 90–98; *VT* 26 (1976) 410–28; *VT* 27 (1977) 36–47.
131 *Quest for the Historical Israel,* 77–81.

Josiah.[132] He finds a unified (southern) geographical perspective, a unified (i.e., Josianic) temporal perspective, a close relationship to Dtr redactional materials, a connection to objects and institutions of high interest for Dtr, and activities pointing directly to the Josianic reformation. Michael David Coogan simply dismisses the entire book of Joshua as "historico-theological fiction" that depicts Joshua as good guy beyond reproach.[133]

Robert Polzin turned in an entirely different direction, examining the book from the perspective of the classical study of literature and its structural elements and devices. He maintains that the book seeks to witness to the method of interpreting the Word of God in general and the law in particular.[134] The themes of God's mercy and justice on the one hand and Israel's identity as both citizen and alien on the other connect the narratives, all pointing back to God's decision in Deut 10:11.

This brief study reveals that a study of Joshua must confront the complex problem of etiological narrative/etiological motif/etiological note in its examination of almost every chapter of the book, requiring an analysis of narrative structure that follows the arc of tension to its resolution. It will involve the study of the function of narrative units rather than simply the appearance of isolated forms. It will determine if within the larger complexes a pattern exists that allows us to speak of the etiological function of the complex and of the redactional function of etiological notes. No unified preconception can cover all etiological elements. Noort claims that a premature characterizing of a narrative or tradition as "etiological narrative" is indeed no longer possible.[135] The exegetical task, then, is to determine the point of entry of the etiological motifs into the narrative complex(es) and the function of these motifs both at the time of entry into the complex and within the final composition.

Ultimately, one must ask if the entire book of Joshua fulfilled an etiological function for an Israel that had lost control of its land and its destiny. We have seen how the traditions played a major part in the land claims between tribes, particularly in Benjamin's troubles with Judah to the south and with Ephraim to the north. Martin Rose's work *Deuteronomist und Jahwist* is important at this point. Rose described the importance of Israel's "legal claim" on the land. Rose claims that the written materials would not have found a function within Israel until the land claim was a matter of major dispute, having already been lost. Thus Rose dates the first written compilation of the narratives to the period after 722 BCE. It is doubtful if one must look so late in Israel's history to find a setting for such a writing. Rather, the period of Saul and David already presents a moment of bitter dispute over land claims, a dispute that was prolonged after the death of Saul.

Was the first conquest narrative formed at Dan on the basis of earlier narrative legitimating the cult? Was such a narrative formulated only on the border territories when they became threatened by outside invaders? Do conquest narratives function as legal claims to land threatened or lost? Is this theme of legal claim to the land the interpretative key for Josh 2–6? Does this point specifically to a time when the entire land is unstable or has been lost?

---

132   *Time, Place*, 120–21.
133   "Archaeology and Biblical Studies," 27.
134   *Moses and the Deuteronomist*, 144.
135   *Das Buch Josua*, 234.

Can one go further with Rose and isolate an oldest traditional layer comprising a relatively unspecific war narrative with spy story, siege, oracle of encouragement, and conquest? Is any historical memory of an event concerning the actual conquest of a city fully secondary at this oldest traditional level? Does the basic literary level then try to demilitarize this narrative? Or must one apply form criticism to a much smaller narrative scope with concrete details and narrative structure to determine the oldest level of tradition?

Daniel Hawk finds three basic categories of materials in the first twelve chapters: battle reports, anecdotes, and reports of ritual observance. The extensive first three campaigns become paradigms for all the following ones, reported in "terse summaries." The anecdotes about Rahab, Achan, and the Gibeonites have common elements: concealment, interrogation, diversion, doxology, petition, response, qualification, battle report of victory assured, victory achieved by miracle, victory accomplished by massacre, etiological note, and curse.

The commentary seeks to find answers to form-critical questions dealing with etiological narratives and with each individual narrative tradition in the book. Are these literary units from the historical era of a generation after Joshua, as argued by Woudstra? Or are there marks of older traditions that have been preserved and interpreted through the long history of Israel's worship before reaching the form God chose to use to teach his people over the succeeding millennia? Could this mean that God used the validating experiences of generations of his people listening to, responding to, and interpreting the ancient stories of the people to give theological and experiential depth to the word he wished to communicate to his people through the many succeeding centuries?

Research into the particular detailed questions will be noted at proper spots in the commentary. The special problems of Josh 13–21 will be reviewed in an introductory section to that portion of the text.

A major question seldom discussed is the genre of the book of Joshua as a whole. Form critics must deal not only with the issue of the component parts but must also raise questions concerning the nature of the final work. Too often, the final work is described as a pastiche of elements from many oral and written sources with emphasis on the variety of the pieces rather than on the character and meaning of the whole.

Lori Rowlett suggests the book presents a "narrative of identity" showing who is included in Israel and who is excluded and why.[136] Rowlett maintains that the text makes the point "absolutely clear": "the punishment for Otherness is death." The text constantly deals with the situation of marginal people: eastern tribes outside the land bordered by the Jordan, the Gibeonites who live inside the land but are of the wrong ethnicity. They face the alternative: death or submission to authority. Both groups will obey Joshua and be his servants. Similarly, the insider Achan, by refusal to obey, becomes an outsider and is sentenced to death.[137] Rowlett concludes: "the true organizing principle of the narrative is not ethnic identity but voluntary submission to authority structures, including the ancestral political arrangement as well as the central ruling establishment represented by Joshua."[138]

---

136 *JSOT* 55 (1992) 15.
137 Ibid., 20.
138 Ibid., 22.

Rowlett finds the audience for such a narrative among the Israelite insiders.[139] The book of Joshua warns readers not to rebel in any way and become outsiders. They need to know the strength of the governing authority (for Rowlett, Josiah).

Richard Hess compares the book of Joshua with Hittite, Akkadian, and Ugaritic land grants.[140] Unlike treaties, land grants protect the vassal landowners, not the kings. Israel talks of land promises, whereas the grants include property deeds. In Joshua, however, God deeds the land and demands loyalty. Hess underlines three areas of resemblance between the book of Joshua and ancient Near Eastern land grants: narrative background leading to the allotment, allotment of specific towns, and repeated stipulations requiring loyalty. This comparison with only one specific document leads Hess to ponder a given form and to state a pre-Deuteronomistic origin.

I attempted to broach this form critical question in a paper—"The Form of the Book of Joshua and Its Significance for Old Testament Research"—presented to the Hebrew Bible Group of the Society of Biblical Literature in 1985. A few earlier studies hinted at possible solutions. Gerhard von Rad in his classic "The Form-Critical Problem of the Hexateuch" attacks the problem only obliquely. He sees the form and purpose of the book centered in Josh 21:43–44, affirming that Yahweh fulfills his promises. The book of Joshua, for von Rad, is a book of promise pointing ahead of itself to the time of future fulfillment, the time of David. Martin Noth worked more with the concept of the Deuteronomistic History than with the final form of Joshua. His basic clue comes in his three-point outline—conquest of Transjordan, distribution of the land, and directions for life in the land—so that for Noth, the land seems to be the central theme of the book, but this says nothing of the form or genre of the book. Hans Wilhelm Hertzberg's commentary takes basically the same approach, as does John Gray.

Soggin writes of the astonishment caused by "the wide range of an attempt at a historical, philosophical, and theological synthesis that is without parallel either in classical antiquity or in the Ancient Near East. Equally astonishing is the strength of a faith which will not be convinced by the evidence that its cause is already lost."[141] Woudstra addresses the Former Prophets as a whole and sees their intent as "to present an intrepretative (prophetical) history of God's dealings with his covenant people Israel."[142] He explicitly denies that biblical historiography focuses on the human agents of the redemptive drama. Thus the final purpose of Joshua is "to stress the truth of the everlasting faithfulness of God."[143]

Robert Polzin speaks of the complicated relationship between the Lord and Israel as it is based on the Mosaic law code with the latter half of the book devoted to "a meditation on how the word of the Lord is fulfilled."[144] Robert Boling, rather, sees a conversation between two Deuteronomistic voices whose final word is the assurance that the promises to the fathers had been fulfilled by the work of Moses and Joshua.[145]

John Hamlin cites similarities between chaps. 1 and 23; a series of summary statements in 10:40, 11:16–20, 11:23, 19:51, 20:9, 21:41–42, and 21:43–45; the impor-

---

139   Ibid., 23.
140   *Bib* 83 (2002) 493–506.
141   Soggin, 5.
142   Woudstra, 3.
143   Ibid., 33.
144   Polzin, 124–26.
145   Boling, 499.

tance of 8:30–35 as the centerpiece looking backward and forward; and the three festivals at the beginning (5:11), midpoint (8:30–35), and end (24:1–18) of the book. These clues show that the book is "a lesson in history for the Israelites of later generations about their responsibilities on the land Yahweh had given them."[146]

This brief survey demonstrates that the surface themes of the book are clear: land, conquest, law, leadership, grace, and covenant obedience. The structure and genre elements that bind these themes together are much less clear. Cultic celebrations in Josh 3–4, 5, 8:30–35, and 24 provide some structure for the book, but the clues they give for genre are not at all clear.

The study of the book of Joshua has traditionally been undertaken in conjunction with the Former Prophets, with the Hexateuch, with the Deuteronomistic History, with the Enneateuch, and with the short historical credos. Certainly, Joshua has important connections with these other literary units. Still, Joshua deserves to be studied for itself and its unique nature. Lost in the maze of interconnections is the basic definition of the material we have at hand, namely the book of Joshua. I must agree with Hertzberg's assessment that Joshua is a "geschlossenen auf Einheitlichkeit angelegtes Werk," a complete work planned to be a unified whole. Joshua has a natural starting point for a literary work, the death of a forerunner and the commissioning and initial exercise of authority by the major character. It, likewise, has a natural conclusion—the burial of the major character after the work for which he was commissioned is as complete as he can make it.

Literary summaries and markers provide conclusions to the smaller literary units comprising the work: 5:1, 11:23, 12:1–24, 19:51, 21:43–45, 24:28, and 24:29–33. A reader can understand the book in and of itself, even though it presupposes the events in a previous literary work: the Pentateuch, especially Deuteronomy. Dividing the book into structural units offers one way to look for the generic structure of Joshua. I find the following:

Table 0.2. Generic Structure of Joshua

Passage	Unit's Central Theme	Central Actor
1:1–9	Joshua is commissioned to succeed Moses.	Joshua/God
1:10–18	Joshua functions as commander of Israel and of East Jordan troops.	Joshua
2:1–24	Joshua sends spies to see the land, and they find Rahab and report back to Joshua.	Joshua/Rahab
3:1–5:1	Joshua directs the crossing of the Jordan and receives the renown of Moses.	Joshua/Priests
5:2–9	Joshua sanctifies the negligent people by circumcising them.	Joshua
5:10–12	The sanctified people celebrate Passover.	People of Israel
5:13–15	Joshua is confronted by the Prince of the Host of Yahweh.	Prince of Host/Joshua
6:1–27	Jericho is given into Joshua's hands.	God/Joshua
7:1–5	Joshua leads a futile attack against Ai after Achan's sin and the spies' foolish advice.	Joshua/Achan/spies

---

146 Hamlin, xvii.

Passage	Unit's Central Theme	Central Actor
7:6–9	Joshua leads a public lamentation ceremony.	Joshua
7:10–26	Joshua obeys God and leads a public trial.	Joshua/God
8:1–29	Joshua captures Ai.	Joshua
8:30–35	Joshua builds an altar and leads a covenant ceremony according to law of Moses.	Joshua
9:1–2	Southern kings gather for war against Joshua.	Kings/ Joshua
9:3–15	Joshua accepts the decision of the men of Israel to make a covenant with Gibeonites.	Men of Israel/Joshua/ Gibeonites
9:16–21	The men of Israel decide not to attack the Gibeonites but to make them cult servants.	Men of Israel/Gibeonites
9:22–27	Joshua curses the Gibeonites and officially makes them cultic servants.	Joshua/men of Gibeon
10:1–14	Joshua defeats the southern kings to fulfill the treaty with the Gibeonites.	Joshua
10:15–43	Joshua directs a punishment and pursuit mission.	Joshua
11:1–15	Joshua captures the northern kings and land following Mosaic commands.	Joshua
11:16–23	Joshua takes the whole land according to God's word through Moses and distributes it as an inheritance.	Joshua
12:1–24	Joshua's accomplishments are listed next to those of Moses.	Moses/Joshua/men of Israel
13:1–7	Yahweh describes for Joshua the land that remains.	God/Joshua
13:8–33	Moses' allotments are summarized.	Moses
14:1–5	Eleazar and Joshua begin the allotments according to law of Moses.	Eleazar/Joshua
14:6–15	Joshua blesses Caleb with his inheritance.	Joshua/Caleb
15:1–17:18	Judah, including Caleb, and Joseph, including Ephraim and Manasseh, receive lots from Eleazar (unmentioned) and from a dispute-settling Joshua.	Joshua (and Elezar)/ tribes
18:1–19:48	From Shiloh, Joshua leads the other seven tribes to spy out and take their inheritance.	Joshua (and Eleazar)/ tribes
19:49–51	Joshua receives an inheritance before Eleazar, and Joshua completes the distribution.	Joshua/Eleazar/Israelites
20:1–9	Joshua follows God's directions in the law of Moses for cities of refuge.	Joshua/Moses/God
21:1–42	Eleazar and Joshua follow God's directions in the law of Moses for cities for the Levites.	Eleazar/Moses/Joshua
21:43–45	God gives the land and fulfills all his promises.	God
22:1–9	Joshua sends the obedient eastern tribes home.	Joshua
22:10–34	Phinehas, the priest, settles an altar dispute between the eastern and western tribes.	Phinehas/officers/ eastern tribes
23:1–16	Joshua delivers his farewell speech.	Joshua
24:1–28	Joshua leads the tribes in a covenant ceremony.	Joshua/tribes of Israel
24:29–33	Joshua, Joseph, and Eleazar are buried.	Joshua/Eleazar

The table shows that the narrative structure of the book of Joshua has a single center. Joshua is the actor on center stage at every important juncture except for the purely cultic elements of land distribution and tribal fighting over cultic disagreements, when Eleazar or Phinehas appear. Even here the priestly duties are split between the two men so that neither can take the starring role away from Joshua. Joshua works with the priest, though, to distribute the land and works apparently without the priest to establish covenant ceremonies (Josh 8:30–35; 24:1–24). Elsewhere, Joshua backs out of the spotlight only when the people do blameworthy acts (7:1–2; 9:14). Content dictates the few places where Joshua disappears or takes a back seat.

The book of Joshua relates the professional career of Joshua as leader of Israel. The subject of the lead sentences of the book is Joshua. As the story unfolds, the fame and glory of Joshua increase. The narrative does not concentrate so much on conquest or on land distribution as it does on the person and work of Joshua in obedience to the law of Moses.

The book of Joshua finds its structure from repeated thematic statements scattered throughout the book.

Table 0.3. Thematic Structures in Joshua

Theme	Passages	Climactic Statement
Divine Promise	1:2, 3, 6, 11, 13, 15; 2:9, 14, 24; 5:5; 6:2,16; 8:1, 7, 18; 9:24; 18:3; warning—23:13; 24:13	21:43
Divine Warrior	10:9, 11, 14, 42; 23:3, 10; 24:8; warning—24:20	10:25
Moses	1:3, 5, 7–8, 13, 17; 3:7; 4:10, 14; 8:31–35; 9:24; 11:12, 15, 20, 23; 12:6–7; 13:8, 15, 24, 29, 32; 14:2, 5, 6, 9; 17:4; 20:2; 21:2; warning—23:6–8	23:6–8
Rest	1:13, 15; 11:23; 22:4; 23:1	21:44
Cult	2:9–11; 4:7, 21–24; 5:1–15; 6:1–26; 7:6–9, 10–26; 8:1, 17, 26–29, 30–35; 9:9–10, 14, 21, 23, 24, 27; 10:6, 7, 9, 12, 43; 11:6; 13:14, 33; 14:1, 3–4; lots in 15–17; 18:1, 7, 8, 10; 19:51; 20:1–9; 21:1–42; 22:1–34	24:1–28

Each of these thematic statements in some way vies for center stage, but no one of them dominates the book. As I stated above the central figure of the book is Joshua in relationship to Moses, to the fulfillment of God's promises of land and inheritance, to the ultimate goal of rest, and to the cultic practices that Joshua constantly promoted and even led.

Table 0.4. Joshua's Central Narrative Role

Chapter/ Parallel Chapter	Elements	Purpose	Role of Joshua
Josh 1/8	Installing Joshua, book of Moses, Joshua's leadership	Show Joshua as respected leader	Commander, subject to the book of Moses, exercises leadership successfully
Josh 2/6	Spy narrative	Joshua as leader echoing Moses' leadership without express command	Joshua follows Moses' pattern and being obeyed

Chapter/ Parallel Chapter	Elements	Purpose	Role of Joshua
Josh 3–4	Cultic crossing and memorializing	Underline chain of command: Yahweh/ Moses/ Joshua/People	Joshua repeats Mosaic water crossing, gains awe from the people
Josh 5	Cultic circumcision, Passover, call	Restore Mosaic practices as before wilderness apostasy	Joshua restores cult, passes test as new leader after Moses
Josh 6/2	Cultic procession, victory	Joshua is victorious warrior like Moses whom people obey, especially in ḥērem, the ban	Show expansion of Joshua's theme throughout the land (earth?)
Josh 7/6	Spy narrative like chap. 2 gone awry	Show results of disobedience	Joshua leads mourning for the people's punishment and punishment of wrong-doer
Josh 8/7	Ambush narrative with modified ban	Show God's willingness to bring victory for repentant, obedient people	Joshua plays Moses' role in battle and gains obedi-ence of the people to new ban conditions
Josh 8:30–35	Covenant ceremony	Show people's obedience to law of Moses	Joshua restores proper worship and loyalty to Yahweh
Josh 9/8:30–35/6	Covenant with foreigners	Show divine wisdom victorious over human cunning; explain contemporary cult	Joshua brings order to the disorderly covenant made by leaders
Josh 10/7	Battle to obey covenant treaty with foreign allies and apply ban	Highlight Joshua's victories in obedience to God	Joshua brings victory by obeying God's com-mands and law and crediting God with fighting for Israel
Josh 11/7	Obeying the ban in battle	Joshua leads in battle that Yahweh wins	Joshua follows the chain of command from Yahweh to Moses to win battle and take and distribute land
Josh 12/ Deut 1–3	Summary of victories	Joshua wins just as Moses did	Joshua is the ideal leader after Moses
Josh 13/11/ Judges	Victories from Moses to David	Joshua leaves work for a new generation as had Moses	Dividing land among western tribes as Joshua's final obedient act in the shadow of Moses
Josh 14–17/11:23	Cultic distribution of land with much that remains	Tribal land distribution begins with some tribes unable to inhabit the land in face of enemies	Joshua fairly distributes land as had Moses and as God commanded and cooperates in leadership with priest
Josh 18–19/2/7	Spy story leads to land distribution	Distribution of land is completed for all tribes	Joshua completes the task God gave him

Chapter/ Parallel Chapter	Elements	Purpose	Role of Joshua
Josh 20–21	Cities of refuge and cities of Levites lists	Special provisions made for people in need	Joshua follows Moses' commands in setting up special cities for accused criminals and for the Levites
Josh 21:43–45	Theological summary	God accomplishes his promises	Joshua is human leader as God fulfills the promises of land and rest
Josh 22/1, 7	Altar dispute	Faithful eastern tribes return home, build altar that brings the wrath of western tribes	Joshua lets the priest settle the cultic dispute
Josh 23/1, 13	Pre-death speech of leader	Joshua reviews God's accomplishments and warns of future disobedience	Joshua sets the agenda for the future
Josh 24/8:30–35	Covenant renewal	The people choose to follow Yahweh and no other gods	Joshua reviews the credo, warns of the results of disobedience, and leads the people to renew the covenant with Yahweh

The central focus on Joshua is thus modified by the way themes and sections are consciously juxtaposed throughout the book to draw attention to concerns beyond the person of Joshua. The themes are not painted in clear black and white strokes but with subtle choices involved. Joshua's office is tied closely to the law and actions of Moses, yet he is given freedom to issue new commands and to interpret the law, particularly the law of the ban, in new situations. The fate of the east Jordan tribes is tied to their obedience to Moses, their obedience to Joshua, and their ability to settle differences with the tribes west of the Jordan. Non-Israelites are under the ban. They represent the chief danger to Israel's total dedication to the worship of Yahweh. Yet isolated examples stand as a reminder of faith, faithfulness, understanding of the Israelite credo, and service to the Israelite cult. The ban is a means to preserve cultic and religious purity, but the intent is that the fame of Israel's God and of Israel's leader be spread over all the land. Flexibility in applying the ban shows the need to follow God's leader, not just to rigidly follow a written law.

The major narrative focuses on the law of Moses as the standard for Israel, but cultic elements constantly remind the reader that the law is more than a call to serve one God in moral purity. The law is also a call to observe the cultic worship regulations of the law. The exemplary life of Joshua as related in the book of Joshua is a description of a past hero, but it is more than that. It also describes the present situation and future potential. The present situation is described in full obedience, but the future potential is one of choice: Joshua's God or the gods of the people who remain in the land, fulfillment of divine promises or of divine threats, life in the totally occupied land with God or death, perishing away from the land God has faithfully given.

The result of a form-critical analysis is that the book of Joshua represents an ancient Near Eastern biography. We are not the first to suggest that biography is the category that best describes the book. Klaus Baltzer devotes a chapter to Joshua.[147] He picks up the pentateuchal references in his discussion of Joshua. Rather than looking at the structure of the book, Baltzer examines the functions and offices exercised by Joshua. He concludes his discussion with a final tantalizing statement:

> I would like to ask if Deuteronomy 31 could have formed the beginning of an Ideal Biography which would have begun with his installation in the 120th year of Moses and would have concluded with his farewell (Josh 23), death, and burial (24:29–30). The biography, however, need not begin in Deuteronomy. Joshua 1 also provides an installation beginning for the biography. But what is a biography in Joshua's cultural setting?[148]

Baltzer concludes that the theme of ancient biography was the office and function of a person. It featured the public life rather than the private, personal life, and thus life and office became practically identical. Ancient biography is interested in the typical rather than the individual fate. It is a complex literary type that can incorporate smaller literary types into itself. Baltzer sees the original setting for ancient biography in the memorial stones for the dead. The topoi of such a biography, for Baltzer, include: securing of peace internally and externally, establishing social justice, and preserving the purity of the cult. The biography becomes a teaching document using the subject as a role model for future generations.

Applying Baltzer's findings to the book of Joshua, we determine that the center of attention is Joshua and the office(s) he occupies. Joshua functions as the leader of the conquest and distribution of the land and of the renewal of the covenant. Carrying out these functions represents the only subject of the book; all private details are omitted. We do not meet Joshua the person. Instead we meet Joshua the national leader. In his official functions Joshua secures peace for and among the people. He lays the demands of the law of Moses before the people to secure social justice. He delivers a divine ultimatum concerning their choice of God in order to ensure the purity of the cult. Christa Schäfer-Lichtenberger shows that the biblical texts picture Joshua as the ideal successor to a charismatic leader in Israel, as opposed to the negative example of Solomon.[149]

Both structure and content thus show the book of Joshua to be biography. John Van Seters looks carefully at ancient Egyptian biographies. He maintains that these "biographies often constitute the most important historical source for these periods."[150] They came to include "an account of how at least some of the offices and honors of the deceased were achieved," were "dominated by the association of the deceased with the king," speak "in a rather conventional fashion of the exemplary behavior of the deceased," and contain "nothing critical about the deceased or the state."[151] Van Seters points to a "perspective on the afterlife" as a dominant characteristic of the biographies. Eighteenth Dynasty examples come from tombs of military men telling their exploits. Later the biographies become didactic, giving lessons in piety and good conduct. Royal inscriptions take up many of these form-

---

147   *Die biographie der Propheten*, 53–61.
148   Ibid., 61.
149   See her *Josua und Salomo.*
150   *In Search of History*, 182.
151   Ibid.

critical elements and combine "a variety of genre elements . . . within the same work."[152] Van Seters then compares the historiography of the Deuteronomistic History with that of Assyrian annals and "letters to the god."[153]

Like the ancient Egyptian biographies, Joshua constitutes the most important historical source for this period and shows how its hero gained his office and his honors among the people. As with the Egyptian sources, so the book of Joshua contains no criticism of Joshua. Certainly, the book combines a number of form-critical genres. It is not a precise parallel to the Egyptian materials. The writer has adapted the form to the culture and religion of Israel. Joshua is viewed in light of his honors, gradually becoming a hero in the shadow of Moses, but he is also viewed in light of his relationships to God, the law God gave Moses, and the cultic worship of Yahweh, the God of Israel.

Lawson Younger (*Ancient Conquest Accounts*) has compared in detail the conquest accounts from Assyria, Hatti, Egypt, and Israel. He concludes that "the conquest account in Joshua 9–12 evinces the same basic ideology as one sees in other ancient Near Eastern conquest accounts. . . . The text of Joshua 9–12 is structured on a transmission code similar to that of other ancient Near Eastern royal inscriptions."[154] Younger's study isolates four chapters of Joshua and shows them to be related in form, content, and cultural presuppositions to the literature of Israel's neighbors. Younger sees the chapters as a literary unity rather than a composite of many separate traditions.[155] It solves many of what have traditionally been viewed as "contradictions" by reverting to the language of hyperbole.[156] As with other ancient Near Eastern records, conquest of a city or land was often temporary rather than permanent, an occupation rather than a subjugation.[157]

"All Israel" for Younger was typical ancient Near Eastern figurative language, probably a synecdoche.[158] Ancient inscriptions show summary accounts comparable to those in Joshua that do not have to be explained as later editorial activity. The texts utilizing this conquest transmission code come from a variety of countries, languages, and dates, not just the Assyrian annals as many scholars, following Van Seters, have alleged. Thus the comparison with Assyrian annals is an incomplete comparison and cannot lead to dating the book of Joshua in the Assryian period. Younger's evidence covers the span 1300 BCE to 600 BCE.

Younger has issued some much needed cautions and shown caution himself in refusing to come to conclusions concerning date and authorship or mode of conquest. He has demonstrated a literary unity in chaps. 9–12. In so doing he has assumed that such a unity obviates the need for underlying traditions or sources and for a larger genre incorporating his conquest account material. He has in the end admitted that Josh 9–12 "cannot be identified as any particular genre *per se*." Indeed, his conquest accounts are found as part of different genres. Thus Josh 9–12, 1–12, and the book as a whole must be studied to find what type of genre has incorporated

---

152 Ibid., 185.
153 Ibid., 330–31.
154 *Ancient Conquest Accounts*, 236–37.
155 Ibid., 241.
156 Ibid., 243.
157 Ibid., 244–45.
158 *Ancient Conquest Accounts*, 249.

material that contains the elements and transmission code of ancient Near Eastern conquest accounts. But the conquest accounts themselves utilize a variety of sources to create their final accounts. Study of these component genres is also an open field, not blocked by the recognition of the conquest-account transmission code.

Knowing Younger's work, Thomas Römer continues the comparison between Assyrian accounts and Joshua, both of which include:[159]

1. Extended reports combined with summary statements;
2. Salvation oracle from God;
3. Voluntary submission of foreign peoples;
4. Enemy coalitions;
5. Miraculous intervention of gods brings victory;
6. Killing enemy kings who often try to escape.

Despite Younger's arguments for a wide chronological context for such similarities, Römer maintains the Assyrian evidence for dating no earlier than the eighth century. The elements he describes belong to conquest accounts but do not form a genre in and of themselves, being widely distributed in Josh 6–12.

The conquest accounts Younger describes all have a purpose. They center on the activities and renown of the ruler—king or pharaoh[160]—in support of a royal ideology.[161] These materials from widely differing dates highlight one area of a king's reign, namely, his battles. Other official acts of the kings are reserved for other types of literature. Chaps. 9–12 represent one part of the presentation of Joshua's biography. Chaps. 1–8 illustrate Joshua's leadership skills in taking over from Moses. Chaps. 13–19 show his administrative skills in distributing the land. Chaps. 20–21 demonstrate his maintenance of the Mosaic tradition in establishing social institutions required by Torah. Chap. 22 shows Joshua can operate through delegation by letting the priest control matters of religious dispute. Chaps. 23–24 depict Joshua preparing Israel for the future without a leader like Moses when they must obey the Torah and maintain the covenant expectations. All of the materials fit together into the larger genre of biography of Joshua.

We must, however, be aware that the book speaks of more than biographical issues. It uses the structure of biography to delve into the biography of the people of Israel themselves, from the fathers with other gods beyond the River to the leader who will complete the conquest to the nation faced with the temptation to desert her heritage and her God in face of peoples who have a different heritage and different gods.

3. Tradition History behind Joshua

Bibliography

Auld, A. G. *Joshua, Moses, and the Land: Tetrateuch—Pentateuch—Hexateuch in a Generation since 1938.* Edinburgh: T&T Clark, 1980. ———. "Tribal Terminology in Joshua and Judges." In *Convegno sul Tema: Le Origini di Israele.* Ed. J. A. Soggin et al. Rome: Accademia Nazionale dei Lincei, 1987. 85–98. **Bieberstein, K.** *Josua, Jordan, Jericho: Geschichte*

---

159 *So-called Deuteronomistic History*, 84.
160 *Ancient Conquest Accounts*, 123, 194.
161 Ibid., 163.

und Theologie der Landnahmeerzählung Jos 1–6. OBO 143. Göttingen: Vandenhoeck & Ruprecht, 1995. **Cortese, E.** *Josua 13–21: Ein priesterlicher Abschnitt im deuteronomistischen Geschichtswerk*. OBO 14. Göttingen: Vandenhoeck & Ruprecht, 1990. **Creangá, O.** "The Silenced Songs of Victory: Power, Gender and Memory in the Conquest Narrative of Joshua (Joshua 1–12)." In *A Question of Sex? Gender and Difference in the Hebrew Bible and Beyond*. Ed. D. W. Rooker. Hebrew Bible Monographs 14. Sheffield: Sheffield Phoenix, 2007. 106–23. **Hawk, L.** *Every Promise Fulfilled: Contesting Plots in Joshua*. Louisville: Westminster John Knox, 1991. **Kaufmann, Y.** "Traditions concerning Early Israelite History in Canaan." In *Studies in the Bible*. Ed. C. Rabin. ScrHier 8. Jerusalem: Magnes; Hebrew University, 1961. 303–34. **Kratz, R. G.** *The Composition of the Narrative Books of the Old Testament*. Trans. J. Bowden. Edinburgh: T&T Clark, 2000. Originally published as *Komposition der erzählenden Bücher des Alten Testaments* (Göttingen: Vandenhoeck & Ruprecht, 2000). **Kraus, H.-J.** *Gottesdienst in Israel: Grundriss einer Geschichte des alttestamentlichen Gottesdienstes*. 2nd ed. Munich: Kaiser, 1962. Translated as *Worship in Israel: A Cultic History of the Old Testament*, trans. G. Buswell (Richmond: John Knox, 1966). **Kuenen, A.** *An Historico-Critical Inquiry into the Origin and Composition of the Hexateuch*. Trans. P. H. Wicksteed. New York: McMillan and Company, 1886. Repr., Wipf and Stock, 2005. **Miller, R. B., II.** "Both Written and Oral: the Dual Nature of Israelite Tradition." Paper read to SBL Orality, Textuality, and the Formation of the Hebrew Bible Section, Atlanta, November 21, 2010. **Mitchell, G.** *Together in the Land*. JSOTSup 134. Sheffield: Sheffield Academic, 1993. **Möhlenbrink, K.** "Die Landnahmesagen des Buches Josua." *ZAW* 56 (1938) 238–68. **Noort, E.** *Das Buch Josua: Forschungsgeschichte und Problemfelder*. EdF 292. Darmstadt: Wissenschaftliche Buchgesellschaft, 1998. **Otto, E.** *Das Mazzotfest in Gilgal*. BWANT 107. Stuttgart: Kohlhammer, 1975. **Ottosson, M.** *Josuaboken: En programskrift för davidisk restauration*. AUU: Studia Biblical Upsaliensia 1. Uppsala: AUU, 1991. ———. "Tradition and History with Emphasis on the Composition of the Book of Joshua." In *The Productions of Time: Tradition History in Old Testament Scholarship*. Ed. K. Jeppesen and B. Otzen. Sheffield: Almond, 1984. 81–106, 141–43. **Polzin, R.** *Moses and the Deuteronomist: A Literary Study of the Deuteronomic History*. Part 1, *Deuteronomy, Joshua, Judges*. Bloomington, IN: Indiana UP, 1980. **Schäfer-Lichtenberger, C.** *Josua und Salomo: Eine Studie zu Autorität und Legitimität des Nachfolgers im Alten Testament*. VTSup 58. Leiden: Brill, 1995. **Schaper, J.** "The Living Word Engraved in Stone: The Interrelationship of the Oral and the Written and the Culture of Memory in the Books of Deuteronomy and Joshua." In *Memory in the Bible and Antiquity: The Fifth Durham-Tübingen Research Symposium (Durham, September 2004)*. Ed. S. C. Barton, L. T. Stuckenbruck, and B. G. Wold. WUNT 212. Tübingen: Mohr Siebeck, 2007. 9–23. **Schmid, H.** "Erwägungen zur Gestalt Joshuas in Überlieferung und Geschichte." *Jud* 24 (1968) 44–57. **Schmid, R.** "Meerwunder und Landnahmetradition." *TZ* 21 (1965) 260–68. **Schmitt, G.** *Du sollst keinen Frieden schliessen mit den Bewohnern des Landes*. BWANT 91. Stuttgart: Kohlhammer, 1970. ———. *Der Landtag von Sichem*. AzTh 1.15. Stuttgart: Kohlhammer, 1964. **Soggie, N. A.** *Myth, God, and War: The Mythopoetic Inspiration of Joshua*. Lanham, MD: University Press of America, 2007. **Stone, L. G.** "Ethical and Apologetic Tendencies in the Redaction of the Book of Joshua." *CBQ* 53 (1991) 25–36. **Tunyogi, A. C.** "The Book of the Conquest." *JBL* 84 (1965) 374–80. **Van Seters, J.** *In Search of History: Historiography in the Ancient World and the Origins of Biblical History*. New Haven, CT: Yale UP, 1983. **Weinfeld, M.** "Historical Facts behind the Israelite Settlement Pattern." *VT* 38 (1988) 324–32. **Whitelam, K. W.** "Israel's Traditions of Origins: Reclaiming the Land." *JSOT* 44 (1989) 19–42. **Younger, K. L., Jr.** *Ancient Conquest Accounts: A Study in Ancient Near Eastern and Biblical History Writing*. JSOTSup 98. Sheffield: JSOT Press, 1990.

The editorial work of this Compiler, to use Noth's term, was not the first effort to gather Israel's traditions. Indeed, it was only the continuation of a process that the cult at Gilgal had carried on for a long time. The activity of this cult is particularly obvious in the cultic additions to chaps. 3 through 6: Josh 3:5, 8, 15–16aαβ; 4:1–3, 8, 15–23; 6:3b, 4, 6b, 8aβ, b, 9*, 13a, 14–16a, 20a. The work of the Gilgal cult probably extended far beyond what we are able to isolate in the book of Joshua. The Compiler had reason to make Gilgal the center of activity in Josh 5:9–10; 9:6; 10:6, 7, 9, 15, 43 (cf. 14:6 and the *Comment* on chap. 22). Though I cannot describe the Gilgal cultic celebrations in as concrete terms as did H.-J. Kraus or E. Otto would like,[162] I do see enough evidence to argue that this Benjaminite sanctuary played a primary role in the gathering and celebrating of the traditions that eventually became the heart of the book of Joshua.

Robert Boling summarizes the work of oral tradition:

> The "Conquest" as Yahweh's gift, a supreme example of divine grace, was a recurring motif in stories told for both edification and entertainment, in which parents and teacher-priests explained to children and worshippers the meaning of their life together as Israelites (Joshua 2–11). It was a theme regularly sung in worship, exalting Yahweh as the ultimate power at work in the world—protecting the weak and breaking the chains of bondage—so that in the Bible love and justice became virtual synonyms, also known as righteousness (see for example, Pss 44:1–8; 78:54–55; 80:8–9, 11; 105:43–45; 106:34–38; 114:1–8; 135:10–12; 136:17–22).[163]

The essence of God's Word began not in the isolation of the scribe's study but in the active worship of the people of God. Thus one element in the mighty mystery of divine inspiration comprehends not just a lone individual, but extends to the entire community in its joyous celebration of worship.

Gilgal had no monopoly on Israelite tradition nor on divine inspiration. Gibeon (chaps. 9–10), Shechem (chap. 24; cf. 8:30–35), and Shilo (chaps. 18–22) also celebrated the greatness of Yahweh and contributed their traditions to the Word of God. Weinfeld begins with Josh 19:50 to argue that the tradition about Joshua centered on Shiloh, not on Gilgal or Shechem.[164] Such a view is difficult to adopt unless one is willing to delete Joshua from most of the tradition concerning him.

Even worship in all its solemn greatness was not the beginning point for the book of Joshua. We can search beyond the ultimate historian, the Deuteronomic editor, the Compiler, and the early worship of Israel to an earlier stage of the tradition. This stage shows great variety: ancient war poetry (10:12b–13aα); a spy narrative report (2:1–9, 12–16, 22–23); holy war catechesis (3:2–4, 6, 9, 11–14, 16b; 4:4–7, 11, 13); a popular anecdote about circumcision (5:2–3, 8); a divine-test narrative (5:13–15); a story of military ruse (6:1–3a, 7, 8aα, 9*, 10–12, 13b, 16b, 20b); an ironical spy narrative introducing a story of military ambush (7:2–6; 8:1, 3–7, 9*, 10–11, 14–17, 19*, 20–22); a polemical narrative of sacral procedure used in face of divine anger (7:13–

162 H.-J. Kraus, *Gottesdienst in Israel*, 179–93 = *Worship in Israel*, 152–65; E. Otto, *Das Mazzotfest in Gilgal*.

163 Boling, 1003.

164 *VT* 38 (1988) 324–32.

14, 16–25); a polemical etiology defending a social position (9:4–5, 8–9a, 11–15a), whose function has been reversed within the tradition (9:15b–21); a holy war miracle story (10:3–6, 8, 9a, 10a, 11b); a popular story of the defeat of five kings at Makkedah (10:16–18, 21–22, 24, 26a); a conquest itinerary (10:31–39*); another narrative of military ruse (11:4–9); and a political list of cities (12:14–24). Common to all of the materials is their roots in the political and military struggles of Israel and her tribes. Holy war theology, which Israel shared with her Near Eastern neighbors, is the common bond holding the traditions together. Here we see another dimension to the process by which God taught his people and directed the formation of his word.

The latter half of the book also contains traditional materials used in Israel long before they were incorporated into the book of Joshua. The major elements comprise three types:

 a. Narratives: Josh 14:6–13; 15:16–19; 17:14–18; 18:3–6, 8–10; 19:47, 49–50; 22:9–34
 b. Political boundary and city lists: Josh 13:15–31; 15:1–12, 20–62; 16:1–9; 17:1–2, 7–11; 18:11–28; 19:1–46, 48; 21:4–42
 c. Notes on Canaanites remaining in the land: Josh 13:13; 15:63; 16:10; 17:12–13

Two other forms of literature must be noted: the law of the cities of refuge in 20:1–7 and the report of the covenant ceremony in 24:1–28. Appended to the book are the burial notices of 24:29–30, 32–33.

These traditions also have roots in the political and military struggles of early Israel, giving us an important clue about the earliest formation of the traditions. Such traditions had their origins in the midst of the struggles of Israel to gain her land, peace with her neighbors, and, importantly, a sense of unity among her various tribes and clans. Such traditions are peculiarly at home in the tribe of Benjamin and its attempts to gain territory from the inhabitants of the land and live in harmony with its tribal colleagues to the northwest, the south, and across the Jordan to the east. Many of these traditions found a home in the cultic celebration, catechetical teaching, and even legal claims of the sanctuary of the Benjaminites in Gilgal. But the sanctity of the holy place was not enough to insure peace even for the traditions.

Other sanctuaries had traditions with other claims. Thus Benjamin and its Transjordan allies faced the claims of Shiloh (Josh 22). Benjamin faced the land claims of an expanding Ephraim (Josh 17:14–18; Judg 12:1–6; 8:1–3; cf. 19–21; Deut 32:17). And the relationships to the south (cf. Josh 7:13–26) eventually burst into the fierce competition between the Benjaminite Saul and the Judean David (1 Sam 16–2 Sam 5). Such fighting within and without gave root to the Joshua traditions. God used even the wars and squabblings of his people to prepare the foundation of his word.

If we are to understand the Joshua tradition in its depths, we must seek to understand how the tradition functioned in this earliest setting, as well as within the later literary settings that provide the present form of the tradition. This understanding dictates our methodology for understanding the meaning of the book of Joshua. The meaning cannot be limited to one level of the story. Rather, we must understand the history of the formation of tradition, a history that leads from ancient military traditions in the earliest life of Israel and her tribes and cults to cultic celebration and recitation to a compiler seeking to unite the traditions to the

Deuteronomic edition of the book of Joshua to the ultimate historical work comprising Joshua, Judges, Samuel, and Kings. The Deuteronomistic editing of Joshua is not the creation of a span of books from Joshua through Kings, for the variety of editorial work on each of the books is too great. Beyond the Deuteronomic editing in Joshua lies an editor who joined Joshua and Judges and eventually joined Samuel and Kings to the collection. Finally, a canonical compiler joined the history with the other parts of the canon.

The interpreter cannot be satisfied at this point. Did this Compiler or the Deuteronomic editor provide the first interpretation to the material? Or can we discover still earlier editors? Admittedly, the work here becomes ever more subjective. Verse divisions attributed to tradition and interpretation are even more tentative. Still, an effort must be made and tentative results reported. An early editing of chaps. 2–11 appears quite evident. Such editing may even have extended into chaps. 14–17. It is most apparent in Josh 2:1, 17–21, 24; 3:1; 4:9; 5:4, 7, 9, 10–12; 6:17–19, 22–25, 27; 7:1a, 10–12, 26; 8:2, 8, 9aβ, 12–13, 23–25, 27–28; 9:1–3, 6–7, 15b, 22–23, 25–27abα; 10:1–2, 7, 9b, 10b–11a, 12a, 13aβ–15, 19–20, 23, 26b–28, 29–39*, 41–43; 11:1–2, 10, 13–14a, 16–20a.

The editing of chaps. 2–11 and chaps. 14–17 created a conquest narrative, often compared to the propagandistic war annals of Near Eastern kings. Younger concludes: "While it remains possible that this section of Joshua (9–12) is a composite of many separate traditions, this may not be the best explanation. It is more likely that the section is a narrative unity exhibiting a typical ancient Near Eastern transmission code commonly employed in the history writing of conquest accounts."[165] Younger underlines the use of hyperbole, making it unnecessary to "maintain that the account in Joshua 9–12 portrays a *complete* conquest. . . . The claims to conquest have been overstated."[166] Similarly, "all Israel" represents "commonly encountered synecdoche found in ancient Near Eastern conquest accounts. . . . [T]he proposal of a pan-Israelite redaction is unnecessary."[167]

Younger compares the procedures of a later international empire run by strong government agencies with a burgeoning group of tribes with little organization, no agencies, and no place to store written materials. The natural conclusion from Younger's work is that a later writer anachronistically described Israel's conquest in the light of Assyrian and Babylonian conquest narratives rather than in the form of tribal warfare with spies and sneak attacks and ambushes. Younger's studies cover professional armies trained to expand land claimed by another international enemy. The book of Joshua reports a landless people seeking to garner a homestead for their families, a place to develop and nurture a new kind of government, and a military base from which they could take the offensive against outside enemies.

Thus we picture the growth of the book of Joshua as beginning with trained narrators who entertained, informed, and worshiped through individual stories, each with a "home" in a local sanctuary. These narratives formed stories of origin for the various tribes or tribal groups. With the formation of the political organization and agencies under David and particularly under Solomon, Israel gained the

---

165 *Ancient Conquest Accounts*, 241.
166 Ibid., 243, 244.
167 Ibid., 248, 249.

scribal base in which oral materials could be collected and reduced to writing. At the same time, government and worship authorities would have been collecting the oral narratives connected to the Judges, Saul, Samuel, and David.

4. Literary (Source) Criticism

Bibliography

Albers, E. *Die Quellenberichte in Josua I–XII: Beitrag zur Quellenkritik des Hexateuchs.* Bonn: Paul, 1891. **Alt, A.** "Judas Gaue unter Josia." *PJ* 21 (1925) 100–116 (= *KS* [1953], 2:276–88). ———. "Das System der Stämmesgrenzen im Buche Josua." In *Beiträge zur Religionsgeschichte und Archäologie Palästina.*, FS E. Sellin, ed. A. Jirku. Leipzig: Deichert, 1927. 13–24 (= *KS* [1953], 1:193–202). **Auld, A. G.** *Joshua, Moses, and the Land: Tetrateuch—Pentateuch—Hexateuch in a Generation since 1938.* Edinburgh: T&T Clark, 1980. **Bieberstein, K.** *Josua, Jordan, Jericho: Geschichte und Theologie der Landnahmeerzählung Jos 1–6.* OBO 143. Göttingen: Vandenhoeck & Ruprecht, 1995. **Blenkinsopp, J.** "The Structure of P." *CBQ* 38 (1976) 275–92. **Blum, E.** *Studien zur Komposition des Pentateuch.* BZAW 189. Berlin: De Gruyter, 1990. ———. *Textgestalt und Komposition.* FAT 69. Tübingen: Mohr Siebeck, 2010. **Colenso, J. W.** *The Pentateuch and Book of Joshua Critically Examined.* London, 1872. **Dietrich, W.** *Prophetie und Geschichte.* FRLANT 108. Göttingen: Vandenhoeck & Ruprecht, 1972. **Eissfeldt, O.** *Hexateuch-Synopse: Die Erzählung der fünf Bucher Mose und des Buch Josua mit dem Anfange des Richterbuches in ihren vier Quellen zerflegt und in deutscher Übersetzung dargeboten saMT einer in Einleitung und Anmerkungen gegebenen Begrundung.* Leipzig, 1922. **Noort, E.** *Das Buch Josua: Forschungsgeschichte und Problemfelder.* EdF 292. Darmstadt: Wissenschaftliche Buchgesellschaft, 1998. **Noth, M.** *Das System der zwölf Stämme Israels.* BWANT 4.1. Stuttgart: Kohlhammer, 1930. Repr., Darmstadt: Wissenschaftliche Buchgesellschaft, 1966. ———. *Überlieferungsgeschichtliche Studien.* Tübingen: Niemeyer, 1943; repr., Darmstadt: Wissenschaftliche Buchgesellschaft, 1957. Translated as *The Deuteronomistic History,* JSOTSup 15. Sheffield: University of Sheffield, 1981. **Rose, M.** *Deuteronomist und Jahwist.* Zürich: Theologischer Verlag, 1980. **Rudolph, W.** *Der "Elohist" von Exodus bis Josua.* BZAW 68. Berlin: Töpelmann, 1938. **Smend, R., Jr.** "Das Gesetz und die Völker." In *Probleme biblischer Theologie: von Rad Festschrift.* Ed. H. W. Wolff. Munich: Kaiser, 1971. 494–509. **Spinoza, B.** *Tractatus theologico-politicus.* Only published volume of *Opera philosophica omnia.* Ed. A. Girörer. 1670. Repr., Stuttgart: Mezleri, 1830. **Otto, E.** *Das Mazzotfest in Gilgal.* BWANT 107. Stuttgart: Kohlhammer, 1975. **Tengström, S.** *Die Hexateucherzählung: Eine literaturgeschichtliche Studie.* ConBOT 7. Lund: Gleerup, 1976. **Veijola, T.** *Die ewige Dynastie.* AASF 193. Helsinki: Suomalainen Tiedeakatemia, 1975. **Wellhausen, J.** *Die Composition des Hexateuchs und der historischen Bücher des Alten Testament.* Berlin: Reimer, 1889. **Younger, K. L., Jr.** "The Rhetorical Structuring of the Joshua Conquest Narratives." In *Critical Issues in Early Israelite History.* Ed. R. S. Hess, G. A. Klingbeil, and P. J. Ray, Jr. BBRSup 3. Winona Lake, IN: Eisenbrauns, 2008. 3–32.

The history of Joshua and the Joshua of history have occupied biblical students at least since the early rabbis admitted that Joshua could not have reported his own death (see *b. B. Bat.* 14b, 15a). In 1564, John Calvin stressed the insignificance of the issue: "Let us not hesitate, therefore, to pass over a matter which we are unable to determine, or the knowledge of which is not very necessary, while we are in no doubt as to the essential point—that the doctrine herein contained was dictated by the Holy Spirit for our use, and confers benefits of no ordinary kind on those who attentively peruse it."[168]

---

168 *Commentarius in Librum Iosue* (Calvina Opera 25) 421; *Commentaries on the Book of Joshua,* xvii–xviii.

John Calvin recognized the probability that Eleazar, the high priest, had compiled a summary of events that provided the materials for the composition of the book.[169] Calvin's translator was uneasy at this point and sought to underline the reasons for accepting the traditional view that Joshua wrote the book. The translator did note that "the authorship, however, is so uncertain that there is scarcely a writer of eminence from the period of the history itself down to the time of Ezra, for whom the honor has not been claimed. Among others may be mentioned Phinehas, Samuel, and Isaiah. The obvious inference is that the question of authorship is one of those destined only to be agitated but never satisfactorily determined."[170]

Friedrich Bleek and Friedrich Tuch,[171] fathers of the supplementary hypothesis theory, drew Joshua into the pentateuchal documentary theories. Julius Wellhausen's climactic synthesis remained ambiguous in its analysis of Joshua. While finding evidence in chap. 24 that E formed the basic source of Joshua, Wellhausen noted basic characteristics of Deuteronomic editing, which, in turn, proved distinct from that in Deuteronomy.[172]

Wilhelm Rudolph later tried to bury E and claim all for J.[173] Kurt Möhlenbrink, on the other hand, traced separate traditions back to Shiloh and Gilgal.[174] For him, these proved to be older literarily, tradition-historically, and thematically than those of the Pentateuch. Indeed, Möhlenbrink claimed that many of the pentateuchal materials had first crystalized around those of Joshua. See the recent discussion by Martin Rose noted below.

Martin Noth's writings illustrate the progression of literary studies in Joshua in the twentieth century. In 1930 he saw no reason to debate the basic E source.[175] By 1937, with the first edition of his commentary, Noth had begun to speak of glosses and expansions of a basic narrative that could not be identified with any pentateuchal source. He remained content to speak generally of a Gilgal collection of etiological narratives formed into a conquest narrative by a collector about 900 BCE. He described the lists in the middle of the book, in agreement with with Alt,[176] as a combination of a premonarchical list of tribal borders with a Josianic list of Judean cities divided into twelve districts. Exilic additions, Deuteronomic redactions, and final Priestly supplements closed the book for Noth.

Noth opened a new epoch in Old Testament scholarship in 1943,[177] suggesting the Deuteronomist as compiler of a history work encompassing Deuteronomy, Joshua, Judges, Samuel, and Kings. The second edition of Noth's commentary in

---

169 *Commentaries on the Book of Joshua,* xvii.
170 Ibid., xviii, n. 1. The sixteenth-century Catholic jurist Andreas Masius, *Iosuae imperatoris historia illustrata atq. explicata* (1574), noted the similarity between literary problems in Joshua and those in the Pentateuch, speaking of compilation and redaction for the first time. In the seventeenth century, Benedict Spinoza attributed compilation to Ezra. See his *Tractatus theologico-politicus,* 164.
171 Bleek, *De libri Geneseos,* 1836; Tuch, *Commentar über die Genesis,* 1858.
172 See Wellhausen, *Die Composition des Hexateuchs.*
173 See Rudolph, *Der "Elohist" von Exodus bis Josua.*
174 Möhlenbrink, *ZAW* 56 (1938) 238–68.
175 Noth, *Das System der zwölf Stämme Israels.*
176 Alt, *PJ* 21 (1925) 100–116; "Das System der Stämmesgrenzen."
177 Idem, *Überlieferungsgeschichtliche Studien.*

1952 officially buried the Priestly source as far as Joshua was concerned and made Deuteronomistic hands responsible ultimately for the basic narrative, for the later incorporation of 13:1–21:42, and for the final addition of chap. 24. A few Priestly elements, but no Priestly strata, were gradually assimilated into the book. Major twentieth century commentaries followed the Nothian perspective with slight alterations of elements and dates. Only recently have steps been taken to refine or make significant shifts away from Noth.[178]

Eckart Otto attempted to demonstrate a Yahwistic strand in Josh 1–11 alongside the Deuteronomistic, both based on ancient celebrations of the Feast of Unleavened Bread at Gilgal during the second half of the twelfth century.[179]

Sven Tengström returned to a supplementary hypothesis, speaking of a Hexateuch that, in its basic constituents, was the work of a premonarchical editor at Shechem.[180] For him, only such a hypothesis can explain the important role of Shechem at major narrative turning points. Deuteronomistic and Priestly supplementation produced first the Deuteronomistic and then Priestly history, though the latter is scarcely evident after Moses.

Marten Woudstra's commentary places the writing of the book in the first generation or so after Joshua. Occasionally, he refers to possibilities of later redactors without affirming their existence or work. In contrast stands the Zurich *Habilitationschrift* of Martin Rose.[181] He seeks to understand the Pentateuch/Hexateuch question from the end, not the beginning. He starts his analysis with Joshua, not Genesis, searching for materials parallel to or related to Tetrateuchal materials. He finds the Joshua materials to be in an older form than the corresponding material in the Tetrateuch. Indeed, for Rose, the Deuteronomistic history with its exclusive focus on existence in the land, proved to be older than the earliest Tetrateuchal strand. Rose concludes that the conquest narrative was the established tradition for which the post-Deuteronomistic Jahwist wrote a *pre-history*.

Klaus Bieberstein[182] describes the work of literary criticism as that of asking about changes that can be determined only by the immanent proof of doublets and tensions in the text. Bieberstein then adds synthetic observations to the tools of the literary critic. Such observations show how different sections belong together.[183]

The literary history of the first books of the Bible continues to intrigue and yet defy scholarship. Edward Noort concludes: "A presentation of the literary history from the oldest stages to the final canonical form that is capable of achieving a consensus remains a task for the future."[184] Similarly, Noort looks to the future for a meshing of synchronic and diachronic studies of Joshua.[185] We have many more theories but hardly any more certainty than did Calvin. In fact, Noort labels literary

---

178 Rudolf Smend ("Das Gesetz und die Völker"), Walter Dietrich (*Prophetie und Geschichte*), and Timo Veijola (*Die ewige Dynastie*) have sought to define more precisely three exilic editions of the Deuteronomistic History.
179 Otto, *Das Mazzotfest in Gilgal*.
180 Tengström, *Die Hexateucherzählung*.
181 Rose, *Deuteronomist und Jahwist*.
182 *Josua, Jordan, Jericho*, 73.
183 Ibid., 80.
184 *Das Buch Josua*, 5; here and elsewhere my translation.
185 Ibid., 5–6.

critical analysis as having no standing in current research.[186] He sets as a research goal the discovery of a consensus solution that explains both the uniqueness of Joshua and its ties to the Pentateuch and to the Deuteronomistic History.[187] The basic evidence for responding to Noort consists of:

- the missing fulfillment of the Pentateuch's goal of receiving the Promised Land
- the Deuteronomic language and teaching inherent in Joshua but not so clear in Judges
- the completion of narratives in Joshua that had their origin in Numbers
- the knowledge of salvation history as shown in the speech of Rahab
- the tie-in of duplicate accounts joining the end of Joshua and the beginning of Judges
- the repetition in Judges of the Caleb narratives in Joshua
- the tie between the installation of Joshua narratives in Deuteronomy and Josh 1
- the place of the law of Moses in the book of Joshua
- the continuation of the priestly line in the book of Joshua
- the fulfillment of Mosaic commands for cities of refuge and Levitical cities

Joshua reaches both back and forward, acting as a hinge between the Mosaic period and a period of anticipating the monarchy. The editing shows knowledge of the basic pentateuchal story and regulations (Josh 24) and sets the foundation for the monarchy and the loss of the land. Such a bridging function does not come from three or four fragmentary written sources such as the long-employed JEDP. Neither does it come as the opening chapters of a history work completed only centuries later. The book of Joshua shows far too much unity of purpose to be classified as a combination of seven or eight redactional stages speaking to different centuries of Israel's preexilic, exilic, and postexilic existence. Deuteronomic editing presupposes the completion of the greater part, if not all, of Deuteronomy and brings the book of Joshua to its completion except for work of an ultimate editor(s) incorporating the completed Joshua into the history collection. Apparently scribes in David's court committed the major portion of Joshua to writing, while scribes in Rehoboam's court created the compilaton known as Judges and tied it to Joshua, perhaps including the Saul, Samuel, and David stories.

5. Narrative Criticism

Bibliography

Albertz, R. "Die kanonische Anpassung des Josuabuches: Eine Neubewertung seiner 'priesterschriftlichen Texte.'" In *Les dernières redactions du Pentateuque, de l'Hexateuque et de l'Ennéateuque.* Ed. T. C. Römer and K. Schmid. BETL 203. Leuven: Peeters, 2007. 199–216. **Alter, R.** *The Art of Biblical Narrative.* New York: Basic, 1981. **Alter, R., and F. Kermode,** eds. *The Literary Guide to the Bible.* Cambridge, MA: Harvard UP, 1987. **Amit,**

---

186 Ibid., 59.
187 Ibid., 91.

Y. *Reading Biblical Narratives, Literary Criticism and the Hebrew Bible.* Minneapolis: Fortress, 2001. **Bar-Efrat, S.** *Narrative Art in the Bible.* JSOTSup 70. Sheffield: Almond, 1980. **Beck, J. A.** *God as Storyteller: Seeking Meaning in Biblical Narrative.* St. Louis: Chalice, 2008. **Chisholm, R. B., Jr.** "History or Story? The Literary Dimension in Narrative Texts." In *Giving the Sense: Understanding and Using Old Testament Historical Texts.* Ed. D. M. Howard, Jr., and M. A. Grisanti. Grand Rapids: Kregel, 2003. **Exum, J. C., and D. J. A. Clines,** eds. *The New Literary Criticism and the Hebrew Bible.* JSOTSup 143. Sheffield: Sheffield Academic, 1993. **Fokkelman, J. P.** *Reading Biblical Narrative: An Introductory Guide.* Louisville: Westminster John Knox, 1999. **Foote, W. A.** ". . . and the Walls Come a Tumblin' Down: A Rhetorical Analysis of the Book of Joshua." Senior honors thesis, 1980. **Gunn, D. M., and D. N. Fewell.** *Narrative in the Hebrew Bible.* Oxford Bible Series. Oxford: Oxford UP, 1993. **Hawk, L. D.** *Every Promise Fulfilled: Contesting Plots in Joshua.* Louisville: Westminster John Knox, 1991. **House, P. R.** "The God Who Gives Rest in the Land: Joshua." *SBJT* 2/3 (1998) 12–33; **House, P. R.,** ed. *Beyond Form Criticism: Essays in Old Testament Literary Criticism.* SBTS 2. Winona Lake, IN: Eisenbrauns, 1992. **Longman, T., III.** *Literary Approaches to Biblical Interpretation.* Foundation of Contemporary Interpretation 3. Grand Rapids: Zondervan, 1987. **Mitchell, G.** *Together in the Land.* JSOTSup 134. Sheffield: Sheffield Academic, 1993. **Oste, G.** "A Prophet Like Moses: The Narrative Shaping of Joshua in the Book of Joshua." Paper read to Old Testament Section of Evangelical Theological Society, Atlanta, November 18, 2010. **Powell, M. A.** *What Is Narrative Criticism?* GBS. Minneapolis: Fortress, 1990. **Ryken, L.** *How to Read the Bible as Literature and Get More Out of It.* Grand Rapids: Zondervan, 1984. **Schnittjer, G. E.** "Narrative Time in the Books of Joshua through Kings." Paper presented at the Evangelical Theological Society, Providence, RI, November 19, 2008.

> Instead of breaking up the text into sources and editorial parts, narrative criticism addresses the unity and coherence of the text. In place of isolating short, form-critical episodes, narrative criticism seeks meaning in the dynamic interplay between a specific passage and the larger literary unit as a whole and focuses on the holistic, temporal experience of an audience . . . seeks to comprehend the "story world" created by the narrative—its characters, events, and settings, its frame of time and space, and its cultural beliefs and values. Narrative critics use a set of literary questions to analyze the various configurations of plot, the means and methods of characterization, and the types and functions of the narrative's settings. In addition, narrative critics address the role of the narrator and the way in which the narrator's point of view encompasses the diverse points of view of the characters. Narrative criticism explores the rhetorical devices employed by the narrator to tell the story, such as repetition, irony, figures of speech, and imagery. From an analysis of the implicit values and beliefs of the narrative, the critic constructs an image of an "implied author" and an "ideal audience" response. Narrative critics seek to infer the ways in which the impact of the narrative may have confirmed, subverted, or transformed the world of ancient audiences.[188]

The book of Joshua appears to make the task of the narrative critic quite simple. Narrative markers quickly separate the text into introduction (chap. 1); part 1, victories over the inhabitants (chaps. 2–12); part 2, land allotments (chaps. 13–

---

188 D. Rhoads, "Narrative Criticism," NIDB, 4:217.

21); and part 3, defining the future (chaps. 22–24). But developing a clear plot or story line from this outline sketch proves more difficult and complex. The first two chapters of the book serve as introductions to the story from God's perspective (1:1–9), Joshua's perspective (1:10–18), and the enemies' perspective (2:1–24). Chaps. 3–6 provide the narrative tension as Israel crosses the river, prepares for battle through cultic activities, and defeats the first enemy. The change occurs as Israel experiences defeat at Ai, obeys God in discovering and punishing the guilty party, gains victory at Ai, and then makes covenant with the cunning Gibeonites (chaps. 7–9). The resolution comes in the extended battle reports as Joshua wins battles in the south and north, defeating all the kings (chaps. 10–12). The extended ending comes as land is allotted, unity affirmed, and the future possibilities set out (chaps. 13–24).

Koorevaar[189] looks in the text for God's initiatives (Josh 1:1–9; 5:13–6:5; 13:1–7; 20:16) and narrative closure (Josh 5:1–12; 11:16–12:24; 19:49–51; 21:43–45; 24:29–33). He then sets forth a complex and imaginative chiasmic structure in the third and most important section (Josh 13:8–21:42) to determine that the setting up of the Tent at Shiloh fulfills Lev 26:11–12 and celebrates the divine presence.

By "initiative of God" Koorevaar means a new act of God in which a specific task given to Joshua has a direct connection with the conquest of Canaan. He finds four such initiatives (Josh 1:1–9; 5:13–6:5; 13:1–7; 20:16). The "narrative closures" bring the divine initiative to a conclusion; Koorevaar finds five of these closures (Josh 5:1–12; 11:16–12:24; 19:49–51; 21:43–45; 24:29–33). Each major block of material is characterized by a key word. This means that the four major blocks of material in Joshua are:

1:1–5:12: CROSS (*'br*, עבר)
    1:1–9 God's first initiative: cross the Jordan
    5:1–12 First closing: circumcision and Passover at Gilgal
5:13–12:24: TAKE (*lqh*, לקח)
    5:13–6:5 God's second initiative: capture Jericho
    11:16–12:24 Second closing: review of the victories
13:1–21:45: DIVIDE (*ḥlq*, חלק)
    13:1–7 God's third initiative: divide Canaan
    19:49–51 Third closing: conclusion of the division of Canaan and the
        inheritance of Joshua
    20:1–6 God's fourth initiative: designate cities of refuge
    21:43–45 Fourth closing: final conclusion
22:1–24:33: SERVE (*'bd*, עבד)
    22:1; 23:1–2; 24:1 Three initiatives of Joshua
    24:29–33 Fifth closing: death and burial of Joshua

Rather than contrive such a long-hidden structure, it would appear better to see the author's ending looking to the future as the central meaning of the book: the call to obedience to Torah and the renewal of covenant. Daniel Hawk[190] moves out of traditional source analysis to find a plot in Joshua that explains the seemingly

---

189 As summarized by Vanoy, NIDOTTE, 4:811–14.
190 In Every Promise Fulfilled; cf. his somewhat different slants in his two commentaries.

contradictory elements and themes. He reads the book as "an enigma" that "plays with the reader's sense that reality is coherent."[191] He explains the various elements of a literary plot and shows their appearance in Joshua. A frame is created with death notices at the beginning and end of the book. Allusions, promises, monoliths, and etiologies connect past, present, and future. In the same vein, speeches interrupt narrative time by referring back to past events and forward to future events, changing from talk of blessing to talk of expulsion. Repetition of elements and the amount of text devoted to a topic reveal the important elements for the author. An ending or goal gives coherence to the narrative. According to Hawk, "The book of Joshua renders powerful obstructions which challenge the promise of fulfillment and threaten hopes for a satisfactory conclusion."[192] He finds that an "ending is presented, but the story remains in suspense."

Gordon Mitchell focuses on the role of the nations in the plot of Joshua. The nations should be destroyed, yet some survive. The theme ties in closely with the land theme. Israel receives the land. The nations are eradicated. Still Israel is threatened with the loss of land to the nations.[193] The main reason to mention the nations is to record their end.[194] Yet some nations receive positive evaluations. "The overriding concern of the narrative is to stress the need to empty the land of foreigners, not to learn how to live with them.[195]" Joshua is marked by ambiguity.

The latest commentaries on the book of Joshua demonstrate a lack of description of plot and structure. Contrasting themes of insiders/outsiders or Israel/the nations reflect a subtheme of the book but do not encompass the entire book. Options are to follow Ernst Axel Knauf's emphasis on the land, use the framework of call to obedience in 1:7–8 and chap. 24, or take up the form-critical work discussed above and build a plot around questions of leadership.

The simplest solution, however, is to build a plot around the structural markers of the final text itself. The final, canonical message of the Joshua traditions is made clear by their structural markers:

   I. Theological prologue: qualification for occupying the land (1:1–18)
  II. Cultic composition: directions for a sinful people occupying the land (8:30–35)
 III. Theological summary: the results of meeting the qualifications (11:23)
 IV. Theological review: program in face of unfinished task (13:1–7)
  V. Theological acclamation: God has been faithful in everything (21:43–45)
 VI. Theological program: a life of obedience beyond the Jordan (22:1–6)
VII. Theological justification: leaving Yahweh loses the land (23:1–16)
VIII. Theological hope: a covenant with God (24:1–28)

This structure reveals both the setting and the message of the final editor's interpretation of the traditions of Joshua. In the hands of an editor joining Joshua to the other history books (Judges through Kings), Joshua becomes a manifesto for a life beyond the Jordan for a people who have lost the land and seek new hope. The

---

191   Ibid., 24.
192   Ibid., 37.
193   Together in the Land, 185.
194   Ibid., 187.
195   Ibid., 189.

final edition of Joshua thus speaks to the exiles beyond the Jordan in Babylon. It outlines four issues that are essential to the survival and future of the people: the land, the leadership, the law, and Yahweh.

In the final analysis, the reader must keep in mind the form-critical results of the book of Joshua. Joshua presents a biography emphasizing the office of Joshua. The biographical form lays out the job description, so to speak, of the Israelite leader. Such a job description is important at two points in Israelite history: the time of David and Solomon as they establish the role of the leader of Israel, and the time of the Babylonian capture and exile. In the exile, without a king, how does Israel model its leadership? How can a leader who is not a king bring hope to a punished people?

6. Redaction History

Bibliography

Albertz, R. "The Canonical Alignment of the Book of Joshua." In *Judah and the Judeans in the Fourth Century B.C.E.* Ed. O. Lipschitz, G. N. Knoppers, and R. Albertz. Winona Lake, IN: Eisenbrauns, 2007. 287–303. ———. "Die kanonische Anpassung des Josuabuches: Eine Neubewertung seiner 'priesterschriftlichen Texte.'" In *Les dernières redactions du Pentateuque, de l'Hexateuque et de l'Ennéateuque.* Ed. T. C. Römer and K. Schmid. BETL 203. Leuven: Peeters, 2007. 199–216. **Becker, U.** "Endredaktionelle Kontextvernetzungen des Josua-Buches." In *Die deuteronomistischen Geschichtswerke: Redaktions- und religionsgeschichtliche Perspektiven zur "Deuteronomismus"-Diskussion in Tora und Vorderen Propheten.* Ed. M. Witte, K. Schmid, D. Prechel, and J. C. Gertz. Berlin: De Gruyter, 2006. 141–61. **Cortese, E.** *Josua 13–21: Ein priesterlicher Abschnitt im deuteronomistischen Geschichtswerk.* OBO 14. Göttingen: Vandenhoeck & Ruprecht, 1990. **Dozeman, T.** "The Relationship of Joshua and Judges in the Late Stages of Redaction History." Paper read to SBL Joshua-Judges Consultation, Atlanta, November 22, 2010. **Haran, M.** "Problems in the Composition of the Former Prophets." *Tarbiz* 37 (1967–1968) 1–14 (Heb.). **Kratz, R. G.** *The Composition of the Narrative Books of the Old Testament.* Trans. J. Bowden. Edinburgh: T&T Clark, 2000. Originally published as *Komposition der erzählenden Bücher des Alten Testaments* (Göttingen: Vandenhoeck & Ruprecht, 2000). **Meer, M. N. van der.** *Formation and Reformulation: The Redaction of the Book of Joshua in the Light of the Oldest Textual Witnesses.* VTSup 102. Leiden: Brill, 2004. **Nihan, C.** "The Literary Relationship between Deuteronomy and Joshua: A Reassessment." Paper read to SBL Deuteronomistic History/Pentateuch Section, Atlanta, November 23, 2010. **Ottoson, M.** "Tradition and History with Emphasis on the Composition of the Book of Joshua." In *The Productions of Time: Tradition History in Old Testament Scholarship.* Ed. K. Jeppesen and B. Otzen. Sheffield: Almond, 1984. 81–106, 141–43. **Römer, T.** "Book Endings in Joshua and the End of the Deuteronomistic History." Paper read to SBL Joshua-Judges Consultation, Atlanta, November 22, 2010. **Rösel, H. N.** "Lässt sich eine nomistische Redaktion im Buch Josua festellen?" *ZAW* 119 (2007) 184–89. **Seebaß, H.** "Josua." *BN* 28 (1985) 53–65. **Spronk, K.** "From Joshua to Samuel: Some Remarks on the Origin of the Book of Judges." In *The Land of Israel in Bible, History, and Theology: Studies in Honour of Ed Noort.* Ed. J. van Ruiten and J. C. de Voss. Leiden: Brill, 2009. 137–49. ———. "Joshua Recapitulated: The Relation between Judges 1–2 and the Book of Joshua." Paper read to SBL Joshua-Judges Consultation, Atlanta, November 22, 2010. **Troyer, K. de.** "The Different Books of Joshua." Paper read to SBL Joshua-Judges Consultation Section, Atlanta, November 22, 2010.

Redaction history seeks to trace the growth of a book in its various literary stages based on different vocabulary and themes that scholars discover within the text. Perhaps the most influential figure in Joshua studies is Martin Noth (see *Literary [Source] Criticism* above).

For Richard Nelson, Josh 1:1–12:24; 21:43–22:6; 23:1–16; and 24:28–31 are part of the Deuteronomistic History, but the book has no evidence of the second Deuteronomist found elsewhere. The Deuteronomist began with a collection of discontinuous stories centered on the fear of the native inhabitants. The stories had an Ephraimite hero and a Benjaminite setting, but were distinctly Judean in outlook. Chaps. 13–21 for Nelson form a separate collection added later but without marks of the Deuteronomist or of Priestly hands. Priestly touches do appear in 3:4; 4:19; 9:15b, 18–21; 13:21b–22; 14:1–2; 17:2–6; 19:51; 21:1–2; and 22:9–34. Chap. 24 remains the center of controversy. Thus, for Nelson, Joshua is built from an ark legend, etiological narratives, a literary testament, genuine administrative documents, artificial scribal compositions, border descriptions, city lists, land-grant narratives, and the purely literary chap. 24.

Recognizing Joshua's extensive literary and thematic connections to the Pentateuch, Jerome Creach still sees stronger connections to Deuteronomy and other Deuteronomic literature, especially in the themes of Torah, the ban, warfare, and all Israel. The book contains doublets that indicate a history of authorship and editing. Some form of Josh 2–11 may have developed at Gilgal. An early form of the book was part of the Deuteronomistic History, whose editing appears clearly in chaps. 1, 12, and 23 and in 21:43–22:6. Sponsored by King Josiah, the book of Joshua was written just before the Babylonian exile. The book was completed during or after the exile. Priestly touches appear in chaps. 14–22. Such additions "temper Joshua's authority."[196] Other later additions to the book deal with the acquisition of land (1:7–9a; 13:1b–6; 23:6–13), making possession of the land dependent on devotion to Torah.

Ernst Axel Knauf describes Joshua as a person who is tribally and genealogically isolated. This leads to the conclusion that his name, Joshua, is actually a constructed variant of Josiah the king (cf. Nelson). This means, for Knauf, that the oldest edition of the story of Joshua comes from the reign of Josiah (640–609 BCE) or later. The book itself is traditional literature, not authored literature, the work of generations of scribes and experts on scripture (*Schriftgelehrten*) as they taught in the scribal schools. Most made small changes affecting only a verse or so. Others reformulated the tradition anew in light of a new political or theological program. The major redaction can be seen in the numerous "book endings" (Josh 10:40–42; 11:16–23; 18:1; 21:43–45; chap. 24).[197]

For Knauf the work began around 600 BCE, centered in either Bethel or Jerusalem. Final redaction came in Jerusalem shortly after 400 except for an anti-Samaritan retouching in the third or second century. Knauf believes he can isolate at least seven book redactions in Joshua:[198]

1. The Exodus-Joshua narrative from about 600 BCE included Joshua as the concluding chapter of a narrative built around the basic parts of Exod 14 and Josh 6 and 10, probably beginning with Exod 2. This added the Exodus narrative to the foundation legend of the Judean monarchy, the story of the house of David (1 Sam 9–2 Kgs 10). Among other things, the narrative sought

---

196 Creach, 11.
197 Knauf, 17.
198 Ibid.

to win the tribe of Benjamin over to the tradition of their new political home. It knew nothing of the theology of the ban.

2. The D- or Pentateuch-redaction included Exod 2 through Josh 11, including legal materials such as the Covenant Code and the Deuteronomic law code. The D-redaction may refer to Deuteronomistic or to the Davidic national religion. The Pentateuch-redaction includes Joshua but not Genesis. The redactor used Josh 11:23 to show that he was already aware of the book of the royal realms (1 Sam–2 Kgs). But the D-book and the realms book were separate entities, not a continuation in two volumes. The redaction history of Joshua gives no indication of being part of a Deuteronomistic History or of a unit conceived as an Enneateuch. Only this stage of the tradition places any value on the ban. The center of attention is the conflict over the importance of the postexilic capital city in Mizpah and the temple in Bethel between returning exiles and the tribe of Benjamin, which remained in Israel. Benjaminites maintained a traditional cult with cult images and a consort for Yahweh and preserved the Moses and Joshua tradition along these lines. Those returning from the exile brought an astounding revolutionary new monotheism without images of any kind. These returnees worked from 520 to 444 BCE to rebuild Jerusalem and restore its political power. By the end of the fifth century, this party had completely edited the Torah and established its authority.

3. The Priestly writing (P) represented a response over against D. It centered everything in the temple and ignored the messianic tradition tied to David and Solomon. D was exclusive, while P used many names for God to represent its inclusiveness. P incorporated ancestral narratives, the myth of origins for those who had not gone into exile. P added the creation narrative in order to bring together the two groups of Jews and to reconcile them to the rest of the world. Knauf lists only parts of six verses in Joshua that he assigns to P. The Priestly writing grew gradually up to 450 BCE.[199]

4. The Hexateuch redaction (H) was undertaken when Jerusalem became the center of Persian provincial rule in 444 and as the priestly group gained control over the D group. H represents the joining of D and P. D theology appears in the language of P and P theology in the language of D. Joshua is introduced into the narrative spanning Exodus through Deuteronomy. In the book of Joshua, H appears most clearly in the crossing of the Jordan (Josh 3–4), in the procession of the ark (chap. 6), and in the basic layer of the land distribution report (chaps. 14–17). H extends from Gen 1 to Josh 18:1 and appears in the D language in Josh 21:43–45. H does not evince any knowledge of a Judges tradition as a bridge to Samuel and Kings.

5. Prophets or Book redaction represents the major redaction of Joshua, rendering it an independent book removed from the Hexateuch traditions. It presupposes the final words of the Torah from Deut 34:10–12. By 400 BCE the larger part of the prophetic tradition was written but was finally formed together under the previously accepted sign (*Vorzeichen*) of the canonized Torah. Josh 1 and 24 become the role model (*Vorbild*) for the prophets after Moses while at the same time explaining and applying the Torah, presuppos-

---

199 Ibid., 20.

ing the incomparable authority of Moses. Josh 1 introduces Joshua as the first in the series of a prophetic canon, while Josh 24 closes the now independent book as a supplement to Torah. All prophetic books thus become a supplement to Torah.

6. The Joshua-Judges redaction is a late event created by Josh 18:2–19:48 and chap. 23. It may have preceded or followed the prophet redaction. Ezekiel may have joined the prophetic canon at this time. Still Knauf (22) finds no indication of a redaction joining only Joshua through Kings or Genesis through Ezra-Nehemiah.

7. The Shechem redaction or the Torah-Prophets redaction represents an anti-Samaritan, pro-Hasmonean work effected by the middle of the second century and perhaps in the third. This appears most clearly in Gen 5 and Jeremiah. About 400 BCE Judeans and Samarians had both accepted the Torah, but at some point the Samarians refused to accept the prophetic canon. The Hasmoneans used the prophetic canon as the justification for their service as high priest and as king, being unable to find such a basis in the Torah.

Hartmut Rösel has transferred the nomistic Deuteronomist of Smend's group into a later Deuteronomist, moving from source criticism to redaction criticism.[200] Robert Hubbard places the events of Joshua in the context of a 1250 BCE exodus but provides a broader historical background reaching back to 1500. The book of Joshua is a "compilation of source materials" edited by a Deuteronomistic Historian whose material "had roots much earlier in Israel" and whose first writing may have occurred in the early monarchy.[201] The book shows a "Judahite perspective." The sanctuary at Gilgal apparently provided source materials, while town and boundary lists date back to Solomon or even to the premonarchical time. Hubbard skips over suggestions of late Priestly editing as materials that "bear other equally plausible explanations."[202]

Michaël van der Meer summarizes redaction studies of Joshua and in so doing reviews the history of the search for literary sources.[203] He points, along with Smend and his students, to a pre-Deuteronomistic layer, the basic Deuteronomistic narrative, a nomistic-Deuteronomistic redaction, and a Priestly redactional layer.[204] After thoroughly examining the study of the Priestly materials, he concludes: "it seems safe to conclude that we can speak of a commonly accepted *redaction* of Joshua breathing the spirit of Priestly ideology."[205] Van der Meer leaves to the side questions of dating, unity, and relationships to the Deuteronomistic school and the Pentateuch.

Magnus Ottosson,[206] representing the Scandinavian approach first developed by Engnell, goes several steps beyond Engnell in his discussion of the Priestly materials in Joshua:

P was a widespread phenomenon attached to priestly circles at the regional sanctuaries in Palestine. . . . We have no indications of a specially delimited

200 *ZAW* 119 (2007) 184–89.
201 Hubbard, 30–31.
202 Ibid., 33.
203 *Formation and Reformulation*, 114–53.
204 Ibid., 120.
205 Ibid., 143.
206 "Tradition and History," 106.

post-Exilic P source, and if it existed at all it will have represented the final stage of the process of tradition. In other words P was a process whose material had acquired its special characteristics at an early date. We discover the language of P in the Book of Joshua when the Deuteronomist makes use of salvation history and of historical materials which must have been employed and preserved in the Temple.

Rainer Albertz finds that the traditional P texts stem from a redactor who wished, by means of them, to bring the presentation of the earlier Book of Joshua concerning the occupation, its extent, and the mode of distribution of the land, etc. into line with the relevant (P and D) directives and announcements of the Pentateuch. This occurred some time between the middle of the fourth century and the beginning of the third century, leading to the canonization of Joshua.[207]

Enzo Cortese attempts to reinstate P as a major source in the book of Joshua,[208] but a P that is supplementary to an original P. Still, this late Priestly source for Cortese had much older documents to hand, especially one going back to the time of Solomon. Cortese labels this as J, thus arguing for a new type of Hexateuch.

This redactional search becomes quite complex when one begins to add multiple stages to a writing as have Smend and his students who speak of a Deuteronomistic Historian, a nomistic DtrN, a prophetic DtrP, plus Priestly additions, etc.

Richard Nelson, on the other hand, sees no second Deuteronomist (against both Cross and Smend) with a distinct vocabulary or theology in Joshua. Dtr had at hand, according to Nelson, a written collection of stories. Another strand of material appears in the geographical allotments which Nelson can classify neither as Deuteronomistic nor as Priestly, but in any case as administrative. The most meticulous study is that of Reinhard Gregor Kratz, who breaks verses up into four or more parts and assigns them to differing editors or editions.[209]

I work with a much simpler redactional pattern for the book, built on a common-sense approach to the growth of literature stemming in great part from text-critical results. Textual study reveals text differences that cannot be explained simply as copying mistakes or changes. Until quite a late date, scribes were willing and apparently free to insert small interpretative phrases into the text as can be seen throughout the textual studies in this commentary. The differences in the texts of Joshua and Jeremiah between LXX and MT show the work of the scribes, even to the point of rearranging the text.

Historical literature may be eyewitness, contemporary reporting, later generations' reconstruction, or centuries later research. It may be preserved in oral traditions and story telling, in political annals, in memorial stele, in political reports, in military records, etc. History writing may be intended to collect and preserve facts and lists. It also can seek to entertain or encourage and give identity to a people. It may represent political or social propaganda. It may even represent

---

207 "Die kanonische Anpassung"; see *OTA* 31 (2008) 383, #1368.
208 *Josua 13–21.*
209 *Composition of the Narrative Books.*

what a writer wished had been the event. History writing orders and sequences source materials, oftentimes using something other than a chronological order. The student of history must, to the best of one's ability, ascertain the nature and intent of the piece of historical literature being examined.

The stories in Joshua appear to come from a limited number of sources: oral stories, administrative lists, battle reports, and cultic materials. Each unit had its own original history and form preserved apart from the other elements that make up the final book of Joshua. One or more collectors gathered the elements into separate collections of battle reports, lists, land allotments, and cultic rituals. The collectors then gave interpretation to the materials by the order in which they placed them and by adding transitional notes to join the individual narratives.

Ultimately, a historian in the time of the united monarchy created the individual book of Joshua as a call to unity between the forces of David and those of Saul and ultimately between David/Solomon and rebellious forces in the northern tribes. Slightly later, the editor of Judges incorporated parts of Joshua into his work and created a pro-Judean work aimed against the revolt of Jeroboam I. Still later, an editor joined Joshua/Judges into an ultimate history reaching through Kings. As these materials came into the hands of scribes to be copied and preserved and then into the possession of translators to spread the message to new audiences, small changes and interpretations entered the text.

Redaction work in this commentary reports on the work of various scholars in each chapter while trying to show evidence of materials at each stage of the book's development and the intentions that lay behind such new settings for the material.

We may be only in the beginning stages of understanding the way in which God worked with human beings to produce his word. It may be that old traditional understandings may eventually be vindicated. The present work can only hope to note a few clues for further research and to emphasize the note raised in Joshua studies at least since the time of Wellhausen, namely the contribution of theologians using language akin to that of Deuteronomy to interpret the work of Joshua.

7. The Rise and Demise of the Deuteronomistic History

Bibliography

Achenbach, R. "Pentateuch, Hexateuch, Enneateuch: Eine Verhältnisbestimmung." *ZABR* 11 (2005) 122–55. **Albertz, R.** "In Search of the Deuteronomists: A First Solution to a Historical Riddle." In *The Future of the Deuteronomistic History*. Ed. T. C. Römer. BETL 147. Leuven: Peeters, 2000. ———. "Die Intentionen und Träger des deueronomistischen Geschichtswerkes." In *Schöpfung und Befreiung*. FS Claus Westermann, ed. R. Albertz, F. W. Golka, and J. Kegler. Stuttgart: Calwer, 1989. 37–53. ———. "Wer waren die Deuteronomisten? Das historische Rätsel einer literarischen Hypothese." *EvT* 57 (1997) 319–38. **Anbar, M.** *Josué et l'alliance de Sichem (Josué 24:1–28).* BBET 25. Frankfurt am Main: Lang, 1992. **Ash, P.** "Jeroboam I and the Deuteronomistic Historian's Ideology of the Founder." *CBQ* 60 (1988) 16–24. **Auld, A. G.** "The Deuteronomists between History and Theology." In *Congress Volume, Oslo 1998*. Ed. A. Lemaire and M. Sæbø. Leiden: Brill, 2000. 353–67. ———. "Narrative Books in the Hebrew Scriptures" *EvT* 119 (2007) 105–10. ———. "What Makes Judges Deuteronomistic?" In *Joshua Retold: Synoptic Perspectives*. Edinburgh: T&T Clark, 1998. 120–26. **Aurelius, E.** *Zukunft jenseits des Gerichts: Eine redactionsgeschichtliche Studie zum Enneateuch.* BZAW 319. Berlin: De

Gruyter, 2003. **Bach, R.** "Deuteronomistisches Geschichtswerk." *RGG,* 2:100–101. **Bartelmus, R.** "The Deuteronomists and the Former Prophets, or What Makes the Former Prophets Deuteronomistic?" In *Those Elusive Deuteronomists.* Ed. L. S. Schearing and S. L. McKenzie. JSOTSup 268. Sheffield: Sheffield Academic, 1999. 116–26. ———. "Forschung am Richterbuch seit Martin Noth." *TRu* 56 (1991) 221–59. **Beck, M., and U. Schorn,** eds. *Auf dem Weg zur Endgestalt von Genesis bis II Regum: Festschrift Hans-Christoph Schmitt zum 65. Geburtstag.* BZAW 370. New York: De Gruyter, 2006. **Becker, U.** "Endredaktionelle Kontextvernetzungen des Josua-Buches." In *Die deuteronomistischen Geschichtswerke: Redaktions- und religionsgeschichtliche Perspektiven zur "Deuteronomismus"-Diskussion in Tora und Vorderen Propheten.* Ed. M. Witte, K. Schmid, D. Prechel, and J. C. Gertz. Berlin: De Gruyter, 2006. 141–61. **Beyerlin, W.** "Gattung und Herkunft des Rahmens im Richterbuch." In *Tradition und Situation: Studien zur alttestamentlichen Prophetie.* FS A. Weiser, ed. E Wirthwein and O. Kaiser. Göttingen: Vandenhoeck & Ruprecht, 1963. **Bieberstein, K.** *Josua, Jordan, Jericho: Archäologie, Geschichte und Theologie der Landnahmeerzählungen Jos 1–6.* OBO 143. Göttingen: Vandenhoeck and Ruprecht, 1995. **Blum, E.** "Beschneidung und Passa in Kanaan: Beobachtungen und Mutmaßungen zu Jos 5." In *Freiheit und Recht.* FS F. Crüsemann, ed. C. Hardmeier, R. Kessler, and A. Ruwe. Gütersloh: Gütersloher Verlag, 2003. 292–322. Repr. in *Text und Komposition,* FAT 69 (Tübingen: Mohr Siebeck, 2010) 219–48. ———. "Der kompositionelle Knote am Übergang von Josua zu Richter: Ein Entflechtungsvorschlag." In *Deuteronomy and Deuteronomic Literature: Festschrift C. H. W. Brekelmans.* Ed. M. Vervenne and J. Lust. BETL 133. Leuven: Leuven UP; Peeters, 1997. 181–212. Repr. in *Text und Komposition,* FAT 69 (Tübingen: Mohr Siebeck, 2010) 249–80. **Briend, J.** "The Sources of the Deuteronomistic History: Resarch on Joshua 1–12." In *Israel Constructs Its History: Deuteronomistic Historiography in Recent Research.* Ed. A. de Pury et al. JSOTSup 306. Sheffield: Sheffield Academic, 2000. 360–86. **Brueggemann, W.** "The Kerygma of the Deuteronomic Historian." *Int* 22 (1968) 387–402. ———. "Social Criticism and Social Vision in the Deuteronomic Formula of the Judges." In *Die Botschaft und die Boten: Festschrift für Hans Walter Wolff zum 70 Geburtstag.* Ed. J. Jeremias and L. Perlitt. Neukirchen-Vluyn: Neukirchener Verlag, 1981. 101–14. **Campbell, A. F.** "Martin Noth and the Deuteronomistic History." In *The History of Israel's Traditions: The Heritage of Martin Noth.* JSOTSup 182. Sheffield: Sheffield Academic, 1994. 31–62. **Campbell, A. F., and M. A. O'Brien.** *Unfolding the Deuteronomistic History: Origins, Upgrades, Present Text.* Minneapolis: Fortress, 2003. **Carr, D. M**. "Empirische Perspektiven auf das deuteronomistische Geschichtswerk." In *Die deuteronomistischen Geschichtswerke: Redaktions- und religionsgeschichtliche Perspektiven zur "Deuteronomismus"-Diskussion in Tora und Vorderen Propheten.* Ed. M. Witte, K. Schmid, D. Prechel, and J. C. Gertz. BZAW 365. Berlin: De Gruyter, 2006. 1–18. ———. *Writing on the Tablet of the Heart: Origins of Scripture and Literature.* Oxford: Oxford UP, 2005. **Carrière, J.-M.** "L'historiographie deutéronomiste: une manière d'écrire l'historie." In *Comment la bible saisit-elle l'histoire: XXIe congrès catholique française pour l'étude de la bible, Issy-les-Moulineaux, 2005.* Paris: Cerf, 2007. 115–54. **Castelbajac, I. de.** "Les juges d'Israel: Une invention du Deutéronomiste?" *RHR* 221 (2004) 83–97. **Coggins, R.** "What Does 'Deuteronomistic' Mean?" In *Words Remembered, Texts Renewed: Essays in Honour of John F. A. Sawyer.* JSOTSup 195. Sheffield: Sheffield Academic, 1995. 135–48. Repr. in *Those Elusive Deuteronomists,* ed. L. S. Schearing and S. L. McKenzie. JSOTSup 268. Sheffield: Sheffield Academic, 1999. 22–35. **Colenso, J. W.** *The Pentateuch and the Book of Joshua Critically Examined.* London: Longman, Green, 1870. **Cortese, E.** *Josua 13–21: Ein priesterschriftlicher Abschnitt im deuteronomistischen Geschichtswerk.* OBO 94. Göttingen: Vandenhoeck & Ruprecht, 1990. ———. "Problemi attuali circa l'opera deuteronomistica." *RivB* 26 (1978) 341–52. ———. "Theories Concerning Dtr: A Possible Rapprochement." In *Pentateuchal and Deuteronomistic Studies: Papers Read at the XIIIth*

IOSOT Congress, Leuven 1989. Ed. C. Brekelmans and J. Lust. BETL 94. Leuven: Leuven UP; Peeters, 1990. 179–90. **Cross, F. M.** "The Structure of the Deuteronomistic History." In *Perspectives in Jewish Learning* 3 (1968) 9–24. ———. "The Themes of the Book of Kings and the Structure of the Deuteronomistic History." In *Canaanite Myth and Hebrew Epic: Essays in the History of Religion of Israel*. Cambridge, MA: Harvard UP, 1973. 274–89. **Davies, G. I.** "The Origin of the History of Israel: Herodotus' Histories as Blueprint for the First Books of the Bible." *JTS* 55 (2004) 805–6. **Davies, P. R.** "The History of Ancient Israel and Judah." *ExpTim* 119 (2007) 15–21. ———. *In Search of "Ancient Israel."* JSOT-Sup 148. Sheffield: Sheffield Academic, 1992. ———. "Whose History? Whose Israel? Whose Bible? Biblical Histories, Ancient and Modern." In *Can a "History of Israel" Be Written?* Ed. L. L. Grabbe. Sheffield: Sheffield Academic, 1997. 104–22. **Dever, W. G.** "Can Archaeology Serve as a Tool in Textual Criticism of the Hebrew Bible?" In *Sacred History, Sacred Literature: Essays on Ancient Israel, the Bible, and Religion in Honor of R. E. Friedman on His Sixtieth Birthday*. Ed. S. Dolansky. Winona Lake, IN: Eisenbrauns, 2008. 225–37. **Dietrich, W.** *Prophetie und Geschichte: Eine redationsgeschichtliche Untersuchung zum deuteronomistischen Geschichtswerk*. FRLANT 108. Göttingen: Vandenhoeck & Ruprecht, 1972. **Dutcher-Walls, P.** "The Social Location of the Deuteronomists: A Sociological Study of Factional Politics in Late Pre-exilic Judah." *JSOT* 52 (1991) 77–94. **Eissfeldt, O.** *Geschichtsschreibung im Alten Testament: Ein kritischer Bericht über die neueste Literatur dazu*. Berlin: Evangelische Verlagsanstalt, 1948. **Fabry, J.-J.** "Spuren des Pentateuchredaktors in Jos 4,21ff.: Anmerkungen zur Deuteronomismus-Rezeption." In *Das Deuteronomium: Entstehung, Gestalt, und Botschaft*. Ed. N. Lohfink. BETL 68. Leuven: Leuven UP, 1985. 351–56. **Fretheim, T. E.** *Deuteronomic History: Interpreting Biblical Texts*. Nashville: Abingdon, 1983. **Friedman, R. E.** "The Deuteronomic School." In *Fortunate the Eyes That See, Festschrift for D. N. Freedman*. Ed. A. B. Beck et al. Grand Rapids: Eerdmans, 1995. 70–80. ———. *The Exile and Biblical Narrative: The Formation of the Deuteronomistic and Priestly Works*. HSM 22. Chico, CA: Scholars Press, 1981. **Galil, G.** "The Chronological Framework of the Deuteronomistic History." *Bib* 85 (2004) 413–21. **Geoghegan, J. C.** *The Time, Place, and Purpose of the Deuteronomistic History: The Evidence of "Until This Day."* BJS 347. Providence: Brown UP, 2006. ———. "'Until This Day' and the Preexilic Redaction of the Deuteronomistic History." *JBL* 122 (2003) 201–27. **Gerbrandt, G. E.** *Kingship according to the Deuteronomistic History*. SBLDS 87. Atlanta: Scholars Press, 1986. **Greenspahn, F. E.** "The Theology of the Framework of Judges." *VT* 36 (1986) 385–96. **Hagedorn, A. C.** "Taking the Pentateuch to the Twenty-First Century." *ExpTim* 119 (2007) 53–58. **Harvey, J. E.** *Retelling the Torah: The Deuteronomistic Historian's Use of Tetrateuchal Narratives*. JSOTSup 403. London: T&T Clark, 2004. **Hjelm, I.** *Jerusalem's Rise to Sovereignty: Zion and Gerizim in Competition*. JSOTSup 404. London: T&T Clark, 2004. **Hoffman, H. D.** *Reform und Reformen: Untersuchungen zu einem Grundthema der deuteronomistischen Geschichtsschreibung*. ATANT 66. Zürich: Theologischer Verlag, 1980. **Hoffman, Y.** "The Deuteronomist and the Exile." In *Pomegranates and Golden Bells: Studies in Biblical, Jewish and Near Eastern Ritual, Law, and Literature in Honor of Jacob Milgrom*. Ed. D. P. Writh, D. N. Freedman, and A. Hurvitz. Winona Lake, IN: Eisenbrauns, 1995. **Hollenberg, J.** "Die deuteronomischen Bestandtheile des Buches Josua." *TSK* 47 (1874) 462–507. **Hurwitz, A.** "The Historical Quest of 'Ancient Israel' and the Linguistic Evidence of the Hebrew Bible: Some Methodological Observations." *VT* 47 (1997) 301–15. **Ibáñez Arana, A.** "La obra deuteronomista del libro de Josuè: el mensaje." *Lum* 29 (1980) 289–310. ———. "La redacción deuteronomista del libro de Josuè." *ScrVict* 28 (1981) 5–38. **Jenni, E.** "Zwei Jahrzehnte Forschung an den Büchern Josua bis Könige." *TRu* 27 (1967) 1–32, 97–146. **Jobling, D.** "Deuteronomic Political Theory in Judges and 1 Samuel 1–12." In *The Sense of Biblical Narrative II: Structural Analyses in the Hebrew Bible*. JSOTSup 39. Sheffield: JSOT Press, 1986. 44–87. **Kaiser, O.** "Pentateuch und Deuteronomistisches Geschichtswerk." In *Studien zur Literaturgeschichte des Alten Testaments.* FB 90. Würzburg: Echter, 2000. 70–133. **Knauf, E. A.** "Does 'Deuteronomistic Historiography' (DtrH) Exist?" In *Israel Constructs Its History: Deuteronomistic Historiography in Recent Research.* Ed. A. de Pury et al. JSOTSup 306. Sheffield: Sheffield Academic, 2000. 388–98. **Knoppers, G. N., and J. G. McConville,** eds. *Reconsidering Israel and Judah: Recent Studies on the Deuteronomistic History.* SBTS 8. Winona Lake, IN: Eisenbrauns, 2000. **Köppel, U.** *Das deuteronomistische Geschichtswerk und seine Quellen: Die Absicht der deuteronomistischen Geschichtsdarstellung aufgrund des Vergleichs zwischen Num 21,21–35 und Dtn 2,26–3, 3.* EHS 23.122. Diss., Lucerne. Berne: Lang, 1979. **Kratz, R. G.** *The Composition of the Narrative Books of the Old Testament.* Trans. J. Bowden. London: T&T Clark, 2005. Originally published as *Die Komposition der erzählenden Bücher des Alten Testaments: Grundwissen der Bibelkritik* (Göttingen: Vandenhoeck & Ruprecht, 2000). ———. "Der vor- und der nachpriesterschriftliche Hexateuch." In *Abschied vom Jahwisten: Die Komposition des Hexateuch in der jüngsten Diskussion.* Ed. J. C. Gertz, K. Schmid, and M. Witte. BZAW 315. Berlin: De Gruyter, 2002. 295–323. **Kraus, H.-J.** "Gesetz und Geschichte: Zum Geschichtsbild des Deuteronomisten." *EvT* 11 (1951–1952) 415–27. **Latvus, K.** *God, Anger and Ideology: The Anger of God in Joshua and Judges in relation to Deuteronomy and the Priestly Writings.* JSOTSup 279. Sheffield: Sheffield Academic, 1998. **Lohfink, N. F.** "Bilanz nach der Katastrophe: Das deuteronomistische Geschichtswerk." In *Wort und Botschaft.* Ed. J. Schreiner. Würzburg: Echter, 1967. 196–208. ———. "Kerygmata des deuteronomistischen Geschichtswerks." In *Die Botschaft und die Boten: Festschrift für Hans Walter Wolff zum 70. Geburtstag.* Ed. J. Jeremias and L. Perlitt. Neukirchen-Vluyn: Neukirchener Verlag, 1981. 87–100. ———. "Was There a Deuteronomistic Movement?" In *Those Elusive Deuteronomists.* Ed. L. S. Schearing and S. L. McKenzie. JSOTSup 268. Sheffield: Sheffield Academic, 1999. 36–66. **Mayes, A. D. H.** "Deuteronomistic Ideology and the Theology of the Old Testament." *JSOT* 82 (1999) 57–82. ———. *The Story of Israel between Settlement and Exile: A Redactional Study of the Deuteronomistic History.* London: SCM Press, 1983. **McCarthy, D. J.** "The Wrath of Yahweh and the Structural Unity of the Deuteronomistic History." In *Essays in Old Testament Ethics.* FS J. P. Hyatt, ed. J. L. Crenshaw and J. T. Willis. New York: Ktav, 1974. 97–110. **McConville, J. G.** *Grace in the End: A Study in Deuteronomic Theology.* Grand Rapids: Zondervan, 1993. **McKenzie, S. L., and M. P. Graham,** eds. *The History of Israel's Traditions: The Heritage of Martin Noth.* JSOTSup 182. Sheffield: Sheffield Academic, 1994. **Meer, M. N. van der.** *Formation and Reformulation: The Redaction of the Book of Joshua in the Light of the Oldest Textual Witnesses.* VTSup 102. Leiden: Brill, 2004. **Miller, R. D., II.** "Deuteronomistic Theology in the Book of Judges?" *OTE* 15 (2002) 411–16. **Moenikes, A.** Zur Redaktionsgeschichte des sogenannten deuteronomistischen Geschichtswerkes." *ZAW* 104 (1992) 333–48. **Moran, W. J.** "A Study of the Deuteronomic History." *Bib* 46 (1965) 223–28. **Mullen, E. T., Jr.** *Narrative History and Ethnic Boundaries: The Deuteronomistic Historian and the Creation of Israelite National Identity.* SemeiaSt. Atlanta: Scholars Press, 1993. **Nelson, R. D.** *The Double Redaction of the Deuteronomistic History.* JSOTSup 18. Sheffield: JSOT Press, 1981. ———. "The Double Redaction of the Deuteronomistic History: The Case Is Still Compelling." *JSOT* 29 (2005) 319–37. ———. "Josiah in the Book of Joshua." *JBL* 100 (1981) 531–40. **Nentel, J.** *Trägerschaft und Intention des deuteronomistischen Geschichtswerks: Untersuchungen zu den Reflexionsreden Jos 1; 23; 24; 1 Sam 12; 1 Kön 8.* BZAW 297. Berlin: De Gruyter, 2000. **Nielsen, F. A. J.** *The Tragedy in History—Herodotus and the Deuteronomistic History.* JSOTSup 251. Sheffield: Sheffield Academic, 1997. **Noll, K. L.** "Deuteronomistic History or Deuteronomic Debate? (A Thought Experiment.)" *JSOT* 31 (2007) 311–45. **Noort, E.** *Das Buch Josua: Forschungsgeschichte und Problemfelder.* EdF 292. Darmstadt: Wissenschaftliche Buchgesellschaft, 1998. **Noth, M.** *The Deuteronomistic History.* Trans. D. Orton. JSOTSup 15. Sheffield: JSOT Press, 1981. ———. *Überlieferungsgeschichtliche Stu-*

dien: Die sammelnden und bearbeitende Geschichtswerke im Alten Testament. 2nd ed. Tübingen: Niemeyer, 1957. ———. "Zur Geschichtsauffassung des Deuteronomisten." In *Proceedings of the Twenty-Second Congress of Orientalists Held in Istanbul, 1951.* Vol. 2, *Communications.* Leiden: Brill, 1957. 558–66. **O'Brien, M. A.** *The Deuteronomistic History Hypothesis: A Reassessment.* OBO 92. Göttingen: Vandenhoeck & Ruprecht, 1989. ———. "Judges and the Deuteronomistic History." In *The History of Israel's Traditions: The Heritage of Martin Noth.* Ed. S. L. McKenzie and M. P. Graham. JSOTSup 182. Sheffield: Sheffield Academic, 1994. 235–59. **Otto, E.** "Das deuteronomistische Geschichtswerk im Enneateuch: Zu einem Buch von Erik Aurelius." *ZABR* 11 (2005) 323–45. ———. *Das Deuteronomium im Pentateuch und Hexateuch: Studien zur Literaturgeschichte von Pentateuch und Hexateuch im Lichte des Deuteronomiumrahmens.* FAT 30. Tübingen: Mohr (Siebeck), 2000. **Ottosson, M.** *Josuaboken: en programskrift för davidisk Restauration.* Acta Universtatis Uppaliensis, Studia Biblica Uppaliensia I. Stockholm: Almquist & Wiksell, 1991. **Peckham, B.** *The Composition of the Deuteronomistic History.* HSM 35. Atlanta: Scholars Press, 1985. ———. "The Significance of the Book of Joshua in Noth's Theory of the Deuteronomistic History." In *The History of Israel's Traditions: The Heritage of Martin Noth.* Ed. S. McKenzie and M. P. Graham. JSOTSup 182. Sheffield: Sheffield Academic, 1994. 213–34. **Plöger, O.** "Reden und Gebete im deuteronomistischen und chronistischen Geschichtswerk." In *Festschrift für Günther Dehn.* Ed. W. Schneemelcher. Neukirchen-Vluyn: Neukirchener Verlag, 1957. 35–49. **Polzin, R.** *Moses and the Deuteronomist: A Literary Study in the Deuteronomistic History.* New York: Seabury, 1980. **Preuß, H. D.** "Zum deuteronomistischen Geschichtswerk." *TRu* 58 (1993) 229–64, 341–95. **Provan, I.** *Hezekiah and the Book of Kings: A Contribution to the Debate about the Composition of the Deuteronomistic History.* BZAW 172. Berlin: De Gruyter, 1988. **Pury, A. de, T. C. Römer, and J.-D. Macchi,** eds. *Israel Constructs Its History: Deuteronomistic Historiography in Recent Research.* JSOTSup 306. Sheffield: Sheffield Academic, 2000. **Rad, G. von.** "The Beginnings of Historical Writing in Ancient Israel." In *The Problem of the Hexateuch and Other Essays.* 1944. Repr., London: SCM Press, 1966. 166–204. **Radjawane, A. N.** "Das deuteronomistische Geschichtswerk: Ein Forschungsbericht." *TRu* 38 NF (1973) 177–216. **Rainey, A.** "Inside, Outside: Where Did the Early Israelites Come From?" *BAR* 34.6 (2008) 45–50, 84. ———. "Shasu or Habiru: Who Were the Early Israelites?" *BAR* 34.6 (2008) 51–55. **Ramsey, G. W.** *The Quest for the Historical Israel.* Atlanta: John Knox, 1981. **Richter, S. L.** *The History and the Name Theology.* BZAW 318. Berlin: De Gruyter, 2002. **Richter, W.** *Die Bearbeitungen des "Retterbuches" in der deuteronomischen Epoche.* BBB 21. Bonn: Hanstein, 1964. **Rofé, A.** "Ephraimite versus Deuteronomistic History." In *Storia e tradizioni di Israele: Scritti in onore di J. Alberto Soggin.* Ed. D. Garrone and F. Isarel. Brescia: Paideia, 1991. 221–35. ———. "Joshua 20: Historico-Literary Criticism Illustrated." In *Empirical Models for Biblical Criticism.* Ed. J. H. Tigay. Philadelphia: University of Pennsylvania Press, 1985. 131–47. **Römer, T. C.** "Entstehungsphasen des 'deuteronomistischen Geschichtswerkes.'" In *Die deuteronomistischen Geschichtswerke: Redaktions- und religionsgeschichtliche Perspektiven zur "Deuteronomismus"-Diskussion in Tora und Vorderen Propheten.* Ed. M. Witte, K. Schmid, D. Prechel, and J. C. Gertz. BZAW 365. Berlin: De Gruyter, 2006. 45–70. ———. "The Form-Critical Problem of the So-Called Deuteronomistic History." In *The Changing Face of Form Criticism for the Twenty-First Century.* Ed. M. A. Sweeney and E. Ben Zvi. Grand Rapids: Eerdmans, 2003. 240–52. ———. "Pentateuque, Hexateuque et historiographie deutéronomiste: Le problème du début et de la fin du livre de Josué." *Transeuphratène* 16 (1998) 71–86. ———. *The So-Called Deuteronomistic History: A Sociological, Historical, and Literary Introduction.* London: T&T Clark, 2005. ———. "Transformations in Deuteronomistic and Biblical Historiography: On »Book-Finding« and other Literary Strategies." *ZAW* 109 (1997) 1–11. **Römer, T. C.,** ed. *The Future of the Deuteronomistic History.* BETL 147. Louvain: Peeters, 2000. **Römer, T. C.,** and **M. Z. Brettler.** "Deuteronomy 34 and the Case for a Persian Hexateuch." *JBL* 119 (2000) 401–19. **Rose, M.** *Deuteronomist und Jahwist: Untersuchungen zu den Berührungspunkten beider Literaturwerke.* ATANT 67. Zürich: Theologischer Verlag, 1981. **Rösel, H. N.** *Von Josua bis Jojachin: Untersuchungen zu den deuteronomistischen Geschichtsbüchern des Alten Testaments.* VTSup 75. Leiden: Brill, 1999. **Rüterswörden, U.** "Erwägungen zum Abschluß des deuteronomistischen Geschichtswerkes." In *Ein Herz so weit wie der Sand am Ufer des Meeres: Festschrift für Georg Hentschel.* Ed. S. Gillmayr-Bucher, A. Giercke, and C. Nießen. ETS 90. Würzburg: Echter, 2008. 193–203. **Sacchi, P.** "Giosuè 1,1–9: dalla critica storica e quelle letteraraia." In *Storia e tradizione di Israele: Scritti in onore di J. Alberto Soggin.* Ed. D. Garrone and F. Israele. Brescia: Paideia, 1991. 237–54. **Schearing, L. S., and S. L. McKenzie,** eds. *Those Elusive Deuteronomists: The Phenomenon of Pan-Deuteronomism.* JSOTSup 268. Sheffield: Sheffield Academic, 1999. **Scherer, A.** "Neuere Forschungen zu alttestamentlichen Geschichtskonzeptionen Beispiel der deuteronomistischen Geschichtswerks." *VF* 53 (2008) 22–40. **Schulte, H.** "Beobachtungen zum Begriff der Zônâ im Alten Testament." *ZAW* 104 (1992) 255–62. **Simpson, C. A.** *The Composition of the Book of Judges.* Oxford: Oxford UP, 1957. **Smend, R.** "Das Gesetz und die Völker: Ein Beitrag zur deuteronomistischen Redaktionsgeschichte." In *Probleme biblischer Theologie: Gerhard von Rad zum 70. Geburtstag.* Ed. H. W. Wolff. Munich: Kaiser, 1971. 494–509. **Soggin, J. A.** "Deuteronomistische Geschichtsauslegung während des babylonischen Exils." In *Oikonomia.* FS O. Cullman, ed. F. Christ. Hamburg-Bergstedt: Reich, 1967. 11–17. **Stahl, R.** "Aspekte der Geschichte deuteronomistischer Theologie: Zur Traditionsgeschichte der Terminologie und zur Redaktionsgeschichte der Redekompositionen." Diss., Berlin, Jenna, 1982. **Stipp, H.-J.** "Ahabs Busse und die Komposition des deuteronomistischen Geschichtswerks." *Bib* 76 (1995) 471–97. **Van Seters, J.** "The Deuteronomist from Joshua to Samuel." In *Reconsidering Israel and Judah.* Ed. G. Knoppers and J. G. McConville. SBTS 8. Winona Lake, IN: Eisenbrauns, 2000. 204–39. **Veijola, T.** "Deuteronomismusforschung zwischen Tradition und Innovation (II)." *TRu* 67 (2002) 391–424. ———. *Die ewige Dynastie: David und die Enstehung seiner Dynastie nach der deuteronomistischen Darstellung.* AASF B193. Helsinki: Suomalainen Tiedeakatemia, 1975. ———. *Das Königtum in der Beurteilung der deuteronomistischen Historiographie: Eine redaktionsgeschichtliche Untersuchung.* AASF B198. Helsinki: Suomalainen Tiedeakatemia, 1975. **Weinfeld, M.** *Deuteronomy and the Deuteronomic School.* Oxford: Oxford UP, 1972. **Weippert, H.** "Das deuteronomistiche Geschichtswerk: Sein Ziel und Ende in der neueren Forschung." *TRu* 50 (1985) 213–49. ———. "The Emergence of the Deuteronomic Movement: The Historical Antecedents." In *Das Deuteronomium Entstehung, Gestalt und Botschaft.* Ed. N. Lohfink. Leuven: Leuven UP, 1985. 76–83. ———. "Geschichten und Geschichte: Verheissung und Erfüllung im deuteronomistischen Geschichtswerk." In *Congress Volume.* Ed. J. A. Emerton. VTSup 43. Leiden: Brill, 1991. 116–31. Repr. as "'Histories' and 'History': Promise and Fulfillment in the Deuteronomistic Historical Work," trans. P. T. Daniels, in *Reconsidering Israel and Judah,* ed. G. Knoppers and J. G. McConville, SBTS 8. Winona Lake, IN: Eisenbrauns, 2000. 47–61. **Westermann, C.** *Die Geschichtsbücher des Alten Testaments: Gab es ein deuteronomistisches Geschichtswerk?* TB 87. Gütersloh: Kaiser, 1994. **Witte, M., K. Schmid, D. Prechel, and J. Christian Gertz,** eds. *Die deuteronomistischen Geschichtswerke: Redaktions- und religionsgeschichtliche Perspektiven zur "Deuteronomismus"-Diskussion in Tora und Vorderen Propheten.* ZAW 365. Berlin: De Gruyter, 2006. **Wolff, H. W.** "Das Kerygma des deuteronomistischen Geschichtswerks." *ZAW* 73 (1961) 171–86. Published in English as "The Kerygma of the Deuteronomistic Historical Work," trans. F. C. Prussner, in *The Vitality of the Old Testament Traditions,* ed. W. Brueggemann and H. W. Wolff. Atlanta: John Knox, 1975. 83–100, 141–43. Repr. in *Reconsidering Israel and Judah,* ed. G. Knoppers and J. G. McConville, SBTS 8. Winona Lake, IN: Eisenbrauns, 2000. 62–78.

Würthwein, E. "Erwägungen zum sogennanten deuteronomistichen Geschichtswerk: Eine Skizze." In *Studien zum deuteronomistichen Geschichtswerk.* BZAW 227. Berlin: De Gruyter, 1994. 1–11.

Research and publication since the first edition of this commentary have raised many more questions than they have answered. We can still establish one clear point as we seek to understand the formation of the book of Joshua. The language of Deuteronomy reappears at many points within the book. This stands in contrast to the book of Judges, in which Deuteronomistic language is minimal. This contrast has led to many new understandings of the origin of the first nine books of the Hebrew Bible as discussed in my introduction to *Judges,* WBC 8. Albert de Pury and Thomas Römer in their report on the history of research on the Deuteronomistic History conclude:

> Research on DH . . . finds itself today in a paradoxical situation. At first sight, we get the impression that the "Deuteronomistic fact" is well established. But after a closer look, it turns out that the definitions of DH are legion and not always compatible with one another. How can we define what is Deuteronomic, Deuteronomistic, and what is not?[210]

Römer and Marc Brettler offer a paradoxical answer: accept both a Hexateuch and the Deuteronomistic History.[211] Deut 34:4, 10–12 represents a pentateuchal redaction incorporating the ancestors and linking them to the Exodus and legal materials. This creates a Mosaic canon that ties the Deuteronomic law to the ancestral materials, not the Deuteronomistic. Deut 34:7–9 becomes a joint Priestly/Deuteronomistic venture, part of a D-P redaction of the Hexateuch.[212] The Hexateuch redactor created Josh 24 to complete the Hexateuch. The book of the Torah of God is the Hexateuch, while the book of Torah of Moses is the Pentateuch. The Hexateuch was central at the time of Nehemiah's reading but eventually gave way to the Pentateuch.

Martin Noth suggested that Joshua is part of a larger historical work, reaching from Deut 1 through 2 Kgs 25. Noth named this the Deuteronomistic History. The history itself may not be the product of one person, at one time. Rudolf Smend and his students Walter Dietrich and Timo Veijola attempted to demonstrate at least three stages in the Deuteronomistic writings, all completed in Jerusalem after 580, that is, during the exile. Frank Cross reduces this to a preexilic Deuteronomist under Josiah and an exilic Deuteronomist who recorded the materials after Josiah and added others. Thomas Römer working off Auld, Knauf, and Lohfink, explores the possibility of two works beginning in the time of Josiah—a propaganda piece covering the first version of Samuel and Kings and a conquest version of Deuteronomy and Joshua. He also speaks of a law collection including parts of Deut 12–25.[213] The primitive version of Joshua would include Josh 5:13–14; 6:2a, 3, 4b, 5, 11, 14–15, 20b–21, 27; 8:1–2, 10–12, 14–16, 19b, 20–21, 23, 25, 27, 29; 9:3–6, 8b, 9–15a; 10:1–5, 8, 10–11, 16–27; 11:23. All this leads to the conclusion that the "so-called 'conquest tradition' is nothing else than an invention by Deuteronomistic scribes".[214] John

---

210   *Israel Constructs Its History,* 24–143.
211   *JBL* 119 (2000) 401–19.
212   See above on Knauf.
213   Römer, *So-Called Deuteronomistic History,* 86–90.
214   Ibid., 90.

Van Seters dismisses any compiler, early sources, or preexilic work.[215] He points to an exilic Deuteronomist who invented the material and to a later P redactor.

A. D. H. Mayes is more cautious, and rightly so, as he speaks of the editing of Deuteronomy as "a process rather than an event or events."[216] He also notes that "there is no doubt but that the work of the deuteronomistic circle represents a process or movement which was not completed in the context of a single editing even incorporating Deuteronomy into the deuteronomistic history."[217] The exact nature of the Deuteronomistic History is a continuing discussion.

Alexander Rofé extends the Deuteronomistic editors' work over a period of almost three hundred years.[218] Michaël van der Meer rightly counters: "One may question Rofé's conclusion that one should stretch out the Deuteronomistic school over such a long period."[219] Still, van der Meer decides that modern historical critical research finds a pre-Deuteronomistic stage, a basic Deuteronomist narrative, a nomistic-Deuteronomistic redaction, and a Priestly redactional layer.[220] In so doing he, basically following Smend and his students, has himself stretched the Deuteronomistic school over a rather long period of time and identified theological tensions within the "school." Römer claims that most German-speaking critics of the Deuteronomistic History remain true to Noth in one point: Deuteronomistic editing began with the exile and was limited to the period of the exile.[221]

Jacques Briend devotes an intensive study to the literary formation of Josh 1–12.[222] He claims the first twelve chapters of the book were a separate written document with its main points in chaps. 3–9, introduced by 1:1–2 and later extended by chaps. 10–12 and then by chap. 2. A postexilic Deuteronomistic redactor then added an all-Israel perspective and a vision of violence showing hatred to the cities and their kings through the introduction of the ban language.

For Robert Coote, Deuteronomy and Joshua have no connection with an original Tetrateuch but begin the new Deuteronomistic History. Joshua's appearances in the Tetrateuch come from additions by scribes in the court of Hezekiah or Josiah.[223] The story of Joshua thus seeks to coerce and intimidate all of Josiah's opponents to submit to the king.

Ernst Axel Knauf provides a short list of arguments against any existence of the Deuteronomistic History.[224] The books show a Deuteronomistic way of composition but were not conceived by one author or by a homogeneous group. Thus many, particularly continental scholars, posit a theory resembling that of Becker, who claims

---

215 *In Search of History*, 324–31.
216 A D. H. Mayes, *Deuteronomy*, NCB (London: Oliphants, 1979) 29.
217 Ibid., 43. For summaries of recent discussion see my introduction to *Judges*, WBC 8; Geoghegan (*Time, Place and Purpose*); Witte et al. (*Die deuteronomistischen Geschichtswerke*, with extensive bibliography); Römer (*So-Called Deuteronomistic History*), and Römer and de Pury (*Israel Constructs Its History*, 24–144). Römer and de Pury point to an independent Joshua with no connection to the following books.
218 "Joshua 20," 145–46.
219 *Formation and Reformulation*, 59.
220 van der Meer, 120.
221 "Entstehungsphasen," 46–47 (but see Knauf's conclusions listed above).
222 "Sources of the Deuteronomistic History."
223 Coote, 560.
224 "Does 'Deuteronomistic Historiography' (DtrH) Exist?" 388; see discussion of his commentary above.

that at the beginning of the development of the book of Joshua the book was not part of a Deuteronomistic History but part of a "Hexateuch" that did not include Deuteronomy and probably not Genesis.[225] Joshua then became part of the Enneateuch.

Paul House argues for a single author because the books in the ultimate history are linked together by death reports, because use of sources brings expected diversity to any history book, because ancient historiography expected one author who used different types of material, and because the one-author approach retains scholarly attractiveness that is based not on a preference for source criticism but on the text itself.[226]

It still appears to me that the evidence points more to a single Deuteronomistic hand than to successive Deuteronomistic editors and that Judges was not involved in the Deuteronomistic editing. In fact, van der Meer notes that "proposals to dismiss the so-called 'Deuteronomistic History' altogether are becoming more and more numerous."[227]

One such proposal to dismiss the Deuteronomistic History comes from Reinhard Gregor Kratz.[228] He finds traditional narratives from before 720 BCE in the early parts of Josh 6 and 8. The seventh century brought three additional works, in Kratz's outline. The exodus narrative stretched from Exod 2 to Josh 12, but from the current book of Joshua only parts of chaps. 2, 3, 4, 6, 8, 10, 11, and 12 were included.[229] This created a "Hexateuch" without Genesis. Editors in the exilic period connected the original part of Deuteronomy to the exodus narrative, followed by the Decalogue. Still later an original Deuteronomistic History developed including parts of Samuel and Kings. The addition of the Deuteronomistic History, Judges, and other Deuteronomistic materials to the exodus narrative created the Enneateuch. That editing incorporated small parts of Josh 1, 5, 6, 11, 12, 23, and 24. Still later came chaps. 13–22. Knauf outlines a similarly tedious process of growth in his commentary. See Redaction History above.

Text-critical study reveals a process of editing, but nothing as elaborate as this. Israelite theologians, seeking to interpret the holy traditions for the people of God, were continually at work under the leadership of God, but they did not start with half verses and add small bits and large bits until the process was finished. Such a process of redaction criticism simply takes critical studies to the brink of the unbelievable.

K. L. Noll cites an extensive bibliography and argues for the improbability of the Deuteronomistic History.[230] He defends the thesis that the "Deuteronomistic History belongs to the history of Jewish and Christian interpretations and not to the history of composition and redactional growth."[231]

Noll reduces Noth's arguments to three issues: the summary speeches, the shared chronology, and the prophecies and fulfilled predictions. End-of-era speeches are a "mixed bag," often having no careful structure. Other speeches do

---

225 Becker, "Endredaktionelle Kontextvernetzungen," 155–56.
226 *SBJT* 2/3 (1998) 16–17.
227 *Formation and Reformulation*, 144.
228 *Composition of the Narrative Books.*
229 Ibid., 323, n. 22.
230 *JSOT* 31 [2007] 312–14, nn. 6–9.
231 Ibid., 345.

not promote the Deuteronomistic program. The chronologies of Judges and Kings do not agree, while Joshua and Samuel are unaffected by the chronology. Many of the prophetic stories do not fit the prophecy/fulfillment pattern. Concerning Noth, Noll notes: "There is no reason to think that the Former Prophets were created as a history narrative. Eventually, they were interpreted as something similar to Greek history writing, but they were not created with this purpose in mind."[232] Noll shows how, beginning with Noth, large and then even larger parts of each of the books have been denied to the Deuteronomist.[233] This means defenders of the Deuteronomistic History must find a new, much later setting, redefine a Deuteronomistic agenda, and describe anew how to identify Deuteronomistic elements.

Noll offers his own simple definition of Deuteronomism as: "the presence of words and phrases from the book of Deuteronomy that seem to affirm the ideology affirmed by Deuteronomy."[234] This at first glance appears to reflect Weinfeld's Deuteronomic vocabulary lists, but Noll adds the concern for ideology, which he demonstrates is a deadly weapon against an extensive Deuteronomistic History. Noll uses Weinfeld's list to isolate glosses (including Josh 4:24; 5:1, 6; 9:27; 10:8; 12:6–7; 14:8–9, 14; 18:3; 21:43–44) from a "very late period."

Noll then offers his own theory. Following Knauf and Lohfink, he speaks of the intermingling of Deuteronomistic and Priestly language and of instances where Deuteronomistic language does not express Deuteronomistic theology. For Noll, this means, "This interesting tendency of the language to intermingle with priestly idiom and to serve multiple theological agendas suggests that the language was not generated by a single 'movement' or 'school,' nor was it all the product of a single, unified redactional plan (or even a succession of one, two, or three individuals). Rather, it was added to pre-existing texts on an ad hoc basis at a time when passages reflecting priestly idiom could be added as well."[235] This theory is built on Lohfink's claim that "books" went through two stages: one copy controlled by the author and only much later multiple copies with some circulation. For Joshua, Noll dates the first stage in the Persian period and the second in the Hellenistic. This leads to the further conclusion that the Former Prophets "did not constitute a semiofficial Jewish tale of origin until Roman times."

One must reply that such extraordinary linguistic theory dismisses any talk of authentic oral tradition, ignores scribal institutions during the monarchy, and leaves Israel without an identity until they have become totally controlled by a distant nation. The language, apart from a few possible poetic examples, had been standardized at some point, quite possibly in the exilic/Persian period. Standardization of a half century or more of linguistic development does not present a conclusion that all literature was composed in the standardized language, only that copyists used the written idiom of the day to record ancient materials.

Noll's solution to this objection is that "the Former Prophets existed for centuries in a predeuteronomistic form."[236] This would relegate this form of the Former

---

232 Ibid., 314, n. 8.
233 Ibid., 315–16 with nn. 16–23.
234 Ibid., 317.
235 Ibid., 323.
236 Ibid., 333.

Prophets to the stage of author control for centuries,[237] rather than seeing a temple or palace institution responsible for maintaining and updating historical writings and national identity. Such institutions may have saved one official copy of the written materials, but certainly they also had copies with which educators taught future scribes. If the books were in any manner tendential or propagandistic, then the writers sought to disseminate them, not simply hold on to past writing for the sake of one's ego or enjoyment. The one-copy-for-centuries idea had to have a social or political function. Noll's retort is that a small group of "like-minded intellectuals"[238] used the books as conversation pieces for their own enjoyment. But how did such conversation continue over centuries, and who was responsible for preserving and overseeing the editing of the one master copy? The theory is interesting but is built on too many assumptions and stands too far from reality to attain wide acceptance.

With respect to Joshua proper, Noll sees construction projects unearthing mammoth Bronze Age structures for which storytellers provided an explanation.[239] Following Van Seters, Noll maintains that Joshua began as an anthology of these stories, emulating Assyrian propaganda. The stories were in no way associated with the Moses tradition. Much later in Noll's first stage of redaction, the narratives became Deuteronomistic and Priestly. Noll's understanding then "divorces the origins of the book of Joshua from any memory, however clouded or unreliable, of actual Bronze Age or Iron Age I battles" (337, n. 75). The earliest, pre-Deuteronomistic Joshua consists, then, of 3*; 5:13–15; 6*; 8*; 9*; 10*; 11*; 24*, and perhaps a few stray verse fragments.[240]

If we insist on disposing of such theories, we must account for the Deuteronomistic language which gives the book of Joshua its basic form and meaning. Such language is most obvious in 1:1–18; 2:9b–11; 3:7, 10; 4:10, 12, 14, 24; 5:1, 5–6; 6:21, 26; 7:7–9, 11*, 15*; 8:18, 26, 29, 30–35; 9:9b–10, 24aB, 27bB; 10:25, 40; 11:3, 11–12, 14b–15, 20b–23; 12:1–13; 13:1–14, 32–33; 14:1–5, 14–15; 15:13–15; 17:3–6; 18:1, 7; 19:51; 20:8–9; 21:1–3, 43–45; 22:1–6; 23:1–16; 24:1, 11aB, 12b–13, 24, 31–32.

The presence of such editorial interpretation built around material from oral tradition is extremely important theologically. It gives us insight into how the inspired canonical writer understood and interpreted the sacred traditions transmitted by the community of faith. These verses unite the book theologically and tie it to the biblical works that precede and follow. They provide the major theological perspective of the book. And they apparently come from a single hand.

8. The History behind the Book of Joshua

Bibliography: Historical Atlases, Geographies, and Histories

Abel, F. M. *Géographie de la Palestine.* Vol. 1, *Géographie physique et historique.* Vol. 2, *Géographie politique: Les villes.* EBib 1, 2. Paris: Librarie Lecoffre, 1933, 1938. **Aharoni, Y.** *The Land of the Bible: A Historical Geography.* Rev. ed. Trans. and ed. A. Rainey. Philadelphia: Westminster, 1979. **Aharoni, Y., and M. Avi-Yonah.** *The Macmillan Bible Atlas.* New York:

---

237 Ibid., 336.
238 Ibid.
239 Ibid., 337.
240 Ibid., 337, n. 77.

MacMillan, 1968. **Ahlström, G. W.** *The History of Ancient Palestine from the Palaeolithic Period to Alexander's Conquest.* Ed. D. V. Edelman. Minneapolis: Fortress, 1993. **Baly, D.** *The Geography of the Bible.* New York: Harper and Brothers, 1957. **Bright, J.** *A History of Israel.* 3rd ed. Philadelphia: Westminster; London: SCM Press, 1981. **Burrows, M.** *Ancient Israel: The Idea of History in the Ancient Near East.* New Haven, CT: American Oriental Society, 1983. **Davies, P. R.** *Memories of Ancient Israel: An Introduction to Biblical History—Ancient and Modern.* Louisville: Westminster John Knox, 2008. **DeVries, L. F.** *Cities of the Biblical World.* Peabody, MA: Hendrickson, 1997. **Donner, H.** *Geschichte des Volkes Israel und seiner Nachbarn in Grundzügen.* Vol. 1, *Von den Anfängen bis zur Staatenbildungszeit.* GAT 4. Göttingen: Vandenhoeck & Ruprecht, 1984; 2nd ed., 1995. **Edwards, I. E. S., C. J. Gadd, N. G. L Hammond, and E. Solleberger,** eds. *History of the Middle East and the Aegean Region c. 1800–1380 B.C.* 3rd ed. CAH 2, part 1. Cambridge: Cambridge UP, 1973. ———. *History of the Middle East and the Aegean Region c. 1380–1000 B.C.* CAH 2, part 2. Cambridge: Cambridge UP, 1975. **Ewald, H.** *Geschichte des Volkes Israel bis Christus.* Vols. 1, 2. Göttingen: Dietrich, 1843, 1845. **Finnegan, J.** *Handbook of Biblical Chronology.* Rev. ed. Peabody, MA: Hendrickson, 1998. **Gunneweg, A. H. J.** *Geschichte Israels bis Bar Kochba.* Theologische Wissenschaft 2. Stuttgart: Kohlhammer, 1972. **Halpern, B.** *The First Historians.* San Francisco: Harper & Row, 1988. **Herrmann, S.** "Autonome Entwicklungen in den Königreichen Israel und Juda." In *Congress Volume, Rome 1968.* VTSup 17. Leiden: Brill, 1969. 266–97. ———. *Geschichte Israels in alttestamentlicher Zeit.* Munich: Kaiser, 1973. Translated as *A History of Israel in Old Testament Times,* trans. J. Bowden. London: SCM Press, 1975. **Hoerth, J. H., F. L. Mattingly, and E. M. Yamauchi,** eds. *Peoples of the Old Testament World.* Grand Rapids: Baker, 1994. **Kaiser, W. C., Jr.** *A History of Israel from the Bronze Age through the Jewish Wars.* Nashville: Broadman & Holman, 1998. **Kallai, Z.** *Historical Geography of the Bible: The Tribal Territories of Israel.* Leiden: Brill, 1986. **Keel, O., and M. Küchler.** *Orte und Landschaften der Bibel: Ein Handbuch und Studien-Reiseführer zum Heiligen Land.* Zürich: Benziger; Göttingen: Vandenhoeck & Ruprecht, 1982. **Kofoeda, J. B.** *Text & History: Historiography and the Study of the Biblical Text.* Winona Lake, IN: Eisenbrauns, 2005. **Lemche, N. P.** *The Israelites in History and Tradition.* Ed. D. A. Knight. Library of Ancient Israel. Louisville: Westminster John Knox, 1998. **Liverani, M.** *Israel's History and the History of Israel.* Trans. C. Peri and P. R. Davies. London: Equinox, 2005. **Long, V. P.,** ed. *Israel's Past in Present Research: Essays on Ancient Israelite Historiography.* SBTS 7. Winona Lake, IN: Eisenbrauns, 1999. **Malamat, A.** *The History of Biblical Israel.* Leiden: Brill Academic, 2004. **Miller, J. M., and J. H. Hayes.** *A History of Ancient Israel and Judah.* 2nd ed. Louisville: Westminster John Knox, 2006. **Na'aman, N.** *Borders and Districts in Biblical Historiography: Seven Studies in Biblical Geographical Lists.* JBS 4. Jerusalem: Simor, 1986. **Noth, M.** *The History of Israel.* Trans. P. R. Ackroyd. New York: Harper & Row, 1960. **Provan, I. V., P. Long, and T. Longman III.** *A Biblical History of Israel.* Louisville: John Knox Westminster, 2003. **Simons, J.** *The Geographical and Topographical Texts of the Old Testament.* Leiden: Brill, 1959. **Smith, G. A.** *The Historical Geography of the Holy Land.* 25th ed. 1894, London: Hodder & Stoughton, 1931. Repr., London: Collins Clear-Type, 1966. **Soggin, J. A.** *A History of Ancient Israel.* Trans. J. Bowden. Philadelphia: Westminster, 1984. **Svensson, J.** *Towns and Toponymns in the Old Testament with Special Emphasis on Joshua 14–21.* ConBOT 38. Stockholm: Almqvist & Wiksell, 1994. **Van Seters, J.** *In Search of History: Historiography in the Ancient World and the Origins of Biblical History.* New Haven: Yale UP, 1983. **Vaux, R. de.** *The Early History of Israel.* 2 vols. Trans. D. Smith. London: Darton, Longman & Todd, 1978. Originally published as *Histoire ancienne d'Israël* (Paris: Gabalda & Cie, 1971). **Weippert, M.** *Die Landnahme der israelitischen Stämme in der neuren wissenschaftlichen Diskussion.* FRLANT 92. Göttingen: Vandenhoeck & Ruprecht, 1967. ———. *The Settlement of the Israelite Tribes in Palestine.* Trans. J. D. Martin. SBT, 2nd ser., 21. London: SCM Press, 1971. **Wiseman, D. J.,** ed. *Peoples of Old Testament Times.* Oxford: Clarendon, 1973.

Bibliography: Ancient Texts Relating to the Old Testament

Hallo, W. H., and K. L. Younger, Jr., eds. *The Context of Scripture.* 3 vols. Brill: Leiden, 1997, 2000. **Pritchard, J. B.** *Ancient Near Eastern Texts Relating to the Old Testament.* Princeton: Princeton UP, 1969. ———. *The Ancient Near East: Supplementary Texts and Pictures Relating to the Old Testament.* Princeton: Princeton UP, 1969. **Thomas, D. W.**, ed. *Archaeology and Old Testament Study: Jubilee Volume of the Society for Old Testament Study 1917–1967.* Oxford: Clarendon, 1967. ———, ed. *Documents from Old Testament Times.* London: Thomas Nelson & Sons, 1958. Repr., New York: Harper & Row, 1961.

a. Studies in the Archaeology of Joshua

Bibliography

Aharoni, Y. *The Archaeology of the Land of Israel.* Trans. A. F. Rainey. Philadelphia: Westminster, 1982. ———. "New Aspects of the Israelite Occupation in the North." In *Near Eastern Archaeology in the Twentieth Century: Essays in Honour of Nelson Glueck.* Ed. J. A. Sanders. Garden City, NY: Doubleday, 1970. 254–65. ———. "Nothing Early and Nothing Late: Rewriting Israel's Conquest." *BA* 39 (1976) 55–76. ———. "Problems of the Israelite Conquest in the Light of Archaeological Discoveries." *AntSur* 2.2–3 (1957) 131–50. **Ahlström, G. W.** "The Origin of Israel in Palestine." *SJOT* 2 (1991) 19–34. ———. "Where Did the Israelites Live?" *JNES* 41 (1982) 133–38. ———. *Who Were the Israelites?* Winona Lake, IN: Eisenbrauns, 1986. **Albright, W. F.** "Archaeology and the Date of the Hebrew Conquest of Palestine." *BASOR* 58 (1935) 10–18. ———. *The Archaeology of Palestine.* Gloucester, MA: Peter Smith, 1971. ———. *The Biblical Period from Abraham to Ezra: An Historical Survey.* New York: Harper, 1963. ———. "A Case of Lèse-Majesté in Pre-Israelite Lachish, with Some Remarks on the Israelite Conquest." *BASOR* 87 (1942) 32–38. ———. "The Israelite Conquest of Canaan in the Light of Archaeology." *BASOR* 74 (1939) 11–23. **Alt, A.** "Erwägungen über die Landnahme der Israeliten in Palästina." *PJ* 35 (1939) 8–63. Repr. in *KlSchr* 1:126–75. ———. *Die Landnahme der Israeliten in Palästina: Territorialgeschichtliche Studien.* Reformationsprogramm der Universität Leipzig, 1925. Repr. in *KlSchr* 1:89–125 = "The Settlement of the Israelites in Palestine," trans. R. A. Wilson, in *Essays on Old Testament History and Religion* (Oxford: Blackwell, 1966) 133–69. **Arata Mantovani, P.** "L'archeologia siro-palestinese e la storia di Israele." *Hen* 9 (1987) 229–48. **Avi-Yonah, M., and E. Stern**, eds. *The New Encyclopedia of Archaeological Excavations in the Holy Land.* 4 vols. London: Oxford UP, 1993. **Bietak, M.** "Der Aufenhalt 'Israels' in Ägypten und der Zeitpunkt der 'Landnahme' aus heutiger archäologischer Sicht." *Ägypten und Levante* 10 (2000) 179–86. **Bimson, J.** *Redating the Exodus and Conquest.* 2nd ed. JSOTSup 5. Sheffield: Almond, 1981. **Blenkinsopp, J.** "The Bible, Archaeology and Politics; or the Empty Land Revisited." *JSOT* 17 (2002) 169–87. **Bloch-Smith, E., and B. A. Nakhai.** "A Landscape Comes to Life: The Iron Age I." *NEA* 62 (1999) 62–92, 101–129. **Brandfon, F.** "The Limits of Evidence: Archaeology and Objectivity." *Maarav* 4 (1987) 5–43. **Brett, M. G.** "Israel's Indigenous Origins: Cultural Hybridity and the Formation of Israelite Identity." *BibInt* 11 (2003) 400–412. **Bright, J.** *Early Israel in Recent History Writing.* SBT 19. London: SCM Press, 1956. **Browning, D. C., Jr.** "'The Hill Country Is Not Enough for Us': Recent Archaeology and the Book of Joshua." *SwJT* 41 (1998) 25–43. **Burrows, M.** *What Mean These Stones? The Significance of Archaeology for Biblical Studies.* New Haven, CT: ASOR, 1941. **Callaway, J. A.** "New Evidence on the Conquest of Ai." *JBL* 87 (1968) 312–20. ———. "A New Perspective on the Hill Country Settlement of Canaan in Iron Age I." In *Palestine in the Bronze and Iron Ages: Papers in Honour of Olga Tufnell.* Ed. J. N. Tubb. London: Institute of Archaeology, 1985. 31–49. **Chavalas, M. W.** "The Context of Early Israel Viewed through the Archaeology of Northern Mesopotamia and Syria." In *Critical Issues in Early Israelite History.* Ed. R. S.

Hess, G. A. Klingbeil, and P. J. Ray, Jr. BBRSup 3. Winona Lake, IN: Eisenbrauns, 2008. 151–61. ———— and **M. R. Adamthwaite.** "Archaeological Light on the Old Testament." In *The Face of Old Testament Studies.* Ed. D. W. Baker and B. T. Arnold. Grand Rapids: Baker, 1999. 59–96. **Coogan, M. D.** "Archaeology and Biblical Studies: The Book of Joshua." In *The Hebrew Bible and Its Interpreters.* Ed. W. Propp. Biblical and Judaic Studies. Winona Lake, IN: Eisenbrauns, 1990. 19–32. **Coote, R. B., and K. W. Whitelam.** *The Emergence of Israel in Historical Perspective.* SWBA 5. Sheffield: Almond, 1987. **Crawford, S. W., et al.**, eds. *"Up to the Gates of Ekron": Essays on the Archaeology and History of the Eastern Mediterranean in Honor of Seymour Gitin.* Jerusalem: IEJ, 2007. **Davies, P. R.** *In Search of "Ancient Israel."* JSOT-Sup 148. Sheffield: Sheffield Academic, 1995. **Dever, W. G.** "Archaeology and the Emergence of Early Israel." In *Archaeology and Biblical Interpretation.* Ed. J. R. Bartlett. New York: Routledge, 1997. 20–50. ————. "Ceramics, Ethnicity, and the Question of Israel's Origins." *BA* 58 (1995) 200–213. ————. *What Did the Biblical Writers Know and When Did They Know It? What Archaeology Can Tell Us about the Reality of Ancient Israel?* Grand Rapids: Eerdmans, 2001. **DeVries, L. F.**, ed. *Cities of the Biblical World.* Peabody, MA: Hendrickson, 1997. **Dornemann, R. H.** *The Archaeology of the Transjordan in the Bronze and Iron Ages.* Publications in Anthropology and History 4. Milwaukee, WI: Milwaukee Public Museum, 1983. **Dorsey, D. A.** *The Roads and Highways of Ancient Israel.* Baltimore: Johns Hopkins UP, 1991. **Drinkard, J. F., Jr.** "The History and Archaeology of the Book of Joshua and the Conquest/Settlement Period." *RevExp* 95 (1998) 171–88. **Faust, A.** *Israel's Ethnogenesis: Settlement, Interaction, Expansion and Resistance.* London: Equinox, 2007. **Finkelstein, I.** *The Archaeology of the Israelite Settlement.* Jerusalem: Israel Exploration Society, 1988. ————. "The Emergence of Early Israel: Anthropology, Environment and Archaeology." *JAOS* 110 (1990) 677–86. ————. "The Emergence of Israel: A Phase in the Cyclic History of Canaan in the Third and Second Millennium B.C.E." In *From Nomadism to Monarchy: Archaeological and Historical Aspects of Early Israel.* Ed. I. Finkelstein and N. Na'aman. Jerusalem: Israel Exploration Society, 1994. 150–78. ————. "The Emergence of Israel in Canaan: Consensus Mainstream, and Dispute." *SJOT* 2 (1991) 47–59. ————. "Ethnicity and Origin of the Iron I Settlers in the Highlands of Canaan: Can the Real Israel Stand Up?" *BA* 59 (1996) 203–9. ————. "The Rise of Early Israel: Archaeology and Long-Term History." In *The Origin of Early Israel—Current Debate.* Ed. S. Ahituv and E. E. Oren. Beersheva: Ben-Gurion University of the Negev Press, 1998. 7–39. ————. "Searching for Israelite Origins." *BAR* 14.5 (1988) 34–45, 58. **Finkelstein, I., and A. Mazar.** *The Quest for the Historical Israel: Debating Archaeology and the History of Early Israel.* Ed. B. B. Schmidt. SBLABS 17. Atlanta: SBL, 2007. **Finkelstein, I., and N. A. Silberman.** *The Bible Unearthed: Archaeology's New Vision of Ancient Israel and the Origin of Its Sacred Texts.* New York: Free Press, 2001. **Finkelstein, I., A. Fanatalkin, and E. Piasetzky.** "Three Snapshots of the Iron IIa: The Northern Valleys, the Southern Steppe, and Jerusalem." In *Israel in Transition.* Vol. 1. Ed L. Grabbe. New York: T&T Clark, 2008. 32–44. **Free, J. P.** *Archaeology and Bible History.* Rev. and expanded by H. Vos. Grand Rapids: Zondervan, 1992. **Fritz, V.** "The Conquest in the Light of Archaeology." *PrWCJewSt* 8 (1982) 15–22. ————. "Conquest or Settlement?" *BA* 51 (1987) 84–100. ————. "Erwägungen zur Siedlungsgeschichte des Negeb in der Eisen-I-Zeit (1200–1000 v. Chr.) im Lichte der Ausgrabungen auf der Kirbet el-Mšaš. *ZDPV* 91 (1991) 30–45. ————. "Die Landnahme der israelitischen Stämme in Kanaan." *ZDPV* 106 (1990) 63–77. **Gal, Z.** *Lower Galilee during the Iron Age.* ASORDS 8. Winona Lake, IN: Eisenbrauns, 1992. **Geus, C. H. J. de.** *The Tribes of Israel: An Investigation into Some of the Presuppositions of Martin Noth's Amphictyony Hypothesis.* SSN 18. Assen: Van Gorcum, 1976. **Gophna, R.** "Archaeological Survey of the Central Coastal Plain." *TA* 5 (1978) 136–47. **Gottwald, N.** *The Politics of Ancient Israel.* Louisville: Westminster John Knox, 2001. ————. *The Tribes of Yahweh.* Maryknoll, NY: Orbis, 1979. **Grabbe, L. L.**, ed. *Israel in Transition: From Late Bronze II to Iron IIa (ca. 1250–850 B.C.E.).* Vol. 1, *The Archaeology.* (A Conference Supported by the Arts and Humanities Research Council). Library of Hebrew Bible/OTS 491. European Seminar in Historical Methodology 7. London: T&T Clark, 2008. ———. "Reflections on the Discussion." In *Israel in Transition*. Ed. L. L. Grabbe. London: T&T Clark, 2008. 1:219–32. **Halpern, B.** *The Emergence of Israel in Canaan*. SBLMS 29. Chico, CA: Scholars Press, 1983. **Hauser, A. J.** "Israel's Conquest of Palestine: A Peasants' Rebellion?" *JSOT* 7 (1978) 2–19. ———. "The Revolutionary Origins of Ancient Israel: A Response to Gottwald." *JSOT* 8 (1978) 46–49. **Hawkins, R. K.** "The Survey of Manasseh and the Origin of the Central Hill Country Settlers." In *Critical Issues in Early Israelite History*. Ed. R. S. Hess, G. A. Klingbeil, and P. J. Ray, Jr. BBRSup 3. Winona Lake, IN: Eisenbrauns, 2008. 165–79. **Herrmann, S.** "Basic Factors of Israelite Settlement in Canaan." In *Biblical Archaeology Today: Proceedings of the International Congress on Biblical Archaeology Jerusalem, April 1984*. Ed. A. Biran. Jerusalem: Israel Exploration Society, 1985. 47–53. **Hess, R. S.** "Early Israel in Canaan: A Survey of Recent Evidence and Interpretations." *PEQ* 125 (1993) 125–42. ———. *Israelite Religions: An Archaeological and Biblical Survey*. Grand Rapids: Baker, 2007. **Hoerth, A. J.** *Archaeology and the Old Testament*. Grand Rapids: Baker, 1998. **Hurvitz, A.** "The Historical Quest for 'Ancient Israel' and the Linguistic Evidence of the Hebrew Bible: Some Methodological Observations." *VT* 47 (1997) 301–15. **Ishida, I.** "The Leaders of the Tribal Leagues: 'Israel' in the Pre-Monarchic Period." *RB* 80 (1973) 514–30. **Isserlin, S. J.** "The Israelite Conquest of Canaan: A Comparative View of the Arguments Applicable." *PEQ* 115 (1983) 85–94. ———. *The Israelites*. London: Thames & Hudson, 1998. **Ji, C. H. C.** "The Israelite Settlement in Transjordan: The Relation between the Biblical and Archaeological Evidence." *NEASB* 41 (1996) 61–70. **Kelm, G. L.** *Escape to Conflict: A Biblical and Archaeological Approach to the Hebrew Exodus and Settlement in Canaan*. Fort Worth: Iar, 1995. **Killebrew, A. E.** "Aegean-Style Pottery and Associated Assemblages in the Southern Levant: Chronological Implications regarding the Transition from the Late Bronze II to the Iron I and the Appearance of the Philistines." In *Israel in Transition*. Ed. L. L. Grabbe. London: T&T Clark, 2008. 1:54–71. **King, P. J.** "Die archäologische Forschung zur Ansiedlung der Israeliten in Palästina." *BK* 2 (1983) 73–76. ———. "The Contribution of Archaeology to Biblical Studies." *CBQ* 45 (1983) 1–16. **Klingbeil, G. A.** "'Between North and South': The Archaeology of Religion in Late Bronze Age Palestine and the Period of the Settlement." In *Critical Issues in Early Israelite History*. Ed. R. S. Hess, G. A. Klingbeil, and P. J. Ray, Jr. BBRSup 3. Winona Lake, IN: Eisenbrauns, 2008. 111–50. **Knauf, E. A.** "From Archaeology to History, Bronze and Iron Ages with Special Regard to the Year 1200 B.C.E. and the Tenth Century." In *Israel in Transition*. Ed. L. L. Grabbe. London: T&T Clark, 2008. 1:72–85. **Kochavi, M.,** ed. *Judea, Samaria, and the Golan: Archaeological Survey 1967–68* (Heb.). Publications of the Archaeological Survey of Israel 1. Jerusalem, 1972. **Lapp, P. W.** "The Conquest of Palestine in the Light of Archaeology." *CTM* 38 (1967) 283–300. **Lemche, N. P.** *Ancient Israel*. The Biblical Seminar 5. Sheffield: Sheffield Academic, 1995. ———. *Early Israel*. VTSup 37. Leiden: Brill, 1985. ———. "'Hebrew' as a National Name for Israel." *ST* 33 (1979) 1–23. ———. *The Israelites in History and Tradition*. Louisville: Westminster John Knox, 1998. ———. "On the Use of 'System Theory,' 'Macro Theories,' and 'Evolutionistic Thinking' in Modern OT Research and Biblical Archaeology." *SJOT* 4 (1990) 73–88. **Leonard, A.** *An Index to the Late Bronze Age Aegean Pottery from Syria-Palestine*. Jonsered, Sweden: Aström, 1994. **Maeir, A. M., and Pierre de Miroschedji, eds.** *"I Will Speak the Riddles of Ancient Times": Archaeological and Historical Studies in Honor of Amihai Mazar on the Occasion of His Sixtieth Birthday*. 2 vols. Winona Lake, IN: Eisenbrauns, 2006. **Master, D. M.** "Israelite Settlement at the Margins of the Northern Hill Country: Connections to Joshua and Judges from Tell Dothan." In *Critical Issues in Early Israelite History*. Ed. R. S. Hess, G. A. Klingbeil, and P. J. Ray, Jr. BBRSup 3. Winona Lake, IN: Eisenbrauns, 2008. 181–89. **Mattingly, G. L.** "The Exodus-Conquest and the Archaeology of Transjordan: New Light on an Old Problem." *GTJ* 4 (1983) 245–62. **Mazar, A.** *Archaeology of the*

Land of the Bible 10,000–586 B.C.E. ABRL. New York: Doubleday, 1990. ———. "From 1200 to 850 B.C.E.: Remarks on Some Selected Archaeological Issues." In *Israel in Transition*. Ed. L. L. Grabbe. London: T&T Clark, 2008. 1:86–120. ———. "The Iron Age I." In *The Archaeology of Ancient Israel*. Ed. A. Ben-Tor. New Haven: Yale UP, 1990. 258–301. ———. "The Israelite Settlement in Canaan in the Light of Archaeological Excavations." In *Biblical Archaeology Today: Proceedings of the International Congress on Biblical Archaeology Jerusalem, April 1984*. Ed. A. Biran. Jerusalem: Israel Exploration Society, 1985. 61–70. ———. "Remarks on Biblical Traditions and Archaeological Evidence Concerning Early Israel." In *Symbiosis, Symbolism, and the Power of the Past: Canaan, Ancient Israel, and Their Neighbors from the Late Bronze Age through Roman Palestine*. Ed. W. G. Dever and S. Gitin. Winona Lake, IN: Eisenbrauns, 2003. 85–98. **Mendenhall, G.** "Ancient Israel's Hyphenated History." In *Palestine in Transition*. Ed. D. N. Freedman and D. F. Graf. Sheffield: Almond, 1983. ———. "The Hebrew Conquest of Palestine." *BA* 25 (1962) 66–87. ———. *The Tenth Generation: The Origins of the Biblical Tradition*. Baltimore: Johns Hopkins UP, 1973. 95–103. **Merling, D., Sr.** *The Book of Joshua: Its Theme and Role in Archaeological Discussions*. Andrews University Doctoral Dissertation Series 23. Berrien Springs, MI: Andrews UP, 1997. ———. "The Relationship between Archaeology and the Bible: Expectations and Reality." In *The Future of Biblical Archaeology: Reassessing Methodologies and Assumptions*. Ed. J. K. Hoffmeier and A. Millard. Grand Rapids: Eerdmans, 2004. 29–42. **Miller, J. M.** "Archaeology and the Israelite Conquest of Canaan: Some Methodological Observations." *PEQ* 109 (1977) 87–93. ———. "Is It Possible to Write a History of Israel without Relying on the Hebrew Bible?" In *The Fabric of History: Text, Artifact and Israel's Past*. Ed. E. V. Edelman. JSOTSup 127. Sheffield: Sheffield Academic, 1991. 93–102. **Na'aman, N.** "The 'Conquest of Canaan' in the Book of Joshua and in History." In *From Nomadism to Monarchy: Archaeological and Historical Aspects of Early Israel*. Ed. I. Finkelstein and N. Na'aman. Jerusalem: Israel Exploration Society, 1994. 218–81. **Nakhai, B. A.** "Contextualizing Village Life in the Iron Age I." In *Israel in Transition*. Ed. L. L. Grabbe. London: T&T Clark, 2008. 1:121–37. **Negev, A.,** ed. *Archaeological Encyclopedia of the Holy Land*. 3rd ed. Jerusalem: Prentice Hall, 1990. **Noort, E.** *Biblisch-archäologische Hermeneutik und alttestamentliche Exegese*. Kamper cahiers 39. Kampen: Kok, 1979. ———. "Geschiedenis als brandpunt: Over de rel van de archeologie bij de vestiging van Israël in Kanaän." *GTT* 87 (1987) 84–102. **Noth, M.** "Der Beitrag der Archäologie zur Geschichte Israels." In *Congress Volume, Oxford, 1969*. VTSup 7. Ed. G. W. Anderson et al. Leiden: Brill, 1960. 262–82. Repr. in *ABLAK*, 1:34–51. ———. "Grundsätzliches zur Deutung archäologischer Befunde auf dem Boden Palästinas." *PJ* 34 (1938) 7–22. Repr. in *ABLAK*, 1:3–16. ———. "Hat die Bibel doch Recht?" In *Festschrift fur Günther Dehn*. Neukirchen, 1957. 7–22. Repr. in *ABLAK*, 1:17–33. ———. *Die Welt des Alten Testaments*. 4th ed. Berlin: Töpelmann, 1964. Translated as *The Old Testament World*, trans. V. I. Gruhn. Philadelphia: Fortress, 1966. **Ortiz, S. M.** "Does the Low Chronology Work? A Case Study of Qasile X, Gezer X, and Lachish V." In *"I Will Speak the Riddles of Ancient Times": Archaeological and Historical Studies in Honor of Amihai Mazar on the Occasion of His Sixtieth Birthday*. Ed. A. M. Meier and P. de Miroschedji. Winona Lake, IN: Eisenbrauns, 2006. 587–612. **Peterson, J. L.** "A Topographical Survey of the Levitical 'Cities' of Joshua 21 and 1 Chronicles 6: Studies on the Levites in Israelite Life and Religion." ThD diss., Seabury-Western Seminary, Evanston, IL, 1977. **Richard, S.,** ed. *Near Eastern Archaeology: A Reader*. Winona Lake, IN: Eisenbrauns, 2003. **Sauer, J.** "Transjordan in the Bronze and Iron Ages: A Critique of Glueck's Synthesis." *BASOR* 263 (1986) 1–26. **Schoors, A.** "The Israelite Conquest: Textual Evidence in the Archaeological Argument." In *The Land of Israel: Cross-Roads of Civilizations*. Ed. E. Lipiński. OLA 19. Leuven: Peeters, 1985. 77–92. **Shanks, H.** "Defining the Problems: Where Are We in the Debate?" In *The Rise of Ancient Israel*. Ed. H. Shanks et al. Washington, DC: Biblical Archaeology Society, 1992. 8–10. **Soggin, A.** "Archaeological Discoveries and the Israelite Conquest of Palestine in the

Thirteenth and Twelfth Centuries." *BO* 29 (1975) 11–30. **Stager, L. E.** "The Archaeology of the Family in Ancient Israel." *BASOR* 260 (1985) 1–35. **Steen, E. van der.** "The Central East Jordan Valley in the Late Bronze and Early Iron Ages." *BASOR* 302 (1996) 41–64. **Steibing, W. H., Jr.** *Out of the Desert? Archaeology and the Exodus/Conquest Narratives.* Buffalo: Prometheus, 1989. **Steiner, M.** "Propaganda in Jerusalem: State Formation in Iron Age Judah." In *Israel in Transition.* Ed. L. L. Grabbe. London: T&T Clark, 2008. 1:193–202. **Thompson, T. L.** *Early History of the Israelite People: From the Written and Archaeological Sources.* SHANE 4. Leiden: Brill, 1994. **Toombs, L.** "Shechem: Problems of the Early Israelite Era." In *Symposia Celebrating the Seventy-Fifth Anniversary of the Founding of the American Schools of Oriental Research [1900–1975].* Ed. F. M. Cross. Zion Research Foundation Occasional Publications. Cambridge, MA: ASOR, 1979. 69–83. **Ussishkin, D.** "The Date of the Philistine Settlement in the Coastal Plain: TheView from Megiddo and Lachish." In *Israel in Transition.* Ed. L. L. Grabbe. London: T&T Clark, 2008. 203–16. **Waltke, B. K.** "Palestinian Artifactual Evidence Supporting the Early Date of the Exodus." *BSac* 129 (1972) 33–47. **Weippert, M.** "The Israelite 'Conquest' and the Evidence from Transjordan." In *Symposia Celebrating the Seventy-Fifth Anniversary of the Founding of the American Schools of Oriental Research [1900–1975].* Ed. F. M. Cross. Zion Research Foundation Occasional Publications. Cambridge, MA: ASOR, 1979. 15–34. **Wood, B.** "Did the Israelites Conquer Jericho? A New Look at the Archaeological Evidence." *BAR* 16.2 (1990) 44–58. ———. *The Sociology of Pottery in Ancient Palestine.* Sheffield: Almond, 1990. **Wright, G. E.** *Biblical Archaeology.* Philadelphia: Westminster, 1979. **Yadin, Y.** "The Transition from a Semi-Nomadic to a Sedentary Society in the Twelfth Century B.C.E." In *Symposia Celebrating the Seventy-Fifth Anniversary of the Founding of the American Schools of Oriental Research [1900–1975].* Ed. F. M. Cross. Zion Research Foundation Occasional Publications. Cambridge, MA: ASOR, 1979. 57–68. **Zertal, A.** "Israel Enters Canaan—Following the Pottery Trail." *BAR* 17.5 (1991) 28–49, 75. ———. *The Manasseh Hill Country Survey.* Vol. 2, *The Eastern Valleys and the Fringes of the Desert.* Culture and History of the Ancient Near East 21.2. Leiden: Brill, 2007. **Zon, V. M.** "Archaeological Evidence of the Joshua and Judges Period." Diss., London, 1969.

Archaeological work provided primary evidence for exegesis of Joshua during the twentieth century. The resulting evidence was been used to prove and disprove the biblical accounts of the conquest. Coote defines the problem: "Of a total of sixteen sites clearly said by the Bible to have been destroyed, only three have produced archaeological evidence for a destruction ca. 1200 BCE: Bethel, Lachish, and Hazor. . . . [S]even . . . either were not occupied in the period or show no trace of a destruction. . . . [S]ix . . . have not been positively located." Coote concludes: "The archaeological evidence today is overwhelmingly against the classic model of Israelite origins, as evidenced in the book of Joshua."[241]

The major issues in using archaeological evidence to verify the historicity of the book of Joshua have been raised in the debate between Martin Noth and John Bright. Noth argued that the nature of the literary traditions must be assessed in and of themselves before archaeological information could be introduced to support the historical character of the traditions. He noted that archaeological findings must be fitted into a larger historical context, and so historical synthesis was necessarily involved. Historians are prone to search too quickly and improperly for direct biblical connections. Noth cautioned that archaeology does not give

---

241 Coote, 615.

evidence of particular historical events unless it yields written documents. Instead, archaeology illuminates the environment and life style of the times. Archaeology may show an event to have been possible but cannot prove it actually occurred.

Bright retorted that Noth had asked the wrong question. We cannot seek absolute proof but must ask where the balance of probability lies. For the conquest, archaeology can distinguish dates and occupants of the various sites. The identities of the towns destroyed in the thirteenth century place the balance of probability on the side of the Joshua narrative.[242]

John Bimson introduced another way of handling the archaeological materials.[243] He questioned the basic presuppositions of archaeologists in comparative pottery dating of sites and in identifying archaeological sites with biblical ones. He pushes the dating of the conquest from the thirteenth century back to the second half of the fifteenth, which he interprets as the end of the Middle Bronze Age. Reviewers have criticized Bimson strongly for his disregard for literary criticism of the biblical sources but have not levied significant criticisms at his archaeological explanations.[244] George Ramsey provides the most extensive and valuable critique of Bimson.[245] Ramsey concludes:

> Although Bimson's method of establishing a biblical chronology as the norm for adjusting the dates of archaeological periods is highly questionable and the particular arguments from the Bible which he employs to re-date the end of the Middle Bronze Age are very weak, his work merits attention. He has summarized well the problem which others have recognized, namely, that the Palestinian cities whose remains from the Late Bronze Age create problems for the theory of a thirteenth century conquest outnumber the cities which do not, and he has given a reasonable alternative archaeological context for consideration.[246]

Alternative solutions to the archaeological questions abound. Joseph Callaway used the Ai evidence to lower the dating of the conquest to the twelfth century.[247] Yohanan Aharoni has rewritten the conquest with "Nothing Early and Nothing Late," thus returning in most essentials to Noth's position.[248]

Manfred Weippert nuanced the Nothian arguments somewhat, identifying the ancestors with Late Bronze Age nomadic settlers in the Palestinian mountains related to the Shoshu known in other texts. Only later did the Shoshu population of Canaan, called Israel, form a twelve-tribe system and still later adopt the Yahwistic religion of the exodus group. Overpopulation forced some to migrate into Transjordan, while others settled into agricultural lives.[249]

---

242   Bright, *Early Israel*; Noth, *PJ* 34 (1938) 7–22 = *ABLAK*, 1:3–16; see the more mediating position of Noth in "Der Beitrag der Archäologie," 262–82.
243   In *Redating the Exodus*.
244   See reviews of Bimson's book: J. M. Miller, *JBL* 99 (1980) 133–35; J. A Soggin, *VT* 31 (1981) 98–99; with more hesitation, W H. Shea, *CBQ* 42 (1980) 88–90.
245   *Quest for the Historical Israel*, 73–77.
246   Ibid., 77.
247   *JBL* 87 (1968) 312–20.
248   Aharoni, *AntSur* 2 (1957) 131–50; *BA* 39 (1976) 55–76.
249   Weippert, *Die Landnahme der israelitischen Stämme*; *Settlement of the Israelite Tribes in Palestine*; "Israelite 'Conquest' and the Evidence from Transjordan," 15–34.

Contributing to the same forum as Weippert, Yigael Yadin has forcefully reasserted the Albright/Bright position:

> I believe everyone will agree that results of thorough archaeological excavations in the last fifty years prove clearly that a certain culture—which we may call the Late Bronze Age culture—based on fortified city-states, had come to a sudden, abrupt end; cities were destroyed, with many of them showing indications of conflagrations and destructions which could not be attributed to famine or earthquakes. Sometime later—stratigraphically speaking—either on the same site or elsewhere, a new, completely different culture developed, having a rather poor architectural concept which could hardly be called urban and which seems most like the first efforts of settlement of a semi-nomadic people. Notwithstanding this remark, some sites—although destroyed in the previous period—were immediately rebuilt and could definitely be regarded as proper cities with fortifications and all the necessary attributes and elements.[250]

Yadin uses the excavations at Hazor to support his conclusions that the Egyptian pharaohs of the fourteenth and thirteenth centuries so weakened the Palestinian city-state system that the seminomadic Israelites could apply the "coup de grâce."

Lawrence Toombs adds one other piece of evidence in examining the Shechem excavations, concluding that

> there was a hitherto unrecognized conquest of Shechem during the Late Bronze Age, probably in the late fourteenth or early thirteenth century. This conquest, which may have come about as a reaction by other city-states to the expansionist policies of the dynasty of Lab'ayu, greatly weakened and impoverished the city and, thus, became an important factor in the subsequent peaceful passage of Shechem into Israelite political control."[251]

Nakhai shows the complexity of village life in various sections of the country, with a number of controlling systems and different mixes of populations.[252] Urban settlements remained or were rebuilt; remnants of the city-state system continued to operate; and some destroyed cities were rebuilt.

Ramsey reminds us of the problem of using archaeological results in dealing with the conquest. He notes that such materials can sometimes falsify the biblical account and at other times show that no known conditions exclude the possibility of the biblical account, but seldom do they explicitly confirm the biblical account. He notes that "the reliability of the biblical witness for the period prior to the monarchy is itself an hypothesis which has not been proved."[253]

Michael Coogan completes his survey with great skepticism: "I strongly doubt that the material culture of settlements known from textual sources to have been Israelite can at present be distinguished from that of settlements known to have been Canaanite (i.e., non-Israelite) in the absence of determinative written evidence." This, of course, assumes that the biblical material is far from determinative

---

250 "Transition from a Semi-Nomadic to a Sedentary Society," 58.
251 "Shechem."
252 "Contextualizing Village Life in the Iron Age I," 121–37.
253 *Quest for the Historical Israel*, 104.

written evidence.[254] For Coogan, then, archaeological results support a date for Joshua late in Iron II. "An archaeological commentary on Joshua would find little if anything to illustrate genuine and exclusively premonarchic traditions."

David Merling surveys five theories of Israel's origins and comes to surprising results.[255] Merling assumes that "without the Book of Joshua there would be few questions about the ethnicity of the Canaanite hill-country inhabitants or discussions about the origins of the Israelites and the nature of their settlement."[256] On the other hand, none of the five theories has received majority support. All five theories make "inadequate and incomplete use of archaeology and the Bible."[257] Each theory has glaring weaknesses:

1. The conquest theory cannot demonstrate responsibility for any one ethnic group for any of the conquests, nor can it explain lack of archaeological evidence for destruction of several cities whose destruction the Bible mentions or lack of biblical testimony to cities archaeology would claim as destroyed in the "conquest period."[258]

2. The peaceful infiltration theory "did not employ archaeology in its development." Its evolutionary foundations have been proved untrue. The theory is built more on extrabiblical data and theory than on biblical evidence.[259]

3. The peasants' revolt theory lets a unique definition of ʿapiru guide its theory as to the essence of the Israelites. It ignores the several migrating groups of the time who "lived in tents and gave little respect to city-dwelling kings." Israel was not ethnically pure, but the revolt theory demands too great a degree of such purity, a degree few if any groups can claim." No biblical evidence points to such a peasant revolt.[260]

4. The theory of Israel's origin in the Late Bronze II and Iron I does not explain the widespread settlement of Israel rather than a confinement to the hill country. The theory "exhibits a serious lack of objective control." One should not expect archaeological uniqueness for the Israelites, Israel not being identified by material culture but rather by self-recognition. Such appearance of new ethnic peoples has no other examples. Those holding this theory get no help from the Bible since they consider its evidence unreliable.[261]

5. The conquest by imagination theory distrusts archaeology, especially evidence like the Merneptah stele that does not fit the theory. The weakest link in the theory is its strong dependence on ancient weather patterns without much study in that area. The theory wants to write a history of Israel without using the Bible.[262]

---

254 "Archaeology and Biblical Studies," 28.
255 *Book of Joshua*, 1–105. Cf. a similar appraisal by Hoppe, 76–81, who sees the narratives as propaganda against religious syncretism in the Davidic period.
256 Merling, 57.
257 Ibid., 59.
258 Ibid., 62–63.
259 Ibid., 66–68.
260 Ibid., 70–79.
261 Ibid., 80–90.
262 Ibid., 91–100.

Since all of the theories exhibit strong flaws, Merling tries a different approach. Working with the present text, whatever editorial history lies behind it, Merling seeks to find the text's "unique message." A survey of archaeological results at the various sites named in Josh 6–11 leads to the conclusion that "no specific information has been found to substantiate the stories of the Book of Joshua."[263] Merling thus proposes that Joshua is written as a book of confirmation not of conquest, that its "primary goal" is "confirming or reconfirming the uniqueness of Israel . . . evidenced . . . by the presence and guidance of YHWH."[264] Merling insists that the writers want the readers to affirm that Yahweh gave the land and determined its boundaries like an oriental ruler. In seeking to prove this thesis, Merling makes interesting observations:

1. Where Israel settled was not as important as how—by God's power. Joshua "does not relate itself in any extensive way to settlement problems."[265]
2. The book of Joshua may be about the conquest of Canaan, but "it says almost nothing about the settling of Canaan."[266] "Israel had no long lasting conquest. The Israelites had only begun a contest to attain the land."[267] They did not control much of the land until David.[268] When they fought, they retuned to Gilgal. Possession (ירש) was much more important than settling (ישב).[269] "I doubt that the 12 tribes, as individual units, were ever able to fully and independently control their territories."[270] A "gap between destruction and settlement more clearly indicates an upheaval of an entire society."[271]
3. Victories did not represent "a final victory," only the first stage.[272]
4. "The act of allotting the land is a confirmation act that pronounces Israel's right to possess it."[273]
5. "The theme of Joshua is promise, not fulfillment."[274]
6. Language about killing everyone and leaving no survivors is used for "different purposes other than to detail the totality of the Israelite casualties." The language applied to those left in the city, not those who fled.[275] Language of the ban (חרם) put moral responsibility on God not on the people.[276]
7. "Archaeology has provided no information as to the origins of Israel. . . . It seems more prudent to accept cautiously the biblical writers' explanation of Israel's origins."[277] Archaeologists too often rely on the absence of evidence, nonevidence, that comes from theories not sites.[278] "Archaeology stops with

---

263 Ibid., 145.
264 Ibid., 155.
265 Ibid., 168.
266 Ibid., 169.
267 Ibid., 181.
268 Ibid., 183.
269 Ibid., 203–4.
270 Ibid., 207.
271 Ibid., 223.
272 Ibid., 173.
273 Ibid., 182.
274 Ibid., 184.
275 Ibid., 188–89; cf. 192.
276 Ibid., 199.
277 Ibid., 230; cf. 238.
278 Ibid., 240–41.

what an archaeologist finds. Beyond that lies speculation."[279] "The biblical writers have provided a theological history. Archaeology cannot determine the trustworthiness of theology."[280] The events of Joshua "might not have been colossal events to a secular historian."[281]

8. A "true monotheism" "could go far in explaining how the Israelites became Hebrews"; "worship of YHWH and monotheism were cocreated."[282] "The purpose, then, of the Book of Joshua is not so much to reveal a sequence of causal events, as to bolster faith in YHWH."[283]

9. Sometime before 1200 BCE "a loosely banded tribal group migrated into the Cisjordan hill country and became associated with the outsiders, the *'apiru*." Such an arrival could go all the way back to the Amarna period. The tribal group chased people from their cities and established YHWH in their minds as a superior god. They carved out "spotty settlements" in the hill country. Many of the native people were eventually adopted into Israel.[284]

Merling's theory calls us to look at strong evidence but does not follow the structural high points of the narrative that emphasize conquest, possession, and distribution of land by Joshua and the Israelites without mention of God's presence or actions, especially the hinge chap. 12.[285]

Mark Brett uses ethnological studies to create a theory of early Israel as a people who formed a loose network by the time of Merneptah.[286] This network had little government or incorporation, nor did it impose culture on the inhabitants of the highlands. The people developed a founding myth in the exodus story, a unique taboo in forbidding the eating of pigs, and a worship of Yahweh that gradually came to be seen as antagonistic to the worship of other gods.

Richard Hess shows elements best or only explained as originating in the second millennium.[287] In an additional note to chap. 6 of the book of Joshua,[288] Hess accepts a thirteenth-century date for the conquest, noting that recent surveys point to earlier occupation in Transjordan. He finds the Amarna letters' references to *hapiru* unhelpful in characterizing the Israelites and admits we have no archaeological evidence of Israel's presence. The biblical witness describes only Jericho and Hazor as having been destroyed and burnt. An early date for the exodus/conquest would seem to require mention of Egyptian control in Palestine. Egyptian authority, particularly in the hill country, weakened in the thirteenth and twelfth centuries. The transition to the Iron Age involved many peoples moving around and resettling, such as the Sea Peoples and the Aramaeans.

Margreet Steiner sees Jerusalem as "the largest town not only in Judah but in the whole region."[289] Whatever king built the strong architectural features of the

---

279 Ibid., 254.
280 Ibid., 259.
281 Ibid., 261.
282 Ibid., 233.
283 Ibid., 272.
284 Ibid., 270–71.
285 Cf. Harris, 74.
286 *BibInt* 11 (2003) 400–412.
287 *Joshua*, 26–31. See enumeration of these under "Studies in the Early History of Israel" below.
288 Hess, 139–43.
289 "Propaganda in Jerusalem," 193–202.

city showed clearly that "Judah was a state." Ann Killebrew uses pottery analysis to move Finkelstein's low chronology up a decade or so and fit the Mycenaean evidence.[290] Philistine evidence still does not yield absolute chronological indicators, but the settlement appears to be more of a process than a one-time event associated with Egypt's defeat of the Sea Peoples.[291]

In his initial essay in this book, Finkelstein reads texts to find more information about the time of the writing than about the time being described.[292] The Deuteronomistic History introduces the idea of Judah claiming control over all Israel, north and south. For the period of conquest and judges, archaeology is "the only source of information."

Biblical narratives here may contain a few "vague memories" of heroic events but are "almost complete expressions of the political and theological ideology of Josianic times."[293] "Early realities" in the Pentateuch and Deuteronomistic History "are beyond recovery."[294] Still, Finkelstein holds, "It is unthinkable that the biblical authors invented stories only in order to serve their aims. Had they done that, they would have lost their credibility among the people of Judah, the target population. It is more reasonable to assume that the authors collected myths, folktales, popular heroic tales, and shreds of memories known to the population of Judah and employed them in their cause."[295]

Finkelstein accuses the conservative camp of not giving archaeology center stage, using it only to support a preconceived theory through circular arguments that had no "actual support in the finds."[296] An idea of oral tradition preserved unchanged through the centuries is unrealistic and naïve.[297] Finkelstein then dates the rise of the kingdom of Judah and "meaningful scribal activity" to shortly before 700 BCE. Only with the fall of the northern kingdom did Judah begin to grow developed administrative systems, and become a meaningful power.[298]

Against the minimalists, Finkelstein claims that literacy and extensive scribal activity were much more influential in seventh-century Jerusalem than in the Persian and Hellenistic periods. Finkelstein is amazed at the minimalist conclusions: "The assumption is inconceivable that in the fifth, or fourth, or even second centuries BCE the scribes of a small, out-of-the-way temple town in the Judean mountains authored an extraordinarily long and detailed composition about the history, personalities, and events of an imaginary Iron Age 'Israel' without using ancient sources."[299] Such a "purely mythic history" would not include the extensive name

---

290 "Aegean-Style Pottery."
291 In "Invited Lectures Delivered at the Sixth Biennial Colloquium of the International Institute for Secular Humanistic Judaism" in Detroit in October 2005, Israel Finkelstein and Amihai Mazar both took mediating, centrist positions between minimalists and maximalists. Both assume the results of historical critical study of the biblical text and authorship centuries after the "conquest and settlement" of Palestine.
292 "Archaeology and the Quest for a Historical Israel in the Hebrew Bible," 15.
293 Ibid., 16.
294 Ibid., 17.
295 Ibid., 18.
296 Ibid., 10.
297 Ibid., 18.
298 Ibid., 49.
299 Ibid., 13.

lists and details of royal administration, some of which archaeology has confirmed. In addition, Finkelstein joins A. Hurwitz in seeing the language of the Deuteronomistic History as late preexilic, not postexilic.[300]

Finkelstein describes archaeological evidence that shows the major theories of Israel's conquest or settlement in Palestine as inadequate.[301] The Canaanite city-state system collapsed over several decades or more, not immediately. Key sites such as Jericho, Ai, Gibeon, Heshbon, and Arad were either uninhabited or only small villages in the Late Bronze Age. Egyptian power in Canaan lasted until after 1150. Late Bronze Age Canaan collapsed as part of a much wider eastern Mediterranean collapse. Israel's rise in the central hill country was one phase in a repeated historical cycle in that area. Still, for Finkelstein, "It is inconceivable that the Conquest stories were invented by the late-monarchic writers. The Deuteronomistic Historian must have taken old folktales and fragmented memories and incorporated them in his compilation" (53–54).

Finkelstein, with Fantalkin and Piasetzky, looks at three distinct areas in Palestine ("Three Snapshots of the Iron IIa," 32–44). They debate Mazar's dating of the transition to Iron II at 970 rather than Finkelstein's dating to after 925. In the south, Shoshenq I's campaign cannot be associated with Arad XII, since Egypt tried to protect the copper industry, not destroy it. In the central area, Jerusalem shows no signs of administrative power and organization until after 900.

Amihai Mazar finds six types of earlier materials and sources in the Deuteronomistic History that may contain "valuable historical information": Jerusalem temple archives, palace archives, public inscriptions, oral renditions of ancient poetry, folk and etiological stories rooted in a "remote historical past," and earlier historiographic writings. Many of the memories "even seem to be pre-Israelite and adapted by the Israelites as part of their heritage."[302]

Mazar identifies Yadin as the last archaeologist "to present Joshua as a real military hero who conquered city after city in Canaan in line with the biblical narrative."[303] Many cities mentioned in the book of Joshua were not inhabited during the supposed time of the conquest. Important cities like Lachish and Hazor were destroyed at least a century apart. Thus all archaeologists realize that archaeology contradicts the biblical account of a conquest under a single leader.[304] Some stories may have historical memories but not be necessarily connected with Joshua or even with Israel. Hazor was burned in this period but possibly by Canaanites, not Israelites. Southern regions around Arad were extensively settled in the tenth century, when the stories may have been created. Mazar locates the Israelites throughout the 250 Iron Age I settlements between Beersheba and the Jezreel Valleys. Thus for Mazar, "The Conquest tradition may be understood as a telescoped reflection of a lengthy, complex historical process in which many of the Canaanite city-states, weakened and impoverished by three hundred years of Egyptian domination, were demolished during the thirteenth and twelfth centuries BCE."[305]

---

300 Ibid., 14.
301 Ibid., 53–55.
302 Mazar, "On Archaeology, Biblical History, and Biblical Archaeology," in *The Quest for the Historical Israel*, 29–30.
303 Ibid., 61.
304 Ibid., 62.
305 Ibid., 64.

Joel Drinkard understands that the cities that might have been taken during an Israelite conquest do not represent the blitzkrieg type of assault credited to Joshua, since the destruction layers are spread over at least fifty years.[306] Admitting that "the genre of historiography was not nearly so rigid during the biblical period as we consider it now,"[307] Drinkard believes archaeological evidence leads far beyond the minimalist position. He finds that the biblical record accurately describes the Philistines, accurately shows a new population in the hill country heartland of Israel, preserves Egyptian names and cities pointing to Israelite contact with Egypt, describes the destruction of several cities that were destroyed in this time frame— Hazor, Lachish, Debir, Tell Beit Mirsim, and Bethel, and attests to the existence of Israel in the land at the time the Merneptah stele witnesses.[308]

David Ussishkin uses evidence from Megiddo and Lachish to challenge Mazar and to hypothesize that "the end of Egyptian hegemony in southern Canaan and the destruction of Lachish Level VI occurred not before c. 1130 BCE."[309] Lachish's absolute lack of Aegean/Philistine pottery means such pottery entered the country after 1130.

Daniel Browning is hard pressed to come to conservative or evangelical conclusions.[310] He recognizes the need for a Late Bronze Age date for the exodus and conquest. He sees the problem of unoccupied cities such as Jericho, Ai, Gibeon, Hebron, and Jarmuth. He finds that archaeology supports the Judges picture over that of Joshua. Any solution to the problem is complex and draws from all the theories of conquest. He concludes, "the book of Joshua is a glorified account of relatively small military encounters with an occasional major victory" with etiological elements, editorial expansions, and elements of Israel coming from within, not without, Canaan.[311]

Ernst Axel Knauf discusses gradual changes in pottery and culture rather than abrupt transitions and concludes that using "historical events" to date archaeological periods is absurd.[312] Why begin the Iron Age at 1200 when nothing important occurred in 1200? He seeks hard statistical evidence and thus looks to the rate of ships lost in shipwrecks as an indication of trade intensity. One finds that Benjamin and Jerusalem flourished long before Shechem, which was absolutely unimportant until about 1000.

Amihai Mazar shows that Canaanite culture continued in the northern plains and apparently only there, until 1000.[313] At best, Sea Peoples constituted a small minority of the population. This means that Finkelstein's talk of a Canaanite renaissance following a gap supports his low chronology but does not have archaeological evidence to verify it. Philistines seem not to have traded their special pottery goods. The decline of Egyptian domination after 1200 made way for Philistine settlement in Palestine. Philistine origins belong to the same historical movement

---

306 *RevExp* 95 (1998) 178.
307 Ibid., 181.
308 Ibid., 182.
309 "Date of the Philistine Settlement," 000
310 *SwJT* 41 (1998) 42–43.
311 Ibid., 42.
312 "From Archaeology to History."
313 "From 1200 to 850 B.C.E."

as the Aegean entrance into Cyprus. Philistine settlers were urbanites from the start. Philistine expansion beyond the core cities occurred after local MycIIIC ware production ceased. The north did not experience transplanted Aegean communities as did the southern coast. Dor's sudden population growth may have come from northern Syria.

Cypriot ware made in Cyprus and found particularly at Beth Shean dates to the twelfth century in Cyprus and must represent either a limited and casual trade with Cyprus or luxury items brought in by Cypriot soldiers. Eleventh-century pottery based on Aegean or Cypriot traditions but locally produced points to Cypriot soldiers in Palestine.

Mazar suggests a modified conventional chronology with the end of Iron I at 980. Jezreel takes the period into the ninth century or Iron IIa.[314] It is not feasible to conflate the several strata at Tel Rehov, Megiddo, and Hazor into one century. C14 dates of Iron IIa strata date to the tenth and ninth centuries. Arad XII is a key site for the south. Processing data on strata points to a transition from Iron I to Iron IIa between 964 and 944. Mazar argues with Finkelstein over the dating and nature of the architecture of Megiddo and Hazor. Mazar sees an urban revival in the tenth century.[315] Recent discoveries have shown that literacy and scribal activity occurred at least by the tenth century, though Finkelstein would reduce it to the eighth. For Mazar, the evidence "supports the existence of contemporary polities mentioned in the biblical narrative relating to David and Solomon."[316] Hubbard sums up the situation succinctly: "What may one glean about Israel from the archaeological record? The short answer is very little about the Conquest but a good deal about the settlement."[317]

Archaeological research thus leaves confusion and unanswered questions. This does not lead us to abandon archaeological research. It reminds us of the great difficulties that stand in our way when we seek to utilize archaeological discoveries for historical reconstruction. Archaeology can rarely name sites. Seldom, if ever, can it determine precisely who destroyed a site. It often cannot tell who occupied a site; it can place only relative dates on sites; and only rarely can one excavate an entire site and secure all the evidence.

Lester Grabbe, then, sums up by expressing frustration at the lack of consistent terminology, at the inability to agree on major divisions of the Late Bronze/Iron I and II cultural periods, at the continually growing number of chronological systems, at the lack of discussion and thought concerning methodology, at archaeologists' continued lack of understanding of technical equipment such as C14 dating, and at the introducton of new designations for various types of Philistine pottery.[318]

Archaeology at the moment appears to leave us with more questions than answers. How does the archaeologist measure different strata chronologically? Who are the Philistines? When did the Egyptians lose control of Palestine? How many infiltrations of Sea People came from the north? How does one explain the

---

314   Ibid., 99.
315   Ibid., 108.
316   Ibid., 109.
317   Hubbard, 40.
318   "Reflections on the Discussion," 220.

diversity of cultural indicators in one town or city? How does one distinguish Isra-elite communities from those of the Canaanites or other groups settled (settling) in Palestine? How does one explain the apparent lack of the spread of Philistine pottery? When did Shoshenq attack Israel, especially the Negev, and why? When and how did Jerusalem become a leading city of a state?

Why are there so many questions raised by archaeology without clear answers? Perhaps the late Anson Rainey had the answer as we stood in the excavations in Beersheba. Anson asked, "What does it take to be an archaeologist?" His answer: "You have to know how to dig a hole and spin a yarn."

Hopefully, we have advanced a bit beyond that, but the fact remains: finding a piece of cultural realia calls on the discoverer to picture the context in which the discovery was found and to explain its use in situ before comparing it with similar finds in different excavations. That explanation then leads to conversations with other archaeologists who have different yarns to connect with the excavations and the concrete finds.

Still, we must acknowledge our deep appreciation for the detailed work archae-ologists have accomplished through long hours of hot, sweaty labor. We must not ignore the large amounts of negative evidence, pointing to periods when the bibli-cal sites were unoccupied. We must not be too quick to identify every destruction layer with the Israelite conquest. Nor can we too rapidly set aside the tradition that Israel was involved in military conquest. Perhaps refined work in pottery chronol-ogy and further excavation and analysis will provide more data for use in exegeting the conquest literary materials. It appears certain that Ai will continue to present the major stumbling block, since it has no signs of occupation during any period which can realistically be set forward as a conquest date. Noort's conclusion still rings true: "Archaeology is a matter of a thematic field from which much is postu-lated and only very little is provable."[319]

b. Studies in the Early History of Israel

Bibliography

Ahlström, G. W. *The History of Ancient Palestine from the Palaeolithic Period to Alexander's Conquest.* Ed. D. V. Edelman. Minneapolis: Fortress, 1993. **Angel, H.** "There Is No Chron-ological Order in the Torah": An Axiom for Understanding the Book of Joshua." *JBQ* 36 (2008) 3–11. ———. "One Book, Two Books: The Joshua-Judges Continuum." *JBQ* 36 (2008) 163–70. **Barr, J.** *History and Ideology in the Old Testament.* Oxford: Oxford UP, 2000. **Barstad, H.** "Israels eldste historie: Omkring den seneste utviklinginnen forskin-gen." *NedTT* 88 (1987) 99–107. **Bienkowski, P.** "Jericho Was Destroyed in the Middle Bronze Age, Not the Late Bronze Age." *BAR* 17.5 (1990) 45–46. **Brodsky, H.** "Bible Lands: Three Capitals in the Hills of Ephraim." *BRev* 5.1 (1989) 38–44. **Burnyeat, J. P.** "Historiography and Hebrew Historical Writing." *EvQ* 50 (1978) 33–37. **Coote, R. B., and K. W. Whitelam.** *The Emergence of Early Israel in Historical Perspective.* SWBA 5. Sheffield: Sheffield Academic, 1987. **Festorazzi, F.** "Il problema storico e il problema teologica delle origini di Israele: In margine al libro di H. Engel: *Die Vorfahren Israels in*

---

319 *Das Buch Josua*, 6. For detailed accounts of the various sites, see the work of Grabbe, Hawkins, Negev, Avi-Yonah and Stern, Svensson, and Hess, the appropriate places in this commentary, and J. M. Miller: "Archaeology and the Israelite Conquest of Canaan: Some Methodological Observations," *PEQ* 109 (1977) 87–93.

Ägypten." *RivB* 29 (1981) 205–22. **Finkelstein, I., and A. Mazar.** *The Quest for the Historical Israel: Debating Archaeology and the History of Early Israel.* Ed. B. B. Schmidt. SBLABS 17. Atlanta: SBL, 2007. **Frendo, A. J.** "Back to Basics: A Holistic Approach to the Problem of the Emergence of Ancient Israel." In *In Search of Pre-Exilic Israel: Proceedings of the Oxford Old Testament Seminar.* Ed. J. Day. JSOTSup 406. London: T&T Clark, 2004. 41–64. **Friis, H.** "Ein neues Paradigma für die Erforschung der Vorgeschichte Israels." *DBAT* 19 (1984) 3–22. **Grabbe, L. L.** *Ancient Israel: What Do We Know and How Do We Know It?* London: T&T Clark, 2007. **Greenspahn, F. E.** "Recent Scholarship on the History of Premonarchic Israel." *JRelJ* 30 (1983) 81–93. **Hagens, G.** "Exodus and Settlement: A Two Sojourn Hypothesis." *SR* 36 (2007) 85–105. **Halpern, B.** *The Emergence of Israel in Canaan.* SBLMS 29. Chico, CA: Scholars Press, 1983. ———. "The Uneasy Compromise: Israel between League and Monarchy." In *Traditions in Transformation: Turning Points in Biblical Faith.* FS F. M. Cross, ed. B. Halpern and J. D. Levenson. Winona Lake, IN: Eisenbrauns, 1981. 59–96. **Hawkins, R. K.** "Propositions for Evangelical Assessment of a Later Date Exodus-Conquest: Biblical Data and the Royal Scarab of MT. Ebal." *JETS* 50 (2007) 31–46. ———. "The Date of the Exodus-Conquest Is Still an Open Question." *JETS* 51 (2008) 245–66. **Hecke, K. H.** *Juda und Israel: Untersuchungen zur Geschichte Israels in vor- und frühstaatlicher Zeit.* FB 52. Würzburg: Echter, 1985. **Heller, J.** "Sozialer Hintergrund der israelitischen Landnahme." *CV* 15 (1972) 211–22. **Hess, R. S.** "Early Israel in Canaan: A Survey of Recent Evidence and Interpretations." *PEQ* 125 (1993) 125–42. **Hoffmeier, J. K.** "What Is the Biblical Date for the Exodus? A Response to Bryant Wood." *JETS* 50 (2007) 225–47. **Ishida, T.** "On the Method of History of Ancient Israel." *Seishogaku ronshwpf* 1.193 (1978) 5–16. **Jeffers, A.** "Ideal versus Real History in the Book of Joshua." *JETS* 12 (1969) 183–87. **Kreuzer, S.** *Die Frühgeschichte Israels in Bekenntnis und Verkündigung des Alten Testaments.* BZAW 178. Berlin: De Gruyter, 1989. **Malamat, A.** "The Proto-History of Israel: A Study in Method." In *The Word of the Lord Shall Go Forth.* FS D. N. Freedman, ed. C. L. Meyers and M. O'Connor. Philadelphia: Fortress, 1983. 303–13. **Mazani, P.** "The Appearance of Israel in Canaan in Recent Scholarship." In *Critical Issues in Early Israelite History.* Ed. R. Hess, G. A. Klingbeil, and P. Ray, Jr. BBSup 3. Winona Lake, IN: Eisenbrauns, 2008. 95–109. **Merrill, E. H.** "The Late Bronze/Early Iron Age Transition and the Emergence of Israel." *BSac* 152 (1995) 145–62. **Metzger, M.** "Probleme der Frühgeschichte Israels." *VF* 22 (1977) 30–43. **Miller, J. M.** "In Defense of Writing a History of Israel." *JSOT* 39 (1987) 53–57. ——— **and J. H. Hayes.** *A History of Ancient Israel and Judah.* 2nd ed. Louisville: Westminster John Knox, 2006. **Neu, R.** "'Israel' vor der Entstehung des Königtums." *BZ* NF 30 (1986) 204–21. **Niditch, S.** *Oral World and Written Word: Ancient Israelite Literature.* Louisville: Westminster John Knox, 1996. **Noll, K. L.** *Canaan and Israel in Antiquity: An Introduction.* Biblical Seminar 83. London: Sheffield Academic, 2001. **Noort, E.** "Klio und die Welt des Alten Testaments: Überlegungen zur Benutzung literarischer und feldarchäologischer Quellen bei der Darstellung einer Geschichte Israels." In *Ernten was man sät: Festschrift für Klaus Koch.* Ed. D. R. Daniels, U. Gleßmer, and M. Rösel. Neukirchen-Vluyn: Neukirchener Verlag, 1991. 533–60. **Otto, E.** "Historisches Geschehen—Überlieferung—Erklärungsmodell: Sozialhistorische Grundsatz- und Einzelprobleme in der Geschichtsschreibung des frühen Israel. Eine Antwort auf N. P. Lemches Beitrag zur Diskussion um eine Sozialgeschichte Israels." *BN* 23 (1984) 63–80. **Prato, G. L.** "Le origini dell'antico Israele nell'analisi socio-religiosa di N. K. Gottwald." *Greg* 62 (1981) 553–61. **Raurell, F.** "The Notion of History in the Hebrew Bible." In *History and Identity: How Israel's Later Authors Viewed Its Earlier History.* Ed N. Calduch-Benages and J. Liesen. Deuterocanonical and Cognate Literature Yearbook. Berlin: De Gruyter, 2006. 1–20. **Schaper, J.** "Auf der Suche nach dem alten Israel? Text, Artefakt und 'Geschichte Israels' in der alttestamentlichen Wissenschaft vor dem Hintergrund der Methodendiskussion in den Historischen Kulturwissenschaften." Part

1, *ZAW* 118 (2006) 1–21; part 2, *ZAW* 118 (2006) 181–96. **Seebaß, H.** "Dialog über Israels Anfänge: Zum Evolutionsmodell von N. P. Lemche." In *Alttestamentlicher Glaube und Biblische Theologie: Festschrift für Horst Dietrich Preuß zum 65. Geburtstag.* Ed. J. Haussmann and H.-J. Zobel. Stuttgart: Kohlhammer, 1992. 11–19. **Sicre, J. L.** "Los origenes de Israel." *EstBib* 46 (1988) 421–55. **Soggin, J. A.** "Le origini d'Israele—problema per lo storiografo?" In *Convegno sul tema: Le origini di Israele.* Ed. J. A. Soggin. Rome: Accademia nazionale dei Lincei, 1987. 5–14. ———. "Probleme einer Vor- und Frühgeschichte Israels." *ZAW* 100 (1988) 255–67. **Strange, J.** "The Transition from the Bronze Age to the Iron Age in the Eastern Mediterranean and the Emergence of the Israelite State." *SJOT* 1 (1987) 1–19. ———. "The Book of Joshua—Origin and Dating." *SJOT* 16 (2002) 44–51. **Tadmor, H.** "The Origins of Israel as Seen in the Exilic and Post-exilic Ages." In *Convegno sul tema: Le origini di Israele.* Ed. J. A. Soggin. Rome: Accademia nazionale dei Lincei, 1987. 15–27. **Velázquez, E., II.** "The Persian Period and the Origins of Israel: Beyond the 'Myths.'" In *Critical Issues from Israelite History.* Ed. R. Hess, G. A. Klingbeil, and P. J. Ray, Jr. BBRSup 3. Winona Lake, IN: Eisenbrauns, 2008. 61–76. **Waltke, B.** "The Date of the Conquest." *WTJ* 52 (1990) 181–200. **Weippert, M.** "Fragen des israelitischen Geschichtsbewußtseins." *VT* 23 (1973) 415–42. **Whitelam, K. W.** "Israel's Traditions of Origin: Reclaiming the Land." *JSOT* 44 (1989) 19–42. **Wood, B. G.** "The Biblical Date for the Exodus Is 1446 B.C.E.: A Response to James Hoffmeier." *JETS* 50 (2007) 249–58. ———. "The Rise and Fall of the 13th-Century Exodus-Conquest Theory." *JETS* 48 (2005) 475–89. **Young, R. C., and B. G. Wood.** "A Critical Analysis of the Evidence from Ralph Hawkins for a Late-Date Exodus-Conquest." *JETS* 51 (2008) 225–44.

As history, Jerome Creach writes, Joshua is part of its ancient environment, trying to establish national identity and support nationalistic goals. It is "composed for theological purposes, not to satisfy the intellectual curiosity of modern readers."[320] This brings a "primary challenge" for modern readers, namely, "to enter Joshua's world and to have our history and our future shaped by it."[321]

Entering that world is not so simple. We do not even know when it began or what it looked like. Patrick Mazani describes the situation: "The history of Israel's appeance in Canaan continues to be an enigmatic puzzle in biblical scholarship. . . . [T]he problem also seems to lie with the scholarly interpretive methodology applied to archaeological finds."[322]

Joachim Schaper summarizes much of the modern search for early Israel.[323] I interpret his German to say: In more or less pronounced form Davies, as well as Lemche, and Thompson, and also Knauf, Niehr, and Uhlinger represent the opinion that all Old Testament texts are secondary or even tertiary sources or are to be understood simply as literary fiction. All these scholars are persuaded that in historical reconstruction preference should be given to primary sources— under which category they understand archaeological witnesses exclusively. They continue to maintain this stance even when many of them recognize that often the secondary sources prepare the interpretational framework for the primary sources.

---

320 Creach, 5.
321 Ibid., 6.
322 "Appearance of Israel in Canaan," 95.
323 *ZAW* 118 (2006) 181.

In similar fashion, Robert Coote finds little possibility of history in Joshua: "it is possible, but unlikely, that this story was recorded as it happened in history."[324] Instead, the reader encounters set speeches, folk narratives, echoes of rituals, excerpts from supposed ancient sources, lists, territorial descriptions, material repeated elsewhere in the Bible but in different form, and a double ending. The presentation of the person of Joshua is sporadic, indicating he may not be an original part of much if any of the materials. Archaeological evidence does not support Joshua's conquests. The book represents a gradual composition two to six hundred years after the events supposedly occurred. It represents the viewpoint of the house of David. Israel was indigenous to Palestine and not attacking outsiders. The tribes of Israel are not genealogical creations but political ones seeking to centralize and reform government. Thus, for Coote, most of Josh 1–9 centers on Gilgal, Bethel, and Gibeon, important to the Davidic monarchy as places where Samuel decided to depose Saul, where Jeroboam I usurped the power of the Davidic kings, and where the overthrow of Saul was played out.

Keith Whitelam decides origin traditions "represent the self-perceptions of much later groups who retroject their own situation or factional disputes into the distant past."[325] Israel's Pentateuch and history books lay claim to the land by those in exile. The Chronicler's work, on the other hand, represents the land claims of those who remained in the land, not going to exile.

John Strange claims "the Book of Joshua is a [*sic*] editorial ploy, a creation by an editor who by writing it turned the whole of the story from Gen 11 to 2 Kings 25 into a 'Hasmonaean manifesto,' and at the same time made the Tetrateuch and the Deuteronomistic History into one single piece of historical literature."[326]

Again, such theories stretch the search for a historical *Sitz im Leben* too far. One does not have to travel to the Hasmonean era to find an absence of hill country names, extreme hatred for the enemy, language from priests, and the importance of Shechem.

A negative attitude toward biblical sources is understandable. Efraín Velázquez offers the straightforward explanation: "the trend in the last decade has been to focus on the Persian period for the origin of Israel."[327] Later, Velázquez notes, "hypercritical approaches to the Bible have made it almost impossible to search for the origins of Israel."[328] Yet Velázquez can point in the opposite direction, against the lure of Persian period origins: "there is no evidence that there was an 'empty land' or massive return of Judahites that formed a new Israel in the southern Levant. Nor is there evidence that the inhabitants of the Judean highlands fabricated their origins in the 6th century BCE."[329]

Richard Hess describes the quagmire of modern study of Israel's historical foundations. He admits that "to write a continuous history of the period is impossible."[330] Still, for Hess, the staging point is David's court, in which the core of the documents behind the Hebrew Scriptures originated.

---

324   Coote, 556.
325   *JSOT* 44 (1989) 36.
326   *SJOT* 16 (2002) 50.
327   "Persian Period," 61.
328   Ibid., 65.
329   Ibid., 74.
330   *PEQ* 125 (1993) 125.

Hess shows that new cultural elements belong to a new area, not to a separate ethnic group.[331] New settlements in the hill country and elsewhere were parts of a larger movement of peoples in this period as seen by the Aramaeans and Sea Peoples. Finding four-room houses, collared-rim pithoi, plaster-lined cisterns, or terraced farming does not identify Israelite occupation, for such items were discovered in earlier strata. Under any theory of origins, Israel remains a member of the West Semitic culture group and should be expected to share many cultural elements. No model of Israelite origins precisely fits the biblical material.

The Bible may provide two perspectives, on the one hand giving victory and prestige to Israel and on the other seeking peace with the neighbors. Hess concludes that aspects of the biblical tradition are not disproven: escaping from Egypt, trekking to the Promised Land, crossing the Jordan, and settling in the hill country where the people had to compete for resources, worshiping of Yahweh, and fighting with other hill country residents.[332] In addition, elements of each of the interpretative models may be true: destroying Hazor; and nomadic peoples, urban peoples, *habiru*, and Middle Bronze Age hill country settlers all becoming part of Israel. Worship at Shechem and Shiloh according to Israelite law codes correlates with biblical narratives. Thus dates and ideologies of texts do not eliminate the possibility of historicity.

The border descriptions of Josh 1:4 match Egypt's understanding of Canaanite borders, the northern border remaining unclear because of conflicts with the Hittites. Josh 2 shows the innkeeper's or prostitute's house as the customary place for spies, conspirators, and such to meet. A three-day pursuit of escapees is also evidenced. At least the Hivites, Perizzites, and Girgashites have distinct third-millennium connections (see Josh 3:10). Gods bring defense walls down for their people in other cultures. Shinar (7:21) does not occur in Babylonian documents after the thirteenth century. The ingot of gold in Josh 7:21 has an Amarna correspondence. The report of the covenant in Josh 24 contains elements unique to second-millennium treaty documents. Hess concludes: "This commentary will not attempt to 'prove' the historicity of any part of Joshua. However, it will accept the work as preserving authentic and ancient sources that attest to events in the late second millennium B.C."[333] He points to nine factors that lead to a second millennium milieu for the stories in the book of Joshua:

- the border descriptions of 1:4
- the use of spies who congregate in a prostitute's house and stay three days
- the naming of the Hivites, Perizzites, and Girgashites
- a god felling city walls (chap. 6)
- the items stolen by Achan and the use of the name Shinar for Babylon
- the importance of Gibeon in Palestine's transition from the Bronze to the Iron Age
- the second-millennium counterparts of the names of the defeated kings in Josh 10–11

---

331   Ibid., 129.
332   Ibid., 138–39.
333   Ibid., 131.

- the connection of the three Anakim in Josh 15:14 with the Hurrian and Canaanite mixed population of southern hill country
- the similarity of the covenant in Josh 24 with second-millennium Hittite treaties rather than seventh-century Assyrian ones

Mazani shows that traditional models of occupation have not served the purpose.[334] They are unable to decide whether early Israel practiced peace or violence, whether they immigrated into Palestine or were indigenous, or whether they had an identifiable pottery or continued Canaanite traditions. Most archaeologists work only with the archaeological finds, not with the biblical text, which they view as a late production, coming no earlier than the seventh century BCE. The challenge for archaeology is to "develop and apply a viable, unbiased, comprehensive, and sustainable methodology for the interpretation of all the related data on the emergence of early Israel in Canaan."[335] But even using the same data, scholars come to vastly contradictory conclusions. It seems that the only ethnic marker that everyone agrees on for Israelites is the absence of pig bones.

The early history of Israel remains almost a blank page in history. It coincided with weak Egyptian leadership, strong southern opposition against Egypt, and the gradual crumbling of the empire. Assyria and Babylonia both lost power and control. Only Merneptah mentions Israel (see below).

Gösta Ahlström states that the Israelites faced Merneptah as "indigenous Canaanites."[336] He claims that biblical texts before the monarchy "were not intended to present the history of the population of Palestine; it was an ideological-theological advocacy that steered the biblical writers. These writers did not know the settlement patterns and religious ideals of the twelfth century B.C.E." For Ahlström the territorial name Israel became a political name only under King Saul.[337]

Baruch Halpern echoes Ahlström's sentiments: "There is no telling exactly when the 'people Israel' came into distinct existence in Canaan."[338] Halpern's description involves an Israelite Hebrew group entering Canaan by way of the Aijalon Pass, entrenching itself in the central hills, and attracting to itself some of the Canaanite population. Through the thirteenth and twelfth centuries, an ethnic consciousness grew, and a full-blown confederacy of tribes developed by the time of the Song of Deborah. The El Berith shrine in Shechem "served as a major cultic center for the earliest Israelite community. . . . [I]t is most prudent to regard Shechem as a centripetal force to which were attracted the more northern and eastern elements of Canaan's non-urban population."[339]

Maxwell Miller and John Hayes emphasize the early disinction between Israel and Judah, neighboring peoples with much in common whose histories "became entangled," Judah being "essentially absent" from Israel until the time of David.[340]

---

334 "Appearance of Israel," 95–98.
335 Ibid., 96.
336 *History of Ancient Palestine*, 285.
337 Ahlström, 423.
338 *Emergence of Israel in Canaan*, 81.
339 Ibid.
340 *History of Ancient Israel and Judah*, 113–17.

Narratives of premonarchical times focus on Ephraim and their neighboring tribes and clans.

Lester Grabbe notes that "no one's idea of the 'united monarchy' bears much resemblance to the biblical description."[341] The first real evidence comes from the time of Omri. "If there was an earlier state, we have no direct information on it except perhaps some memory in the biblical text."[342] Anything that existed was not a state. Still, Grabbe concedes, "The biblical text should always be considered: it is one of the sources for the history of ancient Israel and needs to be treated like any other source."[343]

Keith Whitelam presents the minimalist argument, beginning with the assumption that the historical books of the Bible "are inadequate for historical reconstruction."[344] This is based on identifying the new inhabitants in the northern hill country as Israelites and ignoring the exodus tradition. Whitelam maintains that origin traditions are likely to make ancient claims when the traditions are relatively recent. The traditions are flexible and adaptable. Whitelam tells many tales of origin to illustrate the "late nature of many traditions of origins and their lack of correspondence to historical details and in particular their variance with recent archaeological investigations." [345]

Turning back to Palestine, Whitelam seeks the proper way to read the texts. To set Israel's origins within Palestine "is not to say that the Bible is wrong . . . but rather to challenge the dominant ways of reading these texts as historical records of early Israelite history."[346] Reading must take in the perspective of the social and political forces the author faced. Whitelam places these forces behind pentateuchal and Deuteronomistic traditions in the exilic period as the origin traditions of exiles returning from outside the land to claim the promises, while Chronicles downplays the exodus to make indigenous claims for the land.

Anthony Frendo takes up Newman's call for a "preponderance of probability."[347] This takes into account the multiple texts witnessing to Israel entering from outside the land and accept them until a good reason is found for authors to fabricate them. Reading the texts closely shows that Israel was introduced to Yahweh as God by a group of Kenites in the desert south of Edom. For Frendo, Israel is an anachronism, having been in Canaan before Joshua, Josh 24 portraying the joining of the two groups. This does not eliminate older traditions but shows application and shaping to new conditions of traditions developing between the twelfth and seventh centuries.

Following Hess, Frendo talks of contrasts and hyperbole rather than contradictions in the book of Joshua. He writes, "the biblical evidence regarding the emergence of Israel in Canaan seems to be basically describing the entry (partly peacefully and partly militarily, though not in an unusually violent manner) of Hebrew tribes from the desert who brought the Yahwistic faith with them and who

---

341   *Ancient Israel*, 222.
342   Ibid., 223.
343   Ibid., 224.
344   *JSOT* 44 (1989) 19.
345   Ibid., 27
346   Ibid., 28.
347   "Back to Basics," 42.

settled mainly in the central hills of the country. Early Israel had no memory of the Egyptian armies in the valleys of Canaan simply because it did not form part of the administrative unit of the Egyptian empire."[348] Frendo also cautions against using the evidence of pig bones as an ethnic marker—"Israelites favoured pig prohibition, [but] not every case of pig prohibition reflected in the absence of pig bones is necessarily indicative of an Israelite presence."[349] The most Frendo is willing to acknowledge is that by 1207 a people were settled in a land called Israel. A people living to the southeast of Canaan formed the birthplace of Yahwism. The exploding population statistics point to people coming into the hill country. All proposed models contain some truth to them, but "the Yahwistic faith which the few incoming Hebrew tribes brought with them to Canaan is what transformed the Early Iron Age inhabitants of the hill country of Palestine into a new society as distinct from the Late Bronze Age Canaanites."[350]

In examining early Israel, we must be aware of several claims and pieces of evidence:

- The preserved traditions in the book of Joshua tie everything together into a compact geographical and temporal action by one generation.
- The book of Joshua admits that Joshua had to fight a long time.
- Some "native inhabitants" became part of Israel and much land remained to be conquered.
- The exodus/wilderness stories of origin use hyperbole to describe the size of the people coming out from Egypt.
- Sociological and anthropological models create all sorts of otherwise unknown movements, disputes, and career changes for peoples unassociated with an Egyptian group.
- Archaeological studies find exploding populations and villages in the northern hill country but few if any ethnic markers that distinguish Canaanites and Israelites.
- The biblical text ties early Israel to Gilgal, Mount Ebal, and Shiloh as early worship centers without conquest stories.
- Various theories begin with one piece of the puzzle and build a case for a new model of early Israel. The reality is most likely more complex than any one model and amalgamates parts from each model.

Central to the biblical narrative are people who have a knowledge of Egypt; an identity as former slaves; a memory of an aborted effort to enter Palestine from the south; a faith in Yahweh, the God who led out of slavery and preserved a people in the wilderness with great miracles; a memory of following God across the Reed Sea and the Jordan River, and the experience of setting up markers across Palestine to help a new generation learn about the great works of Yahweh.

Central to archaeological investigations are a large number of new settlements in the hill country; an inability to find evidence of settlement where major biblical narratives describe city destructions, especially Jericho and Ai; few if any ethnic

---

348 Ibid., 47.
349 Ibid., 54–55.
350 Ibid., 59.

markers separating Canaanites and Israelites; and people of different "ethnic" backgrounds living together in the same towns. How does one put these puzzle pieces together? Several decisions must be made before one paints the larger picture:

- How much of a narrative can be traced to oral tradition?
- How does one evaluate the historical reliability of oral tradition?
- How much value does one give to negative archaeological evidence?
- Does one accept the archaeological consensus on the location of the major cities featured in Joshua?
- How far does one equate new populations with Israel? With Canaanites?

Susan Niditch states: "Israelites lived in an essentially oral world. Indeed, the very nature of the epigraphic evidence even in the second half of the monarchy testifies to how fully Israelite society was informed by an oral mentality."[351]

I view oral tradition in two ways: the rote memory of the education and worship systems over against the oral system of storytellers and entertainers. The former emphasizes rote memory, while the latter fits the narrative to the context and reactions of the audience. Oral tradition unrecorded for centuries (i.e., from the exile to the Hellenistic period) can be doubted as to its details. Oral tradition lasting a few generations, especially that used in education and worship, has more probability of "historical accuracy." On the other hand, oral tradition may tend to hyperbole or to condensing or omitting time periods. K. L. Noll speaks of "the fuzzy memories of actual warfare."[352]

Negative evidence from archaeology may not be valuable. The site name may have moved. An incomplete excavation (virtually all excavations being incomplete) may not have unearthed evidence for the particular era. The pottery attribution may not be accurate. The reader may have expected more detail than the biblical narrative affords. Often scholars achieve the result they expected rather than giving the opposing viewpoints any credence. In the case of Israel, Noll concludes, "the Israelites are invisible."[353] Archaeology looks to cultural studies in the northern highlands and finds more of the same, thus not knowing which is Canaanite and which is Israelite.

Archaeology has arrived at a consensus concerning the lack of occupation at Ai and Jericho during the period of the conquest and the increased settlements in the northern hill country. Having agreed on the archaeological "facts," however, scholars still differ in their explanations of the facts. Further excavation and explanation may totally change the "consensus," as with the earlier attribution of terraced farming, collar-rimmed jars, plastered cisterns, and four-room houses exclusively to the Israelites. Scholars must work with the evidence and explanations agreed on at the moment, knowing the future may bring theory-busting evidence.

The biblical narrative limits its perspective to that of affirming "Israel" as a unified people of Yahweh with roots in ancestral origins, Egyptian slavery and deliverance, lessons in Mosaic Torah, wilderness wandering and disobedience, and receipt

---

351 *Oral World and Written Word*, 44.
352 *Canaan and Israel in Antiquity*, 137.
353 Ibid., 140.

of land from Yahweh, the God of the ancestors and of Moses. This perspective sets Israel over against the indigenous residents of Palestine, most frequently identified as Canaanites. Yet the same perspective allows for or alludes to the inclusion of Rahab, the Gibeonites, the Kennizites of Caleb, and the Midianites of Jethro among the Israelites. Since the Israelite narratives do not include other perspectives, the assumption must be made that other groups included in the umbrella term *Canaanites* must have joined Israel in their life style and worship. Josh 24 may be evidence of this.

All Israel means all those who join in worship of Yahweh and respond to the call to arms. The Song of Deborah in Judg 5 apparently shows that those who met these criteria shifted at certain times and allows for the probability that Judah to the south, the tribes to the northwest, and those settled east of the Jordan may have had only loose connections with an Israel centered in Ephraim, west Manasseh, Issachar, Naphtali, and Zebulun. Archaeological investigations have as yet to find determining factors that separate Canaanite and Israelite lifestyle. This means that Israel could have entered the land and settled alongside Canaanites in areas such as Shechem, even though the biblical text preserves no report of it. Many of the Canaanites seemingly did not like the city-state rulers of Canaan or the empire powers of the Egyptians. Seeing an opportunity with the victorious Israelites, dissatisfied Canaanites joined forces with Israel and adopted the confession of faith in Yahweh's military strength just as Rahab did. Israel thus became much more a term of religious devotion than one of a pure ethnic identity.

The final problem in considering evidence results largely from scholars seeking to correlate information from two entirely distinct forms of inquiry. Archaeology provides brief snapshots of the daily life of a people from the farmer's hut to the king's palace. These snapshots tell no story and provide only the broadest of contexts. The biblical narrative tells a long-time-ago, big-picture narrative with brief clues as to the historical context and little interest in normal daily life. The archaeological record provides evidence of the daily activities of the people washing, preparing meals, offering sacrifices, and other daily or regular activies. The biblical narrative provides evidence of the same people as they learn the traditions of the fathers and hand them down to the next generation. Scribal activity then takes up the tradition, joins it with other traditions, and stores it in written form. Archaeology's context may be far too large and complex to give information relating to specific narrative traditions. Bible narrative is much too specific for us to expect confirmation from the daily life and cultic/administrative archaeological finds. Neither biblical scientific study nor scientific archaeological digs and reports will ever sufficiently show the complex relationships of the two types of evidence except for brief, occasional references to biblical characters such as Omri.

c. Studies in Conquest or Settlement

Bibliography

Aharoni, Y. "The Israelite Occupation of Canaan." *BA* 8 (1982) 14–23. ———. *The Settlement of the Israelite Tribes in Upper Galilee.* (Heb.). Jerusalem: Magnes Press, 1957. **Arata Mantovani, P.** "La 'conquista' di Israele." *RivB* 36 (1988) 229–48. **Armerding, D.** *Conquest and Victory: Studies in Joshua.* Chicago: Moody Press, 1967. **Arnaldich, L.** "Conquista de

Canaan." *EstBib* 2 (1963) 477–80. **Bimson, J.** *Redating the Exodus and the Conquest.* JSOT-Sup 5. Sheffield: JSOT Press, 1978. **Borowski, O.** *Agriculture in Iron Age Israel.* Cambridge, MA: ASOR, 2002. **Burney, C. E.** *Israel's Settlement in Canaan.* Oxford, 1908. **Chaney, M.** "Ancient Palestinian Peasant Movements and the Formation of Premonarchic Israel." In *Palestine in Transition: The Emergence of Ancient Israel.* Ed. D. N. Freedman and D. F. Graf. SWBA 2. Sheffield: Sheffield Academic, 1983. **Clarke, T. A.** "One More Time: Was the Conquest Complete or Incomplete?" Paper read for Evangelical Theological Society, 2003. **Coogan, M. D.** "Canaanite Origins and Lineage: Reflections on the Religion of Early Israel." In *Ancient Israelite Religion: Essays in Honor of Frank Moore Cross.* Ed. P. D. Miller et al. Philadelphia: Fortress, 1987. 115–24. **Coogan, M. D.,** ed. *The Oxford History of the Biblical World.* Oxford: Oxford University Press, 1998. **Coote, R. B.** *Early Israel: A New Horizon.* Minneapolis: Fortress, 1990. ———. "Early Israel." *SJOT* 2 (1991) 35–46. **Coote, R. B., and K. W. Whitelam.** *The Emergence of Early Israel in Historical Perspective.* SWBASup 5. Sheffield: Almond, 1987. **Coote, R. B., and K. W. Whitelam.** "The Emergence of Israel: Social Transformation and State Formation Following the Decline in Late Bronze Age Trade." *Semeia* 37 (1986) 107–47. **Crown, A. D.** "Some Factors relating to Settlement and Urbanization in Ancient Canaan in the Second and First Millennium B.C." *AbrN* 11 (1971) 22–41. **Davies, P. R.** *In Search of "Ancient Israel."* JSOTSup 148. Sheffield: JSOT Press, 1992. **Dever, W. G.** "Archaeological Data on the Israelite Settlement: A Review of Two Recent Works." *BASOR* 284 (1991) 77–90. ———. "Ceramics, Ethnicity, and the Question of Israel's Origins." *BA* 58 (1995) 200–213. ———. "Histories and Nonhistories of Ancient Israel." *BASOR* 316 (1999) 89–105. ———. "The Late Bronze–Early Iron I Horizon in Syria-Palestine: Egyptians, Canaanites, 'Sea Peoples,' and Proto-Israelites." In *The Crisis Years: The 12th Century B.C. from beyond the Danube to the Tigris.* Ed. W. A. Ward and M. S. Joukowsky. Dubuque, IA: Kendall/Hunt, 1992. 99–110. ———. "Unresolved Issues in the Early History of Israel: How to Tell a Canaanite from an Israelite." In *The Rise of Ancient Israel.* Ed. H. Shanks. Washington, DC: Biblical Archaeology Society, 1992. 26–60. ———. *Who Were the Early Israelites and Where Did They Come From?* Grand Rapids: Eerdmans, 2003. ———. "'Will the Real Israel Please Stand Up?' Archaeology and Israelite Historiography: Part I." *BASOR* 297 (1995) 61–80. **Dus, J.** "Das Seßhaftwerden der nachmaligen Israeliten im Land Kanaan." *CV* 6 (1963) 263–75. **Edelman, D.** "Ethnicity and Early Israel." In *Ethnicity and the Bible.* Ed. M. G. Brett. Leiden: Brill, 1996. **Engel, H.** "Grundlinien neuerer Hypothesen über die Entstehung und Gestalt der vorstaatlichen israelitischen Stämmegesellschaft." *BK* 38 (1983) 50–53. **Faust, A.** *Israel's Ethnogenesis: Settlement, Interaction, Expansion and Resistance.* London: Equinox, 2007. **Finkelstein, L.** Review of the *Archaeology of Israelite Settlement* by E. L. Esse. *BAR* 14.5 (1988) 6–9. **Finkelstein, I., and A. Mazar.** *The Quest for the Historical Israel: Debating Archaeology and the History of Early Israel.* Ed. B. B. Schmidt. Invited lectures delivered at the Sixth Biennial Colloquium of the International Institute for Secular Humanistic Judaism, Detroit, 2005. SBLABS 17. Atlanta: Society of Biblical Literature, 2007. **Frankel, R.** "Upper Galilee in the Late Bronze–Iron I Transition." In *From Nomadism to Monarchy: Archaeological and Historical Aspects of Early Israel.* Ed. I. Finkelstein and N. Na'aman. Washington: Biblical Archaeology Society, 1994. 18–34. **Gnuse, R.** "Israelite Settlement of Canaan: A Peaceful Internal Process." *BTB* 21 (1991) 56–66, 109–17. **Gottwald, N. K.** "Domain Assumptions and Societal Models in the Study of Pre-monarchic Israel." In *Congress Volume, Edinburgh 1974.* VTSup 28. Leiden: Brill, 1978. 89–100. ———. "Sociological Method in the Study of Ancient Israel." In *The Bible and Liberation: Political and Social Hermeneutics.* Ed. N. K. Gottwald and R. A. Horsley. Maryknoll, NY: Orbis, 1983. 26–37. ———. "Were the Early Israelites Pastoral Nomads?" *BAR* 4.2 (1978) 2–7. **Hawkins, R. K.** *How Israel Became a People.* Nashville: Abingdon Press, 2013. **Isserlin, B. S. J.** "The Israelite Conquest of Canaan: A Comparative Review of the Arguments Applicable." *PEQ* 113 (1983) 85–94. **Noll, K. L.** *Canaan and Israel in Antiquity: An Introduction.* Biblical Seminar 83. London: Sheffield Academic, 2001. **Provan, I. V., P.**

Long, and T. Longman III. *A Biblical History of Israel.* Louisville: John Knox Westminster, 2003. **Rainey, A.** "Inside Outside: Where Did the Israelites Come From?" *BAR* 34.6 (2008) 45–50. ———. "Shasu or Habiru: Who Were the Early Israelites?" *BAR* 34.6 (2008) 51–55. **Schaeffer, F. A.** *Joshua and the Flow of Biblical History.* Downers Grove, IL: InterVarsity Press, 1975. **Schmidtke, F.** *Die Einwanderung Israels in Kanaan.* Breslau, 1933. **Steuernagel, C.** *Die Einwanderung der israelitischen Stämme in Kanaan.* Berlin, 1901. **Stiebing, W. H., Jr.** *Out of the Desert? Archaeology and the Exodus/Conquest Narratives.* Buffalo, NY: Prometheus, 1989. ———. "Should the Exodus and the Israelite Settlement Be Redated?" *BAR* 11.4 (1985) 58–69. **Thompson, T. L.** *The Settlement of Palestine in the Bronze Age.* TAVO B34. Wiesbaden: Reichert, 1979. **Ulrich, D. R.** "Does the Bible Sufficiently Describe the Conquest?" *TJ* 20 (1999) 53–68. **Vaux, R. de.** "A Comprehensive View of the Settlement of the Israelites in Canaan." *Per* 12 (1971) 23–33. **Vieweger, D.** "Überlegungen zur Landnahme israelitischer Stämme unter besonderer Berücksichtigung der galiläischen Berglandgebiete." *ZDPV* 109 (1993) 20–36. **Weippert, M.** "The Israelite 'Conquest' and the Evidence from Transjordan." In *Symposia Celebrating the Seventy-fifth Anniversary of the Foundation of the American Schools of Oriental Research (1900–1975).* Ed. F. M. Cross. Cambridge, MA: Cambridge UP, 1979. 15–34. **Whitelam, K. W.** "Israel's Traditions of Origin: Reclaiming the Land." *JSOT* 44 (1989) 19–42. **Wiener, H. M.** "The Conquest Narratives." *JPOS* 9 (1929) 1–26. **Wood, B. G.** "The Biblical Date for the Exodus Is 1446 B.C.: A Response to James Hoffmeier." *JETS* 50 (2007) 249–58. **Wright, G. E.** "The Conquest Theme in the Bible." In *A Light unto My Path.* FS J. M. Myers, ed. H. N. Bream et al. Philadelphia: Fortress, 1974. 509–18. **Younger, K. L., Jr.** *Ancient Conquest Accounts: A Study in Ancient Near Eastern and Biblical History Writing.* JSOTSup 98. Sheffield: JSOT Press, 1990.

How did the Israelites gain at least a strong foothold in Palestine, the land of Canaanites and Amorites? The biblical narratives emphasize the military-conquest aspect of the story. But too often this military-conquest reading of Joshua reflects a misreading of a book that describes the burning of only three towns—Jericho, Ai, and Hazor.[354] The narratives also emphasize allotting the land to each tribe and expecting the tribe to settle down in the land allotted. Joshua sends the tribes to their territories, but the book of Joshua gives no statement about their occupying the allotted lands and no statement about opposition they found there.

"The book of Joshua itself makes a clear distinction between first gaining the upper hand and then capitalizing on the situation by occupying conquered territory. . . . [A]n important difference exists between subjugation and occupation."[355] Clarke shows how the writer of Joshua carefully qualifies total-conquest statements with a concessive clause using רק or בלתי and depicts troops returning to base camp without leaving a unit to control the captured cities, thus opening the way for a second battle against some cities such as Debir, Hebron, or Jerusalem.[356] The book of Joshua thus does not depict a complete conquest.

Is there another perspective on which the biblical narrative remains virtually silent, a more peaceful settlement in the land? Archaeology suggests a sudden explosion in settlements and population, from under 70,000 in the Late Bronze Age to over 100,000 at the end of Iron I.[357] The settlements show no sign of Egyptian

---

354 Provan et al., *Biblical History,* 140.
355 Ibid., 167.
356 Clarke, "One More Time."
357 See Noll, *Canaan and Israel in Antiquity,* 153–54.

culture, while destruction layers do not appear in cities the Bible describes as destroyed by Joshua. For Noll, this forces abandonment of the conquest model altogether. He concedes that a few of the biblical narratives "might reflect the dim memories of actual warfare at various times from the Late Bronze Age to Iron Age II. . . . Thus, the biblical conquest is a natural—even predictable—result of folklore; it is not an accurate depiction of Israel's entry into Canaan."[358]

In answer Provan, Long, and Longman list three reasons for not jettisoning the Bible so quickly: (1) Late dating of the historical books is far from assured and would not negate a text's capacity to carry historical memory. (2) Having a theological slant does not make void a text's historical content, for all history writing has a slant or bias for which the reader must account. (3) Conclusions drawn from archaeological finds are often far from being obvious.[359]

Concerning a theory built around a peasant revolt against the lowland city-states and taking up life in the highlands, Noll shrewdly remarks, "The Peasant Revolt Model seems to lack any evidence for its most crucial concept, 'revolt.'"[360]

Anson Rainey states, "There is absolutely no relationship" between *habiru* and Hebrew. *Habiru* is not an ethnic designation, and their individual names do not belong to a single linguistic group. They are never pastoralists, nor do they belong to tribes.[361] On the other hand, Rainey links early Israelites and the Shasu, known from Egyptian sources and the Amarna Letters as nomadic pastoralists "who lived in symbiosis with sedentary populations but were prone to violence in times of distress."[362] Rainey concludes: "Israel was simply one group among many *shasu* who were moving out of the steppe lands to find their livelihood in areas that would provide them with food in times of drought and famine."[363]

In a separate article Rainey speaks of the Revolting Peasant Theory as he argues for a Transjordan origin of Israel and the hill-country settlements, pointing to four-room houses, lack of climate for pig raising much less pig consumption, and unpainted pottery east of the Jordan.[364] Finally, Rainey argues that the Hebrew language is more closely related to Transjordan languages than to Canaanite (Phoenician) languages.

Noll offers a symbiosis model formulated in slightly different forms by different scholars. Highland settlers were Canaanites, but did not revolt. Some of the new settlers may have been pastoralists, but only a small percent. Others were farmers from the lowlands. Some see the settlement of the highlands coming from more stringent Egyptian policy. Such a theory cannot group all these on-the-move peoples as Israelites or proto-Israelites. The newcomers established their own unique settlements, mostly isolated, and developed their own lifestyle and culture. Some, but only some, were Israelites.

Hubbard describes exogenous and indigenous models of the conquest and then offers an "Alternate Approach," a variation of the military-conquest model that extended over decades.[365] This model accepts Younger's comparison to Egyptian and Mesopota-

---

358 Ibid., 159.
359 *Biblical History*, 146–47.
360 *Canaan and Israel in Antiquity*, 161.
361 *BAR* 34.6 (2008) 51.
362 Ibid., 53.
363 Ibid., 55.
364 *BAR* 34.6 (2008) 45–50.
365 Hubbard, 35–40.

mian military accounts, admits the limited information the editors chose to use and transmit, and refuses to pit biblical texts against one another since they reflect different genres and a complex reality only partially presented by each text. The accounts then are stereotypical and telescoped, basically historical but "highly simplified."[366]

Archaeology, for Hubbard, helps little with understanding the conquest but a great deal with understanding the settlement in the sparsely populated central hill country.[367] Theologically, *ḥērem* or the ban was limited to the conquest period to remove the temptation of idol worship for Israel. Hubbard justifies the practice in Joshua through "Three Unappealing Realities": some people deserve destruction, an ultimate solution to the problem of violence in Joshua may be elusive, and the sovereignty of God undergirds biblical violence.[368]

Provan, Long, and Longman conclude: "The biblical picture is of a reasonably successful initial conquest of the land—the invading Israelites gaining the upper hand—followed by increasingly unsuccessful attempts to control and occupy the 'conquered territories.' . . . Israel could possibly have been leading a pastoralist existence in Canaan for a very long time (even centuries) prior to being mentioned by Merneptah."[369] This would place settling down, not initial arrival, in the Iron Age, while the Amarna period would reflect the beginning of unsuccessful attempts to occupy and hold the land.

The series of articles in *JETS* featuring Wood, Young, Hoffmeier, and Hawkins shows the evangelical disputes over a fifteenth-century or thirteenth/twelfth-century exodus/conquest.[370] Hawkins provides a thorough discussion of the issues with extensive bibliographies. He understands the Hebrew *gilgalim* to refer to fortified encampments along the Jordan Valley, showing a movement of cult centers by the early Israelites, finally resulting in a massive structure at Mount Ebal that served as a central sanctuary where Israel crystalized its national consciousness.[371]

Hawkins examines the various components that may characterize Israel: (1) a new settlement pattern of small villages outside the traditional city-states with four-room houses on bedrock; (2) houses laid out in a circle facing in with large court-yards, apparently for pastoral nomads settling down; and (3) four-room houses with a courtyard that has rooms on three sides. Such houses have been discovered in Moab, Edom, and Ammon in Iron I strata when these countries and Israel were tribal groups, not nations. Hawkins follows Y. Shiloh, the "discoverer" of four-room houses in claiming the four-room house as marker of Israelites. Hawkins bases his claim on (4) a limited repertoire of pottery with somewhat widespread distribution but basically made in the hill country. The collared-rim jar apparently had its original home among Israelites in Transjordan. And finally, (5) food supplies provide

---

366 Ibid., 40.
367 Ibid., 40–42.
368 Ibid., 44–46.
369 *Biblical History*, 189.
370 Wood, "The Biblical Date for the Exodus," "The Rise and Fall of the 13th-Century Exodus-Conquest Theory"; Young and Wood, "A Critical Analysis of the Evidence"; Hoffmeier, "What Is the Biblical Date for the Exodus? A Response to Bryant Wood"; Hawkins, "Propositions for Evangelical Assessment of a Later Date Exodus-Conquest," "The Date of the Exodus-Conquest Is Still an Open Question."
371 *How Israel Became a People.*

an interdisciplinary way to look at Israel, which grew surpluses rather than living a subsistence-level existence. Using relatively new methods of farming and not eating pork mark two elements by which the new Israelite settlers may be distinguished. Hawkins is hopeful that these five elements will prove to be identity markers for Iron Age I Israelites. Still, the main determinate is what Israel ascribed to itself: a faith community involving a mixed multitude committed to Yahweh and to each other.

Hawkins creates a modified version of the Alt/Noth peaceful-infiltration model of Israel's conquest and settlement. Israelite tribes originated in the Jordan Valley and eastern Manasseh along wadis Far'ah and Malih. From the middle of the thirteenth century to the middle of the twelfth century, the settlers were seminomadic in a sheep-husbandry economy. In this period, several tribes coalesced into a unified group and made military excursions into Canaan, excursions echoed in the ritual-conquest traditions in Josh 1–6. Gilgal was the central camp at this stage, and Israel did not occupy the land of the defeated enemies. The tribes then settled down in the highlands while loosening ties with other groups. Many settlements were in juxtaposition to Late Bronze Canaanite sites, showing cooperation between the two groups. The economy combined sheep raising, wheat and barley farming, and possibly olive and grape groves. Agreements had to be reached with the original inhabitants over the use of water sources. The eleventh and tenth centuries saw expansion into the western and northern hill country, where Canaanites continued to occupy Jerusalem, Hebron, Beth-shean, Ibleam, Dor, Endor, Taanach, Megiddo, and Napheth. The settlers cleared woodlands and settled down to an agricultural economy. For two centuries Israel developed as an egalitarian community with power structures within families and tribal groups defined through genealogical systems. Yahwism held these settlers together from about 1100 BCE or earlier as evidenced in the early poetry. Finally, according to Hawkins, Israel developed into a state-level society and began to dominate the region. This new cultural level does not bring domination to an exploited people. God is king, and the earthly king still represents a kinship society, if a higher-level one.

For Hawkins, then, "Israel's origin resulted from a coalescence of peoples with widely differing backgrounds and experiences and their coming to embrace the decentralized, non-hierarchical social form of early Israel's domestic-scale culture, along with its cult of Yahweh."[372]

Hawkins offers a much more complex model of Israelite origins both militarily and socially than that found in the book of Joshua. He does not feature the person of Joshua and extends the military actions over many generations. He does not establish a time when settlers or slaves gained the name Israel. He does not attempt to solve the mystery of the origin of Yahwism, only placing it in Edom possibly among Kenites. He alludes to a group coming from Egypt, but does not discuss them in his concluding chapters.

Nonetheless, Hawkins has gathered the current information into a single source and has moved our thinking about the origins of Israel into some new interdisciplinary paths. His model develops basically between the books of Joshua and Judges in a biblical "silent spot" centered on Yahwism, even mono-Yahwism. One

---

372   Ibid., 204.

can modify his position a bit and come as close as possible to understanding the complex of conquest and settlement that created biblical Israel. This depicts Israel as a combination of multi-ethnic slaves escaping Egypt, gaining unity and definition on Sinai, showing military power in sorties against the Canaanites, gaining a foothold in Transjordan and the Cisjordan highlands, and finally emerging as the dominant power in Canaan under Saul and David.

d. Studies in Merneptah's (Merenptah's) Stele

Bibliography

Ahlström, G. W. *Who Were the Israelites?* Winona Lake, IN: Eisenbrauns, 1986. **Ahlström, G. W., and D. V. Edelman.** "Merneptah's Stele." *JNES* 44 (1985) 59–61. **Bimson, J.** "Merneptah's Israel and Recent Theories of Israelite Origins." *JSOT* 49 (1991) 3–29. **Coote, R. B.** "Tribalism: Social Organization in the Biblical Israels." In *Ancient Israel: The Old Testament in Its Social Context.* Ed. P. F. Esler. Minneapolis: Fortress, 2006. 35–49. **Engel, H.** "Die Siegestele des Merenptah: Kritischer Überblick über die verschiedenen Versuche historischer Auswertung des Schlussabschnitts." *Bib* 60 (1979). 373–99. **Fecht, G.** "Die Israelstele, Gestalt und Aussage." In *Fontes atque pontes: Eine Festgabe für Hellmut Brunner.* Ed. M. Görg. Ägypten und Altes Testament 5. Wiesbaden: Harrassowitz, 1983. 106–38. **Frendo, A. J.** "Back to Basics: A Holistic Approach to the Problem of the Emergence of Ancient Israel." In *In Search of Pre-Exilic Israel: Proceedings of the Oxford Old Testament Seminar.* Ed. J. Day. JSOTSup 406. London: T&T Clark, 2004. 41–64. **Hasel, M. G.** "Israel in the Merneptah Stele." *BASOR* 296 (1994) 45–62. ———. "Merenptah's Inscription and Reliefs and the Origin of Israel." In *The Near East in the Southwest: Essays in Honor of William G. Dever.* Ed. B. A. Nakhai. AASOR 58. Boston: American Schools of Oriental Research, 2003. 19–44. ———. "Merenptah's Reference to Israel: Critical Issues for the Origin of Israel." In *Critical Issues in Early Israelite History.* Ed. R. S. Hess, G. A. Klingbeil, and P. J. Ray, Jr. BBRSup 3. Winona Lake, IN: Eisenbrauns, 2008. 47–59. ———. "The Structure of the Final Hymnic-Poetic Unit on the Merenptah Stela." *ZAW* 116 (2004) 75–81. **Hjelm, I., and T. L. Thompson.** "The Victory Song of Merneptah, Israel and the People of Palestine." *JSOT* 27 (2002) 3–18. **Kitchen, K. A.** "The Physical Text of Merenptah's Victory Hymn (The 'Israel' Stela)." *JSSEA* 24 (1997) 71–76. **Le Roux, J. H.** "Some Remarks on Sociology and Ancient Israel." *OTE* 3 (1985) 12–16. **Levine, B. A.** "Some Indices of Israelite Ethnicity." In *Ethnicity in Ancient Mesopotamia.* Ed. W. H. van Soldt, R. Kalvelagen, and D. Katz. PIHANS 102. Leiden: Nederlands Instituut voor het Nabije Oosten 2005. 189–97. **Margalith, O.** "On the Origin and Antiquity of the Name 'Israel.'" *ZAW* 102 (1990) 225–37. **Miller, J. M., and J. H. Hayes.** *A History of Ancient Israel and Judah.* 2nd ed. Louisville: Westminster John Knox, 2006. **Morenz, L. D.** "Wortwitz—Ideologie—Geschichte: 'Israel' im Horizont Mer-en-ptahs." *ZAW* 120 (2008) 1–13. **Nibbi, A.** "Some Remarks on the Merenptah Stela and the So-Called Name of Israel." *DE* 36 (1996) 79–102. **Provan, I. V., P. Long, and T. Longman III.** *A Biblical History of Israel.* Louisville: John Knox Westminster, 2003. **Rainey, A. F.** "Israel in Merneptah's Inscription and Reliefs." *IEJ* 51 (2001) 57–75. **Rendsburg, G. A.** "The State of the Exodus and the Conquest/Settlement: The Case for the 1100s." *VT* 42 (1992) 510–27. **Singer, I.** "Merneptah's Campaign to Canaan and the Egyptian Occupation of the Southern Coastal Plain of Palestine in the Ramesside Period." *BASOR* 269 (1988) 1–10. **Sparks, K. L.** *Ethnicity and Identity in Ancient Israel: Prolegomena to the Study of Ethnic Sentiments and Their Expression in the Hebrew Bible.* Winona Lake, IN: Eisenbrauns, 1998. **Spiegelberg, W.** "Der Siegeshymnus des Merneptah." *ZÄS* 34 (1896) 1–25. **Stager, L.** "Merenptah, Israel and the Sea Peoples: New Light on an Old Relief." *ErIsr* 18 (1985) *56–*64. **Whitelam, K. W.** "The Death of Biblical History." In *In Search of Philip R. Davies: Whose Festschrift Is It Anyway?* Ed. D. Burns and J. W. Rogerson. London: T&T Clark,

2010. ———. "The Identity of Early Israel: The Realignment and Transformation of Late Bronze-Iron Age Palestine." *JSOT* 63 (1994) 57–87. Repr. in *The Historical Books*, Ed. J. C. Exum (Sheffield: Sheffield Academic, 1997) 14–45. ———. *The Invention of Ancient Israel: The Silencing of Palestinian History*. London: Routledge, 1996. ———. "'Israel is laid waste; his seed is no more': What if Merneptah's Scribes Were Telling the Truth?" In *Virtual History and the Bible*. Ed. J. C. Exum. Leiden: Brill, 2000. 8–22. **Yurko, F.** "Merenptah's Canaanite Campaign." *JARCE* 23 (1986) 189–215. ———. "Merenptah's Palestinian Campaign." *Society for the Study of Egyptian Antiquities Journal* 8 (1978) 70.

The earliest mention of Israel appears on an Egyptian stele—the Merneptah inscription of his fifth year (ca. 1208 BCE)—after the names of three cities (Ashkelon, Gezer, and Yenoam). Coote states, "The Merneptah Stele suggests that Israel was the main, if not sole, rural power in this region."[373]

Scholars have repeatedly argued over the significance of the word "Israel" on this stele. They have emended the text, devised differing structures of the text, and claimed the section mentioning Israel comes from a separate source. Thus, it is not possible to deduce from the inscription where Israel was located, the range of its territory, nor who was included as part of it. Some 350 years separate this mention of Israel from the next extra-biblical reference to Israel, and by that time, Israel had become an established kingdom. No doubt during that time Israel underwent extensive changes in its ethnic composition, size, and location.

Ludwig Morenz sees Israel as Merneptah's chief opponent in the east, parallel to Libya in the west.[374] For Morenz, the Egyptian author of this text purposely adopted a self-designation of a people in Canaan or in northern Canaan from the thirteenth century BCE.[375] Apparently, certain people outside of the Late Bronze Age cities referred to themselves (nomads, seminomads, and/or outlaws?) precisely not as *habiru*, but rather already in fact as "Israel."

Morenz places the composition of this victory song in the first military campaign of Merneptah's reign as he proved his ability to be king.[376] This would have occurred in his second or third regnal year, for Morenz, 1211 or 1210. The song was then copied in the fifth year onto the stele.

Alessandra Nibbi has tried to dislodge the stele's mention of Israel from any connection to Canaan or biblical Israel.[377] Hjelm and Thompson have attempted anew to translate the term for Israel as Jezreel.[378] Michael Hasel summarizes the simple linguistic case against these and other attempts to eliminate Israel from the stele.[379] Na'aman seeks to locate this Israel in Transjordan, an idea that has gained little favor among archaeologists. Most archaeologists place the Israel referred to on the Merneptah Stele in the hill country of Cisjordan, but this remains a hypothesis until further information appears.

---

373 "Tribalism," 35.
374 *ZAW* 120 (2008) 9.
375 Ibid., 10.
376 Ibid., 12.
377 *DE* 36 (1996) 79–102.
378 *JSOT* 27 (2002) 3–18.
379 "Merneptah's Reference," 48–49.

The Egyptian language uses so-called determinatives to categorize its nouns. The determinative marking Israel is distinct from that marking the names of the three cities preceding it. Israel is marked as a people or, as Hasel phrases it, "a socioethnic entity," distinct from the city-state system familiar to Egypt and the Canaanites. As such, Israel is not connected with nomads by the stele, nor does it incorporate the infamous Shasu.[380]

The reference on the Merneptah puts some kind of Israel in Palestine by 1209 BCE but solves no other chronological problem connected with the exodus and conquest. For an external entity like Egypt to recognize Israel as a people in a distinct geographic location by utilizing a Semitic, not an Egyptian, term suggests that "Israel may have been in Canaan for a very long time as a largely pastoralist people."[381]

Anthony Frendo casts doubts on positive interpretations of the stele.[382] He argues that Ashkelon and Gezer were important cities for the Egyptians and would not have been harmed. Moreover, Merneptah had no opportunity in his first five years to fight in Palestine. The final section of the stele is simply copied from Rameses II. Scribes were notoriously careless in using determinatives. Frendo cites a 1908 article by W. Spiegelberg,[383] who discovered grammatical difficulties and omissions in the text and changed the determinative for Israel to match the determinatives used for the three cities. Gösta Ahlström limits Israel on the stele to the sparsely populated hill country, Israelites being the only people living in that area. No Israelites moved in because outside the territory called Israel, no Israelites existed.[384]

Keith Whitelam states that Egyptian scribes would be "hardly likely to imply that Pharaoh's victory was insignificant."[385] The stele does not say that Israel was a tribal coalition.[386] In fact, Whitelam wants to proceed without reference to the biblical text.[387] Miller and Hayes provide the most honest approach to the stele: "While each of the interpretations . . . is plausible, none of them is compelling. One suspects that they try to extract more information about ancient Israel . . . than the Egyptian scribe . . . intended to give or would have been able to give."[388] Kenton Sparks provides the minimum information to be taken from the stele; namely, Israel was a name by which people identified themselves and referred to a sociocultural unit that shared some common sense of identity, especially the worship of El.[389]

e. Biblical Tradition and History

Bibliography

Albright, W. F. *Archaeology, Historical Analogy, and Early Biblical Tradition.* Baton Rouge: Louisiana State UP, 1966. **Alt, A.** "The Settlement of the Israelites in Palestine." In *Essays on Old Testament History and Religion.* Trans. R. A. Wilson. 1925. Repr., Oxford: Blackwell,

---

380   Ibid., 56–57.
381   Provan, Long, and Longman, *Biblical History*, 170.
382   "Back to Basics," 51–53.
383   "Zu der Erwähnung Israels in dem Merneptah-Hymnus," *OLZ* 11 (1908) 376–78.
384   *Who Were the Israelites?* 39–42.
385   *JSOT* 63 (1994) 69.
386   Ibid., 71.
387   Ibid., 76.
388   *History of Ancient Israel and Judah*, 42.
389   *Ethnicity and Identity in Ancient Israel*, 107.

1966. 133–69. **Blum, E.** *Die Composition der Vätergeschichte.* WMANT 57. Neukirchen-Vluyn: Neukirchener Verlag, 1984. **Coats, G.** *Rebellion in the Wilderness: The Murmuring Motif in the Wilderness Traditions of the Old Testament.* Nashville: Abingdon, 1968. **Cohen, R.** "The Mysterious MBI People: Does the Exodus Tradition in the Bible Preserve the Memory of Their Entry into Canaan?" *BAR* 9.4 (1983) 16–19. **Davies, G. I.** "The Wilderness Itineraries and the Composition of the Pentateuch." *VT* 33 (1983) 1–13. **Fohrer, G.** *Überlieferung und Geschichte des Exodus: Eine Analyse von Ex. 1–15.* BZAW 91. Berlin: Töpelmann, 1964. **Freedman, D. N., and D. F. Graf,** eds. *Palestine in Transition: The Emergence of Ancient Israel.* SWBA 2. Sheffield: ASOR by Almond, 1983. **Fritz, V.** *Israel in der Wüste: Traditionsgeschichtliche Untersuchung der Wüstenüberlieferung des Jahwisten.* Marburger theologische Studien 7. Marburg: Elwert, 1970. **Halpern, B.** "Radical Exodus Redating Fatally Flawed." *BAR* 13.6 (1987) 56–61. **Henige, D.** "Deciduous, Perennial, or Evergreen? The Choices in the Debate over 'Early Israel.'" *JSOT* 27 (2003) 387–412. **Herion, G. A.** "The Impact of Modern and Social Science Assumptions on the Reconstruction of Israelite History." *JSOT* 34 (1986) 3–33. ———. "The Role of Historical Narrative in Biblical Thought: The Tendencies Underlying Old Testament Historiography." *JSOT* 21 (1981) 25–57. **Herrmann, S.** "Israels Frühgeschichte im Spannungsfeld neuer Hypothesen." In *Studien zur Ethnogenese 2.* ARWAW 78. Opladen: Westdeutscher Verlag, 1988. 43–95. **Kilian, R.** *Die vorpriesterlichen Abrahams-Überlieferungen.* BBB 24. Bonn: Hanstein, 1966. **Knight, D. A.** *Rediscovering the Traditions of Israel: The Development of the Traditio-Historical Research of the Old Testament with Special Consideration of Scandinavian Contributions.* SBLDS 9. Missoula, MT: Scholars Press, 1973. **Mowinckel, S.** *Tetrateuch—Pentateuch—Hexateuch: Die Berichte über die Landnahme in den drei altisraelistischen Geschichtswerken.* BZAW 90. Berlin: Töpelmann, 1964. **Nielsen, E.** "The Traditio-Historical Study of the Pentateuch since 1945, with Special Emphasis on Scandinavia." In *The Productions of Time: Tradition History in Old Testament Scholarship.* Trans. F. H. Cryer. Sheffield: Almond, 1984. 11–28. **Noth, M.** *A History of Pentateuchal Traditions.* Trans. B. W. Anderson. 1948. Repr., Englewood Cliffs, NJ: Prentice-Hall, 1972. **Ottoson, M.** "Tradition History, with Emphasis on the Composition of the Book of Joshua." In *The Productions of Time: Tradition History in Old Testament Scholarship.* Trans. F. H. Cryer. Sheffield: Almond, 1984. 81–106. **Rad, G. von.** "The Form-Critical Problem of the Hexateuch." In *The Problem of the Hexateuch and Other Essays.* Trans. E. W. Trueman Dicken. 1938. Repr., Edinburgh: Oliver & Boyd, 1965. 1–78. **Rendtorff, R.** *Das Überlieferungsgeschichtliche Problem des Pentateuch.* BZAW 147. Berlin: Töpelmann, 1977. **Rowley, H. H.** "The Exodus and the Settlement in Canaan." *BASOR* 85 (1942) 27–31. **Schmid, H. H.** *Der sogenannte Jahwist: Beobachtungen und Fragen zur Pentateuchforschung.* Zürich: Theologischer Verlag, 1976. **Schmid, K.** *Erzväter und Exodus: Untersuchungen zur doppelten Begründung der Ursprünge Israels innerhalb der Geschichtsbücher des Alten Testaments.* WMANT 81. Neukirchen-Vluyn: Neukirchener Verlag, 1999. **Schmidt, L.** "Zur Entstehung des Pentateuch: Ein kritische Literaturbericht." *VF* 40 (1995) 3–28. **Tunyogi, A. C.** "The Book of the Conquest." *JBL* 84 (1965) 374–80. **Van Seters, J.** *Abraham in History and Tradition.* New Haven, CT: Yale UP, 1975. **Whybray, R. N.** *The Making of the Pentateuch: A Methodological Study.* JSOTSup 53. Sheffield: JSOT Press, 1987. **Younger, K. L., Jr.** "The Rhetorical Structuring of the Joshua Conquest Narratives." In *Critical Issues in Early Israelite History.* Ed. R. S. Hess, G. A. Klingbeil, and P. J. Ray, Jr. BBRSup 3. Winona Lake, IN: Eisenbrauns, 2008. 3–32.

Five traditions form the backbone of the Exodus-Joshua tradition: the promise to the ancestors, the exodus out of Egypt, Sinai, the wilderness wandering, and the entrance into Canaan. Each tradition finds its climax in Joshua, and each is most closely tied to the ancestors through the promise of land to Abraham and his descendants, a promise fulfilled only through Joshua. The goal of the exodus from

Egypt is the settlement of the Promised Land. The giving of the Torah on Sinai points to a settled people whom God can expect to obey the law as exemplified by Joshua in Josh 1:7–8 and 8:30–35 and available in a book of the Torah in 24:26. The wilderness tradition finds completion in the settled land where a leader and people obey Yahweh and claim the land.

The scholarly questions concern how these traditions came together into one story and in what medium they came together—oral tradition, original writing, various pentateuchal sources, literary creation, or political invention. Martin Noth and Gerhard von Rad set the stage for modern questioning. Noth saw cultic confessions of exodus and entry into the land as foundational to the traditions. The five themes were originally independent of one another and only gradually combined into a basic narrative or *Grundlage* (G). God's guidance into the arable land was central to Israel's confession, with the Sinai covenant tradition coming only later. The wilderness tradition was less important, serving as a connecting link between the exodus and the entry into the land.

Von Rad emphasized a cultic credo that leaves signs of itself behind in Deut 6:20–24; 26:5b–9 and Josh 24:2b–13, the latter described by him as "a Hexateuch in miniature."[390] Only the Sinai tradition is not mentioned in these short credo statements, the Sinai tradition being seen as a separate tradition incorporated into the larger narrative at a "very late date."[391] The credo was tied to the Festival of Weeks in Gilgal and gradually developed into the Yahwist's narrative. Meanwhile, the Sinai tradition was tied to Shechem's Festival of Booths and its covenant renewal.

Ernst Axel Knauf represents a postmodern, particularly German, approach.[392] He sees the confession of Yahweh leading the people out of Egypt as Israel's oldest tradition, dating back to Israel's first identity as the people of Yahweh and Yahweh as the God of Israel. The journey from Egypt to Canaan rested on no tradition but was a theological conclusion from the exodus tradition that had not been evidenced before the eighth century. The land was seen as God's gift at least a century later. The idea of a conquest stands "so good as not at all" in the Bible.[393] The large majority of those whose descendants created Judah and Israel had always occupied the land.

Concerning the exodus, Knauf finds that Merenptah deported Israelite prisoners of war to Egypt before 1208 BCE.[394] The prisoners' descendants then escaped and returned to Canaan about 1150. They created the confession that God had led them out of Egypt. Tribes centered on the hills of Samaria and in Gilead accepted the confession and transmitted it until the ninth century. A break-up of the Canaanite economy in the fifteenth century led to the formation of groups called Habiru who removed themselves from the urban life. These gradually created tribes, made protection treaties with one another, and developed a system of genealogies with founding fathers.

By 1100, according to Knauf, the last Egyptian military post had vanished from Canaan, and thus all of its occupants could claim that "our God has led us out of

---

390   "Form-Critical Problem of the Hexateuch," 8.
391   Ibid., 9.
392   Knauf, 22.
393   Ibid., 23.
394   Ibid., 24.

Egypt." This confession entered the national cult of Israel under Jeroboam I or more likely under Jeroboam II. Jeroboam I is apparently the model on which the biography of Moses was expanded. Moses' name shows he had Egyptian experience. The confession of present land control made the entry tradition unnecessary. Loss of land in 720 did not destroy the exodus tradition but became with Hosea a prophetic tradition.[395]

Assyrian control led to the idea of a vassal treaty as the way to define the relationship of Israel and Yahweh. As Assyria's high god told the king to conquer the world, so Yahweh told Israel to make its land submissive to God, an event that never occurred. Thus came the supplementing of the exodus tradition with a conquest tradition, which represented a theological revolution, not a growth of tradition.

As a literary work of theology, Joshua preserves little material useful for historical reconstruction, says Richard Nelson, who classifies the book form critically as "historiography" but also as etiology.[396] Its "tales" come from folklore and etiology, not memories of Israel's origins. The "overall intention of the book is to strengthen national identity and assert Israel's possession of its ancestral lands."[397] "Disparate materials are not always in complete agreement."[398] Geographical lists and boundary descriptions reflect the history of a much later age. Archaeology does not support Joshua's record since it shows continuity of population rather than discontinuity, not pointing to infiltrators or invaders. Nelson maintains that "emergence of Israel was an indigenous development," and "a shared devotion to Yahweh played an important role in this process of ethnic formation."[399]

David Henige, arguing against Provan, declares any reconstruction of Israel's early history to be "little more than gamesmanship."[400] David Howard, to the contrary, finds "no inherent reason why such stories could not in fact be true . . . not invented to give an etiological explanation for a later phenomenon. . . . The biblical text may indeed preserve the actual reasons for certain names or customs."[401]

K. Lawson Younger notes that understanding the literary techniques of Near Eastern conquest narratives such as backtracking and overlap, parallelism, chiasm, inclusio, stereotyped syntagms, false senses of closure, irony, hyperbole, etc. allows one to see that the book of Joshua "preserves real memories of Israel's early days in Canaan."[402] He agrees with J. G. McConville that "the principal general reason" for seeing real historical memories is "the prominence in the narrative of places that play little part in the periods of the later monarchy, the Exile, and after (Gilgal, Shechem, Shiloh)."[403]

This question of Joshua and tradition history stands at the center of the understanding of the nature of Scripture and of the history behind it. A few things seem obvious:

---

395   Ibid., 25.
396   Nelson, 9, 11.
397   Ibid., 11.
398   Ibid., 5.
399   Ibid., 4.
400   *JSOT* 27 (2003) 387.
401   Howard, 332.
402   "Rhetorical Structuring," 32, n. 29.
403   McConville, "Joshua," *Oxford Bible Commentary* (2001), 159.

1. The majority of the materials in Genesis–Joshua must be based on oral tradition or scribal invention. The narratives as recorded do not represent eyewitness reports.
2. The book of Joshua presupposes a knowledge of traditions from Genesis, Exodus, Numbers, and especially Deuteronomy. Strong source and redaction critics break the narratives into small editions or sources, most of which are then dated centuries after the "event," a dating that is considered proof of the nonhistorical nature of the writings.
3. The original book of Joshua has been seen as connected to the Pentateuch to create an original Hexateuch, including the sources of and giving closure to the themes of the Pentateuch. It has been read as part of the Deuteronomistic History unattached to other "books." Joshua has been dissected and then put back together to join Judges traditions to its own, to complete a literary Enneateuch (Genesis–Kings). Whatever one's literary theory, it appears that Joshua stands in the forefront of research that is attempting, first, to determine the direction of the flow of Israel's traditions and, second, to prove the tradition flow to be an arid wadi without traditional sources to feed it.
4. An understanding of the nature of the history behind these major traditions depends to a great extent on decisions concerning transmission history, the appearance and growth of the Israelite monarchy, the nature of Near Eastern, and especially of Israel's, historiography, and the development of Israelite institutions to create and preserve literature.
5. At one stage in the development of the book of Joshua, a writer tied the narrative tightly to Numbers and to Moses' commandments to Joshua and to Israel. Passages such as chap. 20 on the cities of refuge are virtually impossible to date, even though many employ both D and P language.
6. The editor of Judges has consciously quoted several passages from Joshua and appears to know the Joshua story, since Judges unravels all that Joshua sewed together.
7. D and P language appears to represent contemporaneous scribal and Priestly language that any literate person in Judah or Israel would know. The distinction comes more from the institution in which the language is at home rather than a secret theological sect with its own jargon that no one else could copy.
8. The compiler of Joshua knew in writing or in traditional (oral) form the traditions of promise to the ancestors, the exodus, Sinai, the wilderness, and the entrance into the land.
9. The basic core of Joshua appears to go back to the period of David and Solomon if not earlier. That is the period when tradition was still somewhat fresh and when the Israelites began to have institutions able to support scribes and the education to put tradition into written form and preserve it in archives.
10. No pertinent reason appears to push the origin of the book of Joshua back into the exilic period or later except for a presupposition that D language only appears under Josiah and that P language comes in the exilic period. Joshua underlines Israel's independence from other countries, not their destruction, a theme tied directly to the Sinai/law of Moses tradition that appears at important transitions in Joshua.

f. Studies on Tribal Society

Bibliography

Anbar, M. *The Amorite Tribes in Mari and the Settlement of the Israelites in Canaan* (Heb.). Tel Aviv: University of Tel Aviv, 1985. ———. "Changements des noms des tribus nomades dans la relation d'un méme événenment." *Bib* 49 (1968) 221–32. **Auld, A. G.** "Israel's Social Origins." *ExpTim* 92 (1981) 146–47. **Bartusch, M. W.** *Understanding Dan: An Exegetical Study of a Biblical City, Tribe, and Ancestor.* JSOTSup 379. Sheffield: Sheffield Academic, 2003. **Bender, S.** *The Social Structure of Ancient Israel.* Jerusalem: Simor, 1996. **Bernhardt, K. H.** *Nomadentum und Ackerbaukultur in der frühstaatlichen Zeit Israels: Das Verhältnis von Bodenbauern und Viehzüchtern in historischer Sicht.* VIOF 69. Berlin, 1969. **Boer, R.,** ed. *Tracking the Tribes of Yahweh: On the Trail of a Classic.* JSOTSup 351. Sheffield: Sheffield Academic, 2002. **Coote, R. B.** "Tribalism: Social Organization in the Biblical Israels." In *Ancient Israel: The Old Testament in Its Social Context.* Ed. P. F. Esler. Minneapolis: Fortress, 2006. 35–49. **Faust, A.** "Pottery Talks: What Ceramics Tell Us about the Social World of Ancient Israel." *BAR* 30.2 (2004) 52–55, 62. **Geus, C. H. J. de.** *The Tribes of Israel.* SSN 19. Assen: Van Gorcum, 1976. **Gottwald, N. K.** "Early Israel and the Canaanite Socio-Economic System." In *Palestine in Transition: The Emergence of Ancient Israel.* Ed. D. N. Freedman and D. F. Graf. Sheffield: Almond, 1983. 25–37. ———. *The Tribes of Yahweh.* Maryknoll, NY: Orbis, 1979. **Helm, J.,** ed. *Essays on the Problem of Tribe: Proceedings of the 1967 Annual Spring Meeting of the American Ethnological Society.* Seattle: American Ethnological Society, 1968. **Hoftijzer, J.** "Enige opmerkingen rond het israëlitische 12-stammensysteem." *NedTT* 14 (1959–1960) 241–63. **Katzenstein, H. J.** "Some Remarks concerning the Succession to the Rulership in Ancient Israel (The Period until the Davidic Dynasty)." *PrWCJewSt* 7 (1982) 29–39 (Heb.). **Lemaire, A.** "Asriel, *'sr'l,* Israël et l'origine de la confédération israélite." *VT* 23 (1973) 239–43. **Lemche, N. P.** *Early Israel: Anthropological and Historical Studies on the Israelite Society before the Monarchy.* Trans. F. H. Cryer. Leiden: Brill, 1985. **Martin, J. D.** "Israel as a Tribal Society." In *The World of Ancient Israel: Sociological, Anthropological and Political Perspectives.* Ed. R. E. Clements. Cambridge: Cambridge UP, 1989. 95–117. **McNutt, P. M.** *Reconstructing the Society of Ancient Israel.* Library of Ancient Israel. Louisville: Westminster John Knox, 1999. **Mendenhall, G. E.** "Social Organization in Early Israel." In *Magnalia Dei: The Mighty Acts of God.* FS G. E. Wright, ed. F. M. Cross, W. E. Lemke, and P. D. Miller, Jr. Garden City, NY: Doubleday, 1976. 132–51. **Miller, R. D., II.** *Chieftains of the Highland Clans: A History of Israel in the Twelfth and Eleventh Centuries B.C.* Grand Rapids: Eerdmans, 2005. **Mojola, A. O.** "The 'Tribes' of Israel? A Bible Translator's Dilemma." *JSOT* 81 (1998) 15–29. **Rogerson, J. W.** *Anthropology and the Old Testament.* Oxford: Blackwell, 1978. ———. "Was Israel a 'Segmentary Society'?" *JSOT* 36 (1986) 17–26. **Weinfeld, M.** "Das geographische System der Stämme Israels." *VT* 23 (1973) 76–89.

"No one seems to have asked the most important question: What was an ancient Israelite *shebet* and what were its foundations and functions?"[404] The Bible depicts Israel as a tribal society having twelve members, though the twelve-member lists do not agree completely with one another (see especially Judg 5). The simple truth of this statement hides a multitude of questions. What is a tribe? How does Israel's tribal system relate to the ancestors pictured as the progenitors of the original twelve-son family? When did the tribal system begin? Is it more than a literary

---

404 Mendenhall, "Social Organization," 146.

device to call Israel to unity? What held the system together—politics, religion, adjudicators, common military defense needs? Why do Judges and other books so often narrate troubles among tribes, even war and murder of one or more tribes by the other?

Paula McNutt observes, "The biblical traditions emphasize the tribal structure of this period preceding the rise of the state. Nowhere in this material, however, do we find an explanation of how the notion of tribe was conceptualized, what the composition of tribes was, how the tribes related to one another on the economic and political levels, or the structure of society in general."[405] Robert Coote adds, "I assume instead that social organization referred to as 'Israel,' 'the sons of Israel,' or 'the house of Israel' was changeable and ordinary."[406] George Mendenhall sees a *šēbeṭ* as a "unit of society under the authority of a *nasi*', in other words, an administrative unit."[407]

Norman Gottwald sets up *šēbeṭ* and *maṭṭeh* as synonyms for a loosely organized autonomous social unit, an association of tribes.[408] As McNutt states, "there is no clear consensus on exactly what these terms mean or what level in the organization they refer to."[409]

The tribe had military potency and political self-rule. Together the tribes formed a large entity called the tribes of Israel or the tribes of Yahweh. Each tribe occupied the same organizational level as any other, no one tribe ruling the others though the tribes varied greatly in population and the size of their occupied territory. Tribal Israel was not composed of pastoral nomads but rather of settled agriculturalists who also practiced animal husbandry.[410] Israelite tribalism, for Gottwald, was "a form chosen by people who consciously rejected Canaanite centralization of power and deliberately aimed to defend their own uncentralized system against the effort of Canaanite society to crush the budding movement."[411] Israelite tribalism tried to roll back the zone of political centralization in Canaan to claim territory and peoples for an egalitarian mode of agricultural and pastoral life.

C. H. J. de Geus demonstrated that the people of Israel never were nomads following their flocks.[412] Tribe in the ancient Near East was a vague term referring to a group of clans uniting to meet a specific problem. Genealogies cannot be used as historical evidence, being formed by political relationships as much as by family relationships. Tribal organization did not lead to statehood, but often blocked such a move.

Niels Peter Lemche challenged de Geus and Gottwald and showed that the various family and tribal unit terms have extended, overlapping meaning.[413] The lineage (over fifty people) was the most important political unit. Terms for tribe range from subtribal units down to nuclear families. Israel did not have an egalitarian

---

405 *Reconstructing the Society of Ancient Israel*, 75.
406 "Tribalism," 37.
407 "Social Organization," 146.
408 *Tribes of Yahweh*, 245.
409 *Reconstructing the Society of Ancient Israel*, 76.
410 Gottwald, *Tribes of Yahweh*, 293–94.
411 Ibid., 324–25.
412 See *Tribes of Israel*.
413 See *Early Israel*.

society, but a chiefdom. Lemche eschews textual evidence as too far removed from the events and so depends totally on archaeological evidence, as rare as it proves to be. He, likewise, rejects religion and the covenant as factors in tribal life. Tribal alliances existed, says Lemche, but without stability. No evidence at all suggests a permanent alliance.

McNutt sees the tribe existing "more as a means of providing a range of potential identities than as a base for sustained collective action."[414] Political organization varied from no central power base to a strong leader or chief. In the tribal society egalitarianism rarely existed. Smaller tribal units such as clans "rarely unite with each other politically. When they do, it is normally because of some threat or crisis that requires it."[415] Otherwise, religious and economic ties provided a loose bonding.

Coote emphasizes the flexibility of tribal organization and life: structures and identities were fluid; kinship levels were elastic; kinship functions were blurred; the term Israel rarely if ever referred to a territory; tribal organization and identity tended to be more sharply defined at the higher levels of organization; tribal organizations took shape in relationship to regional powers or states as well as to other tribes; ethnicity did not automatically relate to tribalism; one may doubt seriously that *Israel* was ever used biblically as an ethnic term; genealogical descent was explained by political connections rather than political connections being explained by genealogical descent; tribalism had no direct connection with nomadism; Israel cannot be explained by evolutionary development; and an instrumentalist approach to Israelite tribalism is not to deny the social reality of tribes.[416]

Richard Nelson finds it difficult to separate "historically useful data from later idealism."[417] Clan names often reflect territorial names. Asher, for example, appears quite early in Egyptian texts. The tribe negotiated resource supplies and provided military defense. Tribal borders were not firm, since people of one tribe appear as inhabitants of border cities in other tribes. Names such as Gad appear to refer to a Canaanite god and so reflect a group prior to its becoming part of Israel. Similarly, Ephraim, Judah, and Benjamin represent geographical names in Palestine and so may represent groups who received their names within the Promised Land.

Israel's tribal life does not fit any stable pattern. It has few uniting factors, a life lived separately except in times of danger and threat and need. Aloo Osotsi Mojola decries the problem of defining Israel. He considers Israel to be a tribe. The twelve tribes would each then become a clan. "Israel was basically a peasant society with an acephalous or decentralized political system in which the village was central and self-sufficient. They raised crops and herded animals in their unwalled villages with up to 300 population."[418]

The ancestral narratives point to the naming of the tribal ancestors from inside Palestine. Ancestral cultic sites such as Bethel, Shechem, Hebron, and Mahanaim also played a strong role in the tribal life. Several tribes worshiped at regional sanc-

---

414   *Reconstructing the Society of Ancient Israel*, 81.
415   Ibid., 83.
416   "Tribalism," 40–47.
417   *NIDB*, 5:665–68.
418   *JSOT* 81 (1998) 24.

tuaries such as Mount Tabor, Shilo, Dan, Bethel, Gilgal. Even under the monarchy, tribal associations and identity remained important. According to C. J. H. Wright, the tribe

> was the primary unit of social and territorial organization in Israel. The tribes bore the names of the twelve sons of Jacob/Israel, with Joseph divided into Manasseh and Ephraim. Their varied histories are as complex as the history of the emergence and settlement of Israel in Palestine itself. Although, as the nomenclature shows, a person's tribal identity was important, and in wartime the military levy was on a tribal basis, in terms of practical social impact on ordinary life, the tribe was the least significant of the circles of kinship within which one stood. The secondary and tertiary subdivisions of the social structure were both more socially relevant and also closer to what we could recognize as meaningfully "family" structures.[419]

The study of tribal Israel offers few certainties. Joshua and Judges show us the looseness of the tribal connections as well as the changing identity of constituent members and of political organization. Clans such as Machir and Gilead were at times considered to be tribes. The priestly tribe could be included or excluded from the tribal lists. Central Palestine was controlled by related tribes that could be joined as the Joseph tribes or separately identified as the tribe of Manasseh and the tribe of Ephraim. At least after Joshua's leadership, the tribes seldom had strong, unifying leadership. Judges could serve judicial functions as did Deborah or military functions as did Barak, Gideon, and Jephthah. Connected to the "judges," were elders who apparently formed a decision-making body within individual tribes and acted as tribal representatives in matters reaching beyond the local tribe. Leaders could summon strong armies as did Gideon, work with rag-tag volunteers as did Abimelek, or simply rely on individual skills and strength without any type of army as did Samson. Leaders could have a prophetic bent as did Deborah and Samuel or an almost anti-religious bent as did Abimelek. The book of Judges reveals how the lack of organization and leadership eventually led to vicious infighting and the virtual annihilation of individual tribes.

The tribe is a fluctuating social organization of various sizes that gives its clans collective personnel and negotiating power in the use of resources, protection from enemies, and territorial solvency. Tribes gathered as "all Israel" only when involved in a large mission, in military operations, or in religious celebrations.

g. Studies on the "Amphictyony"

Bibliography

Anderson, G. W. "Israel: Amphictyony: "'Am; Kahal; 'Edah." In *Translating and Understanding the Old Testament.* Ed. H. T. Frank and W. L. Reed. Nashville: Abingdon, 1970. 135–51. **Bächli, O.** *Amphiktyonie im Alten Testament: Forschungsgeschichtliche Studie zur Hypothese von Martin Noth.* *TZ* Sonderband 6. Basel: Reinhardt, 1977. ———. "Miszelle: Nachtrag zum Thema Amphiktyonie." *TZ* 28 (1972) 356. **Celada, B.** "La Anfictionía de las 12 tribus de Israel: Un concepto tan discutible como repetido." *CuBi* 33 (1976) 139–42. **Chambers, H. E.** "Ancient Amphictyonies, sic et non." In *Scripture in Context II: More Essays on*

---

419 *ABD,* 2:761.

the Comparative Method. Ed. W. W. Hallo, J. C. Moyer, and L. G. Perdue. Winona Lake, IN: Eisenbrauns, 1983. 39–59. **Crüsemann, F.** *Der Widerstand gegen das Königtum*. WMANT 49. Neukirchen-Vluyn: Neukirchener Verlag, 1978. **Engel, H.** "Abshied von den frühisraelitischen Nomaden und der Jahwe Amphiktyonie." *BK* 38 (1983) 43–46. **Flanagan, J. W.** "Chiefs in Israel." *JSOT* 20 (1981) 47–73. **Fohrer, G.** "Altes Testament—'Amphiktyonie' und 'Bund'?" *TLZ* 91 (1966) 801–16, 893–904. Repr. in *Studien zur alttes-tamentlichen Theologie und Geschichte 1949–1966*, BZAW 115. Berlin: De Gruyter, 1969. 84–119. **Frick, F. S.** *The Formation of the State in Ancient Israel*. SWBA 4. Sheffield: JSOT Press, 1985. **Geus, C. H. J. de.** *The Tribes of Israel*. SSN 19. Assen: Van Gorcum, 1976. **Gottwald, N. K.** *The Tribes of Yahweh: A Sociology of the Religion of Liberated Israel 1250–1050 B.C.E.* Maryknoll, NY: Orbis, 1979. **Grabbe, L. L.** *Ancient Israel: What Do We Know and How Do We Know It?* London: T&T Clark, 2007. **Hallo, W. W.** "A Sumerian Amphictyony." *JCS* 14 (1960) 88–96. **Hoftijzer, J.** "Enige opmerkingen rond het israëlitische 12-stammensysteem." *NedTT* 14 (1959) 241–63. **Irwin, W. H.** "Le sanctuaire central israélite avant l'établissement de la monarchie." *RB* 72 (1965) 161–84. **James, L.** "An Evaluation of M. Noth's Idea of Amphictyony as Applied to Israel." *ResQ* 19 (1976) 165–74. **Kallai, Z.** "Joshua and Judges in Biblical Historiography." In *Biblical Historiography and Historical Geography*. BEATAJ 44. Frankfurt a.M.: Lang, 1998. 243–60. ———. "Judah and Israel—A Study in Israelite Historiography." *IEJ* 28 (1978) 251–61. ———. "The Twelve-Tribe Systems of Israel." *VT* 47 (1997) 53–90. **Lemche, N. P.** *Early Israel*. VTSup 37. Leiden: Brill, 1985. ———. "The Greek 'Amphictyony'—Could It Be a Prototype for the Israelite Society in the Period of the Judges?" *JSOT* 4 (1977) 48–59. **Mayes, A. D. H.** "Amphictyony." In *ABD*, 1:212–16. ———. *Israel in the Period of the Judges*. SBT, 2nd ser., 29. Naperville, IL: Allenson, 1974. ———. "Israel in the Pre-Monarchy Period." *VT* 23 (1973) 151–70. ———. "The Question of the Israelite Amphictyony." *Herm* 116 (1973) 53–65. **Mendenhall, G. E.** *Law and Covenant in Israel and the Ancient Near East*. Pittsburgh: Bible Colloquium, 1955. ———. "Social Organization in Early Israel." In *Magnalia Dei: The Mighty Acts of God*. FS G. E. Wright, ed. F. Cross and N. P. Lemche. Garden City, NY: Doubleday, 1976. 132–51. ———. *The Tenth Generation: The Origins of the Biblical Tradition*. Baltimore: Johns Hopkins UP, 1973. **Nicholson, E. W.** *Deuteronomy and Tradition*. Oxford: Oxford UP, 1967. **Noth, M.** "Das AMT des 'Richters Israels.'" In *Festschrift für Alfred Bertholet*. Ed. W. Baumgartner et al. Tübingen: Mohr, 1950. 404–17. Repr. in *Gesammelte Studien* 2, TB 39 (Munich, 1969) 71–85. ———. "The Laws in the Pentateuch: Their Assumptions and Meaning." In *The Laws in the Pentateuch and Other Studies*. Trans. D. R. Ap-Thomas. London: SCM Press, 1966. 1–107. ———. *Das System der zwölf Stämme Israels*. BWANT 4.1. Stuttgart: Kohlhammer, 1930. Reproduced by Darmstadt: Wissenschaftliche Buchgesellschaft, 1966. **Orlinsky, H. M.** "The Tribal System of Israel and Related Groups in the Period of the Judges." In *Studies and Essays in Honor of A. A. Neuman*. Ed. M. Ben-Horin, B. D. Weinry, and S. Zeitlin. Philadelphia: Fortress, 1962. 375–87. **Ploeg, J. van der.** "Les Chefs du peuple d'Israël et leurs titres." *RB* 57 (1950) 40–61. **Rad, G. von.** *Der heilige Krieg im alten Israel*. ATANT 20. Zürich: Zwingli, 1951. Translated as *Holy War in Ancient Israel* (Grand Rapids: Eerdmans, 1991). **Rahtjen, B. D.** "Philistine and Hebrew Amphictyonies." *JNES* 24 (1965) 100–104. **Rogerson, J. W.** "Was Early Israel a Segmentary Society?" *JSOT* 36 (1986) 17–26. **Rösel, H.** "Israel—Gedanken zu seinem Anfängen." *BN* 25 (1984) 76–91. ———. *Israel in Kanaan: Zum Problem der Entstehung Israels*. BEATAJ 11. Frankfurt am Main: Lang, 1992. **Sasson, J.** "On Choosing Models for Recreating Israelite Premonarchic History." *JSOT* 21 (1981) 3–24. **Smend, R.** *Yahweh War and Tribal Confederation*. Trans. M. G. Rogers. Nashville: Abingdon, 1970. ———. "Zur Frage der altisraelitischen Amphiktyonie." *EvT* 31 (1971) 623–30. **Speiser, E. A.** "Background and Function of the Biblical Nasi." *CBQ* 25 (1963) 111–17. Repr. in *Oriental and Biblical Studies*, ed. J. J. Finkelstein and M. Greenberg (Philadelphia: Fortress, 1967) 113–23. **Thiel, W.** *Die soziale Entwicklung Israels in vorstaatlicher Zeit*. Neukirchen-Vluyn: Neukirchener Verlag, 1980. **Vaux, R. de.** "La thèse de l'"amphictyonie israélite."' *HTR* 64 (1971) 415–36. **Weber, M.** *Ancient Judaism.* Trans. H. H. Gerth and D. Martindale. Glencoe, IL: Free Press, 1952. **Weingreen, J.** "The Theory of the Amphictyony in Pre-Monarchical Israel." *JANESCU* 5 (1973) 427–33. **Weippert, H.** "Das geographische System der Stämme Israels." *VT* 23 (1973) 76–89. **Zobel, H. J.** *Stammesspruch und Geschichte: Die Angaben der Stammessprüche von Gen 49, Dtn 33 und Jdc 5 über die politischen und kultischen Zustände im damaligen "Israel."* BZAW 95. Berlin: Töpelmann, 1965.

Israel's social organization begins with the father's house (בית אב), the clan, and the tribe. But how do the tribes relate one to the other? Put in another manner, what is the social and political organization that is recognized as Israel? This question deals with the nature of Israel's government in the early stages of life in the Promised Land. Again Martin Noth formulated the hypothesis against which modern scholarship has reacted. Using analogies from Greece and Italy as well as the biblical text, Noth suggested that the twelve-tribe system of Israel operated as an amphictyony.

Such an amphictyony had its supposed historical beginnings in a six-tribe Leah amphictyony with a central sanctuary at Shechem prior to the introduction of Yahwistic worship. Benjamin and the four "concubine" tribes established themselves in Palestine but did not gain entrance into the amphictyony. The Joseph tribes coming from Egypt and Sinai introduced Yahwistic worship to a group already beginning to be formulated only on historical traditions, since Levi, Reuben, and Simeon were quickly becoming mere remnants. The rise of the monarchy spelled doom for the tribal system. Amphictyonic life had centered around the central sanctuary with the ark as its central cult object. *Něśî 'im* or cultic representatives conducted tribal business, based on a form of the book of the covenant. The annual cultic festival brought the tribes together.

A complicating factor was the membership of Judah and Simeon in yet another amphictyony centering in Mamre and comprising Caleb, Othniel, Jerahmeel, and the Kennites. This resulted in split loyalties that plagued Israel throughout her history.[420]

Adamant opposition to the amphictyonic theory has come from a variety of scholars.[421] They find no evidence of one central sanctuary and close tribal cooperation. The twelve-tribe system is seen to be based on genealogical developments reflecting changing political alliances. No political office really joins the tribes, the only abiding feature being common worship of Yahweh, though this was undertaken at separate sanctuaries.

Niels Peter Lemche showed that the Greek had only one original amphictyony, that of Delphi, which only came into existence in the eighth century.[422] Thus it cannot be a model for the much earlier Israelite organization.

The literary theories of Tengström and Otto have produced alternate understandings of the amphictyony, a term Tengström would rather avoid.[423] He

---

420 Noth, *Das System der zwölf Stämme Israels.*
421 See G. Fohrer (*TLZ* 91 [1966] 801–16 = BZAW 115 [1969] 84–119), C. H. J. de Geus (*Tribes of Israel*), S. Herrmann ("Autonome Entwicklungen," 139–51), Mayes (*Israel in the Period of the Judges*), and G. W. Anderson ("Israel: Amphictyony," 135–51), among others.
422 *JSOT* 4 (1977) 48.
423 E. Otto, *Das Mazzotfest in Gilgal* (BWANT 107; Berlin: Kohlhammer, 1975); S. Tengström, Die Hexateucherzählung, (Coniectanea Biblica Old Testament 7; Uppsaia: Gleerup, 1976).

speaks, rather, of a twelve-tribe ideology centering in Shechem and the Rachel tribes. The covenant ceremony of Josh 24 shows the rise of such an ideology. The only outward manifestations of the ideology were the Shechemite Passover, occasional meetings of the tribal representatives, and the foundation of the Hexateuchal narrative. Otto shifts the focus to Gilgal as the only shrine able to involve Judah. Cultic reality became political reality under Saul (1 Sam 15:1–9).

Mendenhall,[424] de Geus, and especially Gottwald have argued for a new sociological understanding of Israel, emphasizing the sociological split between rural farmers and the city-state establishment rather than that between landed Canaanites and immigrating nomadic shepherds. The twelve-tribe system represents, for Gottwald, a political compromise achieved by David in administering his newly established kingdom. Prior to David, Israelite society had formed a confederacy of extended families and tribes cooperating in worship, war, and justice; but "twelve" was not an essential element of the confederacy. Solomon, however, replaced the system with one imposed from above.

Support for Noth has come from two directions. Rudolf Smend underlines the radical distinction between tribal systems and political reality under the monarchy.[425] Thus twelve-tribe Israel must have originated at Shechem when the Leah tribes with an amphictyonic tradition merged with the Rachel tribes with a war-of-Yahweh tradition. The amphictyony must be defined as a sacral institution that does not produce historical narrative. The war-of-Yahweh tradition results in narrative.

Otto Bächli demonstrates the necessity for conclusions by analogy and pleads for a replacement theory rather than a total abandonment of Noth's hypothesis.[426] He admits that Noth's hypothesis must be updated, particularly in eliminating six or twelve as an essential number and in correlating the theory of a Deuteronomistic History with the exegesis of texts crucial to the amphictyonic hypothesis, particularly Josh 24.

A. D. H. Mayes points to an understanding of Noth that is seldom stated or recognized:

Noth[427] acknowledged, that it was not in fact through the amphictyony that the tribes of Israel first came together. Rather, through the accidents of history, such as common invasion of a new land and common opposition to outside forces, the unity of Israel was first established, a unity which the amphictyony was then designed to preserve.[428]

Mayes concludes:

While it must be admitted that, for the present, the evidence in favor of such an organization in Israel is not convincing, the possibility is still open that, within an Israel organized as a segmentary society or an association of chiefdoms, amphictyonic relationships existed between larger or smaller groups of tribes or other social units already united on other grounds. It might be

---

424 *Law and Covenant in Israel*; "Social Organization in Early Israel"; *Tenth Generation*.
425 See *Yahweh War*.
426 See *Amphiktyonie im Alten Testament*.
427 *Das System*, 1930, 55–56.
428 *ABD*, 1:215.

through such relationships that the complex and still uncertain history of the development of Yahwism within Israel will be better understood; but it is unlikely that the analogy will become reestablished as a form by which the nature of the totality of Israel, at any period, is to be expressed.[429]

Lester Grabbe sees the theory as putting too much emphasis on the amorphous group called "tribe."[430] Only the book of Judges gives collective function to the tribes. Small groups carry out collective activities, the tribes being territorial units, that is, geographical and not political entities. The system of twelve tribes may have developed as late as the sixth century.[431] Here Grabbe represents a somewhat extreme position. Land division was an important factor for the tribes, but Judges shows military cooperation among tribes even when such cooperation did not always materialize (Judg 5).

According to Mario Liverani, in the Iron Age, the

members of the state were no longer just the inhabitants of a region, but rather individuals belonging to the same tribe—linked together by birth (or "blood") ties, common language, common traditions (as revealed by genealogies and by etiological stories), and the common worship of a tribal god. . . . The league of the twelve tribes, on the other hand, is a case of pastoral groups giving birth to a larger political unit, to which the term "nation" can be applied—with common leaders (Moses, Joshua, the Judges), with a political structure reproducing the kinship relationships, with the national god Yahweh. The "nation" is already existent before the conquest, so that only a territory is needed to establish a national state. The conquest brings about the inclusion of the former local settlements (villages becoming clans of the Israelite tribes), and the destruction (or more seldom the inclusion) of former polities. After the conquest some areas and cities are "left" outside the Israelite league, so that belonging to the Israelite political unit is (at least tendentially) coincident with the ethnic unit itself. Besides Israel, other national polities exist, the result of foreign immigration (Philistines: but their pentapolis has no political unity) or of parallel developments (Ammon, Moab, Edom).[432]

Liverani is willing to turn the process around for Israel, seeing a move from state to tribal association rather than the normal tribal to state. Thus he concludes: "The very existence of a political entity 'Israel' before the monarchic period must remain a matter of doubt; and even more uncertain is its institutional structure (including the presence or absence of any 'national' self-identification). The solution depends largely on the validity attached to later traditions."[433]

Richard Hess agrees that with the difficulty of importing the term "amphictyony" from later sources to describe Israel but still holds that such evidence does not deny "the possibility of a tribal confederation."[434]

---

429 Ibid., 1:216.
430 *Ancient Israel,* 105.
431 Ibid., 106.
432 *ABD,* 4:1033–34.
433 Ibid., 4:1034.
434 Hess, 34.

Using Greek terminology and a Greek cultural phenomenon to describe Israel in any way must be seen as a scholarly detour. Still, to deny Israel any organization or cooperation prior to the monarchy would replace a detour with a blockade sign, impeding any progress in learning the origins of Israel. Israel does not begin its existence as a powerful, or even not so powerful, monarchy. The people of Israel know their own history. They have two roots. One is an Aramaean contingent who confess that their ancestors came from Syria. The other is a central group who indentify themselves as slaves delivered from Egypt. Scribes in a royal court did not join these two confessions. The joining occurred in the hills of central Palestine in covenant ceremonies. Israelites became people who lived in the land of Israel, worshiped the God of Israel, and sent representatives to the occasional gathering of Israel in times of crisis and/or worship. We may not possess a name for such a politico-religious group tied together somewhat loosely by their confessions and their worship of Yahweh, but we also cannot allow the limitations of our vocabulary erase from history such an association.

h. Studies on Israelite Identity

Bibliography

Albright, W. F. *The Biblical Period from Abraham to Ezra: An Historical Survey.* New York: Harper, 1963. **Besters, A.** "'Israël' et 'Fils d'Israël' dans les livres historiques (Genèse–II Rois)." *RB* 74 (1967) 5–23. **Bienkowski, P.** "La ville de l'époque du Bronze." *MdB* 69 (1991) 15–19. **Bimson, J. J.** *Redating the Exodus and the Conquest.* JSOTSup 5. Sheffield: JSOT Press, 1978. **Bloch-Smith, E.** "Israelite Ethnicity in Iron I: Archaeology Preserves What Is Remembered and What Is Forgotten in Israel's History." *JBL* 122 (2003) 401–25. **Block, D. I.** "'Israel'—'Sons of Israel': A Study in Hebrew Eponymic Usage." *SR* 13 (1984) 301–26. ———. "Israel's House: Reflections on the Use of *Byt Ysr'l* in the Old Testament in the Light of Its Ancient Near Eastern Environment." *JETS* 28 (1985) 257–75. **Bright, J.** *Early Israel in Recent History Writing.* SBT 19. London: SCM Press, 1956. **Bunimovitz, S., and A. Faust.** "Chronological Separation, Geographical Segregation, or Ethnic Demarcation? Ethnography and the Iron Age Low Chronology." *BASOR* 322 (2001) 1–10. **Bunimovitz, S., and Z. Lederman.** "A Border Case: Beth-Shemesh and the Rise of Ancient Israel." In *Israel in Transition.* Ed. L. L. Grabbe. London: T&T Clark, 2008. 21–31. **Davies, P. R.** *The Origins of Biblical Israel.* Ed. Y. Amit et al. Library of Hebrew Bible/Old Testament Studies 485. London: T&T Clark, 2007. 141–48. ———. "The Trouble with Benjamin." In *Reflection and Refraction: Studies in Biblical Historiography in Honour of A. Graeme Auld.* Ed R. Rezetko, T. H. Lim, and W. B. Aucker. VTSup 113. Brill: Leiden, 2007. 93–111. **Day, J.** "Adde Praeputium Praeputio Magnus Acervus Erit: If the Exodus and Conquest Had Really Happened." *BibInt* 8 (2000) 23–32. **Day, J.,** ed. *In Search of Pre-Exilic Israel.* JSOTSup 406. Edinburgh: T&T Clark, 2004. **Dietrich, W.** *The Early Monarchy in Israel: The Tenth Century B.C.* Trans. J. Vette. Vol. 3 of *Biblical Encyclopedia.* Atlanta: Society of Biblical Literature, 2007. Orig published as "Die frühe Königszeit in Israel: 10. Jahrhundert v.Chr.," in *Biblische Enzyklopädie* (1997) vol. 3. ———. "Das Ende der Thronfolgegeschichte." In *Die sogenannte Thronfolgegeschichte Davids: Neue Ansichten und Anfragen.* Ed. A. de Pury and T. Römer. OBO 176. Göttingen: Vandenhoeck & Ruprecht, 2000. **Edelman, D. V.** "Ethnicity and Early Israel." In *Ethnicity and the Bible.* Ed. M. G. Grett. BibInt 19. Leiden: Brill, 2002. 25–55. **Ellis, R. R.** "The Theological Boundaries of Inclusion and Exclusion in the Book of Joshua." *RevExp* 95 (1998) 235–50. **Faust, A.** *Israel's Ethnogenesis: Settlement, Interaction, Expansion and Resistance.* Approaches to Anthropological Archaeology. London: Equinox, 2007. **Finkelstein, I.** *David and Solomon: In Search of the Bible's Sacred Kings and the Roots of the Western Tradition.* New York: Free Press, 2006. 129–38. ———. "Jerusalem in the Eighth and Seventh Centuries BCE: A Reply to Nadav Na'aman." *Zion*

72 (2007) 325–37 (Heb.). ———. "State Formation in Israel and Judah: A Contrast in Context, a Contrast in Trajectory." *NEA* 62 (1999) 35–52. ———. "Temple and Dynasty: Hezekiah, the Remaking of Judah and the Rise of the Pan-Israelite Ideology." *JSOT* 30 (2006) 259–85. **Finkelstein, I., and A. Mazar.** *The Quest for the Historical Israel: Debating Archaeology and the History of Early Israel.* Ed. B. B. Schmidt. Invited lectures delivered at the Sixth Biennial Colloquium of the International Institute for Secular Humanistic Judaism, Detroit, 2005. SBLABS 17. Atlanta: Society of Biblical Literature, 2007. **Finkelstein, I., and N.A. Silberman.** *The Bible Unearthed: Archaeology's New Vision of Ancient Israel and the Origin of Its Sacred Texts.* New York: Touchstone, 2002. 243–45. **Fritz, V.** "Israelites and Canaanites: You Can Tell Them Apart." *BAR* 28.4 (2002) 28–31, 63. **Gonen, R.** "Urban Canaan in the Late Bronze Age." *BASOR* 253 (1984) 61–73. **Gottwald, N.** "Domain Assumptions and Societal Models in the Study of Pre-Monarchic Israel." In *Congress Volume: Edinburgh 1974.* VTSup 28. Leiden: Brill, 1975. 89–100. ———. *The Hebrew Bible in Its Social World and Ours.* Atlanta: Scholars, 1993. ———. "The Hypothesis of the Revolutionary Origins of Ancient Israel: A Response to Hauser and Thompson." *JSOT* 7 (1978) 37–52. ———. "The Israelite Settlement as a Social Revolutionary Movement." In *Biblical Archaeology Today.* Jerusalem: Israel Exploration Society, 1985. 34–46. ———. *The Tribes of Yahweh.* Maryknoll, NY: Orbis, 1979. ———. "Two Models for the Origins of Ancient Israel: Social Revolution or Frontier Development." In *The Quest for the Kingdom of God: Studies in Honor of George E. Mendenhall.* Ed. H. B. Huffmon et al. Winona Lake, IN: Eisenbrauns, 1983. 5–24. ———. "Were the Early Israelites Pastoral Nomads?" *BAR* 4.2 (1978) 2–7. **Grabbe, L. L.** *Ancient Israel: What Do We Know and How Do We Know It?* Edinburgh: T&T Clark, 2007. **Grant, M.** *The History of Ancient Israel.* New York: Charles Scribner's Sons, 1984. **Greenspahn, F. E.** "From Egypt to Canaan: A Heroic Narrative." In *Israel's Apostasy and Restoration: Essays in Honor of R. K. Harrison.* Ed. A. Gileadi. Grand Rapids: Baker, 1988. 1–8. **Halpern, B.** *The Emergence of Israel in Canaan.* SBLMS 29. Chico, CA: Scholars Press, 1983. ———. *The First Historians: The Hebrew Bible and History.* San Francisco: Harper & Row, 1988. **Hawkins, R. K.** "From Disparate Tribes to 'All Israel.'" *NEASB* 50 (2005) 27–39. **Hayes, J. H., and J. M. Miller,** eds. *Israelite and Judean History.* OTL. Philadelphia: Westminster, 1977. **Herrmann, S.** "Israels Frühgeschichte im Spannungsfeld neuer Hypothesen." In *Studien zur Ethnogenese 2.* ARWAW 78. Opladen: Westdeutscher Verlag, 1988. 43–95. **Hess, R. S.** "Asking Historical Questions of Joshua 13–19: Recent Discussion Concerning the Date of the Boundary Lists." In *Faith Tradition and History.* Ed. A. R. Millard, J. K. Hofmeier, and D. W. Baker. Winona Lake, IN: Eisenbrauns, 1994. 191–205. **Hess, R. S., G. A. Klingbeil, and P. J. Ray, Jr.,** eds. *Critical Issues in Early Israelite History.* BBRSup 3. Winona Lake, IN: Eisenbrauns, 2008. **Hjelm, I., and T. L. Thompson.** "The Victory Song of Merneptah, Israel and the People of Palestine." *JSOT* 27 (2002) 3–18. **Hoffmeier, J. K.** "The (Israel) Stele of Merneptah." In *COS.* Ed. W. W. Hallo and K. L. Younger. Leiden: Brill, 2000. 2:40–41. **Hopkins, D. C.** *The Highlands of Canaan: Agricultural Life in the Early Iron Age.* SWBASup 3. Sheffield: Almond, 1985. ———. "Life on the Land: The Subsistence Struggles of Early Israel." *BA* 50 (1987) 178–91. **Kallai, Z.** "The Settlement Traditions of Ephraim—A Historiographical Study." *ZDPV* 102 (1986) 68–74. ———. "Territorial Patterns, Biblical Historiography and Scribal Traditions—A Programmatic Survey." *ZAW* 93 (1981) 427–32. ———. "The Twelve-Tribe Systems of Israel." *VT* 47 (1997) 53–90. **Kaplony-Heckel, U.** "Die Israel-Stele des Mer-en-ptah, 1208 v. Chr." In *Rechts- und Wirtschaftsurkunden: Historisch-chronologische Texte.* Ed. D. Conrad et al. *TUAT* 1. Gütersloh: Mohn, 1985. 544–52. **Kaufmann, Y.** *The Biblical Account of the Conquest of Canaan.* Jerusalem: Magnes, 1953; 2nd ed., 1985. **Kempinski, A.** "How Profoundly Canaanized Were the Early Israelites?" *ZDPV* 108 (1992) 1–7. ———. "The Overlap of Cultures at the End of the Late Bronze Age and the Beginnings of the Iron Age." In *Nahman Avigad Volume.* Ed. B. Mazar and Y. Yadin. *ErIsr* 18 (1985) 399–407 (Heb.). **Killebrew, A. E.** *Biblical Peoples and Ethnicity: An Archaeological Study of Egyptians,*

Canaanites, Philistines, and Early Israel, 1300–1100 B.C.E. Atlanta: Society of Biblical Literature, 2005. ———. "The Emergence of Ancient Israel: The Social Boundaries of a 'Mixed Multitude' in Canaan." In *"I Will Speak the Riddles of Ancient Times": Archaeological and Historical Studies in Honor of Amihai Mazar on the Occasion of His Sixtieth Birthday.* Ed. A. M. Meier and P. de Miroschedji. Winona Lake, IN: Eisenbrauns, 2006. 555–72. **Kitchen, K. A.** *On the Reliability of the Old Testament.* Grand Rapids: Eerdmans, 2003. ———. "The Physical Text of Merenptah's Victory Hymn (The 'Israel' Stele)." *JSSEA* 24 (1997) 71–76. **Knauf, E. A.** "Jerusalem in the Late Bronze and Early Iron Ages: A Proposal." *TA* 27 (2000) 75–90. **Kochavi, M.** "The Israelite Settlement in Canaan in the Light of Archaeological Surveys." In *Biblical Archaeology Today.* Jerusalem: Israel Exploration Society, 1985. 54–60. **Koizumi, T.** "Toward the Establishing of a Scientific History of Israel—From the Nomadic Period to the Organization of the Four Leading Tribes." *AJBI* 12 (1986) 29–76. **Kreuzer, S.** "Max Weber, George Mendenhall und das sogenannte Revolutionsmodell für die 'Landnahme' Israels." In *Altes Testament, Forschung und Wirkung.* FS H. G. Reventlow, ed. P. Mommer and W. Thiel. Frankfurt am Main: Lang, 1994. 283–305. **Lemaire, A.** "Recherches actuelles sur les origines de l'ancien Israël." *JA* 220 (1982) 5–24. **Lemche, N. P.** *Ancient Israel: A New History of Israelite Society.* Sheffield: JSOT Press, 1988. ———. *The Canaanites and Their Land: The Tradition of the Canaanites.* JSOTSup 110. Sheffield: JSOT Press, 1991. ———. *Early Israel: Anthropological and Historical Studies on the Israelite Society before the Monarchy.* VTSup 37. Leiden: Brill, 1985. ———. "'Hebrew' as a National Name for Israel." *ST* 33 (1979) 1–23. ———. "Ideology and the History of Ancient Israel." *SJOT* 14 (2003) 165–91. ———. "Is It Still Possible to Write a History of Ancient Israel?" *SJOT* 8 (1994) 163–88. ———. *The Israelites in History and Tradition.* Library of Ancient Israel. Louisville: Westminster John Knox, 1998. ———. "On the Problem of Studying Israelite History: A Propos Abraham Malamat's View of Historical Research." *BN* 24 (1984) 94–124. ———. "Rachel and Lea: Or on the Survival of Outdated Paradigms in the Study of the Origin of Israel." Part 1, *SJOT* 1 (1987) 127–53; part 2, *SJOT* 2 (1988) 39–65. ———. *Prelude to Israel's Past: Background and Beginnings of Israelite History and Identity.* Trans. E. F. Maniscalco. Peabody, MA: Hendrickson, 1998. **London, G.** "Ethnicity and Material Culture." In *Near Eastern Archaeology: A Reader.* Ed. S. Richard. Winona Lake, IN: Eisenbrauns, 2003.146–49. **Long, V. P.** "Evidence, Argument, and the Crisis of 'Biblical Israel.'" In *Windows into Old Testament History.* Ed. V. P. Long, G. J. Wenham, and D. W. Baker. Grand Rapids: Eerdmans, 2002. 1–22. **Loyd, M. G.** "The Pork Taboo: The Presence and Absence of *sus scrofa* in Ancient Israel." Paper read for Near Eastern Archaeology Society, Atlanta, November 17, 2010. **Machinist, P.** "Outsiders or Insiders: The Biblical View of Emergent Israel and Its Contexts." In *The Other in Jewish Thought and History.* Ed. L. J. Silberstein and R. L. Cohn. New York: NYU Press, 1994. 35–60. **Maisler, B.** "Ancient Israelite Historiography." *IEJ* 2 (1952) 82–88. **Malamat, A.** "The Danite Migration and the Pan-Israelite Exodus-Conquest—A Biblical Narrative Pattern." *Bib* 51 (1970) 1–16. ———. "How Inferior Israelite Forces Conquered Fortified Canaanite Cities." *BAR* 8.2 (1982) 24–35. **Margalith, O.** "On the Origin and Antiquity of the Name 'Israel.'" *ZAW* 102 (1990) 225–37. **Martin, J. D.** "Israel as a Tribal Society." In *The World of Ancient Israel.* Ed. R. E. Clements. Cambridge: Cambridge UP, 1989. 95–118. **Matthews, V. H.** *Studying the Ancient Israelites: A Guide to Sources and Methods.* Grand Rapids: Baker Academic, 2007. **Mayes, A. D.** "Israel in the Pre-Monarchy Period." *VT* 23 (1973) 51–70. **Mazani, P.** "The Appearance of Israel in Canaan in Recent Scholarship." In *Critical Issues in Early Israelite History.* Ed. R. S. Hess, G. A. Klingbeil, and P. J. Ray, Jr. BBRSup 3. Winona Lake, IN: Eisenbrauns, 2008. 95–109. **Mazar, A.** "Iron Age Chronology: A Reply to Israel Finkelstein." *Levant* 29 (1997) 157–67. **McGovern, P. E.** "Central Transjordan in the Late Bronze and Early Iron Ages: An Alternative Hypothesis of Socio-Economic Transformation and Collapse." In *Studies in the History and Archaeology of Jordan, 3.* Ed. A. Hadidi. Amman: Department of Antiquities of Jordan, 1987. **McNutt, P.** *Restructuring the Society of*

Ancient Israel. Louisville: Westminster John Knox, 1999. **Mendenhall, G. E.** "The Hebrew Conquest of Palestine." *BA* 25 (1962) 66–87. **Merling, D., Sr.** *The Book of Joshua: Its Theme and Role in Archaeological Discussions*. Andrews University Doctoral Dissertation Series 23. Berrien Springs, MI: Andrews UP, 1997. **Merrill, E. H.** "The Late Bronze/Early Iron Age Transition and the Emergence of Israel." *BSac* 152 (1995) 145–62. ————. "Palestinian Archaeology and the Date of the Conquest: Do Tells Tell Tales?" *GTJ* 3 (1982) 107–21. **Meyer, E.** *Die Israeliten und ihre Nachbarstämme: Alttestamentliche Untersuchungen*. Halle, 1906. **Milgrom, J.** "Priestly Terminology and the Political and Social Structure of Pre-Monarchic Israel." *JQR* 79 (978) 65–81. ————. "Religious Conversion and the Revolt Model for the Formation of Israel." *JBL* 101 (1982) 169–76. **Möhlenbrink, K.** "Die Landnahmesagen des Buches Josua." *ZAW* NF 15 (1938) 238–68. **Na'aman, N.** "Canaanite Jerusalem and Its Central Hill Country Neighbours in the Second Millennium B.C.E." *UF* 24 (1992) 275–91. ————. "The 'Conquest of Canaan' in the Book of Joshua and History." In *From Nomadism to Monarchy: Archaeological and Historical Aspects of Early Israel*. Ed. I. Finkelstein and N. Na'aman. Jerusalem: Israel Exploration Society, 1994. 218–81. ————. "Habiru and Hebrews: The Transfer of a Social Term to the Literary Sphere." *JNES* 445 (1986) 271–88. ————. "The Israelite-Judahite Struggle for the Patrimony of Ancient Israel." *Bib* 91 (2010) 1–23. ————. "Saul, Benjamin and the Emergence of 'Biblical Israel' (Part 1)." *ZAW* 121 (2009) 211–24. **Netanyahu, B., and B. Mazar, B.,** eds. *The World History of the Jewish People. First Series, Ancient Times*. Vols. 1–4. London: Allen; Jerusalem: Masada, 1964–1979. **Nibbi, A.** "Some Remarks on the Merenptah Stele and the So-Called Name of Israel." *DE* 36 (1996) 79–102. ————. "Some Unanswered Questions Concerning Canaan and Egypt in the So-called Israel Stele." *BN* 73 (1994) 74–89. **Niccacci, A.** "La Stèle d'Israël: Grammaiare et stratégie de communication." In *Études égyptologiques et bibliques à la mémoire du Père B. Couroyer*. Ed. M. Sigrist. Paris: Gabalda, 1997. 41–107. **Niehaus, J. J.** "Joshua and Ancient Near Eastern Warfare." *JETS* 31 (1988) 37–50. **Noll, K. L.** *Canaan and Israel in Antiquity*. Biblical Seminar 83. London: T&T Clark, 2002. **Noort, E.** *Das Buch Josua: Forschungsgeschichte und Problemfelder*. EdF 292. Darmstadt: Wissenschaftliche Buchgesellschaft, 1998. **Noth, M.** *The History of Israel*. 2nd ed. Trans. rev. P. R. Ackroyd. New York: Harper & Row, 1960. Originally published as *Geshichte Israel*, 2nd ed. Gottingen: Vandenhoeck & Ruprecht, 1954. **Otto, E.** "Israels Wurzeln in Kanaan: Auf dem Weg zu einer neuen Kultur- und Sozialgeschichte des antiken Israel." *TRev* 85 (1989) 3–10. **Pitkänen, P.** "Ethnicity, Assimilation and the Israelite Settlement." *TynBul* 55 (2004) 161–82. **Provan, I. V., P. Long, and T. Longman III.** *A Biblical History of Israel*. Louisville: John Knox Westminster, 2003. **Rainey, A.** "Inside, Outside: Where Did the Early Israelites Come from?" *BAR* 34.6 (2008) 45–50, 84. ————. "Israel in Merenptah's Inscription and Reliefs." *IEJ* 51 (2001) 57–75. ————. "Shasu or Habiru: Who Were the Early Israelites?" *BAR* 34.6 (2008) 51–55. ————. "Whence Came the Israelites and Their Language?" *IEJ* 57 (2007) 41–64. ————. "Who Is a Canaanite? A Review of the Textual Evidence." *BASOR* 304 (1996) 1–15. **Ramsey, G. W.** *The Quest for the Historical Israel*. Atlanta: John Knox, 1981. **Rasmussen, C. G.** "Conquest, Infiltration, Revolt, or Resettlement? What Really Happened during the Exodus-Judges Period?" In *Giving the Sense: Understanding and Using Old Testament Historical Texts*. Ed. D. M. Howard, Jr., and M. A. Grisanti. Grand Rapids: Kregel, 2003. 138–59. **Ray, P. J., Jr.** "Classical Models for the Appearance of Israel in Palestine." In *Critical Issues in Early Israelite History*. Ed. R. S. Hess, G. A. Klingbeil, and P. J. Ray, Jr. BBRSup 3. Winona Lake, IN: Eisenbrauns, 2008. 79–93. **Redford, D. B.** "The Ashkelon Relief at Karnak and the Israel Stela." *IEJ* 36 (1986) 188–200. **Rendsburg, G. A.** "The Date of the Exodus and Conquest/Settlement: The Case for the 1100s." *VT* 42 (1992) 510–27. **Rosen, B.** "Early Israelite Cultic Centers in the Hill Country." *VT* 38 (1988) 114–17. **Rowlett, L.** "Inclusion, Exclusion and Marginality in the Book of Joshua." *JSOT* 55 (1992) 15–23. **San Martin, J. A.** "Geschichte und Erzählungen im Alten Orient (I): Die Landnahme Israels." *UF* 17 (1986) 253–82. **Sasson, J.** "On

Choosing Models for Recreating Israelite Premonarchic History." *JSOT* 21 (1981) 13–24. **Shanks, H.** "Israel Comes to Canaan." *BAR* 8.2 (1982) 14–15. **Sharon, I.** "Demographic Aspects of the Problem of the Israelite Settlement." In *Uncovering Ancient Stones: Essays in Memory of H. Neil Richardson.* Ed. L. M. Hopfe. Winona Lake, IN: Eisenbrauns, 1994. 119–34. **Singer, I.** "Merneptah's Campaign to Canaan and the Egyptian Occupation of the Southern Coastal Plain of Palestine in the Ramesside Period." *BASOR* 26 (1988) 1–10. **Skjeggestad, M.** "Ethnic Groups in Early Iron Age Palestine: Some Remarks on the Use of the Term 'Israelite' in Recent Research." *SJOT* 6 (1992) 159–86. **Soggin, A.** "Ancient Israel: An Attempt at a Social and Economic Analysis of the Available Data." In *Text and Context: Old Testament and Semitic Studies for F. C. Fensham.* Ed. W. Claassen. Sheffield: JSOT, 1988. **Sparks, K. L.** *Ethnicity and Identity in Ancient Israel: Prolegomena to the Study of Ethnic Sentiments and Their Expression in the Hebrew Bible.* Winona Lake, IN: Eisenbrauns, 1998. ———. Review of *Israel's Ethnogenesis*, by A. Faust. *RLB* 7 (2008) 5–6. **Spiegelberg, W.** "Der Siegeshymnus des Merneptah auf der Flinders Petrie-Stele." *ZÄS* 34 (1896) 125. ———. "Zu der Erwähnung Israels in dem Merneptah Hymnus." *OLZ* 9 (1908) 403–5. **Spina, F. A.** *The Faith of the Outsider: Exclusion and Inclusion in the Biblical Story.* Grand Rapids: Eerdmans, 2005. **Stager, L. E.** "Forging an Identity: The Emergence of Ancient Israel." In *The Oxford History of the Biblical World.* Ed. M. D. Coogan. New York: Oxford UP, 1998. 123–75. ———. "Merneptah, Israel and Sea Peoples: New Light on an Old Relief." *ErIsr* 18 (1985) 56–64. **Thiel, W.** "Die Anfänge von Landwirtschaft und Bodenrecht in der Frühzeit Alt-Israels." *AoF* 7 (1980) 127–41. ———. *Die Soziale Entwicklung Israels in vorstaatlicher Zeit.* Neukirchen-Vluyn: Neukirchener Verlag, 1980. ———. "Verwandtschaftsgruppe und Stamm in der halbnomadischen Frühgeschichte Israels." *AoF* 4 (1976) 151–65. ———. "Vom revolutionären zum evolutionären Israel." *TLZ* 113 (1988) 313–40. **Thompson, T. L.** *Early History of the Israelite People: From the Written and Archaeological Sources.* Leiden: Brill, 2009. ———. "Historical Notes on Israel's Conquest of Palestine: A 'Peasants' Rebellion.'" *JSOT* 7 (1978) 20–27. **Ulrich, D. R.** "Does the Bible Sufficiently Describe the Conquest?" *TJ* 20.1 (1999) 53–68. **Van Seters, J.** *In Search of History: Historiography in the Ancient World and the Origins of Biblical History.* New Haven, CT: Yale UP, 1983. **Vaux, R. de.** *Histoire ancienne d'Israël.* 2 vols. Paris: Gabalda & Cie, 1971, 1973. Translated as *The Early History of Israel*, 2 vols., trans. D. Smith. London: Darton, Longman & Todd; Philadelphia: Westminster, 1978. ———. "The Settlement of the Israelites in Southern Palestine and the Origins of the Tribe of Judah." In *Translating and Understanding the Old Testament: Essays in Honor of H. G. May.* Ed. H. T. Frank and W. L. Reed. Nashville: Abingdon, 1970. 108–34. **Velázquez, E., II.** "The Persian Period and the Origins of Israel: Beyond the 'Myths.'" In *Critical Issues from Israelite History.* Ed. R. Hess, G. A. Klingbeil, and P. J. Ray, Jr. Winona Lake, IN: Eisenbrauns, 2008. 61–76. **Weinfeld, M.** "Die Eroberung des Landes Kanaan und der Bann seiner Bewohner." *BMik* 12 (1966–1967) 121–27 (Heb.). ———. "Historical Facts behind the Israelite Settlement Pattern." *VT* 38 (1988) 324–56. ———. "The Pattern of Israelite Settlement in Canaan." In *Congress Volume, Jerusalem 1986.* Ed. J. A. Emerton. VTSup 40. Leiden: Brill, 1988. 270–83. ———. "The Period of the Conquest and of the Judges as Seen by the Earlier and Later Sources." *VT* 17 (1967) 93–113. **Weippert, M.** "The Israelite 'Conquest' and the Evidence from Transjordan." In *Symposia Celebrating the Seventy-fifth Anniversary of the Foundation of the American Schools of Oriental Research (1900–1975).* Ed. F. M. Cross. Cambridge, MA: Cambridge UP, 1979. 14–34. ———. "Remarks on the History of Settlement in Southern Jordan during the Early Iron Age." In *Studies in the History and Archaeology of Jordan I.* Ed. A. Hadidi. Amman: Department of Antiquities, 1982. 153–62. ———. *The Settlement of the Israelite Tribes in Palestine.* SBT, 2nd ser., 21. London: SCM Press, 1971. **Weippert, M., and H. Weippert.** "Die Vorgeschichte Israels in neuem Licht." *TRu* 56 (1991) 341–90. **Whitelam, K.** "The Identity of Early Israel: The Realignment and Transformation of Late Bronze-Iron Age Palestine." *JSOT* 63 (1994) 57–87. Repr. in *The Historical Books*, ed. J. C.

Exum. Sheffield: Sheffield Academic, 1997. 14–45. ———. *The Invention of Ancient Israel: The Silencing of Palestinian History.* London: Routledge, 1996. ———. "Israel's Traditions of Origin: Reclaiming the Land." *JSOT* 44 (1989) 19–42. ———. "Recreating the History of Israel." *JSOT* 35 (1986) 45–70. **Wifall, W. R.** "Israel's Origins: Beyond Noth and Gottwald." *BTB* 12 (1982) 8–10. ———. "The Tribes of Yahweh: A Synchronic Study with a Diachronic Title." *ZAW* 95 (1983) 197–209. **Winther-Nielsen, N.** "Fact, Fiction, and Language Use: Can Modern Pragmatics Improve on Halpern's Case for History in Judges?" In *Windows into Old Testament History.* Ed. V. P. Long, D. W. Baker, and G. J. Wenham. Grand Rapids: Eerdmans, 2002. 44–81. **Wood, B. G.** "Pharaoh Merenptah Meets Israel." *Bible and Spade* 18 (2005) 65–82. **Wright, G. E.** "Epic of Conquest." *BA* 3 (1940) 25–40. **Yadin, Y.** "Is the Biblical Account of the Israelite Conquest of Canaan Historically Reliable?" *BAR* 8.2 (1982) 16–23. ———. *Military and Archeological Aspects of the Conquest of Canaan in the Book of Joshua.* El Ha'ayin 1. Jerusalem, 1965. ———. "The Transition from a Semi-Nomadic to a Sedentary Society in the Twelfth Century B.C.E." In *Symposia.* Ed. F. M. Cross. ASOR, 1979. 57–68. **Yeivin, S.** *The Israelite Conquest of Canaan.* Istanbul: Nederslands Historisch-Aarchaeologisch Institut in Het Nabije Oosten, 1971. **Younger, K. L., Jr.** *Ancient Conquest Accounts: A Study in Ancient Near Eastern and Biblical History Writing.* JSOTSup 98. Sheffield: JSOT Press, 1990. ———. "Early Israel in Recent Biblical Scholarship." In *The Face of Old Testament Studies: A Survey of Contemporary Approaches.* Ed. D. W. Baker and B. T. Arnold. Grand Rapids: Baker, 1999. 176–206. **Yurco, F.** "Merenptah's Canaanite Campaign." *JARCE* 23 (1986) 189–215. ———. "Merneptah's Canaanite Campaign and Israel's Origins." In *Exodus: The Egyptian Evidence.* Ed. E. S. Frerichs and L. H. Lesko. Winona Lake, IN: Eisenbrauns, 1997. 27–55. ———. "Merenptah's Palestinian Campaign." *JSSEA* 8 (1978) 70.

Reflection on the history of research forces on us the radical necessity of identifying and defining Israel. How does a people with the divine name El in its own name become identified with the radical devotees of the one God Yahweh? Why do lists and genealogies of tribal units differ both in contents and genealogical relationships? Why do the narratives of the judges depict isolated tribal actions and intertribal battles? Why are Israelite judges named Othni*el* and Jerub*baal*? Why is Shechem, the "amphictyonic center," so closely associated with a temple of Baal-berith? How are the cultic centers such as Shechem, Gilgal, Tabor, Shiloh, Beersheba, Bethel, and Dan connected with the worship practices of early Israel are concerned?

Did Philistine and continued Canaanite or Jebusite occupation of the major valleys allow communication and joint operations among the tribal groups north and south in Palestine? Did the north-south split under Rehoboam have antecedents in the early history of Israel? What explains the dialectical differences between different tribes (Judg 12)? Did a separate northern Exodus theology stand over against a southern Zion theology? Where would a tribal league of any kind have had its early political and cultic roots? Do archaeological discoveries about peoples like the Habiru and Shasu shed light on the origins or antecedents of Israel?

All such questions demand answers before we can confidently describe the political and religious organization of early Israel. Yet, as George Ramsey has shown, "the ambiguity of biblical texts and external evidence make it impossible for one to be categorical in his judgments or interpretations."[435]

The common answer in the last twenty years is that of Gordon McConville:[436] Israel was part of the land's indigenous population emerging from a specific cultural context and only gradually moving from a Canaanite-type religion to one of worship of Yahweh alone. Keith Whitelam goes further: "The terms 'Israelite' and 'Canaanite' are misleading and carry too many implications which the evidence at present does not support."[437]

The description of the early history of Israel continues to feature battles between conservative or maximalist positions and critical scholars representing a minimalist or nihilistic position on recovery of the actual beginnings of the people Israel. Eugene Merrill outlines the problems to solve: "The major issues involved in addressing the matter of Israel's emergence are (a) the historiographical nature and reliability of the Old Testament accounts which describe it, (b) the chronological setting in which it should be placed, and (c) the proper interpretation of both the biblical and extrabiblical data that bear on the matter."[438] These will be considered briefly in that order.

Nature and Reliability of the Accounts. Kenton L. Sparks, in reviewing *Israel's Ethnogenesis* by Avraham Faust, challenges the claim that biblical narratives are as secondary and useless as Faust and so many others claim. He writes, "Because of the Bible . . . we expect to find Israel in the highlands and in Transjordan, the Ammonites, Moabites, and Edomites in Transjordan, and the Philistines along the coast; it is also from the Bible that we learn of Israel's serious conflicts with Philistia. I suspect, too, that we would not think of circumcision and pork consumption as indicative of Israelite identity without the Hebrew Bible."[439] Faust sees Israel developing from nomadic Shasu and highland settlers and struggling against the Egyptians and Canaanites as the Bronze Age gave way to the Iron. The arrival of the Philistines gave "Israel" another challenge to shape its identity in the wake of a new contender for land and cultural superiority. In this way pork abstention, unpainted pottery, and circumcision became marks of the Israelites.

Israel first appears as a group name on the 1205 Merneptah stele. It then becomes the almost exclusive name of the northern tribes and its monarchy. Finally, after the exile of northern "Israel," the name begins to be used for Judah as well.[440]

Nadav Na'aman analyzed the second millennium BCE documentary and archaeological evidence as well as the documentary evidence of the Persian and Hellenistic periods relating to the land of Benjamin's relationship to the territory of Jerusalem. He concludes: "It is obvious that the district of Benjamin always had a southward orientation, toward Jerusalem, and was detached from the political/administrative entity on its north."[441] This would evaluate the David/Saul battles as similar to those of David and his son Absalom—local civil wars or rebellions, not "international war" between separate nations. It would also explain the ease with which Judean scribes could obtain, collect, transmit, and preserve the Benjaminite/Ephraimite materials lying at the base of Josh 1–12.

---

436 McConville, 4–5.
437 *JSOT* 63 (1994) 64.
438 *BSac* 152 (1995) 146.
439 *RBL* 7 (2008) 5–6.
440 See Na'aman, *ZAW* 121(2009) 213.
441 Ibid., 216.

Na'aman looks for historical materials originating in the northern kingdom where the name Israel would be used for the whole people. He finds: "However, it is difficult to demonstrate the northern origin of the biblical historiography; so, except for the story cycle of Jacob, the pre-Deuteronomistic story cycle of the Book of Judges, and some prophetic stories in the Book of Kings, most of the biblical historiography was written by Judahite scribes only after the fall of the Northern Kingdom."[442] At the same time, Na'aman quickly denies the views of Finkelstein and Dietrich, who speak of mass migration into Judah after the fall of the northern kingdom, there being no evidence from text or archaeology to support the theory. Na'aman also sets aside Davies's suggestion that the district of Benjamin was part of the territory of Israel until the late eighth century, when it was turned over to Judah with tension developing between Judah and Benjamin during the monarchical period.

For Na'aman, the rivalry between Saul and David described in the book of Samuel reflects the tension between Israel and Judah in the late monarchical period. As a north-Israelite tribe, according to Davies,[443] Benjamin served as the channel through which northern traditions were passed to the court of Jerusalem.

Na'aman attempts to prove the thesis "that the adoption of the Israelite identity by the Judahite scribes and elite was motivated by the desire to take over the highly prestigious vacant heritage of the Northern Kingdom, just as Assyria had sought to take possession of the highly prestigious heritage of ancient Mesopotamia."[444] This all occurred during Assyria's period of weakness after 630. In his article, Na'aman outlines distinctions between Israel and Judah. On the emergence of "Biblical Israel," he decides that

> as a Religious-Cultural Phenomenon, we must first emphasize the overwhelming superiority of the Kingdom of Israel over Judah in all parameters of statehood—population, urbanization, monumental architecture, administration, economy and trade— from the time of its foundation until its conquest and partial annexation by Tiglath-pileser III in 733/32 BCE. Indeed, most of the territory of Palestine —including all the thickly populated highlands districts (except for the district of Benjamin)—was incorporated into Israel territory. This territory included the Gilead and part of the Mishor, the Upper and Lower Galilee, the Jordan Valley, the northern plains of Jezreel and Beth-shean, the central hill country, the coast between the Carmel and Jarkon River and the northern Shephelah. Included in these districts were the territories of the former Canaanite cities of the Lower Galilee (Chinnereth), the northern plains (Megiddo, Beth-shean, Rehob and Jokneam), the coast (Dor) and northern Shephelah (Gezer). The territories within the Kingdom of Judah, on the other hand— such as the highlands of Judah, the Beersheba Valley and the Upper Shephelah—were largely peripheral and sparsely populated until the late 9th century B.C.E. The Northern Kingdom was a multifaceted state, comprising a heterogeneous population of diversified ethnic origin and cultic and cultural traditions, including many descendants of the former Canaanite population. No

---

442 Ibid., 213.
443 "The Trouble with Benjamin."
444 *Bib* 91 (2010) 17.

wonder, therefore, that Israel absorbed many religious concepts and cultic and cultural elements of Canaanite origin. Moreover, Israel bordered culturally influential kingdoms such as Aram, Damascus, and Tyre, and gradually absorbed cultic and cultural elements from its neighbours.[445]

Judah, on the other hand, was demographically quite homogenous, made up of settled local groups with pastoral roots. It was much more isolated, having a common border with only the two continental Philistine kingdoms of Ekron and Gath. Until the eighth century, it lagged in all aspects of state organization and urban culture far behind its northern neighbor. During the ninth century several major cities in the northern kingdom were fortified (Hazor, Megiddo, Rehob, Jokneam, Jezreel, Dor, and Gezer) and palaces as well as other public structures erected. By the ninth century, the kingdom had evolved into what sociologists call a "mature state": a well-developed territorial-political entity, with a settlement system comprising hundreds of settlements of various sizes. Not surprisingly, Israel is mentioned quite prominently in ninth-century royal inscriptions of the kings of Assyria (Shalmaneser III, Adad-nirari III), Aram (Hazael) and Moab (Mesha). By contrast, only a few dozen small, indigent settlements occupied the territory of Judah in the ninth century.

Excavations in the city of David in Jerusalem have revealed scant traces of settlement during this period. That said, we must not forget the formidable challenges of excavating such a mountainous site continuously inhabited for thousands of years, where each new settlement damaged the remains of its predecessors. Excavations carried out in the territory of Judah have uncovered several fortified cities from the ninth century (Beth Shemesh, Lachish, Tel Beersheba, Arad and Tell en-Nasbeh), indicating the existence of a central government and possibly an administrative apparatus in the kingdom at that time. It also indicates that the Judahite economy and trade were slowly and gradually developing in the second half of the ninth century, both at the primary center of Jerusalem and at the secondary centers of the kingdom's frontiers.

The kingdom—under the name "Beth David"—earned a minor mention in the Aramaic inscription of Tel Dan, in contrast to numerous references to Israel in ninth-century royal inscriptions. Only in the eighth century did a "mature" system of settlements evolve in the kingdom of Judah. During this period large fortifications, public edifices, and items of luxury first appeared in Judah, along with the first mass production of pottery vessels in Judah, manufactured in central workshops and distributed to the periphery of the kingdom. The production of oil and wine similarly developed, progressing from the household level to larger, perhaps even national, scales.

Israel Finkelstein sums up the differences in the environmental and cultural background, and in the growth and development, of the two neighboring kingdoms as follows:

> Israel and Judah were two distinct territorial, socio-political and cultural phenomena. This dichotomy stemmed from their different environmental conditions and their contrasting history in the second millennium B.C.E. Israel was characterized by significant continuity in Bronze Age culture traits, by heterogeneous population, and by strong contacts with its neigh-

---

445 Ibid., 14–15.

bors. Judah was characterized by isolation and by local, Iron Age cultural features, as evidenced by the layout of its provincial administrative towns. Israel emerged as a full-blown state in the early 9th century B.C.E, together with Moab, Ammon, and Aram Damascus, while Judah (and Edom) emerged about a century and a half later, in the second half of the 8th century."[446]

Ann Killebrew reviews the archaeological evidence and the basic theories of the origin of Israel and its identity.[447] Rejecting Joshua's historical account disqualifies the unified military conquest theory. Reliance solely on sociological approaches without textual or archeological evidence invalidates the social revolution theory. The clear-cut division between pastoral and agricultural activities having been discredited by ethnographic studies discredits Finkelstein's pastoral Canaanite theory. Killebrew makes no specific critique of the peaceful infiltration theory but does offer her own mixed multitude theory—"a heterogeneous, multifaceted, and complex process of Israelite ethnogenesis." Based on ethnographic studies, this theory is "rooted in diverse antecedent groups that converge and diverge over time." The binding element for the diverse group is the "empowering narrative of shared experiences, woven into an epic account of primordial deeds, miracles, and genealogies."[448] The original Israelites were a "collection of loosely organized and largely indigenous, tribal, and kin-based groups whose porous borders permitted penetration by smaller numbers from external groups." Archaeology shows distinct settlement and cultural patterns for the twelfth and eleventh centuries in the highlands on both sides of the Jordan.

At this point one is reduced to personal opinion and understanding concerning the date of materials and the reliability of writers and their oral and written sources. Na'aman skips quickly from early oral material to 800 or later written records. We cannot read Joshua, Judges, Samuel, and Kings without seeing some sort of early tribal cooperation and identity, an identity that resulted both in cooperation against enemies and intertribal warfare. We also cannot see the city of Jerusalem losing its prestige and power just coincidently at the time the biblical narratives introduce it as an important city. (See Judg 5, 8–12.)

Chronological Setting. Archaeology and the biblical narrative joined hands for several generations in the mid-twentieth century. But further literary study and expanded archaeological discoveries and discussions yielded a negative tone to the discussions. Many conservatives called for a fifteenth-century exodus and conquest. Others spoke of early thirteenth-century actions. Many dated the writing of the book of Joshua to the period of Josiah and identified many of the Joshua narratives as codes for Josiah's expansionistic program.[449] Others pushed most if not all the literary activity into the exilic period and even into the Persian period.

Now, says David Merling, "modern scholarship is in disarray on the subject of the Israelites. . . . the only thing about which critics of the Bible agree is that the Bible provides little or no evidence about the Israelites."[450] A few quotes will highlight the problem.

---

446 *NEA* 62 (1999) 41.
447 *Biblical Peoples*, 181–85.
448 Ibid., 184.
449 See Nelson.
450 "Foreword," in *Critical Issues in Early Israelite History*, ed. R. Hess, G. A. Klingbeil, and P. J. Ray, Jr. (Winona Lake, IN: Eisenbrauns, 2008) vii.

1. "The Israelite 'conquest' really only ended in the latter years of the reign of David. Until that time there were decades of constant warfare, servitude, and intertribal conflicts."[451]
2. "Whatever the reality, it is clothed in a thick layer of mythical interpretation. . . . [I]t appears that myth has been historicized, and the shades of the dead have been turned into ethnographical entities."[452]
3. "It remains impossible cogently to analyze not just the corpus as a whole, but any individual text within the corpus with a view to extracting editorial (historical) elements from the narrative."[453]
4. "Our biblical traditions are artistically constructed and ideologically shaped entities that are perhaps distanced in time from the past they apparently seek to describe. . . . Our biblical texts simply do not have the appearance of being produced out of the vivid imagination of late postexilic authors."[454]
5. Storytellers "were not describing what happened, but what it meant. . . . The available data is of mixed character. However, used with care and a degree of analytical skepticism, it becomes clear that the ancient Near Eastern texts and the biblical narratives do contain valuable historical information."[455]
6. "Whether the author of the biblical text was an eyewitness or not need not affect our decision concerning whether it is history or not. . . . If the passage is understood as hyperbole, the problem disappears. . . . One encounters very similar things in both ancient Near Eastern and biblical history writing."[456]
7. "As far as ancient Israel is concerned, there can be no doubt that it is an artificial creation of the scholarly world of the modern age. . . . Modern scholars invented ancient Israel not because they wanted to invent something new but simply because of a rather naïve reading of scripture."[457]
8. "What we read in Joshua is prophetic history. It is not just the historical record of a nation. Rather than a mere chronicle, it is a narration of history that preaches God's message of Law and Gospel—human sin and divine grace—from a firm theological perspective."[458]
9. "The biblical picture of an 'Israel' descended from Abraham entering Canaan from without and engaging and defeating various Canaanite forces, but without causing extensive material destruction is the most reasonable and defensible model."[459]
10. "This commentary . . . will accept the work as preserving authentic and ancient sources that attest to events in the late second millennium B.C."[460]

The chronological settings of events and of the records of events become a battle of assumptions—assumptions about oral tradition, the relationship of Israel

---

451 Merling, *The Book of Joshua*, 175.
452 Grabbe, *Ancient Israel*, 84, 87.
453 Halpern, *Emergence of Israel in Canaan*, 19.
454 Provan, Long, and Longman, *Biblical History of Israel*, 34, 60.
455 Matthews, *Studying the Ancient Israelites*, 161, 181.
456 Younger, *Ancient Conquest Accounts*, 250, 251, 265.
457 Lemche, *Israelites in History and Tradition*, 163, 165.
458 Harstad, 3.
459 Howard, 40–41.
460 Hess, 31.

and Judah prior to the monarchy, the history of Jerusalem at the turn of the archaeological ages, the ability for Israelites to produce and preserve written records, the freedom of scribes to change texts as they copied them, the nature of Israelite historical writing with regard to narrative skill and narrative invention.

This commentary assumes a Davidic Jerusalem taken from Jebusite predecessors and having sufficient government institutions to record and store the traditions about Israel's early life. This is one of the few if not the only period when scribes would have relatively easy access to traditions from both the north and the south and could merge them into one continuous narrative. In preserving the traditions, the scribes may well have utilized multiple versions of some traditions resulting in those elements some scholars seize on to dice the text into unnecessarily small pieces. The creation of the book of Joshua appears to come from the united monarchy with final touches possibly added after the split between the north and the south.

This assumption on the chronology of writing also points to a chronology of events. Israel as a people existed long before David and participated in the events the Bible describes. Israel is a real people built around experiences in Egypt and on Sinai. Israel is not an invention of scribes or politicians seeking an identity for a group involved in conflict over control of the local power structure sometime after 538 BCE.

Proper Interpretation of Data. Richard Hess looks at the study of the boundaries in Josh 13–17 and concludes:

> No single population center sufficed to give Israel an identity, for the people were spread across the hill country and beyond, inhabiting numerous small villages. . . . Perhaps . . . the various tribes in Israel could not yet be identified by the one or two cities that served as administrative centers. . . . Could not Joshua 13–19 describe a time when tribal identity was preeminently important and when the topography of this identity, especially in the hill country, could be described only by means of natural landmarks and villages?[461]

Thus for Hess, the lists in Josh 13–17 reflect a covenant document, guaranteed "the integrity of the people's land," and defined "the areas in which they had responsibility."[462] Much of the land allotments were admittedly for Hess idealistic, covering territory not yet conquered. The lists helped Israel discourage competition among tribes or clans for land.

Daniel Hawk centers his reading of Joshua on two questions: "How does Joshua construct an identity for the people of God?" and "What does Joshua hold to be the essential mark(s) of Israelite identity." To answer these questions, Hawk turns to a narrative approach, noting structures, themes, allusions, and especially discontinuities that evince abrupt shifts and contradictory assertions. The latter literary tool comes to expression in seeing the strict obedience of national Israel as opposed to the self-serving, divided picture presented of characters and groups in the smaller stories. Characterization is not a central issue of the plot, but still "in his exemplary execution of the Mosaic commandments" Joshua "represents the national ideal."[463]

Hawk follows the two-voice scheme of Polzin. "A dominant voice trumpets claims

---

461 "Asking Historical Questions."
462 Ibid., 203.
463 Hawk (2010).

of ethnic superiority, military triumphalism, national idealism, divine destiny, and the conviction that Yahweh's might makes right." This voice concludes: "This is who we are: a united nation, devoted to God, a chosen people separate from all others, and destined by God to take this land." A subtle voice whispers back with "a voice of larger visions of Israelite identity, one that dismantles 'us/them' ethnic consciousness, portrays all peoples—invaders and indigenous alike—as recipients of God's mercy, and establishes Israel's identity solely on devotion to a gracious and giving God."[464]

9. Summary of Historical and Archeological Results

Review of the literary, form-critical, and archaeological research has revealed the complexity of describing the history of the conquest. Edward Noort summarizes the issue as follows: "A conquest (*Landnahme*) as far as it is historical is not to be found in the 'total concept' of the Book of Joshua."[465] For Noort, it is not impossible that the joining of settlement and fighting on an east-west axis between Israel and Judah mirrors historical memories. On the other hand, Noort warns against the dangerous task of relying too heavily on archaeological results because of the difficulty of transferring archaelogical data into historical data.[466] He concludes that at the time of his writing (before 1998) we know much more from an archaeological viewpoint while at the same time we know much less about the historical process.[467]

The problem lies, however, with none of these areas of study but rather with one's theological and faith presuppositions. To what degree must the biblical narrative mirror historical events for the truth quality of the narrative to be validated? This is the basic question lying behind all historical research into biblical narratives. The believer does not study the narratives to validate their truth quality. Rather, the narratives proved themselves true for the life of faith long before the believer learned to raise the historical issue. The historical question becomes a means to buttress one's faith or to validate one's doctrine. The issue at hand revolves around a different type of question. Can one objectively raise the historical issue, determine the balance of probability, and then incorporate that balance-of-probability answer into one's growing and maturing faith? Can one truly seek an answer to the historical question without a dominating prior determination already lurking in the soul?

The historical problem lies in several areas. The literary problem is illustrated by a comparison of Josh 11:23; 21:43–45 with 13:1–7; 15:63; 16:10; 17:12–13; 19:47; Judg 1:27–36 or by a comparison of Josh 10:36–39 with 14:13–15; 15:13–19; Judg 1:10–15.

The form-critical problem lies not only in the solution to the question of etiology, but in the deeper determination of the nature and function of the materials within Israelite society prior to their compilation and incorporation into the theologically dominated whole. Was the basic narrative material originally intended to convey raw historical fact, whatever that may be? Did the material attempt to entertain? Did it try to provide material for worship ritual and praise? Or did it seek to defend the political claims of one group against another?

---

464   Ibid., xxiii.
465   *Das Buch Josua*, 226–27.
466   Ibid., 230.
467   Ibid., 245.

To raise such questions risks theological consequences. Was God limited to one methodology to preserve the word for God's people? Or was God willing to take the risk of using the processes that people instituted for preserving tradition to prepare the word for them? Was revelation limited to the interplay between God and one author at one specific moment in history? Or was God able to reveal his word to his people in a protracted period of tradition formation and preservation? Does labeling various stages of the growth of tradition as original narrative, compiler's collection, editor's final book, and ultimate history incorporation mean that only one of the stages can be true history? To put the question another way, does discovery of an editor collecting source materials and creating an extensive history of Israel extending through several centuries exclude that historian's editorial insertions from being historical.

Archaeological results have forced biblical students to raise such theological questions. No one archaeological solution to the question of conquest has satisfied everybody. No matter how many of the cities mentioned in the book of Joshua have provided destruction remains in the thirteenth century, the twelfth century, or the fifteenth century, not all of them have provided the needed remains in any one century. The greatest problems lie precisely with those cities that play the most prominent roles in the Joshua narrative—Jericho, Ai, Gibeon. Proper methodology would force these cities to the center of the investigation and not those which appear more on the periphery of the narrative. This has brought scholars to a variety of answers to the basic historical questions in Joshua. People of faith dedicated to the study of God's Word have understood the nature of the material incorporated into the book in different ways.

W. F. Albright readily admits, "It is no easy task to reconstruct the details of the Conquest, since the extant Israelite tradition is not uniform and our biblical sources vary considerably. . . . The results of excavations are ambiguous and sometimes in apparent conflict with the tradition."[468] He uses the appearance of the name Israel on the Merneptah stele about 1219 (his dating) in correlation with archaeological destruction layers at Tell Beit Mirsim, Bethel, Lachish, and Hazor to date the conquest in the thirteenth century. Still Albright admits that Joshua's military feats were "somewhat exaggerated" by the tradition and that Hebrews who were already in Palestine joined those coming out of Egypt.[469] Albright's student John Bright spoke of Israel as "surely not a race" but a people, "a mixture from the beginning and in no essential distinct from her neighbors."[470]

More recently, Robert Hubbard advocates a military-conduct model of the conquest with the understanding that only two of the nineteen sites mentioned in Joshua suffered destruction and that one cannot determine decisively who caused such damage and destruction.[471] He joins others in seeing Josh 6–11 as a repetitive stereotyped account marked by occasional hyperbole but retaining historical value. The conquest is thus a "complex reality"—"much more complex than a simple short military blitzkrieg."[472] Hubbard agrees with Younger[473] that the conquest is a "long

468 *Biblical Period*, 27.
469 Ibid., 30.
470 *Early Israel in Recent History Writing*, 113.
471 Hubbard, 33.
472 Ibid., 39–40.
473 "Early Israel in Recent Biblical Scholarship," 203.

process of infiltration, fighting (including infighting), and transformation and realignment." The book of Joshua has thus telescoped decades of fighting "into a simplified, selective, focused glimpse."[474]

Albrecht Alt and Martin Noth analyzed the patterns of commerce and settlement in Palestine during the second millennium. They concluded that "Israelite occupation did not ensue from a warlike encounter between the newcomers and the previous owners of the land."[475] Instead, over a period of years Israelite tribes settled areas in the hill country previously not occupied by the Canaanites. The narratives of Joshua represent only the traditions of one tribe—Benjamin. "In time . . . the specific and historically accurate memories of the occupation of the land by the important central Palestinian tribes were imposed on all the tribes of Israel."[476]

Even the most conservative writers temper their discussions when they come to the historical problem of the conquest. John Bimson wants to follow the broad outline of the Old Testament but admits that all of the settling Israelites were not necessarily involved in the conquest of every area, Judg 1 being a truer picture than the Joshua narratives.[477] Marten Woudstra says that the purpose of the story does not depend on a solution to chronological or compositional matters. While maintaining historical accuracy, he recognizes that biblical narrative performs a function "beyond that of the chronological recording of history," i.e., it teaches.[478] He leaves open the possibilities of both oral tradition[479] and later redaction[480] without ever drawing consequences from such statements, though he does say, "one cannot always reconstruct the exact course of events from the biblical record."[481]

Recent sociological study has produced a new approach. C. H. J. de Geus and particularly George Mendenhall and Norman Gottwald propose an entirely different model of Israel, namely that of a peasant's revolt against a repressive city-state governing system. Gottwald thus speaks of "revolutionary Israel: a Canaanite coalition."[482] Using his usual technical jargon, Gottwald concludes: "Consequently, Israel is most appropriately conceived as an eclectic composite in which various underclass and outlaw elements of society joined their diffused antifeudal experiences, sentiments, and interests, thereby forming a single movement that, through trial and error, became an effective autonomous social system. . . . Israel's vehement and tenacious identity as one people under one God has its indisputable axis around an antifeudal egalitarian social commitment."[483]

Each of the views sketched above—peaceful settlement, wars of conquest, and peasant rebellion—is gradually being weighed in ongoing research. As of yet, none has totally achieved "scholarly consensus." Israel Finkelstein believes all modern scholars will reject all theories about the rise of Israel, including the Albright school, the Alt school, and Mendenhall and Gottwald.[484] Sheep and pas-

---

474 Hubbard, 40.
475 Noth, *History of Israel*, 68.
476 Ibid., 75.
477 *Redating*, 30–32.
478 Woudstra, 146–47.
479 Ibid., 159.
480 Ibid., 195.
481 Ibid.
482 *Tribes of Yahweh*, 491.
483 Ibid.
484 Findelstein and Mazar, *Quest for the Historical Israel*, 74–75.

toral nomadism represent an offshoot of sedentary life, not a source for newcomers from the steppe. Archaeology cannot find a shift from the sedentary lowlands to the sedentary highlands. The lowland cities did not have enough people to supply the new highland population. The conquest cannot be seen as a unique event in Palestine history. Indeed, "the rise of early Israel . . . was another repeated phase in long-term, cyclic socio-economic, and demographic processes that started in the fourth millennium B.C.E."[485] Technological advances such as terraced farming, collar-rimmed jars, plastered cisterns, and four-room houses are found earlier than Israel and beyond Israel.

Finkelstein maintains that there is no way to distinguish Canaanite and Israelite culture.[486] He finds the basic significant archaeological fact to rest in the absence of pig bones in the Iron Age I hill country sites.[487] Economic breakdown meant a lack of excess grain for pastoralists to buy, so they had to settle down and raise their own. This means that Israelites were in fact Canaanites.[488]

Amihai Mazar points to greater simplicity in hill-country pottery, creating an assemblage that "as a whole differs widely from both that of the contemporary Canaanite/Philistine culture of the coastal plain and that of the Jezreel Valley."[489] Mazar concludes, "the settlers in the hill county lacked their own pottery-making tradition and initially obtained the most necessary pottery vessels from their Canaanite neighbors." Even Finkelstein's pig-bone evidence does not say much, since "very few pig bones have been found in any of the major Canaanite sites of the lowlands."[490] Mazar contends that "it is therefore questionable that the settlements in the central hill country, the Galilee, the Negev, and the Transjordan should be attributed to a single 'ethnic' entity." On the other hand, "the biblical traditions concerning Transjordan including the emergence of Edom and Moab and the Israelite settlement in Gilead and the valley of Succoth were not completely fictitious, and were partially rooted in actual memories of the past."[491]

Having said this, Mazar still believes that the socio-economic status of the settlers and the historical-geographic data point to these settlers as early Israelites.[492] "The Israelites emerged from unsettled, Late Bronze population groups known from written sources, such as the Shasu attested in Egyptian sources. . . . Nothing in the archaeological findings points to the foreign origin of the hill country settlers."[493] The settlement process stretched over the thirteenth to the eleventh century BCE. For Mazar even religion cannot be isolated as the unifying factor for all the settlers since "this religion was far from being formalized during the Iron I."[494]

Mazar attempts to combine all three theories of settlement.[495] Various clans and groups had to look for new modes of subsistence in the mountains. Some may

---

485 Ibid., 76.
486 Ibid., 77.
487 Ibid., 79.
488 Ibid., 82–83.
489 Ibid., 89.
490 Ibid., 93.
491 Ibid., 98.
492 Ibid., 92.
493 Ibid., 94.
494 Ibid., 91.
495 Ibid., 95–98.

have been local pastoralists; others, Transjordan pastoralists. Some may have been immigrants from Syria or further north; and some, displaced Canaanites. Archaeology, however, still cannot provide an answer to the question of the origin of the Yahwistic religion of early Israel.

Noort maintains that the answers to Israel's settlement and conquest problems are not easy yea or nay answers.[496] Rather "both/and" is closer to reality and reaches over a diachronic period rather than reflecting a simple single moment in history. Both situations of breaks in culture and living conditions and situations of continuity in living patterns appear in the evidence.

Further study must bear in mind basic understandings. The biblical tradition was not a simple invention. The experience of the conquest of the land under divine leadership pervades Israel's entire tradition and must be accounted for by any who posit a theory of Israelite origins. As Noort points out,[497] the Canaanite revolution theory is impossible to prove. An inner Canaanite development seems to have certainly played an important role, based on the visible continuity in the material culture. But against the hypothesis stands the literary tradition in all its parts that states that Israel is not originally at home in the land. And there is no sufficient reason to view this tradition as complete fiction.

The role of Joshua as the lieutenant of Moses and the human agent in Israel's gaining possession of the land is equally pervasive and cannot be ignored. The *El* component of Israel's name and of the ancestral divine titles point to a complex prehistory of the people Israel prior to their conquest of and settlement in the land. The name of the judge Jerubbaal and the sanctuary of El-berith at Shechem point to a continuing complexity, as does the unique tribal listing in Judg 5. Archaeological data cannot be formed into a simplified picture and must be understood as both concrete data and human interpretation of that data. Thus we must continue to investigate the literary nature and the "traditional" nature of the Joshua narratives, as the commentary will seek to do. Such study will reveal a complexity at this level, as well as at the others. Simplified chronological and reportorial conclusions are ruled out for the present state of research, if we follow the rules of the "objective historian" in reaching conclusions. Our theological presuppositions may incline us to go beyond such rules to a statement of faith concerning the historical situation. If this is the case, we must be consciously aware of the nature of the statements we are making.

More important is that we be consciously aware of the nature of the book of Joshua. It is not only a book based on the historical traditions of Israel, but also a book based on the use of those traditions in everyday life, worship, scholarly study, and meditation through many generations Israelites. Hawk emphasizes, "The 'ideal' Israel, marked at the corporate level by unity, victory, and obedience conflicts with a narrated reality, at the individual level, which tells of disobedience, defeat, and diversity."[498] Still, one must contend that the final picture in Joshua is an obedient people blessed by a faithful God. As such, the book represents the mature reflection of the people of Israel upon their own identity. It contains God's revelation to Israel of who they had been, who they were supposed to be, and who they could become.

---

496 *Das Buch Josua*, 12.
497 Ibid., 10.
498 Hawk, (2000) 22.

Israel was one people, formed by one covenant, under one God, destined to live in and control one land. Israel was also a people who still had much to do because they had, even in their best days, refused to follow God completely and carry out his instructions, preferring to argue and feud among themselves and to follow the paths of the gods of the land along with the God of the exodus and conquest. Thus Israel had to look forward to a new Joshua, who would bring the people to follow God all his days and to confess once and for all that this God fulfilled all his promises to his people.

III. Joshua and the Meaning of the Material

Bibliography

Briend, J. "Histoire, historicisme et révélation." *RICP* 24 (1987) 13–23. **Butler, T. C.** "The Theology of Joshua." *RevExp* 95 (1998) 203–25. ———. *Understanding the Basic Themes of Joshua*. Dallas: Word, 1991. **Elßner, T. R.** *Josua und seine Kriege in jüdischer und christilicher Rezeptionsgeschichte*. Theologie und Frieden 37. Stuttgart: Kohlhammer, 2008. **Freitheim, T. E.** "Repentance in the Former Prophets." In *Repentance in Christian Theology*. Collegeville, MN: Liturgical, 2006. 25–45. **Gottwald, N. K.,** ed. *The Bible and Liberation: Political and Social Hermeneutics*. New York: Orbis, 1983. **Green, W. S.** "The Legal Traditions of Joshua and Related Materials." Diss., Brown University, 1974. **Hawk, L. D.** "The God of the Conquest: The Theological Problem of the Book of Joshua." *TBT* 46 (2008) 141–47. **Himpel, F.** "Selbstständigkeit, Einheit, und Glaubwürdigkeit des Buches Josua." *TQ* 464 (1864) 385–444. **House, P. R.** "The God Who Gives Rest in the Land: Joshua." *SBJT* 2/3 (1998) 12–33. **Hubbard, R. L.** "'What do these stones mean?': Biblical Theology and a Motif in Joshua." *BBR* 11 (2001) 1–26. **Ibáñez Arana, A.** "Sugerencias para una lectura cristiana del libro de Josuè." *Lumen* 29 (1980) 385–411. **Kaiser, W. C., Jr.** "The Promised Land: A Biblical-Historical View." *BSac* 138 (1981) 302–13. ———. "The Promise Theme and the Theology of Rest." *BSac* 130 (1973) 135–50. **Knauf, E. A.** "Bundesschlüsse in Josua." In *Les dernières rédactions du Pentateuque, de l'Hexateuque, et de l'Ennéateuque*. BETL 203. Leuven: Leuven UP; Peeters, 2007. 217–24. **Ngan, L. L. E.** "A Teaching Outline for the Book of Joshua." *RevExp* 95 (1998) 161–70. **Noort, E.** "Joshua: The History of Reception and Hermeneutics." In *Past, Present, Future: The Deuteronomistic History and the Prophets*. Ed. J. C. de Moor and H. F. van Roy. Leiden: Brill, 2000. 199–215. ———. "The Traditions of Ebal and Gerizim: Theological Positions in the Book of Joshua." In *Deuteronomy and Deuteronomic Literature*. Ed. M. Vervenne and J. Lust. Leuven: Leuven UP; Peeters, 1997. 161–80. **Rowlett, L. L.** "Inclusion, Exclusion, and Marginality in the Book of Joshua." *JSOT* 55 (1992) 15–23. **Taylor, L. M.** "Theological Themes in the Book of Joshua." *SwJT* 41,1 (1998) 70–85. **Wenham, G. J.** "The Deuteronomic Theology of the Book of Joshua." *JBL* 90 (1971) 140–48.

Noort states: "By the theological evaluation of the Old Testament, the book of Joshua most often ends up in the position of the villain or scoundrel [*Bösewicht*]."[499] The book occupies a key position in the Hebrew Bible. It marks the transition from

---

499 *Das Buch Josua*, 4 (my translation).

Torah to Prophecy. The earliest Greek translation changes this transition to one from Law to History. Either way, Joshua introduces a new kind of literature.

Historically, the book of Joshua marks the transition in the leadership of Israel from Moses to Joshua and the functional transition from wilderness wandering as punishment to land conquest as reward and fulfillment. Thematically, the book brings the transition from the experience of covenant curse to the experience of covenant obedience and renewal.

A book that addresses such important transitions and that raises such controversial issues demands the attention of God's people, particularly a people who claim the Bible as the authoritative ground of all teaching and living. House summarizes Joshua's theology as "the conquest and division grounds Israel's theology in historical reality. . . . War is real, Canaanites are real, and cities are real. Israel's theology does not occur in mythological realms, but in life and death struggles, in mundane affairs, in the real events of history." In other words, "theologically interpreted events should create the impetus for the nation's future."[500]

The text has always claimed in one way or another to be the word of God, a word that comes through the interaction of God and the inspired writer with the historical, cultural, and theological situation of a particular audience. God has been instrumental in all the stages of creating and preserving the Joshua traditions for his people to read and follow through the ages. The oral stage created the basic structure of the individual materials and offered entertainment, inspiration, education, and worship for God's people. The compilation stage gave unity and theological coherence to the individual narratives. At this stage or at a further editorial stage, the material was set in written form. Eventually, the author of the book of Judges used the Joshua material as a backdrop for the intermediate stage between conquest and monarchy, showing Judges dislodging virtually all that Joshua had established territorially and religiously. An ultimate historian incorporated the Joshua/Judges material into the larger history of God's people, creating either a written collection of Genesis through Joshua, one of Genesis through Judges, or one comprising Genesis through Kings. Finally, collections of other types of literature—psalms, wisdom, poetry, prophecy—were joined into the text we now call the Hebrew Bible.

The oral stage of the traditions centers on certain life-and-death questions for God's people as they seek to settle in the land and establish their grip on its territory. These traditions illustrate the weakness of the enemy kings (Josh 2); the miraculous power of Israel's God (chaps. 3–4, 6, 10, 11); the inability even of clever enemy kings to outsmart Israel (chap. 9); and the demand for obedience from Israel itself (chaps. 5, 7–8). Political tensions lie behind the surface of these narratives, particularly chaps. 7, 9, and 10.

Cultic celebration transforms the materials. Now they illustrate the mighty acts of God as he continues the work he began at the exodus (Josh 4:23–24). The role of the priests is underscored; Gilgal assumes center stage; and motifs of polemic and ridicule are sublimated to the praise and adoration of the great acts of Yahweh for his people.

The first literary work is that of the compiler, who continues the process of

---

500 *SBJT* 2/3 (1998) 27.

centering the materials on Gilgal (Josh 5:9; 9:6; 10:7, 9, 15, 43; cf. 14:6). He ties all the materials together explicitly into a continuous narrative emphasizing the conquest of the land. To do so, he uses the theme of pursuit. But past conquest is not his major emphasis. He brings this up to date, showing its present relevance through the use of etiological notations (Josh 4:9; 5:9, 12; 6:25; 7:26; 8:28; 9:27). Israel not only conquered the land, but also gained control over the land that had results and effects still visible in the compiler's day, so that no one could dispute Israel's claim to it.

For the compiler, however, conquest and control were not the only themes. The book of Joshua demonstrates conquest and control by a committed leader and his committed people. Thus the role of Joshua is emphasized with his obedience (Josh 4:9; 5:7; 6:25, 27; 8:1, 27, 28; 9:3, 22–27; 10:1, 14, 26, 41–42; 11:9, 16). Over against this stands the disobedience of the people (Josh 7:1; 9:16–21). We do not know the name of the compiler chosen by God to collect and edit the traditions of his people. We do know that the center of his life was the house of God with its altar (Josh 6:24; 9:23, 27). The location of this house is likewise unknown. In the present context, it appears to be at Gilgal, but it could have been Bethel (Josh 7:2; 8:9, 12, 17) or less probably Gibeon, the center of the climactic battle (chaps. 9–10). It may well have already been Jerusalem. Here, we see that in the process of divine inspiration, the human agent and geographical location are not of primary importance. Above all stands the message God has for his people. That message is summarized in the theological formula of transference: "The LORD has given you the land" (Josh 2:9, 14, 24; 6:2, 16; 8:1, 7; 10:8, 12, 19, 30, 32; 11:6, 8). Both sides of the formula are important for the compiler. Speaking to Israel, he underlines the identity of the giver of the land. Yahweh, not one of the gods of the land, gave the land to Israel. Thus Israel's only allegiance is to Yahweh, the God of Israel. Over against political enemies, the compiler says the land belongs to Israel, having been given to her by Yahweh through the acts of Joshua.

Hebron, the center of David's activities (1 Sam 26:31; 2 Sam 2:1–3), is where Gilgal and the south are brought into confrontation in Joshua (cf. Josh 14:6). David's kingship was troubled by revolt centering again in Hebron (2 Sam 15:7–12). Opposition from Saul and the north had not vanished either (2 Sam 16:5–14; 20:1–22). The great division of the kingdom at Solomon's death brought renewed crisis to the land claims of Israel, with Benjamin the dividing point (1 Kgs 12). At this period Egypt once again threatened Judah (1 Kgs 14:25–27).

Thus the early years of the monarchy in Israel were a time of crisis in which tribes and then kingdoms fought over the land that Yahweh had given Israel. It may well be that early in this era, a Benjaminite compiler sought to set forth the claims of Benjamin over against the Judean monarchy of David. The division of the monarchy thus saw Benjamin joined to the south, so that the southern kingdom could now use the Benjaminite traditions as its base of land claim against the north. Such inner rivalry was not the ultimate meaning of these traditions. God simply used the processes of humanity to maintain the traditions of the people for the use to which God had intended them. Thus the ultimate editor took over the Jerusalem traditions and gave them their canonical interpretation. Here again, God used anonymous scribes to teach his people the divine word.

In such a light, the book of Joshua continues to speak to the people of God with its call for leadership, obedience to the divine will, and loyalty to the God of all the earth who fulfills all his promises. As the people in exile, the people of God today remain waiting for the promises to be fulfilled. We, too, await the day of rest. As we wait, we are given the same program as Joshua, the program of studying the Word of God to search out its depths and embody them in our lives.

The book of Joshua quickly reveals vital issues plaguing the people of God when they first received the book of Joshua. These can be quickly listed and then addressed. The most biting issue is the basic theological one: What kind of God is this? Can we trust him or not?

Other questions raised by God's people and addressed by God in the book of Joshua include: What land belongs to us? Are we assured of possession of this land forever? What leader can we trust? What is the relationship of our written tradition, our cultic worship, and God's promises? What defines membership in the people of Yahweh?

A. An Enigmatic God: Can We Trust Him?

Bibliography

Dietrich, W., and C. Link. *Die dunklen Seiten Gottes: Willkür und Gewalt.* Neukirchen-Vluyn: Neukirchener Verlag, 1995. **Hess, R. S.** "The Divine Name Yahweh in Late Bronze Age Sources?" *UF* 23 (1991) 181–88. **Kennedy, J. M.** "The Social Background of Early Israel's Rejection of Cultic Images: A Proposal." *BTB* 17 (1987) 138–44. **Moor, J. C. de.** *The Rise of Yahwism: The Roots of Israelite Monotheism.* BETL 91. Leuven: Leuven UP; Peeters, 1990. **Sipiliä, S.** "On the Concept of God in the Masoretic Text of Joshua." In *Houses Full of All Good Things: Essays in Memory of Timo Veijola.* Ed. J. Pakkala and M. Nissinen. Publications of the Finnish Exegetical Society 93. Helsinki: Finnish Exegetical Society; Göttingen: Vandenhoeck & Ruprecht, 2008. 95–114, 477–87.

The book of Joshua pulls no punches in its description of God. It preserves the people's traditional view of God:

[Yahweh] is the one who brought us up and our fathers from the land of Egypt, from the house of service, and who did before our eyes these great signs. He protected us in all the way in which we went and among all the peoples through whose midst we passed. Yahweh drove out all the peoples, indeed the Amorite living in the land, from before us. (Josh 24:17–18)

The book of Joshua immediately counters this with what is the Bible's strongest statement about the deity whom Israel served:

A holy God is he, a jealous deity is he, one who will not forgive your sins and transgressions. If you should forsake Yahweh and serve strange, foreign gods, he will turn and do evil to you (pl.). He will finish you (pl.) off after having been so good to you (pl.). (Josh 24:19–20)

Joshua proclaims a similar two-sided view of God in chap. 23:

You know with all your hearts and with all your being that not one word has fallen from all the good words that Yahweh, your God, spoke concerning you. They all have come to pass. . . . And it will be the case that just as every good word that Yahweh, your God, spoke to you has come on you, just so Yahweh will bring on you every evil word until he has destroyed you from upon this good land which Yahweh, your God, has given to you. (Josh 23:14–15)

The people of God face a quandary as they relate to this God. What kind of God is partial to one people over another? Commands the killing of entire races of people? Approves the killing of women and children to achieve his purposes? Fulfills promises of long ago only to threaten to take back the promised gifts in the future? Is so zealous and jealous and holy that he will not forgive sins? But will consume a people after he has done good to them?

Can they really trust him? Or is he as capricious as the gods of their neighbors? When can they expect the loving, giving, promise-fulfilling God to show up, and when must they expect the jealous, holy, unforgiving, destroyer to appear?

The book of Joshua addresses this issue of the complexity of the divine nature with some basic assumptions that it expects its audience to share, serving simply as a review or reminder of what Torah has already taught about God. The readers know their God is named Yahweh. He chose Moses to lead his people out of Egypt and then chose Joshua to take over the leadership duties from Moses. He initiated a covenant relationship with his people, a relationship he expects them to renew periodically. He chose the ancestors from beyond the river Euphrates where they served other gods. He has a history of punishing disobedient people. He has given Israel a book of Torah, or teaching, that he expects them to obey. He gave Israel promises of land and nationhood and victory over enemies. He has claimed Israel for himself with the expectation that they will never in any way countenance worship of or service to any other claimant to deity. He alone is Israel's God.

Israel's enemies often echo the same assumptions:

[Rahab] said to the men, "I know that Yahweh has given to you the land and that the dread of you has fallen upon us and that all the inhabitants of the land have melted away before you, for we have heard that Yahweh dried up the waters of the Reed Sea before you when you came out of Egypt and what you did to the two kings of the Amorites who were beyond the Jordan, to Sihon and to Og, whom you committed to the ban. When we heard, our hearts melted. Spirit remains in no one because of you, for Yahweh your God it is who is God in heaven above and on the earth below." (Josh 2:9–11)

Similarly, the Hivites of Gibeon explain:

From an extremely distant land your servants have come due to the name of Yahweh your God, for we have heard his reputation and all that he had done in Egypt, and all that he did to the two kings of the Amorites who were beyond the Jordan, that is, to Sihon, king of Heshbon, and to Og, king of Bashan, which is in Ashtaroth. (Josh 9:9–10)

When their trickery is discovered, the Gibeonites state:

Since it was clearly reported to your servants that Yahweh your God had commanded Moses, his servant, to give you the whole land and to destroy all the inhabitants of the land from your presence, we feared greatly for our lives before you so that we have done this thing. (Josh 9:24)

The book of Joshua explores quiet assumptions about God shared by author, readers, and enemies. God has all the characteristics of a human being—wrath, jealousy, determination to punish as well as love, self-giving, grace, mercy, and kindness. God communicates with his people. He tells the leader exactly what is expected, and the leader passes the word down through the official chain of command until the people act upon it as illustrated in chaps. 1 and 3.

God gives gifts to his people, specifically the gift of the land. He does this by giving battle instructions to his people and then fighting for them as illustrated in chaps. 6 and 10. God outlines specific teachings and instructions he expects the people to follow if they do not want to face his judgment as illustrated in chaps. 7 and 11. God's great reputation goes before him and frightens the enemies into submission as illustrated in chaps. 2 and 9. God removes all fear from his people as illustrated in chaps. 10 and 11. God has a definite plan for his people so he divides the land he gives into specific portions for each tribe (chaps. 13–19). He calls on the tribes to act as a united front to help one another in land-taking endeavors and in worship as illustrated in chaps. 1 and 22. God fulfills every promise he has ever made (Josh 11:23; 21:45; 23:14).

The climactic chapters of Joshua turn from basic historical narrative to cultic speech, a new kind of speech about God. The positive acts for Israel in history are combined with strong demands on a people not expected to live up to those demands. God takes his own holy nature seriously. Worship of other gods never goes unnoticed. It cannot expect to be forgiven.

Disobedience to God brings the promise of divine punishment. God will fulfill his threats just as he did his promises so that the gift of the land will vanish (23:15–16). This shows a new side of Yahweh, a side that is zealous to protect his name and jealous of worship other gods might receive, and a side that is holy; God cannot abide among a people plagued by sin (Josh 24:19).

Joshua thus gives a balanced picture of God. Israel cannot choose one side of this God without embracing the other. And Israel must choose! Joshua forces the issue (Josh 24:14–15) and then reinforces the choice even more harshly, claiming the people cannot serve the God he has called them to choose to serve. Should they be able to serve him, their God would stand on equal footing with the gods of the enemies. They would know the secrets that secure fertility and blessing. They could meet the god's standards and extract promises even from the capricious nature gods of Canaan.

Yahweh was a different kind of God. He would be no part of a pantheon of gods, not even the king of the gods. He was the only God for Israel. The people must choose to serve him even knowing they would never meet his standards. Still, they had no other viable choice, for no other god had done for them what Yahweh, the God of Israel, had done. Thus they witnessed against themselves and renewed their covenant to obey the God they could not serve because they could not meet his holy covenant standards.

So Israel asked, can we trust this God? They answered, yes, we can trust this God to be who he has always been and who he says he is and always will be. We cannot create this God in our image and serve him according to our standards or according to the traditions of this new country. We can only serve him according to his covenant standards and trust him to be our God as we are God's people.

B. Studies in Land and Rest

Bibliography

Auld, A. G. *Joshua, Moses and the Land.* Edinburg: T&T Clark, 1980. **Benjamin, P.** "The Theology of the Land in the Book of Joshua." Diss., University of Chicago, 1986. **Berg, W.** "Israel's Land, der Garten Gottes: Der Garten als Bild des Heiles im Alten Testament." *BZ* 32 (1988) 35–51. **Boorer, S.** *The Promise of the Land as Oath: A Key to the Formation of the Pentateuch.* BZAW 205. Berlin: De Gruyter, 1992. **Braulich, G.** "Manuach—Die Ruhe Gottes und des Volkes im Lande." *BK* 23 (1968) 75–78. **Brueggemann, W.** "Land: Fertility and Justice." In *Theology of the Land.* Ed. B. Evans and G. Cusack. Collegeville, MN: Liturgical, 1987. 41–68. ———. *The Land: Place as Gift, Promise and Challenge in Biblical Faith.* OBT 1. Philadelphia: Fortress, 1977. ———. "On Land-Losing and Land-Receiving." *Crux* 19 (1980) 166–73. **Davies, E. W.** "Land, Its Rights and Privileges." In *The World of Ancient Israel: Sociological, Anthropological and Political Perspectives.* Ed. R. E. Clements. Cambridge: Cambridge UP, 1989. 349–69. **Diepold, P.** *Israels Land.* BWANT 95. Stuttgart: Kohlhammer, 1972. **Dietrich, W.** "Der heilige Ort im Leben und Glauben Altisraels." In *The Land of Israel in Bible, History, and Theology: Studies in Honour of Ed Noort.* Ed. J. van Ruiten and J. C. de Vos. VTSup 124. Leiden: Brill, 2009. 219–35. **Fanuli, C.** "Terra di Canaan, dono di Jahvé." *PaVi* 18 (1973) 150–54. **Goldingay, J.** *Old Testament Theology.* Vol. 1, *Israel's Gospel.* Downers Grove, IL: InterVarsity Press, 2003. 512–28. **Habel, N.** *The Land Is Mine: Six Biblical Land Ideologies.* OBT. Minneapolis: Fortress, 1995. **House, P. R.** "The God Who Gives Rest in the Land: Joshua." *SBJT* 2 (1998) 12–33. **Jensen, I. L.** *Josué, la tierra de reposo conquistada.* Barcelona: Portavoz Evangélico, 1980. **Johnston, P., and P. Walker,** eds. *The Land of Promise: Biblical, Theological, and Contemporary Perspectives.* Downers Grove, IL: InterVarsity Press, 2000. **Kaiser, W. C., Jr.** "The Promise Theme and the Theology of Rest." *BSac* 130 (1973) 135–50. **Landousies, J.** "Le don de la terre de Palestine." *NRTh* 98 (1976) 324–36. **Levin, Y.** "The Inheritance of the Land according to Joshua, Judges, Samuel, and Kings." Paper read to SBL Deuteronomistic History Section, Atlanta, November 22, 2010. **Macholz, G. C.** "Israel und das Land: Vorarbeiten zu einem Vergleich zwischen Priesterschrift und deuteronomistischen Geschichtswerk." Diss., Heidelberg, 1969. **Miller, P. D.** "The Gift of God: The Deuteronomic Theology of the Land." *Int* 23 (1969) 451–65. **Nel, P.** "Land as Religious Epicentre: The Deuteronomist's Ideology of Inheritance (*nahalah*)." Paper read to Israelite Religion group of Society of Biblical Literature, Edinburgh, 2006. **Noort, E.** *Old Testament Essays.* Pretoria, 1998. **Ohler, A.** *Israel, Volk und Land: Zur Geschichte der wechselseitigen Beziehungen zwischen Israel und seinem Land in alttestamentlicher Zeit.* Stuttgart: Katholisches Bibelwerk, 1979. ———. "Landbesitz—Teilhabe am Gotteserbe." *BK* 36 (1981) 201–6. **Orlinsky, H. M.** "The Biblical Concept of the Land of Israel: Cornerstone of the Covenant between God and Israel." *ErIsr* 18 (1985) 43–55. **Perlitt, L.** "Motive und Schichten der Land theologie im Deuteronomian." In *Das Land Israel in biblischer Zeit: Jerusalem Symposium 1981.* Ed. G. Strecker. GTA 225. Göttingen: Vandenhoeck & Ruprecht, 1983. 46–58. **Rad, G. von.** "Es ist noch eine Ruhe vorhanden dem Volke Gottes" (Eine biblische Begriffsuntersuchung). *ZdZ* 11 (1933) 104–11. Translated as "There Remains Still a Rest for the People of God: An Investigation of a Biblical Conception," in *The Problem of the Hexateuch and Other Essays,* trans E. W. Trueman Dicken. Edinburgh: Oliver & Boyd, 1965. 94–102. ———. "The Promised Land and Yahweh's Land in the Hexateuch." In *The Problem of the Hexateuch and Other Essays.* Trans E. W. Trueman Dicken. Edinburgh: Oliver & Boyd, 1965. 79–93. **Rendtorff, R.** *Israel und sein Land: Theologische Überlegungen zu einem politischen Problem.* TEH NF 188. Munich: Kaiser, 1975. ———. "Das Land Israel im Wandel der alttestamentlichen Geschichte." In *Jüdisches Volk—gelobtes Land: Die biblischen Landverheissung als Problem des jüdischen Selbstverständnisses und die christlichen Theologie.* Ed. W. P. Eckert and N. P. Levinson. Munich: Kaiser, 1970. 153–68. **Robinson, G.** "The Idea of Rest in the OT and the Search for the Basic Character of the Sabbath." *ZAW* 92 (1980) 32–42. **Roshwald, M.** "The Idea of the Promised Land." *Diog* 21.82 (1973) 45–69. **Rost, L.** "Die Bezeichnungen für Land und Volk im Alten Testaments." In *Festschrift Otto Procksch*. Leipzig: Deichert, 1934. 125–48. **Ruiten, J. van, and J. C. de Vos,** eds. *The History of Israel in Bible, History, and Theology: Studies in Honour of Ed Noort*. VTSup 124. Leiden: Brill, 2009. **Scharbert, J.** "The Landverheissung an die Väter als einfache Zusage, als Eid, und als 'Bund.'" In *Konsequente Traditionsgeschichte*. Göttingen: Vandenhoeck & Ruprecht, 1993. **Schwertner, S.** "'Das Verheißene Land': Bedeutung und Verständnis des Landes nach den frühen Zeugnissen des Alten Testaments." Diss., Heidelberg, 1966. **Seebaß, H.** "'Holy' Land in the Old Testament: Numbers and Joshua." *VT* 56 (2006) 92–104. **Smend, R.** "Das uneroberte Land." In *Das Land Israel in biblischer Zeit: Jerusalem-Symposium 1981*. Ed. G. Strecker. GTA 25. Göttingen: Vandenhoeck & Ruprecht, 1983. 91–102. **Timmer, D. C.** "Rest in Joshua: What Is It, and How does It Fit into Biblical Theology." Paper Read to Biblical Theology Section of the Evangelical Theological Society, Atlanta, November 17, 2010. **Townsend, J. L.** "Fulfillment of the Land Promise in the Old Testament." *BSac* 142 (1985) 320–37. **Waldow, H. E. von.** "Israel and Her Land: Some Theological Considerations." In *A Light unto My Path: Festschrift for J. M. Myers*. Ed. H. N. Bream et al. Philadelphia: Fortress, 1974. 493–508. **Weinfeld, M.** "Inheritance of the Land—Privilege versus Obligation: The Concept of 'The Promise of the Land.'" In *The Sources of the First and Second Temple Periods. Zion* 49 (1984) 115–37 (Heb.). ———. *The Promise of the Land: The Inheritance of the Land of Canaan by the Israelites*. The Taubman Lectures in Jewish Studies 3. Berkeley: University of California Press, 1993. **Westbrook, R.** *Property and the Family in Biblical Law*. JSOTSup 113. Sheffield: JOST Press, 1991. **Wildberger, H.** "Israel und sein Land." *EvT* 16 (1956) 404–22. **Wright, C. J. H.** *God's People in God's Land: Family, Land and Property in the Old Testament*. Grand Rapids: Eerdmans, 1990. ———. *Old Testament Ethics for the People of God*. Downers Grove, IL: InterVarsity Press, 2004. 76–99.

Knauf emphasizes Joshua as the book of the land and the land as God's gift to Israel.[501] This leads him to determine what territory is included in God's gift. Knauf finds five or six biblical definitions or descriptions of the land:

1. The entire Grand Israel (*Ganz-Groß Israel*) from the Euphrates to the Nile (Gen 15:18; 1 Kgs 5:4)
2. Grand Israel (*Groß Israel*) (Num 34:1–12) or Land of Israel = Canaan as Egyptian province stretching from the southern Negev to and including southern Syria with Jordan as western boundary, a reality only in the seventh century
3. The twelve tribes of Israel or Israel from Dan to Beersheba (Josh 13/15–19/21)
4. Judea-Israel (Gen 13:14–17) or the Persian province of Judea without Hebron, the Negev, Samaria, and Galilee, which equals the basic layer (*Grundschicht*) of Josh 10:40–42
5. Judea + Samaria = Israel (Josh 15:21–18:1; cf. Gen 28:13–14; 48:4)

Corresponding somewhat to these definitions of the land, Habel isolates six ideologies related to land: the royal, the agrarian, the theocratic, the prophetic, the ancestral household, and the immigrant. For Habel, Joshua illustrates the ancestral household, that is, land claimed by a family tradition as far back as one can tell.

A nation finds identity through many characteristics and traditions in its history. A major identifying characteristic lies in its geography. Possessing land is an essential part of nationhood. Land gives physical reality to a nation. It locates the nation, gives room for homes and government, and determines the occupations

---

501 Knauf, 9–13.

and lifestyles of the people. Land is the identifying physical characteristic that most clearly separates one nation from another as well as the characteristic that tempts one nation to obliterate and replace another.

The book of Joshua's structure suggests that the land has been conquered (Josh 1–12) even though Israel has not been totally obedient (chaps. 7, 9). The land has also been divided among the people (chaps. 13–21). More specifically, the land: (1) was promised to the fathers (1:6; 21:43; cf. 1:3); (2) was given by God (1:2, 3, 11, 13, 15; 9:24; 22:4; 24:11, 13); (3) was to be divided by Joshua as an inheritance for the people (1:6; 13:6–7); (4) actually was divided as an inheritance for the people (11:23; 14:5; 19:51; 21:43; 23:4); (5) was closely connected to the land east of the Jordan (1:12–18; 12:1–6; 13:8–33; 20:8; 21:6–7; 22:1–9, 10–34; 24:8–10); (6) was not difficult to take militarily because God had caused the inhabitants to tremble with fear (2:9, 11; 5:1; 9:9b–10, 24); (7) and was filled with other gods who tempted Israel (23:7, 12, 16; 24:15, 20, 23) because Israel had not possessed all the land or defeated all the peoples (13:1–6; 13:13; 15:63; 16:10; 17:12–13, 18; 19:47; 23:4, 12–13). But the promise remained that God would give this land to Israel (13:6; 23:5; cf. 17:18), but only if the people obeyed (5:5–6; 7:7–9; 23:13, 15, 16; 24:20).

For Israel, land had become a central hope rather than a living reality. As soon as Abraham in faith entered the land to which God directed him, it became the land of promise (Gen 12:7). It remained the land of promise for four hundred years. Only a burial ground marked Israel's foothold in the land (Gen 23). First, Jacob left and returned. Then Joseph's brothers sold him into Egypt. He summoned his family there to escape famine. Years later the pharaoh thrust Israel into slavery. Finally, God acted to bring freedom, but freedom led into the wilderness, not into the land of promise. Only with Joshua does Israel become a nation for the first time, for now Israel has land.

Yet Israel with land must still ask questions. What land belongs to us? Where are the boundaries? Are such boundaries permanent? What if we need more land? What if we cannot conquer part of the Promised Land? What if an enemy takes land away? Does loss of the land mean loss of the land-giver? Has the god of the land-taker become victor over and thus lord of the land-giving God? The book of Joshua reflects long and hard on the theme of land.

Most nations see land as a possession, something won in battle, or something inherited from the forebearers. Israel's forebearers explicitly claimed to be landless. Israel's armies had never been able to seize land by themselves. Land for Israel could never be rightfully claimed as possession. Land was always gift. God possessed the land, for he had created it. In grace God chose to give a particular land to the people Israel. This keynote of Joshua appears in its opening verses (1:2–3), imparting an interesting perspective on the gift of land. The gifting of the land is a present tense activity ("I am giving," v 2 with a Hebrew participle) and a past fact ("I have given," v 3 with a Hebrew perfect). What Israel under Joshua experienced as a gradual process, God claimed to be a one-time past event. The event encompassed not only the land that lay ahead of Joshua, but also the land that lay behind the two and a half tribes east of the Jordan (1:13–15).

Land as gift was at the same time land to be taken. Occupying nations did not want to give up the land. They knew and feared God's promises (see above). Still they strategized and connived to defend and retain their land. This meant land possessed by Israel was land "dispossessed" from other nations (see Num 13:30; 21:24, 32, 35; 33:53; Deut 2:12, 21–22, 24, 31; 4:47; 6:18). Dispossession was God's way of fulfilling promises to the ancestors (Gen 15:7; 22:17; 28:4; Josh 1:11). The gift of land was a call to battle, a call to dispossess the land. While Israel's soldiers fought, God did the dispossessing, the driving out of the enemy (Josh 3:10; cf. 8:7).

The gift of land was a gift to all Israel. The tribes in the east possessed land but had to help the tribes in the west in their fights to gain the land (1:14–15). Land was not fully given to any tribe until all tribes had exercised possession rights (22:4,9). All participated in the rituals and the battles until the gift of land was complete (21:43), even the priestly tribe of Levi, which received cities and grazing lands but no tribal territory (cf. Num 18:20; Deut 18:1–2; Josh 13:14, 33; 14:3–4; 18:7; 21:1–42). The gift of land was suited to the needs of each tribe, but this did not mean the wants of each tribe were fulfilled. Some tribes did not have all they wanted (17:14) and had to labor to gain more land (17:15–18).

Meanwhile, Israel knew that occupying the land was not automatic. Land promised could be land withheld. The experiences of the previous generation in the wilderness had proved that (5:6). Land promised was land promised to an obedient, faithful generation. It was part of covenant, and covenant included proclamation of God's gracious acts and of God's righteous expectations. Only a people willing to be a covenant people could become land people. The experience of presumption and greed proved that again at Ai (chap. 7). Thus Joshua had to pray:

Alas, O Lord Yahweh, why have you so certainly caused this people to pass over the Jordan to give us into the hand of the Amorites to bring about our destruction? If only we had been content to live beyond the Jordan! With your permission, my Lord! Oh, what can I say after Israel has turned its back before its enemies, so that the Canaanites and all the inhabitants of the land will hear and turn themselves about against us and cut our name off from the earth? Then what will you do for your great name? (Josh 7:7–9)

A disobedient nation was thus a nation accursed (7:12). The Israelites had threatened not only their existence in the land but also the glory of God's name on earth. Only an obedient covenant people could expect to receive the gift of the land. Each battle experience began with Yahweh's promise to give the enemy and their land into Israel's hand (Josh 6:2, 16; 8:7, 18; 10:8, 19; 11:6; cf. 11:8; 20:30, 32). When Israel obeyed, God fulfilled the promise, and Israel occupied the land. Now the gift of land could be located in time, space, and human activity. One problem existed, though; the gift was not complete. Much land remained to be claimed (13:1–6).

Even after Israel possessed it, the land remained a gift, not a gift to a nebulous entity called a nation, but a gift to tribes, to clans, to families, a gift to be perpetuated through the generations. Land too easily could become royal fief, royal estate doled out to favorite supporters. This was not to be in Israel. Throughout the generations, the land remained tribal land, clan land, family land, and not royal estate (note how King Ahab learned this lesson, 1 Kgs 21).

The land as gift was also the land as inheritance. God distributed his estate to his children. This was done not in the battle phase but in the distribution phase of the book of Joshua (chaps. 13–22). Moses declared the inheritance to the tribes east of the Jordan (13:8). The right to serve God and sacrifice to him constituted the Levites' inheritance (13:14, 33). Joshua meted out the individual inheritance of each of the other tribes (13:7), not by human will but by divine lot (14:1–2). The inheritance was distributed among each tribe and family, not each nation. This was true to such an extent that daughters also had inheritance rights when no sons existed to receive the inheritance (17:4–6). While not an ideal inheritance, it was concrete real estate whose boundaries could be surveyed and recorded (18:4). Inheritance was the ultimate goal of Joshua's actions, for his last act was to release each of the tribes, clans, and families to occupy and enjoy their inheritance (24:28).

Having occupied the land they inherited from God, Israel enjoyed God's ultimate gift: rest (Exod 33:14; Deut 3:20; 12:9–10; 25:19; Josh 1:13,15).[502] Rest (Heb. *nûaḥ*) included both spiritual and physical elements. It was the condition of the person delivered from trouble (Ps 116:7). It was a change of routine from daily labor (Exod 20:12; Deut 5:14). Rest did not come individually, but to the entire nation after all the tribes cooperated to gain the land for each and every one of the tribes (1:15). Rest meant God had fulfilled for the nation his promise to Abraham (21:44). Larry Taylor writes, "Rest is not a theoretical, spiritual state enjoyed by individuals; it is a 'state of the union' the nation enjoys. Rest is a lasting state measured in months and years (23:1)."[503] That meant rest could be limited; the time of rest could come to an end. It did for Israel when the people refused to listen to Joshua's warnings (chap. 23) and failed to keep their covenant with God (chap. 24). Rest then became something lost and regained over and over in the period of the judges.

The book of Joshua records that land as gift was a promise fulfilled (11:23; 21:43), but it also remained gift to be completely received, for much land remained to be occupied (13:1). Gift remains a goal, a goal for a people committed to the Torah of God (1:7–8) and to the covenant with God (chap. 24). Because of Joshua's advanced age and tribal failure to possess the land (13:13; 15:63; 16:10; 17:12–13; cf. 19:47), the gift remained a goal. Yahweh dispossessed nations and gave the land to a people who loved him (23:11). Israel could quickly transfer allegiance and ally themselves with the surrounding nations rather than with Yahweh and thereby no longer receive the land that remained as gift. As Israel wandered away from God, she would also wander away from land into exile (23:12–13).

The wandering away resulted in more than loss of the land. It resulted in loss of nationhood, self-reputation, and God's reputation. The miracle of the theology of Joshua and of the theology of the Old Testament is that God could remain the Creator God of the universe, sovereign over all nations, all peoples, and all land even when his people lost all claim to the land. God could prove his Godhood both by giving land and by taking it away. In this he exemplified his absolute sovereignty. He was bound to no nation, to no temple, and to no land.

C. Studies in Leadership in Joshua
Bibliography

Beek, M. "Joshua the Savior." In *Voices from Amsterdam.* Ed. M. Kessler. SBLSS. Atlanta: Scholars Press, 1994. 145–53. ———. "Josua und Retterideal." In *Near Eastern Studies in Honour of W. F. Albright.* Ed. H. Goedicke. Baltimore: Johns Hopkins Press, 1971. 35–42. **Bieberstein,**

---

502 See House, *SBJT* 2 (1998) 12.
503 *SwJT* 41 (1998) 49.

K. *Josua, Jordan, Jericho: Archäologie, Geschichte und Theologie der Landnahmeerzählungen Jos 1–6.* OBO 143. Göttingen: Vandenhoeck and Ruprecht, 1995. **Dus, J.** "Moses or Joshua? On the Problem of the Founder of Israelite Religion." *ArOr* 39 (1971) 16–45 = *RadRel* 2 (1975) 26–41. **Eißfeldt, O.** "Führer in der Zeit vom Auszug aus Ägypten bis zur Landnahme." In *Studia biblica et semitica.* FS T. C. Vriezen, ed. W. C. van Unnik and A. S. van der Woude. Wageningen: Veenman, 1966. 62–70. **McCarthy, D.** "The Theology of Leadership in Joshua 1–9. *Bib* 52 (1971) 165–75. **Meer, M. N. van der.** *Formation and Reformulation: The Redaction of the Book of Joshua in the Light of the Oldest Textual Witnesses.* VTSup 102. Leiden: Brill, 2004. **Nelson, R.** "Josiah in the Book of Joshua." *JBL* 100 (1981) 531–40. **Noort, E.** *Das Buch Josua: Forschungsgeschichte und Problemfelder.* EdF 292. Darmstadt: Wissenschaftliche Buchgesellschaft, 1998. **Porter, J. R.** "The Succession of Joshua." In *Proclamation and Presence: Old Testament Essays in Honour of Gwynne Henton Davies.* Ed. J. I. Durham and J. R. Porter. London: SCM Press, 1970. 102–32. **Rowlett, L.** "Inclusion, Exclusion and Marginality in the Book of Joshua." *JSOT* 55 (1992) 15–23. **Schäfer-Lichtenberger, C.** "'Joschua' und 'Elischa'—eine biblische Argumentation zur Begründung der Autorität und Legitimität des Nachfolgers." *ZAW* 101 (1989) 198–222. ———. "Joschua und Elischa—Idealtypen von Führerschaft in Israel." In *Wünschet Jerusalem Frieden: Collected Communications to the XIIth Congress of the International Organization for the Study of the Old Testament, Jerusalem 1986.* BEATAJ 13. Frankfurt am Main; New York: Lang, 1988. 273–82. ———. *Josua und Salomo: Eine Studie zu Autorität und Legitimität des Nachfolgers im Alten Testament.* VTSup 58. Leiden: Brill, 1995. **Schmid, H.** "Erwägungen zur Gestalt Josuas in Überlieferung und Geschichte." *Jud* 24 (1968) 44–57. **Shiryon, M.** "Joshua—The Underestimated Leader: The Use of Psychology in the Book of Joshua." *Journal of Psychology and Judaism* 19 (1995) 205–25.

In a real sense the books of Deuteronomy through Kings wrestle with one major problem for Israel: who has the right to lead Israel? Is it God alone (Judg 8:23)? Is it a human king because of Israel's selfishness and immorality (Judg 17:6; 18:1; 19:1; 21:25)? Is it a son of David (2 Sam 7)? Or must an alternative to a self-centered, foreign god-serving son of David be found (1 Kgs 11–12)? Deuteronomy and Joshua introduce the entire leadership question for Israel in three ways. First, Deuteronomy acknowledges that the day will come when Israel will have a king (Deut 17:14–20). Second, Deuteronomy sets up Moses as the prophetic leader without parallel and declares that Israel must look for a prophet like Moses to give them God's word (Deut 18:15–20; 34:10–12). Third, Deuteronomy describes how God arranged a smooth leadership transition from Moses to Joshua (Deut 1:37–38; 3:21–22, 28; 31:2–8, 14–15, 23; 34:9; Josh 1:2–9). Joshua thereby becomes the example par excellence of leadership after Moses.

Joshua stands as the role model for all Israelite leaders after Moses, thus for all kings of Israel. Israel's king was to be a leader of the nation in maintaining covenant expectations, in having personal trust in God, and in turning to God with heart, soul, strength, and mind. Thus Josh 1:7–8 places Joshua in daily devotion to the law of Moses, and Josh 8:30–35 and chaps. 23–24 show his leadership in covenant loyalty and renewal. Meanwhile, God fights for Israel.

In many ways the book of Joshua becomes a leadership manual for God's people. Joshua is the paradigm of leadership; he holds no permanent, organizational position in an Israelite political hierarchy. He passes no office down to a series of successors. Rather, Joshua exemplifies the leader God's people can trust no matter what the organizational system: charismatic leaders, like judges; hereditary kings, as in the southern kingdom of Judah; consistently changing royal dynasties, as in northern Israel; no political power or position, as in early exilic and postexilic Israel; or an increasingly priestly dominated society as in later postexilic Israel. The system or type of government does not matter. The role of the leader does matter. Israel can trust God to provide the leader they need, and they can follow that leader who acts not like the unparalleled Moses but like Joshua.

Leadership presented a chronic problem and was in many ways the central problem for Israel. In Joshua's time, the issue was that of a successor for Moses. In the monarchy, it was that of a proper king. In the exilic day of the ultimate historian, it was hope for new leadership (cf. 2 Kgs 25:27–30). The book of Joshua depicts the perfect leader after Moses.[504] The primary requisite for leadership proves not to be military might but religious devotion. The leader must be loyal to the law of Moses and his example (Josh 1:1, 5, 13–16; 3:7; 4:10, 14; 8:18, 26, 30–35; 11:11–12, 15, 20, 23; 17:3–6; 21:2–3; 22:2, 5–6; 24:25).

The entire book of Joshua is a call for a leader and people to follow the law (Josh 1:7–8; 22:5; 23:6–8, 11, 16; cf. chap. 24). Hawk summarizes the first twelve chapters as highlighting divine initiative and obedient response.[505] The leader who follows the law of Moses enjoys the presence of Yahweh, which was constantly with Moses (1:5, 9, 17; 3:7, 10). This is grounds for a call to courage in leadership (1:6, 9, 18; 10:25). The leader who follows the law can expect to be followed by the people (1:10, 16–18; 4:10; 24:31). Thus "the Deuteronomistic view of leadership stresses responsibility rather than power and privilege" (Pressler, 14). Leadership does not give privileges, property, or power to the leader. Nor does it provide continuous access to the deity as Moses had. Communication with the divine will now comes not through personal encounter or revelation but through the Torah revealed to Moses.[506]

Nelson, building on the work of Widengren and Porter, attempts throughout his commentary and in his *JBL* article to show that Joshua is basically a cipher for Josiah, picturing all that Josiah accomplished and hoped to accomplish in restoring Judah's land.[507] Rowlett also finds the book to be a piece of propaganda supporting Josiah's rule.[508]

The book, though, in no way pictures Joshua as a royal figure exercising personal privilege and authority. Van der Meer concludes, "One would expect to find a Deuteronomistic evaluation of Joshua in which these links are made explicit, rather than a series of covert allusions."[509] Joshua is totally submissive to the word of God given to Moses. He undertakes his assigned tasks and retreats to the share of land Israel gave him. "The figure of Joshua is a renunciation [*Absage*] of every form of dynastically constituted rulership."[510] Joshua is not an example of inherited monarchy. Moses, his predecessor, was neither a relative nor a monarch, and Joshua had no successor. Thus Schäfer-Lichtenberger concludes that the relationship between

---

504   See the extended discussion by Schäfer-Lichtenberger, *Josua und Salomo.*
505   Hawk (2000) 19.
506   Schäfer-Lichtenberger, *Josua und Solomo*, 200.
507   *JBL* 100 (1981) 531–40.
508   *JSOT* 55 (1992) 15–23.
509   *Formation and Reformulation*, 146, n. 107.
510   Schäfer-Lichtenberger, *Josua und Salomo*, 219; cf. Noort, *Das Buch Josua*, 124; Bieberstein, *Josua, Jordan, Jericho*, 53–54; 384–86.

the literary figure of Joshua and the traditional image of King Josiah is more complex than a simple depiction of Joshua as mirror image and prototype of the king.[511] Indeed, Joshua, the successor to Moses, represents a time of success and prosperity for Israel. Joshua as Israel's leader was able to bring the Torah into reality in everyday living because dynastic interests were never a consideration for him.[512]

Joshua's leadership characteristics do not follow the modern world's picture of strong aggressive leadership. Nor did they imitate the leadership patterns of his day. In Joshua, God provided for Israel a rare leadership model, the model of one who gradually earned the title servant of Yahweh (Josh 24:29).

Outside the book of Joshua we discover a leader who matured into the leadership position, not one who came fully equipped. Young Joshua made mistakes. He misinterpreted what he heard and reported to Moses (Exod 32:17–18). He tried to limit God's Spirit of prophecy (Num 11:28), though later he is described as a man with God's Spirit (Num 27:18). Young Joshua served Moses and was an apprentice to the master leader. He accompanied Moses on the holy mountain (Exod 24:13). He was God's attendant at the tent of meeting (Exod 33:11). He served as Moses' military lieutenant and learned how God directed military operations (Exod 17:8–14). He was one of two faithful spies Moses sent to investigate the Promised Land (Num 13:8; 14:5–9). Joshua was experienced in many areas of Israel's life before he became the people's leader. When he became the leader, he assumed no royal title. He was only the assistant to Moses.

Joshua's major task as the leader of Israel was not planning strategy or leading armies. It was studying and meditating on God's Torah, the Torah of Moses (Josh 1:7–8), as God through Moses had instructed Israel's leaders to do (Deut 17:18–20). All future leaders would be judged on one criterion: Did they follow the Torah of Moses (note 2 Kgs 17:34–40)? Only obedience to the Torah could lead to revival and hope for the people (see 2 Kgs 22–23). Death only transferred Moses' mode of leadership from the mortal human leader to an eternal director through the inspired Torah he left behind. A leader of Israel had to be a leader guided each day by the Torah of Moses.

Israel's best leaders simply followed the tradition of Moses. It was not an impossible dream or an unrealizable task. Joshua heard the command and followed it, and the assistant to Moses became Israel's leader and inherited Moses' title (Exod 4:10; 14:31), "the servant of Yahweh."

The ultimate leader of Israel was not a new Moses, however, but a servant chosen by God, a slave purchased with a price and totally accountable to Yahweh, the God of Israel (cf. Exod 13:3, 14). A servant was a highly responsible official who advised the king and exercised strong authority (Exod 5:15–16; 7:20; 9:20). Moses acted as God's slave. In the eyes of the people of Israel he stood tall, earning their complete trust as Yahweh's highest representative. Joshua acted as God's and Moses' slave; only then could he become Israel's respected, responsible leader. Joshua set the example for Israel's later kings to be called "servant of Yahweh" (2 Sam 3:18; 7:8), and he opened the way for Israel's messianic hope in a suffering servant of Yahweh (Isa 52:13–53:12).

Meditating on Moses' Torah was not Joshua's only source of direction. God appeared to him (Josh 5:13) as he had to Moses (Exod 6). Joshua, like Moses, had to recognize holy ground and remove his shoes. He had to acknowledge that he was

---

511 *Josua und Salomo*, 224.
512 Ibid., 364.

a slave able only to do God's command (Josh 5:14). Humility and obedience to the Torah of Moses and command of Yahweh equipped the assistant of Moses to become the leader of Israel.

Joshua exemplified many leadership characteristics. He was a man of conviction and courage (Josh 1:6, 18). He interceded for a disobedient people (7:6–9); he delegated authority and responsibility to other leaders (1:10; 3:2; cf. 8:33; 23:2); he equipped the leaders to maintain his influence and ministry after his death (24:31); he cooperated with priestly leaders to accomplish tasks beyond his own authority, calling, and competence (chaps. 3–4 and 6; 14:1; 17:4; 19:51; 21:1; 22:13); he taught the people their sacred traditions with God (8:30–35; 23:1–24:27), warning them of the consequences of disobedience (chap. 23); he provided opportunities to worship God, to study the law (8:30–35), and to participate in the rituals God commanded (5:1–12; 24:1–27); and he provided workers for the worship center (9:27).

Joshua's leadership was farsighted. He left memorials and methods for future generations to learn and teach the traditions of God's people (Josh 4; cf. 5:9; 7:24; 8:28–29, 30–35; 9:27; 10:27); he kept God's law before God's people (8:30–35; 23:1–24:27); he followed God's battle plans (except for the tragic case in chaps. 6–7) and acknowledged that God's action, not his own courage and planning, brought about the victory.

By yielding humbly to God but operating with courage and conviction, Joshua defeated the enemies in battle, gained the land promised and given by God, distributed the land to God's people, maintained unity and loyalty among God's people, and renewed God's covenant with God's people. No wonder Joshua's fame was in all the land (Josh 6:27).

We must admit one point of failure in Joshua's leadership. While Moses followed God in selecting, training, and anointing Joshua as the leader after Moses, we have no evidence in the biblical text that Joshua equipped a leader to replace him. Elders certainly could know and teach the ways of Yahweh to a following generation (Josh 24:31), but the next generation had no leader like Joshua who was immersed in the Torah of Moses and yielded to be slave of Yahweh (Judg 2:6–23). The new generation had no one to renew covenant and teach the meaning of memorials and traditions. And so, it eventually began to worship other gods and follow other traditions. This led the way into the tragic generations of Judges, when each person did what was right in his own eyes, no one established effective control over all the tribes, and eventually one tribe (Benjamin) was almost decimated.

Israel needed a leader they could trust. Joshua set the standard for all leaders after Moses: one who was dedicated to Torah of Moses, who was willing to work as the leader of the people, who strove to teach and maintain the holy traditions of the people, and who was courageous enough to lead where God said and do what God commanded. Sadly, as Israel waited for a prophet like Moses, they did not find a leader like Joshua.

D. Studies on Law and Worship in Joshua

Bibliography

DeClaissé-Walford, N. L. "Covenant in the Book of Joshua." *RevExp* 95 (1998) 227–34. **Hahn, S.** "Covenant in the Old and New Testaments: Some Current Research (1994–2004)." *CBR* 3 (2005) 263–92. **Herr, L. G.** "The Role of Law in the Book of Joshua." *Journal of the Association of Adventist Forums* 24 (1995) 8–15. **Mason, S. D.** *Eternal Covenant* *in the Pentateuch: The Contours of an Elusive Phrase.* Library of Hebrew Bible/Old Testament Studies 494. London: Clark, 2008. **Perlitt, L.** *Bundestheologie im Alten Testament.* WMANT 36. Neukirchen-Vluyn: Neukirchener Verlag, 1969. **Widengren, G.** "King and Covenant." *JSS* 2 (1957) 1–32.

Without Joshua or a leader like Joshua, God's people had to fall back on the resources they had: the written Torah of Moses (Josh 24:25–26); the cultic worship traditions of circumcision and Passover (5:1–12); the covenant (8:30–35; 24:1–27) and tribal unity (22:1–34); and God's promises to the ancestors begun with the conquest of the land (11:23; 21:43–45) but yet to be fully realized (13:1–7; 23:4–5). This was Israel's legacy from Joshua.

The God of Israel is a God of covenant. Covenant begins with a confession of the God of history, the God who created people of God in specific historical acts. Covenant continues as the people of God hear the covenant expectations of God and pledge to obey them. Covenant reaches into the future as it promises God's blessings in specific ways on an obedient people and threatens God's curses on a people who refuse to maintain the covenant commitments. For Joshua, this meant looking back at the promises to the ancestors and the saving acts in Egypt and the wilderness. It meant reciting the covenant demands of the Torah and pledging to serve the God who could not be served. It meant knowing that God promised the land to an obedient people but threatened exile and destruction for a people who neglected the covenant and worshiped other gods.

The people of God are people of the Torah. They know covenant and covenant requirements because they know the Torah, and they maintain an existence separate from that of their neighbors because they incarnate the Torah in their lives. The Torah is not something they praise and worship; rather it is a lifestyle on which they meditate and practice. It leads to obeying God and loving God; to loving one's neighbor and observing that neighbor's rights; to solving disputes and unifying the people of God, to humble service of the God that cannot be served; and, eventually, to the creation of a people of God who are called servants of Yahweh.

God's people had another legacy, though—the legacy of the inhabitants of Canaan. For centuries, these people had lived in the land and produced their crops. Surely they knew the secrets of the land. Should Israel not learn from them also? The writer who compiled the book of Joshua had to answer the question: how do we understand God's fulfilled yet unfilled promises in the light of Canaan's history and Joshua's traditions?

The author of Joshua made one thing perfectly clear. Canaan's history, Canaan's worship, and Canaan's fertility practices were to have no meaning for Israel. God had one ominous weapon against these practices, a weapon used by other nations in Israel's environment and yet strongly commanded and endorsed by the God of Israel, a weapon that has caused ethical concern among God's people almost from the time of Joshua. How can a loving, caring God place a holy ban (ḥērem) on the entire population of a country, including its innocent women and children? How does one incorporate such a violent, vengeful practice into one's theology? Should we relegate this practice, recorded in the books of Deuteronomy, Joshua, and Samuel, to the traditions of the ancient past and see it as a borrowed pagan practice that was superceded by the ongoing revelations of God?

Indeed, Israel's ban or ḥērem does not seem to be a legitimate part of biblical theology. But the book of Joshua will not let us adopt such a simplistic theological methodology and approach. Both the Torah of Moses (Deut 7 with its emphasis upon God's love) and the book of Joshua (6:17; cf. 7:1) demand the ban as God's method of warfare in Canaan. Josh 11:20 states that God hardened the Canaanites' hearts so he might annihilate the population of Canaan without mercy. The ban is not just an incidental part of the battle description. It is not just a description of a theology of warfare. It is a basic part of the divine plan to fulfill God's promises to Israel. The plan involves both protection of Israel from the seductive religion of the inhabitants of Canaan (Deut 7:1–5, 16; Josh 23) and the punishment of their wickedness (Deut 9:4–5). This makes the ban significant to the characterization of God himself. We (post) moderns ask, why?

The biblical text relates over and over stories of God using violent means to achieve his judgmental purposes against sin and his saving purposes for his people. One might say that Noah's flood and the total destruction of Sodom and Gomorrah represent the first instances of the ban. God exercised the ban on his own people in the wilderness and came close to the same with the northern kingdom. Mark 13 and Revelation abound with terminology and teaching issuing from ban theology.

Even so, the "ban" narratives in Joshua stand out as distinct. Innocent women and children are slaughtered as part of the ban. How do our modern sensibilities come to grips with such overt inhumanity? The simple answer is, we cannot come to grips. The narratives of the book of Joshua are set in a precarious time in the life of ancient Israel. Israelite men married Canaanite women and corrupted Israel's worship by importing to Israel the religious tradition of Canaan, intermingling worship of Baal with worship of Yahweh. This is precisely what happened in the period of the judges and on a more universal scale in the kingdom of Solomon (1 Kgs 11).

The ban was a method at a point in time in human history to establish a pure people of God in a new land. The ban was never meant to be a universal method of warfare; rather it was God's method for fulfilling his promise of land to the ancestors, of establishing the worship of him and of him alone in that land, and of protecting his people from overwhelming temptations of imitating the religious practices of the Canaanite people. It may be understood as an expression of God's wrath against all types of sin. But, ban theology is not something we are called on to practice today or to condone as permissible in today's warfare.

We are right to ask, then, how does one integrate biblical tradition and worship into modern life? Israel took over ancient worship places such as Shechem, Shiloh, and Jerusalem. The people intermingled with and married Canaanites. Yet they knew that the Torah of Moses demanded total separation from ancient traditions. Was such total separation possible? Was it desirable? Could not God's people learn both from the sacred traditions of the Torah and worship as well as from the practical world's traditions of agriculture and the fertility cult?

The biblical text argues against such universalistic, relativistic, and nonexclusive thinking. Israel is inclusive in the sense that aliens are invited to join in their worship (Josh 8:33), but Israel is totally exclusive when it comes to recognizing the validity of worship practices outside the teaching of Torah. God's people are to hear the word of God and pledge themselves in covenant renewal to obey the entirety of that word. Giving in to exceptions only results in practices that alienate Israel from God and unite them to foreign gods and foreign practices.

The explanation for this is mysterious and yet radically essential for Israel's relationship with God. Israel must choose between the ancient gods of the fathers and the very present Yahweh God of Israel (Josh 24:14–15). Having chosen to serve Yahweh, however, the people of Israel must learn they cannot serve him (24:19). The Canaanites and others knew how to carry out rituals and practices that placated their gods and brought forth the weather and fertility they wanted. They could carry out practices in the fertility cults imitating practices of the gods of their ritual texts and be satisfied they had properly served and worshiped God.

Israel stood in no such secure position. The people of Israel had to come to their God with a confession of their own sinfulness. They could never meet the exclusivistic, perfectionistic covenant demands of their God. They would never be holy as Yahweh is holy. They could not carry out proper worship. They had to humbly come before their God, confess their sins, and bring sacrifices as atonement for their sins. They had to repeatedly renew their covenant vows to a God they could not serve. This radically different attitude to the religions around them separated Israel completely from their neighbors. Israel's first commandment forced them to live apart from and different from their neighbors. Israel had to ask, "Is experiencing the grace and love and salvation of God as well as the holiness and jealousy of God sufficient reason to serve him if only inadequately? Or is the security of knowing how to serve the Canaanite gods, enjoying the sensuality of their worship, and expecting the rewards they promise more inviting?"

The book of Joshua thundered forth answers. Meditate on the Torah of Moses day and night. Learn the commands of your God. Learn the salvation history of your God among you. See the love of your God for you. Trust him even if you cannot serve him. Practice circumcision. Keep the Passover. Go to the place God chooses for your worship. Renew your covenant with him. Believe what he has written for you. Rest assured that God keeps all his promises. Obedience to the written tradition and observance of identity-giving worship practices will lead to an experience with your God in which you will join the book of Joshua in proclaiming: God has fulfilled every one of his promises just as he spoke to Abraham and to Moses.

E. The People of Yahweh

A people who cannot serve their God faces one final basic question: how do we know we are God's people? Or what defines membership in the people of God? This is the summarizing question for the book of Joshua and perhaps for all of biblical theology.

At first glance, membership in Israel seems clear. Israel came from Egypt, a people descended from Abraham and the twelve sons of Jacob who agreed to the covenant at Sinai. They gained new population and identity in the wilderness, and joined Joshua in conquering and inheriting the Promised Land of Canaan. But such a definition ignores the nuances of the biblical narrative, and especially of the book of Joshua. Already with the exodus, a mixed multitude joined Israel (Exod 12:38). Joshua quickly added a number of possibilities of people who may or may not have been part of Israel: ethnic Israelites who lived across Jordan and thus in traditional terms outside the land of Canaan (Josh 1; 22); resident aliens with a history of helping Israel and being devoted to their God (chap. 2); people who met all the qualifications but do not keep covenant (chap. 7); people who deceptively worked their way into the community (chap. 9); families with no males to inherit their land (17:3–6); priests without land (chap. 21); accidental murderers (chap. 20); and members of Israel who feared alienation (chap. 22).

The book of Joshua outlines the qualities that define the people of God. First, they are a people of promise. The traditions of the ancestors of Israel are different from those of other religions. These promises do not describe actions of the innumerable gods, actions that need to be repeated over and over again in the cults. Rather, the ancestors passed down the traditions of divine assurances. God has a plan for his people and lets his people know that plan. The central part of the plan for Joshua's day was the promise of land. Joshua fulfilled that promise, yet land remained to be occupied. Thus, the promise of God is already/not yet in character. The promise of God gives concrete reality and meaning in its fulfillment for the present generation, yet it calls for continued faithfulness and further fulfillment in the future. The people of God are a people of promise.

Second, the people of God are a people of present history. God is a God who acts in sovereign majesty over every aspect of human life. He is not a god who at one time established his dynasty by defeating other gods in battle and then retired as a cult repeated the ritual each year. He is not a god who is constantly changing and evolving as his people learn better language to describe him, or as human achievements demand more of him, or as an expanding universe requires a different kind of god. God was, is, and will be the God who planned human history and directs it toward his eternal goals. For Joshua's day, this meant involvement in the blood and gore of warfare and in the anger and frustration of disagreements among the people of God (see especially Josh 22). God is not a theological ideal whose characteristics a person learns and masters. God is a person who personally involves himself in all human activities. This calls forth all sides of the divine being: love, mercy, and grace as well as holiness, anger, and jealousy. The people of God learn the nature of God because God involves himself in history even to the point of incarnation and death on a cross.

F. Studies on Warfare and Conquest in Joshua

Bibliography

Barrett, L. *The Way God Fights: War and Peace in the Old Testament.* Peace and Justice 1. Scottdale, PA: Herald, 1987. **Bienkowski, P.** "Le rempart de Josué: Énigma pour les archéologues." *MdB* 69 (1991) 22–24. **Bratcher, D.** "Conquest or Settlement? History and Theology in Joshua and Judges." *The Voice.* 2005. Online: http://www.crivoice.org/pdf/conquest.pdf. **Brekelmans, C. H. W.** *De Herem in het Oude Testament.* Nijmegen: Centrale Druccerij, 1959. **Brueggemann, W.** "Revelation and Violence. A Study in Contextualization" (Père Marquette Lecture 17, Milwaukee, 1986). In *A Social Reading of the Old Testament: Prophetic Approaches to Israel's Communal Life.* Ed. P. D. Miller. Minneapolis: Fortress, 1994. 285–318. **Budde, K.** "Die Eroberung Ost-Manasse's im Zeitalter Josua's: Nachtrag zu 'Richter und Josua.'" *ZAW* 8 (1888) 148. **Chaney, M. L.** "Ancient Palestinian Peasant Movements and the Formation of Premonarchic Israel." In *Palestine in Transition: The Emergence of Ancient Israel.* Ed. D. N. Freedman and D. F. Graf. SWBA 2. Sheffield: Almond, 1983. **Coats, G. W.** "The Ark of the Covenant in Joshua." *HAR* 9 (1985) 137–57. ———. "An Exposition for the Conquest Theme." *CBQ* 47 (1985) 47–54. **Colpe, C.** "Zur Bezeichnung und Bezeugung des 'Heiligen Krieges': I, II." *BTZ* 1 (1984) 45–67, 189–214.

Craigie, P. C. "The Conquest and Early Hebrew Poetry." *TynBul* 20 (1969) 76–94. ———. *The Problem of War in the Old Testament.* Grand Rapids: Eerdmans, 1978. **Cross, F. M., Jr.** "The Divine Warrior in Israel's Early Cult." In *Biblical Motifs.* Ed. A. Altman. Cambridge, MA: Harvard UP, 1966. 11–30. **Czajkowski, M.** "Does God Thirst for Human Blood?" *BTB* 40 (2010) 123–36. **Davies, E. W.** "The Morally Dubious Passages of the Hebrew Bible: An Examination of Some Proposed Solutions." *CBR* 3 (2005) 197–228 (bibliography). **Del Monte, G. F.** "The Hittite Herem." In *Memoriae Igor M. Diakonoff.* Ed. L. Kogan et al. Winona Lake, IN: Eisenbrauns, 2005. 21–45. **Ebach, J.** *Das Erbe der gewalt: Eine biblische Realität und ihre Wirkungsgeschichte.* Gütersloh: Gütersloher Verlagshaus, 1982. **Eißfeldt, O.** "Die Eroberung Palästinas durch Altisrael." *WO* 2 (1955) 158–71. **Elbner, T. R.** *Josua und seine Kriege in jüdischer und christlicher Rezeptionsgeschichte.* Theologie und Frieden 37. Stuttgart: Kohlhammer, 2008. **Fredriksson, H.** *Jahwe als Krieger: Studien zum alttestamentlichen Gottesbild.* Lund: Gleerup, 1945. **Galbiati, G.** *La Guerra santa israelitica.* Geneva: Lanterna, 1986. ———. "La guerra santa israelitica: Teoria ed evoluzione (prima parte)." *RBR* 18 (1983) 11–42. **Gangloff, F.** "Joshua 6: Holy War or Extermination by Divine Command (*herem*)." *Theological Review* 25 (2004) 3–23. **Gelin, A.** "Notes bibliques II: Guerre dans l'AT." *AmiCl* 66 (1956) 539–40. **Glock, A. E.** "Warfare in Mari and Early Israel." Diss., University of Michigan, 1968. **Goetz, R.** "Joshua, Calvin, and Genocide." *ThTo* 32 (1975–1976) 263–74. **Good, R. M.** "The Just War in Ancient Israel." *JBL* 104 (1985) 385–400. **Hanson, P.** "War, Peace, and Justice in Early Israel." *BR* 3.3 (1987) 341–62. ———. "War and Peace in the Hebrew Bible." *Int* 38 (1984) 341–62. **Hasel, M. G.** "Assyrian Military Practices and Deuteronomy's Laws of Warfare." In *Writing and Reading War: Rhetoric, Gender, and Ethics in Biblical and Modern Contexts.* Ed. B. E. Kelle and F. R. Ames. SBLSymS 42. Atlanta: Society of Biblical Literature, 2008. 67–81. **Hawk, L. D.** "Conquest Reconfigured: Recasting Warfare in the Redaction of Joshua." In *Writing and Reading War: Rhetoric, Gender, and Ethics in Biblical and Modern Contexts.* Ed. B. E. Kelle and F. R. Ames. SBL SymS 42. Atlanta: Society of Biblical Literature, 2008. 145–60. **Heintz, J. G.** "Oracles prophétiques et 'guerre sainte' selon les archives royales de Mari et l'Ancien Testament." In *Congress Volume, Rome 1968.* VTSup 17. Leiden: Brill, 1969. 112–38. **Helva, G.** "'Pace' e 'guerra' nella teologia israelitica dell'alleanza." In *La Pace nel mondo antico.* Ed M. Sordi. Scienze storice 36. Milan: Vita e pensiero, 1985. 513–28. **Hess, R. S., and E. A. Martens,** eds. *War in the Bible and Terrorism in the Twenty-First Century.* BBRSup 2. Winona Lake, IL: Eisenbrauns, 2008. **Hobbs, T. R.** "Aspects of Warfare in the First Testament World." *BTB* 25 (1995) 79–90. ———. *A Time for War: A Study of Warfare in the Old Testament.* OTS 3. Wilmingon, DE: Glazier, 1989. **Hoffman, Y.** "The Deuteronomistic Concept of the Herem." *ZAW* 111 (1999) 196–210. **Holloway, J.** "The Ethical Dilemma of Holy War." *SwJT* 41 (1998) 44–69. **House, P. R.** "The God Who Gives Rest in the Land: Joshua." *SBJT* 2 (1998) 12–33. **Jenson, P.** *The Problem of War in the Old Testament.* Grove Biblical 25. Cambridge: Grove, 2002. **Jones, G. H.** "The Concept of Holy War." In *The World of Ancient Israel: Sociological, Anthropological, and Political Perspectives.* Ed. R. E. Clements. Cambridge: Cambridge UP, 1989. 299–321. ———. "'Holy War' or 'Yahwe War.'" *VT* 25 (1975) 642–58. **Kang, S.** *Divine War in the Old Testament and in the Ancient Near East.* BZAW 177. Berlin: De Gruyter, 1989. **Kim, W.** "The Rhetoric of War and the Book of Joshua." In *Seeing Signals, Reading Signs: The Art of Exegesis.* FS A. F. Campbell, ed. H. N. Wallace and M. A. O'Brien. JSOTSup 415. London: T&T Clark; JSOT Press, 2004. 90–103. **Klem, J. F.** "A Genre Analysis of Joshua 1–12 as Covenant Military History." ThD thesis, Central Baptist Theological Seminary. **Knierim, R. P.** "Israel and the Nations in the Land of Palestine in the Old Testament." In *The Task of Old Testament Theology.* Ed. R. P. Knierim. Grand Rapids: Eerdmans, 1995. 309–21. **Lind, M. C.** *Yahweh Is a Warrior: The Theology of Warfare in Ancient Israel.* Scottdale, PA: Herald, 1980. **Lingen, A. van der.** *Les guerres de Yahvé: L'implication de YHWH dans les guerres d'Israel selon les livres historiques de l'Ancien Testament].* LD 139. Paris: Cerf, 1990. **Lohfink, N.,** ed. *Gewalt und Gewaltlosigkeit im Alten*

Testament. QD 96. Freiburg: Herder, 1983. **Longman, T. III, and D. G. Reid.** *God Is a Warrior.* Grand Rapids: Zondervan, 1995. **Malamat, A.** "The Ban in Mari and in the Bible." In *Biblical Essays: Proceedings of the Ninth Meeting of die Ou-Testamentiese Werkgemeenschap in Suid-Afrika.* Pretoria, 1966. 40–49. ———. "Israelite Conduct of War in the Conquest of Canaan according to the Biblical Tradition." In *Symposia Celebrating the Seventy-Fifth Anniversary of the Founding of the American Schools of Oriental Research (1900–1975).* Cambridge, MA: American Schools of Oriental Research, 1979. 35–55. **Mendenhall, G. E.** "The Hebrew Conquest of Palestine." *BA* 25 (1962) 66–87. **Merling, D., Sr.** *The Book of Joshua: Its Theme and Role in Archaeological Discussions.* Andrews University Doctoral Dissertation Series 23. Berrien Springs, MI: Andrews UP, 1997. **Michel, D.** *The Divine Warrior in Early Israel.* HSM 5. Cambridge, MA: Harvard UP, 1973. ———. "Probleme der Landnahme." In *Israels Glaube im Wandel: Einführungen in die Forschung am Alten Testament.* Ed. D. Michel. Berlin: Verlag Die Spur Dorbandt, 1968. 149–58. **Miller, P. D.** "God the Warrior." *Int* 19 (1965) 39–46. **Moran, W. L.** "The End of the Unholy War and the Anti-Exodus." *Bib* 44 (1963) 333–42. **Nelson, R. D.** "*Herem* and the Deuteronomic Social Conscience." In *Deuteronomy and Deuteronomic Literature, Festschrift C. H. W. Brekelmans.* BETL 133. Leuven: Leuven UP, 1997. 39–54. **Niditch, S.** *War in the Hebrew Bible: A Study in the Ethics of Violence.* New York: Oxford UP, 1993. **Noort, E.** *Das Buch Josua: Forschungsgeschichte und Problemfelder.* EdF 292. Darmstadt: Wissenschaftliche Buchgesellschaft, 1998. ———. *Geweld in het Oude Testament: Over woorden en verhalen aan de rand van de kerkelijke praktijk.* Delft: Meinema, 1985. ———. "Das Kapitulationsangebot im Kriegsgesetz Dtn. 20:10ff und in den Kriegserzählungen." In *Studies in Deuteronomy in Honour of C. J. Labuschagne.* Ed. F. García Martínez et. al. Leiden: Brill, 1994. 197–222. **Pitkanen, P.** "Memory, Witnesses and Genocide in the Book of Joshua." In *Reading the Law: Studies in Honour of Gordon J. Wenham.* Ed. J. G. McConville and K. Möller. New York; London: T&T Clark, 2007. 267–82. **Prenter, J. A. de.** "The Contrasting Polysemous Meaning of *Herem* in Biblical Hebrew: A Cognitive-Linguistic Approach." Paper read to SBL Biblical Lexicography Section, Atlanta, November 20, 2010. **Rad, G. von.** *Der Heilige Krieg im alten Israel.* ATANT 20. Göttingen, 1951. Repr. in *Holy War in Ancient Israel.* Trans. M. J. Dawn. Grand Rapids: Eerdmans, 1991. **Reinke, L.** "Über das Recht der Israeliten an Canaan und über die Ursache seiner Eroberung und der Vertilgung seiner Einwohner durch die Israeliten, und die verschiedenen Erklärungsversuche darüber." *BEAT* 1 (Münster, 1851) 271–418. **Rodd, C. S.** *Glimpses of a Strange Land: Studies in Old Testament Ethics.* Edinburgh: T&T Clark, 2001. 185–206. **Rowlett, L. L.** *Joshua and the Rhetoric of Violence: A New Historicist Analysis.* JSOTSup 226. Sheffield: Sheffield Academic, 1996. **Sanmartín, J.** "Geschichte und Erzählung in Alten Orient (1): Die Landnahme Israels." *UF* 17 (1985) 253–82. ———. *Las Guerras de Josué: Un estudio de semiótica narrativa.* Valencia: Artes Gráficas Soler, 1982. **Soggie, N. A.** *Myth, God, and War: The Mythopoetic Inspiration of Joshua.* Lanham, MD: University Press of America, 2007. **Stern, P.** *The Biblical* herem: *A Window on Israel's Religious Experience.* BJS 211. Atlanta: Scholars, 1991. **Stolz, F.** *Jahwes und Israels Kriege: Kriegstheorien und Kriegserfahrungen im Glauben des alten Israels.* ATANT 60. Zürich: Theologischer Verlag, 1972. **Stone, L. G.** "Ethical and Apologetic Tendencies in the Redaction of the Book of Joshua." *CBQ* 53 (1991) 25–36. **Tate, M. E.** "Peacemaking and the Book of Joshua." Unpublished paper, April 2008. **Teigen, R. C.** "Joshua's Total Conquest of Canaan: A Theological Rationale." *Consensus* 11 (1985) 23–30. **Thompson, J. A.** "War in Ancient Israel." *BurH* 21 (1985) 61–69. **Vries, S. J. de.** "Temporal Terms as Structural Elements in the Holy War tradition." *VT* 25 (1975) 80–105. **Waldow, H. E. von.** "The Concept of War in the Old Testament." *HBT* 6 (1984) 27–48. **Weinfeld, M.** "The Ban on the Canaanites in the Biblical Codes and Its Historical Development." In *History and Traditions of Early Israel: Festschrift for E. Nielsen.* Ed. A. Lemaiare and B. Otzen. VTSup 50. Leiden: Brill, 1993. 142–60. ———. "Divine Intervention in War in Ancient Israel and in the Ancient Near East." In *History, Historiography and Interpretation: Studies in Biblical and Cuneiform*

Literatures. Ed. H. Tadmor and M. Weinfeld. Jerusalem: Magnes; Leiden: Brill, 1983. 121–47. **Weippert, M.** "'Heiliger Krieg' in Israel und Assyrien." *ZAW* 84 (1972) 460–95. **Yadin, Y.** *The Art of Warfare in Biblical Lands in the Light of Archaeological Discovery.* London: McGraw-Hill, 1963. **Younger, K. L., Jr.** *Ancient Conquest Accounts: A Study in Ancient Near Eastern and Biblical History Writing.* JSOTSup 98. Sheffield: JSOT Press, 1990.

"The book endorses, and even promotes the kinds of attitudes and practices that have generated violence and suffering on a massive scale."[513] This theme has provoked more argument than almost any other theological theme in the book of Joshua and possibly in the Scripture.

Robert Coote approaches the problem head on: Joshua presents "an orgy of terror, violence, and mayhem. . . . It forms a triumphant finale to the Bible's foundational epic of liberation, the savage goal toward which God's creation of Israel and delivery of Israel from slavery in Egypt appears to point from the start."[514] "Thus much about the book of Joshua is repulsive."[515] Only a "sidestepping approach" can rescue the stories of Joshua by letting them "illustrate reliance on the power of God, whose provision both short-term and long-run, does not fail. They illustrate the importance of grace, allegiance, obedience to authority, community solidarity, the family, and deterring hasty revenge."[516] Joshua's values are not pure but are "multifaceted, mixed, and ambiguous."[517] The book may, however, "suggest to us our own affinities with the atrocities, violence, coercion, and prejudicial categorizing as means to social betterment."[518]

Eryl Davies used Josh 6–11 as test case for dealing with "morally dubious passages."[519] He sets forth methods that can be used to redeem such passages from scholarly rejection and restore them to the biblical whole. These methods include an evolutionary approach, the cultural relativists' approach, the canon-within-a-canon approach, the holistic approach, the paradigmatic approach, and the reader-response approach. Davies bends toward the final method but admits its weaknesses also.

Leslie Hoppe argues: "The Holy War theology within Joshua is much more ideology than history." Speaking of the justification of such ideology, Hoppe points to the historical fact that Israel did occupy the land, partly through violence, and that "the ideology of Holy War is not any more difficult to explain than the necessity of Jesus' death. Both are attempts to describe the mysterious ways by which God uses human folly and sin as a means of salvation. . . . The wars that took place during the settlement period were evil—there is no denying that. . . . What the Bible does affirm is that God's purpose was served even by this evil." The Deuteronomistic History was written to "shock Judah into obedience."[520]

Jerome Creach seeks to show the value and definition that the Old Testament

---

513 Hawk, (2010) xi.
514 Coote, 555.
515 Ibid., 578.
516 Ibid.
517 Ibid.
518 Ibid., 579.
519 *CBR* 3 (2005) 197–228.
520 Hoppe, 18.

places on violence as opposed to modern conceptions. For Israel violence "refers principally to actions that tear at the fabric of Israelite society by defying the sovereignty of God."[521] Israel's conquest is not violent because it seeks to instill loyalty to God and human justice on earth. As far as the ban goes, Creach maintains that here the stories and reality part company, for "Israel did not in reality commit genocide."[522] Such stories seek to "present an Israel that was more powerful than it was true historically."[523] The book presents Israel's warfare as mostly a defensive action initiated by the Canaanite enemies. The Canaanites had a chance for peace but rejected it (Josh 11:19).

The thoughts of L. Daniel Hawk are shaped by three ideas: the Bible as a mirror reflecting human nobility and deformity, Joshua as a narrative of origins and thus Israel's identity, and the narrative reflecting on the story of the nation of Israel.[524]

Ernst Axel Knauf devotes much of his commentary to the argument that the conquest and the oath to destroy the enemies in *ḥērem* appear in only one of seven redactional voices in Joshua, that fighting is most usually done by God and not by men, and that stories like Josh 6 and 10 picture divine intervention rather than human action. He concludes that war in Joshua is a mythical war, the conclusion to the primeval (*Urzeitlichen*) wilderness wandering and the entrance into Israel's historical existence.[525] In Josh 11, such warfare is solemnly declared at an end, never to be repeated.

David Merling concludes:

> In the days of Joshua, as portrayed by the Book of Joshua, Israel had no long-lasting conquest. The Israelites had only begun a contest to attain the land. . . . The Book of Joshua is about the Israelites' acquisition and right to the land, not the settlement of the land. The land was claimed in the Book of Joshua, but that does not mean it was necessarily entirely controlled. . . . The act of allotting the land is a confirmation act that pronounces Israel's right to possess it.[526]

Lori Rowlett understands the war language of Joshua as an adoption of Assyrian war ideology and language.[527] Edward Noort backs off this explanation and notes that divine engagement, the role of a central power, and the opposition between chaos and order belongs to the entire ancient Near East and thus as much to Egypt as to Assyria.[528] The question remains about what is unique to Joshua and the neo-Assyrian war descriptions compared to those of other Near Eastern lands.

Noort contends that the war of Yahweh was a theoretical concept practiced for only a very brief time if at all.[529] The whole linguistic grouping of the war of Yahweh and the ban had their true place in the language of the Deuteronomist in the seventh century. Expulsion and ban never really occurred.

---

521 Creach, 15.
522 Ibid., 16.
523 Ibid., 17.
524 Hawk (2010) xi.
525 Knauf, 189.
526 *Book of Joshua*, 181–82.
527 *Joshua and the Rhetoric of Violence*.
528 *Das Buch Josua*, 124.
529 Ibid., 17.

K. Lawson Younger concludes that "one encounters very similar things in both ancient Near Eastern and biblical history writing. . . . The Hebrew conquest account of Canaan in Joshua 9–12 is, by and large, typical of any ancient Near Eastern account."[530] Younger emphasizes the use of hyperbole in ancient history writing, leading to the conclusion that "the claims to conquest have been overstated."[531]

Theologically, Richard Hess discusses holy war and the ban as an ideology Israel shared with the other nations. Israel's distinctive thought might be that God did not approve of all wars and that mercy was extended to foreigners who joined God's covenant. The land as inheritance theme involved a constant tension between God's gift to families and Israel's challenge to occupy the land. Israel had the opportunity to use the land as part of covenant worship. But when misuse of the land signified a breaking of covenant, God's warnings came into effect. Using second-millennium covenant forms, Joshua established the covenant of God with the people in the land, and Israel sets "a standard of faith and unity that will seldom be attained in future generations."[532]

In this "most nationalistic of books" the God of mercy and holiness finds room for foreigners within Israel and its worship.[533] The land distribution documents in Josh 13–21 are part of the treaty tradition and show that "God uses the boundary descriptions to define the fulfilment of promises made to the nation's ancestors in the context of formal covenant ceremonies."[534]

Creach insists: Still, "some Christians reject Joshua because they think it primitive and brutal, promoting a violent god who is surely different from the Father of Jesus Christ."[535] Violence and warfare represent a more modern problem than one of Israel's problems.

Robert Hubbard finds that Yahweh wars means God has enemies whom God chooses to defeat militarily.[536] Participation in a war of Yahweh, a ritual act, requires cultic purity. God alone fights and wins the victory. Only God names things as ḥērem. Items designated as ḥērem have the "highest degree of holiness so that Israel knows no way of returning such items to the secular sphere. Yahweh war as described in the Book of Joshua is time specific and place specific, thus not applicable to any subsequent time or space."

Richard Nelson notes that, theologically, Joshua "touches a raw nerve in most modern readers," speaking of brutal conquest, deliberate acts of genocide, and colonization. Such portraits of a Divine Warrior seem "incompatible with enlightened notions of religion."[537] Still, Joshua deals with contemporary issues: God's gift of peoplehood, responsibilities of peoplehood, kept and unfulfilled promises, and people and land.

Lawson Stone contrasts the Canaanites who resist and those who do not so that

---

530 *Ancient Conquest Accounts*, 265.
531 Ibid., 244.
532 Hess, 51.
533 Ibid., 52.
534 Ibid., 59.
535 Creach, 3.
536 Hubbard, 198–99.
537 Nelson, 2.

a Yahweh war was waged only against the resisters.[538] It is a test of Israel to see if they obey God's instructions in carrying out a Yahweh war. Hubbard extends this to maintain that those not teaching Israel idolatry may remain in the land and that God expects rigorous obedience to his law in this matter as in all others.[539]

Hawk begins bluntly and correctly: "War is evil, and participating in war is participating in evil."[540] He then tries to avoid "all complicity with the state's militaristic endeavors" and asks if we know that we cannot avoid sin and yet can feel compelled to enter into war to resist or halt even greater evils. Hawk continues: "God's election of Israel meant that God would be involved in the mess, broken systems, and violence that entangle nations in a world gone bad."

House reminds his readers that Scripture "prepares the reader from Genesis 15:16 onward for this difficult material. . . . What occurs, then, is not some kind of God-ordained hate mission. Rather it is divine judgment for sin similar to that which God has reluctantly meted out since the Garden of Eden."[541]

Tate admits the violence, war, and theological problems of Joshua but wants to argue that it contains "major elements of peacemaking."[542] This is demonstrated in the emphasis on rest as the goal of the entrance into Palestine. Peacemaking is an important element in the accounts of land allotments that show "a testimony of faith in the divine purpose for Israel seeking to fulfill their need for space, place, and land." Peacemaking appears in the "concern for solidarity between the West Bank tribes and the East Bank tribes." Another peace sign comes in chap. 22 as "the tribes chose to negotiate rather than go to war." Israel's master story, which Joshua concludes, gives another sign of peaceseeking. Tate concludes: "In a strange way the Book of Joshua leads us through violence and war to peacemaking."

Many voices contribute to the discussion of war and violence. In reading the book of Joshua, one can make several admissions:

1. For Joshua's day, war was a normal fact of life with a special season of the year when men go to war.
2. "Normal" warfare in the ancient Near East was unknown. All warfare involved the deity and the reputation of the god(s).
3. The holy war ban was not invented by nor limited to Israel. It was a normal part of any battle in which the gods were involved and the deity had to receive a share of the booty.
4. Both in battle and in gathering spoils of war, the participants acted violently.
5. In Israel, war was one element connected with the anger or wrath of God, a theme that runs through the prophets, the psalms, apocalyptic, the Gospels, and the Pauline writings. Joshua and Judges may in some ways represent the largest grouping of war narratives with its violence and agony, but the theme is prevalent throughout Scripture.
6. Hermeneutically, the commentator must deal with and apply the war and violence of the rest of Scripture using the methodology applied to the books of Joshua and Judges.

---

538 *CBQ* 53 (1991) 25–36.
539 Hubbard, 202.
540 Hawk (2010) 139–40.
541 *SBJT* 2 (1998) 19.
542 "Peacemaking and the Book of Joshua."

7. In no way can the modern military claim the right to engage in violent and
destructive warfare on the basis of the Israelite wars and their reflection of
Near Eastern military practices.

The land is the reward. Leadership is the means of claiming that reward. The
law is the focus of attention. The essential theme remains. That is God himself. This
is the God of all the earth (Josh 2:11; 4:24); the God of the revered name Yahweh
(7:9; 9:9b); the God of the exodus, who led Israel to conquer the kings east of the
Jordan (2:10; 4:23; 9:9–10; 24:1–10, 17); and the God who allowed Israel to conquer
the entire land, thus fulfilling all his promises (10:40; 11:23; 21:43–45; 23:3, 9, 14;
24:11–13, 18).

G. Theological Conclusions

These are the components of the Deuteronomistic theology of Joshua: a conquered land, which could be lost; a model for leadership, which was never again
followed; a law given to Israel as a covenant, but repeatedly disobeyed; and a God
of the universe, who had chosen and helped Israel, fulfilling all his promises and
blessings, but who remained the God holy and jealous (Josh 24:19), ready to fulfill
all his curses (6:26; 23:15–16; 24:20). For the exilic audience, the final author of
the book of Joshua sketched a picture bold with meaning. The curses had been
fulfilled. Israel had lost her land. Israel had not been faithful to her pledge to the
covenant law. God had been faithful to his pledge to curse an unfaithful people.
The books of Judges, Samuel, and Kings sketch Israel's history of unfaithful leadership and rebellious people.

The book of Joshua is not only the historical explanation of why Israel was
punished. It is also a paradigm of hope. Israel must be like the tribes who settled
east of the Jordan (Josh 22:2–3). She must listen again to the law as Israel had done
after her first defeat at Ai (8:30–35). She must pledge anew her obedience to God's
covenant (chap. 24). She must remain totally faithful to Yahweh, the God of Israel
and all the earth, rather than following the temptation of the gods of the ancestors
beyond the river or of the ancestors in the land (chaps. 23–24). A faithful Israel,
even an Israel who had once made a covenant with the foreigners (chap. 9), could
hope for victory once more. The promise to the ancestors could once again be
fulfilled. The land that remained, no matter how large, no matter how mighty its
inhabitants and rulers, that land could once again be Israel's. But it depended on
faithful leadership, loyal to the covenant law.

I. Possessing the Promise (Joshua 1–12)

Bibliography

Assis, E. *From Moses to Joshua and from the Miraculous to the Ordinary: A Literary Analysis of the Conquest Narrative in the Book of Joshua.* Jerusalem: Hebrew University Magnes Press, 2005. **Blum, E.** "Überlegungen zur Kompositionsgeschichte des Josuabuaches." In E. Noort (ed.), *The Book of Joshua.* Leuven: Peeters, 2012. 137–157. **Braber, M. den, and J. W. Wesselius.** "The Unity of Joshua 1–8, Its Relation to the Story of King Keret, and the Literary Background to the Exodus and Conquest Stories." *SJOT* 22 (2008) 253–74. **Briend, J.** "Les Sources de L'Histoire deuteronomique recherches sur Jos 1–12." In *Israël construit son histoire: L'historiograhie deutéronomiste à la lumière des recherches récentes.* Ed. A. de Pury, T. Römer, and J.-D. Macchi. MdB 34. Geneva: Labor et Fides, 1996. Reprinted as "The Sources of the Deuteronomic History: Research on Joshua 1–12," in *Israel Constructs Its History: Deuteronomistic Historiography in Recent Research*, ed. A. de Pury, T. Römer, and J.-D. Macchi, JSOTSup 306 (Sheffield: Sheffield Academic, 2000) 360–86. **Chen, K.** "Torah as Pillar of Cloud: An Intertextual Study of Exod. 13:20–21 and Josh. 1:7–8." Paper read at annual meeting of Evangelical Theological Society, Atlanta, November 18, 2010. **Creanga, O.** "The Silenced Songs of Victory: Power, Gender and Memory in the Conquest Narrative of Joshua (Joshua 1–12)." In *A Question of Sex?* Sheffield: Sheffield Phoenix, 2007. 106–23. ———. "Space, Place and Exile: The Land as 'Third-space' in Joshua 1–12." Paper read to SBL Space, Place, and Lived Experience in Antiquity Section, Atlanta, November 21, 2010. **De Troyer, K.** "'And they did so': following orders given by Old Joshua." In *Her Master's Tools?* Atlanta: SBL; Leiden: Brill Academic, 2005. 145–57. **Dray, S.** "The Book of Joshua." *Evangel* 23 (2005) 2–6, 34–39, 66–71. **Durso, P. R.** "Living in the Interim Time: Lessons to Be Learned from Joshua 1–4." *RevExp* 100 (2003) 257–67. **Gemser, B.** "*Be'ber hayyardën:* In Jordan's Borderland." *VT* 2 (1952) 349–55. **George, D. B.** "Yahweh's Speech at Jos 1,2–6 and Deut 11: Semantics, Intertextuality, and Meaning." *ZAW* 112 (2000) 356–64. **Hess, R. S.** "Joshua 1–12 as a Centrist Document." In *Dort ziehen Schiffe dahin . . . : Collected Communications to the 14th Congress of the International Organization for the Study of the Old Testament, Paris 1992.* Frankfurt am Main: Lang, 1996. 53–67. **Hoffmeier, J. K.** "The Structure of Joshua 1–11 and the Annals of Thutmose III." In *Faith, Tradition, and History.* Ed. A. R. Millard, J. Hoffmeier, and D. W. Baker. Winona Lake, IN: Eisenbrauns, 1994. 165–79. **Mackay, A. B.** *The Conquest of Canaan: Lectures on the First Twelve Chapters of the Book of Joshua.* London, 1884. **Niehaus, J. J.** "The Conquest and Ancient Near Eastern Warfare: The Element of Fear." *Contact* 35 (2006–2007) 26. **Noort, E.** "Josua im Wandel der Zeiten: Zu Stand und Perspektiven der Forschung am Buch Josua." In *The Book of Joshua.* Ed. Ed Noort. BETL 2005. Leuven: Peeters (2012) 21–47. **Roth, W.** "The Deuteronomic Rest Theology: A Redactional Critical Study." *BR* 21 (1976) 5–14. **Rowlett, L.** "Inclusion, Exclusion and Marginality in the Book of Joshua." *JSOT* 55 (1992) 15–23. **Wénin, A.** "Josué 1—12 comme récit." In Noort (ed.) *The Book of Joshua*, 51–63.

Josh 1–12 demonstrates as well as any other portion of Scripture the complex nature of the process in which God worked to produce his inspired word for all future generations. The Word of God did not begin as a book. It began as a story told by people reacting in faith to actions they interpreted as the work of God. Such stories took various forms: spy stories, stories of holy war, cultic catechism, divine call and testing, battle reports, sacral judgment, tribal etiology, and so on. Most were preserved and transmitted in the storytelling venues of Israel—at the campfire, in the family circle, and during tribal and league worship.

The stories did not remain as simple story. They were adopted and adapted by the Israelite cult, particularly the cult at Gilgal. Stories of divine action became the center of cultic celebration. As such, they took on a new form and function but continued to give dynamic life and faith to the people of God through many generations. By hearing these stories and celebrating them in cultic worship, each new generation learned of the faith of their ancestors.

After Israel developed its own political and cultural organizations, liturgy became literature and was used to give identity and hope to the people of God. The breakup of the united monarchy and the ensuing opposition between Rehoboam in the south and Jeroboam I in the north led to propaganda campaigns. The basic source material of both Joshua and Judges came from northern tribes, particularly Benjamin, Manasseh, Naphtali, Zebulun, Issachar, Gad, and Reuben. Judean sympathizers and/or Levites living in the north must have taken the narratives south, where they became central propaganda resources to recount the failure of the folk hero leaders of Judges and the Benjaminite Saul, demonstrating that Israel needed one king, one in the line of David.

The literary collection undergirded its influence by introducing language and narrative from other parts of the canon, so that den Braber and Wesselius can report: "expressed on the literary level: there are few or no other episodes in the Primary History [Genesis–Kings] which exhibit more intertextual connections with other parts of it than precisely these chapters" (Josh 1–8).[1]

In 587, a major crisis confronted Israel—exile, loss of self-government, loss of land, loss of temple worship, apparent loss of the promise and gift of God celebrated so enthusiastically in the sacred text. Now how would Israel react?

At least a portion of the people of Israel were true to their tradition! The exiles in Babylon incorporated the new experiences and new elements of faith into their traditional literature, sometimes transforming old stories into new words of hope for the people as they embarked on a new faith journey. The stories in the "book" of Joshua acted as something of a bridge between the Pentateuch and the former prophets, resulting in the large collection of the Enneateuch or Primary History or ultimate history.

Studies of textual history, particularly of the Septuagint (LXX), show that the content of a number of the books of the Hebrew Bible remained somewhat fluid until the first Christian century. The people continued to transmit and seek to understand the work of God in their lives. Ultimately, the text was stabilized, and today we embrace as authoritative the text of the Hebrew Bible that was preserved for us by the Masoretic tradition.

Thus we interpret the Masoretic text and seek to proclaim its word to our generation. In so doing, we follow a long tradition that has produced a number of Jewish interpretive documents, including the Talmud, and a multitude of Christian commentaries. Even with a stabilized text, the people of God are constantly seeking

---

ways to make the text relevant to new generations through new translations and commentaries.

This commentary tries to demonstrate the dynamic character of the action and word of God in their development and application within the community of the faithful. Just as such growth and use within the community of God revealed the authoritative character of the word for Israel, it is the prayer of the present commentator that the commentary will be used by God to bring forth contemporary confession and testimony to the dynamic power of God to work through his people and his word to give hope and identity to his people.

A. Divine Marching Orders (1:1–18)

Bibliography

Assis, E. "The Choice to Serve God and Assist His People: Rahab and Yael." *Bib* 85 (2004) 82–90. **Auld, A. G.** "Joshua: The Hebrew and Greek Texts." In *Studies in the Historical Books of the Old Testament.* Ed. J. A. Emerton. VTSup 30. Leiden: Brill, 1979. 1–14. **Barth, C.** "Die Antwort Israels." In *Probleme biblischer Theologie.* Ed. H. W. Wolff. Munich: Kaiser, 1971. 44–56. **Barthélemy, D.** *Critique textuelle de l'Ancien Testament.* Vol. 1, *Josué, Juges, Ruth, Samuel, Rois, Chroniques, Esdras, Néhémie, Esther.* OBO 50. Göttingen: Vandenhoeck & Ruprecht, 1982. **Bieberstein, K.** *Josua, Jordan, Jericho: Archäologie, Geschichte und Theologie der Landnahmeerzählungen Josua 1–6.* OBO 143. Göttingen: Vandenhoeck & Ruprecht, 1995. **Blum, E.** "Pentateuch-Hexateuch-Enneateuch? Or: How Can One Recognize a Literary Work in the Hebrew Bible?" In *Pentateuch, Hexateuch, or Enneateuch: Identifying Literary Works in Genesis through Kings.* Ed. T. Dozeman, T. Römer, and K. Schmid. Atlanta: SBL, 2011. 43–72. **Brice, T.** *Kingdom of the Hittites.* New York: Oxford UP, 1999. ———. *Life and Society in the Hittite World.* New York: Oxford UP, 2002. **Brueggemann, W.** *The Land: Place as Gift, Promise and Challenge in Biblical Faith.* OBT 1. Philadelphia: Fortress, 1977. **Chirichigno, G. C.** "The Use of the Epithet in the Characterization of Joshua." *TJ* 8 (1987) 69–79. **Coats, G. W.** "An Exposition for the Conquest Theme." *CBQ* 47 (1985) 47–54. **Collins, B. J.** *The Hittites and Their World.* SBLABS 7. Atlanta: SBL, 2007. **Diepold, P.** *Israels Land.* BWANT 95. Stuttgart: Kohlhammer, 1972. **Dozeman, T.** "Joshua 1.1–9: The Beginning of a Book or a Literary Bridge?" In E. Noort (ed.) *The Book of Joshua.* Leuven: Peeters, 2012. 158–82. **Eissfeldt, O.** *The Old Testament: An Introduction.* Oxford: Blackwell, 1965. **Forrer, E. O.** "The Hittites in Palestine." *PEQ* 48 (1936) 190–203; *PEQ* 49 (1937) 100–115. **George, D. B.** "Yahweh's Speech at Jos 1:2–6 and Deut. 11: Semantics, Intertextuality, and Meaning." *ZAW* 112 (2000) 356–64. **Gerbrandt, G.** *Kingship according to the Deuteronomistic History.* SBLDS 87. Atlanta: Scholars Press, 1986. **Glatt-Gilad, D. A.** "Revealed and Concealed: The Status of the Law (Book) of Moses within the Deuteronomistic History." In *Mishneh Todah: Studies in Deuteronomy and Its Cultural Environment in Honor of Jeffrey H. Tigay.* Winona Lake, IN: Eisenbrauns, 2009. 185–99. **Habel, N.** *The Land Is Mine: Six Biblical Land Ideologies.* OBT. Minneapolis: Fortress, 1995. **Hall, S. L.** *Conquering Character: The Characterization of Joshua in Joshua 1–11.* New York: T&T Clark, 2010. **Harrison, T. P.** "Neo-Hittites in the 'Land of Palestine': Renewed Investigations at Tell Ta'yinat on the Plain of Antioch." *NEA* 72 (2009) 174–89. **Hauch, G.** "Text and Contexts: A Literary Reading of the Conquest Narratives (Jos 1–11)." PhD diss., Princeton University, 1991. **Hawk, L. D.** *Every Promise Fulfilled: Contesting Plots in Joshua.* Louisville: Westminster John Knox, 1991. **Hawkins, J. D.** "Cilicia. The Amuq, and Aleppo: New Light in a Dark Age." *NEA* 72 (2009) 164–73. **Hoffmeier, J. K.** "The Structure of Joshua 1–11 and the Annals of Thutmose III." In *Faith, Tradition, and History*. Ed. A. Millard et al. Winona Lake, IN: Eisenbrauns, 1994. 165–79. **Hoffner, H. A., Jr.** "Ancient Israel's Literary Heritage Compared with Hittite Textual Data." In *The Future of Biblical Archaeology: Reassessing Methodologies and Assumptions*. The Proceedings of a Symposium August 12–14, 2001, at Trinity International University. Ed. J. K. Hoffmeier and A. Millard. Grand Rapids: Eerdmans, 2004. 176–92. **Hölscher, G.** *Geschichtsschreibung in Israel*. Lund: Gleerup, 1952. 259–61, 336. **Howard, D. M., Jr.** "All Israel's Response to Joshua: A Note on the Narrative Framework of Joshua 1." In *Fortunate the Eyes That See*. Ed. A. Beck et al. Grand Rapids: Eerdmans, 1995. 81–91. ———. "The Case for Kingship in Deuteronomy and the Former Prophets." *WTJ* 52 (1990) 101–15.———. "'Three Days' in Joshua 1–3: Resolving a Chronological Conundrum." *JETS* 41 (1998) 539–50. **Jobling, D.** "The Jordan a Boundary: Transjordan in Israel's Ideological Geography." In *The Sense of Biblical Narrative: Structural Analyses in the Hebrew Bible II*. JSOTSup 39. Sheffield: JSOT Press, 1986. 88–134. **Kaiser, W. C., Jr.** "The Promised Land: A Biblical-Historical View." *BSac* 138 (1981) 302–12. ———. "The Promise Theme and the Theology of Rest." *BSac* 130 (1973) 135–50. **Kempinski, A.** "Hittites in the Bible: What Does Archaeology Say?" *BAR* 5.1 (1979) 20–45. **Kitz, A. M.** "Undivided Inheritance and Lot Casting in the Book of Joshua." *JBL* 119 (2000) 604–7. **Klengel, H.** *Geschichte des hethitischen Reiches: Handbuch der Orientalistik*. Vol. 1, *Der Nahe und Mittlere Orient*. Leiden: Brill, 1998. ———. *Hattuschili und Ramses: Hethiter und Ägypter—ihr langer Weg zum Frieden*. Mainz: Zabern, 2002. **Klinger, J.** *Die Hethiter*. Munich: Beck, 2007. **Kratz, R. G.** *The Composition of the Narrative Books of the Old Testament*. Trans. J. Bowden. Edinburgh: T&T Clark, 2000. Originally published as *Komposition der erzählenden Bücher des Alten Testaments* (Göttingen: Vandenhoeck & Ruprecht, 2000). **Latvus, K.** "Tekstin yhtenäisyys ja epäyhtenäiyys hermeneuttisena kysymyksenä (Joos 1)." *Taik* 95 (1990) 394–98. **Lipiński, E.** *On the Skirts of Canaan in the Iron Age: Historical and Topographical Researches*. OLA 153. Leuven: Peeters, 2006. **Lohfink, N.** "Die Bedeutungen von hebr.*jrš* qal und hif. *BZ* NF 27 (1983) 14–33. ———. "Die deuteronomistische Darstellung des Übergangs der Führung Israels von Moses auf Josue." *Scholastik* 37 (1962) 32–44. Translated as "The Deuteronomistic Picture of the Transfer of Authority from Moses to Joshua," in *Theology of the Pentateuch* (Minneapolis: Fortress, 1994) 234–47. ———. *Das Hauptgebot*. AnBib 20. Rome: Pontificio Institutio Biblico, 1963. **Margolis, M. L.** *The Book of Joshua in Greek: According to the Critically Restored Text with an Apparatus Containing the Variants of the Principal Recensions and of the Individual Witnesses*. Part 5, *Joshua 19:39–24:33*. Publications of the Alexander Kohut Memorial Foundation. Paris: Librairie Orientaliste Paul Geuthner, 1931–38. Repr., Monograph Series. Philadelphia: Annenberg Research Institute, 1992. **Mazor, L.** "The Septuagint Translation of the Book of Joshua." *BIOSCS* 27 (1994) 29–38. **McCarthy, D.** "An Installation Genre?" *JBL* 90 (1971) 31–41. ———. "The Theology of Leadership in Joshua 1–9." *Bib* 52 (1971) 228–30. ———. *Treaty and Covenant*. Rome: Pontifical Biblical Institute, 1963. 143–44. **Meer, M. N. van der.** *Formation and Reformulation: The Redaction of the Book of Joshua in the Light of the Oldest Textual Witnesses*. VTSup 102. Leiden: Brill, 2004. ———. "Textual Criticism and Literary Criticism in Joshua 1:7 (MT and LXX)." In *X Congress of the International Organization for Septuagint and Cognate Studies, Oslo, 1998*. Ed. B. A. Taylor. SBLSCS 51. Atlanta: Scholars Press, 2001. 355–71. **Mitchell, G.** *Together in the Land*. JSOTSup 134. Sheffield: Sheffield Academic, 1993. **Mittmann, S.** "*ugebul*—'Gebiet' oder 'Grenze'?" *JNSL* 17 (1991) 37–44. **Moatti-Fine, J.** *Jésus (Josué): Traduction du texte grec de la Septante, Introduction et notes*. La Bible d'Alexandrie 6. Paris: Cerf, 1996. **Möhlenbrink, K.** "Josua im Pentateuch." *ZAW* 59 (1943) 49–56. **Nelson, R.** "Josiah in the Book of Joshua." *JBL* 100 (1981) 531–40. **Nentel, J.** *Trägerschaft und Intentionen des deuteronomistischen Geschichtswerks: Untersuchungen zu den Reflexionsreden Jos 1; 23; 24; 1 Sam 12 und 1Kön 8*. BZAW 297. Berlin: De Gruyter, 2000. **Niemann, H. M.** "Das Ende des Volkes der Perezziter: Über soziale Wandlungen Israels im Spiegel einer Begriffsgruppe." *ZAW* 105 (1993) 233–57. **Nogalski, M.** "Joshua 1:1–9: Only Be Strong and Very Courageous." *RevExp* 95 (1998) 427–35. **Noort, E.** *Das Buch Josua: Forschungsgeschichte und Problemfelder.* EdF 292. Darmstadt: Wissenschaftliche Buchgesellschaft, 1998. ———. "Josua und seine Aufgabe: Bemerkungen zu Jos. 1:1–4." In *Nachdenken über Israel, Bibel und Theologie: Festschrift für Klaus-Dieter Schunck.* Ed. H. M. Niemann, M. Augustin, and W. H. Schmidt. BEATAJ 37. Frankfurt am Main: Lang, 1994. 69–87. **Noth, M.** *Überlieferungsgeschichtliche Studien.* Tübingen: Niemeyer, 1943. 40–41. **O'Connell. K. G.** "The Lists of Seven Peoples in Canaan: A Fresh Analysis." In *The Answers Lie Below: Essays in Honor of L. E. Toombs.* Ed H. O. Thompson. Lanham, NY: University Press of America, 1984. 221–41. **Otto, E.** *Das Mazzotfest in Gilgal.* BWANT 107. Stuttgart: Kohlhammer, 1975. 22–23, 57, 86–88, 135–46. **Plöger, J. G.** *Literarkritische, formgeschichtliche und stilkritische Untersuchungen zum Deuteronomium,* BBB 26. Bonn: Hanstein, 1967. **Polzin, R.** *Moses and the Deuteronomist: Deuteronomy, Judges, Joshua.* New York: Seabury, 1980. **Porter, J. R.** "The Succession of Joshua." In *Proclamation and Presence: Old Testament Essays in Honour of Gwyne Henton Davies.* Ed. J. I. Durham and J. R. Porter. London: SCM Press, 1970. 102–32. **Preuss, H. D.** ". . . ich will mit dir sein!" *ZAW* 80 (1968) 139–73. **Rahlfs, A.** *Septuaginta.* Vol. 1, *Leges et historiae.* Stuttgart: Württembergische Bibelanstalt, 1935. **Rendtorff, R.** *Das überlieferungsgeschichtliche Problem des Pentateuch.* BZAW 147. Berlin: De Gruyter, 1977. **Rofé, A.** "The Devotion to Torah Study at the End of the Biblical Period: Josh. 1:8; Ps. 1:2; Isa 59:21." In *The Bible in the Light of Its Interpreters: Sarah Kamin Memorial Volume.* Ed. S. Japhet. Jerusalem: Magnes, 1994. 622–28. ———. "The Piety of the Torah-Disciples at the Winding-Up of the Hebrew Bible: Josh. 1:8; Ps. 1:2; Isa 59:21." In *Bibel in jüdischer und christlicher Tradition: Festschrift für Johann Maier zum 60. Geburtstag.* Ed. H. Merklein, K. Müller, and G. Stemberger. BBB 88. Frankfurt am Main: Hain, 1993. 78–85. **Römer, T.** "Josué, lecteur de la Torah (Jos 1,8)." In *Lasset uns Brücken bauen: Collected Communications to the XVth Congress of the International Organization for the Study of the Old Testament, Cambridge 1995.* Ed. K.-D. Schunck et al. BEATAJ 42. New York: Lang, 1998. 17–124. ———. *The So-called Deuteronomistic History: A Sociological, Historical and Literary Introduction.* London: T&T Clark, 2005. **Rösel, H. N.** "Lässt sich eine nomistische Redaktion im Buch Josua feststellen?" *ZAW* 119 (2007) 184–89. **Rudolph, W.** *Der 'Elohist' von Exodus bis Josua.* BZAW 68. Berlin: Töpelmann, 1938. 164–65. **Sacchi, P.** "Giosuè 1,1–9: dalla critica storica e quelle letteraria." In *Storia e tradizioni di Israele: Scritti in onore di J. Alberto Soggin.* Ed. D. Garronne and F. Israel. Brescia: Paideia, 1991. 237–54. **Schäfer-Lichtenberger, C.** *Josua und Salomo: Eine Studie zu Autorität und Legitimität des Nachfolgers im Alten Testament.* VTSup 58. Leiden: Brill, 1995. **Schmitt, G.** *Du sollst keinen Frieden schliessen mit den Bewohnern des Landes.* BWANT 91. Stuttgart: Kohlhammer, 1970. 146–47. **Schmitt, R.** *Zelt und Lade als Thema alttestamentlicher Wissenschaft.* Gütersloh: Gütersloher Verlagshaus, 1972. **Simpson, C. A.** *The Early Traditions of Israel.* Oxford: Blackwell, 1948. 280. **Smend, R.** "Das Gesetz und die Völker." In *Probleme Biblischer Theologie.* Ed. H. W. Wolff. Munich: Kaiser, 1971. 494–509. **Springer, B.** "Die Landverheissung im deuteronomistischen Geschichtswerk." *Laur* 18 (1977) 116–57. **Tengström, S.** *Die Hexateucherzählung.* ConBOT 7. Lund: Gleerup, 1976. 143–54. **Tov, E.** "The Growth of the Book of Joshua in the Light of the Evidence of the LXX Translation." In *Studies in the Bible.* Ed. S. Japhet. ScrHier 31. Jerusalem: Magnes, 1986. 321–39. ———. *Textual Criticism of the Hebrew Bible.* 2nd ed. Minneapolis: Fortress, 2001. **Unger, M. F.** "Archeological Discoveries and Their Bearing on Old Testament. Part II: Archaeology and the Resurrection of the Horites and the Hittites." *BSac* 112 (1955) 138–43. **Van Seters, J.** "Joshua's Campaign of Canaan and Near Eastern Historiography." *SJOT* 4 (1990) 1–12. **Veijola, T.** *Die ewige Dynastie: David und die Entstehung seiner Dynastie nach der deuteronomistischen Darstellung.* STT, series B, 193. Helsinki: Suomalainen Tiedeakatemia, 1975. 28–29, 128–29, 141. **Weinfeld, M.** *Deuteronomy and the Deuteronomic School.* Oxford:

Clarendon, 1972. ———. "The Extent of the Promised Land—the Status of Transjordan." In *Das Land Israel in biblischer Zeit*. Ed. D. Strecker. GTA 25. Göttingen: Vandenhoeck & Ruprecht, 1983. 59–75. ———. *The Promise of the Land: The Inheritance of the Land of Canaan by the Israelites*. Taubman Lectures in Jewish Studies 3. Berkeley: University of California Press, 1993. **Wellhausen, J.** *Die Composition des Hexateuchs und der historischen Bücher des Alten Testaments*. 2nd ed. Berlin: Reimer, 1889. 119. **Westermann, C.** *Die Verheissungen an die Väter*. FRLANT 116. Göttingen: Vandenhoeck & Ruprecht, 1976. **Wijngaards, J. N. M.** *The Dramatization of Salvific History in the Deuteronomic Schools*. OtSt 16. Leiden: Brill, 1969. **Wilcoxen, J.** "Narrative Structure and Cult Legend: A Study of Joshua 1–6." In *Transitions in Biblical Scholarship*. Ed. J. Rylaarsdam. Chicago: University of Chicago Press, 1968. 43–70. **Wilhelm, G.,** ed. *Ḫattuša-Boğazköy: Das Hethiterreich im Spannungsfeld des Alten Orients: 6. Internationales Colloquium der Deutschen Orient-Gesellschaft 22.–24. März 2006, Würzburg*. CDOG 6. Wiesbaden: Harrassowitz, 2009. **Winther-Nielsen, N.** *A Functional Discourse Grammar of Joshua: A Computer-Assisted Rhetorical Structure Analysis*. ConBOT 40. Stockholm: Almquist & Wiksell, 1995. **Wüst, M.** *Untersuchungen zu den siedlungsgeographischen Texten des Alten Testaments*. Beihefte zum Tübinger Atlas des vorderen Orients B9. Wiesbaden: Reichert, 1975.

Translation

[1a]*After[b] the death of Moses, the servant of Yahweh,[c] Yahweh said to Joshua, the son of Nun and the official of Moses,* [2]*"Moses, my servant,[a] is dead. Therefore,[b] you are now to get up and cross over[c] this[d] Jordan—you along with all this people—to the land which I am giving to them, to the sons of Israel.[e]* [3]*Every place where the sole of your (pl.)[a] foot may step,[b] to you (pl.) I have given[c] it, precisely as I told Moses.* [4a]*From the wilderness and this Lebanon unto the major river, the River Euphrates, all the land of the Hittites,[b] and across to the Mediterranean Sea at the setting of the sun shall be the territory for you (pl.).*

[5]*No man shall be able to stand his ground before you[a] all the days of your life. Just as I was with Moses, so I will be with you. I will not forsake you, nor will I abandon you.* [6]*Have conviction and courage because it is you who will cause this people to inherit the land[a] which I made an oath with their fathers[b] to give to them.* [7]*Just have great[a] conviction and courage to obey carefully[b] the whole Torah[c] which[d] Moses, my servant, commanded you. Do not turn away from it to the right nor to the left so that you may prudently prosper[e] everywhere you go.[f]*

[8]*This book of the Torah shall not depart from your lips. You shall meditate upon it day and night that you may obey carefully according to[a] everything which is written in it, because[b] then you shall make your paths[c] successful, and then you will be prudently prosperous.* [9]*Have I not commanded you, 'Have conviction and courage. Do not tremble or get all shook up, for with you is Yahweh your God[a] everywhere you go?'"*

[10]*Joshua gave orders to the national officials,* [11]*"Pass through the midst of the camp[a] and order the people, 'Prepare provisions for yourselves,[b] because within three days you (pl.)[c] will be crossing over this Jordan to enter to possess the land which Yahweh your God[d] is giving you to possess it.[e]'"*

[12]*Meanwhile[a] to the Reubenites, Gaddites, and half the tribe of Manasseh, Joshua said,[b]* [13]*"Remember[a] the word which Moses, the servant of Yahweh, commanded you (pl.): 'Yahweh, your God, is giving you rest in that he has given you (pl.) this land.'* [14a]*Your women, children, and herds are to remain in the land which Moses gave to you (pl.) beyond the Jordan,[b] but[c] you (pl.) are to pass over armed[d] before your brothers, all the valiant warriors,[e] so that you (pl.) may help them* [15]*until Yahweh gives rest to your brothers just as to you (pl.). They also are to possess the land which Yahweh your God is giving to them. Then you (pl.) may return to the*

land you (pl.) possess so that you (pl.) may possess that which Moses, the servant of Yahweh,[a] *has given you (p.l) beyond the Jordan at the rising of the sun."*

[16]*They answered Joshua, "Everything which you have commanded us, we will do; everywhere you send us, we will go.* [17]*According to all the way in which we have obeyed Moses, so we will obey you. Only*[a] *may Yahweh your God be with you just as he was with Moses.* [18]*Every man who rebels against your order and does not obey your words, to the last detail which you command us,*[a] *shall be put to death. Only have conviction and courage."*

Notes

1.a. Van der Meer (*Formation and Reformulation,* 161) notes that of about 460 MT lexemes in 1:1–18, LXX does not reproduce 45 of them. He provides (summarized on pp. 245–48) a strong defense of MT by showing LXX eliminating redundancies and presenting a "faithful though not literal translation of the Hebrew original" (246).

1.ab. The book begins with a consec. form of the verb, as do Leviticus, Numbers, Judges, 1 Samuel, 2 Samuel, 2 Kings, Ezekiel, Ruth, Esther, Nehemiah, and 2 Chronicles. GKC §49b, n. 1, attributes this to an attempt to show the close connection of the books to the preceding book. Cf. the discussion of Heb. tenses by W. Schneider, *Grammatik des biblischen Hebräisch* (Munich: Claudius, 1974) §48. The consec. form of היה introduces a temporal clause (cf. discussion of Lambdin, *Introduction to Biblical Hebrew,* §110). See the discussion of *IBHS* 33.2.4.b.

1.bc. The LXX omits "servant of Yahweh." This may be a conscious effort to avoid repetition with v 2 or a later insertion of a familiar biblical idiom into v 1. At no point in chap. 1 does the LXX represent a longer text (see Auld, "Joshua: The Hebrew and Greek Texts," 3). Tov (*Textual Criticism of the Hebrew Bible,* 328) sees this as one of several Deuteronomistic additions. Bieberstein (*Josua, Jordan, Jericho,* 84–85) joins this with 1:15–16; 12:6a; 22:4, finding all are expansions in MT with LXX having the original text. He is most likely correct, though van der Meer (*Formation and Reformulation,* 178–82, 189) sees LXX making a "stylistic shortening."

2.a. ועתה functions as a transitional formula leading to the main point of the dialogue and should be translated "therefore" rather than as a simple temporal adverb "and now" (cf. Schneider, *Grammatik,* §54.1; *IBHS* 38.1e). The imperatives are sg., but the subject is made pl. by adding "and all this people." This is expressed in English translation by subordinating the "people" to Joshua by means of the preposition "along with."

2.b. LXX does include the reference to Moses as servant here, employing the word θεράπων, implying free and honorable service, instead of δοῦλος; cf. 9:4, 6 (= 8:31, 33 MT).

2.c. קום עבר represents "two syntactically coordinate imperatives without a conjunction; so they could be translated 'prepare to cross'" (Harstad, 53).

2.d. LXX omits "this," but retains it in v 11. The presence of the demonstrative adjective could indicate that Jordan is simply a common noun meaning "river" here (Gray, 59). Tov ("Growth of the Book of Joshua," 332, cites this as an MT "small elucidation." Bieberstein (*Josua, Jordan, Jericho,* 87) joins this with 1:3, 4, and 8 and finds that LXX has translated the demonstrative pronouns with topographical antecedents inconsistently. So he retains MT in all cases.

2.e. LXX omits "to the sons of Israel," a phrase as unnecessary in the original Heb. construction as it is in the English translation. Fritz (26) calls this an explanatory gloss, while Tov ("Growth of the Book of Joshua," 332), classifies it as a "small elucidation." Bieberstein (*Josua, Jordan, Jericho,* 86) sees a late MT gloss, but van der Meer (*Formation and Reformulation,* 196) is consistent as he points to LXX shortening. It would appear the tradition would have more reason to delete such a phrase rather than to add it.

vv 2–9. The divine speech is carefully formulated without consec. tenses or the use of ו to connect sentences. V 3, with the direct object opening the sentence, is appositional, specifying the claim of v 2; cf. Andersen, *Sentence,* 47. V 4 continues the specific apposition. V 5a represents a somewhat extended form of what Andersen (*Sentence,* 43) calls "antithesis in apposition," repeating the positive statement of v 3 in a negative form. V 5b is in the form of a comparative clause (cf. GKC §161), but its function in the context is causal (cf. P. Joüon, *Grammaire de l'Hébreu biblique,* 2nd ed. [Rome: Institut biblique pontifical, 1947] 170k). The concluding negative clauses again form an "antithesis in apposition." V 6 changes moods and perspective, forming an "apposition in another perspective" (Andersen, *Sentence*, 44), namely, that of Joshua rather than God. V 7 is an "exclusive clause" limiting the comprehensive statement of the previous clause (Andersen, *Sentence*, 168–77). The meaning is "you cause them to inherit . . . , only just be sure to. . . ." The sentiment is again repeated in a clause of "antithesis in opposition" (*Williams' Hebrew Syntax*, 491, refers to a negated adverbial clause of manner), concluding with a purpose clause that functions similarly to the preceding "exclusive clause." V 8 brings yet another appositional clause, this time from the perspective of the book of Torah, then again from the perspective of Joshua, again ending in a purpose clause. This is all summarized in v 9 through means of a rhetorical question.

3.a. The frequent change of pronouns in the Heb. will be reflected in the translation through use of the "you (pl.)" for the 2nd pers. pl.

3.b. *IBHS* 31.4.e. calls the use of the prefixed tense or imperfect here "the nonperfective of possibility," which "denotes the possibility that the subject may perform an action."

3.c. Syr. reads with a few Heb. MSS, יִהְיֶה, a secondary accommodation to Deut 11:24–25 as shown by Bieberstein (*Josua, Jordan, Jericho*, 88). Compare similar assimilation in 1:4, 5.

4.a. The text of vv 3–4 represents a variant of Deut 11:24 and has provided material for scholarly comment throughout the ages. The most honest approach simply states: "It is impossible to tell how this textual corruption came about" (Soggin, 26). Both verses have been transmitted in various forms by the early versions. The MT of the Deuteronomy passage reads: "Every place where the sole of your (pl.) foot steps will belong to you (pl.), from the wilderness and the Lebanon, from the River, the river Euphrates and across to the western sea will be your (pl.) territory." Compared to Josh 1:4, the Deuteronomy text omits the "this" modifying Lebanon; reads "from the River" rather than "and unto the great river"; omits "all the land of the Hittites"; and refers simply to "the western sea" rather than the "great sea at the setting of the sun," the literal reading in Joshua. Van der Meer (*Formation and Reformulation*, 208–9) thinks the LXX translator picked up the adjective with "the river" from Deut 11:24 rather than rendering the MT.

The LXX in Joshua reads v 4 as the direct object of "I will give" in v 3 (read as future rather than the pf. of the Heb.). This necessitates the omission of the opening preposition of the Heb. text. The LXX reads: "the wilderness and the Antilebanon unto the great river, the river Euphrates, and unto the far sea, from the setting of the sun will be your territory." This represents a quite literalistic translation of the Hebrew but omits "this" modifying Antilebanon, with which LXX always translates Lebanon, and "all the land of the Hittites." The "this" does not make sense in the context. It should point to territory near at hand in the view of the speaker. Such would not be the case for a speaker east of the Jordan. Howard (82) sees the reference as "an ironic one, intended to emphasize the inclusion of this (not-visible) land." Lebanon appears to be of particular interest to at least some part of the late Israelite community (cf. Deut 3:25; Josh 9:1; 11:17; 12:7; 13:5; Zech 10:1). "This" may represent a late gloss into the text (Fritz, 26), what Tov ("Growth of the Book of Joshua," 332) calls a "small elucidation," attempting to underline Lebanon as a vital part of the Promised Land. Van der Meer (*Formation and Reformulation*, 199–200) speaks of a utopian extension of the Promised Land in which Lebanon is now the center of extended Israel so that the pronoun "this" "aims to integrate this territory within the expansionistic view." Gray (59) attaches "this" to wilderness, seeing Lebanon as a later interpolation. Van der Meer (*Formation and Reformulation*, 204–8) thinks the unusual use of Antilebanon "reflects a concern to reserve 'Antilebanon' for the area promised by God and 'Lebanon' for the unconquered territory" (208).

"Unto the major river" in the present context "would in fact include the whole desert region east of Jordan" (Soggin, 26). The idiom is used more logically in Deut 1:7 and may have been taken up into the Joshua tradition due to familiarity with the usage there. Otherwise, it is an attempt to lay claim to the Transjordanian desert regions.

4.b. "All the land of the Hittites" derives from the early Hittite empire in Asia Minor, ca. 1680–1190 BCE, but the geographical reference during Israel's history was to the land of Syria-Palestine, as shown by its frequent use in Assyrian inscriptions. Howard (82) sees it as "a synonym for 'Canaanites,' perhaps designating all of the hill country west of the

Jordan." LXX and Vg. omission of the term may show that this, too, is a later gloss (see Fritz, 26; Gray, 59; Bieberstein, *Josua, Jordan, Jericho*, 86, who speaks of an epexegetical gloss) added to the Heb. text to insure that the land promised by Joshua would be understood as including the land north of that actually controlled by Israel during most of her history. This was made necessary by the fact that Joshua is not credited with conquering nor with apportioning this land. Still the *Preliminary and Interim Report* retains MT. So, too, does van der Meer (*Formation and Reformulation*, (200–203), who sees an LXX omission when the reference to Hittites had "lost its referential function" (203).

5.a. The Heb. returns to the 2nd pers. sg. in direct address to Joshua. The early versions seek to achieve grammatical continuity with the preceding verses by reading the 2nd pers. pl. Bieberstein (*Josua, Jordan, Jericho*, 88) notes the excess use of conjunctions and adverbs in the LXX of 1:5b–8a, correctly attributing them to the stylistic tendencies of the Gk. translator.

6.a. *BHS* notes, where *BHK* did not, that more than twenty Heb. MSS read the preposition אל rather than the sign of the direct object before the land. This goes against all other biblical usage of the *hip'il* of נחל, which regularly has a double object following as here. The use of אל does not appear to conform to rabbinic practice either. Indeed, one might more appropriately expect אל before the "people." Perhaps the later tradition read the promise in the light of the incomplete conquest of Josh 13; Judg 1, etc., and interpreted it to mean "to inherit in the land," thus a portion of the land. Cf. GKC §119g for the use of אל to answer the question "where?"

6.b Consistent with its previous readings, the LXX has the 2nd pers. pl. suffix rather than the 3rd pers., so MT is preferable (see Bieberstein, *Josua, Jordan, Jericho*, 89).

7.a. The LXX has no equivalent for the Heb. adverb מאד. Fritz (26) simply deletes it, but *Preliminary and Interim Report* retains MT. Tov ("Growth of the Book of Joshua," 392) sees MT emphasis here. Van der Meer (*Formation and Reformulation*, 219) sees the LXX translator omitting the adverb to more closely link vv 6 and 7. Bieberstein (*Josua, Jordan, Jericho*, 88–89) sees this as an adverb that would fit the Greek translator's style and so must be a late addition to MT. No reason for the addition or omission of the particle is apparent, unless it is another attempt to maintain consistency by reproducing exactly the formula of v 6.

7.b. MT has two consec. infinitives, which the Gk. reproduces by joining them with a conjunction. In the similar construction in Deut 15:5; 28:1, 15; and 32:46, the LXX has a similar "addition" of the conjunction, but in Deut 24:8 the LXX does not have the conjunction where MT does. (In the latter passage the Heb. מאד appears after לשמר and is translated by the LXX with σφόδρα.) MT joins the pair with the conjunction in Deut 28:13 and Josh 23:6. The evidence points again to a tendency of the Gk. to use a uniform formulation, whereas the Heb. has various formulations.

7.c. "Torah" of MT is called into question in two ways. LXX does not witness it, and the following preposition ממנו has a masc. suffix, whereas a fem. suffix would be needed to agree with Torah. The latter may be explained as a weakening of the gender distinction in Heb. (GKC §135o) or an *ad sensum* reading (van der Meer, *Formation and Reformulation*, 216). The omission of Torah is frequently used as evidence that it is a later interpolation into the Heb. tradition (Noth; Gray, 60; Tov, "Growth of the Book of Joshua," cited from the repr. in *The Greek and Hebrew Bible: Collected Essays on the Septuagint*, VTSup 72 [Leiden: Brill, 1999] 390). The case can be argued both directions. The reference to the whole Torah may have entered from the succeeding verse or may have been omitted in the tradition to avoid repetition. Nelson uses the grammatical argument to opt for LXX. Schäfer-Lichtenberger (*Josua und Salomo*, 192) argues that the masc. pronoun refers to Moses as a prototype of Torah obedience and that the reference to Torah is original to the text. Bieberstein (*Josua, Jordan, Jericho*, 89) finds no reason for the translator to omit or erase Torah, which must represent a Heb. addition. Torah is thus a really unnecessary clarification of "what Moses commanded." Van der Meer (*Formation and Reformulation*, 219–22) finds LXX rewriting the material to bring harmony with the Pentateuch. His theory here as elsewhere may be a bit too clever to explain the work of the translator. Dozeman (177–81) draws wide-ranging canonical conclusions from the absence of Torah in LXX. All the Torah refers to a closed book concept, while omitting the terms shows life experience of certain teachings of Moses. This means that the "question of literary context, specifically whether Josh 1.1–9 functions as the beginning of a book or as a literary bridge to Deuteronomy is not confined to the original introduction of Josh 1.1b, 2.5–6 or the redaction of Josh 111a,3–4.7–9 but continues into the formation of separate canons. The MT of Josh 1.1–9 tends to separate the book of Joshua from Deuteronomy, while the LXX ties Josh 1.1–9 more closely with Deuteronomy, merging the stories of Moses and Joshua into a continuous history."

7.d. LXX omits אֲשֶׁר because of the omission of its antecedent, "Torah."

7.e. The Heb. root שׂכל means "to be wise, clever, to understand, to have success." The translation attempts to incorporate the breadth of the semantic field of the Heb.

7.f. LXX reads ἐν πᾶσιν οἷς ἐὰν πράσσης, "in everything you might do." Bieberstein (*Josua, Jordan, Jericho*, 89) uses the final term and its rare appearance to suggest that LXX is the *lectio difficilior* and thus original. This may simply be a case of the translator taking a bit of freedom in substituting "to do" for "to walk."

8.a. The MT uses the same formulation as in 7a. As there, some MSS read the preposition ב rather than כ. The Gk. tradition is not uniform at this point, with the result that Rahlfs (*Septuaginta*) reads ἵνα συνῇς ποιεῖν πάντα τὰ γεγραμμένα, while Margolis (*Book of Joshua in Greek*) reads ἵνα εἰδῇς . . . . The former picks up the wording of 7b, while the latter repeats that of 7a. Neither reading contains a preposition with "all." The MT is preferable here, representing the traditional Deuteronomic idiom (cf. M. Weinfeld, *Deuteronomy*, 336:17, 17a, 17b; 346:6). Nelson follows MT "as a moderately cumbersome deuteronomistic formulation."

8.b. LXX does not witness the causal conjunction of the MT, expressing the interclausal relationship with the temporal adverb alone. This does not necessarily reflect a different text.

8.c. Whether a sg. or pl. reading is intended by the Masoretic pointing is debatable (GKC §91k). Among the versions, Vg. reads the sg., while LXX and Syr. read the pl.

9.a. Nelson points to the use of the 3rd pers. for Yahweh as a complicating factor that could make everything from v 7 to v 9 words of Moses, not of Yahweh. Nelson chooses to make Yahweh the speaker throughout.

11.a. LXX reads the camp "of the people." Such a phrase never occurs in MT. LXX has copied the addition from the previous or succeeding verse, where "the people" are mentioned.

11.b. "For yourselves" is not stated expressly in LXX but is implicit in the use of the middle voice. Tov ("Growth of the Book of Joshua," 391) finds another MT "small elucidation" here.

11.c. LXX reads the conjunction following the temporal clause, a characteristic of Semitic grammar, not Gk. An original Heb. conjunction may underlie the reading.

11.d. LXX reads "the God of your fathers." Auld has noted the MT preference of the second pl. pronoun attached to "God" ("Joshua: The Hebrew and Greek Texts," VTSup 11–12). Deuteronomy uses the divine title "God of your fathers" eight times, but the Israelite History Books have the title only in Josh 18:3; Judg 2:12; 2 Kgs 21:22. The title is connected with the giving-of-the-land formula in Deut 12:1 and 27:3 and may have entered our text tradition from there. The LXX thus may be a witness to the fluidity of the text tradition in the use of pious idioms.

11.e. "To possess it" is a characteristic Deuteronomistic idiom (Weinfeld, *Deuteronomy*, 342, n. 2) but is missing in the LXX here and in v 15. Both times the expression is redundant and may represent again the fluidity of pious idioms. Nelson says OG lost the phrase by haplography with the start of the next verse. Tov ("Growth of the Book of Joshua," 394) sees an MT expansion under the influence of Deuteronomy. Bieberstein (*Josua, Jordan, Jericho*, 90) calls the phrase a literary critical objectionable interruption of the context. Van der Meer (*Formation and Reformulation*, 224) attributes the MT plus to the "overall emphatic and repetitive style of this deuteronomistic chapter" but sees the LXX rendering as corresponding "to the stylising Greek translation." Thus "the Greek translator was more concerned with a contextually appropriate rendering than a concordant representation of every word of the Hebrew original" (225).

12.a. The section does not begin with a consec. verb form that would indicate action subsequent to the preceding. Rather it begins with a nominal form. This introduces an episode initial circumstantial clause contemporaneous to the preceding (Andersen, *Sentence*, 77–80; compare Howard, "All Israel's Response to Joshua," 83–84). New actors are thus issued onto the scene. But making vv 12–15 simultaneous to vv 10–12 does not then twist the context to make vv 16–18 a response by both the tribal representatives of vv 10–11 and the eastern representatives of vv 12–15. This speech belongs contextually in the mouth of the eastern tribes, not the entire assembly (contra Howard, "All Israel's Response to Joshua," 84–85).

12.b. Van der Meer (*Formation and Reformulation,* 227–32) points to Josh 3:6; 4:3, 22; 9:22; 17:17; 22:24 where LXX does not translate the Heb. discourse marker לאמר. He concludes that "there is no reason to doubt that there existed some variation in the biblical manuscripts regarding the introduction of direct speech in the pre-Masoretic and proto-Masoretic period" (230). LXX omissions at these points represent "stylising the redundant."

13.a. זכור is an infinitive absolute used for the emphatic imperative (GKC §113bb). The Mosaic command employs a participle followed by a pf. verb with the copula. This construction does not appear to have received adequate attention. The present context refers to the command of Moses in Deut 3:18, which presupposes the possession of Transjordan. It must therefore refer to past or present possession and rest, not a future promise. D. Michel in reference to the Psalms says when the pf. appears after an impf. or a participle, it does not carry the action further but rather introduces beside it an explanatory fact (*Tempora und Satzstellung in den Psalmen* [Bonn: Bouvier, 1960] 99; cf. A. B. Davidson, *Hebrew Syntax,* 3rd ed. [Edinburgh: T&T Clark, 1901] 55c, 56; Joüon, *Grammaire,* §§119r).

14.a. It is not clear where the Mosaic "quotation" ends. The language of v 14 comes from Deut 3:19 but speaks of Moses in the 3rd pers., unless one omits the reference to Moses on the basis of the LXX. Nelson accepts OG saying, "MT changes the grammatical subject with a harmonistic expansion from v 15 involving 'Moses has given you across the Jordan.'" Mitchell (*Together in the Land,* 27, n. 4) sees MT harmonizing v 14 with v 15.

14.b. The LXX retains God as the giver of the land rather than Moses and omits the anachronistic localization "beyond the Jordan." Mazor (*BIOSCS* 27 [1994] 37) contends that "LXX seems to exhibit a less hostile view of the Trans-Jordanian territory than that shown by MT." However, LXX itself is not consistent at this point, for in v 15 it, too, speaks of land given by Moses beyond the Jordan. Here is one of many examples of a shorter LXX that may represent a text tradition that avoided repetition of pious terminology. Mitchell (*Together in the Land,* 27, n. 4; compare Tov "Growth of the Book of Joshua," 392) sees MT v 14 harmonizing with the next verse. Bieberstein (*Josua, Jordan, Jericho,* 91–92) resorts to form-critical analysis of Josh 1:13–15 and Deut 3:18–20. MT shows two cases of Yahweh giving the land and two of Moses, the latter limited to land east of the Jordan. This argues for MT as the older text tradition. Van der Meer (*Formation and Reformulation,* 237–39) decides that LXX represents a deliberate avoidance of MT's *lectio difficilior* and "smoothening" of the text to consistently have Yahweh giving the land.

14.c. ואתם introduces a contrast sentence (Andersen, *Sentence,* 150–52). The expectations for the men are contrasted to those of their family and flocks.

14.d. "Armed" "is rather a guess at the meaning" of חלץ (Gray, 61), which comes from Num 32:17 (compare Exod 13:18; Josh 4:12; Judg 7:11). Van der Meer (*Formation and Reformulation,* 244) and Moatti-Fine (*Jésus (Josué),* 53) use this among other examples to show the Gk. translators' impressive command of military vocabulary and willingness to use "contextually appropriate renderings" (van der Meer, *Formation and Reformulation,* 44).

14.e. Nelson notes that "valiant warriors" (גבורי החיל) "are fighters of the highest valor and competence." Gray (61) defines a valiant warrior as "a freeborn Israelite able and liable to defend the community in arms."

15.a. See *Note* 11.e. The MT is repetitive and difficult. LXX opens with "until Yahweh your God," which Nelson attributes to Gk. dittography. The LXX omits וירשתם אותה, as do many modern commentators, seeing dittography of the preceding word (e.g., Holzinger, [1901] 2; Soggin, 27; Fritz, 126; Nelson, 28). Tov (*Textual Criticism of the Hebrew Bible,* 328) calls this an "afterthought" and "a clear addition in the text, disturbing its syntax." *Preliminary and Interim Report* (2:3) defends MT along with Barthélemy (*Critique textuelle,* 1:1) who shows the history of the debate. LXX apparently read איש לירשתו, "each to his own possession" (Margolis, *Book of Joshua in Greek,* 13); however, this may be an attempt to translate a difficult MT. Either the original text or a later reader sought to underline the fact that the Transjordan tribes would actually possess their land, another example of the textual tradition noted in v 4. The possession of territory outside the strict land of

Canaan was important to this tradition. See *Note* 11.e above. Here, the LXX also omits "servant of Yahweh," which is repetitious. See also *Note* 1.b above.

17.a. The particle רק, "only," in vv 17–18 introduces an exclusive sentence (Andersen, *Sentence*, 168–77) placing limits on the total commitment of the people. Such obedience is given to Joshua when God is present with him and Joshua is courageous.

18. a. Fritz (26) sees this phrase, "to the last detail which you command us," as breaking the syntactical pattern and so thus to be regarded as a clarifying addition. This explanation forces the biblical writer into being too much of a linguistic purist.

Form/Structure/Setting

Josh 1 forms a pivotal point in the canon of Scripture. As Knauf shows throughout his commentary, the chapter forms both a conclusion to the Pentateuch, thus creating a Hexateuch, and an introduction to the prophetic books. It also forms a pivotal point in the Deuteronomistic History.

Even though syntactically the impf. consec. of 2:1 ties the two chapters together, Josh 1 sets forth a complete narrative section in and of itself, while chap. 2 turns to an entirely new time and subject, the sending out of spies. We are justified in maintaining, therefore, that a new section begins at Josh 2:1. Chap. 1 opens with divine speech in vv 1–9, followed by Joshua's speech to national officials in vv 10–11. Vv 12–18 form a unit with command (vv 12–15) and response (vv 16–18) between Joshua and the eastern tribes.

Tradition

The tradition history behind Josh 1 cannot be written until the entire book has been exegeted, for the tradition behind this chapter is the tradition behind the entire history of Moses and Joshua. This chapter evinces connections with at least two pentateuchal traditions:

(1) The pentateuchal tradition of Joshua as minister of the prophet Moses (see *Comments*).

(2) The pentateuchal tradition of the appointment of Joshua as successor to Moses.

The older tradition concerning Joshua as minister to Moses reflects some prophetic elements: (1) possession of the spirit (Num 27:18); (2) emphasis upon listening to and obeying the word of the leader (Num 27:20–21); (3) the tent of meeting (Deut 31:14)[2]; and (4) oracular form (compare Deut 31:23).

Josh 1 is a recapitulation of the report of Joshua's appointment in Deut 1:38; 3:21–28; 7:24; 11:24–25; 31:1–8, 14–15, 23; 34:9. This, in turn, is related to the tradition which found written expression in Num 27:12–23. The Joshua "narrator presents Deuteronomy as the lens through which to understand and assess what is to come."[3]

Joshua's appointment tradition may have its origin in prophetic circles that were concerned about the continuity of the prophetic office, as reflected in the story of Elijah and Elisha in 2 Kgs 2:9–15. Such a tradition is formulated in the language

---

2   Cf. M. Haran, "The Nature of the '*'ōhel mô'edh*' in Pentateuchal Sources," *JSS* 5 (1960) 50–65.

3   Hess (2010) 3.

of war, so that both the Deuteronomistic and Priestly forms emphasize the role of Moses as a leader of war (Num 27:17; Deut 31:2). Josh 1 takes up the military element and expands it. Joshua is the military successor to Moses but still dependent on the commands of Moses as well as those of Yahweh.

The tradition of Israelite tribes choosing to live in Transjordan rather than in the land of Canaan is the subject matter of Num 32 and Deut 3. The tradition incorporates the Transjordan narrative into the Israelite conquest tradition to underline the unity of all Israel and the joint responsibility shared by all the tribes (cf. Num 32:20–23). It looks ahead to the crucial narrative of Josh 22.

Deut 3 seeks to remind the Transjordan tribes of their responsibility while encouraging Joshua in his. Num 32 seeks to justify the separation of Israel into Cisjordan and Transjordan territories and to underline the common loyalty of both groups to Yahweh and to one another. Josh 1:12–18 uses the same tradition to demonstrate the total obedience of all Israel to Joshua.

Rösel maintains that a late Deuteronomistic author appropriated the military call, "have conviction and courage," in v 6 and transformed it to another sphere of life, God's encouragement to Joshua to keep the law.[4] For Rösel, the promise of divine presence is placed ahead of the military call rather than behind it, since divine presence is the more important theme in the introduction of Moses' successor.

Source and Redaction

The solution to the literary-critical problems of Joshua is based on somewhat different criteria than those of the Pentateuch. In the Pentateuch critical scholars seek doublets, contradictions, distinctions in divine names, and so on to separate literary strata. Only occasionally are such criteria apparent in Joshua. Here the issue is one of literary style (e.g., shifts from singular to plural address), vocabulary, shifts of content and perspective, theological shifts, and so on. Den Braber and Wesselius concede, "Even if one is in general unwilling to divide the text according to criteria, the validity of which does not appear beyond reasonable doubt, every reader will have to concede that the problems for a reading of these chapters as a coherent work are formidable indeed."[5]

Traditional literary or souce criticism and more recent redaction criticism have sought to show a long literary history in the composition of Joshua. The problem is aptly described by J. Hollenberg.[6] V 11b closely parallels Deut 11:31 and contains Deuteronomic phraseology.[7] שֹׁטְרִים, "officials," appears in Exod 5 and Num 11:16, but is found widely in Deuteronomy. צֵידָה, "provisions," occurs only three times in the Pentateuch (Gen 42:25; 45:21; Exod 12:39), but appears in sources peculiar to the Deuteronomistic or Israelite History (Josh 9:11; Judg 7:8; 20:10; 1 Sam 22:10). In assessing such evidence, one may conclude that where a word itself appears to be archaic, that does not prove that the "literary source" is as well. The most we can

---

4   *ZAW* 119 (2007) 184–89.
5   *SJOT* 22 (2008) 254.
6   "Die deuteronomischen Bestandtheile des Buches Josua," *Theologische Studien und Kritiken* 1 (1874) 476–77.
7   Weinfeld, *Deuteronomy*, 342g, nn. 2, 3.

deduce is that the Deuteronomist may be relying on tradition in these instances (cf. chap. 3).

In chap. 1, source critics point to the following evidence: Moses is called "the servant of Yahweh" three times (vv 1, 2, 7). The audience addressed shifts from singular (vv 2, 5–9) to plural (vv 3–4). The statement in v 3 seemingly makes that of v 5 unnecessary. Vv 7–9 are separated from the verses preceding them grammatically by the particle רק, formally by the variation in the use of the encouragement formula, thematically by insertion of studying the law, and contextually by the placing of a condition on the previous promises.

The most recent source/redaction work on the book of Joshua has been carried out by Knauf and Fritz along with Kratz.[8] Even in his translation Fritz divides the sections into the basic Deuteronomistic literary elements, the redactional additions in Deuteronomistic style, redactional expansions in the style of the Priestly document of the Pentateuch, and redactional additions of various types. The basic Deuteronomistic elements of chap. 1 occur only in vv 1–6; Deuteronomistic redaction appears in vv 7–9; and further supplements come in vv 10, 11, and 12–18. Bieberstein finds a basic Deuteronomistic layer in vv 1–2, 5b–6, 9d–11, 16–17, and some part of v 18.[9] For him, a Reuben or Transjordan redactor added 1:12–15. A law-centered redactor provided vv 3–4 and probably vv 5a, 7–9c. Part of v 18 represents independent additions.

Knauf sets Joshua up as the example for all subsequent prophets of Israel.[10] He maintains that chap. 1 introduces all the major redactional strata that he finds in Joshua except P. Thus for him D appears in vv 1–6*, 16–18; H in vv 12–15; prophetic in vv 7–9; and the Joshua-Judges redaction in v 5a.

Perhaps the most thorough analysis is that of Kratz.[11] His "main passages" are chap. 1; 11:16–23; 12:1–8; 13:1–7; 21:43–45; 22:23–24. He concludes, "redactional passages dominate the structure." His summary isolates independent Joshua legends in chaps. 6 and 8 along with a settlement narrative in chaps. 2–12 based on 6 and 8.[12] This fits easily onto Num 25:1a/Deut 34:5–6 forming a "pre-Deuteronomic Hexateuch." Then come Deuteronomistic and Priestly expansions including 1:1–2, 5–6; 11:16–23; 23–24. Later comes 3–4; 5; 6–11; 1:10–18; 13–22. Next come 1:3–4, 7–9; 11:16–22; 12:1–8; 13:1–6; 23–24.

Dozeman[13] argues against Noth, Smend, and Nentel who use these verses as an important building block for their various theories of a Deuteronomistic historian. Finding these nine verses form a unified text, Noth can describe them as a literary bridge to Deuteronomy. Using a modern redaction critical approach, Smend and Nentel deny the text's unity and use the split to solve the Deuteronomistic contrast between a complete and a partial conquest. Addition of vv 1a, 3–4, 5–6 changes the concept of conquest from total to partial and fits the context of the book of Deuteronomy.

---

8   *Composition of the Narrative Books.*
9   *Josua, Jordan, Jericho,* 100–101.
10 Knauf, 40.
11 *Composition of the Narrative Books,* 186–217.
12 Ibid., 206–7.
13 "Joshua 1.1–9"; see especially pp. 181–82.

Dozeman finds two hands at work in the nine verses with the first composing the opening of a book dated after the formation of the Pentateuch. Dozeman sees themes here that appear in non-Priestly and Priestly materials as well as in Deuteronomy. On this basis, Dozeman argues for Joshua as an independent book.[14] See *Setting* below.

Hess vigorously debates such literary sourcing on the basis of literary and political analyses of the text.[15] Likewise, Den Braber and Wesselius conclude: "the story of the beginning of the conquest of Canaan by the Israelites in Joshua 1–8 in its present form is an extremely well composed literary-religious composition, and there is no reason to assume a complex editorial history."[16]

Literary/source study has produced disparate results, competing theories, an excessively small "original narrative" with little narrative art, and no agreement on definitive criteria for defining original text and sources. Whatever sources one may find, study of vocabulary and tradition reflect a quite ancient tradition.[17] This is only the first indication of many that labeling literature as P or D does not by necessity determine a literary unit's age. P apparently represents the language of the cult and its priestly leaders dating back to the installation of the Jerusalem temple if not from the tent of meeting before the monarchy. D represents to a large extent the language of northern Levites reframing the tetrateuchal tradition and giving it a conclusion. The story of Josiah's temple-restoration discovery of the book of the law is not necessarily a royal claim for an early date for a late writing. The book of Joshua is too closely related to Deuteronomy and to major sections of Numbers for these books to be literary latecomers.

Josh 1:1–9 represents typical Deuteronomic paraenesis. Vv 10–11 form the center of the argument over an earlier or pentateuchal source in Josh 1.[18] The two verses also provide evidence for the Deuteronomistic character of the whole chapter.[19] These nine brief verses reflect much of the language of Deuteronomy but do not create a "doublet" to any section of Deuteronomy or to Num 27. Still, scholars have uncovered abundant evidence of a literary "history" within these nine verses.

How does one describe such a literary history? A variety of solutions is possible:

1. A continuation of pentateuchal sources in chaps. 1–2 with various Deuteronomistic layers added.[20]
2. A Deuteronomic compiler's adaptation of older liturgical-narrative tradition.[21]
3. A unified introduction of the Deuteronomist with a few glosses.[22]

---

14   Cf. more recently Christian Frevel, "Das Josua-Palimpsest. Der Übergang vom Josua- zum Richterbuch und seine Konsequenzen für die These eines Deuteronomistischen Geschichtswerks." *ZAW* 125 (2013) 49–71.
15   Hess (1996) 74, n. 1.
16   *SJOT* 22 (2008) 274.
17   M. Noth, *Überlieferungsgeschichte des Pentateuch* (Stuttgart: Kohlhammer, 1948) 193; K. Baltzer, *Die Biographie der Propheten* (Neukirchen-Vluyn: Neukirchener Verlag, 1975) 55.
18   See Otto, *Mazzotfest*, 86–87; for attribution to E, see Simpson, *Early Traditions*, 280.
19   Wellhausen, *Composition*, 119; Noth.
20   E.g., Holzinger, (1901) 2, xvii; Gressmann, (1922) 134; Tengström, S. *Die Hexateucherzählung.* ConBOT 7. Lund: Gleerup. 1976, 143–54. See also Eissfeldt, O. *The Old Testament: An Introduction.* Trans. P. Ackroyd. Oxford: Blackwell. 1965, 248–57.
21   Gray, 48.
22   Noth, *Überlieferungsgeschichtliche Studien*, 40–41.

4. A succession of Deuteronomistic editors.[23]
5. The solution that is closer to reality, in this author's view, comes from Winther-Nielsen.[24] He writes, "The theme of servanthood and obedience sets the framework for the themes of conquest, distribution, and lifelong success. The promises are motivations for service in a Mosaic fashion. Only arbitrary literary presuppositions can turn this perfect introduction, conclusion and staging into two or more fragmented sources."[25]

One item is clear. The larger part of chap. 1 of Joshua is based on Deuteronomic vocabulary. V 1 takes up the narrative from Deut 34:5, 10–12. The only evidence for an older source might be the expansion משרת משה, "official of Moses," but its use in the earlier literary sources is doubtful (see Comments). The participial נתן, "giving," formula in v 2 is likewise Deuteronomic, and the application of the "servant" title to Moses is widespread in Deuteronomic circles (see Comments), though not confined to them. Vv 3–5a are closely related to Deut 11:24–25a, adding a formula closely related to the Deuteronomic "Promulgationssatz."[26] The motif of divine presence (Josh 1:5b) rests ultimately on the tradition of the call of Moses (Exod 3:12) but is taken up in Joshua directly from the Deuteronomic context of Deut 31:8, 23. Indeed, Deuteronomy never explicitly uses the formula to express the divine presence with Moses, but it is typical of Deuteronomic argument to refer to the divine presence with the ancestors.[27]

The hip'il of נחל, "cause to inherit," the encouragement formula, and the oath formula combine to show that v 6 is Deuteronomic. Every phrase of v 7 is Deuteronomic.[28] V 8 has Deuteronomic tints,[29] but הגה (cf. Ps 1:2) and צלח (Ps 1:3; 1 Chr 22:13; 2 Chr 20:20; 24:20; 31:21) may join it to a later strand of legalistic piety in Israel. V 9 returns to Deuteronomic vocabulary[30] and the promise of presence.

Josh 1:1–9 is thus Deuteronomic in vocabulary and literary connections. It represents one of the many orations by which the Deuteronomistic writer(s) bring theological interpretations to bear on historical materials.[31] "Joshua 1 prepares the reader for the remainder of the book by grounding the conquest and possession of the land in the theological interests of Deuteronomy."[32]

The only question that remains is the number of Deuteronomists who worked on Josh 1. Vv 3–4 might represent an insertion on the basis of Deut 11:24–25. The plural address, however, does not necessarily make it a part of the later redaction.[33] The other point in question comes at v 7, a variation of the encouragement formula that parallels 1 Kgs 2:1–4. Both examples are speeches to new leaders following

---

23   E.g., Smend, "Das Gesetz und die Völker," 494–97; Otto, Mazzotfest, 86; Veijola, Die ewige Dynastie, 28–29.
24   Functional Discourse Grammar.
25   Ibid., 294.
26   Cf. N. Lohfink, Das Hauptgebot, 59–63, 297–98.
27   H. D. Preuss, ZAW 80 (1968) 146, 148.
28   Cf. Weinfeld, Deuteronomy, 336, 339, 343, 346.
29   Ibid., 336, 339.
30   Ibid., 343, 344.
31   Noth, Überlieferungsgeschichtliche Studien, 5.
32   Hess (2000) 20.
33   Lohfink, Das Hauptgebot, 248.

the death of a leader beyond compare. Both contain similar structural elements: external presuppositions for the following speech and the speech composed of introduction, paraenesis, and practical instructions.[34] In each example, a portion of the admonition involves loyalty to the law, a portion Veijola, following Smend, would attribute to a secondary "nomistic" Deuteronomist. Noort insists that when we reach the places in the text where Joshua lays down his commander's mantle and appears as a teacher of Torah (1:7–8; 8:30–35; 23), we have arrived at the literary level on which the final comprehensive lines of the final form of the book of Joshua can be written.[35] Here we have reached the textual horizon that stretches from Exodus to 2 Kings.

Noort's explanation fails to note the structure of the Deuteronomistic work that is determined by the commands to obey the law and commandments given Israel through Moses (the key passages are Deut 1:5; 4:44; 28:69; 31:9; Josh 1:7; 22:2, 4, 5; 23:6; Judg 2:20; 1 Sam 12:14–15; 2 Sam 8:10–11; 1 Kgs 2:3–4; 8:24–25, 56–57; 9:4–7; 11:9–13, 31–39; 14:7–11; 2 Kgs 17:7–20; 18:6–7; 21:2–15; 22:11–20).

From beginning to end, the ultimate history has one theme and one measuring rod—the book of the law given to Moses. Obedience to the law brought rest for Joshua as he succeeded Moses and for Solomon as he succeeded David. Rebellion against it brought destruction upon the generations following Joshua and Solomon and ultimately upon both the northern and southern kingdoms. Neither Moses nor David was enjoined to follow the law; both are pictured as doing so. Their successors were admonished to follow the law. Joshua was able to obey and gained the land. Solomon was not able to obey and lost the kingdom. Thus Pressler can speak of the "bold, active, enlivening character of obedience."[36]

The admonition in v 7 to keep the law is necessary for the structure of the ultimate history. It also follows the covenant/treaty form on which Deuteronomy is structured.[37] Language, structure, and purpose join to attest the literary unity of 1:1–9 with the possible exception of v 8.

Chap. 1 plays a key role in shaping the book of Joshua and the overarching history to which Joshua belongs. The themes it raises—warfare, land, leadership, the unity of the people, and the faithfulness of God—are found throughout the book. Chap. 1 is an elaboration of the commission of Joshua in Deut 31. Key words constantly resound: Moses (vv 1a, 1b, 2, 3, 5, 7); give (vv 2, 3, 6); all (vv 2, 3, 4, 5, 7a, 7b, 8, 9); will be with you (vv 5, 9); and the encouragement formula (vv 6, 7, 9). Different words and phrases are used to reiterate the same thoughts: success in conquest (vv 3a, 4, 5, 6, 7b, 8b, 9b); freedom from fear (vv 5b, 9a, the encouragement formula).

The constant repetition, however, does not express a single, unambiguous statement. Rather, it unfolds a theological dialectic. "YHWH begins the story with announcements of gifts and promises (vv 2b–6) and then informs Joshua of the response necessary to actualize the promises (7–9), namely, the strict and zealous observance of the commandments of Moses."[38]

---

34   Cf. Veijola, *Die ewige Dynastie*, 28–29.
35   *Das Buch Joshua*, 6.
36   Pressler, 15.
37   Cf. K. Baltzer, *Das Bundesformular*, WMANT 4 (Neukirchen-Vluyn: Neukirchener Verlag, 1960) 79.
38   Nelson, 2.

Moses, the receiver and mediator of promise, is dead; now the promise of the land can be fulfilled (vv 1–3). And though he is dead, Moses continues to speak through his officer and his law (vv 1, 7). Everything is done to fulfill the words spoken to Moses (v 3), but the words were originally spoken to the ancestors (v 6). Victory is repeatedly promised (vv 3–9), but victory will only come through human action (vv 2, 3, 5) and obedience (vv 7–9). The Promised Land is described explicitly (v 4), but only what is precisely touched is won (v 3). Victory is certain, but the human leader is admonished repeatedly to have courage and not to fear (vv 5–9). Pressler correctly points out "the verses from Deuteronomy are knit together in a way that stresses continuity in the midst of newness and change. Above all the chapter affirms that the source of both continuity and newness is God, whose word initiates a new epoch for Israel, and whose unchanging faithfulness is the basis for confidence in times of newness and change."[39]

The intention of Josh 1:1–9 is clarified when one further contrast is noted, the formal one. The section is dominated by divine imperative (vv 2b, 5b, 6, 7, 8). The climactic summary (v 9) is not imperative; it is interrogative. God's rhetorical question forces the human leader to respond. Divine imperative, however, is not so overwhelming that response is automatic. The speakers remain in dialogue; the words addressed to the human partner are eliciting rather than intimidating.

Text criticism has revealed the freedom of copyists and scribes to read texts in new ways and to add or subtract elements from them, but such adding and subtracting is not done in the vast quantities that Kratz and other critics suggest; such redaction submerges the original texts into oblivion. Scribal copyists interpreted or retranslated important places in the texts that were unclear or that lent themselves to double readings. They restated texts in the grammar and syntax of their natural languages. They added traditional elements and perhaps composed speeches to clarify precisely the divine interpretation of a text. Still, a working assumption that one can find more creativity from the editor than from the original author demands to be questioned.

Narrative structure reveals the unity of most texts. It also confirms that an author can utilize themes and subthemes creatively so that the introduction of a new theme does not require the hand of a new editor or edition. The most that can be expected is that the person compiling the stories from oral tradition will introduce transition materials and perhaps theological speeches to ensure that the reader will clearly understand the meaning of the new literary production.

Form

Form-critical inquiry has led to different perspectives from which to view chap. 1. Lohfink understands the chapter as the conclusion of the series of narratives found in Deut 1:37–38; 3:21–22, 28; 31:2–8, 14–15, 23; Josh 1:2–9.[40] He describes Josh 1 as the prologue or overture to the book, introducing important motifs, joining the book of Joshua to the first volume of the work (i.e., Deuteronomy) and pointing to the arrangement of the book being introduced. Lohfink assigns this last function to Josh 1:1–9, which introduces the two major themes of the book:

---

39   Pressler, 9–10.
40   *Scholastik* 37 (1962) 32–44.

occupation of the land west of the Jordan (chaps. 1–12) and distribution of the land among the tribes (chaps. 13–21).

Each of the two themes has its own vocabulary. Distribution of the land is noted through the *hip'il* of the verb נחל, "cause to inherit" (Deut 1:38; 3:28; 31:7; Josh 1:6). Occupation of the land utilizes either עבר or בוא—"cross over" or "enter" (Deut 1:38; 3:21, 28; 31:3, 7, 23; Josh 1:2). Lohfink isolates within Josh 1:1–9 two distinct literary forms correlating with the two themes. A legal command to assume the office of commander of the army, an office in which Joshua was installed in Deut 31:23, appears in Josh 1:2–5. The basic elements of this genre comprise a sentence that establishes a fact (v 2a), a command (v 2b), and the necessary basis for implementation of the command (vv 3–5). Such a literary form is rooted in the legal language of Israel.[41]

The second literary form is that of the installation in the office of land distributor. This form appears in Josh 1:6, 9b and includes the following elements: the formula of encouragement, the naming of the task, and the promise of divine presence. This form is also found in Deut 31:7–8; 31:23; 2 Sam 10:12; 2 Chr 19:11b; Hag 2:4.

McCarthy tries to sharpen and expand Lohfink's installation-to-an-office genre, deriving it from cultic practice and expanding its use to civic-religious installations as well as political-military ones.[42] Mitchell comments: "It is a thesis difficult both to prove or [sic] to disprove."[43] Hess finds the genre outline "too general to be of use."[44] Creach shows that "the unit as a whole does not divide neatly along lines created by these [form-critical] elements."[45] Rather, the elements occur more than once and are spread throughout the fuller narrative.

The writer may take up elements from a possible initiation rite but uses them within a form of divine speech and divine instruction. Schäfer-Lichtenberger shows that the promise of divine presence is followed not by an installation into office but by an assigning of tasks.[46]

H. G. Reventlow brings the prophetic call, the installation in office, and the oracle of salvation together into a single form consisting of (a) epiphany of Yahweh, (b) lament, (c) introduction of the oracle of salvation through the messenger formula and its basis in the nature of Yahweh, (d) the oracle of salvation introduced by "Fear not," (e) the commission centering on the key words, "Go, I send you," (f) the objection raised by the one installed, (g) the renewal of the call by Yahweh, (h) the symbolic act, and (i) the word interpreting the symbolic act.[47] Reventlow sees his results verified by the work of Lohfink.[48]

Porter accepts Lohfink's genre conclusions and finds that "the occurrence of צוה, [command] in the passages under discussion indicates that the installation

---

41   Cf. N. Lohfink, "Darstellungskunst und Theologie in Dtn 1:6–3:29," *Bib* 41 (1960) 124–26, esp. 125, n. 2.
42   *JBL* 90 (1971) 31–41.
43   *Together in the Land*, 30.
44   Hess (1996) 72, n. 1.
45   Creach, 23.
46   *Josua und Salomo*, 190–91, n. 214.
47   *Liturgie und prophetisches Ich bei Jeremia* (Gütersloh: Gütersloher Verlagshaus, 1963) 24–77.
48   *Liturgie und Bibel: Gesammelte Aufsätze*, ÖBS 28 (Frankfurt am Main: Lang, 2005) 68, n. 206.

formula in them has its background in the royal practice and administration of the Judaean monarchy. . . . It is from the practice that marked the transmission of the royal office from one king to another that the Deuteronomic presentation would seem to be derived."[49]

Porter finds that the command to obey the law of Moses also reflects the close association of the king and the law. Connection to the king comes further from the correspondence between the admonitions to Joshua and the role of the king in Deut 17:18–20. Joshua's part in the renewal ceremony of Josh 8:30–35 and Josh 24 also come from the king's part in the festival.

Nelson extends this royal connection further. He points to the power to distribute land, the dynastic immediate succession, the people's pledge to follow the king as in the ancient Near Eastern vassal treaties, the similar installations of Solomon and of Joshua, and the double installations—human and divine—of Saul and Joshua. The change from plural to singular in Josh 1:5 shows the royal promise concentrated on Joshua. As Deut 17 commands, Joshua writes his own copy of the law on the altar of Josh 8. For Nelson, Joshua "is a sort of proto-king sketched out along the lines of the ideal deuteronomic monarch."[50]

Nelson narrows the portrait of Joshua down to one king—Josiah—who kept the law, mediated a covenant, and celebrated a Passover. The picture of Joshua then paints characteristics on Josiah: "for Dtr, at least, it could be said of both Joshua and Josiah that every place that the soles of their feet trod upon was given them."[51]

Nelson concludes: "Recognizing that it is Josiah who hides behind the mask of the deuteronomistic Joshua gives us a deeper insight into Dtr's editorial method. His approach to theological history was strongly colored by his hero worship of Josiah."[52] And he adds: "the David who was the prototype of the perfect king was not really the David whom the historian met in his sources but, as in the case of Joshua, an image of Josiah projected back into history."

Coote extends the royal imagery further.[53] He points out that Joshua played the role of monarch throughout the story; his succession followed the royal pattern, not the charismatic-judge pattern; he obeyed the law like a Deuteronomistic king; he led a family of tribes as does a king; he exercised the royal power to partition the land; the victory was attributed to an individual as to a king rather than to the entire nation; and Joshua received a "trust-inspiring oracle" as did the Assyrian kings. The national officials of v 10 represent a monarchy's bureaucracy.[54]

Certainly, Joshua is the prototype for the king, the example of the leader of Israel after Moses. But he is not Josiah retrojected backwards. McConville and Williams state the case simply: "Many have thought that Joshua is a royal figure in all but name. It is not necessary to go so far, however. Rather, the standard for all leaders of Israel is set by these terms."[55] Joshua is the prime example set up for Josiah and all the kings of Israel to follow. Judges shows that without such a leader,

---

49   "Succession of Joshua," 108–9.
50   *JBL* 100 (1981) 534.
51   Ibid., 538.
52   Ibid., 540.
53   Coote, 585–86.
54   See J. J. Niehaus, "Joshua and Ancient Near Eastern Warfare," *JETS* 31 (1988) 37–50.
55   McConville and Williams, 14.

all Israel does what is right in each one's own eyes, creating political anarchy and moral disaster. As Howard concludes, "Joshua fit the model for kings, even though he was not a king himself."[56]

Weinfeld rejects the conclusions of Lohfink and Reventlow, claiming the key formulas "fear not" and "have conviction and courage" do not belong to a ceremony of appointment to office but rather to "the occasion of war and confrontation with a difficult task that must be performed."[57] Weinfeld thus discusses "The Military Oration," finding that early examples have a variety of styles, while those in Deuteronomy are more general and stylized.[58]

Creach notes in passing that chaps. 1–12 of Joshua are patterned after ancient Near Eastern battle reports, except that God, not the king, is the major figure and that the focus is on divine grace not royal results.[59] Following the ancient Near Eastern pattern and this domination by theological themes, "these chapters are not historical records in the modern sense." Rather, chaps. 13–19 and Judg 1 come closer to historical reality. For Creach, then, "Josh 1–12 certainly has some historical roots, but this segment of the book is the product of theologians who collapsed varied and lengthy historical experiences into a story that first and foremost aims to make theological claims."[60]

Here one must ask if the form of the literature determines its historical value and if history telling cannot be done for theological purposes. Do the humorous episodes of the Rahab story eliminate it from historical consideration? Do the cultic activities and priestly language of chap. 5 move it into fiction? Do the miraculous elements in chaps. 6 and 10 that belong to the ancient worldview, if not to the critic's worldview, determine the narrative's historicity? Do stereotyped battle reports built on the form of annals produced by royal armies slip away from historical reports? The form may very well help one determine the setting and purpose of a narrative, but an extremely wide variety of forms may be used to retell historical events even when such forms do not involve self-critique or critique of one's sources.

Josh 1:1–9 cannot be forced into the wide-ranging "form" of Reventlow. Too few of the elements are present. The theory of Lohfink depends on a technical meaning of the formula חזק ואמץ: "Have conviction and courage." The expression occurs precisely in Deuteronomistic contexts introducing Joshua into the narrative (Deut 3:28; 31:6, 7, 23; Josh 1:6, 7, 9, 18). Otherwise, it occurs only in the speech of Joshua in 10:25, in two psalms of mixed *Gattungen* (Pss 27:14; 31:25) and in three passages introduced by the Chronicler (1 Chr 22:13; 28:20; 2 Chr 32:7). Josh 10:25, Ps 27:14, and 2 Chr 32:7 definitely reflect the oracle of salvation given by the commander in battle.

Deut 31:6 reflects the same background, and it is possible that Ps 31:25 is also oracular. Josh 1:7 and 18 reflect a peculiar adaptation of the form by the ultimate historian for his paraenetic interests. The same usage appears in 1 Chr 22:13. Of

---

56 Howard, 85, n. 67. Cf. Gerbrandt, *Kingship according to the Deuteronomistic History*; Howard, *WTJ* 52 (1990) 101–15.
57 *Deuteronomy*, 45, n. 5.
58 Ibid., 45–51.
59 Creach, 19–20.
60 Ibid.

Lohfink's biblical examples of this "form," only Deut 3:28; 31:7, 28; Josh 1:6, and perhaps 1 Chr 28:20 remain for an installation formula. The first four of these do not represent different witnesses to the form; rather they represent one witness repeated four times. The basic conclusion must be that both in the Deuteronomistic literature and in the Chronicler specific language has been so generalized that any form in which it has been embedded no longer plays a role in the extant literature. Thus Nelson concludes: "The suggestion that the structure and language of some sort of traditional 'installation genre' is present in this text is difficult to prove, given the repetitions and circuitous character of deuteronomistic style."[61]

This means that no oral form plays an effective role in the formulation of Josh 1:1–9. Rather, this is a piece of Deuteronomic literature composed specifically as an introduction to the book of Joshua. "We meet little original material: the speeches patch together various bits and pieces of material drawn from Deuteronomy."[62] "The first chapter of Joshua is almost entirely a Deuteronomistic composition, written to demarcate and introduce the period of the conquest."[63]

Does this strengthen Nelson's case for a Josianic Joshua? Certainly not, if Nelson's conclusion is that no Joshua tradition exists, only backward projections from Josiah. But to imagine that original readers saw Josiah in both Joshua and David seems to stretch credulity a bit. Joshua was the ideal leader after Moses.

Josiah and his followers hoped that Josiah could duplicate the success story of Joshua, but the tradition did not provide enough material about Josiah to project him as such a highly successful leader. Josiah obtained his interpretation of the law from a prophet: he moved with limited success into the north; and he died in a foolish adventure against outside forces. Joshua was the leader by whom Josiah was measured, not the reverse. If there were an ideal figure for kings to imitate outside David, then Joshua was that figure, not Josiah.

Josh 1:10–11 plays on terminology from the previous section and carries it further. V 9 summarizes the previous section as a divine command. This command, in turn, centered on obedience to the command of Moses (v 7). V 10 describes Joshua obediently commanding the national officials to command the people. The section (vv 1–11) introducing the military occupation of the land (see *Comments*) does so through a "divine chain of command": God>Joshua>officials>Israelites.

Just as God commanded Joshua to pass over the Jordan River (v 2), in v 11 the officials pass over the camp and command the people to pass over the Jordan. The divine command to Joshua involved "cross[ing] over this Jordan . . . to the land which I am giving" (v 2). The entire section (vv 1–11) centers on the promises and provision of God in giving the land as well as the encouragement of the leader of the people.

Joshua's command to the officials centers on the human provisions needed for the task of taking possession of the land God is giving. V 11 places the reference to the land in a subordinate clause with unnecessary repetition of the root ירשׁ, "possess," emphasizing the military participation of the people.[64]

---

61   Nelson, 29.
62   Hess, *Every Promise Fulfilled*, 56.
63   Pressler, 9.
64   For an understanding of עַם, "people," as showing dependence upon Yahweh, see Waltraut

Vv 12–18 conclude the introductory theological narrative. It is not independent literature, but, rather, it quotes from other biblical literature. As such, it is classified as a collection of quotations. The quotations, however, are not strung together loosely; they are embedded in a particular form. Christoph Barth has called this the "Answer of Israel" or "Declaration of Readiness."[65] From examples in Exod 19:7–8; 24:1–7; Ezra 10:10–12; Neh 8:2–6, joined with Deut 27:11–26; 1 Kgs 18:17–40; Josh 24:14–28; 2 Kgs 23:1–3; Num 32:28–32; Deut 31:9–13 and the present section, Barth has isolated elements of the structure of Israel's answer.[66] The entire people speak unanimously in true dialogue with God, stating that they will follow the directions given by God. Such directions are issued through a mediator to the people.

The people pledge themselves to obey the divine directions through the use of a verb of action in the first person plural imperfect. This represents a declaration of readiness to follow God's directions. The place of such an event is the cultic liturgy, says Barth, but it is not any specific festival. It is rather a celebration *sui generis*, wherein the congregation is confronted with the expressed will of God. This ritual grew out of the Deuteronomic paraenesis, particularly in the seventh century BCE.[67]

Barth's suggestion is somewhat problematic, particularly in light of his restriction of the literary form to Deuteronomic theology. As with so many exegetical questions hovering over discussion of Deuteronomic theology, Deuteronomistic History, and Deuteronomic traditions, this attribution to Deuteronomic theology hangs together with the question of the liturgical practices, apparently in northern Israel, which lay behind the Deuteronomic paraenesis.

Gray suggests that the center of action in vv 12–18 is Gilgal, which he sees as the early border sanctuary of Reuben, Gad, Ephraim, Benjamin, and Manasseh.[68] The suggestion is illuminating for our passage. The form of the passage rests on a liturgy between man and God. The content reports vows between man and men. The leaders of Israel pledge to Joshua what men normally pledge to God. Joshua's responsibility is to show the two basic requirements of Israelite leadership (see 1:1–9). God must be with him. He must be a man of great conviction and courage.

Josh 1:12–15 virtually quotes Deut 3:18–20. The few distinctions can be explained from the new historical context given the tradition and from the particular theological interests in the Joshua narrative.[69] Thus v 12 sets the context for what follows even if this involves an abrupt shift in the Joshua narrative. Or one can describe the speech of the eastern tribes as an "ironic rendition," replaying Yahweh's opening exhortations in a minor key and foreshadowing "the reversal of other expectations," thus hinting at "the possibility of other, less desirable conclusions."[70]

The call to remembrance sets the stage for the quotation from Deut 3. Signifi-

---

Schulz, "Stilkritische Untersuchungen zur deuteronomistischen Literatur," diss., Tübingen, 1974, 45–68.

65   "Die Antwort Israels," 52–56.
66   Ibid., 48–53.
67   Ibid., 53, 55.
68   Gray, 61.
69   See Hess (1996) 77.
70   Hess, *Every Promise Fulfilled*, 58–59.

cant changes occur in v 13, where Joshua adds "is giving you (pl.) rest" to introduce the key word of promise for this section. The "servant of Yahweh" attribution again takes up a theological refrain of the chapter (see 1:1–9). In v 14 Joshua substitutes "in the land" for Deuteronomy's "in your cities." This must be viewed in light of the change in v 15 from Deuteronomy's picture of each man returning to his possession (3:20) to all the tribes returning to their collective possession. Here the book of Joshua is consistent in introducing Joshua as the leader of the conquest of united Israel seeking a united land. This is also seen in the addition of "to help them" in v 14. The Joshua text goes its own way in introducing חמשים, "in battle array" (v 14), for חלוצים, "armed" (Deut 3:18), and substituting גבורי, "warriors" (v 14), for בני, "sons" (Deut 3:18). The significance of the changes is uncertain if they are not an attempt to make the military tone of the passage even stronger. They do not indicate source distinctions.

Vv 16–17 are related to the content but not the phraseology of Num 32. The language itself may rather be that of liturgy. Verse 18 stems certainly from the author of the chapter and ties it together. The entire section is thus dependent on Deut 3:18–20, but goes its own way to make specific points.

Structure

Contemporary narrative criticism would look for an opening exposition, a complication, a change or crisis, an unraveling or resolution, and an ending.[71] Josh 1:1–9 contains only a set of speeches marking the transition from Deuteronomy to Joshua, from the wilderness to the Promised Land, from Moses' leadership to that of Joshua. Chap. 1 is thus a major part of the larger story but not essentially a narrative in and of itself. The only hint of crisis and resolution is that the eastern tribes will stay with the western armies. This is not really presented in narrative, crisis format, however.

Coats attempts to show that these opening chapters create an exposition for the conquest theme in similar fashion as earlier verses form an exposition for the patriarchal theme of promise (Gen 12:1–3), the exodus theme (Exod 1:1–14), and the wilderness theme (Exod 13:17–22).[72] One may accept Coats's argument on the pentateuchal theme even though it leaves Coats no choice but to subject the Sinai materials and the conquests of Numbers to the wilderness theme. Coats's "exposition" section in Joshua, however, clearly covers too large a body of material to be compared to the much smaller expositions of the other themes. Moreover, Coats underlines only two themes in Josh 1–5 as leitmotifs, namely, the fear of the Canaanites and the divine gift of the land. This clearly omits the major themes of the presence of God, the participation of the people in taking the land, and leadership of Joshua in obeying the Torah of Moses, among others.

One must find more exact structural markers than did Coats. These theological and literary markers have been delineated in the introduction to the commentary. Chap. 1 is such a marker, forming the transition between Deuteronomy and Joshua

---

71   Y. Amit, *Reading Biblical Narratives: Literary Criticism and the Hebrew Bible*, trans. Y. Lotan (Minneapolis: Fortress, 2001) 46–47.

72   *CBQ* 47 (1985) 47–54.

by continuing the literary theme of the departure of Moses from Deuteronomy and picking up the narrative themes of the first half of Joshua.

Hawk gives another perspective, seeing chap. 1 as the exposition that introduces the main characters—God, Joshua, and representatives of the nation—initiates the plot of conquest, and presents a perspective to connect the events that will follow. Hawk's reading focuses on the book of Joshua and its unique narrative, but he recognizes "that Joshua does not stand in isolation but is to be read within the context of the much larger story that extends back to the early chapters of Genesis."[73]

Chaps. 1–12 present the conquest of the land under Joshua's leadership. Within this larger section, chaps. 1–5 introduce preparations for the conquest, while chaps. 6–12 describe the various encounters involved in the conquest. Van der Meer notes that "the narrative of the installation of Joshua by YHWH in Josh. 1:1–6:9 forms both a direct continuation and an expanded repetition of these passages from Deuteronomy."[74] He points explicitly to the themes of encouragement, the call not to fear, and divine assistance.

Hall sets out the following structure of chaps. 1–11, 12–21, and 22–24: entrance into the land, distribution of the land, and proper worship in the land.[75] Josh 11:23 would serve as a concluding transition to 13:1 if chap. 12 were not present. The major problem with Hall's analysis is that chap. 12 gives no impression of being an introduction. Rather, it presents a concluding summary of all that chaps. 1–11 describe. A similar problem arises when Hall subdivides chaps. 1–11 into 1:1–5:12, 5:13–8:35, and 9:1–11:23. The problem hinges on one's understanding of Josh 5:1. See the structural discussions there.

Hess finds that 1:2–5 provides the following outline for the book:[76]

- crossing the Jordan, 1:1–5:12
- conquest, 5:13–12:24
- distribution of the land, 13:1–22:34
- all the days of Joshua's life, 23:1–24:33

In this sense, chap. 1 functions as an epilogue to the Pentateuch and a prologue to Joshua.[77] George contends, however, that the "narrator uses these words [1:2–5] to mark an allusive dependence of his account of the story upon another account of a related story (Josh 1,2–5 = Deut 11, 23–25)."[78] Now "Yahweh talks to Joshua directly."[79]

The chapter itself has two sections. The first nine verses are given in the form of divine speech addressed to the new leader. They set the theological tone for Josh 1–12. The remaining verses pick up the narrative sequence from Deuteronomy and give the first illustration of the theological themes of 1:1–9 being actualized.

The structure of chap. 1 must then be categorized as a literary transition. The chapter presupposes the pentateuchal story and prepares for the conquest and

---

73   Hess (2000) 1; cf. Hall, *Conquering Character*, 10.
74   *Formation and Reformulation*, 173.
75   *Conquering Character*, 1.
76   Hess (1996) 68.
77   Hall, *Conquering Character*, 10.
78   *ZAW* 112 (2000) 358.
79   Ibid., 359.

land-allotment reports. It also transfers Israel from a group of unsettled tribes to a league of dispersed tribes seeking to define their relationship to one another. Here we see the specific Hebrew method of letting narrative progress through speeches and dialogue rather than through narration and action.

Narrative criticism is concerned with more than just the structural elements of a piece of literature. It also investigates how the narrative presents characters. Chirichigno shows how the book of Joshua develops Joshua's character. Starting a bit secretively, the narrator manipulates the telling of the story of Joshua so that Joshua could remain somewhat of a "mystery-character" until the narrator felt it was the right point in the story to reveal Joshua's Joshua.[80] The mystery that surrounds Joshua is partly solved when the reader encounters the remark concerning Joshua's name change. Joshua now becomes the authoritative leader bringing deliverance. See *Comments* on v 1.

Another method of determining narrative characterization comes from Hall, who reduces narrative methodology to that which isolates character traits, particularly those of Joshua.[81] Character traits are revealed in epithet, dialogue, contrast, perspective, narrative pace, structure, repetition, narrative analogy, delimitation criticism, comparison with ancient Near Eastern materials, and intertextual considerations. Hall's employment of these legitimate tools does not bring us much further along in defining Joshua's character. Who has neglected the "unique" traits of eager obedience, despair in the face of defeat, failed diplomacy, prophetic utterances, military oracles, astronomical pronouncements, and tangible commitment to Israel's corporate memory?[82] Many Joshua scholars would debate the appropriateness of a couple of these, especially "despair in the face of defeat," based on the lament of chap. 7. See the discussion there.

Setting

The narrated setting of chap. 1 is taken over from Deuteronomy without explicit description. Joshua and Israel stand on the east side of the Jordan ready to invade the west side. The literary setting is that of the author of Joshua, who appropriates a large amount of language from Deuteronomy to present Joshua and his preparation to complete Moses' tasks as the leader of the people of Israel as they enter the Promised Land.

The editor of Joshua and his point in time challenges scholars from many perspectives.[83] Ideas about the time frame of his work range from the premonarchic period through the Persian period after the return from exile.

H. J. Koorevaar points to a new model of the development of the Hebrew canon that places important texts about Torah at the seams of the tripartite canon. One such seam is Josh 1:7–8. He concludes: "we should ask ourselves whether the mentions of the Torah in Jos 1,7f. and Mal 3,22 actually refer to the Pentateuch. From the context in the preceding book of Deuteronomy, the Book of Law mentioned in

---

80   *TJ* 8 (1987) 69–79.
81   *Conquering Character*, 6.
82   Ibid., 9.
83   See discussion of Knauf, Kratz, Bieberstein, and Fritz above under *Source and Redaction*.

Jos 1,8 is not the Pentateuch, but the Deuteronomic Book of Law."[84] With specific regard to Josh 1, Koorevaar finds that "Jos 1,1–9 would have formed part of the book of Joshua long before the closure and finalization of the canon. In that case, we have a text (in a book) at the beginning of a canon block that is not the product of a macrostructural intervention in the canonical final editing."[85] Writing more simply, Koorevaar notes: "Joshua, Judges, Samuel, and Kings are all separate works. Starting with the Book of Deuteronomy, each book was written in succession and attached to the precious one, without making any changes to it. . . . There is no overarching, unifying structure. Each book is structured differently from a literary point of view. The method of historiography varies greatly."[86]

This author places the authorial time frame in the time of Rehoboam as a talented, inspired writer presents the accomplishments of Joshua as a model for Judah's new king and as a call for the northern tribes to see that their own traditions point to a covenant union of the people of Israel whether the threat to unity comes from north to south or as in Joshua from east to west. This dating of the Joshua corpus falls in line with the author's dating of Judges in a slightly later time period. Joshua must have been the first of the two writings, since Judg 1–2 reveals knowledge of Joshua.[87]

Comments

1 The death of Moses "divides Israel's early history into two distinct epochs of salvation (Deut 1:37–38): Moses' leadership in the exodus/wilderness with a stubborn people lacking faith and Joshua's leadership in the conquest/occupation of the land with an obedient people."[88] Thus the book opens with a contrast between Moses as the עֶבֶד, "servant," of Yahweh and Joshua as the מְשָׁרֵת, "official," of Moses.

Knauf reminds us that a servant is not a hired servant but a slave without rights just like an animal.[89] The servant is not free but is a family member treated no worse than women and children, and whose social status depends on the social status of the family. Servant of the king is thus a high social position, with the highest position being servant of God. "Joshua may erect a new nation on the promised soil, but its architect remains Moses."[90]

The servant-of-God terminology is not unique to the Joshua narratives. Hess identifies uses of the term in the Amarna letters and elsewhere in the ancient Near East.[91] Gray points to a Ugaritic royal title "servant of El," so that the title could well go back to Mosaic times.[92] It was one element used to define the Mosaic office as prophetic and thus to help authenticate contemporary prophecy.

---

84   "The Torah Model as Original Macrostructure of the Hebrew Canon: A Critical Evaluation," *ZAW* 122 (2010) 77.
85   Ibid., 73.
86   "The Book of Joshua and the Hypothesis of the Deuteronomistic History: Indications for an Open Serial Model." In Ed Noort, ed. *The Book of Joshua*. Leuven: Peeters, 2012. 231.
87   See Butler, *Joshua*, WBC 8.
88   Creach, 21.
89   Knauf, 42.
90   Hubbard, 77.
91   Hess (1996) 67.
92   Gray, 59.

Israel may have borrowed the ancient Near Eastern term for Moses, who is called the servant of Yahweh in Exod 4:10; 14:31; Num 11:11; 12:7–8. The first two occurrences of the term form a theological arc joining Exod 1–14 into a larger theological unit.[93] Disciples of Isaiah also picked up the theme, creating the formal similarities between Isa 7 and Exod 14 as well as the theme of belief in the prophetic word.[94] The prophetic call form of Exod 4 would also fit into this pattern. Similarly, Num 11–12 centers on the prophetic office of Moses (cf. Num 11:23; 12:6–8).

The author of Joshua took up the motif and formed it into a dominant element in his presentation of Israel's history, thereby giving honor to Moses and authenticity and authority to his words (Deut 34:5; Josh 1:1, 2, 7, 13, 15; 8:31, 33; 11:12, 15; 12:6; 13:8; 14:7; 18:7; 22:2, 4–5; compare 1 Kgs 8:53, 56; 2 Kgs 18:12; 21:8).[95] Only occasionally is the motif used in the later literature (Ps 105:26; Neh 1:7–8; 9:14; 10:30; 1 Chr 6:34; 2 Chr 1:3; 24:6; Isa 63:11; Dan 9:11; Mal 3:22).

Hawk asserts, "Moses may be dead, but the strongly Mosaic cast of this first chapter intimates that his presence will remain with Israel, both through his words and through the person of his successor. . . . Moses' death will mean the transformation of Israel—from a community propelled by the energy of an original, unitary vision to a people now motivated by essentially conservative impulses," that is the maintenance of the Mosaic tradition and teaching."[96]

Over against the great "servant" of the deity stands Joshua as the "minister" or "official" of Moses. The tradition appears only in Josh 1 and three times in the Pentateuch: Exod 24:13; 33:11; Num 11:28. It utilizes a well-chosen term. משרת indicates a youthful page serving his master freely and never implies slavery.[97] Joshua is thus introduced as the young page waiting on Moses. In some way this is a further qualification for him to succeed Moses.[98]

Where did such a picture develop? Exod 24:13 is a literary bridge to Exod 32; in 32:17–18 Joshua abruptly appears to announce the sound of war in the camp to Moses, and is just as abruptly silenced by the superior knowledge of the master. In Exod 33:11, Joshua's role switches to that of a minister at the oracular tent of meeting in the absence of Moses. In Num 11:26–30, a narrative likewise centering on the tent of meeting, Joshua is again introduced abruptly as he pleads with Moses to punish unauthorized prophets. Once again he is abruptly silenced by the master.

Outside Josh 1, the term is applied to Joshua in cultic contexts, twice in connection with the tent of meeting. Deut 31:14 also connects Joshua with the tent. Num 11 makes the context a little more specific. The tradition is at home among "circles of ecstatic 'prophecy.'"[99] The understanding of Joshua as minister of Moses as well as that of Moses as servant of the Lord has arisen in prophetic circles.

The repeated emphasis on Moses' superiority and Joshua's inferiority lends credence to the theory that such a tradition arose in circles seeking to demonstrate

---

93   Cf. R. Rendtorff, *Das überlieferungsgeschichtliche Problem*, 71, 155.
94   Cf. H. H. Schmid, *Der sogenannte Jahwist* (Zürich: Theologischer Verlag, 1976) 54–55.
95   See I. Riesener, *Der Stamm* עבד *im Alten Testament*, BZAW 149 (Berlin: De Gruyter, 1979) 184–91.
96   Hess (2000) 5.
97   C. Westermann, "שרת—dienen," *THAT* 2:1019–20.
98   Hess (1996) 68.
99   Noth, *Numbers*, trans. J. D. Martin (Philadelphia: Westminster, 1968) 89.

the superiority of Moses as a prophet of God. In this tradition Joshua appears as an ignorant warrior ready to condemn and destroy.

Chirichigno argues strongly against this characterization of Joshua:[100]

> The deuteronomic historian has made Joshua subordinate but not stupid, and demonstrated that Joshua's willing submission to Moses is the mark of greatness. . . . [W]e have demonstrated above that Joshua was very protective of the authority of Moses in Num 11:28. . . . [T]he term "minister" does not carry any idea of inferiority in the case of Elisha who was Elijah's "attendant" and who succeeds Elijah as prophet. . . . Therefore, rather than seeing in the term משרת "minister," a reference to the inferiority of Joshua, it is better to understand the term as an illustration of the disciple-like service which prepared Joshua for his own service to Yahweh as leader of the people of Israel. Therefore, the "traditions" which appear in Exodus-Numbers are consistent with the deuteronomic traditions found in Deuteronomy-Joshua. Furthermore, the development of the term משרת in the characterization of Joshua provides the reader with an analogy from which one can interpret Elisha's "ministry" to Elijah as both a physical and spiritual service, which also extends to Elisha's service to God.

Perhaps I made too much of too little in the first edition of this commentary, but Chirichigno appears to do the same in order to defend the opposite position. Num 11 surely does not honor Joshua's zeal for Moses and lack of insight into what Israel truly needed from its prophets. The minister vocabulary separates Joshua from slavery, but also suggests his position is the last one to which Israel would look for a successor to Moses. The reader observes the same development in the relationship between Elisha and Elijah. One would like to accept Chirichigno's pious picture of Joshua, but the texts simply do not present him in that way, showing, rather, how much Joshua had to learn and how far he came before God appointed him as Moses' successor.

On the positive side, Chirichigno finds the development of the character of Joshua can be seen as a progression from becoming a משרת ("attendant") of Moses to a עבד יהוה ("servant of God"). In this regard, the term "minister," in addition to referring to secular service, refers to spiritual service in much the same way as the term עבד, "slave, servant" does.

Hubbard repeatedly tries to place Joshua on an equal status with Moses in receiving revelation and leading the people. But he maintains that Joshua was mistaken in sending spies to Jericho and to Ai and in dealing with the Gibeonites. The text, however, underlines Yahweh's presence with Joshua and Joshua's courage and leadership, painting Joshua as virtually the perfect leader for Israel after Moses. It also paints Joshua as dependent on the kind of presence that was with Moses and on the law Moses prepared. The subordination of Joshua to Moses is an important, if secondary, theme in the book of Joshua. Hubbard himself concludes that "Moses shapes all that Joshua does. . . . Moses remains the gold standard to guide Joshua."[101]

In the book of Joshua the term "minister" appears in quite a different manner.

---

100   *TJ* 8 (1987) 78.
101   Hubbard, 81.

Joshua is subordinate to the law of Moses, his dead but authoritative master. Joshua's willing submission to Moses is the mark of greatness. His authority is simply limited as authority delegated from Moses and as authority subject to and limited by Torah.[102]

2 The Jordan crossing narrative raises questions. Knauf maintains that the Jordan was never Israel's border and that the narrative represented a passage from the mythical antiquity of the "wilderness" placed in historical time.[103] Such a statement can come only from Knauf's presumptuous reading in which the wilderness theme is concocted to account for the distance from Egypt to Canaan. For Knauf the land God promised west of the Jordan is not separated from the land for which the Transjordan tribes asked, knowing it was not part of the original Promised Land. For another text in which the Jordan becomes an important boundary, see Josh 22.

Central to the book of Joshua is the land given by God, inherited by Israel, and conquered by Joshua.[104] "All references to the Lord's gift of land occur in speeches and not in battle reports."[105] Mitchell's insistence that "the primary concern of chap. 1 is that the land is a divine gift, and this establishes Israel's right to it" is an overstatement.[106] The gift of the land is an early and important motif in this chapter, but the central issue is Joshua's leadership after Moses, not divine gift. H. Rösel discovers that the formula "the land which I am giving . . ." ceases to appear after this chapter, a piece of evidence that chap. 1 was composed to connect Deuteronomy and Joshua and that the Book of Joshua is not related in any way to the following books of history.[107]

In contrast to the superpowers of her environment, Israel did not claim possession of the land from primeval times on. The land belonged originally to the Canaanites (Gen 11:31; 12:5; Deut 1:7; etc.) or to a long list of former inhabitants (e.g., Exod 3:17). Israel claimed the land only because Yahweh chose to punish the original inhabitants (Gen 15:16; Deut 9:4–5) and to promise the land to Abraham.

The motif of the promise of land to the patriarchs may rest on traditions preserved by nomadic shepherds connected to divine direction during the regular change of pasture land.[108] It has been applied specifically to the land of Canaan as early as the settlement.[109] It is used to link the various sections of the Pentateuch together theologically (Gen 50:24; Exod 3:8; 6:4; 13:5, 11; 32:13; 33:1; Num 11:12; 14:16, 23–24; 32:11–12; Deut 1:8; 4:38; 6:3, 10, etc.). The language of such theological editing is closely related to that of the book of Deuteronomy.[110] The book of Joshua takes up the land theme in dependence on Deuteronomy and brings the theme to its completion. The promise to the ancestors is realized; the punishment

---

102   See Schäfer-Lichtenberger, *Josua und Salomo*, 371. For a comparison of the ministries of Joshua and Moses, see Harris (20–22).
103   Knauf, 42.
104   See "Meaning of the Material": "Studies in Land and Rest," with bibliography, in the Introduction.
105   Mitchell, *Together in the Land*, 27.
106   Ibid., 28.
107   H. Rösel, 29.
108   V. Maag, "Der Hirte Israels," *SThU* 28 (1958) 2–28; idem, "Malkût JHWH," In *Congress Volume: Oxford, 1959*, VTSup 7 (Leiden: Brill, 1960) 129–53.
109   C. Westermann, *Die Verheissungen*, 133–38.
110   Cf. Rendtorff, *Das überlieferungsgeschichtliche Problem*, 40–45, 51–70, 75–79.

of the inhabitants is carried out; the hope of the Pentateuch is fulfilled; and the inheritance from Yahweh is received. Yet much land remains (chaps. 13–19).

3 Nelson suggests that walking over a stretch of land may have been a way of laying legal claim to the land (compare chap. 18).[111] God has already given Israel the land, land they have yet to touch. "It is as though Israel already possessed legal title to the land (ever since Abraham's day), but they were awaiting God's timing for the actual possession."[112]

Ann Kitz refers to a common ancient Near East practice of undivided inheritance before inherited property was divided among the heirs.[113] This situation required an administrator of the property, a role Joshua exercised. Walter C. Kaiser, Jr., raises the issue of the loss of the promise by subsequent disobedient generations. He concludes: "Neither the days of Joshua nor of David were any kind of blank check for their descendants to rest on their father's laurels. The word of promise could also be theirs, if they would appropriate it by faith. If not, they were the losers, however, the promise was not thereby revoked, withdrawn or thereby nullified for any succeeding generation: rather that word was eternal!"[114]

4 Israel has two sets of borders, that in which her own people live and that which is the land of promise. The first can be described simply as from Dan to Beersheba (2 Sam 24:2–8, 15; 2 Kgs 4:25; cf. Deut 34:1–3), including land beyond the Jordan (2 Sam 24:5–6). The land of promise stretches from the Brook of Egypt to the Euphrates and from the Jordan River to the Mediterranean (Gen 15:18; Exod 23:21; Num 13:21; 34:1–12; Deut 1:7; 11:24, 1 Kgs 5:1 [4:21]; 8:65; 2 Kgs 14:25; 1 Chr 13:5; 2 Chr 7:8; Amos 6:14). Coote maintains that the boundary of promise corresponds to the system of Assyrian provinces in Palestine, making the Jordan a boundary that it never was in the real life of the people, as seen by the divided tribe of Manasseh.[115]

Kaiser examines the borders and states: "Even though a number of evangelical scholars have wrongly judged the southern boundary of the 'River Egypt' to be the Nile River, it is more accurately placed at the Wadi el-'Arish which reaches the Mediterranean Sea at the town of El-'Arish, some ninety miles east of the Suez Canal and almost fifty miles southwest of Gaza (cf. Num 34:2, 5; Ezek 47:14, 19; 48:28)."[116]

Amos 6:14 likewise points to the same limits for the southern boundary: the "brook of the Arabah" that flows into the southern tip of the Dead Sea. Other indicators of the southern boundary are the end of the Dead Sea (Num 34:3–5), Mount Halak (Josh 11:17), the Wilderness of Zin (Num 13:21; 34:3), Arabah (Deut 1:7), Negev (Deut 34:1–3), and Shihor opposite Egypt (Josh 13:3–5; 1 Chr 13:5).[117]

The book of Joshua refers both to the boundaries of the land where the people actually lived and to the boundaries of the land promised. The conquest narrative covers only the first (Josh 10:41; 11:17, 22; 13:2–7), but the promise was for more. Behind each of the border descriptions stood a specific historical reality.

---

111 Nelson, 33.
112 Howard, 76; note his excursus on the giving of the land in Joshua, 77–81.
113 "Undivided Inheritance and Lot Casting in the Book of Joshua," *JBL* 119 (2000) 604–7.
114 *BSac* 130 (1973) 145.
115 Coote, 586; cf. Römer, *So-called Deuteronomistic History*, 134.
116 *BSac* 138 (1981) 304.
117 On the tension surrounding the inclusion or exclusion of Transjordan in the promised land, see Mitchell, *Together in the Land*, 34–35.

Dan to Beersheba represented the land actually occupied by Israelites and governed directly by the Israelite kings. The land promised represented the traditional description of the land of Canaan by Egyptian sources of the fourteenth and thirteenth centuries (compare Gen 10:19; Num 13:17, 21–22; 34:3–12). Likewise, Hess shows that the territory described in Joshua is identical in usage and territorial boundaries to the land called Canaan in Egyptian New Kingdom texts from 1550 to 1150.[118]

The description, adopted by the Israelite tradition, still has the Jordan as the eastern boundary until farther north into Syria and on toward the Euphrates.[119] Despite the efforts of Mitchell to make the boundaries in Josh 1:4 include and emphasize the Transjordan, in either boundary description the land of the Transjordan tribes is viewed as not belonging to the land of the Lord (see Josh 22:9–34).[120] On the few occasions when Israel controlled the territory of the land promised, they governed territory outside the Dan-to-Beersheba limits through a system of tributary states (1 Kgs 5:1). "God's promise of land becomes the challenge for future generations."[121]

Creach demonstrates that the Joshua delineation of the promised borders is more than a transcription of Deut 4. Joshua features the land as all the land of the Hittites and creates an east-west emphasis with indefinite northern and southern borders. Still, the major portion of the description is of the northern part of the land—Lebanon to Euphrates. "Joshua's authors intended to make a magnificent claim in this verse about the territory to be captured now by military prowess of the people empowered by the Lord. . . . Joshua's author was placing Israel in a category with these large, dominant empires of their day."[122]

The "Promised Land" was land already controlled by enemies, not by Israel. "Rather than settling an uninhabited area, which will offer no opposition, Israel will have to overcome opponents if it is to acquire the land."[123] This is also the land David would control and in so doing build a memory celebrated as past achievement and future hope within Israel itself.

Reference to the Hittites creates some confusion. Hattusa, the capital of the Bronze Age Hittite Empire, was deserted between 1200 and 1180 BCE. That leaves the burning question of the identity of the people Joshua refers to as Hittites.

Howard cites different meanings for Hittites through the Bible.[124] In the book of Joshua, he finds the term to be a synonym for Canaanites, perhaps designating all the hill country west of the Jordan. For a discussion of Hittites, see H. A. Hoffner, Jr., who tries to separate the Hittite country in Syria and the Hittite people with Semitic names in Canaan.[125] Hess maintains this separation fits the biblical evidence the best.[126] In a later publication, Hess says people we call Hittites from

---

118   Hess (2009) 2:15.
119   Cf. Y. Aharoni, *Land*, 58–72; Hess (1996) 26.
120   *Together in the Land*, 34–35.
121   Harris, 18.
122   Creach, 24–25.
123   Hess (2000) 9.
124   Howard, 82.
125   "Hittites," in *Peoples of the Old Testament World*, ed. A. J. Hoerth, G. L. Mattingly, and E. M. Yamauchi (Grand Rapids: Baker, 1994) 127–56.
126   Hess (1996) 70–71, n. 2.

southern Anatolia did not refer to themselves as Hittites, the Hittite land thus being northern Canaan, as it was so designated by the Egyptians and Assyrians.[127]

Recent archaeological reports have located a network of neo-Hittite states in Karkamish, Tarhuntassa, Aleppo, the Amuq Valley, and Cilicia between 1000 and 700 BCE.[128] Hawkins finds this to be a "powerful Philistine" kingdom in the Amuq Plain during the period 1100–1000 BCE controlling Aleppo, Hama, Unqi, Aarpad, and Hammath whose center was at Tell Ta'yinat. These entities may have comprised the group Joshua refers to as Hittites.

The motif of land as נחלה, "inheritance," is central for Deuteronomy.[129] The word has usually been translated "inheritance" and used as the basis of a theology. G. Gerleman calls such theologizing into question by showing that the term means "home, place of residence, security of home."[130] The verb means "to settle, to cause to occupy a territory." Goldingay defines נחלה not as land but as "the rightful possession of those who live on it."[131] *DCH* retains the traditional "inherit, take possession of, hold as a possession" for the meaning of the verb and thus gives a meaning of "inheritance, possession, inalienable hereditary property" for the noun.[132] Deuteronomy uses the term in a unique way, referring to the home of all Israel, whereas other sources speak of the homestead of individuals or individual tribes (e.g., Mic 2:2; 1 Kgs 21:3; Num 16:14).

The term נחלה thus unifies the nation into a homeland for Deuteronomic theology, a homeland never before experienced by the wandering, landless, homeless Israelites. At the same time, the term limits the claim of Israel, for it shows that the homeland comes from God, not from natural rights nor from human claims of possession or power.[133]

Still another theological motif of importance to the Deuteronomic movement appears in v 3b: the fulfillment of prophecy given through Moses.[134] The force of the prophetic word was not created by the Deuteronomic theologian(s). It is implicit in the patriarchal promises of Genesis and explicit in the work of the prophets at least from Nathan onward. "The Deuteronomist's [or Deuteronomic writer's] innovation was to make this prophetic word of God the focal point of his history."[135]

Josh 1:3 is the first reference to fulfillment of prophecy given to Moses. It refers back to the specific commissions Moses gave Joshua, commands that appear only in Deuteronomy and not in the Tetrateuch (Deut 3:21, 28; 31:3–8; cf. 1:38; 31:23). The motif appears to be another element in the picture of Moses as the great prophet painted by the author of Joshua on the basis of earlier traditions.[136]

5 Howard calls this verse "the spiritual climax and highlight of the first part of

127 Hess (2009) 2:15.
128 See J. David Hawkins, "Cilicia, The Amuq, and Aleppo: New Light in a Dark Age," *NEA* 72.4 (2009) 164–73 and other articles in the issue with bibliography.
129 G. von Rad, "Promised Land," in *The Problem of the Hexateuch and Other Essays*, trans. E. W. T. Dicken (Edinburgh: Oliver & Boyd, 1966) 91.
130 "Nutzrecht und Wohnrecht," *ZAW* 89 (1977) 313–25.
131 *Old Testament Theology*, 1:516, n. 133. Cf. N. C. Habel, *Land Is Mine*, esp. 35.
132 *DCH* 5:655–56, 659.
133 See P. Diepold, *Israels Land*, 81–84.
134 Cf. G. von Rad, *Studies in Deuteronomy*, trans. D. Stalker (London: SCM Press, 1953) 83–91.
135 Weinfeld, *Deuteronomy*, 21.
136 Cf. L. Perlitt, "Mose als Prophet," *EvT* 31 (1971) 588–608.

God's charge to Joshua."[137] Mitchell tries to prove that "unlike territorial descriptions found later in the narrative, the primary concern of chap. 1 is that the land is a divine gift, and this establishes Israel's right to it. The unmilitaristic character of the chapter is also noticeable in the way the notion of 'rest' is employed."[138] In a similar tone, Earl contends that "ultimately Joshua is not concerned with conquest, but with finding rest in peaceful covenantal life with YHWH."[139]

A less idealistic reading of the chapter suggests that in every part of it, the people are preparing for warfare and conquest. Leading into war is Joshua's task. Reading the Torah prepares him to face an enemy who will not be able to take a military stand before Joshua. Rest without warfare is the goal, but the only path to the goal is warfare. Mitchell offers a weak defense here, acknowledging that the understanding of rest includes an element of warfare and, by admitting that the phrase "men of valor armed for war" in 1:14 suggests warfare, that "chap. 1 is still some distance from the enemy and the clamour of battle."[140] This is simply to say that chap. 1 is not a battle report but a theological introduction explaining the purpose and plan for warfare.

Nelson notes the plethora of divine war vocabulary here and the relationship to the uplifiting rallying cry of Deut 20:1–4.[141]

The vb. יצב, take one's stand, exclusively in the hitp. often functions in a military context, comparable to the English "mobilize" or "poised to strike" (e.g., Goliath, 1 Sam 17:16; Jer 46:4). God's promise to Israel, oft repeated, is that no one will be able to stand against (יצב) them in warfare (Deut 7:24; 11:25; Josh 1:5), a promise illustrated historically in Jehoshaphat's experience (2 Chron 20:17; cf. Exod 14:13).[142]

God's promise of presence comes in positive and negative forms: He will not forsake nor abandon, and he will be with. The double statement לֹא יַרְפְּךָ וְלֹא יַעַזְבֶךָ comes from Deut 31:6, 8 (compare 4:31) and is taken up in 1 Chr 28:20. The single statement appears in Gen 24:27; 28:15; 1 Kgs 6:13; Isa 41:17; 42:16; Pss 9:10 (Heb. 11); 16:10; 37:28, 33; 94:14; Ruth 2:20; Ezra 9:9; Neh 9:17, 19, 31. לֹא יַעַזְבֶךָ, "he will not forsake you," "constitutes the basis for an appeal to both the nation (Deut 31:6) and individuals (Joshua, Deut 31:8 [cf. Josh 1:5; Heb 13:5]; Solomon, 1 Chron 28:20) to be strong and courageous."[143]

The motif of divine presence has its roots in the nomadic lives of the ancestors, particularly in the Isaac, Jacob, and Joseph narratives.[144] It expresses the divine promise to accompany the ancestor on a fearful journey (e.g., Gen 28:15; 31:3; Exod 3:12). The motif is taken up into the holy war ideology of Israel (Judg 6:11–16; Num 14:43; 1 Sam 17:37; 2 Sam 7:9). The law corpus of Deuteronomy uses the motif only

---

137 Ibid., 83.
138 *Together in the Land*, 27–28.
139 Earl, 122.
140 *Together in the Land*, 29.
141 Nelson, 33–34.
142 E. Martens, *NIDOTTE*.
143 R. Wakely, *NIDOTTE*.
144 H. D. Preuss, *ZAW* 80 (1968) 139–73; "את עם," *TWAT*, 1:485–500; C. Westermann, *Die Verheissungen*, 130–32; D. Vetter, "עם-mit," *THAT*, 2:325–28.

in the laws for battle (Deut 20:1–4), while the framework of the book uses it in reference to guidance through the wilderness (2:7) and in Joshua's preparation for conquest (31:6, 8, 23). The motif thus expresses one of the basic roots of Israelite faith, the belief that Yahweh is the God of Israel who accompanies, leads, protects, fights, and goes with the people he has chosen for his work.[145]

The book of Joshua takes up the ancient motif and claims it for Joshua, but again a characteristic modification is made. God's presence with Joshua is the same as that which was with Moses (vv 5, 17). This presence "is the only essential factor of a leader's authority."[146] The presence is not limited to a brief blitzkrieg of a few days or weeks, but rather the presence is for a lifetime, intimating that the battle will be a long-lasting reality. The descriptions at the beginning of chaps. 13 and 23 that Joshua has become advanced in years seem to confirm this.

6 "Possession of the land, though legitimated . . . by God's gift, can continue to be legitimate only when it is held according to God's law."[147] The phrase "have conviction and courage" (חֲזַק וֶאֱמָץ) is spoken by God to Moses and then by Moses to Joshua in Deut 31:6–7, 23, the narrative of Joshua's ordination as Moses' successor. George, however, ties the words closer to Deut 11.[148] They resound as an echo in Joshua 1 (compare 10:25), and though common in holy war instructions, are much more than a battle cry. They "are not really a call to be vigorous in waging war. Rather, they are primarily an injunction to trust and depend upon the Lord."[149] Schäfer-Lichtenberger shows how the phrase is tightly tied to Joshua.[150] George finds the phrase to mean "keep the law for then you will succeed in leading the people into the land."[151]

The words reappear in the cultic lamentations (Pss 27:14; 31:24 [25]) and in David's commissioning of Solomon (1 Chr 22:13; 28:20). Hezekiah uses the phrase to encourage his officials as they wait for Sennacherib to attack Jerusalem (2 Chr 32:7). "God effects the fulfillment of his promise; man's part is to hold fast to his faith."[152] Howard advocates for an alteration in meaning, maintaining "courage" in vv 6–9 but using "resoluteness" in vv 7–8.[153] Hess finds the term used in a "variety of circumstances but always within a context of God's presence and support."[154] Nelson maintains that "as the plot unfolds, this call for courage on the part of Israel will contrast with the enemies' chronic terror (2:9, 24; 5:1; 10:2)."[155]

This commissioning and encouraging formula applies to the people as well as to Joshua. "Both the people as a whole and Joshua, who will assume the lonely role of leader, are urged to be strong and courageous, not because of any innate abilities they may possess, but because Yahweh their God will be with his obedient

---

145 Cf. Preuss, *ZAW* 80 (1968) 157.
146 Pressler, 13.
147 McConville and Williams, 14.
148 *ZAW* 112 (2000) 361–62.
149 Hess (2000) 24.
150 *Josua und Salomo*, 203, n. 506.
151 *ZAW* 112 (2000) 362.
152 Gray, 60.
153 Howard, 84.
154 Hess (1996) 72.
155 Nelson, 34.

servants and will never fail or forsake them."[156] Josh 1 uses the term to describe warfare (v 6) and allegiance to Torah (v 7).[157] "The unexpected application of the phrase as a connecting device suggests that the two tasks are inseparable. The same militant resolve that must attend Israel's conquest of the land must also characterize Joshua's strict observance of the words of Moses."[158] Pressler states: "The words are both exhortation and command. They speak to an attitude, a willingness to step out into the future that God makes available. Divine agency does not call for passivity but for bold and courageous action."[159] McConville and Williams sharply delineate the theological issue: "Possession of the land, though legitimated first of all by God's gift, can continue to be legitimate only when it is held according to God's law."[160]

The final part of v 6 makes clear what has been established to this point. Joshua is the leader who will be responsible for taking the land. Kitz, however, overstates the case, "Joshua's primary function . . . that of estate administrator . . . (who) must complete two tasks: (1) remove squatters from the land, that is, conquer it; and (2) divide and distribute the inheritance among the legitimate co-heirs so that they may take full possession by dwelling on the landed property."[161]

The land becomes an inheritance for Israel throughout the generations, each family bequeathing land to the next generation, not selling it off or having it taken away by the government. The inherited land (נחלה) is the land of a tenant farmer or fief (*Lehen*) that does not belong to the farmer. Israel's land does not belong to the family or the clan or the tribe or the nation. It belongs to God and remains the property of the deity even as Joshua distributes it among the tribes (chaps. 15–21).[162] The terms of inheritance of the land are not new; they go back to the promise to Abraham in Gen 12:7. The Promised Land is a divine gift, not human wages or human spoils of war.

7–8 The commissioning and encouraging formula appears again, in an unexpected context as we encounter "the strongest statement in the chapter."[163] The command to Joshua reflects God's command concerning the future king of Israel in Deut 17:18–20, but this does not make Joshua a royal figure. "Rather the standard for all leaders of Israel is set by these terms."[164]

These verses render the introduction of the book of Joshua as an introduction to the entire prophetic corpus, with Joshua standing as an example for all future prophets.[165] They also provide the chief evidence for Smend's introduction of a DtrN redactor.[166] While Lohfink thoroughly refutes his evidence on rhetorical and structural grounds,[167] van der Meer can still claim, "Smends's DtrN thesis

---

156   R. Wakely, *NIDOTTE.*
157   See Knauf, 40–41.
158   Hess (2000) 10.
159   Pressler, 12.
160   McConville and Williams, 14.
161   *JBL* 119 (2000) 608.
162   See Knauf, 43.
163   Mitchell, *Together in the Land*, 29.
164   McConville and Williams, 24.
165   Knauf, 40.
166   "Das Gesetz und die Völker."
167   "Deuteronomistic Picture," 239–41; cf. Schäfer-Lichtenberger (*Josua und Salomo*, 197–99).

with respect to Josh. 1:7ff. has found common acceptance."[168] Van der Meer states that the repetition of the v 6 imperatives only make sense as a redactional device.[169] He lists authors, however, who "tend to regard verses 7–8 as an integral part of the chapter."[170] Rösel describes chap. 1 as differing in literary terms –"in author, content, and character" –from chap. 2.[171] Deuteronomistic sections exist in Joshua but not in chap. 1. Chap. 1 confines itself "to the realm of the book of Joshua; this is not the broad horizon of the so-called Deuteronomistic history. The infrequent use of "the land which I am giving to . . ." calls forth the conjecture that chap. 1 was composed "to connect the book of Joshua to Deuteronomy, and on the other hand that Josh. 1 is not related to the subsequent historical books (Joshua-Kings)."

Rather than a redactional device, the imperatives serve as a rhetorical device, tying together the military and the religious task. "The same militant resolve that must attend Israel's conquest of the land must also characterize Joshua's strict observance of the words of Moses. Failure of pursuit of either task will compromise the rich life the nation seeks across the Jordan."[172] Torah is not the sole possession of a DtrN redactor. It is the central identifying theme of the Deuteronomic preaching and of the message of Joshua.

The final motif that underlines Josh 1 is Torah, specifically the Torah commanded by Moses. Often the mention of the Torah in texts is seen as a late interpolation of a secondary Deuteronomistic editor (see *Notes*), but Mitchell, among others, argues for the Torah passages as "an integral part of its context."[173] Gebhardt defends the thesis that "the correct question with which to confront the Deuteronomist . . . is not whether he was anti-kingship or pro-kingship. Rather, we need to ask what kind of kingship he saw as ideal for Israel, or what role kingship was expected to play for Israel."[174] His answer is strong and on target: the king was "to lead Israel by being the covenant administrator; then he could trust Yahweh to deliver. At the heart of this covenant was Israel's obligation to be totally loyal to Yahweh."[175] The practical result would be a king who meditated on Torah and instituted it in the life of the nation.

Law and land have an integral connection as shown by Diepold.[176] Josh 1 is constructed around the issue of obedience, beginning with obedience to Torah.[177] But obedience to Torah changes the leadership equation for Israel and for Joshua. No figure like Moses presenting God's commandments is ever again needed. In a real way, Torah replaces the need for a leader like Moses.[178] Moses and Torah are the enduring leaders of Israel, while Joshua and all other leaders are merely transitional.

---

168 *Formation and Reformation*, 174, n. 28.
169 Van der Meer, 217.
170 Ibid., 175, n. 29.
171 Rösel, 27–30.
172 Hess (2000) 10.
173 *Together in the Land*, 30–31.
174 Gebhardt, 41.
175 Gerald Eddie Gerbrandt, *Kingship According to the Deuteronomistic History* (SBLDS 87; Atlanta: Scholars Press, 1986) 102; cf. the review by David Howard, *WTJ* 52 (1990) 101–15.
176 *Israels Land*, 90–96; cf. Brueggemann, *Land*, 59–67.
177 Compare Hess, 74, n. 1.
178 Schäfer-Lichtenberger, *Josua und Solomo*, 214.

In basic usage Torah designated the teaching of the priests (Jer 18:18; Ezek 7:26; Hos 4:6). Particularly important here was the information given members of the community who asked questions of the priests (e.g., Hag 2:11–13). But, Torah was not confined to the priests. Isaiah's teachings were Torah for his disciples (8:16). The wise man also produced Torah (Prov 13:14), a task which may have ultimately had its roots in the family (Prov 1:8; 4:4, 11). Chaps. 4 and 8 of Hosea introduce the idea of a collected body of traditions called Torah, perhaps reflecting a similar tradition found infrequently in the Tetrateuch (Gen 26:5; Exod 13:9; 16:4, 28). Torah is attributed to Moses in the Tetrateuch only in Exod 18:16–20; 24:12. Even the central chapters of Deuteronomy use Torah infrequently.[179]

Torah, particularly Torah written in a book, becomes a central theological motif for the ultimate historian behind Joshua (Deut 1:5; 4:8, 44; 29:20, 28; 30:10; 31:9–12, 24–26; 32:46; 33:4, 10; Josh 1; 8:31–35; chaps. 22–24; 1 Kgs 2:3; 2 Kgs 10:31; 14:6; 17:13, 34, 37; 21:8, 11; 23:24, 25). The Torah to which he refers is uniformly the one given to Moses after he defeated Sihon and Og (Deut 1:1–5). It was written down by Moses and placed in the ark of the covenant entrusted to the Levitical priests (Deut 31:24–26). By this Torah the kings of Israel and Judah were judged (e.g., 2 Kgs 17:37). Apparently this Torah sparked the Josianic reformation (2 Kgs 22–23).

By means of the Torah motif, Josh 1 connects primarily with Moses and only secondarily with Joshua, yielding important structural implications (Josh 1:7–8; 8:31–32, 34; 22:5; 23:6; 24:26). Joshua and his people are to be thoroughly grounded in the Torah that Moses commanded from the book of the Torah. Joshua builds an altar based on the book of the Torah of Moses, writes on stones the Torah of Moses, and reads aloud the words of the law according to what was written in the book of the Torah. The final section of chap. 1 begins with admonition to obey the command and the Torah that Moses commanded. In chap. 23, Joshua insists that the new generation obey all that stands written in the book of the Torah of Moses. Chap. 24 completes the theme: Joshua wrote these things in the Torah of God (v 26). This statement brings the theme to a close with a crescendo. The Torah becomes the Torah of Moses and ends as the Torah of God.

The contrast between the Torah of Moses and the Torah of God leads Erhard Blum to see the Torah of Moses as a reference to the Pentateuch, while the Torah of God comes through Joshua and concludes the Hexateuch.[180] If such a hypothesis could be substantiated, the importance of Joshua's transitions would be even more significant for Old Testament studies in canon, exegesis, and theology.

This Torah is more than a collection of laws. Torah is the form that divine authority has assumed in the reality of Israel.[181] It is the way of life corresponding to the order of the created universe, the only way promising success. Joshua and all of the later leaders of Israel stand under the authority of Torah.[182] "Law gives shape to the life of faith, drawing the parameters within which healthy communal existence is possible. . . . The Bible does not regard law as burden or wrath, but as gift."[183]

---

179   For the appearances in chaps. 17, 27, 28, cf. Lohfink, *Das Hauptgebot*, 58.
180   Blum, "Pentateuch-Hexateuch-Enneateuch."
181   Schäfer-Lichtenberger, *Josua und Solomo*, 107.
182   See Knauf, 43.
183   Pressler, 18.

To meditate (הגה) basically means "to make a sound" and can be applied to all types of sound-makers: the cooing of pigeons (Isa 38:14; 59:11); the growling of lions (Isa 31:4); human beings uttering sounds in their throats (Job 27:4; Pss 1:2; 2:1; 35:28; 37:30; 38:12 [13]; 59:3; 63:6 [7]; 71:24; 77:12 [13]; 115:7; 143:5; Prov 8:7; 15:28; Isa 16:7; 33:18; Jer 48:31). "The range of meaning is broad, ranging from the inarticulate sounds of a cooing dove (Isa 38:14) to the articulate praise of Yahweh (Ps 35:28). . . . [T]he righteous meditate not only for the purpose of encouragement, but also that their life may actually conform to the object of such meditation."[184] In the present context "meditate" apparently represents the sounds of a person reading slightly aloud to oneself. Howard says it includes a focus on God. God permits the king to have a copy of the law and read it continually to avoid becoming despotic, proud, or cruel (Deut 17:19–20).

Neither Joshua nor a king actually rules over God's people. God's Torah, his teaching, rules over the people and shows them the boundaries of life with Yahweh, their God. Political power and injustice may appear to be the prudent path to gaining personal power and prosperity, but God points his people to the law to find the way to true prosperity and success. K. L. Sarles, reminds us:[185]

> The context of God's promise to Joshua that He would make his way prosperous and give him good success is military, not financial. It specifically relates to the conquest of the Promised Land by Israel as the outworking of the land promises given unconditionally in the Abrahamic Covenant. The Book of Joshua traces Joshua's successes in conquering Canaan. Joshua was a general, not a banker; financial prosperity is simply not in view here.

"Israel's struggle in Canaan begun under Joshua was to be moral and religious and not just military."[186] Creach notes, "Joshua's 'meditation' is not casual (or quiet) reflection but active reading and study. . . . [T]he Lord commands Joshua to meditate not on a lifeless legal code but on precepts that have the purpose of liberating the oppressed, ensuring justice for the weak, and forging an egalitarian society."[187]

9 Schäfer-Lichtenberger demonstrates that Noth is wrong in finding a secondary hand here.[188] Rather such artistic rhetoric represents the goal and high point of this section.[189] The new element here is the call not to tremble or get all shook up. Only here in the Hebrew Bible are these terms (ערץ, חתת) so paired. The first is often paired with ירא, "to fear." The two verbs "are the antithesis of 'be strong and of good courage,' indicating the deuteronomistic view of the history of Israel as under God's control."[190] The verb ערץ occurs fifteen times in the OT (Deut 1:29; 7:21; 20:3; 31:6; Josh 1:9; Isa 2:19, 21; 8:12–13; 29:23; 47:12; Pss 10:18; 89:8; Job 13:25; 31:34). George summarizes: "If Joshua were to turn from the law, then he would tremble and be dismayed. To be strong and courageous is to observe the law; to

184 M. V. Van Pelt and W. C. Kaiser, Jr., *NIDOTTE.*
185 "A Theological Evaluation of the Prosperity Gospel," *BSac* 143 (1986) 338.
186 Auld, VTSup, 11.
187 Creach, 27–28.
188 *Josua und Salomo*, 196.
189 Ibid., 203.
190 Gray, 60.

discard it is to tremble and be dismayed. But Joshua will keep the law so he will not be dismayed."[191]

The occurrence of these verbs in Joshua is tied to their appearances in Deuteronomy, each followed by a clause promising Yahweh's presence. "The earlier uses in Deut and Josh are related to these later instances in that the early prohibitions against being terrified are further grounded in the later testimony that Yahweh is the ultimate object of astonishment for his people and the supreme terror against the wicked."[192] Joshua and the people of Israel face an overwhelming task against overwhelming odds, but it is no reason for alarm. God's presence should be sufficient to drive away all terror at the thought of the enemy. God is the victor. The people simply follow obediently to collect the spoils God gives them, the land of promise.

"The obedience and the success will be enjoyed in the presence of the Lord God who gave both the law and the promises. Joshua will not succeed because he obeys God's instruction; he will succeed because God is with him to enable him to obey his instruction."[193] Nelson notes, "Joshua illustrates the correlation between obedience and success, while Judges follows with the contrasting association between disobedience and disaster."[194] Success is achieving God's goals for his people, not gaining human desires for personal bragging rights or personal estates. "In the Old Testament 'prosperity' is not financial in its primary orientation, if at all. Rather, it refers to succeeding in proper endeavors. Also, it comes only when it is not the focus of one's efforts. . . . It comes when one's focus is on God and one's relationship with him."[195]

10 Joshua demonstrates his immediate obedience to God's command and his respect for the military ordinances set up in Deut 20.[196] שטרים, "officials," reflects the tradition of Exod 18:24–25, Num 11:16, and Deut 1:15, wherein Moses appointed tribal officials to assume part of the responsibility that had become burdensome for him. Gray sees the term signifying "either field officers or, as in Dt. 20:5, officials who had charge of conscription and exemption from service."[197] Pressler sees a wide range of meaning, but with the military in focus in this verse.[198] Hess[199] maintains the term refers to secular counterparts to the priests, while Howard[200] emphasizes the term's administrative rather than military function.[201] The tradition is closely tied to the reorganization of the military and legal system by Jehoshaphat (2 Chr 19:5–11).[202] For the Chronicler, the term is tied closely to the legal duties of the Levites (1 Chr 23:4; 26:29; 27:1; 2 Chr 19:11; 26:11; 34:13).

191 *ZAW* 112 (2000) 361.
192 *NIDOTTE*.
193 Hess (1996) 73.
194 Nelson, 31.
195 Howard, 90.
196 See Schäfer-Lichtenberger, *Josua und Salomo*, 204.
197 Gray, 60.
198 Pressler, 15.
199 Hess (1996) 75.
200 Howard, 90.
201 Cf. M. Weinfeld, "Judge and Officer in Ancient Israel and in the Ancient Near East," *IOS* 7 (1977) 65–88.
202 Cf. R. Knierim, "Exodus 18 und die Neuordnung der mosaischen Gerichtsbarkeit," *ZAW* 73

Deuteronomy assumes the tetrateuchal tradition of civil administration set up by Moses and closely connects the officers' duties to the military (Deut 20:5–9) as well as to legal issues (Deut 16:18). The one appearance of the term in wisdom literature appears to presuppose a position of some political power (Prov 6:7). The editor behind Joshua takes up the term in a stereotyped fashion to speak of administrators of the people prior to the monarchy (Deut 1:15; 29:9; 31:28; Josh 8:33; 23:2; 24:1). This may well reflect tribal organization and terminology later adapted into the monarchical system, but the details remain unclear.

11 "Pass through" (עבר) is a key term in Joshua (Josh 1:2, 11, 14; 2:23; 3:1–2, 4, 6, 11, 14, 16–4:1; 4:3, 5, 7–8, 10–13, 22–23; 5:1; 6:7–8; 7:7, 11, 15; 10:29, 31, 34; 15:3–4, 6–7, 10–11; 16:2, 6; 18:9, 13, 18–19; 19:13; 22:19; 23:16; 24:11, 17), especially in reference to crossing the Jordan, marching to battle, breaking the covenant, and boundaries passing specific points. It plays a similarly important role in Exodus (Exod 12:12, 23; 13:12; 15:16; 17:5; 30:13–14; 32:27; 33:19, 22; 34:6; 36:6; 38:26). Hess characterizes the term as "the key activity in the opening chapters."[203]

A new theological element emerges in v 11 expressed by the root ירשׁ. The precise meaning of the term is broad, and its basic meaning disputed. L. A. Snijders studies Mic 6:15; Deut 28:42; and Isa 63:18 and concludes that the basic meaning is "to tread upon."[204] H. H. Schmid examines Gen 15:3–4; 21:10; 2 Sam 14:7; Jer 49:1–2 and concludes that the original meaning was "inherit."[205] J. G. Plöger speaks of a technical military term.[206] *DCH* lists a wide-range of meanings: "take possession of, inherit from, displace from property, dispossess, drive out."[207]

The usage of ירשׁ underlying our passage has its apparent roots in a traditional popular blessing formula transmitted in Gen 24:60.[208] Deuteronomy's meaning becomes clear in Deut 2:12, 21, 22, 24, 31; 4:47; 6:18. A similar meaning is confirmed in Num 13:30; 21:24, 32, 35; 33:53. Thus Lohfink speaks of "legal succession" in family contexts and "one people or nation succeeding another in ruling over a territory by right of conquest."[209] Mitchell writes that the use of the word indicates that "the right to land is grounded in the authority resulting from victory legitimized by divine intervention."[210]

Israel's military possession of the land becomes the basis of paraenesis in Deuteronomy (e.g., chap. 4; 5:31; 6:1, 18; 28:21, 63; 30:5, 16, 18; 31:13; 32:47; almost fifty times in all). "The people will take possession. Yes, but only of what the Lord their God gives them to possess."[211] Military possession of the land also becomes a link between the ancestral promises and the conquest narratives (Gen 15:7; 22:17; 28:4; Num 33:53; Deut 1:8, 21, 39; 3:12, 18, 20; 31:3; Josh 1:11). Our text is thus the

---

(1961) 146–71; G. Macholz, "Zur Geschichte der Justizorganisation in Juda," *ZAW* 84 (1972) 314–40.

203 Hess (1996) 75. Cf. Koorevaar, 117.
204 "Genesis XV: The Covenant with Abram," in *Studies on the Book of Genesis*, OtSt 12 (Leiden: Brill, 1958) 267–71.
205 "ירשׁ *beerben*," *THAT*, 1:780–81.
206 *Literarkritische*, 83.
207 *DCH*, 4:302–2.
208 Cf. H. W. Wolff, "Das Kerygma des Jahwisten," *EvT* 24 (1964) 84–85.
209 *TDOT*, 6, 371–72.
210 *Together in the Land*, 32.
211 Auld, 12.

final link in the fulfillment of the land promise to the ancestors, a fulfillment that includes the gift from God but also the military participation of the people.[212] Mitchell reminds readers that Israel's actions in crossing the Jordan represent "a belligerent act" of "encroachment on someone else's property."[213]

"Three days" causes chronological confusion. The spies also took at least three days (Josh 2:16, 22). After three days the officers went through the camp (3:2) alerting the people about what would happen the next day (3:5). How can Joshua tell the officials to say they would cross in three days (1:11)? Gray suggests the span of three days refers to a ritual procession from Gilgal to Shittim or is taken from the three days of the spies' absence.[214] Hess notes the relationship to the crossing of the Reed Sea by Moses with a major difference: "The second crossing was not to be done in haste and in flight from an enemy. Instead, it would be done with sufficient preparation. The second crossing takes the appearance of a ceremonial act of worship."[215]

Madvig maintains that understanding the three days in context is virtually impossible.[216] Hess postulates that the three days of 2:16, 22 and 3:2 are all the same three days.[217] Howard sees the possibility the people would "merely be setting out from their present encampment within three days, not actually crossing within three days. Or it may indicate that his estimate of when they would be able to set out simply was erroneous."[218] Woudstra understands the three days of 1:11 as an "indefinite period," including the mission of the spies, which may have taken as many as four or five days.[219] The three days in Josh 3:2 begin with the departure from Shittim. This is the most straightforward reading of the text. D. Howard reviews previous solutions and then offers his own, seeing two three-day periods and a seventh day:[220]

Day One: Instructions for officers; officers deliver instructions; two spies commissioned, go out and spend first night in hills in hiding.
Day Two: Spies in hiding; people begin preparations.
Day Three: Spies return; people's preparations concluded.
Day Four: Travel from Shittim to Jordan; spend the night.
Day Five: At Jordan with ritual preparations.
Day Six: Officers instruct camp on actual crossing; Joshua instructs on sanctifying themselves.
Day Seven: River Jordan crossed; stone altars raised on tenth day of first month.

In the above schema Howard has to assume a very short part of three days for the spies to accomplish their task and has to assume a morning-to-morning day rather than an evening-to-evening one. Even those scholars he quotes as offering

---

212   See Plöger, *Literarkritische*, 83–87; P. Diepold, *Israels Land*, 88–89.
213   *Together in the Land*, 32.
214   Gray, 60–61.
215   Hess (1996) 76.
216   Madvig, 257. Cf. Nelson, 55.
217   Hess (1996) 95.
218   Howard, 91. Cf. Woudstra 65, n. 2.
219   Woudstra, 79; cf. Harstad, 92.
220   "Three Days in Joshua 1–3: Resolving a Chronological Conundrum," *JETS* 41 (1998) 539–50.

optimistic solutions cannot squeeze all the events into seven days. The main problem is with 1:11. Howard's only conclusion seems to be that Joshua was mistaken, and his timetable was delayed by the length of the spies' mission. This is not a solution to the problem, but rather a surrender to the impossibility of the problem. With all the *waw* consecutives that Howard rightly sees as sequential, the numbers still do not add up to crossing the Jordan in three days, and the many activities cannot be so easily squeezed into the seven-day timetable.

Knauf simply states that the overnight stay of the spies in Jericho and their hiding for three more days (2:22) cannot be joined with the time reckoning of chap. 1.[221] Perhaps Nelson explains it best: "Chapter 2 has its own parallel three-day schema (2:16, 22), and the reader must assume that somehow these two run concurrently."[222] Or we might follow Hubbard in seeing "a symbolic rather than a chronological sense. . . . It [the three-day time period] denotes the stylized biblical time period to mark momentous events."[223] Den Braber and Wesselius, writing about chaps. 1–8, maintain, "We will see that on the basis of the indications of time provided in the text, if we take them completely seriously, we can indeed reconstruct one single chronological scheme which must underlie these chapters, which also makes it less likely that the discontinuities in the text are to be explained from its supposed history."[224]

The Jordan River travels about two hundred miles as it covers a sixty-five-mile distance from the Lake of Galilee to the Dead Sea, from six hundred feet below sea level to thirteen hundred. It is generally quite shallow and narrow with numerous places where it can be forded. Below Galilee, came a broad, flat plain—the Ghor (Arabic for depression). Inside this valley is the jungle-like Zor, hiding wild animals and called "the pride of Jordan" (Jer 12:5, 49:19, 50:44, Zech 11:3). Bordering the southern Jordan is the fertile Kikkar. It offered no opportunity for navigation and little for settlement. It simply separated the land of Canaan from Transjordan and made control of the fords a military necessity.[225]

The word translated "provisions" (צידה) represents food and other supplies needed by people on a journey or a military expedition away from home (Gen 27:3; 42:25; 45:21; Exod 12:39; Josh 1:11; 9:11; Judg 7:8; 20:10; 1 Sam 22:10; Ps 78:25). Harris notes, "With this order, Joshua changed the wilderness habits of the tribes. . . . This operations order heralded a new period in the life of the people."[226] Mitchell finds tension here with 5:11–12, but no tension need exist.[227] Provisions for the time of crossing the Jordan and establishing a base in Cisjordan differ from those needed for a people who have completed the first stage of the occupation, have celebrated their rituals, and are "at home in the land" for better or for worse. Pre-

221 Knauf, 44.
222 Nelson, 34.
223 Hubbard, 84.
224 *SJOT* 22 (2008) 254.
225 Cf. D. Baly, *The Geography of the Bible* (New York: Harper & Brothers, 1957) 193–210; Y. Aharoni, *Land*, 29–32; S. Cohen, "Jordan," *IDB*, 2:973–78; E. G. Kraeling, *Rand McNally Bible Atlas* (New York: Rand McNally, 1956) 25–29; N. Glueck, *The River Jordan* (Philadelphia: Westminster, 1946).
226 Harris, 23–24.
227 *Together in the Land*, 33.

paring provisions covers a short time period. Eating the fruit of the land covers the rest of Israel's existence in the land. Gathering provisions means abandoning the camp east of the Jordan once and for all.[228]

12 This final section (vv 12–18) cannot be isolated as a later addition as is frequently done. Rather, it completes the themes of the chapter, especially the unity of all Israel and the authority of Joshua, as Schäfer-Lichtenberger has shown.[229] Themes from vv 1–9 continue to reappear: Moses (vv 13, 14, 15, 17a, b); give (13, 14, 15a); land (13, 14, 15a, b). Each verse then has its own emphasis. V 12 includes the tribes east of the Jordan. V 13 introduces the new theme of rest (cf. v 15). V 14 uses repeated references to military preparations. V 15 speaks of possessing the land. Vv 16–17a underline the obedience of the people, while v 18a speaks of the consequences of disobedience. Enumeration of these themes points to the typical emphasis on the divine gift of the land to an obedient people through the mediation of Moses. A shift in form and context, though, uses these familiar themes for a radically distinct purpose. The context is a call to battle, not worship, a call issued by Joshua, not Moses. The form indicates a call to obedience to a divine command, but is utilized for an oath of allegiance to Joshua, which in turn is modified by the final exclusive clauses in vv 17 and 18, calling for obedience by Joshua.

13 Judges will show how disunified Israel actually was after the conquest. Joshua tries to show the ideal unity of the people. The main distinction in Joshua involves east and west, while the main distinction in the remainder of the Old Testament history books, starting in Judg 1, will run north and south. Joshua presupposes knowledge of the settlement of two and a half tribes east of the Jordan, though one may argue whether this knowledge comes directly from the narrative of Num 32. Nelson points out that "the literary relationship between Joshua's version and that of Numbers chapter 32 is complex and disputed."[230]

The writer of Joshua at least knew the tradition of part of Israel living outside the limits of the Promised Land and having to fight for recognition as part of Israel. This can be seen especially in 4:12–13, in chap. 22, and in the Gideon and Jephthah narratives in Judges. "Whether . . . the Transjordan area is part of the Promised Land in the strict sense is always somewhat in doubt."[231] These eastern tribes "are highlighted in order to emphasize the 'all Israel' theological schema of Joshua."[232]

One sentence (1:13; compare v 18) sets out the goal of the book of Joshua (compare 11:23; 12:7–24; 21:43–45). God wants to give the land to his people and let them find rest in that land. Hess has shown the important differences between vv 13–16 and the verses they seem to quote from Deut 3:18–20.[233] Two major differences involve the promise of rest and the call to help "brothers." נוח, "rest," is the new word of promise in this section. "Land can be given by Moses, only YHWH gives rest."[234] The term has a variety of contexts within the OT. Kaiser observes concerning the *hipʿil* construction of נוח: "This rest is a place granted by the Lord

---

228   Schäfer-Lichtenberger, *Josua und Salomo*, 204.
229   *Josua und Salomo*, 205–7.
230   Nelson, 35, n. 12.
231   McConville and Williams, 16.
232   Nelson, 35.
233   Hess (1996) 76–77.
234   Mitchell, *Together in the Land*, 29.

(Exod 33:14; Deut 3:20; Josh 1:13, 15; 22:4; 2 Chron 14:5), a peace and security from all enemies (Deut 12:10; 25:19; Josh 21:44; 23:1; 2 Sam 7:1, 11; 1 Kings 5:18 [5:4]; 1 Chron 22:9, 18; 23:25; 2 Chron 14:6; 15:15; 20:30; 32:22—probable reading?) or the cessation of sorrow and labor in the future (Isa 14:3; 28:12)."[235]

The cult speaks of "divine deliverance" given to the individual as bringing rest (Pss 23:2; 116:7; Jer 45:3; compare Job 3:13, 26; Exod 33:14) with the cult as the place of divine resting (Ps 132:8, 14; 1 Chr 28:2; compare the earlier ark tradition of Num 10:33, 36; contrast the later prophecy of Isa 66:1). The early Sabbath commandments spoke of human rest (Exod 23:12; cf. Deut 5:14), which priestly language reinterpreted to speak of divine rest (Exod 20:11; cf. Gen 2:2–4, שבת). The term appears also to have roots in early legal language (2 Sam 14:17).

Isaiah uses the term to describe the life God desired for the people, who rejected it (Isa 28:12). Prophecy then eschatologized the term (Isa 14:3, 7; 11:20; 32:18; cf. Dan 12:13), and prophetic schools used the term to speak of the gift of the divine spirit (Num 11:25–26; 2 Kgs 2:15), a usage that also became eschatologized (Isa 11:2; 63:14; Zech 6:8).

Nelson says the definition of נוח comes in vv 13 and 15: "Giving rest (נוח) is defined as giving a homeland."[236] But it is more than just having a homeland. In Deuteronomic speech the term was so widely used to speak of peace and rest from the problems of life that it received a specific theological meaning: rest from war and enemies (Deut 3:20; 12:9–10; 25:19). Thus Nelson is on target when he states that "'rest' is the security established by the defeat of the enemy."[237] Hawk concludes: "all Israel still seeks the promised rest, and the entire nation lives within the tension of a land that YHWH has already given and will yet give. Rest and land are both accomplished fact and future promise. The land which has been given must also be taken. One part of the nation cannot rest until all find rest."[238]

Our passage takes the line of Deut 3:20 and moves rest a step forward to its eventual realization (Josh 21:44; 22:4; 23:1). Even realization is not a static thing. It can be lost (Judges) and regained (2 Sam 7:1, 11; 1 Kgs 5:18; 8:56). The people of Israel regard the exile of 587–586 BCE as the time when they, through their disobedience, lost their rest (Deut 28:65; Lam 1:3). The connection between rest and salvation history is also taken up by other schools of thought in Israel (1 Chr 22:9, 18; 23:25; 2 Chr 14:5; 15:15; 20:30; Neh 9:28; Ps 95:11; Isa 63:14).

Rest is an attainable reality for Israel. It can be a goal lost and looked forward to again; that is, it can be a goal regained. In whatever stage Israel finds herself, rest is a concept with concrete content. It represents freedom from enemy oppression and deadly war. It represents life lived with God as a gift from God.[239] "For a little nation regularly subjugated by rapacious empires and frequently devastated by war, to live in peace and security in a land of their own must have seemed something like heaven."[240]

---

235   *BSac* 130 (1973) 139.
236   Nelson, 35.
237   Ibid., 31.
238   Hawk (2000) 15.
239   See G. von Rad, "Es ist noch eine Ruhe vorhanden dem Volke Gottes," *ZdZ* 11 (1933) 104–11 = *Gesammelte Studien zum Alten Testament* (Munich: Kaiser, 1958) 1:101–8 = *The Problem of the Hexateuch and Other Essays*, trans. E. W. T. Dicken (Edinburgh; Oliver & Boyd, 1966) 94–102.
240   Pressler, 16; cf. Matties, 455–58.

Josh 1 thus portrays Israel in Transjordan looking across the river into the Promised Land. Surrounded by the memory of the difficult years in the wilderness and by the reports of giants in the land, Israel must choose to enter and fight or to turn back to the wilderness (cf. Josh 7:7). Motivation to fight comes from the divine promise of rest first uttered by Moses and now repeated by Joshua. Such rest may be the possession of a part of Israel in Transjordan, but that is not enough. Guarantee of that rest depends upon the conquest of the whole gift of God so that the whole people of God can have rest. Rest, not war, is the ultimate goal of Israel. "Such 'rest' will be the consummation of this campaign and of Joshua's career (21:44; 22:4; 23:1)."[241] But rest will not come in the book of Judges.

The author sees the dialectic that rest can be won only through war. This is best seen in the following outline:

1. Call to remember the Mosaic marching orders (vv 12–15)
2. Response of loyalty to loyal Joshua (vv 16–18)

14–15 Joshua stands at a crisis point. He "is in a potentially precarious position with respect to the Transjordanian tribes. They had already received their land by the authority of Moses; they had made their pledge and agreements with Moses; and their families and their claim to land lay to the east of the Jordan River, not to the west. Before verse 12 it is not clear that Joshua has any authority over them. He exercises his authority as the figure who will lead Israel to claim the land west of the Jordan. No mention is made of his role east of the river. . . . Joshua must appeal to the agreement between these warriors and Moses, for he has no other basis on which to claim their loyalty and participation in the battles yet to come."[242]

Joshua lets the eastern tribes know the procedure they must follow to show loyalty to himself and to greater Israel. The men must leave possessions and family in their chosen home east of the Jordan and join the fight for the other tribes' territories west of the Jordan. This calls for a faithful people who trust God to protect the families they have left behind.

Such action also shows a strong commitment to a unified Israel, a level of commitment the western tribes may not share. In spite of overstating his case, Hawk is correct when he writes: "Unlike their kindred, the easterners will settle land that they have asked for and received through negotiation and compromise. It is not the land Yahweh has chosen to give but rather the land Moses gave in order to preserve the unity of the people."[243]

The easterners know that their land is just as much a gift from God as is the western land and the traditional land of Canaan. Part of the duty of a tribe of Israel was to participate in wars with the other tribes. In Judges this sense of duty will deteriorate as Jephthah decimates the tribe of Ephraim, and the other eleven tribes reduce Benjamin to an endangered species.

The eastern tribes must participate in the war in the west until it is finished. Only then can they cross the Jordan to the land that God gave to them. And only then will east and west enjoy God's rest. Hawk goes a bit far in his contrast of

---

241 Nelson, 31.
242 Hess, 77.
243 Hawk (2010) 10.

eastern tribes owing allegiance to Moses and western tribes to Joshua: "They have claims to the Mosaic tradition that the rest of the nation does not share, yet they will be marked as outsiders, those who live on the other side of the Jordan."[244] But the book of Joshua and the history of Israel clearly deny this contrast. The eastern tribes clearly participate in the conquest. They received land directly from Moses, but the western tribes received land from Joshua following the precedent and command of Moses. At times (ch 22) western tribes showed suspicion of the eastern ones, but such suspicion is not validated or shared by the narrator of Joshua.

16–18 Joshua has admonished the eastern tribes to support the western tribes in their battle with the Canaanites west of the Jordan. Some scholars try to expand the speakers here to include all Israel, not just the eastern tribes.

Hall acknowledges that the eastern tribes are speaking, but she maintains that the words function more broadly.[245] The eastern tribes "serve here as a sort of Greek chorus speaking the mind of the whole people."[246] Auld understands vv 16–18 as the response of the loyal officers whom Joshua commissioned in vv 10–11.[247] Howard sees both the officers of vv 10–11 and the eastern tribal representatives speaking here.[248] In his emphasis on the potential division between east and west, Hawk reads the prayer for God's presence as a relationship or leadership condition that puts Joshua on trial.[249]

Though he isolates vv 12–15 as a later addition, Knauf suggests that legitimation from above is completed with acceptance from below, making the military leaders or the entire army as speakers here instead of the east Jordan tribes that the present text has answering.[250] The attempts of Noth and Steuernagel to find redactional work here miss the point of the text that conditions must be set and met as Schäfer-Lichtenberger shows.[251] Hess explains the text more forthrightly: "The context requires that it is only the Transjordan tribes who respond here. Their response of loyalty exemplifies that of the other tribes."[252] While the author's statement may represent the understanding of the commitment of every member of Israel, the literary context here has only the eastern tribes committing themselves to the conquest program Joshua has laid out.

In their conversation with Joshua, the eastern tribes make only one condition: they must see evidence that God is with Joshua as he was with Moses. The text has the easterners acknowledge by their loyalty that Joshua is the chosen and capable model of the leader after Moses, whatever office that leader may hold. They pronounce ahead of time the sentence for anyone who repeatedly fails to obey and follow Joshua. Such a traitor will face execution. Thus Knauf can conclude: disobedience over against a prophet is dangerous to one's health from then on.[253]

244   Ibid., 15–16.
245   *Conquering Character*, 16.
246   Nelson, 35.
247   VTSup, 14.
248   Howard, 93; cf. Polzin, *Moses and the Deuteronomist,* 79; Schäfer-Lichtenberger, *Josua und Salomo,* 207. Cf. also D. Howard, "All Israel's Response to Joshua," 81–91, where he includes representatives of the entire nation.
249   Hawk (2010) 11.
250   Knauf, 40.
251   *Josua und Salomo,* 196.
252   Hess (1996) 79, n. 3.
253   Knauf, 45.

The Transjordanian tribes acknowledge Joshua's authority and commit themselves to follow his leadership. This commitment remains steadfast throughout the book. Only with Judges does the leadership issue come under question as first one tribe and then another provides a leader that various numbers of tribes will follow. Repeatedly, Ephraim demands a leadership role, enters warfare with its covenant brothers, and suffers great defeats.

The eastern tribes conclude their answer with the command to Joshua that Yahweh has repeatedly given him: have conviction and courage. Hess correctly sees the words as a confession and prayer on behalf of Joshua.[254] This rather veiled questioning or slight hedging on Joshua's qualifications for leadership—that he demonstrate divine presence and personal conviction and courage—"makes the subsequent demonstration of these realities all the more convincing."[255]

"Rebels" (מרה) appears only here in Joshua but plays off of Deuteronomy (1:26; 9:7, 23, 24; 21:18–21; 31:27). As Hess notes, it appropriately describes Israel's actions in the past, actions Joshua could well expect to see repeated.[256] Howard notes, "If their promise was to obey Joshua in the same way they had obeyed Moses, the prospects were not as bright as they might first appear, since, of course, they did not 'fully obey' Moses. Quite to the contrary!"[257]

The people of Israel did not fully follow through on their obligations in Joshua's day either. Both Howard and Hawk emphasize the lack of obedience.[258] The biblical narrator says nothing about such lack. He points to Israel's obedience and God's faithfulness in fulfilling his promises. The lack-of-obedience motif comes in the book of Judges. "The theme upon which all the rest of the theology of Joshua is based is the faithfulness of God."[259]

Explanation

At the narrative level, Josh 1:1–9 introduces the narrative of the conquest of the land. At this level the threefold task given to Joshua corresponds to the three major sections of the book: (a) Conquer the land, chaps. 1–12; (b) distribute the land, chaps. 13–19; (c) and obey the law, chaps. 20–24. The section thus functions as a formal introduction to the book, giving in summary fashion a brief survey of the contents. More than that, it sets the tone for the book, a tone dominated by the divine imperative, directing, demanding, and yet encouraging his people into action.

The Israelite historian behind Joshua 1:1–9 was not content to remain at the narrative level. He used the introduction of this portion of his history to make an important theological statement. For Israel's historians the story of Israel centered around the great leaders of Israel—Moses, Joshua, Samuel, David, Solomon, Hezekiah, Josiah, and so on. What did one expect of such leaders? Deut 17:14–20 gives a legal standard by which to measure Israel's leaders. Josh 1:1–9 gives a correspond-

---

254   Hess (1996) 79.
255   Nelson, 36; cf. Hess (2000) 17, who speaks of "an element of contingency," an element denied
      by Hess (1996) 78–79.
256   Hess (1996) 79.
257   Howard, 94–95.
258   *Every Promise Fulfilled.*
259   Pressler, 18.

ing paradigm. The remainder of the book gives flesh and blood to that paradigm in the figure of Joshua. The paradigm of Israelite leadership begins in Israel's unique context of leadership. All leadership in Israel occurs in the shadow of Moses. He has died, but his example and teaching stand before every successor. The Israelite leader must be an official, a minister, of Moses.

Leadership in Israel is tied to the promised gift of the land. The leader may not multiply emblems of power for self-gain but must remain on equal footing with the rest of his fellow Israelites (Deut 17:16, 17, 20). The task of the leader is to gain control of and maintain the land for Israel. In so doing, the leader maintains the true identity of Israel, the people of the promise to Moses (v 3) and to the ancestors (v 6).

The explicit command to each generation may be different. For the author of Joshua, it was the conquest of the whole land. For a later editor, the emphasis seems to have been on Lebanon and the land of the Hittites, the northern territory beyond Dan, so that the editor inserted these territorial names into the border description (see *Notes*). No matter what the specific command, it was simply a specification of the general command given to Moses. Israelite leadership fulfilled the command to Moses to possess the land for Israel. "The real obstacle to fulfillment is therefore not the formidable resolve of the Canaanites but a potential lack of resolve on the part of Joshua and Israel. . . . [S]uccess also depends on Israel's determination to obey YHWH as they enter the land."[260]

The biblical historian is well aware of the consequences of obedience to the divine command. The command, in human perspective, leads to danger and risk. The danger is counterbalanced by the promise of divine presence. This promise is as old as the ancestors. For the historian, however, everything is based on the promise to Moses (v 5). The Israelite leader stands not only in the shadow of Moses but also in the shadow of the presence that led Moses from Egypt into the wilderness and on to the plains of Moab. Such presence guarantees fulfillment of the command. It stands as the basis of the call to courage and certainty (v 6).

The divine gift of consolation has a human corollary, the call to obedience to the Torah of Moses. For the historian, the path was clearly marked in the Torah of Moses. The leader of Israel, whether king (Deut 17) or conqueror (Joshua), had no claim to a new revelation. The word to Moses sufficed and was the path to success in leadership. Only he who obeyed Moses, the leader of Israel, could expect success in his leadership endeavors.

The final element of Israel's theology of leadership is the call to response. In a rhetorical question, God summarizes all that he had said and called upon the leader to reflect upon and respond to the divine word. Was the leader willing to walk in the shadow of Moses beneath the larger shadow of divine presence, fulfilling both the promise and the Torah? The historian saw a positive response in the person of Joshua, and God sought similar responses among his people beyond the Great River, the River Euphrates. Could the promise once again be fulfilled, the land once again received as gift by a people who were once again walking in the shadow of Moses and his larger Shadow?

The historian's dialectic has constantly plagued the people of Israel. The tendency is ever to place the emphasis on one side or other of the dialectic and thus

---

260 Hess (2000) 2.

destroy the delicate balance achieved here. Promise and presence frame the section and its thought. Yet they are offered only to a people willing to abide in the shadow of the divine and his human representative. Historian, prophet, priest, and sage form a great biblical chorus calling the people to accept the divine gift through human obedience. The New Testament witnesses point to an even greater representative who completed the task given him in total obedience and called all humanity to follow him in similar obedience.

The opening section of Joshua introduces a specific understanding of Israelite leadership. The remainder of the book plays on the theme of Joshua as the example of Israelite leadership in the shadow of Moses. This first section transposes traditions and interrupts chronology to show that Joshua obeyed the divine command immediately without question. The motif of "within three days" belongs to chap. 3, introducing the need to cleanse the camp prior to the great cultic procession through the Jordan (cf. 3:2). It totally ignores the tradition of the spies sent out (chap. 2). It also transforms the cultic tradition into a battle tradition through the insertion of ירשׁ, "possess," and the emphasis upon preparation of provisions for a long journey. Joshua thus interprets the divine command as a command to lead the nation into battle and responds accordingly. He is the military commander par excellence in Israel by the very fact that he carries out the command of the heavenly general.

The text shifts abruptly from preparations to march to an admonition to fulfill a former pledge to fight. Here specific pieces of tradition have been joined without logical consistency or narrative harmony to illustrate a theological teaching that incorporates all the important themes of the book of Joshua.[261]

"Taken together the speeches (of chap 1) implicitly communicate a unanimity between God, Joshua, and the nation and reiterate Deuteronomy's insistence that integrity is at heart of all that Israel is and does."[262] Israel is defined as a unified body. The Jordan River does not divide Israel. Threat to Israelite unity lies not in geography but in loyalty. The Israelites outside the narrow confines of the land promised by Yahweh must be loyal and support the Israelites within the land. Despite geographical separation, Israel must remain one body dedicated to one land.

Israel is the people of the Torah of Moses living in the land promised to Moses. Such a definition of Israelite unity is based on the words of Moses given to Israel outside the land. This definition of Israelite unity is personified in response to the man who has taken over the Mosaic office in the land. Each Israelite generation must decide on a leader named by God who will call them back to loyalty to the leader of God in the land of God. Any part of Israel living outside the land must help those in the land.

The Christian church has taken up much of this identity for itself. The leadership has changed from Moses and Joshua to Jesus and his present-day interpreters. The geography has changed from one small piece of land to all the earth. The intention of the text still points to the identity of the people of God. People of God must have strong leadership from leaders loyal to the incomparable pioneer of the

---

261 Schäfer-Lichtenberger, *Josua und Salomo*, 190.
262 Hess (2000) 1.

faith. Such leadership must face the task given by God with strong conviction and courage. Such leadership gains its authority only from God. Only then can such leadership expect a declaration of readiness to follow from the congregation.

Leaders and congregations look for the free gift of God; yet they must be prepared to go to war to win that gift. God is giving, but he gives only to an obedient people. This dialectic remains in the New Testament call to accept justification by faith without any works of the law coupled with the call to follow after Christ in perfect obedience demonstrating faith through works.

The book of Joshua deals extensively with the dialectic of unity in geographical divergence. The Christian church may face this as its biggest hurdle. Released from identity with one geographical spot, the church continues to struggle with the problem of expressing its loyalty to the one body when it is separated by so many different conditions produced by its historical development.

B. Prostitute's Profession (2:1–24)

Bibliography

Abegg, M., Jr., P. Flint, and E. Ulrich. *The Dead Sea Scrolls Bible.* San Francisco: Harper San Francisco, 1999. 201–7. **Abel, F. M.** "L'anathème de Jéricho et la maison de Rahab." *RB* 57 (1950) 321–30. ———."Les stratagèmes dans le Livre de Josué." *RB* 56 (1949) 321–39. **Acosta, M.** "Dos espías secretos en Josué 2: El éxito de un fracas." *Kairós* 44 (2009) 9–32. **Anbar, M.** "History of the Composition of the Story of Rahab and the Spies." *BMik* 29 (1993–1994) 255–57 (Heb.). ———. "La 'Reprise.'" *VT* 38 (1988) 385–98. **Arayaprateep, K.** "A Note on *yr'* in Jos. IV 24." *VT* 22 (1972) 240–42. **Assis, E.** "The Choice to Serve God and Assist His People: Rahab and Yael." *Bib* 85 (2004) 82–90. ———. "The Sin at Kadesh as a Recurring Motif in the Book of Joshua." *JANESCU* 31 (2008) 1–14. **Astour, M.** "Bené-lamina et Jéricho." *Sem* 9 (1959) 5–18. **Bächli, O.** "Zur Aufnahme von Fremden in die altisraelitische Kultgemeinde." In *Wort-Gebot-Glaube.* Ed. H. J. Stoebe. ATANT 59. Zürich: Zwingli, 1970. 21–26. **Barnes, P.** "Was Rahab's Lie a Sin?" *RTR* 54 (1995) 1–9. **Barstad, H.** "The Old Testament Feminine Personal Name *raḥab:* An Onomastic Note." *SEÅ* 54 (1989) 43–49. **Beek, M.** "Rahab in the Light of Jewish Exegesis." In *Von Kanaan bis Keral.* FS J. P. M. van der Ploeg, ed. W. C. Delsman. AOAT 211. Neukirchen-Vluyn: Neukirchener Verlag, 1982. 37–44. **Benjamin, C. D.** *The Variations between the Hebrew and Greek Texts of Joshua: Chapters 1–12.* Thesis, University of Pennsylvania. Leipzig: W. Drugulin, 1921. **Bieberstein, K.** *Josua, Jordan, Jericho: Archäologie, Geschichte und Theologie der Landnahmeerzählungen Josua 1–6.* OBO 143. Göttingen: Vandenhoeck & Ruprecht, 1995. **Bienkowski, P.** "Jericho Was Destroyed in the Middle Bronze Age, Not the Late Bronze Age." *BAR* 17.5 (1990) 45–46, 69. **Billmayr-Bucher, S.** "'She Came to Test Him with Hard Questions': Foreign Women and Their View in Israel." *BibInt* 15 (2007) 135–50. **Bimson, J.** *Redating the Exodus and Conquest.* 2nd ed. JSOTSup 5. Sheffield: Almond, 1981. **Bird, P.** "The Harlot as Heroine: Narrative Art and Social Presumption in Three Old Testament Texts." *Semeia* 46 (1989) 119–39. ———. "To 'Play the Harlot': An Inquiry into an Old Testament Metaphor." In *Gender and Difference in Ancient Israel.* Ed. P. L. Day. Minneapolis: Fortress, 1989. 75–94. **Brenner, A.** "Wide Gaps, Narrow Escapes: I Am Known as Rahab, the Broad." In *First Person: Essays in Biblical Autobiography.* Ed. P. R. Davies. Biblical Seminar 81. Sheffield: Sheffield Academic, 2002. 47–48. **Briend, J.** "Le Dieu d'Israël reconnu par des étrangers: Signe de l'universalisme du salut." In *Ouvrir les Écritures.* Paris: Cerf,

1995. 65–76. ———. "Une épopé de fiction: Josué 2.6–12." In *Comment la Bible saisit-elle l'histoire? XXIe Congres catholique française pour l'étude de la Bible (Issy-les-Moulineaux, 2005)*. Ed. D. Doré. Paris: Cerf, 2007. 57–71. **Campbell, K. M.** "Rahab's Covenant: A Short Note on Joshua 2:9–21." *VT* 22 (1972) 243–45. **Chaney, M. L.** "Ancient Palestinian Peasant Movements and the Formation of Premonarchic Israel." In *Palestine in Transition: The Emergence of Ancient Israel*. Ed. D. N. Freedman and D. F. Graf. Sheffield: Almond, 1983. 67–69. **Cohen, A.** "The Cord of Scarlet Rope." *BMik* 86 (1981) 278 (Heb.). **Cross, F. M.** "A Response to Zakovitch's 'Successful Failure of Israelite Intelligence.'" In *Text and Traditions: The Hebrew Bible and Folklore*. Ed. S. Niditch. Atlanta: Scholars Press, 1990. 99–104. **Culley, R.** "Stories of the Conquest: Joshua 2, 6, 7, 8." *HAR* 8 (1984) 25–44. **Daniélou, J.** "Rahab, figure de l'Église [Josh 2; 6:22–25]." *Irén* 22 (1949) 26–45. **Davis, E. F.** "Critical Traditioning: Seeking an Inner Biblical Hermeneutic." *AThR* 82 (2000) 733–51. **Deurloo, K. A.** "Spiel mit und Verweis auf Torah-Worte in Jos 2–6, 9." *DBAT* 26 (1989–1990) 70–80. **Du Preez, R.** "A Holocaust of Deception: Lying to Save Life and Biblical Morality." *Journal of the Adventist Theological Society* 9 (1998) 187–220. **Felber, A.** "Ecclesia ex Gentibus Congregata: Die Bedeutung der Rahabepisode (Jos 2) in der Patristik." Diss., der Karl-FranzUniversität, Graz, 1992. **Fields, W. W.** "The Motif 'Night as Danger' Associated with Three Biblical Destruction Narratives." In *'Sha'arei Talmon': Studies in the Bible, Qumran, and the Ancient Near East Presented to Shemaryahu Talmon*. Ed. M. Fishbane and E. Tov with W. W. Fields. Winona Lake, IN: Eisenbrauns, 1992. 17–32. **Floß, J.** *Kunden oder Kundschafter? Literaturwissenschaftliche Untersuchung zu Jos 2*. 2 vols. ATAT 16, 26. St. Ottilien: EOS, 1982, 1986. **Fry, E.** "Dual Pronouns in Jos 2." *BT* 29 (1978) 247–48. **Frymer-Kensky, T.** "Reading Rahab." In *Tehillah le-moshe: Biblical and Judaic Studies in Honor of Moshe Greenberg*. Ed. M. Cogan, B. L. Eichler, and J. H. Tigay. Winona Lake, IN: Eisenbrauns, 1997. 57–67. **García Bachmann, M.** "Evaluación de la prostitución desde los textos bíblicos." *Cuadernos de teología* 19 (2000) 23–35. **Gillmayr-Bucher, S.** "She Came to Test Him with Hard Questions: Foreign Women and Their View in Israel." *BibInt* 15 (2007) 135–50. **Grant, R.** "Literary Structure in the Book of Ruth." *BSac* 148 (1991) 438–39. **Gunn, D.** "The 'Battle Report': Oral or Scribal Convention?" *JBL* 93 (1974) 513–18. **Haarmann, V.** *JHWH-Verehrer der Völker: Die Hinwendung von Nichtisraeliten zum Gott Israels in alttestamentlichen Überlieferungen*. ATANT 9. Zürich: Theologischer Verlag, 2008. 100–131. **Hanson, A. T.** "Rahab the Harlot in Early Christian Tradition." *JSNT* 1 (1978) 53–60. **Hawk, L.** "Problems with Pagans." In *Reading Bibles, Writing Bodies: Identity and the Book*. Ed. T. K. Beal and D. M. Gunn. London: Routledge, 1997. 153–63. ———. "Strange Houseguests: Rahab, Lot, and the Dynamics of Deliverance." In *Reading between Texts: Intertextuality and the Hebrew Bible*. Ed. D. Fewell. Louisville: Westminster John Knox, 1982. 89–97. **Hawkins, P. S.** "God's Trophy Whore." In *Women of the Hebrew Bible and Their Afterlives*. Vol. 1 of *From the Margins*. Sheffield: Sheffield Phoenix, 2009. 52–70. **Heller, J.** "Die Priesterin Rahab." *CV* 8 (1965) 113–17. **Hoffman Y.** "The Deuteronomistic Concept of the *Herem*." *ZAW* 111 (1999) 196–210. **Hölscher, G.** "Zum Ursprung der Rahabsage." *ZAW* 38 (1919–20) 54–57. **Horn, P. H.** "Josua 2,1–24 im Milieu einer 'dimorphic society.'" *BZ* NF 31 (1987) 264–70. **Howard, D. M., Jr.** "Rahab's Faith: An Exposition of Joshua 2:1–14." *RevExp* 95 (1998) 271–77. **Jost, R.** "Von 'Huren und Heiligen': Ein Sozialgeschichtlicher Beitrag." In *Feministische Hermeneutik und Erstes Testament: Analysen und Interpretationen*. Stuttgart: Kohlhammer, 1994. 126–37. **Klassen, J. H.** *A Reading of the Rahab Narrative (Joshua 2:1–24) Based on a Text-Linguistic and Narrative Analysis*. Vancouver: Regent College, 1998. **Kramer, P. S.** "Rahab: From Peshat to Pedagogy, or: the Many Faces of a Heroine." In *Culture, Entertainment and the Bible*. Ed. G. Aichele. Sheffield: Sheffield Academic, 2000. 156–72. **Langlamet, F.** "Josué II et les traditions de l'Hexateuque." *RB* 78 (1971) 5–17, 161–83, 321–54. **Leith, M. J. W.** "The Archaeology of Rahab." *BAR* 33.4 (2007) 22, 78. **Liptzin, S.** "Rahab of Jericho." *DD* 9 (1993) 111–19 (Heb.). **Lock-**

Wood, P. F. "Rahab: Multi-faceted Heroine of the Book of Joshua." *Lutheran Theological Journal* 44 (2010) 39–50. **Louw, T. A. W. van der.** "Translator's Competence and Intention in LXX-Joshua 2." In *The Land of Israel in Bible, History, and Theology.* FS E. Noort, ed. J. van Ruiten and J. C. de Vos. VTSup 124. Leiden: Brill, 2009. 3–18. **Lyons, W. L.** "Rahab through the Ages: A Study of Christian Interpretation of Rahab." *SBL Forum.* No pages. Cited July 2008. Online: http://www.sbl-site.org/publications/article.aspx?articleid=786. **Marcus, D.** "Prolepsis in the Story of Rahab and the Spies (Joshua 2)." In *Bringing the Hidden to Light: The Process of Interpretation.* FS S. A. Geller, ed. K. F. Kravitz and D. M. Sharon. Winona Lake, IN: Eisenbrauns, 2007. 249–62. **Marx, A.** "Rahab, Prostituée et Prophétesse: Josue 2 et 6." *ETR* 55 (1980) 72–76. **Matties, G. H.** "Reading Rahab's Story: Beyond the Moral of the Story (Joshua 2)." *Direction* 24 (1995) 57–70. **McCarthy, D. J.** "Some Holy War Vocabulary in Joshua 2." *CBQ* 33 (1971) 228–30. ———. "The Theology of Leadership in Joshua 1–9." *Bib* 52 (1971) 165–75. **McKinlay, J. E.** "Rahab: A Hero/ine?" *BibInt* 7 (1999) 44–57. **Mendenhall, G.** "The Amorite Heritage in the West." In *Inspired Speech: Prophecy in the Ancient Near East.* FS H. B. Huffman, ed. J. Kaltner and L. Stulman. London: T&T Clark, 2004. 12–16. **Merling, D.** "Rahab: la mujer que cumplió las palabras de YHWH." *Theologika* 16 (2001) 128–53. ———. "Rahab: The Woman Who Fulfilled the Word of YHWH." *AUSS* 41 (2003) 31–44. **Millard, A.** "Amorites and Israelites: Invisible Invaders—Modern Expectations and Ancient Reality." In *The Future of Biblical Archaeology: Reassessing Methodologies and Assumptions. Proceedings of a Symposium August 12–14, 2001, at Trinity International University.* Ed. J. K. Hoffmeier and A. Millard. Grand Rapids: Eerdmans, 2004. 148–60. **Mitchell, G.** *Together in the Land.* JSOTSup 134. Sheffield: Sheffield Academic, 1993. **Moran, W. L.** "The Repose of Rahab's Israelite Guests." In *Studi sull'Oriente e la Bibbia offerti al P. Giovanni Rinaldi.* Genoa: Studio e Vita, 1967. 273–84. **Mowinckel, S.** *Tetrateuch-Pentateuch-Hexateuch.* BZAW 90. Berlin: Töpelmann, 1964. 13–15. **Newman, M. L.** "Rahab and the Conquest." In *Understanding the Word: Essays in Honor of Bernhard W. Anderson.* Ed. J. Butler et al. JSOTSup 37. Sheffield: JSOT Press, 1985. 167–81. **Niehaus, J. J.** "The Conquest and Ancient Near Eastern Warfare: The Element of Fear." *Contact* 35 (2005–2006) 26. **Nogalski, J. D.** "Preaching from Joshua in Canonical Contexts." *RevExp* 95 (1998) 263–69. **Orlinsky, H. M.** "The LXX Variant *katepausan* in Josh. II.1." *JBL* 63 (1944) 405–6. **Otto, E.** *Das Mazzotfest in Gilgal.* BWANT 107. Stuttgart: Kohlhammer, 1975. 86–88. **Ottosson, M.** "Rahab and the Spies." In *Dumu-E2-Dub-Ba-A.* FS Å. W. Sjöberg, ed. H. Behrens et al. Philadelphia: Samuel Noah Kramer Fund, 1989. 419–27. **Rhee, V.** "Chiasm and the Concept of Faith in Hebrews 11." *BSac* 155 (1998) 337–38. **Riegner, I. E.** *The Vanishing Hebrew Harlot: The Adventures of the Hebrew Stem ZNH.* Studies in Biblical Literature 73. New York: Lang, 2009. **Robinson, B. P.** "Rahab of Canaan—and Israel." *SJOT* 21 (2009) 257–73. **Rudolph, W.** *Der 'Elohist' von Exodus bis Josua.* BZAW 68. Berlin: Töpelmann, 1938. 165–69. **Runions, E.** "From Disgust to Humor: Rahab's Queer Affect." *Postscripts* 4 (2008) 41–69. **Schulte, H.** "Beobachtungen zum Begriff der Zona in Alten Testament." *ZAW* 104 (1992) 255–62. **Sheldon, R. M.** "Spy Tales." *BRev* 19 (2003) 12–19, 41–42. **Sherwood, A.** "A Leader's Misleading and a Prostitute's Profession: A Reexamination of Joshua 2." *JSOT* 31 (2006) 43–61. **Simpson, C. A.** *The Early Traditions of Israel.* Oxford: Blackwell, 1948. 280–83. **Soggin, J. A.** "Gerico: anatomia di una conquista." *Protest* 29 (1974) 193–213. ———. "Giosue 2 alla luce di un testo di Mi." *RSO* 39 (1964) 7–14. **Spina, F. A.** *The Faith of the Outsider: Exclusion and Inclusion in the Biblical Story.* Grand Rapids: Eerdmans, 2005. ———. "Reversal of Fortune: Rahab the Israelite and Achan the Canaanite." *BRev* 17 (2000) 24–30, 53–54. **Stark, C.** *'Kultprostitution' im Alten Testament?: Die Qedeschen der Hebräischen Bibel und das Motiv der Hurerei.* OBO 221. Göttingen: Vandenhoeck & Ruprecht, 2006. **Steinberg, N.** "Israelite Tricksters, Their Analogues and Cross-Cultural Study." *Semeia* 42 (1988) 1–13. **Stek, J. H.** "Rahab of Canaan and Israel: The Meaning of Joshua 2." *CTJ* 37 (2002) 28–48. **Stolz, F.** *Jahwes und*

Israels Kriege. ATANT 60. Zürich: Theologischer Verlag, 1972. 80–81. **Stone, L. G.** "Ethical and Apologetic Tendencies in the Redaction of the Book of Joshua." *CBQ* 53 (1991) 25–36. **Tov, E.** "4QJosh^b." In *Intertestamental Essays in Honour of Jósef Tadeusz Milik.* Ed. Z. J. Kapera. Karków: Enigma, 1992. 205–12. **Tucker, G. M.** "The Rahab Saga (Joshua 2): Some Form-Critical and Traditio-Historical Observations." In *The Use of the Old Testament in the New and Other Essays.* Ed. J. M. Efird. Durham, NC: Duke UP, 1972. 66–86. **Vattioni, F.** "Il filo scarlatto di Rahab nella Bibbia e nei Padri." In *Atti della settimana Sangue e antropologia Biblica nella Patristica (Roma 23–28 novembre 1981).* Ed. F. Vattioni. Centro studi sanguis Christi 2. Roma, 1982. 1:81–117. **Vincent, A.** "Jéricho, une hypothèse." *MUSJ* 37 (1960–61) 81–90. **Wagner, S.** "Die Kundschaftergeschichten im Alten Testament." *ZAW* 76 (1964) 255–69. **Weippert, M.** *Die Landnahme der israelitischen Stämme in der neueren wissenschaftlichen Diskussion.* FRLANT 92. Göttingen: Vandenhoeck & Ruprecht, 1967. 32–34. **Wellhausen, J.** *Die Composition des Hexateuchs und der historischen Bücher des Alten Testaments.* 2nd ed. Berlin: Reimer, 1889. 119–20. **Wilcoxen, J. A.** "Narrative Structure and Cult Legend: A Study of Joshua 1–6." In *Transitions in Biblical Scholarship.* Ed. J. C. Rylaarsdam. Chicago: University of Chicago Press, 1968. 43–70. **Windisch, D. H.** "Zur Rahabgeschichte, zwei Parallelen aus der klassischen Literatur." *ZAW* 37 (1917–18) 188–98. **Winther-Nielsen, N.** *A Functional Discourse Grammar of Joshua: A Computer-Assisted Rhetorical Structure Analysis.* ConBOT 40. Stockholm: Almqvist & Wiksell, 1995. 105–62. **Wiseman, D.** "Rahab of Jericho." *TynBul* 14 (1964) 8–11. **Wood, B.** "Dating Jericho's Destruction: Bienkowski Is Wrong on All Counts." *BAR* 16.5 (1990) 45, 47–49, 68–69. ———. "Did the Israelites Conquer Jericho? A New Look at the Archaeological Evidence." *BAR* 16.2 (1990) 44–59. **Wright, S.** "Salvation and the House of a Harlot." *Kerux* 21 (2006) 37–44. **Wu, R.** "Women on the Boundary: Prostitution, Contemporary and in the Bible." *Feminist Theology* 28 (2001) 69–81. **Zakovitch, Y.** "Humor and Theology or the Successful Failure of Israelite Intelligence: A Literary-Folkloric Approach to Joshua 2." In *Text and Traditions: The Hebrew Bible and Folklore.* Ed. S. Niditch. Atlanta: Scholars Press, 1990. 75–104. **Zevit, Z.** "The Problem of Ai: New Theory Rejects Battle as Described in Bible but Explains How Story Evolved." *BAR* 11.5 (1985) 58–69.

Translation

[1]*Then Joshua, the son of Nun, sent out from Shittim two men for secret spying,[a] saying,* "*Go, see the land and Jericho.*"[b] *So they went and came[c] to the house of a woman, a prostitute. Her name was Rahab. They bedded down there.* [2]*It was then reported to the king of Jericho,* "*Two men have just[a] come here tonight[b] from the Israelites to spy out the land.*" [3]*So the king of Jericho sent to Rahab,* "*Bring out the men who have come to you, who have come[a] to your house,[b] for they have come to spy out all[c] the land.*" [4]*The woman took[a] the two[b] men and hid them.[c] She said,[d]* "*Certainly you are right.[e] The men came to me, but I did not know from where they came.[f]* [5]*When the gate was to close[a] at dark, the men went out. I do not know where the men[b] went. Pursue quickly[c] after them because you can overtake them.*"

[6]*Now[a] she had brought them up to the roof and concealed them in the flax stalks arranged by her on the roof.* [7]*But, meanwhile, the men pursued after them the way of the Jordan on[a] the crossings. They had closed the gate[b] just as[c] the pursuers went out after them.* [8]*But they were still not bedded down when she came up to them on the roof.*

[9]*She said to the men,* "*I know that Yahweh has given to you (pl.) the land and that[a] the dread of you (pl.) has fallen upon us and that all the inhabitants of the land melt away before you (pl.),[b]* [10]*for we have heard that Yahweh[a] dried up the waters[b] of the Reed Sea before you when you came out of Egypt[c] and what you (pl.) did[d] to the two kings of the Amorites who*

were beyond the Jordan, to Sihon and to Og whom you committed to the ban. [11]*We heard, and our heart melted. Spirit remains in no one because of you (pl.), for Yahweh your God it is*[a] *who is God in heaven above and on the earth below.* [12]*Now*[a] *make an oath with me in the name of Yahweh. Since I have treated you graciously, you, yes you (pl.), shall deal graciously with the house of my father. You shall give me a sign of the truth.*[b] [13]*You shall save alive my father*[a] *and my mother and my brothers and my sisters*[b] *and all that belongs to them.*[c] *You shall deliver our lives from death."*

[14]*The men said to her, "Our lives are in place of yours even to death! If you (pl.)*[a] *do not report this business of ours,*[b] *then*[c] *when Yahweh gives*[d] *us the land,*[e] *we will treat you with kindness and faithfulness."*

[15]*Then she let them down with rope*[a] *through the window because her house was in the city wall. Thus she was living in the wall.*[b] [16]*She said to them, "Go to the mountain lest the pursuers encounter you. Hide yourselves there three days until the pursuers*[a] *return. Afterwards you may go your way."*

[17]*The men said to her, "We are exempt from this oath of yours*[a] *which you have caused us to swear.*[b] [18]*Right as we are entering the land,*[a] *this cord of*[b] *scarlet thread you shall tie in the window from which you let us down. Your father, mother, brothers, and all the house of your father you shall gather to yourself to the house.* [19]*Everyone who shall go out from the doors of your house to the outside shall have his blood on his own head. We shall be exempt.*[a] *But everyone who is with you in the house, his blood shall be on our head if a hand should be laid on him.*[b] [20]*Now if you report this*[a] *business of ours, then we will be exempt from your oath*[b] *which you caused us to swear."*[c]

[21]*She said, "According to your words, thus it shall be." Then she sent them away, and they left. And she tied the scarlet cord in the window.*[a] [22]*So they left and came to the mountain. They remained there three days until the pursuers had returned.*[a] *The pursuers searched in all the way, but found nothing.* [23]*The two men returned and came down from the mountain. They passed over and came to Joshua, the son of Nun, and reported to him all their findings.* [24]*They told Joshua that "Yahweh has given into our hand*[a] *the whole land. All the inhabitants of the land even melt before us."*

Notes

Van der Louw ("Translator's Competence," 3–6) points out the features in LXX that are inelegant, unnatural, and very exotic for Gk. narrative and sees the translator employing "an economy of labour" rather than a "principle of curtailment" (17). Van der Louw thus sees the translator as "a native speaker of Greek, but without rhetorical education, and thus lacking professional text awareness" (18).

1.a. MT has a participle and adverb. It is not clear whether the adverb relates to Joshua's action or to that of the spies. LXX and Syr. omit the adverb. The Masoretic accentuation has connected it with לֵאמֹר, the Hebrew quotation marks. Benjamin (*Variations*) explains the adverb as a later corruption from an original הָאָרֶץ, "the land," admitting that other Greek evidence represents a guess. It is probable that the corruption resulted in the more common word הָאֹר, while the earlier Gk. tradition may have refused to guess at the meaning of the *hapax*. Fritz (32) sees the adverb as superfluous and so eliminates it as a gloss. Nelson (38) sees it as MT expansion in a revision emphasizing secrecy. Hess may be right in deciding "that the original meaning of the occurrence in Joshua 2 may have been lost" (83). Bieberstein (*Josua, Jordan, Jericho*, 107) gives a complicated explanation supporting the MT as original and the LXX as representing an expanded Hebrew text adding a second mention of the two spies and of Jericho. Bieberstein (*Josua, Jordan, Jericho*, 108–9) then looks at the designations for the spies as "young men" and as "men" (2:1, 2, 3, 4, 5, 9, 14, 17, 23; 6:17, 22, 23, 25). He finds the Gk. original in designating them as "young men" in the presence of Joshua and as "men" when they are anonymous within the city. Similarly, Rahab is named only within the framework, while she remains simply a woman in interchange with the spies. MT is then seen as a later leveling (*Nivellierung*) to the context. Winther-Nielsen translates, "sent two men spying secretly" (*Functional Discourse Grammar*, 117). Van der Louw ("Translator's Competence," 15) says the Gk. κατασκοπεύω includes meaning related to both spy and secret, making translation of the Heb. adverb superfluous.

1.b. "And Jericho" is awkward in the context. Syr., Tg. frag., and Vg. give evidence for reading "the region of Jericho," but this is most likely an attempt to interpret the present MT in a less awkward fashion. Fritz (32) sees the term as senseless in this context and thus eliminates it as a gloss. Text criticism cannot solve the problem. This is a matter of Hebrew grammar and syntax. Winther-Nielsen points to Josh 7:2 as evidence for this "double argument construction" (*Functional Discourse Grammar*, 117).

1.c. LXX adds "the two men came into Jericho." This may represent an original reading that has fallen from the Heb. tradition through homoioteleuton (cf. Benjamin, *Variations*; Fritz, 32; Nelson, 36, 38), but note Bieberstein's strong argument in *Note* 1.a above for MT as original. Van der Louw ("Translator's Competence," 13–14) reads LXX as "having gone, the two young men entered Jericho and entered the house of a prostitute woman," seeing the LXX as protecting the spies from the charge of ignoring their task and of sexual misdeeds by substituting "lodged" for "sleep."

2.a. הנה expresses immediacy, action happening right now within the narration. See *IBHS* 40.2.1; Lambin, *Introduction to Biblical Hebrew*, 168. LXX does not translate הנה. Van der Louw ("Translator's Competence," 12) attributes this to preventing a problem of logic, in that the king has nothing to "see," the translator's normal rendering of הנה.

2.b. LXX does not witness "tonight" here but does in v 3. This represents a smoothing out of narrative style within the tradition. Nelson (38) believes MT moved "tonight" from v 2 to v 3 "to emphasize the secrecy motif and to reduce sexual implications." Van der Louw ("Translator's Competence," 12) sees Gk. νύξ as referring only to the darkness of night, which would not be appropriate here where the Heb. term is more extensive in its meaning. The term was added by LXX in v 3, where it was more appropriate to the conditions there.

3.a. LXX and Syr. represent separate traditions here. LXX omits "to you," while Syr. omits "who have come to your house." Fritz (32) calls the MT reading a clarifying addition, pointing to Noth's description of it as an attempt to avoid a possible misunderstanding in this context. MT probably represents a conflation of traditions. Nelson (38) sees Syr. as original, being "more difficult, offensive, and morally ambiguous." Similarly, Bieberstein (*Josua, Jordan, Jericho*, 110) sees MT as the common source for both MT and LXX but accepts Syr. as the oldest reading. Van der Louw ("Translator's Competence," 15–16) finds that LXX has condensed the MT's redundancy.

3.b. LXX adds "tonight." See *Note* 2.b above.

3.c. A few Heb. MSS, LXX, Syr. omit "all." This is a traditional idiom that may easily have worked its way into the textual tradition as a theological heightening. It does not fit the original context well. Still, Hess ([1996] 85, n. 1) argues for the originality of MT since "there is no other explanation for its appearance only here." Van der Louw ("Translator's Competency," 16) makes the "all" implicit.

4.a. These verbs are often interpreted as examples of "dischronologized narratives" and rendered as past perfects: "had taken" and "had hidden." See Howard (100, n. 111) and W. J. Martin, "Dischronologized Narrative in the Old Testament," in *Congress Volume, Rome, 1968*, VTSup 17 (Leiden: Brill, 1969) 179–86. Harstad (110) sees a flashback here. I agree with Hubbard (116, n. 27) in seeing the normal consec. tenses here. For the repeated references to hiding, see Hess ([1996] 85–86).

4.b. "Two" is redundant and omitted by LXX and Vg. The form is different here than that in v 1. The numeral does not reappear until the close of the narrative (v 23). It may represent a gloss from the tradition here.

4.c. The versions read the expected pl. suff. here. MT may represent dittography of the following *waw* (Delitzsch, Bieberstein) or a scribal error in copying the suff. Fritz (32) and Nelson (38) read pl. with the versions. *Preliminary and Interim Report* (2:4) decides the sg. suff. is impersonal and interprets the verse to mean: "she hid the fact of having received the men into her house." Barthélemy (*Critique textuelle*, 1:1–2) retains MT, seeing LXX as change necessitated by receptor language. Bieberstein (*Josua, Jordan, Jericho,* 110) removes the suff. completely and explains Syr., LXX, Tg. as supplying the unnamed object.

4.d. LXX adds "to them" unnecessarily, "causing confusion" (van der Louw, "Translator's Competence," 10). For כן LXX reads the difficult λέγουσα, "saying."

4.e. The sentence attempts to reproduce the Heb. כן "right, true," either omitted or misunderstood by LXX.

4.f. "But I did . . ." is omitted by LXX, possibly in view of the explanation following in v 5. Bieberstein (*Josua, Jordan, Jericho,* 118) finds no way to decide between the two readings. There is no apparent reason for its being added later to the Heb. Nelson sees it as "an important part of Rahab's defense" (38).

5.a. The inf. const. here is one of obligation (Williams, *Williams' Hebrew Syntax,* 196). *IBHS* 36.2.1 notes the passive aspect of the inf. here.

5.b. "Men" does not appear in the versions and may represent a growth in the textual tradition seeking to make the subject explicit. Van der Louw ("Translator's Competence," 16) finds "men" redundant and thus unneeded in Gk.

5.c. "Quickly" does not appear in LXX, which may represent a loss due to the similarity of the following word (Benjamin, *Variations*).

6.a. Nelson (38) points to the disjunctive clauses in vv 6–7 as "somewhat perplexing." He sees them as contrastive, highlighting each subject in turn. He is certainly correct in seeing a "flashback perfect" here.

7.a. That Ugaritic usage can prove a meaning of "as far as" for the Heb. על is at best doubtful (contra Soggin, 36–37). The logical meaning of the text is that the men were on the crossings of the Jordan. It may be a simple confusion with אל or עד (cf. Noth; Fritz, 32).

7.b. Nelson sees a need for "resolving the lack of a direct object marker before 'gate'" (38). He thus follows LXX in construing the verb as passive and connecting the end of v 7 with v 8. Nelson thus reads: והשער שגר ויהי כאשר יצאו, "and the gate was shut. As soon as the pursuers went out after them [8]and before they lay down . . ." This is a complex way to ensure a Hebrew scribe used 'proper Hebrew.'"

7.c. The construction כאשר אחרי is "singular" (Noth) but not impossible (C. Brockelmann, *Hebräische Syntax* [Neukirchen: Erziehungsvereins, 1956] §163b). LXX apparently read the more usual temporal construction with ויהי. The more complicated theory of abbreviations and variant textual traditions proposed by Benjamin is at least worthy of further study. Bieberstein (*Josua, Jordan, Jericho,* 112–13) finds five distinct forms in MT, Heb. MSS, Tg., Syr., LXX: אחרי כאשר, כאשר, אחרי אשר, ויהי כאשר, and אחריהם כאשר. He sees the last three as unable to produce the other readings and so opts for אחרי כאשר or כאשר, seeing no distinct change in meaning and no way to resolve the issue. The single word seems less likely to produce the compound expression than vice versa.

9.a. LXX has gone its own way with the end of the verse, reading γάρ for the Heb. וכי, thus transforming the relative clause into a result clause.

9.b. LXX could make the interpretation noted in *Note* 9.a because it did not have the parallel result clause with which MT concludes the verse. This expression occurs also in v 24, which served either as the basis for addition to MT (Nelson, 38 pointing also to Exod 15:15–16) or for omission from the LXX tradition. Again, traditional phrases are easily added to the tradition. Compare Bieberstein (*Josua, Jordan, Jericho,* 118–19).

10.a. LXX adds "God." Auld, "Joshua: The Hebrew and Greek Texts," 12–13) implies the originality of the LXX reading in all ten cases of such LXX additions. Such is hard to prove in view of the fluidity of the text particularly in the use of such traditional pious phrases.

10.b. LXX omits "waters." The expression ים-סוף, "Reed Sea," appears twenty-four times in the MT, only here and Deut 11:4 with "waters." LXX reads "waters" in Deut 11:4. It is possible that textual corruption has changed an original אלוהים into את-מי. Van der Louw ("Translator's Competence," 13) suggests that in Gk. καταξηραίνω "does not normally collocate with ὕδρ."

10.c. LXX adds "from the land" before "Egypt." Benjamin (*Variations*) calls this a "tendency to full phrase" within the ongoing textual tradition. Van der Louw ("Translator's Competence," 9–10) is more precise in explaining the LXX reading as taken from the Pentateuch, which the translator knew well.

10.d. LXX reads 3rd masc. sg., attributing the action to God, a much easier reading than the MT and so probably secondary. Actually the theological statement is implicit in either reading.

11.a. Gk. does not witness the copula. Van der Louw ("Translator's Competence," 11) points to the translator's seeking to avoid ungrammatical Gk.

12.a. 4QJosh[b] appears to read, "and she said" instead of "Now." See Abegg, *Dead Sea Scrolls Bible*, 203.

12.b. LXX omits "you shall give to me a true sign." LXX does mention a "sign" in v 18, where MT does not. Fritz (32) and Nelson (38) say the sentence is a later addition. LXX is the easier reading, since the red thread in the window is more easily interpreted as a sign than is the saving alive of Rahab's family. The same problem is apparent in Exod 3:11–12. "Sign" may cover a broader semantic and temporal field than in Western culture. Bieberstein (*Josua, Jordan, Jericho*, 119) points to other requests for grace involving Rahab's whole family and to lack of reference to the sign in the following dialogue to decide that MT has added the sentence to parallel 2:14. But the spies ignore the request for a concrete sign ironically as they turn the conversation from their responsibilities to Rahab's. Van der Louw ("Translator's Competence," 14) sees the omission as a means to avoid "an interpretational difficulty." V 14 does not serve as a parallel to v 12. Rather LXX did not see the irony of the sentence and thus omitted it.

13.a. LXX expands to "house of my father," copying v 12 (compare Bieberstein, *Josua, Jordan, Jericho*, 113–14). The expression is not apt for the present list of relatives. Coote sees LXX as original, representing "the social unit responsible for covering family debts" (594), Coote's favorite theme in this section.

13.b. The traditional Heb. text reads "my sister." The Masoretic pointing suggested "my sisters." LXX referred to "all my house," reflecting the reading of v 18. The pl. corresponding to "brothers" would be expected. That the Gk. reading is to be preferred because it would make the list correspond to that of v 18 is doubtful (contra Benjamin, *Variations*). Nelson (39) sees both the LXX and MT expressions as expansions and so reads, "my brothers and everything they have and deliver my life [with LXX; MT our lives] from death."

13.c. Heb. אשר can mean either "all which" or "everyone who." Perhaps both readings are comprehensible here.

14.a. Fritz (32) follows strong Heb. evidence in addition to Origen and the Vg. in reading the 2nd fem. sg. This is the easier reading. MT tradition is to be retained and applied to the entire family of Rahab just mentioned.

14.b. LXX does not witness the entire clause "if . . . ours." Nelson (39) sees two divergent traditions in v 14, labeling the clause as an MT expansion concerned with secrecy. Bieberstein (*Josua, Jordan, Jericho*, 120) sees a MT expansion seeking to modify the otherwise unconditional promise of vv 17–20. This avoids the duplication with v 20, but it also misses the subtle change of direction given the conversation over against the woman's statement of the agreement in v 12. Here the spies ironically take away the advantage in the negotiations from the woman, an argument not followed by the LXX.

14.c. LXX changes the subject to Rahab. Nelson thinks this is an OG correction after "to us" became "to you (pl.)" in the tradition. Bieberstein (*Josua, Jordan, Jericho*, 114–15) opts for MT, though seeing both as possibilities. He proposes MT offers more meaningful dialogue. Soggin (37) characterizes this as meaningless repetition. It could be original, showing Rahab's acceptance of the agreement as stated by the men. In the textual transmission, this was misunderstood and changed to continue the speech of the spies.

14.d. *IBHS* 32.2.6 shows that "sometimes the future time is emphasized by the addition of היה."

14.e. LXX reads "city" rather than land. Again, this fits the story itself more aptly. Rahab's concern is with the city and its walls in which she lives. "The land" represents the ongoing theological interpretation of the story. Nelson (39) finds a "pedantic OG correction."

15.a. LXX omits "rope," probably an accident in textual transmission. Van der Louw ("Translator's Competency," 16) finds the LXX translator omitting the term as subtly implicit in the verb.

15.b. LXX omits "because . . . in the wall." Vg. also omits the final sentence. Tov (*Textual Criticism of the Hebrew Bible*, 328) sees MT plus as an exegetical addition. Nelson sees

MT expansions in all the differences in the textual tradition, seeing MT as a "conflated doublet of two alternative explanations." Coote sees the MT as a "late explanatory addition that accords poorly with the fall of Jericho's walls and survival of Rahab's house (6:20, 22)" (594). The sentence is problematic in light of chap. 6. This has caused the tradition to omit the clause. Compare Bieberstein, *Josua, Jordan, Jericho,* 116, followed by van der Louw, "Translator's Competency," 15.

16.a. LXX adds "after you" following the expression "those pursuing." Heb. also has the prepositional phrase in vv 5, 7. Participial forms are not used there, however. Here it is an explanatory addition on the basis of the pattern in vv 5, 7.

17.a. The verbless clause with predicate first classifies or describes the subject, in this case "we." See *Williams' Hebrew Syntax,* 579.

17.b. The verse contains problems in its grammatical forms. The masculine זה, "this," does not agree with the fem. noun "oath." So Nelson (39) vocalizes as a fem. Also, the noun has a pronominal suff. The demonstrative pronoun following such nouns does not ordinarily take the article. *Williams' Hebrew Syntax,* 74b, n. 117, calls this instance a "rare occasion" where "a noun with a pronominal suff. is followed by a demonstrative with the article. In such cases the demonstrative is considered to be a demonstrative adjective rather than a demonstrative pronoun in attributive position." The form for the 2nd pers. sg. fem. verb is slightly irregular (note GKC §59h). The LXX simply omits the last clause "which . . . swear" here and in v 20. Bieberstein (*Josua, Jordan, Jericho,* 116–17) shows that Gk. consistently eliminates the "figura etymologica," so that MT is the older reading.

18.a. LXX reads "outskirts of the city" for land. Fritz (32) says this is an assimilation to the text. Nelson (39) thinks MT represents the scouts' perspective. Coote (594) sees this as part of the original folk narrative, along with 6:17, 25, dealing only with the city. LXX again (see *Note* 14.d) fits the story better. MT represents a theologizing of the tradition.

18.b. Nelson (39) omits "cord of" as doublet or expansion of v 21 and notes LXX use of "sign" as misreading of MT marker of direct object. *Preliminary and Interim Report* (2:4) retains MT, seeing LXX as assimilation to other passages.

19.a. LXX mentions "this oath of yours" here as in vv 17 and 20. Again familiar language has intruded into the textual tradition.

19.b. LXX transfers the concluding condition to the next verse, changing the object of injury to the spies: "If anyone should wrong us . . ." This is done in the textual transmission to relieve the spies of any shadow of blame.

20.a. The demonstrative without the article modifying a noun with a suff. is a demonstrative pronoun in attributive position (*Williams' Hebrew Syntax,* 74b, 117b).

20.b. The versions read "this" as in v 17 (also v 19 LXX). The originality of such "familiar" language cannot be decided.

20.c. LXX omits the last clause "which . . . swear," as in 17. The phrase agrees with the tenor of tradition in attributing initiative to Rahab but control of the situation to spies. Cf. *Notes* 14.b* c.

21.a. LXX lacks "and she . . . window." This is a rather clear case of homoioteleuton (cf. Benjamin, *Variations,* 27) or haplography. Nelson (39) thinks the omission might be caused by a scribe thinking Rahab's action was premature at this point. Bieberstein (*Josua, Jordan, Jericho,* 120), on the other hand, suggests the fulfillment of the promise to place the cord in the window comes from a scribe who thought the fulfillment was missing and placed it too early in the text. The fulfillment of the promise is a needed part of the characterization of Rahab and so cannot be omitted.

22.a. LXX omits "until . . . returned," a duplication of the command in v 16. This may reflect later expansion in MT or haplography in the LXX (Nelson, 39; Bieberstein, *Josua, Jordan, Jericho,* 123). Van der Louw ("Translator's Competence," 13) says Gk. omission sought to avoid two logical problems: how could hidden spies know pursuers had returned, and why is search mentioned only after the return?

24.a. Some Heb. MSS, Syr., Tg. frag., and Vg. change "hand" into the pl. MT, witnessed by LXX, is the more difficult reading.

Form/Structure/Setting

The setting changes to Shittim (v 1) and the interest shifts from crossing the Jordan (e.g., 1:11) to spying out Jericho (e.g., 2:1). Chap. 2 then carries out a complete narrative from Joshua's commission of the spies (v 1) to their report back to Joshua (vv 23–24). Chap. 3 returns to the narrative of the Jordan crossing. Thus chap. 2 must be handled as a complete unit within itself, a prelude to chap. 6, where an epilogue or denouement for chap. 2 appears (6:22–25).

Tradition

The chapter displays all the characteristics of a story, not theology. Fritz correctly sees oral tradition behind the story but finds its final form in the time of the monarchy, explaining the taking of the land and the survival of a group of Canaanites. Chap. 2 "employs irony, humor, and folkloric qualities to create an irresistible plot in which a prostitute outsmarts two groups of men in order to preserve herself and her family during the Israelite attack on Jericho. The narrative has suspense, sexual innuendo, and an underdog who triumphs."[263]

Nelson contends that "there can be no doubt that the text has had a complicated prehistory."[264] Its three-day motif and loose tie to the fall of Jericho show this. He thus finds three stages in the story's development: an independent tale, a part of the pre-Deuteronomistic book, and a part of the Deuteronomistic History. For Nelson, the independent tale whose reconstruction is quite speculative tells of "a clever act of treachery," akin to Gen 19; Judg 1:23–26; 4–5; 19; and to classical tales adduced by Windisch.[265] This stage represents an ethnological saga in which "a wily ancestor helps herself and her kinfolk through shrewdness and presence of mind." The saga "provides an etiology for the continued existence of a non-Israelite group . . . in or near Jericho."[266] The second stage for Nelson connects it to chaps. 2–11 as a pre-conquest story of spying.[267] Here Rahab rather than Yahweh "asserts the divine will." The narrative at this stage shows "this land is ours because Yahweh, the divine warrior, has given it to us." In Nelson's third stage, that of the Deuteronomistic History, the story of Rahab "becomes the story of a conversion," introducing the holy ban and illustrating Israel's obedience to the law of Deuteronomy. Throughout the history of the narrative we have "a tale of a woman who is both cunning trickster, securing her family's future, and praiseworthy host, protecting her endangered guests in accordance with ancient norms of hospitality."[268]

Certain elements in the narrative lead to popular folklore: sexual innuendo, a prostitute hero, men dangling on a rope from a window, a prostitute's concern for family, inept king and messengers, and wily negotiations. Thus Pressler concludes "just what the ancient tale included is hard to say. . . . [T]he tale's humor attests to its folk origins, as do several of its motifs: the harlot with a heart of gold; the trickster who wins by wit, not power; the underdog who bests a powerful lord. All are typical folkloric themes."[269]

Other elements apparently originated in cultic worship and celebration, especially the Israelite confession of faith in the mouth of a prostitute. The standard-

---

263 Creach, 31.
264 Nelson, 41.
265 *ZAW* 37 (1917–18) 188–98.
266 Nelson, 43.
267 Ibid., 45.
268 Ibid., 46.
269 Pressler, 21.

ized formulations in vv 9–10 and 24 may well point to cultic usage as Wagner and Wilcoxen insist.[270] With such a story Israel celebrated and reaffirmed Yahweh's gift of the land.

Scholars who support some form of the Deuteronomistic History interpretation see the standard formulations of confession as contributions of the Deuteronomistic historians. Such language in cultic forms may show a close connection between cult and Deuteronomists, a connection formed perhaps via Levite worship leaders and/or ancient storytellers. Judges 17—21 reveals the vagabond life of Levitical priests, seeking employment wherever they could find it. Part of their responsibilities was to maintain Israel's identity-giving traditions and to implant them in the lives of worshipers.

A literary stage in the tradition appears in the spy framework (vv 1a, 23b–24) and in the epilogue in chap. 6. These may represent the same stage or a literary collection stage and a final book of Joshua stage.

Tradition-historical analysis has revealed a complex tradition behind the present narrative. Originally, the narrative elements arose in popular folklore. The popular story was taken up by the cult to explain its procedure in conquering the entire land and to testify to the unique power of Israel's God. This transformed the popular folk narrative into an Israelite spy story.

The literary narrative forms an introduction to the story of the conquest of Jericho. The spies spell out the conditions of the oath (vv 18–21a), and Joshua faithfully fulfills his promises (6:17, 22–23, 25). The final historian's literary interpretation of the story, including chap. 6, becomes an illustration of holy war theology both as it is carried out (albeit imperfectly) and how it allows for exceptions.

Source and Redaction

Knauf calls the Rahab narrative one of the latest supplements in the book of Joshua with traces of post-classical Hebrew in vv 16d, 17b, 20a.[271] He finds no trace of older or local tradition. Rather, he maintains that the story represents a theological construction. Only one with Knauf's redactional assumptions could come to such a conclusion about the obvious descendant of popular storytelling.

The chapter is a critical battleground for the entire question of a "hexateuch." Langlamet gives an extensive history of research with appropriate charts. He also provides detailed word statistics.[272] Evidence of literary unevenness is self-evident. The linguistic evidence of Langlamet simply proves that the story represents typical Israelite narrative language, not that it represents vocabulary that is exclusively J.[273]

Shittim (v 1) is at home in the Tetrateuch (Num 25:1; 33:49; cf. Mic 6:5), but not in Deuteronomic literature. Doublets appear in vv 4 and 6; 1b and 8 with reference to 17; שׁכב and 19–20. Contradictions appear in the emphasis on the location of the house on the wall (v 15) and the later total destruction of the walls (6:20); in the chronology of vv 16 and 22 with 1:11 and 3:1; and in the unconditional and conditional oaths of vv 14 and 19. The narrative sequence of vv 15–21 leaves questions,

270 Wagner, *ZAW* 76 (1964) 268–69; Wilcoxen, "Narrative Structure," 56.
271 Knauf, 46.
272 *RB* 78 (1971) 5–17, 161–83.
273 Ibid., 61–83, 353–54.

since the men are depicted as entering into extended haggling over details of the agreement while dangling from the end of a rope. Finally, one may infer a double interpretation of the scarlet cord as the rope on which the men are swinging (v 18) with a smaller string (v 21). Such evidence has led to repeated efforts to isolate two narrative strands in the material. Such evidence does not necessarily lead, however, to the conclusion of parallel narratives. In fact, scholarly discussion assumes a rather unified narrative with some secondary accretions.[274]

Narrative technique explains most of the difficulties.[275] The geographical and chronological difficulties do point to a different literary origin from that of chaps. 1 and 3. Reinterpretation within tradition, whether oral or literary, accounts for the sequential problems of vv 15–21 as well as the problem of the house on the wall. The basic narrative unit is thus explicable without reference to differing literary parallel narratives. This does not answer, however, the question of the literary origin itself.

The one major clue is the geographical reference to Shittim. The origin of the Shittim reference lies in Josh 2.The reference reappears in Josh 3:1, where the compiler or redactor uses it to tie chaps. 3–6 with chap. 2. This compiler uses Shittim as knowledge presupposed by the listener or reader. This literary employment of Shittim may be explained as a part of a larger oral tradition or, more likely, as a conscious literary reference back to Num 25, where Israel became harlots (25:1). Here Israel is saved by a harlot.

Num 25 begins the conquest narrative in the Tetrateuch with a narrative of holy war carried out in disobedience (Num 25:16–18; 31). Josh 2 begins the story of the conquest itself, a narrative of holy war carried out in obedience (Josh 6). Shittim appears to form a literary bridge spanning the Deuteronomic or literary materials.[276] As such, it may well point to an early literary source of the materials, a source that incorporated Joshua and the conquest of Jericho into the tetrateuchal tradition, or at least into the wilderness tradition. The exact nature and dating of such a source remains open until new light is shed on the nature of the literary origins of the Pentateuch as a whole.

Seebaß separates Num 25 from Josh 2:1; 3:1.[277] The register of names in Num 26 has no equivalent in Joshua. The land possession expected in Numbers does not occur in Joshua, only battles that later led to tribes gaining land possession. The contact between Josh 13 and Num 32 does not bring reference in one to the other and gives separate names to the parties involved. God's commission in Num 34 points to land borders related to that of the Egyptian New Kingdom in the thirteenth and fourteenth centuries, but has no counterpart in Joshua. With regard to Levites, the traditions in Num 35 appear older than those behind Num 21, while those in Josh 20 appear older than those in Num 35. Seebaß concludes that the Book of Joshua certainly does not correspond to the expectations the Book of Numbers arouses but rather is independently composed.

Bieberstein lists the elements that call for literary analysis of the text: the quick

---

274 Cf. Rudolph, *Elohist*, 165–69; Langlamet, *RB* 78 (1971) 353–54; Otto, *Mazzotfest*, 87–88.
275 Moran, "Repose," 273–84.
276 Cf. Fritz, 35.
277 "Das Buch Joshua als nicht zu erwartende Fortsetzung des Buches Numeri." In Noort, ed. *The Book of Joshua*, 249–257.

change of venue (vv 2–3), the repeated bedding down of the spies (vv 1, 8), the apparent disagreement in the chronology (vv 2, 5), the repeated mention of hiding the spies (vv 4, 6), an apparent conflict of the place of meeting (vv 6, 8, 15), the noticeable Deuteronomistic language in the woman's central speech (vv 9–11), and the long conversation the spies have after they have been let down on the city wall (vv 17–21).[278] Also, the story in Josh 2 seems to lead to a capture of the city through betrayal, while chap. 6 tells of the capture through a miracle.

Fritz represents the latest redaction-history approach, reducing the original narrative to vv 1–3, 4b, 5–7, 15–17a, 18, 19, 21–23.[279] Römer maintains that the Rahab story interrupts the chronology and thus represents a later, non-Deuteronomistic addition inserted in the Persian period to counter the Deuteronomistic ideology of segregation.[280]

Such piecemeal approaches to the text demonstrate scholarly arrogance by ignoring the artistic creativity of Israelite narrators and demanding absolute consistency in literary characters and from storytellers. Such approaches are too complex and reflect more of the university ivory tower than the Israelite campfire where such stories originated. Granted, stories gained new elements as they moved from individual oral narration, to compilation, to canonical incorporation; but the additions certainly were not as drastic as the redaction critics suggest.

One item that does seem to be clear is that the ultimate editor, following ancient Near Eastern practice, has introduced his own or his cult's theological conception in the words of Rahab in vv 9–11. The tradition of the fear of the nations, the drying up of the waters (יבש *hipʿil*), the two kings of the Amorites, and the divine title (v 12b) all bear a Deuteronomic stamp. V 24 stems from the same source. Here then is pre-Deuteronomic literature given a Deuteronomic stamp.

Form

Many issues arise in an examination of the form and structure of this unit. Winther-Nielsen states "the issue is whether Joshua 2 is a spy drama, a reinterpretation of the law of Moses, an exposition on the difficulties of obedience or even a condemnation of Joshua and Yahweh."[281]

Gunkel describes the story of Rahab as typical of a common type of saga characterized by foreign travelers finding hospitality and protection with a compassionate woman.[282] Greek and Latin parallels led Hölscher to narrow the category to an etiological saga of a Jericho cult served by cult prostitutes descended from Rahab.[283] This presupposed an original ending that described the fall of Jericho through betrayal in Josh 6:25. Creach states "Joshua 2 does have a clear etiological purpose," but he then offers a theological explanation of the ban as central to the story's genre.[284] Knauf classifies the theological construction as an antiwar report.

278   *Josua, Jordan, Jericho*, 105.
279   Fritz, 33–35.
280   *So-called Deuteronomistic History*, 134, 182.
281   *Functional Discourse Grammar*, 109.
282   *RGG*, 4:2019.
283   *ZAW* 38 (1919–1920) 54–57.
284   Creach, 41.

The etiological form in Josh 6:25 has received the most attention in discussions of the text. (Compare "Form Criticism" in the Introduction above.) F. Golka still classifies Josh 2 and 6 as an etiological narrative in which the etiology is identical with the arc of tension.[285] Yet he admits that 6:25 represents an etiological motif not identical with the arc of tension.[286] Rather the motif is based on old clan tradition and is much more a theological epilogue to the story.[287] The etiological element encompasses both chap. 2 and chap. 6. The red cord in the window certainly gives rise to etiological speculation. The cord appears and disappears without explanation. Etiology represents editorial comment and connections, not the original narrative form.

Wagner suggests a different understanding of the narrative, even though he maintains its etiological character. He includes the story among "spy narratives," whose form he described as having six elements: (1) selection or naming of the spies; (2) dispatching of the spies with specific instructions; (3) report of the execution of the mission, along with confirmation through an oracle or reference to the context of salvation history; (4) notice of return and results; (5) a perfect-tense formula confirming the gift of the land by Yahweh; and (6) conclusions derived from vv 1–5, namely, action of entering or conquering the land.[288]

The form, Wagner finds, appears in Num 13–14; 21:32, 33–35; Deut 1:19–46; Josh 14:7–8; Judg 18.[289] He places the *Sitz im Leben* of the spy narratives in the ritual surrounding holy war.[290] This ritual serves as the basis for the proclamation that Yahweh has given the land to Israel.[291] In a study independent of Wagner, Wilcoxen also places Josh 2 in the Israelite cult, but in a more elaborate fashion, as part of the Gilgal Passover/Feast of Unleavened Bread celebration involving all of Josh 1–6 as a cultic legend.[292]

The enthusiasm for etiological explanations was seriously dampened, however, by B. O. Long, B. Childs, and C. Westermann.[293] F. Langlamet applies these findings concerning etiologies specifically to Josh 2, and asserts that Josh 6:25 provides a narrative epilogue but not an etiological conclusion to the story and, perhaps in connection with 2:12ff., allows us to catch a glimpse of the original etiology of the legend.[294] Langlamet agrees with Wagner that it is a spy story and notes that it is related to Judg 18 in being very regional.[295]

D. J. McCarthy moves in a slightly different direction, claiming that what is of interest in stories is not the etiology but the stories themselves and the general

285 "The Aetiologies in the Old Testament," *VT* 26 (1976) 416.
286 Ibid., 419.
287 Cf. Langlamet, *RB* 78 (1971) 323–28.
288 *ZAW* 76 (1964) 261–62.
289 Ibid., 255–62.
290 Ibid., 263–67.
291 *ZAW* 76 (1964) 267–69; cf. G. von Rad, *Der Heilige Krieg im alten Israel*, ATANT 20 (Zürich: Zwingli, 1952) 7, 9.
292 "Narrative Structure," 64.
293 Long, *The Problem of Etiological Narrative in the Old Testament*, BZAW 108 (Berlin: Töpelmann, 1968); Childs, "A Study of the Formula, 'Until This Day,'" *JBL* 82 (1963) 279–92; Westermann, "Arten der Erzählung in der Genesis," in *Forschung am Alten Testament*, vol. 1, TB 24 (Munich: Kaiser, 1964) 39–47.
294 *RB* 78 (1971) 323–28, 353.
295 Ibid., 330–33, 337.

social attitudes they reveal.[296] He demonstrates that the vocabulary in Josh 6:17, 22–23, 25 is decisively distinct from that of chap. 2.[297] The story in chap. 2 reveals for McCarthy all the elements of the popular folktale.[298]

Without reference to Langlamet, McCarthy, or Wagner, G. Tucker shows that chap. 2 has its own conclusion in v 24 and owes its existence to the theological conception and cultic institution of holy war.[299] The literary form given by the pre-Deuteronomistic redactor, however, is etiological. F. Stolz sees all the spy stories as a feature contributed by the Deuteronomistic historian.[300]

Floß reduces the original oral tale to a story of two customers visiting a prostitute and their eventual flight, all without giving proper names to people or places.[301] Bieberstein asks the natural question: Who might have told such a story to whom and for what purpose?[302] Mitchell reviews work on holy war and battle report elements and finds the latter to be part of theological reflection.[303] He, along with Gunn, points out a resemblance of Israelite battle reports to those of Assyria but emphasizes the unique literary presentation of each of the biblical reports.[304] Thus Mitchell writes: "comparisons with the campaign reports of the annals can often serve a valuable heuristic function, but . . . the narrative of Joshua has a dynamic of its own and offers a unique literary presentation."[305]

Hawk[306] identifies the chapter as an "anecdote," which Long defines as "a particular kind of report that records an event or experience in the life of a person. Anecdote may also show a tendency toward storylike features, such as conversation and imaginative description. It is the private 'biographical' focus . . . that is characteristic of anecdote."[307]

Certainly, the focus on Rahab may allow the story to be considered an anecdote, but one would expect to be able to classify various types of anecdotes, given such a generalized definition. Hawk maintains that the stories of Rahab, Achan, and the Gibeonites each "concerns some form of forbidden contact with Canaan," raising fundamental questions of national identity.[308] He provides a closer description of the common elements of these "anecdotes": concealment (2:1, 4); interrogation (2:2–3); diversion (2:4b–5, 7); doxology (2:8–11); petition (2:12–13); response (2:14); qualification (2:17–20); battle report of victory assured (6:2), of victory achieved by miracle (6:20), and of victory accomplished by massacre (6:21); etiological note (6:27); and curse (6:26).[309]

296 *Bib* 52 (1971) 165–75.
297 Ibid., 169–70.
298 Ibid., 171–72.
299 "Rahab Saga," 71–83.
300 *Jahwes und Israels Kriege: Kriegstheorien und Kriegserfahrungen im Glauben des alten Israel.* ATANT 60 (Zürich: Theologischer Verlag, 1972) 81.
301 *Kunden oder Kundschafter.*
302 *Josua, Jordan, Jericho,* 104.
303 *Together in the Land,* 23–26.
304 *JBL* 93 (1974) 513–18.
305 Mitchell, 26.
306 Hess (2000) 19.
307 *I Kings: With an Introduction to Historical Literature,* FOTL 9 (Grand Rapids: Eerdmans, 1984) 243.
308 Hess (2000) 20.
309 Ibid., 25–26.

Hawk admits that the Rahab anecdote is framed by elements that make it a spy story (vv 1a, 23–24) but understands the major part of the narrative as building on the convention of "the shrewd woman who prevails over men."[310] More recently he suggests that the story is more about salvation than spying and that "the ambiguous nature of the story allows it to be read from many different angles."[311]

This brief survey of the history of research shows the complications involved in the form-critical study of the chapter. Several stages of work are called for. First, the form of the present written narrative must be determined. Second, editorial elements or other additions in the growth of the tradition must be removed to determine if earlier oral forms served as sources for the present literary product. Third, the nature and function of such earlier forms must be described where possible. At each stage, we must remember the words of C. Westermann, who wrote that narrative material must lead from the opening through narrative tension to a resolution.[312] Where possible, we can test the insights of W. Dommershausen, that narrative begins with a statement in the perfect tense or with a noun clause; builds tension through imperfect consecutive clauses; climaxes with speech or dialogue that leads to a denouement in imperfect consecutive clauses; and ends in a formulaic construction.[313]

Josh 2 is, according to Wagner, an Israelite spy story.[314] Recall that he maintains that spy stories consist of six elements: (1) selection or naming of the spies; (2) dispatching of the spies with specific instructions; (3) report of the execution of the mission, along with confirmation through an oracle or reference to the context of salvation history; (4) notice of return and results; (5) a perfect-tense formula confirming the gift of the land by Yahweh; and (6) conclusions, namely, action of entering or conquering the land.

The selection of the spies is not mentioned in Josh 2. Rather the narrative begins with Joshua sending them out with specific instructions (v 1). The major portion of the narrative is devoted to the execution of the mission, whose confirmation is found in the actions and confession of Rahab (particularly vv 9–11). The last three elements of Wagner's form are concentrated in the final two verses with the return and report of the results (v 23) and the perfect-tense formulation of the gift of the land (v 24). The conclusion, the act of entering and conquering the land, comes only in the following chapters.

Wagner's outline fits our text. In fact, it doubly fits the text, for complication and resolution come at two points: the entrance and dismissal of the royal messengers and the spies bedding down and then dangling on a rope against the city wall before being dismissed to hide in the mountains and return to Joshua (see chart below). At the literary level, the narrative is a complex, ironic spy narrative. A simple spy report frames the Rahab narrative.[315]

Tucker is certainly correct in pointing to the diversity of traditions that have

310 Ibid., 35. Cf. Zakovitch, "Humor and Theology."
311 Hess (2010) 22–23.
312 *The Promises to the Fathers*, trans. D. Green (Philadelphia: Fortress, 1980) 1–94.
313 *Die Estherrolle: Stil und Ziel einer alttestamentlichen Schrift* (Stuttgart: Katholisches Bibelwerk, 1968).
314 *ZAW* 76 (1964) 261–62.
315 See Frymer-Kensky, "Reading Rahab," 57.

contributed to the final form of the narrative.[316] Interestingly, the elements that form the story into a cultic spy report can be removed, and the narrative form remains intact. Here we have a true spy story complete with folklore elements, humor, and narrative tension.[317] But still, with Hawk, we must consider the nature of the canonical story, which focuses on a non-Israelite whose cunning brings salvation to herself and her family. Hawk thus concludes: "the biblical writer prompts us to see the humanity of those who will be slaughtered without mercy."[318]

Structure

Gillmayr-Bucher identifies the crisis point of the narrative. When Rahab begins to speak in v 9, "the readers have no idea why Rahab acted as she did, why she offered hospitality to her enemies. In this way the dramatic tension of the story is increased and has to be released in the following speech."[319] Harstad notes the elements that create intense drama: "spies, a prostitute, a king in panic, cover blown, a cover-up, the dark cover of night, men covered by flax on a roof, a misguided wild chase, and a quick closing gate that squeaks of Canaanite fears."[320]

The narrative is dominated by ironic humor. Assis compares its irony with that in the story of Deborah and Jael. Concerning the Rahab narrative, he writes:[321]

> The behaviours of the men is [sic] presented ironically compared with that of the women. The king and his soldiers seem pathetic when they immediately believe the harlot that her customers are not in the house. . . . The assistance that Rahab provides the spies also presents them in an ironic light. The spies are passive in comparison with Rahab who actively hides them, allowing them to escape from the city. . . . Both Yael and Rahab are in control of the men they want to subdue and the men whom they plan to help. It is in their power to decide who will triumph and who will fail. The encounters of Yael and Rahab with men are presented in a similar fashion. In the Rahab story the soldiers are sent to her to find the spies and she disrupts their mission when she sends them out of the city.

The setting of the story in the house of prostitution lends itself to such an ironic style. The spies do just what one expects them to do in such a house: they bed down (vv 1, 8; cf. v 6). Each time the lady of the house has other business. H. Rösel sees the expression to bed down as intentionally ambiguous, leading the audience to a wrong conclusion by playing with different meanings of the Hebrew שכב.[322]

The king's intelligence system is so thorough it knows when strange men enter a prostitute's house, but so ignorant that it follows the advice of the prostitute without even searching the house or watching the window to discover the spies, who dangle tantalizingly within reach for such a long time (vv 15–21).

---

316 "Rahab Saga," 82.
317 McCarthy, *Bib* 52 (1971) 171–72.
318 Hess (2000) 25.
319 *BibInt* 15 (2007) 144.
320 Harstad, 119.
321 *Bib* 85 (2004) 84–85.
322 Rösel, 47.

When the lady of the house comes to the men in their beds, her bedtime story for them is just what is expected in such an establishment: a confession of religious faith, an act of religious conversion (vv 8–11). This leads to the prolonged bargaining between the woman and spies. She appears to gain the advantage from them (vv 12–16). Suddenly the tables are turned. Jericho's intelligence agents may fall for Rahab's tricks, but not Israel's spies. They are innocent. They set the conditions of the agreement (vv 17–21).

The burden of proof is upon Rahab and her family for their future actions, not upon the spies because of the past graces of Rahab. Such irony is built into the speech forms found in the narrative. The report to the king uses the impersonal passive voice, subtly underlining the inevitability of such a report (v 2). Winther-Nielsen dismisses this statement, however, saying the "passivization demotes the unidentifiable subject actor," an interesting grammatical category that says little in this context, since the unnamed royal intelligence agent could hardly be further demoted.[323]

Over against this is the naming of the prostitute (v 1). Rahab is able to move back and forth between the spies and the royal messengers without arousing suspicion (vv 4, 6). Whatever the original role of the sign in the tradition, it now occupies an ironically mysterious place. The prostitute demands it of the spies (v 12). She appears to define the sign as a future event, the rescue of her family (v 13).

The spies then subtly change the nature of the sign. It is a cord that she must tie in her window (v 18). Her family can be saved only if she obeys their commands (vv 18–20). The very form of Rahab's speech to the messengers mimics legal defense speech, as Rahab claims to tell the truth while in reality telling the biggest lie possible (vv 4–5).[324] She is so persuasive that the royal messengers are transformed into "pursuers," though what they pursue lies behind them, at the starting gate.[325] The story, then, ridicules the enemies of Israel represented by the king and his messengers. It also ridicules Canaanite enclaves remaining within Israel, as represented by the clever prostitute tricked by the spies.[326]

Sherwood suggests, however, that Joshua is at fault in the story.[327] For him, building on Hawk's work, "the episode seems to function on at least two competing levels, one focused upon Joshua and the Israelite spies, the second upon Rahab."[328] In no way can one compare narrative levels of the Joshua narrative and Rahab narrative. The Joshua emphasis comes from the 24-chapter Joshua narrative. In no way does the narrative of chap. 2 give focus on Joshua to the extent it gives focus on Rahab. The story itself belongs to Rahab and no one else.

Hawk, Sherwood, and Hubbard try to find reasons to criticize Joshua, but the narrative simply reports Joshua's actions without passing any judgment on them. Sherwood would be prudent to stick with his statement, "Joshua is primarily a background presence for the episode" and go no further. Surely one cannot attribute the "primary interest perspective" to Joshua.[329] Sherwood overly emphasizes the story's

---

323 *Functional Discourse Grammar*, 119.

324 Moran, "Repose," 280–81.

325 Cf. M. Weiss, "Einiges über die Bauformen des Erzählens in der Bibel," *VT* 13 [1963] 462–63.

326 For other rhetorical tricks, see Moran, "Repose"; Langlamet, *RB* 78 (1971) 338–43.

327 "A Leader's Misleading and a Prostitute's Profession."

328 *JSOT* 31 (2006) 44.

329 Ibid., 47.

very passive presentation of Joshua and the spies. Only in the larger context of the story could they claim a part of the action. Sherwood seeks to examine that larger context carefully, reading Josh 1–12 as a mirror image of the Exodus narrative. In this weak parallel Sherwood compares the structure of the exodus narrative with Joshua.

1. Ten conquest narratives parallel 10 plague stories (defeat of cities versus miracles of nature).
2. The victory at Jericho gives the people the land and parallels the defeat of Egypt and taking the people out of the land of oppression (battle with one town requiring a new series of battles before part of the land is settled over against a series of miracles that provide divine victory over a nation's entire army).
3. The new institution of Passover (with circumcision in Joshua) parallels the institution of Passover and consecration of the first-born (comparing adult rite with childhood rite).
4. God leads people across the divided Jordan and into land parallels God leading Israel out of a land of oppression through the divided Reed Sea (entering land after 40 years compared with entering wilderness).
5. God charges Joshua to keep Torah over against God giving Torah on Sinai (brief charge to leader compared to long chapters defining law).
6. God promises divine presence with new leader compared with God tabernacling among his people.

The comparison can be challenged based on the type of literature and the number of chaps. or vv used:

Joshua Passage/Literary Type	*Exodus Passage/Literary Type*
1. 6 chaps., 6–11, battle reports	6 chaps., 7:13–12:32, contest narratives
2. 1 chap., 6, holy war narrative	12 chaps., 1–12, holy war narrative
3. 11 vv, 5:2–12, ritual report	1 chap., 13, ritual regulations
4. 2 chaps., 3–4, cultic ritual report	2 chaps., 14–15, prophetic salvation oracle, battle report, victory song
5. 2 vv 1:7–8, divine instruction	5 chaps., 19–23, theophany, establishment of law
6. 2 half-verses, 1:5b, 9b, divine promise	5 vv 34–38, theophany

Sherwood misreads what I intended in the first edition of the commentary when he says I find no theological coherence in the narrative.[330] The coherence comes in the praise and acceptance of the Canaanite prostitute and her confession, not in a judgment of Joshua's misleading. Oral elements make up the story, but they are assembled into a coherent narrative.

Coote reminds us that Josh 2 is the introduction to the fall of Jericho and is "plaited out of numerous thematic strands and interconnected plots, which intertwine like the multiple plots of an effective television drama."[331] Coote claims the master plot relates not to battle but to the keeping of the Passover.

---

330 *JSOT* 31 (2006) 46, n. 8; 54–55, n. 46.
331 Coote, 588.

Winther-Nielsen describes the chapter's structure as follows:[332]

Staging	Spies sent and arrive	Introduction	2:1
Episode 1	Arrival is reported	Inciting incident	2:2
Episode 2	Dialogue 1	Complication	2:3–8a
Episode 3	Dialogue 2	Climax	2:8b–14
Episode 4	Dialogue 3	Resolution	2:15–21
Episode 5	Rescue of the spies	Lessening tension	2:22
Closure	Spies return and report	Conclusion	2:23–24

This result of esoteric grammatical study and description differs only slightly from McCarthy's descriptions and from my own narrative conclusions.

The literary opening (exposition) consists of command and obedience (v 1). Tension builds (complication) through a report to the king (v 2). Dialogue between king and Rahab brings the crisis of royal intervention (vv 3–6). A resolution appears to come as the soldiers are persuaded to join in a wild goose chase (v 7), but the plot is further complicated by the continued plight of the spies bedded down in the city (v 8). The crisis then reappears and the tempo slows in the confession of faith joined to the demands of the prostitute and the counterproposal of the spies dangling from the wall (vv 9–20). Finally, the real resolution comes (vv 21–23) as both parties agree on oath to the plan to save Rahab's family and as the royal messengers return home unsuccessful. The formulaic denouement appears with a conveyance formula (v 24).

Setting

Josh 2 is a narrative unit built around the intrigue and conspiracy of betrayal, similar to Judg 1:22–26. Such a story would be told around military campfires or at the city well accompanied by snickers and sneers and laughter. Perhaps it was called "The Harlot Helped Us Do It."

Narrative			Genre: Ironic spy narrative		
Element	Passage	Marker	Element	Passage	Marker
Exposition (pf. or disjunctive)	vv 1–2a (impf. consec.); Rahab (disjunctive)	New time; new location; new characters— Rahab and king	Select, commission spies	v 1	Sent two men
Complication (impf. consec.)	vv 2b	Intervention by king	Dispatching of the spies with specific instructions	v 1	Commissioning formula: go, look at land and Jericho

---

332 *Functional Discourse Grammar*, 111–13.

Narrative		
Element	*Passage*	*Marker*
Change or crisis (speech or dialogue)	vv 3–6	Dialogue between Rahab and royal messengers
Resolution (impf consec.)	v 7	Royal messengers leave
Renewed complication (disjunctive)	v 8	Spies inside city
Change or crisis (speech or dialogue)	vv 9–20	Bargaining for future safety
Resolution (impf. consec.)	vv 21–23	Oath of agreement; royal messengers return home; spies return and report to Joshua
Ending/denouement (formulaic)	v 24	Conveyance formula

Genre: Ironic spy narrative		
Element	*Passage*	*Marker*
Ironic execution of mission	v 1	Bedded down in harlot's home
Execution of mission 2, by Harlot	vv 2–7	Hiding spies; leading king's men astray
Confirmation through an oracle or reference to the context of salvation history	vv 8–13	Conveyance formula: God has given; holy panic formula; salvation history confession; personal declaration for Yahweh; call for oath
Response to oracle with oath and bargaining	vv 14–21	Oath response on both sides with stipulations of "treaty"
Notice of return and results	vv 22–23	Return to camp
A pf.-tense formula confirming the gift of the land by Yahweh	v 24	Conveyance formula; holy panic report

Comments

1 Joshua here, as throughout the book, takes center stage and initiates the action. The imperfect consecutive opening the narrative is unusual as Tucker notes.[333] Winther-Nielsen seeks to use discourse theory to justify the opening imperfect consecutive but, in the end, only demonstrates that his normal expectations have exceptions.[334]

Joshua sends the spies to see the whole land just as Moses did in Num 13, though Numbers uses תור instead of Joshua's רגל to describe the scouting activity. The secret nature of Joshua's action in sending the spies certainly does not attempt to hide something from the people of Israel.[335] Joshua followed the normal part of sending spies without public announcement. Another normal part of the spy

---

333 "Rahab Saga," 71.
334 *Functional Discourse Grammar*, 114–15.
335 Sherwood, *JSOT* 31 (2006) 50; see Hall, *Conquering Character*, 35.

business is the time of sending—in the darkness.[336] Robinson interprets Joshua's sending of spies as a sign that he is a faithful disciple of Moses.[337]

No comparison with other spy stories or other evidence leads the reader to think Joshua has overextended himself.[338] Sending spies would allow Joshua to find the lay of the land. But, interestingly, Joshua gives the spies no specific instructions.[339]

The scouting narrative is limited to the two spies entering a prostitute's house in Jericho. This location seems to separate Rahab from "sacred prostitutes" connected to a sanctuary.[340] "In the Hebrew Bible spying precedes conquest almost as a matter of course" without a hint of this being seen as weakness or unbelief.[341] Rather, the obedient spies enhance "the status of Joshua as leader and coordinator of the advance plans for the military expedition."[342]

The narrative centers on Jericho. The city has been excavated as extensively as any in Palestine, and it has several distinctions. Its elevation is the lowest of any town on earth, 250 meters or about 750 feet below sea level. It is the earliest fortified town known to scholarship, with settlements dating to ca. 8,000 BCE and fortifications to 7,000. The seventy-foot-high Tell es-Sultan, six miles north of the Dead Sea, first felt the excavator's shovel in 1867. Major excavations were carried out by Sellin and Watzinger between 1907 and 1909. J. Garstang dug there from 1930 to 1936 and thought he had found the Late Bronze Age walls destroyed by Joshua. Finally, Dame Kathleen Kenyon led an expedition to Jericho from 1952 to 1958.[343] She demonstrated that the large Early Bronze Age walls represented settlement between 2900 and 2300 BCE. Middle Bronze Age walls reflect a series of building stages. The final stage featured a new type of rampart-wall defense system. This was destroyed, according to Kenyon, ca. 1560. The site was abandoned during most of the sixteenth and fifteenth centuries. Scanty evidence shows some occupation but no walls for a few decades after 1400. From before 1300 until the eighth or even seventh century, the site was again abandoned. This leads Fritz to conclude: "The settlement history shows that the king of Jericho in the period of the conquest is a fiction."[344]

J. J. Bimson has tried to reinterpret the archaeological evidence.[345] He associates the Israelite entrance into Palestine with the destruction of cities between 1450 and 1400. He, therefore, rejects any association with the so-called Hyksos movement, moves the destruction date from the sixteenth-century dates proposed by archaeologists to the fifteenth century, and revolutionizes the pottery chronology, the basic tool of archaeological dating.

Hess points to Lachish and especially Megiddo as towns said to have walls by Egyptian texts, although excavations have not discovered any.[346] Hess thus suggests erosion as the explanation for the problems surrounding Jericho.

---

336   Sherwood, *JSOT* 31 (2006) 54.
337   *SJOT* 21 [2009] 263.
338   Contra Sherwood, *JSOT* 31 (2006) 50.
339   Frymer-Kensky, "Reading Rahab," 59.
340   Robinson, *SJOT* 21 (2009) 265.
341   Nelson, 47.
342   Hess 81.
343   *The Bible and Recent Archaeology* (Atlanta: John Knox, 1978) 36–40.
344   Fritz, 36.
345   *Redating the Exodus.*
346   Hess (2009) 19.

For those attempting to uphold the veracity of the biblical text, the most we can conclude is that the interpretation of the archaeological evidence from Jericho is an open question, requiring an immense amount of new examination and interpretation in light of current archaeological knowledge and theories. The alternative, as stated by J. M. Miller, is that "archaeological evidence from Jericho, Ai, and Gibeon conflicts with the narratives in Joshua 1–9."[347]

Archaeological and form-critical evidence bring the historical question of the Rahab narrative into sharp focus. At the core of the account is an entertaining folk narrative about the Israelite spies in Jericho. It presupposes the city at the height of its power and strength and its purpose in its present setting is to ridicule the original inhabitants of the land. From the perspective of a people settled in a land that does not belong to them, Israel looks back and draws an intentionally one-sided portrait of their enemies to glorify their God.

Shittim "has ominous connotations."[348] The Old Testament places Shittim (or Acacia Wood) in Moab, across the Jordan from Jericho (Num 33:48–49), and names it as the place where Moabite women led Israel astray (Num 25:1–5). The precise site of Shittim is not known. It has been identified traditionally with Tell el-Kefrein, seven miles east of the Jordan and six miles north of the Dead Sea. Most modern commentators, however, accept the identification made by N. Glueck.[349] Glueck argues that Shittim was located at present-day Tell el-Hammam es Samri, located one and a half miles (two and a half kilometers) east of Tell el-Kefrein. Tell el-Hammam is a much larger site and more important militarily and economically. Knauf identifies Shittim with Akazien-Hain across the Jordan from Jericho.[350]

Hawk writes, "The brief reference to the spies' starting point thus reminds the reader of the danger represented by Canaan and its women."[351] Sherwood takes the connection too far when he concludes that "the narrator apparently implies that the spies quitted one place of prostitution only for another, to the neglect of their mission."[352]

The narrative's location at the prostitute's house simply provides a great opportunity for ironic language replete with double meanings and a platform for the prostitute to participate in unexpected business. The spies have not neglected their mission. They have gone to a place where information may be easily obtained without causing too great a stir.

The name Rahab may represent a confession of faith that the god has opened the womb, with the name of the god missing.[353] The "house of a woman, a prostitute," apparently inserts the grammatically superfluous term *woman* to emphasize the unusual situation of a woman owning the house.[354] "The house is hers (not

---

347 "The Israelite Occupation of Canaan," in *Israelite and Judean History*, ed. J. H. Hayes and J. M. Miller (London: SCM Press, 1977) 260.
348 Robinson, *SJOT* 21 (2009) 264.
349 "Some Ancient Towns in the Plains of Moab," *BASOR* 91 [1943] 13–18; cf. A. F. Rainey, R. S. Notley, et al., *The Sacred Bridge: Carta's Atlas of the Biblical World* [Jerusalem: Carta, 2006] 124; *NIDB*, 5:240; 5:1223.
350 Knauf, 47.
351 Hawk (2000) 40.
352 *JSOT* 31 (2006) 51.
353 See Hess (2009) 17.
354 Against Coote (593), who emphasizes the father's poverty in trying to maintain control of the house.

some man's) and she is the one who takes responsibility for her family—brothers and father included."[355] Hess accepts the argument suggested by Josephus and others that the house in question is an inn, tavern, or hostel rather than a brothel, but such a view is not necessary to protect the reputation of the spies nor does it allow for the folklore way of telling this story with humor and irony.[356]

Rahab is a prostitute, though Stark (*Kultprostitution*) has argued against cult prostitution in Canaan. *KB* defines the Hebrew *zōnāh* as: "a woman occasionally or professionally committing fornication, prostitute, harlot."[357] The term "has two related but distinct meanings: to fornicate or have illicit sex, and to practice prostitution, i.e., offer sex for hire.[358] Knauf remarks that prostitution could have been the only chance a single woman living alone had to make a living.[359]

In the OT, fornication expressed by the Hebrew *zōnāh* describes illicit sex by a female that violates a relationship with a male, either a husband or father, for which the penalty is death (Gen 38:24; Lev 21:9; Deut 22:21; Hos 2:3).[360] The *qal* participle זֹנָה unequivocally refers to a prostitute, especially when preceded by אִשָּׁה "woman of prostitution" (Gen 38:15—Tamar; Lev 21:7; Josh 2:1; 6:17, 22, 25—Rahab; Judg 11:1—Jephthah's mother; Judg 16:1—Samson's friend; 1 Kgs 3:16; Prov 6:26). "זָנָה normally occurs with feminine subjects. It is used with masculine forms only when referring to a nation (Deut 31:16; Ezek 23:43) or in the *hip'il* stem (Lev 19:29)."[361] Creach effectively argues against any cult prostitution interpretation in Josh 2.[362] Still, "the name 'Rahab,' coupled with the epithet 'prostitute,' reminds the reader that the goodness of the land itself may seduce Israel from covenantal obedience to YHWH (Deut 6:10–15; 8:11–20; 32:11–15)."[363]

Despite many commentators' attempts to redefine Rahab's occupation, Pressler contends, "the fact that Rahab is a prostitute is integral to the story. . . . [H]er profession is important to its plausibility on several levels."[364] While one may describe Rahab as an independent business woman, a hostess, perhaps an innkeeper, and to some extent an advisor to the king, Gillmayr-Bucher hits the target: "the roles in which Rahab appears are ambiguous, creating a manifold portrayal of this woman."[365] These roles include dangerous strange woman, unreliable prostitute, faithful and wise theologian, and capable informant.

Rahab may well have joined her profession out of economic necessity and thus have easily sided with the incoming Israelites rather than with the economically elite Canaanite rulers. The first activity of the spies in Jericho was to bed down in the prostitute's home. Sexual allusions to sexual activity help drive the narrative

---

355   Nelson, 48.
356   Hess (1996) 83, cf. 26–27; Howard, 98–99. Cf. also Winther-Nielsen, *Functional Discourse Grammar*, 117 with n. 16.
357   Cf. P. Bird, "To 'Play the Harlot,'" 75–94, and H. Schulte, "Beobachtungen zum Begriff zona im Alten Testament," *ZAW* 104 (1992) 255–62.
358   Hall, *NIDOTTE*, 1048.
359   Knauf, 47.
360   Cf. Bird, "To 'Play the Harlot.'"
361   Hall, *NIDOTTE*.
362   Creach, 33; cf. Nelson, 44.
363   Hess (2000) 41.
364   Pressler, 24.
365   *BibInt* 15 (2007) 142.

and "hint at an intimate affair between Rahab and the Israelite spies."[366] Robinson decides "the men are perhaps to be taken to be furthering their work of spying at the same time as indulging their carnal desires."[367]

The narrator does not describe or report sexual activity by the spies,[368] and Rahab is not depicted as a temptress.[369] Howard's strong denial of any sexual overtones in the story represents too flat a reading of the folklorish narrative and ignores the artistic skill of surrounding a story in a prostitute's house with sexual innuendo without sexual activity.[370]

2–3 Howard and others note that "the action in vv 2–9 moves along quickly and is described in rather choppy Hebrew."[371] "The king of Jericho" is the enemy who never appears on the scene. He is a city-state king ruling the territory connected to the city of Jericho or is at least responsible for its security while answerable to a higher authority such as the pharaoh of Egypt or the ruler of a larger nearby city-state.[372] His intelligence forces trace the spies' entrance, and the king sends forces to arrest the intruders.

Sherwood goes to great lengths to establish a "calamity motif" at this point in the story, setting up readers to expect disaster for the spies.[373] This may well be true, but it is not a negative point in the narrative. It is simply a clever way to reach the crisis point that must be resolved.

4–5 The woman prostitute could not know the history of all the men who came to her establishment, nor could the royal messengers expect her to. As Assis explains:[374]

> Rahab rejects any suspicion that she has cooperated with the spies, suggesting rather that they came, like most of her visitors, for sexual satisfaction, and, when their desires were met, they left. If she had not lied, but rather claimed that there had been no sexual intercourse, and that the spies had come to lodge at the inn, she could not have claimed that they had already left. The apparent sexual intentions of the spies constitute a good alibi for Rahab's claim that she did not know where they came from (v. 4).

Hawk notes "a sequence of rapid shifts during which the narrator takes the reader from Rahab and the king's men (v. 3) to the spies (v. 4a), back to the king's men (vv. 4b–5), then again to the spies (v. 6), and back a final time to the king's men (v. 7), before ending on the roof with the spies (v. 8)."[375] He interprets this as a "technique" that "creates an energetic sense of suspense by keeping the two scenes directly in the reader's view."

Rahab could easily hide the men and send the king's messengers away on a wild

---

366 Creach, 32; cf. Nelson, 43–44.
367 "Rahab of Canaan," *SJOT* 21 (2009) 265.
368 See Hess (1996) 83 and n. 2.
369 Mitchell, *Together in the Land*, 165.
370 Howard, 98; cf. Harstad, 108.
371 Howard, 99.
372 Hess (2009) 17–18.
373 *JSOT* 31 (2006) 50–53.
374 *Bib* 85 (2004) 83.
375 Hawk (2010) 27.

goose chase. Her actions show "the foolishness of the king's men and the wiliness of the woman. Rahab uses trickery, the power of the powerless, to outwit the king."[376] Sherwood's conclusion that the "spies'" lives are ironically safer in the hands of a Jericho native than in Joshua's is not based on the narrative structure of the account, but rather on weak exegesis.[377] Certainly, the narrator wants the hearers to marvel at the extent to which Rahab goes to protect the spies and misdirect the royal messengers. But the larger message of the book of Joshua remains the way in which Joshua serves as a role model for all other leaders after Moses.

The narrator accepts Rahab's lying as necessary in the emergency situation. Harris explains, "Rahab's deception is the way God rescues the blundering spies and ensures that the tribes will possess Canaan. Deception remains the weapon of the marginal and helpless."[378]

Howard includes an extensive excursus on Rahab's lie and the various ethical positions on it.[379] He opts for "nonconflicting absolutism" that claims all lying is sin, and thus concludes that Rahab should have sought a way to trust in God that involved telling the truth and believing God would still protect the spies and Rahab's house. Hess argues, "It is best not to excuse Rahab's actions, but neither to be troubled by them. In so far as they were wrong, the narrator and Israelite readers would understand that her acceptance among the people of Israel would also provide the means for forgiveness of such sin."[380] Hess's continuing argument that the narrator was not really concerned about the ethical issue at this point but was concentrating on her heroic personal risk in committing treason among her own people to help Israel is more to the point.[381]

Hawk maintains that the narrator highlights "Rahab's differences while transforming her from enemy to protagonist."[382]

6–7 Winther-Nielsen sees this "explanatory background satellite" (in vv 6–8) as a flashback.[383] Apparently, the woman had cultivated flax and was drying the stems on her roof or allowing the morning dew to "soak the plants as preparation to spread their fibers."[384] Howard[385] follows Boling[386] in thinking flax was not cultivated at this early period in history, so that Rahab just happened to have some wild flax on her roof. Such a theory is far from certain. Knauf sees here an indication that Rahab ran an inn and also produced linen.[387]

The roof with the flax proved a natural place to unbed and rebed the spies. Flax

---

376 Pressler, 26.
377 Sherwood, *JSOT* 31 (2006) 54.
378 Harris, 28.
379 Howard, 106–12.
380 Hess (1996) 86.
381 Contrast O. H. Prouser, "The Truth about Women and Lying," *JSOT* 61 (1994) 15–28). Frymer-Kensky makes the interesting observation, "Hiding and lying is the way biblical women demonstrate their loyalty" ("Reading Rahab," in *Tehillah le-Moshe*, 59). She points to 2 Sam 17:17–22; Judg 4:18–20.
382 Hess (2000) 42.
383 *Functional Discourse Grammar*, 126.
384 Creach, 33.
385 Howard, 100, n. 114.
386 Boling, 145.
387 Knauf, 48.

was laid out just before the barley harvest, the harvest connected with Passover.[388] "The stalks were used for fiber, sails, cloth (Israelite priests wore linen [flax] garments), curtains, wicks for lamps, mummy wrappings, cartonnage (linen and papyrus) used for mummy masks, and thread. The seed produced linseed oil, an edible oil when cold-pressed. Medicinally, the seed were prescribed as a demulcent, emollient, and laxative; it was also used as a remedy for burns."[389]

The royal messengers followed the prostitute's orders and chased the culprits to the mountains, carefully shutting the gate behind them, thus locking their prey in the city while they hunted outside the city, leaving the spies "at the mercy of the woman who has just saved them."[390] Hubbard may be right in locating the Jordan crossings or fords at the "silt sandbar known today as Al-Maghtas, eight miles southeast of Jericho."[391]

8–11 Amid all the confusion, the men still have not bedded down for the night. This appears to stand in tension with v 1. Nelson sees the simplest solution as the men lying down in v 1 and being relocated to the roof in v 4, v 6 giving a flashback, and finally settling down after the action of v 8.[392] Hess sees the roof as "the most private and secret part of the house, away from any unwanted listeners."[393]

The prostitute gives them the late night news: the city is in a state of panic and terror, knowing the God of the Israelites has given his people the land. The people of Jericho have cause to fear because they know the story of Israel's deliverance from Egypt through the Reed Sea (Exod 14–15) and of the total defeat of Sihon and Og (Num 21). "Rahab confesses that what was foretold by the celebrants of the exodus (Exod 15:1–18) has come to pass."[394] She confesses what she heard, though the source of the message is not given. Rahab becomes the first prophetic figure in the historical books as well as the first inhabitant of the land to join Israel and Israel's God.[395]

Knauf dismisses the historicity of a king of Heshbon, of Sihon, and of Og, the latter a totally mythical figure.[396] Hesbon is normally located at "Tell Hesban (M.R. 226134), a mound which rises 895 m above sea level, guarding the NW edge of the rolling Madaba (Moabite) plain where a southern tributary to the Wadi Hesban begins to cut down sharply toward the Jordan River about 25 km to the W. It is about 55 km E of Jerusalem, 20 km SW of Amman, 6 km NE of Mount Nebo."[397] L. T. Geraty notes the lack of excavation findings at Tell Hesban before 1200 BCE and suggests "its (seminomadic) impermanent nature left no trace to be discovered."[398]

The news that the inhabitants of the land hear plays a recurring role in the structure of Joshua (5:1; 6:27; 7:9; 9:1–2; 9:3–4, 9–10, 16–17; 10:1–3; 11:1–5; 22:11–12,

---

388 Coote, 593.
389 I. Jacob and W. Jacob, "Flora," *ABD*, 2:815.
390 Creach, 34.
391 Hubbard, 118.
392 Nelson, 49, n. 21. See Moran, "Repose."
393 Hess (1996) 87.
394 Ibid., 88.
395 Frymer-Kensky, "Reading Rahab," 62.
396 Knauf, 49.
397 *ABD*, 3:181.
398 Ibid., 3:182.

30–31).[399] The expression "I know that" appears repeatedly in the confessions of foreigners (Exod 18:11; 1 Kgs 17:24; 2 Kgs 5:15; Isa 45:3).[400]

The enemies' fear also plays a structural, connecting role in Joshua (2:9, 11, 24; 5:1; 9:24; 10:2).[401] In contrast to the nations, Israel is told not to fear (Josh 8:1; 10:8, 25; 11:6). Rather Israel sees God at work (Josh 5:13; 6:2; 8:1, 8; 23:3; 24:7) and knows God's purposes and intentions (Josh 3:4, 7, 10; 14:6; 22:22, 31; 23:13–14; 24:31). The pattern can be reversed to show Canaanites coming into the same category as Israelites, knowing God's power and actions (Josh 2:9–11; 4:24).

The monotheistic confession in v 11 occurs also in Deut 4:39, with similar language found in 1 Kgs 8:23. The ultimate editor of Joshua seeks to emphasize the unique authority of Yahweh compared to other gods. Israel's neighbors had high gods with functions in the heavens and other gods whose chief functions were on earth. Israel had one God, who exercised authority over all spheres of existence.

The writer here maintains that such clarification is not needed. From Egypt onwards, Yahweh had proved himself more powerful than any other claimants to deity. The irony of the situation existed in the fact that Israel's enemies recognized this when Israel did not.

Coote's attempt to define the inhabitants of the land (v 9b) as rich landowners in opposition to poor debt servants like Rahab is overstating the case on the basis of supposed sociological evidence and a particular way of reading Deuteronomy.[402] Rahab is making a statement about all those living in the land of Canaan, not just the rich. Both rich and poor had everything to fear and everything to lose as Israel invaded their homeland. See Mitchell for the uniqueness of the phrase כל־ישבי ארץ, "all the inhabitants of the earth (or land or territory)."[403]

Rahab's speech echoes the elements of covenant language found in Deuteronomy.[404] The elements are: preamble (v 11), prologue (vv 9–11), stipulations (vv 12–13, 18–20), sanctions (vv 18–20), oath (vv 14,17), and sign (vv 18–21). Campbell's analysis too often separates individual elements into two parts in order to assert a covenant form here.

Israel's hope lay in the divinely commanded חרם, "ban" (10b). This term is central to the "deuteronomistic" theory of holy war.[405] Such war was permitted only against the cities in the Promised Land (Deut 20:15–18) and explained for the Deuteronomic editors how Yahweh had fulfilled his promises to the ancestors and why many peoples on the lists of nations no longer existed. (See Introduction, "Joshua and the Meaning of the Material, Studies on Warfare and Conquest in Joshua.") Knauf insists that this ban theology depends on the war theory of the Assyrian Empire and so makes this a late narrative.[406] He does indicate that the ban first appears here in Joshua and appears for the last time in 23:12–13, both instances of the ban not being carried out in full. H. Rösel reminds readers that

---

399 Cf. Knauf, 91, who finds "hear" as the structuring element of chap. 1–12.
400 See Mitchell (*Together in the Land*, 142–44) for discussion of this connecting link.
401 See also Deut 2:25 and *Together in the Land*, 144–48.
402 Coote, 594.
403 *Together in the Land*, 122–23.
404 Frymer-Kensky, "Reading Rahab," 62–63; cf. Campbell, *VT* 22 (1972) 243–45.
405 See N. Lohfink, "חרם," *TWAT*, 3:192–213.
406 Knauf, 49.

the ban was never realized historically and that it was a late concept probably a part of Deuteronomistic theology.[407] For Knauf, this means that ban theology troubled the original writer and audience.

Hoffman finds a way around the troublesome ban theology through Deuteronomistic layers:[408]

> The two conflicting concepts of the conquest found in these books [Joshua and Judges] . . . cannot be harmoniously reconciled. The only reasonable explanation is that the Deuteronomistic author/editor imposed his concept of the *herem* and the complete conquest on the entire story in Joshua, at the same time being tolerant enough not to force this concept on each individual source intertwined within his work. Thus, the Deuteronomist (whether one person, two, or a school) who inserted the law of the *herem* in the book of Deuteronomy is also responsible for the portrayal of the conquest as a process which concluded with the complete annihilation of the autochthonic population of Canaan. Hence, a significant difference exists between the textual position of the *herem* writings in Deuteronomy compared with that of the historiographical Deuteronomistic block in the book of Joshua. Whereas in the former it is a secondary layer, in the book of Joshua it is an integral part of the context, both philologically and conceptually.

Hoffmann places the *ḥērem* materials into the time of Ezra and maintains that they, along with Ruth, are a protest against anti-foreigner populations: "the entire concept of the conquest in the book of Joshua, including the very formulation of the figure of Joshua as a super military commander reflects the same approach. Its covert, indirect message is: in order to conquer and rule a land, a people needs a strong, organized army, which we don't have now. Therefore, let us forget overly grandiose national ambitions."[409]

Inventing *ḥērem* so late in Israel's history is a desperate step to protect God and the Bible from "bad theology." *Ḥērem* appears in the Moabite stone, showing a concept much earlier than Hoffmann chooses for Israel's concept. It is a concept used by a people truly at war, not one simply in an ideological conflict. Israel knew their obligation to enforce the ban. As much as modern theologians would like to dismiss in one way or another the existence and meaning of ban theology, too much biblical and ancient Near Eastern evidence prevents any simple or complex theory of dismissal.

Again the irony of Josh 2 is apparent. The foreign harlot knows the Israelite laws and reacts accordingly. She is clever enough to make herself an exception to the Israelite law. Her exceptional status is important for the Israelite identity. It was obvious to later generations that people of Israel comprised a "mixed multitude" (Exod 12:38). The introduction to the conquest narrative explains this part of Israel's population. Israel included those Canaanites who had treated Israel with grace and helped them conquer the land. Even such Canaanites could not appeal to their great social status. They were descended from a prostitute.

Other Canaanites faced destruction under the ban. Why? The inhabitants of

---

407 Rösel, 8–9.
408 *ZAW* 111 (1999) 202–3.
409 *ZAW* 111 (1999) 208.

Canaan had defiled the land with their sexual perversity, bringing Yahweh's judgment down on them. Their deeds were so detestable that the very land is depicted as vomiting them out (Lev 18:24–28). These nations were guilty of idolatry (1 Kgs 21:26) and child sacrifice (2 Kgs 16:3). Yahweh gave Israel the land because of the wickedness of the native population (Deut 9:4–5). In short, Israel was Yahweh's instrument of judgment in bringing this corrupt civilization to an end. "The hardening of its kings was an important element in this divine judgment, for it expedited Yahweh's purposes and forced Israel to launch its military campaign in full force, rather than delaying and risking the possibility of being assimilated into Canaanite culture."[410]

12–21 The precise nature of the relationship between the Israelites and the remaining Canaanites is described in a clever bargaining session. "Rahab is a character who inhabits a boundary, radically non-Israelite in ethnicity and occupation but distinctively Israelite in loyalties and behavior."[411] The prostitute claims that Israel is indebted to her because she has done חסד (acted graciously) for Israel (v 12); that is, she has preserved and enriched Israel's life as a community with enduring results[412] or she has given "aid in keeping alive one's family for future generations."[413] In this situation חסד means protecting the life of another by endangering one's own life.[414] As Gillmayr-Bucher states, the narrative portrays Rahab as the "exemplary Israelite spy."[415]

Rahab wants a sign with enduring quality, that is, a promise that will be confirmed as a true sign in the future fulfillment.[416] She wants an agreement tantamount to a covenant treaty. The spies swing on her cord below her window at her feet. They know that God has forbidden agreements with the Canaanites (Exod 23:32–33; Deut 7:2–5; 20:16–18), but they must accept her terms. They have hit bottom.[417]

In a text focused on feminine wiles and powers in gaining safety and a new citizenship, "the spies opt for survival over obedience."[418] They are apparently willing to enter into a treaty with a Canaanite if it proves the way to save their own lives. Hawk asks if there is "flexibility in the interpretation of the law if circumstances warrant."[419] Hess asserts that the covenant agreement makes Rahab and her family Israelite and no longer Canaanite.[420]

Dangling from her window on a rope, the spies turn the tables. They set out the conditions—Rahab the Canaanite must carry out חסד (act graciously) in the future. She must put out the sign (v 18). She must be responsible for gathering her family to safety. She must prove trustworthy (v 20). Otherwise, the spies will be released from their oath. The Hebrew word (נקי) means free from blood guilt and its result, death.[421]

---

410   R. B. Chisholm, Jr., "Divine Hardening in the Old Testament," *BSac* 153 (1996) 43.

411   Hess (2000) 47.

412   Cf. H.-J. Zobel, "חסד," *TWAT*, 3:48–71.

413   Hess (1996) 91; cf. G. R. Clark, *The Word Hesed in the Hebrew Bible*, JSOTSup 157 (Sheffield: JSOT Press, 1993) 73–75, 262.

414   Fritz, 40.

415   *BibInt* 15 (2007) 147; cf. Earl, 126–27.

416   Cf. A. Jepsen, "אֱמֶת," *TWAT*, 1:334.

417   Nelson, 49.

418   Hess (2000) 46.

419   Hawk (2010) 31.

420   Hess (1996) 92; cf. Howard, 106.

421   Fritz, 38.

In the end she capitulates to their terms (v 21a). She follows their orders and ties the scarlet cord in her window. "The spies thus reconstitute the issue of culpability by placing the decision squarely within the context of obligations that Rahab and her house (as opposed to the spies) must exercise."[422]

Robinson objects to this interpretation because the cord is not called a sign (אות), the passive spies suddenly take the initiative, and the interpretation somehow lessens the heroism of Rahab.[423] The sign responds to Rahab's request for a sign (v 12). The spies give the sign, but ironically the sign sets out something Rahab must do. The spies have had to be passive while hiding in the prostitute's house. They may have shown some courage by daring to enter a building in Jericho. Rahab remains the central hero of the story through her heroism in protecting the spies and in confessing faith. She will retain that heroic position by meeting the spies' demand. Still the positioning of the spies' demands on Rahab show that for a time they take center stage and control the action.

Fritz insists the cord, visible only from outside the city, played a significant role in an earlier version of the narrative dealing with invading the city through the place the cord marked.[424] Such a theory requires the modern commentator to cast a spy story into an entirely different type of narrative—a betrayal story.

Seeking to solve the problem of how the parties communicated while hanging out the window on a rope, Hess maintains that the answer lies in the narrative technique: "It was not necessary to follow a linear sequence of events or to mention an event or a statement only once."[425] The conversation actually took place before they went out through the window. This is the logical answer to the problem, but it may not be in keeping with the folklorish nature of this story with its wry irony and intentional humor. The narrator here constantly makes characters do the unexpected, even the foolish, to make a point of God's protection and guidance.

Coote understands the cord as "intentionally reminiscent of the blood of the pascal lamb which protected the Israelite debt slaves in Egypt (Exod 12:7, 13)."[426] Creach is much more cautious in observing that the Hebrew term means "cord of thread," that is, "a strand of material from which cloth could be woven."[427] Creach goes on to surmise that the cord shows that Rahab's house "was more than a brothel. It contained a private industry by which Rahab clothed members of her household," so that the harlot can be compared to the virtuous woman of Prov 31. "She shows herself a woman of worth by doing whatever it takes to preserve them (her family)." This interpretation stretches the text just a bit.

Israel claims that certain "foreigners" dwell among them because they have met Israel's demands, not because Israel has met theirs. The details of the demands are not outlined; they have already been fulfilled. Any foreigner who lived among Israel had to adopt Israel's creed.

One cannot follow Nelson's statement regarding Rahab: "She is not the Gentile convert that later tradition would make of her, but rather one of those foreigners in

---

422   Hess (2000) 48.
423   *SJOT* 21 (2009) 269.
424   Fritz, 38.
425   Hess (1996) 93.
426   Coote, 594; cf. Hess (2000) 49.
427   Creach, 38.

the Hebrew Bible whose acknowledgment that Yahweh is God underscores the self-evident power and glory of Yahweh (Balaam, Naaman, Nebuchadnezzar, Darius)."[428] Those with whom Nelson compares Rahab differ entirely, though, in that they never became part of Israel in any way. The intent of the Joshua narrative is to provide an acceptable reason why a Canaanite was rescued and made part of Israel. Rahab even stands apart from the Gibeonites who become temple slaves; nothing in the text indicates that Rahab does not enjoy full alien freedom among Israel. Howard is on target with the bold assertion that Rahab is "a prostitute and the first Canaanite convert to belief in Israel's God."[429]

22–23 The spies follow the prostitute's orders, heading for the hills and lying quiet for three days. Knauf maintains that this chronology would place Joshua already in Gilgal.[430] For the three-days problem, see *Comments* on 1:10. Hawk decides the three days here "serves as a stylistic rather than chronological purpose," linking the story "to the events of Josh 1 and to the climactic event of the Jordan crossing."[431] Hall understands chap. 2 as a chronological parenthesis.[432] Nelson advocates a flexible approach, taking Josh 1:11 as day one, 3:1 as day two, and 3:2 as day three with the spy narrative being contemporaneous but sees problems for this in chap. 3.[433] Auld finds the three days to be a "round number for the same brief period."[434] Pressler interprets the dating loosely to mean "a few days."[435]

The royal messengers return home, having to report their failure to the king. The spies return back across the Jordan River and report to their commander, Joshua. Again Joshua's authority as the leader after Moses is confirmed.

24 Safely back at camp, the spies report to Joshua. They cannot really report "mission accomplished." All they have seen of the land is the roof of a prostitute's house and a hill country hideout. Rahab "effectively prevents them from carrying out their original assignment as spies."[436]

Hall argues on the basis of contrast with the intertextual reference in Num 13–14 that the narrator's main concern was to bring encouragement to the people.[437] Concluding statements are important in determining the meaning of a passage, but one cannot read the passage's entire message from the conclusion. The narrative surely has a much broader meaning than encouragement. Had encouragement been the central focus, then the narrative conclusion would picture the reaction of the people to the spies' report.

The report of the spies sounds like a prophetic oracle. But the words do not come from the mouth of an Israelite prophet; they come from experiences with a Canaanite prostitute. The prostitute had to give Israel evidence for her basic conviction. Just as the Canaanites had no right to lay claims on Israel, so Israel could not make claims for itself. Israel had, in the final analysis, to confess her own lack

---

428   Nelson, 50.
429   Howard, 97.
430   Knauf, 50.
431   Hess (2000) 47, n. 14.
432   *Conquering Character*, 35.
433   Nelson, 41, n. 4.
434   Auld, 16.
435   Pressler, 27; cf. Hess (2009) 20.
436   Nelson, 51.
437   *Conquering Character*, 30.

of faith. She, too, had learned in the process of history to believe Yahweh. Part of the knowledge came from most unlikely sources. A prophetic prostitute gave Israel courage to carry out the divine command and conquer the land.

Explanation

What a spy story! "The spies do no reconnaissance, and they do not return with any strategically useful information, and they are not criticized for this."[438]

"The narrative of the conquest of the Canaanites and the life of the chosen people in their land begins with the faithful words and saving deeds of a Canaanite whore."[439] "The quintessential Canaanite whose very occupation epitomized Canaanitism from the Israelite perspective has become an Israelite. The scarlet thread (*tiqvāh*) that once hung in her window as a sign of hope (*tiqvāh*) for new customers comes to represent her hope for salvation as a part of Israel."[440] Hawk ientifies a central element of the narrative: "The story is a calculated attempt to dismantle the reader's stereotypes about Canaanites before the first blow has actually been struck."[441] McConville and Williams ask if the spies' inefficient efforts raise the issue of "whether Israel's occupation of Canaan will run as smoothly as hoped."[442] The story thus proves to raise unexpectedly complex issues.

The author of Joshua has taken a popular story form centering around the ability of a prostitute to trick a king and gain freedom for two men and used it as the prelude for the conquest of Jericho. The two men are spies sent out by Israel to conquer the land, that is, the city-state ruled by the king of Jericho. The newly-formed story stands at the front of the conquest narratives as a whole to introduce the theology of conquest.

Coote pictures the characters as "stock figures rather than nuanced individuals."[443] Still, one sees the strength of character and leadership of Rahab. The ultimate editor has made the story the basis for his theological creed. "The story highlights the question of how Israel will treat those living in the land. Specifically, the story alerts the reader that implementing the ban, the destruction of all the residents of Canaan, will be much more difficult and complex than the deuteronomic law seems to indicate."[444] Knauf gives three reasons for letting Rahab escape the ban:[445]

1. She is not a citizen of the country (v 9).
2. She acknowledges the one God (11).
3. She has delivered the spies from the king of Jericho and shown them mercy (חסד).

Each generation of Israelites has learned something new about themselves and their God through telling and retelling the story of Jericho's prostitute. Creach sees the story as saying all Canaanites had opportunity for hope if they acted like

---

438 Earl, 124–25.
439 Pressler, 20.
440 Spina, *BRev* 17 (2000) 53.
441 Hawk (2010) 36.
442 McConville and Williams, 18.
443 Coote, 592–93.
444 Creach, 31.
445 Knauf, 47.

Rahab.[446] At the same time he reads the story as an example of Israel's lack of faith. Such a view comes mainly from casting the teaching of Moses' spy story onto Joshua's. The two illustrate widely-opposed teachings. Joshua was adept at preparing for battle and testing his people's loyalties to himself, while Moses did not exercise faith while sending out spies. Pressler notes, "The story [in Joshua] has to do with the difference between human expectations and divine decisions. . . . Rahab, a Canaanite, a woman, and a prostitute, is three times 'other,' three times despised. Yet she is a deliverer of Israel, the first in the promised land to confess the sovereignty of God."[447]

Conquest narratives begin in Israel with the dispatch of spies (Num 13–14; Judg 1:22–26; 18, etc.). And spy stories only occur in the conquest narratives, suggesting that the intent of spy stories is to show that God has given the land into the hands of his people.

Human spying and divine gift are not self-exclusive realities. God sends human spies. Why? The obvious explanation would be that spies should help develop military strategy. That is not the case with the biblical materials in every case. Rather, the biblical spies convince Israel that God can and will give the land to Israel. God uses human spies to convince his people to do what he has called them to do.

This is very evident in the present context. The first chapter of Joshua demonstrates the need for strong, courageous leadership through both divine (vv 1–9) and human (vv 16–18) exhortation. The second chapter gives a concrete example of such obedient leadership showing how God is fulfilling his promises and the weakness of Israel's opposition. As Hess states, in "Joshua 2 the role of Joshua is magnified as one who follows God and who leads the people. Joshua 2 thus justifies the character of Joshua as a leader concerned for his people, for he gathers intelligence before leading them into hostile territory."[448]

A common prostitute is more intelligent than the intelligence agents of the king. Yet even she is no match for Israel's spies. Israel can easily get their opponents to chase shadows while they occupy the enemy fortresses. Israel, with strong, courageous leadership, will face an enemy king without intelligence and an enemy people who "melt in fear" (v 9) in the face of Israel and their mighty God.

The basis for Jericho's fear lies in common gossip. The grapevine has brought news of God's mighty deeds for Israel to Jericho. No prophet or preacher has been there. God has simply used the mysterious manner of human beings in which they learn the important events of the day from sources they can no longer identify. The source is not important but rather, the message and the response. The resulting story of Rahab "confirms God's welcome to all people, whatever their condition."[449]

The message itself is couched in terms of holy war theology, which has become a Yahwistic creed. The full form of the creed is found in Deut 26:5–9; 6:21–23; Josh 24:2–13. The version spoken by Rahab centers on the action at the Egyptian sea (cf. Exod 14) and on the battles with the Amorite kings (Deut 3:8; 4:47; 31:4: Josh 5:1; 9:10; 10:5–6; 24:12; cf. Deut 1:4; 2:26–3:11; Pss 135:11; 136:19–20). In Num 21:21–35

---

446 Creach, 42–43.
447 Pressler, 25.
448 Hess, 80.
449 Hess (1996) 81.

only Sihon is called king of the Amorites. God's mighty acts in the history of his people have two immediate results. Future opponents are afraid, and intelligent ones confess Yahweh, the God of Israel, as God of heaven and earth. Thus we can conclude, along with Hess, "Joshua 2 affirms a theology of the mission of Israel. . . . Together these [Rahab's confession and the scouts' conditional promise] provide the justification for war, the provision of mercy for deliverance, and the expectations of Israel."[450]

The NT understands the story of Rahab as an example of faith. She is one of three women, all with tarnished reputations, included in the ancestors of the Messiah (Matt 1:5–6). She is enshrined in the faith hall of fame (Heb 11:31). Jas 2:25 praises Rahab as the prime example, alongside Abraham, of justification through works. Both Hebrews and James emphasize the role and significance of Rahab. The present OT context uses the narrative to give identity and courage to Israel, particularly to Israel without land and power. That Israelite identity includes the ironic fact that God uses not only his own prophets and leaders to bring faith and courage to disconsolate Israel, but also the most unexpected and immoral persons to further his purposes in the world.

The leadership of Joshua dependent upon Moses is one side of the picture. The power of God to convince even the enemy is the other side. People of God must be open to learn from all sources that God uses. They must always be aware of their own prejudiced tendencies to look to powerful leaders for direction and to fear powerful enemy leaders. Throughout the Bible and church history, God has opened new doors and new opportunities for his people through the most unlikely people. Through it all, God has shown himself able to fulfill the promises he made to our ancestors in the faith. He has indeed proved to be the God of heaven above and earth below without competition.

From a Canaanite perspective, Rahab shows that Israel has an open door into the country. Israel will walk through the river and into the land. But "the account has now raised the question whether Israel's occupation of Canaan will run as smoothly as hoped."[451]

C. Crossing to Conquer (3:1–5:1)

Bibliography

Abegg, M., Jr., P. Flint, and E. Ulrich. *The Dead Sea Scrolls Bible.* San Francisco: Harper San Francisco, 1999. **Abel, F. M.** "Les stratagèmes dans le Livre de Josué." *RB* 56 (1949) 323–25. **Alfrink, B. J.** "De litteraire compositie van Jos 3 en 4: De overtocht over de Jordaan." *StC* 18 (1942) 185–202. **Anbar, M.** "La 'Reprise.'" *VT* 38 (1988) 385–98. **Aryaprateeb, K.** "A Note on YR' in Jos IV 24." *VT* 22 (1972) 240–42. **Assis, E.** "A Literary Approach to Complex Narratives: An Examination of Joshua 3—4. In *The Book of Joshua.* Ed. E. Noort. Leuven: Peeters, 2012. 401–13. **Auzou, G.** *Le don d'une conquête.* Paris: Éditions de l'Orante, 1964. 70–79. **Ballhorn, E.** "Did Gestaltung des Gilgal (Josua 3—4): Das Buch

---

450 Ibid., 80–81.
451 McConville and Williams, 18.

Josua als Heterotopie." In *The Book of Joshua*. Ed. E. Noort. Leuven: Peeters, 2012. 415–29. **Beck, J. A.** *God as Storyteller: Seeking Meaning in Biblical Narrative*. St. Louis: Chalice, 2008. 121–26. ———. "Why Do Joshua's Readers Keep Crossing the River? The Narrative-Geographical Shaping of Joshua 3–4." *JETS* 48 (2005) 689–99. **Bennett, B. M., Jr.** "The Search for Israelite Gilgal." *PEQ* 104 (1972) 111–22. **Bieberstein, K.** *Josua, Jordan, Jericho: Archäologie, Geschichte und Theologie der Landnahmeerzählungen Josua 1–6.* OBO 143. Göttingen: Vandenhoeck & Ruprecht, 1995. **Briend, J.** "La traversée du Jourdain dans la geste 'Israël.'" *MdB* 65 (1990) 21–22. **Campbell, A. F.** *Joshua to Chronicles: An Introduction.* Louisville: Westminster John Knox, 2004. ———. "Yahweh and the Ark: A Case Study in Narrative." *JBL* 98 (1979) 31–43. **Ceuppens, M. F.** *Le Miracle de Josué, Études religieises.* Liege, 1944. **Coats, G.** "The Ark of the Covenant in Joshua: A Probe into the History of a Tradition." *HAR* 9 (1985) 137–57. **Cody, A.** "When Is the Chosen People Called a *goy?*" *VT* 114 (1964) 1–6. **Cross, F. M.** "The Divine Warrior." In *Canaanite Myth and Hebrew Epic.* Cambridge, MA: Harvard UP, 1973. 91–111. **Davies, G. H.** "The Ark of the Covenant." *ASTI* 5 (1967) 30–47. **Dozeman, T. B.** "The *yam-sûp* in the Exodus and the Crossing of the Jordan." *CBQ* 58 (1996) 407–16. **Dus, J.** "Die Analyse zweier Ladeerzählungen des Josuabuches (Jos. 3–4 und 6)." *ZAW* 72 (1960) 107–34. ———. "Der Brauch der Ladewanderung im alten Israel." *TZ* 17 (1961) 1–16. ———. "Noch zum Brauch der Ladewanderung." *VT* 13 (1963) 126–32. ———. "Zur bewegten Geschichte der israelitischen Lade: Zum Problem der sogenannten Thronvorstellung." *AION* 41 (1981) 351–83. **Fabry, H.-J.** "Spuren des Pentateuchredaktors in Jos 4,21ff." In *Das Deuteronomium: Entstehung, Gestalt und Botschaft.* Ed. N. Lohfink. BETL 68. Leuven: Leuven UP, 1985. 351–56. **Fernández, A.** "Crítica histórico-literaria de Jos 3, 1–5, 1." *Bib* 12 (1931) 93–98. **Fohrer, G.** "Altes Testament-'Amphiktyonie' und 'Bund'?" *TLZ* 91 (1966) 801–16, 893–904. Reprinted in *Studien zur alttestamentlichen Theologie und Geschichte (1949–1966),* BZAW 115 (Berlin: De Gruyter, 1969) 84–119. **Geoghegan, J. C.** *The Time, Place, and Purpose of the Deuteronomistic History: The Evidence of 'Until This Day.'* BJS 347. Providence: Brown Judaic Studies, 2006. **George, A.** "Les récits de Gilgal en Josué (5:2–15)." In *Mémorial J. Chaine.* Lyon: Facultés Catholiques, 1950. 169–86. **Görg, M.** "Zur 'Lade des Zeugnisses.'" *BN* 2 (1977) 13–15. **Gressmann, H.** *Die Anfänge Israels.* Göttingen: Vandenhoeck & Ruprecht, 1922. 137–40. **Hall, S. L.** *Conquering Character: The Characterization of Joshua in Joshua 1–11.* New York: T&T Clark, 2010. **Hawkins, R. K.** "The Gilgal Traditions in Joshua and Recent Archaeology in the Jordan Valley." Paper read to SBL Joshua-Judges Consultation, Atlanta, November 22, 2010. **Hill, A.** "The Ebal Ceremony as Hebrew Land Grant?" *JETS* 31 (1988) 399–406. **Hostetter, E. C.** "Geographical Distribution of the Pre-Israelite Peoples of Ancient Palestine." *BZ* 38 (1994) 81–86. ———. *Nations Mightier and More Numerous: The Biblical View of Palestine's Pre-Israelite Peoples.* BDS 3. North Richland Hills, TX: BIBAL, 1995. **Hubbard, R. L., Jr.** "What Do These Stones Mean? Biblical Theology and a Motif in Joshua." *BBR* 11 (2001) 1–26. Online: www.ibr-bbr.org/files/bbr/BBR_2001a_01_Hubbard_StonesJoshua.pdf. **Hulst, A. R.** "Der Jordan in den alttestamentlichen Überlieferungen." *OtSt* 14 (1965) 162–88. **Ishida, T.** "The Structure and Historical Implications of the Lists of Pre-Israelite Nations." *Bib* 60 (1979) 461–90. **Jastrow, M.** "Joshua 3:16." *JBL* 36 (1917) 53–62. **Jobling, D.** "The Jordan a Boundary: Transjordan in Israel's Ideological Geography." In *The Sense of Biblical Narrative: Structural Analyses in the Hebrew Bible.* 2nd ed. Vol. 2. JSOTSup 39. Sheffield: JSOT Press, 1986. 88–134. **Kaiser, O.** *Die mythische Bedeutung des Meeres in Ägypten, Ugarit und Israel.* BZAW 78. Berlin: Töpelmann, 1959. 135–40. **Keller, C. A.** "Über einige alttestamentliche Heiligtumslegenden." *ZAW* 67 (1955) 141–68; 68 (1956) 85–97. **Kitchen, K. A.** *On the Reliability of the Old Testament.* Grand Rapids: Eerdmans, 2003. **Kraus, H. J.** "Gilgal: Ein Beitrag zur Kultusgeschichte Israels." *VT* 1 (1951) 181–99. ———. "Zur Geschichte des Passah-Massot-Festes im Alten Testament." *EvT* 18 (1958) 47–67. **Krause, J. J.** "Der Zug durch den Jordan nach Josua

3—4: Eine neue Analyse." In *The Book of Joshua*. Ed. E. Noort. Leuven: Peeters, 2012. 383–400. **Kuhnert, G.** *Das Gilgalpassah: Literarische, überlieferungsgeschichtliche und geschichtliche Untersuchungen zu Josua 3–6*. Mainz, 1982. **Lamaire, A.** "Hiwwites, Perizzites et Girgashites: Essai d'identification ethnique." In *Stimulation from Leiden: Collected Communications to the XVIII Congress of the International Organization for the Study of the Old Testament Leiden 2001*. Ed. H. M. Niemann and M. Augustin. BEATAJ 54. Frankfurt am Main: Lang, 2006. 219–24. **Langlamet, F.** *Gilgal et les récits de la traversée du Jordain*. CahRB 11. Paris: Gabalda, 1969. ———. "La traversée du Jourdain et les documents de l'hexateuque." *RB* 79 (1972) 7–38. **Lauha, A.** "Das Schilfmeermotiv im Alten Testament." In *Congress Volume, Bonn 1962*. Ed. G. W. Anderson et al. VTSup 9. Leiden: Brill, 1963. 32–46. **Lewis, J. P.** "In Search of Gilgal." *ResQ* 11 (1968) 137–43. **Long, B. O.** *The Problem of Etiological Narrative in the Old Testament*. BZAW 108. Berlin: Töpelmann, 1968. 78–86. **Loza, J.** "Les catéchèses étiologiues dans l'Ancien Testament." *RB* 78 (1971) 481–500. **Maier, J.** *Das altisraelitische Ladeheiligtum*. BZAW 93. Berlin: Töpelmann, 1965. 18–32, 76–80. **Mann, T. W.** *Divine Presence and Guidance in Israelite Traditions: The Typology of Exaltation*. Baltimore: Johns Hopkins UP, 1977. 196–212. **Margolis, M. L.** "τῶν ἐνδόξων—Josh iv:4." In *Studies in Jewish Literature in Honour of Prof. K. Kohler*. Berlin, 1913. 204–9. **Mayes, A. D. H.** *Israel in the Period of the Judges*. SBT, 2nd ser., 29. London: SCM Press, 1974. 47–53. **Meer, M. N. van der.** *Formation and Reformulation: The Redaction of the Book of Joshua in the Light of the Oldest Textual Witnesses*. VTSup 102. Leiden: Brill, 2004. **Mitchell, G.** *Together in the Land*. JSOTSup 134. Sheffield: Sheffield Academic, 1993. **Möhlenhrink, K.** "Die Landnahmensagen des Buches Josua." *ZAW* 56 (1938) 254–58. **Mowinckel, S.** *Tetrateuch, Pentateuch, Hexateuch*. BZAW 90. Berlin: Töpelmann, 1964. 33–43. **Muilenburg, J.** "The Site of Ancient Gilgal." *BASOR* 140 (1955) 11–27. **Nelson, R.** "The Role of the Priesthood in the Deuteronomistic History." In *Congress Volume, Leuven 1989*. VTSup 43. Leiden: Brill, 1991. 134–35, 144. **Nielsen, E.** "Some Reflections on the History of the Ark." In *Congress Volume, Oxford 1959*. VTSup 7. Leiden: Brill, 1960. 61–74. **Noort, E.** *Das Buch Josua: Forschungsgeschichte und Problemfelder*. EdF 292. Darmstadt: Wissenschaftliche Buchgesellschaft, 1998. **Noth, M.** "Der Jordan in der alten Geschichte Palästinas." *ZDPV* 72 (1956) 123–48. **Otto, E.** *Das Mazzotfest in Gilgal*. BWANT 107. Stuttgart: Kohlhammer, 1975. 4–57, 104–75, 186–91, 306–11, 323–65. **Ottosson, M.** "Tradition and History with Emphasis on the Composition of the Book of Joshua." In *The Productions of Time: Tradition History in Old Testament Scholarship*. Ed. K. Jeppesen and B. Otzen. Sheffield: Almond, 1984. 81–106, 141–43. **Peckham, B.** "The Composition of Joshua 3–4." *CBQ* 46 (1984) 413–31. **Porter, J. R.** "The Background of Joshua 3–5." *SEÅ* 36 (1971) 5–23. **Rudolph, W.** *Der 'Elohist' von Exodus bis Josua*. BZAW 68. Berlin: Töpelmann, 1938. 169–78. **Saydon, P. P.** "The Crossing of the Jordan." *CBQ* 12 (1950) 194–207. **Schäfer-Lichtenberger, C.** *Josua und Salomo: Eine Studie zu Autorität und Legitimität des Nachfolgers im Alten Testament*. VTSup 58. Leiden: Brill, 1995. **Schmid, R.** "Meerwunder- und Landnahme-Traditionen." *TZ* 21 (1965) 260–68. **Schmitt, R.** *Zelt und Lade als Thema alttestamentlicher Wissenschaft: Eine kritische forschungsgeschichtliche Darstellung*. Gütersloh: Mohn, 1972. 60–65, 76–78, 91, 133, 161, 166, 280–81. **Schunck, K.-D.** *Benjamin*. BZAW 86. Berlin: Töpelmann, 1963. 39–48. **Seitz, O. J. F.** "'What Do These Stones Mean?'" *JBL* 79 (1960) 247–54. **Sellin, E.** *Gilgal: Ein Beitrag zur Geschichte der Einwanderung Israels in Palestina*. Leipzig, 1917. **Simpson, C. A.** *The Early Traditions of Israel*. Oxford: Blackwell, 1948. 283–86. **Sipilä, S.** "The Septuagint Version of Joshua 3–4." In *VII Congress of the International Organization for Septuagint and Cognate Studies, Leuven 1989*. Ed. C. E. Cox. SBLSCS 31. Atlanta: Scholars Press, 1991. 63–74. **Soggin, J. A.** "Gilgal, Passah und Landnahme." In *Volume du congrès, Genève, 1965*. VTSup 15. Leiden: Brill, 1965. 263–77. ———. "Kultätiologische Sagen und Katechese im Hexateuch." *VT* 10 (1960) 341–47. **Speiser, E. A.** "'People' and 'Nation' of Israel." *JBL* 79 (1960) 157–63. **Stevenson, W. E.** "'Adam, that is beside Keriat,' Jos III,16." *PEFQS* 28 (1896) 82–83.

————. "The Stoppage of the River Jordan, a.d. 1267." *PEFQS* 27 (1895) 334–38. **Stolz, F.** *Jahwes und Israels Kriege.* ATANT 60. Zürich: Theologischer Verlag, 1972. 60–62. **Tengström, S.** *Die Hexateucherzählung.* Lund: Gleerup, 1976. 58–65. **Thigpen, J. M.** "Lord of All the Earth: Yahweh and Baal in Joshua 3." *TJ* NS 27 (2006) 245–54. **Thompson, L.** "The Jordan Crossing: Ṣidqot Yahweh and World Building." *JBL* 100 (1981) 343–58. **Tov, E.** *Textual Criticism of the Hebrew Bible.* 2nd ed. Minneapolis: Fortress, 2001. **Vaux, R. de.** *Histoire ancienne d'Israël.* Vol. 1. Paris: Gabalda, 1971. 552–59. Translated as *The Early History of Israel,* trans. D. Smith (London: Darton, Longman & Todd, 1978) 598–608. **Vogt, E.** "Die Erzählung von Jordanübergang. Josue 3–4." *Bib* 46 (1965) 125–48. **Vries, S. J. de.** "The Time Word *mahar* as a Key to Tradition Development." *ZAW* 87 (1975) 65–79. **Wagenaar, J. A.** "Crossing the Sea of Reeds (Exod 13–14) and the Jordan (Josh 3–4): A Priestly Framework for the Wilderness Wandering." In *Studies in the Book of Exodus.* Ed. M. Vervenne. Leuven: Leuven UP, 1996. 461–70. **Watson, C. M.** "The Stoppage of the River Jordan in 1267." *PEFQS* 27 (1895) 253–61. **Weinfeld, M.** *Deuteronomy and the Deuteronomic School.* Oxford: Clarendon, 1972. **Wellhausen, J.** *Die Composition des Hexateuchs und der historischen Bücher des Alten Testaments.* 2nd ed. Berlin: Reimer, 1889. 120–22. **Wiesmann, H.** "Israels Einzug in Kanaan." *Bib* 11 (1930) 216–30; 12 (1931) 90–92. **Wijngaards, J. N. M.** *The Dramatization of Salvific History in the Deuteronomic Schools.* OtSt 16. Leiden: Brill, 1969. **Wilcoxen, J. A.** "Narrative Structure and Cult Legend: A Study of Joshua 1–6." In *Transitions in Biblical Scholarship.* Ed. J. C. Rylaarsdam. Chicago: University of Chicago Press, 1968. 43–70. **Wildberger, H.** *Jahwes Eigentumsvolk.* ATANT 37. Zürich: Zwingli, 1960. 40–62. **Winther-Nielsen, N.** *A Functional Discourse Grammar of Joshua: A Computer-Assisted Rhetorical Structure Analysis.* ConBOT 40. Stockholm: Almqvist & Wiksell, 1995. ————. "The Miraculous Grammar of Joshua 3–4." In *Biblical Hebrew and Discourse Linguistics.* Winona Lake, IN: Eisenbrauns, 1994. 300–319. **Woudstra, M. H.** *The Ark of the Covenant from Conquest to Kingship.* Philadelphia: Presbyterian and Reformed, 1965. 103–33. **Yeivin, S.** "Zaaredah—Zererah—Zarthan." *BJPES* 14 (1947–1949) 85–90. **Zertal, A.** "Israel Enters Canaan—Following the Pottery Trail." *BAR* 17.5 (1991) 38–47.

Translation

[1]*Joshua set out early*[a] *in the morning from Shittim and came to the Jordan, he and all the sons of Israel.*[b] *They spent the night there before they crossed over.* [2]*At the end of three days the officials crossed through the midst of the camp.* [3]*They commanded the people, "When you see the ark of the covenant*[a] *of Yahweh your God with the Levitical priests*[b] *carrying it, then you shall set out from your place and march after it.* [4]*Still, there shall be some distance between you and it, about a thousand yards in length.*[a] *You shall not approach it so that you may know the way which you are to follow, since you have never crossed over in the way."*[b]

[5]*Then Joshua told the people, "Sanctify yourselves,*[a] *for tomorrow Yahweh will perform wonders among you."* [6]*Then Joshua told the priests, "Carry the ark of the covenant*[a] *and cross over before the people." Then they*[b] *carried the ark of the covenant*[a] *and marched before the people.* [7]*Yahweh told Joshua, "Today I will begin to make you great in the eyes of all Israel that*[a] *they may know that just as I was with Moses, I am with you.* [8]*As for you,*[a] *command the priests who carry the ark of the covenant, 'When you come to the edge of the waters of the Jordan, in the Jordan you shall take your stand.'"*

[9]*Then Joshua told the sons of Israel, "Come over here and listen to the words*[a] *of Yahweh your God."* [10]*Then Joshua said,*[a] *"By this you shall know that the living God is among you*[b] *and that he will certainly drive out from before you the Canaanites, the Hittites, the Hivites, the Perizzites, the Girgashites, the Amorites, and the Jebusites.* [11]*Right now*[a] *the ark of the*

covenant of[b] *the Lord of all the earth*[c] *is crossing over before you into the Jordan.* [12]*Therefore,*[a] *take for yourselves twelve men from the tribes of Israel, one man per tribe.* [13]*As the soles of the feet of the priests, who bear the ark of Yahweh, the Lord of all the earth, rest in the waters of the Jordan, then the waters of the Jordan will be cut off, that is the waters going down from above, so that they will stand as one heap."*[a]

[14]*When the people set out from their tents to cross over the Jordan, with the priests who carry the ark of the covenant*[a] *in front of the people,* [15a]*and while* [b]*the ones carrying the ark came to the Jordan, the feet of the priests who carry the ark having dipped in the edge of the waters, the Jordan being full over all its banks all the days of harvest,*[b] [16]*then* [a]*the waters going down from above stood up; they formed one heap a great distance at Adam,*[a] *the city which is at the side of Zarethan, while those waters going down into the Sea of Arabah,*[b] *the Sea of Salt, were completely cut off. During all this the people crossed over opposite Jericho.* [17]*The priests who carry the ark of the covenant of Yahweh stood firmly*[a] *on dry ground in the middle of the Jordan while all Israel was crossing over on dry ground until all the nation had completed crossing over the Jordan.*

[4:1]*When*[a] *all the nation had completed crossing over the Jordan, Yahweh told Joshua,* [2]*"You (pl.) take for yourselves from the people twelve*[a] *men, one per tribe.* [3]*You (pl.) command them, 'Carry for yourselves from this place,*[a] *from the midst of the Jordan, from the place where the feet of the priests stood firm,*[b] *twelve stones. You shall cause them to cross over with you, and shall cause them to rest in the lodging place where you lodge tonight.'"*

[4]*Then Joshua called to the twelve men whom he had appointed*[a] *from the sons of Israel, one man per tribe,* [5]*and Joshua told them, "Cross over before the ark of Yahweh your God*[a] *to the middle of the Jordan. Each man shall hoist a stone on his shoulder according to the number of the tribes of the sons of Israel,* [6]*that this may be a sign in your midst*[a] *when your children ask on the morrow, 'What do these stones represent for you?'*

[7]*"You shall tell them that the waters of the Jordan were cut off before the ark of the covenant of Yahweh: when it crossed over the Jordan, the waters of the Jordan were cut off.*[a] *These stones shall be an eternal memorial to the sons of Israel."* [8]*The sons of Israel acted just as Joshua*[a] *had commanded. They*[b] *carried twelve stones from the middle of the Jordan just as Yahweh had spoken to Joshua, according to the number of the tribes of the sons of Israel.*[c] *They made them cross over with them to the lodging place and caused them to rest there.*

[9]*(Meanwhile, Joshua had raised up the twelve stones*[a] *in the middle of the Jordan in the place of the standing place of the feet of the priests who carry the ark of the covenant.) They have been there until this day.*[b]

[10]*But the priests who carry the ark were standing in the middle of the Jordan until everything was complete which Yahweh commanded Joshua to speak to the people according to all which Moses commanded Joshua. The people hurried and crossed over.*[a] [11]*As soon as all the people had finished crossing over, the ark of Yahweh along with the priests*[a] *crossed over in the presence of the people.*[b] [12]*The sons of Reuben and the sons of Gad and half the tribe of Manasseh crossed over armed before the sons of Israel just as Moses had spoken to them.* [13]*Approximately forty thousand*[a] *armed for battle crossed over before Yahweh for battle to the plains of Jericho.*

[14]*In that day Yahweh made Joshua great in the eyes of all Israel. They stood in respectful awe of him just as they had stood in respectful awe*[a] *of Moses all the days of his life.*

[15]*Yahweh told Joshua,* [16]*"Command the priests who carry the ark of testimony*[a] *so that they may come up from the Jordan."* [17]*Joshua commanded the priests, "Go up out of the Jordan."* [18]*When the priests who carry the ark of the covenant of Yahweh went up from the middle of*

the Jordan, the soles of the feet of the priests having been drawn up to the dry ground, then the waters of the Jordan returned to their place. They flowed as always over all its banks.

[19]*Now it was on the tenth day of the first month when the people went up from the Jordan. They camped at Gilgal on the eastern edge of Jericho.* [20]*It was precisely these twelve stones which they*[a] *had taken from the Jordan that Joshua raised up in Gilgal.* [21]*He told the sons of Israel, "When*[a] *your sons ask their fathers*[b] *on the morrow, 'What are these stones?'* [22]*you shall instruct your sons, 'On dry ground Israel crossed over this Jordan,* [23]*when*[a] *Yahweh your God dried up the waters of the Jordan before you (pl.) until you crossed over just as Yahweh your God did to the Reed Sea which he dried up before us until we crossed over,* [24]*so that all the peoples of the earth might know the hand of Yahweh that it is strong in order that you may have*[a] *respectful awe before Yahweh your God all the days."* [5:1]*When all the kings of the Amorites, who were beyond the Jordan to the west*[a] *and all the kings of the Canaanites who were beside the sea heard that Yahweh had dried up the waters of the Jordan before the sons of Israel until we*[b] *had crossed over, their heart melted. Spirit was no longer in them because of the sons of Israel.*

Notes

3:1.a. Nelson (54) translates "rose early in the morning" and calls it an "alternate translation." BDB (1014) lists "rise early, make an early start." *KB* (4:1492–94) lists both "to do early" and "to do eagerly." Concise *DCH* says, "when followed by other verbs, perh. as auxiliary verb, do early," an understanding that lies behind the translation above. R. Bartelmus (*TWAT*, 7:1327–34) argues against a meaning of rising up early and supports "to do in a hurry, to do eagerly." Setting the action in the morning probably shows that the term includes both nuances.

1.b. The Heb. syntax is a bit awkward with the shift from the sg. "he rose early" to the pl. "they set out." (But see the attempt of Winther-Nielsen, *Functional Discourse Grammar*, 173, to show that "cosubordination can explain why the first verb shifts to pl.") Heb. manages the shift by inserting "he and all the sons of Israel" after "to the Jordan." LXX omits the inserted subject and reads "he set out," but then adapts the pl. verbs for the remainder. Fritz (43) sees the phrase as a later insertion in the MT seeking to more clearly define the subject. Langlamet (*Gilgal*, 44–45) is correct here in seeing an attempt at harmonization on part of the Gk. changing the verb to sg. and a glossator's insertion in the Heb. Compare Bieberstein (*Josua, Jordan, Jericho*, 147).

3.a. Knauf (54–55) sees "ark of the covenant" (*Bundeslade*) as a mistranslation and so renders *Vertragskasten* or "cask of the treaty."

3b. Strong textual support is found for dividing the priesthood into two branches—priests and Levitical servants. This represents a later understanding than that of Deuteronomy and the books influenced by Deuteronomy, wherein all priests are Levites (cf. Deut 18:1–8; 21:5; 1 Kgs 12:31). Fritz (43) concludes that the missing *waw* before "Levites" shows that the word is a gloss. This evidence is a bit tenuous and sounds like a theory of the priesthood's development lurking behind the decision.

4.a. The Jerusalem Bible and Soggin (47) transpose the two halves of v 4. Without textual support, this is precarious. For the Qere-Kethib problem with the preposition בֵין, cf. GKC §103o.

4.b. The Heb. reads literally "because you have not crossed over in the way yesterday or the day before," an idiom meaning any time previous to the present.

5.a. LXX reads ἀγνίσασθε εἰς αὔριον, "purify yourselves for tomorrow." Bieberstein (*Josua, Jordan, Jericho*, 147) finds a decision difficult to make here. The Gk. reading apparently comes from the same phrase in MT and LXX in Num 11:18 and Josh 7:13. LXX may well have added the familiar phrase here.

6.a. The LXX adds κυρίου to the title of the ark both times in this verse. See Bieberstein (*Josua, Jordan, Jericho*, 145) for cases where this recurs in this chapter. Syr. shares this tendency to add familiar phrases to the text.

6.b. LXX clarifies the indefinite subject as "the priests."

7.a. The אשר clause designates purpose here (*Williams' Hebrew Syntax*, 466, 523; Howard, 124, n. 191).

8.a. LXX reads the logical connective ועתה, "now, therefore," instead of the MT 2nd masc. pl. pronoun. The two terms sound alike, so an error could have occurred in copying from dictation. MT represents a contrast sentence (cf. Andersen, *Sentence*, 150–53; Lambdin, *Introduction to Biblical Hebrew*, §132).

9.a. The versions give strong support for reading sg. "word." Soggin (48) argues for LXX as reflecting early use of an abbreviation for the divine name later incorporated into the word דבר as pl. const. ending. Langlamet (*Gilgal*, 45–46) decides that LXX is the easier reading following the prophetic formula, admitting that no criteria are decisive here. It would appear, however, that changing to דבר יהוה, the prophetic formula for "word of Yahweh," would be the most likely event in the textual history.

10.a. The repetition "and Joshua said" is unnecessary in the context and does not appear in LXX. No reason appears why it would be added to Heb., so LXX has omitted it on stylistic grounds.

10.b. The syntax of vv 10–11 is not clear. To what does "by this" refer? Winther-Nielsen refers to it as a "cataphoric dummy pronoun" that "prepares for an elaboration in a future participle clause" (*Functional Discourse Grammar*, 185). A conditional particle usually follows (Gen 42:15; Num 16:28; Mal 3:10; cf. Ps 41:12). Exod 7:17 uses the construction with the הנה clause introducing the apodosis (see Langlamet, *Gilgal*, 111). It is probable that the הנה clause opening v 11 introduces the apodosis here. (Compare Winther-Nielsen, *Functional Discourse Grammar*, 185.) Hubbard (153, n. 20) thinks בְּזֹאת, "by this," refers to the ark, a possible interpretation that would include Joshua pointing toward the holy object.

11.a. The הנה clause expresses the immediate presence of an object or idea, what Hubbard (153, n. 20) explains as "a presentative exclamation." Cf. Lambdin, *Introduction to Biblical Hebrew*, §§125, 135; Joüon, *Grammaire*, §177i.

11.b. The Masoretes placed a strong disjunctive accent (*zāqēp parvum*) on הברית, "covenant," thus separating it from the divine title which follows. Soggin (48) prefers the Syr. insertion of "Yahweh" after ברית as in v 13. Barthélemy (*Critique textuelle*, 1:2–3) finds vestiges of literary amplification in reference to the ark. Fritz decides the divine title is a gloss since it lacks a reference word. Langlamet (*Gilgal*, 46–47) notes that this still contains a grammatical irregularity with the article before the *nomen regens* and that the Syr. may represent a correction based on v 13. Nelson (53–54) seeks to take the article seriously and translates, "Here is the ark of the covenant! The Lord of the whole earth is going to cross [in front of you] in the Jordan." Gray (62) explains MT as "an obvious deuteronomic interpolation." Langlamet is certainly correct in seeing here "a unification of terminology." His further conjecture that a glossator sought to create a series of seven uses of different formulas is more open to question but worthy of further study. *Preliminary and Interim Report*, 2:5–6, prefers the reading: "the ark of the covenant, <i.e. that> of the Lord of all the earth." Howard (120) insists on "the ark of the covenant, the Lord of all the earth," equating the two. Text criticism cannot solve the issue. Only study of the sources, forms, and redaction can begin to do so.

11.c. Only in the phrase אֲדוֹן כָּל-הָאָרֶץ does אָדוֹן refer to God in the sg. (*IBHS* 7.4.3.b).

12.a. LXX reads vv 10 and 11 together and could not see a logical connection with v 12. Thus it omitted the "before you" of v 11 as well as reading a long genitive construction there, while it omitted the opening conjunction of v 12. The "therefore" of MT is certainly preferable. Nelson (54) follows Gk. in reading "sons of Israel," claiming MT's "tribes of Israel" is an attempt to clarify an unclear text. The two terms are too distinct to find explanation in a copying error. Insertion of "tribes" may represent the tradition's attempts to call for unity among the various tribes of Israel.

13.a. This verse concludes the quotation begun in v 10, though the Heb. has no means of denoting this fact. LXX includes "of the covenant" after "ark," but omits "from above" and the following conjunction. "One heap" also lacks an LXX equivalent, and as Bieberstein (*Josua, Jordan, Jericho*, 151) notes, gave translators problems.

Fritz (43) sees "the waters going down from above" as an explanatory gloss. Nelson (54) follows the LXX reading, saying MT "supplements from v 16, creating some puzzling grammar in the process." Bieberstein (*Josua, Jordan, Jericho*, 149–50) finds a tendency in LXX to drop a Heb. clause-opening *waw* and attach the clause to the subject of the previous free-standing construction. Williams (*Williams' Hebrew Syntax*, 29a) lists this and 8:11 as two of the rare occasions when a word in const. state bears the article.

The textual tradition has attempted to make the prophecy of v 13 correspond exactly to the fulfillment of v 16. The LXX parallelism may represent a close proximity to the original text.

14.a. Howard (120) insists the Heb. must be read, "the ark, the covenant," the article being on "ark" rather than on "covenant."

15.a. The syntax of vv 14–16 is overloaded. LXX appears to have simplified it a bit (Bieberstein, *Josua, Jordan, Jericho*, 152). V 14 begins with a temporal clause followed by a disjunctive clause indicating contemporaneous action, in effect continuing the temporal clause. V 15 then adds another temporal clause followed by two contemporaneous disjunctive clauses. Only with v 16 does a main clause appear. This is then followed by an apposition sentence (Andersen, *Sentence*, 36–60). The following disjunctive clauses again give contemporaneous action. The Heb. consecution of tenses finally takes up again in v 17, but there the subject matter repeats that of 14–16.

15.b-b. LXX reads: ὡς δὲ εἰσεπορεύοντο οἱ ἱερεῖς οἱ αἴροντες τὴν κιβωτὸν τῆς διαθήκης ἐπὶ τὸν Ιορδάνην καὶ οἱ πόδες τῶν ἱερέων τῶν αἰρόντων τὴν κιβωτὸν τῆς διαθήκης κυρίου ἐβάφησαν εἰς μέρος τοῦ ὕδατος τοῦ Ιορδάνου—ὁ δὲ Ιορδάνης ἐπλήρου κάθ' ὅλην τὴν κρηπῖδα αὐτοῦ ὡσεὶ ἡμέραι θερισμοῦ πυρῶν, which may be translated: "As the priests who were carrying the ark of the covenant entered on the Jordan and the feet of the priests who were carrying the ark of the covenant of the Lord were dipped into the edge of the water of the Jordan, the Jordan filled against all its banks just as the days of wheat harvest." LXX has added explicit nouns for priests and for "of the covenant of the Lord."

Nelson (54) follows the LXX in restoring the final phrase from MT's כֹּל יְמֵי קָצִיר, "all the days of harvest," to LXX's כִּימֵי קָצִיר, "according to the days of harvest." 4QJosh^b supports this with בימי as well as joining LXX in adding wheat. Bieberstein (*Josua, Jordan, Jericho*, 152–53) says Gk. has no reason to limit the harvest just to the time of the wheat harvest, while MT needed to stretch the time to include Feast of Weeks, Passover, and Unleavened Bread.

16.a-a. Neither the Masoretic tradition nor the versions were agreed on the precise readings of v 16's geographical descriptions. Langlamet (*Gilgal*, 48–50) has ingeniously restored a primitive text: הרחק מאד מאדם ועד קצה צרת, translating "at a very great distance from Adam to the edge of Zarethan." Nelson (54) retroverts the LXX reading to במאד ער אשר קץ עדתן. Compare the lengthy discussion of Bieberstein (*Josua, Jordan, Jericho*, 154–57). The textual diversities reflect two early problems: (a) the geographical location of Adam and (b) the need to intensify the miraculous. Here, as often, textual history is exegetical history.

The entire tradition here is fraught with the scribal or storyteller's tendency to add or not use traditional phrases and titles, so determining an original text becomes difficult. *Preliminary and Interim Report* (2:6–7) could not decide between the reading tradition Qere's מאדם and the written tradition Kethib's באדם. See the discussion of van der Meer (*Formation and Reformulation*, 99–103) reviewing proposals of Tov, Greenspoon, Lucassen.

16.b. The Arabah is the depression running from the Sea of Galilee to the Gulf of Aqabah. The Sea of Arabah and the Salt Sea are both biblical names for what we call the Dead Sea. Fritz (43) sees "the Salt Sea" as an explanatory gloss.

17.a. The Heb. word הכן, "firmly," appears to be the *hip'il* infinitive absolute of כון. LXX does not translate it. Noth (28) and Soggin (49) see it as meaningless in the context, being a composite of כן, "here," and the article used in a demonstrative sense. KBL (427) is more likely correct in seeing the inf. used as an adverb (compare Nelson, 54). Bieberstein (*Josua, Jordan, Jericho*, 159) leaves the question open after suggesting the Gk. and Syr. translators may have not found an answer here and left the word untranslated, though they translated the term in Josh 4:3.

Again, as in v 11, the formulation of "the carriers of the ark" contains a grammatical anomaly. Here textual observation may lead to the literary decision that a later gloss has entered the text in the words "covenant of Yahweh" (see Langlamet, *Gilgal*, 50). Howard (120) concludes that the meaning is "the ark, the covenant of the LORD."

4:1.a. 4QJosh^b has "Joshua" above the line, apparently reading, "When Joshua and all the nation . . ." See Abegg et al., *Dead Sea Scrolls Bible*, 203. Tov ("Joshua," in *Qumran Cave 4. IX: Deuteronomy, Joshua, Judges, Kings*, DJD 14 [Oxford: Clarendon, 1995] 155–56) finds the "reconstruction of the text for these lines (vv 1–3) is problematic." Tov then reconstructs the fragments on the basis of the LXX, saying a reconstruction on the basis of the MT is impossible. He eliminates "all the nation" (v 1); "twelve men" and "one man" (v 2); and "saying" and "the standing place of the priests" (v 3). Hess ([1996] 107) says the verse describes the following events as taking place "as the people crossed the river. The verb *finished* (Heb *tmm*) does not suggest that everyone had crossed before the next event took place. It is better understood as something still taking place and translated 'were finishing the task.'"

2.a. The LXX renders the command of v 2 in masc. sg. participle as appropriate to the context of v 1, i.e., God speaking to Joshua. MT continues the pl. from v 1 as well as the dative pronoun into the impvs. in vv 2–3a. The LXX is clearly harmonizing. The MT reading does not result from textual criticism.

LXX also omits the "twelve" in v 2 and the phrase "place where the feet of the priests stood" in v 3. The number may have been omitted in the LXX tradition as redundant or supplied by the Heb. tradition for explicitness. The latter phrase may be a gloss seeking to underline the prophetic element (cf. v 9) or a Gk. simplification. Bieberstein (*Josua, Jordan, Jericho*, 159) sees Gk. and Syr. adjusting the text to the context so that MT is original. Again we see that transmitting the text involved interpreting the text.

3.a. Literally, "from this." Nelson (64) finds it missing from OG and 4QJosh^b and so declares it an MT expansion.

3.b. הכן presents a problem similar to that of 3:17. Here the inf. const. form appears but seems to function similarly to the inf. absolute. LXX omitted the word in 3:17 but refers it here to the stones as "prepared stones," having omitted the priestly reference of MT. Steurnagel called the term meaningless. Fritz thinks "from the place where the feet of the priests stood" is a later addition and הכן means "therefore" or "in that place." Nelson (64) finds "from where the feet of the priests stood" to be an MT expansion absent from OG and probably from 4QJosh^b. He takes הכן as relating to the stones as does LXX. Bieberstein (*Josua, Jordan, Jericho*, 158) finds no parallels available and so makes no decision.

4.a. Bieberstein (*Josua, Jordan, Jericho*, 158) shows LXX reading MT הֵכִין, "he appointed," as the adjective הַכִּין, "eminent, established," Gk. ἐνδόξων, giving positions of honor to the twelve stone bearers.

5.a. Gk. omits the repetition of Joshua's name, adds "before me" while omitting reference to the ark, and specifies twelve as the number of tribes, an item it omitted in v 2. Here the Gk. tries to simplify the tradition (cf. Soggin, 49–50). Textual transmission is textual interpretation. Fritz finds "your God" is to be deleted on the basis of LXX evidence.

6.a. LXX reads "a sign laid down through the hole," a reading Nelson (64) correctly identifies as having "no obvious explanation."

7.a. LXX has changed "sons" into sg. in vv 6–7 with corresponding grammatical changes: adding "river" to "Jordan" and "of all the earth" to "Yahweh," omitting the second mention of Jordan and of the waters of the Jordan being cut off. Fritz (43) uses this evidence to delete "the waters of the Jordan were cut off" as superfluous repetition.

Syntactically, one may ask where the words of the fathers to the sons end and where the instructions of Joshua to the children of Israel take up. Nelson (64) decides MT represents "an expansion ('in the Jordan') followed by dittography ('The water of the Jordan was cut off')." Bieberstein (*Josua, Jordan, Jericho*, 160–61) claims that MT never adjusts the text to the context whereas LXX often does, and so he follows MT here. He sees homoioteleuton in the Gk. tradition skipping from one mention of the Jordan to the next. Bieberstein thinks the original Heb. thus utilized chiasm with vv 7b and 7c.

8.a. LXX reads "just as the Lord commanded Joshua," again a different theological interpretation of the text within the transmission tradition. Bieberstein (*Josua, Jordan, Jericho*, 162–63) sees the possibility of MT homoioarkton switching from the יהו starting "Yahweh" to the same letters starting "Joshua." LXX, on the other hand, has a tendency to insert divine names and titles. Bieberstein refuses to make a final decision. It appears more likely that the LXX tradition inserted the divine reference.

8.b. The indefinite subject here must refer to the twelve men appointed in 4:4. Winther-Nielsen (*Functional Discourse Grammar*, 179) seeks to explain: "For discourse semantic reasons, it must be a departure from the usual pronominalization rules"—the execution language repeating the order language of v 3 (compare v 20).

8.c. Instead of "according to the number of the tribes," LXX reads "at the completion of the crossing over," again an interpolation of a different traditional formula within the transmission of the text. Nelson (64) sees no explanation for LXX.

9.a. Nelson concludes: "Since there is no definite article, it is most natural to understand these as a second set of stones. The OG translator characterized them as 'other stones,' as did V" (64). The lack of the article is curious here, but writers did not always follow the grammatical rules we set up. (See Winther-Nielsen, *Functional Discourse Grammar*, 180 and n. 35.) Hubbard (158, n. 41) sees the disjunctive clause beginning with the direct object as representing contemporary action as presented in the translation above.

9.b. *IBHS* 33.3.1c sees the *wayyqtl* form of the final clause here as signifying a pf. state after suffixed verb (pf.) forms and so translates: "and they are there until this day."

10.a. LXX adds the traditional "of the covenant" to ark, and says Joshua finished all which Yahweh had commanded him to announce to the people. LXX omits the reference to all which Moses commanded Joshua. Fritz (43) finds this to be a disturbance in the text and so an addition of the seemingly incompetent editors. Tov (*Textual Criticism of the Hebrew Bible*, 328–29) finds an afterthought added here in MT. Nelson (64) sees this as an MT expansion "perhaps based on Deut 27:4." Van der Meer (*Formation and Reformulation*, 184) sees a "stylistic shortening" in LXX. Langlamet (*Gilgal*, 51) explains the latter as an Hebraic gloss in an attempt to have exactly forty uses of the word צוה, "command." This misses, however, the theological ordering of Yahweh—Moses—Joshua made explicitly in the book (see *Explanation*). LXX and MT have gone different ways in their interpretation of the text with the shorter LXX perhaps the earlier text as Bieberstein (*Josua, Jordan, Jericho*, 163) decides.

The syntax of the verse also deserves comment. The verse begins with a disjunctive clause pointing to contemporary action or explanation of what has preceded. The impf. consec. then refers to the continuation of the action, the priests crossing only after everything else has been completed.

11.a. MT has a sg. verb for "the ark of Yahweh" (LXX, "of the covenant of Yahweh") and the priests "crossed over." LXX has "stones" for MT "priests." This may be explained grammatically (GKC §146f). It may be combined with the LXX reading "and the stones were before them" instead of "before the people" to see the later correction of a partially erased text (Langlamet, *Gilgal*, 51). The latter may be explained as a LXX interpretation of a contradiction in content (Steuernagel). Nelson (64) sees LXX trying to clear up confusion over the stones. Fritz (43) finds the phrase "the priests before the people" as disturbing the text and as unnecessary for the content in the context. Thus it is a correcting remark. Again the ongoing tradition sought to copy and to explain the text. Bieberstein (*Josua, Jordan, Jericho*, 164) objects that the reference to stones makes no logical connection. He then keeps MT as the more difficult reading and sees it as drawn from 3:6, 11, 14 without thinking of its fit with the context. LXX represents an attempt to correct the text. See *Comments*.

11.b. לִפְנֵי הָעָם can be translated with NRSV "in front of the people," but the context does not appear to allow that, particularly in light of vv 17–18. The Heb. term must mean "in the presence of" or "in the sight of." (See Winther-Nielsen, *Functional Discourse Grammar*, 182.) The action of leaving the waters begins here and is completed in vv 17–18.

13.a. See Hess ([1996] 113 with n. 1) for translation of "thousand" as "groups," with perhaps as few as five people in each.

14.a. Nelson notes that OG lacks "they had respectful awe," "apparently to create a smoother translation" (64).

16.a. עדות, "testimonies," has waved a red flag for source critics to find the Priestly source here. This commentary is not convinced that Priestly language necessarily means exilic/postexilic language rather than language of an operating cultus.

Langlamet (*Gilgal*, 52) sees the term as an attempt of a late editor to mark the sixteenth of thirty occurrences of the word "ark" in Joshua, an attempt that replaces an original ברית, "covenant." Whatever the case, we see again the textual tradition interpreting the text.

20.a. The Gk. sg. verb is the more difficult reading, the MT adjusting to the pl. context (Bieberstein, *Josua, Jordan, Jericho*, 165).

21.a. Williams (*Williams' Hebrew Syntax*, 469) shows the ambiguity between a rare real conditional sentence beginning with אשר and a temporal clause. The translation may be "when" or "if," but either translation speaks of something that is expected to occur. Thus Williams (515) translates "If/when in the future your sons ask their fathers."

21.b. Fritz (43) deletes "their fathers" as an explanatory addition to a stereotyped phrase. LXX reads, "when your sons ask you," a reading Nelson (64) accepts, seeing MT as expansion and "correction." Bieberstein (*Josua, Jordan, Jericho,* 165) thinks LXX represents a simplified text. The two readings represent different emphases.

Inclusion of their fathers generalizes the prediction for all generations. Maintaining 2nd pers. throughout spotlights the present generation and appears to represent the older text.

23.a. Williams (*Williams' Hebrew Syntax,* 468) sees this as a causal clause with אשר rather than a temporal clause.

24.a. The MT change of persons is cause for pause. Langlamet (*Gilgal,* 54) follows a host of witnesses in reading the inf. with 3rd pl. suffix without textual support. Soggin is correct in saying "the remedy is no better than the malady, which is not very great in any case" (50). Nelson (64) says the MT fits Deuteronomic usage and context. Bieberstein (*Josua, Jordan, Jericho,* 167–68) prefers MT here.

5:1.a. LXX omits "westwards." Fritz (56) sees this as MT gloss. Bieberstein (*Josua, Jordan, Jericho,* 168–69) sees MT reading as unneeded gloss with simple LXX text the older. The Heb. most often employs some phrase to indicate "westwards" with "beyond the Jordan," when this is meant, since the term is most often used to refer to the territory east of the Jordan (BDB, 719). LXX may also show its own historical setting in interpreting the Canaanites by the sea as Phoenicians.

1.b. The textual tradition witnesses a confusion between 1st pl. and 3rd pl. suffix on the inf. Grammar in the context would demand 3rd pl. Cultic usage of the text would give rise to 1st pl. Bieberstein (*Josua, Jordan, Jericho,* 168) finds LXX, multiple Heb. MSS, Targum, Syriac, and many Gk. MSS retaining the oldest reading, while Leningrad has taken up its reading from 4:23.

Form/Structure/Setting

The section begins with an imperfect consecutive rather than a normal structural indicator. The same imperfect consecutive appears at Josh 6:12, 15; 7:16; 8:10, 14, opening subsections or episodes of a narrative but not the narrative itself. Still, the closure at 2:24 indicates that a new narrative section begins here. The change of location and narrative content confirms 3:1 as the opening of a new narrative. The temporal clause of 4:1 appears to open a new narrative, but it repeats the final temporal clause of 3:17, showing a binding of narrative content, not a closure. The catechetical confession of 4:22–24 appears to offer closure, but again the following verse (5:1) takes up the theme of the confession and shows its beginning realization among the kings of the Canaanites and Amorites. Thus Josh 5:1 may readily be tagged the concluding statement of the narrative.

On the other hand, the parallel opening at Josh 9:1, also with a temporal clause, may point to its function as a discourse marker opening the next narrative section.[452] I take the temporal clause at Josh 5:2 as the opening marker, as it changes content completely, moving from connection to the crossing of the Jordan to the observance of ritual to prepare for battle.

Tradition

Josh 3:1–5:1 presents a complex prose report incorporating a complex oral tradition. Involved in the history of tradition in this passage are Gilgal, Jericho, a

---

452 See Winther-Nielsen, *Functional Discourse Grammar,* 165.

camp near Jericho, two question-and-answer catechetical questions, the ark of the covenant, and the crossing of the Jordan River. Inserted in this is the tradition of Joshua's recognition by God and the people.

The obvious tradition here is cultic. Priests and the ark of the covenant are the featured performers. Cultic parade is the manner of military maneuvers, that is priests lead out with cultic horns and cultic objects with a military purpose. Personal purity and sanctification represent the central pre-battle preparations. Prophetic orations are the motivating materials prior to action. Cultic trumpets sound the keynotes for the story. Cultic stones mark the points of victory. The enemy turns out to be a river, not an army. Children's cultic catechism becomes a central function of the narrative. In the end, dispirited enemy armies acknowledge the power of the God of Israel. The cultic site of Gilgal is the final destination of the story of the exodus, thus connecting this narrative to the salvation history of the exodus. Still, Krause is most likely correct in concluding that the traditions of the Sea and of the Jordan have originated independently from one another.[453] The common elements represent a two-way growth of tradition influencing one another.

The climax of the narrative comes with setting up stones in Gilgal. This portion of the narrative could easily have its origin in a *hieros logos*, telling a story to show the origin of a holy place through an event that made it holy.[454] Two separate catechisms within the narrative point to the importance of the crossing narrative and increases the probability of its historical roots. The ties to Jericho in the tradition show that a military tradition of preparation for battle with Jericho had become part of the tradition. The military role of the ark of the covenant along with the battle-equipped East Jordan tribes enhances the military aura of the tradition.

Source and Redaction

Chaps. 3 and 4 provide a happy hunting ground for source and redaction critics. Bieberstein offers the honest evaluation of the situation: Doublets and tensions create literary critical problems that are hardly capable of being solved.[455] Such problems involve chronological inconsistencies (3:6//3:7–8), opposing instructions (3:6//3:7–8), multiple mentions of the crossing of the Jordan (3:16–17//4:10), the setting up of twelve stones at different places (4:8//4:9//4:20), and the functionless repetition of so-called children's questions (4:6–7//4:21–24).[456] For Bieberstein these point to a complex origin for this unit (3:1–5:1), which prompts him to give a brief history of research.[457] From such evidence Assis concludes: "Synchronic approaches to these passages do not resolve the problems."[458] In spite of such evidence, McConville and Williams conclude: "Most of the perceived discrepancies, however, are intelligible within the progress of the narrative."[459] Assis determines

---

453   Krause, 399.
454   Cf. Gen 28:10–22; 33:18–20; 35:1–7; 35:9–15. See G. Coats, *Genesis*, FOTL 1 (Grand Rapids: Eerdmans, 1983) 318.
455   *Josua, Jordan, Jericho*, 136.
456   See Assis ("A Literary Approach," 401) for another list of the literary critical problems.
457   See Campbell, *Joshua to Chronicles*, 38–41, for a discussion of the "numerous lumpy bits, knots, and twists . . . rough spots" needing attention.
458   Assis, 403.
459   McConville and Williams, 19.

that "the redactor was a composer in his own right, and that the tensions in the text are not a sufficient tool with which to determine the sources of a text."[460]

The passage underscores the necessity of historical critical study of the OT. No reading of the narrative can overlook duplications and chronological contradictions. Howard concedes "the chronology becomes difficult to follow in several places. However, the author's primary concern is not chronology but theological reflection."[461]

Nelson concludes: "Too many topics have been crammed into too constricted a narrative space so that the thematic threads have tangled and knotted. . . . The text seeks simultaneously to enhance the standing of Joshua, to include various personnel, to define the processional order, to boost the wonder of the event, and to explore its theological meaning."[462]

The three days' wait of Josh 1:11 occurs twice (2:22; 3:2) plus two more nights, one camping (3:1) and one in cultic purification (3:5), though the latter is never actualized (cf. v 6). Structural elements of the narrative recur: crossing the river (3:16b; 4:10); the priests leaving the river (4:11, 18); the selection of men to carry the stones (3:12; 4:2); the setting up of the stones at the camping place (4:8), in the middle of the Jordan (4:9), and at Gilgal (4:20); and the command to teach the children (4:6–7; 4:21–24).

The duplication of structural elements suggests duplicate sources rather than simply duplicate motifs and traditions. Any reconstruction of sources, though, has not obtained consensus among scholars.[463]

Fritz reduces the original edition to Josh 3:1, 14a, 15a, 16; 4:11a, 18, 19, a straightforward telling of the crossing of the river with no explanations or interpretations.[464] Such a story, however, would have no *Sitz im Leben* for its preservation. He discovers an ark addition, a secondary insertion of the setting up of the stones, a post-Priestly insertion, and further redactional additions.[465]

Nelson finds an "original story" in 3:1, 5, 11, 13–17.[466] Most of the rest comes from the Deuteronomistic historian. He then separates out two stories: memorial stones (4:1–10, 20–24) and miraculous crossing (3:1–17; 4:11–19), the former being added to the latter, which could not have existed independently.[467]

For Knauf, the major editing of chaps. 3 and 4 is the work of post-Priestly editors who presuppose the post-Priestly Torah.[468] A minute portion may be credited to Knauf's Exodus-Joshua story.[469] Knauf takes his clues from the confusingly complicated (*verwirrenden*) terminology for the treaty chest and the complicated and distorted architecture of the narrative.

---

460   Assis, 405.
461   Howard, 118.
462   Nelson, 55; cf. Hawk: "Nowhere else in Joshua does the narrative lapse into such disarray" (2000) 54.
463   See the lists by Langlamet, *Gilgal*, 21–38, along with his own unique solutions and later ones by Otto, *Mazzotfest*, 26–57, and Mann, *Divine Presence*, 196–212.
464   Fritz, 46.
465   Ibid., 49.
466   Nelson, 56.
467   Ibid, 57.
468   Knauf, 54.
469   Ibid.

Hubbard discusses the "complex literary piece" and explains "an appearance of disorder" as "the incorporation of an original cultic ceremony."[470] Nelson finds attempts to reconstruct literary history "doomed to failure."[471]

Creach contends that "the story's attempt to instruct is primary and overrides its effort to report. . . . [T]he entire event is presented as elaborate ritual. . . . Joshua 3:1–5:1 was shaped for the purpose of creating a proper memory of the Jordan crossing and instructing each generation as to its importance in Israelite history."[472]

The fusion of different versions of the narrative still seems most true to the evidence if not to some of our presuppositions and expectations concerning Scripture. To say that different versions exist is not to applaud attempts to find different literary sources. It is to say that oral tradition almost by definition produces parallel narratives built around central events described from different perspectives and used in different arenas for different purposes.

Precise delineation of the sources is made difficult by the lack of vocabulary evidence to connect the accounts to traditional "hexateuchal sources."[473] Nelson insists the two-source approach is "untenable" because the water is stopped only once (but note Josh 3:16a and 3:16b) and reversed only one time (4:18, but the first story is complete when the people cross).[474] Nelson isolates Deuteronomistic History contributions in 3:2–4, 6–10 and then tries to read the story as a whole since "by using moderate effort the reader actually has no trouble making sense out of the story line. The basic pattern of chapters 3 and 4 is one of scene setting (3:1–2) followed by command and prediction (3:3–13) followed by obedience and miracle (3:14–17; 4:11–19)."[475] The remainder of the narrative features the ark. The story of the memorial stones is supplemental to the crossing of the ark. Hawk notes, "The various features of the narrative—the awkward style, the disjointed chronology, the narrator's interruptions, and the multiple viewpoints—work together to produce a sense of disorientation in space, time, and perspective."[476]

Some authors do attempt to find unity in the passage. Thus Peckham maintains that the narrative has two major parts—3:1–17 and 4:1–24.[477] Each part has four corresponding sections related logically rather than chronologically. A complex analysis of the relationship and structure of the two parts and their sections leads Peckham to conclude:[478]

> The consistency and coherence of the account are evident from an analysis
> of its grammar, style, and organization. Disjunction is normal, and conse-
> cution is confined to the pattern of command and obedience. Prolepsis

---

470 Hubbard, 148–49.
471 Nelson, 57.
472 Creach, 44–45.
473 Note that Simpson's extensive lists affect only five verses, two of which he attributes to
       sources in direct contradiction to his own vocabulary evidence and two of which he refers
       to redactors (*Early Traditions*, 283–86), while Weinfeld's Deuteronomic vocabulary (*Deuter-*
       onomy, 320–59) appears only in Josh 4:24–5:1.
474 Nelson, 56.
475 Ibid., 57.
476 Hess (2000) 57.
477 *CBQ* 46 (1984) 418–19.
478 Ibid., 423.

and resumption are typical of the logical arrangement that has replaced narrative sequence. The parts and paragraphs are connected by a system of iteration that subjects narrative development to argument and interpretation. This balanced and bipartite composition of the account is the literary evidence for the two editions of the Dtr history and illustrates their relationship as narrative and as commentary.

Peckham disects his consistency and coherence, however, into two Deuteronomistic authors with the original comprising only 3:5, 10b, 16b. Winther-Nielsen attempts to build on Peckham to show unity.[479] He discovers the "peak climax of the priests' crossing into the river . . . (3:14–17) and the peak resolution of their crossing out again . . . (4:15–18). . . . The front-position of the ark and its rich symbolism, the miracles and the commemoration by the stones all witness to the deeds of Yahweh (3:6) through Joshua (3:7; 4:14)."[480] This analysis may point to some structural elements the author used but does not provide sufficient evidence to declare this a unified narrative.

J. Krause centers his study on the two catechetical statements. He discovers three editorial layers: a Deuteronomic basic text and two post-Priestly editorial layers. He finds 4:6–7 younger than 4:21–24. The catechesis in 4:21–24 seeks to glorify Yahweh in the presence of the nations.[481] The Rahab narrative and 5:1 were inserted into the basic narrative, joining to 1:11; 3:1–2, 9–11, 13. Unlike the original story set as a miracle narrative to bring trust in Joshua, these inserts have no interest in Joshua's leadership.

Krause finds 4:6–7 seeking to describe the miraculous force of the Ark. This post-Priestly addition includes 3:4, 17; 4:3, 9. Krause's study comes to the redactional history of a basic Deuteronomic layer comprising 3:2–3, 4b, 6–8, 14–15, 16a; 4:1b–3*, 5, 8, 10a, 12, 14–19a, 20. The first post-Priestly editorial layer comprises 3:1, 5, 9–11, 13, 16*; 4:21–5:1. The final editorial layer spans 3:4*, 17*; 4:3*, 6–7, 9. Even later additions come in 3:12, 16a, 17b–4:1a, 4a*, 13, 19a. Over against this stands Assis with the understanding that the two catecheses represent separate dimensions of the same event, one directed toward Israel featuring the Ark and the other directed to the nations with Israel's acts as the featured attraction.[482] Assis finds a third purpose as magnifying Joshua. Thus Krause and Assis come to the same conclusions as to aims of the catecheses while following strongly different literary methods and presuppostions. Assis encourages exegetes "first and foremost" to "examine how inconsistencies, repetitions, and tensions in the text shape a text's meaning."[483]

We are left with only internal consistencies as criteria for source division. The climactic catechetical statements provide clues concerning content. The first (Josh 4:6–7) centers on the ark cutting off the waters and the memorial stones. The second (4:21–23) centers on the miracle that Israel crossed on dry ground. We would expect the other narrative material to point toward these climactic statements. Closer observation proves that it does.

479   *Functional Discourse Grammar*, 169–90.
480   Winther-Nielsen, 190.
481   Krause, 391.
482   Assis, 406.
483   Ibid., 413. Cf. Ballhorn, 416–17.

Despite Nelson's disclaimers, certain markers are given. Josh 3:1 connects to chap. 2, while 3:2 reaches back to 1:11. One narrative appears to point toward a camping place near Jericho (3:16), while the other points to Gilgal (4:19–20). One version is painted in terms used in Exod 14–15 to describe the crossing of the Reed Sea and climaxes in a catechetical statement (4:21–23) explicitly connecting the two events. The other version describes only the crossing of the Jordan river by the ark, again climaxing in a catechetical statement using these terms (4:6–7).

A reexamination of the two chapters shows that the ark cutting off the waters of the Jordan is the central emphasis of Josh 3:2–4, 6–7, 9, 11–14, 16b; 4:1–8, 10, 12–17. The second version centers on the action of the priests with the ark allowing Israel to cross on dry ground and appears in Josh 3:1, 5, 8, 10, 15–16a, 17; 4:9, 11, 18–24; 5:1. Thus we find two oral sources, each with its own structure, intention, and cultic use. Form-critical study should provide us with more information about each of these sources.

Form

Dozeman isolates the two catechisms as Josh 4:6b–7 and Josh 4:21–24 and maintains that each provides its own interpretation of the twelve stones.[484] Josh 4:6b–7 memorializes the twelve stones for the Jordan's being cut off. Josh 4:21–24 shifts the focus to Israel as the second generation of those who left Egypt now crossing the Jordan on dry ground. Dozeman sees the first catechism as the older, supplemented with 4:21–24, since the horizon of the first catechism and its answer are more limited than those of the second, the first addressed to an immediate audience, the second to coming generations. The symbolism of the first is confined to the ark cutting off the waters with Israel playing no role. The second catechism has a more exact location, not the middle of the river but at Gilgal, with the focus totally on river-crossing Israel.[485]

> This shift in location transforms their symbolic significance in Josh 4:21–24. The horizon is no longer limited to the Jordan River and Yahweh's power over it. Instead, the significance of the stones now reaches back to the exodus, as they memorialize Yahweh's power over both the *yam-sûp* and the Jordan River.

Granting the presence of mythic overtones, Dozeman still finds that the combination of the river and sea is an innovation going beyond the first catechism in two ways—placing the crossing of the Jordan in the larger framework of a salvation history and outlining a history of salvation from the exodus to the conquest.

Our musings on the tradition history behind these two catechisms have revealed basically two complete oral sources. The first involves Joshua, the ark cutting off the waters, a camp near Jericho, military undertones, and the fulfillment of orders given by Moses. It centers on the present generation of Israelites, the preservation of testimony to God's miracle at the Jordan, and the recognition of Joshua's prowess as a general leading the battle. The story apparently served as preparation for the battle of Jericho. Its basic purpose in its present form is to move the nation and its armed soldiers across the Jordan so that they can set up camp to fight Jericho. Its theological purpose is to expand the reputation of Joshua as the chosen leader

---

484 *CBQ* 58 (1996) 412.
485 Dozeman, *CBQ* 58 (1996) 412.

after Moses and to show the miraculous power of God as sufficient for anything the people faced in the new land.

The second narrative involves Gilgal, dry ground, etiology, the power of the Jordan waters, God's universal control over all nations and all history, and a connection of exodus miracle with Jordan miracle to show the connectedness of salvation history. It thus reaches out to a new generation with we-and-you language and with teachings about the power of the living God over all nations and all history.

Passage	Hebrew Source 1	Hebrew Source 2
3:1		¹ וַיַּשְׁכֵּם יְהוֹשֻׁעַ בַּבֹּקֶר וַיִּסְעוּ מֵהַשִּׁטִּים וַיָּבֹאוּ עַד־הַיַּרְדֵּן הוּא וְכָל־בְּנֵי יִשְׂרָאֵל וַיָּלִנוּ שָׁם טֶרֶם יַעֲבֹרוּ
3:2–4	² וַיְהִי מִקְצֵה שְׁלֹשֶׁת יָמִים וַיַּעַבְרוּ הַשֹּׁטְרִים בְּקֶרֶב הַמַּחֲנֶה ³ וַיְצַוּוּ אֶת־הָעָם לֵאמֹר כִּרְאוֹתְכֶם אֵת אֲרוֹן בְּרִית־יְהוָה אֱלֹהֵיכֶם וְהַכֹּהֲנִים הַלְוִיִּם נֹשְׂאִים אֹתוֹ וְאַתֶּם תִּסְעוּ מִמְּקוֹמְכֶם וַהֲלַכְתֶּם אַחֲרָיו ⁴ אַךְ רָחוֹק יִהְיֶה בֵּינֵיכֶם וּבֵינוֹ כְּאַלְפַּיִם אַמָּה בַּמִּדָּה אַל־תִּקְרְבוּ אֵלָיו לְמַעַן אֲשֶׁר־תֵּדְעוּ אֶת־הַדֶּרֶךְ אֲשֶׁר תֵּלְכוּ־בָהּ כִּי לֹא עֲבַרְתֶּם בַּדֶּרֶךְ מִתְּמוֹל שִׁלְשׁוֹם	
3:5		⁵ וַיֹּאמֶר יְהוֹשֻׁעַ אֶל־הָעָם הִתְקַדָּשׁוּ כִּי מָחָר יַעֲשֶׂה יְהוָה בְּקִרְבְּכֶם נִפְלָאוֹת
3:6–7	⁶ וַיֹּאמֶר יְהוֹשֻׁעַ אֶל־הַכֹּהֲנִים לֵאמֹר שְׂאוּ אֶת־אֲרוֹן הַבְּרִית וְעִבְרוּ לִפְנֵי הָעָם וַיִּשְׂאוּ אֶת־אֲרוֹן הַבְּרִית וַיֵּלְכוּ לִפְנֵי הָעָם ס ⁷ וַיֹּאמֶר יְהוָה אֶל־יְהוֹשֻׁעַ הַיּוֹם הַזֶּה אָחֵל גַּדֶּלְךָ בְּעֵינֵי כָּל־יִשְׂרָאֵל אֲשֶׁר יֵדְעוּן כִּי כַּאֲשֶׁר הָיִיתִי עִם־מֹשֶׁה אֶהְיֶה עִמָּךְ	
3:8		⁸ וְאַתָּה תְּצַוֶּה אֶת־הַכֹּהֲנִים נֹשְׂאֵי אֲרוֹן־הַבְּרִית לֵאמֹר כְּבֹאֲכֶם עַד־קְצֵה מֵי הַיַּרְדֵּן בַּיַּרְדֵּן תַּעֲמֹדוּ
3:9	⁹ וַיֹּאמֶר יְהוֹשֻׁעַ אֶל־בְּנֵי יִשְׂרָאֵל גֹּשׁוּ הֵנָּה וְשִׁמְעוּ אֶת־דִּבְרֵי יְהוָה אֱלֹהֵיכֶם	
3:10		¹⁰ וַיֹּאמֶר יְהוֹשֻׁעַ בְּזֹאת תֵּדְעוּן כִּי אֵל חַי בְּקִרְבְּכֶם וְהוֹרֵשׁ יוֹרִישׁ מִפְּנֵיכֶם אֶת־הַכְּנַעֲנִי וְאֶת־הַחִתִּי וְאֶת־הַחִוִּי וְאֶת־הַפְּרִזִּי וְאֶת־הַגִּרְגָּשִׁי וְהָאֱמֹרִי וְהַיְבוּסִי

Passage	Hebrew Source 1	Hebrew Source 2
3:11–14	¹¹ הִנֵּה אֲרוֹן הַבְּרִית אֲדוֹן כָּל־הָאָרֶץ עֹבֵר לִפְנֵיכֶם בַּיַּרְדֵּן ¹² וְעַתָּה קְחוּ לָכֶם שְׁנֵי עָשָׂר אִישׁ מִשִּׁבְטֵי יִשְׂרָאֵל אִישׁ־אֶחָד אִישׁ־אֶחָד לַשָּׁבֶט ¹³ וְהָיָה כְּנוֹחַ כַּפּוֹת רַגְלֵי הַכֹּהֲנִים נֹשְׂאֵי אֲרוֹן יְהוָה אֲדוֹן כָּל־הָאָרֶץ בְּמֵי הַיַּרְדֵּן מֵי הַיַּרְדֵּן יִכָּרֵתוּן הַמַּיִם הַיֹּרְדִים מִלְמָעְלָה וְיַעַמְדוּ נֵד אֶחָד ¹⁴ וַיְהִי בִּנְסֹעַ הָעָם מֵאָהֳלֵיהֶם לַעֲבֹר אֶת־הַיַּרְדֵּן וְהַכֹּהֲנִים נֹשְׂאֵי הָאָרוֹן הַבְּרִית לִפְנֵי הָעָם	
3:15–16a		¹⁵ וּכְבוֹא נֹשְׂאֵי הָאָרוֹן עַד־הַיַּרְדֵּן וְרַגְלֵי הַכֹּהֲנִים נֹשְׂאֵי הָאָרוֹן נִטְבְּלוּ בִּקְצֵה הַמָּיִם וְהַיַּרְדֵּן מָלֵא עַל־כָּל־גְּדוֹתָיו כֹּל יְמֵי קָצִיר ^{16a} וַיַּעַמְדוּ הַמַּיִם הַיֹּרְדִים מִלְמָעְלָה
3:16b	^{16b} קָמוּ נֵד־אֶחָד הַרְחֵק מְאֹד בָּאָדָם הָעִיר אֲשֶׁר מִצַּד צָרְתָן וְהַיֹּרְדִים עַל יָם הָעֲרָבָה יָם־הַמֶּלַח תַּמּוּ נִכְרָתוּ וְהָעָם עָבְרוּ נֶגֶד יְרִיחוֹ	
3:17		¹⁷ וַיַּעַמְדוּ הַכֹּהֲנִים נֹשְׂאֵי הָאָרוֹן בְּרִית־יְהוָה בֶּחָרָבָה בְּתוֹךְ הַיַּרְדֵּן הָכֵן וְכָל־יִשְׂרָאֵל עֹבְרִים בֶּחָרָבָה עַד אֲשֶׁר־תַּמּוּ כָּל־הַגּוֹי לַעֲבֹר אֶת־הַיַּרְדֵּן
4:1–8	¹ וַיְהִי כַּאֲשֶׁר־תַּמּוּ כָל־הַגּוֹי לַעֲבוֹר אֶת־הַיַּרְדֵּן פ וַיֹּאמֶר יְהוָה אֶל־יְהוֹשֻׁעַ לֵאמֹר ² קְחוּ לָכֶם מִן־הָעָם שְׁנֵים עָשָׂר אֲנָשִׁים אִישׁ־אֶחָד אִישׁ־אֶחָד מִשָּׁבֶט ³ וְצַוּוּ אוֹתָם לֵאמֹר שְׂאוּ־לָכֶם מִזֶּה מִתּוֹךְ הַיַּרְדֵּן מִמַּצַּב רַגְלֵי הַכֹּהֲנִים הָכִין שְׁתֵּים־עֶשְׂרֵה אֲבָנִים וְהַעֲבַרְתֶּם אוֹתָם עִמָּכֶם וְהִנַּחְתֶּם אוֹתָם בַּמָּלוֹן אֲשֶׁר־תָּלִינוּ בוֹ הַלָּיְלָה ⁴ וַיִּקְרָא יְהוֹשֻׁעַ אֶל־שְׁנֵים הֶעָשָׂר אִישׁ אֲשֶׁר הֵכִין מִבְּנֵי יִשְׂרָאֵל אִישׁ־אֶחָד אִישׁ־אֶחָד מִשָּׁבֶט ⁵ וַיֹּאמֶר לָהֶם יְהוֹשֻׁעַ עִבְרוּ לִפְנֵי אֲרוֹן יְהוָה אֱלֹהֵיכֶם אֶל־תּוֹךְ הַיַּרְדֵּן וְהָרִימוּ לָכֶם אִישׁ אֶבֶן אַחַת עַל־שִׁכְמוֹ לְמִסְפַּר שִׁבְטֵי בְנֵי־יִשְׂרָאֵל ⁶ לְמַעַן תִּהְיֶה זֹאת אוֹת בְּקִרְבְּכֶם כִּי־יִשְׁאָלוּן בְּנֵיכֶם מָחָר	

Passage	Hebrew Source 1	Hebrew Source 2
4:1–8 continued	לֵאמֹר מָה הָאֲבָנִים הָאֵלֶּה לָכֶם ⁷וַאֲמַרְתֶּם לָהֶם אֲשֶׁר נִכְרְתוּ מֵימֵי הַיַּרְדֵּן מִפְּנֵי אֲרוֹן בְּרִית־יְהוָה בְּעָבְרוֹ בַּיַּרְדֵּן נִכְרְתוּ מֵי הַיַּרְדֵּן וְהָיוּ הָאֲבָנִים הָאֵלֶּה לְזִכָּרוֹן לִבְנֵי יִשְׂרָאֵל עַד־עוֹלָם ⁸ וַיַּעֲשׂוּ־כֵן בְּנֵי־יִשְׂרָאֵל כַּאֲשֶׁר צִוָּה יְהוֹשֻׁעַ וַיִּשְׂאוּ שְׁתֵּי־עֶשְׂרֵה אֲבָנִים מִתּוֹךְ הַיַּרְדֵּן כַּאֲשֶׁר דִּבֶּר יְהוָה אֶל־יְהוֹשֻׁעַ לְמִסְפַּר שִׁבְטֵי בְנֵי־יִשְׂרָאֵל וַיַּעֲבִרוּם עִמָּם אֶל־הַמָּלוֹן וַיַּנִּחוּם שָׁם	
4:9		⁹ וּשְׁתֵּים עֶשְׂרֵה אֲבָנִים הֵקִים יְהוֹשֻׁעַ בְּתוֹךְ הַיַּרְדֵּן תַּחַת מַצַּב רַגְלֵי הַכֹּהֲנִים נֹשְׂאֵי אֲרוֹן הַבְּרִית וַיִּהְיוּ שָׁם עַד הַיּוֹם הַזֶּה
4:10	¹⁰ וְהַכֹּהֲנִים נֹשְׂאֵי הָאָרוֹן עֹמְדִים בְּתוֹךְ הַיַּרְדֵּן עַד תֹּם כָּל־הַדָּבָר אֲשֶׁר־צִוָּה יְהוָה אֶת־יְהוֹשֻׁעַ לְדַבֵּר אֶל־הָעָם כְּכֹל אֲשֶׁר־צִוָּה מֹשֶׁה אֶת־יְהוֹשֻׁעַ וַיְמַהֲרוּ הָעָם וַיַּעֲבֹרוּ	
4:11		¹¹ וַיְהִי כַּאֲשֶׁר־תַּם כָּל־הָעָם לַעֲבוֹר וַיַּעֲבֹר אֲרוֹן־יְהוָה וְהַכֹּהֲנִים לִפְנֵי הָעָם
4:12–17	¹² וַיַּעַבְרוּ בְּנֵי־רְאוּבֵן וּבְנֵי־גָד וַחֲצִי שֵׁבֶט הַמְנַשֶּׁה חֲמֻשִׁים לִפְנֵי בְּנֵי יִשְׂרָאֵל כַּאֲשֶׁר דִּבֶּר אֲלֵיהֶם מֹשֶׁה ¹³ כְּאַרְבָּעִים אֶלֶף חֲלוּצֵי הַצָּבָא עָבְרוּ לִפְנֵי יְהוָה לַמִּלְחָמָה אֶל עַרְבוֹת יְרִיחוֹ ¹⁴ בַּיּוֹם הַהוּא גִּדַּל יְהוָה אֶת־יְהוֹשֻׁעַ בְּעֵינֵי כָּל־יִשְׂרָאֵל וַיִּרְאוּ אֹתוֹ כַּאֲשֶׁר יָרְאוּ אֶת־מֹשֶׁה כָּל־יְמֵי חַיָּיו ¹⁵ וַיֹּאמֶר יְהוָה אֶל־יְהוֹשֻׁעַ לֵאמֹר ¹⁶ צַוֵּה אֶת־הַכֹּהֲנִים נֹשְׂאֵי אֲרוֹן הָעֵדוּת וְיַעֲלוּ מִן־הַיַּרְדֵּן ¹⁷ וַיְצַו יְהוֹשֻׁעַ אֶת־הַכֹּהֲנִים לֵאמֹר עֲלוּ מִן־הַיַּרְדֵּן	
4:18–5:1		¹⁸ וַיְהִי בַּעֲלוֹת הַכֹּהֲנִים נֹשְׂאֵי אֲרוֹן בְּרִית־יְהוָה מִתּוֹךְ הַיַּרְדֵּן נִתְּקוּ כַּפּוֹת רַגְלֵי הַכֹּהֲנִים אֶל הֶחָרָבָה וַיָּשֻׁבוּ מֵי־הַיַּרְדֵּן לִמְקוֹמָם וַיֵּלְכוּ כִתְמוֹל־שִׁלְשׁוֹם עַל־כָּל־גְּדוֹתָיו ¹⁹ וְהָעָם עָלוּ מִן־הַיַּרְדֵּן בֶּעָשׂוֹר לַחֹדֶשׁ הָרִאשׁוֹן וַיַּחֲנוּ בַּגִּלְגָּל בִּקְצֵה מִזְרַח יְרִיחוֹ

Passage	Hebrew Source 1	Hebrew Source 2
4:18–5:1 continued		20 וְאֵת שְׁתֵּים עֶשְׂרֵה הָאֲבָנִים הָאֵלֶּה אֲשֶׁר לָקְחוּ מִן־הַיַּרְדֵּן הֵקִים יְהוֹשֻׁעַ בַּגִּלְגָּל 21 וַיֹּאמֶר אֶל־בְּנֵי יִשְׂרָאֵל לֵאמֹר אֲשֶׁר יִשְׁאָלוּן בְּנֵיכֶם מָחָר אֶת־אֲבוֹתָם לֵאמֹר מָה הָאֲבָנִים הָאֵלֶּה 22 וְהוֹדַעְתֶּם אֶת־בְּנֵיכֶם לֵאמֹר בַּיַּבָּשָׁה עָבַר יִשְׂרָאֵל אֶת־הַיַּרְדֵּן הַזֶּה 23 אֲשֶׁר־הוֹבִישׁ יְהוָה אֱלֹהֵיכֶם אֶת־מֵי הַיַּרְדֵּן מִפְּנֵיכֶם עַד־עָבְרְכֶם כַּאֲשֶׁר עָשָׂה יְהוָה אֱלֹהֵיכֶם לְיַם־סוּף אֲשֶׁר־הוֹבִישׁ מִפָּנֵינוּ עַד־עָבְרֵנוּ 24 לְמַעַן דַּעַת כָּל־עַמֵּי הָאָרֶץ אֶת־יַד יְהוָה כִּי חֲזָקָה הִיא לְמַעַן יְרָאתֶם אֶת־יְהוָה אֱלֹהֵיכֶם כָּל־הַיָּמִים 1 וַיְהִי כִשְׁמֹעַ כָּל־מַלְכֵי הָאֱמֹרִי אֲשֶׁר בְּעֵבֶר הַיַּרְדֵּן יָמָּה וְכָל־מַלְכֵי הַכְּנַעֲנִי אֲשֶׁר עַל־הַיָּם אֵת אֲשֶׁר־הוֹבִישׁ יְהוָה אֶת־מֵי הַיַּרְדֵּן מִפְּנֵי בְנֵי־יִשְׂרָאֵל עַד־עָבְרָנוּ וַיִּמַּס לְבָבָם וְלֹא־הָיָה בָם עוֹד רוּחַ מִפְּנֵי בְּנֵי־יִשְׂרָאֵל

Passage	Source 1	Source 2
3:1		[1]Joshua got up early in the morning. They set out from Shittim and came to the Jordan, he and all the sons of Israel. They spent the night there before they passed over.
3:2–4	[2]At the end of three days the officials passed through the midst of the camp. [3]They commanded the people, "When you see the ark of the covenant of Yahweh your God with the Levitical priests carrying it, then you shall set out from your place and march after it. [4]Still, there shall be some distance between you and it, about a thousand yards in length. You shall not approach it so that you may know the way which you are to follow, since you have never passed over in the way."	
3:5		[5]Then Joshua told the people, "Sanctify yourselves, for tomorrow Yahweh will perform wonders among you."

Passage	Source 1	Source 2
3:6–7	⁶Then Joshua told the priests, "Carry the ark of the covenant and pass over before the people." Then they carried the ark of the covenant and marched before the people.⁷Then Yahweh told Joshua, "Today I will begin to make you great in the eyes of all Israel that they may know that just as I was with Moses, I am with you.	
3:8		⁸"As for you, command the priests who carry the ark of the covenant, 'When you come to the edge of the waters of the Jordan, in the Jordan you shall take your stand.'"
3:9	⁹Then Joshua told the sons of Israel, "Come over here and listen to the words of Yahweh your God."	
3:10		¹⁰Then Joshua said, "By this you shall know that the living God is among you and that he will certainly drive out from before you the Canaanites, the Hittites, the Hivites, the Perizzites, the Girgashites, the Amorites, and the Jebusites."
3:11–14	¹¹Right now the ark of the covenant of the Lord of all the earth is passing over before you into the Jordan. ¹²Therefore, take for yourselves twelve men from the tribes of Israel, one man per tribe. ¹³As the soles of the feet of the priests, who bear the ark of Yahweh, the Lord of all the earth, rest in the waters of the Jordan, then the waters of the Jordan will be cut off, that is the waters going down from above, so that they will stand as one heap." ¹⁴When the people set out from their tents to pass over the Jordan, with the priests who carry the ark of the covenant in front of the people,	
3:15–16a		¹⁵and while the ones carrying the ark came to the Jordan, the feet of the priests who carry the ark having dipped in the edge of the waters, the Jordan being full over all its banks all the days of harvest, ¹⁶ᵃthen the waters going down from above stood up.
3:16b	¹⁶ᵇthey [the waters] formed one heap a great distance away at Adam, the city which is at the side of Zarethan, while those waters going down into the Sea of Arabah, the Sea of Salt, were completely cut off. During all this the people passed over opposite Jericho.	

Passage	Source 1	Source 2
3:17		¹⁷The priests who carry the ark of the covenant of Yahweh stood firmly on dry ground in the middle of the Jordan while all Israel was passing over on dry ground until all the nation had completed passing over the Jordan.
4:1–8	⁴:¹When all the nation had completed passing over the Jordan, Yahweh told Joshua, ²"You (pl.) take for yourselves from the people twelve men, one per tribe. ³You (pl.) command them, 'Carry for yourselves from this place, from the midst of the Jordan, from the place where the feet of the priests stood firm, twelve stones. You shall cause them to pass over with you and shall cause them to rest in the camp where you camp tonight.'" ⁴Then Joshua called to the twelve men whom he had appointed from the sons of Israel, one man per tribe, ⁵and Joshua told them, "Pass over before the ark of Yahweh your God to the middle of the Jordan. Each man shall hoist a stone upon his shoulder according to the number of the tribes of the sons of Israel, ⁶in order that this may be a sign in your midst when your children ask on the morrow, 'What do these stones represent for you?' ⁷You shall tell them that the waters of the Jordan were cut off before the ark of the covenant of Jahweh: when it passed over the Jordan, the waters of the Jordan were cut off. These stones shall be an eternal memorial to the sons of Israel." ⁸The sons of Israel acted just as Joshua had commanded. They carried twelve stones from the middle of the Jordan just as Yahweh had spoken to Joshua, according to the number of the tribes of the sons of Israel. They passed them over with them to the camp and caused them to rest there.	
4:9		⁹Meanwhile Joshua raised up twelve stones in the middle of the Jordan underneath the standing place of the feet of the priests who carry the ark of the covenant. They have been there until this day.
4:10	¹⁰But the priests who carry the ark were standing in the middle of the Jordan until everything was complete which Yahweh commanded Joshua to speak to the people according to all which Moses commanded Joshua. The people hurried and passed over.	

Passage	Source 1	Source 2
4:11		[11]As all the people completed passing over, the ark of Yahweh and the priests passed over before the people.
4:12–17	[12]The sons of Reuben and the sons of Gad and half the tribe of Manasseh passed over armed before the sons of Israel just as Moses had spoken to them. [13]Approximately forty thousand armed for battle passed over before Yahweh for battle to the plains of Jericho. [14]In that day Yahweh made Joshua great in the eyes of all Israel. They stood in respectful awe of him just as they had stood in respectful awe of Moses all the days of his life. [15]Yahweh told Joshua, [16]"Command the priests who carry the ark of testimony so that they may come up from the Jordan." [17]Joshua commanded the priests, "Go up out of the Jordan."	
4:18–5:1		[18]When the priests who carry the ark of the covenant of Yahweh went up from the middle of the Jordan, the soles of the feet of the priests having been drawn up to the dry ground, then the waters of the Jordan returned to their place. They flowed as always over all its banks. [19]Now it was on the tenth day of the first month when the people went up from the Jordan. They camped at Gilgal on the eastern edge of Jericho. [20]It was precisely these twelve stones which they had taken from the Jordan that Joshua raised up in Gilgal. [21]He told the sons of Israel, "When your sons ask their fathers on the morrow, 'What are these stones?' [22]you shall instruct your sons, 'On dry ground Israel passed over this Jordan, [23]when Yahweh your God dried up the waters of the Jordan before you (pl.) until you passed over just as Yahweh your God did to the Reed Sea which he dried up before us until we passed over, [24]so that all the peoples of the earth might know the hand of Yahweh that it is strong in order that you may have respectful awe before Yahweh all the days. [5:1]When all the kings of the Amorites, who were beyond the Jordan to the west and all the Kings of the Canaanites who were beside the sea heard that Yahweh had dried up the waters of the Jordan before the sons of Israel until we had passed over, their heart melted. Spirit was no longer in them because of the sons of Israel.

The first narrative (Josh 3:2–4, 6–7, 9, 11–14, 16b; 4:1–8, 10, 12–17) cannot be classified in any category of popular stories and sagas. It has no arc of tension with which the narrator could hold the attention of the audience. Instead, it seeks to teach the audience the nature of the ark. It is a catechetical example showing how the divine presence in the ark led the people when they followed obediently.

In this commentary, true narrative chapters will have tables reflecting both the structural elements and the form-critical elements of the particular section of Joshua. Such a chart has proved beyond the author's ability to construct for this chapter, precisely because the chapter fits liturgy and catechesis rather than narrative with exposition, complication, crisis, resolution, and ending. Certainly those involved in the narrative will have experienced crisis and complication, but the narrative is not constructed in that manner.

The catechetical form includes the miracle story, theological explanations (if these are not editorial), the designation of a sign, the children's question, the parental explanation, and a conclusion of the narrative. The narrative thus appears to stand at a distance removed from the event. Rather, the event has become a subject of reflection. It can be used as an example from history to help the present generation, no matter how far removed in time and territory from the original event. The event does not give rise to only one kind of reflection, but differing reflections lead to differing ways of telling the story and explaining its meaning to the next generation.

The nature of the story as reflection is demonstrated by several details. The picture of Joshua as both prophet (3:9–11) and military commander (3:6; 4:4–5) shows a development of the understanding of the office of Joshua.

The narrative of the crossing of the ark has been supplemented with a traditional catechism of the ark. Gressmann noted long ago that a military crossing of the river does not allow time for stopping to carry heavy rocks and dedicate them.[486] The rocks themselves may well have represented an altar or an open-air sanctuary in their original context. The present context interprets them as a roadside monument. This first narrative source behind Josh 3:1–5:1 thus reveals itself as a composite of many motifs bound together into a catechetical example for parents to use in reflecting on the history of Israel with their children.

The second narrative (Josh 3:1, 5, 8, 10, 15–16a, 17; 4:9, 11, 18–24; 5:1) is of a quite different nature. The cult dominates it. Ottosson observes that "although the choice of language and phraseology in these materials is foreign to the Deuteronomistic vocabulary, it is nevertheless clear that the segment is a Deuteronomistic composition which contains liturgical materials attached to the cult site at Gilgal."[487] We must ask, however, how a foreign vocabulary and theme become a Deuteronomistic piece of literature. That defies logic.

Cultic sanctification is the first order of business (Josh 3:5). The entire story is a narration of God's wonders (3:5b, נִפְלָאוֹת), a cultic expression reappearing in Pss 9:2, 26:7; 40:6; 72:18; 86:20; 98:1; 106:22; 111:4, altogether fifteen times in the book of Psalms and nine more in psalmic literature found in the book of Chronicles. Narrative uses of this term in Exod 3:20 and 34:10 may witness an earlier use in the

---

486   Gressmann, 140.
487   "Tradition History," 87.

traditions of Israel, but not necessarily a place in the Gilgal cultus of the magnitude imagined by Otto.[488]

The emphasis is on the priests standing in the edge of the water (Josh 3:8, 15) changing the riverbed to dry ground (3:17), and going up out of the water onto dry ground (4:18). This is an entirely different type of catechetical statement, one filled with cultic confession. The site is an explicitly named sanctuary at a specific festival time (4:19–20).

Like the first narrative, the second cannot be classified in any category of popular story or saga, since it has no arc of tension. Instead it may be classified as cultic teaching or proclamation. Several details show that the proclamation is itself a developed piece of tradition within Israel's cultic history. The catechetical piece (4:21–23) uses different Hebrew terminology for dry ground (יַבָּשָׁה) than does the narrative (חָרָבָה). The theme of crossing on dry ground has tied two originally different motifs together. The development of a catechetical statement linking the experiences at the sea with those at the river indicate a period of cultic reflection, as does the development of the catechetical statement into a personal confession involving you and we language. Nelson denies connection with any cultic legend by omitting stones, priests, and catechetical instruction from the earliest level of the materials.[489] Such radical editorial deletions rob the narrative of its basic form and structure and leaves neither a folk tale nor a cultic legend as the original format.

Harris states: "The silence of Scripture about this celebration makes it unlikely that an annual covenant renewal festival was celebrated at Gilgal, near Jericho."[490] Such argument from silence leads to admitting total ignorance about the worship of Israel. Fritz goes further in saying that one cannot prove either that Gilgal was the permanent residence of the ark nor that it was the cultic center of the tribes.[491]

Noort maintains that the cultic interpretation has no grounding, since the texts on which it is based are the product of late editorial work.[492] Again, this places a lot of weight on redaction-critical work and robs the narrative of any true *Sitz im Leben*. Thus Noort calls for future studies to look again at the question of *Sitz im Leben* and sees a supplementary model as the basis for that future work.

Hess concludes: "It is important to remember that this text is part of a ceremonial action on the part of Israel."[493] Hawk states acutely, "The account of the Jordan crossing is rendered both as an historical event and as a timeless experience that transcends the historical moment."[494] One must ask about the nature and origin of cultic ceremony and literature. Does the catechetical story, whether parental or cultic, derive from historical tradition based on historical event? Or does such material simply represent the fertile and imaginative mind of professional scriptwriters desperate for material to be used in liturgy?

The origin of the present form of the second catechism is still in question. The obvious answer is that Gilgal and its cult played the dominant role in the formation

---

488   *Mazzotfest*, esp. 133–34.
489   Nelson, 66–67.
490   Harris, 38–39.
491   Fritz, 46.
492   *Das Buch Josua*, 163.
493   Hess (1996) 98.
494   Hawk (2000) 61.

of the cultic legend adapted into the present cultic cathechetical confession. The heyday of the sanctuary at Gilgal was the reign of King Saul (cf. 1 Sam 7:16; 10:8; 11:14–15; 13:4–15; 15:12–33). Even then Gibeah, not Gilgal, was Saul's headquarters (1 Sam 10:26; 13:2, 15; 14:16; 15:34; 26:1). Gilgal was only one of many important sanctuaries (cf. 1 Sam 7:16–17).

A cultic legend of the founding of Gilgal lies at the roots of this narrative, but it cannot be isolated in its full form from the present narrative. "The text portrays the episode as a ceremonial invasion of Canaan" as seen in the need to sanctify the people repeatedly.[495] The ark of the covenant represents Yahweh's presence as it dominates the scene and leads Israel into "Yahweh's war." The ark's place in the water becomes perpetually remembered by the stones.

Otto argues against the attempts of Keller, Dus, Vogt, Maier, and Langlamet to isolate a number of early oral traditions within the material.[496] None of the proposed traditions meet form-critical criteria. This does not mean such traditions did not exist, but that signs of development within both narrative sources show that earlier material must have been at hand for both sources. The early sources were reshaped to communicate the word of God to a new time and place.

The explicit etiological nature of the stone materials reveals a development in the tradition. No set phrase marks this as etiology. Rather, the narrative climaxes with the setting up of the stones in the cultic place of Gilgal at the cultic festival time. Hess demonstrates that "until this day," the supposed marker of etiologies, "has a wide range of uses in Joshua, . . . does not reveal any consistent literary form, helps the writer apply the story to a contemporary generation, allows no conclusions concerning historicity or lack of historicity, and allows no conclusions as to when the book was written."[497]

It appears that the traditions in Josh 3–4 come from Israel's early cult before Gilgal lost its esteemed reputation among early Israelite cult places. The catechesis statements provided Gilgal worshipers and visitors an opportunity to review their history with God and to renew their promises to serve him. Surely the material provided a "script" for some type of worship drama reliving the Jordan crossing and opening celebration of the taking and settling of the land. Notations about the greatness of Joshua probably came from the ultimate editor of the history with his emphasis on Israel's need for leadership.

Structure

The final narrative does not fit the normal narrative pattern of a crisis leading to resolution. No armies appear to contest the crossing. No Israelites rebel and want to retrace steps to Egypt. The raging river gains no new victims. No foreign god rises to contest Yahweh. The narrative presents a unified people in a unified plan to achieve a unified goal with no opposition.

The final unit thus becomes a teaching narrative with a slow tempo that leads to one catechetical confession of faith after another. Israel leaves Shittim (3:1)—tying it to chap. 2—and travels towards the river before spending the night. Three days

495   Hubbard, *BBR* 11 (2001) 5.
496   *Mazzotfest*, 104–18.
497   Hess 110–11.

then pass as described in chap. 1. The officials of chap. 1 give instructions and then disappear from the scene. The people are to remain a distance from the ark. Joshua then commands ritual sanctification before the action the following day.

The people receive a promise that Yahweh will do miracles; the priests receive instructions about navigating the ark and carry out their instructions. Finally, God promises to enhance Joshua's position among the people (3:4–7). The story thus far sounds like a preparation for a holy war.

Next, Joshua instructs the priests concerning the ark and speaks to the people, assuring them of the presence of the living God among them as they enter into battle against the peoples of the Promised Land. Attention focuses again on the priests and the ark with the universal notation as ark of the covenant of the Lord of all the earth, yet another teaching moment about the nature of God. In a foreshadowing note, God instructs Joshua to select twelve men for no stated task (3:6–13).

God promises that when the feet of the priests touch the Jordan River, its water will stop. A detailed narrative describes the crossing of the Jordan, as the priests carrying the ark lead and the people follow. The Jordan stands in a heap as promised, and the priests remain standing with the ark in the middle of the riverbed until all of the people have safely crossed. Finally, the people pass over the Jordan. A summary of the event follows, featuring priests in the middle of the Jordan on dry ground and the entire people passing over. Past reflection then looks back to the people passing over the Jordan before giving the chosen twelve a duty to perform. Then the twelve whom God commanded Joshua to select are given their task—to collect and lay down twelve stones (3:14–4:3). First Yahweh explains to Joshua who then tells the twelve their task.

Joshua explains the purpose of the stones—they are to be a memorial to help the children of this generation know the miracle of the Jordan. The narrative describes how the twelve carried out the task of stone retrieval. In 4:19, the reader learns that Joshua also sets up twelve stones in the Jordan where the priests still stood. An etiological note leads to the priests exiting the Jordan, the nation having accomplished all Moses' commands. The details of the crossing are summarized, and a special additional note records the crossing of the east Jordan tribes armed for battle, another indication that the story appears to point to battle, not just river crossing.

God fulfills his promise of making Joshua great, even though, as yet, no battle has occurred. Then Joshua, following divine command, seemingly a bit belatedly, orders the priests out of the water, and they obey. When priests' feet hit dry ground, the waters return to normal flood stage. The people camp at Gilgal near Jericho, and Joshua raises up the twelve stones retrieved from the Jordan in Gilgal. Thus future generations can use the stones to remind their children about the Jordan crossing and relate it to the Reed Sea crossing, thereby remembering the salvation history Yahweh carried out with his people, a history that will come to be known by all the peoples of the earth. This becomes immediate reality as the Canaanites and Amorites lose hope in the face of Yahweh's power.

Chaps. 3–4 thus tell a simple story in a complex, infinitely slow manner to highlight Israel's belief in Yahweh as the living God of Israel, the commander of Israel's armies, the guarantor of Israel's victories, and the God of salvation and of all the earth, who was feared by all Israel's enemies. In the larger picture, the narrative joins chap. 1 with chap. 6, interrupted by the cultic interlude of chap. 5, preparing Israel emotionally, spiritually, and geographically for the battle of Jericho.

Crossing the Jordan is the narrative meat, but instructions about God form the central function of this narrative. God is the universal God of the ark of the covenant of the LORD of all the earth. God brings success to the Israelites and fear to the nations. The catecheses present the glorious deeds of God.

Thus, describing the narrative structure of chap. 3 and 4 is difficult. It is more of an extended report or a tempo-slowing transition than a literary narrative. In the larger picture Knauf finds that the two water crossings (Exod 14 and Josh 3–4) break the Hexateuch into three sections, fulfilling the three promises to Abraham in Gen 17:4–8:[498]

> Abraham's descendants become a nation (Exod 1)
> Moses' God becomes Israel's God (Exod 40)
> Israel receives its land (Josh 5–21)

Since this narrative has no arc of tension, the reader may look for a chronological report pattern, but chronology does not control the narrative either. Hall finds "dischronologized narrative" here, where thematic concerns outweigh chronological ones.[499] Chap. 3 provides a concise version, while chap. 4 elaborates the event. Joshua narratives supposedly then alternate between action and interpretation. That exact alternation can be discovered is debatable, but that theological interpretation dominates the passage is clear.

Nevertheless, Winther-Nielsen posits a chronological outline based on the macrostructure of the narrative:[500]

Staging	March to Jordan	Exposition	3:1
Episode 1	Preparatory orders	Inciting incident	3:2–5
Episode 2	Crossing orders	Mounting tension	3:6–13
Episode 3	Descent	Climax	3:14–17
Episode 4	Stone orders	Inter-peak tension	4:1–10
Episode 5	Crossing lead	Lessening tension	4:11–14
Episode 6	Ascent	Resolution	4:15–18
Closure	Arrival at Gilgal	Conclusion	4:19–24

Winther-Nielsen further explains recurring elements in the narrative:[501]

A. Josh 3:2 is a "resumptive flashback," the three days referring to "facets of preparation."

B. Crossing the river (Josh 3:16b; 4:10) makes Josh 4:10 a repetitive summary.

---

498   Knauf, 53.
499   *Conquering Character*, 60–63.
500   *Functional Discourse Grammar*, 90.
501   Ibid., 173 with n. 14.

C. The priests leaving the river (Josh 4:11, 18) reflects movement starting and its completion.

D. The selection of men to carry the stones (Josh 3:12; 4:2) involves preparation and actual selection.

E. The setting up of the stones at the camping place (Josh 4:8), in the middle of the Jordan (4:9), and at Gilgal (4:20) points to one set of stones set up by Joshua, picked up by the twelve men, and placed in the camp at Gilgal.

F. The command to teach the children (Josh 4:6–7; 4:21–24) involves immediate teaching for the twelve men and nighttime teaching for the entire congregation.

Pitkänen uses similar analysis to decide that "little, if any, inconsistency remains."[502] The complexities of the many suggested grammatical/literary readings make one wonder how early listeners or readers were able to understand such complex grammatical, syntactical, and discourse rules with a few rare and unexpected forms thrown in. Could they really distinguish at first hearing between narrative succession, repetitive summary, and literary flashback? Why does the outline ignore the two dominant forms in the text—the catechisms—as well as the confessions about Yahweh and about Joshua?

Perhaps the following structure will stimulate further discussion on this question:

I. Preparing for Yahweh's miracle
   A. Geographical preparation (3:1)
   B. Cultic preparation (3:2–5)
   C. Personnel preparation (3:6–8)
   D. Motivating preparation (3:9–11)
   E. Ritual preparation (foreshawdowing) (3:12)
   F. Predictive preparation (3:13)
II. Experiencing Yahweh's miracle
   A. Aligned for miracle march (3:14)
   B. Conditions for miracle march (3:15)
   C. Waters split for miracle march (3:16a)
   D. People take miracle march (3:16b)
   E. Priests stand firm on dry ground for miracle march (3:17)
III. Memorializing the miracle march
   A. Selecting stones for the memorial (4:1–5)
   B. Purpose of the memorial—teach your children (4:6–7)
   C. Obedient setting up of the memorial (4:8–9)
   D. Completing the miracle march (4:10–11)
   E. The unity of the miracle march and the army (4:12–13)
   F. Memorializing the leader's greatness (4:14)
IV. Reviewing the miracle march
   A. Exit of the priests and return of the flood waters (4:15–18)
   B. Chronological and geographical review of the miracle march (4:19)

502 Pitkänen, 131.

C. Stone review (4:20)

D. Cultic review connecting to salvation history (4:21–24)

E. Reaction of the nations to the miracle march (5:1)

This outline centers attention on the divine miracle, its purpose, and its continuing significance rather than on narrative form or on chronology and thus affirms the text as a catechetical tool, rather than a time-driven story.

Setting

Where and when would such a teaching task as we find in 3:1–5:1 arise in Israel? Knauf relates the twelve stone carriers to the twelve spies sent by Moses into the Promised Land.[503] He thus posits that this portion of Joshua was written in the fifth century BCE after the returned Babylonian exiles tried to restore the power of Jerusalem.

An early form of the tradition of the river crossing apparently provided a foundation legend for Gilgal, an early cultic center. The tradition was then expanded two ways in oral tradition. One tradition emphasized the ark cutting off the Jordan and the establishing of a military camp near Jericho. This tradition informed Israelite parents as they taught their children the meaning of the Jordan crossing. The second tradition became the cultic catechism for Gilgal, expanding the association of the Jordan crossing to include the Reed Sea crossing and thus encompassing Israel's salvation history. Such a narrative became the focus for Israel's teachers in a wider educational system. Interweaving the two narratives and placing them in the Joshua narratives created a story that at the literary level easily fit into the exodus narrative and the conquest of the land, especially of Jericho.

This ultimate setting involves the entire question of Israel's "holy war" or "Yahweh war" theology and its development, which has been the object of much research.[504] Certainly the full-blown schema set out by von Rad represents a rather late development, but the understanding of Yahweh as a warrior fighting for Israel with his ark as a battle emblem has deeper roots.[505] Where in that history of development the present story originated is at present impossible to pinpoint. It could have developed and served many different eras of Israel's history to remind the people of the nature of warfare with Yahweh.

The developed state of the present narrative and its relation to the sea narrative make it possible that any of the cultic centers of Israel could have taken up and reflected upon earlier material, formalizing it into the present shape. The central role of the ark might indicate that Shiloh or even Jerusalem has influenced the material.

The literary narratives did not become items for Israelite archives. Rather they functioned within the community as instruments to teach what God had done for his people. As such, they became the object of continuing study and exegesis. The community continually sought to explain what the passages meant to the new generations and in new contexts. The two narratives became one and served "less

---

503   Knauf, 59.

504   See "Studies on Warfare and Conquest in Joshua" above in Introduction.

505   *Der Heilige Krieg im alten Israel*, ATANT 20 (Zürich: Zwingli, 1951) 6–14; G. H. Jones, "'Holy War' or 'Yahweh War'?" *VT* 25 (1975) 642–58.

an etiology for a circle of stones than an etiology for the group identity of Israel."[506] This is evident at several points within the text.[507]

The editor who inserted the tradition into the larger literary context joined it to Josh 2 by means of the itinerary item of Shittim (Josh 3:1), which itself was based on a tradition that is also found in Mic 6:5 and Num 22:1; 25:1; 33:48–49. This gave geographical staging and continuity to the tradition. The editor of Joshua in its basic form took up the theological and thematic motifs of Josh 1 and gave them a further formulation here. Thus he showed the greatness of Joshua based on the divine presence begun with Moses (Josh 3:7; 4:10a, 14). The greatness of Joshua was reinforced by showing that the Transjordan tribes kept their word and obeyed his command (4:12–13). The holy war (Yahweh war) theology of Josh 2:9–11 is extended further in the concluding verses of this section (4:24–5:1). The entire composition thus has become something quite distinct from its original components. It is a narrative with a parallel theological construction. First, God promises to make Joshua great (3:1–7). Then he promises to reveal his own greatness (3:8–17). He then makes Joshua great (4:1–14) before bringing greatness to himself before all the kings (4:15–5:1). God promises victory over the remaining peoples in Canaan (3:10) and then shows the Amorites and Canaanites cowering before his power (5:1).

Comments

3:1 The problems begin in the first verse with the change from singular "Joshua rose" to the plural "they set out." Here the final editor seeks to emphasize two points. First, he shows that Joshua is the leader, who initiates all action, thereby building toward his summary statement in v 7. Second, he shows that Joshua acted immediately upon the return of the spies. When God opened the opportunity, Joshua acted. He moved immediately to the goal, the Jordan River. Here, Knauf finds the first trace of the old Moses-Joshua narrative from the seventh-century BCE that might be joined to an original part of Josh 1:1–2 and continued in 3:1; 4:13; 6:1.

Except in flood season, the Jordan has never served as a real political or communication barrier. It is much more a theological symbol defining for Israel the promise of God. The Jordan was the last obstacle Israel had to cross to escape the wilderness and enter the land of promise. Auld claims that the Jordan, even in flood stage from winter rain and melting snow, does not create a barrier to fording the river.[508] They "only increase discomfort at the fords." As so often, God intervened in a marvelous fashion to help Israel overcome its obstacles. See Harstad's excursus on the Jordan.[509]

The first verse ends with the term עבר, "cross over." This becomes the chorus for the following passage, appearing twenty-two times in this section.[510] The emphasis is not, however, on the simple fact of crossing. The emphasis in the present text is on the subjects making the crossing possible.

506 Nelson, 68.
507 See "Studies on Israelite Identity" in Introduction above.
508 Auld, 23; cf. Mitchell, *Together in the Land*, 41–43.
509 Harstad, 159–63.
510 Hertzberg, 24.

2 The שטרים, "officials," appear unexpectedly in v 2. Their inclusion may be part of the history of the tradition, but it serves an explicit theological purpose in our text by connecting it to Josh 1:10, a passage in which Joshua's command is carried out. Joshua's leadership is effective. His time schedule (1:11) works. His commands are obeyed.

3 The ark surprises us here. We are not prepared for its appearance. To this point, Joshua has not mentioned the ark. Deuteronomy describes it as the home of the Decalogue (10:1–5) and the Deuteronomic law (Deut 31:26) and as the identifying mark of the Levitical priests (Deut 10:8; 31:9, 25). The ark appeared for the first time in the Exodus account of the construction of the wilderness sanctuary (Exod 25–31; 35–40), where it is set up in the holiest place where God met Moses (Exod 25:22; 30:6; cf. Num 7:89). Later Aaron was allowed to enter the holiest place, but only on the Day of Atonement (Lev 16). Among the priests, the Kohathites were set apart to care for the ark and sanctuary (Num 3:31), particularly while the Israelites traveled (Num 4:5–15).

Exodus describes the ark as a portable gold-plated wooden chest containing holy objects and covered with a lid adorned with two cherubim. The container's lid, the mercy seat, was crafted entirely of gold and adorned by two winged cherubim. Num 10:33–35 outlines a role for the ark different from that in Deuteronomy. Here it leads Israel in her wilderness journeys and wars. Such a role is enacted only once in Numbers and then negatively (Num 14:44). Josh 3 is the first time the ark explicitly leads Israel in the biblical narratives. "The ark was the most holy physical possession of Israel since it symbolized God's very presence (Exod 25:22; Num 7:89; 10:35–36; 1 Sam 4:4)."[511] Howard points to three symbols in the ark expressing Israel's relationship with God: the Ten Commandments, Aaron's rod, and a jar of manna.

The titles given the ark in Josh 3–4 represent a sample of the many titles given the ark throughout the biblical literature. "The ark of the covenant" is primarily restricted to Deuteronomic literature (Deut 10:8; 31:9, 25, 26; Josh 6:6, 8; 8:33; Judg 20:27; 1 Sam 4:3–5; 2 Sam 15:24; 1 Kgs 3:15; 6:19; 8:1, 6; Jer 3:16) and is used later by the Chronicler. The only possible exceptions appear to be Num 10:33 and 14:44 and any traditions that lay behind Josh 3–4. To use these exceptions, however, as a basis for a wide-ranging theory of covenant theology at Gilgal, as does Otto, is going beyond what the evidence allows.[512]

Knauf insists that the best translation for *běrît* (ברית) is *Vertragskasten* or "treaty chest," and that "covenant" is not a proper translation for what he understands as a political term.[513] He places any historical reality connected to the chest in the time of Solomon, when the king led the Judean and Israelite tribal god, Yahweh, into the temple as another of the sons of the father god, El. Knauf's theory is based on the Septuagint version of 1 Kgs 8:12–13, and he maintains that all the previous narratives about the chest may well be the speculation and historical reconstruction of the biblical authors.[514]

R. Albertz comes closer to historical reality as he posits that the ark was a kind

---

511   Howard, 120.
512   *Mazzotfest*, 199–202.
513   Knauf, 56.
514   Ibid.

of military standard that guaranteed the presence of Yahweh in battle and then in Shiloh was a cultic object before being understood as part of God's throne in the Jerusalem temple.[515] P. D. Miller maintains that the ark traveled among several sanctuaries before finding a final home in Jerusalem.[516] Bruce Wells notes the debate over the ark's function as throne or footstool of God and points to international treaties that refer to depositing a treaty in a box at the feet of the deity.[517]

A second title given the ark is that of the "ark of testimony" (4:16), one that should not be dismissed through text-critical procedures as would Langlamet.[518] *DCH* offers "royal protocol, document given to king at coronation" as one definition.[519] This title is at home in priestly, cultic literature, based on the understanding that the testimony of God, that is, his law, was placed in the ark (Exod 25:16, 21; cf. 25:22; 26:33, 34; 30:6, 26; 31:7; 39:35; 40:3, 5, 21; Num 4:5; 7:89).

Finally, the ark is called "the ark of Yahweh" (e.g., Josh 3:13), a title also found frequently in the narrative of the ark in 1 Sam 4–6 and 2 Sam 6. These different titles of the ark appear to reflect different stages in its history and function within Israel. These titles provide another indication of the history of theological reflection that lies behind the present passage. Each of the narratives in our section shows a stage of that reflection. The first narrative shows the ark as the divine symbol leading the armies of Israel into battle, performing miracles, and promising victory over the enemies. In the second narrative the ark has been reduced to a secondary role, that of a cultic object carried by the priests. In this narrative the feet of the priests, the standing place of the priests, and the actions of the priests are significant. The ark has become a customary cult object that one presupposes but whose role is no longer a matter of reflection or real significance. The final editor adds nothing about the ark. His interests lie elsewhere, in the question of the leadership of Israel. Notice Pitkänen's excursus on the ark.[520]

Josh 3:3 mentions the Levitical priests for the only time in the section. The role of the Levites has been much discussed by scholarship. They play a significant role in Deuteronomic literature.[521] The inclusion of the Levites in this narrative is usually taken as a mark of Deuteronomic editing. Howard sees all legitimate priests as Levites and thus maintains that the expression Levitical priests is "redundant," perhaps an attempt to emphasize the legitimacy of the priests at this important juncture of Israelite history.[522] M. D. Rehm posits, probably correctly, "apparently by the time the book of Joshua was written, there was in Israel still the memory of a tradition that connected the Levites with the ark of the covenant and the public

515 *A History of Israelite Religion in the Old Testament Period*, vol. 1, *From the Beginnings to the End of the Monarchy*, trans. J. Bowden, OTL (Louisville: Westminster John Knox, 1994) 57.

516 *The Religion of Ancient Israel*, Library of Ancient Israel (Louisville: Westminster John Knox, 2000) 50.

517 "Exodus," in *Genesis, Exodus, Leviticus, Numbers, Deuteronomy*, Old Testament vol. 1 of *Zondervan Illustrated Bible Backgrounds Commentary* (Grand Rapids: Zondervan, 2009) 248.

518 *Gilgal*, 51–54.

519 *DCH*, 6:279.

520 Pitkänen, 144–46.

521 G. von Rad, *Studies in Deuteronomy*, trans. D. Stalker (London: SCM Press, 1953) 66–69; E. W. Nicholson, *Deuteronomy and Tradition* (Philadelphia: Fortress, 1967) 73–76; R. Abba, "Priests and Levites in Deuteronomy," *VT* 27 (1977) 257–67.

522 Howard, 121.

reading of the law in the very earliest period of the tribal league."[523] We see no reason to deny the Levites a priestly position in Israel at a very early period.

4 In v 4, the "officials" call on Israel to follow the Ark, but at a specified distance. We expect the instruction to be followed by a theological statement about why the people must remain at a distance. The ark could be explained as the symbol of divine presence. Israel would be warned to keep its distance from the danger of the divine holiness (e.g., Exod 33:17–23). But no reason is given to the people.

The problem is one of transportation. Israel is entering foreign territory. They must have a guide. That is the ark, but they must not get too close. The actual distance, however, is rather significant, the length of a pasture (Num 35:4), the eventual distance for Judaism of a Sabbath's walk. Such great distance does not derive from the need to follow the ark to find one's way.

Again we have signs of theological reflection. The concept of keeping a distance from divine holiness has entered the passage. Hess compares this 1,000 yard distance to that maintained by ancient Near Eastern armies in relationship to their king.[524] Our text thus gives two emphases to the ark. It shows God's people God's way into the Promised Land, but it also represents a royal, holy presence from which the people must keep their distance. Nelson dismisses the verse as an extraneous interruption probably from Priestly hands.[525] The verse is not extraneous. It sets the entrance into the land in an aura of holiness and divine presence.

5 The same concept of divine holiness carries over to v 5. Israel is to sanctify itself, literally, "make yourselves holy." A purification ritual prepared a person to enter the divine presence (e.g., Exod 19:22; 1 Sam 16:5; cf. Exod 22:30 [31]). Such a ritual required time, so it was often done the day before.[526] This may explain why an extra day appears in the narrative at this point, though it is not mentioned in the remainder of the narrative.

The purification is not depicted as simply cultic. It is also purification for battle, in accordance with the law of Deut 23:15 (14). When God leads his people into the land of the enemy, their battle camp must be purified. Ottosson says the language of v 5 is "obviously not Deuteronomistic," pointing to the P language of Exod 19:10,14; Num 11:18; Josh 7:13.[527] Again, Priestly language in connection with ancient battle customs seems not to have first appeared in Israel with the publication of an exilic or postexilic document. Purification for battle is a millennia-old practice connected with priests and cults. It is language used in oral rituals long before its appearance in written documents.

6 Having made all the necessary preparations, Joshua issues the long-awaited order: Forward. The priests obey immediately. The picture of Joshua the leader after Moses is thus complete. God's order to Joshua (1:2) has been carried out. Joshua is leading the people over the Jordan. Joshua has purified the camp according to the rules established by Moses (cf. Josh 1:7–8). The officials and priests have responded to Joshua's leadership. The ground is laid for the first divine word of the section.

---

523   *ABD*, 4:297. For a fuller discussion of the Levites, see T. Butler *Judges*, WBC 8 (Nashville: Nelson, 2009) 385–88.

524   *ZIBBC*, 2, 22.

525   Nelson, 60; cf. Fritz.

526   Cf. Num 11:18; Josh 7:13; cf. S. de Vries, *ZAW* 87 (1975) 65–79.

527   "Tradition History," 88.

7 The divine word is closely related to chap. 1. God promises to validate the leadership of Joshua for the people and thus to fulfill his promise to Joshua (1:5). The miracle at the Jordan becomes the basis of Joshua's claim for divine authority and divine presence. Joshua's claim to power does not rest on anything he has accomplished. It rests on what God has promised and accomplished at the Jordan, and it rests on the obedience of Joshua to the words and example of Moses. Joshua thus inherits the Mosaic presence and Mosaic office through obedience to the divine word and the Mosaic word. Joshua is the true, chosen leader after Moses and a true prophet.[528]

9–10 Joshua again takes the speaking role. Now the goal is different. All that follows points to what God is going to do while the priests are standing (v 8), the people listening (v 9), and Joshua explaining (v 10). God's actions will reveal God's power and person. The living God is in the midst of Israel. This designation for God appears in Hos 2:1; Pss 42:3; 84:3. Slightly different formulations occur in 1 Sam 17:26; Deut 5:23; Jer 10:10; 23:36; Dan 6:21, 27; 2 Kgs 19:4, 26. The acclamation "Yahweh lives" appears in Ps 18:47. Israel's God is thus contrasted to the other claimants to the title. Only Yahweh is active and alive. Only Yahweh intervenes in the affairs of his people. God's actions for his people prove his power and demonstrate the nature of his person in contrast to the nations' gods made with human hands.[529]

In our context God's actions are quite specific. He will drive out the inhabitants of the Promised Land and give it to his chosen people, Israel, as a gift. Such a gift comes at a price, though: "The act of possessing is at the same time a dispossession of the population of Canaan."[530]

The order of the peoples who inhabit the land in v 10 is distinctive within the OT.[531] The list of the peoples inhabiting the Promised Land reflects a long tradition. City-states and ethnic identities had separated inhabitants of Canaan for centuries. Israel did not march in to face only one enemy. The Amarna letters demonstrate clearly that the political and cultural makeup of Palestine was exceedingly diverse and lacking in unity long before Israel entered it. Israel faced a number of small city-states, each with its own tradition, people, culture, and god. None of these was any match for the living God of Israel.

Identifying each of the groups proves difficult.[532] Harstad maintains that the number seven used for the number of nations in the list functions as a symbol of completeness, the seven members of the list standing for all of Israel's enemies.[533] The list is related to other lists of pre-Israelite inhabitants in the land.[534] Nadav Na'aman argues that most of these groups migrated into Palestine from the north.[535]

---

528 See Hall (*Conquering Character*, 51–54) for discussion of Joshua's prophetic role.
529 Cf. H. Ringgren, "חיה," *TWAT*, 2:891–93.
530 McConville and Williams, 21.
531 Langlamet, *Gilgal*, 109–11.
532 See Harstad's excursus on "The Seven Peoples of Canaan" (175–79).
533 Ibid.
534 See Gen 10:15–18; 13:7; 15:19–21; 34:30; Exod 3:8, 17; 13:5; 23:23, 28; 33:2; 34:11; Num 13:29; Deut 7:1; 20:17; Josh 3:10; 5:1; 9:1; 11:3; 12:8; 24:11; Judg 1:4–5; 3:5; 1 Sam 27:8; 1 Kgs 9:20; 1 Chr 1:13–16; 2 Chr 8:7; Ezra 9:1; Neh 9:8.
535 "The 'Conquest of Canaan' in the Book of Joshua and in History," in *From Nomadism to Monarchy: Archaeological and Historical Aspects of Early Israel*, ed. I. Finkelstein and N. Na'aman (Jerusalem: Israel Exploration Society, 1994) 218–81.

Archaeological data cannot separately identify any of the groups in this list of "native peoples."[536]

Fritz surmises the list as totally unhistorical.[537] Mitchell suggests that to be on the list is to be a candidate for destruction and that all of the lists of peoples in the book of Joshua have the same literary function being one of those people Israel is to destroy. At the same time the lists "serve as a constant reminder of the presence of the enemy."[538] Hess correctly points out that "there was no single list that was used to construct the narratives, but that the names of these peoples have their place in the origins of the narratives."[539]

Canaanites is a broad umbrella term for the inhabitants of Syria-Palestine from the Early Bronze period onward. Egyptian texts refer to the region as Canaan. The ancestors of the Canaanites may have emigrated into the land earlier, but the evidence is not clear at this point. The name became the general term for all pre-Israelite inhabitants, though population diversity is evidenced by burial and cultic practices.[540] Numbers 13:29 appears to limit the Canaanites of Israel's early experience to the sea coast. Some research would place the Canaanites as that part of the Amorite population living in the coastal cities, especially the dominating merchant class. Genesis 26:2–3 states that Esau married Canaanite women, but the individuals named are Hittite, Hivite, and Ishmaelite.[541] On the other hand, Canaanites can be distinguished from Amorites as inhabitants of the plain (Deut 1:7; Josh 5:1; 11:3; 13:3, 4). Much of Israel's culture, language, and material culture came from the Canaanites. The book of Joshua, in distinction from Judges, Samuel, and Kings, does not list the Canaanites as a religious temptation for Israel.

The Hittites are discussed in the *Comment* at 1:4.

The Hivites apparently lived in the northern mountains near Shechem (Gen 34; Josh 11:3; Judg 3:3), near Gibeon north of Jerusalem (Josh 9:7; 11:19), up toward Lebanon and Mount Hermon (Josh 11:3; Judg 3:3; 2 Sam 24:7). Gen 36:2 locates them in Transjordan. They are unknown outside the biblical lists though Harris points to an Amarna letter in which they may be mentioned.[542] Hess associates the Hivites with the Hurrians, who were city leaders in fourteenth-century Palestine and whose names appear in Jerusalem at the same time.[543]

The Perizzites were based in the central Palestine forests near Samaria (Gen 13:7; Josh 17:15) but have left little if any mark in materials outside Scripture. Kitchen finds a Mitannian envoy with a similar Hurrian name in cuneiform and

---

536 See E. C. Hostetter, *Nations Mightier and More Numerous: The Biblical View of Palestine's Pre-Israelite Peoples*, BIBAL Dissertation Series 3 (Richland Hills, TX: BIBAL Press, 1995); T. Ishida, "The Structure and Historical Implications of the Lists of Pre-Israelite Nations," *Bib* 60 (1979) 461–90; R. Drews, "Canaanites and Philistines," *JSOT* 81 (1998) 39–61; N. P. Lemche, *The Canaanites and Their Land*, JSOTSup 110 (Sheffield: JSOT Press, 1991).

537 Fritz, 50.

538 *Together in the Land*, 125–26.

539 Hess, 102. Cf. K. G. O'Connell, "The Lists of Seven Peoples in Canaan: A Fresh Analysis," in *The Answers Lie Below: Essays in Honor of Lawrence Edmund Toombs*, ed. H. O. Thompson (Lanham, MD: University Press of America, 1984) 221–41.

540 A. E. Killebrew, *Biblical Peoples and Ethnicity*, SBLABS 9 (Atlanta: SBL, 2005) 12–13.

541 Cf. Ezek 16:3.

542 Harris, 35.

543 Hess 27.

Egyptian sources.[544] Hess locates them originally in the northern part of Syria.[545] Fritz points to Hebrew פרזי (Przi) meaning "driven from the city and living in the open fields," thus suggesting that they occupied a lower social class.[546] Hess further associates the Hivites and the Perizzites with the Hurrians, all of whom apparently migrated south from their homelands.[547]

The Girgashites may belong in the northern part of Palestine by default, other names on the list covering the remainder of the territory. They are mentioned only in the Bible. Kitchen points to a name from Ugarit and in Egyptian sources that might be akin to the Girgashites.[548]

The Amorites are well known from Mesopotamian sources, in which they are referred to as the westerners, having entered Mesopotamia from Syria in the west as nomads about 2000 BCE. The Amarna letters and Ugaritic texts refer to a kingdom of Amurru in Syria between Lebanon and Damascus. Since the material culture in Palestine evinces few distinctions, archaeologists have not been able to distinguish when various groups entered "Canaan." Num 13:29 places the Amorites in the hill country, perhaps both east and west of the Jordan. Moses defeated them in the area east of the Jordan and took over their land (Josh 2:10; 9:10; 12:1–2; 13:8–12; 13:21; 24:8), but their gods continued to threaten Israel (Josh 24:15).

The Jebusites were, according to the biblical text, the original inhabitants of Jerusalem (Josh 15:8; 18:28). No other literature refers to them.[549]

Mitchell dismisses all the nations listed in 3:10 as literary creations used to symbolize primordial opposition to Yahweh.[550] Much of his theory rests on seeking meaning for these nations during the exilic writing of the Deuteronomistic History rather than giving credence to historical traditions sourcing the Deuteronomist's materials.

Too many of the nations, however, appear in other ancient Near Eastern texts, and the various listings must reflect something besides a willy-nilly group of names pulled from a writer's hat at various times without distinctions. We may not understand the origins and meanings of each of the groups, but we must find in each of them a definite ethnic group who in one way or another met Israel in the land of Canaan.

11 Israel can know the living God is active on their behalf, driving out their enemies, because they can see his present action. He is present in the ark of the covenant. He is present as "Lord of all the earth." This divine epithet is yet another indication of the theological reflection and development within the first of the narratives used as sources for this section. The Hebrew term ארץ means either "land" or "earth" or "planet" depending upon the context. Its meaning in the present context is debated because its original context is debated. The divine epithet

544 *On the Reliability of the Old Testament*, 175.
545 Hess (1996) 27.
546 Fritz, 50. Cf. H. M. Niemann, "Das Ende des Volkes der Perizziter: Über soziale Wandlungen Israel im Spiegel einer Begriffsgruppe," *ZAW* 105 (1993) 233–57.
547 Hess (2009) 23–24.
548 *On the Reliability of the Old Testament*, 175. See M. Görg, "Hiwwiter im 13. Jahrhundert v. Chr.," *UF* 8 (1976) 53–55; R. Hess "Cultural Aspects of Onomastic Distribution in the Amarna Texts," *UF* 21 (1989) 209–16.
549 See M. Miller, "Jebus and Jerusalem: A Case of Mistaken Identity," *ZDPV* 90 (1974) 64–81.
550 *Together in the Land*, 131.

appears also in Mic 4:13; Zech 4:14; 6:5; Pss 97:5; 114:7 (the latter following the emendation of Kraus). The epithet may have been at home in the Gilgal cult.[551] Kraus suggests a Jebusite or Canaanite origin of the epithet.[552] Langlamet,[553] working on the Ugaritic parallels drawn by Maier[554] and biblical studies of E. Lipiński,[555] sought to demonstrate that material taken over from a Canaanite cult was shorn of mythical elements and reduced to the concerns of Israel, namely, the possession of the land of Canaan. Gray, on the other hand, views the phrase as a late Deuteronomistic elaboration of Deut 10:14.[556]

The earliest history of the phrase "Lord of all the earth" in Israel is not clear. It seems to reflect one of the many epithets appropriated by Israel from its Canaanite heritage and baptized into service to proclaim the greatness of Yahweh, the God of Israel. A limitation of its meaning to the land which Israel sought to possess is possible within an early framework. In the present text we may well have Israel's appropriation of the material within the Jerusalem cult, from which spring all other uses of the epithet.

We have evidence in the several divine idioms of a growth of tradition and a reflection upon the theological significance of the material. When the terminology was read and used by the late Israelite community as it was threatened and finally captured by the nations of the world, the confession of Josh 3:11 would certainly have been seen in a universalistic context, giving hope that Yahweh would once more lead Israel out of the wilderness of the east over the Jordan into the Promised Land.

12 The transition to Josh 3:12 is abrupt and unexpected, giving rise to many theories of textual disruption. In the final context, the material represents a part of the divine command preparing Israel for its great moment and testing the leadership of Joshua. It shifts the focus from the present to the future and to the storyline of the stones that will follow in chap. 4.[557] Thus it is placed in the section where Joshua is acting as a prophet and relaying to Israel the words of Yahweh (cf. v 9). As such, it points forward as foreshadowing to the action of 4:2.

Hess points to three groups acting simultaneously in the following verses—the priests, twelve chosen men, and the people.[558] "In the present form of the text, this isolated command creates suspense and signals that there will be more to this story than the report of a miraculous crossing."[559] As Howard sees the evidence, "it shows a skilled author at work, who will repeat himself at different points or suspend his story and then resume it, in the interests of weaving an ordered, intricate story."[560]

13–14 Josh 3:13 introduces a complicated Hebrew sentence structure. It makes all the action described in vv 13–15 contemporary with and subordinate to the

551　H.-J. Kraus, *Psalmen*, 2nd ed., BKAT 15 (Neukirchen-Vluyn: Neukirchener Verlag, 1961) 2:781; Otto, *Mazzotfest*, 150, 187–88.

552　*Psalmen*, 1:199.

553　*Gilgal*, 112–15.

554　*Ladeheiligtum*.

555　*La royauté de Yahwé dans la poésie et le culte de l'ancien Israël* (Brussels: Paleis der Academiën, 1965) 173–275.

556　Gray, 62.

557　Hess (2000) 65.

558　Hess (1996) 103.

559　Nelson, 61.

560　Howard, 128.

great action of v 16, the formation of a great heap of waters. "The syntax of 3:14–17 and 4:18 gives descriptive force to a miraculous situation. It is a dramatic pause of the sort that occurs at peak climaxes. All dialogue is faded out, and action is described by turbulent predicate functions."[561]

The waters, the Jordan and the waters going down to the sea are mentioned ten times in 3:1–5:1. They are the center of attention. Everything and everyone else is subordinate to the miracle at the waters. Whereas the opening section of the chapter centers on the person and office of Joshua, the final verses center on the words and actions of Yahweh for Israel at the waters. The living God, the Lord of all the earth, moves before his people and makes good his claims to universal dominion. The author intricately prepares for this climactic moment and then piles up language at the critical moment to highlight the miracle.[562]

15 The miracle of the Jordan is heightened in the last half of v 15. At many seasons of the year, the Jordan is a mere trickle of water that could easily be forded. During the spring harvest, melting snows from the northern mountains flood the riverbed. Only resulting landslides or divine miracles allow crossing at this time of year (cf. 4:19). Harstad admonishes scholars not to spend time "speculating on what the Scriptures do not say at the expense of believing and being edified by what they do say."[563]

16–17 The complex syntax of v 16 slows the action to a snail's pace. "The actions of the people and the priests and the state of the Jordan are all syntactically subordinated to form the temporal background for the real center of narrative interest, the cessation of the water."[564] The tradition has tried to locate the miracle quite exactly in 3:16, though this has not always resulted in a clear understanding even for the early versions (see *Notes*, 3:16.a-a). The MT text states the names of two cities and two names for what we call the Dead Sea. The first city is Adam, associated by scholarship with Tell ed-Dāmiyeh, on the eastern shore of the Jordan, a mile south of the junction of the Jordan with the Jabbok and about eighteen miles south of Jericho. The location of the second city, Zarethan, is greatly disputed. Recent excavations at Tell es-Sa'idiyeh have not confirmed or denied Glueck's identification[565] with Zarethan.[566] Thus some like Fritz follow Aharoni and point to Tell Umm Hamid, three miles north of Adam as the likely location of Zarethan.[567] Hess uses the location of Adam to estimate that the Jordan flooding involved 29 percent of the Jordan Valley.[568]

The early tradition appears to have connected the miracle with Jericho, rather than with Gilgal (3:16). Again we can see a development within the tradition. This may indicate that the narrative of the conquest of Jericho was later taken up in a Gilgal cultic celebration. Israel is here identified as a גוֹי, "a nation." In the late history of Israel and Judaism, the word took on a negative character and was applied only

561 Winther-Nielsen, *Functional Discourse Grammar*, 165.
562 See Howard, 130–31.
563 Harstad, 186.
564 Nelson, 62.
565 "Three Israelite Towns in the Jordan Valley: Zarethan, Succoth, Zaphon," *BASOR* 90 (1943) 2–23.
566 J. B. Pritchard, "Tell es-Sa'idiyeh," *EAEHL* 4 (1978) 1028.
567 Fritz, 48. See R. Hess "*adam* as 'Skin' and 'Earth,'" *TynBul* 39 (1988) 148; H. O. Thompson, *ABD*, 6:1041–43; J. N. Tubb, *ABD*, 5:900–904.
568 Hess (2009) 25.

to the foreign nations. The biblical witness, however, shows that Israel knew herself as one nation among many, a status she owed to the greatness of her God (cf. Exod 19:6; Gen 12:2; Deut 32:8–9).[569] Our text thus testifies that the Israel that crossed the Jordan under Joshua was a unified nation. Israel was the גוי that God had promised they would become. "For Israel crossing the Jordan symbolized the means to enter the 'new world' of God's promises."[570] "They ceased to be a wandering band and became a landed people who would have to be dealt with as a political entity."[571]

4:1–3 Repeating the last line of chap. 3 freezes the ark's action in midstream to emphasize the simultaneous action of lifting the stones (4:1–11). Narrative action unfreezes with the resumptive repetition in 4:10–11.[572] The tradition presupposes Israel as a unified league of twelve tribes as distinguished from the seven divergent people now occupying the land (3:10) and interprets the stone monument in this light. Hall suggests the stones represent for the writer "a theological concern for enduring memory."[573] Sadly, too soon Israel lost that enduring memory (Judg 2:6–10).

The twelve selected men take the stones from the midst of the Jordan, the standing place of the priests. Josh 3:8, 15 emphasize the edge of the waters as the standing place of the priests. Only Josh 3:17 places them in the middle of the Jordan. In Josh 4:9 the stones are set up in the middle of the Jordan. Again, a development of and reflection upon the tradition is seen. The original tradition appears to associate the priests with the edge of the waters, emphasizing the miracle that ensued. Another tradition, though, associates the stones with the middle of the waters, either as the place of their collection or of their deposit. Combining the traditions enhances the role of the priests. The memorial stones not only memorialize what Yahweh has done; they also show precisely where the sacred priests stood. The exact location of the stones remains obscure in 4:1–3, designated only as the camping place for the night.

4–5 Joshua responds immediately to the divine command and proves himself an obedient leader. But he is something more. By setting up the stones and establishing the catechesis for future generations of children, Joshua functions as an interpreter of the divine will and the founder of later teaching practice, just as Moses had been.

6–7 The explanation for the taking of the stones from the Jordan is given in the form of an answer to a question posed by children to their parents:[574]

> Twice in two embedded instructions, Joshua teaches the people how to explain events to their children. The first occurs in an address to the twelve men in the presence of all the people . . . (4:6–7), the second in a devotional at the night camp in the closure (4:21–24). Both concern the twelve stones to be carried to Gilgal (4:20) as . . . "a sign among you" (4:6a).

This form of discourse appears also in Exod 12:26–27; 13:14–15; Deut 6:20–21; Josh 4:21–23, always in connection with cultic materials with which a child would

---

569   R. E. Clements, "גוי," *TWAT,* 1:965–73.
570   Hess (1996) 109.
571   Creach, 52.
572   Nelson, 65.
573   *Conquering Character,* 63–64.
574   Winther-Nielsen, *Functional Discourse Grammar,* 187.

not be familiar.[575] The form represents the cultic practice of teaching adults specific formulas they were to teach their children concerning the meaning of God's history with his people.[576] Joshua thus institutes the later practice of the priests, who must look to him as their founding father. The teaching itself, however, is confined strictly to the Jordan event interpreted as a miracle of God without mention of priests.

8 The people follow their leader precisely, doing just what Joshua commanded in v 2. This action is the theological point of the text. God has raised up a leader who listens to the divine word and to whom the people listen obediently.

9 The stones spoken of in this verse cause the reader to ponder. How are they related to the twelve stones of v 7? Saydon chooses to omit the reference to the stones in this verse as unnecessary.[577] Boling maintains that they represent a platform for the priests to stand on.[578] Knauf sees the stones in v 9 as a version of the foundation legend of Gilgal for times in which the sanctuary did not actually exist.[579]

Hess points to the repetitive style of the section on the stones and the unlikelihood of introducing a new subject here.[580] He thus argues for only one set of stones, translating v 9: "Joshua set up the twelve stones that had been in the middle of the Jordan." Similarly, Howard posits only one set of stones, maintaining that v 9 is a "parenthetical aside, telling us Joshua himself had set up the stones initially. . . . [T]he twelve men . . . were taking up the twelve stones that Joshua had set down previously."[581] Winther-Nielsen sees v 9 as the "major interpretative crux of the story" and asks, "Why would a later scribe want to add them (the second set of stones) in the first place?"[582]

V 9 does represent a disjunctive clause since it does not begin in the waw plus verb form of the consecutive clauses. Such a clause either interrupts the narrative sequence in either a flashback or an explanation or expansion of v 8. The verb הֵקִים may well indicate past perfect.[583] This would indicate that Joshua had set up the particular stones and made them easy to recognize for the twelve men to pick up and carry. Such an interpretation certainly removes a clumsy editor from the scene, takes invisible stones in the river out of play, and emphasizes the role of Joshua and the importance he placed on the stones. To get to this result, Winther-Nielsen offers a "very turbulent grammar. Yet the discourse context seems to favor it." He then sets up another exception to his own grammatical rules, creating "a very unusual discontinuous . . . construction."[584]

The etiological formula "until this day" appears here for the first time in the book of Joshua (Josh 4:9; 5:9; 7:26; 8:28–29; 9:27; 13:13; 14:14; 15:63; 16:10; 22:3; 23:8–9.)[585] Geoghegan finds direct connections here in Josh 4:9 to the southern part of the country, to Levitical priests, the Ark of the Covenant, all "central

---

575 Soggin, *VT* 10 (1960) 341–47.
576 See Otto, *Mazzotfest*, 131–33.
577 *CBQ* 12 (1950) 203.
578 Boling, 175. See Creach (47) for a defense of two groups of stones.
579 Knauf, 60.
580 Hess (1996) 109.
581 Howard, 136.
582 *Functional Discourse Grammar*, 179–81.
583 Cf. Boling, 174.
584 *Functional Discourse Grammar*, 180–81.
585 See the Introduction for various viewpoints on this formula.

concerns for Dtr."[586] One must question whether the preponderance of appearances of the formula in Joshua, Judges, and 1 Samuel does not point to early usage of the formula in the sources rather than in the latest layer of unified editing. One must also ask why one Dtr editor used so many different forms of the formula rather than mechanically introducing the same form in each instance.

10–11 These verses make it specifically clear that the people have crossed the Jordan, bringing to a climax the narrative of Josh 3:17–4:1. Tradition-history suggests the material may have referred originally to the crossing by the priests, who are the subjects of the opening disjunctive clause in v 10. As theological material, the verse climaxes all that has gone before. "This retelling of the crossing is not the result of clumsy editing but rather an expansion which develops the significance of the event."[587]

Joshua had commanded the priests to stand in the water while the people crossed (Josh 3:8). The command is obeyed in Josh 4:10. The Israelites obeyed what God commanded their leader, which corresponded precisely to what Moses had commanded him. Schäfer-Lichtenberger maintains that in v 10, Joshua's leadership is firmly grounded in the authority of Moses.[588] That is, Joshua remains the example of the leader after Moses, not of a leader per se.

When Israel followed the Mosaic commandment mediated through their God-given leader, Israel experienced the miraculous leadership of God. This was mediated through the ark, the tangible symbol of divine presence.

12 A "flashback" interrupts the action in vv 12–13.[589] Quite unexpectedly the tradition from Josh 1:12–18 appears. Again the word of Joshua based on the word of Moses is totally obeyed (cf. 1:13). The Transjordan tribes keep their promise (1:16–18), thereby preserving the unity of Israel. The authority of Joshua is proven. Knauf isolates vv 12–13 as the only verses that use military language rather than that of cultic procession to describe the Jordan crossing.[590]

13 Knauf recognizes here a fragment of an old (seventh-century) Exodus-Joshua narrative which in his view may have known the Song of Deborah.[591]

V 13 appears to summarize the preceding verses, but to what extent? Does it relate only to v 12 and the Transjordan tribes? Its vocabulary is closely related to that of Num 32, particularly v 27, another tradition of the Transjordan tribes, but it is not related to the vocabulary of Josh 4:12.[592] If v 13 relates only to v 12, then it simply repeats the information of v 12. The disjunctive sentence structure breaking the series of imperfect consecutives may indicate that v 13 forms the conclusion of the entire preceding narrative. The verse would thus indicate that the Israelite army marched across the Jordan forty thousand strong to fight Jericho, which would point forward to the narratives of chap. 5. Thus, the verse could represent the original conclusion of an early tradition of the crossing of the Jordan and be a conclusion to the first narrative source of this chapter. In the present context, how-

---

586 *Time, Place, and Purpose,* 120–122.
587 Hess (2000) 71.
588 *Josua und Salomo,* 212.
589 Nelson, 66.
590 Knauf, 61.
591 Ibid.
592 See Langlamet, *Gilgal,* 136–37.

ever, v 13 underlines the obedience of Israel preparing to fight the wars of Yahweh. "Here was not merely a religious ritual empty of significance. The crossing was the first part of the movement to occupy Canaan, and this was done with the necessary appearance of military preparedness."[593]

Hubbard finds the "forty thousand" to be a "round number meaning huge army (Judg 5:8; 2 Sam 10:18//1 Chron 19:18; 1 Kings 4:26; 1 Chron 12:36)."[594] Hess points out that the Hebrew *'lep* (אלף), usually translated a thousand, can also refer to a unit or squad of soldiers with no specific number.[595]

14 V 14 concludes and summarizes the first half of the chapter. The divine command (vv 1–3) has resulted in perfect obedience by Joshua (vv 4–7) and the people. The actions of Joshua (v 9), the priests (v 10a), and the people (v 10b) have brought forth the sign of the divine presence (v 11). Finally, the tribes least affected by the action have demonstrated their loyalty to Joshua and Moses (v 12). Israel is prepared to fight for their God-given land (v 13).

The great event of the Jordan under the leadership of Joshua has the same ending as the great event at the sea under the leadership of Moses (Exod 14:31). The people hold in awe the divinely appointed leader. Joshua has become the new Moses.[596] The promise of 3:7 is realized. But the narrator "is careful to elevate Joshua in a manner that discourages hero worship," by featuring the priests and the ark.[597] The story does not end here, however. Only half the purpose has been realized. The greatness of Yahweh must be underlined.

15–18 Again the divine command is followed by human command. The result is human obedience (v 18a), but now this is only expressed in a temporal clause. The major result is miracle (v 18b), the waters returning to their place. The situation of Josh 3:15b is restored. God's action, rather than human obedience, is again the center of focus. All this occurs outside strict chronological consistency, the action belonging before v 11,[598] in what Hubbard sees as a "flashback."[599] Hess maintains that "religiously, this action places the entire crossing in the context of a divinely ordained ceremony."[600] In a unique blending of forms and content, worship and warfare come together. כִּתְמוֹל, "as always," points back to מִתְּמוֹל, "before," in Josh 3:4, suggesting the uniqueness of the crossing of the Jordan. The people experienced something they had never witnessed before, while the river returned to what it always had been. This is "the end of the wonder" and the "return to normal existence."[601]

19–20 The cultic, priestly interest reaches its climax in v 19. The date formulation given in v 20 places the event in April, the beginning of the year according to the Babylonian calendar and in accordance with the traditional observance of the exodus passover ritual in Exod 12, the tenth day being the day for selection of

---

593 Hess (1996) 113.
594 Hubbard, 159.
595 Hess (2009) 27.
596 Cf. D. J. McCarthy, "The Theology of Leadership in Joshua 1–9," *Bib* 52 (1971) 175.
597 Hess (2010) 49.
598 Howard, 140. See also for the "ark of the testimony" language.
599 Hubbard, 159.
600 Hess (1996) 114.
601 Hess (2000) 72.

lambs (Exod 12:3).[602] Jordan crossing and sea crossing thus converge in the cultic calendar. The cultic site also becomes clear.

Gilgal is mentioned for the first time in the book of Joshua, being located even here in reference to Jericho.[603] Knauf maintains that Gilgal was never a settlement but only an ancient, beloved sanctuary whose location is no longer known.[604] Hess states that Gilgal was simply a temporary camp that would have left no remains for excavators.[605]

The stones become a cultic memorial to the deeds of God who led Israel across the Jordan to Gilgal. Ottosson sees a "censored etiology" in these verses, since they lack the traditional marker "until this day."[606] The story of the Jordan crossing has been used to authorize the cult practices of Gilgal.

21–23 The cultic teaching form reappears (see Josh 4:6–7). The emphasis is no longer the cutting off of the waters before the ark (Josh 3:2–4, 6–7, 9, 11–14, 16b; 4:1–8, 10, 12–17). Now the basic theme is the appearance of dry ground allowing Israel to pass over the river (Josh 3:1, 5, 8, 10, 15–16a, 17; 4:9, 11, 18–24; 5:1.) This catechetical statement includes reference to the crossing of the sea, providing a basis for scholars to make a comparison with the exodus event.[607] The Reed Sea reference is now the climax of the second narrative, but its distinctive vocabulary shows that it had a separate origin from the Jordan-crossing tradition. A parallel vocabulary distinction for dry land also appears in the crossing-of-the-sea tradition (Exod 14–15). There the early narrative tradition uses חרב, while the cultic, Priestly tradition uses יבשׁ to describe the drying up of the sea.

The present context uses the drying-of-the-waters motif to underline the mighty acts of God for Israel. Hubbard sees echoes of a cultic ceremony here linking back to the exodus, "making the experience of his audience as crucial as that of their ancestors."[608] Knauf shows that the narrative of the wilderness wandering ends here and a new theme—the conquest—begins.[609]

The text uses an interesting device to define Israel. "You (pl.)"—the sons—are the Israel who crossed the Jordan. "We"—the fathers—are the Israel who crossed the sea. Thus time is stopped; geographical space is ignored, creating a single history; and divergent generations are connected.[610] Hubbard goes further to claim that the reference to the nations ("all the peoples of the earth") hints at Yahweh wanting to relax the ban and invite the nations, like Rahab and the Gibbeonites, to join in his salvation.

Hubbard may be stretching the text a bit much in seeking to align it to modern sensitivities, but the message demonstrates the nation's uncertainty. Liturgical teaching dramatizes the event and transforms it into personal confession and involvement. The church has participated similarly in singing together, "Were you there when they crucified my Lord?" Such cultic language brings each generation

---

602   Cf. D. J. A. Clines, "New Year," *IDBSup*, 625–29.
603   See C. U. Wolf. "The Location of Gilgal," *BR* 11 (1966) 42–51.
604   Knauf, 57.
605   Hess (2009) 28.
606   "Tradition History," 89.
607   See A. R. Hulst, *OtSt* 14 (1965) 162–88; R. Schmid, *TZ* 21 (1965) 260–68.
608   Hubbard, 161–62.
609   Knauf, 61.
610   Hubbard, *BBR* 11 (2001) 9.

back to the point where its faith originated and forces it to relate personally to the God of the beginnings. In this the greatness of God is recognized not just by Israel, but also by all the peoples of the earth (compare 5:1).

4:24–5:1 The final two verses of the section present grammatical problems. The sentence that begins in Josh 4:22 is continued by a temporal clause in 4:23 and a result clause in 4:24. This demonstrates the reflection of later generations on the meaning of the cultic teaching. The content of the result clause is precisely the editorial teaching concerning holy war or Yahweh war. The teaching is aimed on the surface level to two audiences—Israel and the nations. It seeks to demonstrate to all the enemies of Israel that Israel's God controls the military power to win any battle for Israel and thus is truly Lord of all the earth. By their reaction the nations should then teach Israel to stand in worshipful awe of their God forever, no matter what happens. The material is not written and given to the nations. It is written and taught only to Israel to bring the people of Israel to reflect upon their history and to respond with reverence and awe to Yahweh, the God who has brought the nations to their knees. The knowledge about God results not in pride and dogmatism but in worship and service.

The final verse of the section demonstrates that God had done his part. "Tranquility rules and gives the Israelites an opportunity for preparation of activities in the land."[611] The nations whom Israel faced in the Promised Land hear the report of Yahweh's action and fear for their lives, unable to react in any way. They have lost all spirit. Before Israel has fought a single battle, the entire land is theirs for the taking. "Rahab's analysis proves true."[612] This is the message of the book of Joshua (cf. the "giving" motif of chap. 1; the confession of 2:9–11). Later generations of Israelites heard the story and applied the message to their own day. If God gave his people the land once, he could do it again, if the people have leaders and obedience as in the day of Joshua.

Explanation

The experience at the Jordan River proved theologically fruitful to many generations of Israelites. Two cultic sources eventually expressed Israel's understanding of what the miracle at the river had meant and what it continued to mean to the worshiping community. These sources incorporated many Israelite traditions to express the total meaning of the event. The sources were in turn incorporated into an even greater literary context to continue proclaiming the meaning of the Jordan event centuries after the event itself. "The narrative as a whole focuses on worship and wonder."[613]

"Several levels of proclamation occur simultaneously. The narrative intends to exalt Joshua as model and hero (v. 14), to remind readers of Yahweh's saving deeds in giving the land, to hold up the Jordan crossing as foundational to Israel's identity and faith, and to encourage obedience and fidelity to Yahweh."[614]

The central focus of both sources and the final biblical context is the action of God and its meaning for Israel. The presence of God, symbolized by the ark, cut

---

611 Winther-Nielsen, *Functional Discourse Grammar*, 165.
612 Harris, 40.
613 Hess (2010) 43.
614 Nelson, 67.

off the waters and allowed Israel to enter the Promised Land. The people crossed the Jordan on dry land. It was another exodus miracle. The God of the exodus was also the God of the land. With the crossing complete, "now the history of Israel in the land under the authority of the book of the law (Deut 31:9–13) can begin."[615]

The miracle of the Jordan asserts that Yahweh is a living God and has defeated Baal at the height of the presence of his power. Yahweh's life and presence among his people are seen not in the recurring annual cycles of nature, but in the fulfillment of prophecy. Although the ark serves as a symbol of Yahweh's presence, his power and life are proven in the miracle. The miracle defines Yahweh not just as Lord, but as Lord of all the earth. Universal and local, Yahweh exerts his sovereignty over Egypt and its deities in the plagues, over the sea in the exodus, and over the land of Canaan and its deity Baal in the crossing of the Jordan.[616]

"The ideological focus is on Israel's national identity and their claim to the land. Both center on Yahweh's act. . . . Crossing the Jordan means to begin to take control of the land Yahweh is giving."[617] In the land of Egypt, a great international power, and in the land of the numerous kingdoms vying for possession of Israel's promised territory, Yahweh proved himself to be Lord of all the earth. No matter where the Israelites found themselves, they could depend on their God to deliver them. God controls the natural powers of the universe. He can control any enemy facing Israel.

One qualification must be made. Israel must see themselves as the people of Yahweh. The people of God must realize that God does not help them automatically. God helps them when they obey his commands given through his leader. The final context makes certain of these commands important. First, Israel must follow the symbol of divine presence among them. Only God could lead the way Israel was to walk. Second, the people of Israel must sanctify themselves, for the holy God did miracles only for a holy, purified people. And third, they must remember their tradition and devise means to teach it to their children. Israel was responsible that the reputation of God live on. God did not do miracles of the proportion of the exodus or the Jordan in every generation. Yet every generation could devise teaching and ritual situations in which Israel could experience anew what God had done for them.

For the people who followed, sanctified, remembered, and taught, God would raise up leaders in the Mosaic tradition who would teach the people the things to do to be the people of God. Joshua was the unique successor to Moses showing, under Torah and with obedience, Israel could succeed in the land as a nation without a king. When miracle was needed again, God could prove that his hand was still strong, that he could still bring fear upon the nations, and that he was still worthy of the reverential awe of his people.

Such teaching may trouble the contemporary people of God. We in Jesus Christ have been stripped of national identity. We do not look for a warrior God to freeze our enemies with fear and give us a land. Our hero won the victory through self-giving and suffering. Still, we can learn from the story of the Jordan the nature of

---

615   Nelson, 60.
616   See Thigpen, *TJ* NS 27 (2006) 252.
617   Nelson, 59.

the people of God. Whatever the historical setting, the people of God still face a life confronted with opposition and are tempted to find other gods who can please for the moment. We are called again to confess that there is only one Lord of all the earth. We need not seek out new gods. We do need to renew our quest for the identity God would give us as his people and for the leaders God raises up to lead his people in the way of Moses and in the way of Jesus through our modern difficulties.

D. Cultically Correct for Conquest (5:2–15)

Bibliography

Abegg, M., Jr., P. Flint, and E. Ulrich. *The Dead Sea Scrolls Bible.* San Francisco: Harper San Francisco, 1999. **Abel, F. M.** "L'apparition du chef de l'armée de Yahveh à Josué (Jos. V, 13–15)." In *Miscellanea Biblica et Orientalia R. P. Athanasio Miller, O.S.B., Completis LXX Annis, Oblata.* SA 27–28. Rome: Herder, 1951. 109–13. **Alexander, T. D.** "The Passover Sacrifice." In *Sacrifice in the Bible.* Grand Rapids: Baker, 1995. 1–24. **Arenhoevel, D.** "Ursprung und Bedeutung der Beschneidung." *Wort und Antwort* 14 (1973) 167–72. **Auerbach, E.** "Die Feste im Alten Israel." *VT* 8 (1958) 1–5. **Auld, A. G.** "Joshua: The Hebrew and Greek Texts." In *Studies in the Historical Books of the Old Testament.* VTSup 30. Leiden: Brill, 1979. 1–14. ———. "Le texte hébreu et le texte grec de Josué: Une comparaison à partir du chapitre 5." Tr. P. Rolin. *FV* 97 (1998) 67–78. **Balzaretti, C.** "L'angelo del censimento (1 Cr 21:15–16)." *RivB* 54 (2006) 29–44. **Bar-On, S.** "Zur literarkritischen Analyse von Ex 12,21–27." *ZAW* 107 (1995) 18–30. **Bergant, D.** "An Anthropological Approach to Biblical Interpretation: The Passover Supper in Exodus 12:1–20 as a Case Study." *Semeia* 67 (1994) 43–62. **Bernat, D. A.** *Sign of the Covenant: Circumcision in the Priestly Tradition.* Ancient Israel and Its Literature 3. Atlanta: Society of Biblical Literature, 2009. **Bieberstein, K.** *Josua, Jordan, Jericho: Archäologie, Geschichte und Theologie der Landnahmeerzählung Josua 1–6.* OBO 143. Göttingen: Vandenhoeck & Ruprecht, 1995. **Blaschke, A.** *Beschneidung: Zeugnisse der Bibel und verwandter Texte.* Texte und Arbeiten zum neutestamentlichen Zeitalter 28. Tübingen: Francke, 1998. **Blum, E.** "Beschneidung und Pessach in Kanaan: Beobachtungen und Mutmassungen zu Jos 5." In *Freiheit und Recht: Festschrift für Frank Crüsemann zum 65. Geburtstag.* Ed. C. Hardmeier, R. Kessler, and A. Ruwe. Gütersloh: Kaiser; Gütersloher, 2003. 292–322 cited here from *Textgestalt und Komposition.* FAT 69. Tübingen: Mohr Siebeck, 2010. 219–38. **Brekelmans, C.** "Joshua v 10–12: Another Approach." In *New Avenues in the Study of the Old Testament: A Collection of Old Testament Studies Published on the Occasion of the Fiftieth Anniversary of the Oudtestamentisch Werkgezelshap and the Retirement of Prof. Dr. M. J. Mulder.* Ed. A. S. van der Woude. OTS 25. Leiden: Brill, 1989. 89–95. **Briend, J.** "La Pâque Israèlite." *MdB* 43 (1986) 4–15. ———. "The Sources of the Deuteronomic History: Research on Joshua 1–12." In *Israel Constructs Its History: Deuteronomistic Historiography in Recent Research.* Ed. A. de Pury, T. Römer, and J.-D. Macchi, JSOTSup 306. Sheffield: Sheffield Academic, 2000. 360–86. Orginally published as "Les Sources de L'Histoire deuteronomique recherches sur Jos 1–12," in *Israël construit son histoire: L'historiograhie deutéronomiste à la lumière des recherches récentes,* ed. A. de Pury, T. Römer, and J.-D. Macchi, MdB 34 (Geneva: Labor et Fides, 1996). **Collins, J. J.** "A Symbol of Otherness: Circumcision and Salvation in the First Century." In *'To See Ourselves as Others See Us': Christians, Jews and 'Others' in Late Antiquity.* Ed. J. Neusner and E. S. Frerichs. Chico, CA: Scholars Press, 1985. 163–86. **Cooper, A., and B. R. Goldstein.** "Exodus and *Massôt* in History and Tradition." *Maarav* 8 (1992) 15–37. **Deurloo, K. A.** "Om Pesach te kunnen vieren in het land (Joz.

5, 2–9).” In *Verkenningen in een Stroomgebied*. FS M. A. Beek, ed. M. Boertien et al. Amsterdam: University of Amsterdam, 1974. 41–50. **Diebner, B. J.** “Das Mazzen-Passa zu Gilgal.” *DBAT* 17 (1983) 123–25. **Elder, W. H.** “The Passover.” *RevExp* 74 (1977) 511–22. **Fahr, H., and U. Gleßmer.** *Jordandurchzug und Beschneidung als Zurechtweisung in einem Targum zu Josua 5 (Edition des MS T.-S. B 13,12)*. Orientalia Biblica et Christiana 3. Glückstadt: Augustin, 1991. **Finkel, J.** “The Case of the Repeated Circumcision of Josh. 5, 2–7: An Historical and Comparative Study.” In *Annals of the Jewish Academy of Arts and Sciences*. New York: MSS Information, 1974. 177–213. **Fox, M. V.** “The Sign of the Covenant: Circumcision in the Light of the Priestly *'oth* Etiologies.” *RB* 81 (1974) 537–96. **Füglister, N.** *Die Heilsbedeutung des Pascha*. SANT 8. Munich: Kösel, 1963. 27–28, 67, 87, 112, 202, 216, 244. **Geoghegan, J. C.** “The ‘Biblical’ Origins of Passover.” In *Sacred History, Sacred Literature: Essays on Ancient Israel, the Bible, and Religion in Honor of R. E. Friedman on His Sixtieth Birthday*. Winona Lake, IN: Eisenbrauns, 2008. 147–62. **George, A.** “Les récits de Gilgal en Josué (5:2–15).” In *Recherche sur l’étude des Traditions: Mémorial J. Chaine*. BFCTL 5. Lyon: Facultés Catholiques, 1950. 169–86. **Gertz, J. C.** “Die Passa-Massot-Ordnung im deuteronomischen Festkalender.” In *Das Deuteronomium und seine Querbeziehungen*. Ed. T. Veijola. Göttingen: Vandenhoeck & Ruprecht, 1996. 66–67. **Gooding, D. W.** “Traditions of Interpretation of the Circumcision at Gilgal.” In *Proceedings of the Sixth World Congress of Jewish Studies I*. Ed. A. Shinan. Jerusalem: World Union of Jewish Studies, 1977. 149–64. **Gradwohl, R.** “Der ‘Hügel der Vorhäute’ (Josua V,3).” *VT* 26 (1976) 235–40. **Greenspoon, L.** “The Book of Joshua—Part 1: Texts and Versions.” *CBR* 3 (2005) 229–61 (with bibliography). **Gressman, H.** *Die Anfänge Israels*. Göttingen: Vandenhoeck & Ruprecht, 1922. 140–41, 143–44. **Grünwaldt, K.** *Exil und Identität: Beschneidung, Passa, und Sabbat in der Priesterschrift*. BBB 85. Frankfurt am Main: Hain, 1992. **Guggisberg, F.** “Die Gestalt des Mal’ak Jahwe im Alten Testament.” Dissertation, Neuenburg, 1979. **Gunkel, H.** “Über die Beschneidung im Alten Testament.” *APF* 2 (1903) 13–21. **Haag, H.** *Vom alten zum neuen Pascha: Geschichte und Theologie des Osterfestes*. SBS 49. Stuttgart: KBW, 1971. 67–71. **Halbe, J.** “Erwägungen zum Ursprung und Wesen des Massotfestes.” *ZAW* 87 (1975) 324–46. ———. “Passa-Massot im deuteronomischen Festkalender.” *ZAW* 87 (1975) 148–51. **Hall, S. L.** *Conquering Character: The Characterization of Joshua in Joshua 1–11*. New York: T&T Clark, 2010. **Hermisson, H. J.** *Sprache und Ritus im altisraelitischen Kult*. WMANT 19. Neukirchen-Vluyn: Neukirchener Verlag, 1965. 66–67. **Hertog, G. C.** “Jos 5,4–6 in der griechischen Übersetzung.” ZAW 110 (1998) 601–05, **Hollenberg, J.** *Der Charakter der alexandrinischen Übersetzung des Buches Josua und ih textkritischer Werth*. Moers: Eckner, 1876. **Holman, J.** “An Approach from biblical theology of the Passover: a critical appraisal of its Old Testament aspects.” In *Christian feast and festival: the dynamics of western liturgy and culture*. Ed. L. van Tongeren. Leuven: Peeters, 2001. 167–84. **Hölscher, G.** *Geschichtsschreibung in Israel*. Lund: Gleerup, 1952. 338–39. **Humbert, P.** *La ‘terou'a’: Analyse d’un rite biblique*. Neuchâtel: Secrétariat de l’Université, 1946. **Isaac, E.** “Circumcision as a Covenant Rite.” *Anthropos* 59 (1964) 444–56. **Jacob, E.** “Une théophanie mystérieuse: Josué 5,13–15.” In *Ce Dieu qui vient: Mélanges offerts à Bernard Renaud*. Ed. R. Kuntzmann. Paris: Cerf, 1995. 131–35. **Jeremias, J.** *Theophanie: Die Geschichte einer alttestamentlichen Gattung*. WMANT 10. Neukirchen-Vluyn: Neukirchener Verlag, 1965. **Jóder Estrella, C.** “Jos 5,13–15: ensayo sobre la coherencia textual.” *Estudios bíblicos* 59 (2001) 243–279. **Johnstone, W.** “The Two Theological Versions of the Passover Pericope in Exodus.” In *Text as Pretext*. Sheffield: JSOT Press, 1992. 160–78. **Keel, O.** “Erwägungen zum Sitz im Leben des vormosaischen Pascha und zur Etymologie von פסח.” *ZAW* 84 (1972) 414–34. ———. *Wirkmächtige Siegeszeichen im Alten Testament*. OBO 5. Freiburg: Universitätsverlag, 1974. 82–88. **Keller, C. A.** “Über einige alttestamentliche Heiligtumslegenden II.” *ZAW* 68 (1956) 85–97. **King, P. J.** “Circumcision—Who Did It, Who Didn’t, and Why.” *BAR* 32.4 (2006) 48–55. **Klauck, H.-J.** “Erinnerung—Übergang—

Alltag: Eine Besinnung zu Josua 5,9–12." In *Was die Bibel mir erzählt*. FS F. Laub, ed. H. Stettberger. Münster: LIT, 2005. 33–39. **Kraus, H. J.** "Gilgal." *VT* 1 (1951) 181–99. ———. *Gottesdienst in Israel*. 2nd ed. Munich: Kaiser, 1962. 64–67, 179–93. ———."Zur Geschichte des Passah-Massot-Festes im Alten Testament." *EvT* 18 (1958) 47–67. **Kuhnert, G.** *Das Gilgalpassah: Literarische, überlieferungsgeschichtliche und geschichtliche Untersuchungen zu Josua 3–6*. Mainz, 1981. **Kutsch, E.** "Erwägungen zur Geschichte des Passafeier und des Massotfestes." *ZTK* 55 (1958) 10–21. **Laaf, P.** *Die Pascha-Feier Israels: Eine literarkritische und überlieferungsgeschichtliche Studie*. BBB 36. Bonn: Hanstein, 1970. 86–91, 103–15, 131, 167. **Lehmann, R.** "Bemerkungen zu einer neuen Begründung der Beschneidung." *Sociologus* NS 7 (1957) 57–75. **Lemche, N. P.** "Det revolutionäre Israel: En praesentation af en moderne forskningsretning." *DTT* 45 (1982) 16–39. **Leonhard, C.** "Die Erzählung Ex 12 als Festlegende für das Pesachfest am Jerusalemer Tempel." In *Das Fest: Jenseits des Alltags*. Ed. M. Ebner et al. JBT 18. Neukirchen-Vluyn: Neukirchner Verlag, 2004. 233–60. **Long, B. O.** *The Problem of Etiological Narrative in the Old Testament*. BZAW 108. Berlin: Töpelmann, 1968. 54–55. **Lubsczyk, H.** *Der Auszug Israels aus Ägypten*. ETS 11. Leipzig: St. Benno, 1963. 135–37. **Maiberger, P.** *Das Manna: Eine Literarische, etymologische naturkundliche Untersuchung*. ÄgAT 6. Wiesbaden: Harrassowitz, 1983. **Maier, J.** *Das altisraelitische Ladeheiligtum*. BZAW 93. Berlin: Töpelmann, 1965. 24, 33–39. **Malina, B. J.** *The Palestinian Manna Tradition: The Manna Tradition in the Palestinian Targums and Its Relationship to the New Testament Writings*. AGJU 7. Leiden: Brill, 1968. **McConville, J. G.** "Deuteronomy's unification of Passover and Massot: a response to Bernarad M. Levinson." *JBL* 119, 2000. 47–58. **McKay, J. W.** "The Date of Passover and Its Significance." *ZAW* 84 (1972) 435–47. **Meer, M. N. van der.** *Formation and Reformulation: The Redaction of the Book of Joshua in the Light of the Oldest Textual Witnesses*. VTSup 102. Leiden: Brill, 2004. **Miller, P. D.** *The Divine Warrior in Early Israel*. HSM 5. Cambridge, MA: Harvard UP, 1973. 128–31. **Möhlenbrink, K.** "Die Landnahmensagen des Buches Josua." *ZAW* 56 (1938) 262–68. **Morgenstern, J.** *Rites of Birth, Marriage, Death, and Kindred Occasions among the Semites*. Cincinnati: Hebrew Union College Press, 1966. **Mowinckel, S.** *Tetrateuch, Pentateuch, Hexateuch*. BZAW 90. Berlin: Töpelmann, 1964. 36. **Müller, H.-P.** "Die kultische Darstellung der Theophanie." *VT* 14 (1964) 183–91. **Noort, E.** "The Disgrace of Egypt: Joshua 5.9a and Its Context." In *Wisdom of Egypt*. Ed A. Hilhorst and G. H. van Kooten. Leiden: Brill, 2005. 3–19. **Otto, E.** *Das Mazzotfest in Gilgal*. BWANT 107. Stuttgart: Kohlhammer, 1975. 57–65, 158–59, 175–86, 189–91, 195–98, 311. **Ottosson, M.** "Tradition and History with Emphasis on the Composition of the Book of Joshua." In *The Production of Time: Tradition History in Old Testament Scholarship*. Ed. K. Jeppesen and B. Otzen. Sheffield: Almond, 1984. 81–106, 141–43. **Porter, J. R.** "The Background of Joshua 3–5." *SEÅ* 36 (1971) 5–23. **Power, E.** "Josue 5:9 and the Institution of Circumcision." *ITQ* 18 (1951) 368–72. **Prosic, T.** *Development and Symbolism of Passover until 70 ce*. JSOTSup 414. London: T&T Clark, 2004. ———. "Passover in Biblical Narratives." *JSOT* 82 (1999) 45–55. **Rösel, M.** "The Septuagint-Version of the Book of Joshua." *SJOT* 16 (2002) 5–23. **Rothschild, M.** "Gilgal Site of the First Passover." *DD* 6 (1977) 137–40 (Heb.). **Röttger, H.** *Mal'ak Jahwe—Bote von Gott: Die Vorstellung von Gottes Boten im hebräischen Alten Testament*. RST 13. Frankfurt am Main: Lang, 1978. **Rudolph, W.** *Der 'Elohist' von Exodus bis Josua*. BZAW 68. Berlin: Töpelmann, 1938. 178–82. **Ruprecht, E.** "Stellung und Bedeutung der Erzählung vom Mannawunder (Ex 16) im Aufbau der Priesterschrift." *ZAW* 86 (1974) 269–306. **Ruwe, A.** "Beschneidung als interkultureller Brauch und Friedenszeichen Israels: Religionsgeschichtliche Überlegungen zu Genesis 17, Genesis 34, und Josua 5." *TZ* 64 (2008) 309–42. **Sasson, J. M.** "Circumcision in the Ancient Near East." *JBL* 85 (1966) 473–76. **Schmidt, L.** 'Die vorpriesterliche Darstellung in Ex 11,1–13,16." *ZAW* 117 (2005) 171–88. **Schmitt, R.** *Exodus und Passah: Ihr Zusammenhang im Alten Testament*. OBO 7. Freiburg: Universitätsverlag, 1975. 51–53. **Schur, J.**

G. *Wesen und Motive der Beschneidung im Lichte der alttestamentlichen Quellen und der Völkerkunde.* Helsinki, 1937. **Segal, J. B.** *The Hebrew Passover from the Earliest Times to a.d. 70.* London Oriental Series 12. London: Oxford UP, 1963. **Sierksma, F.** "Quelques remarques sur la circoncision en Israel." *OtSt* 9 (1951) 136–69. **Simpson, C. A.** *The Early Traditions of Israel.* Oxford: Blackwell, 1948. 286–88. **Soggin, J. A.** "Gilgal, Passah und Landnahme: Eine neue Untersuchung des kultischen Zusammenhangs der Kap. III–VI des Josuabuches." In *Volume du congrès Genève 1965.* VTSup 15. Leiden: Brill, 1966. 263–77. ———."La 'negazione' in Gios. 5:14." *BeO* 7 (1965) 75. Reprinted in *Old Testament and Oriental Studies* (Rome: Biblical Institute Press, 1975) 219–20. **Stade, B.** "Der 'Hugel der Vorhäute' Jos 5." *ZAW* 6 (1886) 132–43. **Štrba, B.** *Take Off Your Sandals from Your Feet! An Exegetical Study of Josh 5,13–15.* ÖBS 32. Frankfurt am Main: Lang, 2008. **Tabory, J.** "Towards a History of the Paschal Meal." In *Passover and Easter.* Notre Dame, IN: University of Notre Dame Press, 1999. 62–80. **Tov, E.** "Literary Development of the Book of Joshua as Reflected in the MT, the LXX, and 4QJosh^A." In *The Book of Joshua.* Ed. E. Noort. Leuven: Peeters, 2012. 65–85. **Van Seters, J.** "The Place of the Yahwist in the History of Passover and Massot." *ZAW* 95 (1983) 175. **Vaux, R. de.** *Histoire ancienne d'Israël.* Vol. 1. Paris: J. Gabalda, 1971, 557–59. Translated as *The Early History of Israel,* trans. D. Smith (London: Darton, Longman & Todd, 1978) 605–8. **Veijola, T.** "The History of Passover in the Light of Deuteronomy 16,1–8." *ZABR* 2 (1996) 54–55. **Wagenaar, J. A.** "The Cessation of Manna: Editorial Frames for the Wilderness Wandering in Exodus 16,35 and Joshua 5,10–12." *ZAW* 112 (2000) 192–209. ———. "Post-Exilic Calendar Innovations: The First Month of the Year and the Date of Passover and the Festival of Unleavened Bread." *ZAW* 115 (2003) 3–24. **Wagner, V.** "Profanität und Sakraelieierung der Beschneidung im Alten Testament." *VT* 60 (2010) 447–64. ———. *Profanität und Sakralisierung im Alten Testament.* BZAW 352. Berlin: De Gruyter, 2005. **Wambacq, B. N.** "Les Massôt." *Bib* 61 (1980) 44–46. ———. "Les origines de la Pesah israélite." *Bib* 57 (1976) 216, 223, 305–9. **Weimar, P.** "Ex 12,1–14 und die priesterschriftliche Geschichtsdarstellung." *ZAW* 107 (1995) 196–214. ———. "Pascha und Massot: Anmerkungen zu Dt 16,1–8." In *Recht und Ethos im Alten Testament—Gestalt und Wirkung.* Neukirchen-Vluyn: Neukirchener Verlag, 1999. 61–72. ———. "Zum Problem der Entstehungsgeschichte von Ex 12,1–14." *ZAW* 107 (1995) 1–17. **Weiss, C.** "A Worldwide Survey of the Current Practice of Milah (Ritual Circumcision)." *Jewish Social Studies* 24 (1962) 30–48. **Wellhausen, J.** *Die Composition des Hexateuchs und der historischen Bücher des Alten Testaments.* 2nd ed. Berlin: Reimer, 1889. 122–23. **Westermann, C.** "Arten der Erzählung in der Genesis." In *Forschung am Alten Testament.* TB 24. Munich: Kaiser, 1964. 84–85. **Wijngaards, J. N. M.** *The Dramatization of Salvific History in the Deuteronomic Schools.* OtSt 16. Leiden: Brill, 1969. 60, 104–5, 120. **Wilcoxen J. A.** "Narrative Structure and Cult Legend: A Study of Joshua, 1–6." In *Transitions in Biblical Scholarship.* Ed. J. C. Rylaarsdam. Chicago: University of Chicago Press, 1968. 43–70. **Wildberger, H.** *Jahwes Eigentumsvolk.* ATANT 37. Zürich: Zwingli, 1960. 40–62. **Winther-Nielsen, N.** *A Functional Discourse Grammar of Joshua: A Computer-Assisted Rhetorical Structure Analysis.* ConBOT 40. Stockholm: Almqvist & Wiksell, 1995. **Wyatt, N.** "Circumcision and Circumstance: Male Genital Mutilation in Ancient Israel and Ugarit." *JSOT* 33 (2009) 405–31. **Zenger, E.** *Die Sinaitheophanie.* FB 3. Würzburg: Echter, 1961. 136–47.

Translation

[2a]*At that time Yahweh said to Joshua, "Make for yourself flint knives*[b] *and circumcise again*[c] *the sons of Israel a second time."*[d] [3]*Joshua then made for himself flint knives and circumcised the sons of Israel on*[a] *the hill of the foreskins.* [4]*This is the reason for Joshua's circumcising: all the people*[a] *coming out from Egypt, the males, all the warriors had died in the*

wilderness on the way when they came out from Egypt. [5]*Indeed, all the people coming out were circumcised, but all the people who were born in the wilderness on the way when they came out from Egypt they had not circumcised.* [6]*Because forty years*[a] *the Israelites were on the move in the wilderness until all the nation,*[b] *the men of war coming out from Egypt, were finished off,*[c] *those who did not listen obediently to the voice of Yahweh*[d] *when Yahweh swore to them that they would not see*[e] *the land which Yahweh had sworn to their fathers to give to us, a land flowing with milk and honey.* [7]*But it was their sons whom he set up in their stead that Joshua circumcised, since uncircumcised were they because they did not circumcise them in the way.*[a] [8]*When all the nation was finished being circumcised, they remained in their place in the camp until they recovered.*[a] [9]*Then Yahweh said to Joshua, "Today I have rolled the disgrace of Egypt away from you." So he called the name of that place Gilgal until this day.*[a]

[10]*Then the sons of Israel camped in Gilgal.*[a] *They kept the Passover on the fourteenth day of the month in the evening in the plains of Jericho.* [11]*They ate from the produce of the land on the day after Passover*[a]*—unleavened bread and parched grain—on that very same day.* [12]*Then the manna stopped the morrow*[a] *of the day when they ate from the produce of the land. Manna was never again available for the sons of Israel. They ate the crops of the land of Canaan that year.*[b]

[13]*When Joshua was at*[a] *Jericho, he lifted his eyes and watched. Right before his face, a man was standing with his sword drawn in his hand. Joshua went to him and said to him, "Do you belong to us or to our enemies?"*[b] [14]*He said, "No!*[a] *Because I am the prince of the host of Yahweh, I have now come." Joshua fell on his face to the ground and worshiped*[b] *him. He said to him, "What will my lord say to his servant?"* [15]*Then the prince of the host of Yahweh said to Joshua, "Loosen your sandal from upon your foot for the place on which you are now standing is holy." Joshua obeyed.*[a]

Notes

LXX forces the interpreter of this section, particularly vv 4–6, to consider the implications of textual variants and textual criticism. LXX offers not only a much shorter text, but a different interpretation of the events. Thus Pitkänen finds that this evidence "suggests that the text was malleable in its transmission." He hurries to assure readers that "there are no major differences between the two versions in this case, which itself speaks for the basic reliability of the transmission process" (149).

This textual problem provides clear evidence that textual transmission involved interpretation as late as the translation into Gk. and beyond as each new scribal generation explained the meaning of the cultic practices for its own worship, teaching, and self-identity as heirs of the tradition.

Greenspoon (*CBR* 3 [2005] 239) explains the complexity of the situation: (1) Gk. pays more attention to the knives; (2) Gk. says nothing about "second time" circumcision; (3) Gk. has most of the men coming from Egypt uncircumcised, while Heb. has all the men circumcised; (4) Gk. has forty-two years in the wilderness, while Heb. has the traditional forty; and (5) Gk. does not have etiological explanation for Gilgal. Greenspoon concludes: "It is no less arduous to imagine that the text always contained something of a jumbled, even confused character, reflecting in its very structure the scene that Joshua and his fellow Israelites are portrayed as experiencing" (240).

Nelson (72) prints both an "unrevised text" of vv 2b–6a and an MT revision, concluding that "application of standard text-critical principles reveals that the MT of vv. 2–9 and 10–12 represents revisions of the earliest recoverable text. These revisions reflect an interest in harmonization and concerns about orthodoxy" (74).

Van der Meer (*Formation and Reformulation*, 249–315) tries to demonstrate that the differences are so massive and consistent that one must look for "a well-considered reworking of one version into the other," not "a series of unconscious scribal corruptions." Bieberstein (*Josua, Jordan, Jericho*, 206) finally decides that MT preserved the older

Vorlage. He sees LXX based on scholarly research and attempts at chronological agreement with texts such as Exod 12:38; Num 10:11; 11:4; 14:29, 33–34.

The notes below show that the text-critical conclusions cannot be so easily made in favor of one text tradition over the other so that an earliest recoverable text is much more complex than Nelson's statement would lead one to believe. Even Nelson must footnote the debate with Holmes and Auld on his side and Gooding vigorously opposed to such conclusions. Nelson admits (74, n. 1) that 4QJosh[a] supports MT.

2.a. 4QJosh[a] does not appear to preserve 5:1 but has 8:34–35 and a unique text followed by 5:2. The unique text talks of "after that," apparently referring to the reading of the covenant law in 8:34–35. The Qumran reading also refers to "the book of the Torah" and to "the bearers of the ark." Abegg et al., *Dead Sea Scrolls Bible* (204), translates: "After they had removed [their feet from the Jordan, . . .], the book of the law. After that, the ark-bearers . . ." and suggests that "MT, LXX lack this verse and have the secondary traditional wording of 5:1 in its place." Thus at this place 4QJosh[a] is viewed as superior to MT and LXX. Compare Howard (p. 146 with n. 254). Nelson, however, notes that just because the Qumran text is so much more logical, "it is also less likely to be original than the order of MT or OG" (73).

2.b. LXX expands the description of the knives to μαχαίρας πετρίνας ἐκ πέτρας ἀκροτόμου, "rock knives out of hard [or sharp] rock." Van der Meer (*Formation and Reformulation*, 338–39) explains this reading as Gk. interpretation: "the Greek translator sought to modify the crude notion of a circumcision with such primitive instruments as stone knives. . . . [T]he purpose of the phrase is to clarify that the painful operation on the adult population was at least performed by sharp knives."

2.c. LXX read וְשֵׁב, "sit down," rather than וְשׁוּב, "again." For the MT double imperative, see GKC §120g. LXX may reflect an older circumcision practice wherein youth were circumcised at puberty in community ritual (cf. *ANEP*, no. 629). Nelson (73) sees LXX as preferable, deciding MT represents harmonizing with its understanding of a second circumcision. Bieberstein (*Josua, Jordan, Jericho*, 203–6) concludes that an ambiguous original reading gave opportunity for each of the differing interpretations in LXX and MT. Here we see the need of the translators to clarify the text for their readers and listeners. The more difficult MT may well be original.

2.d. As van der Meer (*Formation and Reformulation*, 339–40) shows, the best Gk. witnesses omit שֵׁנִית, "a second time" (contra Otto, *Mazzotfest*, 58; Gooding, "Traditions of Interpretation," 149–64) as apparently does 4QJosh[a] according to Tov ("Joshua," in *Qumran Cave 4. IX: Deuteronomy, Joshua, Judges, Kings*, DJD 14 [Oxford: Clarendon, 1995], 147; Abegg et al., *Dead Sea Scrolls Bible*, 204). MT represents interpretation of the tradition in light of Gen 17 and Exod 12:43–49. Bieberstein (*Josua, Jordan, Jericho*, 204) objects to the inclusion of Gen 17 on the self-evident grounds that Joshua was not yet alive. We are making a literary comparison, not a real-life depiction. Gen 17 shows the first general circumcision, including adults. Gk. has no place in its logical narrative for a second circumcision (van der Meer, *Formation and Reformulation*, 340). Indeed, for van der Meer, the LXX represents "deliberate efforts by the Greek translator to avoid the literal understanding of a second circumcison of adult males that had already been circumcised" (341). Bieberstein (*Josua, Jordan, Jericho*, 206) decides this is one of few times LXX has the older reading. Apparently, different copyists/translators interpreted the text in different ways.

3.a. Here and v 14, MT reads אֶל, "toward," in the sense of עַל, "upon."

4.a. LXX reads "purified" for "circumcised." This shows the Gk. translator's understanding of the function of circumcision (compare van der Meer, *Formation and Reformulation*, 347). Gk. ὃν δὲ τρόπον indicates "manner," showing "the unusual instruments" Joshua used (van der Meer, *Formation and Reformulation*, 345).

LXX omits v 4b referring to the death of a generation in the wilderness and v 5a stating that all people leaving Egypt were circumcised. LXX thus reports the circumcision of those born in the wilderness and those not circumcised in Egypt and makes the older generation "directly responsible for the uncircumcised state of their sons" (van der Meer, *Formation and Reformulation*, 296). Van der Meer (344) finds that the Gk. with all its differences from MT still "forms a cogent literary unit in itself."

MT again is more in line with tradition of Gen 17 and Exod 12 (cf. Auld, "Joshua," 9). Nelson (72) follows LXX in his "Unrevised," that is, "pre-MT" text. Bieberstein (*Josua, Jordan, Jericho*, 200) sees both renditions as viable. MT could have viewed as offensive the Gk. claim that the younger part of the exodus generation crossed the Jordan and so deleted it.

LXX could have seen the MT version of a whole generation dying in the wilderness as incorrect and so altered it. M. Rösel correctly sees all LXX reconstructions and retroversions to a Heb. *Vorlage* "as so speculative that I refrain from working with them" (*SJOT* 16 [2002] 16).

6.a. LXX reads "forty-two years," interpreting the tradition in Num 10:11–12; 12:16; 13:3; 14:33–34 and counting two years spent in Kadesh-Barnea. (See van der Meer, *Formation and Reformulation*, 296.) LXX describes the wilderness twice, first translating Heb. מדבר (*midbār*) and then transliterating it to get "the desert of Midbaritis." This appears to represent a doublet in the Heb. text used by the Gk. translator (van der Meer, *Formation and Reformulation*, 358–59). LXX also witnesses the unexpected verb from ἀναστρέφω, "to live" or "to dwell," rather than MT's חלך, "to walk" or "to travel." MT follows the chronology of Deut 1:3; 2:14 (cf. Margolis, *Book of Joshua in Greek*, 69–70). Nelson (73) sees OG as dittography. Howard suggests "the forty-year sentence on the rebellious Israel must be seen as a round number that included the first two years before their rebellion at Kadesh Barnea in Numbers 14" (149, n. 264).

6.b. Many Heb. MSS and some Targum MSS insert the reading כל הדור, "all that generation," from Deut 2:14 (compare van der Meer, *Formation and Reformulation*, 300–301). See the detailed list of variant interpretations of the Gk. passage and a new theory by van der Meer (*Formation and Reformulation*, 360–78).

6.c. LXX reads "therefore many of them were uncircumcised" instead of "until all the nation were finished off," consistent in both text traditions with the interpretations of vv 4–5. Van der Meer contends, as usual, that LXX in this chapter is "a product of intensive exegesis, slight harmonization with the Pentateuch, and well-considered translation . . . clearly distinguishing between guilty fathers and innocent children" (*Formation and Reformulation*, 373).

6.d. LXX reads οἱ ἀπειθήσαντες τῶν ἐντολῶν τοῦ θεοῦ, "who were disbelieving the commandments of God" for MT לֹא־שָׁמְעוּ בְּקוֹל יהוה, "who did not listen to [or obey] the voice of Yahweh." Van der Meer (*Formation and Reformulation*, 373) sees the Gk. translator distinguishing the older and younger generations through use of the more definite commandments.

6.e. Or "that he would not let them see." 4QJosh[a] reads the *qal* inf. const. without the 3rd pl. suffix for MT's *hip'il* inf. const. with the suffix, joining LXX in reading "they would not see." Van der Meer (*Formation and Reformulation*, 381) finds that the *qal* formation implies not just seeing but also entering the land, while *hip'il* indicates seeing from a distance.

7.a. LXX changes MT to read "because the ones born along the way were uncircumcised." Van der Meer (*Formation and Reformulation*, 384) sees a free formulation of the translator based on v 5 and an attempt to reduce redundancy.

8.a. LXX has obviously shortened the text through use of Gk. participles for the Heb. clauses. In so doing it may well have emphasized "the idea of the recuperation of the Israelite adult warriors after such a painful operation" (van der Meer, *Formation and Reformulation*, 386).

9.a. LXX does not record the formulaic "until this day," again perhaps reflecting continued interpretation within the Heb. tradition. Here the explanation by van der Meer (*Formation and Reformulation*, 391–93) rests more on his theory of Gk. freedom and creativity than on any textual or literary evidence.

10.a. LXX does not record the encampment in Gilgal, which is repetitious of Josh 4:19. MT specifically connects Gilgal and Passover. LXX reads the last part of the verse as "from evening at sunset at [or in the western part of] Jericho on the Beyond the Jordan in the plain," expanding the identification of the locale, using "Beyond the Jordan" to indicate territory west of the Jordan rather than east. Hollenberg (*Der Charakter*, 18) concluded that what we now read in the LXX is "clearly meaningless and full of contradictions." Nelson (73) sees a haplography in Gk. omission of Gilgal and a doublet in the geographical expansion. Van der Meer decides the Gk. translator made a successful attempt "to provide a sensible translation for a problematic Hebrew phrase" (*Formation and Reformulation*, 400). Bieberstein (*Josua, Jordan, Jericho*, 206) acutely finds homoioteleuton in the Heb. of the Gk. *Vorlage*.

11.a. LXX appears to reflect a differing chronological order, omitting "on the day after Passover," and placing "on that day" at the end of v 11, where it may have been understood either as closing the previous sentence or opening the following, and not translating בעצם, "on the same."

Van der Meer (*Formation and Reformulation*, 391–97) says the Gk. translator merged the elements of Passover and Unleavened Bread into a single unified festival. This made the division into separate days meaningless. Hubbard (184, n. 27) supports the two-day reading of MT.

The LXX reading appears to place the eating of unleavened bread and corn on Passover itself over against the festival calendars in Num 28 and Lev 23. If, however, LXX relates the eating to v 12, then the eating is done at an indeterminate time seemingly without contradicting the festival calendars. This understanding leads Bieberstein (*Josua, Jordan, Jericho*, 217–19) to declare the two temporal adverbs in the MT as secondary insertions under Priestly influence with v 11b leading to v 12 but then to argue against any attempts to excise corn or "the very same day" as later additions. Blum (*Beschneidung und Passa*, 229; original 301) points out that Josh 5:10–11 offers something like an appropriate application of priestly Torah decisions concerning Passover/Unleavened Bread to a one time circumstance of entry into the land. He thus categorizes this passage as Midrash.

MT makes clear that the regulations of Deut 3:1 were followed. There is no indication, however, that the Feast of Unleavened Bread was celebrated (contra Otto, *Mazzotfest*, 62–63, 185). Bieberstein (*Josua, Jordan, Jericho*, 219) sees the shorter Gk. using the last clause with בעצם, "the very same," to refer to v 12.

12.a. LXX is consistent in not translating ממחרת, "the morrow," which Bieberstein (*Josua, Jordan, Jericho*, 219) omits as a later insertion. The entire section is built around an understanding of the timing of the cultic calendar for Passover and Unleavened Bread.

12.b. LXX renders "land of Canaan" with the unexpected χώραν τῶν Φοινίκων, "region of the Phoenicians." Van der Meer (*Formation and Reformulation*, 404–5) reads the Gk. term as a common noun φοῖνιξ meaning "date palm," a much more apropos term for the context but without textual support.

13.a. Howard argues correctly that though the preposition ב most frequently means "in," it can also mean "at," which "fits the scenario easily" (155, n. 281).

13.b. Williams (*Williams' Hebrew Syntax*, 282) calls the prepositions here *lameds* of partisanship or assistance or advantage, showing whose side someone takes.

14.a. MT לא, "no," represents the most difficult reading and should be retained against the evidence of Heb. MSS, LXX, Syr., which read the Heb. homonym לֹו, "to him." Nelson (73; compare Barthélemy, *Critique textuelle*, 1:4, who says LXX assimilates to the formula of vv 13 and 14. *Preliminary and Interim Report* (2:10) sees Gk. employing the easier reading as does Bieberstein (*Josua, Jordan, Jericho*, 226).

14.b. LXX does not have "worshiped him," probably, as Nelson notes, "to avoid an offense against piety" (74).

15.a. LXX does not have "and Joshua obeyed," an important part of the book's depiction of Joshua, which Nelson (74) sees as an expansion in MT along with 10:23.

Form/Structure/Setting

The Gilgal and Ebal units in Josh 5:2–12 and 8:30–35 are at the beginning and end of a Jericho and Ai section delimited by *wayehî kišmōaʿ* (וַיְהִי כִשְׁמֹעַ) clauses, "as he (they) heard." For the argument for beginning this section at 5:2, see the opening structural comments on chapter 4. The ending of this section can also be debated. Certainly, the temporal clause of Josh 9:1 begins the next major section or discourse, thus tying chaps. 5–8 together as a unit.

Hall argues that the syntax of Josh 5:1 starts a new pericope and the content connecting to 5:2–12, providing the occasion for Israel to "incapacitate" their army.[618] Howard ties 5:1 to the preceding section, though in a footnote admitting it serves as a hinge between the two sections.[619] Other scholars offer differing views about the function of 5:1 because it contains a temporal clause and is followed by a temporal phrase in v 2. The phrase in v 2 changes time and moves to talk about

---

618 *Conquering Character*, 65–66.
619 Howard, 144.

circumcision, while the content of 5:1 remains focused on the Jordan crossing. Thus, this writer maintains that v 2 opens the new section.

The temporal clause of Josh 5:13 changes time and location and introduces military language for preparing for the battles in chaps. 6–8. Yet the content is still part of the cultic ("holy ground") language of 5:2–12, preparing Israel cultically or ritually for the battle ahead. As vv 2–12 made the people cultically clean for battle, so vv 13–15 show Joshua, the commander of the armies being made pure for battle.

Hall boldly states that "any reading that treats 5:13–15 and 6:1–5 as two distinct episodes is untenable."[620] She argues that 6:1 is a parenthetical clause rather than a disjunctive one and that the four participles of 6:1 make "an odd introductory statement."[621] We are permitted, though, to see this as normal predicate usage of participles.[622] The participle "as a predicate usually indicates a continuing action, one in progress, and is best translated with the English progressive tense."[623] This places 6:1 as an introductory disjunctive clause beginning a new pericope that sets up the siege predicament of Jericho.

The defensive sealing of Jericho in Josh 6:1 is more than "a digression."[624] The disjunctive construction marks both a "temporal shift" and a shift in location. The commander's appearance came "in Jericho," which is now sealed off to Joshua. The new unit starts with the disjunctive clause of 6:1 pointing to a location outside Jericho for the ensuing dialogue. Thus the unit for study here becomes 5:2–15.

Tradition

Chap. 5 introduces some of the oldest practices of early Israelite religion without putting them in any oral literary structures. Here we do not look for exposition, conflict, resolution. Here we look to literary reports describing cultic acts. Tradition here then refers not to the transmission (*Überlieferung*) of oral literary forms but to the content of the tradition itself (*Tradition*). Here we will look at circumcision as a religious tradition as well as at Passover and Unleavened Bread as elements of early Israelite worship. We will then examine briefly the oral transmission behind the theophanic report closing out the chapter.

Israel traces its circumcision back to the sign of the covenant God made with Abraham (Gen 17). Circumcision is not a unique practice in the ancient Near East. J. H. Walton cites evidence of circumcision prior to 2000 BCE in west Semitic and Egyptian cultures (not in Mespotamia, though), with varying procedures, life stages, and purposes.[625] Central among the purposes were fertility, virility, maturity, and genealogy. In some instances circumcision represented a rite of passage into adulthood and so was performed as a prepuberty or prenuptial rite.

---

620 *Conquering Character,* 80–81.
621 Ibid.
622 See *IBHS,* 37.6.
623 Lambdin, *Introduction to Biblical Hebrew,* §19.
624 Winther-Nielsen suggests the words of the Lord's commander are contained in Josh 6:2–5. His opinion comes from a need to place the words of the commander somewhere and the ability to pass over 6:1 with its clear disjunctive opening of a new section in a new location (*Functional Discourse Grammar,* 193).
625 "Genesis," in *Genesis, Exodus, Leviticus, Numbers, Deuteronomy, ZIBBC* (Grand Rapids: Zondervan, 2009) 1:89.

Circumcision gained central meaning for Israel's identity when it was tied to the event of the Abrahamic covenant. As so often in the history of religions, new interpretations raise old rites to new significance. Though not mentioned in the Deuteronomic law, circumcision plays an important role in the early narratives in distinguishing Israel from other nations aspiring to dominate the land (Judg 14:3; 15:18; 1 Sam 14:6; 17:26, 36; 31:4; 2 Sam 1:20, cf. Gen 34:14). The Joshua narrative appropriately has Israel take up circumcision in the land of the circumcised, not in Mesopotamia in the east where the rite was apparently unknown. Of course, scholars such as Wagner argue that Israel did not practice circumcision until late in the first millennium and thus that it had no cultic connections.[626] Wagner and Bieberstein find in Josh 3–5 a typology of the return from Babylon rather than an older tradition. Too much of Wagner's argument, however, is built on absence of evidence rather than on positive documentation in the text.

The basic evidence for Passover comes from sociological study and exegesis of eight passages—Exod 12; Num 9:4–6; Josh 5:10–12; 1 Kgs 9:25 and 2 Chr 8:12–13; 2 Chr 30; 2 Kgs 21–23 and 2 Chr 35:1–19; and Ezra 6:19–22—a task we cannot undertake here. Israelites in Egypt may well have included both farmers and shepherds. Quite surely the nomadic shepherds who went to Egypt maintained that vocational tradition in coming from Egypt. On the borders and in the hill country of Palestine with their flocks, they encountered agriculturalists who entered into a Yahwistic covenant with them (Josh 8:30–35; 24:1–27). Joining of two occupations also joined two festivals: the shepherds' one-day celebration of Passover sacrifice (Exod 12:14; Num 18:16) and the agriculturalists' seven-day blessing of a new crop of barley by eating unleavened bread (Exod 23:15; 34:18; Lev 23:6, 10–15; Num 28:17; Deut 16:9). Bokser explains, "The experiences and hopes of both groups would have been given new meaning in terms of the Exodus experience as a celebration of God's liberation of Israel."[627] Deuteronomy 16 represents the joining of the two festivals and the centralization of the celebration in the place God chooses rather than in family groups.

Whatever the original setting of the tradition—nomadic or agricultural—Passover is the festival referred to in this passage.[628] Such elements as the ritual knives and the family Passover certainly rest on ancient tradition. *Maṣṣôt* or Unleavened Bread with its connections to agricultural life stands faintly in the background. Apparently, Passover does involve eating unleavened bread, offering a natural linguistic and ritual connection of Passover to the *maṣṣôt* festival.

Passover thus moves from a family celebration of nomadic or seminomadic shepherds to a week-long combination with *maṣṣôt* connected to the exodus-from-Egypt tradition, to a national festival of Passover and Unleavened Bread at the central sanctuary, to a forgotten tradition revived by Hezekiah (2 Chron 30:1–19) and Josiah (2 Kings 23:21–23).

John Van Seters sets forth arguments against the antiquity of the Passover celebration and its constituents.[629] Wambacq states that Arabic blood rituals celebrate

---

626   *VT* 60 (2010) 447–64.

627   AB 6, 756.

628   Halbe, *ZAW* 87 (1975) 330–31; contra Wildberger, *Jahwes Eigentumsvolk*, 52.

629   *The Life of Moses: The Yahwist as Historian in Exodus-Numbers* (Louisville: Westminster John Knox, 1994) 113–27. See too the works of Wambacq; Halbe; and J. Goldingay, *Israel's Life*, vol. 3 of *Old Testament Theology* (Downers Grove, IL: IVP Academic, 2009) 164–65.

arrival, not departure.[630] Similarly, Israel finds protection in the house, not outside (Exod 12:22). S. I. L. Norin shows Hebrew הַמַּשְׁחִית (*hammašḥît*), "destroyer" may refer to Yahweh or Yahweh's messenger, not necessarily a demon.[631] For Van Seters, the great difference between the Priestly and Deuteronomic sources points to a lack of evidence for practice from antiquity. Van Seters finds that the J account does not appear in Exod 12:1–17 and its account in chap. 11 has no need for a slaying of the firstborn. For Van Seters the blood rite originates in the Diaspora as a development of priestly cultic blood rites.

Van Seters begins with an assumption that the Pentateuch literature derives from late sources. Israel's written witness is set aside in favor of anthropological data from Arabic tribes of an even later date. The emphasis on staying in the house remains temporary, for the staying in the house is not preparation for daily life. It is preparation for departure on a long journey.

The word normally translated "destroyer" (Exod 12:23) becomes a key witness because in Exod 12 it is applied to Yahweh and to Yahweh's messenger. The destructive force may well represent Yahweh's actions, but still the unusual title "destroyer" must be explained. Its use in early versions of the tradition is as strong an interpretation as any. In such tradition it represented an evil force opposing the people just as it represented an evil force for the Egyptians. Against these arguments we would still contend that Passover represents the practice of the wandering Israelites joining a feast from their (semi-?) nomadic background with new cultural and religious realities in the settled land of the farmer.[632]

Hess uses structural and anthropological arguments to deny that two originally separate rites have been joined in Israel's celebration. The settled population in the hill country "could have been both (enclosed) nomads and settled village dwellers, changing their lifestyle according to the challenges of political and environmental forces."[633] Quite rightly, the hill country population may have possessed the flexibility to live out either lifestyle.

The claim here is that the Israelites were involved in one lifestyle or the other at any given stretch of time. Israel's ability to come in and settle the hill country hints strongly at a time when challenges were few and settlement in the country was not strongly opposed. At such a time incoming shepherd people may have begun to adapt to the agricultural life and found it convenient to incorporate major parts of an agricultural festival into their own pastoral one, tying the new combination to the historical event in Egypt.

Bruce Wells sums up the arguments: "Certain elements in the Passover suggest that at its roots may be a nomadic herdsmen's ritual in which they sought both protection from demonic attack as they moved to summer pasture and fertility for the herds in the new breeding season."[634] Wells points to the family nature of the

---

630   *Bib* 57 (1976) 206–24.

631   *Er spaltete das Meer: Die Auszugsüberlieferung in Psalmen und Kult des alten Israel,* ConBOT 9 (Lund: LiberLäromedel; Gleerup, 1977) 171–204.

632   Cf. L. Rost, "Weidewechsel und altisraelitischer Festkalender," *ZDPV* 66 (1943) 205–16; reprinted in *Das kleine Credo und andere Studien zum Alten Testament* (Heidelberg: Quelle & Meyer, 1965) 101–12; though Knauf, 66, would deny any connection to nomadic life.

633   Hess (1996) 124–25.

634   "Exodus," in *Genesis, Exodus, Leviticus, Numbers, Deuteronomy,* ZIBBC (Grand Rapids: Zondervan, 2009) 1:205.

original celebration, negating the need for access to a sanctuary or altar. Mesopotamian *namburbi* rituals involve similar blood rituals smearing doorposts and keyholes for protection.

Manna was part of the wilderness tradition seen in both a postive (Exod 16:30–35; compare Neh 9:20; Ps 78:24) and a negative light (Exod 16:1–4; Num 11:6). Deut 8 pictures manna as a testing and teaching element, leading Israel to see that the divine word is more important than meeting human hunger. Though Israel at times could not see or understand what God was doing, the provision of manna with its testing qualities was intended for Israel's good (Deut 8:16).

The meshing of traditions apparently took place in the vicinity of Jericho and its surrounding territory, which the tradition has connected with Gilgal. "The celebration identifies Israel at the Jordan with Israel at the exodus and Israel at Sinai. Israel at the Jordan inherits the covenantal promises of the previous generation."[635] Thus Hall underlines the commemorative side of Passover that looks backward and frames the narrative of the wilderness wandering.[636] "Passover strengthens the identity of the people as a community whose roots go deep into history and commemorates the saving mercy of God."[637]

The narrative looks forward as well as backward. It qualifies the new generation to be the people of God (compare Exod 12) living in purity in God's pure land. The narrative and the tradition behind it, however, do not qualify Joshua as the prophet like Moses with authority equal to Moses' as Štrba tries unsuccessfully to prove.[638]

Chap. 5 thus unites ancient traditions (circumcision, Passover, unleavened bread, and manna) into a liturgical unit that qualifies the people and their leader cultically for the task ahead. Ottosson sees the union of cultic acts as "intended to emphasize Israel's distinctiveness from the Canaanite population."[639]

Source and Redaction

Three independent units constitute this section (Josh 5:1–9, 10–12, 13–15) and appear to have been joined together by the biblical editor without any transitional material. Traditionally, scholars divide the material in chap. 5 into sources. By identifying repetitive materials in each section. Wagenaar explains: "These repetitions may indicate that the text is the result of a long literary history. In the history of research the identification of sources or literary strands in Jos 5,10–12 has resulted in a multitude of opinions. The presence of elements that betray the hand of P, e.g. the exact date of the fourteenth of the month in v. 10b has been widely recognized. The assessment of these elements for the attribution of vv. 10–12 to a literary strand varied."[640] Wagenaar embraces the new redaction criticism, which maintains late dates for all the Pentateuchal/Hexateuchal "sources." He writes: "The Yahwist in Jos 5,12a can, therefore, be identified as a post-dtr editor in the Book of Joshua, linking the conquest to the wilderness wandering by an editorial note on the ces-

---

635   Hess (1996) 123.
636   *Conquering Character,* 71.
637   Pressler, 41.
638   *Take Off Your Sandals from Your Feet!*
639   "Tradition History," 90.
640   *ZAW* 112 (2000) 199.

sation of the manna."[641] He adds: "both the Yahwist and the Priestly writer have framed the wilderness wandering in their own way with a note on the cessation of manna in respectively Ex 16,35a + Jos 5,12acc and Ex 16,35b + Jos 5,12abb."[642]

Fritz finds that only vv 2–3, 8, 13–15 belong to the original "deuteronomistic historian." The majority of the text thus becomes "redactional," and even the basic narrative is seen as a literary creation without any foundation in old tradition. Briend, rather, finds a truncated text at the end of the chapter with a natural ending in Josh 6:2 provided by his "Joshua redactor," although he admits that 5:13–14 probably came from an earlier source.[643] Such painstaking analysis leaves a story without narrative art or narrative connection.

Bieberstein[644] points out that Y. Thorion has shown that Hebrew *kî* (כי) clauses can be explanatory rather than always being causal.[645] Bieberstein thus shows the parallel structure of Josh 5:4–8 in the use of גוי (nation) and עם (people).[646] The former is used elsewhere in the biblical text to depict the view of an outsider who sees Israel as a nation among other nations.

The uses of the different names for Israel and the artistic use of כי clauses point to conscious formulations, not redactional changes. This evidence does away with any need for literary division as far as Bieberstein is concerned. The subject matter leads Bieberstein to place vv 2–8 in the hands of a post-Priestly redactor, while 5:9 may be attributed to an etiological redactor.

The second narrative, vv 10–12, describes the first Passover in the land. Again literary problems arise. The opening reference to Gilgal is missing in LXX (see *Notes*); duplicates, if not contradicts, Josh 4:19; and stands in tension with the end of v 10: "in the plains of Jericho." Bieberstein tries to remove the tension by stating that the site of Gilgal according to the entire context is assumed to be completely in the region of Jericho.[647] But where in the region? In Gilgal, in a camp near Jericho? Bieberstein then attempts to remove the dating formula in v 10 as using circular argument.[648]

In v 11 the phrase "on the day after Passover" stands in tension with the concluding notice "on that very same day" and is lacking in LXX. The notice may be explained as a later generation's reading the text and seeing two festivals celebrated, Passover and Unleavened Bread (cf. Lev 23:6; Num 28:17; Exod 12:14–20). The Joshua text knows only implicitly of a seven-day celebration.[649] The date given for the celebration of the Passover reflects Ezek 45:21; Num 28:16; Lev 23:6 and could be interpreted in light of later celebrations, though this is not certain.[650]

MT has Israel eat unleavened bread and roasted corn on the day after Passover, that is, the first day of Unleavened Bread. The final phrase ("on the same day")

---

641   Ibid., 207.
642   Ibid., 208.
643   "Sources of the Deuteronomic History," 370.
644   *Josua, Jordan, Jericho*, 207–8.
645   *Studien zur klassischen hebräischen Syntax*, Marburger Studien zur Afrika- und Asienkunde B6 (Berlin: Reimer, 1984).
646   *Josua, Jordan, Jericho*, 208–9.
647   Ibid., 220–21.
648   Ibid., 221–22.
649   Cf. Halbe, *ZAW* 87 (1975) 332.
650   Cf. Soggin, 74.

refers again to the eating of unleavened bread and roast corn. Manna stopped on the (sixteenth day of the first month) after Israel first ate the unleavened bread and corn.

The expression עשה את־הפסח, "keep the Passover" appears only in the "priestly" strata of the Pentateuch (Num 9:2, 5) and in the Chronicler's work (2 Chr 35:17; Ezra 6:19; cf. Exod 12:47; Num 9:3, 11, 12.)[651] Van der Meer says numbering the months, the specific dating system, and the ties to "priestly" parts of Pentateuch—especially dependence on Lev 23—all show that vv 10–12 are a late Priestly addition.[652] Laaf is surely correct in arguing that late Priestly circles did not invent such vocabulary.[653] One also doubts that counting the months and setting dates for major festivals came late in Israel's cultic life after the opportunities for major celebrations had passed. Descriptions of ancient traditions must have a foothold in ancient history when Israel had opportunity to go to a central sanctuary and follow the instructions for celebrating Passover, Unleavened Bread, and other festivals.

The third narrative in this chapter (vv 13–15) has been subject to a plethora of source analyses. See especially the review by Bieberstein, who points out that more recent commentators find a unified narrative here.[654] Working off Keel, Tim, Groß, and Rouillard, Bieberstein compares vv 13–15 with Exod 3:2–5; Num 22:23, 31–32; and 1 Chr 21:16–17.[655] He determines that Joshua stands between Exodus and Numbers in language, drawing from both sides, while Exodus and Numbers do not borrow language from each other. For Bieberstein, then, Josh 5:13–15 contains no old local tradition but is a late composition from the scribal desk built off the Pentateuch.[656] Similarly, he finds a connection between Joshua's circumcision narrative and Exod 12:48–50 and between Joshua's Passover narrative and Exod 12:1–28. All the Exodus traditions are deemed earlier than those in Joshua. A post-Priestly scribe completed an arch from Exodus to Joshua, tying the two traditions together in what Bieberstein calls a *Fortschreibung* or continuation of the writing.

Prosic demonstrates the futility of employing traditional source criticism to find the original character of Passover.[657] Such four-source (JEPD) searches resulted in a number of self-contradictory explanations—pastoral and agricultural ritual, apothropaic rite, thanksgiving festival, harvest festival, sanctification ritual, and ritual drama. Thus one realizes the difficulty in presenting yet another opinion.

Prosic points to Segal's objection to literary criticism, especially in regard to Passover narratives, namely, that words and phrases are always employed as the context requires and that they are not "stock-in-trade" of individual sources. This understanding of language strikes at the core of the source hypothesis and certainly provides us with a good argument for its rejection. At the same time, such an understanding of language points to the differentiation of meaning as words and

---

651 Laaf, *Pascha-Feier,* 87–89.
652 *Formation and Reformulation,* 318–22.
653 Contra Otto, *Mazzotfest,* 184.
654 *Josua, Jordan, Jericho,* 229.
655 Ibid., 415.
656 Ibid.
657 *JSOT* 82 (1999) 46.

idioms travel through history, pairing with new linguistic partners and assuming wider or narrower or even opposite meanings.

Prosic joins Van Seters and others whose theories dispute the traditional notion that J is the oldest stratum in the Old Testament. In relation to Passover, these theories raise doubts as to whether the J version can be taken as a firm starting point in a quest for its pagan, pre-Yahwistic prototype.

Thus attempts to discover the original character of Passover poses a methodological question. What methods does one bring to reading and interpreting the biblical text? I would argue against Prosic's assumption that "the so-called historical narratives which deal with the early history of the Israelites . . . constitute a sacred history which does not have much in common with the real history of Israelites."[658]

Passover appears at important junctures in the so-called Deuteronomistic History (Deut 16; 2 Kgs 23:21–23; compare 2 Chr 30). Geography, subject, and possibly even chronology separate the narratives, but they share an interesting link. All point to the cultic correctness of Israel and their leader as they view the conquest of the land. That Israel was actually cultically correct was never self-evident within her history, as the Israelite historian(s) takes pains to prove in the remainder of the Enneateuch. But the period of Joshua, and then later of each of the Judges, is painted as an example of cultic correctness.

These brief vignettes of Israelite rituals show the various ways Israel and their leader are prepared to join in Yahweh war. They are built on ancient traditions of Israel's self-identifying cultic rites. In their present canonical form, these brief vignettes represent a scribal or editorial transition uniting the crossing of the Jordan and the battle of Jericho. They carry no narrative tension but represent the resolution of much cultic tension within Israel's developing identity.

Form

As to literary form, vv 1–8 constitute a report about Joshua and the problems resulting from circumcision (thus the conclusion in v 8). The report represents a "brief, self-contained prose narrative, usually in third-person style, about a single event or situation in the past" with "no developed plot or imaginative characterization" but usually with some type of action.[659] They are presented in the command-and-obedience conversation style familiar in much Israelite narrative.

This report could well have been used in Israel's cultic and/or teaching tradition to encourage the faithful to keep up the tradition of circumcision despite the pain. The report has become part of a larger literary setting, interpreted and transmitted in at least two forms as seen in LXX and MT. LXX reflects a setting in which the report is used to explain how Joshua had to purify the disobedient wilderness generation, with possibly a few exceptions such as Joshua himself and Caleb. MT represents a different literary setting. Circumcision had once been universal for Israel as exemplified by the exodus generation (v 5a), but that generation had disobeyed (v 6b) and died (vv 4b, 6a). A new people had come of age, but they were not Israel, for they were uncircumcised (vv 5b, 7b). Thus Israel had to be circumcised again, a second time (v 2; cf. *Notes*).

---

658 Ibid.
659 B. Long, *2 Kings*, FOTL 10 (Grand Rapids: Eerdmans, 1991) 312.

Only a circumcised Israel could become a conquering Israel. This is the present literary setting. Textual notes give clues that this may not have been the original literary setting. Vv 5b and 7b are apparent doublets, as are vv 4b and 6a. The narrative continuation of v 4 would thus appear in v 7. The original literary piece may have encompassed vv 2–4, 7–8. The editors who placed it in the book clarified the historical background and made the picture more explicit by tying it closer to the pentateuchal narrative.

This doublet reading is not the only valid reading of these verses. Van der Meer argues strongly for a literary unity in vv 4–7, saying "The arguments for distinguishing between layers have not been very convincing or applied consistently."[660] Such literary theories "point to a remarkably complex literary history for such a small piece of text."[661] One might add that repetitive style is typical of much Israelite narrative.

One section has not yet been discussed. V 9 forms the etiological conclusion on which Noth lays so much emphasis. Even here Noth had to attribute the etiological language to the Compiler, who, according to Noth, omitted the original ending of the geographical etiology, replacing it with the story of circumcision.

B. S. Childs shows form critically that the present etiology is only a fragment originally unconnected with the preceding.[662] The LXX even omits the etiological formula. V 9 thus does not belong to the original report. It does belong to the original literary piece (with Noth), for the etiology connects the narrative to Gilgal rather than to the anonymous "camp" of v 8. The etiology here, like many Childs discusses, represents an editiorial addition to the narrative joining the circumcision tradition to the Gilgal sanctuary.

Vv 10–12 represent a literary production presupposing a much larger context, namely, the context of the entire saving history. In a real way, this is the literary climax to the entire exodus-wilderness narrative. The people who celebrated Passover in Egypt prior to experiencing the exodus celebrate Passover again prior to taking the land. Wars of conquest may lie ahead to achieve political control, but the produce of the land has been given into the hands of those who celebrate Passover.

The interesting point here is the climax of the narrative. No further remark is made about festival celebration. The conclusion centers on life in the land. This has consequences for understanding the type of narrative under discussion. The brief report signals the end of the Pentateuch promise of land and prosperity in the land, for it reports the beginning of a life that will rely on the resources of the land rather than on the wilderness manna resources from heaven.

Josh 5:13–15 shifts subjects and locale in a startling fashion. The transition to the unit is marked by Josh 5:10a, showing how Israel had time and security for such cultic activities. Whereas Joshua was not mentioned in the preceding notice about Passover, he alone is the subject here "at Jericho" (v 13). Nelson recognizes a plot movement from unrecognition through question and answer to recognition and goes on to categorize the passage as a commissioning story in the tradition of divine war.[663] Nelson also connects the narrative to ancient Near East stories whose purpose is to build up the confidence of a king or military leader going into

---

660   *Formation and Reformulation*, 304.
661   Ibid.
662   "A Study of the Formula, 'Until This Day,'" *JBL* 82 (1963) 285.
663   Nelson, 81. Cf. Štrba, *Take Off Your Sandals*, who sees Joshua commissioned as the prophet like Moses.

battle, as exemplified in the text in which Ishtar appears with a drawn sword and gives Ashurbanipal a promise of victory.[664]

This story centers on Joshua and his actions, not on Israel and its army or on the nations and their reaction to Israel's powerful presence. Joshua is surprised to see a mysterious figure standing before him with a sword. As Moses went to investigate the bush (Exod 3:3), Joshua goes to investigate the mysterious figure confronting him (5:13b). Joshua even goes so far as to speak first (v 13b). The figure refuses to answer Joshua's question (v 14a; see *Notes*) but does identify himself. In fact, he starts to tell his mission (v 14aβ; cf. the same form in 2 Sam 14:15) but does not finish his sentence.

The form of the narrative connects it to Exod 3 (note particularly Josh 5:15 and Exod 3:5) but has caused trouble for commentators since it appears to be incomplete. The form of this narrative appears to call for a final commissioning line. This has led commentators repeatedly to speak of a broken form and an original ending that was quite distinct. Thus Nelson suggests "perhaps the original announcement was cut out as offensive to theological sensibilities."[665] He adds that it could have been duplicated by Josh 6:2.

We must ask if this search for an ending is not precisely the intended reaction. Joshua, not the figure that appears to him, occupies center stage. The purpose of the narrative is not to hear words from the messenger but to show Joshua's obedient reaction. This is not a commissioning narrative but a readiness narrative. Will Joshua show himself to be a prototype of the leader after Moses by recognizing and responding to the presence of the holy? Joshua does not wait to see the messenger's mission, that is, to hear why God sent the messenger. Joshua knows the proper reaction and falls on his face in awe (note that Moses allowed Yahweh to identify himself fully before covering his face [Exod 3:6]). Hess notes that distinctions between messengers and the deity are not clearly maintained in Hebrew narrative.[666]

Having expressed proper reverence, Joshua asks the figure before him to continue his introduction. The answer is both a demand for yet another sign of reverence and a revelation that the spot of ground is holy.

The expected conclusion would be for the figure to instruct Joshua to establish a new cultic practice or change an existing one.[667] That is not the case here. One might expect the instruction to the man chosen by God as appears in the Moses narrative (Exod 3). That is unnecessary here, having been given in Josh 1 and in Deut 31. The conclusion is simply the obedience of Joshua. Whatever the original form of the narrative, the present form is that of divine test. The divine messenger appears and places demands upon the human recipient. In Gen 17:22–27, Abraham's obedience to God's command is described in great detail. In Josh 5, Joshua's response to God's command is a simple statement of fact—he obeyed. The result will be that the Lord's commander will lead Joshua's armies even if this is not explicitly stated. The brief, enigmatic narrative thus functions as a qualification of Joshua as God's commander and "Joshua's authorization to begin the campaign and a guarantee that it will be successful."[668]

---

664 *ANET*, 451.
665 Nelson, 82.
666 Hess (2009) 30.
667 Noth, 23.
668 Nelson, 83.

Joshua 5 Form and Narrative Elements

Narratives: Legitimate land, food, and leader			Genre: Cultic Report: Circumcision, Passover, theophany		
Element	Passage	Marker	Element	Passage	Marker
Exposition (pf. or disjunctive)	v 2	Disjunctive	Divine cultic command to circumcise second time	v 2	Imperatives
Complication (impf. consec.)	v 3	Impf. consec.: Joshua obeyed	Command executed with etiological hint	v 3	
Change or crisis (speech or dialogue)	vv 4–8	Disjunctive narration by narrator	Explanation	vv 4–7	This is reason why
Resolution (impf. consec.)	v 9a	Impf. consec.: disgrace rolled away	Reaction of circumcised	v 8	Temporal clause pointing to period of healing
Ending/ denouement (formulaic)	v 9b	Etiological formula	Divine reaction to circumcision	v 9a	Divine speech
			Etiology	v 9b	Etiological formula
Exposition (pf. or disjunctive)	v 10	Syntactically tied to previous unit; narrative exposition introducing new settiing	Report	v 10	Impf. consec. reporting on camping and keeping Passover
Complication (impf. consec.)	v 11	Impf. consec.: eating from land	Chronological report on eating land's produce	v 11	Impf. consec. with repetition of eating and time
Change or crisis (speech or dialogue)	v 12a	Manna stopped; narrator's monologue	Report of manna ceasing	v 12a	Impf. consec. for ceasing
Resolution (impf. consec.)	v 12b	Ate from produce of land	Report of manna disappearing forever	v 12b	Disjunctive negative on availability of manna
Ending/ denouement (formulaic)		(No explicit formula)	Report of depending on fruit of land	v 12c	Impf. consec. of eating
Exposition (pf. or disjunctive)	v 13	Temporal clause laying setting	Report of appearance of unexpected warrior	v 13a	Disjunctive temporal clause with impf. consec.
Complication (impf. consec.)	v 13b	Impf. consec.	Report of approach to and questioning of warrior	v 13b	Impf. consec. plus interrogative

Narratives: Legitimate land, food, and leader			Genre: Cultic Report: Circumcision, Passover, theophany		
Element	*Passage*	*Marker*	*Element*	*Passage*	*Marker*
Change or crisis (speech or dialogue)	vv 13c–14a	Dialogue: interrogative	Report of warrior's response	v 14a	Impf. consec. plus negative plus self-introduction
Resolution (impf. consec.)	v 14b	Impf. consec.: Joshua fell to ground	Joshua's response	v 14b	Impf. consec. plus interrogative
Ending/ denouement (formulaic)	v 15	Theophanic formula			
			Theophanic revelation and command	v 15	Theophanic formula
			Report of obedience	v 15b	Obedience formula

Structure

Knauf notes that the exodus began with the observance of Passover, while the entrance into the Promised Land begins with *maṣṣôt* or Unleavened Bread.[669] Thus Josh 5 fits structurally into the larger context of the Pentateuch. One can explain this larger structure as a growth of independent sources. It might be explained as the result of a series of editors capped by a Priestly or a post-Priestly/Deuteronomic final editor. One can speak of an Enneateuch developed backward so that the Pentateuch is the final literary piece and is composed in light of the Joshua-Kings narratives. Or one can posit an early editor who knew Israel's major traditions and created this structure tying together Exodus and Joshua structure if not the complete Pentateuch. The decision at this point rests as much on one's theological understanding of the nature of the Bible as authoritative canon as it does on scholarly investigation and evidence. One can look for minute redactional inserts and changes. One can look for seams marking transition or for repeated elements indicating *Wiederaufnahme* or literary resumption after an inserted section. One can also seek literary elements that show artistry in using repetition and synonyms to achieve a literary unity that explains away seeming doublets or contradictions or theological nuances.

Narrative structures tracing movement from crisis to resolution do not assist the analyst in examining this chapter. The only tension is produced by the unexpected appearance of the commander of God's armies, and this is plot surprise rather than a narrative resolution. The structure is threefold: circumcision report, Passover report, messenger test story.

I. Circumcision report
   A. Divine instructions for circumcision "a second time"
   B. Joshua's obedience in circumcising
   C. Historical reason for second circumcision

---

669 Knauf, 65.

  D. Rest after circumcision
  E. Naming of Gilgal with etiology
 II. Passover report
  A. Camping in Gilgal
  B. Observing Passover on fourteenth of month in plains of Jericho
  C. Day after Passover eating fruit of land consisting of unleavened bread and parched grain
  D. Cessation of manna, and persistence of Israel in eating fruit of the land
III. Messenger test story
  A. Exposition (pf. or disjunctive): Joshua in Jericho on the alert (disjunctive)
  B. Complication (impf. consec.): Man standing with drawn sword ("surprise clause")
  C. Change or crisis (speech or dialogue): Joshua approaches and speaks, seeking man's identity; man answers, "No. But I am . . ."
  D. Resolution (impf. consec.): Joshua fell face to the ground; man said place was holy.
  E. Ending/denouement (formulaic): Etiological formula

The final unit in chap. 5 proves to be a Hebrew crisis-resolution narrative with the resolution coming with the obedience of Joshua. It is thus a test narrative seeing if the leader after Moses would obey divine orders.

The chapter has, then, three units only loosely tied together syntactically but tightly joined by their ritual interests and by their concern with cultic purification. They do not constitute a storyline or plot line as much as they do three brief vignettes that transition Israel from a wandering people to a people ready to reside in the Promised Land.

Setting

The word *setting* may be used in different ways and in different contexts when applied to this chapter. Nelson underlines the literary redaction that joins the materials in the chapter, arguing against their origin or preservation in any cultic presentation.[670] Literary redaction understands the chapter as brief reports followed by a brief testing narrative. The third element featuring Joshua and the mysterious messenger may well have its home in the Gilgal/Jericho cult celebration of the crossing of the Jordan and/or the Israelite preparations to move into the land to fight the enemies. As such it would have served as the introduction to Yahweh war narratives.

The circumcision report rests on a tradition of Israel's longtime ritual, perhaps at one time a rite of passage into adulthood but transformed by Abraham's covenant actions into a sign of God's covenant with Israel and Israel's covenant obedience. In carrying out circumcision, Joshua thereby binds covenant obedience and land possession.

The circumcision report is located on the "hill of foreskins" (v 3). The action itself obviously involved a painful healing process (v 8; cf. Gen 34:25). No chronological statement is made (v 2). It is a time when iron knives are known, so that flint knives have to be specifically prescribed if they are to be used.

Originally the oral story referred to the problems suffered by grown men under-

---

going a child's operation (cf. Gen 34). It may have been told tongue in cheek to get a good laugh at the sufferers' expense. Transformed in the biblical context it has taken on new meaning.

We see, then, that an original report about Joshua bringing soreness upon the men of Israel has been taken up by the theological tradition to show that Israel under Joshua was theologically and cultically prepared to begin the conquest of Jericho. Later interpretation made explicit that the people in Egypt had followed the command to Abraham and had been circumcised; only the generation born in the wilderness had not been circumcised. That courageous generation had to endure the pain and harassment of infant surgery just as they celebrated entering the land and preparing for conquest.

The Passover report in Josh 5 is rooted in centuries of cultic celebration, that, most likely, presupposed the joining of Passover and Unleavened Bread. The setting for the report is not cultic but literary, formulated in writing for just this place in the ultimate history. The focus of the narrative is not so much on Passover as much as on the possession of the crops of the land as a gift from God and the assurance that Israel will possess the land.

Finally, the test narrative binds Josh 5 closely to the Exodus tradition by forming a narrative arc from Exod 3 to Josh 5. At home in the Gilgal cult, the narrative shows that the Israelite leader is prepared spiritually to command the invading armies and that he and the newly circumcised men are cultically prepared for battle.

Comments

2 The book of Joshua continues as a dialogue between Yahweh and human leader. Yahweh commands Joshua to make flint knives and use them to circumcise the people. Hess suggests that the knives were made of obsidian and states "the smooth and sharp surface of this sort of knife enjoyed popularity for ritual and non-ritual purposes long after the development of metal knives."[671] Josh 5 indicates what "'new life' for Israel will look like and what is central to its construction."[672]

Metal knives were forbidden in the construction of Israelite altars (Exod 20:25; Deut 27:5; Josh 8:31) so the notice here is perhaps "intended as a polemic against the use of metal knives."[673] The use of flint knives represents a common ritual phenomenon, since time-honored, old-fashioned materials are used in the cult even when more "modern" equipment is available. The use of such utensils lends an awesome aura to the cultic event.[674] Exod 4:25 shows a similar connection of flint utensils to circumcision, and thus Howard maintains that the command to use the knives intentionally recalled the incident of Abraham and his son in Gen 17 and that the knives were special instruments used only for ritual purposes.[675]

Knauf sees circumcision, like the water crossings, as literary markers of the fulfillment of divine promises:[676]

---

671 Hess (1996) 119; cf. A. R. Millard, "Back to the Iron Bed: Og's or Procrustes'?" *Congress Volume Paris 1992*, VTSup 61 (Leiden: Brill, 1995) 197.

672 Earl, 133.

673 Nelson, 76.

674 Cf. van der Meer, *Formation and Reformulation*, 292.

675 Howard 148; cf. Nelson, 76.

676 Knauf, 64.

Table. 5.1. Knauf's Ritual/Promise Table Expanded

Bible Passage	Rite	Promise
Genesis 17	Circumcision in Abraham's family	Promise of nation, God, and land
Exodus 1		Fulfillment of nation promise
Exodus 4:24–26	Circumcision in Moses' family	Preparation to face Pharaoh
Exodus 12:43–49	First national Passover with circumcision required	Preparation for escape from Egypt
Exodus 40	[Beginning of wilderness wandering]	Fulfillment of God's presence promise
Joshua 5:2–8	Second circumcision; end of wilderness wandering	
Joshua 6–24		Fulfillment of land promise

Circumcision is performed on adult males, as is also the case in Egypt. It may have once been a rite of passage into puberty for Israel, but the biblical record knows it only as a religious ritual by which Israel shows her loyalty to Yahweh (Gen 17; 21:4; Exod 12:43–49; Lev 12:3). Many of Israel's neighbors may have practiced circumcision (cf. Jer 9:24–25), but this is not the narrative point. God sought a people who obediently carried out what he commanded, even Abraham at age ninety-nine (Gen 17:24). Circumcision and the Israelite(s) became identical (Gen 17:13–14). In the exilic period, this mark of differentiation became essential, since the Babylonian overlords were not circumcised.

Knauf argues that the rite became important only in the Babylonian exile from whence it was brought back to Canaan.[677] Prior to the exile it was a custom that did not unconditionally require a divine command. Such an argument again lays too much weight on refined redaction-critical methodology and on a quite negative view of Israel's religious history and historical sources prior to the exile.

The physical rite helped identify one's own flesh, and thereby one's own children, as belonging to Israel's God and not to the culture and gods of the environment. The historian realized, too, that the ritual was not enough in itself. It demanded more—a circumcised heart (Deut 10:16; 30:6; cf. Lev 26:41; Jer 9:4).

The Hebrew text says Joshua is to "circumcise again the sons of Israel a second time." (See *Notes*.) Questions run rampant concerning this second circumcision. Hall argues vigorously that the first circumcision has to be that of the exodus generation in Egypt.[678] Failure to continue the practice signifies rebellion or negligence. The wilderness generation had not maintained the rite as had the Exodus participants. No one was circumcised twice. Rather the nation's men had been circumcised in light of the covenant with Abraham and through the generations in Egyptian captivity. In the wilderness the Exodus generation died out, so that Joshua is supposed to return Israel to the ancient practice.

Josh 5:2 makes clear that Joshua had not initiated circumcision into Israel. He was only restoring Israel to her previous covenant relationship. The present text

677   Ibid., 65.
678   *Conquering Character*, 66–67.

traces the practice of circumcision back to Egypt (v 5a), while the pentateuchal tradition traces it back to Abraham (Gen 17) while affirming the circumcision of those in Egypt (Exod 12:43–49). God led Joshua to reimpose "the rite after it had lapsed after the 'first time.'"[679] Such reimposition constituted Israel as a people eligible to participate in the cultic rites of Yahweh before they received the gift of the land.[680]

3 True to his promise in chap. 1, Joshua is obedient to the divine command. He accomplishes the task at the "hill of foreskins." Van der Meer interprets the story here as fiction describing Joshua's work of creating a hill of foreskins, a detail given "to stress the extraordinary character of the event narrated."[681] Yet such intimate, folkloristic details as flint knives and foreskin hills are what maintains itself in oral narrative.

No location is given for the ritual of circumcising, though v 9 attaches the whole scene to Gilgal. The hill most likely originally represented the site, cultic in nature, where the community practiced circumcision and buried the foreskins.[682] It is now identified with the area of Gilgal. The story itself was not, however, an etiology of this hill, for the conclusion does not come in v 3.

4 The story is no longer simply a report. It now is an important part of sacred history. It describes Israel's atonement (cf. LXX) for a whole generation's neglect, a neglect caused in part at least by the sins of the previous generation. The fathers left Egypt circumcised, identified as people of God, experiencing the saving act of God.

5 But circumcision, the identifying mark of the people of God, was not passed to the next generation. Thus under Joshua Israel obeys the obligation implied by Exod 13:5.

6–7 Forty years passed until the condemned generation died in the wilderness. The Hebrew text makes an interesting play on two words. The older generation left Egypt as an עַם, a "people" of God (v 4), indeed a circumcised people (עַם, v 5a). It died, however, as a גּוֹי, a "nation" of God's enemies (v 6).[683] The younger generation was born an עַם (people) in the wilderness (v 5b). It became a גּוֹי (nation, v 8) until it was circumcised. Both גּוֹיִם (nations) were "finished off" (Heb. תם) by God, the first by death (v 6), the second by circumcision (v 8). Turning from a nation to a people was the goal of Israel in the book of Deuteronomy (Deut 4:6). But Israel sought to be like the גּוֹיִם, "nations" (e.g., Deut 17:14–20; 1 Sam 8:5).[684]

The writer makes clear how the circumcised people of God came to be a nation opposed to God. Here is the Deuteronomistic theme. God has clearly revealed his will to his people in the Deuteronomic law. They have refused to listen and act. This brings immediate action from God. He swears an oath that the disobedient generation will not have part of the oath he has sworn to the fathers. Here is an important statement about the nature of God's promises to his people. He has made a promise that directs the history of his people, but that promise can be realized only by an

679   Nelson, 77; cf. van der Meer, *Formation and Reformulation,* 292–93.
680   Fritz, 58.
681   *Formation and Reformulation,* 294.
682   Cf. Soggin, 69–70; Bright, 573; Gradwohl, *VT* 26 (1976) 235–40; Fritz, 58.
683   Cf. R. E. Clements, "גּוֹי," *TWAT,* 1:972; A. Cody, "When Is the Chosen People Called a Goy?" *VT* 14 (1964) 1–6; Hess 46.
684   See opposition to this view by van der Meer, *Formation and Reformulation,* 299.

obedient people. A disobedient generation finds itself under an oath counteracting for a time the promise of God (cf. the blessings and cursings of Deut 27–28). The promise itself is maintained and transmitted among the people in the first-person plural. It is an oath sworn to us.

Flowing with milk and honey "describes the agricultural and pastoral abundance of Canaan."[685] Pitkänen points to a large apiary found at Tel Rehov from about 900 BCE regarded as the earliest apiary found in the ancient Near East.[686]

8 Winther-Nielsen finds a flashback here to the circumcision.[687] This is not necessary. The temporal clause sets the chronological location as immediately following completion of the circumcision of the nation. The new generation receives new life. The root חיה has the basic meaning "to live, be alive." But ancient humanity did not consider themselves to be fully alive when they were ill. Thus the psalmists often describe themselves as dead (Pss 33:19; 56:14).[688] In a real sense Israel the nation had to let her God make the people sick before they could be healed. This proved to be true not only in the ritual of circumcision but also on the plain of history.

9 Circumcision delivered Israel from the reproach of Egypt. The text assumes that readers know precisely what is meant. Such precise knowledge eludes modern commentators, giving rise to many theories. Gen 34:14 calls uncircumcision "a reproach." The present biblical context makes this impossible, for the Israelites were circumcised while in Egypt (5:5).[689] So Nelson stretches the meaning to the wilderness generation's uncircumcised state.[690] It might be the "disobedience of the previous generation (the generation of Egypt) which brought about the period of wandering and death in the desert."[691] Howard sees the reproach as the scorn the Egyptians heaped on Israel (compare Zeph 2:8).[692] Creach generalizes it to "shame borne by the Israelites in the wilderness."[693] Hall points to Egyptian mockery of Israel's wandering in the wilderness.[694] Knauf connects it to Jer 42:18; 44:8, 12 to find here a summons (*Aufforderung*) to the Egyptian Diaspora in the Persian period to return to the Promised Land.[695] Hawk sees the context pointing to the uncircumsised wilderness generation but also suggests the possibility of a metaphor for the "shame and degrading condition of slavery in Egypt."[696]

The reproach or disgrace of Egypt refers to the insulting social position as slaves to which Israel was degraded in Egypt.[697] Note Hubbard's insistence that the reproach must be something the present generation had experienced, but this is a

---

685 Hess (1996) 121.
686 Pitkänen, 150.
687 *Functional Discourse Grammar*, 167.
688 Cf. C. Barth, *Einführung in die Psalmen*, BibS(N) 32 (Neukirchen-Vluyn: Neukirchener Verlag, 1961) 56–62.
689 Cf. van der Meer, *Formation and Reformulation*, 313–14.
690 Nelson, 76; Cf. Blum, *Textgestalt und Komposition, 235*="Beschneidung und Passa in Kanaan," 307.
691 Hess (1996) 122.
692 Howard, 151.
693 Creach, 56.
694 *Conquering Character*, 69–70.
695 Knauf, 65.
696 Hawk (2010) 60; cf. McConville and Williams, 27.
697 Cf. Gray, 69–71; Hertzberg, 33; Harris, 41; Fritz, 59; Pressler, 40; McConville and Williams, 27; and the uncertainty of Soggin, 72.

reference to national history, not personal history.[698] Pharaoh had degraded the nation of Israel in the sight of all the nations by enslaving them. The cultic symbol of Abraham's covenant renewed the nation in their own land and removed any weapons of reproach Egypt might have. Hubbard[699] sees the reproach connected to Israel's life in the wilderness, which gave Egypt opportunity to ridicule them as having been promised much that Yahweh could not deliver.

Such social reproach is not relieved through political or military maneuvers, however. Only cultic ritual in obedience to Yahweh removes social disgrace. Hawk concludes: "Whatever the precise sense, the comment clearly asserts that Egypt and everything associated with it have been exorcized from Israel."[700] The stay in Gilgal thus becomes a new beginning, which includes not only the action of circumcising the people but also freeing the nation from an unseemly condition.[701] "Divine deliverance of the Hebrews is not complete until the former slaves are settled on their own land as God's free, covenant people."[702]

The theological conclusion is transformed into an etymological wordplay and etiology in v 9b: גלותי, (*galôtî*) "I have rolled away," is connected to Gilgal. This ensures that the narrative is understood in the context of chaps. 3–4. Circumcision stands in continuity with the cultic traditions of the crossing of the Jordan and the teachings of what God has done for Israel. At Gilgal, Israel both learned the catechism and endured the circumcision. This sanctifies Gilgal as an important cultic place for Israel throughout the generations, "until this day."

The "I" of "I called the name" could refer to either Yaweh or Joshua. Hall is most likely correct in maintaining that humans—not the gods—name places.[703]

10 The connection to Gilgal is repeated by the interpreters of vv 10–12, assuring the explicit unity of the context. This also transforms the circumcision narrative into a ritual prelude for Passover, meeting the requirements of Exod 12:43–49. Passover itself is celebrated on the proper day of the calendar (Deut 16:1; Exod 12:4; Num 9:3; Lev 23:5).[704] The dating here can be confusing as van der Meer shows.[705] It can be interpreted as three separate days in vv 10–12, or vv 11–12 may be the same day, or even vv 10–12 could be one twenty-four-hour period from sunset to sunset.

Interestingly, "Joshua has disappeared as the main agent," as van der Meer notes in arguing against Nelson's theory that Joshua stands as a prototype of King Josiah.[706] The emphasis on the camp seems to repeat Josh 4:19 and is not needed here. Van der Meer finds a *Wiederaufnahme* here in which an editor inserts a passage (here 5:10–12) and introduces it by repeating an earlier phrase.[707] Such a literary theory sounds logical, but it is hard to prove since it begins with a presupposition that it then proves with the evidence that led to the presupposition. A presuppposition for unity of the text will follow the same logical path to prove the unity.

---

698 Hubbard, 182.
699 Hubbard builds on Howard, 151–52, and Noort, "The Disgrace of Egypt," 18–19.
700 Hess (2000) 81.
701 Fritz, 59; cf. van der Meer, *Formation and Reformulation,* 314.
702 Pressler, 40.
703 *Conquering Character,* 77.
704 For general orientation on the biblical calendar, see S. J. de Vries, "Calendar," *IDB,* 1:483–88.
705 *Formation and Reformulation,* 394; cf. Wagenaar, *ZAW* 115 (2003) 3–24.
706 *Formation and Reformulation,* 315.
707 Ibid., 317.

11 The point of interest for the original tradition is not the Passover as such, but the transition in lifestyle. Israel can now eat the produce of the land rather than the manna of the desert.[708] The language used to express this requires attention. מעבור, "produce," occurs only in this passage (vv 11–12) in the entire Hebrew Bible. The root קלה appears nine times in the Bible, in reference to roasted grain (Lev 2:14; 23:14; Josh 5:11; 1 Sam 17:17; 25:18; 2 Sam 17:28; Ruth 2:14). The biblical texts do not support the claim that this represented a delicacy.[709] Rather it signifies food able to be sent easily to those away from home from a supply readily available. The Passover took place at the time of barley harvest, and barley was the basic staple of Canaanite and then Israelite diets. For newcomers from the wilderness, though, it may have been considered a delicacy. The Israelites are not pictured eating it in relation to a harvest festival, but simply eating grain ready to hand, growing wild in fields they had not planted. The same applies to מצות, "unleavened bread." This is the typical bread for a journey, that to which a wandering people would be accustomed. The point is not that Israel denied themselves the use of yeast for festival regulations. Rather, the point is one of joy. They could eat their normal diet with the prospect of much more to come because the whole land lay before them.

Josh 5:10–12 shows one stage in the development of Israel's cultic history, a stage when Passover was celebrated on one day and included the eating of the crops of the new land in celebration of God's gift of the land. The seven-day festival of Unleavened Bread does not appear to fit into the time frame given here. The separate history of the two festivals is revealed in the early cultic calendars, where only Unleavened Bread is mentioned (Exod 23:15; 34:18) and in the exodus narrative where each of the festivals is given a separate origin (Exod 12:21–27; 13:3–9). At some point in its history, Israel's cultic calendar united the two festivals (Deut 16:1–8; Lev 23:5–8). Israelites celebrating Passover under these new cultic conditions did not read the Josh text with the same understanding in which it had been composed. For them the reference to מצות could mean nothing else than the seven-day festival immediately following Passover. Thus they interpreted the text by adding "on the day after Passover" (see *Notes*). Nelson finds that "Joshua celebrates a centralized national Passover like the one envisioned in Deuteronomy 16 and carried out by Josiah (2 Kings 23:21–23)."[710] But the Joshua text does not emphasize Passover. It emphasizes the produce of the land. It does not emphasize leadership, for Joshua does not appear in vv 10–12. Josiah may later have read the Joshua tradition and patterned his action after his interpretation of "Joshua's Passover," but Joshua's Passover is much more than a model invented to foreshadow Josiah's actions.

12 The manna tradition is taken up from the pentateuchal traditions (Exod 16:13–35; cf. Num 11:4–9; Deut 8:1–20). Israel has not conquered the land, but she can live off its bounty and no longer needs special divine provision. McConville and Williams think the "actual transition . . . may in practice have been gradual."[711] "To

---

708   Cf. Segal, *Hebrew Passover*, 237.
709   G. Dalman, *Arbeit und Sitte in Palästina*, vol. 3 (Gütersloh: Bertelsmann, 1933) 265; Halbe, *ZAW* 87 (1975) 333.
710   Nelson, 79.
711   McConville and Williams, 29.

eat the yield of the land of Canaan is to claim the land."[712] Yahweh proved himself to be the giver of the fruit of the land before he gave the fortifications of the land to Israel.

13 The introductory temporal clause sets this off as a new narrative, one that proves "cryptic" with an "unmotivated, puzzling shift in locale."[713] How did Joshua get to Jericho and why? How does the episode fit chronologically?[714] "This was a threatening sight."[715] Thus Hess concludes: "A figure with a drawn sword is one not to be toyed with. He is one who threatens divine judgment."[716] Compare Num 22:23; 1 Chr 21:16. "Joshua reacts like an alert sentry."[717]

The reader may locate the Israelite encampment in Jericho if one takes the most natural reading of the text or perhaps "at" Jericho (see *Notes*). This ties the text both to the previous location "in the plains of Jericho" and to the site of the following chapter, though it is unlikely that the present context means to place Joshua inside the walls of the city. Thus McConville and Williams conclude, "'In Jericho' can hardly be taken at its face value, since, in the logic of the narrative, Joshua has not yet even approached it to give battle. It must be taken to mean 'in the region of Jericho.'"[718] Unlike the previous sections (vv 9b, 10a), the writer makes no attempt to tie the material here to Gilgal. Rösel is certainly on target as he concludes that "in Jericho" is original.[719] But then he explains the location in Jericho as the result of a possible later sanctuary in Jericho "which could explain the emergence of the tradition."[720]

The Bible consistently pictures Joshua as a rather brash young man asking questions and giving opinions in the most unlikely circumstances (Exod 32:17; Num 11:28). Here he boldly confronts the visitor and demands proper identification before permitting him to enter the camp.

14 The visitor answers quickly and simply: "No." "Joshua was asking the wrong question."[721] Joshua sought the visitor's military allegiance. The visitor sought Joshua's reverent obedience. The messenger put Joshua to the test. Joshua could not put the messenger to the test. The messenger was on God's side. Was Joshua on the same side? "The Lord remains independent and will judge what side to support by how the people obey or do not obey their orders from God."[722] "The 'man' initially answers, 'No' or 'Neither one' in order to turn down Joshua's alternative between his own or the enemy's forces."[723]

"The prince of the host of Yahweh" appears only here and in Dan 8:11, where the reference is to God himself. Our passage is more closely akin to the figure of the messenger of Yahweh who appears fifty-eight times in the OT, with eleven further

712 Nelson, 80.
713 Ibid.
714 See Hubbard, 185.
715 Howard, 155.
716 Hess (1996) 126.
717 Harris, 42.
718 McConville and Williams, 29.
719 Rösel, 87–88.
720 Ibid.
721 Howard 156, n. 285.
722 Harris, 43.
723 Winther-Nielsen, *Functional Discourse Grammar,* 204.

occurrences of "messenger of God." (See the excursus on "The Identity of the Angel of the Lord" by Howard, 159–60.) Such a messenger commissions Gideon (Judg 6:11) and even appears briefly in the narrative of Moses' commissioning (Exod 3:2). Another brief appearance comes in the deliverance at the sea (Exod 14:19; cf. Num 20:16). Seeing the messenger can be equated with seeing God (Judg 13:22). As a military figure, the messenger destroys God's enemies (Num 22:23; 2 Sam 24:16–17; 2 Kgs 19:35). Howard concludes: "The exact nature or personality of this divine self-revelation are [sic] not known precisely because the Scriptures are silent on the question."[724]

O. Keel argues on the basis of Near Eastern art that the scene here is one of commissioning in which the messenger hands the javelin in his hand to Joshua (see Josh 8:18, 26, and the "rod" of Moses in Exod 4:17; 17:9).[725] Whatever the scene imagined here, the present narrative has drastically altered it. The prince is never given the opportunity to commission Joshua or hand over anything to him. Joshua continues talking and acting. The scene thus pictures Joshua as the totally obedient servant doing precisely what the divine messenger requires. He needs no commission in addition to the one he received in Chap. 1. What he does need is (a) a personal confrontation with deity that confirms his commission; and (b) a personal devotion to the deity that confirms his readiness for the task ahead. These are provided here. Without bidding, Joshua falls to the ground in reverence for God's presence in the divine messenger. He stops grilling the messenger and asks simply for the divine word brought to him. He sees that the divine commander is not automatically tied to either army. The question is always, which army is devoted to the divine commander? "The angelic commander is part of no human army. Joshua needs to broaden his perspective to include Yahweh's supernatural resources."[726] "The enigmatic words of the commander challenge any attempt to tie national aspirations too closely to YHWH's purpose."[727] "The narrative ends with a barefoot Joshua—like Moses at the burning bush (Exod 3:1–6)—who has been given nothing to do."[728]

15 The messenger's words may have originated in the stories of the founding of sanctuaries,[729] but their present literary function is distinct. The words are borrowed from the experience of Moses to attest once more the dependence of Joshua on Moses. Hubbard argues that Joshua is equal in authority to Moses.[730] Such a view raises Joshua's stature a bit too high. Joshua remains tied to the law of Moses and to doing exactly what Moses commanded. The book of Joshua praises Joshua as the perfect successor to Moses, but does not indicate that Joshua shared the same stature, power, and authority as did Moses.[731]

Even his "call experience" with the divine messenger is simply a replica of the Moses' call. Wherever he turns, Joshua cannot escape the Mosaic shadow. In that shadow he does precisely what Moses commanded Israel to do. As Moses slipped off his sandals on holy ground (Exod 3:5), so did Joshua. But what ground was holy,

---

724 Howard, 160.
725 *Wirkmächtige Siegeszeichen*, 85–88.
726 Nelson, 81.
727 Hess (2000) 75.
728 Creach, 50.
729 See Noth.
730 Hubbard, 186.
731 Contra Štrba, *Take Off Your Sandals*.

that of Gilgal near Jericho, that of Jericho itself, or that of the entire land? Has God now declared Palestine, the Promised Land, holy because a holy people will take it in God's holy way of the ban (חרם)?

Israel's enemies are divided into only two groups: the Amorite land lovers and the Syrians and the Canaanite inhabitants of the coast or Phoenicians.[732] The theme connected to the enemies throughout Joshua is that of lack of courage (compare Josh 2:11; chap. 9; 10:2).

Joshua has passed the divine test. The literary form is complete. The theological message has been delivered. Nothing more is needed. This small section "easily stands alone as God's final encouragement . . . to Joshua."[733]

Explanation

The ending of chap. 5 marks a "decisive change" not only in Israel's geographic position but also in its theological position. The people of Israel have "passed from a condition of disgrace, and they bear once again in themselves the marks of their covenant standing before God."[734]

All three scenes in chap. 5, each in its own way, give the same signal: the wilderness wandering is complete; Israel has arrived at home.[735] Pressler summarizes the theological connections clearly:[736]

> Key themes voiced in chaps 1 through 4 continue to weave through chap 5: Yahweh's agency, Israel's call to obedience, Joshua's leadership, and the identity of Israel as God's covenant people. . . . A less dominant voice, heard in Rahab's story, that the Lord who fights for Israel is nonetheless not owned by Israel, sounds in the chapter's closing vignette: the commander of the armies of Yahweh is neither Israelite nor Canaanite.

"God's suppport and victory in battle demand that the tribes prepare liturgically and religiously for battle."[737] One can read the theological intentions at different levels of composition and usage. The first level comprises three isolated incidents. The example of Joshua's generation stands as testimony that the people of God undergo even the pain and inconvenience of ritual, perhaps enduring gentle ridicule from their friends, to demonstrate loyalty to their God. The celebration of Passover provides an opportunity to enjoy the fruits of the land and look in anticipation to the fuller bounty God will provide. The experience of the prince of God's armies assures the leader of his role in leading God's people into battle and shows that the land is holy because God is present in it and is giving it to Israel. Nelson states that possession of the land ties the sections together thematically, while the locale of Gilgal/Jericho ties them together geographically.[738]

Set in a literary context, the materials charge one another theologically.

---

732 Knauf, 63.
733 Howard, 159.
734 McConville and Williams, 27.
735 Knauf, 63.
736 Pressler, 36.
737 Harris, 40.
738 Nelson, 75.

Circumcision is proper preparation for the observance of Passover. God's people demonstrate that they are responsible in their preparations to celebrate what God has done. In turn, the act of circumcision testifies that God is active among them, rolling away their reproach and shame and establishing them as at least equals in the councils of the nations. The action also provides a name and a basis of authenticity for the sanctuary where Israel's history of worship in the land began. Passover is the end of the story of God's saving history with his people, an end that repeats the beginning of that story. History has come full circle. The people who escaped the deadly visit of God in Egypt through observance of the Passover now observe the Passover to celebrate the bountiful gifts of God's presence in the new land. The miracle of manna is replaced by the miracle of fertility provided by God in the as-yet-unconquered land. The land will be conquered, however, for the prince of the divine host has appeared to the commander of the host of Israel, and the human commander has proved himself worthy of the task given him. "Israel transformed is now prepared to wrest the land from its inhabitants."[739]

For the later exiled readers of the history, the story takes on a new meaning. Circumcision was not unique in Canaan, but it is unique when carried out in the land of captivity. In Babylon the ritual of circumcision is certainly cause for ridicule and physical suffering. Passover is once more celebrated in hope rather than in celebration of a gift already given.

After the return from exile, the narrative continues to speak to the people of God. Their own cultic celebration is now undergirded. To be circumcised again may be a call to portions of the community who had, like the wilderness generation, neglected the rituals of the people in a foreign land or under persecution and hopelessness. It is certainly a prerequisite for participation in the rituals of the new temple. Observing Passover at God's chosen sanctuary on the proper date, followed by eating unleavened bread on the day after Passover, is a reminder for the Second Temple community to celebrate again God's gift of the land, this time after a journey across a different wilderness. Such celebration for the Second Temple community would involve both the Feast of Passover and the Feast of Unleavened Bread. After such proper worship, Israel could expect renewed opportunity to enjoy the fruits of the land. Perhaps then the prince of the heavenly hosts would again appear, even to a new Joshua (cf. Hag 1:1, 12; 2:2, 4; Zech 3; etc.).

Josh 5 thus functioned for many generations as a testimony to God's greatness in enduring the unfaithfulness of one generation of Israelites and stirring new hopes in a new generation. It stood as a call to each generation to cultic faithfulness even when the result might be shame, reproach, or suffering. It stood as a call to remember God's gift of fertility, a gift given to a faithful people. It stood as a promise of divine appearance and divine protection for a leader ready to worship and obey.

(See *Excursus: Yahweh War in Tradition and Theology*)

---

739 Hess (2000) 75.

E. Faith Fells Fortifications (6:1–27)

Bibliography

Abel, F. M. "L'anathème de Jéricho et la maison de Rahab." *RB* 57 (1950) 321–30. ———. "Les stratagèmes dans le Livre de Josué." *RB* 56 (1949) 321–39. **Anbar, M.** "La 'Reprise.'" *VT* 38 (1988) 385–98. **Baars, W.** *New Syro-Hexaplaric Texts.* Leiden: Brill, 1968. 101–3. **Bartfeld, H.** "Different Pictures Have Been Integrated into the Narrative of the Conquest of Jericho." *BMik* 53.2 (2008) 27–56 (Heb.). ———. "Uncovering the Latest Stratum Added to the Composition Describing the Conquest of Jericho (Jos. 6) by Text-Critical Research." *BMik* 53.1 (2008) 5–30 (Heb.). **Bartlett, J. R.** *Jericho.* Cities of the Biblical World. Grand Rapids: Eerdmans, 1982. **Bar-Yosef, O.** "The Walls of Jericho: An Alternative Interpretation." *Current Anthropology* 27 (1986) 157–62. **Begg, C. T.** "The Crossing of the Jordan according to Josephus." *AcT* 26 (2006) 1–16. ———. "The Fall of Jericho according to Josephus." *EstBib* 63 (2005) 323–40. **Benjamin, C. D.** *The Variations between the Hebrew and Greek Texts of Joshua: Chapters 1–12.* Thesis, University of Pennsylvania. Leipzig: W. Drugulin, 1921. **Bieberstein, K.** *Josua, Jordan, Jericho: Archäologie, Geschichte und Theologie der Landnahmeerzählung Josua 1–6.* OBO 143. Göttingen: Vandenhoeck & Ruprecht, 1995. **Bienkowski, P.** *Jericho in the Late Bronze Age.* Warminster: Aris & Phillips, 1986. ———. "Jericho Was Destroyed in the Middle Bronze Age, Not the Late Bronze Age." *BAR* 16.5 (1990) 45–49, 69. ———. "Le rempart de Josué: Enigme pour les archéologues." *MdB* 69 (1991) 22–24. **Bimson, J. J.** *Redating the Exodus and Conquest.* JSOTSup 5. Sheffield: University of Sheffield, 1978. Esp. 115–45. **Blake, I. M.** "Jericho ('Ain es-Sultan): Joshua's Curse and Elisha's Miracle. One Possible Explanation." *PEQ* 99 (1967) 86–97. **Bliss, F. J.** "Notes on the Plain of Jericho. *PEFQS* (1894) 175–83. **Boling, R. G.** "Enigmatic Bible Passages: Jericho Off Limits." *BA* 46 (1983) 115–16. **Braber, M. den.** "'They keep on going . . .': Repetition in Joshua 6:20." In *The Book of* Joshua. Ed. E. Noort. Leuven: Peeters, 2012. 489–500. **Braber, M. den, and J.-W. Wesselius.** "The Unity of Joshua 1–8, Its Relation to the Story of King Keret, and the Literary Background to the Exodus and Conquest Stories." *SJOT* 22 (2008) 253–74. **Brekelmans, C. H. W.** *De Ḥerem in het Oude Testament.* Nijmegen: Centrale Drukkerij, 1959. 86–92. ———. "Le Ḥerem chez les prophètes du royaume du Nord et dans le Deutéronome." In *Sacra Pagina: Miscellanea Biblica Congressus Internationalis Catholici de Re Biblica.* Ed. J. Coppens, A. Descamps, and E. Massaux. Vol. 1. BETL 12. Gembloux: Duculot, 1959. 377–83. **Briend J.** "Bible et Archéologie en Josué 6,1–8:29: Recherches sur la composition de Josué 1–12." Dissertation, Paris, 1978. ———. "Le Trésor de YHWH en Jos 6.19.24b." *Transeu* 20 (2000) 101–06. ———. "The Sources of the Deuteronomic History: Research on Joshua 1–12." In *Israel Constructs Its History: Deuteronomistic Historiography in Recent Research.* Ed. A. de Pury, T. Römer, and J.-D. Macchi, JSOTSup 306. Sheffield: Sheffield Academic, 2000. 360–86. Orginally published as "Les Sources de L'Histoire deuteronomique recherches sur Jos 1–12," in *Israël construit son histoire: L'historiograhie deutéronomiste à la lumière des recherches récentes,* ed. A. de Pury, T. Römer, and J.-D. Macchi, *MdB* 34 (Geneva: Labor et Fides, 1996). **Broshi, M.** "Troy and Jericho." *BAIAS* 7 (1987–1988) 3–7. **Bruins, H. J., and J. van der Plicht.** "Tell Es-Sultan (Jericho): Radiocarbon Results of Short-Lived and Multiyear Charcoal Samples from the End of the Middle Bronze Age." *Radiocarbon* 37 (1995) 213–20. **Burgmann, H.** "Der Josuafluch zur Zeit des Makkabäers Simon (143–34 v. Chr.)." *BZ* 19 (1975) 26–40. **Cobet, J.** "Troia, Jericho und die historische Kritik." In *Archäologie und historische Erinnerung: Nach 100 Jahren Heinrich Schliemann.* Ed. J. Cobet and B. Patzek. Essen: Klartext, 1992. 117–35. **Colenso, J. W.** *The Later Legislation of the* Pentateuch (vol 6 of *The Pentateuch and Book of Joshua Critically Examined.* London, 1871. 114–15. **Coogan, M. D.** "Archaeology and Biblical Studies: The Book of Joshua." In *The*

Hebrew Bible and Its Interpreters. Ed. W. H. Propp, B. Halpern, and D. N. Freedman. Winona Lake, IN: Eisenbrauns, 1990. 19–32. **Cova, G. D.** "Popolo e vittoria: L'uso di תרועה e הריע in Gios 6." *Bib* 66 (1985) 221–40. **Culley, R. C.** "Stories of the Conquest: Joshua 2, 6, 7 and 8." *HAR* 8 (1984) 25–44. **Delcor, M.** "Le trésor de la maison de Yahweh des origines à l'exil." *VT* 12 (1962) 353–77. **De Prenter, J.** "The Contrastive Polysemous Meaning of חרם in the Book of Joshua: A Cognitive Linguistic Approach." In *The Book of Joshua*. Ed. E. Noort. Leuven: Peeters, 2012. 473–88. **Dus, J.** "Die Analyse zweier Ladeerzählungen des Josuabuches (Jos 3–4 und 6)." *ZAW* 72 (1960) 107–34. **Eissfeldt, O.** *The Old Testament: An Introduction*. Ed. P. Ackroyd. Oxford: Blackwell, 1965. **Ernst, S.** "Jahwe als Kriegsherr in den Eroberungsberichten von Jericho und Ai: ein Vergleich der erzählerischen Middel von 'Schreibtischstrategen." In *Kulte, Priester, Rituale*." Ottilen: EOS Verlag, 2010. 159–74. **Eshel, H.** "The Historical Background of the Pesher Interpreting Joshua's Curse on the Rebuilder of Jericho." *RevQ* 15 (1992) 409–20. **Fleming, D. E.** "The Seven-Day Siege of Jericho in Holy War." In *Ki Baruch Hu*. FS B. A. Levine, ed. R. Chazan, W. W. Hallo, and L. H. Schiffman. Winona Lake, IN: Eisenbrauns, 1999. 211–28. **Franken, H. J.** "Tell es-Sultan and Old Testament Jericho." *OTS* 14 (1965) 189–200. **Frost, K. T.** "The Siege of Jericho and the Strategy of the Exodus." *ExpTim* 18 (1907) 464–67. **Garstang, J.** "The Date of the Destruction of Jericho." *PEFQS* 59 (1927) 96–100. ———. "The Fall of Bronze Age Jericho." *PEFQS* 67 (1935) 61–68. ———. "The Story of Jericho: Further Light on the Biblical Narrative." *AJSL* 58 (1941) 368–72. **Garstang, J., and B. E. Garstang.** *The Story of Jericho*. London: Hodder & Stoughton, 1940. **Gevirtz, S.** "Jericho and Shechem: A Religio-Literary Aspect of City Destruction." *VT* 13 (1963) 52–62. **Greenspoon, L.** "The Book of Joshua—Part 1: Texts and Versions." *CBR* 3 (2005) 229–61 (with bibliography). **Hachmann, R.** "Die 'Befestigungen' des keramischen Jericho." *BaghM* 25 (1994) 19–74. **Hall, S. L.** *Conquering Character: The Characterization of Joshua in Joshua 1–11*. New York: T&T Clark, 2010. **Hamiel, H., and H. N. Rösel,** "Are the Conquest Narratives of Joshua 6—11 Shaped According to Traditions in the Books of Judges Samuel, and Kings?" In *The Book of Joshua*. Ed. E. Noort. Leuven: Peeters, 2012. 211–17 **Heller, J.** "Die Mauern von Jericho." *CV* 12 (1969) 203–10. **Hertog, C. G. den.** "Ein Wortspiel in der Jerichoerzählung (Jos 6)?" *ZAW* 104 (1992) 99–100. **Hess, R. S.** "The Jericho and Ai of the Book of Joshua." In *Critical Issues in Early Israelite History*. Ed. R. S. Hess, G. A. Klingbeil, and P. J. Ray, Jr. BBRSup 3. Winona Lake, IN: Eisenbrauns, 2008. 33–46. **Horn, S. H.** "Jericho in a Topographical List of Ramesses II." *JNES* 12 (1953) 201–3. **Hulse, E. V.** "Joshua's Curse and the Abandonment of Ancient Jericho: Schistosomiasis as a Possible Explanation." *Medical History* 15 (1971) 376–86. ———. "Joshua's Curse: Radioactivity or Schistosomiasis?" *PEQ* 102 (1970) 92–101. **Humbert, P.** *La 'terou'a': Analyse d'un rite biblique*. RTFL 23. Neuchâtel: Universitéde Neuchâtel, 1946. **Joüon, P.** "Notes philoloqiquessur le texte hébreu de Josuè 6,18; 10,13; 23,13." *Bib* 9 (1928) 161–66. **Kaminsky, J.** "Joshua 7: Holiness Violation and Corporate Punishment." In *Corporate Responsibility in the Hebrew Bible*. JSOTSup 196. Sheffield: Sheffield Academic, 1995. 67–95. ———. "Joshua 7: A Reassessment of Israelite Conceptions of Corporate Punishment." In *The Pitcher is Broken: Memorial Essays for Gösta W. Ahlström*. Ed. S. W. Holloway and L. K. Handy. JSOTSup 190. Sheffield: Sheffield Academic, 1995. 315–46. **Kaufman, A. S.** "Date of Jericho's Destruction—Archaeologically and Biblically." *BAR* 16.5 (1990) 73. **Kenyon, K. M.** *The Architecture and Stratigraphy of the Tell*. Vol. 3 of *Excavations at Jericho*. Ed. T. A. Holland. London: British School of Archaeology in Jerusalem, 1981. ———. *Digging Up Jericho*. London: Benn, 1957. ———. "Excavations at Jericho, 1952." *PEQ* 84 (1952) 62–93. ———. "Excavations at Jericho, 1953." *PEQ* 84 (1953) 81–96. ———. "Excavations at Jericho, 1954." *PEQ* 84 (1954) 45–63. ———. "Excavations at Jericho, 1955." *PEQ* 84 (1955) 108–17. ———. "Excavations at Jericho, 1956." *PEQ* 84 (1956) 67–82. ———. "Excavations at Jericho, 1957–58." *PEQ* 84 (1957–1958) 88–

119.———. "Jericho." *EAEHL* 2 (1976) 550–64, 575. ———. "Some Notes on the History of Jericho in the Second Millennium B.C." *PEQ* 83 (1951) 101–38. **Kratz, R. G.** *The Composition of the Narrative Books of the Old Testament.* Trans. J. Bowden. Edinburgh: T&T Clark, 2000. Originally published as *Komposition der erzählenden Bücher des Alten Testaments* (Göttingen: Vandenhoeck & Ruprecht, 2000). **Kraus, H. J.** *Gottesdienst in Israel.* 2nd ed. Munich: Kaiser, 1962. 185–89. **Maier, J.** *Das altisraelitische Ladeheiligtum.* BZAW 93. Berlin: Töpelmann, 1965. 32–39. **Margot, J.-C.** "La structure du cortège d'Israël autour de Jéricho d'apres Josué 6." In *Literary Structure and Rhetorical Strategies in the Hebrew Bible.* Ed. L. J. de Regt, J. de Waard, and J. P. Fokkelman. Assen: Van Gorcum, 1996. 199–210. **Mazor, L.** "A Nomistic Reworking of the Jericho Conquest Narrative Reflected in LXX to Joshua 6:1–20." *Text* 18 (1995) 47–62. ———. "The Origin and Evolution of the Curse upon the Rebuilder of Jericho." *Text* 14 (1988) 1–26. **McKenzie, J. L.** *The World of the Judges.* Englewood Cliffs, NJ: Prentice-Hall, 1966. 52–54. **Meer, M. N. van der.** *Formation and Reformulation: The Redaction of the Book of Joshua in the Light of the Oldest Textual Witnesses.* VTSup 102. Leiden: Brill, 2004. ———. "'Sound the Trumpet!' Redaction and Reception of Joshua 6:3–25." In *The Land of Israel in Bible, History, and Theology: Studies in Honour of Ed Noort.* Ed. J. van Ruiten and J. C. de Vos. VTSup 124. Leiden: Brill, 2009. 19–44. **Mely, F. de.** "Les trompettes de Jéricho et la grêle d'aérolithe de Gabaon." *RAr* 33 (1931) 111–16. **Mitchell, G.** *Together in the Land.* JSOTSup 134. Sheffield: Sheffield Academic, 1993. **Möhlenbrink, K.** "Die Landnahmensagen des Buches Josua." *ZAW* 56 (1938) 258–59. **Müller, H.-P.** "Die Kultische Darstellung der Theophanie." *VT* 14 (1964) 183–91. **Muszynski, H.** "Sacrificium fundationis in Jos 6,26 et 1 Reg 16,34?" *VD* 46 (1968) 259–74. **Niehaus, J. J.** "Joshua and Ancient Near Eastern Warfare." *JETS* 31 (1988) 37–50. ———. "*paʿam ʾehat* and the Israelite Conquest." *VT* 30 (1980) 236–38. **Noort, E.** *Das Buch Josua: Forschungsgeschichte und Problemfelder.* EdF 292. Darmstadt: Wissenschaftliche Buchgesellschaft, 1998. ———. "De val van de grote stad Jericho: Jozua 6. Kanttekeningen bij diachronische en synchronische benaderingen." *NedTT* 50 (1996) 265–79. **North, R. S. J.** "The 1952 Jericho-Sultan Excavation." *Bib* 34 (1953) 1–12. **Noth, M.** "Der Beitrag der Archäologie zur Geschichte Israels." In *Congress Volume: Oxford, 1959.* VTSup 7. Leiden: Brill, 1960. 262–82. Reprinted in *Aufsätze zur biblischen Landes- und Altertumskunde* (Neukirchen-Vluyn: Neukirchener Verlag, 1971) 1:34–51. ———. "Grundsätzliches zur geschichtlichen Deutung archälogischer Befunde auf dem Boden Palästinas." *PJ* 34 (1938) 7–22. Reprinted in *Aufsätze zur biblischen Landes- und Altertumskunde* (Neukirchen-Vluyn: Neukirchener Verlag, 1971) 1:3–16. ———. "Hat die Bibel doch recht?" FS G. Dehn, ed. W. Schneemelcher. Neukirchen-Vluyn: Neukirchener Verlag, 1957. 7–22. Reprinted in *Aufsätze zur biblischen Landes- und Altertumskunde* (Neukirchen-Vluyn: Neukirchener Verlag, 1971) 1:17–33. **Olmo Lete, G. del.** "La Conquista de Jericó y l leyenda ugarítca de KRT." *Sef* 25 (1965) 3–15. **Otto, E.** *Das Mazzotfest in Gilgal.* BWANT 107. Stuttgart: Kohlhammer, 1975. 65–86, 191–98. **Ottosson, M.** "Tradition and History with Emphasis on the Composition of the Book of Joshua." In *The Productions of Time: Tradition History in Old Testament Scholarship.* Ed. K. Jeppesen and B. Otzen. Sheffield: Almond, 1984. 81–106, 141–43. **Peters, N.** "Hiels Opfer seiner Söhne beim Wiederaufbau Jerichos: Ein Blatt aus dem Kommentaren des Spatens." *TGl* 1 (1909) 21–32. **Riesner, R.** "Die Mauern von Jericho: Bibelwissenschaft zwischen Fundamentalismus und Kritizismus." *TBei* 14 (1983) 79–86. **Robinson, B. P.** "Rahab of Canaan—and Israel." *SJOT* 23 (2009) 257–73. **Robinson, J.** "Who Cares about Jericho?" *ExpTim* 78 (1966) 83–86. **Robinson, R.** "The Coherence of the Jericho Narrative: A Literary Reading of Joshua 6." In *Konsequente Traditionsgeschichte.* Ed. R. Bartelmus et al. OBO 126. Stuttgart: Vandenhoeck & Ruprecht, 1993. 311–35. **Rösel, H.** "Studien zur Topographie der Kriege in den Büchern Josua und Richter." *ZDPV* 91 (1975) 159–90; 92 (1976) 10–46. **Rösel, M.** "The Septuagint-Version of the Book of Joshua." *SJOT* 16 (2002) 5–23. **Rowe, A., and J.**

Garstang. "The Ruins of Jericho." *PEFQS* 68 (1936) 170. **Rudolph, W.** *Der 'Elohist' von Exodus bis Josua.* BZAW 68. Berlin: Töpelmann, 1938. 182–88. **Savignac, R.** "La conquète de Jéricho (Josué VI, 1–20)." *RB* NS 7 (1910) 36–53. 18. **Schottroff, W.** *Der altisraelitische Fluchspruch.* WMANT 30. Neukirchen-Vluyn: Neukirchener Verlag, 1969. 150–52, 212–14. **Schoville, K.** "Jericho Falls." *BR* 9, 1993. **Schwienhorst, L.** *Die Eroberung Jerichos: Exegetische Untersuchung zu Josua 6.* SBS 122. Stuttgart: Kohlhammer, 1986. **Schwienhorst-Schönberger, L.** "Josua 6 und die Gewalt." In *The Book of Joshua.* Ed. E. Noort. Leuven: Peeters, 2012. 433–71. **Seidel, H.** "Der Untergang Jerichos (Jos 6) Exegese ohne Kerygma?" *ThV* 8 (1977) 11–20. **Sellin, E., and C. Watzinger.** *Jericho: Die Ergebnisse der Ausgrabungen.* WVDOG 22. Leipzig: Hinrich, 1913. **Semkowski, L.** "La data della distruzione di Gerico." *Bib* 13 (1932) 354–57. **Smith-Christopher, D. L.** "Gideon at Thermapolae? On the Militarization of Miracle in Biblical Narrative and 'Battle Maps.'" In *Writing and Reading War: Rhetoric, Gender, and Ethics in Biblical and Modern Contexts.* Ed. B. E. Kelle and F. R. Ames. SBLSymS 42. Atlanta: SBL, 2008. 197–212. **Soggin, J. A.** "The Conquest of Jericho through Battle: Note on a Lost Biblical Tradition." *ErIsr* 16 (1982) 215–17. ———. "Gerico: anatomia di una conquista." *Protest* 29 (1974) 193–213. ———. "Gilgal, Passah und Landnahme: Eine neue Untersuchung des kultischen Zusammenhangs der Kap. III–VI des Josuabuches." In *Volume du congrès Genève 1965.* VTSup 15. Leiden: Brill, 1965. 263–77. ———. "Jericho, Anatomie d'une conquête." *RHPR* 57 (1977) 1–18. **Sternberger, J. P.** "Jéricho: Jugement ou Carnaval." *FV* 91 (1992) 27–33. **Stolz, F.** *Jahwes und Israels Kriege.* ATANT 60. Zürich: Theologischer Verlag, 1972. 66–68. **Stone, L.** "Ethical and Apologetic Tendencies in the Redaction of the Book of Joshua." *CBQ* 53 (1991) 25–36. **Tushingham, A. D.** "Excavations at Old Testament Jericho." *BA* 16 (1953) 46–67. **Ussishkin, D.** "Die Mauern von Jericho." In *Archäologie und historische Erinnerung: Nach 100 Jahren Heinrich Schliemann.* Ed. J. Cobet and B. Patzek. Essen: Klartext, 1992. 105–15. ———. "The Walls of Jericho." *BAIAS* 8 (1988–1989) 85–90. **Vaux, R. de.** *Histoire ancienne d'Israël.* Vol. 1. Paris: Gabalda, 1971. 560–63. Translated as *The Early History of Israel,* trans. D. Smith (London: Darton, Longman & Todd, 1978) 608–12. **Vilar, V.** "Las excavaciones de Jericó y el Antiguo Testamento." *CB* 18 (1961) 373–76. **Vincent, A.** "Jéricho, une hypothèse." *MUSJ* 37 (1960–61) 81–90. **Vincent, L. H.** "L'aube de l'histoire à Jéricho." *RB* 47 (1938) 561–89; 48 (1939) 91–107. ———. "The Chronology of Jericho." *PEFQS* 63 (1931) 104–5. ———. "Jericho et sa chronologie." *RB* 44 (1935) 583–605. **Wächter, L.** "Die Mauern von Jericho." *ThViat* 11 (1979) 33–43. **Warren, C.** *Notes on the Valley of the Jordan and Excavations at Ain es Sultan.* London, 1869. **Watzinger, C.** "Jeriko i belysning av de nya fynden och forskningarna i Orienten." *SOÅ* 1 (1923) 100–105. ———. "Zur Chronologie der Schichten von Jericho." *ZDMG* 80 (1926) 131–36. **Weippert, H., and M. Weippert.** "Jericho in der Eisenzeit." *ZDPV* 2 (1976) 105–48. **Wellhausen, J.** *Die Composition des Hexateuchs und der historischen Bücher des Alten Testaments.* 2nd ed. Berlin: Reimer, 1889. 122–25. **Wendel, A.** *Das freie Laiengebet im vorexilischen Israel.* Leipzig: Pfeiffer, 1931. **Wénin, A.** "Josué 1—12 comme récit." In *The Book of Joshua.* Ed. E. Noort. Leuven: Peeters, 2012. 109–35. **Wilcoxen, J. A.** "Narrative Structure and Cult Legend: A Study of Joshua 1–6." In *Transitions in Biblical Scholarship.* Ed. J. C. Rylaarsdam. Chicago: University of Chicago Press, 1968. 43–70. **Winther-Nielsen, N.** *A Functional Discourse Grammar of Joshua: A Computer-Assisted Rhetorical Structure Analysis.* ConBOT 40. Stockholm: Almqvist & Wiksell, 1995. **Wood, B.** "Dating Jericho's Destruction: Bienkowski Is Wrong on All Counts." *BAR* 16.5 (1990) 45–49, 68–69. ———. "Did the Israelites Conquer Jericho? A New Look at the Archaeological Evidence." *BAR* 16.2 (1990) 44–58. **Wright, G. E.** *Biblical Archaeology.* 2nd ed. Philadelphia: Westminster, 1962. 76–80. **Yadin, Y.** *The Art of Warfare in Biblical Lands in the Light of Archaeological Study.* Vol. 1. New York: McGraw-Hill, 1963. **Zakovitch, Y.** "A Study of Precise and Partial Derivations in Biblical Etymology." *JSOT* 5 (1980) 31–50.

Translation

[1a]*Now Jericho was totally sealed off in face of the sons of Israel.*[b] *No one could leave or enter.* [2]*Then Yahweh said to Joshua, "Look, I have given into your hand Jericho and her king, valiant warriors.*[a]

[3]*You (pl.) shall encircle the city, all the warriors marching*[a] *around the city one time. So you shall do six days.*[b] [4]*Seven priests shall carry seven trumpets of rams*[a] *horns before the ark. But on the seventh day you (pl.) shall encircle the city seven times while the priests blow on their trumpets.* [5]*With the prolonging of the ram's horn, when you (pl.) hear the sound of the trumpet,*[a] *all the people shall shout the great war cry. Then the walls of the city will fall down under it. The people will go up,*[b] *each straight ahead."*

[6]*Joshua, the son of Nun, called to the priests and said to them, "Raise the ark of the covenant while seven priests raise seven trumpets of rams' horns before the ark of Yahweh."*[a] [7]*They said*[a] *to the people, "Cross over and encircle the city while the armed men*[b] *cross over before the ark of Yahweh."* [8]*As Joshua spoke to the people,*[a] *the seven priests carrying seven trumpets of rams' horns before Yahweh*[b] *crossed over and blew in the trumpets. All the while the ark of the covenant of Yahweh was moving along behind them.* [9]*Meanwhile, the armed men were moving*[a] *along before the priests, who were blowing the trumpets, while the rear guard*[b] *was moving along after the ark, blowing the trumpets continuously.* [10]*But as for the people, Joshua commanded them, "Do not shout nor cause your voices to be heard. Do not let a word go out from your mouth*[a] *until the day when I*[b] *tell you (pl.) to shout. Then you shall SHOUT!"* [11]*Then he made*[a] *the ark of Yahweh encircle the city, marching around one time. They came*[b] *to the camp and spent the night in the camp.*

[12]*When Joshua rose early in the morning,*[a] *the priests carried the ark of Yahweh* [13]*while seven priests carrying seven trumpets of rams' horns before the ark of Yahweh were moving along. They blew on the trumpets continuously.*[a] *But the armed men were moving before them while the rear guard was marching behind the ark of Yahweh, blowing continuously on the trumpets.*[b] [14]*They encircled the city on the second day one time, and then*[a] *they returned to camp. So they did six days.*

[15]*Early on the seventh day as the dawn came up, they encircled the city, following this procedure seven times.*[a] *Only on that day did they encircle the city seven times.* [16]*On the seventh time, the priests blew on the trumpets. Then Joshua said to the people, "SHOUT! for Yahweh has given to you the city.* [17]*The city shall be put under the ban, it and all that is in it, to Yahweh.*[a] *Only Rahab, the harlot, shall live, she and all that is with her in the house, for she hid the messengers whom we sent out.*[b]

[18]*"Only you (pl.) be sure to keep away*[a] *from the banned goods lest you (pl.) should set up the ban*[b] *and then you would take something from the banned goods. You would then set up the camp of Israel for the ban and would make it taboo.* [19]*Indeed, all the silver and gold and the vessels of bronze and iron are sanctified for Yahweh. The treasury of Yahweh*[a] *it shall enter."*

[20]*Then the people shouted.*[a] *They blew on the trumpets. When the people heard the sound of the trumpet, the people shouted out the great cry. Then the wall fell under it, and the people went up to the city, each straight ahead, and they captured the city.*[b] [21]*They*[a] *set everything in the city under the ban; male and female, young and old, cattle, sheep, and donkey were devoted to the sword.*

[22]*But to the two men who had spied out the land, Joshua said, "Enter the house of the woman, the prostitute, and bring out from there the woman and all that belongs to her just as you swore to her."*[a] [23a]*The young spies entered and brought out Rahab and her father and*

her mother and her brother[b] *and all that belonged to her. All her clan*[c] *they brought out. They let them rest outside the camp of Israel.* [24] *But the city they burned with fire and everything which was in it. Only the silver and the gold and the utensils of bronze and iron they gave to the treasury house*[a] *of Yahweh.* [25] *As for Rahab the harlot and her father's house and all that belonged to her,*[a] *Joshua saved them all alive. She has dwelt in the midst of Israel until this day because she hid the messengers*[b] *whom Joshua sent to spy out Jericho.*

[26] *Joshua swore at that time, "Cursed be the man before Yahweh*[a] *who should raise and build this city, namely, Jericho.*[b] *With his firstborn shall he lay its foundation, and with his youngest shall he establish its gates."*[c] [27] *Yahweh was with Joshua, and his reputation was in all the land.*

Notes

1.a. Two items in the text of chap. 6 are of particular interest. The LXX is considerably shorter than MT—lacking equivalents for 92 of about 350 Heb. words (van der Meer, *Formation and Reformation*, 72–73)—and the Heb. syntax appears to go to great lengths to avoid the normal consecution of tenses. The basis of the first problem must be examined in individual detail (compare Steuernagel). Nelson (83–85) prints two texts. The first is his unrevised pre-MT text based on LXX. The second is the MT seen as a revision. The "early" text lacks much of the Priestly, processional air of the MT. Mazor points to the LXX as correcting the MT in line with the Pentateuch, especially Num 10:8–9. Van der Meer (*Formation and Reformation*, 75) prefers to speak of the LXX translator taking literary initiative at this and most other points. In "Sound the Trumpet!" van der Meer asserts that textual and literary criticism do not overlap in the case of Josh 6: "The Greek version should rather be seen as another example of stylistic shortening of a redactionally layered Hebrew text" (22–23). Van der Meer concludes the article by asserting that "the tensions and doublets in the text are the result of a single coherent priestly redaction of the text (6:4, 6, 8–9, 12–13, 16a, 18–20a, 24b). . . . [T]his redaction transformed an older narrative into the present cultic ceremony. . . . [T]he translator deliberately reshaped the narrative in order to stress the military elements in the narrative and enhance the dynamics of the repetitive story" ("Sound the Trumpet!" 43).

Bieberstein also credits the Gk. translator for the differences in chap. 6 (*Josua, Jordan, Jericho*, 79), seeing the Greek translator aiming at a free rendition of the Heb. rather than a literal one. For Bieberstein, the translator made no effort to maintain identical translations for Heb. terms or for repeated Heb. phrases or clauses. The Gk. text has protected the priests' prerogatives of blowing the trumpets and leading the precession.

Greenspoon also notes that the Gk. text is 10 percent shorter than Heb. in this chapter. He decides one can easily "strip away supposed accretions to arrive at a 'primitive' text" but imagines "that the text always contained something of a jumbled, even confused character, reflecting in its very structure the scene that Joshua and his fellow Israelites are portrayed as experiencing" (*CBR* 3 [2005] 240). Pitkänen notes that commentators point out "errors and inconsistencies in the text." Pitkänen dismisses this: but he states "the problems do not seem to be particularly serious" (155). Is it not particularly serious that 10 percent of the text is not evidenced in a major textual source? What would be considered a particularly serious problem?

A pressing need exists for the study of Heb. word order in relationship to syntactical meaning. The present translation relies heavily on principles set out by T. O. Lambdin (*Introduction to Biblical Hebrew* [New York: Charles Scribner's Sons, 1981]) and F. I. Andersen (*Sentence*). Often the narrator is attempting to present several scenes with contemporaneous action rather than the more normal Heb. manner of describing events in succession.

1.b. "In face of the sons of Israel" is lacking in the LXX. It may well be an "explanatory" plus in the later Heb. tradition (compare Benjamin, *Variations*, 34).

2.a. The concluding phrase "valiant warriors" fits the Heb. syntax no better than the English, there being no conjunction or possessive pronoun. The expression appears only in the Deuteronomistic History (Josh 1:14; 6:2; 10:7; 2 Kgs 15:20; 24:14) and often in the Chronicler. In the sg. the phrase appears only in Ruth 2:1 outside the two histories. It is a synonym for "warriors" in v 3 and may originally have been placed there as a marginal gloss on the text (compare Noth; Benjamin, *Variations*; Fritz, 67; Nelson, 86). But the *Preliminary and Interim Report*, 2:10) reminds that text-critical evidence is not sufficient to delete the phrase.

3.a. *IBHS* 35.3.2a discusses the inf. absolute here as an "adverbial complement." The inf. is not joined to the main verb by a copula and "describes the manner or the attendant circumstances of that situation."

3.b. The two major verbs are both 2nd pers., but the first is pl. and the second sg. The text thus switches from speech to Joshua (v 2) to speech to the warriors (v 3) to speech to Joshua (v 3b). Bieberstein (*Josua, Jordan, Jericho*, 258) decides the decision here must be left to the realm of literary criticism, which shows ambiguity of the syntax (269), as to what verb has all the men of war as subject. Bieberstein's answer is late language inserted into the passage late. He finds vv 3 and 4a belong to the same redactional hand, necessitating reading the sg. of v 3b as a pl.

Fritz (67) wants to read all in 2nd pers. pl. with the versions to fit the context. LXX reads sg. throughout but represents a much shorter text in vv 3–5, lacking any equivalent to vv 3aβ, b, 4, which Nelson (86) takes to be a late addition to the text. This heightens both the military and the miraculous (compare walls that fall αὐτόματα, "by themselves, of their own accord," v 5). LXX preserves narrative tension, while MT describes minute divine commandments precisely followed. The latter may represent later scribal interpretation and expansion. The emphasis on the miraculous element in LXX may represent similar expansion.

4.a. The Heb. יובל, translated "ram" throughout this chapter, has that meaning only here and in Exod 19:13. Elsewhere, it refers to the year of release or Jubilee (compare Lev 25 and 27; Num 36:4). LXX never translates the term (compare Benjamin, *Variations*, 35). The horns here are short instruments for signaling rather than musical trumpets (Hertzberg, 40). Fritz (67) finds the use of both יובל and שופר meaningless and so wants to delete יובל. Van der Meer ("Sound the Trumpet!" 40) sees the Gk. translator reducing everything to a military stratagem of Joshua, including the changing of pl. verbs to sg.

5.a. "When you hear the sound of the trumpet" is lacking in LXX and may represent expansion on the basis of v 20 (Nelson, 86). Fritz (67) wants to delete, "with the prolonging of the ram's horn." Bieberstein (*Josua, Jordan, Jericho*, 272) sees the phrase as later interpretation.

5.b. LXX and 4QJosh[a] read the verb as sg. collective rather than MT's pl. The Gk. ὁρμήσας enhances the Heb. term from "to go up" to "rush upon." Van der Meer ("Sound the Trumpet!" 37) sees a Gk. connection with 4:18, giving new nuances and color to the narrative and raising the dramatic tension.

6.a. Joshua's statement in v 6b is lacking in LXX, while MT (Kethib) has the speaker of v 7 in the pl., perhaps representing a tradition in which the priests mediated between Joshua and the people. Nelson (86) relegates v 6b to his MT revision but notes its presence in 4QJosh[a].

MT of v 6 again represents the tendency to have Joshua spell out every detail prior to execution (compare vv 8, 13). Bieberstein (*Josua, Jordan, Jericho*, 273) points to the full name of Joshua, i.e., "Joshua, the son of Nun," here as opposed to mere "Joshua" in v 2 as marking a new redactional opening. The name does introduce a new section of the narrative, but that this must be redactional and not original is not so clear.

7.a. 4QJosh[a] has explicit mention of Joshua as the subject. The verb is not preserved in this tablet, but apparently used the sg. verb rather than the MT's written (Ketib) pl. (Ulrich, "Joshua," in *Qumran Cave 4. IX: Deuteronomy, Joshua, Judges, Kings*, DJD 14 [Oxford: Clarendon, 1995] 148). Many Heb. MSS, Syr., Tg., Vg., and the Heb. reading tradition marked Qere have a sg. verb, which Fritz (67), Hall (*Conquering Character*, 94), Bieberstein (*Josua, Jordan, Jericho*, 253), and Nelson (86) accept, Nelson reading LXX's impv. verb.

7.b. LXX adds ἐνωπλισμένοι, "armed with weapons," giving a stronger military tone to the passage and showing, according to van der Meer ("Sound the Trumpet!" 37–38), the translator's initiative in varying translation equivalents.

8.a. LXX lacks reference to Joshua's speaking, a statement in tension with the pl. verb of v 7 (Kethib) but in accord with the sg. tradition of Qere, MSS, and versions. LXX presents further instructions, while MT describes the beginning of the action. MT thus initiates action before the conclusion of the instructions. LXX inserts εὐτόνως, "vigorously," the Greek translator taking the initiative to strengthen the trumpet sounds. (See van der Meer, "Sound the Trumpet!" 38.) This is further evidence of the ongoing scribal interpretation of the tradition as command and immediate fulfillment (cf. v 4).

8.b. Fritz (67) thinks "ark" has fallen out before "Yahweh" and so restores it, with MSS and versions. But MT is definitely the more difficult reading, corrected theologically by the other witnesses.

9.a. LXX continues v 9 (compare v 13) as instruction, but knows only two groups: warriors in the lead followed by a rear guard of priests with the ark in the middle. This appears to contradict the LXX order in v 8. Bieberstein argues, however (*Josua, Jordan, Jericho*, 248–49) that the Gk. is ambiguous, capable of two interpretations. This means that Greek and MT differ in the order of march but that each is internally consistent. Nelson "tentatively follows OG, uncertainly reconstructed" and translates: "and the armed soldiers were going before him and the priests were a rear guard after the ark, continuously blowing trumpets" (86). Bieberstein (246) decides that תָּקְעוּ הַשּׁוֹפְרוֹת represents an addition to the Heb. tradition inserted after the tradition behind the LXX had branched off. The original tradition apparently sought to surround the holy place with military guard. LXX sought rather to underline the role of the priests and the ark. See Bieberstein, *Josua, Jordan, Jericho*, 245–46.

9.b. The Tg. variant noted by Soggin (81) identifies the house of Dan as the rear guard. MT with its pl. participle leaves the subject of "blowing the trumpets continuously" somewhat ambiguous, though apparently referring to the closest noun, the priests. Fritz (67) adopts the reading tradition Qere's *qal* impf. pl. It appears that both priests and rear guard had trumpet-blowing assignments. L. Mazor (*Text* 18 [1995] 47–62) argues that the LXX was attempting to attribute all horn-blowing to priests in accordance with Torah. Hall (*Conquering Character*, 105) points to Num 10 to show that special silver trumpets were reserved for the priests. Hall then lists a number of examples of lay hornblowers.

10.a. Nelson (87) thinks MT and 4QJosh[a] have "conflate doublet readings" and so removes "do not let a word go out from your mouth" from his Unrevised Text.

10. b. LXX has the 3rd-pers. subject with redundant subject pronoun, based on a misreading of the unpointed text and later interpretation awaiting direct command from God.

11.a. The causative form is not represented by the versions, where the ark is subject. MT represents continued emphasis on the role of Joshua. (See Nelson, 87.) MT switches from sg. here to pl. with the ending verbs, while LXX maintains sg. throughout the verse. Bieberstein (*Josua, Jordan, Jericho*, 259) points to unconscious adaptation to the context by LXX.

11.b. LXX adds εὐθέως, "immediately," emphasizing the abruptness or unexpectedness of the action. See van der Meer, "Sound the Trumpet!" 38–39.

12.a. LXX adds "second day" here, while MT waits until v 14. MT is probably original. V 11 is unprepared for in LXX so that reference to a second day in v 12 makes clear that v 11 depicts day one. See Bieberstein, *Josua, Jordan, Jericho*, 256.

13.a. LXX changes the marching order, the priests being in front of the warriors, apparently contradicting its own order in v 9, though Bieberstein sees consistency in LXX but accepts MT as older reading. Nelson (87) sees LXX haplography. MT repeats the trumpet blowing, the second being without clear subject. LXX omits the first reference and makes the priests clearly the subject of the second. Fritz (67) seeks to bring uniformity to the verbal readings.

13.b. LXX reads καὶ ὁ λοιπὸς ὄχλος ἅπας περιεκύκλωσε τὴν πόλιν ἐγγύθεν, "and the rest of the crowd encircled the city close by." Van der Meer ("Sound the Trumpet!" 39) suggests this Gk. addition seeks to heighten the narrative tension and shows the growing security of the Israelite army.

14.a. LXX uses v 13b to describe encircling the city, omitting that action here but adding πάλιν, "again," after ἀπῆλθεν, "he went back." Van der Meer ("Sound the Trumpet!" 39) sees this as an intentional addition in Gk. from v 11 to show "ease with which the Israelites returned to their camp." It may rather simply represent a way to translate Heb. וַיָּשֻׁבוּ, "and they turned around."

15.a. LXX omits "according to this procedure" (deleted by Fritz, 67, as a gloss) and mentions only six times, leaving the seventh for the next verse. It lacks v 15b, which Fritz (67) sees as a later expansion, making explicit reference to obedience to command, though Nelson (87) finds homoioteleuton in the OG. Bieberstein (*Josua, Jordan, Jericho*, 256–57) shows the Gk. different readings cannot incorporate the Heb. readings in a sensible fashion so that MT is the preferred reading throughout the verse.

17.a. LXX adds "sabaōth," transliterating the divine title "Lord of hosts." This is one of several examples where titles of divine objects and of deity are expanded in the written as well as the oral tradition. Compare references to the ark in this chapter.

17.b. LXX lacks "for she . . . sent out," preserving the clause for v 25, from which it has probably entered MT at this point. See Nelson, 87.

18.a. Fritz (67) agrees with *BHS* in reading *nip'al* for *qal.* Bieberstein (*Josua, Jordan, Jericho,* 260) accepts this reading without textual support based on normal usage of שמר.

18.b. Fritz (67), Nelson (87), *Preliminary and Interim Report* (2:11), Bieberstein (*Josua, Jordan, Jericho,* 260), and *BHS* change תחרימו to תחמדו, "you would covet," on basis of LXX and 7:21 and nearby verses. Barthélemy (*Critique textuelle,* 1:4) reports a split in the committee vote on this issue, giving support for each side.

19.a. Without a preposition, the "accusative of place" marks the goal of movement (*IBHS* 10.2.2b).

20.a. Bieberstein (*Josua, Jordan, Jericho,* 251) shows the tensions in this verse: people cry in response to Joshua's command or the trumpet signal, horns in sg. or pl., and the people shouting twice. For Bieberstein, this represents a redactional seam between the two halves of the verse, MT representing the older reading. "The people shouted" is premature in the context and missing from LXX. It may represent a copyist's error based on the second half of the verse (Fritz, 67; Nelson, 87), but *Preliminary and Interim Report* (2:11) shows two ways to explain and maintain MT. Barthélemy (*Critique textuelle,* 1:4) shows reasons for each side and then closes by noting—quite probably correctly—that v 20 may represent a synthetic presentation of what will be explained in more detail later. Thus Harstad sees the shouting as proleptic, being the same shouting as recorded later in the verse. See *Comments.* Hall suggests a small-scale example of "progressive elaboration, summarizing the event and then giving fuller detail" (*Conquering Character,* 95). This may represent a Heb. literary tool, but it may also represent the type of work that copyists do on a text.

Explicit reference to the priests as the ones blowing the trumpet (LXX) is not essential to the context. Simultaneity of the war cry (LXX) also reflects expansion. The sg. verbs of LXX and Syr. contrast to MT's pl., but no textual evidence or reasoning solves this problem. See Bieberstein, *Josua, Jordan, Jericho,* 261.

20.b. LXX lacks the final clause that may be expansion. Margolis (*Book of Joshua in Greek,* 95) suggests the possibility of homoioteleuton. Bieberstein (*Josua, Jordan, Jericho,* 261) sees the Gk. scribal error at this point leading to following verbs in sg.

21.a. LXX's errors and changes (see *Note* 20.b) result in making Joshua the subject, joining the tradition of expanding his role.

22.a. LXX lacks reference to the oath, another example of MT expansion emphasizing precise fulfillment of command, though Nelson (87) sees OG homoioteleuton.

23.a. LXX offers an expanded translation:

καὶ εἰσῆλθον οἱ δύο νεανίσκοι οἱ κατασκοπεύσαντες τὴν πόλιν εἰς τὴν οἰκίαν τῆς γυναικὸς καὶ ἐξηγάγοσαν Ρααβ τὴν πόρνην καὶ τὸν πατέρα αὐτῆς καὶ τὴν μητέρα αὐτῆς καὶ τοὺς ἀδελφοὺς αὐτῆς καὶ πάντα, ὅσα ἦν αὐτῇ, καὶ πᾶσαν τὴν συγγένειαν αὐτῆς καὶ κατέστησαν αὐτὴν ἔξω τῆς παρεμβολῆς Ισραηλ.

And the two young men who spied out the city entered into the house of the woman and brought out Rahab the prostitute, and her father and her mother and her brothers and everything, as much as was hers and all her family and they settled them outside the camp of Israel.

LXX explicitly identifies Rahab as a πόρνην, "prostitute," and the spies as two young men who spied out the city. They also have the two men explicitly enter the house. All these additions seek to clarify the text by reference to previous information.

23.b. Bieberstein (*Josua, Jordan, Jericho,* 262) refers to the literal Heb., "all her families," as meaningless, taking over the pl. form thoughtlessly from the pl. "brothers." Here the LXX sg. must be original.

23.c. The LXX employs a different syntax and so does not repeat "they brought out." Bieberstein shows that the MT is to be preferred in all cases in this verse. Fritz (67) and *BHS* regard "all her clan they brought out" as a later addition without citing evidence for this judgment.

24.a. Fritz (67) and Nelson (87) follow *BHS,* a Heb. ms, LXX, and Vg. in deleting "house" as an anachronism.

25.a. Fritz (67) sees "and all that belonged to her" as a superfluous gloss from v 22 to be deleted. The inclusive statement may underline the keeping of the oath to bring out all the family.

25.b. Nelson (87) notes that LXX translates "messengers" as "spies." Bieberstein (*Josua, Jordan, Jericho*, 108), probably correctly, finds LXX conforming the reading to the surrounding context, while MT represents the older text.

26.a. Fritz (67) sees "before Yahweh" as a clarifying gloss lacking in a Heb. ms, LXX. Nelson (86) brackets it, noting OG gets support from 4QTest. *Preliminary and Interim Report* (2:12) sees the deletion as a simplification of the text. Such a simplification would come from theological grounds not wanting to place curse and Yahweh together. See the full discussion by Bieberstein (*Josua, Jordan, Jericho*, 264–65). M. Rösel (*SJOT* 16 [2002] 10–11) finds a feature in Gk. Joshua that more often occurs in Gk. Pentateuch, namely, that "very explicit references to God were avoided." His immediate impression is to see that MT is secondary, but he can argue the other side just as well.

26.b. Fritz (67) deletes "namely, Jericho" as a clarifying gloss; *BHS* notes its lack in the LXX. Again Nelson (86) brackets it, noting OG gets support from 4QTest. But again *Preliminary and Interim Report* (2:12) is most likely correct when it sees the deletion as a simplification of the text.

26.c. LXX adds explicit reference to the fulfillment of the curse, taken from 1 Kgs 16:34, another example of scribal interpretation of the text to show explicit fulfillment. M. Rösel (*SJOT* 16 [2002] 11) says the Kings reference looks like an addition, but the issue cannot really be "reliably verified nor falsified."

Excursus: Yahweh War in Tradition and Theology
(See "Studies on Warfare and Conquest in Joshua" in the Introduction)

Bibliography

Colpe, C. "Zur Bezeichnung und Bezeugung des 'Heiligen Krieges.'" *BTZ* 1 (1984) 45–57, 188–214. **Craigie, P.** *The Problem of War in the Old Testament.* Grand Rapids: Eerdmans, 1978. **Jones, G. H.** "'Holy War' or 'Yahweh War'?" *VT* 25 (1975) 642–58. **Kang, T. S. M.** *Divine War in the Old Testament and in the Ancient Near East.* BZAW 177. Berlin: De Gruyter, 1989. **Lind, M.** *Yahweh Is a Warrior: The Theology of Warfare in Ancient Israel.* Scottsdale: Herald, 1980. **Longman, T. III, and D. G. Reid.** *God Is a Warrior.* Grand Rapids: Zondervan, 1995. **Miller, P. D., Jr.** *The Divine Warrior in Early Israel.* Cambridge: Harvard UP, 1973. **Mitchell, G.** *Together in the Land.* JSOTSup 134. Sheffield: Sheffield Academic, 1993. **Niditch, S.** *War in the Hebrew Bible.* Oxford: Oxford UP, 1993. **Niehaus, J. J.** "Joshua and Ancient Near Eastern Warfare." *JETS* 31 (1988) 37–50. **Schwally, F.** *Semitische Kriegsaltertümer.* Vol. 1, *Der heilige Krieg im alten Israel.* Leipzig, 1901. **Stolz, F.** *Jahwes und Israels Kriege: Kriegstheorien und Kriegserfahrungen im Glauben des alten Israel.* ATANT 60. Zürich: Theologischer Verlag, 1972. **Waldow, H. von.** "The Concept of War in the Old Testament." *HBT* 6 (1984) 36–37. **Weinfeld, M.** "Divine Intervention in War in Ancient Israel and in the Ancient Near East." In *History, Historiography, and Interpretation: Studies in Biblical and Cuneiform Literature.* Ed. H. Tadmor and M. Weinfeld. Jerusalem: Magnes, 1983. 121–47. **Weippert, M.** "'Heiliger Krieg' in Israel und Assyrien." *ZAW* 84 (1972) 486.

"An orgy of terror, violence, and mayhem!" So Coote describes the Joshua narrative.[740] He summarizes: "It forms a triumphant finale to the Bible's foundational epic of liberation, the savage goal toward which God's creation of Israel and delivery of Israel from slavery in Egypt appears to point to from the start."[741] Later Coote adds: "Much about the book of Joshua is repulsive, starting with ethnic cleansing, the savage dispossession and genocide of native peoples, and the massacre of women and children—all not simply condoned but ordered by God."[742]

To such a portrait of Joshua, Dallaire asks, "How can we then reconcile God's love for humanity with the concept of genocide in the book of Joshua?" She offers a beginning point for an answer: "The book of Joshua introduces no new theological concept. It simply depicts God fighting on behalf of his people."[743] This response leads to the issue of Holy War."

The scheme of holy war is based on Deuteronomic theology (Deut 7, 20) and yet

---

740 Coote, 555.
741 Ibid.
742 Ibid, 578.
743 Dallaire, 842.

is not a Deuteronomistic invention. Holy war is mentioned in ancient Near Eastern inscriptions.[744] In Josh 6, holy war appears in its strongest cultic dress. The transferral formula of v 2 marks the entire following narrative as holy war under divine direction. See the brief review of research in Mitchell.[745]

G. von Rad brought holy war talk to the forefront of Old Testament scholarship.[746] He saw the tribal league (he used the term amphictyony, borrowed from Noth) as a group of tribes that safeguarded and protected its clans. For von Rad, the political/military function of the league "was not secular, but cultic . . . and subject to definite laws and ideas." This cultic institution of worship and warfare, von Rad called the holy war.[747] The institution originated and died with the tribal league in Palestine prior to the monarchy.

Holy war involved consultation with the deity to determine God's readiness to become involved, trumpet calls, war cries, restrictions on the warriors, the putting away of anything that would pollute or offend God, the charisma of the human leader, an offering of himself by the leader to God, an exaggerated numerical disparity in the numbers of participants to honor God in victory, a climatic terror sent by God that causes the enemy to panic and bring about their own destruction.[748]

The central core of holy war was the belief that Yahweh was the only warrior and deserved all the credit for victory. Von Rad even finds the origin of biblical faith in the holy war.[749] The ban requirements differ on different occasions but function to acknowledge Yahweh as the victor. "Destroying is not the main point of the legislation; remaining loyal is."[750]

R. Smend investigated the relationship between what he termed "Yahweh war" and the tribal league by whatever name one wanted to call the Israelite assemblies prior to the monarchy.[751] He sees the term *Israel* meaning "El fights," making Yahweh the "fighting El after whom the people named itself."[752] The war of Yahweh could be termed "the dynamic principle of the earliest history and history of the religion of Israel."[753]

Held together in some respect by the Yahweh war, Israel's wars cannot be compared to Greek wars, which followed legal processes and punished legal offenders.[754] Smend agrees with von Rad that the war of Yahweh "is a cultic event with cultic forms involved."[755] Smend then backs up to note that priests are not "essentially prominent" and that the "historical action is completely uncultic."[756] He quotes von Rad's statement that a theory of holy war develops with much schematization and

---

744   "Moabite Stone," *ANET*, 320–21.
745   *Together in the Land*, 23–26.
746   *Der Heilige Krieg im alten Israel* (Zürich, 1951).
747   *Studies in Deuteronomy*, trans. D. Stalker, SBT 9 (London: SCM Press, 1953) 45.
748   Ibid., 47–48.
749   *Studies in Deuteronomy*, 48.
750   Hess (2010) 72.
751   *Yahweh War and Tribal Confederation: Reflections upon Israel's Earliest History*, trans. M. G. Rogers (Nashville: Abingdon Press, 1970).
752   *Yahweh War*, 27.
753   Ibid., 28.
754   Smend, *Yahweh War*, 33.
755   Ibid., 36.
756   Ibid., 37.

stiffness of form but that the event "in its essential and intended form has histori-cally never fully appeared."[757] Smend determines that "the event is chiefly and pri-marily 'the war of Yahweh,' only secondarily 'holy war.'"[758] Thus "the war of Yahweh indeed is not derived from the national status, but it leads to the national status."[759]

R. Albertz picks up Smend's "war of Yahweh" terminology and distinguishes its use of rudimentary weapons and military organization from the purely miraculous deliverance at the Sea of Reeds.[760] Yahweh wars were small battles of liberation, not major battles of conquest, thus apparently eliminating the battles of Joshua. Wars of Yahweh involved a divine and human synergy and were limited to the period before the monarchy. Yahweh Wars lacked any form of compulsory recruitment.

"The occasion had to be so important that a large number of those involved were convinced of the need for military conflict; thus the presupposition for a Yah-weh war is usually a bitter or long-drawn-out political or economic emergency. The aim of the war was limited to ending this emergency and again allowing everyday life to continue without disruption."[761] Yahweh found charismatic leaders, in whom he placed the spirit of Yahweh. The leaders were "political nobodies" raised by Yahweh to mobilize the troops. Yahweh gave the war oracle promising support and victory and then provided tactics and panic to bring victory.

Albertz maintains that "the scholarly discussion on Yahweh's war has tended to go wrong," pointing to the elements of such war in Assyrian royal inscriptions. He notes that Weippert "left out of account the sociological and technical peculiarities of the early wars of Israel and completely leveled out the differences between wars before the state and wars under the state."[762]

J. Goldingay emphasizes the variety of war and the "various perspectives and frameworks for thinking about war."[763] Mitchell[764] responds to Van Seters' attempt[765] to equate biblical battle reports with those of Assyrian scribal conventions. Mitchell concludes: "The comparisons with the campaign reports of the annals can often serve a valuable heuristic function, but . . . the narrative of Joshua has a dynamic of its own and offers a unique literary presentation." He makes the eye-catching but quite apt observation that "this complex of ideas [connected with holy war] is in the foreground of the early chapters of Joshua, while the concept of warfare itself remains in the background."[766]

Den Braber and Wesselius add "a long list of similarities [that] connects the sto-ries of King Keret at Udum with those of Joshua taking Jericho."[767] They conclude that "unless the similarity is completely accidental, [the transformation in the two

---

757 Ibid.
758 Ibid., 38.
759 Ibid., 40.
760 *From the Beginnings to the End of the Monarchy*, vol. 1 of *A History of Israelite Religion in the Old Testament Period*, OTL, trans. J. Bowden (Louisville: Westminster John Knox, 1994) 79–82.
761 Albertz, *From the Beginnings*, 80.
762 *From the Beginnings*, 272, n. 71.
763 *Israel's Gospel*, vol. 1 of *Old Testament Theology* (Downers Grove, IL: InterVarsity Press, 2003) 475–76.
764 *Together in the Land*, 26.
765 "Oral Patterns or Literary Conventions in Biblical Narrative," *Semeia* 5 (1976) 139–54.
766 *Together in the Land*, 26.
767 *SJOT* 22 (2008) 263.

stories] must almost certainly have a literary background, with one story alluding to the other one."[768]

While a few of the story elements between Josh 6 and King Keret at Udum are similar, the differences in the plot are so overwhelming that it is difficult to see one serving as the literary or traditional model for the other. A large gulf separates the harlot Rahab and the royal wife of Keret as well as the mission of Joshua and that of Keret. The authors admit we have "two texts which are separated by religion, literary culture, location and probably by at least a few centuries of time."[769] They conclude, nonetheless, that "we will probably never know what exactly was behind our present text of Joshua, but the conclusion that there must have been a case of literary emulation certainly seems rather likely."[770]

Matties begins with an against the grain approach that finds Joshua is not a conquest account and that the faithfulness of God, not warfare, is the theological center.[771] Biblical writers "lived in a context informed by a warfare worldview that assumed divine involvement in earthly warfare."[772] Israel's God "vanquishes the cosmic and historical forces of chaos . . . and maintains order by seeing that justice is done?"[773] Matties summarizes in a succinct line: "A biblical theology of warfare is one that places God's sovereignty at the center, that creates space for human freedom to engage in warfare, yet invites participation in a vision of cosmic salvation and transformation that the Bible calls *shalom*."[774]

K. L. Younger analyzes a number of Near Eastern sources and argues strongly for the unity of conquest accounts and against any use of the term "holy war." He decides that "many of the terms and concepts of so-called 'holy war' which many biblical scholars have attributed to Israelite origin must be re-evaluated in light of a comparison with ancient Near Eastern conquest accounts. . . . One cannot help but wonder why such scholars would argue that 'fear' and 'panic' are essential elements in 'holy war', when fear and panic are common in every war."[775] Younger cites numerous examples of gods bringing such panic. He concludes, along with Craigie, that "the label 'holy war' is best not employed."[776]

Stone works at tradition history and redactional levels to show within the final text a "disquiet" with "holy war." He finds "the term 'holy war' inadequately grasps the precise character of the Hebrews' religio-military ideology" but decides to use the term "merely by convention, though the objections to it are considerable."[777] He maintains that Josh 2:10, 5:1, 9:1–2, 10:1, and 11:1 "construe the entire military campaign after Ai as a defensive reaction. . . . Thus the Israelites are depicted as destroying the southern and northern coalitions exclusively as the result of the

---

768   Ibid., 265.
769   Ibid., 265.
770   Ibid., 266.
771   Matties, 458–62.
772   Ibid., 459.
773   Ibid., 460.
774   Ibid., 461.
775   *Ancient Conquest Accounts: A Study in Ancient Near Eastern and Biblical History Writing*, JSOTSup 98 (Sheffield: JSOT Press, 1990) 258.
776   *Ancient Conquest Accounts*, 260.
777   *CBQ* 53 (1991) 25 with n. 3.

Canaanites responding aggressively to Israel's presence in the land. Only Jericho and Ai are directly attacked by Israel."[778]

Stone thinks that Josh 11:19 "comes close to suggesting that war would not have been necessary had the Canaanite response been more cooperative." He concludes:[779]

> The destruction of the Canaanites is not because they are religiously decadent, nor is it because they have perpetrated economic oppression on the landed peasantry. They have resisted the action of Yahweh and thus have perished. . . . The Israelites are depicted not as a savage, unstoppable war machine blazing over Canaan, but as reacting to the Canaanite kings' opposition to Yahweh.

Stone focuses on clearly Deuteronomistic redactional additions in Josh 1, 8:30–35, and 23. This switches unusable past tradition to a call to Torah. "For the reader, holy war cannot ultimately be a matter of territory or warfare; it is about uncompromising obedience to Yahweh's law understood as a normative text." The ethical conclusion for Stone then is that "clear moves were made to guide the reader to a nonmilitaristic, nonterritorial actualization of the text in which the conquest first illustrated the necessity of an affirmative response to Yahweh's action, then became a paradigm of obedience to the written Torah."[780]

What then, might we conclude about Yahweh war? Ancient Near Eastern powers seldom if ever fought "secular" wars. They simply did not separate the political and military spheres of life from the religious. The term "holy war" resonates in a postmodern world, forcing contemporary listeners to stop and contrast current ideas of war with Israel's radically different preunderstanding of the nature and process of war.

Weippert, Younger and others have shown the similarities of "holy war" motifs in a number of ancient Near Eastern sources. Their evidence makes it virtually impossible to argue for Israel's uniqueness in the use of these motifs or even of what Younger constantly refers to as "transmission codes." The motifs are neither unique nor original to biblical writers who use these cultural motifs to describe how Israel conducted warfare in the premonarchic period.

Here we come back to Smend's sociological distinctiveness of Israel. Israel's reports come from a small group of people who will eventually become a small nation facing major powers like Egypt, Assyria, and Babylon. Israel's battles show tactics a small group utilized to defeat much stronger armies. The fear and panic God sends are distinct from fear and panic that characterize all people involved in every war throughout history. This is a panic caused by God that overwhelms the enemy army and brings defeat, an unreasonable, inexplicable panic far beyond the fear and trepidation of marching into battle. The motif is shared with neighbors but Israel uses it to show the superiority of Israel's God over all other gods.

An idea or term does not have to be unique to Israel to be true to Israel. Thus Nelson continues to speak of a "divine war" tradition.[781] For Pressler, Israel and the nations surrounding it saw no split between the spheres of religion and war.

---

778   Ibid., 33.
779   Ibid., 34.
780   Ibid., 36.
781   Nelson, 93.

God was Israel's sovereign; as king, God waged war. "The conduct of war, under divine command, involved seeking a divine word to initiate battle, consecrating the human warriors to the service of God, and attributing victory to Yahweh."[782] Pressler continues that early and late the divine warrior fought with and for Israel, spreading panic among its enemies. The practice of holy war found systematization in Deuteronomy and the ensuing history.

How does a contemporary commentator deal with the Yahweh-war tradition as a contemporary theological issue? A great starting place is Elmer Martens' essay "Toward Shalom: Absorbing the Violence."[783] Martens argues for nonviolence while granting the biblical picture of a God who both commands violence and partici- pates in violence while working toward "Shalom." God-commanded wars become, for Martens, opportunities to teach people to have faith in God, to see God involved in history as sovereign king and warrior, and to let God do the work of fighting and redressing wrongs. God must do so to be true to his holiness and justice, and God will engage in human history to the point of suffering martyrdom. This leaves a picture for Christ followers that leads to absorption of violence, not to engendering violence. Martens concludes: "The fact that Yahweh our God is a powerful warrior, whose passion for holiness and justice is intense and who will deal decisively with evil, means that his followers can afford to leave the righting of wrongs in God's hands."[784]

Yahweh war is much more than a strong metaphor or a time-limited reality. It is, rather, an element of Israelite experience and a strong factor in Israelite under- standing of their God, Yahweh. It is common to both testaments in many distinct literary genres, and its meaning can be found in the very nature of God, a holy nature that reacts against human sinfulness, unfaithfulness, and lack of trust. Yah- weh war evokes human faith, incites human participatory action, and yet eliminates need for human initiative in seeking to use violence to right wrongs.

---

782 Pressler, 49.
783 In *War in the Bible and Terrorism in the Twenty-first Century*, ed. R. S. Hess and E. A. Martens (Winona Lake, IN: Eisenbrauns, 2008) 33–58.
784 Ibid., 55.

Form/Structure/Setting

The chapter is a "self-contained plot unit" with an opening disjunctive clause—supplying background information and introducing the central location—and a closing statement.[785] It thus does not represent in any way a continuation of the previous narrative quoting the instructions from the commander of the Lord's army.[786] Hubbard understands the speaker in 6:2–5 to be the commander of Josh 5:14–15.[787] This ignores the disjunctive opening at 6:1 that introduces a new narrative and the shift of speakers from Yahweh's commander to Yahweh himself. The representative of Yahweh, as so often in the Hebrew Bible, appears, has his say, and disappears. Blum interprets 5:13–15 as a scenic introduction to the divine speech in chapter 6, though 6:1 must be explained as a later addition to the scenic introduction.[788]

The problem actually lies in chap. 7, which begins with an imperfect consecutive continuing the theme of חרם (the ban). Similarly, chap. 8 begins with another imperfect consecutive, taking up the battle-at-Ai theme again. Josh 8:29 is an etiological formula that ends the larger unit, a new section beginning in 8:30 with a simple temporal clause introduced by אז, "then." For convenience, I have broken the material into chapter units, but realize that the syntax and themes mark off a full narrative unit only from 6:1 to 8:29.

Tradition

Robinson provides a quick overview of the history of interpretation of Josh 6 and comes to a "skeptical conclusion that no developmental schema can provide an adequate account of the continuity between Joshua and the Pentateuch."[789] He points out the obvious, that if critics are to trace the tradition through history, they must come to a conclusion that shows "that at every point in time the text must make sense synchronically."[790] Over against this "is the tendency of historical study to relate features of the text to earlier stages in a historical reconstruction rather than to other features of the contemporaneous text. This sort of analysis makes it very difficult to see how a text could have been understood at any one moment."[791]

Our task is to determine as closely as possible how the growth of tradition occurred and why. In so doing, we must be constantly aware of the cultic interests that are so evident in the material and must constantly ask what role the cult played both in preserving and interpreting the traditions. Thus Ottosson echoes the common scholarly recognition that "the people's circuits round about the city reflect a liturgical procession rather than a military procedure."[792] The community's celebration of the Jericho victory has left elements of its processional ritual on the

---

785   Nelson, 90.
786   See Howard, 168, n. 5, and the opposite argument from Winther-Nielsen, *Functional Discourse Grammar,* 192, who maintains that this major discourse starts at Josh 5:13. He states on p. 193, "It is not easy to determine the beginning and end of the Jericho story." But note my argument in the previous chapter on *Form/Structure/Setting* of 5:2–15.
787   Hubbard, 187.
788   *Textgestalt und Komposition,* 236–37.
789   "Coherence of the Jericho Narrative," 316; cf. Bieberstein, *Josua, Jordan, Jericho,* 230–40.
790   Robinson, 317.
791   Ibid.
792   "Tradition History," 90.

oral and written versions of the tradition. Coote rightly modifies this assertion: "the language of war and the language of liturgy merge into a common diction."[793] That is, liturgy serves both worship and strategic purposes. Bieberstein maintains that there are two editions of the narrative, one militaristic and the other cultic.[794] Yet he questions the very possibility of discovering oral materials behind the present layers of editorial insertions and points to a literary construction.[795]

Analysis of the growth of tradition can best begin by isolating the important traditional elements involved. Of primary importance are Joshua, the holy war scheme, Rahab, the ark, the treasury house of God, the siege of Jericho, and the priestly celebration. One can simply ignore such tradition history issues with the claim that one can make sense of the Hebrew text on its own merits.

Certainly, one can make sense of the final text as is attempted in the comments below, but one needs also to face the evidence beginning with text-critical matters onward that Israelite texts had a more complex history of tradition than simply being written down at one time with no trace of oral usage behind them or any trace of multiple usage in various contexts after the major written collection. Tracing tradition history informs us as to how steadfast God was in producing materials to guide and inspire his people and how relevant he was in letting each generation continue to incorporate more interpretative insight into their stories and their canon until the time came for completion of the canon itself.

Nelson posits "an earlier divine warrior conquest narrative" with the ark, trumpet-blowing priests, and Joshua missing. He concludes quite astutely: "It is methodologically fruitless to pursue these speculations beyond the evidence offered by the text."[796] Still, he sees Rahab and the unrestricted חרם (holy ban) as "obviously redactional." Later, he states that a "ritual background . . . is difficult to evaluate . . . because there is no way to determine whether trumpet-blowing priests or the processional ark were part of the narrative's most primitive configuration."[797] Still, he concludes that the central thematic core of the narrative focuses on "the ideology of the Divine Warrior" that it is "basically a tale of miraculous conquest, but redactionally staged with the trappings of liturgical procession." It represents "the most radically theocentric of Joshua's conquest stories."[798]

The ban is part of the original Yahweh war tradition and is connected to the capture of Jericho. It is also connected to the Rahab tradition and its roots in Israelite experience. The reporting and interpreting of the conclusion of the Rahab tradition in chap. 6 comes from the hand of the editor who collected the traditions rather than from the original tradition.

The ark tradition presents an element of mystery and intrigue in the study. Nelson dismisses it as a late addition used to connect chap. 6 with chaps. 3 and 4.[799] It is present in the narratives of the encircling of the city (v 11), the armed men (v 6), and the priests (vv 7, 12); but it disappears during the climax of the story. In other

---

793　Coote, 613.
794　*Josua, Jordan, Jericho*, 231.
795　Bieberstein, 304–5 and 316, 318.
796　Nelson, 89.
797　Ibid., 90.
798　Ibid., 93.
799　Nelson, 89.

texts, it is directly connected with war tradition (Num 10:35; 14:44; 1 Sam 4:3), but for Deuteronomy it is simply the repository of the law (chaps. 10, 31). In Josh 6 we may have a rather early element of the tradition, connecting the ark with battle. This was one way in which the ark symbolized Yahweh's leadership of Israel.[800] The interesting element in this narrative is that the ark does not lead, it follows.

The siege of Jericho offers a possible clue to the earliest tradition. V 1 states that the city defended itself against siege in typical ancient Near Eastern fashion. Other elements of siege warfare also appear. A prophetic oracle promises victory (v 2); the army surrounds the city (vv 3, 14); an attack signal is planned (v 5); men armed for war lead the divine symbol into battle (vv 7b, 13bα); a rear guard follows (vv 9b, 13bβ); priests blow horns of war (v 9bβ; compare *Notes*, 13bγ); the troops have a base camp to which they return (v 14); and, finally, the signal is given and the city taken (v 20). Behind such a tradition of military siege and capture may lie a story of military ruse and stratagem such as hinted at in the story of Rahab (chap. 2) or narrated concerning the Romans.[801]

The house-of-God tradition (v 24) is peripheral here, but quite important, even though LXX has ignored it. It is part of the holy-war tradition. Certainly the Israelites had no house of God ready as they sought to gain a foothold in the land. Here again we see a clue that Israel updated her tradition as she told it, making it fit the circumstances and practices of the generation telling the story. For later Israel, spoils of war were to be taken to the house of God, that is, the Jerusalem temple. Howard works hard to avoid the obvious designation of the later temple here.[802] Howard suggests this may be reference to Gilgal (see 9:23), Shiloh (1 Sam 1:7), the tabernacle (Ps 27:4,6). His opening remark at this point is more to the point: "Since no temple stood in Joshua's day, the exact nature and location of this treasury is unknown." Van der Meer traces the designation of 19b and 24 as later interpolations back to Colenso in 1871.[803]

Yet in line with Yahweh-war tradition, the military element of the tradition most likely included priestly elements and actions in relating the story. The ark functioned in its most ancient role as a guide into warfare representing God's presence in leading Israel to war.

Priestly celebration dominates the present text. At some point Israel's cult, probably first at Gilgal, incorporated the Jericho-siege tradition into its ritual celebrating the miraculous gifts of Yahweh to Israel. Priests spearheaded the celebration and transformed military marches into ritual processions featuring priests blowing horns.

Four basic elements comprise the festive ritual: First, the priests may belong to the original story as bearers of the divine symbol. In the present text, they, not the rear guard, carry and blow the trumpets. Cultic celebration calls for a strong role for the priests in leading ritual remembrance.

The trumpets constitute the second festive element. Robinson sees the horns in the text as serving both cultic ceremonial functions and military signaling functions (Josh 6:5, 16). "Little regard is paid to the fact that the two functions stand in

---

800 Cf. H.-J. Zobel, "אָרוֹן," *TWAT*, 1:391–404.
801 Y. Yadin, *Art of Warfare*, 99–100.
802 Howard, 174.
803 "Sound the Trumpet," 29 and n. 32.

some tension with one another." Thus for Robinson, the horns "are not employed in the narrative as accurate descriptions of an event but as literary figures to characterize the cultic and climactic nature of different moments in the event."[804]

But we are also permitted to interpret the blowing of the trumpets as part of the original battle narrative in the hands of the rear guard. Cult drama transforms them into cultic trumpets that accompany the drama and lend fanfare and excitement to it. No longer can they remain simply instruments to relay battle signals. Now they must be blown constantly, as occurs in cultic drama. The military need for silence is incorporated as a final element, quieting the people so that they will be able to hear the trumpet signal and Joshua's voice signal. The silence motif contrasts with the trumpet motif, but, nonetheless, the cultic ritual seeks to stir emotions and evoke praise.

The third festive element is the shout of the people. This may well have its basis in the war narrative as a signal of attack and an attempt to frighten the unsuspecting enemy, but the cult drama has heightened and transformed it. The shout of the people serves simultaneously to mark the moment of victory and to initiate the cultic shouts of praise. The command of silence prepares for the moment of tumultuous call to action and praise.

The fourth element of celebration is the seven-day scheme. It could possibly have a basis in the battle narrative as part of the ruse.[805] It is most probable that the description of the second day's activities goes back to the original narrative since it is somewhat disruptive in the present context (v 14 [LXX 12]). The present seven-day scheme reflects something entirely different—the week of cultic festival. But which festival originally? And where? The present narrative links the material to Passover (Josh 5:10) at Gilgal.

This presents the problem of a seven-day Passover, something not apparently known in early Israel, unless this is our only clue. It also presents the problem of the relation of Gilgal to the tradition. One stage of tradition interpreted the festival as a combination of the Feast of Passover and the Feast of Unleavened Bread. Such a connection could come about in one of two ways. Either the popular narrators chose Gilgal as the center of Israel's early history and worship on the basis of geography and some early tradition, or Gilgal actually played such a cultic role in early Israel. The latter is the much more likely alternative.

Early in the history of Israel, then, the cult of Gilgal celebrated the greatness of Yahweh and his gift of the land during a seven-day festival. Along with the Exodus Passover (Exod 12–13), this became the example for later Israel's cultic celebration.

Eventually, instructions for the celebrations were reduced to writing, probably in connection with the collection of the basic conquest tradition. Here began a process that would not be complete for centuries, as LXX witnesses. What had once been popular narrative and then cultic drama became sacred, written treaties (vv 22–23). The collector may well have inaugurated the ongoing process of underlining every element as commandment and obedience. The MT reflects this in several places. Cultic celebration was reflected in the priestly activities of v 13. This became command and fulfillment in the literary version (vv 4, 6, 8). The silence motif (vv 5,

---

804 "Coherence of the Jericho Narrative," 327.
805 Cf. Yadin, *Art of Warfare*, 100.

20) became total prohibition, faithfully observed (vv 10, 16, 20aα). The ark is now carried by the priests obeying Joshua (vv 6a, 12).

Source and Redaction

The first chapters of Joshua add one wrinkle to source and redaction studies, namely, as den Braber and Wesselius note:[806]

> On the literary level: there are few or no other episodes in the Primary History which exhibit more intertextual connections with other parts of it than precisely these chapters (i.e. Josh 1–8). Without attempting to be exhaustive, we mention the well-known cases of the crossing of the river Jordan (Joshua 4), to be compared with the crossing of the Red Sea (Exodus 14), and ultimately with Elijah's and Elisha's crossing of the same Jordan (2 Kings 2,8 and 14); the three-day search for the spies (Joshua 2,22) and the three-day search for Elijah (2 Kings 2,17); the command to Joshua to take off his shoes (Joshua 5,15) and a similar order to Moses at Horeb (Exodus 3,5); Joshua's curse on the eventual rebuilder of Jericho (6,26), which is connected with 1 Kings 16,34, and the description of the way in which Ai is taken in Joshua 8,3–28 as compared with the taking of Gibeah in Judges 20,29–48.

These data show how deeply immersed the historians were in the traditions— oral and written—of their people. Ties to the Jordan crossing and the call of Moses at the burning bush may be, as source critics continually point out, late editorial additions tying Israel's story into a literary and theological whole. Or this evidence may well reflect the work of early historians, who know the Israelite traditions up through the time of Solomon, tying Joshua and his work back to that of his mentor Moses.

Reading Joshua without the overt connections to the pentateuchal narrative as context leaves one searching for the introduction to the story. Rahab's confession, in whatever version one accepts as original, makes no sense apart from knowledge of the earlier traditions. Observance of circumcision and Passover make literary and historical sense only in light of the Pentateuch. The significance of the Jordan crossing comes across only in light of the sea crossing under Moses. The battles for the land gain context only in light of the patriarchal promises.

Individual stories may be told in an entertaining manner without such backward glances, but collection of the narratives into a larger whole makes sense only as the "hexateuchal" climax to an all-Israel narrative during a period in which the identity of Israel as a twelve-tribe group or a north-plus-south entity is a reality under fire. Most likely, this would point to the kingdom of Solomon or Rehoboam as the north begins its departure.

The early historian who committed the material to writing brought a further introduction to and interpretation of the Rahab narrative (vv 17b, 25). Finally the historian prepared for his story of the rebuilding of Jericho (1 Kgs 16:34) by reciting the ancient tradition of the curse on Jericho (v 26). The historian also interpreted the whole narrative as one giving glory to Joshua by proving God's presence with Joshua (v 27; compare chap. 1).

---

806 *SJOT* 22 (2008) 253–54.

The long transmission process has produced a literary creation with its own characteristics and purposes. "The events that comprise the chapter thus bring together and complete the two opposing plot lines we have encountered thus far, Israel's expression of fidelity through ritual and Rahab's exemption from the Mosaic ban."[807]

Closer literary study reveals stages in the ongoing interpretation process. Here we must be careful in light of our personal tendencies and presuppostions and of recent, especially German, redaction criticism. Knauf reduces the original unit to Josh 6:1, 2b–3a, 5b–d, 7a–c, 10b–f, 12a, 15b*, 16c–d, 20a, e–g, and 27a and assigns it to the time of Ahab when Jericho was again fortified.[808] Knauf sees an earthquake as the originating force causing walls to fall. Kratz honors Josh 6 and 8 as basic sources behind the book, but reduces chap. 6 to vv 1–3aα, 5, 12a, 14aα, 20b.[809] Neither Knauf nor Katz retains sufficient material for an oral narrative and certainly not sufficient material for literary artistry. They reduce ancient memories and practices to a simple battle report featuring cultic warriors rather than military ones with no narrative tension. Briend finds a "command and execute" source for the compiler, who introduces Joshua, after which a Deuteronomistic editor enfuses the text with the ban theology.[810]

Bieberstein works with doublets and tensions in the text to isolate a basic narrative in Josh 6:1–3, 4b, 5, 11, 14–15, 20c–21. A first redactor adds cultic images: ark, priests, advance guard (vv 4a, c, 6–9, 12–13, 16a, b). A third literary layer brings command-and-obedient fulfillment (vv 10, 16c, d, e, 20a, b, 22–23). Finally, for Bieberstein, an etiological redactor added vv 17–18 and 25, while vv 19 and 24 represent the late style of Chronicles.[811] Bieberstein isolates a DtrP with prophetic interests in v 26 and a final redaction in v 27. Even then Bieberstein must remove four more elements from the first editorial layer (his layer B) to avoid two presentations of the order of march and five other elements from vv 2–7.[812] Such finely tuned surgical skills make great scholarship but appear to stretch a bit beyond editorial reality.

Van der Meer reminds us that the "one point these reconstructions [of the literary history] have in common is that they tend to reduce the narrative to a very small textual core narrative, while on the other hand they postulate a large number of subsequent redactions."[813] Van der Meer then isolates his own version of priestly additions: 4, 6, 8–9, 12–13, 16a, 18–20a, 24b.[814] This leaves as pre-priestly vv 2–3, 5, 7, 10–11, 14–15, 16b–17, 20b–24a, 25 with no priest, one trumpet or shofar. This interpretation sees a military emphasis but no cultic indications in the pre-priestly layer, while the priestly layer underlined the importance and roles of the priest as compared to the laity, linked the book of Joshua to Sinai, and removed all military language.[815]

Several elements of the narrative do demand explanation. How does the total

---

807   Hess (2000) 87.
808   Knauf, 70.
809   *Composition of the Narrative Books*, 284, 294.
810   "Sources of the Deuteronomic History," 372.
811   *Josua, Jordan, Jericho*, 293–94.
812   Ibid., 296–97.
813   "Sound the Trumpets," 29.
814   Ibid., 30–31.
815   Ibid., 34.

silence of the people (v 10) relate to the constant blaring of the horns (vv 8, 9, 13)? Do not vv 4–5 presuppose that the priests will blow the horns only on the seventh day? What is the difference, if any, in duty and in marching order between the men of war (v 3), the armed men (vv 7, 9, 13), the rear guard (vv 9, 13), and the priests? Why is the final priestly signal recorded twice (vv 16, 20)? Why is the destruction of the city reported twice (vv 21, 24)?

Scholars have formulated various theories to answer these questions. Eissfeldt[816] found three literary sources, while Otto[817] posited two. Noth spoke of a growth of tradition and final redaction. Dus[818] and Kraus[819] sought to reconstruct a cultic ritual that gave rise to the tradition. Wilcoxen opted for three slightly different forms of cultic ritual as the basis for the story.[820]

Coogan finds two sources: 1) "a walls came a-tumblin' down source" (Josh 6:3–21) originally not attached to Jericho and 2) a source with a siege resulting in the murder of Jericho's king (6:1; 24:11).[821] Joining the Rahab narrative to the latter, he finds a story of betrayal within the city. The original source, according to Coogan, is a written account of Ahiel's rebuilding of Jerusalem under Ahab, a kind of rebellious succession the Deuteronomists did not like.[822] Added to this was an ancient tradition about Jericho's walls.

Fritz finds at least five layers of literary activity in the original narrative (vv 1, 2a, 3*, 4aβ, 5, 7a, 14, 15a, 20b, 21–24a).[823] DtrH carefully constructed this miracle story out of an older version of the taking of the city by betrayal. Thus, he maintains, contemporary scholars have no reason to ask historical or archaeological questions of the story, according to Fritz. In this view a Deuteronomistic redactor inserted the ark into the narrative. A cultic procession featuring rams' horns came from a redaction layer encompassing vv 4aαb, 6, 8, 9, 12, 13, 16a, and 20aβ. A further editorial addition recorded the oath of destruction involving vv 17–19, 24b, and 25, shifting the focus from the destruction of Jericho to the fate of Rahab. Next comes the addition of the curse of Jericho (v 26) and finally an emphasis on Joshua's role in vv 10, 16b, and 27.

Schwienhorst[824] raises the number to seven redactions, causing Winther-Nielsen[825] to call for a new method that shows the unity of the discourse. Schwienhorst's result is a macrostructure:

Staging	Commander	Introduction	5:13a–c
Episode 1	Divine command	Inciting incident	5:13d–6:5
Episode 2	Execution day 1	Mounting tension	6:6–11
Episode 3	Execution day 2–6	Unfolding	6:12–14

816   *Old Testament*, 252–53.
817   *Mazzotfest*, 84–86; cf. Wellhausen, *Composition*, 122–25.
818   *ZAW* 72 (1960) 119–20.
819   *Gottesdienst*, 187–89.
820   "Narrative Structure," 52–53.
821   "Archaeology and Biblical Studies," 20.
822   Ibid., 22.
823   Fritz, 67–69.
824   *Die Eroberung Jerichos*, 23–28.
825   *Functional Discourse Grammar*, 192.

Episode 4	Execution day 7	Climax	6:15–20b
Episode 5	Miracle	Resolution	6:20c–21
Episode 6	Rahab	Lessening tension	6:22–25
Conclusion	Closure	Curse on Jericho	6:26

Van der Meer raises the major problem with this source/redactional method: "One wonders how such a massive and paper consuming process of text accretion would fit into the general picture of text production in Antiquity that can be established on the basis of parallels from the scribal culture from neighbouring civilizations."[826]

Certainly strict literary-source solutions are difficult to sustain when employing the traditional methodology, for it assumes that the various sources differed only on points of cultic acts, the basic narrative of the fall of the city being the same in all of them and thus not producing doublets in the final redaction. Nelson states the problem succinctly: "Although division into written sources has often been suggested, this hypothesis is unlikely because the climactic collapse of the wall is referred to only once."[827] Still, the LXX reveals that literary interpretation continued to produce differences in the material until a quite late date. Such new interpretation is, in the final analysis, only a continuation of the growth of tradition posited by Noth. We cannot overlook the conclusion of den Braber and Wesselius that the "story of the beginning of the conquest of Canaan by the Israelites in Joshua 1–8 in its present form is an extremely well composed literary-religious composition, and that there is no reason to assume a complex editorial history."[828]

Tradition-history study has shown the complexity of traditional elements that were incorporated into the text and the intertwining of battle report and cultic celebration. The intertwining has given rise to the questions at the top of this section. Easy answers only engender further inquiry.

How does the total silence of the people (v 10) relate to the constant blaring of the horns (vv 8, 9, 13)? Silence belongs to siege or ambush military strategy in order to prevent the enemy from knowing the movement of the attacking forces. It also can appear in the attack phase in order to enable people to hear clearly the signal—voice or trumpet—to attack. It may have served a military function in the early tradition, but when joined with the cultic overlay it functions to delay the celebration and create an eerie, mysterious atmosphere among Jericho's besieged inhabitants. As such, it coordinates with the priestly trumpets that seek to create a raucous atmosphere of encouragement for Israel and of fear for the enemy.

Do not vv 4–5 presuppose that the priests will blow the horns only on the seventh day? This can be one interpretation of the text. What is the difference, if any, in duty and in marching order between the men of war (v 3), the armed men (vv 7, 9, 13), the rear guard (vv 9, 13), the people, and the priests? This is a question whose answer lies partly in the tradition history of the material. Men of war or warriors represent the tradition's earliest emphasis on a military account, with a focus on warriors in general. The "people" may be a term for the army or warriors, not the entire population of Israel. The priests also belong to the early Yahweh-war tradi-

---

826 "Sound the Trumpet!" 30.
827 Nelson, 88.
828 *SJOT* 22 (2008) 274.

tion as bearers of the ark, while the cultic celebration has elaborated their participation so they now have responsibilities for cultic celebration and military signal. The armed men probably belong to the early military tradition, either representing another term for warriors or constituting an elite group within the warriors whose armed presence would impress or even terrify the besieged citizens. The rear guard was again a special element among the warriors with a specific assignment. They may have had original responsibility for the military signal horns. This explanation would set a strict order for march as: warriors, that is, armed guard; seven priests with trumpets; priests carrying the ark; and warriors, that is, rear guard.

Do the various conversations reflect a chain of command, or are various groups and individuals the recipients of divine command?[829] This depends on one's reading of several text questions. See *Notes* above. The *Translation* understands Yahweh giving commands (vv 2–5), Joshua relaying shortened commands to the priests (v 6), who relay audience-specific commands to the people, most likely the army or warriors (v 7). After the commands are followed, Joshua speaks directly to the people (warriors) (v 10). V 16 complicates the issue as Joshua gives the warriors the signal to shout and then introduces the issues of Rahab and the ban, thereby postponing the people's shout until v 20, where it is reported and then explained.

Why is the final priestly signal recorded twice (vv 16, 20)? The insertion of the ban material between the command to shout and the actual shout brings about the two shouts. The insertion is a literary maneuver to report the shout in v 20a and then put it in a clearer context in v 20b. See *Notes*. Why also is the destruction of the city reported twice (vv 21, 24)? V 21 reports the initial defeat of Jericho as the walls fall, allowing Israel to capture the city. V 24 reports the carrying out of the ban and destroys the city so human occupancy is no longer possible.

Form

Cultic language and cultic activity so pervade the Jericho story that one must see in the narrative a strong influence of cultic material that results in liturgy. The priests play an important role in the development of the narrative itself. Their role is to transform the narrative from battle story to cultic drama. Preservation of the story has moved from the popular narrators of the community to the cult and has thus not remained narrative, becoming instead cult drama, a means of remembering the great acts of God and of worshiping God. The narrative thus includes not only the original battle elements but also the description of the ritual elements used to remember and retell the battle.

Pressler uses the liturgical shape to claim the genre "is not historical or military reporting, but theological, even doxological, literature. Its purpose is not to recount 'what really happened' but to extol the God who brought Israel into being and gave the nation its land."[830] Still, at the root of the cultic narrative lies a historical event. Something happened to give rise to such popular narrative and cultic drama.

Noort places cultic language, personnel, and objects into the category of ele-

829 See Hess (2010) 65.
830 Pressler, 44.

ments of younger layers, though the age of such layers remains in question.[831] At the same time he denies the creative role of etiology in the origin of the tradition. He finds basically all issues concerning the narrative unresolved and as the subject for further study.

The form of chap. 6 can be variously designated, depending on the context chosen. Connected back to chap. 2, its form is the conclusion of a spy report encompassing a Yahweh war story. B. Long defines a "battle story" as telling of a military encounter with more sophistication than a battle report.[832] It emphasizes a "historical" aim. Much of its information comes from popular culture, and it contains at least the confrontation of forces, the battle, and the consequences for battle.

Bieberstein points out elements of Yahweh-war ideology that appear in the extended narrative:[833]

1. Call to sanctification (3:6; compare Jer 51:27–28)
2. Oracle from Yahweh with conveyance formula (6:2)
3. Signal from shophar with battle cry (6:5, 20)
4. Divine miracle victory (6:5, 20)
5. Ban (6:21)

He thus decides that chap. 6 represents a stylized literary presentation, not an oral or historical presentation, of common ancient Near Eastern military practice.[834]

Israel's battle story is transformed into a war-of-Yahweh story, minimizing battle description and maximizing cultic parade, cultic trumpets, cultic celebration, cultic consequences, and command and obedience. As such, it stretches beyond a traditional battle report, using some elements common to the ancient Near East but isolating them so that divine action overshadows battle action. See the table below.

Chap. 6 becomes the climax of the first 6 chapters of Joshua, which begin with the divine presence and the divine gift of the land promised in chap. 1 and climax with the exchange between Rahab and Joshua. In the context of chaps. 1–12, chap. 6 becomes the narrative resolution prior to chaps. 7–9 as the first internal complication and resolution to the narrative that then has two additional internal complications (Ai and Gibeon) and two external complications (chaps. 10–11: Jerusalem and south plus Hazor and north).

As an isolated single narrative, chap. 6 is a cultic-laden Yahweh-war battle story as outlined above. The literary whole is a paradigm of victory for the nation and especially for its leader. The paradigm is carefully constructed, following the plan of chap. 1 to a large degree, thus signalling "a new beginning" and reconfirming "the unity of YHWH, Joshua, and the people."[835] The divine command is given (vv 1–5), but nothing else is heard from the deity. All is in the hands of the leader. He issues the battle plans (vv 5–7), which are immediately (v 8a) obeyed (vv 8–9). A final command (v 10) closes the opening section of the narrative and silences the

---

831   *Das Buch Josua*, 172.
832   *2 Kings*, FOTL 10 (Grand Rapids: Eerdmans, 1991) 293.
833   *Josua, Jordan, Jericho*, 319–20.
834   Ibid., 323, 331.
835   Hess (2000) 92.

people prior to the battle itself (vv 11–16). It is executed precisely as planned, with Joshua as the causative agent.

At the precise moment of victory (v 16), the action is halted. Victory plans are given (vv 17–19) in a tone of warning, demanding obedience. The section closes with the brief statement of victory (v 20). The final section illustrates obedience in victory as well as in battle (vv 21–25). The conclusion is an etiological narrator's aside to the audience, not the central genre determinative element of the narrative. The section closes with an example of the curse of disobedience (v 26) and the blessing of obedience (v 27).

Joshua 6 Form and Narrative Elements

Structure: Promises fulfilled (without narrative elements)			Genre: Yahweh war battle report/etiology		
Element	*Passage*	*Marker*	*Element*	*Passage*	*Marker*
Exposition (pf. or disjunctive)	v 1	Disjunctive	Situation	v 1	Disjunctive
			Divine oracle	vv 2–5	Conveyance formula
Promise (divine oracle)	v 2	Conveyance formula			
Directions (oracle)	vv 3–5a				
			Oracle mediated to people	vv 6–7	
Divine promise (oracle)	v 5b				
Commander's orders	vv 6–7				
Commander's orders obeyed	vv 8–9		Battle (cultic) parade	vv 8–9	
Commander's orders to people	v 10		Commander's orders completed	v 10	
First-day maneuvers	v 11		First-day parade	v 11	
Second-day maneuvers as exemplary	vv 12–14		Second-day parade as example	vv 12–14	
Yahweh's seventh-day "battle action"	vv 15–16	Conveyance formula	Seventh-day battle activities	vv 15–16	
Commander's ban orders	vv 17–19		Victory orders: the ban	vv 17–19	
Yahweh's seventh-day "battle action" resumed	v 20a		(Cultic) battle	v 20	

Structure: Promises fulfilled (without narrative elements)			Genre: Yahweh war battle report/etiology		
Element	Passage	Marker	Element	Passage	Marker
Victory promise fulfilled	v 20b		(Cultic) consequences of battle	vv 20–27	
Ban orders obeyed	v 21		Ban consequences	v 21	
Promise to Rahab fulfilled	vv 22–23		Rahab consequences	vv 22–23	
Ban orders completed	v 24		Jericho consequences	v 24	
Rahab promise completed	v 25a		Rahab's family consequences	v 25	
Rahab family etiology	v 25b		Rebuilding consequences	v 26	Curse
Curse on rebuilder of Jericho	v 26		Leader's consequences	v 27	See chap. 1
Chapter 1 promises fulfilled	v 27				

Structure

Nelson finds a common structure in the accounts of chaps. 6, 8, 10, and 11: initial situation and confrontation; military actions; Israelite victory; and the victory's consequences.[836] Nelson's structure may work if one follows a totally reconstructed text. It does not work in chap. 6, however, since the text features cultic procession and does not describe at any length military confrontation or military actions. Each of the three stories has its own structure, its own genre, and its own theme and even Nelson has to admit, "Jericho is unique, however, because it serves as a paradigm for the entire conquest."[837]

Robinson explains the synchronic method:[838]

Literary features of the text gain their significance from the constellation of relationships in which they stand with other features of the immediate text and with other texts. The mode of explanation is relational or, though this term may mislead, structural. Particular literary features derive their value and significance from their position in a pattern, and from the specific relationships they establish with other features that make up the pattern.

Applied to Josh 6, Robinson's method admits that "Jos 6 in its present form fails to describe a sensible plan of attack on a city or consistent rubrics for a cultic procession. . . . The present interpretation does not insist on a self-consistent historical

---

correlate for the text. Rather, it seeks intelligibility in patterns of intertextual and intra-textual relationships."[839] Thus, according to Robinson, "Military and sacral images are held in a very rich, unresolved tension which sets the stage for the account of the conquest of the city itself."[840] Robinson then describes how the apparent military attack is transformed into a cultic process by the addition of "one time" (v 3) and the leading role of the priests. He concludes, "the cultic procession forming has no obvious military purpose."[841] A partial explanation comes when one realizes that "battle is sacred ritual."[842] The equation between God and the ark is a simple, unexplained assumption.[843] This means "the cultic procession retards movement toward the military climax of the story but does not deny the martial character of the event at Jericho."[844]

Robinson's methodological argument makes theoretical sense, particularly with a modern text, even one in which an author provided several versions or editions through time. The *Notes* have shown here, as elsewhere through Joshua and Judges, the extensive interpretation given the material in its use in Israel prior to the fixing of the written text. That means that the tradents and copyists of the text did not see themselves bound unfalteringly to the transmitted version of the text.

Hall finds in vv 3–9 a "three-fold repetition of the Jericho procession," each repetition giving more detail.[845] This is one structural component used to underline Joshua's obedience and authority.

The table above outlines the structural elements of the present text. Such elements are not taken from the standard story structure, for chap. 6 shows no narrative movement to or from a literary tension toward resolution. The battle report moves quickly through various elements that show both God and his leaders keep their promises. It ties the narrative back to the patriarchal promises and forward to the promise of the land in the rest of the book of Joshua.

Setting

The setting of Josh 6 stands in the middle of scholarly debate as views of the origin and purpose of the material are argued vigorously. Bieberstein, building on the work of Perlitt and others, sets the literary construction in the aftermath of the fall of Israel in 722 BCE.[846]

As seen above, the setting for chap. 6 is cultic memory and representation. The material seems to be at home in the early history of the Gilgal cult, gradually becoming part of the cult history of the house of God in Jerusalem. The historian completes the narrative with the etiology of Rahab's family and the curse on the rebuilder of Jericho.

The Rahab narrative is specifically tied to Jericho and nearby Gilgal and seems to have originated among elements whose descendants identified themselves with Israel. It may, in its early forms, have had religious elements within it, but it was not clothed in full cultic dress. The form of the narrative would not be etiological

839 "Coherence of the Jericho Narrative," 320.
840 Ibid., 321.
841 Ibid., 322–23.
842 Ibid., 323.
843 Ibid., 324.
844 Ibid., 325.
845 *Conquering Character*, 93.
846 *Josua, Jordan, Jericho*, 341–43.

saga but popular war narrative, ridiculing the enemy while encouraging the local populace by reporting how easily victory had been won with God's help.

Comments

1 Hess's attempt, along with others such as Coote, to make Josh 5:13–15 the introduction to chap. 6 fails in many respects, particularly in its dealing with 6:1 as a "narrative obstacle."[847] Josh 6:1 is an obstacle introducing a new narrative and separating 5:13 from 6:2. Josh 5:13–15 prepares Joshua for the entire military campaign ahead, not just for chap. 6. These verses characterize Joshua as the obedient servant of God rather than as a one-time, temporary leader in battle.

Jericho "represents a paradigm for the entire enterprise of conquest (8:2; 10:1; 24:11)."[848] The battle is completely an offensive attack by Israel. Jericho is totally shut off, unable to counterattack. The people of Jericho depend on strong walls to repel the attackers. From Israel's perspective, "the act of shutting forms a physical barrier to Israel's divinely ordained movement to take possession of the land."[849]

Jericho "was strategically located between both east and west and north and south" in the land of Canaan.[850] Jericho is also a crux for archaeological interpretation, the discussion of which was opened anew by Bimson, who fails, however, to discuss the literary and tradition history problems involved (see *Form/Structure/Setting* in Josh 2 in this commentary).[851] Coogan notes that the archaeological findings present no evidence for occupation at Jericho from the middle of the Late Bronze Age to the end of Iron Age I.[852]

Pressler echoes the standard critical position, "Even allowing for the effects of erosion, had there been a fortified town at that time, some signs of its existence would remain. At best, Jericho was a poor, small, unwalled village when Joshua was supposed to have conquered it."[853] On the other hand, "when the deuteronomistic historians compiled their work, Jericho was an important city, dominating its region and guarding the route to Jerusalem."

Hess deals with the situation behind the texts and finds that the Hebrew for city, 'îr (עִיר), can simply designate a fort or military outpost, small enough that the Israelite army could march around it seven times in one day and still have time to fight a battle.[854] He determines that Jericho may have been a forward post to protect road passes to Bethel or Jerusalem or both larger settlements. The walls would be "a small circle of mud-brick houses that form a continuous wall around the center."[855] Such walls would rise no more than two stories. Even major cities such as Hazor and Megiddo had gates but no attached walls. Thus failure to find massive walls says nothing about the historicity of Josh 6.

---

847 Hess (1996) 126–28.
848 Nelson, 89.
849 Hess (1996) 128; cf. A. van der Lingen, "*bw'-yṣ'* ('to go out and to come in') as a Military Term," *VT* 42 (1992) 59–66.
850 McConville and Williams, 31.
851 *Redating the Exodus*, 52–53, 115–45.
852 "Archaeology and Biblical Studies," 21.
853 Pressler, 45.
854 "The Jericho and Ai of the Book of Joshua," 35.
855 Ibid., 37.

For Hess, Rahab was apparently one of few women in the outpost, but the story is more about her and the salvation of her family than it is about the fall of Jericho. Hess also argues that the Hebrew word *melek* (מֶלֶךְ) does not always mean "king" in the sense of a powerful monarch controlling a large territory. It can refer to an administrator subject to a more powerful ruler or "of anyone holding influence over others."[856] The "king of Jericho" then, could be understood as the military commander of the fort who answered to administrators in Jerusalem or Bethel.

Studying the Amarna letters, Hess finds city-state leaders asking Pharaoh for only twenty to four hundred extra soldiers to defend a large city. The fort at Jericho may well have had only a hundred soldiers or fewer in its army.[857] Finally, the biblical writer devotes such a large part of the narrative to Jericho because it represents the all-important first battle for Joshua, one he must win to gain the respect of his soldiers and of the enemies. This realistic view of Jericho lets one find more history within the account than archaeologists and commentators typically find.

Howard contends that "the problem of erosion" creates a serious problem for either a fifteenth-century or a thirteenth-century dating of the conquest.[858] He follows K. Kitchen in explaining the lack of excavation results as being due to "washed-out remains . . . now lost under the modern road and cultivated land."[859] Howard also looks favorably at B. Wood's attempt to reinterpret the pottery and date the city's fall to 1400 BCE.[860] Howard readily admits, though, that J. Bimson has not found much scholarly following.[861]

Hubbard reminds us that Jericho is among the oldest cities of the world, dating back to 8,000 BCE.[862] The great city burned to the ground about 1550 BCE, and erosion washed away most of the layers between 1400 and 1200. Ultimately, Hubbard would like to follow Wood but cannot find enough evidence to do so.

Jericho remains, then, a conundrum. The biblical writer leaves the reader with the impression of a mighty, masterful victory over a large city, but the best evidence points to the taking of a small fort that guarded the roads to larger cities and stood under the command of one or more of those cities. Still, the Jericho tradition is preserved in a spy story, in a military siege tradition, in a preserve-the-prostitute tradition that goes against Yahweh war legislation, and in a cultic reenactment tradition. The isolation of such multiple preservations provides strong evidence for the importance of victory at Jericho for God and the chosen people Israel.

Fleming argues on the basis of the Keret text from Ugarit that a seven-day period represents the work of the deity, and that the siege was transformed into a ritual procession by the introduction of the ark.[863] Seven-day language belongs to the activity of the gods, not to that of human armies.

God's miraculous working in the situation left the impression of a victory of great importance no matter the actual size of the opposition army. God had prom-

---

856 Ibid., 40.
857 Ibid., 42.
858 Howard, 77.
859 "Jericho," *NBD*, 555.
860 Howard, 178; *BAR* 16.2 (1990) 44–58; *BAR* 16.5 (1990) 45–49, 68–69.
861 Bimson, *Redating the Exodus*.
862 Hubbard, 202–3.
863 Fleming, "The Seven-Day Siege."

ised to give the land. He had promised to give the city. Now he that had given the city, could the gift of the land be far behind?

2–3 "Given into your hand . . ." Repeated in Josh 8:1–2, 18; 10:8, 19; and 11:6, this conveyance formula also belongs to the ancient Near Eastern climate. Creach argues that the story shows initiative strictly on God's part so that it cannot be considered a prophetic oracle, but the typical oracular form (v 2) most likely points to a prophetic inquiry that the listeners would assume occurred.[864] See *Comments* on 2:24.

Mitchell notes that the divine instruction makes the information gathered in the visit to the prostitute "irrelevant":[865]

> The instruction for the ceremonial procession and the description of its execution are undeniably confusing. . . . The complexity is of such a magnitude that it resists resolution into consistent strands. . . . Yet the complexity is not so entangled that it defies literary interpretation. . . . Precisely those elements of the text that cannot be read as mutually consistent descriptions of a real event force the reader to seek literary explanations.

Robinson's solution is to see the horns and the climactic shout doing both military and cultic duty, with the final blowing of the horn recalling the language of Sinai (Exod 19:13) and representing a theophany: "There are not two separate events at Jericho, a theophany and a battle. There is but one event, a theophany which captures the city."[866] This would be quite a stretch for listeners or readers unless they were totally familiar with the entire language of Torah. Certainly, the writers intended here more than a literary masterpiece that would cause listeners to marvel at the rather obscure cross-references to other literature. It was the work of well-educated scribes who listened closely to the traditions of Israel's origins. They sought to describe God's perfectly executed battle plan for the chosen people, a plan that incorporated military elements to confuse the enemy but also featured worship and ritual to remind Israel of the true source of victory.

The conveyance formula appears overloaded with three objects: Jericho, her king, and the valiant warriors. Bieberstein argues that the king reference comes from references back to the king of Jericho in later layer(s): Josh 8:2; 10:1, 28, 30; 12:9.[867] He argues that other biblical uses of the conveyance formula testify overwhelmingly against the use of the king as object and that "valiant warriors" appears only in late literature. Such a literary argument forces the writer into a literary straitjacket limiting the writer to a limited vocabulary and cutting off any literary creativity. It appears that the writer has consciously gone against normal usage to emphasize the city of Jericho as having a king and to describe the enemy as having a valiant army. This exalts Israel and her God for their victory.

Following the conveyance formula, Yahweh provides "marching orders" for Joshua. These involve a ritual element. Even Hess cannot find a pre-battle ritual in the ancient Near East comparable to this one.[868] The Babylonian New Year's

---

864   Creach, 62.
865   *Together in the Land*, 51.
866   "Coherence of the Jericho Narrative," 326, 328.
867   *Josua, Jordan, Jericho*, 268.
868   Hess (1996) 129.

festival involves elements not found in the Joshua narrative: incantations, ritual confessions by the king, and a parade of the god's image from temple to temple.[869]

4 The horns carried by the priests are variously named in the Hebrew text: שׁוֹפְרוֹת הַיּוֹבְלִים (*šôpĕrôt hayyôbĕlîm*, 6, 8, 13); הַשּׁוֹפְרוֹת (*haššôpĕrôt*, vv 4, 8, 9, 9, 13, 13, 16, 20); קֶרֶן הַיּוֹבֵל (*qeren hayyôbēl*, v 5); הַשֹּׁפָר (*haššôpār* vv 5, 20). For יוֹבֵל, see *Notes*. קֶרֶן (*qeren*) is used to refer to an animal horn often (e.g., Gen 22:13), but as a musical instrument only here and possibly in 1 Chr 25:5; compare Aramaic קַרְנָא in Dan 3:5, 7, 10, 15. The term קֶרֶן may be archaic and derive from the original military version of the story. The שׁוֹפָר (*šôpār*) is the most frequently named instrument in the Hebrew Bible and was basically used for signaling.[870] It was more of a noisemaker than a music maker.[871]

Here we see the ritual element dominating the military element in the narrative.[872] Yet the military element remains, as Hess clearly shows.[873] The parade is more than ritual. It also involves inspection of enemy defenses and morale and a show of force to let Jericho know of Israel's military intent.[874]

The seven-day seige reflects a theme found in Akkadian and Ugaritic literature, as exemplified in the Gilgamesh Epic.[875] This emphasis on the calendar may reflect the full components of a single day Passover followed by the Feast of Unleavened Bread.[876] If so, then Creach correctly notes: "The first two weeks of Israel's life in Canaan were occupied with religious celebrations."[877] Hess continues this line of thought: "The battle becomes part of the Passover celebration, a memorial of the first exodus, and a victory over enemies in the Promised Land."[878]

5–6 The shout of the people, "the great war cry" (יָרִיעוּ תְרוּעָה), has a double meaning, as does much of the vocabulary here. It refers to the call to battle in war (Num 23:21; 31:6; Jer 20:16; Amos 1:14; 2:2; Zeph 1:16) and to the shout of religious joy (1 Sam 4:5–6; 2 Sam 6:15; Ezra 3:11–13; Ps 33:3). Both overtones are meant to be heard in the final form of the narrative.

7–10 Exactly which people—priests or rear guard—are blowing the horns here is "difficult to pin down."[879] In verse 9 the literal reading is "And the ones being equipped [for battle] are walking before the priests; they blow the horns and the ones gathered together [as a rear guard] are walking after the ark, walking and blowing in the horns." This text could easily refer to the rear guard, but the priests are the more likely subjects. Knauf understands the reference to the priests as an archaic asyndetic relative clause, while reference to the heavily armed or those

869 Ibid., 131.
870 E. Werner, "Musical Instruments," *IDB*, 3:473.
871 Cf. further, A. L. Lewis, "Shofar," *EncJud*, 14:1442–47; 12:565; G. Cornfeld, *Pictorial Biblical Encyclopedia* (New York: Macmillan, 1964) 537–42; M. Weippert, *ZAW* 84 (1972) 486.
872 Howard, 169.
873 Hess (1996) 129–30.
874 See Ibid., 130.
875 See Fritz, 70; S. E. Loewenstamm, "The Seven Day Unit in Ugaritic Epic Literature," *IEJ* 13 (1963) 121–33.
876 Creach, 63.
877 Ibid.
878 Hess (1996) 130.
879 Winther-Nielsen, *Functional Discourse Grammar*, 199, but note his critique of the first edition of this commentary, 198, n. 20.

equipped for battle indicates postclassical Hebrew.[880] In v 9b, Knauf sees only the rear guard blowing the horns. According to him, the command for silence is constitutive of the original narrative but sounds unusual in the later edition.[881] Knauf also assumes the original narrative only included one day's actions, not seven.

The Hebrew term עבר, "to cross over, to pass over," is often used in contexts connected with the celebration of Passover (Exod 12:12, 23) and is a key verb in Joshua (Josh 1:2, 11; 2:23; 3:1–2, 4, 6, 11, 14, 16–4:1; 4:3, 5, 8, 10–13, 22–23; 6:7–8; 7:11, 15; 10:29, 31, 34; 15:3–4, 6–7, 10–11; 16:2, 6; 18:9, 13, 18–19; 19:13; 22:19; 24:11, 17), although it is not related to the Hebrew word for Passover (פסח).

11 The assemblage moves to Jericho, marches around the city one time, and returns to camp. Any army besieging a walled city established a camp as a base of supplies and defense against surprise attacks from allies of their enemy. Our narrative never states where the camp is located. The compiler of the Joshua narratives expects the reader to understand the camp to be at Gilgal.

12–15 The notice that Joshua rose early in the morning serves two functions. It introduces the second day (compare LXX, v 14), but more importantly it underlines the commanding role of Joshua in all that follows, even though he does not specifically appear until v 16b. Knauf suggests the similar language in Josh 3:1 demonstrates a literary tie between the Jordan crossing and the first conquest in the oldest narrative.[882] He also finds in the cultic and military actions on the seventh day an indication of Joshua's authority to supplement Torah and its Sabbath laws where the Torah text is not explicit.

Meanwhile, the marchers take center stage with the ark of Yahweh and lots of loud noise-making trumpets. Again (see verse 9), exactly who is blowing the trumpets is not always clearly indicated. At the end of v 13 two infinitive absolutes emphasize the continual blowing of the trumpets without giving a clear subject.[883] The text creates clamor without naming precisely who is causing all the noise. Imagine the perspective of the inhabitants of Jericho. The people see a crowd of troops and priests and hear the clamor of the shofars or animal horns being continuously blown to make noise, not music. Not just once, but six times they endured this sight and sound, all the while being shut up behind their walls and unable to reach their crops or engage in normal traffic and trade.

רק (only) appears fifteen times in Joshua (Josh 1:7, 17–18; 6:15, 17–18, 24; 8:2, 27; 11:13–14, 22; 13:6, 14; 22:5), most often as part of imperative, jussive, or instructional constructions. רק heading a clause is restrictive and shows that the clause describes an exception or limitation to another clause.[884]

16 Joshua uses the conveyance formula and confesses what God has already promised him (compare vv 2, 16), even when the victory is not yet clearly in hand. This is part of the paradigm of the divinely blessed leader. Winther-Nielsen sees vv 16–19 as a "flashback" that "repeats what Joshua must have told them earlier. . . . This speech . . . may very well have been delivered before the start of the march ear-

---

880 Knauf, 71.
881 Ibid.
882 Ibid.
883 See GKC §§113s, 113u.
884 *Williams' Hebrew Syntax*, 390.

lier that day, but is placed here to mark a climax with immediacy and heightened suspense."[885] Winther-Nielsen has to exercise a "twisting" of his own rules to get to this conclusion, particularly in view of the temporal clause opening this verse. V 16 may emphasize laity—if עַם refers to the people in general and not to the army, as is quite possible. The עַם participate in the divine miracle through silence and shouting along with God fulfilling the divine promises of chap. 1.

17–18 The city is set under the "ban" (חרם). The term "has a variety of functions and possibly numerous levels of meaning."[886] Hubbard explains that "Joshua's declaration of Jericho as *ḥērem* affirms that Yahweh owns it exclusively and seals the fate of everything in it."[887] As God's "exclusive property, *ḥērem* enjoys the highest degree of holiness."[888] (See *Excursus on* חרם, *ḥērem, the Ban*)

18 חרם, "ban," was not only a program for Israel to carry out. It was also a temptation in Israel's way (compare 1 Sam 15). They, too, could be placed under חרם if they violated the program of חרם set out for them by their leader. Violation endangered not just an individual, but the entire community. This is demonstrated clearly in the narrative of chap. 7. The danger lay in the fact that "the items to be banned were the Lord's portion. As such these items were holy and should not be handled carelessly."[889]

19 Placing "banned" booty in the treasury of Yahweh after Solomon's day meant placing it in a special compartment of the temple (1 Kgs 7:51). Thus Coote claims anachronism here.[890] He also suggests the dedication of all enemy spoil is an institution of the monarchy, not of the tribes, showing that the text here stems from Josiah's reform.[891] "However, since no temple stood in Joshua's day, the exact nature and location of this treasury is unknown. . . . [I]t may have been associated with the 'house of God' at Gilgal mentioned in 9:23. . . . [T]he reference here in Joshua may have been to the tabernacle as the Lord's house, not the temple."[892] Whatever the narrator considered the Lord's house in Joshua's time, the basic understanding is clear: חרם goods belonged to Yahweh, not to Israel as a nation or to any individual Israelite. God provided victory. God got the spoils of victory.

20 Israel does not enter the city, according to Robinson, as a "conquering army rushing through breached walls but as cultically prepared people going up to the place of theophany. The city falls to God alone."[893] The marching language of the verse carries strong military overtones. It is no longer procession language. The people march up to the city in military order and capture the city.

The order of events is a bit confusing if one retains the MT. See *Note* 20.a above. The people shout, the trumpets sound, the people hear the trumpets, the people shout a loud shout, and the walls fall down flat. V 20a connects back to Joshua's command in v 16, while the second shout connects back to v 5. The first appears to be a shout of celebration, while the second is a part of the "battle strategy" prior

885 *Functional Discourse Grammar*, 200.
886 Mitchell, *Together in the Land*, 57; cf. Kaminsky, "Joshua 7: A Reassessment," 329.
887 Hubbard, 192.
888 Ibid., 198.
889 Creach, 65.
890 Coote, 614.
891 Ibid., 615.
892 Howard, 174.
893 "Coherence of the Jericho Narrative," 329.

to Yahweh's knocking down the walls. Again Winther-Nielsen tries to provide a discourse analysis solution:[894]

> This episode [vv 20c–21] releases the tension built up in the preceding episode. It is the resolution of the story. A discourse grammar solves the apparent problem of how the people can shout and then blow, and after that hear the blast and then shout again. These repetitive statements are distributed over separate episodes marked by turbulent grammar. The apparent conflict stems from overlooking a skillfully marked boundary between 20a–b and 20c.

Hall finds alternation between destruction and salvation in vv 16–25, all of which are "not disjunctive but emphatic."[895] She seems to be saying that an episode or boundary introduction skillfully repeats the conclusion of the previous episode. How it solves the "apparent problem" is not clear. Somehow, the Hebrew syntax must indicate a statement of the action of the people followed by an explanation of exactly how that happened chronologically: the people shouted and the shofars were blown; that is, just at the time when the people heard the sound of the shofar, then the people shouted a great shout, and then the wall fell in on itself.

21 Implementation of חרם follows the prescriptions of Deut 20 (compare Deut 2:34; 3:6). Hess alleviates some of the problem of ḥērem by suggesting that the extensive listing of categories here may be "stereotypical and synonymous with 'all, everyone' rather than an indication of killing of noncombatants."[896] To accept Hess's suggestion as a solution to such a theological, moral problem, though, requires much stronger linguistic evidence. The text has already encompassed all who were in the city and then sets out to categorize those included in smaller categories: gender, age, and valuable animals. Other texts in Deuteronomy spell out the disposal of spoils differently. In Deut 2:34 and 3:6 enemy people—the entire families—were devoted to God but livestock were not. In Deut 20:13–14 only males are devoted to death. But Deut 20:16–18 deals with cities in Palestine, where every living being is to die.

22–23 The reappearance of the Rahab tradition brings closure to chap. 2 as the spies keep their oath and rescue Rahab and her family. Her house on the wall is basically incompatible with the chap. 6 tradition where the walls come tumbling down before she is rescued unless "he said" (the Hebrew suffixed verb אמר) takes a perfect meaning here: "he had said."

Chap. 2 is complete in itself. The distinct vocabulary of Josh 6:17, 22–23, 25 shows that these verses represent a later interpretation.[897] In fact, they function in the same way as much of the interpretation discovered in textual analysis (see *Notes*), in that they attempt to make explicit the connection between the original command or promise and the final execution. In chap. 6 the Rahab materials portray the ban command as the context for Rahab's rescue (vv 17–19, 24). Ottosson

---

894 *Functional Discourse Grammar*, 202.
895 *Conquering Character*, 103.
896 Hess (2009) 31.
897 D. J. McCarthy, "The Theology of Leadership in Joshua 1–9," *Bib* 52 (1971) 169–70; cf. B. S. Childs, "A Study of the Formula, 'Until This Day,'" *JBL* 82 (1963) 286.

sees non-Deuteronomistic regulations here, differing from the Deuteronomistic rules of Josh 8:2, and connects the narrative to 1 Sam 15 to show that the "draconic form was attached to the sanctuary at Gilgal."[898]

Israel did nothing to threaten the holiness of their war operations and bring חרם upon themselves. They kept the foreign heroes outside the camp so that they would not bring cultic impurity upon the people.[899] The foreigner(s) may have made a confession of faith, but they certainly had not gone through the purity rituals needed to become part of Israel in any manner. They were "unclean" both as non-Israelites and as spoils of war placed under the ban. Creach notes that "she [Rahab] is placed outside the camp because as the Lord's possession, she could not be kept as a slave, taken as a wife, or 'owned' in any sense by an Israelite. Moreover, as a 'devoted thing' Rahab must remain at a distance so the Israelites do not become infected with the sacred nature that required her destruction."[900] Hawk argues that "the violation of an oath sworn in the name of YHWH would be a more serious matter than allowing pious Canaanites to live. . . . Joshua then assigns her and her household a place outside the Israelite camp and thus to a marginal status befitting their ambiguous identity."[901] Hall gives the interesting, simplistic suggestion that this was a pattern for anyone involved in battle.[902] Earl underscores the "rest" that comes to Rahab and her family. They "found rest just like the rest that Israel sought," thus characterizing Rahab as a true Israelite without explicitly stating her status.[903]

Certainly Israel does not preserve and feature the story to condemn Rahab to a place of in-betweenness. She represents much of the identity of the nation Israel, a mixed multitude incorporating many outsiders.

24–25 Life outside the camp is not the final word, however. Rahab and her family come to live in the midst of Israel. But what does this mean? Coote sees them as perpetual aliens who "do not become Israelites."[904] Auld maintains that they remain at the margins of Israel, never totally absorbed but always protected.[905] Hawk seeks to show this as a sign that the Canaanites were never assimilated into Israel and maintained their own community.[906] Such an assessment appears to go against all the book of Joshua is teaching. Hess is on target: "She [Rahab] is not distinguished from, but is part of, Israel. She has ceased to be a Canaanite or non-Israelite and has now become an Israelite."[907] Becoming an Israelite, however, occurs fully only after the Israelites have returned to normal life and away from the holy state of dedication required for war time. Rahab must join all Israel in purification rituals following the holy state of battle preparedness. Earl approaches the situation from the reverse angle. Israel changes its identity and stretches itself

---

898 "Tradition History," 90.
899 Cf. Fritz, 73.
900 Creach, 66.
901 Hawk (2000) 103–4.
902 *Conquering Character*, 107.
903 Earl, 144.
904 Coote, 619.
905 Auld, 42.
906 Hawk 104.
907 Hess, (1996) 134.

by changing the status accorded a Canaanite prostitute who makes a confession for Yahweh.[908]

The etiological formula indicates something of the lasting effects of the agreement the two spies had made with Rahab. Here the formula takes the "imperfect consecutive form" but conforms otherwise quite closely to Childs' original formula until it adds the explanatory כי clause.[909] This gives the formula the feel of a narrator's explanation rather than serving as the determining factor of the genre of the material. Still, the subject matter appears to be much too old to be of interest to people in the time of Josiah or later. It must be part of an oral presentation rather than that of a scribal editor. The editorial addition comes with the following sentence, which ties ahead to another part of the history.

26 חרם is depicted as complete, not only for Joshua's day, but forever. "In light of Deuteronomy 13 and 20, the destruction of Jericho must be understood as punishment upon the people for their refusal to worship the God of Israel."[910]

Jericho "was used as a place of habitation on occasion (see Josh 18:21; Judg 3:13; 2 Sam 10:5), but Hiel's actions [1 Kgs 16:34] represented the first time that someone actually attempts to rebuild the city in a systematic way, restoring its foundations and its gates, in violation of the curse."[911] Whoever seeks to rebuild the city placed under חרם by Joshua will find his own family placed under חרם. An ancient curse formula, alive among the inhabitants of the region, is incorporated by the historian to illustrate his theological point. This is made perfectly clear in 1 Kgs 16:34. The book of Joshua in its written form thus must have been available to the writer/editor of 1 Kings.

27 The first sentence here is key for Knauf who claims that out of this authorizing of Joshua, the later redactors have developed and connected on all of chaps. 1–4.[912] Knauf's author whom he places at the end of the monarchy had the Jericho in mind that Ahab had fortified.[913] The falling of the walls Knauf connects with the earthquake tendency of the Jordan Valley. In spite of his redaction-critical analysis of the text, Knauf still emphasizes the authorization of Joshua as well as the occupation of the land, underlining the divine act rather than human participation.[914] Thus he can maintain that the author deemphasized holy-war theology in favor of Priestly tendencies, leading him to claim that in the time of the Second Temple Jericho was the home of a priestly family.

The book's focus on Joshua (see Introduction) comes through clearly here. Having won his first battle in the land, he established himself as a God-ordained leader and victorious commander. Coote's observation is correct if one ignores his reference to Josiah: "The entire first quarter of the book of Joshua may be said to be dedicated to verifying that Joshua and his royal successor Josiah represent the authority of Yahweh."[915]

---

908   Earl, 146–47.
909   "A Study of the Formula, 'Until This Day,'" *JBL* 82 (1963) 286.
910   Hess (1996) 135.
911   Howard, 176.
912   Knauf, 70.
913   Ibid.
914   Ibid.
915   Coote, 613.

Explanation

Finally, the fight begins. The story of Jericho entertained and instructed Israel for many generations. Each new historical situation added another dimension of meaning to the narrative. "The main themes of Joshua 1–12 are concentrated in the account of Jericho . . . including the sovereign agency of Yahweh, who gives Israel the land; the obedience and the worship that constitute Israel's role in the conquest; the importance of Joshua as mediator and leader; the image of God as warrior and war as sacred; and the command to devote the enemy to destruction."[916]

"Chapter 6 is closely woven into the fabric of the book and plays a pivotal role in its plot,"[917] a plot that, as Knauf points out, involves conquest in only five of twenty-four chapters.[918] Worship looms as important here as war.[919]

> Worship provides the occasion for God's people to align themselves with and participate in God's victory over those forces that stand in the way of Yahweh's purposes in the world. Through worship—the praise of God, the celebration of God's mighty acts, the confession of God's supremacy in the world—Israel was united with Yahweh's ongoing work in the world and God's victory over hostile powers.

Hawk may be stretching interpretation a bit when he tries to tie the sevens of Jericho into the sevens of Jubilee.[920]

Throughout the long history of telling and interpretation, one message continued to ring out loud and clear: God fights for his people. The people of God testified repeatedly that what they possessed came from the hand of God, not the strength of men. Israelite audiences never lost the captivating awe and mystery of the lesson. The most ancient city of the land, with its seemingly impregnable fortifications, fell easily before Joshua and his God.

Such a wonderful testimony could not be left in the domain of the popular storytellers. It became part of worship, in fact, the central part of the main worship experience of the year. The very identity of the worshiping community derived from the victory of God over the enemy. The audience no longer simply listened, laughed, and learned. Now they marched, made music, and marveled at the miracle. They remembered anew that the food they ate depended on the victory God had given and the protection he continued to give. The trumpets—calling the Israelites to battle and to worship—guaranteed the people of Israel that they never again had to cower in fright before such foreboding sounds. Their God protected them just as surely as he had given them the land.

Liturgy became literature, expanding again the audience to whom it could speak. Thus, Israel again embattled in international politics and turned back to her roots for help. Again she found her identity. The identity still rested in the God who gave victory to his people. Thus the people were called on to see that being the people of God meant obeying the word of God. Battle plans and life plans were

---

916 Pressler, 44.
917 Nelson, 91.
918 Knauf, 70.
919 Hess (2010) 70.
920 Ibid., 94–95; but see Earl, 142.

laid out not by humanity but by God. Even the general of the army had to get his battle plans from the Commander-in-Chief. This lesson became even more profound when Israel lost her land and marched into exile. Were the odds now more overwhelming than those faced by Joshua? Had God failed his people? Or had the people failed God? Might not a new obedient commander with an obedient people find anew that God would give the land into their hand? Was not the curse of God still upon those who rebuilt what he had destroyed?

Yet not every foreigner stood under the curse. Long ago Rahab had seen the deeds of God and confessed him as her God. Her reward lasts to this day. Was it not still possible for Israel to do mighty deeds in the power of their God which would win the nations to their God? Rahab stood beside Joshua as an example of the blessing of God upon an obedient person, no matter what their racial origin. Over against them stood the warning of a curse to whomever would dare disobey.

"Jericho falls because of the power of God and the faithfulness of the people instead of battlefield strategy or skills."[921] The Jericho story provided an illustration of God's promises fulfilled. He had promised to Joshua that he would receive the gift of the land and the presence of God if he were obedient to the command of God (chap. 1). Chap. 6 shows that Joshua listened to the command of God, carried out the command of God, received the land of God, experienced the presence of God, and enjoyed the acclaim of the people. What God said, he did.

Yet the manner in which God commanded the Israelites to act raises questions for a modern generation plagued and horrified by violence. Can one find a way around the literal text so that God is the loving God of the New Testament rather than the fierce divine warrior of Joshua? The apocalyptic notes of the New Testament forbid such a Marcionite dichotomy. Explaining the original narrative as simply an age-old etiology or an anti-Assyrian propaganda piece without footings in history still cannot avoid the clear biblical teaching that God expresses anger at sinful people and punishes sin—often violently—in foreign enemies and in his own chosen people. A biblical believer has to find a way to accept the so-called dark side of God with its refusal to accept sin and its sometimes violent expression of tough love against sinners trying to prevent further sin.

---

921 Harris, 47.

Excursus on חרם, ḥērem, the Ban

Bibliography

(See surveys of the meaning and usage of חרם in Rösel, 8–14; J. A. de Prenter, "The Contrastive Polysemous Meaning of חרם in the Book of Joshua: A Cognitive, Linguistic Approach." In *The Book of Joshua*, ed. E. Noort. Leuven: Peeters [2012] 473–88.)

Fretz, M. "*Cherem* in the Old Testament: A Critical Reading." In *Essays on War and Peace: Bible and Early Church*. Ed. W. M. Swartley. Occasional Papers, Institute of Mennonite Studies 9. Elkhart, IN: Institute of Mennonite Studies, 1986. 7–44. **Gangloff, F.** "Joshua 6: Holy War or Extermination by Divine Command (*herem*)." *Theological Review* 25 (2004) 3–23. **Hoffman, Y.** "The Deuteronomistic Concept of the *Cherem*." *ZAW* 111 (1999) 196–210. **Kaminsky, J.** "Joshua 7: A Reassessment of Israelite Conceptions of Corporate Punishment." In *The Pitcher is Broken: Memorial Essays for Gösta W. Ahlström*. Ed. S. W. Holloway and L. K. Handy. JSOTSup 190. Sheffield: Sheffield Academic, 1995. 315–46. **Malamat, A.** "The Ban in Mari and in the Bible." In *Mari and the Bible: A Collection of Studies*. Jerusalem: Hebrew UP, 1975. 52–61. **Mitchell, G.** *Together in the Land*. JSOTSup 134. Sheffield: Sheffield Academic, 1993. 55–66. **Nelson, R.** "*Ḥērem* and the Deuteronomic Social Conscience." In *Deuteronomy and Deuteronomic Literature*. FS C. H. W. Brekelmans, ed. M. Vervenne and J. Lust. BETL 133. Leuven: Leuven UP; Peeters, 1997. 39–54. **Niditch, S.** *War in the Hebrew Bible: A Study in the Ethics of Violence*. New York: Oxford UP, 1993. 28–77. **Schäfer-Lichtenberger, C.** "Bedeutung und Funktion von Herem in biblisch-hebräischen texten." *BZ* NS 38 (1994) 270–75. **Schmitt, G.** *Du sollst keinen Frieden schliessen mit den Bewohnern des Landes*. BWANT 91. Stuttgart: Kohlhammer, 1970. **Stern, P. D.** *The Biblical Cherem: A Window on Israel's Religious Experience*. Atlanta: Scholars Press, 1991. **Weinfeld, M.** "The Ban on the Canaanites in the Biblical Codes and Its Historical Development." In *History and Traditions of Early Israel: Studies Presented to Eduard Nielsen, May 8th 1993*. Ed. A. Lemaire and B. Otzen. Leiden: Brill, 1993. 142–60. **Younger, K. L.** *Ancient Conquest Accounts: A Study in Ancient Near Eastern and Biblical History Writing*. JSOTSup 98. Sheffield: JSOT Press, 1990.

The term for the holy ban—*ḥērem* (חרם)—has two major contexts—military and cultic—both commanding the transfer of the banned items or persons into Yahweh's possession.[922] It rests on ancient Near Eastern military practice, as evidenced for Moab by the Moabite Stone, though how extensive the practice was in the ancient Near East "is not known."[923] חרם is also a strong part of Deuteronomy's theology (Deut 7:20; 20:6–18). In the Moabite Stone and in Deuteronomy, חרם remains closely tied to religious motivations. Deuteronomy uses the term in relationship to religious threats, not military ones. Joshua, on the other hand, does not

---

922 Hess (2010) 66.
923 Coote, 614.

relate חרם to foreign religious practice or objects. Rather it is a test of obedience (compare 1 Sam 15).[924]

Mitchell states that a search of Assyrian annals yields "nothing that quite matches the function that חרם has in the narrative of Joshua."[925] H. W. F. Saggs, as noted by Mitchell, claims that biblical accounts of חרם "depict brutality that is difficult to parallel in the literature of surrounding nations."[926]

Hess, however, maintains that "similar customs occurred among the Egyptian and Mesopotamian civilizations."[927] Younger points to a stele of Thutmoses III, the Merneptah Israel Stele, and the Moabite Stone, all of which include total destruction themes, but uses them as illustrations of ancient Near Eastern hyperbole or exaggeration, referring to "the hyperbolic nature of the various syntagms."[928]

Hawk reminds us that "these campaigns of extermination are usually presented as a response to a divine decree and place the conduct of war within the context of the nation's relationship with YHWH. The massacres of populations are cast as acts of careful obedience to the divine decrees and enhance the sense of Israel's covenant loyalty."[929] Hess describes Israel's understanding of חרם "as returning to God what belonged to him but had departed from his sovereignty through accumulated sin."[930]

Earl speaks in neo-structuralist terms of the narrative function of ḥērem.[931] The Achan and Rahab stories depend on the ḥērem element for their existence. Israel's identity becomes based on doing ḥesed as did Rahab and avoiding ḥemed, the desire that destroys the person or object desired (see KBL). Thus ḥērem closes out the Rahab narrative and opens the Achan narrative by setting limits for the characters.

The term is used primarily against the pre-Israelite occupants of the Promised Land.[932] It applied to anyone who sacrificed to another god (Exod 22:20). The חרם object is so holy no ritual act can redeem it or recall it (Lev 27:28).[933]

חרם in Josh 6:17 is the only instance in the OT where humans and goods are included. Everywhere else the verb, not the noun, is used in reference to humans.[934] חרם refers to the cultic dedication of these humans and things, so that God, not humanity, receives glory and profit. How often Israel actually practiced the חרם is questionable.[935]

Schmitt sees the ban as a rare exception prior to the Deuteronomistic literature.[936] What is of importance for the present text is that חרם is understood as the

---

924   Mitchell, *Together in the Land*, 58.
925   Ibid., 54.
926   "Assyrian Prisoners of War and the Right to Live," in *28. Recontre Assyriologique Internationale, Wien 6–10 Juli 1981* (Horn, Austria, 1982) 85–93; Mitchell, 54–55.
927   Hess (2009) 31.
928   *Ancient Conquest Accounts*, 227–28.
929   Hess (2000) 99.
930   Hess (2009) 31.
931   Earl, 143.
932   Mitchell, *Together in the Land*, 54.
933   Compare Auld, 40–41.
934   N. Lohfink, *TWAT*, 3:199.
935   Cf. Ibid., 3:207.
936   *Du sollst keinen Frieden*, 122–23.

goal of the entire conquest operation (compare Josh 11:14, 20). Jericho's conquest is set up as the prime example of obedience to divine command (compare the negative example of Ai that follows). What causes a person or community or object to be חרם? The object becomes devoted through an act of disobedience. "The primeval occupants of the land are to be exterminated because they are in the land that Israel must occupy."[937] Thus many interpret the total devotion of Jericho to God as a type of firstfruits sacrifice acknowledging God's ownership of all the land to be conquered.[938]

Howard reminds the reader:[939]

> The instructions to Israel to annihilate the Canaanites were specific in time, intent, and geography. That is, Israel was not given a blanket permission to do the same to any peoples they encountered, at any time or in any place. It was limited to the crucial time when Israel was just establishing itself as a theocracy under God, to protect Israel's worship, as well as to punish these specific peoples. Thus, harsh as it is to our sensibilities, we should remember that it was for very clearly stated reasons, and it was carefully circumscribed.

חרם is not carried out totally. Rahab and her family escape. They certainly did not represent any threat to Israel.[940] The importance of this is underlined by the etiological formula placed at the conclusion of the story (v 25). That certain elements might be rescued from the ban and devoted to the treasury of God (v 19) is a specification not mentioned in Deuteronomy and represents one stage in Israel's interpretation of the ban. Lev 27:27 prohibits the rescue or ransom of any person under the ban. Deut 20 sets out regulations for an invading enemy who seeks terms of peace.

Israel blatantly goes against this teaching in rescuing Rahab from banned Jericho. Pressler explains: "Joshua determines that upholding the spies' covenant obligations to Rahab is more important than carrying out the law."[941] Creach, however, explains it as Joshua's freedom and the dynamic quality of the word of God. Israel "essentially treated Rahab as one who accepted terms of peace, but she dwelt in a city that was not to have such terms offered."[942] Israel understands its own identity to be that of mixed blood (compare Exod 12:38). At least implicitly, Israel's theologians understood that foreigners were welcome in Israel when they confessed the God of Israel (Josh 2:9–11) and helped the people of Israel (compare Josh 6:25). Still, they must remain outside the camp until fully integrated through purification and ritual.

---

937 Mitchell, *Together in the Land*, 64.
938 Creach, 64–65; Mitchell, *Together in the Land*, 61–62, points to 1 Sam 15 to argue for a bit of ambiguity here.
939 Howard, 186.
940 Mitchell, *Together in the Land*, 66.
941 Pressler, 48.
942 Creach, 67.

F. Consequence of Covenant Curse (7:1–8:29)

Bibliography: Archaeology and Geography

(See "Studies in the Archaeology of Joshua" in the Introduction)
Albright, W. F. "The Israelite Conquest of Canaan in the Light of Archaeology." *BASOR* 74 (1939) 11–23. **Allen, L.** "Archaeology of Ai and the Accuracy of Joshua 7:1–8:29." *ResQ* 20 (1977) 41–52. **Alonso Schökel, L.** "*(YDH) tôdâh* = confesión de pecados en Ps 50:14, 23, Jos 7:19, Esd 10:11." In *Treinta salmos: poesía y oración.* Estudios de Antiguo Testamento 2. Madrid: Cristiandad, 1981. 210–11. **Amit, Y.** "And Joshua stretched out the *kjdwn* which was in his hand." *Shnaton* 5/6 (1982) 11–18, lxiii (Heb.). **Anbar, M.** "La critique biblique à la lumière des Archives royales de Mari: Jos 8." *Bib* 75 (1994) 70–74. **Begg, C. T.** "The Function of Josh. 7:1–8:29 in the Deuteronomistic History." *Bib* 67 (1986) 320–34. **Bimson, J. J.** *Redating the Exodus and Conquest.* JSOTSup 5. Sheffield: University of Sheffield, 1978. 60–65, 215–25. **Blizzard, R. B., Jr.** "Intensive Systematic Surface Collection at Livingston's Proposed Site for Biblical Ai." *WTJ* 36 (1974) 221–30. **Briend, J.** "Bethel et Beth-Awen." *Salm* 28 (1981) 65–70. ———. "Le récit biblique face à l'archéologie: La conqête de Ai." *BTS* 151 (1973) 16–17. ———. "The Sources of the Deuteronomic History: Research on Joshua 1–12." In *Israel Constructs Its History: Deuteronomistic Historiography in Recent Research.* Ed. A. de Pury, T. Römer, and J.-D. Macchi. JSOTSup 306. Sheffield: Sheffield Academic, 2000. 360–86. Orginally published as "Les Sources de L'Histoire deuteronomique recherches sur Jos 1–12," in *Israël construit son histoire: L'historiograhie deutéronomiste à la lumière des recherches récentes,* ed. A. de Pury, T. Römer, and J.-D. Macchi, MdB 34. Geneva: Labor et Fides, 1996. **Briggs, P.** "Testing the Factuality of the Conquest of Ai Narrative in the Book of Joshua." *Global Journal of Classical Theology* 3 (2003). Reprinted in *Beyond the Jordan: Studies in Honor of W. Harold Mare.* Ed. G. A. Garnagey. Eugene, OR: Wipf & Stock, 2005. 157–96. **Butticaz, S.** "Josué et la rhétorique de la violence: Le cas de la prise d'Aï en Jos 8/1–29." *ETR* 77 (2002) 421–27. **Callaway, J. A.** "'Ai (et-Tell)." *RB* 72 (1965) 409–15. ———. "Ai." *EAEHL* 1 (1975) 36–52. ———. "Ai (et-Tell): Problem Site for Biblical Archaeologists." In *Archaeology and Biblical Interpretation: Essays in Memory of D. Glenn Rose.* Ed. L. G. Perdue, L. E. Toombs, and G. L. Johnson. Atlanta: John Knox, 1987. 87–99. ———. *The Early Bronze Age Citadel and Lower City at Ai (et-Tell).* Report of the Joint Archeological Expedition to Ai (et-Tell) 2. Cambridge, MA: ASOR, 1980. ———. "Excavating Ai (et-Tell): 1964–1972." *BA* 39 (1972) 18–30. ———. "New Evidence on the Conquest of Ai." *JBL* 87 (1968) 312–20. ———. "A New Perspective on the Hill Country Settlement of Canaan in Iron Age I." In *Palestine in the Bronze and Iron Ages: Papers in Honour of Olga Tufnell.* Ed. J. N. Tubb. London: Institute of Archaeology, 1985. 31–49. ———. "Village Subsistence at Ai and Raddana in Iron I." In *The Answers Lie Below.* Ed. H. O. Thompson. Lanham, MD: University Press of America, 1984. 51–66. **Conrad, E. W.** *Fear Not, Warrior: A Study of 'al tîrā' Pericopes in the Hebrew Scriptures.* BJS 75. Chico, CA: Scholars Press, 1985. **Coogan, M. D.** "Archeology and Biblical Studies: The Book of Joshua." In *The Hebrew Bible and Its Interpreters.* Ed. W. H. Propp, B. Halpern, and D. N. Freedman. Biblical and Judaic Studies from the University of California, San Diego. Winona Lake: IN: Eisenbrauns, 1990. 19–32. **Couturier, G.** "Sens de *tôdah* en Jos 7,19 et Esd 10,11." In *La vie de la Parole: De l'Ancien au Nouveau Testament. Études d'exégèse et d'herméneutique bibliques, Fs. P. Grelot.* Paris: Desclée, 1987. 121–27. **Cross, F. M.** "A Footnote to Biblical History." *BA* 19 (1956) 12–17. **Dorsey, D. A.** "Shechem and the Road Network of Central Samaria." *BASOR* 268 (1987) 57–70. **Dussaud, R.** "Le nom ancien de la ville de Ay en Palestine." *RHR* 115 (1937) 125–41. **Eissfeldt, O.** "Gilgal or Shechem? (Dtn 11,29–32; 27,11–13; 27,1–8; Jos 8:30–35." In *Proclamation and Presence. FS G. H Davies,* ed. J. I. Durham and J. R. Porter. Richmond: Knox, 1970. 90–101. **Getz, G. A.** *Joshua:*

Defeat to Victory. Glendale, CA: Gospel Light, 1979. **Greenspoon, L.** *Crimes And Punishments: Joshua 7 as Literature*. Studia Hebraica 3. Bucharest: Goldstein Goren Center for Hebrew Studies, 2003. 311–24. **Grintz, J. M.** "'Ai which is beside Beth-Aven.'" *Bib* 42 (1961) 201–16. **Guest, T. H.** "On the Site of Ai." *PEFQS* 10 (1878) 194–96. **Hess, R. S.** "Achan and Achor: Names and Wordplay in Joshua 7." *HAR* 14 (1994) 89–98. **Humbert, P.** "'Étendre la main.'" *VT* 12 (1962) 383–95. **Kaminsky, J. S.** *Corporate Responsibility in the Hebrew Bible*. JSOTSup 196. Sheffield: Sheffield Academic, 1995. ———. "Joshua 7: A Reassessment of Israelite Conceptions of Corporate Punishment." In *The Pitcher Is Broken: Memorial Essays for Gösta W. Ahlström*. Ed. S. W. Holloway and L. K. Handy. JSOTSup 190. Sheffield: Sheffield Academic, 1995. 315–46. **Kasten, D. L.** "Narrator Devices in Joshua's Ruse: Translating Joshua 8:15." *JOTT* 13 (2000) 1–13. **Keel, O.** *Wirkmächtige Siegeszeichen im Alten Testament: Ikonographische Studien zu Jos 8,18–26; Ex 17,8–13; 2 Kön 13,14–19; and 1 Kön 22,11*. OBO 5. Freiburg: Universitätsverlag, 1974. **Kelso, J. L.** *The Excavations of Bethel (1934–1960)*. AASOR. Cambridge, MA: ASOR, 1968. **Kitchener, H. H.** "The Site of Ai." *PEFQS* 10 (1878) 74–75. **Klem, J. F.** "Joshua 7–8 and the Covenant Ideology of Military History: A Genre Analysis." Unpublished paper. **Knauf, E. A.** "Beth-Aven." *Bib* 65 (1984) 251–53. **Köhlmoos, M.** *Bet-El—Erinnerungen an eine Stadt: Perspektiven der alttestamentlichen Bet-El-Überlieferungen*. FAT 49. Tübingen: Mohr Siebeck, 2006. **Kuschke, A.** "Hiwwiter in ha Ai?" In *Wort und Geschichte*. Ed. H. Gese and H. P. Rüger. Neukirchen-Vluyn: Neukirchener Verlag, 1973. 115–19. **Livingston, D.** "Further Considerations on the Location of Bethel at el-Bireh." *PEQ* 126 (1994) 154–59. ———. "Is Kh. Nisya the Ai of the Bible?" *Bible and Spade* 12 (1999) 13–20. ———. *Khirbet Nisya: The Search for Biblical Ai, 1979–2002*. Manheim, PA: Associates for Biblical Research, 2003. ———. "Locating Biblical Bethel." *Bible and Spade* 11 (1998) 77–84. ———. "Location of Biblical Bethel and Ai Reconsidered." *WTJ* 33 (1970) 20–44. ———. "One Last Word on Bethel and Ai—Fairness Requires No More." *BAR* 15.1 (1989) 11. ———. "Remarks on Blizzard's Investigation." *WTJ* 36 (1974) 231–32. ———. "Traditional Site of Bethel Questioned." *WTJ* 34 (1971) 39–50. **Lods, A.** "Les fouilles d'Aï et l'époque de entrée des Israélites en Palestine." In *Mélanges Franz Cumont*. Brussels: Secrétariat de l'Institut, 1936. 847–57. **Malamat, A.** "Die Eroberung Kanaans: Die israelitische Kriegsführung nach der biblischen Tradition." In *Das Land Israel in biblischer Zeit*. Ed. G. Strecker. GTA 25. Göttingen: Vandenhoeck & Ruprecht, 1983. 7–32. **Marquet-Krause, J.** *Les fouilles d'Aï (et-Tell) 1933–35*. Paris: Geuthner, 1949. **Mazor, L.** "A Textual and Literary Study of the Fall of Ai in Joshua 8" (Heb.). In *The Bible in Light of Its Interpreters: Sarah Kamin Memorial Volume*. Ed. S. Japhet. Jerusalem: Magnes, 1994. 73–108. **Na'aman, N.** "Beth-aven, Bethel and Early Israelite Sanctuaries." *ZDPV* 103 (1987) 13–21. **Noth, M.** "Bethel und Ai." *PJ* 31 (1935) 7–29. Reprinted in *Aufsätze zur biblischen Landes- und Altertumskunde*, vol. 1. Neukirchen-Vluyn: Neukirchener Verlag, 1971. 210–28. ———. "Grundsätzliches zur geschichtlichen Deutung archäologischer Befunde auf dem Boden Palästinas." *PJ* 34 (1938) 7–22. Reprinted in *Aufsätze zur biblischen Landes- und Altertumskunde*, vol. 1. Neukirchen-Vluyn: Neukirchener Verlag, 1971. 3–16. **Pitkänen, P.** "The Archaeology of Ai." 182–84. **Rainey, A. F.** "Bethel Is Still Beitin." *WTJ* 33 (1971) 175–88. ———. "Looking for Bethel: An Exercise in Historical Geography." In *Confronting the Past: Archaeological and Historical Essays on Ancient Israel in Honor of William G. Dever*. Ed. S. Gitin, J. E. Wright, and J. P. Dessel. Winona Lake, IN: Eisenbrauns, 2006. 269–73. **Rösel, H.** "Studien zur Topographie der Kriege in den Büchern Josua und Richter I–III." *ZDPV* 91 (1975) 159–90. **Ross, J.** "Loosening the Gordian Knot: A Contextual Critical Investigation of the Second Battle of Ai." Paper read for Old Testament Narrative Section of Evangelical Theological Society, November 17, 2010. **Tricot, A.** "La prise d'Aï (Jos 7,1–8:29): Notes de critique textuelle et d'histoire biblique." *Bib* 3 (1922) 273–300. **Vincent, L. H.** "Les fouilles d'et-Tell-Ai." *RB* 36 (1937) 231–66. **Weippert, M.** *Die Landnahme der israelitischen Stämme*. FRLANT 93. Göttingen:

Vandenhoeck & Ruprecht, 1967. 28–36. **Wolf, C. U.** "The Location of Gilgal." *BR* 11 (1966) 42–51. **Wood, B. G.** "Khirbet el-Maqatir, A Proposed New Location for the Site of Joshua's Ai: The 2009 and 2010 Seasons." Paper Read to Near Eastern Archaeology Society, Atlanta, November 18, 2010. ————. "The Search for Joshua's Ai." In *Critical Issues in Early Israelite History*. Ed. R. S. Hess, G. A. Klingbeil, and P. J. Ray, Jr. BBRSup 3. Winona Lake, IN: Eisenbrauns, 2008. 205–40. ————. "The Search for Joshua's Ai: Excavations at Kh. El-Maqatir." *Bible and Spade* 12 (1999) 21–30. **Zevit, Z.** "Archaeological and Literary Stratigraphy in Joshua 7–8." *BASOR* 251 (1983) 23–35.

Bibliography: Exegesis

Abegg, M., Jr., P. Flint, and E. Ulrich. *The Dead Sea Scrolls Bible.* San Francisco: Harper San Francisco, 1999. **Abel, F. M.** "Les stratagèmes dans le Livre de Josué." *RB* 56 (1949) 329–32. **Alfrink, B. J.** "Die Achan-Erzählung (Jos 7)." *SA* 27/28 (1951) 114–29. **Auld, A. G.** "Joshua: The Hebrew and Greek Texts." In *Studies in the Historical Books of the Old Testament.* VTSup 30. Leiden: Brill, 1979. 1–14. **Baltzer, K.** *Das Bundesformular.* 2nd ed. WMANT 4. Neukirchen-Vluyn: Neukirchener Verlag, 1964. 66–67. **Begg, C.** "The Function of Josh. 7:1–8:29 in the Deuteronomistic History." *Bib* 67 (1986) 320–34. **Benjamin, C. D.** *The Variations between the Hebrew and Greek Texts of Joshua: Chapters 1–12.* Thesis, University of Pennsylvania. Leipzig: W. Drugulin, 1921. **Boecker, H. J.** *Redeformen des Rechtslebens im Alten Testament.* WMANT 14. Neukirchen-Vluyn: Neukirchener Verlag, 1964. 115–16, 141–42, 147–48. **Geoghegan, J. C.** *The Time, Place, and Purpose of the Deuteronomistic History: The Evidence of 'Until This Day.'* BJS 347. Providence: Brown Judaic Studies, 2006. **Hermisson, H. J.** *Sprache und Ritus im altisraelitischen Kult.* WMANT 19. Neukirchen-Vluyn: Neukirchener Verlag, 1965. 39–42. **Holmes, S.** *Joshua, the Hebrew and Greek Texts.* Cambridge: Cambridge UP, 1914. **Hölscher, G.** *Geschichtsschreibung in Israel.* Lund: Gleerup, 1952. 340–42. **Kaminsky, J.** "Joshua 7: Holiness Violation and Corporate Punishment." In *Corporate Responsibility in the Hebrew Bible.* JSOTSup 196. Sheffield: Sheffield Academic, 1995. 67–95. **Keel, O.** *Wirkmächtige Siegeszeichen im Alten Testament.* Freiburg: Universitätsverlag, 1974. 13–34, 77–88. **Knierim, R.** *Die Hauptbegriffe für Sünde im Alten Testament.* Gütersloh: Gerd Mohn, 1965. 21–22, 27, 38–41, 106. **Latvus, K.** *God, Anger, and Ideology: The Anger of God in Joshua and Judges in Relation to Deuteronomy and the Priestly Writings.* JSOTSup 279. Sheffield: Sheffield Academic, 1998. **Long, B. O.** *The Problem of Aetiological Narrative in the Old Testament.* BZAW 108. Berlin: Töpelmann, 1968. 6–7, 25–26. **Macholz, G. C.** "Gerichtsdoxologie und israelitisches Rechtsverfahren." *DBAT* 9 (1975) 52–69. **McKenzie, J. L.** *The World of the Judges.* Englewood Cliffs, NJ: Prentice-Hall, 1966. 54–58. **Meer, M. N. van der.** *Formation and Reformulation: The Redaction of the Book of Joshua in the Light of the Oldest Textual Witnesses.* VTSup 102. Leiden: Brill, 2004. **Mitchell, G.** *Together in the Land.* JSOTSup 134. Sheffield: Sheffield Academic, 1993. 55–66. **Möhlenbrink, K.** "Die Landnahmensagen des Buches Josua." *ZAW* 56 (1938) 259–62. **Mowinckel, S.** *Tetrateuch, Pentateuch, Hexateuch.* BZAW 90. Berlin: Töpelmann, 1964. 37–38. **Otto, E.** *Das Mazzotfest in Gilgal.* BWANT 107. Stuttgart: Kohlhammer, 1975. 89, 193. **Ottosson, M.** "Tradition and History with Emphasis on the Composition of the Book of Joshua." In *The Productions of Time: Tradition History in Old Testament Scholarship.* Ed. K. Jeppesen and B. Otzen. Sheffield: Almond, 1984. 81–106, 141–43. **Roth, W.** "Hinterhalt und Scheinflucht: Der stammespolemische Hintergrund von Jos 8." *ZAW* 75 (1963) 296–304. **Rudolph, W.** *Der 'Elohist' von Exodus bis Josua.* BZAW 68. Berlin: Töpelmann, 1938. 189–98. **Scharbert, J.** *Solidarität in Segen und Fluch im AT und in saner Umwelt.* BBB 14. Bonn: Hanstein, 1958. 115–19, 249. **Schmitt, G.** *Du sollst keinen Frieden schliessen mit den Bewohnern des Landes.* BWANT 91. Stuttgart: Kohlhammer, 1970. 144–47. **Schwienhorst, L.** *Die Eroberung Jerichos: Exegetische Untersuchung zu Josua 6.* SBS 122. Stuttgart: Kohlhammer, 1986. **Shanks, H.** "Jerusalem Roundup." *BAR* 37.2 (2011) 35–45. **Simpson, C. A.** *The Early Traditions of Israel.* Oxford: Blackwell, 1948. 293–301. **Stec, D.** "The Mantle Hidden by Achan." *VT* 41 (1991) 356–59. **Stolz, F.** *Jahwes und Israels Kriege.* ATANT 60. Zürich: Theologischer Verlag, 1972. 81–84. **Tov, E.** *Textual Criticism of the Hebrew Bible.* 2nd ed. Minneapolis: Fortress, 2001. **Tricot, A.** "La prise d'Ai (Josh 7, 1–8, 29)." *Bib* 3 (1922) 273–300. **Vaux, R. de.** *Histoire ancienne d'Israël.* Vol. 1. Paris: Gabalda, 1971. 563–70. Reprinted in *The Early History of Israel,* trans. D. Smith (London: Darton, Longman & Todd, 1978) 612–20. **Veijola, T.** "Das Klagegebet in Literatur and Leben der Exilsgeneration am Beispiel einiger Prosatexte." In *Congress Volume: Salamanca 1983.* Ed. J. A. Emerton. VTSup 36. Leiden: Brill, 1985. 286–307. **Vries, S. J. de.** "The Time Word *mahar* as a Key to Tradition Development." *ZAW* 87 (1975) 73–79. **Wagner, S.** "Die Kundschaftergeschichten im Alten Testament." *ZAW* 76 (1964) 255–69. **Weinfeld, M.** *Deuteronomy and the Deuteronomic School.* Oxford: Oxford UP, 1972. **Wellhausen, J.** *Die Composition des Hexateuchs und der historischen Bücher des Alten Testaments.* 2nd ed. Berlin: Reimer, 1889. 125–26. **Westermann, C.** *Das Loben Gottes in den Psalmen.* 4th ed. Göttingen: Vandenhoeck & Ruprecht, 1968. **Wilson, R. R.** "Enforcing the Covenant: The Mechanisms of Judicial Authority in Early Israel." In *The Quest for the Kingdom of God: Studies in Honor of George E. Mendenhall.* Ed. H. B. Huffmon, F. A. Spina, and A. R. W. Green. Winona Lake, IN: Eisenbrauns, 1983. 59–75. **Winther-Nielsen, N.** *A Functional Discourse Grammar of Joshua: A Computer-Assisted Rhetorical Structure Analysis.* ConBOT 40. Stockholm: Almqvist & Wiksell, 1995. **Zevit, Z.** "Archaeological and Literary Stratigraphy in Joshua 7–8." *BASOR* 251 (1983) 23–35. ———. "The Problem of Ai." *BAR* 11.2 (1985) 58–67.

Translation

[1]*The sons of Israel were not faithful*[a] *in regard to the ban. Achan,*[b] *the son of Carmi, the son of Zabdi, the son of Zerah of the tribe of Judah, took part of the banned goods. Then the anger of Yahweh burned against the sons of Israel.*

[2]*Joshua sent men from Jericho*[a] *to The Ruin,*[b] *which is beside Bethaven,*[c] *east of Bethel. He told them, "Go up and spy out the land." The men went up and spied out The Ruin.* [3]*They returned to Joshua and told him, "Do not make all the people go up. About two or three thousand men should go up to attack The Ruin. Do not make all the people exert themselves there, since they are insignificant."* [4]*So about three thousand of the people went up there, and they fled before the inhabitants of The Ruin.* [5]*The inhabitants of The Ruin killed about thirty-six of them and chased them away before*[a] *the gate clear to The Breaking Points.*[b] *They smote them at the Descent. The heart of the people melted and became water.* [6]*Then Joshua tore his clothes and fell on his face to the ground in front of the ark*[a] *of Yahweh until evening, he and the elders of Israel. And they placed dust on their head.* [7]*Then Joshua said, "Alas, O Lord Yahweh, why have you so certainly caused*[a] *this people to pass over the Jordan to give us into the hand of the Amorites to bring about our destruction? If only*[b] *we had been content to live beyond the Jordan!* [8]*With your permission,*[a] *my Lord! Oh, what can I say after Israel has turned its back before its enemies* [9]*so that the Canaanites and all the inhabitants of the land will hear and turn themselves about against us and cut our name off from the earth? Then what will you do for your great name!"*

[10]*Yahweh said to Joshua, "Get up! What is the reason that you are falling on your face?* [11]*Israel has sinned. They*[a] *have transgressed my covenant which I commanded them. They have taken from the banned goods, stolen, deceived, and put them among their own things.*[12]*Unable to stand before their enemies,*[a] *the sons of Israel turn their backs*[b] *to their enemies because they have become banned goods. Never*[c] *again will I be with you (pl.) if you (pl.) do not banish the*

banned goods from your midst. [13]Get up, sanctify[a] the people, and say, 'Sanctify yourselves for tomorrow, for thus says Yahweh, the God of Israel, "Banned goods are in your[b] midst, O Israel. Thus you are not able to stand before your enemies[c] until you have removed the banned goods from your midst." [14]You (pl.) must appear in the morning by your tribes. Then[a] the tribe which Yahweh captures must draw near by clans, while the clan which Yahweh captures must appear by houses,[b] and the house which Yahweh captures must appear individually. [15]The one captured with the banned goods[a] will be burned with fire, he and everything which belongs to him, because he has transgressed the covenant of Yahweh and[b] because he has committed a sacrilege in Israel.'"

[16]Then early in the morning, Joshua caused Israel to approach by tribes.[a] The tribe[b] of Judah was taken. [17]He caused the clan[a] of Judah to approach, and he captured[b] the clan of the Zerahites. He caused to approach the Zerahite clan individually,[c] and Zabdi was captured. [18]He caused his house to approach individually, and Achan, son of Carmi, son of Zabdi, son of Zerah of the tribe of Judah, was captured. [19]Then Joshua said to Achan, "My son,[a] set forth glory to Yahweh, the God of Israel, and give him praise. Then tell me what you have done. Do not hide anything from me!"

[20]Achan answered Joshua, "Truly,[a] I have sinned against Yahweh, the God of Israel. Here are the details of what I have done. [21]I saw among the spoils a lovely robe from Shinar,[a] two hundred shekels of silver, a bar of gold weighing fifty shekels.[b] Then I coveted them and took them; they are right there hidden in the ground in the center of my tent.[c] The silver is underneath."[d]

[22]Joshua sent messengers. They ran to the tent.[a] It[b] was right there hidden in his tent with the silver underneath. [23]They took them from the center of the tent and brought them to Joshua and to all the sons[a] of Israel and poured them out before Yahweh. [24]Then Joshua took Achan, the son of Zerah, and the silver[a] and the robe and the bar of gold, and his sons and his daughters and his oxen and his donkey, and his sheep and his tent, and everything which belonged to him. All Israel was with Joshua. They brought them up to the Valley of Aching.

[25]Joshua said, "For what reason have you made us ache?[a] May Yahweh make you ache today!" Then all Israel stoned him with stones and burned[b] them in the fire and threw rocks at them. [26]They raised over him a great heap of stones until this day.[a] Then Yahweh repented of his burning rage. Therefore, he called the name of that place the Valley of Aching until this day.

[8:1a]Yahweh said to Joshua, "Do not fear nor be terrified. Take with you (pl.) the warriors. Get up and go to The Ruin. See, I have given into your hand the king of The Ruin and his people[b] and his city and his land. [2]Treat The Ruin and its king[a] just as you treated Jericho and its king, with the exception that its booty and its animals you shall plunder for yourselves. Set up for yourselves an ambush behind[b] the city." [3]Joshua and all the warriors got up to go to The Ruin. Joshua chose thirty thousand men, valiant heroes, and sent them by night. [4]He commanded them, "Look! You are setting an ambush for the city behind the city. Don't move exceedingly far away from the city so that you, all of you, may be prepared.[a] [5]But I and all the people with me will approach the city. When they[a] come out to meet us, just like the first time, we will flee before them [6]so that they will come out after us until we have lured them from the city because they will say, 'They're fleeing[a] before us just like the first time.' We will flee before them,[b] [7]but you (pl.) shall rise up from ambush[a] and take possession[b] of the city. Yahweh[c] your God will give it into your hand. [8]As you seize the city, you shall set the city on fire. According to the word of Yahweh,[a] you shall act. See, I have commanded you."

[9]Joshua sent them, and they went to the ambush and settled down between Bethel and The Ruin, west of The Ruin. Joshua[a] lodged that night in the midst of the people.[b]

[10]*Early in the morning, Joshua summoned the people. Then he and the elders*[a] *of Israel went up at the head of the people to The Ruin.*

[11]*Indeed, all the army who were with him had gone up*[a] *and approached and come near the city. They had camped*[b] *north of The Ruin with the valley between it and The Ruin.* [12a]*He had taken about five thousand men and set them as an ambush between Bethel and The Ruin, west of the city.* [13]*Then the people had set up the camp which was north of the city and its "heel" west of the city. Joshua had gone*[a] *that night into the midst of the Valley.*

[14a]*When the king of The Ruin took notice, the men of the city*[b] *hurriedly got out of bed and went out to meet Israel in battle, he and all those with him going to the Assembly Point in front of the Arabah.*[c] *But he did not know that an ambush waited*[d] *for him behind the city.*[e] [15]*Joshua*[a] *and all Israel feigned defeat before them and fled*[b] *the way of the wilderness.* [16]*Then all the people who were in the city were called out to pursue them. They pursued Joshua*[a] *and were lured away from the city.* [17]*Not a man was left in The Ruin or in Bethel*[a] *who did not go out after Israel. They left the city open and pursued after Israel.*

[18]*Yahweh said to Joshua, "Stretch out the sword*[a] *that is in your hand toward The Ruin, for into your hand I will give it."*[b] [19]*Joshua stretched out the sword in his hand to the city, whereupon the ambush arose hurriedly from its place and ran just when he stretched out his hand. They entered the city and captured it. They hurriedly set the city afire.* [20]*Then the men of The Ruin made an about-face and saw that right in front of them smoke from the city went up toward heaven. But they did not possess strength to flee in any direction. Meanwhile,*[a] *the people fleeing to the wilderness turned back to the pursuit.* [21]*When Joshua and all Israel saw that the ambush had captured the city and that smoke from the city ascended,*[a] *then they turned and smote the men of The Ruin.* [22]*At the same time this group came out from the city to meet them. They were thus in the midst of Israel, one group on one side and the other on the other side. They smote them until there remained nothing to them,*[a] *neither survivor nor remnant,* [23]*but the king of The Ruin they seized alive. They brought him before Joshua.*

[24]*When Israel completed killing all the inhabitants of The Ruin in the field, in the wilderness,*[a] *into which they pursued them, all of them fell*[b] *before the sword until their total extermination. Then all Israel*[c] *returned to The Ruin. They smote it with the sword.* [25]*Now all who fell that day both men and women numbered twelve thousand, all the people of The Ruin.* [26]*But*[a] *Joshua did not return his hand which he had stretched out with the sword until he had put to the ban all the inhabitants of The Ruin.* [27]*The only exceptions were the animals and the booty of that city. Israel plundered them for themselves, according to the word of Yahweh, which he commanded Joshua.* [28]*Then Joshua burned*[a] *The Ruin. He set it up as a tell forever, desolate until this day.* [29]*But the king of The Ruin he hung on the tree until evening time. As the sun set, Joshua commanded, and they brought his corpse down from the tree and cast it out to the opening of the gate*[a] *of the city. Then they set up over it a circle of boulders until this day.*

Notes

1.a. Nelson (97) follows J. Milgrom, *Leviticus 1–16,* AB 3A (New York: Doubleday, 1991) 345–56 (compare *NIDOTTE*) in translating מעל as "committed sacrilege." *HALOT* translates "to be untrue, violate one's legal obligations." *DCH* most often uses "sin, commit sin," but notes "esp. commit sacrilege as redressed by the אשם reparation offering." See *Comments.*

1.b. "Achan" is read as "Achar" in 1 Chr 2:7. LXX consistently reads "Achar" in all occurrences. This makes the play on the name of the Valley (v 26) more exact (cf. L. Koehler, "Hebräische Etymologien," *JBL* 59 [1940] 38–39), but MT is the more difficult reading. Hess (*HAR* 14 [1994] 95–96) attributes the change of name to the writer of

Chronicles, who wanted to make the wordplay between the names clear as well as that with the Valley.

2.a. LXX lacks "from Jericho," which demonstrates how one tradition has made explicit that which was implicit.

2.b. The city name Ai means "The Ruin" and is so translated throughout this commentary to give the proper "color" of the narrative. Zevit (*BASOR* 251 [1983] 32) argues that the name would have been pronounced with a ghayin, thus ġay. This "would have mitigated any association between it and the word for ruin 'iy." Winther-Nielsen (*Functional Discourse Grammar*, 215, n. 11) agrees, but modern lexicographers do not even note the article (*DCH*, 6:352–53, 871; *HALOT*, 2:815–16). W. Osborne decides, "the names Ai and Beth Aven used for the locations in the narrative may have been designed more for theological impact, in much the same way as Hosea's use of Beth Aven for Bethel, than to serve as geographical guides" (*NIDOTTE*, 4:369).

2.c. LXX lacks "Beth-aven, east of." Fritz (77) sees a gloss here. Nelson (97) sees Gk. haplography responsible for the loss. *Preliminary and Interim Report* (2:13) concludes, "it would appear that the omission is facilitating. For it is possible that Beth-aven and Bethel are not the same place." Hosea uses the term Beth-aven, literally translated "house of iniquity," as a derogatory reference to the royal sanctuary at Bethel (Hos 4:15, 5:8, 10:5, cf. Josh 18:12). In 1 Sam 13:5, 14:23, it may represent actual geography, but this is uncertain (cf. H. J. Stoebe, *Das erste Buch Samuelis*, KAT 8 [Gütersloh: Gütersloher, 1973] 244). Our text may also represent a writer's view of geography (Albright, *BASOR* 74 [1939] 15–17; Grintz, *Bib* 42 [1961] 210–16), LXX representing scribal homoioarchton.

5.a. Fritz (77–78) follows Noth (38) in reading מלפני, adding a mem as a victim of haplography.

5.b. The meaning of the geographical term is uncertain. LXX appears to have read it as a military term meaning total destruction (cf. 2 Chr 14:12). Nelson (97) sees LXX with Syr. and Tg. as meaning "until they were broken," which was then combined with נכה to mean "they destroyed." He notes with some approval Zevit's proposal (*BASOR* 251 [1983] 31) to read "a historicizing suggestion, "to the broken walls" of the city. NRSV simply transliterates the MT; NEB translates "quarries," while Soggin (93) suggests "ravines." I have tried to retain the ambiguity of the MT based on the root שבר, "to break in pieces." The connotation of מורד, "descent," is equally ambiguous and might be rendered, "the dropping-off point."

6.a. LXX lacks "ark," and probably is based on a text in which ארון, "ark," had become אדון, "Lord."

7.a. LXX reads "your servant caused . . . to give him (= people)," for the rare inf. form (GKC §113x) of MT. The double "correction" represents a theological interpretation of the tradition, avoiding any judicial charges lodged by man against God. Compare Nelson (97).

7.b. For לו, "if only, would that," introducing an unreal condition, here without an apodosis, compare Lambdin, *Introduction to Biblical Hebrew*, §278; *Williams' Hebrew Syntax*, 548; *IBHS* 38.2e. Williams notes that such desire clauses with לו often indicate a desire for something that did not or could not happen. Lambdin (*Introduction to Biblical Hebrew*, §173 (238–239) notes the use of לו in verbal hendiadys. Cf. GKC §120e.

8.a. בי, "with your permission," is an idiom used in addressing a superior and accepting responsibility for the result of the conversation (cf. *KB*, 3:117; W. Schneider, *Grammatik des biblischen Hebräisch* [Munich: Claudius, 1974] 265). Nelson (97) notes the Gk. omission here "to avoid a near repetition of the start of v. 7."

11.a. The series of וגם clauses defies English translation. They form an "inclusive sentence" (Andersen, Sentence, 154) joining the parts into a whole. LXX has "people" for "Israel," so MT is perhaps making specific the more original general term. LXX also lacks "stolen, deceived," later liturgical amplification of the text (cf. Josh 24:7; Hos 4:2) or with Nelson (98), haplography caused by repeated וגם clauses.

12.a. 4QJosh³ has 3rd pers. sg. rather than MT's 3rd pers. pl. suff.

12.b. 4QJosh³ has "and not their faces" as a unique reading here, an addition of a familiar phrase. *IBHS* 10.2.2 calls the use of "neck" here an accusative of limitation.

12.c. 4QJosh³ has the conjunctive waw before the negative, which MT does not have, apparently an easing of the grammar by the Qumran text.

13.a. Nelson (98) sees verbal hendiadys here with קום meaning, "to start," so "start to satisfy the people." See Lambdin, *Introduction to Biblical Hebrew*, §173.

13.b. MT fluctuates between sg. and pl. "you(r)." The versions harmonize. 4QJosh[a] and LXX have pl. suff. here, while MT has sg. Nelson (98) sees pl. as preferred reading, "O Israel" having led to the sg. readings.

13.c. 4QJosh[a] has 2nd pl. suff. with LXX, while MT has sg. See Note 7:13.b above.

14.a. The Heb. disjunctive clauses (Lambdin, *Introduction to Biblical Hebrew*, §§162–65) present the process as one continuous act with its parts rather than a series of acts in temporal sequence.

14.b. 4QJosh[a] does not have "will appear by clans, and the clans which Yahweh captures." Ulrich ("Joshua," in *Qumran Cave 4. IX: Deuteronomy, Joshua, Judges, Kings*, DJD 14 [Oxford: Clarendon, 1995] 149) explains this as parablepsis or distorted vision causing the copyist to omit materials between similar words (see E. Tov, *Textual Criticism of the Hebrew Bible*, 238–40; van der Meer, *Formation and Reformulation*, 97, calls this homoioteleuton). For defense of MT over against LXX and Qumran, see Nelson (98).

15.a. LXX lacks "with the banned goods," which the tradition added to make explicit what the original text implied. 4QJosh[a] reads "with them" (בהם) rather than "with the banned goods" (בַּחֵרֶם), a first step in the expansion. See Nelson (98), who agrees this is MT expansion and gives alternate translation possibilities as "in a state of being devoted" or "even 'caught in the net.'"

15.b. 4QJosh[a] does not have the conjunctive waw, "and."

16.a. Vv 16–18 do not carry out exactly the instructions of v 14. LXX has achieved grammatical harmony but lacks reference to vv 17bβ, 18aα, processing of the house of Zabdi, as a result of scribal homoioteleuton, skipping from the first to the second "individually." This proves, however, that it read the MT "inconsistent" tradition of bringing both clan and house "individually" over against the instructions of v 14. Syr. and Vg. show that tradition tried to harmonize completely, reading "by houses" for the first "individually."

16.b. 4QJosh[a] brings syntactical consistency by reading the sign of the direct object, not evidenced in MT.

17.a. "Clan" of Judah is an anomaly. Total consistency would require "tribe." LXX reads the pl. Fritz (78) says the context, the LXX, and some MSS demand the pl. here. Nelson (98) says the sg. is to be construed as a pl. *Preliminary and Interim Report* (2:13) sees assimilation to another passage and so prefers the pl. reading. The reading may represent a tendency of the narrative itself to polemicize, reducing the tribe of Judah to clan status.

17.b. "He captured" represents the more common verb form and is probably a scribal error for the passive form used elsewhere in the sequence. Cf. LXX, Syr., Tg.

17.c. Literally, "by warriors." *Preliminary and Interim Report* (2:13–14) retains MT text with a low degree of certainty citing simplification and assimilation. Fritz says social order requires reading with a few MSS לבתים, "by houses," but Nelson (98) correctly goes with MT as the more difficult reading, explaining that "once the level of family is reached, Joshua deals with individuals rather than groups," pointing to Barthélemy, *Critique textuelle*, 1:6–8. For history and complexity of the textual problems in this verse, see these same pages in Barthélemy .

19.a. LXX read Heb. כיום, "today," rather than בני , "my son," due to scribal confusion of letters (Benjamin, *Variations*).

20.a. *IBHS* 39.3.4b labels אמנה an adverbial disjunct. Disjuncts "modify a clause in relation to the act of speaking."

21.a. LXX and Vg. show that early translators were not sure of the meaning, resulting in a tradition of a coat of many colors here (cf. Gen 37:3). Nelson (98) says "it would be peculiar for the construct 'robe of Shinar' to signify place of origin," so he translates "a robe made of Shinar fabric."

21.b. Fritz (78) sees "and a bar of gold weighing fifty shekels" as a gloss since it does not reappear in the narrative.

21.c. MT article + pers. suff. causes grammatical purists to change the text (see Fritz, 78; *BHS*), but the tradition followed its rules and habits, not ours. Williams (*Williams' Hebrew Syntax*, 82c) points to this as one of the rare occasions where a word with a pronominal suff. takes the article (compare 8:33). Nelson (98) decides MT represents a conflation of "the tent" and "my tent," pointing to *IBHS* 13.6b. He also suggests LXX did not witness "weighing" and "in the ground" through Heb. copying mistakes involving similar words.

21.d. Fritz strikes the last clause as dittography from the following verse, seeing the expressions without reference in this verse. The Heb. narrator enjoys such repetition, so the words should not be so quickly stricken.

22.a. LXX adds "into the camp," an example of later exegesis explaining why the entire community was polluted (cf. reference to camp in Josh 6:18).

22.b. Fritz (78) is not satisfied with the indefinite subject and wants to add האדרת, "robe."

23.a. LXX reads "elders" for "sons," perhaps in light of later practice and of other references in the context (Josh 7:6, 8:10). *Preliminary and Interim Report* (2:14) retains MT, citing simplification and assimilation as the causes of the alternative reading.

24.a. LXX lacks list of banned goods, including only his other possessions. MT is later expansion in light of v 21 (compare Nelson, 98). Fritz (78) calls the list an addition that is inappropriate to the context. LXX repeats the leading into the valley at beginning and end of verse. The first reference may point to earlier text tradition without any list at all.

25.a. The verb used is a play on the name Achan and the Valley of Achor, using the root of the latter. The meaning is "to trouble, to make taboo, bring destruction upon." The translation seeks to imitate the wordplay. Nelson translates "make taboo" (97) and names the valley "Taboo Valley" (99).

25.b. The versions omit redundancy, ending the verse after stoning (LXX) or burning (Vg., Syr.). MT represents expansion to bring total agreement with command of v 15 and prepare for stone heap of v 26, thus understanding sequence of burning, covering of remains by stoning, and setting up of stone heap (cf. Soggin, 94; Fritz, 78; Pressler, 59; Nelson, 98, who also sees possibility of inner-Gk. haplography). Kaminsky ("Joshua 7," 319) sees first reference to stoning as a "later interpolation." *Preliminary and Interim Report* (2:14–15) sees the versions as simplifying an original text that uses specific vocabulary to describe the situation. Barthélemy (*Critique textuelle*, 1:8–10) offers a history of opinions and suggestions but still favors MT, referring to homoioteleuton.

26.a. LXX lacks first "until this day," a MT expansion making explicit that both the heap and the name survived (see Fritz, 78).

8:1.a. Chap. 8 witnesses several minuses in the LXX. Prominent scholars such as Fernández, Benjamin, Auld, Greenspoon, Holmes, and Tov see LXX as original. (See van der Meer, *Formation and Reformulation*, 429–31, who claims a majority of scholars see LXX as representing deliberate omissions to avoid logical problems of MT.) Mazor finds 4QJosh[a] as reflecting the earliest text, followed by LXX, and MT (see van der Meer, *Formation and Reformulation*, 434). Van der Meer, however, ascribes "the main divergences in this chapter between the Hebrew (MT and 4QJosh[a]) and Greek texts to the interpretative, harmonising and stylising skills of the Greek translator" (*Formation and Reformulation*, 467).

1.b. LXX lacks "and his people and his city." MT represents amplification for completeness. Nelson (108) sees haplography in the LXX.

2.a. LXX lacks "and its king," an amplification in light of the following reference to Jericho. The LXX pls. for MT sgs. are harmonizations to the context.

2.b. Or "west of"; see Williams (*Williams' Hebrew Syntax*, 359).

4.a. Nelson (108) finds MT expansions in "look" and "exceedingly" "generally supported" by 4QJosh[a]. Neither Abegg et al., *Dead Sea Scrolls Bible*, nor Ulrich, "4QJosh[a]," in *Qumran Cave 4. IX: Deuteronomy, Joshua, Judges, Kings*, DJD 14 [Oxford: Clarendon, 1995] mention this.

5.a. LXX adds "inhabitants of Ai" as explicit subject.

6.a. A verbless clause with a participle as predicate often does not have an explicit subject as this clause does not in the Heb. (*Williams' Hebrew Syntax*, 359). Compare *IBHS* 37.6a.

6.b. LXX lacks "we will flee before them," possibly dittography from v 5b (Margolis, *Book of Joshua in Greek*, 126; Nelson, 108; Fritz, 87; van der Meer, *Formation and Reformulation*, 471), or possibly a clause placed in contrast to v 7a but not understood by later tradition (cf. *Preliminary and Interim Report*, 2:15). Barthélemy (*Critique textuelle*, 1:10) notes the committee's great hesitation in finally accepting MT. Van der Meer (*Formation and Reformulation*, 459) finds by counting spaces in the 4QJosh[a] scroll frg. 1 that the scroll apparently supports the longer MT reading.

7.a. Fritz (87) changes the articular part to the simple noun.

7.b. Nelson (109) follows Gk. in reading ונגשתם אל, "approach to," for MT והורש תם את, "take possession of," seeing Gk. as less theological. But one expects theological language in Joshua. Van der Meer *(Formation and Reformulation,* 472) sees the alteration as anticipation of v 19.

7.c. LXX lacks vv 7b, 8α, the first a later insertion of a traditional formula and the latter harmonization with v 19. Nelson (109) sees inner haplography in Gk. tradition.

8.a. For MT "word of Yahweh," LXX reads "this word," representing the more original tradition. MT reflects prophetic tradition. Nelson (109) says LXX misreads an abbreviation for the divine name, which is also quite possible. *Preliminary and Interim Report* (2:15–16) retains MT, seeing LXX as simplification. Van der Meer notes *(Formation and Reformulation,* 96) that 4QJosh[a] supports MT.

9.a. LXX lacks v 9b, which gives narrative preparation to v 10a and narrative contrast to v 13b, but still may be the product of the ongoing tradition seeking to harmonize and make explicit every detail. Van der Meer *(Formation and Reformulation,* 423) credits Gk. translator with making all the action occur in a night and the following day.

9.b. 4QJosh[a] seems to allow space only for the shorter LXX text of vv 7–9, not that of the longer MT (Ulrich, "4QJosh[a]," in *Qumran Cave 4. IX: Deuteronomy, Joshua, Judges, Kings,* DJD 14 [Oxford: Clarendon, 1995], 50). From this, Nelson (109) suggests this is MT expansion and clarification. Fritz (87) simply changes העם to העמק, "the people" becoming "the valley" on the basis of v 13. MT certainly represents the more difficult reading.

10.a. 4QJosh[a] (compare LXX) does not have the const. pl. form of "elders" and so apparently does not read "of Israel." Nelson (109) correctly speaks of MT expansion.

11.a. 4QJosh[a] reads only "and they returned" for MT's "went up and drew up and entered." This seems to indicate simplification in the tradition.

11.b. Nelson (109) sees "and camped" as MT expansion anticipating v 13. LXX simplifies the geography and contextual contradictions in vv 11–13 by reading "on the east side with the ambush west of the city." Auld ("Joshua," 4–5) argues that "small is beautiful" and earlier, but the tendency of the ongoing tradition is to harmonize, which is precisely what LXX has done, omitting the contradiction in numbers between vv 3 and 12 and placing the two companies exactly opposite of one another, while MT sets one to the north and the other to the west. Nelson (109) detects haplography in Gk. tradition. Van der Meer *(Formation and Reformulation,* 423, 443) says Gk. simply has Israelite force arrive from the east without camping, the MT description making more sense than LXX's simplified idea. It is also apparent to many scholars that the Egyptian-based LXX translator was not familiar with Palestinian geographical details.

12.a. 4QJosh[a] does not appear to have space for vv 12–13.

13.a. Several Heb. MSS read ילן for MT ילֶךְ, thus "he spent the night" rather than "he went." Fritz (87) reads יָלֶךְ here on the basis of v 9. This makes the contrast to v 9b exact. An easy interchange of letters is involved, and another explicit example of different Heb. traditions becomes evident. Syr. makes the parallelism complete, reading "people" for "Valley." Nelson (109) concludes that "the MT expansions in vv. 9 and 13 emphasize the timetable by explicitly reporting the nights that preceded the mornings of vv. 10 and 14." *Preliminary and Interim Report* (2:16–17) translates: "And the army (lit. the people, i.e., the soldiers) pitched the entire camp which <was> to the north of the city, and the rearguard <which was> to the west of the city. But Joshua went that night into the midst of the valley." Barthélemy *(Critique textuelle,* 1:11) strongly supports MT, showing statistics on LXX omissions. Howard (200) points to the disjunctive syntax of v 13 to argue for a flashback here extending the description in vv 3–9. The translation above follows this understanding.

14.a. LXX reads all verbs in the sg., omitting "got out of bed," "men of the city," and the geographical details. The latter reflects the tendency seen in vv 11–13. The verbal changes and omission of the men of the city as co-subjects is "more logical" (Soggin, 95; compare Fritz, 87, who also deletes "got out of bed"), which may show its character as later simplification and harmonization. Nelson (109) finds LXX preferable, deciding "MT gives the subject as 'the men of Ai' with attendant plural verbs, anticipating 'all his people.'" Fritz (87) says sg. must be read, but the text often combines a leader as sg. subject with his army or people using pl. subjects. The emphasis here is on the army going to battle, not the king.

14.b. LXX reads, "and it came to pass as the king of Ai saw, he hurried and went out for a meeting with them immediately into battle, he and all the people who were with him, and he could not know that an ambush was against him outside the city." 4QJosh[a] also witnesses "to meet them" rather than "to meet Israel," an indication that MT may represent a clarifying expansion (compare Nelson, 109). LXX fits narrative to its context omitting "early in the morning" because it had Joshua and troops arriving from Gilgal, not camping.

14.c. Nelson (109; compare Fritz, 87) calls "going to the Assembly Point in front of the Arabah" an "MT expansion or gloss to clarify the geographical situation." He gives no evidence for this. *Preliminary and Interim Report* (2:17) decides on "for the encounter in the direction of the Arabah." Barthélemy (*Critique textuelle*, 1:11–12) accepts MT. Van der Meer (*Formation and Reformulation*, 448) changes לְמוֹעֵד, "Assembly Point" or "Meeting Place," to לְמוֹרָד, "of the Descent," in line with Josh 7:5, but the text often repeats information without copying word for word.

14.d. "Waited" supplied, MT having no verb.

14.e. At the end of v 14 in 4QJosh[a], a secondary hand has added יָדְךָ אל העי, "your hand to Ai," without a space between the last two words. This seems to reflect part of v 18.

15.a. LXX adds "saw," making the obvious explicit.

15.b. LXX lacks vv 15b–16a, "and fled . . . to pursue them," due to homoioteleuton (Holmes, *Joshua, the Hebrew and Greek Texts*; Margolis, *Book of Joshua in Greek*, 131; compare Nelson, 109). Van der Meer (*Formation and Reformulation*, 468) credits Gk. translator with avoiding a doublet of pursuit here.

16.a. LXX reads "sons of Israel" for "Joshua," harmonizing with the context.

17.a. LXX lacks "Bethel," an amplification making the conquest complete (see Noth, 46; Fritz, 87) in light of contextual references to Bethel (Josh 7:2; 8:9, 12), the notices in Josh 12:9, 16, and the greater importance of Bethel in later tradition. (But see Albright, BASOR 74 [1939] 15–17; *Preliminary and Interim Report* [2:17–18]; Barthélemy [*Critique textuelle*, 1:12–13].)

18.a. LXX reference to "sword" is gramatically awkward and may reflect late addition (Benjamin, *Variations*; cf. Keel, *Wirkmächtige Siegeszeichen*, 20–21; Nelson, 109).

18.b. LXX adds καὶ τὰ ἔνεδρα ἐξαναστήσονται ἐν τάχει ἐκ τοῦ τόπου αὐτῶν, "and the men in ambush will rise quickly from their place," an expansion in light of v 19 underlining the theme of prediction and fulfillment. Van der Meer (*Formation and Reformulation*, 423) sees the divine speech as strengthening the signal function of the sword.

20.a. LXX lacks the last part of the verse, an expansion making the obvious explicit and dependent upon v 15b, which may itself be an expansion. Compare Nelson, who chooses the shorter reading but admits LXX could represent a "deliberate" omission "to create a more coherent narrative" (109). Van der Meer (*Formation and Reformulation*, 423) sees Gk. avoiding a doublet.

21.a. LXX adds "into heaven," from v 20. *Preliminary and Interim Report* (2:18) sees LXX as an assimilation to parallel passages. It may simply be the addition of traditional idiom.

22.a. MT apparently has collective sg. pronoun, but English translation requires pl. as found in some MSS and Tg. See Fritz (87).

24.a. For "in the wilderness," LXX reads "in the mountain, at the descent." All may be later explication of "in the field" (Noth; Soggin, 96), but LXX at least reflects Heb. tradition, reading בהר במורד based on Josh 7:5 (Margolis, *Book of Joshua in Greek*, 138). Nelson reads "in the open country on the slope," saying LXX's rendering of Heb. בהר, "mountain," "must be an expansion or gloss" while Heb. במדבר, "in the wilderness," represents a misreading and transposition of "the more difficult original," 109) במורד). Fritz (87) simply omits "in the wilderness" as a gloss dependent on the description of the escape path.

24.b. LXX lacks "all of them fell before the sword," a later explication duplicating the end of the verse, though van der Meer (*Formation and Reformulation*, 470) calls it an LXX omission avoiding duplication.

24.c. Van der Meer (*Formation and Reformulation*, 470) ties this to omission of v 26 allowing Joshua to resume as military commander. LXX may be original in reading "Joshua" instead of "all Israel" as the subject of the final action, thus giving prominence to Joshua at the conclusion of the narrative as in v 28 and the other narratives in this section. MT represents a harmonization to the context.

26.a. LXX lacks entire verse either due to inner-Gk. homoioteleuton (Margolis, *Book of Joshua in Greek*, 140; Nelson, 110) or because it was doublet to v 24b. Van der Meer (*Formation and Reformulation*, 470) thinks Gk. saw sword as signal to ambush only and thus was not needed once ambush was called up, thus deleting v 26.

28.a. LXX adds the obvious "with fire."

29.a. LXX reflects Heb. פחת, "pit," a transposition of פתח, "gate," showing two early Heb. variants, later expanded to "the opening of the gate of the city." This may find Qumran verification, according to Callaway (*JBL* 87 [1968] 319–20). Nelson (110) sees פתח, "gate," as the more difficult and so original reading that caused the expansion. Consistent with his theories, van der Meer (*Formation and Reformulation*, 470) says the translator reasoned from v 28 that the city gate had been burned to the ground.

Form/Structure/Setting

The opening of the section is well marked by the concluding formula in Josh 6:27 and the opening transition in 7:1. The ending is open to debate. Winther-Nelson[943] points with Schwienhorst[944] to the opening וַיְהִי construction in 6:27 as a discourse marker in 9:1, 10:1, and 11:1. This fails to observe that the three compared texts (as also 4:1; 5:1) have introductory temporal clauses introducing action that initiates the narrative. No temporal clause appears in 6:27. Rather, a narrator's summary statement describes the state of affairs after the Jericho victory. A *waw* consecutive action verb begins the narrative in 7:1 as well as in 2:1 and 3:1.

A concluding formula appears in Josh 7:26 but concludes only the episode of Achan, not the fate of defeated Israel and Ai. The latter ends with the concluding etiological formula of 8:29. The narrative section ends here, but it is not theologically complete. Theological completion occurs in 8:30–35. That section, however, completes not only the present section, but the first major division of the book as a whole. We will consider it in a separate section of the commentary.

Tradition

The structure of chap. 7 is clear and interesting. The opening verses take away any narrative arc of tension.[945] Ottosson understands Jos 7 as "an independent section without visible signs of Deuteronomistic reworking" but dominated by the archaic P style, which for Ottosson means traditions "must derive from priestly circles attached to the shrine at Gilgal."[946] Fritz finds an artful composition in which numerous literary topoi have been assimilated.[947] For Fritz this means the absence of oral tradition or other sources and posits a Deuteronomistic creation.

The vast number of stories that present Israel's heroes of antiquity negatively suggests that these stories were cemented in tradition, rather than that some scribe or priest invented them. Spy stories such as this one forge a strong part of Israel's ancient tradition. The stories are frequently told in ironic, humorous tones as in chap. 2. Here tradition turned the spy story genre upside down to explain what God requires in order for Israel to defeat an enemy whose headquarters was aptly named "The Ruin." No battle for God was simple or could be carried out without the united work of all Israel and its fighting forces. The end of the story demonstrates

---

943   *Functional Discourse Grammar*, 214–15.
944   *Die Eroberung Jerichos*, 89.
945   Fritz, 78.
946   "Tradition History," 87–88.
947   Fritz, 78.

how a defeated nation could find new hope and help from Yahweh. Tying the two Ruin narratives together are a long national lament and a judgment scene in which the guilty party who caused Israel's defeat is discovered and punished.

Israel's tradition contained stories that elevated leaders such as Abraham, Moses, Joshua, Deborah, and David to hero status. Amid the heroic stories, though, interruptions take center stage, attesting to the weaknesses and wrongs that marked the heroes' lives. These are often told in campfire style with unexpected twists and turns and artfully inserted ironic elements. The capture-of-Ai tradition interrupted by the punishment-of-Achan narrative represents one more example of the rich traditions that provided real, honest identity to Israel as a nation and as individuals.

Source and Redaction

The Achan tradition is complex and has been interpreted in differing ways. Knauf finds chaps. 7–8 to be an interruption of the Exodus-Joshua narrative but contributing essentially to the Joshua sections of the old narrative that eventually became the book of Joshua.[948] In the narrative strata, including his Hexateuch redaction, Knauf sees Joshua more as a successor of Moses. In Josh 7–8, on the other hand, Knauf finds Joshua to be more of a battlefield commander and hero like the leaders in Judges and Samuel.

According to Briend,[949] the preexilic composer began with Josh 7:2–5 and continued with 8:10. This editor contributed 7:6–26 while the Dtr hand introduced the ban theology in 7:1b, 26aβ. A Priestly editor contributed 7:1a, 18.

Having misnumbered the the latter part of the Scripture text and chart, Knauf finds six acts, each with two or three scenes:[950]

Table 6.3 Knauf's Literary Analysis

Parts/Scripture	Act/Narrative Function	Scene	Content
I vv 1a–c	Exposition: God's anger and its basis		The Problem
II vv 2a–5b	Act 1: The shattered conquest of Ai	1	Sending of Spies (2a–f); Joshua's speech (2c–d)
		2	Report and counsel of the spies (3a–g); speech of spies (3c–g)
		3	The Defeat (4a–5e)
III vv 6a–15d	Act 2: What now?	1	Joshua's lament (6a–9d); speech of Joshua (7b–9d)
		2	Yahweh's answer (10a–15d); Yahweh's speech (10b–15d)
IV vv 16a–23c	Act 3: The investigation	1	Identification of the criminal (16a–18b)
		2	Trial (19a–21e); Joshua's speech (19b–f); Achan's speech (20c–21e)
		3	The conviction (22a–23c)

---

948   Knauf, 73.
949   "Sources of the Deuteronomic History," 364.
950   Knauf, 76.

Parts/Scripture	Act/Narrative Function	Scene	Content
V vv 24a–26a	Act 4: The punishment	1	Procession to the place of execution (23a–c)
		2	The verdict (25a–c); Joshua's speech (25b–c)
		3	Carrying out the verdict (25d–26a)
VI v 26b	Conclusion: Solving of the problem—God's anger appeased		
Late addition v 26c			

Knauf maintains that chaps. 7–8 interject a retarding element to the narrative.[951] The readership in all ages knows who is going to win; these chapters simply add to the narrative tension or suspense.

Auld suggests that chap. 8 begins where 7:10 leaves off. "Attentive readers may scratch their heads as they try to reconstruct what might have happened. Even in ancient times rather different versions were available."[952]

Here again we have a history of literary questions as listed by van der Meer: a doublet of men sent into ambush; repetitive phrases in vv 9b and 13b; a triple narration of the inhabitants of Ai pursuing Israel; a lack of clarity concerning appointed place in v 14; the appearance of Bethel in 17; the unexpected use of the sword in v 18; and the double reversal of pursued and pursuers in vv 20–21.[953] The problem is heightened by the absence of many of the problematic passages from the LXX. Van der Meer calls 8:14–19 the original version and 8:5–8 the alternative version.[954] Fritz trims the original narrative down to vv 10–12, 14, 15, 19, 21, 23, 29.[955]

Nelson suggests that the Achan narrative has been inserted into the Ai plot, but that the union of the two with the Jericho story shows no Deuteronomistic features so that the larger narrative span must be pre-Deuteronomistic.[956] For Nelson, Deuteronomistic editing does appear in vv 11 and 15.[957] Latvus points out all the "priestly" connections in Josh 7:1, 6–26 but finally decides the narrative must be located "in the open terrain between deuteronomistic, priestly and chronistic traditions," leading to a dating about 500 BCE.[958]

Other considerations point to the separate nature of the two narratives. The first is topographical and geographical. The Achan narrative is localized in the tribe of Judah at Achor.[959] The Ai narrative points to a site near Bethel about thirty kilometers or eighteen miles across rugged hill country from Achor. Literary criteria include the fact that each narrative has its own concluding etiology pointing to a pile of stones over a man's body (7:26; 8:29). Further, Joshua's lamentation

---

951 Knauf, 73.
952 Auld, 55.
953 *Formation and Reformulation*, 421–23.
954 Van der Meer, 444–45.
955 Fritz, 87–89.
956 Nelson, 99.
957 Ibid., 102.
958 *God, Anger and Ideology*, 48–50.
959 Cf. F. M. Cross, "El-Buqeia,'" *EAEHL*, 1:267–70.

presupposes only the defeat of Ai and is answered by the salvation oracle of Josh 8:1–2. Vv 10–12 consciously tie the two units together.

The questions, then, are: How did the two narratives arise individually? How did they come to be joined? And how do they function in the present context?

Form

Chapter 7 is introduced by a general theological problem (7:1a): Israel has been unfaithful to divine prohibition. All that follows must be understood in light of that statement. Fritz maintains that Josh 7 is simply an instructional narrative created by the Deuteronomistic Historian.[960] From a slightly different perspective, Pressler explains, "The story of Ai is a cautionary tale, urging obedience lest one suffer the fate of Achan."[961]

The narrative is full of literary topoi and serves as an instructional narrative, but that does not preclude its having strong historical roots and literary or oral sources. V 1b adds the specific details to the general introduction and states the divine reaction. The problem is addressed through six narrative scenes:

- self-confident attack and defeat at Ai (7:2–5)
- national lamentation (7:6–12)
- public trial (7:13–26)
- salvation oracle (8:1–2)
- obedient battle against Ai (8:3–23)
- destruction of Ai (8:24–29)

Each of the component narratives contains its own form, which must be understood if the unit as a whole is to be fully appreciated. Yet, as Ottosson points out, "the unity of the chapter can hardly be doubted" with only the final etiology coming into question as a later element.[962]

The defeat at Ai is presented as a spy narrative much more than as a battle report.[963] Coogan finds literary dependence on Judg 20:19–48, including the sending of the spies (Josh 7:2); the commissioning with a specific task (7:2aβ); the report of the mission itself (7:2b); the return and report of the spies (7:3); and the attack (7:4).[964] Forms with much the same vocabulary are found in Num 13–14; Josh 2; Judg 18; cf. Num 21:32–35; Deut 1:19–25. In Josh 7, though, certain important elements are absent. The spies are neither named nor given specific qualifying credentials (cf. Num 13:2; Judg 18:2; Deut 1:23). Nothing is done to establish certainty that the task will succeed (Josh 2:9–11; Judg 18:5–6; cf. Num 13:30; 14:6–9; 21:34). Most important, the climactic formula of transference—"Yahweh has given them into our hand"—is missing (Num 14:8; 21:34; Deut 1:25; Josh 2:24; Judg 18:10).

On the other hand, the narrative has unexpected additions to the spy-narrative form. The spies plot battle strategy without reference to the deity or his appointed

---

960 Fritz, 78.
961 Pressler, 54.
962 "Tradition History," 91.
963 Cf. Wagner, ZAW 76 (1964) 258.
964 "Archaeology and Biblical Studies," 24.

leader (Josh 7:3). The battle plan is unsuccessful (7:4b–5a), and the concluding formula (v 5b) belongs in the mouths of Yahweh's enemies (Josh 2:11; 5:1; cf. Deut 1:28; Isa 13:7; 19:1; Ezek 21:12; Nah 2:11). An Israelite spy narrative has been ironically transformed into an explanation of how the people of God become defeated enemies of God. It thus is set in exact contrast to Josh 2.

The liturgical element dominates Josh 7:6–12. Defeated Israel falls to the ground in national lamentation. Joshua tears his clothes and puts dust on his head, expressing both that he has been humiliated and that he is humbling himself before God.[965] Joshua's prayer is based on the typical lament pattern, beginning with the address and introductory cry for help to God; the reference to God's earlier saving deeds; and the lament proper with regard to the people, the foes, and God himself.[966]

Here, too, subtle changes are noticeable and informative. The reference to God's earlier saving deeds is not a motif "which should move God to intervene."[967] Rather it is part of the introductory cry for help. The history of God's salvation for his people is pictured as the reason for lamentation, not the basis of future hope. The confession of trust is absent entirely, but so is the petition, "the most constant of all parts."[968] Lamentation has been transformed from trusting pleas to God for intervention into hopeless complaint against the saving acts of God. The lament can include or allude to an oracle of salvation within "prophetic liturgy."[969] Josh 7:10 introduces the salvation oracle here, but again a dramatic shift occurs. Salvation is not announced. Rather, a lawsuit ensues.

Joshua is called to court to plead his case (cf. Ezra 10:4; Mic 6:1) rather than lie on the ground complaining (v 10). Yahweh makes a specific accusation against Israel (v 11). The accusation is justified by the evidence of history: Israel lost the battle (v 12). This gives the basis for the legal decision: They have become banned (חרם). That is, they are guilty and must be dedicated in sacrifice to the Lord.[970]

Speech forms change again in Josh 7:12b. Words of a cultic prophet address Israel directly in second person, describing the process of ridding Israel of the guilt. The prophetic-messenger formula of v 13 reveals the prophetic nature of the speech. The suggested procedure is concluded in v 15b with a renewed double pronouncement of guilt.

The procedure of the sacred lot is carried out (Josh 7:16–18). This is the only type of divination to find the will of God that Israel may employ.[971] The procedure concludes with the call for the doxology of judgment.[972] The call ends the court proceedings by letting the defendant admit his guilt while, at the same time,

---

965 Cf. E. Kutsch, "'Trauerbräuche' und 'Selbsminderungsriten' im Alten Testament," in *Drei Wiener Antrittsreden* (Zürich: EVZ, 1965) 25–42.

966 Cf. C. Westermann, *Loben*, 39–48.

967 Westermann, *Loben*, 41.

968 Ibid., 39.

969 Ibid., 46–48. Note that Winther-Nielsen, *Functional Discourse Grammar*, 220, n. 22, misreads the earlier edition of this commentary, which did not say that a salvation oracle must follow the lamentation liturgy.

970 Cf. Boecker, *Redeformen*, 141–42, 147–48; Knierim, *Hauptbegriffe*, 21–22; Kaminsky, "Joshua 7."

971 Knauf, 79.

972 Cf. G. von Rad, "Gerichtsdoxologie," in *Schalom*, ed. K. H. Bernhardt (Stuttgart: Calwer, 1971) 28–37; reprinted in *Gesammelte Studien zum AT*, vol. 2 (Munich: Kaiser, 1973) 245–54; see also Macholz, *DBAT* 9 (1975) 52–69.

confessing the justice of the divine judge and of the announced punishment.[973] The confession is substantiated by the messengers (vv 22–23), and the sentence is carried out (vv 24–26).

An etiological interpretation concludes the narrative (Josh 7:26). Geoghegan attributes the etiological formula "until this day" to Dtr because of the following "do not fear nor be terrified" in Josh 8:1.[974] The Achan narrative is Noth's classic example of an etiological narrative. It is one of the few "pure, unbroken" forms found by B. Childs, but even he is reluctant to see etiology as the primary focus of the tradition here.[975] Long details how the etiology differs from primary etiological material: (a) the valley, not the pile of stones, is named; (b) the narrative points to burning (v 15), not stoning, which is central to the etiology (v 26); (c) the etiology relates to a minor theme, not the major narrative tension; (d) the etiological form is disturbed and does not compose an integrated unit; and (e) the name of the etiology is not essential to the narrative.[976] Nelson still continues to claim that a "clear etiological purpose must be admitted" and that the narrative is "a cautionary tale with an etiological background."[977]

We must conclude that etiology is not the primary setting for the Achan narrative. Instead, the narrative proceeds from the anger of God (Josh 7:1) to the discovery of the reason for that anger (v 13), to the removal of the anger (v 26a). The Achan narrative is an example narrative teaching Israel how to deal with divine anger. The earliest form we can discover is at home in Israel's cult, where such sacral processes were carried out.

The salvation oracle (8:1–2) belongs to the prophetic liturgy. The liturgy has been interrupted by the long public trial. Only after the trial is complete can the word of salvation be delivered. Over against the spy narrative, the salvation oracle places the directions for battle solely in the mouth of God.

The battle is presented in the form of a pretended flight leading to ambush.[978] An almost exact parallel appears in Judg 20:18–48: salvation oracle (Josh 8:1–2// Judg 20:18, 23, 28); preparation of ambush (8:3–9//20:29); attack and flight before the enemy (8:10–17//20:30–36); signal to ambush (8:18//—); attack from ambush (8:19//20:37); signal of smoke from city (8:20–21//20:38–41); and victory accomplished (8:21b–23//20:42–48). The lamentation in Judg 20:23, 26–27 is paralleled in the Joshua context by 7:6–9. Further, this larger context includes the initial defeat prior to the ambush tactics (7:2–5//20:19–25).

This suggests that the narrative of Ai represents a separate unit that is interrupted by the Achan materials. Such an assumption is strengthened by the fact that the Achan material is separated from its introduction (7:1) by the rather abrupt transition to the Ai battle in Josh 7:2. Form critically then we have two major units: (a) the story of Ai given in the form of a spy narrative introducing a battle of pretended flight leading to ambush and (b) the sacral procedure against Achan. The

973 Cf. F. Horst, "Die Doxologien im Amosbuch," ZAW 47 (1929) 50–51; reprinted in Gottes Recht (Munich: Kaiser, 1961) 162–64.

974 Time, Place, and Purpose, 122.

975 "A Study of the Formula 'Until This Day,'" JBL 82 (1963) 281–82, 285, n. 18.

976 Problem of Aetiological Narrative, 25–26.

977 Nelson, 99.

978 Abel, RB 56 (1949) 329–32; Roth, ZAW 75 (1963) 296–97.

two are joined by the lamentation liturgy, which is a component of the pretended flight and ambush narrative.

For Geoghegan, the etiological formulas of Josh 8:28–29 represent Dtr editorial work, being attached to Deuteronomistic materials featuring fulfillment of the altar command of Deut 27, Levitical priests, the ark of the covenant of Yahweh, and the Torah of Moses.[979] Winther-Nielsen states the obvious: "It is doubtful that the naming of a place is the primary focus or the departure for the tradition."[980] The concluding etiological element represents the editor's conclusion, tying the story to his own era and audience and underlining the completeness and significance of Joshua's victory over The Ruin.

Structure

The Ai story represents narrative mastery. Every element is chosen with the proper touch of sarcasm. Forms are transformed to give them the ironic note. Israel has forsaken her dependence on God's oracles and her trust in his salvation history to fight her own battles. In so doing she cannot even conquer The Ruin, with its few inhabitants. This has incredible results. The name of God himself may be cut off from the face of the earth (Josh 7:9). All this threatens because thirty-six Israelites were killed (7:5).

Winther-Nielsen finds a constituent structure with the following elements:[981]

Staging	Theft of Achan	6:27–7:1
Episode 1	Defeat at Ai	7:2–5
Episode 2	Conviction of Achan	7:6–25 [*sic*, 26?]
Episode 3	Divine instruction	8:1–2
Episode 4	Departure of ambush	8:3–9b
Episode 5	Departure of main army	8:9c–13a
Episode 6	Apparent defeat	8:13b–17
Episode 7	Victory at Ai	8:18–23 (peak)
Episode 8	Capture of Ai	8:24–27 (post-peak)
Closure	The execution of the king	8:28–29

Winther-Nielsen understands the story as "a remarkable case of how intertwined sub-stories can merge into one," so that "the combination of three stories and their intricate embedding in the episode structure of the Ai story will inevitably result in a complicated story line."[982] Through his functional-discourse grammar, he claims to demonstrate that "the story line is entirely homogeneous."[983]

The narrative itself centers around the elements of the wars of Yahweh.[984] The

979 *Time, Place, and Purpose*, 122.
980 *Functional Discourse Grammar*, 213.
981 *Functional Discourse Grammar*, 215–18.
982 Ibid., 211, 219.
983 Ibid., 228.
984 Cf. R. Smend, *Jahwekrieg und Stämmebund*, FRLANT 84 (Göttingen: Vandenhoeck & Ruprecht, 1963).

questions raised are Israel's dependence on Yahweh for victory, Israel's gratitude for her salvation history, and Israel's willingness to follow the battle plan of Yahweh rather than that of humanity. The story is at home in those circles that instructed Israel about her basic identity as the people of Yahweh, dependent on him for their very existence as a nation. But it is also at home where their identity as the people of Yahweh comes from the crossing of the Jordan (Josh 7:7). Thus it is akin to one strata of Josh 3–4 (cf. 4:7). This is evidently the cult at Gilgal.

The battle-of-Ai narrative has been combined with two elements, and thus it is both an etiology and the finale to the Achan episode. The etiological element shows the long-range effects of Joshua's action. Ai is nothing but two heaps of stones. Why is this significant? It stands over against the narratives of Judg 19–21. The two stories "are examples of the same stock plot" with "intertextual contacts."[985]

Winther-Nelson speaks of two embedded stories (Josh 7:2–5 and 7:6–25) in the narrative of the defeat at Ai.[986] The two stories were joined into a new whole and then were introduced into the larger conquest narratives of Israel. Their purpose was to give Israel claim to the territory of Ai and Bethel "until this day," while demonstrating over against Josh 6 what happens when God's people try to conduct war without his leadership. For the ultimate historian, such narratives spoke to an exilic audience without land and home. For them the narrative exemplified hope for a landless people seeking once more the leadership of God in giving into their hands the land. Such hope rested not on their numbers or those of the enemies, but upon leadership and people obedient to the directions of God.

Setting

The content of the etiology that concludes Josh 7 offers the best clue to its setting. Rather than being a direct play upon the name Achan, the etiology plays on the root עכר, "trouble." Such a name is not given with patriotic feeling toward one's homeland. Rather it represents a negative reaction. Thus Nelson decides that the Achan grave material began as "an anti-Judah polemic by Benjamin" but that in its present context the narrative is "minatory and parenetic."[987] Certainly, the narrative would not be told by members of the family of Achan or of the tribe of Judah. It is a narrative told by Judah's enemies.

The action in Josh 8 is on Benjaminite soil. The tribe of Benjamin and Benjamin's major sanctuary stand behind the tradition. Benjamin uses the same tactics as those in Judg 20 but with more lasting effect. Israel, particularly Judah (Judg 20:18), had practically destroyed Benjamin, but Benjamin survived with its towns and inheritance (21:23). Josh 7 concludes with a polemical etiology against a piece of land in Judah. The story in Judg 20 is about a traitor from the tribe of Judah. The union of the Achan tradition with the Ai tradition forms a narrative showing the superiority of Benjamin to Judah. It could point to the time of the conflict between the Judean David and the Benjaminite Saul.[988]

Knauf sets the temple disputes that occurred between Bethel and those who

---

985   Nelson, 111.
986   *Functional Discourse Grammar*, 211, 216.
987   Nelson, 100.
988   But see K.-D. Schunck, *Benjamin*, BZAW 86 (Berlin: Töpelman, 1963).

did not go into exile and Jerusalem and those who returned from exile as the time of origin of these materials.[989] These disputes led to the destruction of the Bethel temple about 450 BCE. Knauf's conclusions demand acceptance of his redaction-critical arguments that remain far from conclusive.

Comments

7:1 "The chapter opens with an ominous tone that alerts us to spiritual and physical disaster."[990] Israel's sin lies in *maʿal*, "disregarding" (מעל) the חרם (*ḥērem*). The term מעל (*mʿl*) refers to the trust relationship between persons or with God and signifies a break in that relationship, an encroachment by humans into the realm set aside for the sacred. Often it has marriage connections. "Matrimonial unfaithfulness becomes an image, a figure of speech for human breach of faith towards God."[991] Josh 7:1 is the only passage where the verb's linguistic reference is to a thing (the ban) rather than to persons.

Here the ban represents the divine-human relationship that stands behind the actual ban.[992] The relationship is not individual; Israel as a nation receives the guilty verdict. Creach writes, "the categories of individual and community, though clearly present in the story, are blurred at numerous points. Indeed, in Joshua 7 the questions of who is guilty, who should be punished, and why are sometimes difficult to answer."[993] Nelson is more in line with the meaning of the narrative: "For Israel to permit any individual to commit apostasy is to share in a collective sin and risk collective disaster."[994]

Knauf maintains that the author's audience needed instruction in a custom long out of practice.[995] The term *ḥērem*, for Knauf, has three levels of meaning: (1) the action of making the oath to destroy in v 1; (2) the goods determined by the oath in vv 1b and 15b; and (3) the persons placed under the curse of the ban in v 12. Thus *ḥērem* as a taboo is contagious; the action of one individual can contaminate the entire people.

Divine anger dominates the opening narrative (cf. v 26). It represents the divine reaction to the human breach of trust and threatens the very existence of the nation. A basic Deuteronomic theme is taken up (cf. Deut 6:15; 7:4; 11:17; 29:26; 31:17; Josh 23:16; compare Judg 2:14, 20; 3:8; 10:7; 2 Sam 6:7; 24:1; 2 Kgs 13:3: 23:26). Israel cannot take its position as the people of God or its possession of the land of God for granted. They are constantly under obligation to God, and when they disregard that, his anger burns, and Israel's position and possessions are threatened.

2 The geography ignores the destruction of Jericho and the camp at Gilgal (cf. Josh 5:10). Joshua sends spies from Jericho to the city of Ai. Modern archaeologists have searched the ruins of et-Tell for traces of Joshua's Ai.[996] They found a city covering twenty-seven and a half acres dating from 3100 to 2400 BCE, when Ai

989 Knauf, 76–77.
990 Harstad, 303.
991 Auld, 51.
992 Cf. R. Knierim, "מעל-treulos sein," *THAT*, 1:920–22 = *TLOT*, 2:680–82.
993 Creach, 70–71.
994 Nelson, 103.
995 Knauf, 75.
996 Marquet-Krause and Callaway, *EAEHL*, 1:36–52.

was the largest settlement in southern Palestine with thousands of inhabitants.[997] Archaeologists also found a two-and-a-half acre village without fortifications that was occupied from 1220 until 1050.

These findings have led to the conclusion that "at the time when the Israelites arrived in Canaan, there was certainly no town at Ai, nor was there a king of Ai. All that existed there was an ancient ruin of a town destroyed about 1200 years before."[998] The archaeological conclusions have led to attempts to show that Bethel, not Ai, was the town really involved.[999] Others dismiss the narrative as another etiological invention.[1000]

Two suggestions may be noted. Callaway[1001] suggested that the narrative refers to the late stage of the Iron Age village of Ai, but this has been dismissed by de Vaux.[1002] Howard determines that the biblical evidence forces us to look elsewhere than et-Tell for the location of Ai, an approach which then forces a new look at the location of Beth-el.[1003] Grintz,[1004] Wood,[1005] and Harstad[1006] attempt to locate Ai away from et-Tell, identifying it with Beth-Aven. Soggin[1007] hints at a relocation of Bethel. Livingston seeks to show that Bethel should be located at modern el-Bireh, Ai being at an unnamed tell nearby.[1008] Despite Rainey's objections,[1009] Bimson suggests keeping this theory as an option.[1010]

Coogan finds the archaeological evidence deafening in its silence.[1011] For him, the best option is to read the story as an etiology of the ruin par excellance. He states that the story represents a late tradition, "a kind of historical fiction that incorporated topographic elements of the unoccupied city's remains."

Hess persists in locating the towns at their traditional sites, placing Ai a mile east-southeast of Bethel and Beth Aven 3.3 miles south of Ai.[1012] He says the most likely scenario is that the broken walls of Ai, "the Ruin," served as a strategic fortress for the inhabitants of Bethel. "Ai was more important to the narrator because of the wordplay on its name, the reversal of the defeat of Joshua 7, and perhaps because this was where the inhabitants of Bethel made their greatest defense."[1013]

Whatever view one holds, the fact remains that archeology has not clarified the background of our narrative. As yet, we cannot locate it in time nor space. It remains interesting that the two cities are named Ai ("The Ruin") and Beth-Aven ("House of Sin,") both quite negative and yet quite relevant for biblical narrators.

---

997 Knauf, 76.
998 de Vaux, *Histoire ancienne*, 565; *Early History*, 614.
999 Vincent, *RB* 46 (1937) 231–66; Albright, *BASOR* 74 (1939) 15–17.
1000 Noth.
1001 *JBL* 87 (1968) 312–20.
1002 *Histoire ancienne*, 568; *Early History*, 617; Bimson, *Redating*, 60–65, and Kuschke, "Hiwwiter," 115–19.
1003 Howard, 179–80.
1004 *Bib* 42 (1961) 208–16.
1005 "Search for Joshua's Ai."
1006 Harstad, 301–2.
1007 Soggin, 99.
1008 *WTJ* 33 (1970) 20–44; *WTJ* 34 (1971) 39–50.
1009 *WTJ* 33 (1970) 175–88.
1010 *Redating*, 215–25.
1011 "Archaeology and Biblical Studies," 23.
1012 Hess (1996) 144–45.
1013 Ibid., 158–59.

3–4 The spies demonstrate that "poor reconnaissance is worse than no reconnaissance."[1014] Their judgment of numbers is as far below reality as the spies' estimate in Moses' day (Num 13:16–14:4) was beyond reality. The spies suggest that two or three thousand men should go up. In fact, three thousand are sent (v 4). Knauf points to Deut 32 and Josh 1:12–15 as evidence that Israel here broke the law because the entire nation was expected to fulfill their God-given task.[1015]

Great alarm breaks out when thirty-six are killed (Josh 7:5). The second time around, Joshua takes ten times as many soldiers (8:3) just for the ambush. Later, only five thousand are set in ambush (8:12). The battle destroys twelve thousand citizens of The Ruin (8:25).

The numbers in the narrative require comment. P. J. Budd declares: "The central difficulty here is the impossibly large number of fighting men recorded. The historical difficulties in accepting the figure as it stands are insuperable."[1016] Howard states that no proposed solution "is without its problems" and that "absolute certainty is not possible."[1017] Fritz cites Judg 15:11; 1 Sam 13:2; 24:3; 26:2 in his claim that this is the general idea of the size of a fighting force and so expresses nothing about actual relationships.[1018]

Hess suggests the Hebrew term *'elep* (אלף) should be read as a military company or unit, not as a thousand.[1019] R. B. Allen sees exaggeration:[1020]

> But these real numbers (in terms of their addition) are numbers that are used for effect. I personally believe there is a deliberate exaggeration of the sums for each tribe and hence for the total, as a rhetorical device. By deliberately magnifying these numbers by a common factor (ten, the number of the digits), the writer was able to use them as power words. That is, the ancients who were the recipients of these words knew what we may forget, that numbers can be used for purposes other than merely reporting a given datum. I suggest, as noted in the Introduction, that we should possibly regard these sums as a deliberate exaggeration by the factor of ten, a rhetorical device used to give praise to God and hope to his people.

K. L. Younger speaks repeatedly of hyperbole, overstating claims for political and theological purposes. For him hyperbole is "the use of exaggerated terms for the purpose of emphasis or heightened effect; more is said than is literally meant."[1021] Peter J. Naylor reminds us, "We must be careful not to reject a literal interpretation simply because we cannot fully understand it."[1022] M. Barnouin, rather, offers

1014 Harris, 53.
1015 Knauf, 77.
1016 *Numbers*, WBC 5 (Waco, TX: Word, 1984) 6.
1017 Howard, 189, n. 76.
1018 Fritz, 80.
1019 Hess (1996), 146.
1020 "Numbers," in *Genesis, Exodus, Leviticus, Numbers*, ed. F. E. Gaebelein, EBC 2 (Grand Rapids: Zondervan, 1990) on Num 1:46; cf. Pressler, 57.
1021 *Ancient Conquest Accounts: A Study in Ancient Near Eastern and Biblical History Writing*, JSOTSup 98 (Sheffield: JSOT Press, 1990) 323, n. 11.
1022 "Numbers," in *New Bible Commentary: 21st Century Edition*, ed. D. A. Carson et al. (Leicester: Inter-Varsity Press, 1994) 170.

numbers from planetary periods as calculated by Babylonian astronomers that lead to the division of each number by 100.[1023]

The IVP Bible Background Commentary explains:[1024]

> The most probable solution at this point is to understand that the numbers given here are mixtures. Since the Hebrew word translated "thousand" (*'lp*) looks the same as the word translated "military division," a number like 74,600 (v. 4) may be read as 74 military divisions, (totaling) 600 men. The total in verse 32 would originally have been written 598 military divisions (*'lp*), 5 thousand (*'lp*) and 5 hundred men. But at some point in the transmission of the text the two words were confused and added together to make 603 thousand. If this solution is correct, the size of the Israelite group that left Egypt would have been about 20,000.

E. W. Davies seeks to refute other theories and show that "far from attempting to preserve historically accurate information from Israel's past, it seems more probable that the numbers are purely fictitious and were simply invented."[1025] This widespread literary convention emphasized that God was beginning to fulfill his promise to the patriarchs.[1026]

D. M. Fouts provides history of research and ancient Near Eastern usage and concludes, "If the numbers are simply reflective of a rhetorical device common in ancient Near Eastern literature, however, one may no longer question the integrity of the record by use of this argument. The large numbers are often simply figures of speech employed to magnify King Yahweh, King David, or others in a theologically-based historiographical narrative."[1027]

C. J. Humphreys assumes the number in Num 3:46 to be "entirely reasonable."[1028] From there he shows that *'lp* "was used with two different meanings": "troop" or "team" and "thousand."[1029] Each troop comprised about ten men. T. R. Ashley may have the most open and honest approach: "We lack the materials in the text to solve this problem. . . . Perhaps it is best to take these numbers as R. K. Harrison has done—as based on a system familiar to the ancients but unknown to moderns."[1030] Howard, however, falls back on an "early copyist's error" without any textual support, changing 5,000 to 30,000.[1031]

Several factors are at work here. First, *'lp* may well have represented a military or work unit in Israel. The unit at one time may have had a complement of 1,000 members, but the actual number recruited at any one time may have been much

---

1023 "Les recensements du livre des Nombres et l'astronomie babylonienne," *VT* 27 (1977) 280ff.

1024 J. H. Walton, V. H. Matthews, and M. W. Chavalas, *The IVP Bible Background Commentary: Old Testament* (Downers Grove, IL: InterVarsity Press, 2000) 144.

1025 "A Mathematical Conundrum: The Problem of the Large Numbers in Numbers I and XXVI," *VT* 45 (1995) 466.

1026 Ibid., 469.

1027 "A Defense of the Hyperbolic Interpretation of Large Numbers in the Old Testament," *JETS* 40 (1997) 377–87.

1028 "The Number of People in the Exodus from Egypt: Decoding Mathematically the Very Large Numbers in Numbers i and xxvi," *VT* 48 (1998) 196–213.

1029 Ibid., 206–7.

1030 *The Book of Numbers,* NICOT (Grand Rapids: Eerdmans, 1993) 67.

1031 Howard, 203–4; cf. Woudstra, 137; Winther-Nielsen, *Functional Discourse Grammar,* 22, n. 34.

less. Second, deliberate overstatement or hyperbole may well have been one of the narrative tools of the storyteller and writer as Younger has shown. Third, to reduce the numbers in a troop to five to ten men, as Humphreys claims, may be unnecessarily low. Finally, God normally tests Israel's faith by reducing their army so that glory can go only to God and not to humans, as seen in the Gideon narrative (Judg 7:1–8; compare Deut 20:1–8). The present narrative reverses the situation, showing that Israel cannot win without God no matter how large and superior the army. The contrast between Israelites sent and Israelites killed is part of the narrative art that seeks to ridicule the self-confident, self-reliant Israel.

The original battle narrative may well have shown the faith of Israel that enabled the five thousand in ambush to destroy the city of twelve thousand. The twelve thousand also stands over against the spies' ridiculing of the city of Ai as having only a very few people or soldiers (Josh 7:3). In actuality, the narrator says, one city proved to have a population equal to more than a fourth of Israel's army (cf. 4:13). The task of taking the land was no small one. Self-reliant Israel could not do it. This explanation shows the narrator's art in using numbers to make a theological or practical point. It does not "reject all the figures of the story as inaccurate" as Winther-Nielsen claims.[1032]

5 "The heart . . . melted" represents Deuteronomic vocabulary.[1033] One of the few Deuteronomic flourishes in the narrative, it vividly expresses the fact that Israel has become the enemy rather than the people of God (cf. 2:11; 5:1). "Blithe confidence was not matched by performance."[1034]

6–8 Joshua had fallen on his face once before, when he confronted the divine messenger (Josh 5:14). That was in the humility of worship. This time it is in the humility of defeat and lament before God. "Eastern laments describe the loss and its consequences as God's problem and hope that God will be moved to resolve the situation."[1035] The lament is not a sign "of resignation but of confrontation. In the face of defeat, Israel demands that Yahweh act like God!"[1036]

"This manner of addressing the Lord may seem manipulative: it is certainly not a type of prayer familiar to most modern Christians. It makes sense, however, and is perfectly acceptable in light of the contractual nature of ancient Israelite society and the assumption that God, too, acted in contractual ways," claims Creach.[1037] But does this viewpoint make the covenant relationship too mechanical?

Howard accurately describes the situation: "Joshua's words were bitter ones, ones that echoed various complaints by the Israelites in the wilderness (see Exod 16:3; 17:3; Num 11:4–6; 14:2–3; 30:3–5)."[1038] In a time of crisis and uncertainty, not knowing Achan's sin, Joshua acted emotionally, not rationally, fearfully, not faithfully. He expressed a basic doubt concerning Yahweh's promise of deliverance.[1039]

He approached the situation from a human perspective, not a divine one. "The

1032 *Functional Discourse Grammar*, 224 n. 34.
1033 Weinfeld, *Deuteronomy*, 344, n. 15.
1034 McConville and Williams, 38.
1035 Harris, 53.
1036 Hoppe, 51.
1037 Creach, 69.
1038 Howard, 191.
1039 Fritz, 81.

certainty of the past was preferable to the difficulties of the present and the uncertainty of the future."[1040] The promise of divine presence (Josh 1:5–9) vanished in the reality of defeat. Still, is lament inappropriate or even wrong here?[1041] Is an emotional cry to God out of ignorance and frustration appropriate? Do we try to solve the problem before turning to God, or do we turn to him in desperation and anger rather than directing that anger to fellow humans? The ark plays no subsequent role in the narrative and may represent an element that entered the tradition when the ark was the central sanctuary symbol for Israel.

The "elders of Israel" have not appeared earlier in the book.[1042] They are included here to show what was taking place was national lamentation rather than individual lament. The elders represented tribal, then city and political leaders at different periods of Israel's development with fairly wide-ranging functions (cf. Judg 8:14, 16; 11:5–11; Ruth 4:1–12; 1 Sam 11:3; 16:4; 2 Sam 3:17; 5:3; 17:4; 19:12–13).[1043] The elders appear again in Josh 8:10, but their cameo appearances do not provide sufficient evidence to reconstruct a history of tradition behind this chapter without Joshua being part of the tradition.

אהה "Alas." This Hebrew word is a cry of shock and hopelessness (Judg 11:35; 2 Kgs 3:10; 6:5, 15). It is most often used in addressing God (Judg 6:22; Jer 1:6; 4:10; 14:13; Ezek 4:14; 9:8; 11:13). The lamentation ritual contrasts sharply with the festal rites of chaps. 3–5. Israel has become God's enemy, having to turn the back of their necks and flee (Exod 23:27).[1044] "Apart from the presence and guidance of YHWH, Israel bears an uncanny resemblance to the peoples of the land."[1045]

9 Joshua fears that the names of Israel and of Yahweh will disappear from the land. The word "name" refers to reputation and esteem. Behind it lies an important theological development in Deuteronomic literature, where God chooses to reveal his name, not his glory or his person to humanity. He chooses to allow his name to dwell in the temple while he dwells in heaven (Deut 12:5–28; 1 Kgs 8; compare Deut 26:15; 4:12; 2 Kgs 23:27).[1046]

Israel's temptation was to connect the name of Yahweh with themselves, their temple, and their power. The historian writes to show that Yahweh's power is not diminished even though his temple, where he has chosen to put his name, disappears. Israel depends for her name on Yahweh. Yahweh does not depend for his name upon Israel.

How does one interpret this central moment of Joshua's lament? Hawk suggests that even Joshua "has been affected by the community's sin and rebellion. . . . [H]e speaks like one who has lost hope."[1047] Similarly, P. J. Kissling finds that "It does not seem even to occur to Joshua that Israel's defeat might be due to some-

---

1040 Howard, 191.
1041 Pressler, 58.
1042 For the elders in this context, see Harstad, 309.
1043 J. Conrad, "זקן," *TWAT*, 2:644–50 = *TDOT*, 4:122–24; H. Reviv, *The Elders in Ancient Israel: A Study of a Biblical Institution* (Jerusalem: Magnes, 1989).
1044 Cf. Hess (1996) 149.
1045 Hess, 114.
1046 Cf. G. von Rad, *Studies in Deuteronomy*, trans. D. Stalker (London: SCM, 1953) 37–44; Weinfeld, *Deuteronomy*, 193–209; and the opposing view of A. S. van der Woude, "שם-Name," *THAT*, 2:953–55 = *TLOT*, 3:1348–67.
1047 Hess 115.

thing other than Yahweh's failure to protect Israel. He blames Yahweh because he has no knowledge of Achan's sin and he can see nothing wrong in the approach he took to the planning and the execution of the battle."[1048] A. Malamat provides a military explanation: "breakdown in discipline" and "over confidence," combined with Joshua's "fear of loss of image."[1049] Hess understands Joshua's lament as an appeal seeking protection for God's great name "transforms the complaint from a self-serving whine, such as occurred in Numbers, to a concern for the honor of God," thus preventing the punishing, destructive divine anger.[1050]

10 Van der Meer finds vv 10–13 to be a duplicate of vv 3–9.[1051] God's rhetorical question snaps Joshua to attention, ending his string of questions.[1052]

11 Israel's sin lies first and foremost in transgressing God's covenant. The verb used here is the same as used to refer to Israel crossing over the Jordan (cf. Josh 3–4; 7:7). The people of Israel did not want to cross over the Jordan. They, however, did want to cross over the covenant, that is, break its demands.

The origin and meaning of covenant theology continues to be the center of contemporary scholarship.[1053] A fully developed covenant theology appears in the Deuteronomic literature based on a pattern developed over long centuries of cultic worship.[1054] According to the canonical pattern, God made a covenant with Noah (Gen 9) and with Abraham (Gen 15, 17). Both involved a promise of God, while the latter enjoined circumcision on males. Sinai represented the climax, where God set his covenantal obligations upon his people while promising to continue the special relationship with them (Exod 19; 24; 34). Deuteronomy sees the covenant based on the Ten Commandments (Deut 4:13; 5:2; 9:11), particularly the first two commandments (Deut 4:23; 17:2). God is thus pictured as the loving God who keeps covenant (4:31; 7:9), but also as the God who remembers to punish those who break covenant (Deut 7:10–11; 8:19–20; 29:15–28). Josh 7 then presents the first example of the people of Israel—in the land—breaking the covenant. Immediately they discover the consequences: death. Israel becomes banned goods before God (7:12).

12–13 The key promise to Joshua in the book is the presence of God (Josh 1:5,

---

1048 *Reliable Characters in the Primary History: Profiles of Moses, Joshua, Elijah, and Elisha* (Sheffield: Sheffield Academic, 1996) 73.

1049 *History of Biblical Israel: Major Problems and Minor Issues* (Leiden: Brill, 2001) 78.

1050 Hess (1996) 148.

1051 *Formation and Reformulation*, 442.

1052 Cf. Nelson, 105.

1053 Cf. L. Perlitt, *Bundestheologie im Alten Testament*, WMANT 36 (Neukirchen-Vluyn: Neukirchener Verlag, 1969); E. Kutsch, *Verheissung und Gesetz*, BZAW 131 (Berlin: De Gruyter, 1972); idem, "ברית/Verpflichtung," *THAT*, 1:339–52 = *TLOT*, 1:256–66; M. Weinfeld, "ברית," *TWAT*, 1:781–808 = *TDOT*, 2:253–79; D. J. McCarthy, *Treaty and Covenant*, 2nd ed., AnBib 21A (Rome: Pontifical Biblical Institute, 1978); J. Barr, "Some Semantic Notes on Covenant," in *Beiträge zur Alttestamentlichen Theologie*, ed. H. Donner, R. Hanhart, and R. Smend (Göttingen: Vandenhoeck & Ruprecht, 1977) 23–38; G. J. McConville, "ברית," *NIDOTTE*, 1:746–55; S. Hahn, "Covenant in the Old and New Testaments: Some Current Research (1994–2004)," *CBR* 3 (2005) 263–92; J. Goldingay, *Old Testament Theology*, vol. 1, *Israel's Gospel* (Downers Grove, IL: InterVarsity Press, 2003) 369–450; P. R. Williamson, *Sealed with an Oath: Covenant in God's Unfolding Purpose*, New Studies in Biblical Theology 23 (Downers Grove, IL: InterVarsity Press, 2007).

1054 McCarthy, *Treaty and Covenant*, 15–16.

9; 3:7). Divine presence is the prayer of the people for Joshua (1:17), the basis of Joshua's exaltation (3:7), and the hope of possessing the land (3:10). Transgressing the covenant has let all this pass away. But all is not totally hopeless. There is a big "if." If the obedient people will destroy the banned goods in their midst, they can again experience divine presence. Israel must choose between the presence of God (v 12) and the presence of חרם (ḥērem, v 13). Here ḥērem is employed in the sense of Deut 13 "against fellow Israelites with a severity and thoroughness unparalleled in the accounts of it being used against the nations."[1055]

14 Criminal investigation is not left to humanity. God captures the thief. The process involves the casting of the sacred lot (cf. 1 Sam 10:20–21; 14:42).

15 The captured sinner faces the horrific punishment of being burned to death along with all his possessions. The latter apparently includes his children. The guilty verdict is based on two charges: "because he has transgressed the covenant of Yahweh and because he has committed a sacrilege in Israel." Keeping the covenant marked Israel as God's people ready to accomplish God's purpose and receive God's promises. Crossing over the covenant meant disobeying God and forfeiting the right to be part of his chosen people. Committing a sacrilege "refers to disorderly and unruly action in breaking a custom. Achan violated the covenant of the Lord and committed 'sacrilege in Israel' by taking from the banned spoil, which, according to customary law of the holy war, was the Lord's property (Josh 7:15)."[1056] M. Saebo concludes: "All passages concern a fateful breach of Israel's 'firmly ordained ethical code'; these abominations bring only disaster and dishonor on the perpetrators."[1057] Knauf maintains that the writer of Joshua supplements the Torah here, since becoming unclean through embezzlement of goods dedicated to the ban is not mentioned in Torah.[1058]

16–18 Hess suggests that each tribe sends one representative to Joshua.[1059] Knauf understands a competition between Jerusalem on one side and Bethel (or Mizpah) and Ai on the other between 520 and 445 BCE as the background of this narrative.[1060] He posits a foundational layer coming from perhaps the sixth-century Exodus-Joshua strata of Joshua collected in Bethel and including the kernel of the book of Judges, the so-called Book of Deliverers (*Retterbuch*). This represents another of many examples in Knauf of extremely low dating of narratives and of extremely high regard for the literary and political creativity of Israelite postexilic scribes.

19 "The command to confess is a call to self-condemnation."[1061] The culprit discovered in the sacral process is called upon to confess his guilt, which gives praise and glory to God by showing that the divine judgment has been just.

20 The confession is given in general terms. The details are added only in the following verse, causing many scholars to regard it as an unnecessary secondary insertion into the narrative (cf. Noth). Hess points to ancient Near Eastern

---

1055 Mitchell, *Together in the Land*, 75.
1056 C.-W. Pan, *NIDOTTE*, 3:11.
1057 *TLOT,* 2:712.
1058 Knauf, 79.
1059 Hess (1996) 151.
1060 Knauf, 83.
1061 Hess (2000) 121.

examples of reluctant admissions of military defeat.[1062] When people did admit defeat, they listed catalogs of sins that might have caused such defeat, hoping they had included the one that fit the present occasion. But, says Hess, Israel had a different attitude toward sin: one listens to the word of God, obeys it, confesses the exact sin committed, and bears the consequences. Earl states that the confession is inadequate precisely because Achan does not give glory to God.[1063] The inadequate confession confirms his death sentence. Here Earl may well be on the right track.

21–23 "The plunder is luxuriant and exotic."[1064] The first item that caught Achan's eye was "one fine luxury mantle from Shinar." This could be a piece of clothing imported from lower Mesopotamia, the area of the city of Babylon.[1065] The shekel represented part of the ancient Near Eastern weight system. Israel seems to have had at least two systems.[1066] A shekel weighed approximately four ounces or eleven and one-half grams. Hess sets the weights at 560 grams or 1.25 pounds of gold and 2.7 kilograms or 6 pounds of silver. Hess sees the reference to Shinar and to a "wedge" of gold as pointing to a date before 1000 BCE.[1067]

Winther-Nielsen points to the repeated reference to the family abode as anticipating "the astonishing procedure when the sentence is carried out" (vv 24–25).[1068] The Israelites took Achan's son and daughters (v 24a)—his wife must be excluded as either gone or not guilty. Or the wife may have had more freedom as an individual than did the children.

24 The Lord instructs that all that belongs to the guilty party must be destroyed (v 15), now interpreted as meaning his family and possessions. Interestingly, his wife is never mentioned. The principle of community solidarity may be involved here so that the social focus is on the group rather than the individual, the sins of the individual being seen as involving the group. Creach maintains that "Israel's communal identity, particularly the identity of members of a household to each other, was so strong that the individual could not be conceived as completely autonomous. . . . The sins of one family member affected every other member, especially in the case of the head of the household, who embodied the values and actions of the entire group."[1069]

A more likely explanation may be found in the conception of holiness. The spoils of war are devoted to God and are holy (cf. Josh 6:19). As such, they must be given over to God. Their holiness contaminates humanity. If they are brought into the camp, they contaminate the entire camp so that it must be sanctified, made

---

1062 Hess (1996) 153.
1063 Earl, 149.
1064 Hess (2000) 121.
1065 Cf. D. Kellermann, "Überlieferungsprobleme alttestamentlicher Ortsnamen," *VT* 28 (1978) 424–25.
1066 Cf. O. R. Sellers, "Weights and Measures," *IDB*, 4:828–33.
1067 Hess (1996) 28–29, 152.
1068 *Functional Discourse Grammar*, 222.
1069 Creach, 72; cf. H. Robinson, "The Hebrew Conception of Corporate Personality," in *Werden und Wesen des Alten Testament*, ed. P. Volz, F. Stummer, and J. Hempel, BZAW 66 (Berlin: Töpelmann, 1936) 49–62; reprinted in *Corporate Personality in Ancient Israel* (Philadelphia: Fortress, 1964) 1–20; J. Kaminsky, "Joshua 7," 321–22 with n. 17 and with bibliography.

holy (7:13). Anyone who had come into contact with the goods was contaminated and had to be removed from the community to protect the community.[1070]

Hess suggests that the emphasis is on the family name and all that it represented. By including the children in the capital punishment, Israel wiped out the family name and future.[1071] Kaminsky concludes that "the action was taken because ritual violations, inasmuch as they endangered the community as a whole, were considered a criminal offence punishable by the human legal system."[1072] He later attributes "the necessity for eliminating Achan's family and his chattels primarily to the idea that the tabooed status of the items that he illicitly procured was transmitted to him and to his whole household."[1073] Finally, Kaminsky ties the taboo element of חרם, or the ban, to the larger concepts of individual and communal holiness and covenant membership.[1074]

Hess tentatively locates the Valley of Achor as the Buqei'ah Valley about eight miles from Jericho. Such a location "would emphasize the concern to remove the impurity from Israel's midst."[1075]

25 Two stonings are described, one of the individual and the other of the group. Hess suggests that the first stoning killed the victim(s) while the second piled up stones on the victims' remains.[1076]

26 The point of the narrative lies in the action of Yahweh. He has turned aside or turned back from his anger. The relationship Israel did not regard (v 1) has been restored by obedience to the divine directions and removal of the contaminating sin from its midst. With the חרם, "ban," no longer in Israel (v 13), Yahweh can once more move about in her midst without destructive anger. Only as a holy people can Israel have the holy God with her. The relationship restored must not be forgotten, therefore it is memorialized in a geographical name.

Knauf connects the introduction of the etiological note to the operation of a temple school, whose students took every possible opportunity to show the geographical connotations of sites connected to the events of salvation history.[1077] Every time Israel approaches the Valley of Achor, it remembers the example of Achan and dedicates itself once more to be the holy, obedient people of God.

8:1 God changes the direction of the narrative, renewing the promise of deliverance with the call not to fear and to resume military activity because the transferral formula "I have given into your hand" is still valid, even after the Achan incident. Knauf uses the picture of Joshua as warrior to differentiate the basic narrative from editorial additions.[1078] Through to the final redaction, Joshua is pictured, according to Knauf, as one doing all of and only what God has ordered. This, however, paints too simplistic a picture of the complex figure of Joshua. He is throughout the book

---

1070 See J. R. Porter, "The Legal Aspects of the Concept of 'Corporate Personality' in the Old Testament," *VT* 15 (1965) 361–80.
1071 Hess (1996) 154.
1072 "Joshua 7," 327–28.
1073 Ibid., 338.
1074 Kaminsky, 342–46.
1075 Hess (1996) 154–55.
1076 Ibid., 155.
1077 Knauf, 80.
1078 Ibid., 83.

pictured as obedient minister of Moses, strong leader of the army, obedient follower of Yahweh, interpreter and giver of Torah, and prophetic guide to the future.

2 The king of Jericho is not mentioned in chap. 6. He is introduced here to underline the total obedience of Israel in light of the large role played by the king of Ai in this narrative.

Specific regulations are given now for the ban, in contrast to the instructions in chap. 6 (15–19). The Hebrew word *raq* (רַק) meaning "only," sets apart this ban narrative.[1079] Mitchell notes that taking booty "enables a king to pay for his military escapades, his bureaucracy, his building projects, and to honour his gods with his gifts . . . Nevertheless, booty is never the goal of victory but the consequence."[1080]

Deut 20 lists only people to be destroyed since the aim of Deuteronomy is to prevent disobedience of the first commandment, not to be specific in all details. War itself brought various vows and various interpretations of the ban as can be seen in Num 21:2; 1 Sam 15:3, 9–10. "This divine instruction signifies a flexibility on the meaning of the ban, which could be interpreted by God according to the particular needs of the people."[1081] The present oath is attested in Deut 2:35; 3:7; compare 20:12–14. The narrative sets forth a definite understanding of the banned goods so that it can be demonstrated that Israel was totally obedient (v 27). It also shows God's concern for the identity of and relationship with his people, not with enriching his treasuries.[1082]

3–6 Van der Meer sets up Josh 8:3–9 as an alternative version and 8:10–14, 16, 18–20, 26 as the older, pre-Deuteronomistic version.[1083] He suggests the alternative version is implausible militarily but seeks to stress Israel's superiority. The view goes against the basic message of Joshua that God wins battles, not human superiority.

Nelson points to the complexity of the chronology.[1084] He maintains an original narrative had Josh 8:3–9 at night, vv 10–13 the next morning, followed on the same day by the king of Ai's initiative, the battle, and the slaughter lasting until evening (vv 14–29). Two textual additions to MT (vv 9b and 13b) transform this, according to Nelson with a first night (vv 3–9), a first day (vv 10–13a), a second night (v 13b) and a second day (vv 14–29).

Howard, using a sound syntactical explanation, determines that there was only one ambush and one night.[1085] Preparations come in vv 3–9; v 10 gives the start of the battle the next morning; vv 11–13 represent a flashback expanding on vv 3–9; and v 14 continues the narrative. Winther-Nielsen sees the ambush taking place a day before the battle with Josh 8:12 representing "a summarizing recapitulation with a past perfect force 'he had taken.'"[1086] Then v 13a must be a flashback. Thus vv 11, 12, and 13 repeat the same information three times.

6 "The central phrase, around which the entire speech is constructed, is that of v 6: 'until we have lured them away from the city.'"[1087]

1079 Howard, 202.
1080 *Together in the Land*, 77–78.
1081 Hess (1996) 160.
1082 Hess (2010) 88.
1083 *Formation and Reformulation*, 443–52.
1084 Nelson, 112; cf. Howard, 200.
1085 Howard, 200.
1086 *Functional Discourse Grammar*, 223.
1087 Hess (1996) 164.

7 "Joshua's resourceful military strategy is of the essence."[1088] The war strategy of humanity may work. They may possess the city, but the praise goes to God, not humanity. The ultimate source of victory is for the divine warrior, who gives the city into the hands of his obedient people.

8 Such obedience is demonstrated when the people do everything according to the word of Yahweh (v 8), which comes only through the divinely chosen spokesperson. Here again we see the emphasis on the person and role of Joshua. Hess explains, "the text is framed within Joshua's commands that the people are to see."[1089]

9–13 Hess suggests a literary technique at work so that the temporal markers are not to be taken literally.[1090] Instead, they serve to position each of the involved groups and to repeat and expand the narrative theme. They show that all the Israelite forces were placed in the right spot at the right time. Winther-Nielsen maintains that it is more likely "that the ambush was sent ahead one day beforehand and sat tight and lay in wait (9a–b) while Joshua spent the night among the people."[1091]

One approach to the problem of Joshua's nighttime activities may be to understand the Hebrew word 'am (עַם) as referring to the army in a technical sense so that Joshua spent the night with his troops.

14–17 The events turned out just as Joshua planned. Josh 8:14 forms a summary of the action that will be detailed in vv 15–17. For the textual problem of Bethel, see *Notes*. Hess claims Bethel is necessary for the story.[1092] The people of Bethel would have seen Joshua and the ambush attack Ai and would have rushed to help them against Israel. The text underscores the understanding that Joshua defeated not only Ai but Bethel at this time. In forsaking their city to battle retreating Israel, "the army [of Bethel] has disregarded its primary duty."[1093]

18 "Verse 18 forms the turning point in the battle and the narrative."[1094] The momentum for victory obviously swings to Israel. The Ruin is defeated. Clean-up work remains. Israel wins the victory, but that is not all. "The taking of Ai is symbolic of what would have had to be a more extensive campaign than is actually described."[1095]

The role of the sword in the narrative is not clear. Certainly it was not large enough to be seen by the ambushers on the other side of the city. V 19 refers to an outstretched hand, not a sword. Hess states that the action served some signaling function, arguing that the main army was close enough to see the signal, and the ambushers watched for the movement of the army.

Josh 8:26 (see *Notes*) understands the function to be one similar to the hands of Moses in Exod 17:8–13, where the rod of Moses is also mentioned (v 9). Keel located the motif in Egyptian art, where the sword is raised in the hand of the victorious god.[1096] The OT places the sword in the hand of the general appointed by the

---

1088 McConville and Williams, 42.
1089 Hess (1996) 164.
1090 Ibid.
1091 *Functional Discourse Grammar*, 223.
1092 Hess (1996) 166.
1093 Ibid.
1094 Ibid., 167.
1095 McConville and Williams, 44.
1096 *Wirkmächtige Siegeszeichen*, 51–76.

deity. This demonstrates the power of the deity working on behalf of his warring people. The motif may well be used with Joshua here to show yet another way in which he continued the work and ways of Moses. Keel states that the sword itself was a curving sickle-shaped sword used in the ancient Near East between 2400 and 1150 BCE.[1097]

22 "Verse 22 is complicated and obscure."[1098] The reader must picture a storyteller pointing to one group and then another to understand precisely who is involved. The new group here is apparently the ambushers returning from Ai and joining in the fray against the retreating enemy.[1099]

29 Israel carries out the execution of the king according to the law in Deut 21:22–23. The people have learned their lesson. They will not defile the land Yahweh is giving them. Israel knows the consequences. In executing the king, Israel follows both Torah and custom, for ancient Near Eastern armies treated kings in the same manner Joshua treated the king of Ai. Victory brings Israel away from the periphery of the land on the Jordan River to the center of the central hill country. The conquest is becoming a reality.

Explanation

"There was disobedience from the very beginnings of life in the promised land—and nowhere other than in the often favoured tribe of Judah."[1100] Creach finds it "difficult to determine any positive message Joshua 7 might have for the church."[1101] The two chapters show the reverse sides of warfare led by Yahweh. Warfare carried out in thoughtless self-confidence leads to disaster. Warfare carried out in obedience to God's commands leads to victory and possession of the land. The narrative of a sacred process illustrated to the people of Israel how they must act when they bring the anger of God upon themselves. "In the Achan story the external threat caused by other nations with their gods has turned to the internal question of how to worship Yahweh in an appropriate way."[1102] This then sets up the following verses (Josh 8:30–35) that demonstrate proper worship.

These two chapters play a key role in defining the identity of the people of God. In so doing they stand in stark contrast to the preceding chapters, where the people of God are pictured in all their festal gaiety and victorious jubilation. Here the people of God return to the reality of life, learning to deal with defeat. They learn that even the people of God face God's anger when they act in self-confidence, refusing to look to God for direction or give him the glory for victory.

"God would not favor his own people when they blatantly disobeyed any more than he would favor wicked Canaanites."[1103] The lesson learned by the ancestors in the wilderness had no effect on the children in the Promised Land. They had to learn it all over again. "Joshua 6 is encouragement in the face of fears—Joshua 8 an encouragement in the face of failure."[1104]

1097 Ibid., 34.
1098 Nelson, 115.
1099 Ibid.; but contrast REB.
1100 Auld, 52.
1101 Creach, 75.
1102 Latvus, *God, Anger, and Ideology*, 52.
1103 Howard, 199.
1104 Winther-Nielsen, *Functional Discourse Grammar*, 232.

From their experiences with the anger of God, the people of Israel developed rituals to deal with such times of defeat. One ritual was that of the sacral lot, whereby God captured the guilty party and demanded from him a confession of guilt and an admission of the justice of God. The books of Psalms and Lamentations show us that Israel incorporated this lesson into their worship. They recognized the signs of God's anger against them and learned to express their own anger to God. The NT continues this picture as it shows Jesus in Gethsemane and at Golgotha declaring his deepest feelings and even his sense of being forsaken to God. The people of God cannot always be the people marching through the Jordan and around Jericho. Often they are the people in utter defeat falling before God with pleas for mercy and renewal. Still, "the tension between divine promise and the need for human planning and action is not dissolved."[1105]

The people of God do not only have problems relating to God. They often have problems relating to one another. When one group feels slighted by other groups, tribal warfare can be the result. Tribal polemic is the literary result. Amazingly, even this can be taken up by the community and used as the word of God. As it is, the tribal polemic recedes into the background, but it stays clear enough to remind us hauntingly that even the people of God have their struggles for power and need to learn from them.

Through the agonies of defeat and intertribal polemic, the people of God learned one major lesson. They learned what it meant to be the covenant people of God under God's chosen leader. Covenant meant more than simply accepting the promises of God to multiply the nation and extend its power in the land. It meant more than going through the ritual of circumcision and the celebration of the yearly festivals. Being the people of God meant accepting certain obligations set down by God. It meant adopting the divinely ordered lifestyle. It meant making each decision of life in the light of divine leadership, not in the light of personal self-confidence. Even The Ruin could not be captured by a few of God's people relying on their own power and marching forth with no thought of divine leadership. Being the covenant people of God meant looking back at salvation history with gratitude, not regret. It meant recognizing that God could undo the elements of the saving history, but he did it when he chose to punish his people, not when his people chose to retreat from hardship and setback.

God did all this through his obedient leader. Hess points to four ways chap. 7 enhances Joshua's leadership position.[1106] Joshua does not appear in the narrative of the disastrous assault on Ai (vv 4–5). But he leads in penitence before God, receives God's instructions on discovering and dealing with the cause of the problems, and leads in carrying out God's punitive instructions (vv 6–26). "Thus," says Hess, "Joshua's religious and political leadership is not marred by the incident with Achan."

In summary, then, the story recorded in chaps. 7–8 taught Israel the meaning of life in the divine presence. Only the covenant people could experience the divine presence, but they had to learn that that presence was demanding as well as promising. They had to learn how to react to a punishing as well as a promising God. They

---

1105 Nelson, 113.
1106 Hess (1996) 24.

had to learn to value the divine presence above material prosperity. And they had to learn that the acts of humans were only temporary, whereas the acts God gave lasted to this day.

Thus God assured the greatness of the name of his people and of his own name, an important issue to the ultimate historian's original audience. These people were in the midst of defeat and wondered why divine anger had replaced the divine presence. They worried that the destruction of the temple, where God had chosen to make his name dwell, meant the destruction of the sovereignty of their God. They were tempted instead to worship the victorious gods. Josh 7–8 reminded them of their covenant with God and of their ways of admitting their own guilt and God's justice. Victory could lie just around the corner for them, just as it had for Joshua. God's anger was not his last word. He waited for the people's word of lamentation, confession, and petition. Then the salvation oracle would again resound among the people of God.

G. Fulfilling Moses' Orders (8:30–35)

Bibliography

Abegg, M., Jr., P. Flint, and E. Ulrich. *The Dead Sea Scrolls Bible.* San Francisco: Harper San Francisco, 1999. **Anbar, M.** "La critique biblique à la lumiére des Archives royales de Mari: Jos 8*." *Bib* 75 (1994) 70–74. ———. "The Story about the Building of an Altar on Mount Ebal: The History of Its Composition and the Questions of the Centralization of the Cult." In *Das Deuteronomium: Entstehung, Gestalt und Botschaft.* Ed. N. Lohfink. BETL 68. Leuven: Leuven UP, 1985. 304–9. **Campbell, A. F.** "Tribal League Shrines in Amman and Shechem." *BA* 32 (1969) 104–16. **Coogan, M. D.** "Archeology and Biblical Studies: The Book of Joshua." In *The Hebrew Bible and Its Interpreters.* Ed. W. H. Propp, B. Halpern, and D. N. Freedman. Biblical and Judaic Studies from the University of California, San Diego. Winona Lake: IN: Eisenbrauns, 1990. 19–32. **De Troyer, K.** "Building the Altar and Reading the Law: The Journeys of Joshua 8:30–35." In *Reading the Present in the Qumran Library.* Atlanta: Society of Biblical Literature, 2005. 141–62. **Eissfeldt, O.** "Gilgal or Shechem?" In *Proclamation and Presence.* Ed. J. I. Durham and J. R. Porter. London: SCM Press, 1970. 90–101. **Hawkins, R. K.** "The Iron Age Structure on Mount Ebal: Excavation and Interpretation." Diss., Andrews University Seventh Day Adventist Seminary, 2007. **Hill, A.** "The Ebal Ceremony as Hebrew Land Grant?" *JETS* 31 (1988) 399–406. **Hollenberg, J.** "Die deuteronomischen Bestandtheile des Buches Josua." *TSK* 1 (1874) 478–81. **L'Hour, J.** "L'Alliance de Sichem." *RB* 69 (1962) 178–81. **Keller, C. A.** "Über einige alttestamentliche Heiligtumslegenden." *ZAW* 67 (1955) 143–48. **Kempinski, A.** "Joshua's Altar—An Iron Age Watchtower." *BAR* 12.1 (1986) 42–48. ———. "'When History Sleeps, Theology Arises': A Note on Joshua 8:30–35 and the Archaeology of the 'Settlement Period.'" In *Avraham Malamat Volume.* Ed. S. Ahituv and B. A. Levine. ErIsr 24. Jerusalem, 1993. 175–83, 237 (Heb.). **Kuenen, A.** "Bijdragen tot de critiek van Pentateuch en Jozua: V. De godsdienstige vergadering by Ebal en Gerizim (Deut. XI:29,30; XXVII; Joz. VIII:30–35)." *ThT* 12 (1878) 297–323. **McCarthy, D. J.** *Treaty and Covenant.* 2nd ed. AnBib 21A. Rome: Pontifical Biblical Institute, 1978. 197–99. **Meer, M. N. van der.** *Formation and Reformulation: The Redaction of the Book of Joshua in the Light of the Oldest Textual Witnesses.* VTSup 102. Leiden: Brill, 2004. **Möhlenbrink, K.** "Die Landnahmensagen des Buches Josua." *ZAW* 56 (1938) 241–45. **Mowinckel, S.** *Psalmenstudien* 5. Oslo: Dybwad,

1924. 97–107. **Nielsen, E.** *Shechem.* Copenhagen: Gad, 1955. 74–85. **Nihan, C.** "The Torah between Samaria and Judah: Shechem and Gerizim in Deuteronomy and Joshua." In *The Pentateuch as Torah: New Models for Understanding Its Promulgation and Acceptance.* Ed. G. N. Knoppers and B. M. Levinson. Winona Lake, IN: Eisenbrauns, 2007. 187–223. **Noort, E.** *Een plek om te zijn: Over de theologie van het land van Jozua 8:30–35.* Kampen: Kok, 1993. ———. "The Traditions of Ebal and Gerizim: Theological Positions in the Book of Joshua." In *Deuteronomy and Deuteronomic Literature.* FS C. H. W. Brekelmans, ed. M. Vervenne and J. Lust. BETL 133. Leuven: Leuven UP; Peeters, 1997. 161–80. **Noth, M.** *Das System der zwölf Stämme Israels.* Stuttgart: Kohlhammer, 1930. 140–51. **Ottosson, M.** "Tradition and History with Emphasis on the Composition of the Book of Joshua." In *The Productions of Time: Tradition History in Old Testament Scholarship.* Ed. K. Jeppesen and B. Otzen. Sheffield: Almond, 1984. 81–106, 141–43. **Rad, G. von.** *Das formgeschichtliche Problem des Hexateuch.* Stuttgart: Kohlhammer, 1938. 33–34. Reprinted in *Gesammelte Studien zum Alten Testament,* vol. 1. TB 8. Munich: Kaiser, 1958. 44–45. **Rudolph, W.** *Der 'Elohist' von Exodus bis Josua.* BZAW 68. Berlin: Töpelmann, 1938. 198–99. **Schäfer-Lichtenberger, C.** *Josua und Salomo: Eine Studie zu Autorität und Legitimität des Nachfolgers im Alten Testament.* VTSup 58. Leiden: Brill, 1995. **Sellin, E.** *Gilgal.* Leipzig: Deichert, 1917. 40–41, 50–53. **Soggin, J. A.** "Zwei umstrittene Stellen aus dem Überlieferungskreis um Schechem." *ZAW* 73 (1961) 82–87. **Tengström, S.** *Die Hexateucherzählung.* Lund: Gleerup, 1976. 153–54. **Tov, E.** *Textual Criticism of the Hebrew Bible.* 2nd ed. Minneapolis: Fortress, 2001. **Ulrich, E.** "4QJoshua[a] and Joshua's First Altar in the Promised Land." In *New Qumran Texts and Studies: Proceedings of the First Meeting of the International Organization for Qumran Studies, Paris 1992.* Ed. G. J. Brooke and F. G. Martínez. STDJ 15. Leiden: Brill, 1994. 89–104. **Vaux, R. de.** *Histoire ancienne d'Israel.* Vol. 1. Paris: Gabalda, 1971. 570. Translated as *The Early History of Israel,* trans. D. Smith. London: Darton, Longman & Todd, 1978. 620. **Vink, J. G.** "The Date and Origin of the Priestly Code in the Old Testament." *OtSt* 15 (1969) 77–80. **Weinfeld, M.** *Deuteronomy and the Deuteronomic School.* Oxford: Oxford UP, 1972. **Wood, B. G.** "The Role of Shechem in the Conquest of Canaan." In *To Understand the Scriptures: Essays in Honor of William H. Shea.* Ed. D. Merling. Berrien Springs, MI: Institute of Archaeology; Siegfried H. Horn Archaeological Museum, 1997. 245–56. **Zertal, A.** "Has Joshua's Altar Been Found on MT. Ebal?" *BAR* 11.1 (1985) 26–43. ———. "How Can Kempinski Be So Wrong?" *BAR* 12.1 (1986) 43, 49–53. **Zevit, Z.** "Archaeological and Literary Stratigraphy in Joshua 7–8." *BASOR* 251 (1983) 23–35. ———. "The Problem of Ai." *BAR* 11.2 (1985) 58–69.

Translation

[30a] *Next Joshua builds[b] an altar to Yahweh, God of Israel, in Mount Ebal,* [31]*just as Moses, the servant of Yahweh, commanded the sons of Israel as it is written in the book[a] of the law of Moses, "An altar of stones which are intact, on which no one has wielded[b] an iron tool." They[c] sent up burnt offerings to Yahweh and sacrificed peace offerings.* [32]*He[a] wrote there on the stones a duplicate[b] of the Torah of Moses which he wrote[c] in the presence of the sons of Israel.* [33]*Meanwhile, all Israel, including its elders, officers,[a] and its judges, were standing[b] on each side of the ark in front of the Levitical priests,[c] who carry the ark of the covenant of Yahweh. Both citizens and aliens were there, half before Mount Gerizim and half[d] before Mount Ebal, just as Moses, the servant of Yahweh, had commanded to bless the people of Israel[e] formerly.[f]* [34]*Afterwards he[a] read out all the words of the[b] Torah, the blessing and the curse, according to all which was written in the book of the Torah.[c]* [35]*There was not a word from all which Moses commanded[a] that Joshua did not read out before all the assembly of Israel, including[b] women and children, and the aliens active among them.[c]*

Notes

30.a. LXX places the section after Josh 9:2, where it disrupts the narrative sequence even more than in MT. 4QJosh[a] places this material before 5:2 with its own introduction in place of 5:1. See *Notes* there. Sellin (*Gilgal*, 40–41, 50–53), Soggin (241–42), and others seek to connect this section with chap. 24 because of the similar subject matter. Tov thinks the entire section is based on Deut 27 and was possibly "added at a later period in different places within the framework of the deuteronomistic editing of Joshua" (*Textual Criticism of the Hebrew Bible*, 332), the positioning by OG being more plausible. Later, he notes that 4QJosh[a] "probably reflects the original story" (346). Van der Meer (*Formation and Reformulation*, 513; compare Nelson, 117) argues that MT reflects original positioning and that a scribe saw that Deut 27:2 was not explicitly fulfilled in Joshua and so copied part of Josh 8:30–35 into the position represented in 4QJosh[a]. Gk., meanwhile, connected more logically Josh 9:1 to 8:29. I will try to demonstrate the theological purpose in its present context.

30.b. The use of the impf. after אָז, "then," has often been noted (e.g., C. Brockelmann, *Hebräische Syntax* [Neukirchen: Moers, 1956] 42a; P. Joüon, *Grammaire*, §113i; W. Schneider, *Grammatik des biblischen Hebräisch* [Munich: Claudios, 1974] 197–98), but never adequately explained. Williams calls this the "preterite in prose after אָז," saying this particle "is often followed by a verb that is spelled like the imperfect but appears to have a past-time meaning. Such verbs might be preterite rather than imperfect. One difficulty with this view is that the verb . . . is not shortened as the preterite is thought to be" (*Williams' Hebrew Syntax*, 177c). See the discussion in *IBHS* 31.6.3b; I. Rabinowitz, "*'az* Followed by Imperfect Verb Form in Preterite Contexts: A Redactional Device in Biblical Hebrew," *VT* 34 (1984) 53–62. Compare Josh 10:33.

31.a. Here and in v 34, LXX lacks "book," which the MT tradition added to bring the text "up-to-date" with their practice. Again, van der Meer (*Formation and Reformulation*, 504–5) credits the Gk. translator with intensifying stress on Torah by omitting "book."

31.b. The Heb. verb נוּף, "wielded," has no explicit subject.

31.c. Van der Meer (*Formation and Reformulation*, 506) emphasizes the substitution of a sg. verb in LXX to credit Joshua with performing the offerings.

32.a. LXX adds the explicit subject "Joshua."

32.b. LXX translates מִשְׁנֶה, "duplicate," as "Deuteronomy," which means literally "second law."

32.c. "Which he wrote" is missing in the best Gk. tradition. Its subject is not clear in the Heb. The immediate antecedent is Moses, but the intention appears to be to emphasize the work of Joshua. Nelson (116) follows Rahlfs in seeing the words present in the OG but not in LXX[B]: "The reference to Joshua's obedience to Deut. 17:18 was not understood and dropped as awkward" (with reference to Margolis, *Book of Joshua in Greek*, 146). *Preliminary and Interim Report* (2:18) sees the omission as simplification of the text and translates "which he had written" (compare Barthélemy, *Critique textuelle*, 1:13).

33.a. Fritz (94) strikes "officers" as a gloss because it lacks the pronominal suffix. This is not a sufficient reason to delete material.

33.b. LXX appears to have read עָבַר, "cross over," instead of the similar appearing עָמַד, "standing." LXX may represent an original cultic procession.

33.c. LXX read the text to refer to priests and Levites. Deuteronomic literature repeatedly speaks of Levitical priests. Fritz (94) deletes "Levitical" as a gloss. The latter is based on a popular critical understanding of the history of development of the priesthood by which the postexilic period saw a definite break between Levites and priests.

33.d. *BHS* and Nelson (116) point to the merged reading here from וְהַחֵצִי and וַחֲצִיו. Fritz (94) strikes the article to avoid the double determination. See Williams (*Williams' Hebrew Syntax*, 82c) and *Note* on 7:21.

33.e. LXX omits "Israel," an addition in MT tradition representing traditional vocabulary and concern to make the definition of "people of God" explicit.

33.f. Fritz (94) omits "formerly" or "at first" as a later addition. See Nelson (116) for translation options.

34.a. LXX makes Joshua the explicit subject. 4QJosh[a] has vv 34–35 at the beginning of chap. 5. See *Notes* there.

34.b. LXX reads "this" law, again pointing to explicitness.

34.c. Rather than "book of the Torah," LXX reads "law of Moses," repeating its reading of v 31. Nelson (116) may be correct in seeing both readings as expansions of an original "law."

35.a. LXX and 4QJosh^a limit the commandments to that which was commanded "to Joshua." 4QJosh^a reads "all" rather than "all that."

35.b. LXX completes the list by adding "men." Originally, the "assembly of Israel" was probably understood as being composed of men. In the postexilic period women were admitted (Ezra 10:1; Neh 8:2), so the tradition added "men" to this text. 4QJosh^a reads "before all [. . .] the Jordan and the women and children" with room for about two words in the blank. See Abegg et al., *Dead Sea Scrolls Bible*, 204.

35.c. LXX makes "Israel" explicit here as MT tradition did in v 33.

Form/Structure/Setting

The section is a literary accumulation of citations from Deuteronomy:

v 30 = Deut 27:4–5

v 31a = Deut 30:10; cf. 31:24; 17:18; 28:58, 61; 29:19–20; 26; 31:24, 26(!); Josh 1:8

v 31aβ = Deut 27:5; cf. Exod 20:25

v 31b = Deut 27:6–7; cf. 12:13–14, 27

v 32a = Deut 17:18; cf. 27:8; Josh 24:26

v 32b = Deut 31:9; cf. 4:13; 5:22; 10:2, 4; 17:18; 31:24

v 33 = periphrastic combination of Deut 29:9–14 and 27:12–13; cf. 11:29; 31:9–13; Exod 12:49; Lev 19:34; 24:22; Num 9:14; 15:29; Josh 23:2; 24:1

v 34 = Deut 31:11; cf. 17:19; 11:26–29; 27:13; 28:2, 15, 45; 29:26; 30:1, 19; Josh 8:31

v 35 = Deuteronomistic summary of Josh 8:30–34 based on Deut 4:2; 12:32; cf. 26:16–19; 27:1, 10; 17:18–20; 28:13–14, 58; 30:1, 8; 32:46, Josh 1:7

The citations from the Deuteronomic imperatives have been transformed into narrative, leading Pressler to state: "Historically, the passage has little claim to reliability."[1107] Knauf attributes the narrative to a fifth-century polemic in Jerusalem against the Samaritans and their altar on Mount Gerizim.[1108]

Taking wording from a previous text does not preclude the narrative's historical reality but rather reveals the source materials and theological concerns of the narrator who created the narrative. Howard states that "almost every statement in this passage has roots in the Pentateuch" and points to the above list to support the statement.[1109] Ottosson sees Deuteronomistic reworking of "old traditional material."[1110]

Joshua fulfills each of the commandments of Moses: building an altar, offering sacrifices, writing down the Mosaic law on stones, assembling the people, reading the law to them, and outlining the blessings and the curses that could befall them. The section is not oral narrative. It is a literary composition of the ultimate editor of the book. It may well echo the cultic traditions of Shechem, but only the study of chap. 24 will allow for a definite conclusion on that point. The major question

---

1107 Pressler, 64; compare Knauf, 87.

1108 Knauf, 87.

1109 Howard, 214, n. 136.

1110 Ottoson, "Tradition History," 87–88.

for the present text is not the traditions behind the passage but the function of the passage in its literary context.

The passage 8:30–35 interrupts the narrative, moving the action suddenly and unexpectedly from the newly conquered Ai to the previously unmentioned Shechem, twenty miles to the north. In the midst of warfare, the narrative switches to construction and cult. The sudden switch has consistently baffled interpreters. In the middle of the nineteenth century, commentators noted the fragmentary nature of 8:30–35 and its unsuitability for the present context.[1111] In 1874, Hollenberg assumed as a generally accepted fact that the unit did not fit the present context.[1112] Soggin moves it from its present context to chap. 24, without the evidence of any manuscript attestations.[1113] Van der Meer maintains that Josh 8:30–35 is a relatively late redactor's work based on Deut 27 and that its concern to emphasize Torah is a strong possiblity.[1114] Creach plausibly argues, "When we consider these statements to Israel [Deut 28:1, 7, 10], the placement of 8:30–35 before 9:1–2 is quite logical. The Canaanite rulers recognize that Israel is declaring international superiority for itself, and universal sovereignty for its God."[1115]

The geographical and chronological difficulties may be resolved by understanding the importance of Israel gaining control of much of the central hill country (Ai and Bethel). Israel's previous relationships with Shechem as depicted in Gen 34 may have given Israel easy access to that important city-state. Whatever the explanation, the important task is to look for theological explanations. The preceding section contrasted the experiences of a disobedient people of God with those of an obedient people of God. It introduced covenant terminology into the book of Joshua for the first time and demonstrated the punishment required of any person who brought trouble on Israel. In that narrative, one theological question remains unanswered: How could the congregation that transgressed the divine covenant restore that relationship?

This theological question is so vital that the biblical editor ignored problems of geography, unconquered territory, chronology, and even literary unity to supply the vital theological answer. A people of God who have transgressed the divine covenant go to the place where God has chosen and renew their commitment to the law that Moses has set out for them in the book of Deuteronomy. Joshua 8:30–35 is the answer to the burning theological issue of the narrative. The reader must recognize the narrative's integral role as the closing verses of the first major section of the book of Joshua, connecting the story-line back through Josh 1 to the book of Deuteronomy, especially chaps. 17, 27–31. It thus presents Shechem in a positive light in contrast to its later role as "the archrival power in Israel to the house of David."[1116]

1111 E.g., Hauff, *Offenbarungsglaube und Kritik der biblischen Geschichtsbücher am Beispiele des Buchs Josua in ihrer nothwendigen Einheit* (Stuttgart: Belser, 1843), 142–43; Knobel (1861) 388–90.

1112 *Der Charakter der alexandrinischen Übersetzung des Buches Josua und ih textkritischer Werth* (Moers: Eckner, 1874) 478–81.

1113 Soggin, 222.

1114 *Formation and Reformulation*, 504.

1115 Creach, 80.

1116 Coote, 635; compare 1 Kgs 12.

Comments

30 Altars play only a minor role in the book. This is the first reference; the others are in Josh 9:27 and chap. 22. The editor recognizes the legitimacy of the sacrificial worship and of Israel's worship in various places prior to David's establishment of Jerusalem as the central sanctuary. He faces the problem that in his own time the altars of Yahweh have been destroyed, and thus complex sacrificial worship is not possible. What is possible is adherence to the law of Moses.

The particular altar is built on Mount Ebal, which is mentioned only in Deut 11:29; 27:4, 13; and here. The Deuteronomic literature portrays Mount Ebal as the place of the altar but also as the place of the curse. The Samaritan Pentateuch places the altar on Mount Gerizim in Deut 27:4. This would be more consistent, but it also represents the regard of the Samaritans for their major sanctuary on Mount Gerizim. Polemic between postexilic Jews and Samaritans has most likely influenced the text tradition, but the original reading cannot be ascertained. In any case, Ebal, the great northern mountain overlooking the crucial east-west trade route, is pictured as an important point of early Israelite worship. Since Israel was never credited with fighting for or capturing Shechem, "the location of the ceremony confronts the reader with the gap between what the reader knows and what the narrator wishes to disclose."[1117]

31 As was seen clearly in Josh 1, authority for Israel is based on the law of Moses. Joshua gains his authority only as he follows that law. This section underlines the authority of Joshua by showing how he carries out the Mosaic commands.

Joshua's care to obey the Mosaic commands is demonstrated in that he follows primitive construction techniques rather than following the trends of modern architecture. The law shows that it originated among an Iron Age people. Normally, Joshua himself is dated to the Late Bronze Age, so that the passage may be anachronistic in attributing to Joshua the possibility of utilizing instruments of iron. In any case, the law is not an editorial invention, for it appears in the Covenant Code (Exod 20:25), possibly Israel's earliest collection of laws. Similar altars appear in 1 Sam 14:33–35 and 1 Kgs 18:31–32. Zertal[1118] has discovered what he considers an altar at el-Barnat, a conclusion to which even Coogan[1119] concurs, with the caveat that it probably was not Israelite.

Two types of sacrifices are mentioned. "Burnt offerings" (עֹלוֹת) represents the offering of a whole animal in fire (cf. Exod 29:18).[1120] "Peace offerings" (שְׁלָמִים) are always mentioned in connection with the burnt offerings (עֹלוֹת). Peace offerings are offered on the altar at occasions of particular public significance.[1121] The precise meaning of the Hebrew term is debated. From the time of the early versions on, various translations have been rendered salvation offering, peace offering, thanksgiving offering, welfare offering, offering of friendship or alliance. L.

1117 Hess (2010) 92; for archaeological information, see Pitkänen's excursus, 192–204; Hawkins's dissertation, "The Iron Age Structure on Mount Ebal."

1118 *BAR* 11.1 (1985) 26–43; cf. R. Hawkins, *How Israel Became a People*.

1119 "Archaeology and Biblical Studies," 26.

1120 R. Rendtorff, *Studien zur Geschichte des Opfers im alten Israel*, WMANT 24 (Neukirchen-Vluyn: Neukirchener Verlag, 1967) 74–118; L. Rost, "Erwägungen zum israelitischen Brandopfer," in *Von Ugarit nach Qumran*, BZAW 77 (Berlin: Töpelmann, 1958) 177–83.

1121 Rendtorff, *Studien*, 123–26.

Köhler[1122] suggests a translation of "concluding" or "final" sacrifice and is followed by Rendtorff.[1123] G. Gerleman suggests a derivation from a verbal meaning to "pay," the sacrifice consisting of the fat pieces brought as a substitution for the entire animal (שׁלם—"genug haben").[1124]

Whatever the meaning, Joshua is pictured as bringing the two major types of sacrifices on a special occasion and thus fulfilling the teaching of Moses. Such an offering may present Joshua in a kingly function (cf. 2 Sam 6:17–18; 24:25; 1 Kgs 3:15; 8:64; 9:25) but not as a paradigm or cipher for Josiah.[1125] Howard underlines the importance of atonement underlying these sacrifices, thus reestablishing a sense of relationship and well-being.[1126]

32 The function of the stones suddenly changes from altar to writing tablet. In Deut 27:1–8, plaster stones are set up for writing the law (vv 2–4), an altar is built for sacrifice (vv 5–7), and the command to write the law on the stones is given in the summary conclusion (v 8). The author of Joshua has conflated the material and describes only one set of stones, serving both for altar and for writing. Thus he reveals his own emphasis—preserving and obeying the law is much more important than building an altar and offering sacrifices. Joshua also practices what ancient Near Eastern rulers commonly did, namely, set up a stele with the law inscribed on it to remind the people of the ruler's beneficence and of their commitment to obey the law.[1127]

The reference to the duplicate copy of the law has its literary base in Deut 17:18, the Deuteronomic description of the role of the king. The two passages have several points of contact which reveal another side to the image being painted of Joshua. He is a royal figure. Thus Weinfeld speaks of a "quasi-regal figure" and notes that David was the first ruler after Joshua to implement the Deuteronomic laws.[1128] Joshua thus becomes a paradigm of monarchy, not only in the manner in which he leads Israel into battle but also in his worship and his reaction to the sin of the people.

The final words of v 32 are ambiguous and lack a real basis in Deuteronomy. They represent another emphasis of the author. The actions of the regal representative are not only performed in seclusion, as might be inferred from Deut 17, but are also to be done publicly before the people. The leader of Israel is not only an example, but he is also a teacher of the people.

33 V 33 goes to great lengths to list the participants, but the list is not exhaustive, as a comparison with Deut 29:9–10 shows. The first words, "all Israel," are the important ones. No member of the people of God is exempt from the worship service that among other components outlines the duties of the people of God.

The worship service meets all Deuteronomic requirements, having the ark and the Levitical priests at its center. The inclusion of aliens rests on a particular Deuteronomic concern. The alien included anyone living outside his own clan and thus not protected by clan law. Thus the ancestors were "aliens" in the Promised Land (Gen 12:10; 19:9; 20:1; 21:23, 34; 26:3; 32:5; 47:4, 9). The Deuteronomic law viewed such aliens as eco-

---

1122 *Theologie des Alten Testaments* (Tübingen: Mohr [Siebeck], 1935) 178.
1123 *Studien*, 133.
1124 *THAT*, 2:932 = *TLOT*, 3:1340–41.
1125 Rendtorff, *Studien*, 78–81.
1126 Howard, 215.
1127 Schäfer-Lichtenberger, *Josua und Salomo*, 221.
1128 *Deuteronomy*, 170–71.

nomically underprivileged and provided special means of support for them (Deut 14:29; 16:11, 14; 24:17, 19–21; 26:12–13; 27:19; cf. 24:14). Special protection (Deut 1:16; 5:14; 24:17; 27:19) and even privilege (14:21; cf. Lev 17:15) were granted them. Their presence in the cult was assumed and commanded (Deut 16:11, 14; cf. Lev 23:42), based on Yahweh's love for them (Deut 10:18–19). Still, one of the curses facing a disobedient Israel was that the tables would be turned so that citizens depended upon aliens for livelihood (Deut 28:43–44).[1129] Josh 8:33 builds on the Deuteronomic understanding to assure the aliens a place within the cultic life of Israel (cf. Deut 31:12).

The immediate purpose of the assembly is to bless the people of Israel. This is based on the cultic instructions of Deut 27:12–13, but a significant shift of emphasis occurs. In Deuteronomy, the emphasis is on the curses (cf. Deut 27:16–26). The Joshua context makes clear that the blessings are to be given first, thereby shifting the focus of the section from threat to promise. Israel, which has transgressed the covenant, is still the subject of divine promise and blessing before any mention of curse (Josh 8:34) appears. The promise of Deuteronomy (cf. Deut 7:13; 12:7; 14:22–27; 15:4–18; 16:9–17; 24:19; 26:15; 28:1–14; 30:16) is secured for Israel through the ritual ceremony even after her transgression. The people who respond properly to the call of Yahweh to worship and to renewal of the covenant are accepted and blessed by him.

No other OT passage connects the ark with Shechem. This has led Eissfeldt to suggest that the present passage was originally a Gilgal tradition seeking to join the book of the covenant with a pre-Deuteronomic Hexateuch.[1130] A later editor, on the basis of the Shechem traditions of Deut 11:29–32 and 27:11–13 interpreted Josh 8:30–35 as the fulfillment of the Deuteronomic commands. The ark motif here, however, does not identify our passage as a Gilgal tradition. Rather, it shows the constant Deuteronomic concern for the ark as the divine symbol from the wilderness period until the time of the dedication of the Solomonic temple (1 Kgs 8). The presence of the ark is only one more sign of the Deuteronomic character and theological importance of this passage. Joshua included the proper priests and the proper divine symbol in his major act of dedicating the people of Yahweh in the Promised Land. The Shechemite location derives from Deut 27 in its present literary form, as is demonstrated also by the retention of the function of the stones.

34 Only after the emphasis on blessing does the text return to follow the ritual of Deut 27. Joshua reads the law to the people. Here another shift is made. Moses spoke to the people and taught the people. Moses had the direct word for the people from their God. Joshua's word is secondhand. It comes through Moses. Here is the paradigm for Israelite leadership (cf. Josh 1). Joshua acts as the Israelite king was supposed to act (Deut 17:18–20).

35 The total obedience of Joshua concludes the section. The original context of Deut 27 referred only to a small number of blessings and cursings. The context in Deut 4:13 and 5:22 referred only to the Ten Commandments as being written down. Deut 31:24–26 expanded the writing to include all the book of Deuteronomy. The canonical tradition then expanded this to include the entire Pentateuch. Josh 8 takes the process one step further. Not only is the entire corpus of material to be written down for

---

1129 See further D. Kellermann, "גור," *TWAT*, 1:979–91 with bibliography = *TDOT*, 2:439–49; *NIDOTTE*, 1:839.
1130 "Gilgal or Shechem," 96.

Israel, it is to be read to them in an annual ceremony and is to be written on the altar. Here is the extreme to which the biblical writer felt compelled to go to enforce the teachings upon the community. The community must know the entire law and must be reminded of it and pledge themselves to observe all of it. Why? Because to be the people of God means to be an obedient people, following the divinely-given lifestyle.

Explanation

Josh 8:30–35 does not fit the present geographical, chronological, or narrative context. It was not supposed to. Rather, it gives a theological summary of the first major division of the book of Joshua and reveals the nature of the literature preserved in the book. It also underscores the major teachings of the book to this point.

The final editor of Joshua inserted this section to speak directly to his contemporaries. He saw them standing in the same confused condition as Israel after the battle of Ai. They had suddenly faced the faith-shaking fact that victory was not automatic for the people of Yahweh. An identity based on possession of the land as fulfillment of the promises of God was not enough. Another element was necessary.

This element had been given in the imperative mode in chap. 1. It is given in the paradigm of historical narrative in chap. 8. Here Israel sees the real meaning of the command to obey, to live the divine lifestyle.

Israel learns an even greater lesson: how to find its way back to its identity as the people of God once that identity is lost. This must come through purification. "Placing such a ceremony after the story of Achan's covenant violation shows that restoring the breach that sin causes in the community's relationship with God is both possible and necessary."[1131]

Chaps. 3 through 6 outlines the victorious identity of the people of God in cultic terms. Chap. 7 caricatures cultic terms to show the loss of such identity. The concluding verses of chap. 8 continue in the cultic framework to show that identity regained. The people who transgressed the divine covenant, disregarding the divine will, must return to the place of God's choice. As Deut 11:29, 27:1–26, and Josh 24 show, that place is Shechem with a tradition of a ceremony of blessing and cursing understood as covenant theology. The sinful nation must again stand under the blessing and the cursing, must again hear the whole law of Moses, and must again renew their pledge to Yahweh by bringing him the proper sacrifices.

If the people were cultically obedient, the blessing would again ring out loud and clear, drowning out the cursing. The fight for the land could be taken up anew in the assurance that the identity of the people of God had been restored and so the oracle of salvation would again come to their armies. Israel would be once again the people of the covenant. Yahweh would be in her midst to bless rather than to express anger. All of this was possible because God had given to Israel two gifts. The first was the Torah of Moses showing the proper lifestyle with God. The second was a new leader, one who was certainly no Moses, speaking face to face with God, but one who followed the law for leaders by reading the Torah of Moses, teaching it to his people, and embodying it in his own life as an example to all the people. With the law of Moses and the leadership of Joshua, Israel could again pass over

---

1131 Pressler, 64.

into the covenant, be the people of God, and enjoy the blessings of God. This was gospel for a people who had lost their land and temple, the symbol of God's presence with them. Having experienced the curse, they needed desperately to hear the directions to blessing. After the ceremony Israel is a new people of God.[1132]

H. Covenant Compromise (9:1–27)

Bibliography

Alt, A. "Neue Erwägungen über die Lage von Mizpa, Ataroth, Beeroth, und Gibeon." *ZDPV* 69 (1953) 1–27. **Auld, A. G.** "Joshua: The Hebrew and Greek Texts." In *Studies in the Historical Books of the Old Testament.* VTSup 30. Leiden: Brill, 1979. 1–14. **Bächli, O.** "Zur Aufnahme von Fremden in die altisraelitische Kultgemeinde." In *Wort, Gebot, Glaube.* Ed. H. J. Stoebe. ATANT 59. Zürich: Zwingli, 1970. 21–26. **Bekkum, K. van.** "De Belofte van het land vervuld: Goddelijk en menselijk handelen in Jozua 9–12." *Schrift* 226 (2006) 116–19. **Bimson, J. J.** *Redating the Exodus and Conquest.* JSOTSup 5. Sheffield: University of Sheffield, 1978. **Blenkinsopp, J.** "Are There Traces of the Gibeonite Covenant in Deuteronomy?" *CBQ* 28 (1966) 207–19. ———. *Gibeon and Israel: The Role of Gibeon and the Gibeonites in the Political and Religious History of Early Israel.* Cambridge: Cambridge UP, 1972. **Boer, R. T.** "Green Ants and Gibeonites: B. Wongar, Joshua 9, and Some Problems of Postcolonialism." *Semeia* 75 (1996) 129–52. **Briend, J.** "The Sources of the Deuteronomic History: Research on Joshua 1–12." In *Israel Constructs Its History: Deuteronomistic Historiography in Recent Research.* Ed. A. de Pury, T. Römer, and J.-D. Macchi. JSOTSup 306. Sheffield: Sheffield Academic, 2000. 360–86. Orginally published as "Les Sources de L'Histoire deuteronomique recherches sur Jos 1–12," in *Israël construit son histoire: L'historiograhie deutéronomiste à la lumière des recherches récentes,* ed. A. de Pury, T. Römer, and J.-D. Macchi, MdB 34 (Geneva: Labor et Fides, 1996). **Ceuppens, P. F.** *Le Miracle de Josué.* Liège: Soledi, 1944. **Coats, G. W.** *Rebellion in the Wilderness.* Nashville: Abingdon, 1968. 40–43. **Conder, C. R.** "Notes on Bible Geography: 3. The Battle of Gibeon." *PEFQS* 37 (1905) 72–74. **Culley, R. C.** "Structural Analysis: Is It Done with Mirrors?" *Int* 28 (1974) 176–77. ———. "Themes and Variations in Three Groups of OT Narratives." *Semeia* 3 (1975) 3–13. **Day, J.** "Gibeon and the Gibeonites in the Old Testament." In *Reflection and Refraction: Studies in Biblical Historiography in Honour of A. Graeme Auld.* Ed. R. Rezetko, T. H. Lim, and W. B. Aucker. VTSup 113. Leiden: Brill, 2007. 113–37. **Demsky, A.** "Geba, Gibeah, and Gibeon, an Historico-Geographic Riddle." *BASOR* 212 (1973) 26–31. **Dus, J.** "Gibeon—eine Kultstätte des Šmš und die Stadt des benjaminitischen Schicksals." *VT* 10 (1960) 353–74. **Edenburg, C.** "Joshua 9 and Deuteronomy: An Intertextual Conundrum, the Chicken or the Egg?" Paper read to SBL Deuteronomistic History/Pentateuch Section, Atlanta, November 23, 2010. **Fensham, F. C.** "The Treaty between Israel and the Gibeonites." *BA* 27 (1964) 96–100. **Geoghegan, J. C.** *The Time, Place, and Purpose of the Deuteronomistic History: The Evidence of 'Until This Day.'* BJS 347. Providence: Brown Judaic Studies, 2006. **Geraty, L. T.** "Heshbon: The First Casualty in the Israelite Quest for the Kingdom of God." In *The Quest for the Kingdom of God: Studies in Honor of George E. Mendenhall.* Ed. H. B. Huffmon, F. A. Spina, and A. R. W. Green. Winona Lake, IN: Eisenbrauns, 1983. 239–48. **Gordon, R. P.** "Gibeonite Ruse and Israelite Curse in Joshua 9." In *Covenant as Context: Essays in Honour of E. W. Nicholson.* Ed. A. D. H. Mayes. Oxford: Oxford UP, 2003. **Grintz, J. M.** "The Treaty of Joshua with the Gibeonites." *JAOS* 86 (1966)

1132 See McConville and Williams, 46; Earl, 145.

113–26. **Halbe, J.** "Gibeon und Israel: Art, Veranlassung und Ort der Deutung ihres Verhältnisses in Jos. IX." *VT* 25 (1975) 613–41. ———. *Das Privilegrecht Jahwes.* FRLANT 114. Göttingen: Vandenhoeck & Ruprecht, 1975. 247–50, 341–46. **Hall, S. L.** *Conquering Character: The Characterization of Joshua in Joshua 1–11.* New York: T&T Clark, 2010. **Halpern, B.** "Gibeon: Israelite Diplomacy in the Conquest Era." *CBQ* 37 (1975) 303–16. **Haran, M.** "The Gibeonites, the Nethinim, and the Sons of Solomon's Servants." *VT* 11 (1961) 159–69. **Hawk, L. D.** *Every Promise Fulfilled: Contesting Plots in Joshua.* Louisville: Westminster John Knox, 1991. **Herr, L. G.** "The Search for Biblical Heshbon." *BAR* 19.6 (1993) 36–37, 68. **Huesman, J. E.** ". . . For Gibeon Was a Great City." *TBT* 1.12 (1964) 761–67. **Ibáñez Arana, A.** "El pacto con los Gabaonitas (Jos 9) como narración etiológica." *EstBib* 30 (1971) 161–75. **Kearney, P. J.** "The Role of the Gibeonites in the Deuteronomic History." *CBQ* 35 (1973) 1–19. **Kissling, P. J.** *Reliable Characters in the Primary History: Profiles of Moses, Joshua, Elijah, and Elisha.* Sheffield: Sheffield Academic, 1996. **LaBianca, Ø. S.** *Sedentarization and Nomadization: Food System Cycles at Hesban and Vicinity in Transjordan.* Hesban 1. Berrien Springs, MI: Institute of Archaeology; Andrews UP, 1990. **Liver, J.** "The Literary History of Joshua IX." *JSS* 8 (1963) 227–43. **Leuchter, M.** "The Cult at Kiriath Yearim: Implications from the Biblical Record." *VT* 58 (2008) 526–43. **Mayes, A. D. H.** "Deuteronomy 29, Joshua 9, and the Place of the Gibeonites in Israel." In *Das Deuteronomium.* Ed. N. Lohfink. BETL 68. Leuven: Leuven UP, 1985. 321–25. ———. "The Gibeonites as a Historical and Theological Problem in the Old Testament." *PIBA* 10 (1986) 13–24. **Mitchell, G.** *Together in the Land.* JSOTSup 134. Sheffield: Sheffield Academic, 1993. **Möhlenbrink, K.** "Die Landnahmensagen des Buches Josua." *ZAW* 56 (1938) 241–45. **Mowinckel, S.** *Tetrateuch, Pentateuch, Hexateuch.* BZAW 90. Berlin: Töpelmann, 1964. 38. **Noth, M.** *Das System der zwölf Stämme Israels.* Stuttgart: Kohlhammer, 1930. 140–51. **Otto, E.** *Das Mazzotfest in Gilgal.* BWANT 107. Stuttgart: Kohlhammer, 1975. 89–92, 96–97, 309–11, 318–22. **Pritchard, J. B.** "Gibeon's History in the Light of Excavation." In *Congress Volume: Oxford, 1959.* Ed. G. W. Anderson et al. VTSup 7. Leiden: Brill, 1960. 1–12. ———. *Gibeon Where the Sun Stood Still: The Discovery of the Biblical City.* Princeton: Princeton UP, 1962. ———. "Gibeon Where the Sun Stood Still." In *Archaeological Discoveries in the Holy Land.* New York: Holy Land Archaeological Institute of America, 1967. 139–46. **Rainey, A. F., R. S. Notley, et al.** *The Sacred Bridge: Carta's Atlas of the Biblical World.* Jerusalem: Carta, 2006. **Richardson, A. T.** "The Battle of Gibeon." *ExpTim* 40 (1929) 426–31. **Rösel, H.** "Anmerkungen zur Erzählung von Bundesschluss mit den Gibeoniten." *BN* 28 (1985) 30–35. ———. "Wer kämpfte auf kanaanäischer Seite in der Schlacht bei Gibeon, Jos. 10?" *VT* 26 (1976) 505–8. **Rudolph, W.** *Der 'Elohist' von Exodus bis Josua.* BZAW 68. Berlin: Töpelmann, 1938. 200–204. **Sapin, J.** "Josué 9–10: Gabon—Israël." *Etudes Théologiques et Religieuses Montpellier* 54 (1979) 258–63. **Schäfer-Lichtenberger, C.** "Das gibeonistische Bündnis im Lichte deuteronomistischer Kriegsgebote: Zum Verhältnis von Tradition und Interpretation in Jos 9." *BN* 34 (1986) 58–81. **Schmitt, G.** *Du sollst keinen Frieden schliessen mit den Bewohnern des Landes.* BWANT 91. Stuttgart: Kohlhammer, 1970. 30–45. **Schottroff, W.** *Der altisraelitische Fluchspruch.* WMANT 30. Neukirchen-Vluyn: Neukirchener Verlag, 1969. 80–84. **Schunck, K.-D.** *Benjamin.* BZAW 86. Berlin: Töpelmann, 1963. 38–39. **Stephenson, F. R.** "Astronomical Verifications and Dating of Old Testament Passages Referring to Solar Eclipses." *PEQ* 107 (1975) 119. **Stolz, F.** *Jahwes und Israels Kriege.* ATANT 60. Zürich: Theologischer, 1972. 84–85. **Sutherland, R.** "Israelite Political Theories in Joshua 9." *JSOT* 53 (1992) 65–74. **Vaux, R. de.** *Histoire ancienne d'Israel.* Vol. 1. Paris: Gabalda, 1971. 571–76. Translated as *The Early History of Israel,* trans. D. Smith. London: Darton, Longman & Todd, 1978. 621–26. **Winther-Nielsen, N.** *A Functional Discourse Grammar of Joshua: A Computer-Assisted Rhetorical Structure Analysis.* ConBOT 40. Stockholm: Almqvist & Wiksell, 1995. **Yeivin, S.** *The Israelite Conquest of Canaan.* Istanbul: Nederlands Historisch-Archaeologisch Instituut in het Nabije Oosten, 1971. 80–81. **Younger, K. L.** *Ancient Conquest Accounts: A Study in Ancient Near Eastern and Biblical History Writing.* JSOTSup 98. Sheffield: JSOT Press, 1990. **Zertal, A.** "Israel Enters Canaan—Following the Pottery Trail." *BAR* 17.5 (1991) 28–47.

Translation

[1]*When all*[a] *the kings*[b] *who were beyond the Jordan in the hill country and in the Shephelah and on all the Mediterranean coast in front of the Lebanon mountains, namely, the Hittites, Amorites, Canaanites, Perizzites, Hivites, and Jebusites, heard,* [2]*they assembled together to make war with Joshua and with Israel in complete accord.*[a] [3]*But the inhabitants of Gibeon, having heard what Joshua*[a] *had done to Jericho and to Ai,* [4]*were the very ones*[a] *who acted with cunning. They went and prepared supplies.*[b] *Then they took dilapidated sacks for their donkeys*[c] *and dilapidated wineskins which had been cracked and mended.* [5]*They put dilapidated sandals*[a] *which they had patched up on their feet and dressed in dilapidated clothing. All*[b] *their bread supply was dried out and crumbling.* [6]*So they came to Joshua to the camp at Gilgal and said to him and to the man*[a] *of Israel, "From a far distant land we have come. Therefore, sign a covenant agreement with us."* [7]*And they*[a] *said, that is, the men of Israel, to the Hivites, "It could just be the case that you live nearby. How then could I sign a covenant agreement with you?"*

[8]*They replied to Joshua, "We are your servants."*

Joshua said to them, "Who are you? From where do you come?"[a]

[9]*They said to him,*[a] *"From an extremely distant land your servants have come due to the name of Yahweh your God, for we have heard his reputation*[b] *and all that he had done in Egypt,* [10]*and all that he did to the two*[a] *kings of the Amorites who were beyond the Jordan, that is, to Sihon, king of Heshbon,*[b] *and to Og, king of Bashan, which is in Ashtaroth.*[c] [11a]*Our elders and all the inhabitants of our land said to us, 'Take supplies in your hands for the way and go to call on them and say to them, "We are your servants; therefore sign a covenant agreement with us."'* [12]*This is our bread. It was piping hot when we packed it among our supplies at our homes*[a] *the day of our leaving to come to you. Right here it is, all dried out. It has become crumbly.* [13]*These are the wineskins which we filled when they were new. But look here, they are split open. This is our clothing and our sandals. They have become dilapidated from the great distance of our journey."*

[14]*The men*[a] *accepted*[b] *the evidence of the supplies, but of Yahweh*[c] *they did not inquire.* [15]*So Joshua made peace with them and signed a covenant agreement with them to let them live. The chiefs of the congregation swore an oath with them.*

[16]*Three days after*[a] *signing the covenant agreement with them, they heard that they were from the vicinity, that in fact they were living quite near to them.* [17]*Then the sons of Israel set out and came to their cities on the third day.*[a] *Their cities included Gibeon, Cephirah, Beeroth, and Kiriath-Jearim.* [18]*But the sons of Israel did not kill them because the chiefs of the congregation*[a] *had sworn an oath to them in the name of Yahweh, the God of Israel. Then all the congregation grumbled against the chiefs.*

[19]*All the chiefs explained to all the congregation, "We have sworn to them by Yahweh, the God of Israel; therefore we are not able to touch them.* [20]*But this we will do to them, preserving them alive*[a] *without the wrath coming upon us due to the oath which we have sworn to them."*

[21]*The leaders said to them,*[a] *"Let them live." Then they became gatherers of firewood and drawers of water for all the congregation,*[b] *just as the chiefs said to them.*

[22]*Joshua called to them and spoke to them, "Why have you deceived us,*[a] *saying, 'We are a long way away from you (pl.),'*[a] *when you (pl.) live right in the vicinity?* [23]*Therefore, you are*

accursed! Servitude shall never be eliminated from you (pl.). Rather, you will be gatherers of firewood and drawers of water[a] for the house[b] of my God."

[24]They answered Joshua and said, "Since it was clearly reported to your servants[a] that Yahweh your God had commanded Moses, his servant, to give to you (pl.) the whole land and to destroy[b] all the inhabitants of the land from your presence, we feared greatly for our lives before you (pl.) so that we have done this thing. [25]Now here we are in your[a] hands. Whatever is good and right in your eyes to do to us, do."

[26]Then he acted accordingly and rescued them from the hand of the sons of Israel and did not kill them. [27]Joshua appointed them that day gatherers of firewood and drawers of water for the congregation[a] and for the altar of Yahweh[b] to the place which he chose until this day.[c]

Notes

1.a. LXX lacks "all," possibly an interpretation in the MT tradition in light of the all-inclusive conquest.

1.b. LXX adds "of the Amorites," using the term for all pre-Israelite occupants. They are then listed after the Hivites as one among many inhabitants at the end of the verse. Here the LXX adds Girgashites (compare Gen 10:16; 15:21; Deut 7:1; Josh 3:10; 24:11).

2.a. LXX understood the Heb. idiom "with one mouth" in a temporal sense. It transposed Josh 8:30–35 here, thus showing Israelite devotion to divine law even in the face of mounting danger and of the Canaanite kings' immediate response to the destruction of Ai. LXX gave an added emphasis on the aliens living among them (see Younger, *Ancient Conquest Accounts,* 377, who still holds the Heb. order to be original).

3.a. LXX reads "Lord" for "Joshua," refusing to give a man credit for divine actions. MT is the superior reading in line with the consistent aim of the book to define Joshua's role and underline his achievement. LXX, Vg., and a few MSS underscore the divine achievement by noting that all that had been done was heard.

4.a. "Very ones" renders גם המה. Younger (*Ancient Conquest Accounts,* 377–78) sees an ironic twist in referring back to what Joshua had done at Jericho and Ai. Having used trickery, the Israelites become victims of deception.

4.b. MT has the *hitpaʿel* of ציר, which occurs nowhere else. The noun derivative is "messenger," so that the verbal root could mean "disguise oneself as a messenger" (Abel; Soggin, 108; Nelson, 122; *Preliminary and Interim Report,* 2:18–19). LXX translates with two terms meaning "to prepare" or more specifically "to prepare food." This appears to witness, with many MSS and versions, to the verb ציד, "to go hunting, to prepare provisions for a hunt," which appears to be the original reading (Fritz, 100), though Nelson (122; compare Barthélemy, *Critique textuelle,* 1:13–14) sees this as an assimiliation to vv 5, 12. Younger (*Ancient Conquest Accounts,* 378) prefers the emended text and interprets וַיִּצְטַיָּרוּ וַיֵּלְכוּ as a hendiadys, "they went as a delegation."

4.c. Confusion in dictation has produced an inner Gk. variant, reading, ὤμων, "shoulders," or ὄνων, "donkeys." There is no reason to change MT.

5.a. The Gk. tradition witnesses a double expression for footware, perhaps reflecting changing fashions in the ancient world.

5.b. For כול, "all," LXX lacks an equivalent but appears to have two equivalents for נקדים, "crumbling" or "moldy" (appearing again only in 1 Kgs 14:3). Nelson (122) says authentic OG does not have doublet for "crumbling." LXX represents an attempt to parallel the reading with v 12, where MT duplicates v 5, but Gk. does not (see Margolis, *Book of Joshua in Greek,* 153–54). Fritz (100) deletes נקדים from v 12 as a gloss.

6.a. LXX reads "to Joshua and to Israel." Here textual history has sought to alleviate problems introduced into the text in its literary development (compare Nelson, 122). "Man of Israel" appears in vv 7–8, while "men" appear in v 14. The Masoretic tradition added "men of Israel" to v 6 to prepare for v 7. LXX then smoothed out tradition by eliminating the role of "man of Israel" altogether and explicitly underscoring the role of Joshua. Other Gk. traditions underscored Israel by reading "all Israel."

7.a. Kethib has a pl. verb form, interpreting "man of Israel" collectively, as is normally the case. Qere suggests sg. reading to secure strict grammatical agreement. LXX changed the subject to "sons" of Israel and so read pl. Manuscript, Targum, and version support can be shown for both Heb. interpretations. Fritz (100) supports Qere.

8.a. *IBHS* 31.3b describes "progressive non-perfective" time reference that represents the situation as ongoing. Thus Joshua sees the Gibeonites as on a journey and not having reached their goal, whereas the Gibeonites see themselves as having reached the goal in their meeting with Joshua. Joshua sees the place of origin for their journey.

9.a. LXX lacks "to him," an addition in MT making the obvious explicit.

9.b. LXX repeats "name," whereas Heb. changes from שֵׁם, "name" to שמע, "reputation." MT represents original tradition.

10.a. LXX lacks "two," perhaps because it was written as β and dropped out before the same letter beginning the following word (Margolis, *Book of Joshua in Greek,* 156; Nelson, 122), or the Heb. tradition may have added it as a common phrase (Deut 3:8, 4:47; Josh 2:10; 24:12).

10.b. The LXX copyist has taken "Amorite" over from the preceding line instead of "Heshbon."

10.c. LXX added the verb "who lived in," which is not necessary, but possible, in Heb. LXX also added "and in Edrei," a popular phrase taken over from Deut 1:4; Josh 12:4; 13:12, 31 (compare Num 21:33; Deut 3:1, 10).

11.a. LXX added the interpretive note "Having heard . . ." Younger (*Ancient Conquest Accounts,* 378) follows MT here, seeing OG as amplification in light of v 10.

12.a. "At our homes" does not appear in LXX and may be amplification in the Heb. tradition.

14.a. A simple transposition has changed Heb. האנשים, "the men," to הנשאים, "the chiefs," in LXX tradition, but this is anticipatory to v 15. Barthélemy (*Critique textuelle,* 1:15) says it is not certain that LXX read הנשיאים here and so supports MT (compare Younger, *Ancient Conquest Accounts,* 378; compare similar error in Judg 8:15). *Preliminary and Interim Report* (2:19) sees a translational adjustment to the text by the Gk. translator.

14.b. The literal translation would be "took from their supplies." This may be interpreted either as eating, based on the evidence of closing a covenant agreement with a meal, or as testing the evidence of the supplies. The latter seems more fitting with the present narrative since the point is that the supplies were old, the food inedible (compare Schmitt, *Du sollst keinen Frieden,* 34–35).

14.c. LXX avoids the anthropomorphic "mouth of Yahweh" (Margolis, *Book of Joshua in Greek,* 159–60; Nelson, 122).

16.a. Williams (*Williams' Hebrew Syntax,* 501) shows that a temporal clause beginning with אהרי indicates something that happened before the main clause.

17.a. LXX lacks the date formula, which may be added in the Heb. in light of similar formulas in Josh 1:11; 2:16; 3:2; 9:16. *Preliminary and Interim Report* (2:19) notes that the two references to three days must not be added together, a warning observed in the translation above.

18.a. LXX reads "all the chiefs," underlining the Israelite commitment. The LXX's reason for omitting "congregation" is not obvious. In v 19, MT has "all," lacking in LXX.

20.a. LXX has introduced a doublet: "having let them live, we will preserve them for ourselves." This is an interpretation of the Heb. inf. absolute construction (compare GKC §113z).

21.a. The opening words are unnecessary in light of v 19 and are omitted by LXX. MT tradition has introduced the verse as a summary, as is shown by the impf. consec. "and then they became," which the versions have changed to the future to incorporate the statement in the quotation. See Nelson, 122–23. Compare *Preliminary and Interim Report* (2:19). Barthélemy (*Critique textuelle,* 1:15–17) provides a long discourse on the history of interpretation and the weak vote of the committee for MT.

21.b. Strong Gk. evidence supports the reading, "for all the congregation" before "just as." This was necessary when the previous sentence was read in the future rather than the past. Compare *Preliminary and Interim Report* (2:19). Syr. introduces the etiological formula "to this day," even while reading the entire quotation as future. This shows how the tradition could insert the etiological formula at a very late date to interpret the material.

22.a. LXX reads sg. pronouns "me" and "you," for the Heb. pls., thus intensifying the role of Joshua as representative of the community.

23.a. LXX makes some radical modifications. "Servitude" is understood as a single servant, so that the description becomes "a hewer of wood," with no reference to drawers of water.

23.b. The anachronistic reference to the temple is observed, resulting in the change to "cutter for me and my God" (see Nelson, 122). Fritz (100) eliminates "gatherers of firewood and drawers of water" as an insertion from v 21. Nelson (123) adopts OG, reading, "there will not be cut off from you a slave, that is a woodcutter," saying MT fills out the formula from vv 21 and 27.

24.a. Williams (*Williams' Hebrew Syntax,* 59) sees a "determinative accusative here with the word following a verb, being the logical subject of the verb and preceded by the accusative marker אֵת. Such an accusative usually lacks concord with the verb and is most often passive. He translates here "what YHWH had commanded . . . was correctly told to your servants."

24.b. LXX dramatizes the scene, adding "us and" as the object of "destroy."

25.a. Reversing the pattern of v 22, LXX has pl. pronouns for MT sg. This continues in v 26a, where LXX pluralizes the verb, before introducing Joshua as explicit subject of "rescued," to which the etiological formula is added.

27.a. LXX continues the pattern of vv 18, 19, and 21 by referring to "all" the congregation. Fritz (100) deletes reference to the congregation as an intrusion brought about by the insertion of vv 18–21.

27.b. LXX has "God" rather than the personal name Yahweh. LXX then introduces Yahweh at the end of the verse where MT has no divine name. Auld should be followed in arguing for LXX originality here ("Joshua," 12–13; compare Fritz, 100; Younger, *Ancient Conquest Accounts,* 379).

27.c. LXX has an explicit etiological statement, "Through this the inhabitants of Gibeon became woodcutters and drawers of water of the altar of God until today." This may well have dropped from the MT through homoioteleuton (C. D. Ginsburg, *Introduction to the Massoretico-Critical Edition of the Hebrew Bible* [London: Trinitarian Bible Society, 1897] 175–76). Nelson (123) calls the addition "an expansion intended to fill out and relieve the awkwardly compacted phraseology" and refers to Margolis, *Book of Joshua in Greek,* 167, as does Younger (*Ancient Conquest Accounts,* 379) with the quote: "The plus was introduced by the Greek translators to mitigate the zeugma."

Form/Structure/Setting

The first two verses of chap. 9 clearly form a transition from the previous section, but they introduce a subject that appears not in chap. 9 but in chap. 10. The larger unit for the editor is thus chaps. 9 and 10. By itself, chap. 9 is a complete narrative with its own purpose, as shown by the concluding formula in v 27. Its character as an independent narrative unit is witnessed also by Josh 10:1–2, which refers back to it. Thus the unit we study here is 9:1–27, recognizing that vv 1–2 represent an introduction to the larger narrative in chaps. 9 and 10. As Winther-Nielsen notes, "The treaty made with Gibeon in Joshua 9 clearly prepares for the following regional wars and thus opens a new unit in the story of conquest."[1133]

Tradition

Coote, along with many others, sees little if any tradition behind the final chapters of the conquest reports in Joshua, calling them "literary compositions rather than historical reports." He bases his claim on the parallels between chaps. 10 and 11 and between these chapters and ancient Near Eastern campaign accounts. The accounts are too lacking in particulars of battle, being marked by "spare formulaic prose of scribal war diaries, royal campaign annals, and monarchic Egyptian

---

1133 *Functional Discourse Grammar,* 163.

'day books.'" These feature "grandiose claims of victories . . . rich only in stereo-typed hyperbole."[1134] In similar mode, Pressler claims the account of chap. 9 "is not historicallly reliable. . . . Both archaeological and textual evidence suggest that Joshua 9 is an ideologically-shaped story, not a historical report" and is "inherently implausible."[1135]

Such claims and expectations are unrealistic for Joshua's day. They look for a non-ideological report that defies human composition and goes against the nature of biblical literature. Such claims force the scholar to push the writing of Joshua forward into a period when Israel possessed the resources and institutions to pro-duce scribes and annals, and day books. Israel produces sparse accounts based on the nature of swift-told tales preserved by master storytellers, not by royal scribes.

Coote likewise compares the social setting of the book of Joshua with that of the Amarna letters and decides "the picture of society in Joshua offers a poor match for the Amarna era" with the mention of iron, too many kings, every town having its own idealized king responsible to no one else.[1136] Likewise, tribes are positively idealized to represent Josiah's policies but correspond to no earlier reality. Coote's picture is built on a negative assumption of the nature of premonarchic Israel and on a scholarly idealization of Josiah. Certainly, later generations and administra-tions could learn much from Joshua, but they did not clone Josiah in the person of Joshua.

Younger uses Assyrian, Hittite, and Egyptian documents to show that chaps. 9–12 reflect the components of ancient campaign accounts. From the Assyrian accounts he isolates a series of "syntagms" and some of their identifying compo-nents, fitting them into all types or genres of Assyrian documents:[1137]

1. Spatio-temporal coordinates
2. Disorder inducing the Assyrian king to act—to rise against, rebel
3. Divine aid
4. Gathering of the troops—to assemble chariots and troops
5. Move from place to place
6. Presence of the terrifying god or king, the siege of the enemy city, the passing of the night—to overwhelm, to fear, to surround
7. Flight of the enemy from the Assyrian king—trust in their own strength, hiding oneself, assembling the troops without fleeing, to escape, to go up, occupy, save one's life
8. Pursuit—after him, after them, to explore
9. Combat
10. Outcome of the combat—to bring about defeat, conquer the city, make a great havoc, description of booty, take hostages or prisoners, to take alive, to deport, take possession of horses, take away their gods, physical destruction of the city
11. Submission—by enemy king with tribute, seizing the feet
12. Exemplary punishment—on enemies who resisted stiffly, flaying alive,

---

1134 Coote, 637–38.
1135 Pressler, 68.
1136 Coote, 637.
1137 *Ancient Conquest Accounts*, 72–79.

impalement, cutting or excising body parts, burning alive, smashing, to scatter, piling up heaps of corpses or heads, removal of corpses

13. Consequences—belong to Assyria, corvée, taxes
14. Acts of celebration—make, inscribe, and erect statue or stele of Assyrian king, founding or reconstructing cities, offerings to the deity
15. Return to base camp or to Assyria with booty and prisoners (seldom used)—to return to camp, to pass the night
16. Supplemental royal activities—killing wild animals, capturing wild animals, cutting down trees
17. Summary statement
18. Geographic note

Younger concludes: "In the Assyrian historical accounts, it is clear that we are dealing with a series of narratives of homologous structure, the product of a single scribal environment over a short period of years (for individual kings)."[1138]

These elements or syntagms form episodes with "a typical structural pattern"; yet "the sequential order may be altered" and each event may represent a virtual beginning.[1139] Thus Younger finds "variations in the structure . . . easily explained in terms of expansion, amplification, replacement, ellipsis, or deletion."[1140] Summary texts or display texts do not show, however, the "iterative scheme" of the annals and may telescope many wars into one year.[1141]

Hittite texts prove to have the same syntagms as the Assyrian with the exceptions of a lack of exemplary punishment, supplemental royal activities, and geographical notes. A "report" is attached at the end. The linguistic keys to each of the elements differ in the two cultures, probably because of differing linguistic bases and different cultural practices. Younger maintains that the Hittite "Ten Year Annals of Muršili II" "were the end product of an editorial process of selection and arrangement of narrative material from a larger corpus of written records" but still form "a literary unity."[1142]

Younger insists that the accounts from the Assyrians, Hittites, and Egyptians were all "figurative accounts" featuring strong rhetorical elements such as hyperbole and metonymy.[1143] He concludes his view of Egyptian conquest accounts: "The Egyptian scribes were selective with their material and constructed their accounts from their particular point of view."[1144] The response at this point is to note that all scribes are "selective with their material and constructed their accounts from their particular point of view."

Returning to Josh 9–12, Younger's discussion leads us to expect heavily formulaic, repetitive language using an editor's choice of content and figurative language to express a particular viewpoint. Younger finds this in 9:1–2, repeated in 9:3, 10:1, and 11:1 with a final resolution in 12:1 and 12:7. He decides that vv 1–2 "produce a

1138 Ibid., 72.
1139 Ibid., 71.
1140 Ibid., 82; cf. 124.
1141 Ibid., 122.
1142 Ibid., 141.
1143 Ibid., 190, 192.
1144 Ibid., 194.

general introduction to the account, with 9:3, 10:1, and 11:1 introducing the particular detailed accounts." Thus he finds a unitary composition in chaps. 9–12.[1145]

The distinctive Hebrew contribution is the dependence on direct speech. "This feature creates a more sophisticated surface to the narrative, but does not necessarily add significant information."[1146] Younger admits that "the syntagmic iterative scheme is encountered primarily in chapters 10 and 11,"[1147] and thus he must find a way to include the framing chapters in his scheme, since "there does not appear to be an exact parallel to the biblical account [chap. 9] in the Assyrian material per se."[1148] He discusses an Assyrian account and two Hittite accounts to illustrate chap. 9.[1149] Finally, he uses the submission code to conclude, "through analogy chapter 9 might be considered as an integral part of the Joshua conquest narratives."[1150]

Several questions must be raised at this point. Is Younger dealing with conquest accounts or with royal wars? The ancient Near Eastern parallels he draws on deal with kings seeking to punish recalcitrant vassals, for the most part, not with a tribal group trying to conquer land to live on. Do the opening and closing formulas or syntagms Younger examines in chaps. 9–12 really demand that the work is a literary unit by one author? Are these unifying elements rather the work of an editor who has chosen several independent, probably oral, narratives and placed them together into a whole? Are syntagms and transmission codes truly the trellis for a biblical account? Are they not rather traditional military language scribes or even storytellers used to relate all types of military actions in all kinds of genres? Furthermore, must not form criticism attempt to define the individual units apparent in a longer campaign narrative, while redaction or literary criticism shows the work of the collector or compiler or editor in tying the narratives into a whole and the narrative critic traces the line of tension through to resolution?

Also, does not the content of chaps. 9–10 tie them together into a larger literary unit even if traditional syntagms are missing in chap. 9? Does discovering smaller literary units break up the narrative of Joshua so much that we must "dismiss it as history writing"?[1151] Or do the smaller units simply point to original oral materials and to form-critical units within those oral stories so that one can reach beyond the literary editor to see the historical components available for composition using the syntagms and other traditional linguistic tools available in Israelite and to an extent in ancient Near Eastern culture? Should one speak of editorial activity on the one hand and then dismiss the work of redactors?[1152] Finally, one might ask how many times one may repeat the same syntagm with effect before it becomes trite and is ignored.[1153]

Younger derives an Israelite ideology from his study, underlining the contrast of comrades and the enemy, the use of terror tactics to soften up enemies, and a

---

1145 Ibid., 197–98.
1146 Ibid., 198.
1147 Ibid., 199.
1148 Ibid., 201.
1149 Ibid., 201–3.
1150 Ibid., 204.
1151 Ibid., 204.
1152 Ibid., 141, 232.
1153 Ibid., 233.

stress on revenge. All these have parallels in other ancient Near Eastern cultures. Ultimately, he can conclude, "it would appear that the conquest account in Joshua 9–12 evinces the same basic ideology as one sees in other ancient Near Eastern conquest accounts."[1154] Hess, however, finds "no precise parallels" to this account in the ancient Near East. Still "major parts of the text do have their correspondent in the annals of the great powers of the ancient world."[1155]

I would like to modify Younger's conclusion. First, Younger's detailed attention to "transmission codes" within chaps. 9–12 might well turn out quite differently had he included chaps. 1–8 in his analysis. Then he would have found greater appreciation for, rather than denial of, the truth in Brueggemann's references to different types of communication employed by egalitarian Israel and the imperial nations of kings. W. Brueggemann rightly refers to "narratives of a playful kind."[1156]

Second, Younger's descriptions of warfare and practicing war depend on the linguistic limits and the technological capabilities of a culture. Israel's land seekers stood far distanced in culture from the culturally and technologically superior nations. Still, in a broad sense Israel did not live in isolation but belonged to the cultural milieu of the ancient Near East. One would expect to find Israel using the same terminology and technology to describe and conduct war.

At least since B. Albrektson's work we have known of similar language and ideology expressed by Israel and her neighbors.[1157] However, just because Israel shares much vocabulary with her neighbors does not mean we should not talk of holy war. But G(g)od-caused holy-war panic—Israelite or Assyrian—still differs from modern fear and panic in war.

Similarly, pursuit is one episode of any depiction of a victorious campaign.[1158] But it is also a literary styntagm or element. When repeated and/or placed in emphatic parts of the narrative, this literary usage becomes an author's tool to present an important part of the message. It is not just a note in passing. Pursuit is an opportunity to see God at work winning victories. It becomes an important literary theme, not just a repetitive syntagm.

"In Joshua 9 the ban is perceived as an act of justice; its purpose is to ensure Israel a pure environment, free from the influences of polytheistic cults. In contrast Joshua 6 presents the ban primarily as an act of sacrifice in which Israel devotes the first fruits of Canaan to the Lord."[1159] The elements of holy war came to Israel from her neighbors, possibly from her predecessors as inhabitants of Canaan. Israel found several ways to utilize the ban theme from holy-war tradition to apply to specific situations.

Israel in its "conquest days" did not have the institutional structures to maintain annals and daily reports and diaries of its actions. Israel until the Solomonic days probably relied on oral storytellers to preserve its historical memories. In this sense,

---

1154 Ibid., 236.
1155 Hess (2009) 40.
1156 *Revelation and Violence: A Study in Contextualization* (Milwaukee: Marquette UP, 1986) 38, cited by Younger, *Ancient Conquest Accounts*, 254–55.
1157 *History and the Gods: An Essay on the Idea of Historical Events as Divine Manifestations in the Ancient Near East and in Israel*, ConBOT 1 (Lund: Gleerup, 1967).
1158 Younger, *Ancient Conquest Accounts*, 260.
1159 Creach, 87.

Israel's ideology is not a royal, imperialistic ideology. It is an ideology of warfare that can be expressed only through the language, culture, and technology of its day. Such tools of expression are not necessarily limited to a royal, imperial form of government. An upstart, loosely-knit society of settlers can also use the common vocabulary of war to describe its military actions. Such descriptions have ideological components and functions, but they do not reach the grand international scale of the royal battles of Assyria, the Hittites, and Egypt. Nor do the new settlers have the government organization and institutions available to the international powers to preserve the information.

Israel's unique contribution comes in the biblical writers' understanding of Yahweh as the only necessary God for all facets of life and in the oral form of conversation and dialogue to preserve the tradition. Israelite writers tie warfare syntagms to obedience to Torah and revelation. Such obedience elements were surely tied to warfare elements of language while Israel retained its own independent systems of religion and justice.[1160]

Chap. 9 consists of two narratives—vv 3–15 and 16–27— which have been editorially tied together.[1161] Nelson notes "a complicated history of composition" but then admits "a completely satisfying explanaton for these irregularities is impossible."[1162] He also writes, "the concepts of Deuteronomy are not required to make this story work. Violence against the local population is obviously part of the pre-deuteronomistic plot of Joshua."[1163] Nelson points to Exod 23:32; 34:12 to show that agreements such as the one made here with the Gibeonites were part of the pre-Deuteronomic law.[1164]

Younger claims his work "seriously questions the prevailing opinion that the section [Josh 9–12] is a composite of many different independent traditions."[1165] He calls the section "a narrative unity exhibiting a typical ancient Near Eastern transmission code commonly employed in the history writing of conquest accounts."[1166] At the same time he concedes, "obviously, the writer utilized source material (war reports, diaries (?), the Book of Yashar, etc.) so that in one sense separate accounts were collected."[1167] Utilizing source material makes the conquest account composite, so his only real argument is against the "long time period." But a period of time is precisely what is required to explain the preservation of the materials.

The unity comes then from the editorial artistry found especially in the introduction and conclusion that are the major elements Younger uses to argue for unity in chaps. 9–12. My conclusion in a way simply uses different terminology from that Younger uses. Both of us see a collection of materials put into a holistic report by a writer using language and technology and cultural practices of the ancient Near East to create a final report. My work emphasizes the development process behind the sources, while Younger emphasizes the unifying work of the final writer.

The summary statements on which Younger lays so much emphasis as the sign of unity come from the final editor and do not determine how many sources the

---

1160 See *Comments* on 1:7–8.
1161 Cf. Halbe, *VT* 25 (1975) 629–30.
1162 Nelson, 123.
1163 Ibid., 124, n. 2.
1164 Ibid., 126.
1165 *Ancient Conquest Accounts*, 242.
1166 Ibid.
1167 Ibid., 321, n. 1.

editor has used or how much of the "syntagmatic" language comes from the writer and how much comes from the sources collected to create the campaign account. All the while, the nature of conquest used in Younger's title and the nature of conquest by Israel remain two separate kinds of wars, one initiated by a major king controlling many vassals and military resources and the other by a military upstart with few resources seeking to conquer a land and settle it.

In the end, I agree with Younger at one significant point: "Whether the author of the biblical text was an eyewitness or not need not effect our decision concerning whether it is history or not."[1168] In some sense the oral stories of Joshua do go back to eyewitnesses, not to exilic creators of a new Israelite identity. But the form of the stories preserved and transmitted results from the artistic rendering of generations of storytellers and compilers.

Source and Redaction

Israelite tradition developed a two-part narrative. The opening part of the story is not told from Israel's perspective. Rather it reflects Gibeon's.[1169] They laugh at Israel, the mighty military power who allows a foreign army into the midst of its camp (v 6). There the all-victorious commander receives them and gives them the customary military order for name, rank, and serial number (v 8), yet never receives an answer in any explicit terms (v 9a).

On the other hand, the commands of the Gibeonite elders (v 11) are followed to the letter (vv 6, 8). Gullible Israel immediately accepts the evidence and takes their provisions (v 14). Here a play on Hebrew words in v 14 allows for an understanding that the Israelites both accepted the provisions as evidence and ate them (compare above, *Note* 14.b).[1170] Such eating can symbolize acceptance of the strangers into the camp and provide a basis for temporary protection.[1171] This not being enough, Israel makes a permanent treaty with them, something always done in the name of the god(s), but Israel never turned to inquire of her own God (v 14b). Joshua made peace, as the leaders swore an oath to let the enemy soldiers live.

History changed things fast. Solomon enslaved the foreigners in his kingdom (1 Kgs 9:20–21; compare Ezra 2:43–58; Neh 7:46–60).[1172] The people of Israel took over the story and used it to explain the new situation. To do so, they added their own ending, preserved in vv 16–21.[1173]

The second half of the narrative shows Israel's perspective when the truth is revealed (v 16) so that Israel pursues the Gibeonites, realizing they could not do battle because they had sworn in Yahweh's name that they would not do so. Internal grumbling led to a plan B, turning the enemies into permanent servants of Israel's temple. With Gibeon's pool (2 Sam 2:13) and its alliance with a town named Beeroth, "wells," the assignment to water duty appears to be suitable if ironic punishment.[1174]

1168 Ibid., 250.
1169 Cf. Hertzberg, 68; Gray, 97.
1170 Cf. Hertzberg, 67.
1171 Cf. Halbe, *VT* 25 (1975) 620, n. 50.
1172 Haran, *VT* 11 (1961) 159–69.
1173 See Nelson, 127–28.
1174 Harstad, 379.

"The two parts of the story fit nicely together in present form, with verses 16–27 forming the natural sequel to verses 3–15,"[1175] while the second section "could never have constituted an independent story" since it relies "on vv 3–15 to provide background and narrative tension."[1176]

Knauf sees the D tradition as setting the problem or crisis in the chapter and the P tradition providing the solution.[1177] The language points Knauf to editors later than the P tradition of the Pentateuch. Pitkänen appears more in line when he argues for an early, integral place for "P" elements of the story, with a Deuteronomistic writer integrating the P elements into the story.[1178]

Briend begins his study with chap. 9 and its unique references to the "man of Israel," which provide Briend the clue to the original source prior to a "Joshua redactor" who knew chaps. 6–8.[1179] A Deuteronomistic redactor inserted his "rhetoric of conquest" in vv 1–2, 9–10, 16, 17, 24a, 26, and 27; a second Dtr hand inserts centralization language in v 27b; and a Priestly editor adds vv 15, 18–21, 27 (community).

In my understanding, the ultimate historian uses the two parts of the traditional materials, especially utilizing the two references to the etiological formula (vv 26–27) to show the greatness of Joshua.[1180] The final verses are not the only contribution of the historian. He has also expanded the confession of faith in the opening narrative with his own particular interests (vv 9bβ–10).

Form

Knauf refers to the narrative as an example story (*Beispielerzählung*) that explains the position of Gibeon among Israel, a position of treaty partner protected by the might of Israel's army.[1181] The basic Gibeonite narrative does not employ a narrative pattern. Rather, it depends on a legal pattern, that of gaining revenge for a crime through cursing, a pattern found also in Gen 4:9–16.[1182] Guilt is established through a question (v 22) that uses the language of both narratives. The verdict is given in the form of a curse (v 23a) and sentence (v 23b). The convicted criminals do not appeal the verdict (compare Gen 4:13–14) but submit to it (vv 24–25). The narrative has no etiological formulas, yet functions etiologically.[1183]

Finally (v 22), Joshua examines the enemy witnesses and pronounces sentence against them (v 23). The Gibeonites use Israel's confession of salvation history to explain why they did what they have done and then accept their sentence. Joshua then imposes the sentence, stated in the form of etiologies.

1175 Creach, 85; cf. Nelson, 128.
1176 Nelson, 127.
1177 Knauf, 92.
1178 Pitkänen, 207.
1179 "Sources of the Deuteronomic History," 361.
1180 See Geoghegan, *Time, Place, and Purpose*, 122.
1181 Knauf, 93.
1182 Cf. Halbe, *VT* 25 (1975) 623–24.
1183 Ibid., 628.

Structure and Form of Joshua 9

Structure: Ruse narrative and trial				Genre: Negotiation story and etiology		
Element	Passage	Marker		Element	Passage	Marker
Editorial introduction: Kings unite against Israel	vv 1–2	Temporal clause		Editorial introduction	vv 1–2	Temporal clause
Exposition: (pf. or disjunctive)	v 3	Disjunctive with perfect		The ruse	vv 3–5	Disjunctive; deceptively
Complication (impf. consec.): Gibeonite ruse	vv 4–5	Impf. consec.		The offer	v 6	Claim of travel; request for covenant
				Examination of witness	v 7	Opposing proposition
				Defendants surrender	v 8a	Surrender speech
				Renewed examination of witness (defendant)	v 8b	Interrogative
				Defendants' testimony	vv 9–13	Personal situation; Israel's salvation history
				Treaty made	vv 14–15	Ate provisions without God; made a treaty; swore an oath
Change or crisis (speech or dialogue): treaty negotiation	vv 6–13	Dialogue		Counter testimony unveiled	v 16	Truth discovered
				Pursuit	v 17	Israel pursues
				Attack prevented by oath	v 18a	Oath in divine name
				Community response	v 18b	Murmuring
Resolution (impf. consec.): Agreement made without consulting God	v 14	Impf. consec.		Leaders' response with counter plan	vv 19–21a	Let guilty live because of oath
Ending/ denouement (formulaic): Joshua makes peace	v 15	Formulaic		Verdict	v 21b	Serve the community

Structure: Ruse narrative and trial			Genre: Negotiation story and etiology		
Element	Passage	Marker	Element	Passage	Marker
Renewed exposition: Ruse uncovered	v 16	Temporal clause	Joshua's cross-examination and sentence	vv 22–23	Slaves for God's house
Complication (impf. consec.): Israel pursues deceivers but cannot attack	vv 17–18	Impf. consec.	Admission of guilt	vv 24–25	We heard so we did; passive sentence
Change or crisis (speech or dialogue): Decision to let Gibeonites live	vv 19–21	Dialogue	Sentence enforced	vv 26–27	Installed as temple slaves; etiology
Resolution (impf. consec.): Verdict delivered and accepted	vv 22–25	Impf. consec. and dialogue verdict			
Ending/ denouement (formulaic): Punishment enforced	vv 26–27	Formulaic language: etiology			

Structure

Chaps. 9–10 join chap. 11 to "expand the horizons of the book's action. Whereas previously, Israel's opposition came from individual cities, now it came from coalitions of cities."[1184] Knauf sees the final form of this chapter as critical of the ban theology and so places its writing between his Hexateuch redaction and his final redaction.[1185] The material, for Knauf, began as a brief notice in the Exodus-Joshua narrative, tying chap. 6 to chap. 10. This underscores Knauf's dedication to finding a theology opposing the ban a dominant theme in Joshua.

The first unit comprises vv 3–15. The disjunctive clause (v 3) is a typical narrative introduction setting forth the point of view of the Gibeonites, who react to the startling victories of Israel over their neighbors. Imperfect consecutives in vv 4–6a build up the narrative tension around the deception of the Gibeonites. Dialogue then takes over to form the narrative climax. This climbs slowly to its height in v 14, where the tension is resolved. Israel has fallen for the deception without inquiring of Yahweh. The denouement appears in typical imperfect consecutive, formulaic fashion in v 15. Gibeon has received life. But still "the Gibeonite ruse remains undiscovered."[1186]

As so often in biblical Hebrew, a temporal clause opens the second narrative

---

1184 Howard, 218.
1185 Knauf, 90.
1186 Nelson, 126.

beginning in verse 16 and introduces the point of tension—a covenant with neighbors, not foreigners (v 16b). Imperfect consecutives build up narrative tension (vv 17–18) and reverse the direction of march from the earlier narrative (compare v 6). Dialogue forms the climax (vv 18b–21a) and centers on the point of tension, the covenant with neighbors. The extended dialogue places Israel in a real dilemma. It cannot follow the law and kill them (Deut 7:2; Exod 34:12a; compare Deut 20:16–18), since it has made a covenant with them. Israel must preserve them alive, and yet they must know once and for all Israel's superiority. Finally, the plan evolves (v 21) and is carried out (vv 22–27).

Setting

When and where would such a story be told? Fritz argues that we cannot recognize any evidence of editorial work on an older tradition (*Überlieferung*) so we must conclude that the narrative cannot be seen as old; thus Fritz attributes the narrative to the Deuteronomistic Historian.[1187] We gain hints from 2 Sam 21:1–4 that send us in another direction. In the days of Saul and David, the Gibeonites exerted their own pressures and enjoyed their own privileges. This was too much for Saul, so he tried to exterminate them, only later to have Gibeon gain revenge on his family. Gibeon then served as a major sanctuary for the nation until Solomon completed the Jerusalem temple (1 Kgs 3:4–5). Quite likely in the period of prosperity under David, the Gibeonites would have used this story to illustrate their superiority over their politically superior neighbors. Its earlier origin appears from the "tribal democracy" reflected in the predominate use of the collective "man of Israel."[1188]

The final composition in chap. 9 is thus composed of three units, each with its own setting and purpose, yet the three have been combined into a remarkable whole. The first section reports the trickery of the Gibeonites, setting them in a bad light through the following context, while picturing Joshua as a peacemaker (v 15a). The second unit (vv 16–21) concerns only Israel. The Gibeonites are referred to but never appear. Nor does Joshua. Israel decides its fate. Joshua then appears as mediator to announce the verdict to the Gibeonites, while protecting them from the Israelites (v 26). This is the peaceful conclusion to the desperate battle begun under Saul and David and brought to a climax under Solomon. Insertion in Josh 2–11 (12) showed the Gibeonite story as another form of victory for Israel and their God over the native inhabitants of the land. Eventually the historian used the narrative to show the leadership of Joshua and the guilt of Gibeon.

Comments

The scene of action widens unexpectedly. No longer does Israel face simply one city-state and its army. She has become so important that coalitions are formed against her. The threat presented by Israel is pictured as being so great that it forces the racially diversified former enemies to join together against Israel. Yet they do so without the fear and panic previous enemies have shown. "No longer are the Canaanites cowed by the Israelites."[1189]

1187 Fritz, 101–2.
1188 Nelson, 127.
1189 Hess, 175.

1 The expression "beyond the Jordan" here refers to the area west of the Jordan, as the following description shows. The more usual referent is the area east of the Jordan as in v 10. Of the nineteen lists of nations, only Deut 20:17 corresponds to this one.[1190] "These verses (1–2) portray the ultimate issue: that Israel lays claim to the whole land and is therefore in conflict with all its peoples."[1191]

The geographical description includes only the southern part of the country and the Mediterranean coast, preparing for the conquest summary in Josh 10:40, where the list is expanded to include the southern Negev but does not include the coastal plain up to Lebanon. The many lists in Joshua "all have a similar literary function, while differing in particular details. . . . [They] serve as a constant reminder of the presence of the enemy."[1192]

The root שָׁמַע (šĕmaʿ), "hear," "creates a narrative structure that connects the stories. It recalls an earlier stage in the narrative and, simultaneously, introduces the next stage, which serves to keep up pace" (see Josh 2:10, 11; 5:1; 7:9; 9:1, 3, 9, 16; 10:1; 11:1; 22:11–12).[1193] This linguistic theme of hearing (שמע) often introduces enemy kings into the narrative and marks the beginning of a new narrative, often introduced by the editor to create a framework for the narratives. Hearing leads to the nations fearing, while Israel sees what God has done and knows.[1194] The goal appears to be for foreigners and the nations to know God (Josh 2:9–11; 4:24).

2 The editor makes two points in the second verse. The kings were unanimous, and they fought against Joshua as well as Israel. Again the role of Joshua is highlighted.

Hawk repeatedly emphasizes that from this point the initiative moves from Israel to the enemy kings. For Hawk, the narrator "attempts to redirect the stark brutality of Israel's conquests by suggesting that Israel had to fight in order to defend itself against the belligerent kings of Canaan."[1195] This is one more ingenuous way to attempt to shift blame away from Israel for its violence.

The kings were only protecting their homeland from the strong military onslaught of Israel. Israel's aim is never anything less than conquering the entire country. Israel is not fighting a defensive war trying to make the enemy armies retreat to their home bases. Rather, Israel is pursuing the foreign kings to the borders of the "Promised Land." The enemies' fearful initiative only mirrors Israel's military prowess and the overwhelming power of Israel's God.

3 Not everyone joined the coalition. Joshua's reputation caused part of the population to attempt devious means to escape the Israelite threat. Gibeon is identified with el-Jib, five and a half miles (nine kilometers) northwest of Jerusalem in the territory of Benjamin (Josh 18:25) and seven miles southwest of Ai. Pritchard's excavations revealed extensive occupation in Early Bronze I (ca. 3150–2850), Middle Bronze II (2000–1750), and early Iron Age I (1200–1150), when the first city wall was built.[1196] The peak of prosperity came in Iron Age II (1000–586). Fritz leaves

---

1190 Blenkinsopp, *CBQ* 28 (1966) 207.
1191 McConville and Williams, 47.
1192 Mitchell, *Together in the Land*, 126.
1193 Ibid., 143.
1194 Ibid., 145–46.
1195 Hess (2010) 103.
1196 "Gibeon's History," 8–12.

open the questions of occupation in the Late Bronze Age and in the period after Solomon.[1197] Bimson finds no evidence for a Late Bronze settlement and so uses Gibeon as evidence for redating the conquest.[1198] For recent archaeological findings, refer to Pitkänen.[1199] Hess looks to further excavation and to Late Bronze tombs to suggest the possibility of Late Bronze occupation at Gibeon.[1200]

Knauf sees Gibeon as a city *in* Israel but not a city *of* Israel.[1201] Rather, for Knauf, Gibeon before the time of Saul was not a strong enough political entity to carry out war.[1202] Nor was Gibeon a Canaanite royal city. Instead, a citizens' assembly directed the town. It was larger than Jerusalem and relatively independent from both Judah and Israel. The picture of the Gibeonites in chap. 9 is based, for Knauf, on their status at the time of the Second Temple. In the First Temple period they were anything but drawers of water and gatherers of firewood. This is simply one of the several assumptions that leads Knauf to push all the Joshua materials to a late dating without true historical foundations.

4–5 The Gibeonites thus acted with "cunning." The verbal form of the root ערם occurs five times in the OT, being applied by Saul to David in 1 Sam 23:22 in a two-sided meaning. From Saul's perspective it is a bad characteristic, while from the narrator's it is admirable. The term is cast in a bad light in Job 5:13 and Ps 83:4, while a good connotation appears in Prov 15:5 and 19:25. Outside our passage the adjective occurs four times, negatively in Exod 21:14 but positively in Prov 1:4; 8:5, 12. Double entendre is used in our passage as in 1 Samuel. From the Gibeonite point of view, they were quite wise in what they did, whereas the Israelites saw their actions as deceptive and wrong. The modern reader tends to take the Israelite perspective so that "contemporary readers may need some help to comprehend the worldview that could see such trickery as laudable."[1203] For the language here, compare Deut 29:5, 11.[1204]

Knauf finds the Gibeonites playing their roles too well to be believable and notes that meal, not bread, would be taken on a long journey.[1205] This makes it improbable that Joshua and Israel's leaders should not have seen through the Gibeonite charade. Knauf thus joins chaps. 2 and 9 to conclude that Joshua accepted almost any reason not to carry out the oath of destruction. Hawk emphasizes the theme of disobedience: "By shaping the story of the Gibeonite emissaries according to this Deuteronomic text, the narrative expresses the opposing plot of disobedience and once again disrupts movement toward fulfillment." For the narrator, no word of either condemnation or reconciliation comes forth at this time. It is not that the narrator "represses the sense of Israel's disobedience once again."[1206] Rather, the Gibeonite episode in chap. 9 becomes the occasion for the defeat of the southern kings in chap. 10.

1197 Fritz, 102.
1198 *Redating*, 205–6.
1199 Pitkänen, 214–16.
1200 Hess (2009) 41–42.
1201 Knauf, 90.
1202 Ibid., 97.
1203 Creach, 84.
1204 See Hess, *Every Promise Fulfilled*, 88–89.
1205 Knauf, 91–92, 93.
1206 Ibid., 90.

6 Israel is located back at Gilgal rather than Shechem as in Josh 8:30–35. The story is thus tied to the earlier narratives of the book. While this does not show that the story itself originated or was used in the sanctuary at Gilgal, the possibility cannot be totally excluded. Howard sees this location as requiring a twenty-five- to thirty-mile journey and so suggests a location nearer Ebal and Gerizim for another village named Gilgal.[1207]

Kotter assumes the traditional location near Jericho and equates this location with that mentioned in Deut 11:29–30.[1208] Hess, however, points to El-'unuq east of Shechem as a possible location for a second Gilgal.[1209] I concur with Hubbard's judgment that "the book seems everywhere to presuppose the same well-known Gilgal."[1210]

The Gibeonites claim to have come from "an extremely distant land." They seek a treaty with Joshua and the Israelites (literally, the man of Israel). "To the unwary Israelites the Gibeonites must have seemed to fit the Mosaic rules for the treatment of distant enemies quite precisely (Deut. 20:10–15). The only way they differed from Moses' scenario is that the Gibeonites came to Israel seeking peace while Moses legislated for circumstances when Israel was on the verge of attacking a distant enemy, but first offered it peace for forced labor (Deut. 20.10, 11)."[1211]

The term, the "man of Israel" (אִישׁ יִשְׂרָאֵל) is introduced here (see *Note* 6.a) and has driven numerous attempts to find parallel sources.[1212] Such attempts have failed to note the two distinct narrative structures (9:1–15; 9:16–27), while being unable to find complete parallel accounts. The expression "man of Israel" is a collective (a judgment to which Fritz, 103, and Howard, 224, agree) often referring to the Israelite army (Judg 7:23; 9:55; 20:11–48; 1 Sam 13:6; 14:22; 17:2, 19–25; 2 Sam 17:24; 23:9). A military undertone may be present in all uses of the term, but a few passages (Judg 8:22; 21:1; 2 Sam 16:18; 17:14; 19:42–44) may support Schmitt's contention that the expression represents more clearly than others the democratic element in Israel's society.[1213] Sutherland finds it to be the marker of the original oral story based in Gilgal and referring to the military in Benjamin. Schmitt could be correct in saying that the expression is used in the early years of the monarchy and then again in Deuteronomistic literature, though the understanding of what constitutes Deuteronomistic literature is still debated.

Hall suggests two possibilities.[1214] These men of Israel are a narrative device to take away some of Joshua's guilt, or they belong to Israel's authentic historical political scene. The first alternative is dismissed because the writer does not completely erase Joshua's part in the guilt. This passage, joined with Josh 22, may indicate that the "man of Israel" had the responsibility for such negotiations.

In Josh 9 the expression "man of Israel" appears only in vv 6–7 and represents

---

1207 Howard, 224; cf. Hess (1996) 178.
1208 *ABD*, 2:1022.
1209 Hess (2009) 42.
1210 Hubbard, 284, n. 11.
1211 Kissling, *Reliable Characters*, 91.
1212 Cf. the attempts by Schmitt, *Du sollst keinen Frieden*, 30–37, and Otto, *Mazzotfest*, 89–92; Sutherland, *JSOT* 53 (1992) 65–74.
1213 *Du sollst keinen Frieden*, 38. See also Knauf, 92, who equates the collective with Israel's elders.
1214 *Conquering Character*, 158–59.

the work of tradition history in joining the narrative of vv 3–15 with that of vv 16–21 and shifting blame away from Joshua. In so doing, the tradition shows that Israel, not Joshua, violated the ancient law of Exod 34:12. Hubbard, however, puts blame on Joshua here and in chap. 7 for taking initiatives that produce "problematic results."[1215] The ultimate historian read this in light of Deut 20:15–18. "The people of the promised land were too dangerous to Israel by their very presence, by their different religious practices, for them to be offered terms of peace."[1216]

The Hivites are not documented in extrabiblical texts and may reflect early linguistic confusion with the Horites or Hurrians.[1217] Fritz simply states, "Origin and meaning of the name are not known."[1218] Crawford suggests that the Hivites inhabited the central and northern hill country of Palestine, in locales as far north as Lebo-Hamath (Judg 3:3), down to Shechem (Gen 34:2), Gibeon (Josh 9:3, 7), and environs (2 Sam 24:7).[1219] Esau's marriage to a Hivite (Gen 36:2) suggests connections with Edom as well.

In the Shechem massacre (Gen 34) and the Gibeonites' ruse (Josh 9), the Hivites represent a group with whom the Israelites make covenants that are soon broken when one of the parties acts deceitfully. At Shechem, circumcision forms the cultural barrier between Israel and the Shechemites/Hivites. In the Gibeon narrative, the Hivites trick Joshua and the Israelites into thinking that they have traveled from a distant land and thereby secure a peace treaty. In Josh 9:27, the trickery found out, Joshua appoints them as woodcutters and water drawers for the sanctuary as a punishment for their deception. Later, they are part of Solomon's conscripted slave labor for his building projects (1 Kgs 9:20).

The LXX calls into question the Hebrew evidence for the Hivites. In the Greek of Gen 34:2, Hamor is not a Hivite but a Horrite, as are the inhabitants of Gibeon in Josh 9. In Josh 11:19, the Hebrew notes that the Hivites were spared because of the pact of Josh 9, while the LXX registers no such report. This discrepancy has prompted a debate over whether the Hivites are a distinct ethnic group or the term is merely a corruption of "Horrite." Orthographic similarity in the Hebrew forms is likely at the heart of the confusion. Scholars have had difficulty connecting the Hivites with any extrabiblical group. Some hold that they are connected somehow with the Hurrians because of the LXX evidence (above).

Crawford points out that the word Hivite is etymologically connected with the Achaeans known from Homer's *Iliad*. Crawford then points to a similar, more plausible connection between the Hivites and Cilicia (southeastern Turkey) on the basis of Egyptian, Akkadian, and Luwian terms for Cilicia. This connection suggests that the Hivite homeland was located in the northeastern Mediterranean, and that some moved down into northern Palestine.[1220]

1215 Hubbard, 278.
1216 Auld, 65.
1217 E. A. Speiser, "Hivite," *IDB*, 2:615; R. North, "The Hivites," *Bib* 54 (1973) 43–62.
1218 Fritz, 103.
1219 *NIDB*, 2:831.
1220 See Baruch Halpern, "Gibeonite Israelite Diplomacy," 303–16; M. Margalith, "The Hivites." *ZAW* 100 (1988) 60–70; N. Na'aman, "The Conquest of Canaan in the Book of Joshua and History." In *From Nomadism to Monarchy: Archaeological and Historical Aspects of Early Israel*. Ed. I. Finkelstein and N. Na'aman. Jerusalem: Israel Exploration Society, (1994): 218–81.

Originally at home in Armenia, the Hivites travelled far and wide in the ancient Near East between ca. 2200 and 1000 BCE. They entered Syria-Palestine early enough for Hivite groups to be among the "native" population when the Israelites entered the land. The Bible connects them especially with Shechem (Gen 34:2), Gibeon (Josh 11:19), and the northern mountains (Judg 3:3; Josh 11:3).[1221] Howard points to Exod 34:11, Deut 20:17, and Josh 3:10 to credit the narrator with providing his own evaluation of the Hivites in Gibeon as among those supposed to be destroyed, and certainly not to become treaty partners of Israel.[1222]

The expression כרת ברית ל, "to make a covenant agreement with," refers to an agreement between an overlord and his vassals.[1223] Such an agreement would place obligations on the vassals with promises given by the overlord.[1224] The treaty would be sealed with an oath, equivalent to a self-curse and would seek to establish peace between the two parties (compare v 15). In Joshua's context the reference would be to the political treaty by which Gibeon obtained favored status while living among the people of Israel. It would presuppose a time when Israel had sufficient power to be in a political position to be the overlord of a political treaty. Deuteronomy would negate the treaty as a covenant with foreign nations forbidden by the law (Deut 7:2) and in conflict with the covenant tying Israel as a vassal to Yahweh, its divine overlord (Deut 7:4).

8 The Gibeonites use the polite language of ancient Near Eastern diplomacy by referring to themselves as Joshua's servants. The later tradition understood the term literally as referring to the servile status of the Gibeonites over against Israel. Howard contrasts the Gibeonites' use of the Hebrew בוא, "to come," in the perfect tense (v 6) with Joshua's use in the imperfect tense (v 8) to reflect a misunderstanding.[1225] The Gibeonites say they have arrived at a stopping place while Joshua asks from where they are coming as they pass through on their way.

9 The divine promise is again seen at work, as the inhabitants of the land tremble in fear before Yahweh and his great reputation (compare Josh 2:9; 5:1). God continues to do his part. The writer has taken the opportunity to give content to the confession in vv 9b–10. For the original collector, the fame of Yahweh rested on his victories over Jericho and Ai, but for the historian the victories in Egypt and the Transjordan formed the basis for Yahweh's reputation. Harstad suggests that the cunning Gibeonites do not mention recent victories at Jericho and Ai so as not to reveal their acquaintance with nearby happenings when they claim to come from so far.[1226]

10–13 As often occurs in Hebrew narrative, a historical flashback repeats or paraphrases what has already been narrated (compare vv 4–5). The Gibeonite travelers claim to be legitimate representatives of their people, commissioned by

---

1221 See further, Speiser, "Hurrians," *IDB*, 2:664–66; H. A. Hoffner, "The Hittites and Hurrians," in *Peoples of Old Testament Times*, ed. D. J. Wiseman (Oxford: Oxford UP, 1973) 221–28; F. W. Bush, "Hurrians," *IDBSup*, 423–24; D. W. Baker, "Hivites," *ABD*, 3:234; C. D. Crawford, *NIBD*, 2:831.
1222 Howard, 225.
1223 Cf. M. Weinfeld, "ברית," *TWAT*, 1:784; Knauf, 92.
1224 Cf. E. Kutsch, *Verheissung und Gesetz*, BZAW 131 (Berlin: De Gruyter, 1973) 53.
1225 Howard, 225.
1226 Harstad, 386.

the ruling elders and all the citizens. They thus reveal a political system similar to Israel's, not one with a city-state king.[1227] Israel makes a covenant not with the political authorities but with representatives whose only credentials are their own testimony and their dilapidated condition. Howard refutes the idea that Israel sat down to a covenant-ratifying meal. Instead, he maintains "the Israelites took from the Gibeonites' provisions in order to inspect them, to confirm the Gibeonites' words."[1228] One may wonder, however, if the writer did not intend, in ironic fashion, to plant the idea of a covenant meal in the minds of the readers.

14 The climactic verse condemns Israel for not following the normal pattern of seeking the divine will before making such an agreement.[1229] "As with Ai, the Israelites are deceived when they rely upon their own perceptions rather than upon divine direction."[1230] From the Gibeonite point of view, this represented the superiority of Gibeonite cunning. For the biblical narrator, it was Israel's sin. "The Gibeonites have acknowledged YHWH and claim that YHWH's deeds have drawn them to Israel. But the Israelites seem for the moment to have forgotten YHWH."[1231] "The narrative now intimates that responsibility for dealing with the pact and its consequences lies with the Israelite leaders. In this manner the text safeguards Joshua's character as a leader zealous for carrying out the Mosaic commands to annihilate the Canaanites. (The leaders, not Joshua, make the decision to spare them.)"[1232]

15 Quite surprisingly, this verse apparently condemns Joshua. Hall notes that "Joshua's role in this oversight and the degree of his responsibility for Israel's neglect is less clear. . . . He does not deliberately violate the law. . . . Any responsibility he does bear is shared by others."[1233] One may question Hall's contention that Joshua did not seek the will of God because he was accustomed to Yahweh initiating encounters and speaking directly with Yahweh.[1234] Such a crucial moment was a time to seek God. Even Israel without Joshua did that (Judg. 1:1). McConville and Williams suggest that the "alternation of agents . . . is scarcely to protect Joshua from blame, but rather to signify a certain division and lack of purposeful leadership."[1235] Sutherland sees Joshua as the marker of a supplemental layer to the "man of Israel" tradition, setting up an example of the king consulting with the representatives of the people as in the days of Josiah (following Nelson).[1236]

Joshua makes the covenant and establishes peace. The verse makes sense only on Gibeonite tongues, where the authority of Joshua is claimed for Gibeonite privileges. The later editor counterbalances this through the addition of vv 22–27, where v 15 gives reason for Joshua's curse. V 15b is the literary link by which vv 16–21 are joined to the preceding narrative by introducing the chiefs of the

---

1227 Knauf, 93.
1228 Howard, 226.
1229 Cf. L. Eslinger, *Into the Hands of the Living God*, JSOTSup 84 (Sheffield: Sheffield UP, 1989) 24–54.
1230 Hess 180; cf. Hall, *Conquering Character*, 153.
1231 Hess (2000) 143.
1232 Ibid., 146.
1233 *Conquering Character*, 156–57.
1234 Iibd., 157.
1235 McConville and Williams, 48.
1236 *JSOT* 53 (1992) 65–74.

community (נְשִׂיאֵי הָעֵדָה) into the narrative. These chiefs of the community are often used to cite priestly redaction, but this has been seriously challenged by M. Noth.[1237] Sutherland uses this term (נְשִׂיאֵי הָעֵדָה) to separate out a source of elite postexilic leaders who did not share power with representatives of the people.

Howard uses the absence of Joshua's name in vv 16–21 as evidence the narrator lays all guilt at the leaders' feet and downplays Joshua's guilt.[1238] Yet Joshua's actions in v 15 confirm his guilt. Hawk cleverly describes the situation: "the Israelites divide"—men sampling provisions, Joshua making peace with the enemy, and the congregational leaders swearing an oath to them. The first half of the narrative ends with Israel going all directions at once and the Gibeonites holding steady on the course to survival. Again Hawk notes in his interpretation of the words "to let them live" or "to spare them": the phrase "foreshadows grave consequences. Sparing Canaanites will ensure a plurality in the land that may lead the nation away from YHWH (Deut 20:18)."[1239]

16–17 The Gibeonites are exposed as more than a small group of isolationists. They control a whole group of cities. Three satellites of Gibeon are included in the list of Benjamite cities in Josh 18:25–28. Kephirah is mentioned in Ezra 2:25; Neh 7:29; 1 Esdr 5:19 and is usually located at Khirbet el-Kefirah about four miles (seven kilometers) west-southwest of Gibeon. This has, however, been disputed by K. Vriezen.[1240]

Beeroth means "wells." The city is mentioned in 2 Sam 4:2, Ezra 2:25, and Neh 7:29 and has been variously located at el-Bireh, seven kilometers northeast of Gibeon; tell en-Nasbeh, twelve kilometers north of Jerusalem; Nebi Samwil, a mile south of Gibeon; Khirbet el-Burj, on the ridge above Nebi Samwil; Biddu, the modern city near Khirbet el-Burj; and Khirbet Raddana in the outskirts of Bireh. A. Kuschke claims, on the basis of reports from Z. Kallai-Kleinmann, that the location of Beeroth, based on discoveries at Ras et-Tahune, is on the northwest edge of el-Bireh.[1241] In *Sacred Bridge*, Rainey seems to accept Khirbet el-Burj, admitting the archaeological evidence is against it.[1242] Finally, D. Dorsey can only conclude: "At present, therefore, the site of biblical Beeroth remains a matter of dispute."[1243] Hess gives a weak vote for el-Bireh.[1244] Harris exclaims: "Beeroth's location remains a mystery."[1245]

1237 *Das System der zwölf Stämme Israels*, 102–3, 151–62; cf. O. Calberini, "Il nāsi biblico nell' epoca patriarcale e arcaio," *BeO* 20 (1978) 64–74; Blenkinsopp, *CBQ* 28 (1966) 211; J. Milgrom, "Priestly Terminology and the Political and Social Structure of Pre-Monarchic Israel," *JQR* 69 (1978) 65–76.

1238 Howard, 228.

1239 Hess (2000) 143.

1240 "Hirbet Kefire—Eine Oberflächenuntersuchung," *ZDPV* 91 (1975) 149–58.

1241 "Gibeon," in *Biblisches Reallexikon*, 2nd ed. (Tübingen: Mohr, 1977) 97; cf. Bimson, *Redating*, 219; S. Cohen, "Beeroth," *IDB*, 1:375; A. F. Rainey, "Beeroth," *IDBSup*, 93; Y. Aharoni, "Khirbet Raddana and Its Inscription," *IEJ* 21 (1971) 133–35; S. Yeivin, "The Benjamite Settlement in the Western Part of Their Territory," *IEJ* 21 (1971) 141–54; J. A. Callaway and R. E. Cooley, "A Salvage Excavation at Raddana, in Bireh," *BASOR* 201 (1971) 9–19.

1242 Rainey, 126.

1243 "Beeroth," *ABD*, 1:646–47.

1244 Hess (2009) 43.

1245 *NIDB*, 1:415.

Kiriath-Jearim appears under slightly different names in Josh 15:9, 11, 60; 18:14; Judg 18:12; 2 Sam 6:2; 1 Chr 13:6; Ezra 2:25; Neh 7:29. It is usually located at Tell Deir el-Azhar, a little over ten kilometers or seven miles northwest of Jerusalem.

18 The theme of leadership, which has so dominated the book of Joshua, appears again. The community murmurs just as they had done in the wilderness (Exod 15:24; 16:2, 7; 17:3; Num 14:2, 36; 16:11). "Divided Israel now stands in sharp relief to unified Gibeon."[1246] The murmuring is directed against the leaders who have prevented them from carrying out the divine command (cf. v 7, which ties the two units together) and from killing the Gibeonites (18a).[1247] Younger points to the irony here.[1248] Following the great victories at Jericho and Ai and the great covenant renewal at Shechem, the people stop to murmur, not to praise.

The leadership question thus becomes acute. How do leaders who have allowed themselves to be tricked into disobedience work their way out of the situation and justify themselves before their own congregation? Here the wilderness motif is turned upside down. In the wilderness the leaders were justified, while the congregation was guilty. Here the congregation is justified, while the leaders are at fault.

19–20 The immediate reaction by the leaders is that an oath cannot be broken, a basic tenet of ancient treaties. The ironic element is that the oath was sworn in the name of Yahweh, and thus binding, though the action had been carried without consulting Yahweh. McConville and Williams find the leaders facing an extremely difficult situation: "They are forced either to break the fundamental terms of the mandate to occupy the land by letting these inhabitants live or to break an oath before Yahweh by which they were equally bound."[1249]

Breaking the treaty would not only result in human wrath; it would also bring about divine wrath. Latvus represents many critical scholars in interpreting וְלֹא־יִהְיֶה עָלֵינוּ קֶצֶף, "without the wrath coming upon us," on the basis of two appearances of the term in Numbers (1:53; 18:5).[1250] This phrase is thus seen as late language which leads to the conclusion that "it is quite possible that the role of the Gibeonites was critical in the exilic/postexilic period for one reason or another."[1251] Similarly, Knauf finds the leading men to represent the self-governing body formed under Persian rule in the days of Nehemiah.[1252] Such dating represents a rather radical conclusion from so little evidence.

21 The leaders go one step further and develop a plan of action, just as cunning as that of the Gibeonites. "The leaders' rhetoric is a fine piece of persuasion, carefully laid out and calculated to appease the congregation's outrage."[1253] Unable to kill the foreigners in their midst, they reduce them to insignificant service (compare Deut 29:11 = Heb 29:10).

This was certainly not the Gibeonite understanding. They sought military protection in exchange for military loyalty. Israel turns the tables by reducing them

---

1246 Hess (2000) 145.
1247 Cf. Coats, *Rebellion*, 40–43.
1248 *Ancient Conquest Accounts*, 378–79.
1249 McConville and Williams, 49.
1250 *God, Anger, and Ideology*, 65.
1251 Ibid, 69.
1252 Knauf, 94.
1253 Hawk, *Every Promise Fulfilled*, 86.

to slaves doing menial tasks for the community. The solution presents a problem, letting foreigners enter the temple. "The role of the Gibeonites in the temple is no less of a problem than their confession of faith."[1254]

The leaders regain the confidence of the community, resulting in their word being carried out. This is a different understanding of leadership from that connected with Moses in the Pentateuch. It calls for leaders to be responsive to the complaints of the people and to justify their own actions. Such justified complaint, though, is based on the authority of the Mosaic law. Here "is a realistic reckoning that Israel must pursue its vocation in the midst of the imperfections of life, including the consequences of disobedience and compromise."[1255]

22–23 The theme changes drastically in the final section of the chapter. No longer is the guilt of the leaders in question. The Gibeonites are brought to trial before Joshua.[1256] As is proper in treaty violations, the condemnation comes in the form of a curse (compare Deut 27), which condemns the descendants to servitude. "Joshua's sentence is even more surprising than the making of the covenant. The wily Gibeonites, a people cursed, will not be separated from Israel but will serve at the very site which signifies the heart of Israel's covenant relationship with Yahweh."[1257]

The precise definition of this servitude in v 23b appears anachronistic for the time of Joshua—when Israel had yet to build a house for God, unless they had one in Shiloh in connection with the ark and the tabernacle—and is loosely connected syntactically to the sentence. Thus v 23b may represent a later updating or literary foreshadowing in light of the Jerusalem temple. Knauf contends that the verse presupposes Ezra 2:41–58 (= Neh 7:60–83).[1258]

24–25 The Gibeonite defense shows their Yahwistic piety, as they paraphrase the Israelite credo. Their inadequate confession deals with what they fear, not with who Yahweh is, as Earl points out.[1259] They are no different from all the other kings in their reaction to Israel. Terribly frightened, they seek to save their scalps with a clever plan. They submit to Joshua and his judgment (v 25) and finally tell the truth.[1260] In a play off the concluding Judges refrain of 17:6 and 21:25, the Gibeonites tell Joshua to do what is right in his eyes. Thus they throw themselves on Joshua's mercy, setting the stage for Joshua to become a hero of non-Jews who make statements of faith in Yahweh.[1261]

Knauf continues to emphasize Joshua as a prophet, able to decide disputes through correct interpretation or application of the Torah.[1262] Joshua certainly plays a prophetic role, but I suggest that is not so evident here, where he acts more like a royal figure or a judicial one.

26 The action of Joshua is thus justified by the accused and, he does not have to justify himself before the Israelite citizens. Hawk maintains that the expression

---

1254 Mitchell, *Together in the Land*, 172.
1255 McConville and Williams, 50.
1256 Cf. Creach, 86; Mitchell, *Together in the Land*, 171.
1257 Hess, *Every Promise Fulfilled*, 87.
1258 Knauf, 95.
1259 Earl, 158.
1260 Nelson, 131.
1261 See D. M. Howard, Jr., "The Case for Kingship in Deuteronomy and the Former Prophets," *WTJ* 52 (1990) 110–11.
1262 Knauf, 95.

"rescued from the hand of" (וַיַּצֵּל אוֹתָם מִיַּד) is usually an expression of God's work (Judg 6:9; 9:17; 1 Sam 4:8; 7:3; 10:18; 12:11; 14:48; 17:37) but here refers to Joshua's work. He concludes: "In sparing the Gibeonites, Joshua stands with the cursed inhabitants of the land against those who would adhere to Yahweh's commands and exterminate them [i.e., the Gibeonites]."[1263]

Having placed the Gibeonites under Joshua, Joshua prevents Israel from killing them, in contrast to the crafty plan which the chiefs of the community had to devise to regain community confidence. He simply condemned the Gibeonites to menial service at the sanctuary in conformity. "Those who were subject to the 'holiness' command of the 'ban' are now made to serve the holiness of Yahweh in this different way."[1264]

The story in Josh 9 explains the position of the Gibeonites. They are foreigners permitted to live within Israel, but their very presence is a living lesson for both Israel and for foreigners. Foreigners learn that they cannot trick their way into dwelling among the people of Yahweh, even with pious confessions of faith. Israel learns the supreme danger that threatens its life and leadership when decisions are made without consulting Yahweh and when the Mosaic law is not followed.

Knauf insists that the amount of water and wood the Gibeonites could carry suited only the Second Temple.[1265] This stands over against any size and importance of the First Temple, assuming the Levitical laws are native to the Second Temple without roots in First Temple practice. Thus, Knauf dates this chapter to 425 BCE or later, near the final redaction.

27 The final phrase of the verse is syntactically awkward and apparently represents Deuteronomistic phraseology referencing the Jerusalem temple (compare 1 Kgs 8:14–21).[1266] If the language suggests a Deuteronomistic editor for Joshua, then the editor must stand at the back of the editorial line behind the original oral storytellers, behind the people and institutions who collected the stories into larger clusters, behind the collector/editor who assembled the major part of the book into a whole probably just before or just after the division of the united monarchy, and behind the person who created a Hexateuch by tying Joshua onto the Pentateuch. The Deuteronomist, then, was either the ultimate editor who tied the Hexateuch into the ultimate history (Genesis through Kings) or someone who used the book of Deuteronomy to give a late update to the completed work.

The leadership of Joshua thus provided servants for the temple God planned in Jerusalem. Where such servants served prior to Solomon remains unclear. At least one stage of the tradition probably set this house of God in Gibeon. An even earlier stage of the tradition may have been connected with Gilgal, though this is less certain.

Explanation

"The shadow of possible disobedience to the law and the problematic presence of unconquered peoples left in the land (15:63; 16:10; 17:12–13; 23:4, 7, 12–13) has started to loom over the book of Joshua, in spite of protestations to the contrary (11:23)."[1267] Chap. 9 looks backward and forward as it seeks to teach Israel its iden-

---

1263 *Every Promise Fulfilled*, 88.
1264 McConville and Williams, 49.
1265 Knauf, 91.
1266 Weinfeld, *Deuteronomy*, 324, n. 1.
1267 Nelson, 132.

tity. It recalls the story of Rahab, in which foreigners were allowed to become part of the people of God, dwelling in their midst (Josh 6:25). It looks forward to chap. 10, where the existence of foreigners in her midst forces Israel into war, but thus enables her to carry out her program of conquest. Thus chap. 9 raises the question of Israel and foreigners. Hawk asks, "What is the good and right thing to do with peoples of the land who look like Israelites, act like Israelites, and talk like Israelites?"[1268]

From one point of view, chap. 9 lets the Gibeonites "put a human face on the annihilation policy. . . . Seen up close, at least some Canaanites are not the whoring, incorrigible idolaters of popular impression. Rather, they are ordinary people who know a little about Yahweh."[1269]

As it glimpses the human face of the land's residents, chap. 9 "demonstrates Israel's continued susceptibility to chicanery."[1270] "The narrative suggests that Israel must coexist with other peoples, to live and let live, but that sometimes the nations remain objects of distrust and even oppression."[1271] Here "is a realistic reckoning that Israel must pursue its vocation in the midst of the imperfections of life, including the consequences of disobedience and compromise."[1272]

How to deal with foreigners was an acute issue for Israel throughout its history. The exodus tradition states that Israel included a "mixed multitude" (Exod 12:38). And despite the conquest, Canaanite enclaves remained among her (Judg 1:21–36; Josh 13:1–7, 13). In the exile, Israel lived in the midst of foreign people, a situation that did not change when they returned to Palestine (Ezra 9:1–10:44). The book of Joshua allows some pious foreigners who prove their loyalty to Israel to be accepted into the community (6:25), but warns that those who seek to deceive the people, those who entice them after other gods (Deut 7), those whose piety is out of self-interest, face the judgment of Yahweh and his people.

The book of Joshua also addresses leadership in Israel. Leaders are not allowed to act on their own authority without consulting the deity and the Torah of Moses. They cannot assume the loyalty of the people when they act in such a godless manner, not consulting Yahweh. They cannot ignore divine law. If they do so, they find themselves trapped by their own actions. The leader is required to execute justice by proper legal channels. Only then can he expect the loyalty of the people. Such acts of loyalty then become part of Israel's sacred tradition and prepare the way for the service of God at the holy temple in which God chooses to dwell.

I. The Southern Sweep (10:1–43)

Bibliography

Abel, F. M. "Les stratagèmes dans le Livre de Josué." *RB* 56 (1949) 332–35. **Ahlström, G. W.** "Is Tell ed-Duweir Ancient Lachish?" *PEQ* 112 (1980) 7–9. **Alfrink, B.** "Het 'Still Staan' van Zon en Maan in Jos. 10:12–15." *StC* 24 (1949) 238–68. **Alonzo Díaz, J.** "La detencíon

---

1268 Hess (2010) 103.
1269 Hubbard, 291.
1270 Hess (2000) 134.
1271 Pressler, 68.
1272 McConville and Williams, 50.

del sol por Josué." *CB* 24 (1967) 259–65. **Alt, A.** "Josua." In *Werden und Wesen des Alten Testaments.* Ed. P. Volz, F. Stummer, and J. Hempel. BZAW 66. Berlin: Töpelmann, 1936. 13–29. Reprinted in *Kleine Schriften zur Geschichte des Volkes Israel,* vol. 1 (Munich: Beck, 1953) 176–92. **Anbar, M.** "La 'Reprise.'" *VT* 38 (1988) 385–98. **Anonymous.** "In the Study." *ExpTim* 27 (1916) 559–66. **Auld, A. G.** "Joshua: The Hebrew and Greek Texts." In *Studies in the Historical Books of the Old Testament.* VTSup 30. Leiden: Brill, 1979. 1–14. **Badger, W. C.** "The Standing Still of the Sun upon Gibeon." *PEFQS* 31 (1899) 270–71. **Badger, W. C., and W. F. Birth.** "The Sun Standing Still on Gibeon." *PEFQS* 32 (1900) 283–85. **Balaban, M.** "Kosmische Dimension des Wunders von Gibeon." *CV* 12 (1969) 51–60. **Barr, J.** "Mythical Monarch Unmasked? Mysterious Doings of Debir King of Eglon." *JSOT* 15 (1990) 55–68. **Benjamin, C. D.** *The Variations between the Hebrew and Greek Texts of Joshua: Chapters 1–12.* Thesis, University of Pennsylvania. Leipzig: W. Drugulin, 1921. **Bimson, J. J.** *Redating the Exodus and Conquest.* JSOTSup 5. Sheffield: University of Sheffield, 1978. 210–15. **Birch, W. E.** "The Standing Still of the Sun upon Gibeon." *PEFQS* 32 (1900) 165–66. **Blenkinsopp, J.** *Gibeon and Israel.* Cambridge: Cambridge UP, 1972. 41–52. **Boling, R. G.** "Where Were Debir 2 and Gilgal 3?" *BASOR* (July-August 1976) 1–2, 7–8. **Bourlier, J.** "Josué a-t-il arrêté le soleil." *Revue du clergé français* 12 (1897) 44–56. **Breytenbach, A. P. B.** "Die letterlike vertolking van metaforiese taal in Josua 10:12–14" ("The Literal Understanding of Metaphoric Language in Joshua 10:12–14"). *HvTSt* 58.4 (2002) 1337–55. **Campbell, A. F.** *Joshua to Chronicles: An Introduction.* Louisville: Westminster John Knox, 2004. **Ceuppens, P. F.** *Le Miracle de Josué.* Liége: Soledi, 1944. **Christensen, D. L.** *Transformations of the War Oracle in Old Testament Prophecy.* HDR 3. Missoula, MT: Scholars Press, 1975. 41–43, 49–50. **Clarke, T. A.** "Complete v. Incomplete Conquest: A Re-Examination of Three Passages in Joshua." *TynBul* 61 (2010) 89–104. **Cortivo, J. B.** *Dissertatio de prodigo stationis solis et lunae imperante Josua in consessu theolgico dicta et subinde aucta.* Vienna, 1755. **Curnock, G. N.** "Another Neglected Parallel (Joshua 10:12–13 and *Iliad* II:410–17)." *ExpTim* 50 (1938) 378. **Dafne, A.** "*šdwm* (Jos 10,12)." *BMik* 25–26 (1965) 127–28 (Heb.). **David, R.** "Jos 10,28–39, temoin d'une conquête de la Palestine par sud?" *ScEs* 42 (1990) 209–29. ———. "Récits de conquête du Sud de la Palestine." Diss., Université de Montréal, Montreal, 1987. **Davies, G. I.** "Tell Ed-Duweir = Ancient Lachish: A Response to G. W. Ahlström." *PEQ* 114 (1982) 25–28. ———. "Tell Ed-Duweir: Not Libnah but Lachish." *PEQ* 117 (1985) 92–96. **De Troyer, K.** "Did Joshua Have a Crystal Ball? The Old Greek and the MT of Joshua 10:15, 17, and 23." In *Emanuel: Studies in Hebrew Bible, Septuagint, and Dead Sea Scrolls in Honor of Emanuel Tov.* Ed. S. M. Paul, R. A. Kraft, L. H. Schiffman, and W. W. Fields. VTSup 94. Leiden: Brill, 2003. 571–89. ———. "'Is This Not Written in the Book of Jashar?' (Joshua 10:13c): References to Extra-Biblical Books in the Bible." In *The Land of Israel in Bible, History, and Theology: Studies in Honour of Ed Noort.* Ed. J. van Ruiten and J. C. de Vos. VTSup 124. Leiden: Brill, 2009. 45–50. ———. "Reconstructing the Older Hebrew Text of the Book of Joshua: An Analysis of Joshua 10." Paper delivered to Joshua and Judges Consultation, Atlanta, Georgia, 2010. ———. *Rewriting the Sacred Text: What the Old Greek Texts Tell Us about the Literary Growth of the Bible.* SBLTCS 4. Atlanta: SBL, 2003. **Dorsey, D. A.** "The Location of Biblical Makkedah." *TA* 7 (1980) 185–93. **Dus, J.** "Gibeon—eine Kultstätte des Šmš und die Stadt des benjaminitischen Schicksals." *VT* 10 (1960) 353–74. **Eisler, R.** "Joshua and the Sun." *AJSL* 42 (1926) 73–85. **Elliger, K.** "Josua in Juda." *PJ* 30 (1934) 47–71. **Elssner, T. R.** Wer fürchtet sich? Eine Anmerkung zu *wayyîr'û* in Jos 10,2." *BN* 118 (2003) 24–26. **Feldman, S.** "'Sun Stand Still'—A Philosophical-Astronomical Midrash." In *Proceedings of the Ninth World Congress of Jewish Studies.* Ed. C. Goldberg. Division C. Jerusalem: World Union of Jewish Studies, 1986. 77–84. **Fraine, J. de.** "De miraculo solari Josue, Jos. 10,12–15." *VD* 28 (1950) 227–36. **Frantz, I.** "Dissertatio super illo Jos 10,12: Sol contra Gabaon ne movaris, ubi quaeritur an Scriptura repugnet astronomorum sententiae in systemate Copernicano." Olmüss, 1755. **Fuller, R. C.** "Sun, Stand Thou Still (Joshua X,12)." *Scr* 4 (1951) 305–13. **Galling, K.** "Zur Lokalisierung von Debir." *ZDPV* 70 (1954) 135–41. **Gilead, H.** "Towards the Meaning and Etymology of Sefer Hayyashar." *BMik* 25 (1980) 281–83. **Giles, T., and W. J. Doan.** *Twice Used Songs: Performance Criticism of the Songs of Ancient Israel.* Peabody, MA: Hendrickson, 2009. **Görg, M.** "Südpalästinische Ortsnamen." *BN* 12 (1980) 18–19. **Greenspoon, L. J.** "The Qumran Fragments of Joshua: Which Puzzle Are They Part of and Where Do They Fit?" In *Septuagint, Scrolls and Cognate Writings: Papers Presented to the International Symposium on the Septuagint and Its Relations to the Dead Sea Scrolls and Other Writings (Manchester, 1990).* Ed. G. J. Brook and B. Lindars. SBLSCS 33. Atlanta: Scholars Press, 1992. 149–94. ———. *Textual Studies in the Book of Joshua.* HSM 28. Chico, CA: Scholars Press, 1983. **Gruenthaner, M. J.** "Two Sun Miracles of the Old Testament." *CBQ* 10 (1948) 271–90. **Hall, S. L.** *Conquering Character: The Characterization of Joshua in Joshua 1–11.* New York: T&T Clark, 2010. **Halpern, B.** "Doctrine by Misadventure: Between the Israelite Source and the Biblical Historian." In *The Poet and the Historian: Essays in Literary and Historical Biblical Criticism.* Ed. R. E. Friedman. HSS 26. Chico, CA: Scholars Press, 1983. 41–73. ———. "Gibeon: Israelite Diplomacy in the Conquest Era." *CBQ* 37 (1975) 303–16. **Heller, J.** "Der Name Eva." *ArOr* 26 (1958) 636–56. ———. "Die schweigende Sonne." *CV* 9 (1966) 73–78. **Hess, R. S.** "Joshua 10 and the Sun That Stood Still." *BurH* 35 (1999) 26–33. ———. "Rhetorical Forms in Joshua 10:4." In *'Und Moses schrieb dieses Lied auf': Studien zum Alten Testament und zum Alten Orient.* FS O. Loretz, ed. M. Dietrich and I. Kottsieper. AOAT 250. Münster: Ugarit, 1998. 363–67. **Holladay, J. S.** "The Day(s) the Moon Stood Still." *JBL* 87 (1968) 166–78. ———. "Khirbet El-Qom: Notes and News." *IEJ* 21 (1971) 175–77. **Hollenberg, J.** "Die deuteronomischen Bestandtheile des Buches Josua." *TSK* 1 (1874) 497–99. **Hom, M. K.** "A Day Like No Other: a Discussion of Joshua 10:12–14." *ExpTim* 115 (2004) 217–23. **Hoonacker, A. van.** "Das Wunder Josuas." *TGl* 5 (1913) 454–61. **Houston, W. J.** "Misunderstanding or Midrash? The Prose Appropriation of Poetic Material in the Hebrew Bible." *ZAW* 109 (1997) 342–55. **Jacobs, L.** *Jewish Biblical Exegesis.* New York: Behrman, 1973. 92–99. **Jericke, D.** "Die Landnahme im Süden: Archäologische und exegetische Studien." Diss., KiHo Berlin, 1992. **Jones, G. H.** "'Holy War' or 'Yahweh War'?" *VT* 25 (1975) 653–55. **Joüon, P.** "Notes philologiques sur le texte hébreu de Josuè 6,18; 10,13; 23,13;. . . ." *Bib* 9 (1928) 161–66. **Kallai, Z.** "Some Scribal Conventions in Biblical Narrative: A Study in Historiography." *ZAW* 115 (2003) 38–53. **Kallai, Z., and H. Tadmor.** "Bet Ninurta = Bet Horon—On the History of the Kingdom of Jerusalem in the Amarna Period." *ErIsr* 9 (1969) 138–47. **Keel, O.** *Die Geschichte Jerusalems und die Entstehung des Monotheismus.* Ort und Landschaften der Bibel 4. Göttingen: Vandenhoeck & Ruprecht, 2007. **Kissling, P. J.** *Reliable Characters in the Primary History: Profiles of Moses, Joshua, Elijah, and Elisha.* Sheffield: Sheffield Academic, 1996. **Kleber, A.** "Josue's Miracle." *AER* 56 (1917) 477–88. **Knauf, E. A.** "Jerusalem in the Late Bronze and Early Iron Ages: A Proposal." *TA* 27 (2000) 75–90. **Kochavi, M.** "Khirbet Rabud = Debir." *TA* 1 (1974) 2–33. **Kruger, H. A. J.** "Sun and Moon Grinding to a Halt: Exegetical Remarks on Joshua 10:9–14 and Related Texts in Judges." *HvTSt* 55 (1999) 1077–97. ———. "Sun and Moon Marking Time: A Cursory Survey of Exegetical Possibilities in Joshua 10:9–14." *JNSL* 26 (2000) 137–52. **Lambert, G.** "Josué à la bataille de Gabaon." *NRTh* 76 (1954) 374–91. **Lance, H. D.** "Gezer in the Land and in History." *BA* 30 (1967) 34–47. **Latvus, K.** "From Army Campsite to Partners in Peace: The Changing Role of the Gibeonites in the Redaction Process of Josh. X 1–8; xi 19." In *'Lasset uns Brücken bauen . . .': Collected Communications to the XVth Congress of the International Organization for the Study of the Old Testament, Cambridge, 1995.* Ed. K.-D. Schunk and M. Augustin. BEATAJ 42. Frankfurt am Main: Lang, 1998. 111–15. ———. *God, Anger, and Ideology: The Anger of God in Joshua and Judges in Relation to Deuteronomy and the Priestly Writings.* JSOTSup 279. Sheffield: Sheffield Academic, 1998. **Levine,**

Y. "'From Goshen to Gibeon' (Joshua 10:41): The Southern Frontier of the Early Monarchy." *Maarav* 10 (2003) 195–220. **Love, W.** *Did the Sun Stand Still? An Interpretation of Joshua Chapter 10, Verses 12–13.* Boston, 1945. **Margalit, B.** "The Day the Sun Did Not Stand Still: A New Look at Joshua x 8–15." *VT* 42 (1992) 466–91. **Matthes, J. C.** "Das Solstitium Jos. 10:12–14." *ZAW* 29 (1909) 259–67. **Maunder E. W.** "A Misinterpreted Miracle." *Exp* 36 (1910) 359–72. **Meer, M. N. van der.** *Formation and Reformulation: The Redaction of the Book of Joshua in the Light of the Oldest Textual Witnesses.* VTSup 102. Leiden: Brill, 2004. **Mierlo, J. van.** "Das Wunder Josues." *ZKT* 37 (1913) 895–911. **Miller, P. D.** *The Divine Warrior in Early Israel.* HSM 5. Cambridge, MA: Harvard UP, 1973. 123–28. **Miroschedji, P. de.** "Yarmuth: The Dawn of City-States in Southern Canaan." *NEA* 62 (1999) 2–19. **Mitchell, G.** *Together in the Land.* JSOTSup 134. Sheffield: Sheffield Academic, 1993. **Möhlenbrink, K.** "Die Landnahmensagen des Buches Josua." *ZAW* 56 (1938) 264–65. **Mowinckel, S.** "Hat es ein israelitisches Nationalepos gegeben?" *ZAW* 53 (1935) 130–52. ———. *Tetrateuch, Pentateuch, Hexateuch.* BZAW 90. Berlin: Töpelmann, 1964. 39–40. **Na'aman, N.** "Cow Town or Royal Capital? Evidence for Iron Age Jerusalem." *BAR* 23.4 (1997) 43–47, 67. ———. "Sennacherib's Campaign to Judah and the Date of the *lmlk* Stamps." *VT* 29 (1979) 61–86. **Niehaus, J.** "*pa'am 'ehat* (Jos 10:42) and the Israelite Conquest." *VT* 30 (1980) 236–39. **Noort, E.** "Joshua and Copernicus: Josh 10:12–15 and the History of Reception." In *Flores Florentino: Dead Sea Scrolls and Other Early Jewish Studies in Honour of Florentino García Martínez.* Ed. A. Hilhorst et al. JSJSup 122. Leiden: Brill, 2007. 387–401. ———. "Zwischen Mythos und Rationalität: Das Kriegshandeln Yhwhs in Josua 10:1–11." In *Mythos und Rationalität.* Ed. H. H. Schmid. Gütersloh: Gütersloh (Mohn), 1988. 149–61. **Noth, M.** "Die fünf Könige in der Höhle von Makkeda." *PJ* 33 (1937) 22–36. Reprinted in *Aufsätze zur biblischen Landes- und Altertumskunde.* Vol. 1. Neukirchen-Vluyn: Neukirchener Verlag, 1971. 281–93. ———. "Zur historischen Geographie Südjudäas." *JPOS* 15 (1935) 35–50. Reprinted in *Aufsätze zur biblischen Landes- und Altertumskunde.* Vol. 1. Neukirchen-Vluyn: Neukirchener Verlag, 1971 197–209. **Otto, E.** *Das antike Jerusalem: Archäologie und Geschichte.* Munich: Beck, 2008. ———. *Das Mazzotfest in Gilgal.* BWANT 107. Stuttgart: Kohlhammer, 1975. 92–93, 318–19. **Ottosson, M.** *Josuaboken: En programskrift för davidisk restauration.* AUU, Studia Biblica Upsaliensis 1. Uppsala: AUU; Stockholm: Almqvist & Wiksell, 1991. 85–92. **Peels, H. G. L.** *The Vengeance of God: The Meaning of the Root NQM and the Function of the NQM Texts in the Context of Divine Revelation in the Old Testament.* OtSt 31. Leiden: Brill, 1995. **Phythian-Adams, W. J.** "A Meteorite of the Fourteenth Century bc." *PEQ* 78 (1946) 116–24. **Pritchard, J. B.** "Gibeon's History in the Light of Excavation." In *Congress Volume: Oxford, 1959.* Ed. G. W. Anderson et al. VTSup 7. Leiden: Brill, 1960. 1–12. **Quell, G.** "Das Phänomen des Wunders in Alten Testament." In *Verbannung und Heimkehr.* Ed. A. Kuschke. Tübingen: Mohr, 1961. 259–61, 273–74. **Rainey, A. F., R. S. Notley, et al.** *The Sacred Bridge: Carta's Atlas of the Biblical World.* Jerusalem: Carta, 2006. **Reid, J.** "Did the Sun and Moon Stand Still?" *ExpTim* 9 (1898) 151–54. **Richardson, A. T.** "The Battle of Gibeon." *ExpTim* 40 (1929) 426–31. **Richter, W.** *Traditionsgeschichtliche Untersuchungen zum Richterbuch.* BBB 18. Bonn: Hanstein, 1963. 181–86. **Roehrs, W. R.** "The Conquest of Canaan according to Joshua and Judges." *CTM* 31 (1960) 746–60. **Rösel, H.** "Anmerkungen zur Erzählung von Bundesschluss mit den Gibeoniten." *BN* 28 (1985) 30–35. ———. "Wer kämpfte auf kanaanäischer Seite in der Schlacht bei Gibeon, Jos. X?" *VT* 26 (1976) 505–8. **Rudolph, W.** *Der 'Elohist' von Exodus bis Josua.* BZAW 68. Berlin: Töpelmann, 1938. 204–9. **Sawyer, J. F. A.** "Joshua 10:12–14 and the Solar Eclipse of 30 September 1131 bc." *PEQ* 104 (1972) 139–46. **Schmid, H.** "Erwägungen zur Gestalt Josuas in Überlieferung und Geschichte." *Jud* 24 (1968) 55. **Schunck, K.-D.** *Benjamin.* BZAW 86. Berlin: Töpelmann, 1963. 18–39. **Scott, R. B. Y.** "Meteorological Phenomena and Terminology in the Old Testament." *ZAW* 64 (1952) 11–25. **Seligmann, I. L.** "Menschliches Heldentum und göttliche Hilfe."

TZ 19 (1963) 385–411. **Shanks, H.** "Jerusalem Roundup." *BAR* 37.2 (2011) 35–45. ———. "Newly Discovered: A Fortified City from King David's Time." *BAR* 35.1 (2009) 38–43. **Starkey, J. L.** "Excavations at Tell el-Duweir, 1933–34: Wellcome Archaeological Research to the Near East." *PEQ* 66 (1934) 164–75. ———. "Excavations at Tell el-Duweir, 1934–35: Wellcome Archaeological Research to the Near East." *PEQ* 67 (1935) 198–207. ———. "Excavations at Tell el-Duweir, 1935–36: Wellcome Archaeological Research to the Near East." *PEQ* 68 (1936) 178–89. ———. "Excavations at Tell el-Duweir." *PEQ* 69 (1937) 228–41. ———. "Lachish as Illustrating Bible History." *PEQ* 69 (1937) 171–79. **Steiner, M. L.** "The Notion of Jerusalem as a Holy City." In *Reflection and Refraction: Studies in Biblical Historiography in Honour of A. Graeme Auld.* Ed. R. Rezetko, T. H. Lim, and W. B. Aucker. VTSup 113. Leiden: Brill, 2007. 447–58. **Stephenson, F. R.** "Astronomical Verification and Dating of Old Testament Passages Referring to Solar Eclipses." *PEQ* 107 (1975) 117–20. **Stolz, F.** *Jahwes und Israels Kriege.* ATANT 60. Zürich: Theologische, 1972. 85–87. **Taylor, J. G.** *Yahweh and the Sun: Biblical and Archaeological Evidence for Sun Worship in Ancient Israel.* JSOTSup 111. Sheffield: JSOT Press, 1993. **Thils, G.** "De solis institione secundum Iosue 10, 12–14." *Collectanea Mechliniensia* 30 (1945) 153–56. **Thoburn, C. S.** "Joshua's Long Day." *ExpTim* 47 (1936) 373–77. **Tufnell, O.** *Lachish (Tell Ed-Duweir): The Bronze Age.* Vol. 4. New York: Oxford, 1958. **Ussishkin, D.** "Lachish—Key to the Israelite Conquest of Canaan." *BAR* 13.1 (1987) 18–41. **Van den Bussche, H.** "Het zogenaamd zonnewonder in Jos. 10:12–15." *Collationes Gandavenses* 1 (1951) 48–53. **Van Seters, J.** "Joshua's Campaign of Canaan and Near Eastern Historiography." *SJOT* 4 (1990) 1–12. **Vaux, R. de.** *Histoire ancienne d'Israel.* Vol. 1. Paris: Gabalda, 1971. 576–82. Translated as *The Early History of Israel*, trans. D. Smith (London: Darton, Longman & Todd, 1978) 627–35. **Vèronnet, A.** "L'arrêt du soleil par Josué." *Revue du clergé français* 41 (1905) 585–603. **Wallace, G. P.** "Joshua and the Miracle of the Sun." *ExpTim* 33 (1922) 187–89. **Walton, J.** "Joshua 10:12–15 and Mesopotamian Celestial Omen Texts." In *Faith, Tradition, and History.* Ed. A. Millard et al. Winona Lake, IN: Eisenbrauns, 1994. 181–90. **Weimar, P.** "Die Jahwehkriegserzählungen in Exodus 14, Josua 10, Richter 4, und I Samuel 7." *Bib* 57 (1976) 38–73. **Weinfeld, M.** "'They fought from heaven'—Divine Intervention in War in Ancient Israel and in the Ancient Near East." *ErIsr* 47 (1978) 23–30. **Wellhausen J.** *Die Composition des Hexateuchs und der historischen Bücher des Alten Testaments.* 2nd ed. Berlin: Reimer, 1889. 128–29. **Wilson, R. D.** "What Does 'the Sun Stood Still' Mean?" *PTR* 16 (1918) 46–54. **Wright, G. E.** "The Literary and Historical Problem of Joshua 10 and Judges 1." *JNES* 5 (1946) 105–14. ———. "A Problem of Ancient Topography: Lachish and Eglon." *BA* 34 (1971) 76–86. Also published in *HTR* 64 (1971) 437–50. **Yeivin, S.** *The Israelite Conquest of Canaan.* Istanbul: Nederlands Historisch-Archaeologisch Instituut in het Nabije Oosten, 1971. 80–83. **Younger, K. L.** *Ancient Conquest Accounts: A Study in Ancient Near Eastern and Biblical History Writing.* JSOTSup 98. Sheffield: JSOT Press, 1990. ———. "The 'Conquest' of the South (Josh 10:28–39)." *BZ* 39 (1995) 255–64. ———. "The Rhetorical Structuring of the Joshua Conquest Narratives." In *Critical Issues in Early Israelite History.* Ed. R. S. Hess, G. A. Klingbeil, and P. J. Ray, Jr. BBRSup 3. Winona Lake, IN: Eisenbrauns, 2008. 3–32. **Zwickel, W.** "Die Landnahme in Juda." *UF* 25 (1993) 473–91.

Translation

[1a]When Adoni-Zedek,[b] the king of Jerusalem, heard that Joshua had captured The Ruin and put it to the ban, that just as he had done to Jericho and to its king, so he had done to The Ruin and to its king and that the residents of Gibeon had made peace[c] with Israel[d] and were living among them,[e] [2]then he[a] feared exceedingly, because[b] Gibeon was a great city, comparable to one of the city-state capitals, and because it was greater than The Ruin,[c] all

its men being mighty warriors. ³*So Adoni-Zedek, king of Jerusalem, sent to Hoham,*ᵃ *king of Hebron, and to Piram, king of Jarmuth, and to Japhia, king of Lachish, and to Debir, king of Eglon, saying,* ⁴*"Come up*ᵃ *to me and help me so that we may punish Gibeon, for they have concluded a peace treaty with Joshua and with the sons*ᵇ *of Israel."* ⁵*The five kings of the Amorites*ᵃ—*the king of Jerusalem, the king of Hebron, the king of Jarmuth, the king of Lachish, the king of Eglon*—*they and all their armies assembled*ᵇ *and encamped against Gibeon. They battled against them.*

⁶*The men*ᵃ *of Gibeon sent to Joshua to the camp*ᵇ *at Gilgal, saying, "Do not abandon your vassals. Come up to us quickly. Save us! Help us! for all the kings of the Amorites, who live in the hill country, have gathered themselves against us."* ⁷*So Joshua went up from Gilgal, he and all his combat troops with him and all the valiant warriors.*

⁸*Then Yahweh said to Joshua, "Have no fear of them, for into your hand I have given them. Not one man of them shall stand before you."*

⁹*Joshua came to them suddenly, traveling*ᵃ *all night from Gilgal.* ¹⁰*Then Yahweh threw them into a panic before*ᵃ *Israel. He*ᵇ *inflicted a crushing defeat on them in Gibeon, then pursued them on the road ascending to Beth Horon,*ᶜ *and defeated them clear to Azekah and Makkedah.* ¹¹*While they were fleeing before Israel, being on the descent from Beth Horon, Yahweh hurled down on them huge*ᵃ *stones from heaven unto Azekah, and they died.*ᵇ *More died from the hailstones than the sons of Israel killed*ᶜ *with the sword.*ᵈ

¹²*Then*ᵃ *Joshua spoke to Yahweh before the sons of Israel in the day of Yahweh's*ᵇ *giving over the Amorites, and he said in the sight of Israel:*ᶜ

"'O sun, in Gibeon stand still:

O moon, in the valley of Aijalon.'

¹³*Still stood the sun,*

*And the moon remained*ᵃ

*Till the nation*ᵇ *took vengeance on its enemies.*ᶜ

*"Is it*ᵈ *it not written in the book of the Upright?*ᵉ *The sun remained at the halfway point of the heavens and did not hurry to set for about a whole day.* ¹⁴*There has never been a day like it before or since when Yahweh listened to the voice*ᵃ *of a man, for Yahweh fought for Israel."*

¹⁵ᵃ*Joshua and all Israel with him returned to the camp at Gilgal.* ¹⁶*These five kings fled and hid in the cave at Makkedah.* ¹⁷*It was reported to Joshua, "The five kings have been found hidden in the cave in Makkedah."*

¹⁸*Joshua said, "Roll large*ᵃ *boulders into the mouth of the cave, and station men in front of it to guard it.* ¹⁹*But you (pl.) should not stand around. Pursue after your enemies. Destroy*ᵃ *them. Do not give them a chance to enter into their cities, for Yahweh, your God,*ᵇ *has given them into your hand."*

²⁰*As Joshua and the sons*ᵃ *of Israel completed inflicting the crushing defeat upon them, almost totally destroying them, a remnant did remain*ᵇ *from them and entered the fortified cities.* ²¹*All the people returned to the camp*ᵃ *to Joshua at Makkedah*ᵇ *unharmed. Not a single man threatened*ᶜ *the sons of Israel.* ²²*Joshua said, "Open the mouth of the cave and bring out to me*ᵃ *these five kings from the cave."* ²³*They obeyed. They brought out to him these five kings from the cave—the king of Jerusalem, the king of Hebron, the king of Jarmuth, the king of Lachish, the king of Eglon.* ²⁴*As a man was bringing them—these kings*ᵃ—*to Joshua, Joshua called out to all the men*ᵇ *of Israel and said to the commanders of the troops who*ᶜ *had gone with him, "Come near. Place your feet on the necks of these kings."*ᵈ *They came near and placed their feet on their necks.*

²⁵*Joshua said to them, "Be not afraid*ᵃ *nor terrified. Be strong and brave, for Yahweh will act accordingly against all your enemies whenever you (pl.) are fighting them."* ²⁶*Afterward,*ᵃ

Joshua struck them and killed them and hung them on five trees. They were hanging on the trees until the evening. ²⁷*At sunset, Joshua issued the command, and they brought them down from the trees and threw them into the cave where they had hidden. They placed large boulders on the mouth of the cave until this very day.*

²⁸*But as for Makkedah, Joshua*ᵃ *captured it that day and smote it with the sword and its king.*ᵇ *He put them*ᶜ *to the ban, including everything alive in it. He did not let anything remain.*ᵈ *He did to the king of Makkedah just what he had done to the king of Jericho.* ²⁹*Joshua and all Israel with him passed over from Makkedah to Libnah. He battled Libnah.* ³⁰*Yahweh also gave it into the hand of Israel*ᵃ *along with its king. He smote it with the sword and everything alive in it. He did not let anything in it*ᵇ *remain. He did to its king just what he had done to the king of Jericho.*

³¹*Joshua and all Israel with him crossed over from Libnah to Lachish. He encamped against it and battled against it.* ³²*Yahweh gave Lachish into the hand of Israel. He captured it on the second day and smote it with the sword and everything alive*ᵃ *in it according to all which he had done to Libnah.* ³³*Then Horam, king of Gezer, went up to help Lachish. Joshua smote him*ᵃ *and his people until nothing at all remained for him.* ³⁴*Joshua and all Israel with him crossed over from Lachish to Eglon. They encamped against it and battled against it.* ³⁵ᵃ*They captured it on that day and smote it with the sword and everything alive in it. In that day*ᵇ *he set out the ban according to all that he had done to Lachish.* ³⁶*Joshua and all Israel with him went up from Eglon*ᵃ *to Hebron. They battled against it.* ³⁷*They captured*ᵃ *it and smote it with the sword and its king and all its cities and everything alive in it. He did not let anything remain, according to all that he had done to Eglon. He put it to the ban and everything alive in it.*

³⁸*Joshua and all Israel with him turned to Debir. He battled against it.* ³⁹*He*ᵃ *captured it and its king and all its cities.*ᵇ *They smote them with the sword and put everything alive in it to the ban. He did not let anything remain. Just as he had done to Hebron,*ᶜ *so he did to Debir and its king and just as he had done to Libnah and to its king.*ᵈ

⁴⁰*Joshua smote all the land, the hill country and the Negev and the Shephelah and slopes and all*ᵃ *their kings. He did not let anything remain. Everything that breathed he put to the ban just as Yahweh, the God of Israel, commanded.* ⁴¹*Joshua smote*ᵃ *them from Kadesh-Barnea to Gaza, along with all the land of Goshen and unto Gibeon.* ⁴²*All these kings and their land Joshua captured at one time because Yahweh, the God of Israel, fought for Israel.* ⁴³ᵃ*Joshua and all Israel with him returned to the camp at Gilgal.*

Notes

1.a. Despite the evidence presented here, Margalit (*VT* 42 [1992] 487) finds the text of Josh 10:1–15 "perfectly sound."

1.b. LXX renders the royal name "Adoni-bezek," which appears in Judg 1:5–7. Noth, followed provisionally by Soggin (119), adopts LXX reading here. Hertzberg (72) is more probably correct in rejecting this. Adoni-bezek is original to Judg 1 and related to an otherwise unknown locality of Bezek. Late textual tradition did not understand this and sought to identify him with the king of Jerusalem in Josh 10. Wright (*JNES* 5 [1946] 108; compare Younger, *Ancient Conquest Accounts*, 379) sees lack of mention of Bezek as a town in other sources and the lack of a divine name in the second element pointing to Adoni-zedek as the original name. Bezek would certainly provide the more difficult reading but most likely represents an attempt to bring agreement between the two passages.

1.c. LXX interpreted the Heb. root לסמ to mean "deserted."

1.d. LXX adds "Joshua" along with "Israel" as object of the action, another element in the tradition's continued effort to glorify Joshua. But the original text apparently used this to blame Israel and remove Joshua from responsibility for making a peace treaty with Gibeon. Still Boling (275) and Younger (*Ancient Conquest Accounts*, 379) argue for haplography based on Josh 9:2 and 10:4 along with the pl. verb, reading "with Joshua and with Israel." But "Israel" as a collective may take a pl. verb.

1.e. LXX lacks "and were living among them," a motif used in Josh 9:7 (compare 9:22) to connect the two narrative elements and added here by even later tradition to make the connection with chap. 9 explicit. Nelson (136) holds out possibility of MT haplography. The expression "living among them" or "were in their midst" (קֶרֶב) refers in Joshua to the camp or people of Israel. The expression, "they were living in their midst," means the Gibeonites (Hivites) were living in Israel's territory among Israelites.

2.a. Many translators read the subject of the Heb. pl. verb as a collective sg. or as an error, making the king of Jerusalem either the subject or the spokesman for the city's populace (NRSV). net inserts "all Jerusalem" as the subject. NLT, NIV, NASB, JPS, REB, GWT and Message (compare CEV and HCSB) read "he and his people." NAB reads, "and there was great fear abroad." NJB has "there was consternation at this." *Preliminary and Interim Report* (2:21) sees an impersonal pl. here to be translated "and there was a great fear." Barthélemy (*Critique textuelle*, 1:17) strongly supports the MT. Younger (*Ancient Conquest Accounts*, 379) points to the pl. suffix ending v 1 to support MT. The 3rd pers. pl. does carry over from the previous verse and refer to the people under Adoni-zedek. See *Note* 1.d above.

2.b. LXX reads ᾔδει γὰρ ὅτι, leading Boling (275) to restore כי ידע כי עיר, but Younger (*Ancient Conquest Accounts*, 379) correctly follows Margolis, *Book of Joshua in Greek* (170), in seeing Gk. amplification here.

2.c. LXX lacks "and because it was greater than The Ruin," an addition to the MT to enhance the ensuing achievement (Benjamin, *Variations*) and to make the tie to the larger tradition explicit.

3.a. The names are transmitted quite differently by LXX: Hoham becomes Ailam, a name reappearing in LXX for Horam in v 33. Pir'am becomes Phidon, through faulty Heb. transmission. Japhia becomes Jephthah. Eglon becomes Odollam (cf. Margolis, *Book of Joshua in Greek*, 172; Barr, *JSOT* 15 [1990] 58–59). Barr concludes: "the Greek was not produced by mere misreading of the Hebrew of MT, but is evidence of a stage of Hebrew tradition in which the word used was 'Adulam.'" At the same time Barr sees Eglon as a personal name, not a place name. He decides that "later biblical traditions sometimes provided persons with names by borrowing known place names," a process he calls "mythical creativity" (64). For Barr, LXX represents a different set of guesses (65), and Debir is a city, not a king.

4.a. LXX gives a dynamic equivalent, adding δεῦτε, "hurry up."

4.b. 4QJosh^a does not have "sons of," another case of the tradition's introduction of familiar phrases.

5.a. LXX reads "Jebusite" for MT "Amorite," connecting the tradition more closely to Jerusalem (cf. Josh 15:8, 63; 18:28; Judg 1:21; 2 Sam 5:6).

5.b. LXX lacks "they assembled," an addition in the tradition showing that the appeal of v 4 was carried out.

6.a. LXX read "inhabitants" for "men," thus repeating the expression of v 1.

6.b. LXX adds the redundant "of Israel," whereby the tradition makes the identity explicit.

9.a. 4QJosh^a reads הלך for MT וַיָּבֹא. Nelson (137) notes the "adverbial noun clause" here, referring to *IBHS* 38.8d (compare Younger, *Ancient Conquest Accounts*, 379; Williams, *Williams' Hebrew Syntax*, 491, 576). The clause has no explicit adverb or copula joining the two clauses.

10.a. LXX adds "the sons," which may have fallen out after the similar לפני, "before." This recurs in v 11.

10.b. LXX makes Yahweh the explicit subject, while Syr. and Tg. evidence show a pl. subject, a phenomenon witnessed by Gk., Syr., and Tg. frg. for the following verbs. This seeks to avoid the picture of God pursuing and striking. Nelson says "Yahweh can hardly be intended as the subject of 'pursued' and 'struck down'" (137). Younger (*Ancient Conquest Accounts*, 380) makes Israel the subject of each of the verbs. The natural syntactical reading would place Yahweh as the subject. The slight ambiguity helps the Heb. writer describe divine causality within human actions.

10.c. For Beth-Horon, LXX reads Ωρωνιν, "Horonaim," otherwise a Moabite city (Isa

15:5; Jer 48:3, 5, 34; Moabite stone). Dittography of the final נ (*nun*) may be the ultimate cause of confusion. LXX is more difficult reading but cannot be accepted. Boling (276) sees a pl. term representing the upper and lower Beth-Horon.

11.a. LXX reads "hail," anticipating the following line. 4QJosh[a] does not have "huge," perhaps a later expansion (compare Nelson, 137). Greenspoon (*Textual Studies*, 69–70), followed by Younger (*Ancient Conquest Accounts*, 380), sees an original "stones" modified in two directions by MT and OG, an unmodified "stones" representing the original text.

11.b. Nelson (137) notes OG reading of "and there were" for MT's "and they died."

11.c. LXX redundantly adds "in the battle," perhaps reflecting an early textual variant (Benjamin, *Variations*).

11.d. The verse is a verbless clause with two אשר clauses being compared to one another, the "relative pronoun" having no antecedent. See *IBHS* 19.1.d.

12.a. For the use of אז to unite a clearly recognizable unit to the context loosely, see Dus, *VT* 10 (1960) 358, n. 1. Williams (*Williams' Hebrew Syntax*, 177c) notes preterite meaning after אז. See *Note* on 8:30.

12.b. LXX reads "God" for "Yahweh" and continues "gave over the Amorites into the hands of Israel, when he shattered them in Gibeon and they were shattered before the sons of Israel, and Joshua said. . . ." Younger (*Ancient Conquest Accounts*, 380) and Boling (276) see OG as amplification. C. D. Ginsburg (*Introduction to the Masoretico-Critical Edition of the Hebrew Bible* [London: Trinitarian Bible Society, 1897] 176), Benjamin (*Variations*), Soggin (119), and Nelson (137) are right in seeing this as homoioteleuton. Nelson retroverts this as ביד ישראל כי הכם בגבעון ויכו, "into the power [lit. hand] of Israel, when he had struck them down at Gibeon and they were struck down."

Auld ("Joshua," 13) is probably correct in seeing "God" here and in v 14 as the original reading, explaining the corruption of ἔθνος, "nation," to θεός, "god," within the Gk. transmission of v 13.

12.c. LXX lacks "in the sight of Israel," which may have entered the tradition after the previous line was omitted in the Heb. tradition. Nelson (137) calls it a "misplaced gloss."

13.a. To restore the Joshua text, Margalit (*VT* 42 [1992] 480–81) uses Hab 3:11: שֶׁמֶשׁ יָרֵחַ עָמַד זְבֻלָה, "sun, moon, stand silent." He uses a rare Gk. ms of Hab 3 to give a new meaning to זְבֻלָה and then repoints the Heb. term to get the meaning "radiance."

13.b. The use of גוי, "nation," to refer to Israel is somewhat rare and is often changed to מגוי on the basis of haplography of the preceding מ (Delitzsch; Noth; Hertzberg, 74; Gray, 110; etc.). Israel is pictured as גוי in Josh 5:6, and R. E. Clements ("גוי," *TWAT*, 1:970–73) finds that Israel was often referred to as גוי prior to the postexilic priestly writings. Emendation without textual support is not in order here. LXX reads "until God took vengeance," a reading Howard (241) accepts, but that appears to be a simplification of the message of the text.

13.c. The poem offers good examples of the principle that "the article is not consistently used even according to the best established patterns" (*IBHS* 13.7a–b).

13.d. Note fem. pronoun used as neuter: "with respect to some vague action or circumstance" (*IBHS* 16.3.5.c).

13.e. The interrogative particle creates a rhetorical question here. The quotation formula is lacking in LXX. Nelson (137; compare Auld, "Joshua," 13) sees it as "expansion, probably on the basis of 2 Sam 1:18." Alfrink (*StC* 24 [1949] 238–68), Sawyer (*PEQ* 104 [1972] 140), and Benjamin (*Variations*) argue for priority of LXX, while most commentators ignore the fact. The citation interrupts the context. The later tradition would have had no reason to omit the reference.

14.a. LXX omits "voice" to tone down the anthropomorphism (Benjamin, *Variations*).

15.a. V 15 does not appear in LXX, nor does the corresponding v 43. Knauf (101) concludes that the missing verses belong to his "Hasmonean redaction" since they describe Joshua and Gilgal according to the figure of Judas Maccabeus and his defense stand at Modein. Younger (*Ancient Conquest Accounts*, 380–81) provides a long defense of MT as possibly a part of the quote from the Book of the Upright (Jashar). He speaks of resumptive repetition in the mention of the return to Gilgal. Mitchell says "the scene retrogresses in time and links what follows to the theme of flight" (*Together in the Land*, 88). Howard (251; compare Hall, *Conquering Character*, 165 n. 5) gives four options and decides either the verses were intentionally included as structural conclusions to sections or that v 43 is original and v 15 is a scribal duplication. Hubbard (282, n. 3) dismisses the verse as a copyist's error. De Troyer uses these two duplicate verses to "reconstruct the history of the Biblical text, from the Old Hebrew text as witnessed in the Old Greek to the (proto-) Masoretic text"—MT emphasizing "with him," "camp," and "Gilgal" ("Reconstructing the Older Hebrew Text").

These two summary verses probably represent the work of the later tradition tying the entire tradition to Gilgal (cf. Auld, "Joshua," 13; Benjamin; *Variations*; Nelson, 137; Boling, 277).

18.a. "Large" does not appear in LXX in vv 18 and 27 and may represent later amplification of the narrative.

19.a. זנב derives from the noun "tail." It is used here and in Deut 25:18 to mean "seize and destroy" or "attack the rear guard" (cf. LXX).

19.b. LXX reads "our God" in both instances in this verse, following a regular pattern of differentiation from MT (Auld, "Joshua," 11–12). This may reflect liturgical usage of the tradition personalizing references to deity.

20.a. LXX reads "every son," an attempt of the later tradition to underline the total involvement of the community. See Greenspoon (*Textual Studies*, 70–71) for full textual evidence and defense of "Israel" alone as original reading, expanded by other textual traditions.

20.b. שריד, "remnant, survivor," is used in two formulaic expressions in Joshua: "until no remnant at all remained for him" (8:22; 10:33; 11:8; cf. Deut 3:3; 2 Kgs 10:11; Num 21:35); "he did not cause a remnant to remain" (10:28, 30, 37, 39, 40; cf. Deut 2:34). Only in Josh 10:20 does a verbal form of the root appear: "a remnant did remain." LXX's free rendering abbreviates the sentence but reflects the rare verbal usage.

21.a. LXX lacks "to the camp," a regular LXX feature by which the camp is never located outside Gilgal (cf. Josh 8:13; 18:9). *Preliminary and Interim Report* (2:21) calls this a simplification of the original MT. Barthélemy (*Critique textuelle*, 1:17) finds homoioarchton in the *Vorlage* of the Gk., while Boling speaks of haplography (277).

21.b. MT lacks article before Makkedah. "Unharmed" renders Hebrew בְּשָׁלֹם in peace or wholly or as a complete unit.

21.c. The final element of the verse is an idiom elsewhere associated with a dog (Exod 11:7) and translated literally "to point [or sharpen] the tongue at," meaning "to threaten." LXX translates "to grumble, murmur." The function of לְאִישׁ, literally "to a man," in the present text is debated. The initial ל is usually deleted as dittography, making "man" the indefinite subject, but Nelson (137) takes it as an "emphatic lamed." It could be read adverbially, meaning "totally, unanimously." The indefinite subject would then be expressed by the verb form. The older suggestion to supply "dog" as subject as in Exodus is represented by Fritz (109) but otherwise is no longer taken seriously.

22.a. "To me" is lacking in LXX and may have been added as the tradition underscored the authority of Joshua. Similarly, LXX lacks "to him" in v 23 as well as the introductory formula of obedience there.

24.a. "These kings" is superfluous and is omitted by LXX. Later tradition underlines the explicit obedience to Joshua.

24.b. LXX reads συνεκάλεσεν Ἰησοῦς πάντα Ισραηλ καὶ τοὺς ἐναρχομένους τοῦ πολέμου τοὺς συμπορευομένους αὐτῷ λέγων αὐτοῖς . . . , "Joshua called together all Israel and the chief commanders of the battle who went out with him, saying to them . . . ." "Man of Israel" in MT may have been inserted on the basis of chap. 9. A few Heb. MSS do not witness it, nor does the Syr. MT makes explicit that the address was only to the commanders and may reflect later tradition. Younger (*Ancient Conquest Accounts*, 381) thinks OG did not have "man of" in the text he was translating or copying and so introduced "all." Van der Meer sees in the LXX "a stylistic condensation of the two groups of Joshua's addressees" (*Formation and Reformulation*, 232). One continues to wonder just how much literary ability and freedom to give the translator.

24.c. The pf. verb beginning a relative clause may have an article. See Williams (*Williams' Hebrew Syntax*, 91; *IBHS* 13.5.2d.24; 19.7c; BDB, 208).

24.d. LXX lacks "these kings," having only the possessive pronoun "their." The text may have had the suffix הם, which later copyists took for the initial letters of המלכם, "kings," or later tradition may have sought to formulate command and execution exactly alike.

25.a. LXX has not understood the general form of the oracle of salvation and has applied it to the specific case. "Do not fear them."

26.a. LXX omits "afterward he struck them." The text is redundant and perhaps represents later tradition's attempts to unite the text with v 24 after the intrusive note in v 25. Nelson (137), however, finds inner Gk. haplography.

28.a. LXX has the indefinite "they" as subject. Later tradition again underscored the role and authority of Joshua.

28.b. "And its king" is out of place in the formulary style of the section and is omitted by LXX. Later tradition sought to make all the formulaic statements complete. The addition included "them" in the following clause. See Fritz, 115, and discussion of Younger, *BZ* 39 (1995) 259.

28.c. Nelson (137; compare Fritz, 115) uses Heb., Tg. and LXX*L* to read "it" for MT "them," whose pl. comes from addition of "and its king." See *Note* 28.b.

Younger emends to fem. sg. on the basis of "syntagmic structure" (*Ancient Conquest Accounts*, 381–82). E. Merrill writes, "Many MSS and some LXX and Targumic readings prefer אֹתָה for MT אוֹתָם ("them") thus requiring the translation, 'he put it under the ban and every person in it; he left no survivor.' While this may be attractive in some ways, the *lectio difficilior* would retain MT and . . . [t]he *waw* on וְאֶת could well be a *waw explicativitum* (GKC §154a note), yielding the meaning, 'he put them (the population and king) under the ban; that is, every person in it—he left no survivor'" ("Palestinian Archaeology and the Date of the Conquest: Do Tells Tell Tales?" *GTJ* 3 [1982] 121, n. 16). Nelson correctly notes that "in vv 28–38 both MT and OG have a large number of secondary readings intended to harmonize the repeated formulas, making textual reconstruction of these verses uncertain" (137). Such variations may go back to repetition in oral tradition and use of memory to create texts.

28.d. LXX also witnesses tendency to complete the formulaic expressions by adding καὶ διαπεφευγώς = וּפָלִיט (cf. Josh 8:22; Jer 42:17; 44:14; Lam 2:22). A similar tendency appears in LXX in vv 30, 33.

30.a. Younger (*Ancient Conquest Accounts*, 382) restores וילכדו אותה on the basis of OG and appearance of this syntagma in other passages as he charted out (205–6). Younger (*BZ* 39 [1995] 259; compare Boling, 290) sees haplography as the cause for the MT omission. Younger may well be correct in his assessment, but the attacks on different cities employ different manners of description and should not be automatically reduced to one system.

30.b. Fritz (115) follows many Heb. MSS in deleting "in it" as dittography. This may be correct, but the Heb. language can be expansive and redundant.

32.a. "And everything alive in it" does not appear in LXX and represents tendency to full formula. LXX, on the other hand, has pl. subjects (cf. v 28), avoiding any possibility of understanding "Yahweh" as the subject of such human activities. The Heb. subject is ambivalent, being capable of interpretation as Yahweh, Israel, or Joshua. Israel is most likely in the context. Gk. completes the formula with "he utterly destroyed it." Nelson (137) is most likely right in seeing the MT and OG readings as "harmonizing additions." Younger (*Ancient Conquest Accounts*, 382) looks to repeated structures and finds contrasting omissions in OG and MT here so that he restores to ויחרם אותה ואת כל הנפש אשר בה, "and he put it to the ban and every soul that was in it." Again, one must be careful not to establish a rigid pattern and expect every instance to fit it.

33.a. LXX adds formulaically "with the edge of the sword."

35.a. LXX adds "and Yahweh gave it over into the hand of Israel," again inserting the full formulation (Benjamin, *Variations*, suggests homoioteleuton in MT). Younger (*Ancient Conquest Accounts*, 382) follows Boling (290) and Margolis (*Book of Joshua in Greek*, 196) in seeing an "obvious haplography" and restoring, ויתן יהוה את ביד ישראל, "and Yahweh gave it into the hand of Israel." The tradition knew the formula and completed it here, while the original author may have shortened the formula in various occurrences.

35.b. LXX (compare Syr.) avoids repetition of "in that day," which may have been added by the tradition to underscore the miraculous. See Fritz (115).

36.a. LXX omits "from Eglon," which may again represent full formulation in the tradition. Younger (*Ancient Conquest Accounts*, 382) finds inner-Gk. haplography here.

37.a. LXX lacks "they captured it" and changes the subject to sg. Younger (*Ancient Conquest Accounts*, 382) claims the clause was lost in LXX via haplography. LXX makes no mention of the king, since his death was presupposed in v 26. This omission drew with it the following "and its cities." Nelson (137) may well be right when he sees LXX omissions as MT expansions from v 39.

39.a. Evidence from a few Heb. manuscripts and a Tg. support the pl. subject. Younger (*Ancient Conquest Accounts*, 382) argues vigorously with Boling, against Orlinsky, claiming a sizable Gk. haplography.

39.b. Nelson (137) finds OG using the "less problematic" "its precincts . . . , perhaps in harmony with 15:48–51."

39.c. Filling out the form, LXX adds "and its king," but then omits the final "just as . . ." clause, which is syntactically awkward but which rounds off the section vv 29–39 as a literary unit and which would not have been added by the later tradition. Nelson (138) sees haplography at work in the Gk. tradition.

39.d. Fritz (116) omits "and just as he had done to Libnah and to its king" as missing in LXX and not fitting the context and so representing a later addition. Younger (*Ancient Conquest Accounts*, 383) correctly follows Boling (291) and numerous Gk. MSS in retaining the MT reading.

40.a. LXX lacks "all," which has been added by tradition to underline the completeness of the conquest.

41.a. "Joshua smote" does not appear in LXX and may reflect later amplification.

43.a. Cf. *Note* 15.a.

Form/Structure/Setting

The temporal clause in v 1 marks a transition to a new section, in addition to tying the material both to the preceding narrative and to Josh 9:1–2. The MT has a concluding formula in v 15a, but the LXX gives the more original reading (*Notes* 15.a and 43.a). By inserting v 15, the tradition notes that a narrative unit is complete at that point. The following material is closely tied, however, to vv 1–14 by the compiler and continues his theme. This is concluded by the summary formula of v 42. The tradition has also marked the end of the unit by adding v 43. A new transition is made in Josh 11:1, paralleling in form that of Josh 10:1. Thus the unit for study is Josh 10:1–42 (43).

Tradition

Israel's strength is in narrative reporting, creating from a variety of ancient (oral) sources accounts of its earliest days. The extended battle reports from chaps. 6–11 are built on these earlier traditions.

Chap. 10 is an artistic unit, but it is also an individual narrative, separated from chaps. 9 and 11 by introductory and concluding formulas and built up from various sources that are described below. The narrative features Joshua's valor and piety. The tradition uses a poetic fragment to tell how Joshua marched all night to defeat a coalition opposing Gibeon. Five kings meet their death in a cave, and tells how Joshua and his army pursue the other coalition partners and put their cities under the ban.

What lies behind these materials? The list of theories is almost endless.[1273] The form-critical surprise is that each of the component narratives had its own genre before being included within the larger conquest narrative, a narrative that must be seen as reaching back beyond chap. 9 or 10 to chap. 6. How and when the individual narratives were joined into a whole is an open question needing further investigation.

How did each of the component narratives receive its present form? Again, ideas conconcerning the tradition history behind the battle of Gibeon are myriad.

1273 See Hess (1996) 197–99.

Alt sees it as the one battle in which Joshua was firmly anchored.[1274] Noth expresses doubts about Joshua's anchorage in the tradition but holds to the historical battle between Israel and Canaanite city-states. Sawyer dates the material exactly to an eclipse of the sun that lasted four minutes on 30 September 1131 BCE, beginning at 12:40 p.m.[1275] Rösel limits the action to Jarmuth and Azekah against Gibeon.[1276] Gruenthaner argues strongly for the unity of the passage.[1277] He concludes: "Our study of the text shows that the sun is depicted as occupying the same position from noon or afternoon of one day until approximately sunrise of the next day. This phenomenon must have been observed at least in the area of the pursuit; how far it extended beyond this district we do not know. It may have been visible in the whole Promised Land."[1278] Weimar transposes the narrative to a battle pitting Gibeon against Israel.[1279] Schunck moves in the opposite direction and posits a coalition of Ephraimites, Benjaminites, and Judahites joining forces against the Amorites.[1280] For Dus, the story is an etiological invention of the compiler to explain a heroic song, whose true origin lay in a polemical curse against the cities of the sun and moon god.[1281]

Margalit reworks the material and downplays the author's knowledge and skill. For him, the writer got his material from "an ancient source" "known to him but vaguely from oral tradition." Part of this "hoary tradition" appears in the dominant role Jerusalem plays.[1282] So, for Margalit, we are "much closer to the realm of literature than to 'history.'"[1283]

Knauf traces the tradition to the time of Saul (and Ishbaal) and David, finding that after Merneptah and before Saul, Israel was not an independent political entity capable of conducting warfare.[1284] Hess sees chap. 10 as having more ancient Near Eastern parallels than any other chapter in the book of Joshua.[1285] His conclusion seems to result from the length and details of the chapter with its multiple battles rather than the individual city battles up till this place in the narrative.

Hess finds an overall structural similarity to Late Bronze Age royal annals that include accounts of major victories followed by stereotyped, repetitive reports of enemy city after enemy city being defeated. Of course, the annals cover years as opposed to the Israelite extended campaign. The annals were created by specially trained scribes supported by the royal court. One continues to doubt that Israel at that time had such trained and educated scribes, supporting infrastructure, or available writing materials to emulate the Mesopotamian system. Only with David and Solomon did Israel gain the resources and institutions to preserve oral traditions into continuous written accounts.

1274 "Josua," in *Kleine Schriften*, 1:187–89.
1275 *PEQ* 104 (1972) 139.
1276 *VT* 26 (1976) 506–7.
1277 *CBQ* 10 (1948) 271–90.
1278 Ibid, 284.
1279 *Bib* 57 (1976) 61–62.
1280 *Benjamin*, 37–39.
1281 *VT* 10 (1960) 360–61.
1282 *VT* 42 (1992) 486–87, n. 45.
1283 Ibid., 486, n. 45.
1284 Knauf, 97.
1285 Hess (2009) 43–44.

Younger outlines the "iterative scheme" here as elements repeat over and over and compares it to ancient Near Eastern parallels.[1286] He attributes the similarities to "a common ancient Near Eastern transmission code."[1287] Similarly, though not iterated in Joshua, "the narrative of the miracle of the hailstones is a notable ingredient of the transmission code for conquest accounts."[1288]

A few facts appear clear. Several traditional units have been joined together here. These include the coalition of kings, traditional poetic fragments, a Makkedah tradition, an etiological tradition, and a series of annal-like reports. They appear united as a battle report, but "the cities named in the account do not correspond exactly to those that formed the alliance."[1289] Thus I agree with McConville and Williams that "some of the 'gaps' in the narrative serve . . . to remind us that the historical actuality was probably less tidy than a superficial reading of the account appears."[1290]

McConville and Williams further insist: "Joshua is said to have made war on these nations for 'a long time' [11:18]. This sits a little oddly with the narratives of swift victory."[1291] The pursuit narrative is thus chronologically telescoped for literary and theological purposes. The writer wants to underline the ease of the battle when Yahweh fights for Israel and so speeds up the narrative tempo and brings uniformity to the various victory reports.

Together the independent traditions include most of the elements in Younger's ancient Near Eastern conquest scheme, pointing to a compiler or writer familiar with literary patterns from neighboring cultures. This suggests that the Solomonic period was the time of composition, when Israel began strong political contacts and probably had Egyptian and Mesopotamian scribes as part of the royal court.

The first narrative (vv 1–11) rests on an old Jerusalem tradition of a king of Jerusalem whose name contained the divine component Zedek (cf. Gen 14:18). Its locus is confined to the area of Gibeon and Beth-Horon. At least the kings of Jarmuth and Azekah, whose cities play no role in the following traditions, were included.[1292] The tradition tells how the coalition against Gibeon was defeated by a nighttime march of Joshua.

The poetic fragments (vv 12b–13a) reach back beyond the ancient Book of Jashar. The editor's framework stands in vv 12a, 13b–14 + 15. The tradition of five kings occupies vv 16–27, while vv 28–39 preserve the formulaic pursuit narrative. The theological summary appears in vv 40–42.

The Makkedah tradition takes a list of victories and presents them as a pursuit narrative. The order of the cities mentioned reflects a conquest itinerary used by ancient empires marching against Jerusalem. That Libnah, Lachish, and Eglon formed an original unity is possible, but not proven.[1293] The unit represents a logi-

1286 *Ancient Conquest Accounts*, 204–28.
1287 Ibid., 210.
1288 Ibid., 211.
1289 McConville and Williams, 55.
1290 Ibid., 56.
1291 Ibid., 59.
1292 So Rösel, *VT* 26 (1976) 506–7.
1293 Schunck, *Benjamin*, 31–33; Weimar, *Bib* 57 (1976) 52–53.

cal pattern of conquest in Judah, one quite possibly followed by Sennacherib and Nebuchadnezzar.[1294] It is thus a typical conquest summary. Campbell describes the section as "an independent fragment of traditions . . . skillfully inserted into the account of Joshua's campaign against the southern coalition."[1295]

Younger objects to my emphasis on the pursuit narrative, wanting to list "panic-stricken flight" as a "common motif" in ancient accounts and to dismiss pursuit as a part of holy-war theology, a term he wants to discard.[1296] Pursuit, of course, does not differentiate holy from secular or Israelite from Assyrian war strategy.

The original author/compiler of the book of Joshua chose pursuit as a literary theme to display Israel's obedience to God's ban (חרם) orders. In so doing, the pursuit became not just a denouement or ending to the narrative but a major narrative in and of itself, given more narrative space than any other literary element in chap. 10. Literary emphasis on the pursuit portion rather than on the original battle encounter does not necessarily make the narrative "fabricated, secondary, non-historical, etc.," as Younger interprets my discussion of chapter 10.[1297] Use of ancient tradition does not immediately classify a narrative as non-historical. An editor can just as well add historical elements as can an original author. Such emphasis does show the central point of the inspired person creating the literature, namely, an emphasis on Israel's obedience in light of what might be considered questionable actions in accepting Rahab, in not controlling the greed of Achan, and in signing a treaty with the Gibeonites without consulting God. By extending the pursuit motif to such an extent, the author/compiler repeatedly showed Israel's total obedience. Chap. 10–11 fit Younger's scheme more clearly than other parts of Joshua because they represent annalistic genres most clearly related to ancient Near Eastern sources.

Source and Redaction

Chap. 10 is difficult for source critics. While few portions of the narrative can be classified as doublets or contradictory materials, some continue to try to identify sources.

Fritz continues the Noth tradition, seeing the opening narrative as a combination of several parts with nothing coming from history but all resulting from the Deuteronomistic Historian and later editors.[1298] According to Fritz vv 17–27 do go back to an etiology while the stereotyped formulations show vv 28–43 as a purely literary formation apart from any older traditions.[1299] Vv 1a, 2a, 3–6, 7abα, 8, 9a, 10, and 12–15 constitute the original narrative. Redactional additions appear in vv 1b, 2b, 7bβ, 9b, and 11. Vv 16–23a and 24–27 are original to the kings in the cave text, with only v 23b representing a later addition. The conquest of the cities has additions only in vv 33 and 41.

1294 Cf. Wright, *JNES* 5 (1946) 109–12; Halpern, *CBQ* 37 (1975) 314–15; N. Na'aman, *VT* 29 (1979) 61–86.
1295 *Joshua to Chronicles*, 49.
1296 *Ancient Conquest Accounts*, 221–23, 260.
1297 *Ancient Conquest Accounts*, 220.
1298 Fritz, 109.
1299 Ibid., 110, 115.

Nelson finds Deuteronomistic language only in vv 25 and 40 and the repeated phrase: "he did not let anything remain" or "he left no survivors."[1300] "Deuteronomistic orthodoxy" is represented in vv 13b–14 and 27. The names of the five cities and the poetic fragment come from other sources.

Margalit isolates three parts of the chapter:[1301]

1. A heroic saga (*Heldensage*) in vv 1, 3–7, 9a, 10αβb, 16, 22–27
2. The "War of Yahweh" in vv 2(?), 8, 10aα, 11, 12b, 13aα, 14b, 16
3. Compiler in vv 12a, 13aβγ, 14a, 17–21, 25

He sees no reason for a salvation oracle in v 8 since the story is a heroic saga, not a war of Yahweh to this point.[1302] Thus Margalit continues to separate elements of human heroism and leadership from elements of divine intervention. This separation, however, does not correspond to Israelite thinking, in which human cooperation and divine action are both parts of warfare. Again Margalit senses geographic problems and redundancy in the shift of the battle scene to the Lachish area since the miracle apparently took place at Gibeon. The camp for nighttime rest remains in Gilgal, far from the battle area. Elimination of v 15 textually then makes vv 17–19 "unintelligible."[1303]

Knauf finds the conclusion to his Exodus-Joshua history here.[1304] It featured three battles: the battle report by the exodus from Egypt (Exod 14), the entrance into Canaan (Josh 6), and the battle over all the kings of Canaan (Josh 10:40a, 42a). In each of these battles, as opposed to Josh 8 and 11, Israel stands as mere spectators while Yahweh fights the battle.

Younger argues against such analysis, eliminating sources because he finds elements of an ancient Near Eastern transmission code throughout the narrative.[1305] Younger does not, however, go the extra step and analyze the various episodes or individual narratives form critically. He has discovered the transmission code of ancient royalty reports appearing in various genres of materials. He is correct in seeing Josh 10–11 as closely related linguistically to different examples of ancient Near Eastern battle reports. That he has proved the case for chap. 9 and even for chap. 12 may be questioned.

His examples most clearly related to Joshua represent royal annals or campaign reports, but he does not examine the sources of each episode of the account. He also does not distinguish between reports from royalty seeking to preserve territory and authority and initial thrusts from new settlers seeking new land under a new type of government. His assumptions work best if the biblical accounts stem not from premonarchical Israel but from a time of aggressive monarchy so that the syntagms correspond to the time of writing, not to the time of happening. His repeated underlining of the hyperbolic element of the narrative takes him quite close to those who deny any historicity to the stories.

1300 Nelson, 138.
1301 *VT* 42 (1992) 489.
1302 Ibid., 468–69.
1303 Ibid., 472.
1304 Knauf, 97.
1305 *Ancient Conquest Accounts*, 220.

Mitchell ties the theme of total destruction to that of the kings' hearing and "suggests that the stories are best understood as a corpus"[1306] and points to Noort[1307] "for a convincing argument that sources have been so thoroughly reworked that it is virtually impossible to extricate them."[1308] Traditions came down to the Israelite compiler or ultimate author relating to the time of conquest and to southern geography. The Israelite compiler transformed the tradition(s) into an example of holy-war narrative. To do so, he utilized yet another tradition of Israelite battle on the descent of Beth-Horon going toward Azekah (v 11). No other contours of the tradition are apparent. To put the proper theological perspective on the narratives, the compiler inserted into the original Gibeon narrative the Israelite holy-war narrative elements: great fear of the enemy (v 2), the salvation oracle (v 8), and the theological summary (v 11b).

The conquest itinerary has been described by Knauf:[1309]

1. Joshua and all Israel move from station *x* to *y*.
2. They battle *y*.
3. Yahweh delivers the city and its king to Israel.
4. Joshua or Israel strikes with the edge of the sword everything alive in the city.
5. Joshua carries out the dedication to the ban on the city or on its king.
6. No survivor remains.
7. He does to *y*'s king just as he had done with *z*'s king.

The resulting narrative includes the extended elements of a battle report:

1. Summoning forces (vv 1–5)
2. Treaty partner's call for help (vv 6–7)
3. Salvation oracle (v 8)
4. The battle: Yahweh wins with miracles (vv 9–11)
5. Joshua speaks to Yahweh telling sun and moon to stop, and they do (vv 12–13)
6. Summary interpretation (v 14)
7. Return to camp (v 15)
8. Battle consequences (v 16)
    a. Canaanites flee to cave in Makkedah (v 16)
    b. Joshua and army close Canaanites in cave (vv 17–18)
    c. Pursuit leaves remnant of other enemies (vv 19–20)
    d. Israel returns to camp unscathed (v 21)
    e. Joshua makes symbol of five encaved kings and kills them (vv 22–27)
    f. Pursuit destroys enemy cities (vv 28–39)
9. Battle summary (vv 40–42)
10. Israel returns to camp (v 43)

This battle story, featuring the pursuit narrative, assures readers that God fights for and protects his obedient people.

1306 *Together in the Land*, 87.
1307 "Zwischen Mythos und Rationalität," 149–61.
1308 *Together in the Land*, 87, n. 2.
1309 Knauf, 105.

Form

As has long been recognized, the unit has several traditional components. In his "The Book of Joshua as a Land Grant," Hess uses an Alalakh land-grant document as a point of comparison with chaps. 10–11.[1310] Common elements include:

1. Opening with names of chief enemy and his city-state
2. Enemy exciting other towns into battle
3. Divine weapons with meteorological ties
4. Peace or rest as final outcome

In his commentary, Hess speaks of a battle report (vv 1–10) developed in three panels: "God's assistance (vv. 11–15), Joshua and Israel's defeat of the enemy (vv. 16–27), and the systematic destruction of southern towns (vv. 28–39)."[1311]

Margalit divides the material into a heroic saga and a war-of-Yahweh narrative.[1312] The prototype of the war-of-Yahweh narrative appears in Exod 14. It has three parts:[1313] Israel walks into a trap, cries to Yahweh for help, and watches Yahweh fight for Israel. Human skill, fortitude, or heroism play no role in such stories.[1314]

The war-of-Yahweh material is, for Margalit, closely connected to the day-of-the-Lord tradition with its daytime darkness theme.[1315] To achieve this interpretation, Margalit has to redefine a word based on an isolated Greek fragment of Hab 3, move the poetic fragment to a later slot in the narrative, and call on solar eclipse language.[1316] He works too hard to separate works of Yahweh and works of humans.

Younger argues against the formula עַד־עֶצֶם הַיּוֹם הַזֶּה, "until this very day" (v 27), as an indicator that the previous narrative is an etiology.[1317] He writes: "in a great majority of the cases is a formula of personal testimony added to, and confirming a received tradition."[1318] Younger shows from the Annals of Thutmose III that the "biblical phrase refers to the time at which the account was written."[1319] Hawk, however, points to the stock elements used with variety to give each account uniformity and uniqueness.[1320]

Formally, the chapter contains a holy-war narrative to which is attached a poetic fragment with prosaic introduction and conclusion. They are used as the introduction to a narrative fragment. Another addition (v 27) transforms the whole into a secondary etiology to illustrate holy-war technique. This shows that the narrative is not simply an etiology without historical tradition behind it. Etiology is, rather, a narrative technique that ties the ancient narrative to the world of the narrator's present audience. A typical conquest itinerary and a theological summary conclude the chapter.

1310 *CBQ* 83 (2002) 501.
1311 Ibid., 187.
1312 *VT* 42 (1992) 477.
1313 Ibid., 475.
1314 Ibid., 476.
1315 *VT* 42 (1992) 481.
1316 Ibid., 482–83.
1317 Younger, 224–25.
1318 Ibid., 318, n. 93.
1319 Ibid., 225.
1320 Hawk (2010) 126.

Structure and Form of Joshua 10

Structure: Facing a coalition attack			Genre: Holy war story		
Element	Passage	Marker	Element	Passage	Marker
Exposition (pf. or disjunctive): Leading enemy fearful	vv 1–2	Temporal clause	Troops gather for war	vv 1–5a	When king heard . . . , he feared . . . so he sent
			1st battle	v 5b	Coalition battles Gibeon
			Gibeon calls to Israel for help	v 6	Sent. . . . "Do not abandon"
Complication (impf. consec.): Coalition gathers	vv 3–5	Impf. consec.	Israel gathers for battle	v 7	Went up
			Salvation oracle	v 8	Fear not: Conveyance formula
Change or crisis (speech or dialogue): Gibeon calls for help	vv 6–7	Dialogue	2nd battle report	vv 9–13	Joshua and God defeat unsuspecting coalition; God obeyed Joshua's poetic call
			Editorial summary	v 14	Unique day: God obeyed man
Resolution (impf. consec.): Salvation oracle	v 8	Impf. consec./ dialogue	Consequences: Israel	v 15	Return to camp
			Consequences: Enemy	v 16	Fled
			3rd battle plan	vv 17–18	Double command: Roll stone, pursue and destroy
Ending/ denouement (formulaic): Joshua and Yahweh defeat coalition	vv 9–14	Poetic fragment; God obeying Joshua and summary description	3rd battle report	v 20a	Crushing defeat on enemy
Editorial summary	v 15	Formulaic: return to camp	Battle consequences: Enemy	v 20b	Remnant in fortified cities
Exposition (pf. or disjunctive) leading enemy fearful	Missing		Battle consequences: Israel	v 21	In camp unharmed

Structure: Facing a coalition attack			Genre: Holy war story		
Element	*Passage*	*Marker*	*Element*	*Passage*	*Marker*
			Battle consequences	vv 22–24	Symbolic consequences showing Israel's superiority
Complication (impf. consec.): Enemy kings flee to caves	v 16	impf. consec.	Salvation oracle	v 25	Prophetic Joshua issues oracle
			Battle conclusion report	vv 26–27a	Kings killed; corpses handled according Dtn law
Change or crisis (speech or dialogue): Joshua hears report	vv 17–19	Dialogue: report to Joshua, who gives orders	Etiology	v 27b	"Until this very day"
			Pursuit narrative	vv 28–39	Formulaic series of battle reports
Resolution (impf. consec.): Israel gains crushing victory	v 20	Temporal clause serves double duty as resolution and exposition	Battle summary	vv 40–42	Joshua smote all
			Formulaic closure	v 43	Return to camp
Ending/ denouement (formulaic): People return safely	v 21	Formulaic conclusion of victorious unharmed army			
Exposition (pf. or disjunctive): Remnant remains after victory	vv 20–21	Temporal clause			
Embedded crisis (dialogue)	vv 22–25	Dialogue picks up vv 18–19 narrative, showing defeat symbol; salvation oracle			
Complication (impf. consec.):	Missing				
Change or crisis (speech or dialogue): Joshua slays, shames kings	vv 26–27a	impf. consec. + command			
Resolution (impf. consec.):	v 27b	Eternally encaved kings			

Structure: Facing a coalition attack			Genre: Holy war story		
Element	Passage	Marker	Element	Passage	Marker
Ending/ denouement (formulaic): Buried until this day	v 27c	Etiological conclusion			
Final resolutions: Pursuit force wins victories	vv 28–39	Formulaic series showing remnant destroyed			
Editorial summary	vv 40–43	God brings total victory and return to camp			

Structure

Knauf finds the structure to include:[1321]

Exposition: Overthrow of Gibeon (9:3a–15a*)
Reaction: Jerusalem organizes coalition against Gibeon (10:1–4) marked by Adoni-zedek's speech
Crisis: Siege of Gibeon (10:5–7) with speech of Gibeonites
Resolution: Battle of Gibeon (10:8–10, 14) with speech of Yahweh

Knauf maintains that the narrative was quickly expanded by the song fragment of vv 12c–13c, but that we cannot tell if this was narrated from a Jerusalem or Gibeon perspective.[1322] He claims that the certain item about the narrative fragment is that it is polytheistic, calling on enemy gods not to enter the fray. Knauf isolates a basic layer describing the conquest of the entire land in one attack but without mention of the oath to destroy everything.[1323] Rather his Deuteronomistic layer introduced the ban into the narrative at a later time while composing a veritable campaign report.

Harstad explains vv 15 and 43 in two possible ways.[1324] First, v 15 may be proleptic, describing what took place after v 42, vv 15 and 43 forming an inclusion. This view sees a thematic arrangement, not a chronological one. Second, if the narrative intends to be sequential, then an unmentioned time lapse allows Joshua and his men to move their military camp to Makkedah. V 43 shows the return of the camp to Gilgal.

Hall divides the structure into three "scenes":[1325]

1–15	Yahweh's help in battle
16–27	Israel's pursuit of enemies
28–43	Israel's campaign in the south

1321 Knauf, 97.
1322 Ibid., 98.
1323 Ibid., 105.
1324 Harstad, 431–32.
1325 *Conquering Character*, 166.

She reads the parts as dischronologized narrative, with some of the material overlapping in time.

Coote understands the defense of Gibeon in three stages: attack against five kings, pursuit and execution of kings, dedication and destruction of towns.[1326] Younger emphasizes the chiastic structure forming a palistrophe with hyperbole, creating a structure that is simulated or artificial so that "the narrative only approaches a representation of the reality it purports to describe" as "is the case with any historical narrative."[1327]

Looking at the larger picture, Hawk describes Josh 10:28–11:23 as a series of reports and summaries that "create a sense of unity and totality in the conquest of the land."[1328] He comments that "the historical reality was likely much different," a judgment he supports by reference to Josh 11:18, which points to a much more complex situation.[1329]

Younger shows parallel narrative patterns between Josh 9:3–10:43 and 11:1–15, each with an introductory setting, an oracle of assurance, a victory in one decisive open-field battle, a pursuit of the retreating enemy to the extreme southern or northern boundary, the capture of the leading city(ies), and a summary of the campaign.[1330]

I maintain that vv 1–11 represent a typical miraculous Yahweh war narrative, introduced by the temporal clause (vv 1–2), leading to the imperfect consecutives building up narrative tension. These are skillfully augmented by parallel dialogue sections (vv 4, 6b) by which both sides expand the action to their allies. The climax occurs in the salvation oracle (v 8), the expected resolution then being described in vv 9–11. The formulaic conclusion comes in v 11b.

Traditional poetry then appears in vv 12bβ–13aα, with an introduction in v 12a–bα and a summary conclusion in vv 13aβ–b and 14. The poetry describes a battle and its results either as another perspective on the previous battle or more likely as an introduction to the pursuit narratives.

A new narrative begins in v 16. It presents an unexpected variant ending to the previous narrative, having no narrative introduction of its own. It does have a distinctive setting, however. While vv 1–11 center on Gibeon (v 10) and the descent of Beth-Horon (v 11), vv 16–27 center on Makkedah (v 16). The two are linked through the appearance of Makkedah in the first narrative (v 10).

The second narrative reaches its climax quickly in the report to Joshua (v 17) and his response (v 18) with orders that are assumed to be followed but not explicitly said to be. The continuation confuses the issue and complicates the plot. Thus Nelson sees a chronological backtrack and overlap in vv 18–20, suggesting that the two stories concerning the five kings were originally independent.[1331]

A new issue arises—the remnant. Joshua's orders are supplemented (v 19). Only these supplementary orders are carried out and then only by a temporal clause

---

1326 Coote, 646.
1327 "The 'Conquest' of the South," *BZ* 39 (1995) 260–61.
1328 Hess (2010) 124.
1329 Ibid, 125.
1330 "Rhetorical Structuring," 5.
1331 Nelson, 138.

rather than a main clause (v 20a). The main clause features the remnant returning to fortified cities.

The scene then shifts back to the starting point at the cave (v 21), where new orders (v 22) are carried out (v 23), giving rise to yet another command (v 24) and then a general formula of encouragement (v 25). An apparent concluding formula appears in v 26, only to be followed unexpectedly by the etiological ending (v 27). Narrative form has disintegrated, and narrative tension disappears. The narrative sidetrack in vv 19–20 prepares for the formulaic list of vv 28–39, while the narrative continuation in vv 21–27 illustrates Yahweh war technique and theology with the etiological formula being secondary interpretation.[1332] Vv 29–39 form a unit as shown by the summary formula (vv 40–42) concluding the section and pointing back to its beginning.

Setting

The original home of the Gibeonite war tradition may well have been the same as that of chap. 9: Gibeon. The Gibeonites used it to explain how Israel's great hero Joshua showed himself true to the treaty that bound Israel and Gibeon together. They used it to protest against the treatment they received at the hands of Saul and Solomon.

Knauf traces the tradition back to the days of Saul and David when, according to him, for the first time Israel became strong enough to conduct a military campaign.[1333] The opening verses of chap. 10 join the original kernel of vv 40–43 to form the conclusion for Knauf's Exodus-Joshua narrative. This narrative joins Exod 14, Josh 6, and the conclusion in Josh 10 to illustrate God fighting on Israel's behalf.

Margalit denies Noth's compiler any connection to the material and places the author in the Babylonian exile as one who had never set foot on Palestinian soil and who spoke royal Aramaic rather than classical Hebrew.[1334] Kallai, however, refutes Margalit's position: "It is not lack of familiarity with the geography and inadequate command of the language of an Aramaic-speaking Israelite in the Babylonian exile that caused the unconformities in this narrative, but the manner of compilation and redaction."[1335]

The tradition behind the list in vv 28–39 can probably never be recovered. Certainly it would only explain the preservation, not the creation of the story. The final part of Josh 10:27 states why the narrative was preserved at one stage of the development of the larger text and how it functioned at that stage

The Israelite compiler transformed the tradition into a holy-war narrative. To do so, he utilized yet another tradition of Israelite battle on the descent of Beth-Horon going toward Azekah (v 11). He inserted into the original Gibeon narrative the Israelite holy-war narrative elements: great fear of the enemy (v 2), the salvation oracle (v 8), and the theological summary (v 11b).

The compiler used the poetic fragment to make the miracle more promi-

---

1332 B. Childs, "A Study of the Formula, 'Until This Day,'" *JBL* 82 (1963) 288.
1333 Knauf, 97.
1334 *VT* 42 (1992) 484–85.
1335 *ZAW* 115 (2003) 40.

nent. The poem may well be related to compositions such as Exod 15:21; Judg 5; Num 21:14–15; and 21:27–30, which commemorate early military achievements. Its precise context cannot be known, however. It could well be related originally to the same context as the core of vv 1–10a. As such, it would be a prayer for the sun not to rise and for the moon to remain in control.[1336] The compiler, though, interprets it in a different perspective. He creates a chapter of pursuit by introducing v 10b. The miracle is one of extended daylight for him (v 13b). In v 14 he reiterates the holy-war theme, while also underlining the unique position of Joshua.

Listing differences in the cities of vv 1–15, 16–27, and 28–43, Pressler points to "different memories of Israel's acquisition of the land . . . woven together . . . [into] a coherent narrative, closely and logically linked to the story of the Gibeonite-Israelite alliance."[1337]

The Makkedah tradition concerned five kings buried in a cave there, quite possibly the five kings listed in v 23. The compiler has inserted his pursuit motif to transform the burial story into a lesson for holy war. Burial in the cave is only a temporary measure while Israel pursues the remnant. He also added the etiological formula to show the validity of his holy-war lesson for the contemporary generation.

Finally, the compiler used a conquest itinerary to create the final leg of his pursuit, used by Younger to argue that its written style represents ancient Near Eastern conquest accounts. He concludes: "the account is simulated or artificial in its structure. . . . The narrative only approaches a representation of the reality which it purports to describe."[1338]

Younger's illustrations of ancient Near Eastern examples of campaigns reporting the killing of everyone with no survivors may indicate a hyperbolic literary element that Israel also used.[1339] This leads to the conclusion that hyperbole lets us see "there is no reason to maintain that the account in Joshua 9–12 portrays a complete conquest."[1340] Thus "the Israelites may very well have 'conquered' the land as generally described in the narrative. But this 'conquest' was in many instances temporary, not permanent. It did not mean the complete subjugation of the land" (compare Josh 11:18; 13:1–2).[1341]

The compiler thus gives the chapter its basic form, that of a conquest campaign against rebelling kings. Repeated redactional levels are not evident.[1342] Rather, a few modest changes may have been introduced to underline the totality of the destruction (cf. v 20, the total destruction refrain in vv 28, 30, 33, 37, 39, 40, and perhaps v 25). Younger's conclusions pull back from the text's emphasis on the great extent of Israel's conquest. Hyperbole and other literary devices are employed, but the final teaching is the great power of God to win victories.

1336 Gray, 110.
1337 Pressler, 79.
1338 *BZ* 39 (1995) 226–27.
1339 Ibid., 227–28.
1340 Ibid., 243.
1341 Younger, 244.
1342 Contra Weimar, *Bib* 57 (1976) 51–62.

Comments

1 The opening verse ties the conquest narratives together into a unit, referring back to Jericho (chap. 6), Ai (chaps. 7–8), and Gibeon (chap. 9). Readers must remember with Howard that "Jerusalem became the most important city in Israel, but this did not happen until many years later, under David (2 Sam 5:6–19)."[1343] Pressler estimates that "pre-Israelite Jerusalem had a population of roughly one thousand and occupied about fifteen acres."[1344] Hess finds in the Amarna letters evidence that Jerusalem was a regional administrative center with some literary sophistication.[1345]

Knauf maintains that Gibeon was bigger and stronger than Jerusalem up until the campaign of the Egyptian pharaoh Shishak (1 Kgs 14:25–25) in the days of Rehoboam and that Gibeon was relatively independent from Israel and Judah, having enough independence to be attacked by a Canaanite coalition and to call on Joshua for help.[1346] The biblical text apparently insists that by this time Gibeonites were indentured by the Jerusalem temple. Yet Gibeon served as a worship place and confirmation site for Solomon (1 Kgs 3:4–15). This may indicate, as seen in the comments on the previous chapter, that the temple references connected to Gibeon's servitude represent foreshadowings of the days of Solomon and Rehoboam rather than immediate results under Joshua.

Knauf further maintains that the treaty obligations placed on the Israelites to protect a vassal were influenced by seventh-century international legal treaties and not by Torah from the Persian period.[1347] They may also reflect Hittite treaty forms from the era prior to the conquest.

Margalit states that the description of Gibeon here does not fit with the image of the Gibeonites in the previous chapter, but we must recall that the Gibeonites intentionally built a false image of themselves and their city, while the narrator of chap. 10 wants to show how strong Yahweh is to be able to defeat such a city.[1348] Margalit also searches chap. 9 for explicit references to the duty to defend the partner in a friendship pact, such a duty would have been an understood element of such treaties that need not be spelled out for original writer, reader, or listeners.[1349]

2 V 2 introduces the holy-war ideology that dominates the chapter. In so doing, it harks back to the theme of Josh 2:9—the fear of the inhabitants of the land before the mighty acts of Yahweh. Despite the covenant made with inhabitants of the land, Israel remains in proper relationship to Yahweh. Joshua's measures have been sufficient. The plural verb form has no antecedent in the present context. It may represent an earlier form of the narrative (Noth) or simply refer to the inhabitants of Jerusalem without specifically introducing them into the narrative. The comparison of Gibeon with Ai may represent the Gibeonite city at the time of

---

1343 Howard, 234.
1344 Pressler, 80.
1345 Hess (2009) 44. See excursus by Harstad, 443–48.
1346 Knauf, 97.
1347 Ibid.
1348 *VT* 42 (1992) 467.
1349 Ibid., 468.

the Israelite monarchy.[1350] The description serves to emphasize the even greater power of Israel and God. It appears to imply that Gibeon had the power of one of the city-states but did not have a king. It is often surmised that a council of elders ruled the city (cf. Josh 9:11).

Excavations in Jerusalem and references in ancient Near Eastern documents show that Jerusalem occupied a prominent place in Palestine by the nineteenth century (execration tablets). Apparently the city wall erected in that era lasted until the seventh century. The city's wide range of influence in the southern hill country is well documented in the Amarna letters, seven of which come from its king, Abdi-Khepa. It became Israelite only with its capture by David (2 Sam 5:6–10). Hess believes that "Jos 10 preserves a distinct and authentic early memory of a city-state that had "controlled the Benjaminite plateau and influenced events in the towns of the Judean Shephelah."[1351]

The Jerusalem king and his southern cohorts had reason to fear, for now "Israel controlled the Benjaminite plateau, the crossroads between the hill country and the Judean wilderness," thus controlling access to the coastal plains and lowlands.[1352] "Adoni-Zedek must regain control of the area of Gibeon for his own security."[1353] The Jerusalem leader thus selected allies who would help him control the western and southern trade routes into the Shephelah and the coast. Hawk focuses on the kings as the initiators of battle rather than on the plot of the entire book that shows Israel conquering and occupying land they wanted to possess and settle.[1354]

3 Gen 23:1–7; 13:18; 18:1; and Num 13:22 preserve ancestral traditions concerning Hebron. Its conquest is attributed to Caleb in Josh 15:13 and Judg 1:20. It is located at Tell er-Rumeideh about nineteen miles (thirty kilometers) south of Jerusalem, controlling the road south to Beersheba and two passes to the coastal plain.[1355] A travel itinerary of Rameses II seems to verify the location despite dispute among archaeologists and geographers over Late Bronze occupation.

Jarmuth is generally identified with Iermochos, a Byzantine village on Tell Jarmuth (Khirbet el-Yarmuk = M.R. 147124) in the Shephelah, three miles (five kilometers) southwest of Beth Shemesh and sixteen miles (twenty-five kilometers) west-southwest of Jerusalem. A brief trial excavation has revealed only Early Bronze Age remains (ca. 2650–2350 BCE). Thus its location is not certain.[1356] The town was allotted to Judah (Josh 15:35) and reoccupied after the return from exile (Neh 11:29). An Amarna age letter found at Tell el-Hesi mentions Jarmuth.

Lachish has a long history reaching back to prehistorical times. It is known for its expansionist policies in the fourteenth century as evidenced in the Amarna letters, eighteen of which have been discovered there. Three kings are named: Zimreda, Shipti-Balu, and Yabni-Ilu. The city is mentioned here for the first time in the Bible. The Lachish letters confirm its location at Tell ed-Duweir (= M.R.

1350 Cf. J. B. Pritchard, "Gibeon's History," 4–5, 11–12.
1351 Hess (1996) 188, n. 1.
1352 Ibid., 187–88.
1353 Ibid., 188.
1354 Hawk (2010) 111.
1355 Fritz, 116.
1356 See Rainey, *Sacred Bridge*, 86; P. de Miroschedji, *ABD*, 3:644–45.

135108), eighteen miles (thirty kilometers) southeast of Ashkelon and fifteen miles (twenty-five kilometers) west of Hebron.[1357] Late Chalcolithic and Early Bronze Age settlements are followed by signs of eighteenth-century settlement, with an extensive Late Bronze Age settlement representing the city's prime, even without defensive walls.[1358] This thirteenth-century city was destroyed by fire and abandoned for a considerable period. A recent excavator attributes the burning to Joshua.[1359]

Eglon is a center of archaeological debate. The supplement to the *Interpreter's Dictionary of the Bible* includes two articles, one by A. Rainey[1360] supporting Tell 'Aitun (M.R. 143099), seven miles (twelve kilometers) southeast of Lachish and ten miles (seventeen kilometers) southwest of Hebron, and one by D. G. Rose[1361] supporting Tell el-Hesi (M.R. 124106), seven miles (eleven kilometers) west-southwest of Lachish. Tell el-Hesi was destroyed in the thirteenth century and reoccupied in the tenth.[1362] Outside the present context, the Bible mentions Eglon only in Josh 12:12 and 15:39. Capturing Eglon gave Israel immediate access to the southern trade routes.

Debir is the name of a king in v 3. In Josh 10:38–39; 11:21; 12:13; 15:7, 15, 49; 21:15; Judg 1:11, and 1 Chr 6:43, however, it is the name of a city. Its location is a matter of scholarly debate. Proposals include Tell Beit Mirsim, thirteen miles (twenty kilometers) southwest of Hebron; Khirbet Tarrameh, five miles (nine kilometers) southwest of Hebron; or Khirbet Rabud, seven and a half miles west of Hebron. M. Kochavi calls it the largest and most important Canaanite city south of Hebron.[1363] Rainey[1364] and Fritz[1365] strongly support Khirbet Rabud. Hess also agrees.[1366]

For the significance of the kings' names, see especially Hess.[1367] Knauf suggests the kings' names are supplementary to the text inserted by the speculation of creative scholars.[1368] Barr concludes that Debir, king of Eglon, never existed but is a product of tradition and literary activity.[1369] See Younger[1370] and Greenspoon[1371] for conclusive arguments opposed to Barr.

4–5 Israel's movements into the land threaten the stability of the establishment. The king of Jerusalem takes drastic measures, calling together the major city-state chieftains of the south. The Amarna letters illustrate such tactics well.

1357 See Fritz, 116; Rainey, *Sacred Bridge*, 127–28; D. Ussishkin, *ABD*, 4:125–26.

1358 D. Ussishkin, "Excavations at Tel Lachish," *TA* 5 [1978] 91; Fritz, 116.

1359 Ussishkin, 92.

1360 *IDBSup*, 252; see now *Sacred Bridge*, 128; Hess 189; Fritz, 116.

1361 *IDBSup*, 252–53.

1362 For other suggested locations, cf. Gray, 108; Bimson, *Redating*, 212; C. S. Ehrlich, *ABD*, 2:320–21.

1363 "Debir," *IDBSup*, 222.

1364 *Sacred Bridge*, 128–29.

1365 Fritz, 116.

1366 Hess (2009) 45.

1367 "Non-Israelite Personal Names in the Narratives of the Book of Joshua," *CBQ* 68 (1998) 205–14.

1368 Knauf, 99.

1369 *JSOT* 15 (1990) 66.

1370 *BZ* 39 (1995) 263–64.

1371 *Textual Studies*, 170–71; "Qumran Fragments of Joshua," 185.

There we see Shuwardata of Hebron protesting against the strong-arm policies of ʿAbdu-Heba of Jerusalem,[1372] but then we learn that the same two kings have joined together against Hapiru opposition.[1373] Amarna letters show the king of Jerusalem constantly appealing to the pharaoh for help against his enemies. Hess finds the note in v 4 represents "authentic style of this period."[1374]

So now Jerusalem attacks Canaanite-turned-Israelite Gibeon while the Israelite invaders march all night to deliver the deceitful Canaanite converts.

6 Gibeon responds in kind, calling on a new ally for protection in the face of invasion. Joshua maintains his headquarters at Gilgal (cf. v 10), so that Gilgal may be the eventual source of the Israelite tradition. The appeal of Gibeon employs the typical ploy of exaggeration.[1375] Now "all the kings of the Amorites," not just five, are involved.

Howard maintains that vv 6–11 and 12–15 to be parallel accounts, "not successive stages. . . . [T]hey both describe different facets of the battle of Gibeon."[1376] This could be correct. See *Form* above. McConville and Williams point out, "in common with ancient Near Eastern vassal-treaties generally, it [the treaty with Gibeon] had committed Israel to act against the enemies of its 'servants' the Gibeonites as if they were the enemies of Israel itself."[1377]

7 Joshua proves true to his commitment, even when the commitment was made under false pretenses. He takes his entire fighting force with him. The army must climb up to the highest point in that part of the hill country.[1378] Hess points out the frequent appearance of "all Israel" in this episode and defines it as "the whole army under Joshua's command."[1379] This may be true, but the term still implies a united Israel with all tribes fighting together, much in contrast to what is found later in Judges.

De Troyer points to the lack of collaboration outside vv 7, 20, and 24, Joshua often being conspicuously absent, whereas in the three verses he and Israel go up from Gilgal.[1380] From v 28 onwards Joshua and Israel work together in a second part of the narrative following the Gibeon emphasis of the first part. The summary in vv 40–42 returns all the work to Joshua.

8 The victory does not rest upon Joshua and his power. The victory, rather, depends upon the divine word and divine action. A prophetic oracle of salvation insures victory for God's commander. Hall reads a lot into the text when she sees Yahweh affirming Joshua's "foreign- policy decision."[1381]

9 Divine assurance does not exclude human wit and action. Joshua stages a surprise dawn attack after an all-night march. Hall states: "Divine and human

---

1372 Letter 280, *ANET*, 487.
1373 Letter RA, xix, *ANET*, 487.
1374 Hess (2009) 46.
1375 See the extensive discussion of figurative language and hyperbole in ancient Eastern "conquest accounts" by Younger, *Ancient Conquest Accounts*, accepted by Hess 192; Hess 151.
1376 Howard, 236.
1377 McConville and Williams, 52.
1378 Hess (1996) 193.
1379 Ibid., 193–94.
1380 De Troyer, "Reconstructing the Older Hebrew Text."
1381 *Conquering Character*, 166.

agency are inseparable."[1382] From Gilgal to Gibeon would entail a march of about eighteen miles (thirty kilometers). Soggin claims it could be carried out in eight to ten hours.[1383] The Hebrew text of Josh 9:17 claims that it took three days for Joshua to reach Gibeon the first time. The notice there may intentionally point to the present verse to underline the remarkable achievement of Joshua and his men here.

10 Yahweh sends the enemy into a panic before the unexpected reinforcements. This panic, in Heb. המם, is a technical term in holy-war narratives, binding Exod 14, Josh 10, Judg 4, and 1 Sam 7 together.[1384] It is closely tied to storm phenomena (cf. Exod 14:24; 1 Sam 7:10; Josh 10:11).[1385] Nelson calls panic "Yahweh's characteristic weapon," an emotion more than the normal human fear of fighting and dying.[1386] This is God-sent unnatural despair and hopelessness that makes fighting unimaginable and so sends the victim in helter-skelter retreat.

The narrative may well have ended at one time with the great victory at Gibeon (v 10a), but the present context uses the narrative as an introduction to its real theme, the pursuit resulting in the destruction of enemy fortified cities. This begins on the ascent of Beth Horon and covers fifty kilometers or about thirty miles. The name Beth Horon probably represents an early Canaanite sanctuary for the god Horon/Hoton, who is mentioned in the execration texts and in Ugaritic materials. The city is actually in two parts, an upper and a lower, dominating the northern pass to the Shephelah. Upper Beth Horon (Beit 'Ur el-Foqa = M.R. 16143) is five miles (eight kilometers) northwest of Gibeon, while the Lower Beth Horon (Beit 'Ur et-Tahta = M.R. 158144) lies six and a half miles (eleven kilometers) northwest of Gibeon.

Azekah is usually located at Tell-ez-Zakariyeh (= M.R. 143123), fifteen miles (twenty-five kilometers) south of Beth Horon and fifteen miles (twenty-five kilometers) northwest of Hebron. It has always been a strategic military outpost as shown by its appearance in the Lachish letters[1387] and in an inscription of Sennacherib.[1388] Its capture opened the way through the Elah Valley to Lachish. Excavations carried out at the turn of the twentieth century have been subject to varying interpretations.[1389] It certainly had a long history prior to the Israelite occupation.

Makkedah is introduced into the text in a rather awkward fashion to join the narrative to that which follows. The main tradition centers on the cave (vv 16–27), while v 28 turns the attention to a city. Its location is generally placed at Khirbet el Qôm (M. R. 146104). W. R. Kotter refuses even a guess at a location.[1390] Rainey gives a definite location at Khirbet el-Qom (= M.R. 146510) in the Shephelah

---

1382 Ibid., 167.
1383 Soggin, 127.
1384 Cf. Richter, *Traditionsgeschichtliche Untersuchungen*, 52–53; Weimar, *Bib* 57 (1976) 38–39, 70–73.
1385 Cf. further, H.-P. Müller, "המם," *TWAT*, 2:449–54.
1386 Nelson, 141.
1387 *ANET*, 322.
1388 N. Na'aman, *VT* 29 (1979) 61–86.
1389 Cf. E. Stern, "Azekah," *EAEHL*, 1:141–43; E. Stern, *ABD*, 1:538; Rainey, *Sacred Bridge*, 147.
1390 *ABD*, 4:478.

twelve miles west of Hebron.[1391] Hubbard locates Makkedah at twenty miles from Gibeon.[1392] The pursuit goes southward. Dorsey points to Khirbet Beit Maqdum (M. R. 147104) eleven kilometers southeast of Beit Jibrin and eleven kilometers east-southeast of Lachish.[1393]

11 The center of interest for the compiler is the act of God. Israel's experience has shown that God provides victory for his people in battle. The people of Israel do not have to depend upon their own power. They can rely on their God, when their God can rely on them. The point made is that the victory was much more due to the power of God than to that of Joshua. Younger provides a text from Sargon to conclude that the miracle of hailstones is a part of ancient Near Eastern transmission code for conquest stories.[1394] The people of Israel would not have accepted such a description, for they believed that their God controled the natural world of hail as well as the personal world of war. As McConville and Williams recognize: "the point is to assert the concordance between the forces of nature under God and the human capacities of Joshua and Israel."[1395]

This was a message of real comfort to the readers of the ultimate history when in exile they found themselves in a much weaker position militarily than did Joshua. R. B. Y. Scott has shown that such hailstorms in the Palestinian spring can produce stones two inches in diameter.[1396]

12–14 The precise context of the original poem prior to its incorporation into the Book of Jashar (the Upright) will probably never be known. Hall points to "the indeterminacy of the text itself," and suggests that the quotation may reach from vv 12–15, or may not exist at all.[1397] Hall prefers the traditional interpretation that Joshua asked for the day to be lengthened, but then states that the roles of Yahweh and Joshua are more important in the text than defining the miracle.

Younger states, "It would be foolhardy to believe that a definite explication can be given here."[1398] He seeks to understand the phenomenon as polemic against Canaanite understanding of omens, showing Yahweh controls everything they consider to be omens.[1399] Hawk notes the poetic form and decides, "None, however, can sufficiently define the event, and perhaps that is what the narrator intends. . . . [The narrator's method] preserves its marvel and mystery, leaving the details to the reader's imagination."[1400] Auld refers to hailstones in v 11, to a stopping of sun and moon in vv 12–14, and to an earthquake in Isa 28:21 as three alternative memories of divine action.[1401]

Margalit maintains that the poetic fragment means "the precise opposite of what the prose framework presupposes, viz., a celestial blackout in daytime." The

1391 *Sacred Bridge*, 127; cf. Fritz, 113, 116; Hess (1996) 195; W. G. Dever, *EAEHL*, 2nd ed., 4:1233–35; Compare Pitkänen, 233; Mc Cormick, *NIDB*, 3:753.
1392 Hubbard, 293.
1393 Dorsey, 188.
1394 "Rhetorical Structuring," 10–12; cf. Hess (2009) 47.
1395 McConville and Williams, 53.
1396 *ZAW* 64 (1952) 19. See also Halpern, "Doctrine by Misadventure," 55.
1397 *Conquering Character*, 172.
1398 *Ancient Conquest Accounts*, 212.
1399 Ibid., 216; cf. Walton, "Joshua 10:12–15."
1400 Hess (2000) 153.
1401 Auld, 69–70.

fragment belongs before v 10 and points to "a stratagem used by the divine warrior to throw the enemy into panic."[1402]

Other questions are more important for theological exegesis, though. The emphasis is on Yahweh uniquely listening to the voice of a human person. Here again we see a way to exalt Joshua. God listens to him. "'Listen' is a word that often connotes obedience. The strange happening at Gibeon gives Joshua an extraordinary authority."[1403]

"The narrator's summation of the event magnifies Joshua's heroism and prestige, imbuing him with a unique eminence previously reserved only for Moses."[1404] This "cannot mean that God has never answered a prayer; it probably means that God has never taken orders from anyone in battle."[1405] Hall compares this passage with others where God has listened to a human and concludes that unlike other instances, here "Joshua's petition is both public . . . and a request for something specifically miraculous."[1406]

If one does not emend the text, the poem is a direct address to the heavenly bodies. This is normal for Israel's neighbors, where the moon and sun would be seen as gods. It is astounding in Israel, where even the creation story refuses to name the sun and moon, being content to refer to the greater and lesser lights (Gen 1:14–19). Such language could easily be interpreted as worship of and prayer to the heavenly deities, but the biblical writer carefully avoids this. Joshua speaks to Yahweh through such language (v 12a). In so doing, he shows the impotence of the gods of Canaan and underscores the importance of Joshua. He is a man of prayer empowered to command the great "gods" of Israel's neighbors. But he can do so only because Yahweh listens to him (v 14).

Tradition has understood the poem to be an excerpt from an ancient collection (v 13; cf. *Notes*) called the Book of Jashar (= Upright) here and in 1 Sam 1:18. The LXX in 1 Kgs 8:12–13 refers to a book of Song, which represents a transposition of two letters in the Hebrew from ישר to שיר. Knauf dates this old poetic collection to the tenth or ninth century.

Younger maintains that the work is premonarchic and that it does not include any contributions from David or Solomon.[1407] Howard suggests that no actual quotation from the Book of Jashar appears here at all, similar to sources referred to later in Kings.[1408] De Troyer finds the title not mentioned in Old Greek and given a different name in 2 Samuel, leading to the decision that the quotes are old but the title not well known.[1409]

The name and content of the book are not the most important issue. What is noteworthy is that the Hebrew tradition understood that its Scripture was based on even more ancient sources. This implies the removal of the final authors of Scripture from eye witnesses to compilers of early traditions and sources, just as critical

---

1402 *VT* 42 (1992) 487.
1403 McConville and Williams, 53.
1404 Hess (2000) 154.
1405 Coote, 647.
1406 *Conquering Character*, 174.
1407 *Ancient Conquest Traditions*, 380.
1408 Howard, 239.
1409 "Is This Not Written," 50.

scholarship has shown on other grounds. The criteria for authority and canonicity in the OT is not that of having been an eyewitness of the events. Rather, it is that of having been inspired by God to use the traditions of the nation to interpret the identity of the nation for the future. The book of Joshua is based on old traditions and sources, but its ultimate form was achieved only by later editors or compilers, perhaps even into the exilic period. Even as comparison with the LXX and other versions quickly shows, the text was not fixed until quite late. The material was authoritative, but open for new interpretation in light of new experiences with God. Only at a quite late date was the canon seen as unchangeable text. Even then the process of interpretation continued, giving rise to the oral traditions recanonized by the Jewish community into the Talmud.

The compiler of the text uses the poetic fragment to give further witness to his theme, that God fights for Israel. In fact, "YHWH so thoroughly shocks the Canaanite troops that no military engagement takes place."[1410] This is the central motif of holy-war theology. Here for the only time the book of Joshua speaks of the nation taking vengeance (נקם) on its enemies.

Mitchell places the term in the context of ineffectual judicial institutions so that the highest authority—king or God—must step in.[1411] All happened in "about a whole day."[1412] Younger sees this language as part of the ancient Near Eastern conquest accounts and thus figurative and hyperbolic.[1413]

However one interprets the details of this section of Joshua, Kissling offers a telling comment:[1414]

Even though Joshua takes the initiative in a more direct way in this passage, he also displays a greater reliance on Yahweh's intervention than elsewhere. . . . There is nothing in the narrative to indicate that Joshua gets the balance wrong between using his own initiative, on the one hand, and relying on Yahweh to act on the other hand.

Yahweh may listen to a human, but the human must first trust in and have a relationship with the all-powerful God.

If the book of Joshua is, in its final form, addressed to the exilic community, it does not encourage the people to retrace the steps of Joshua by totally destroying all their enemies, but by trusting Yahweh to fulfill his promises to his people and to do the necessary fighting for them, even against overwhelming odds. The people of Israel are not to waste their time planning battle strategy and gathering armies. They are to spend their energy finding and doing the will of God.

The nature of the poetic miracle is another subject of wide debate. See the extended discussion by Howard,[1415] Nelson,[1416] Hom,[1417] and Hubbard.[1418] How-

---

1410 Hess (2000) 152.
1411 *Together in the Land*, 88.
1412 Younger, *Ancient Conquest Accounts*, 215.
1413 Ibid., 216.
1414 *Reliable Characters*, 77, 78.
1415 Howard, 241–49.
1416 Nelson, 142–45.
1417 *ExpTim* 115 (2004) 217–23.
1418 Hubbard, 96–97.

ard eventually decides the language is figurative. Nelson finds that "originally these two heavenly entities were being called upon [by the poet] to stand frozen or fixed, or perhaps silent, in stunned reaction to an awe-inspiring victory."[1419] Hubbard prefers to see Israel finding an omen, aligning the heavenly bodies to signify victory.[1420] Israel, according to Hubbard, receives about a full day to take revenge on their enemies, a phrase that may "draw on an ancient hyperbolic literary convention."[1421] "In sum," decides Hubbard, "in Joshua 10 the sun and moon personify the cosmic sovereignty of Yahweh, for whose intervention Joshua appeals."[1422]

Hom follows Howard in a survey of theories:[1423]

Sun and moon literally stopped.
Sun's light was suppressed through eclipse or cloud covering.
Sun's light persisted through refraction by a meteorite or other heavenly object.
The sun and moon represented cultic deities.
Sun and moon are referred to astrologically in attempts to find omens from the deity.
Sun and moon are referred to figuratively.
Poetry is misinterpreted or purposely ignored by compiler.

By studying genre, vocabulary and idioms, and significance, Hom concludes that no one explanation fully addresses all the issues. According to Hom, Joshua prays to God, God responds in v 12b, and v 13a records the result. This refers to the all-night march of v 9 (the moon) and the all-day battle until sunset (v 27). Symbolically, the heavenly bodies are stationed to cover the entire battle field. Reference to the Book of Jashar legitimizes the entire day's march and battle. An overall summary appears in v 13c.

Knauf sees the poet calling on the enemy G(g)od not to join in. Knauf then shows both Jerusalem and Gibeon with sun-god connections and claims that the original poem must have been polytheistic.[1424] Knauf declares the astronomical explanation of the Old Testament text to be physically impossible.[1425]

The last half of v 12a certainly is an editorial link with the present context.[1426] The text begins with אָז, usually translated as "then." "The particle אָז is often followed by a verb that is spelled like the imperfect but appears to have a past-time meaning. Such verbs might be preterite rather than imperfect."[1427] Younger understands the construction "as a type of flashback—simply introducing a section of the text which narrates material which chronologically belongs between verse 9

1419 Nelson, 145.
1420 Hubbard, 297.
1421 Hubbard, 295; cf. Younger, *Ancient Conquest Accounts*, 215–16.
1422 Hubbard, 298.
1423 *ExpTim* 115 (2004) 217–23.
1424 Knauf, 98.
1425 Ibid., 101.
1426 Cf. Nelson, 141.
1427 *Williams' Hebrew Syntax*, 77c; cf. *IBHS* 33.3.3; I. Rabinowitz, "*'az* followed by imperfect verb form in preterite contexts: A redactional device in biblical Hebrew" (*VT* 34 [1984] 53–62).

and 10. . . . [T]he biblical writer relates the principal incident which is connected to the battle (namely, the hailstones) first, before he then proceeds to the special point to be cited from the book of Yashar."[1428] Howard maintains that v 12a is a description of an "important action that took place at the same time as that of vv. 6–11, not something that happened later. . . . That is, somehow the hailstorm of v. 11 and the phenomena of vv. 12–13 either were one and the same thing or (more probably) they happened at the same time, as part of the larger miracle of deliverance for Israel."[1429]

Howard suggests that the subject of "he said" may well be Yahweh and not Joshua so that the Old Greek is then correct in saying God took vengeance on his enemies.[1430] Howard finds a tension between Joshua speaking to Yahweh while the statement seems directed to the sun and moon. Such an interpretation weakens the major thrust of the passage, that God listened to, obeyed, heeded the word of a human.

The original context for the first part of the verse is debated. It could well have been linked to the poem in the original source. Knauf is uncertain whether the poem represents the vantage point of Jerusalem or of Benjamin/Gibeon.[1431] He also maintains that the address to the sun and moon reflects a polytheistic view of the heavenly bodies as deities.[1432] Knauf finds such an entreaty of the natural bodies at home about 650 BCE under the Assyrians.

The Hebrew verb דמם can mean "to be motionless" or "to be silent." It may have meant that the heavenly bodies did not shine (Noth) or that the sun stood still and did not move, as it is interpreted by the compiler (v 13b). Explanations for the phenomenon include a cosmic eclipse,[1433] a Palestinian hailstorm,[1434] and an understanding of heavenly signs and portents by which proper positions of the heavenly bodies are important for earthly events.[1435]

15 See *Note* 15.a.

16–28 Creach calls Josh 10:16–11:23 "one of the most gruesome accounts in the book."[1436] The compiler continues his pursuit motif, though all opposition appears to be destroyed. His reason appears in v 19. Israel must complete their assigned duties. God fights for Israel. He also fights with and through Israel. Israel cannot expect the victory, thus, if they do not do their part. Israel did not carry out God's battle plan at Ai and so was defeated (chap. 7). The people of Israel risked their identity as the people of God by letting the Gibeonites trick them (chap. 9). Now Israel faces another challenge. God has given the enemy into their hands, but Israel must take the enemies. Israel cannot celebrate victory when total victory and total obedience are not yet realities.

Younger maintains that chap. 10 uses "backtrack and overlap" in two scenes (vv

1428 *Ancient Conquest Accounts*, 211; cf. Nelson, 141.
1429 Howard, 238.
1430 Ibid., 240; but see Nelson, 141.
1431 Knauf, 98.
1432 Ibid., 100.
1433 Sawyer, *PEQ* 104 (1972) 139–46.
1434 Scott, *ZAW* 64 (1952) 19–20.
1435 Holladay, *JBL* 87 (1968) 176; cf. Halpern, "Doctrine by Misadventure," 55.
1436 Creach, 93.

1–15 and 16–43).[1437] The latter develops three tensions: captured but not killed kings, survivors in fortified cities, and a temporary camp at Makkedah. The final three episodes of scene 2 then each resolve one of the tensions in order.

20 Israel lost valuable time and did not totally achieve their objective. A remnant remained.

Auld understands the Hebrew here as ambiguous and states, "Israel completed all it could immediately after the battle and only when no more could be done (because any enemies still alive were now behind walls) did they return to their chief outside Makkedah."[1438] The biblical emphasis, however, is not on what Israel could not do but on the massive defeat Israel inflicted on the enemy.

21 The pursuit must continue. But first, Israel must learn another lesson. After the battle, the people return to camp in שָׁלוֹם (peace, v 21). The people who follow God's orders and complete the battle for God are led back to the camp and find they have wholeness, safety, health. This state, not that of battle, is the goal for the people of God, the gift of God to obedient people. They will overcome enemies (Deut 2:26; 20:10), and no one will speak ill of them (v 21).

Interestingly, here (v 21) the camp is at Makkedah. The exclusiveness and importance of the camp at Gilgal gives way to a temporary field base for the army.[1439]

The writer uses a folk saying to describe the situation: "Not a single man threatened the sons of Israel." Fritz, echoing Exod 11:7 translates v 21b as "not a dog had barked against the Israelites" (my translation from German). See *Note* 21.b. Fritz further states that the saying refers to "peace and security along with the dominance [or superiority, *Überlegenheit*] that comes to expression through an undertaking."[1440] Knauf maintains that a suitable translation is uncertain but interprets the phrase to mean that since Israel had destroyed the Amorites but the land still contained people, none of those people dared "bark" at Israel.[1441] Hess interprets the people of Israel as the subject and compares their lack of complaint here with their strong murmuring in the wilderness.[1442] Hubbard suggests the reference is to Israel's escaping battle without a scratch in contrast to her enemies.[1443] Howard interprets it to mean: "things had come to such a peaceful, satisfying conclusion that 'no one uttered a word'" against Israel.[1444] Knauf uses the verse to build a case that the original text knew nothing of a commandment to totally destroy or drive out the Canaanite inhabitants.[1445] His claim is supported, however, only when one pulls the verse out of its larger context.

22–27 The obedience of the Israelites is further illustrated when Joshua issues commands and the people obey. At the same time, the section illustrates the authority of Joshua, the leader of Israel, since the military commanders are obedient to the authority of Joshua. The present context depicts a man of God's choosing, obe-

---

1437 "Rhetorical Structuring," 7.
1438 Auld, 72.
1439 Cf. McConville and Williams, 53; see too *Notes* to v 15*, 21*.
1440 Fritz, 113.
1441 Knauf, 103.
1442 Hess (1996) 201 with n. 2.
1443 Hubbard, 299.
1444 Howard, 253.
1445 Knauf, 103.

dient to the Mosaic law (chap. 1) having power over the military strongmen. Thus, priorities in leadership are set up for Israel.

Placing the foot on the neck of the enemy was a sign of triumph—see Ps 18:41 (= 2 Sam 22:41).[1446] Fritz states that the act was a demonstration of power, in which one nation gained power over another with no conditions.[1447] Hubbard notes the propaganda purposes of such actions—the discouragement of other enemies.[1448] The "commanders" (*qĕṣînîm*) are military or civil leaders who have decision-making authority.

25 Knauf combines v 25, somewhat of a Testament of Joshua, with vv 42–43 as a preexilic compositional conclusion expanded in the exile.[1449] A second conclusion comes from postexilic Dtr or a *ḥērem* layer with Josh 10:1*, 26c–27c, 28–39* leading to the conclusion of chap. 11. A base layer of vv 16–27 proves older for Knauf than the *ḥērem* layer.[1450]

V 25 is not meant simply to report the events of the past. It is, rather, a message of courage and comfort for the people of Israel. The words delivered to Joshua as he took up his task (1:7, 9, 18) are now given by him to Israel. "Joshua was demonstrating his leadership qualities. He now had the authority to give the same encouraging exhortation to others with which the Lord had encouraged him."[1451]

The people of God have no need to fear their enemies. God fights for his people; he protects and guides them with his presence. The conquest was not a once-and-for-all event. It is typical of God's work for his people. Whenever an obstacle stands before the people of God, they need not fear. God is there to conquer for his people.

26 Knauf attributes the method of killing—public display and hanging on trees—to the Assyrians in the eighth century.[1452] The Assyrian evidence may be only what has been discovered and so interpreted (compare Gen 40:19).

27 Even as Joshua speaks words of encouragement and promise of future victory, he exemplifies the other half of the equation. He obeys the law that God gave Moses, in this instance Deut 21:22–23. The land God is giving to the people must not be defiled by a body hanging overnight (Deut 21:23). Joshua thus takes the bodies down and buries them fittingly in the hole they tried to use for refuge. Howard states, "The place they had thought would be their refuge ended up as their tomb."[1453]

The place of refuge is important for Israel as a reminder of what God has done for them and of the significance of that act for the present day. The people who experience divine victory are all too prone to forget even though Israel has constant reminders to remember and to obey.

28–39 Knauf dismisses vv 28a–29a as a *ḥērem* secondary expansion. Hawk finds

---

1446 Cf. G. Schmuttermayr, *Psalm 18 und 2 Samuel 22*, SANT 25 (Munich: Kösel, 1971) 160; M.
   Dahood, *Psalms I*, AB (Garden City, NY: Doubleday, 1966) 116; cf. Exod 23:27; Isa 51:23;
   ANEP, no. 393.
1447 Fritz, 113.
1448 Hubbard, 301.
1449 Knauf, 102.
1450 Ibid., 103.
1451 Howard, 254.
1452 Knauf, 102.
1453 Howard, 254.

a major structural change at this point so that in the following narratives "Joshua, rather than Israel, gradually becomes the exemplar for the themes of initiative and response. . . . Joshua and the kings thus personify the continuing conflict between Israelite integrity and Canaanite plurality."[1454] Nelson[1455] sees the conquest itinerary as "a literary construction rather than an authentic vestige of popular tradition" but points to R. David[1456] for an alternate explanation.

Hoffmeier argues that Num 33 represents the real itinerary form and that Josh 10:28–42 cannot be so classified, or "if an itinerary lay behind Josh 10:28–42, it has been embellished to such an extent that its original character is no longer discernible."[1457] Hoffmeier studies seven episodes (Makkedah, Libnah, Lachish, Eglon, Hebron, Debir, and Hazor [in chap. 11]) and charts eleven repeated phrases (departure from conquered city, all Israel, arrival at next city, brief report on military encounter, Yahweh giving city into hand, date of campaign or its duration, smiting city with sword, extent of destruction of enemy people, comparison with previous victory, additional note, and booty taken) in each of the episodes. The conveyance formula, an additional note about the fighting, and the taking of booty are elements that appear only rarely.[1458] Hoffmeier argues that behind the materials lies an Egyptian scribal "daybook" tradition illustrated by the first campaign of Thutmose III to Megiddo.[1459] This tradition of battle reports combines long and short reports in a similar manner as do the first eleven chapters of Joshua. Joshua apparently shares with the Egyptian account at least six elements:[1460] divine commission, intelligence report, march through significant topographical feature, setting up camp and preparing for war, siege and battle, and victory with presentation of tribute or collection of booty. The ritual at Shechem (Josh 8:30–35) parallels land-grant stelae set up by Egyptian and Mesopotamian rulers to mark land ownership, especially on international borders. The summary of Josh 10:40–42 has parallels in Egyptian and Assyrian sources. Arguing against Weinfeld and Van Seters, Hoffmeier concludes that both first- and second-millennium sources from Egypt as well as Mesopotamia must be brought into consideration and that the New-Kingdom period when Israel departed from Egypt was likely when she embraced the daybook tradition of Egypt. This dating may be correct, but the David/Solomon united monarchy with its strong ties to Egypt and its much stronger administrative structures may also be a plausible time for undertaking the practice.

That seven cities are listed leads Howard to suggest this as "a summarizing account, showing the destruction of representative cities and not intended to be comprehensive."[1461] He finds a "balanced structure around Gezer" without note of its destruction to be in line with the historical reality of Josh 16:10 and Judg 1:29.[1462]

1454 Hawk (2000) 157–58.
1455 Nelson, 147.
1456 *ScEs* 42 (1990) 209–29.
1457 "Structure of Joshua 1–11," 167.
1458 Ibid., 168.
1459 Ibid., 169, 176.
1460 Ibid., 174.
1461 Howard, 256.
1462 Ibid.; cf. Hubbard, 302.

Lachish and Eglon do not say the king was killed, that having been reported in Josh 10:3, 26.[1463]

The pursuit list follows a formula, though every element does not appear in each entry. Hubbard details the formulas as:

The city's capture (vv 28, 32, 35, 37, 39)
The siege and attack (vv 29, 31, 34, 36, 38)
Everyone put to the sword (vv 28, 30, 32, 35, 37, 39)
No survivors remain (vv 28, 30, 33, 35, 37, 39)
Israel implements the "ban" (vv 28, 35, 37, 39)
The king suffers the same fate as the king of city X (vv 28, 30, 32, 25, 37, 39)

"The campaign against the cities of southern Canaan is rendered in an annalistic style reminiscent of other ancient Near Eastern literatures. By use of this form, as opposed to the narrative style of the previous accounts, the narrator elevates Israel's status by linking it with the great powers of the ancient world. Israel too is a mighty nation with an impressive catalogue of victories."[1464] Still, "the list displays a variation in vocabulary and content that stresses the distinctiveness of each victory."[1465]

The formulaic elements use figurative language and hyperbole. The cities are each only six to seven miles from the preceding city. Still, the entire campaign must have taken several weeks, even months, to complete.[1466]

The conquest list completes the history of pursuit. As Joshua has obeyed, so Israel sets out again to follow God into battle. The people are not satisfied with victory. They must obey the divine command to totally obliterate any in the land who might tempt them to follow other gods (Deut 20:16–18). The present formulation of the list shows that Israel did precisely what the law commanded (cf. vv 30, 32, 33, 35, 37, 39, 40). Thus after the catastrophe at Ai and the foolhardy action with Gibeon, Israel once again assumes her place as the totally obedient people of Yahweh, fulfilling the command of Yahweh to the letter. At the same time, Yahweh has shown himself to be a God who accepts a people who follow him despite their past mistakes.

Interpreters often point to discrepancies between the fate of the cities in Josh 10; 13–21 and in Judg 1. Coote attributes the discrepancies to "differing deuteronomistic concepts of the two eras, one of Joshua, the other of the judges and saviors."[1467] Joshua emphasizes complete conquest while Judges "the troubling presence everywhere of Israel's opponents."[1468] "Joshua 11:3 implies that none of these major southern towns was put to the torch."[1469] Hess[1470] follows Younger,[1471] whose comparisons with the Mesha stele and the Merenptah stele show that the claims of

---

1463 Howard, 257.
1464 Hess (2000) 167.
1465 Ibid., 168.
1466 Hubbard, 302.
1467 Coote, 646.
1468 Ibid.
1469 Hess (1996) 202.
1470 Ibid., 203.
1471 *Ancient Conquest Accounts*, 227.

each to complete destruction of Israel is really military hyperbole not to be taken at face value.

The listing follows ancient Near Eastern royal annals in using the syntagms or traditional military linguistic patterns to describe each of the "conquests" with a slightly different combination of syntagms each time. This allows the preservation of some detail while succintly showing that God wins over all enemies as God had promised.[1472]

Libnah appears unexpectedly for the first time here, suggesting that the list is independent from the original narrative. Its location is disputed. The meaning of the name is "white," which has often led to an identification with Tell es-Safi. A. Rainey, however, has correctly argued that Tell es-Safi can no longer be considered.[1473] Elliger has suggested Tell Bornat (= M.R. 138115), nine kilometers southeast of Tell es-Safi, three kilometers west of Tell Judeideh.[1474] Rainey[1475] agrees but says the identification is still not confirmed. Tell el-Judeideh (= M.R. 141115) has also been suggested,[1476] but this is more commonly identified with Moresheth-Gath, the home of the prophet Micah.[1477] Wright suggests that Tell Bornat/Burnat began in the Late Bronze Age and would have been only a small fortified outpost.[1478] J. L. Peterson examines each suggested site and concludes: "Although Tell Bornat cannot be absolutely identified with biblical Libnah, the evidence strongly supports this association."[1479]

33–39 Gezer is located at Tell Jezer (Tell el-Jazari = M.R. 142140) on the boundary of the Judean hills guarding the road leading from the way of the sea to the Valley of Ajalon and on to Jerusalem. It is referred to frequently in Egyptian sources and plays an important role in the Amarna correspondence. Hess posits that Gezer was an Egyptian military base.[1480] In the Egyptian sources, it is depicted responding to the distress of a neighboring city-state just as the king of Jerusalem called for help from his neighbors. "The 'help' provided by King Horam serves as a contrasting foil to Israel's successful 'help' of Gibeon (v. 6)."[1481] The defeat does not include destruction of the city (cf. Josh 16:10; Judg 1:20; 1 Kgs 9:15–17).[1482] "Gezer, it seems, occupying a key position between coastal plain and hill country, was always disputed territory."[1483]

40–43 Knauf considers this the conclusion of the Exodus-Joshua narrative, which was then expanded with three to four times more material. That literary works in Israel or elsewhere developed in such piecemeal fashion remains to be proven. One can see the necessity for accounting for an oral tradition phase prior to the development of an all-Israel stabilized government and remaining in play

---

1472 See Hess (1996) 203–4.
1473 "Libnah," *IDBSup*, 546.
1474 *PJ* 30 (1934) 47–71.
1475 *Sacred Bridge*, 127; cf. Fritz, 116; Rösel, 383; Fritz, 256; Hess, 227.
1476 "Judeideh [Tell El-]," *AEHL*, 176.
1477 M. Broshi, "Judeideh, Tell," *EAEHL*, 3:694.
1478 *HTR* 64 (1971) 444.
1479 *ADB*, 4:323–24; cf. Hawkins, "Libnah," *NIDB* 3: 654.
1480 Hess (2009) 48.
1481 Nelson, 147.
1482 See W. G. Dever, *ADB*, 2:1002–3.
1483 McConville and Williams, 56.

even after a compiler collected the individual narratives into a larger whole. That long itineraries and independent narratives would be added to the collection after its written form must be placed in doubt. Text-critical study shows the text was not firm and stable, but the changes represent only small interpretations or different readings of the text, not wholesale rewriting and addition of materials.

The concluding summary is "somewhat repetitive," giving regions in v 40, boundaries or limits in v 41 and kings in v 42.[1484] The section echoes the common themes of the chapter: "battle success, elimination of survivors, defeated kings, and Yahweh's combat for Israel."[1485] The compiler has a different geographical span in view—that of the Davidic empire.[1486] Here is the land that belongs to Israel. Israel's persistent pursuit has reaped rewards. Nelson makes an important differentiation at this point: "Both Joshua and these [ancient Near Eastern] campaign reports seek to increase the wonder of the accomplishments they report and to promote a certain religious and political ideology. For Israel the ideology being advanced was not the power of the king as in the texts from Assyria or Egypt, but their own national identity as the people of a powerful God and as the legitimate masters of Canaan."[1487]

The hill country refers to the Judean hills. The Negev or steppe is the arid country south of the Judean hills. The Shephelah is the low hills leading down from the western mountains. No mention of the coastal plain occurs, probably because the Philistines controlled it. The "slopes" (אשדות) seem to refer to the mountain spurs on the eastern border of the Judean hills leading down to the Dead Sea, though reference to western slopes leading toward the Mediterranean is possible.[1488]

The traditions do not include all the land involved. "The historical actuality was probably less tidy than a superficial reading of the account appears."[1489] The editor draws from the available traditions the conclusion that God has fulfilled his promises and given all the southern territory to his people. In so doing, he does not note that his sources speak at best of a "victorious raid" rather than a battle of conquest that should result in leaving settlers behind in each conquered city.[1490] The land reaches from Kadesh-Barnea to Gaza in its southern boundary and up to Gibeon, the site of the major conflict in this section. Kadesh-Barnea is situated on 'Ain el-Qudeirat nearly midway on the east-to-west southern border.[1491] Gaza is the southernmost Philistine city located at the modern city of Gaza. The land of Goshen often refers to a location in Egypt where Joseph settled his family, but the reference here is to an unknown locality. Fritz suggests a location between the southern edge of the Judean hills and the Negev (compare Josh 11:16; 15:51).[1492]

"Although land has been conquered, there is no sense in which it is occupied."[1493] Coote concludes that "this obvious exaggeration was not even intended to be

---

1484 Howard, 258.
1485 Nelson, 139.
1486 Note that Knauf, 109, sees here the territory of the king of Judah just before 600 BCE.
1487 Nelson, 139.
1488 Hess, 205. On this geography, see Fritz, 116; Howard, 261.
1489 McConville and Williams, 56.
1490 Soggin, 132.
1491 Rainey, *Sacred Bridge*, 35, 121.
1492 Fritz, 118.
1493 Mitchell, *Together in the Land*, 92.

consistent with other parts of Joshua and Judges. Its purpose is to contribute to the deuteronomistic idealization of the era of Joshua."[1494] Howard sees a picture that is "unequivocally one of complete and swift annihilation of people throughout the region," a "stylized summary of sorts" giving a broader, more general perspective with hyperbole over against a detailed perspective showing much more work to do.[1495] The picture thus has a "complex texture": "what was a sweeping conquest on one level involved much hard work—and failure—on another."[1496]

Clarke examines three summary passages—Josh 10:40–43; 11:16–23; 21:43–45—to show they are not in conflict with other sections of the book.[1497] Most commentaries and articles on the book of Joshua take as a starting point an apparent contradiction between a complete and an incomplete conquest. Kitchener observes that there has not been a "careful and close" reading of the passages taken as evidence of a complete conquest (i.e., Josh 10:40–43; 11:16–23; 21:43–45).[1498] This article seeks to fill that gap in the literature. A close reading of these passages suggests that the author carefully describes the extent of the conquest, suggesting that the apparent contradiction regarding these passages may be overstated.

Hawk synthesizes the theological development here:[1499] "The language of totality configures all the material in this section. The Hebrew particle כול (kûl) ('all, every, whole')" asserts

> Israelite integrity, comprehensive conquest, and obedience to YHWH and the commands of Moses. . . . This tendency to depict the conquest in hyperbolic terms follows ancient Near Eastern conventions for report conquests but also affirms that the nation now embodies the holistic view of Deuteronomy. The narratives and summaries bring closure to Israel's campaign of conquest by confirming the final collapse of Canaanite resistance and the complete obedience of Israel to the God who has given the land.

The writer "telescoped events in order to magnify the achievement of Israel and particularly its God."[1500] This is unimportant for the writer. He looks back on a history of Israel with God, a history in which Israel occupies the land. He seeks to use the traditions available to him to show how Israel has gained this land. The traditions give him every right to talk about the great military victories of Joshua and Israel, but this is precisely what he does not emphasize. He speaks of the great victories of God fulfilling his promises to his people. Yahweh has fought for his people and given them the land. Now Joshua is ready to distribute that land.[1501]

Explanation

The compiler uses a complex set of traditions as he sets out the fulfillment of

1494 Coote, 648.
1495 Howard, 258–59.
1496 Ibid., 260.
1497 *TynBul* 61 (2010) 89–104.
1498 *PEFQS* 10 (1878) 74–75.
1499 Hawk (2000) 158–59.
1500 Pressler, 82.
1501 Fritz, 117.

God's promises to Israel and the way in which God fulfills those promises. Latvus maintains that "the aim of the writer is to prove that on some occasions it is acceptable for the foreigner to live among the Israelites and even work in the temple."[1502] To so emphasize what the Gibeonites gained is to miss the thrust of the narrative, for it shows much more what the Gibeonites lost—political and personal freedom in becoming temple slaves. The narrative much more underlines Israel's faithfulness to their commitments than it does the acceptance of foreigners. Hawk states that in Josh 10, "Israel's disobedience, and the threat it elicits, is once more repressed, and the narrative continues toward fulfillment. . . ."[1503] Creach addresses the misuse of royal power and authority and the establishment of an egalitarian society.[1504] Hawk sharpens the focus. By contrasting Gibeonites taken into the community with kings eliminated from life, the writer highlights "the consequences of responding positively and negatively to Yahweh."[1505] Later Hawk shows that the writer used literary devices and "transforms annalistic accounts of military victorious *[sic]* into a striking example of the great things Yahweh can accomplish through those who are obedient."[1506]

A basic tradition of Israel's faithfulness to their commitment to Gibeon is transformed in the introduction to a story of pursuit. The story of physical pursuit is interspersed with teachings about Israel's pursuit of spiritual identity as people of Yahweh. The pursuit is pictured on the physical plain as the conquest of the southern territory. Such a conquest is made possible through the use of a basic tradition of victory at Gibeon, punishment at Makkedah, and a list of cities on the conquest itinerary. These sources are transposed into a spiritual pilgrimage of the people of God. This is done via "exaggeration used for dramatic effect. . . . Both forces in the conflict are presented in dimensions much larger than life, and the outcome is a total victory in which the enemy is completely annihilated."[1507]

The identity given the people of God has several components. As throughout the early chapters of the book, particular emphasis is laid on the role of Israel's leader. Joshua is depicted as a leader without parallel, since God listened to his command. Such a definition of leadership is not left without modification. Joshua is pictured as the leader who carries out the divine commands, but he does not tarry to celebrate victory. Rather, he continues the pursuit until the battle is won. Fulfilling the role given him in the first chapter, he displays the fearless courage of leadership and admonishes his generals to do likewise. He can convert the near tragedy of the covenant with foreigners living in the land into an example of the obedience and victory of God's people.

Obedience to the divine law is a second component. The law of holy war is spelled out in Deuteronomy. The law placed particular emphasis on the total annihilation of the enemy. While this requirement bring shivers to the modern conscience, the editor of Joshua knew that such a program had not been carried out

---

1502 *God, Anger, and Ideology*, 67.
1503 *Every Promise Fulfilled*, 91, 93.
1504 Creach, 94.
1505 Hawk (2010) 111.
1506 Ibid, 125.
1507 Mitchell, *Together in the Land*, 64, summarizing Noort, "Zwischen Mythos und Realität."

consistently. Too many people remained in the land. Chap. 10 is careful to avoid any mention that Jerusalem was destroyed. The motif has aims far beyond pure historical description. It shows the great lengths to which Joshua and his people went to obey God. It underlines the total victory God gave them, thereby spelling hope that an exiled Israel might win back their land that is once again occupied by foreigners. An Israel punished because they trusted covenants with foreign powers more than they did covenant with Yahweh could receive another chance if they could find leadership like that of Joshua and obedience like that of the nation in the period of conquest. The message succinctly put says, "When Israel is faithful, God is faithful, allowing Israel to triumph regardless of the odds."[1508] Would the exiled nation pursue God as steadfastly as Joshua pursued his opponents and God's law? Or would they continue their pursuit of the enemy's gods? Would Israel again allow Yahweh to fight for Israel? Would the day come again when Israel returned to camp in safety with no one threatening?

J. Northern Annihilation (11:1–23)

Bibliography

Abel, F. M. "Les stratagèmes dans le Livre de Josué." *RB* 56 (1949) 335–38. **Aharoni, Y.** "New Aspects of Israelite Occupation in the North." In *Near Eastern Archaeology in the Twentieth Century.* Ed. J. A. Sanders. Garden City, NY: Doubleday, 1970. 254–67. ———. "Problems of the Israelite Conquest in the Light of Archaeological Discoveries." *Antiquity and Survival* 2 (1957) 131–50. **Alt, A.** "Erwägungen tiber die Landnahme der Israeliten in Palästina." *PJ* 35 (1939) 17–19. Reprinted in *Kleine Schriften zur Geschichte des Volkes Israel.* Vol. 1. Munich: Beck, 1953. 134–35. **Bardtke, H.** *Bibel, Spaten und Geschichte.* Göttingen: Vandenhoeck & Ruprecht, 1969. 200–209. **Batten, L. W.** "The Conquest of Northern Canaan: Joshua xi 1–9; Judges iv–v." *JBL* 24 (1905) 31–40. **Becker, U.** "Endredaktionelle Kontextvernetzungen des Josua-Buches." In *Die deuteronomistischen Geschichtswerke: Redaktions- und religionsgeschichtliche Perspektiven zur 'Deuteronomismus'-Diskussion in Tora und Vorderen Propheten.* Ed. M. Witte, K. Schmid, D. Prechel, and J. C. Gertz. Berlin: De Gruyter, 2006. 141–61. **Ben-Ami, D.** "Early Iron Age Cult Places—New Evidence from Tel Hazor." *TA* 33 (2006) 121–33. ———. "The Iron Age I at Tel Hazor in Light of the Renewed Excavations." *IEJ* 51 (2001) 148–70. ———. "Mysterious Standing Stones: What Do These Ubiquitous Things Mean?" *BAR* 32.2 (2006) 38–45. **Benjamin, C. D.** *The Variations between the Hebrew and Greek Texts of Joshua: Chapters 1–12.* Thesis, University of Pennsylvania. Leipzig: W. Drugulin, 1921. **Ben-Tor, A.** "Excavating Hazor—Solomon's City Rises from the Ashes." *BAR* 25.2 (1999) 26–37. ———. "The Fall of Canaanite Hazor—The 'Who' and 'When' Questions." In *Mediterranean Peoples in Transition.* Ed. S. Gitin, A. Mazar, and E. Stern. Jerusalem: Israel Exploration Society, 1998. 456–67. ———. "Hazor—A City State between the Major Powers: A Rejoinder." *SJOT* 16 (2002) 303–8. ———. "Hazor and Chronology." *Aegypten und Levante* 14 (2005) 45–67. ———. "Hazor Excavations in Memory of Yigael Yadin—Aims and Preliminary Results." *ErIsr* 25 (1996) 67–81. **Ben-Tor, A., and D. Ben-Ami.** "Hazor and the Archaeology of the 10th Century b.c.e." *IEJ* 48 (1998) 1–37. **Ben-Tor, A., and M. T. Rubiato.** "Excavating Hazor—Part Two: Did the Israelites Destroy the Canaanite City?" *BAR* 25.3 (1999) 22–39, 60.

1508 Pressler, 81.

Ben-Tor, A., and S. Zuckerman. "Hazor at the End of the Late Bronze Age: Back to Basics." *BASOR* 350 (2008) 1–6. **Bienkowski, P.** "The Role of Hazor in the Late Bronze Age." *PEQ* 119 (1987) 50–61. **Bimson, J. J.** *Redating the Exodus and Conquest.* JSOTSup 5. Sheffield: University of Sheffield, 1978. 185–200. **Briend, J.** "Akshaph et sa localisation à Tell Keisan." *RB* 79 (1972) 239–46. **Bright, J.** *The Authority of the Old Testament.* Nashville: Abingdon, 1967. 241–51. **Brueggemann, W.** *Divine Presence amid Violence Contextualizing the Book of Joshua.* Carlisle: Paternoster, 2009. **Caessens, G. E. B.** "A History of Northwest Palestine in the Middle Bronze II–Late Bonze I Period." PhD thesis, University of Cambridge, 1990. **Camillo, C. C.** "A Contexted Conquest: Joshua and the Destruction of Hazor." Paper read to Near East Archaeology Society of Evangelical Theological Society, Atlanta, November 17, 2010. **Chisholm, Robert B., Jr.** "Divine Hardening in the Old Testament." *BSac* 153 (1996) 411–34. **Clermount-Ganneau, C.** "Le dieu Mifsenus et Mispheh de Joshué 11,8." *Recueil d'archéologie orientale* 5 (1903) 79–84. **Coogan, M. D.** "Archeology and Biblical Studies: The Book of Joshua." In *The Hebrew Bible and Its Interpreters.* Ed. W. H. Propp, B. Halpern, and D. N. Freedman. Biblical and Judaic Studies from the University of California, San Diego. Winona Lake: IN: Eisenbrauns, 1990. 19–32. **DeVries, L. F.** *Cities of the Biblical World.* Peabody, MA: Hendrickson, 1997. 182–88. **Dothan, M.** "Ashdod at the End of the Late Bronze Age and the Beginning of the Iron Age." In *Symposia Celebrating the 75th Anniversary of the Founding of the American School of Oriental Research (1900–1975).* Ed. F. M. Cross. Cambridge, MA: American Schools of Oriental Research, 1979. 125–34. **Dothan, T., S. Zuckerman, and Y. Goren.** "Kamares Ware at Hazor." *IEJ* 50 (2000) 1–15. **Eissfeldt, O.** "Die Eroberung Palästinas durch Altisrael." *WO* 2 (1955) 158–71. Reprinted in *Kleine Schriften,* vol. 3 (Tübingen: Mohr [Siebeck], 1966) 367–83. **Finkelstein, I., and A. Mazar.** *The Quest for the Historical Israel: Debating Archaeology and the History of Early Israel.* Ed. B. B. Schmidt. Archaeology and Biblical Studies 17. Atlanta: SBL, 2007. **Finkelstein, I., and N. A. Silberman.** *The Bible Unearthed.* New York: Simon & Schuster, 2001. **Fritz, V.** "Das Ende der spätbronzezeitlichen Stadt Hazor Stratum XIII und die biblische Überlieferung in Jos. 11:1–15 und Ri. 4:1–3, 23, 24." *UF* 5 (1973) 123–39. **Görg, M.** "Dor, die Teukrer und die Girgasiter." *BN* 28 (1985) 7–14. **Gover, W.** "The Waters of Merom." *PEFQS* (1890) 50–53. **Gray, J.** "Hazor." *VT* 16 (1966) 26–52. **Greenspoon, L. J.** *Textual Studies in the Book of Joshua.* HSM 28. Chico, CA: Scholars Press, 1983. **Hall, S. L.** *Conquering Character: The Characterization of Joshua in Joshua 1–11.* New York: T&T Clark, 2010. **Hallo, W., and H. Tadmor.** "A Lawsuit from Hazor." *IEJ* 27 (1977) 1–11. **Holmes, S.** *Joshua, the Hebrew and Greek Texts.* Cambridge: Cambridge UP, 1914. **Horowitz, W.** "A Combined Multiplication Table on a Prism Fragment from Hazor." *IEJ* 47 (1997) 190–97. ———. "Two Late Bronze Age Tablets from Hazor." *IEJ* 50 (2000) 16–28. **Horowitz, W., and T. Oshima.** "Two More Cuneiform Finds from Hazor." *IEJ* 52 (2002) 179–186. **Kallai, Z.** "The Conquest of Northern Palestine in Joshua and Judges." *PrWCJewSt* 5 (1969) 129–34. **Lohfink, N.** "Geschichtstypologisch orientierte Textstrukturen in den Büchern Deuteronomium und Josua." In *Deuteronomy and Deueronomic Literature: Festschrift C. W. Brekelmans.* Ed. M. Vervenne and J. Lust. Leuven: Leuven UP, 1997. 133–60. **Maas, F.** "Hazor und das Problem der Landnahme." In *Von Ugarit nach Qumran.* Ed. J. Hempel and L. Rost. BZAW 77. Berlin: Töpelmann, 1958. 105–17. **Maeir, A.** "The Political and Economic Status of MB II Hazor and MB Trade: An Inter- and Intra-Regional View." *PEQ* 132 (2000) 37–58. **Malamat, A.** "Hazor, the Head of All Those Kingdoms." *JBL* 79 (1960) 12–19. ———. "Mari and Hazor—Trade Relations in the Old Babylonian Period. In *Biblical Archaeology Today, 1990: Proceedings of the Second International Congress on Biblical Archaeology—Supplement. Pre-Congress Symposium: Population, Production and Power.* Jerusalem: Israel Exploration Society, 1993. 66–70. ———. "The Period of the Judges." In *The World History of the Jewish People.* Series 1, vol. 3. Ed. B. Mazar. Tel-Aviv: Massada, 1971. 135–40. **Margolis, M. L.** "Τετροπωμένους: Joshua 11:6." *JBL* 33 (1914) 286–89. **Mazar, B.**

"Beth She'arim, Gaba, and Harosheth of the Peoples." *HUCA* 24 (1952–1953) 75–84. **Miguens, E.** "Eaux de Merom: Dernière étape de la conquête." *TS(F)* 4 (1965) 100–105. **Mitchell, G.** *Together in the Land.* JSOTSup 134. Sheffield: Sheffield Academic, 1993. **Mowinckel, S.** *Tetrateuch, Pentateuch, Hexateuch.* BZAW 90. Berlin: Töpelmann, 1964. 40–41. **Na'aman, N.** *Borders and Districts in Biblical Historiography.* Jerusalem Biblical Studies 4. Jerusalem: Simor, 1986. **Niehaus, J.** *"Pa'am 'Ehat* and the Israelite Conquest." *VT* 30 (1980) 236–39. **Noth, M.** "Der Beitrag der Archäologie zur Geschichte Israels." In *Congress Volume: Oxford, 1959.* Ed. G. W. Anderson et al. VTSup 7. Leiden: Brill, 1960. 272–73. Reprinted in *Aufsätze zur biblischen Landes- und Altertumskunde,* vol. 1 (Neukirchen-Vluyn: Neukirchener Verlag, 1971) 43–44. ————. "Hat die Bible doch recht?" In *Festschrift für Günther Dehn.* Ed. W. Schneemelcher. Neukirchen-Vluyn: Neukirchener Verlag, 1957. 14–15. Reprinted in *Aufsätze zur biblischen Landes- und Altertumskunde.* Vol. 1. Neukirchen-Vluyn: Neukirchener Verlag, 1971 25–26. **Otto, E.** *Das Mazzotfest in Gilgal.* BWANT 107. Stuttgart: Kohlhammer, 1975. 93–95. **Petrovich, D.** "The Dating of Hazor's Destruction in Joshua 11 by way of Biblical, Archaeological, and Epigraphical Evidence." *JETS* 51 (2008) 489–512. **Polak, F.** "Joshua 11,23, 'Joshua conquered the whole country . . . and gave it to Israel as inheritance.'" *Shnaton* 9 (1985) 234–35 (Heb.). **Provan, I. V., P. Long, and T. Longman III.** *A Biblical History of Israel.* Louisville: John Knox Westminster, 2003. **Rainey, A. F., R. S. Notley, et al.** *The Sacred Bridge: Carta's Atlas of the Biblical World.* Jerusalem: Carta, 2006. **Rösel, H.** "Studien zur Topographie der Kriege in den Büchern Josua und Richter." *ZDPV* 91 (1975) 171–83. **Rudolph, W.** *Der 'Elohist' von Exodus bis Josua.* BZAW 68. Berlin: Töpelmann, 1938. 209–11. **Schäfer-Lichtenberger, C.** "Hazor: A City between the Major Powers." *SJOT* 15 (2001) 104–22. **Schmid, H.** "Erwägungen zur Gestalt Josuas in Überlieferung und Geschichte." *Jud* 24 (1968) 56. **Schunck, K.-D.** *Benjamin.* BZAW 86. Berlin: Töpelmann, 1963. **Soggin, J. A.** "On Joshua 11:7." In *Old Testament and Oriental Studies.* Ed. J. A. Soggin. BibOr 29. Rome: Biblical Institute, 1975. 227–28. **Stolz, F.** *Jahwes und Israels Kriege.* ATANT 60. Zürich: Theologischer, 1972. 88. **Sweeney, M. A.** *King Josiah of Judah: The Lost Messiah of Israel.* Oxford: Oxford UP, 2001. **Tur-Sinai, N. H.** "How Far Did the Fighting against the Kings of Canaan Extend after the Battle of the Waters of Merom?" *BIES* 24 (1959–1960) 33–35 (Heb.). **Vaux, R. de.** *Histoire ancienne d'Israel.* Vol. 1. Paris: Gabalda, 1971. 599–605. Translated as *The Early History of Israel,* trans. D. Smith (London: Darton, Longman & Todd, 1978) 655–67. **Vries, S. J. de.** "Temporal Terms as Structural Elements in the Holy-War Tradition." *VT* 25 (1975) 80–83. **Waltke, B.** "The Date of the Conquest." *WTJ* 52 (1990) 181–200. **Weippert, M.** *Die Landnahme der israelitischen Stämme.* FRLANT 92. Göttingen: Vandenhoeck & Ruprecht, 1967. 40–43. Translated as *The Settlement of the Israelite Tribes in Palestine,* trans. J. D. Martin (London: SCM Press, 1971) 33–37. **Winther-Nielsen, N.** *A Functional Discourse Grammar of Joshua: A Computer-Assisted Rhetorical Structure Analysis.* ConBOT 40. Stockholm: Almqvist & Wiksell, 1995. **Wright, G. E.** "Hazor and the Conquest of Canaan." *BA* 18 (1955) 106–8. **Yadin, Y.** *Hazor I–IV.* Ed. A. Ben-Tor. Jerusalem: Magnes, 1958–1961, 1989. ————. "Hazor and the Battle of Joshua: Is Josh 11 Wrong?" *BAR* 2.1 (1976) 3–4, 44. ————. *Hazor: The Head of All Those Kingdoms.* London: Oxford UP, 1972. ————. *Hazor: The Rediscovery of a Great Citadel of the Bible.* New York: Random House, 1975. **Yeivin, S.** *The Israelite Conquest of Canaan.* Uitgaven van het Nederlands historisch-archeologisch insttuut te Istanbul 27. Leiden: Brill, 1971. ————. "The Israelite Settlement in Galilee and the Wars with Jabin of Hazor." *Mélanges bibliques rédigés en l'honneur de André Robert.* Travaux de l'institut catholique de Paris 4. Paris: Bloud & Gay, 1957. 95–104. **Younger, K. L.** *Ancient Conquest Accounts: A Study in Ancient Near Eastern and Biblical History Writing.* JSOTSup 98. Sheffield: JSOT Press, 1990. **Zarzeki-Peleg, A.** "Hazor, Jokneam, and Megiddo in the Tenth Century B.C.E." *TA* 24 (1997) 258–88. **Zuckerman, S.** "Anatomy of a Destruction: Crisis Architecture, Termination Rituals and the fall of Canaanite Hazor." *Journal of*

Mediterranean Archaeology 20 (2007) 3–32. ———. "Where Is the Hazor Archive Buried?" *BAR* 32.2 (2006) 28–37.

Translation

[1]*When Jabin, king of Hazor, heard, he sent to Jobab, king of Madon,*[a] *and to the king of Shimron and to the king of Achshaph,* [2]*and to the kings who were in the northern*[a] *hill country and in the Arabah south*[b] *of Chinneroth and in the Shephelah and in the hills*[c] *of Dor on the west.*[d] [3]*Now the Canaanites from east and west and the Amorites and the Hittites and the Perizzites and the Jebusites in the hill country, and the Hivites under Hermon in the land of Mizpah* [4]*came out—they and all their armies*[a] *with them, a multitude as numerous as the sands on the seashore—along with horses and chariots of immeasurable number.* [5]*All these kings assembled together according to their agreement and came and encamped together at the waters of Merom to do battle with Israel.*

[6]*Yahweh said to Joshua, "Do not fear them, for tomorrow at this time I am giving all of them*[a] *dead to Israel—while their horses you will hamstring, and their chariots you shall burn with fire."* [7]*Joshua came and all the warriors with him*[a] *against them beside the waters of Merom suddenly and attacked them.*[b] [8]*Yahweh gave them into the hand of Israel. They smote them and pursued them unto Great Sidon and unto Misrephoth-mayim and unto the valley of Mizpeh*[a] *to the east. They smote them until nothing at all remained for them.* [9]*Joshua did to them just what Yahweh said to him. Their horses he hamstrung, and their chariots he burned with fire.*

[10]*Joshua turned at that time and captured Hazor, and its king he smote*[a] *with the sword because Hazor had previously been the head of all these kingdoms.* [11]*They*[a] *smote every person in it with the edge of the sword, applying the ban.*[b] *Nothing remained of all that breathed. Hazor he burned with fire.* [12]*All the cities of these kings and all their kings Joshua captured. He smote them with the edge of the sword, putting them to the ban, just as Moses, the servant of Yahweh, commanded.* [13]*The only exception was that all the cities standing on their tell,*[a] *Israel did not burn, with the exception of Hazor alone, which Joshua*[b] *did burn.* [14]*At the same time, all the spoil of these cities*[a] *and the cattle the sons of Israel appropriated for themselves. It was only all the people that they smote with the edge of the sword until they had utterly destroyed them. They did not leave anything breathing.* [15]*Just as Yahweh commanded Moses, his servant, thus Moses commanded Joshua, and thus Joshua did. He did not leave one thing undone from all that Yahweh*[a] *commanded Moses.*

[16]*Joshua took all this land, the hill country and all the Negev and all the land of Goshen and the Shephelah and the Arabah and the hill country of Israel and its Shephelah.* [17]*From Mount Halak going up to Seir clear unto Baal-Gad in the valley of the Lebanon under Mount Hermon, all their kings he captured. He smote them and killed them.*

[18]*For many days Joshua did battle with all these kings.* [19]*There was not a city which made peace*[a] *with the sons of Israel except for the Hivites dwelling in Gibeon. They captured absolutely everything in battle.* [20]*For it had been Yahweh's idea to harden their hearts to encounter Israel in battle in order that they could put them to the ban without their having opportunity to plead for mercy. Indeed, this was so that they might annihilate them just as Yahweh commanded Moses.*

[21]*Joshua came at that time and cut off the Anakim from the hill country, from Hebron, from Debir, from Anab, and from all the hill country of Judah and from all the hill country of Israel.*[a] *With*[b] *their cities, Joshua put them to the ban.* [22]*None of the Anakim remained*

in the land[a] *of the sons of Israel with the exception that in Gaza, Gath,*[b] *and Ashdod, they remained.* [23]*Joshua took all the land according to all which Yahweh spoke to Moses. Joshua gave it out for a possession of Israel according to their lots by their tribes. Meanwhile, the land had rest from battle.*

Notes

1.a. LXX transliterates the geographical references in this chapter in unexpected ways, but Nelson (150) sees Gk. spellings as original. Madon becomes Marrōn, identified with Merom in vv 5 and 7, which Nelson finds in Egyptian and Assyrian sources. Shimron becomes Sumoōn (LXX[A]-Somerōn-Samaria) or *Shim'on.* Achshaph becomes *Aziph. Preliminary and Interim Report* (2:22) decides on Shimeon and Maron/m, but gives the lowest probability rating to each of these readings as does Barthélemy (*Critique textuelle,* 1:18). Rainey (*Sacred Bridge,* 129) calls the Heb. Madon, Shimron, and Merom in v 5 "ghost words," the superior Gk. tradition showing the originals to be Mērôn and Šim'ôn. Compare Josh 12:20 and 19:15.

2.a. LXX reads צפון, "northern," as צדון, "Sidon," as in v 8, and then added "the great" as in v 8.

2.b. LXX reflects a confusion of letters in the Heb. copying tradition, reading נגד, "over against," for MT נגב, "south." *Preliminary and Interim Report* (2:22) and Barthélemy (*Critique textuelle,* 1:20) follow MT. Fritz (119) refuses to emend the text because the Arabah is the designation for the Jordan Valley (Josh 12:3). Nelson (150) finds support for MT in Deut 1:7; Josh 11:16; 12:8. Boling shows how LXX anticipated v 8 and lost an *ayin* in ובערבה.

2.c. The Heb. נפות, "hills," occurs only here and in 1 Kgs 4:11, both times with Dor. Its meaning is uncertain, possibly referring to sand dunes near Dor (Soggin, 134). Boling (301) follows the versions and Josh 12:23 in reading the sg. Naphath-dor. Nelson (152) interprets the MT as signifying "the region under the administrative control of Dor." Hess simply admits: "No one knows to what Naphoth in Naphoth Dor refers" (210).

2.d. "On the west" was taken by LXX with the next verse to achieve parallelism, translating the word "seacoast" first of the Canaanites and then of the Amorites. Younger follows Boling (303) in seeing a chiastic construction of east and west and so reading: "Naphath Dor on the west, to the Canaanites in the east and on the west the Amorites, the Hittites, the Perizzites, and the Jebusites in the hill country" (*Ancient Conquest Accounts,* 383).

4.a. Copying mistakes have transformed MT מחניהם, "armies," into LXX סמלכי, "kings," parallel to v 5. This led to the dropping of "all" by LXX.

6.a. LXX reads the sign of the direct object with a suffix rather than MT sign of direct object plus "all of them." The MT may result from dittography of the following חללים. See Nelson (150).

7.a. LXX lacks "with him against them," which may have entered the text as dittography of the following על־מי. Nelson (150) finds an MT conflated doublet with עם and עם.

7.b. LXX amplifies the narrative with specific geography: בהר, "in the hill country," which may have arisen in confusion with the preceding בהם.

8.a. Fritz (119) changes the Heb. spelling to mirror v 3. For the Gk. evidence, see Greenspoon (*Textual Studies,* 45–46).

10.a. LXX lacks "he smote with the sword," perhaps through haplography (Holmes, *Joshua, the Hebrew and Greek Texts*; Benjamin, *Variations*). Nelson (150) sees no explanation for the LXX minus.

11.a The textual tradition is confused in the uses of sg. and pl. subjects in this verse (cf. *BHS*).

11.b. LXX emphasizes the extent of the ban by adding πάντας, "all."

13.a. LXX reads tells, pl., as opposed to MT with "their tell," a case of differing pointing. Younger (*Ancient Conquest Accounts,* 383) follows Boling (303) in opting for the pl.

13.b. LXX reads "Israel" for Joshua, continuing the confusion of subjects (cf. 11.a.). MT may reflect continued tendency of tradition to emphasize the role of Joshua.

14.a. LXX and Syr. lack "of these cities and the cattle," possibly an addition by the later tradition to limit the case to this time and not let it be understood as a general practice. A similar tendency is at work in MT addition of אדם, "people," not attested by LXX. Nelson finds this to be a "tendentious MT specification of the difference between that which was devoted to destruction and allotted plunder" (150).

15.a. LXX reads "Moses commanded him," which may reflect simple mistakes in copying (Benjamin, *Variations*), but more probably reflects the later tradition's refusal to leave the last command to Moses. Nelson considers this "a theologizing improvement" (150).

19.a. LXX abbreviates the verse: "there was not a city which Israel did not take. They took them all in battle." This makes Israel the controlling subject, rather than the enemy city and eliminates the concept of making peace. The omission of the reference to the Gibeonites may reflect the original tradition, which later was augmented to make explicit connection to chap. 9. Nelson decides this is a "MT supplement for clarification" (150).

21.a. LXX reads "from all the family of Israel and from all the hill country of Judah." Here the tradition has intensified the meaning while missing the geographical distinction between the two kingdoms. That more than a copyist's error is involved (Benjamin, *Variations*) is seen in the transposition of Israel before Judah. Nelson (150) finds no obvious explanation for the LXX reading.

21.b Williams (*Williams' Hebrew Syntax*, 333) shows that עִם can signify "along with" or "as well as."

22.a. LXX lacks "in the land" and interprets Israel as the agent of the action.

22.b. LXX lacks "Gath," which later tradition may have added or which may have dropped out within the Gk. tradition (Margolis, *Book of Joshua in Greek*, 225–26). Nelson (150) follows Margolis in seeing an "inner-Greek haplography" (150).

Form/Structure/Setting

An introductory formula parallel to that of Josh 10:1 marks the opening of the section. Its conclusion is problematic. Josh 11:9 is a formulaic conclusion, but v 10 obviously seeks to continue the previous narrative. V 15 contains yet another concluding formula. Vv 16–20 form a summary parallel to Josh 10:40–43. The summary can be taken as an independent unit, but the parallel in 10:40–43 shows that it is intended to be read with the preceding narrative. V 20 then gives the concluding formula. This leaves vv 21–23 isolated as a small unit consisting of a specific notation (vv 21–22) and a general summary transitional statement (v 23). Though these might be treated in isolation, it is easier in the present format to include them with the preceding section to which they are loosely connected.

Tradition

Traditions behind the narrative are difficult to delineate because of the obscurity concerning the group that burned the great city and because of the form of the narrative.

Josh 11 may be related to the destruction of the massive Late Bronze Age Hazor, the largest city of Canaan.[1509] Another candidate would be Pharaoh Seti I, who reports an expedition against Hazor and other cities about 1290 BCE. Bimson, on the other hand, dates the destruction of Hazor by Joshua to the last decades of the fifteenth century BCE.[1510] Coogan maintains that the perpetrators of the destruction were anonymous and that the story is dependent on Judg 4 and 5.[1511]

1509 Cf. Yadin, *Hazor: The Head of All Those Kingdoms*, 129–34; Maas, "Hazor," 113–17; Gray, 117, 120–21; Schunck, *Benjamin*; Benjamin, *Variations*, 27–28; Ben-Tor and Rubiato, *BAR* 25.3 (1999) 22–39, 60; etc.

1510 *Redating*, 185–200.

1511 "Archaeology and Biblical Studies," 24.

Zuckerman attributes the destruction to an internal revolt.[1512] Petrovich dates the conquest to April 26, 1406 BCE, finding two destructions, the first by Joshua about 1400 and the second, the fiery destruction of Hazor in 1234, by Deborah and Barak.[1513]

Ben-Tor and Rubiato suggest a destruction date of fourteenth or thirteenth century BCE based on pottery evidence, noting that Yadin's 1230 date was "overly confident."[1514] They admit that identifying the group that destroyed the city is a historical and to some extent theological issue and that the biblical account is "not entirely accurate" since several sites in addition to Hazor were burned at the end of the Late Bronze Age.[1515]

Ben-Tor and Rubiato reduce the candidates for the burning of the city to four groups: Sea Peoples, another Canaanite city, Egypt, or Israel. They eliminate the Canaanites and Egyptians because they would have had to destroy statues of their own kings and gods. The Sea Peoples would not be interested in an inland city. And they offer the interesting observation that other city-states would be too weak to capture the mighty Hazor. They ignore the possibility of a fire caused by the inhabitants of Hazor itself and thus leave open the possibility of a miraculous victory by Israel and their God. They conclude: "with what we now know, the 'Israel' of the Merneptah Stele seems to be the most likely candidate for the violent destruction of Canaanite Hazor."[1516]

Provan et al. cautiously state, "the archaeology of Hazor seems reasonably compatible with a thirteenth-century conquest."[1517] Having summarized Bimson's view of a late fifteenth-century conquest, Provan et al. decide that "reasonable cases can be made for several scenarios, though none without loose ends."

If one posits a connection between Josh 11 and the destruction of Hazor based on excavations, the commentator must remain cautious. The biblical account reports the long fight Israel had to wage to conquer the area (v 18) and the fact that only Hazor of all the major cities was burned (v 13). The loose literary connection between vv 1–9 and 10–15 (cf. "at that time," v 10) cautions against making firm chronological statements. At best, we have an old Israelite tradition preserved by the settlers of Iron Age Hazor describing the destruction of the city. The important point for the tradition was not when and why. The question was how. The answer reverberates even today: God gave it into our hands.

Fritz, however, posits a destruction of Hazor by the Sea Peoples and reduces Josh 10–11 and Judg 4 to the free creation of tradition based on the existence of the ruins of Hazor. His tradition-history studies appear to assume a unilinear growth of tradition in which related traditions cannot circulate at the same time.

The compiler of the conquest narratives most likely collected the wide range of traditions and used them to create the picture of how God gave Israel the land. A list of cities, as in Josh 12, and the ruins of Hazor do not create the narrative traditions behind Josh 10–11.

1512 *BAR* 32.2 (2006) 37.
1513 *JETS* 51 (2008) 495 with n. 26.
1514 *BAR* 25.3 (1999) 36.
1515 Ibid., 38.
1516 Ibid., 39.
1517 *Biblical History of Israel*, 180.

Fritz warns against assuming that other city-states or other groups could not have taken Hazor and that only a tribal confederation under Joshua could have.[1518] The veracity of the tradition is not based on the size of Hazor, but rather on the nature and growth of traditional narrative itself. The correlation between tradition and excavation has not been proved but has more probability than a reconstruction without literary support. The description of Hazor as "the head of all these kingdoms" (v 10) originates prior to the great destruction of Hazor, for it would not be labeled on the city any time thereafter.

Nelson maintains that the parallel form in Josh 5:1, 9:1, and 10:1 shows that "the basic form of the chapter goes back to the pre-deuteronomistic book of Joshua." Still, he finds "little in this chapter can be attributed to genuine early tradition. It is largely a literary composition."[1519]

A response to Nelson is founded on two uncertainties: the nature of the tradition behind these materials and the method of the compiler. Neither issue can be ultimately solved. I would argue for faithful tradition and a compiler who handed down tradition in a collected form rather than creating tradition in an unhistorical form.

An idea of oral tradition preserved unchanged through the centuries is unrealistic and naïve, according to Finkelstein in his discussions with Mazar.[1520] He is not willing, however, to go with the minimalists who date the materials as very late (14–15). Mazar concedes that all archaeologists realize that archaeology contradicts the biblical account of the conquest with one leader.[1521] Some stories may have historical memories but not be necessarily connected with Joshua or even with Israel. Hazor was burned in this period but possibly by Canaanites, not Israelites.

The issue at this point is how much early information such stylized, hyperbolic, annalistic campaign reports can preserve. The northern conquest tradition of chap. 11 does not provide a true narrative with crisis and resolution. Its opening verses are stylized like those of chaps. 9 and 10. Then follows a brief battle report resembling annals more than narrative. The final part of the chapter involves formulaic, theological language, not oral narrative. Thus the tradition has been handed down in list and formula fashion, not in the earlier form of stories with individual battle tactics, pursuit stories, and narrative suspense.

Source and Redaction

Knauf considers the chapter to be an attempt to bridge the discrepancy between the land described as having been conquered in chap. 10 and that described as to be conquered in Josh 1:4.[1522] For Knauf, the language ties directly to his D-layer in Josh 10:29–39. Compared to the Jabin story of Judg 4, the Joshua version proves to be the later one for Knauf.[1523]

Fritz understands an unusually large part of the chapter to be original—with vv 2, 3, and 13 forming redactional additions, vv 16–20 belonging to a Deueronomistic

1518 *UF* 5 (1973) 123–39.
1519 Nelson, 151.
1520 *Quest for the Historical Israel*, 18.
1521 Ibid., 62.
1522 Knauf, 111.
1523 Ibid., 112.

redactor, and vv 21–23 a final late addition (*Nachtrag*).[1524] Vv 1, 3, and 13 expand the geographical spread of the story beyond the area of the original story. Vv 16–20, for Fritz, provide a summary of the previous story in Deuteronomistic language and themes.[1525] The final verses of the chapter explain the continued existence of the Anakim in the land.

Nelson finds chap. 11 to be "a literary mirror of chapter 10."[1526] While this is true for the opening verses, chap. 11 lacks a narrative plot and any semblance of a pursuit narrative. Chap. 10 has a story line or plot, while chap. 11 is a basic theological report and interpretation.

The simple explanation is that a compiler received the annalistic tradition and molded it into a report showing Yahweh's incomparable strength and power.

Form

The opening verses (vv 1–9) form a concise and terse battle report with confrontation, battle, and consequences as in the table below. Though the chapter centers on Hazor's defeat, the actual battle form applies to the battle against the combined forces, not against Hazor. The latter appears as a subplot tacked onto the major report. Its mention is basically an editorial footnote.

Brueggemann categorizes vv 1–15 as a true narrative with vv 1–14 forming a "general theological summary."[1527] Winther-Nielsen compares vv 12a–15d with Josh 10:40–42 and seeks to deny the parallel structure of 11:16–20 with 10:40–43. This demands a closer look.[1528]

Josh 10:38–39 ends the battle with Debir just as 11:9–15 completes the victory over Hazor and its allies. Whereas the southern campaign involved a series of victories that had to be summarized, the northern campaign included only one major battle, the battle of Hazor and its allies, and thus it required only one summary statement. Josh 10:40–42 summarizes the southern campaign parallel to the summary in 11:16–20 of the entire conquest from southeast to northwest. Notice the parallel openings in 10:40 and 11:16 and the parallel of 11:20 with 10:40. Similarly, both summaries focus on Gibeon, the northernmost point of the southern campaign.

Nelson points to הַהִיא בָּעֵת, "at that time," in Josh 11:10, 21 as evidence that the three sections (vv 1–9, 10–20, and 21–23) are to be read as "coordinated or overlapping in time rather than as purely sequential."[1529] The phrase "at that time" places all the narratives in a broad chronological timespan. While Hebrew narrative does not always employ chronological sequence as its major organizing principle, it seems clear that these three distinct military actions against the coalition, against Hazor, and against the Anakim occupy three definite time slots and cannot overlap in time. The first two sections are in expected chronological order. The final section concerning the Anakim may be out of chronological order, just as it is out

---

1524 Fritz, 118.
1525 Ibid., 124.
1526 Nelson, 151.
1527 *Divine Presence amid Violence*, 14, n. 5.
1528 *Functional Discourse Grammar*, 248–49, n. 24.
1529 Nelson, 151.

of geographical order, to emphasize the importance of this victory and its ties to events that lay ahead for Hebron and its related towns.

Vv 16–20 are formulated by the compiler to provide a parallel summary to that of Josh 10:40–41. Vv 21–23 take up the special tradition of the Anakim, who are mentioned in Num 13:22, 28, 33; Deut 1:28; 2:10–11, 21; 9:2; Josh 14:12, 15; 15:13, 14; 21:11; Judg 1:20. They are described as "giants" who possessed the land Israel desired. They centered in Hebron, from which they were driven out by Caleb (Josh 14:12–15; 15:13–14; Judg 1:20).

Our passage, again given in theological report style, attributes their destruction to Joshua. The sudden geographical switch from north to south, the loose literary connection ("at that time," v 21), and the report in Deut 9:2 lead to the assumption that these verses are a literary construction of the ultimate historian filling out his picture of Joshua (so Pressler, Creach, Rösel, Fritz). The switch can also mean that the writer placed this as his final battle report to emphasize God's ability to gain victory over even the fiercest opponent. The constant return to battle at Hebron also shows this same power exercised by the enemy there. The final verse is a literary summary and transition pointing back to chaps. 1–11 and forward to chaps. 13–21.

Younger shows the relationship of chap. 11 to the various stereotyped, even hyperbolic syntagms of ancient Near Eastern royal campaign reports. His diagram (without the breakdown by verbs and formulas used) displays the text in a complex language to expose its "iterative code":[1530]

Table 11.1. Younger's Syntagms for Joshua 11

Passage	Iterative Code Syntagms
v 1a	Temporal collocation
vv 1b–3	Non-flight, assembling troops, numerical quantification
v 4	Non-flight, assembling the troops
v 5	Non-flight, battle action
v 6a	Obtaining divine guarantee through oracle
v 6b	Divine aid, numerical quantification
v 6c	Outcome of the combat
v 6d	Exemplary punishment
v 7a	Move from place to place
v 7b	Outcome of the combat = destruction
v 8a	Divine aid/divine intervention
v 8b	Outcome of the combat = capture
v 8c	Pursuit
v 8d	Outcome of the combat = destruction
v 8	Outcome of the combat with hyperbole
v 9a	Divine aid/divine intervention

1530 *Ancient Conquest Accounts.*

Passage	Iterative Code Syntagms
v 9b	Exemplary punishment
v 10a	Temporal collocation
v 10b	Outcome of the combat = acquisition
v 10c–d	Outcome of the combat = destruction
v 11a	Outcome of the combat = destruction
v 11b	Outcome of the combat = destruction
v 11c	Outcome of the combat = destruction
v 11d	Outcome of the combat = destruction
v 12a	Outcome of the combat = acquisition
v 12b	Outcome of the combat = acquisition
v 12c	Outcome of the combat = destruction
v 12d	Divine aid with explicit divine guarantee
v 13a	Outcome of the combat = destruction
v 13b	Outcome of the combat = destruction
v 14a	Outcome of the combat = acquisition
v 14b	Outcome of the combat = destruction
v 14c	Outcome of the combat = destruction
v 14d	Outcome of the combat = destruction
v 15	Divine aid/oracle
v 16	Outcome of the combat = acquisition
v 17b	Outcome of the combat = acquisition
v 17c	Outcome of the combat = destruction
v 18	Outcome of the combat = destruction
v 19a	Non-flight
v 19b	Flight in difficult places
v 19c	Outcome of the combat = acquisition
v 20a	Divine aid/divine intervention
v 20b	Outcome of the combat = destruction
v 20c	Outcome of the combat = destruction
v 20d	Divine aid/oracle
v 21a	Temporal coordinate
v 21b–c	Outcome of the combat = destruction
v 21d	Outcome of the combat = destruction
v 22a	Outcome of the combat = destruction
v 22b	Outcome of the combat = destruction
v 23a	Outcome of the combat = acquisition
v 23b	Divine aid/intervention
v 23c	Consequences
v 23d	Consequences

Structure and Form of Joshua 11

Structure: Holy war battle narrative		
Element	*Passage*	*Marker*
Exposition (pf. or disjunctive): personnel, problem	vv 1–3	Temporal clause
Complication (impf. consec.): Enemies attack	vv 4–5	Impf. consec.
Change or crisis (speech or dialogue): Salvation oracle	v 6	Speech
Resolution (impf. consec.): Joshua's surprise attack	v 7	Impf. consec.
Ending/ denouement (formulaic)	vv 8–9	Conveyance formula
Theological summary	vv 10–23	No narrative tension or structure

Genre: Battle report		
Element	*Passage*	*Marker*
Confrontation: armies gather at waters of Merom	vv 1–5	He heard, he sent, they came out
Battle: Salvation oracle and surprise attack	vv 6–8a	Salvation oracle; they fell on them; conveyance formula; pursuit motif
Consequences: no survivors; hamstrung horses; burned chariots	vv 8b–9	Struck them down; obedience formula

Genre: Battle report		
Element	*Passage*	*Marker*
Battle	vv 10–11ab	Took Hazor; struck king
Consequences	v 11b	No survivor; city burned
Concluding exposition	vv 10b–15	Hazor's importance; all cities destroyed; obedience formula; only Hazor burned; ban regulations obeyed
Editorial summary: Joshua	vv 16–19	Joshua took all land
Editorial summary: Yahweh	v 20	Harden hearts
Editorial summary: Anakim	vv 21–22	
Editorial summary: chaps. 1–11	v 23	

Structure

A holy-war narrative describing the victory of Joshua and Israel over a Canaanite coalition near the waters of Merom forms the center of the chapter. The introduction in v 1 has no real reference point. We are not told what was heard.

The narrative begins with the temporal clause in v 1, builds dramatic tension through the imperfect consecutive clauses of vv 4 and 5, reaches its climax in the dialogue of v 6, and is resolved in the formulaic imperfect consecutive clauses of vv 7–9.

Certain interpretive elements appear in the narrative, particularly the long list in v 3. The conclusion of the battle (v 8aβ, b) is placed in the same pursuit thematic characteristic of chap. 10. The obedience theme of v 9 may be attributed to the theological interpretation of the compiler. The compiler has shaped the narrative into the same pattern as that of chap. 10.

V 10 opens a new section of the narrative, one even more closely patterned on chap. 10. No narrative tension is established. Rather, battle reports are summarized in theological terms. Such a structure is suited to form-critical review, not to narrative-structure analysis.

Setting

The oral setting for these materials is difficult to determine. The tradition is not tied to Gilgal or any other Israelite site, and no direct clue is available for detecting the original home of the tradition. It may have been preserved and transmitted by the northern tribes, possibly the later Israelite inhabitants of Hazor. The compiler of the book of Joshua joined it to other traditions to formulate the original conquest narrative. Vv 11–23 seem to be a theological interpretation by the compiler summarizing the northern conquest and the complete conquest by emphasizing Joshua's obedient leadership.

Comments

1 The conquest of the north, as that of the south (chap. 10), is pictured as Israel's response to enemy attack. Brueggemann insists the enemy had to attack Israel because of their competing social systems. With Gottwald, Brueggemann describes Israel's system as antimonarchic, "hostile to every concentration, surplus, and monopoly."[1531]

Israel's victories over Jericho and Ai led Gibeon to seek a peace agreement, but led the two dominant kings—those of Hazor and Jerusalem—to form military alliances with their erstwhile enemies to resist the new military power emerging on the scene. Note that the northern coalition involves more people and is larger than the southern coalition.[1532] McConville and Williams find that the "accent is on the exceptional size and might of the army that gathers at Merom."[1533]

Hazor, located at Tell el-Qedah about ten miles north of the Sea of Galilee, is among the largest tells or mounds of city remains in Israel with a base of twenty-

---

1531 *Divine Presence amid Violence*, 20.
1532 See the discussion by Hall, *Conquering Character*, 184–85.
1533 McConville and Williams, 57.

six acres and, according to Hubbard, a total of two hundred acres.[1534] Hazor (= M.R. 203269) is known from the nineteenth century onward as a major city in Palestine. The Mari letters describe its extensive trade relationships. Egyptian correspondence from the sixteenth to the fourteenth century BCE reveals Hazor as a city of importance for the Egyptian empire. The Amarna correspondence shows its troubled relationships with its Palestinian neighbors, its declared loyalty to the Egyptian pharaoh, and friendly relations with the Habiru. The ruler of Hazor is given the title of "king," an unusual occurrence in the Amarna correspondence for Palestinian city-state heads.

Excavations headed by Yadin at Tell el-Qedah have traced the city's history back to the twenty-seventh century BCE.[1535] In the fourteenth and thirteenth centuries, the city covered 175 acres, ten times the area of Jerusalem, Megiddo or any other Palestinian city excavated. The population may have numbered 40,000. The city met violent destruction and was replaced in the twelfth and eleventh centuries BCE by an unfortified, temporary settlement resembling others of the period in Galilee, often identified as Israelite settlements.

Hess notes the problem caused by the role Hazor plays in Judg 4.[1536] There the chief ruler is Jabin of Hazor, who seems to dominate northern Canaan when Stratum 12 following Stratum 13 in archaeological excavations shows no fortifications or public buildings. This could mean that the Jabin dynasty continued to claim power over the area without rebuilding the city. Rainey remarks that "Canaanite Hazor had been destroyed violently and subsequently occupied by a new and less sophisticated culture in the early Iron Age."[1537] He maintains that Hazor's reputation as head of all the kingdoms goes back to a Middle Bronze Age early arrival by groups later called Naphtali.[1538]

But who destroyed Hazor? Fritz attributes its destruction to the Sea People.[1539] Hess[1540] implies that Israel caused the destruction, while Howard[1541] simply states that Israel did. Schäfer-Lichtenberger[1542] points to Rameses II of Egypt. Aharoni attributed the burning to Deborah and Barak.

Jabin appears as king of Hazor in Judg 4:2, 7, 17, 23, 24, and Ps 83:10. Since Jabin is not involved in the action of Judg 4, does not appear at all in the parallel account in Judg 5, and is said to have been killed in Josh 11, the tradition of his activity has aroused great scholarly interest. W. Richter provides evidence for the secondary role of Jabin in the Judges narrative.[1543] Fritz attempts to prove that Jabin is secondary to Judg 4 but still tradition historically prior to his appearance in Josh 11 (see his commentary, 120, where Jabin becomes a free creation of the writer).[1544] Fritz's attempt assumes a unilinear development of tradition. Bimson, on the other hand,

---

1534 Hubbard, 324.
1535 *Hazor: Head of All Those Kingdoms*, 23–26.
1536 Hess (1996) 14, n. 1.
1537 *Sacred Bridge*, 135.
1538 Ibid., 137.
1539 Fritz, 120.
1540 Hess (1996) 214.
1541 Howard, 269–70.
1542 "Hazor: A City between the Major Powers," *SJOT* 15 (2001) 104–22.
1543 *Traditionsgeschichtliche Untersuchungen zum Richterbuch*, BBB 18 (Bonn: Hanstein, 1963) 56–63.
1544 *UF* 5 (1973) 123–39.

argues on the basis of Mari evidence that Jabin was the dynastic name of several kings of Hazor.[1545]

The text names only three of Hazor's allies, each of which appear much earlier in Egyptian texts and each of which is located about twenty-five to thirty-five miles southwest of Hazor.[1546] The town of Madon appears only in the Egyptian texts and in the list of Josh 12:19. It is usually located at modern Khirbet Madin due to the similarity of names. This would place it five miles west of Tiberias on the mountain called Qam Hattin. Y. Aharoni argues for the LXX reading, locating the city by the waters of Merom.[1547] Rainey also follows LXX and places Maron at Tell el-Khureibeh, "just over 2 miles south of Marûn er-Râs."[1548] Na'aman points to Tell Qarn Hattin or Tel Qarnei Hittin five miles west of modern Tiberias.[1549] Nelson[1550] follows Rösel[1551] in intepreting *mrwm* as simply a height. Hess sees a reference to Marom, it being possible for both names to refer to the same site.[1552] Hess locates the Waters of Merom at Wadi el-Hamam.[1553] Gal suggests Tel Qarnei Hittin.[1554]

Shimron appears in the Egyptian texts, in Josh 12:20, and in the list of cities of Zebulon in Josh 19:15. The original name may have been Shim'on.[1555] It is usually identified with Khirbet Sammuniyeh (= Tel Shimron) five miles (eight kilometers) west of Nazareth in the Esdraelon Valley,[1556] but Gray[1557] suggests Marun er-Ras, ten miles (seventeen kilometers) northwest of modern Safed, north of the Sea of Chinneroth (or Galilee).

Achshaph appears in the Egyptian texts, in Josh 12:20, and in the list of Asher cities in Josh 19:25. It is generally identified with Tell Keisan, six miles (ten kilometers) southeast of Acco.[1558] Hess,[1559] and Rainey[1560] posit Khirbet el-Harbaj—Tel Regev—at the southern end of Plain of Acco, while Gray[1561] suggests Tell Iksif, five and a half miles (nine kilometers) east of Marun er-Ras.

If the traditional identifications are correct, then the Canaanite coalition is depicted as covering the area between the Jordan River and the Mediterranean Sea north of Megiddo. Gray's suggestions would narrow the area to the immediate vicinity of Hazor and the Sea of Chinneroth, the city of Chinneroth being at Khirbet el-'Ureima (Tel Kinirot). In either case, the great northern stronghold trembles and plots before the fame of Israel and her God.

1545 *Redating*, 195. Cf. Yadin, *Hazor: Head of All Those Kingdoms*, 5–6; Howard, 265; Hess (1996) 208, n. 1. See T. C. Butler, *Judges*, WBC 8 (Nashville: Nelson, 2009) 88–89.
1546 Hubbard, 325.
1547 *Land*, 106.
1548 *Sacred Bridge*, 129.
1549 *Borders and Districts*, 119–43; Hess (1996) 209; cf. Hubbard, 324.
1550 Neslon, 153.
1551 *ZDPV* 91 (1975) 179–80.
1552 Hess (1996) 208, n. 4.
1553 Ibid., 211.
1554 "The Late Bronze Age in Galilee: A Reassessment," *BASOR* 272 (1988) 79–83; see J. Drinkard, Jr., *NIDB*, 4:51.
1555 Aharoni, *Land*, 106; see *Note* 1.a.
1556 Rainey, *Sacred Bridge*, 129.
1557 Gray, 118.
1558 Fritz, 120.
1559 Hess (1996) 209; cf. (2009) 50.
1560 *Sacred Bridge*, 129.
1561 Gray, 118.

2 V 2 employs general geographical terms that are normally associated with the south to extend the coalition. The kings are neither named nor given specific location. From this evidence, Nelson concludes, "the authorial perspective is thoroughly Judahite."[1562] Brueggemann finds the list of mobilized kings to be "generalized and stylized" and so "not historically literal."[1563] One cannot disprove such a theory, but any battle story must have combatants. An author with sources describing the battle will have used those sources rather than creating an enemy coalition. The question remains as to when the book is written and what sources were available for the compiler who put the material together in the first place.

While the northern hill country is the mountainous area northwest of the Sea of Chinneroth, the Arabah south of Chinneroth is not a precise geographical area. Arabah usually refers to the Jordan River Valley between the Sea of Chinneroth and the Dead Sea. Occasionally, it refers to the continuation of the depression south of the Dead Sea to the Gulf of Aqabah. In v 2 it may refer either to the area immediately south of the Sea of Chinneroth or to the area near the sea immediately south of the city of Chinneroth on the northwestern shore of the sea. If the latter is meant, it is unique in OT usage.

Unique language certainly appears in "the Shephelah." The term occurs twenty times and always refers to the area between the Philistine plain and the southern hill country (e.g., Josh 9:1; 10:40).[1564] The reference here may be to its northern continuation between Mount Carmel and Shechem even though this area is more hilly than the southern Shephelah.[1565] Rainey speaks of the "north-south foothills of western Galilee extending up to the coastal plain of Tyre in southern Lebanon."[1566] Fritz[1567] dismisses the term as a meaningless later gloss, but see I. Finkelstein.[1568]

Dor (compare *Note* 2.c) is identified with Khirbet el-Burj, twelve miles (twenty kilometers) south of Mount Carmel. For a discussion of Naphoth, see M. Ben-Dov.[1569] An inscription of Ramses II from the thirteenth century BCE is the first mention of Dor. The Bible mentions it only here, Josh 12:23; 17:11; Judg 1:27; 1 Kgs 4:11; and 1 Chr 7:29. Located in the territory of Asher, it was assigned to Manasseh but was not captured (Josh 17:11–12; Judg 1:27). The account of Wen-Amon[1570] lists its ruler as Beder (ca. 1100) and identifies him as a member of the Sea Peoples, who are closely related to the Philistines. Limited excavations in 1923–1924 revealed that the city was founded in the Late Bronze Age and destroyed in the thirteenth-century, possibly by the Sea People.[1571] Rainey has no explanation for "Naphoth."[1572] *HALOT* defines it as "yoke."

The biblical writer thus depicts the forces opposing Joshua as in control of the

---

1562 Nelson, 152.
1563 *Divine Presence amid Violence*, 15.
1564 Cf. D. Baly, *The Geography of the Bible* (New York: Harper & Row, 1957) 142.
1565 Cf. G. A. Smith, *The Historical Geography of the Holy Land* (London: Hodder & Stoughton, 1894) 203; Baly, *Geography*, 144.
1566 *Sacred Bridge*, 129.
1567 Fritz, 122.
1568 "The Shephelah of Israel," *TA* 8 (1981) 84–94.
1569 "נפה: A Geographical Term of Possible 'Sea Peoples' Origin," *TA* 3 (1976) 70–73.
1570 *ANET*, 26.
1571 Cf. G. Foerster, "Dor," *EAEHL*, 1:334–37.
1572 *Sacred Bridge*, 176.

land from the Esdraelon plain north at least to Dan and stretching from the Jordan Valley to the Mediterranean Sea. Their defeat means Israelite control of the north.

3 Not only the whole territory but also all its peoples are involved (compare Josh 9:1). The Canaanites are located by the Mediterranean Sea and the Jordan River and the Hittites, Jebusites, and Amorites in the hill country in Num 13:29. Elsewhere, the Jebusites are closely identified with Jerusalem (Josh 15:8, 63; 18:28; Judg 1:21; 19:10–11; 2 Sam 5:6, 8; 24:16, 18; cf. Josh 18:16). The Hivites are located in the northern extremities of the land in Judg 3:3 and 2 Sam 24:7.[1573] The Hittites in Palestine appear to have had one center at Tell Taʻyinat near the northern bend of the Orontes River. Excavations evidence buildings from the twelfth to the eighth century BCE, suggesting cultural and political continuity with the Anatolian Hittite empire that was destroyed at the end of the Late Bronze Age. T. P. Harrison calls the new entities "diminished 'rump' states ruled by dynastic lines with direct ancestral links to the royal family in Hattusa" (that is, the classical Hittites).[1574]

Rainey states that "the idea in the description of the allies is to present a picture of the main centers of non-Israelite settlement in the northern part of the country, all of them presumably subordinate to the king of Hazor. There must have been a longer list of towns, but it has been intentionally truncated and summarized in terms of the general area."[1575]

The use of the extended list of nations rests on an old tradition and serves a specific theological function. The territory occupied by these nations is promised to Abraham (Gen 15:18–21) and again to the Israelites in Egypt (Exod 3:8, 17). The promise becomes the basis of divine demand in Exod 13:5; 23:23; 34:11 and can be used to exemplify the seriousness of divine anger (Exod 33:2). Deuteronomy attests the list of nations to demonstrate the necessity that the nations in the land be totally exterminated (Deut 7:1; 20:17). Victory over the peoples becomes the sign that God fulfills his promises (Josh 3:10). This is brought to reality in Josh 9:1; 11:3; 12:8 and serves again as the basis for the divine command (Josh 24:11). The reality is that Israel has not completely fulfilled the divine command (e.g., Josh 15:63; Judg 1:21, 27, 36; 3:1–5). Solomon fulfilled the command by enslaving the peoples (1 Kgs 9:20–21).[1576] The listing of the nations serves rhetorically to "cast a dark cloud of impending doom over the Israelites."[1577]

4 The holy-war narrative emphasizes the impossible task facing the people of God. Israel had to face an innumerable army that had the best modern equipment. Horses and chariots were well-known and widely used in the ancient Near East, but Israel did not gain the wealth or necessary institutional control to manufacture and use such weaponry until the days of Solomon. "A multitude as numerous as the sands on the seashore" is traditional hyperbolic language pointing to overwhelming numbers (Judg 7:2; 1 Sam 13:5; 2 Sam 17:11; 1 Kgs 4:20). The odds were insurmountable. Such hyperbole "not only heightens the suspense but also presents the

1573 See T. C. Butler, *Judges*, WBC 8 (Nashville: Nelson, 2009) 61.

1574 "Neo-Hittites in the 'Land of Palistin' *[sic]*: Renewed Investigations at Tell Taʻyinat on the Plain of Antioch," *NEA* 72 (2009) 174–89.

1575 *Sacred Bridge*, 129.

1576 For study of the lists and literature see J. Halbe, *Das Privilegrecht Jahwes*, FRLANT 114 (Göttingen: Vandenhoeck & Ruprecht, 1975) 140–47.

1577 Howard, 265.

coming conflict in climactic terms, as though all the kings and peoples of the land are gathering for a final attack against Israel."[1578] Yet, for Israel, God by himself was a force so great in number that no army was large enough to defeat him.

5 As in the case of the Jerusalemite coalition, the northern kings overcame a history of fighting one another to join forces against the Israelite threat. They camp at the waters of Merom, mentioned only here in the biblical literature. Egyptian texts from about 1500 BCE include Merom in a list of Palestinian cities.[1579] Ramses II (ca. 1300) also mentions it.[1580] It is generally identified with Meiron, four miles west of Safed, but Aharoni argues that a suitable tell is lacking there.[1581] He prefers to understand the name as being preserved in Jebel Marun and Marun er-Ras, so that the site of the town would be the nearby Tell el-Khirbeh about fourteen miles northwest of Hazor.[1582] Fritz[1583] and Rösel[1584] suggest Merom simply means Heights. Rainey says the Canaanites mustered their forces at "a well-known water source near Marun er-Ras" so that the battle took place on "relatively level ground" and calls Mount Meiron "a modern invention."[1585] Hess points to Wadi el-Hamam.[1586] The battle site is thus quite close to Hazor.

6 The central feature of the holy-war narrative is the intervention of Yahweh by means of an oracle of salvation that promises victory and encourages the people not to fear. The oracle here also gives battle directions. Israel is to cut the hamstrings of the horses, thus taking away the advanced weaponry of the enemy.[1587] Such action is cruelty to animals (Gen 49:6) but is good battle strategy for a people who do not have chariots (2 Sam 8:4).[1588]

Brueggemann's book, *Divine Presence amid Violence*, which outlines a "theology of violence" is based on this single verse that references divine speech and the destruction of the effective use of the technology a domineering unjust political power exercises over a group with a vision from God for an egalitarian state. Brueggemann finds revelation "is not an act extrinsic to the social process, but it is an act precisely embedded in the social continuity. Instead of suggesting that revelation comes down to intrude in the community, I submit that this revelation arises up out of the hurt and the hope of this community so that the dream is understood as certified from heaven," thus receiving "enormous credibility in the life of the community on earth."[1589] Brueggemann relies heavily on the sociological readings of Gottwald (egalitarian community) and on an understanding of revelation where quoted divine speech gains superiority over other parts of Scripture.

7 As in the attack on the southern coalition, surprise is Joshua's best weapon (cf. 10:9). Throughout the book, the biblical writer sees no discrepancy between

---

1578 Hess (2000) 169.
1579 *ANET*, 243, 256; Aharoni, *Land*, 150.
1580 *ANET*, 243.
1581 *Land*, 206.
1582 Cf. Hubbard, 326.
1583 Fritz, 121.
1584 *ZDPV* 91 (1975) 180.
1585 *Sacred Bridge*, 129.
1586 Hess (2009) 51.
1587 Hess (1996) 211.
1588 Cf. Nelson, 153.
1589 *Divine Presence amid Violence*, 26.

attributing the victory to Yahweh and describing clever human military tactics. Israel tells her military history as a history directed by God. Human tactics may be described, but the ultimate glory and praise is given to Yahweh.

8 As in chap. 10, the battle narrative is transformed into a pursuit narrative. The pursuit leads to Great Sidon. Knauf takes this as reference to the governing policies under Persian rule.[1590]

Sidon is the ultimate limit of the tribe of Asher (Josh 19:29), twenty-five miles (forty-two kilometers) north of Tyre on the Mediterranean coast. Asher could not conquer it (Judg 1:31). Only 2 Sam 24:6 hints that Israel ever controlled the region. Josh 13:1–6 states that the land of the Sidonians, including Misrephoth-maim, was not conquered by Joshua. The latter is the traditional frontier city between Lebanon and Palestine[1591] and is identified with Khirbet el Musheirefeh at the northern end of the Plain of Acco,[1592] but Aharoni says excavations there do not reveal remains from the Late Bronze or Early Iron Age.[1593] Aharoni notes the possibility of identifying it with the river Litani, which Fritz accepts.[1594]

Mizpeh is a common Palestinian place name since the word means "watchtower." The precise place meant here cannot be determined.[1595] It represents the eastern extreme, just as Sidon and Misrephoth-maim represent the western boundaries. Fritz locates it on the southern foothills of Hermon at either the Valley of Merom or the lower course of the Wadi et-Tem.

The book of Joshua states that Joshua and the Israelite army beseiged the entire northern territory promised to Abraham and finally conquered by David. The understanding is that Joshua did not gain permanent control, but he showed that God had fulfilled his promises by giving victory throughout the territory. This parallels the conception of Josh 10:41. Not only was God faithful in fulfilling his promises, but Joshua was also faithful in carrying out the divine commands. He destroyed various peoples of Palestine (cf. Josh 10:40).

9 The tradition may have understood the act here as the surprise strategy which enabled Israel to win the battle. This made sure the enemy could never use these advanced weapons against Israel in any future battle. Joshua's obedience even extended to the manner in which he dealt with the horses and chariots (cf. v 6). The narrative shows that Yahweh can be trusted and that obedience leads to fulfilled promises.[1596] The interest underlining the obedience of Joshua makes the chronological order of events somewhat unclear. The command in v 6 indicates the battle strategy. Israel is to hamstring the chariot horses so that chariots could not be used against them. The fulfillment of the command represents the final act in the victory celebration (cf. 2 Sam 8:4). The animals are booty to Yahweh as a part of the holy-war ban requirements in obedience to Yahweh's commands.[1597]

Surprising is the lack of detail about the battle of Hazor. "The narrator has

---

1590 Knauf, 114.
1591 Soggin, 135.
1592 Hubbard, 328.
1593 *Land*, 216; cf. Rainey, *Sacred Bridge*, 129, "near Musheirefeh"; Nelson, 153, "unknown."
1594 Fritz, 121.
1595 Nelson, 153, "unidentifiable."
1596 McConville and Williams, 58.
1597 See Fritz, 121.

been more concerned to convey the meaning of the battles than to relate the details of what happened. . . . [T]he battles become object lessons for the reader and illustrate a powerful message: YHWH's initiative joined with faithful obedience brings victory over Canaanite power."[1598]

10 Biblical tradition remembers the greatness that was Hazor, evidenced by archaeological excavations and inscriptions. The largest tell in Palestine, Hazor controlled the northern country for centuries. Hubbard infers from the phrase "head of all these kingdoms" that Hazor "sustained its lengthy, regional hegemony by violent oppression," but nothing absolutely demands this.[1599] Her proud history and strong army did not save her when Yahweh decided to give the land to his people.

11 Thus Hazor fell to the fate commanded by God for all cities in the land (Deut 7:2; 20:17).

12 A similar fate met all the kings who had conspired with Hazor against Israel. Joshua thus completed the task set out for him in chap. 1. He stood tall as the example of leadership for the people of God. That example was not to be seen simply in his military prowess. Rather, it was epitomized in his fulfillment of the Mosaic law. God's perfect leader chose to follow God's perfect command and thus reap God's perfect victory.

13 The people of Israel tried to be honest and face facts in their use of tradition to create a self-understanding. Israel did not claim to be perfect. Israel had failed. Israel had not burned all the cities. In fact, of the major cities of the north, only Hazor was burned. Nelson maintains that the point of v 13 is "that other visible ruin mounds, either deserted or now occupied by Israelite towns, did not result from Israelite destruction, but already existed as such at the time of the conquest. Israel did not destroy captured towns, but appropriated them, thus realizing the principle of Deut. 6:10–11 and Jos. 24:13."[1600] Hess posits that the text assumes the reader knows Ai and Jericho were burnt without mentioning them here.[1601] McConville and Williams see here that the ban of Yahweh war "could admit of variations of rigor."[1602] Still what was destroyed most significantly was the power system of Canaan.[1603]

Much remained to do (Josh 13:1–6). Joshua had fulfilled the task given him. Israel had not. Israel could set Joshua up as the example for all later leaders to follow. But even in the conquest, Israel had not gone far enough. When Israel recited her history, she confessed the greatness of God, who fulfilled his promises to Israel. She also confessed her own sins in not living up to the demands made upon her by God.

14 As at Ai (Josh 8:2, 27), the people of Israel are allowed to take booty to enrich themselves. This is a rather loose interpretation of the rules in Deut 20. It shows that even at this early date, the legal material was interpreted in differing ways rather than being seen as strict legalism with no exceptions. The continuing word of God was the dominant factor (Josh 8:27; 11:15).

1598 Hess (2000) 170.
1599 Hubbard, 329.
1600 Nelson, 154.
1601 Hess, 215.
1602 McConville and Williams, 58.
1603 Ibid.

15 The major emphasis of the section is found in the repetition in v 15 of what was already made clear in v 12. The conquest narratives from the story of the spies sent to Jericho to the destruction of Hazor and the north stand as a monument to the great faithfulness of Joshua to the Mosaic law. His faithfulness thus stands as a goal for all future leaders of Israel. Rather than being lawmakers, the kings of Israel are law takers and law keepers.

16 V 16 marks an important point in the narrative structure of Joshua. Knauf isolates the entire section vv 16–23 as the conclusion to his D-edition with P-tradition still not known.[1604] He also maintains that this section completes the larger narrative from Exodus, including the Covenant Code (Exod 20–23) and the Deuteronomic law (Deut 6–28). This larger narrative thus forms the prologue to the history of the monarchy in Samuel and Kings.

V 16 is a linguistic parallel to Josh 10:40, but it functions in a different way. Whereas 10:40 summarizes the conquest of the immediately preceding narrative unit, 11:16 summarizes the entire conquest, north and south.[1605] "The extent of the lands conquered is not as ambitious as the 'map' of lands that God was giving to Israel in 1:4, but even this description is programmatic and schematic in light of the lands that still had not been taken (see 13:1–5)."[1606]

The hill country, the Negev, the land of Goshen, the Shephelah, and the Arabah are southern geographical features. A question remains concerning the precise territory designated by Goshen. Is it the Nile Delta where the family of Joseph settled in Gen 45–50; Exod 8:18 (Eng. = 8:22); 9:26? Does it refer to a part of the southern territory conquered by Israel (Josh 10:41 and 11:16)? Or is it, as in Josh 15:51, a city in the hill country assigned to the tribe of Judah? Aharoni states that the Judean land of Goshen is "the broad intermediate zone designated as a border region between the hill country and the Negeb."[1607] The description of the northern territory is interestingly brief in light of the preceding narrative. Only the hill country and its Shephelah are mentioned. The latter appears to have the same referrent as in v 2.

17 V 17 gives a more precise geographical description. Mount Halak is identified with Jebel Halaq, about forty miles (sixty-seven kilometers) southwest of the Dead Sea and thirty miles southeast of Beersheba. It marks the southern end of Israel's activities.[1608] Seir normally refers to the major mountain range of Edom, though Josh 15:10 and Deut 1:44 point to a Seir in Judah. The reference here is to Edom. It represents the southern limit of the Israelite victory march, corresponding to the reference to Kadesh-Barnea in 10:40.

The northern limit is described as Baal Gad. Aharoni states simply, "the exact identification of Baal-gad is not known."[1609] Eissfeldt equates it with modern Baalbek.[1610] The Valley of Lebanon includes at least the Beqa Valley running north and south between Mount Hermon and Mount Lebanon and possibly also the Litani

1604 Knauf, 116.
1605 See Howard, 271.
1606 Ibid., 272.
1607 *Land*, 38.
1608 Hess (2009) 52.
1609 *Land*, 217; cf. Hess, 216.
1610 "Die ältesten Bezeugungen von Baalbek als Kultstatte," *FF* 12 (1936) 51–53.

River Valley.[1611] Joshua's victory march is depicted as reaching the limits of the Davidic kingdom. Whereas Josh 10:40 gave the east-west boundary, 11:16 gives the north-south boundary of Joshua's triumphs.

18 V 18 reveals clearly the nature of the biblical tradition. Joshua fought a long time with these kings. Only exemplary narratives have been preserved by the biblical tradition.[1612] The conquest and occupation of the land were long and complicated affairs. The narratives preserved show that God fulfilled his promises and gave the land to his people, defeating its occupants against overwhelming odds. The book of Judges describes more of Israel's attempts to occupy and protect the Promised Land from internal and external enemies.

19 In this verse, the tradition attempts to give a summary picture. Israel learned her lesson after one mistake. The people did not sign peace agreements with any of the other inhabitants of the land. They responded to God's faithfulness by fulfilling the divine command. Yet the reminder of Gibeon's ruse along with the unexpected statement of v 18 "sensitize the reader to the rhetorical character of the language of totality and raise again the larger issues of inclusion and exclusion from the Israelite community and land."[1613]

20 Nelson explains:[1614]

> Yahweh's plan to destroy them leads to divine intervention in the choices made by the enemy. Their choices may not necessarily be to their advantage, but are to the advantage of Yahweh's scheme. Seemingly negative realities such as incessant enemy attacks and the protracted struggle were actually opportunities for Israel to obey the law faithfully. At the same time, Israel's faithful obedience in destroying the enemy turned out to be the very mechanism by which Yahweh kept the promise to him. Thus the gracious action of Yahweh, hidden behind human choices and the fidelity of Israel worked together to bring the divine will to fruition.

God made Israelite obedience easier by causing the inhabitants of the land to resist any temptation to plead for peace. As Hess explains, "the hearts of the Canaanites, sunk with fear, need to be hardened so that their inclination can become a firm resolve to fight the Israelites."[1615]

The Egyptian plague narratives in Exod 4:21–14:18 also contain "hardening of the heart" language. There, the motif serves to "describe the resistance which prevented the signs from achieving their assigned tasks."[1616] Pressler sees in both passages a "difficult notion . . . because of its incompatibility with what Scriptures elsewhere teach about God's love for all creation."[1617] Pressler maintains this view "reflects the authors' efforts to hold together their belief that nothing is outside God's power with their recognition that some people resist God's will."[1618]

1611 See Rainey, *Sacred Bridge*, map on p. 38; Hess (1996) 216.
1612 Cf. Nelson, 155.
1613 Hess (2000) 173.
1614 Nelson, 152.
1615 Hess (1996) 218.
1616 B. S. Childs, *The Book of Exodus* (Philadelphia: Westminster, 1974) 174; cf. his discussion and literature, 170–75.
1617 Pressler, 85–86.
1618 Ibid., 86.

Auld states that "the story-teller may want to suggest that there was high motivation and even religious fanaticism on both sides. He draws attention to this by stating that both sides were encouraged by God."[1619] Thus for Auld, "God is doing the same, not something different, to both sides. Joshua and the kings of Canaan are affected by the works of God in order that a battle would take place which he will win and they will lose."[1620]

Here the motif serves to force Israel to obey, rather than to be merciful.[1621] "Thus, the text is stark and harsh: the idea and activity of hardening originated with God himself, and it was for the purpose of destroying the Canaanites through battle."[1622] On the other hand, "God's hardening of their hearts, then, was due, at least in part, to their own stubbornness and resistance of Israel's God."[1623] The biblical teaching keeps these two sides of God's action in tension without trying to solve the dialectical teaching. Hawk explains hardening in this way: "By hardening the hearts of (the enemy) kings, Yahweh demonstrated his dominion over human power and authority in Canaan just as he did in Egypt."[1624]

In the book of Deuteronomy, God commanded Israel to obey him, to destroy the inhabitants of the land, to have no mercy, to make no covenant, and to make no marriages (Deut 7:1–3). The commands had a divine purpose—to remove the temptation to follow other gods. From the days of the Judges and especially from the period of Solomon, making political alliances through covenants and political marriages between royal families was a great temptation (1 Kgs 11:1–8; 16:31; 20:30–43). To protect Israel against the sin of idolatry, God commanded it not to show mercy to the enemy. To enable the people to keep his commandment, God caused their enemies to fight rather than seek mercy and peace.

21–22 Anab is probably located at Khirbet ʿUNNAB ets–Tsaghir, fifteen miles southwest of Hebron.[1625] Debir and Hebron proved to be strong opponents for Israel. Israel destroyed them in Josh 10:36–39 and Caleb and Othniel destroyed them again in Josh 14:6–15 and 15:15–17. Howard places the campaign in Josh 11 in the context of the campaign in chap. 10 with the importance of the Anakim leading the writer to place the account at this concluding point.[1626] Howard sees that the "exterminations of 10:36–39 and 11:21–22 were less than complete, or, perhaps more likely in this case, that the area was resettled by Anakim shortly thereafter."[1627]

The Anakim are the villains of the spy narratives (Num 13:28, 33; Deut 1:28). God promised specifically to destroy them (Deut 9:1–3). Hess identifies the Anakim as an ethnic group, not a race, who are best understood as mighty warriors who fell in battle against Israel.[1628] Hess points to Papyrus Anastasi I, which refers to some Canaanites who are almost nine feet tall. The conquest narrative thus concludes

---

1619 Auld, 82.
1620 Ibid., 81.
1621 Cf. Hertzberg, 83.
1622 Howard, 273.
1623 Ibid., 274.
1624 Hawk (2010) 130.
1625 Hess (1996) 218–19; Rainey, *Sacred Bridge*, 218.
1626 Howard, 275.
1627 Ibid.
1628 Hess (2009) 52.

with the specific fulfillment of the promise. The destruction of the Anakim "provides a commentary on the conquest as a whole, and recalls the legendary power of an enemy that has been destroyed with such ease."[1629]

Interestingly, an exception clause is appended to the report in v 22. The Anakim remained in the territory of the Philistines. This prepares the reader for the future narratives of combat with the Philistines in the Samson narratives and the books of Samuel (1 Sam 17:4; cf. 2 Sam 21:18–22). Verse 22 "intimates that the overall program has not yet been achieved. The coastal plain of Canaan is part of the land promised to Israel (Num 34:1–12; Josh 1:4). . . . Israel has succeeded in obliterating indigenous peoples from the land." The notes "also caution against viewing this operation as the end of the program. Israel may have taken 'the whole land,' but what is the whole land?"[1630] Hawk later answers his own question: the land is not the traditional land of Canaan but only that which eventually became Israel's possession.[1631]

23 The final verse of the chapter summarizes the conquest and the work of Joshua. "It captures almost every important element of the book's theology— Joshua's leadership, the taking and giving of the land in the fulfillment of God's promises, and the tribes' peaceful settlement of the land in their allotted territories."[1632] Becker sees 11:23* with Judg 2:8–9 as the oldest transition from Joshua to Judges with Josh 24:28 possibly standing between the two sections, joining the people's history (*Volksgeschichte*) with the history of the monarchy.[1633]

At the same time, in the book of Joshua "the totality of the conquest is held in tension with the concept that some land and peoples remained unconquered (13:2–6; 15:63; 16:10; 17:12–13, 16, 18)."[1634] Younger defines conquest in the context of ancient Near Eastern military campaigns: gaining temporary control represents a conquest. Thus he concludes: "The Israelites may very well have 'conquered' the land as generally described in the narrative. But this 'conquest' was in many instances temporary, not permanent. It did not mean the complete subjugation of the land" (compare Josh 11:18; 13:1–2; 15:63; 16:10; 17:12).[1635] For Younger, such an understanding removes any need to pit Josh 1–12 against Judg 1 to decide which is historical. Both are historical within an ancient Near Eastern context in which occupation does not mean subjugation or total replacement.

Chap. 1 has been realized. With strength and courage, Joshua has conquered the whole land, the land promised to Abraham and eventually ruled by David and Solomon. Every promise and every command given by Yahweh to Moses has been fulfilled. Joshua gives out the land to the people, who had rest from fighting. Hess reminds us, however, that, "The Book of Joshua does not portray a conquest of every square metre of land west of the Jordan."[1636]

Kaiser discusses the difference between the two common Hebrew words for

1629 Mitchell, *Together in the Land*, 95.
1630 Hawk (2000) 174.
1631 Hawk (2010) 131.
1632 Howard, 275–76.
1633 "Endredaktionelle Kontextvernetzungen," 151.
1634 Nelson, 156.
1635 *Ancient Conquest Accounts*, 244.
1636 Hess (1996) 220.

rest: "Even the repeated notices of 'rest' in Judges (3:1, 30; 5:31; 8:28) reflect שָׁקְטָה periods which were not the permanent rest promised in the *nuaḥ* group of words. The same שָׁקְטָה type is observed in Joshua 11:23 and 14:15 where the land is given this type of 'rest' from war. It is a temporary lull in the continuous surge of the restless sea, Isaiah 57:20, a 'respite' from days of trouble, Psalm 94:13."[1637]

In v 23, the identity of Israel is realized. Israel is the obedient people of God dwelling in the land given them by God. They no longer need to fight because they have totally subdued the enemies of God. But Israel does not maintain the ideal, as the biblical historian knows only too well (Josh 24:31; Judg 2:6–15). The example of Joshua thus looms ever larger in the history of Israel. He was the obedient leader serving as the example for all his successors. He embodied the leader after Moses.

Explanation

Using the tradition of a victory over a coalition led by the king of Hazor, the biblical writer describes how God gave the northern territory to Israel. In so doing, he carefully retains the traditions that suggest that only Hazor of all the cities was burned and that the battle for the Promised Land lasted a long time. Thus he reveals much about his historical procedures and sources. He has not attempted to preserve all the details. On the basis of his faith and the word of God entrusted to him, he has testified to the greatness of God in providing the entire land for Israel. God devised a strategy for Israel's entire life, a strategy revealed in the book of Deuteronomy. This strategy was then entrusted to the human agent Joshua. The command-execution pattern that previously confirmed Israel's obedience now is applied to Joshua (11:6, 9), and the narrator emphatically relocates the theme of obedience to Joshua through repeated comments that he did all that he was commanded to do (11:9, 12, 15, 23; cf 1:9). Joshua is thus for Hawk "the epitome of the Deuteronomic ideal."[1638] Hubbard maintains that the writer's "particular concern is to bring a literary crescendo to one of the book's major themes—Joshua's attainment of Mosaic-like stature through exemplary, faithful leadership."[1639]

Divine encouragement and instruction combine with human faithfulness to accomplish the total victory. Even though much remains to be done (Josh 13:1–6), the victory is described as total because the work of Joshua has been carried out in total faithfulness. The task for the historian is not to describe every detail of what had been done, nor every detail of what remained to be done. Rather, the historian seeks to demonstrate how Israel obtained its land. Throughout the years of monarchy, of exile, and even through the years of the postexilic period, the story could be read as a call to similar obedience awaiting the act of God again fulfilling his promises to his people.

1637 "The Promise Theme and the Theology of Rest," *BSac* 130 (1973) 139.
1638 Hawk (2000) 158.
1639 Hubbard, 323.

K. Victory's Victims (12:1–24)

Bibliography

Aharoni, Y. "Nothing Early and Nothing Late: Rewriting Israel's Conquest." *BA* 39 (1976) 55–76. **Albright, W. F.** "The Site of Tirzah and the Topography of Western Manasseh." *JPOS* 11 (1931) 241–51. **Barr, J.** "Mythical Monarch Unmasked? Mysterious Doings of Debir, King of Eglon." *JSOT* 15 (1990) 55–68. **Benjamin, C. D.** *The Variations between the Hebrew and Greek Texts of Joshua: Chapters 1–12.* Thesis, University of Pennsylvania. Leipzig: W. Drugulin, 1921. **Ben-Tor, A., D. Ben-Ami, and A. Livneh.** *Yokneʿam III: The Middle and Late Bronze Ages: Final Report of the Archaeological Excavations (1977–1988).* Qedem Reports 7. Jerusalem: Institute of Archaeology, Hebrew University of Jerusalem, 2005. **Bimson, J.** *Redating the Exodus and Conquest.* 2nd ed. JSOTSup 5. Sheffield: Almond, 1981. **Biran, A.** "Aroer Which Is in the Negev." *ErIsr* 15 (1981) 250–73 (Heb.). **Boras, R. S., and S. H. Horn.** "The First Campaign at Tell Hesban." *AUSS* 7 (1969) 97–117. **Briend, J., and J.-B. Humbert,** eds. *Tell Keisan (1971–1976): Une Cité Phénicienne en Galilée.* Paris: Gabalda, 1980. **Brooke, A. E., and N. McLean,** eds. *The Old Testament in Greek, according to the text of Codex Vaticanus.* Vol. 1, part 4, *Joshua, Judges and Ruth.* Cambridge: Cambridge UP, 1917. **Dever, W. G.** "Iron Age Epigraphic Material from the Area of Khirbet el-Kom." *HUCA* 40–41 (1969–1970) 139–204. **Dothan, T.** "Apek on the Israel-Aram Border and Aphek on the Amorite Border." *ErIsr* 12 (1977) 63–65 (Heb.). **Fritz, V.** "Die sogenannte Liste der besiegten Könige in Josua 12." *ZDPV* 85 (1969) 136–61. **Gerarty, L. T.** "Heshbon: The First Casualty in the Israelite Quest for the Kingdom of God." In *The Quest for the Kingdom of God: Studies in Honor of George E. Mendenhall.* Ed. F. A. Spina, H. B. Huffmon, and A. R. W. Green. Winona Lake, IN: Eisenbrauns, 1983. 239–48. **Gilboa, A., and I. Sharon.** "Between the Carmel and the Sea: Tel Dor's Iron Age Reconsidered." *NEA* 71 (2008) 146–70. **Glueck, N.** "Three Israelite Towns in the Jordan Valley: Zarethan, Succoth, Zaphon." *BASOR* 90 (1943) 2–23. **Greenspoon, L. J.** *Textual Studies in the Book of Joshua.* HSM 28. Chico, CA: Scholars Press, 1983. **Herr, L. G.** "The Search for Biblical Heshbon." *BAR* 19.6 (1993) 36–37, 68. **Hollenberg, J.** "Die deuteronomischen Bestandtheile des Buches Josua." *TSK* 1 (1874) 499–500. **Kellermann, D.** "ʿAstarot-ʿAstʿrot-Qarnayim-Qarnayim: Historisch-geographische Erwägungen zu Orten in nördlichen Ostjordanland." *ZDPV* 97 (1981) 45–61. **Knauf, E. A.** "Hesbon, Sihons Stadt." *ZDPV* 106 (1990) 135–44. **Lapp, P.** "Taanach by the Waters of Megiddo." *BA* 30 (1967) 2–27. **Lemaire, A.** "Heshbon = Hisban." *ErIsr* 23 (1992) 64–70 (Heb.). **Meer, M. N. van der.** *Formation and Reformulation: The Redaction of the Book of Joshua in the Light of the Oldest Textual Witnesses.* VTSup 102. Leiden: Brill, 2004. **Merling, D., Sr.** *The Book of Joshua: Its Theme and Role in Archaeological Discussions.* Andrews University Doctoral Dissertation Series 23. Berrien Springs, MI: Andrews UP, 1997. **Miller, J. M.** "Site Identification: A Problem Area in Contemporary Biblical Scholarship." *ZDPV* 99 (1983) 124–25. **Mitchell, G.** *Together in the Land.* JSOTSup 134. Sheffield: Sheffield Academic, 1993. **Na'aman, N.** *Borders and Districts in Biblical Historiography.* Jerusalem Biblical Studies 4. Jerusalem: Simor, 1986. **Ottosson, M.** *Gilead.* Lund: Gleerup, 1969. 117–19. **Rainey, A.** "The Toponymics of Eretz-Israel." *BASOR* 231 (1978) 10. **Rainey, A. F., R. S. Notley, et al.** *The Sacred Bridge: Carta's Atlas of the Biblical World.* Jerusalem: Carta, 2006. **Rast, W. E.** *Taanach I: Studies in the Iron Age Pottery.* Cambridge, MA: American Schools of Oriental Research, 1978. **Ring, Y.** "The Biblical List of 31 Kings in the Book of Joshua against Parallels in Mycenaean Greek Tablets." *Tarbiz* 46 (1976–1977) 141–44 (Heb.). **Rowe, A.** "Tell Keisan." *Quarterly of the Department of Archaeology in Palestine* 5 (1936) 207–9. **Schmitt, G.** *Du sollst keinen Frieden schliessen mit den Bewohnern des Landes.* BWANT 91. Stuttgart: Kohlhammer, 1970. 116–20. **Tsaferis, V., and G. Edelstein.** "Tel ʿAitun." *RB* 76 (1969) 578–79. **Wüst, M.** *Untersuchungen zu den siedlungsgeographischen Tex-*

ten des Alten Testaments. Wiesbaden: Reichert, 1975. 12–24, 28–57. **Younker, K. L.** *Ancient Conquest Accounts: A Study in Ancient Near Eastern and Biblical History Writing.* JSOTSup 98. Sheffield: JSOT Press, 1990. ———. "The Rhetorical Structuring of the Joshua Conquest Narratives." In *Critical Issues in Early Israelite History.* Ed. R. S. Hess, G. A. Klingbeil, and P. J. Ray, Jr. BBRSup 3. Winona Lake, IN: Eisenbrauns, 2008. 3–32. **Younker, R. W.** "The Emergence of Ammon: A View from the Rise of Iron Age Polities from the Other Side of the Jordan." In *The Near East in the Southwest: Essays in Honor of William G. Dever.* Ed. B. A. Nakhai. AASOR 58. Boston: American Schools of Oriental Research, 2003. 153–76.

Translation

[1]*Now these are the kings of the land whom the sons of Israel smote and then possessed their land beyond the Jordan toward the sunrise, from the valley of the Arnon unto Mount Hermon and all the[a] Arabah eastward:*

[2]*Sihon, the king of the Amorites whose residence was in Heshbon. He was ruling from Aroer,[a] which is upon the bank of the River Arnon, and the middle of the river[b] and half of the Gilead on unto the River[c] Jabbok, the border of the sons of Ammon.* [3]*And the Arabah unto the Sea of Chinneroth eastward and unto the Sea of the Arabah, the Salt Sea eastward, the way of Beth[a]-jeshimoth and southward[b] under the slopes of Pisgah.*

[4]*The boundary[a] of Og, the king of Bashan, one of the remnant of the Rephaim,[b] who resided in Ashtaroth and in Edrei.* [5]*He ruled over Mount Hermon and Salecah and all Bashan unto the border of the Geshurites[a] and the Maacathites and half of Gilead,[b] unto[c] the border of Sihon, king of Heshbon.*

[6]*Moses, the servant of Yahweh, and the sons of Israel smote them. Moses, the servant of Yahweh,[a] gave it for an inherited possession to the Reubenites and to the Gaddites and to half the tribe of Manasseh.*

[7]*Now these are the kings of the land[a] whom Joshua and the sons of Israel smote beyond the Jordan westward from Baal-gad in the Valley of Lebanon unto Mount Halak going up to Seir, the land which Joshua gave to the tribes of Israel for a possession according to their lots,* [8]*in the hill country, and in the Shephelah, and in the Arabah, and in the slopes and in the wilderness and in the Negev, the Hittites, the Amorites, the Canaanites, the Perizzites, the Hivites, and the Jebusites:*

[9]*the king of Jericho, one:[a] the king of Ai, which is beside Bethel, one;*

[10]*the king of Jerusalem, one; the king of Hebron, one;*

[11]*the king of Jarmuth, one; the king of Lachish, one;*

[12]*the king of Eglon, one; the king of Gezer, one;*

[13]*the king of Debir, one; the king of Geder,[a] one;*

[14]*the king of Hormah, one; the king of Arad,[a] one;*

[15]*the king of Libnah, one; the king of Adullam, one;*

[16]*the king of Makkedah,[a] one; the king of Bethel,[b] one;*

[17]*the king of Tappuah, one; the king of Hepher, one;*

[18]*the king of Aphek, one; the king of Lashsharon,[a] one;*

[19]*the king of Madon,[a] one; the king of Hazor, one;*

[20]*the king of Shimron-meron,[a] one; the king of Achshaph, one;*

[21]*the king of Taanach, one; the king of Megiddo, one;*

[22]*the king of Kedesh,[a] one; the king of Jokneam by Carmel, one;*

[23]*the king of Dor in Haphath-Dor, one; the king of Goiim in Gilgal,[a] one;*

[24]*the king of Tirzah, one;*

all the kings were thirty-one.[a]

Notes

1.a. LXX transliterated Arabah, but added "land of" before it. This may represent a confused dittography from the preceding τήν in the Gk., since in vv 3 and 8 the transliteration is made properly. LXX does have trouble understanding Arabah (Benjamin, *Variations*), as seen in Josh 4:13; 5:10; 8:14; 11:16; 13:32; 18:18.

2.a. Aroer has been confused in part of the Gk. tradition with Arnon.

2.b. Fritz (127) says "in the middle of the River," makes no sense and so adds הָעִיר אֲשֶׁר בְּ, "the city which is in," to read in analogy to Josh 13:16: "the city which is in the middle." See *Comments.*

2.c. LXX lacks "River," though the word occurs in the parallel passage Deut 3:16.

3.a. LXX lacks בֵּית, literally "house of," a component of many geographical names reflecting the presence of sanctuaries. In Josh 13:20, LXX renders the בֵּית.

3.b. The Heb. תֵּימָן can mean "south," as in Job 39:26; Zech 9:14; Isa 43:6. It can also refer to Edom or the southern part of Edom (compare R. de Vaux, "Téman, ville ou région d'Édom?" *RB* 76 [1969] 379–85). LXX interprets it in the latter sense for our passage, being followed by NEB. The term is missing from the parallel passage in Deut 3:17 and is probably a directional addition by the editors here in parallel to the earlier reference to the "east."

4.a. LXX lacks "boundary," being followed by most modern commentators. Fritz (127), following Barthélemy (*Critique textuelle*, 1:21–22), who gives a lengthy explanation, thinks it originally belonged to the previous territorial description, as does Nelson (158), pointing to 13:23, 27; 15:12, 47; Num 34:6; Deut 3:17; and the *Preliminary and Interim Report* (2:24). In this instance, LXX may have been as good a form critic as modern commentators who notice that a territorial list is not called for by the introduction in vv 1–2. MT is the more difficult reading and must be accounted for.

4.b. LXX interprets Rephaim as "giants."

5.a. LXX^B has confused Geshurites with more common Girgashites. See Greenspoon, *Textual Studies*, 136–37.

5.b. Nelson (158) refers to the "equivocal nature of MT." He sees "Og's dominion" reaching "southward down to the boundary of Sihon's half of Gilead." *Preliminary and Interim Report* (2:24) reads, "as far as the territory of the Geshurites(s) and the Maacathite(s) and 'as far as' half of Gilead."

5.c. "Unto" is lacking in MT but present in LXX. It has fallen out due to haplography with the previous word. Fritz (128) adds the Heb. עַד to restore the agreement with Josh 12:2. Compare Harstad, 475. Barthélemy (*Critique textuelle*, 1:22) preserves MT as original, giving history of interpretation.

6.a. LXX and Vg. lack the second "servant of the Lord," possibly an addition of traditional terminology within the Masoretic tradition, though van der Meer (*Formation and Reformulation*, 195]) would see LXX as a stylistic shortening to avoid redundancy.

7.a. LXX read "Amorites" for "land." The words evidence some similarity in Heb., leading to confusion of the two traditional phrases in the Heb. textual transmission.

9.a. LXX simply lists the kings without using the schematic "one" throughout the list. Nelson (159) sees an original list without the repeated "one" and without the repeated "king of." All he is left with is a city list. That changes the complexion and meaning of the list entirely.

13.a. LXX^B reads "Asei" for "Geder," but the original Gk. tradition reflected MT (compare Margolis, *Book of Joshua in Greek*, 237).

14.a. LXX^B has given two variant forms of "Arad" (compare Fritz, *ZDPV* 85 [1969] 142, n. 27).

16.a. LXX has transmitted "Makkedah" in several corrupt forms (compare Brooke and McLean, *Old Testament in Greek*; Margolis, *Book of Joshua in Greek*, 238).

16.b. LXX makes no reference to Bethel, perhaps because of previous mention in v 9 (Margolis, *Book of Joshua in Greek*, 238–39; Nelson, 158). Nelson also points to Judg 1:22–26. It is more probable that the reference to Bethel entered the textual tradition at a quite late stage, but Barthélemy (*Critique textuelle*, 1:25) supports originality of "Bethel."

18.a. The MT לְשָׁרוֹן is evidently to be understood as the preposition לְ plus the noun "Sharon" (compare Isa 33:9; 35:2; 65:10; 1 Chr 5:16; 27:29; Song 2:1). The MT uses the prepositional construction only here. G (Rahlfs) apparently read "the king of Aphek of Sharon" (Margolis, *Book of Joshua in Greek*, 239–40), though LXX[B] reads "the king of Ephek tē Arōk," which Rahlfs, Margolis, and Nelson take as Aphek of Sharon, an original reading distinguishing this Aphek from at least two others, a process also followed in vv 22–23. *Preliminary and Interim Report* (2:26) follows a conjectural reading: "the king of Aphek-in-Sharon, one." Barthélemy (*Critique textuelle*, 1:26) finds an early stage in the LXX preceding MT's false insertion of אחד מלך, "king of." Younger ("Rhetorical Structuring, 31, n. 28) supports the Old Greek king of Aphek of the Sharon.

LXX[A] omits v 18b entirely. The first modification of the simple king of a city-state form in the list led the later tradition to modify the text. MT divided the double name into two, while LXX[A] tradition omitted the unusual form.

19.a. LXX omits "the king of Madon," probably understanding it as a doublet of "the king of Maron," which it lists in the following verse (Fritz, *ZDPV* 85 [1969] 142), though Nelson sees this as an MT plus added by copyists familiar with Josh 11:1. *Preliminary and Interim Report* (2:26) omits it as assimilation (compare Barthélemy, *Critique textuelle*, 1:24).

20.a. "Shimron-meron" occurs only here in the OT. LXX read two separate cities, though the spellings of both have suffered in the LXX transmission. Elsewhere the two distinct cities appear in the MT and are to be presupposed as original here (Nelson, 158), though MT does represent the more difficult reading (Howard, 282, n. 292, sees MT as full name). Fritz (128) says "Meron" here is disturbing, the name not being included in the final count. So he sees "Meron" as scribal error or as clarification of the previous village, Shimron. *Preliminary and Interim Report* (2:26–27; compare explanation of Barthélemy, *Critique textuelle*, 1:26) points to conjectural emendation in reading: "the king of Shimeon, one; the king of Meron, one."

22.a. LXX transposed "Kedesh" before "Taanach" in v 21.

23.a. MT translates literally, "the king of the nations of Gilgal." LXX reads "the king of goiim of Galilee," which is most often taken as the correct reading since the list deals with kings in the region of Galilee (Nelson, 158). Fritz (*ZDPV* 85 [1969] 143; and his commentary, 128) says MT cannot be understood, being a distortion probably of חרשת הגוים, "Harosheth Haggoyim." *Preliminary and Interim Report* (2:27; compare Barthélemy, *Critique textuelle*, 1:27) conjectures: "the king of Goiim in Galilee." Fritz (128) also reads Gilgal as לגליל, of Galilee. Hess sees "Galilee" and "Gilgal" as possibly variants of the same name or as the same as Harosheth Haggoyim as a region in the north that served the pharaohs as the site of royal estates (228, n. 1). The MT tradition represents an attempt to bring Gilgal, the central point of the early tradition, into the list.

24.a. Corresponding to its transmission of the tradition, LXX reads the number as twenty-nine. Nelson (159; compare Barr, 65–66) reconstructs the list to read the conventional number of thirty instead of MT's thirty-one. Barr (*JSOT* 15 [1990] 65) thinks LXX had its own list and counted for itself rather than simply translating.

Form/Structure/Setting

The introductory formula of v 1 marks a new beginning, while the concluding formula in v 24b brings the unit, indeed chaps. 1 through 12, to a close. While Howard calls chap. 12 "an appendix of sorts to the first major section."[1640] Hess states that, "Joshua 11:12–23 summarizes the whole of Joshua 1–11, so chapter 12 provides a summary of all the conquests, those of Moses as well as those of Joshua."[1641] Knauf maintains that the chapter seeks to reconcile the discrepancies between the conquered land and the distributed land by inserting all places mentioned in chaps. 1–11 and adding others such as the Israelite hill country.[1642]

The chapter has two clear subdivisions marked by similar introductory formulas in v 1 and v 7. They are structured in close parallelism to one another. The

---

1640 Howard, 277.
1641 Hess (1996) 221.
1642 Knauf, 120.

striking differences between them, thus, call for explanation. V 1 states that the Israelites "possessed their land," while v 7 offers a parallel statement at the end of the sentence but modifies it to "the land which Joshua gave to the tribes of Israel for a possession according to their lots." The latter prepares the way for the following chapters, which detail the giving of the land to the tribes and which note areas that were not yet conquered, but of which the tribes had to take possession for themselves.

Tradition

Hess examines three areas of comparison with ancient Near Eastern annals from Assyria and Egypt: summary texts, selectivity in lists, and use of itinerary lists.[1643] He points out that Neo-Assyrian summary lists of towns conquered use phraseology similar to the Joshua text. Josh 12:7–24 shows the same type of selectivity since some cities do not appear in the preceding narratives. Egyptian lists correspond to Josh 12:9–24. Younger studies the Assyrian texts and concludes: "Summarizing statements and lists of defeated lands following accounts of military campaigns are common in the Assyrian royal inscriptions. . . . [T]hese lists are partial. They are very selective."[1644] He states that the inclusion of Megiddo in chap. 12 is an example of the selectivity of the list.

Younger argues against the involvement of redactors, and assumes that a contemporary scribe assembled the material on the battlefield.[1645] I question whether Israelite armies had accompanying scribes until David and Solomon organized the monarchy and staffed royal institutions. I maintain that in Israel's case, the repeated "one" represented a memory device that gave a rhythmic quality to the list.

Source and Redaction

During the period of oral transmission some selectivity surely took place. One must leave open the possibility of an even more complex process of compiling various parts of Joshua and/or various parts of the larger history until the final product appeared. In this way one accounts for the varied types of battle reports and stories, the somewhat uniform pattern of compilation, the additions of both "Priestly" writers and "Deuteronomistic" ultimate historian(s). On the other hand, the extended process of seven to ten redactors plus other hands contributing small pieces is dismissed as too complex and as using too small a set of materials for an original source.

Vv 1–6 list the territories of two conquered kings, while vv 7–24 list the entire territory (v 8) and various kings. The most likely explanation is that the editor had two types of material available to make the descriptions. The first came from Deut 1–3 and summarized the eastern conquest.[1646]

The other material comprises a list of towns in the western sector. Fritz attributes parts of v 1 with vv 2, 4, 5, and 7 to a Deuteronomistic redactor with further

---

1643 Hess (2009) 53.
1644 *Ancient Conquest Narratives*, 230.
1645 Ibid., 232.
1646 That the geographical descriptions developed in the highly complex literary reflections described by Wüst (*Untersuchungen*, 12–24) is doubtful.

redactional additions in part of v 1 with vv 3, 6, and 8.[1647] He concludes that the list taken up by the Deuteronomistic Historian is not a historical document but rather a literary compilation whose origin and significance cannot be determined.[1648] Fritz depends on archaeological discoveries to claim that the listed cities did not exist during the same time frame.

I contend that the document may be a literary compilation but that it used dependable sources. Archaeology may tell us when a site had been populated, but without excavating the entire area, archaeology cannot prove the nonexistence of a site. The stories of the defeat of Ai, Jericho, and other cities may well show us that the lists here give cities that Joshua conquered but intermix city descriptions from the time of each city's historical heyday.

Form

Since vv 1–6 (as well as vv 7–8) represent the ultimate editor's summary of the material in both Deut 1–3 and Josh 11, I will focus form-critical interest on vv 9–24. The towns here appear in order of mention in the book, not in the order of battles, and significantly, Shechem does not appear in the lists.[1649] Fritz attempted to show that vv 10–24 represent a list of cities fortified by Solomon, with v 9 simply being a résumé of chaps. 6–8.[1650]

Schmitt, on the other hand, assumes that all the names come from conquest reports either preserved in Numbers and Joshua or available to the editor but not preserved for us.[1651] Soggin argues that the list must be "very ancient" because it disagrees with the "official version" of chaps. 1–11 and because "the picture of Palestine which it presents gives the best description, though it is not always complete, of the city states of the region as they appear a century and a half earlier in the el-Amarna archives."[1652]

Younger suggests a parallel in form and language with royal Assyrian campaign reports concluding in summaries of cities conquered.[1653] Examining two Assyrian lists tied to the same campaign leads Younger to the conclusion that "lists of conquered cities in the ancient Near East were often selective or partial."[1654] Hubbard notes, however, that Israelite lists are in third person compared to first-person royal voice in ancient Near Eastern lists.[1655] Josh 12 focuses on kings, not just captured cities. Hubbard examines royal lists of conquests and lists of names or items followed by numbers or tally marks and posits that the list in Josh 12 may derive from an ancient source that gave the basic outline to the conquest narrative.[1656]

Creach maintains that the list derives from Josiah's or David's conquests and that the Joshua account is a theological history.[1657] Knauf compares the list to taxa-

---

1647 Fritz, 129.
1648 Ibid., 137.
1649 Knauf, 122–23.
1650 *ZDPV* 85 (1969) 136–61.
1651 *Du sollst keinen Frieden*, 116–20.
1652 Soggin, 143; cf. Hubbard, 363.
1653 *Ancient Conquest Accounts*, 230–32.
1654 Ibid., 231.
1655 Hubbard, 359.
1656 Ibid., 363.
1657 Creach, 95.

tion lists, distribution lists (*Spendenlisten*), and recruiting decisions (*Rekrutierungs-bescheide*) from the Judean monarchy or Persian provincial government.[1658] They represent examples of various types of documents that a scribal student had to master.

Certainly v 9 summarizes chaps. 6–8. Vv 10–12a follow precisely Josh 10:3 (= 10:5, 23). Despite the arguments of Noth and Fritz, it is doubtful that the names were introduced into chap. 10 on the basis of chap. 12. Rather, the procedure in vv 1–9 suggests the literary dependence of the editor of chap. 12 on earlier literature.

Note that Gezer follows Eglon in v 12. This, too, shows dependence on Josh 10:33, where Gezer is closely related to the defeat of Lachish and then Eglon. Debir follows (12:13) just as in Josh 10:38, omitting Hebron (10:36), which has already been listed (12:10). It appears that the information in Josh 12:14–24 is dependent on a source outside Joshua. It is possible that the results of Fritz apply to this list, but Mitchell notes, "in its present context it [the list in vv 9–24] serves to provide a powerful summary of the conquest which unites the events of Joshua 6–11. . . . The kings of the sixteen towns that are included in the list, which are not mentioned in the earlier accounts of conquest, create the impression of a victory on an even grander scale than at first envisaged."[1659] Hess reminds us that the list includes defeated, not necessarily destroyed, towns, so that many will not evidence a destruction layer for archaeologists.[1660] Some regions are not mentioned, preparing, Hess says, for the recitation of the land not conquered in the next chapter.[1661] He suggests that Bethel, which lies outside the counting system, may have had the same leader as Ai.

Nelson provides perhaps the best explanation for chapter 12, stating that it is "a topographical list from an unidentifiable source" that "clearly reflects to some degree a genuine source with a previous history of its own."[1662]

Form critically, then, it seems that chap. 12 joins together two lists. Vv 1–6 represent a literary composition based on Deut 3. It is presented as a king's list but shows dependence on a narrative rather than on a previous list, having only two kings in the list and concluding with a narrative summary preparing for chap. 13. Vv 7–8 introduce the list found in vv 9–24, which appear to be dependent on a list that is no longer available. This is a list of kings who are identified by town, not by name. The list thus functions as a summary of towns defeated similar to the Egyptian and Assyrian summaries discussed by Younger and Hess. This is not a concluding summary, however, but a transition to land distribution. The list does not glorify the conquering king, but rather points to the promises made and fulfilled by the conquering God.

Structure

See *Form*. The list form and the narrative structure cannot be separated, since this is not a narrative with narrative tension. It is a literary compilation in list form.

1658 Knauf, 121.
1659 *Together in the Land*, 96–98.
1660 Hess 226.
1661 Ibid., 229.
1662 Nelson, 159, 162.

Two structural elements tie chaps. 12 and 13 together, reflecting again a unified editorial perspective behind the whole book. Hawk maintains that territorial descriptions and the transference formula "God gave," along with the phrase "for a possession," ties chap. 12 to chap. 1 and forward to chaps. 13–21.[1663]

In these chapters, two distinctive forms appear. The first begins with the demonstrative pronoun—"this, these," parallel to Josh 13:1:

Josh 12:1: kings defeated east of the Jordan
Josh 12:7: kings defeated west of the Jordan
Josh 13:2: land remaining to be possessed
Josh 13:23b: inheritance of Reuben
Josh 13:28: inheritance of Gad
Josh 13:32: inheritance distributed by Moses

The second uses the verb נתן to describe the gift of land to the people, parallel to Josh 11:23aβ:

Josh 12:6a: Moses gave east Jordan to the two and a half tribes.
Josh 12:7b: Joshua gave west Jordan to the tribes of Israel.
Josh 13:8b: Moses gave the land to the two and a half tribes, who now possess it (cf. 12:1aβ; 13:12bβ).
Josh 13:15: Moses gave to the sons of Reuben.
Josh 13:24: Moses gave to Gad.
Josh 13:29: Moses gave to half of Manasseh.

Setting

The original setting of chap. 12 may well have been the early educational system of Israel, where students learned lessons by rote memory. This chapter can easily be memorized by students to help them recall the gist of Deuteronomy through Josh 12. It might also represent a device to teach the worshiping community the outline of their history and thus the reason to praise God. These settings preserved documents that the historian modified to form a transition point in the story of Israel's entry into the land.

Comments

1 For the writer of Joshua, possession of the land beyond Jordan is an established fact. He summarizes it here to demonstrate God's leadership of Israel in taking the land and to prepare for the distribution of the land in the following chapters. In so doing, he uses a form of superscription familiar from the superscriptions of Deuteronomy (1:1; 4:44; 28:69).[1664] The territory extends from the River Arnon in the south to Mount Hermon in the north (compare Deut 3:8). The Arnon separated Moab from the kingdom of Sihon (Num 21:13, 26).

Knauf states that allotting the eastern territory to only two kings is simply a schematic theory since these territories never belonged to Israel at the same

---

1663 Hawk (2010) 133.
1664 Cf. G. Seitz, *Redaktionsgeschichtliche Studien zum Deuteronomium*, BWANT 93 (Stuttgart: Kohlhammer, 1971) 31.

time.[1665] This assumes negativity toward any historical reality of Joshua and Judges and towards the Davidic/Solomonic monarchy.

Mount Hermon rises 9,232 feet above sea level and supplies the headwaters for the Jordan River. "All the Arabah" is a summarizing term related to Deut 4:49, intending to show that Israel controlled all the eastern Jordan Valley.

2 The notice of Sihon's capture is taken from the tradition of Num 21:21–30, which is repeated in Deut 1:4; 2:24–37; 29:6–7 (Eng. 7–8). Rumors of the defeat paved the way for Israelite victories west of the Jordan (Josh 2:10; 9:10). Sihon's capital was Heshbon. Hess contributes an "additional note" concerning the location of Heshbon.[1666] Heshbon lay between Ammon and Moab fourteen miles southwest of modern Amman, Jordan. Its king fought Moab and gained control of Moab to the Arnon River (Num 21:26). Tell Hesban (= M.R. 226134) across the Jordan River from Jericho retains the name but has no remains earlier than the seventh century BCE.[1667] Still Rainey insists, "There can be hardly any doubt that this is the ancient biblical site of Heshbon."[1668] He joins this with other evidence to point to a twelfth- to eleventh-century BCE conquest. Hess suggests a possible shift of the name from an earlier site such as Tell Jalul or Tell el-Umeiri (= M.R. 235142). Horn submits nearby Jalul as a good candidate.[1669] Knauf sees it as a small town of the eighth to fifth centuries BCE that was never large enough to serve as the center of a Transjordanian kingdom.[1670] Howard states that since Heshbon is marked as a Levitical city in the tribal territory of Gad rather than Reuben, as in 13:17, 26, the text evidences overlapping of some of the territorial descriptions.[1671] The Moabites later controlled the city (Isa 15:2, 4; 16:8–9).

Sihon's kingdom is described as reaching from Aroer on the Arnon to the Jabbok. Aroer was not a town, but a fortress guarding an important highway.[1672] Ancient Aroer is identified with the site of a small Arab village—and its imposing tell—named 'Ara'ir (= M.R. 228097), three miles southeast of Dhiban (biblical Dibon) and two and a half miles east of the so-called King's Highway. Evidence of Late Bronze Age settlement has been excavated.[1673]

"And the middle of the river" is a phrase found in Josh 13:16 and in Deut 2:36, where a city is mentioned. Gray suggests that Josh 12 has lost an original reference to the city or "watchpost."[1674] Wüst notes, however, that chap. 12 gives geographical boundaries while chap. 13 traces border cities and that Josh 12 thus places the boundary in the middle of the river valley.[1675] The territory is understood to include half of Gilead, a geographical term that denotes a vague area east of the Jordan, north and south of the Jabbok.[1676] Our text sees the Jabbok as dividing

1665 Knauf, 121.
1666 Hess (1996) 225–26.
1667 S. H. Horn, "Heshbon," *EAEHL*, 2:510.
1668 *Sacred Bridge*, 124.
1669 "Heshbon," *IDBSup*, 410.
1670 Knauf, 130.
1671 Howard, 311.
1672 E. Olávarri, "Aroer," *EAEHL*, 1:98.
1673 G. L. Mattingly, *ABD*, 1:399.
1674 Gray, 124.
1675 *Untersuchungen*, 12.
1676 Cf. Ottosson, *Gilead*, 9.

Gilead into two halves. Wüst's detailed syntactical and literary arguments for a complicated literary development constantly reinterpreting the boundaries are at their weakest here.[1677] The stereotyped Deuteronomistic phraseology shows a conception that the land of the Ammonites extended east of the Jordan between the Arnon and the Jabbok (compare Judg 11:12). The victory over Sihon, king of the Amorites, gives Israel control of the land of the Ammonites.

3 V 3 describes the land of Sihon from a perspective that is not quite clear. While v 2 describes the northern and southern boundaries, v 3 appears to outline its east and west limits. But only the western boundary is delineated, the Jordan Valley between the Sea of Chinnereth, later called the Sea of Galilee, and the Sea of the Arabah or the Salt Sea, later called the Dead Sea. This is more precisely defined with the addition of "the way of Beth-jeshimoth," a city whose exact location is unknown but has been sought in the area at the north end of the Dead Sea at least since the time of Eusebius of Caesarea (ca. 324 CE). Nelson sees a road running from the Jordan to Heshbon.[1678] Hess notes the possibility of Tell 'Azeimeh (= M.R. 208132).[1679]

"Southward under the slopes of Pisgah" offers more information about the location of Heshbon. Pisgah is located at Ras es-Siyagha (= M.R. 218130), according to Hess and is the mountain of Moses' death (Deut 34:1; compare 3:27).[1680] It was also the scene of the confrontation between Balaam and Balak (Num 23:14). Otherwise, the name occurs only in geographical lists (Num 21:20; Deut 3:17; 4:49; Josh 13:20). The twice-repeated "eastward" is the only indication of the eastern boundary (compare v 1). It is interesting that in giving the imprecise east-west boundary, the description extends the north-south boundary north of the River Jabbok, perhaps to underline the completeness of Israel's conquest of the Transjordan territory.

4 Compare Deut 3:10–11. Having ended the reference to Sihon with a long territorial description, the text introduces the "boundary of Og" rather than the expected introduction of the person of Og. He ruled Bashan, the northern portion of Transjordan, which was renowned for its fertility (Amos 4:1), forests (Isa 2:13), and mountains (Isa 33:9). Only at the height of her power did Israel maintain control of Bashan.

Og was among the remnant of the Rephaim, ancient inhabitants of the land (Gen 14:5; 15:20) who gave their name to the land of Bashan (Deut 3:13; compare Josh 17:15) as well as to a valley separating Judah and Benjamin west of the Jordan (Josh 15:8; 18:6). Tradition identifies several groups who were renowned for their stature as the Rephaim (Deut 2:11, 20), but Og came to be recognized as the last survivor of the group (Deut 3:11; Josh 13:12).

Ashtaroth, the first of Og's royal cities, is usually identified with tell 'Ashtarah (= M.R. 243244), twenty-four miles (forty kilometers) south of modern Keneitra and twenty miles (thirty-nine kilometers) east of the Sea of Chinneroth.[1681] It is mentioned in Gen 14:5; Deut 1:4; Josh 9:10; 13:12, 31; 1 Chr 6:56, in the Amarna letters,[1682] and other Egyptian texts.[1683]

1677 *Untersuchungen*, 12–24.
1678 Nelson, 160.
1679 Hess (2009) 55; cf. Rainey, *Sacred Bridge*, 124.
1680 Hess (1996) 223.
1681 Cf. S. Cohen, "Ashteroth-Karnaim," *IDB*, 1:255; cf. Rainey, *Sacred Bridge*, 114.
1682 Cf. Ottosson, *Gilead*, 12.
1683 *ANET*, 242, 329, 486.

Edrei is the battle scene in Num 21:33 and is mentioned in connection with Og (Deut 1:4; 3:1, 10; Josh 13:12, 31). The Egyptians also refer to it.[1684] It is identified with modern Dera (= M.R. 253224) near the Yarmuk River halfway between Damascus and Amman.

5 Meager traditional evidence is used to describe the borders of Og. The northern border is Mount Hermon (compare v 1). Salecah is the extreme eastern border of Bashan, possibly identified with modern Salkhad (= M.R. 311212), the defensive center of the Jebel el-Druze. The Geshurites and Maacathites represented peoples Israel could not drive out of the land (Josh 13:2, 13) until the time of David (1 Sam 27:8; 2 Sam 10:6–14). Their territory furnished a border point for Israel to the east (Deut 3:14; Josh 13:11). Later, David entered into a marriage alliance with the king of Geshur (2 Sam 3:3), and Absalom fled there for refuge (2 Sam 13:37–15:8). The southern boundary is simply taken from v 2. See *Comments* on 13:2.

6 This verse is a summary statement of the work of Moses. Transjordan has been given the two and a half tribes (Deut 3:12–13; compare Josh 13:8–32). Moses set the example which Joshua followed.

7 That Joshua followed Moses' example is made clear in v 7, which combines the language of vv 1 and 6 with the information of 11:17, given in reverse order, with one modification made. Joshua distributes the territory according to lots, which harmonizes this narrative with Josh 18:10. Pitkänen thus states, "It is very possible that verses 7–24 in particular telescope some events that happened somewhat later, citing Joshua and the Israelites of the initial conquest and settlement as their ultimate cause."[1685] Again, such a literary process is possible in Israel and the ancient Near East. We do not have stories of conquest from all the sites listed. Those who preserved the literature may well have identified themselves in cultic worship with the earlier generations and may have equated their conquest as the continuation of what Israel first began. On the other hand, Israel may have faced several groups of city-state coalitions and not preserved the story of each encounter except for including the city in the summary of defeated kings.

8 V 8 geographically details Joshua's distribution of all the land he and Israelites had conquered.[1686] Here again the picture becomes clear that Joshua first conquered the major part of the land in battle but then later gave it out to the tribes to possess, even though much work remained to be done in conquering the land (Josh 13:2–6), the task being completed only by David. For a discussion of the six nations, see Josh 3:10.

9 Chaps. 1–12 do not tell the story of the conquest of Bethel, yet the city is so important that it comes in for specific mention in the text in a manner unlike any other city (Josh 7:2; 8:9, 12, 17). The original list here may not have included the king of Bethel (v 16; compare *Note* 16.b.). In a dramatic fashion the extent of the conquest is forced upon the reader via the list of kings. Most of the cities have been discussed previously, and the addition of cities not previously mentioned may suggest that chap. 10 "may have been merely a schematic list."[1687]

1684 Ibid., 242.
1685 Pitkänen, 238.
1686 Cf. Nelson, 161.
1687 Howard, 281.

13 Geder is graphically close to Gezer and could be an early scribal error (compare Gray). Aharoni suggests the error is for Gerar, "the most important Canaanite city in the western Negeb."[1688] Hess suggests that Geder is Khirbet Jedur (= M.R. 158115).[1689]

14 Hormah was the scene of Israelite defeat (Num 14:45; compare Deut 1:44) and victory (Num 21:3). The territory lay in the southern end of Judah (Josh 15:30) and was allotted to Simeon (Josh 19:4). Judah and Simeon joined to conquer it (Judg 1:17). Later David gained support there (1 Sam 30:30). Egyptian texts also refer to Hormah.[1690] Its exact location is a matter of scholarly debate. Aharoni, suggests Tell Masos (= M.R. 146069) eight miles (twelve kilometers) east of Beersheba and seventeen miles south of Hebron.[1691] Excavation evidence shows occupation from the end of the thirteenth century until a major destruction in ca. 1000 BCE. Defensive walls appear never to have been built. Fritz maintains it must be north of Beersheba.[1692] Bimson uses Middle Bronze evidence from Tell Masos to date the Israelite destruction of Hormah to the fifteenth century.[1693]

Arad is tied closely to Hormah in Num 21:1–3 and was settled by the Kenites according to Judg 1:16. Harstad (479) posits two Arads. Aharoni has suggested that Israelite Arad is to be identified with Tell Arad, eighteen miles (thirty kilometers) east-northeast of Beersheba. The site was settled, however, only in the Early Bronze Age and then again about the eleventh or twelfth century. Aharoni thus locates the Arad mentioned in Numbers at Tell Malhata (= M.R. 152069), where Middle Bronze (ca. 1550 BCE) fortifications were found followed alongside an Israelite fortress of the tenth century.[1694] Bimson takes this as further support for his dating.[1695] The lack of Late Bronze and Early Iron evidence for Tell Arad is a key in Fritz's dating of the list in Josh 12 to the period of Solomon. See especially Y. Aharoni, "Arad: Its Inscriptions and Temple."[1696]

15 Adullam is a city in southern Judah (Josh 15:35; Neh 11:30) that is mentioned in an oracle of doom by Micah (1:15). A nearby cave served as a hiding place for David (1 Sam 22:1; 2 Sam 23:13), and its traditions go back to Jacob (Gen 38). On the basis of Eusebius and a nearby locality that has preserved the name, Adullam is identified with esh-Sheikh Madhkur (= M.R. 150117), nine and a half miles (sixteen kilometers) east-northeast of Beit Jibrin and twelve miles northwest of Hebron. Surface explorations have revealed Iron Age remains.

16 Makkedah may be located at Khirbet el-Kum (= M.R. 146104) eight miles west of Hebron.[1697]

17 Tappuah is the name of two cities, one in Judah (Josh 15:34) and the other on the boundary of Ephraim and Manasseh (Josh 17:7–8; 16:8). Josh 12 suggests

---

1688 *Land*, 210; "The Land of Gerar," *IEJ* 6 (1956) 27.
1689 Hess (2009) 56.
1690 Aharoni, *Land*, 133.
1691 *BA* 39 (1976) 71–72; cf. Hess (2009) 56.
1692 "Arad in der biblischen Überlieferung [Num 21:1–3] und in der Liste Schoschenks I," *ZDPV* 82 (1966) 340–41.
1693 *Redating*, 203–4.
1694 *BA* 39 (1976) 56–57.
1695 *Redating*, 204–5.
1696 *BA* 31 (1968) 2–32.
1697 Harstad, 479; Hess (1996) 227.

that the latter is meant here. It is located at Tell Sheikh Abu Zarad (= M.R. 172168) nine miles (fifteen kilometers) southeast of Nablus. Surface explorations indicate settlement in the Late Bronze Age and in the Iron Age.

Hepher is the personal name of one of the clans of Manasseh (Num 26:33; 27:1; Josh 17:2–3). The only other geographical reference is 1 Kgs 4:10. It has been identified with et-Tayibeh, three and a half miles south of Tulkarm, by Alt[1698] but with Tell el-Muhaffar (= M.R. 171205) by Wright[1699] and with Tell Ibshar eight miles (thirteen kilometers) northwest of Tul Kerm by B. Maisler.[1700] Harstad locates it at el-Ifshar (Tell Hefer) twenty-five miles north-northeast of Joppa and three miles from the Mediterranean coast.[1701] Uncertainty of location makes a description of the occupational history impossible.

18 Aphek is identified with Ras el-ʾAin (= M.R. 143168) at the mouth of the Yarmuk River just east of Tel-Aviv. The city appears in the nineteenth-century execration texts from Egypt.[1702] That it was settled in the fourth millennium and was a walled city in the early third millennium has been demonstrated by excavations.[1703] A Middle Bronze Age palace and a Late Bronze Age occupation evince a massive destruction layer around 1200 BCE, with Iron Age settlement also destroyed by fire.[1704]

The excavator suggests that the thirteenth-century destruction can be attributed to the Sea Peoples and reports that in the Israelite layer a cult site has been discovered which was destroyed in the eighth century.[1705] During the days of Samuel and Saul, Aphek served as a mustering point for Philistine troops (1 Sam 4:1; 29:1; 31:1–7).[1706]

Lashsharon probably is to be connected with Aphek and referred to the Plain of Sharon (compare *Note* 18.a). Harstad sees Sharon as referring to the Plain of Sharon, a "large territory" or an otherwise unknown city.[1707]

20 See *Comments* on 11:1. Shimron-meron is probably the same city as Shimron in Josh 11:1 and 19:15.

21 Taanach was a Levitical city in western Manasseh (Josh 21:25; compare 17:11) but was not immediately conquered (Judg 1:27). It was the site of the famous battle by the waters of Megiddo (Judg 5:19) and is mentioned in the list of Solomon's taxation districts (1 Kgs 4:12) and is well known in Egyptian sources.[1708] It is located at Tel Taʿanakh (= M.R. 171214) five miles (eight kilometers) southwest of Megiddo. Excavation has revealed occupation reaching back into the Early Bronze Age, ca. 2700. A long gap is followed by a Middle Bronze settlement beginning about 1700. Some destruction evidence closes the Middle Bronze settlement. A

1698 "Das Institut im Jahre 1925," *PJ* 22 (1926) 68–69.
1699 "The Provinces of Solomon," *ErIsr* 8 (1967) 63*; cf. Hess (2009) 56.
1700 "Die westliche Linie des Meerwegs," *ZDPV* 58 (1935) 82–83.
1701 Harstad, 479.
1702 *ANET*, 329; cf. 242, 246.
1703 M. Kochavi, "Tel Aphek (Ras el-ʿAin)," *IEJ* 22 (1972) 238–39.
1704 M. Kochavi, "Tel Aphek," *IEJ* 23 (1973) 245–46; M. Kochavi, "Tel Aphek," *IEJ* 24 (1974) 261–62; cf. R. Giveon, "Two Unique Egyptian Inscriptions from Tel Aphek," *TA* 5 (1978) 188, n. 1.
1705 M. Kochavi, "Tel Aphek," *IEJ* 26 (1976) 51–52.
1706 *IEJ* 27 (1977) 54.
1707 Harstad, 479.
1708 *ANET*, 235–36, 243, 490.

Late Bronze settlement was interrupted by Thutmose III about 1468. Significant occupation resumed in the late thirteenth century only to be destroyed about 1125 BCE.[1709]

"The inclusion of Megiddo in the list of chapter 12 means only that the account of the conquest of the north is selective and does not include the account of that city's capture," parallel to Assyrian lists introducing certain cities not mentioned previously.[1710] Megiddo was a vital defense station that controlled the entrance of the international highway Via Maris into the Jezreel Valley. It appears repeatedly in Egyptian texts and is located at Tell-el-Mutesellim (= M.R. 167221).[1711]

The territory of Megiddo was given to Manasseh (Josh 17:11), but it was not conquered (Judg 1:27). Deborah and Barak battled Sisera and the kings of Canaan by its waters (Judg 5:19). Solomon strengthened its defenses (1 Kgs 9:15) and levied taxes on it (1 Kgs 4:12). Ahaziah of Judah died from battle wounds there (2 Kgs 9:27), and Josiah was slain by Pharaoh Neco (2 Kgs 23:29–30). Excavations have revealed that its defenses date to the Early and Middle Bronze Ages and its settlement into the Chalcolithic (before 3300 BCE). The pottery evidence for dating the Middle Bronze Age strata of Megiddo forms one of the central links in Bimson's arguments for dating the conquest in the fifteenth century.[1712] A destruction level at the end of the Late Bronze Age is evident.

22 Kedesh is a common geographical name and may have been used by several different towns. The one specified here is the subject of debate.[1713] Hess locates it at Tel Qedesh (= M.R. 170218) between Taanach and Megiddo, but notes that various options have been suggested.[1714]

Jokneam lies near the border of Zebulon (Josh 19:11) at Tell Qeimun (= M.R. 160230) and was a Levitical city (Josh 21:34). Thutmose III mentions it.[1715] Recent excavation has shown Late Bronze Age and Iron Age settlement. S. Zuckermann reports: "Strata of the Middle and Late Bronze Iron ages attest to the existence of a thriving Canaanite city. The succeeding Israelite city was a well-planned settlement with sophisticated fortifications and a water system."[1716]

23 The meaning of גוים לגלגל (Goiim of Gilgal or nations of Gilgal or emended to Goiim of Galilee) is uncertain (see *Note* 23.a). The locality meant here is unknown, though Hess suggests Jiljuliyey (= M.R. 145173), just north of Aphek.[1717]

24 Tirzah is located at Tel el-Farah north (= M.R. 182188), seven miles (eleven kilometers) northeast of Nablus, on a major highway. It belongs to a group of cities in the central highlands (vv 16b–17) and is somewhat out of place in this list. The name is used for a woman in the genealogy of Manasseh (Num 26:33; 27:1; 36:11; Josh 17:3). Later the city served briefly as the royal residence of the northern king-

---

1709 A. Glock, "Taanach," *EAEHL* 4 (1978) 1138–47.
1710 Younger, *Ancient Conquest Accounts*, 231.
1711 *ANET*, 228, 234–38, 242–43, 477, 485, cf. 263–64.
1712 *Redating*, 151–65.
1713 Cf. Fritz, *ZDPV* 85 (1969) 152–53.
1714 Hess (1996) 227.
1715 Cf. A. Ben-Tor and R. Rosenthal, "The First Season of Excavations at Tel Yoqne'am, 1977," *IEJ* 28 (1978) 60.
1716 *NIDB*, 3:374; cf. *IEJ* 28 (1978) 57–82.
1717 Hess (2009) 57.

dom (1 Kgs 14:17–16:23; compare 2 Kgs 15:14–16) and was renowned for its beauty (Song 6:4).

Excavations reveal settlements dating to the Neolithic and Chalcolithic periods and continuing in the Early Bronze Age. Middle Bronze Age II occupancy follows six hundred years of desolation. A strong city wall was built about 1700 BCE. Late Bronze Age evidence is poorly preserved but is shown by pottery to have continued until 1400 and possibly into the thirteenth century. Signs of destruction are attributed by the excavator to the Israelites. The Iron Age period saw continued use of the sanctuary first used in the Middle Bronze Age.[1718] The city's Iron Age pottery dates from the tenth and ninth centuries, but de Vaux does not want to exclude earlier Israelite occupation.[1719]

Baal-gad stands at the opposite end of Lebo-Hamath (Josh 11:17) and of Mount Halak (Josh 11:17; 12:7). Na'aman thinks Baal-gad probably lies on a watershed, and "it is clear that the border passed along the southern foot of Mount Hermon, then turned northwards and encompassed both the source of the Jordan River and the Valley of Marj-'ayyun."[1720]

Table 12.1 shows the location of many of the cities and villages mentioned in Josh 1–12, but note the uncertainty of many of the locations.

Table 12.1. Cities and Villages in Joshua 1–12

Passage in Joshua/City	*Modern Location— Arabic/Israeli*	*Map Reference*	*Distance Locations*	*Late Bronze / Early Iron Evidence*	*Alternate Location(s)/ Conquest Date*
12:2/Heshbon	Tell Hisban (Hesban)	226134	34.2 mi E of Jerusalem; 12.4 mi SW of Amman; 3.7 mi NE of Mt. Nebo	LB-No; EI-disturbed	Tell Jalul/Tell el-Umeiri 1150–1051
12:2/Aroer	'Ara'ir	228097	3 mi SE of Dhiban; 2.5 mi E of King's Highway	Occupied LB and EI	
12:2/ Beth-jeshimoth	Tell el 'Azeimeh	208132	In Syria		
12:4/Ashtaroth	Tell 'Ashtarah	243244	Tell 'Ashtara in S Syria	LB and EI	
12:4/Edrei	Der'a	253224	60 mi S of Damascus	LB	
12:5/Salecah	Salkhad	311212			

1718 Cf. R. de Vaux, "El-Far 'a, Tell, North," *EAEHL* 2 (1976) 395–404.
1719 "Tirzah," in *Archaeology and Old Testament Study*, ed. D. W. Thomas (London: Oxford UP, 1967) 376; cf. Fritz, *ZDPV* 85 (1969) 155.
1720 *Borders and Districts*, 43; cf. P. Skehan, "Joab's Census: How Far North? [2 Sam 24:6]," *CBQ* 31 (1969) 46–47.

Passage in Joshua/City	Modern Location— Arabic/Israeli	Map Reference	Distance Locations	Late Bronze / Early Iron Evidence	Alternate Location(s)/ Conquest Date
12:7/ Baal-gad=Baal Hermon	Perhaps Banias (?)		Valley of Lebanon below Mount Hermon; north boundary of the territory conquered by Joshua		Called Mount Baal-Hermon (Judg 3:3)
12:9; 2:1; chap. 6/Jericho	Tell es-Sultan	192142	9.9 mi NW of Dead Sea's N shore	Some LB ca. 1300; no walls; some Iron I pottery	
12:9; chaps. 7–8/Ai	Khirbet et-tell	174147	Next to Bethel, which is 9 mi S of Shiloh	EI-large village; abandoned; destroyed ca. 2400; unwalled village ca. 1200	
12:10; 10:1/ Jerusalem	el-Quds/Jeru-salem	172131		Yes	
12:10; 10:3/ Hebron/ Kiriath-arba	Jebel er-Rumeideh/ El-Khalil	160104	19 mi SSE of Jerusalem; 23 mi NE of Beersheba		
12:11; 10:3/ Jarmuth	Khirbet el-Yarmuk/ Yarmut	147124	10 mi N of Beth Govrin; 15.5 mi SW of Jerusalem	Abandoned 2300; resettled LB	1050
12:11; 10:3/ Lachish	Tell ed-Duweir/ Tell Lachish (Lachish letters; Sennacherib relief)	135108		No walls in LB; maybe unoccupied ca. 1130–1000	ca. 1200 fire; fire also about 1130
12:12; 10:3/ Eglon	Tell 'Aitun Tell 'Eton	143099 124106			Tell el-Hesi Tell Beit Mirsim
11:12; 10:33/ Gezer	Tell Jezer Tell Gezer = Tell el-Jazari	142140	5 mi SSE of Ramleh	LB outer wall built; EI = Philistines	1482—Thutmose III; ca. 1200 Merneptah burned part of city
12:13; 10:38/ Debir/Kiriath Sepher	Khirbet er-Rabud (Kiriath-sannah)	151093		LB-occupied	
12:13/Geder = Gedor	Khirbet Jedur	158115	Between Bethlehem and Hebron		

Passage in Joshua/City	Modern Location— Arabic/Israeli	Map Reference	Distance Locations	Late Bronze / Early Iron Evidence	Alternate Location(s)/ Conquest Date
12:14; Num 14:45/Hormah	Khirbet el-Meshash Tell Masos	146069	7.5 mi E of Beersheba	No LB; occupation in EB	Tell el-Milh (Tel Malhata); Tell esh-Sheri'ah; Tel Ira
12:14; Num 21:1–3/Arad	Tel-Milh Tell Malhata	152069	20 mi from Hebron	LB occupation	Tell 'Arad 162076
12:15; 10:29/ Libnah	Tell Bornat Tell Burna	138115	4.9 mi NE of Lachish	LB, EI occupation	Tell es-Safi (135123)
12:15/Adullam	Tell esh-Sheikh Madhkur; Khirbet Adullam	150117	Halfway between Bethlehem and Gath		
12:16 10:10/ Makkedah	Khirbet el-Qom; Tell 'Abyad	146104	6.8 mi ESE of Lachish	No LB; EI occupation	
12:16; 8:9/ Bethel; Luz	Beitin	172148	8 mi N of Jerusalem	LB occupation	El-Bireh; 1200
12:17/Tappuah	Sheikh Abu Zarad	172168	7.5 mi S of Nasblus; 12 mi N of Bethel		
12:17/Hepher	Tell el-Muhaffar	170205	S of Megiddo	LB lost population; flourished in EI	Et-Tayibeh Tell Ibshar
12:18/Aphek	Ras el-'Ain Tell Afeq	143168			
Lashsharon [of Sharon=Sharon Valley]					
12:19; 11:1/ Madon (= Merom?)	Qarn Hattin; Tell Qarnei Hittin	19345			Khirbet Madin
12:19; 11:1/ Hazor	Tell el-Qedah Tell Hazor	203269	4 mi SW of Huleh basin on N border of Palestine	LB declining; EI limited occupation	ca. 1250
12:20; 11:1/ Shimron-meron (= Shimron?)					
[Shimron] [Shim'on]	Khirbet Sammuniyeh Tell Shimron	170234	5 mi W of Nazareth		
[Maron]	Tell el-Khureibeh				
12:20; 11:1/ Achshaph	Tell Keisan Tell Kison	164253	6 mi SE of Acco; 4.9 mi from Mediterra-nean	LB; EI remains	Khirbet el-Harabaj (158240); LB/EI destruction (Sea Peoples?); 1000 fire

Passage in Joshua/City	Modern Location—Arabic/Israeli	Map Reference	Distance Locations	Late Bronze / Early Iron Evidence	Alternate Location(s)/ Conquest Date
12:21/Taanach	Tell Ti'innik Tell Ta'anakh	171214	4.9 mi SE of Megiddo; 6.2 mi NW of Jenin	14th-cent. remains; limited EI remains	
12:21/Megiddo	Tell el-Mutesellim; Tell Megiddo	167221	Close to foot of Mt. Carmel overlooking Jezreel Valley	LB and EI occupation	LB fire
12:22/Kedesh	Tell Abu Qudeis; Tell Qades	170218 or NEAEHL 170622	NW of Lake Huleh; 9.9 mi N or Safed	LB, EI occupation	Kedesh in Galilee (Howard)/fire before 1150
12:22/Jokneam	Tell Qeimun Tel Yoqneam	160230	6 mi from Acco	LB unfortified; abandoned until ca. 1100; EI remains	LB strong destruction
12:23; 11:2/ Dor	Khirbet el-Burj, Tell Dor	142224	N of Tantura; 12 mi S of Carmel; 9 mi from Caesarea	Founded in LB; EI occupation	Destroyed after 1300 (Sea Peoples?)
11:2/ Naphath-Dor=Dor					
12:23/Goiim in Gilgal (or Galilee of the nations)					
12:24/Tirzah	Khirbet Tell el-Far'ah North	182188	NE of Shechem	LB, EI occupation	

Explanation

Using the available sources, the final editor of Joshua describes the victory of Moses and Joshua over the kings of Canaan east and west of the Jordan. Thus the writer ties together the work of Moses and Joshua into a single whole and the territories east and west of the Jordan into a single nation.[1721]

The writer clearly shows that enemy leaders are defeated but their towns are not necessarily destroyed.[1722] Neither the battle reports nor the summary lists, however, include all the conquered cities. The conquest of the hill country is not recorded in the book of Joshua.[1723] Shechem is not mentioned, and the hills of Ephraim are sparsely represented, as is the territory north of Hazor. Completeness is not the

---

1721 Cf. McConville and Williams, 60.
1722 Hess (1996) 226.
1723 Ibid., 228.

object. Rather than chronicling "the adventures of Israel under Joshua," the writer's purpose is "theological."[1724]

Hubbard rightly concludes that "the chapter draws together the book's central thematic threads and motifs":[1725]

Unity of Moses and Joshua
Resistance from Canaan's kings
List of enemy peoples
Echoes of Yahweh War
Unity of eastern and western tribes
Land distribution

Hubbard claims that "a united Israel" is "in full possession of all the land on both sides of the Jordan." Howard states that the importance of this summary list is that of "confirming the veracity of the claims elsewhere that these lands were indeed conquered, in confirming the tribes' claims to the lands mentioned here, and in confirming that God was faithful to his promises to give these lands to his people."[1726] Still, for Howard, "the book's central message concerns Israel's inheritance of the Promised Land in fulfillment of God's promises."[1727] This inheritance came not from human military encounters based on military superiority, for all the battles were "sacred exercises."[1728]

Merling argues that the purpose of Josh 1–12 is to confirm the presence of Yahweh with his people.[1729] Such an argument rests on a few statements in the chapters rather than on an analysis of their entire structure, which concentrate on Yahweh doing what is necessary for Israel to conquer the entire land, east and west as one united nation.[1730] The confirmation of Israel's claim to the land is shown through rallying east and west troops; through spying out the land; through crossing the Jordan into the land of Canaan; through getting the people cultically correct for conquest; through divine appearance to the chosen military leader; and through conquest of Jericho, Ai, and both the southern and northern coalitions. The conclusion is not a simple one, that Yahweh was with Israel, but a complex explanation that Yahweh hardened hearts so he might destroy the enemies of Israel and confirm that Joshua followed Yahweh's instructions to Moses and destroyed the enemies and their towns and conquered the entire land before giving the land to Israel (Josh 11:18–23). This concluding summary thus showed beyond doubt the central place of conquest and distribution of land in the purpose of Joshua. Josh 12 reinforces this purpose with its listing of the kings Joshua and the Israelites defeated, taking over their land.

Hawk suggests there is more complexity in the narrative content. He writes:[1731]

The stories of Rahab, Achan, and the Gibeonites take place on the individual level and contest notions of identity based on ethnic separation,

---

1724 Ibid., 229.
1725 Hubbard, 359.
1726 Hubbard, 278.
1727 Howard, 286.
1728 Ibid., 278.
1729 *Book of Joshua.*
1730 See Howard, 277.
1731 Hawk (2000) 157.

obedience to the commands of Moses, and possession of territory; peoples
of the land survive to live among Israel while Israelites who have entered
the land are put to death. . . . [T]he narrator creates a series of destabilizing
tensions. Israel enjoys life in the land to the extent that it executes divine
directives. Yet YHWH continues to fight for Israel, even when the commandments of Moses are broken. The Israelites annihilate the peoples of the land
but also permit some to live among them. Israel takes the entire land but
allows territory to remain in the possession of indigenous people.

Succinctly, for the book, conquering lands is of upmost meaning. The writer
brings together threads from the whole book: Moses and Joshua, divine war, east
and west together, land distribution, and victory over enemy kings, and compiles
a list that will impress readers with the greatness of the feat of God in working for
Israel and of the greatness of the leadership of Joshua in following the example of
Moses and completing the task given to him. As Hess concludes: "The covenanted
blessings of inheritance become Israel's (chaps. 13–19) because of their faithfulness to God through all the battles and because of the faithfulness of Moses and
Joshua."[1732] This is a much stronger conclusion than Merlin's direction toward the
presence of God and Israel's lack of need to act.

The writer is aware, however, that much remains to be done. Israel has not
achieved rest and accomplishment. The people bask in the glory of victory and obedience, but they face a new task ahead. They have won the territory; now they must
drive out the remaining inhabitants and settle the land. They have not been called
to a life of constant warfare and celebration of victory. They have been called to a
life in the land that God has given them, a life to be lived in accordance with the
lifestyle prescribed by God. The first step in fulfillment of that calling is the division of the land. That follows immediately. When that is complete, the people will
have their identity set before them, an identity of life in the land obeying Yahweh,
the giver of the land and of the law.

Still suspended over the list of kings, the hanging of kings at Makkedah, and
the fear spread across all of Canaan is the threat of violence, war, and killing. One
cannot concentrate on possession and neglect the result of possession for those
deposed. Thus Hawk warns: "God's election of Israel meant that God would be
involved in the mess, broken systems, and violence that entangle nations in a world
gone bad. God's participation in, and even initiation of, the evil of war seems to fly
in the face of God's goodness, righteousness, and love."[1733]

The problem of such a conclusion lies in its limitation of God to One who does
what we call righteous. We cancel God's anger, wrath, and fight for justice. We must
live with this tension between God's creative goodness and God's re-creating a just
society for his kingdom. The life of the believer will remain caught in this tension.

1732 Hess (1996) 221.
1733 Hawk (2010) 140.

Scripture Index

Subject Index

Author Index

CPSIA information can be obtained
at www.ICGtesting.com
Printed in the USA
JSHW040237211021
19686JS00004B/2